ENCYCLOPEDIA

THE COMPREHENSIVE GUIDE TO THE STAR WARS GALAXY

ENCYCLOPEDIA

THE COMPREHENSIVE GUIDE TO THE STAR WARS GALAXY

Written by
Dan Brooks   Megan Crouse   Kelly Knox   Amy Ratcliffe
Amy Richau   Brandon Wainerdi   Dan Zehr   Matt Jones

Cover design by
Brian Rood

CONTENTS

Introduction	6
Foreword by Rosario Dawson	8

CHARACTERS AND CREATURES 10–235

Obi-Wan Kenobi	22
Qui-Gon Jinn	23
Darth Sidious (Sheev Palpatine)	24
Padmé Amidala	25
Jar Jar Binks	27
R2-D2	30
Maul	31
Darth Vader (Anakin Skywalker)	32
C-3PO	33
Jabba the Hutt	37
Yoda	40
Mace Windu	41
Bail Organa	48
Clone Trooper	52
Boba Fett	53
Darth Tyranus (Count Dooku)	56
Captain Rex	59
Asajj Ventress	60
General Grievous	61
Ahsoka Tano	62
Mon Mothma	67
Grand Moff Tarkin	73
Chewbacca	74
Bo-Katan Kryze	75
Saw Gerrera	84
Luke Skywalker	87
Leia Organa	88
Han Solo	100
Stormtrooper	101
Qi'ra	102
Lando Calrissian	107
Cassian Andor	113
Kanan Jarrus	122
Hera Syndulla	123
Chopper (C1-10P)	124
Garazeb "Zeb" Orrelios	125
Sabine Wren	126
Ezra Bridger	127
Alexsandr Kallus	129
The Grand Inquisitor	130
Thrawn	136
Jyn Erso	140
Doctor Chelli Aphra	152
Din Djarin	172
Grogu	175
Poe Dameron	194
BB-8	195
Captain Phasma	203
Finn	207
Kylo Ren (Ben Solo)	208
Rey	209
Armitage Hux	210
Snoke	213
Rose Tico	217

LOCATIONS 236–319

Naboo	240
Tatooine	243
Mos Espa	244
Watto's Shop	245
Mos Espa Grand Arena	246
Coruscant	247
Jedi Temple	248
Kamino	251
Geonosis	253
Lars Moisture Farm	255
Geonosis Execution Arena	256
Jabba's Palace	257
Mustafar	258
Alderaan	261
Mos Eisley Spaceport	262
Dagobah	266
Kashyyyk	269
Lothal	280

Yavin 4	286
The Death Star	287
Darth Vader's Fortress	288
Endor	296
Nevarro	299
Starkiller Base	305
Colossus Platform	307
Jakku	308
Maz Kanata's Castle	310

TECHNOLOGY 320–369

Battle Droid	323
Super Battle Droid	328
Skywalker Lightsaber	331
Darksaber	338

VEHICLES 370–435

Boba Fett's Starship	379
Y-wing Starfighter	389
Millennium Falcon	394
TIE Fighter	395
Ghost	401
Red Five	410
Index	436
Acknowledgments	448

INTRODUCTION

If you're familiar with Ric Olié, porgs, U-wings, IG-88, Constable Zuvio, and Ewoks, you must be a fan of *Star Wars*. But if you recognize any of those names, that's remarkable because none are mentioned in the *Star Wars* movies themselves, so you must have gained that knowledge elsewhere, possibly from toy packages, comics, books, or pure osmosis.

It can be quite challenging for fans to learn more about specific topics, because numerous droids, starships, weapons, and locations are never identified on screen. How does one go about looking up a subject in an encyclopedia if one doesn't know the name of the subject? That's almost as difficult as trying to pinpoint the origin of an unusually lethal dart for which no records exist in the Jedi Archives.

Fortunately, the authors, editors, and designers of the *Star Wars Encyclopedia* are here to help. This unique compendium features a wealth of images and information about many characters, creatures, locations, technology, and vehicles, and each one is organized by its first significant appearance in official *Star Wars* lore, whether they be from movies, live-action series, animated series, or other sources. You can also refer to the index at the back of the book to find any entry you wish.

So, if you're familiar with the *Star Wars* saga, you should have little difficulty finding what you're looking for. And if you're new to *Star Wars*, I encourage you to delve into a galaxy far, far away. Soon, you'll be an expert, too!

RYDER WINDHAM

FOREWORD BY ROSARIO DAWSON

Once a rebel always a rebel.

Taking up the mantle of the wandering, stoic warrior Ahsoka Tano has been one of the greatest joys of my life. As a fan of the character from her animated beginnings, I was beside myself with excitement to put in those ice-blue contacts and hold her two lightsabers. But more than anything, it was donning her new costume that thrilled and moved me beyond measure because it meant that we would all get to join her on yet another adventure. A story that reconnected her with old friends (and foes!) while accepting new positions and confrontations that provoked her to grow and develop in ways that, in my opinion, make her arc continue to be one of the greatest ever told.

Despite the challenges and setbacks she faces, Ahsoka is consistently loyal, steadfast in her beliefs, and fiercely passionate. A beacon of faith, hope, and wisdom, I believe she embodies what it means to be a Jedi. She is a consummate master of her craft, and yet always wants to be better—something we can all aspire to. This experience has been so deeply fortifying and beyond exceptional, which is only that much more stirring because it is only the beginning...!

And what an unforgettable beginning, as *Star Wars* has been a part of my life for as long as I can remember. To be included in this galaxy is such a privilege, one that we're all indebted to its creator for, the brilliant George Lucas, who envisioned and captured this expansive world. I continue to be awed and inspired by it, and especially by Ahsoka herself. *Star Wars* has sparked the imagination of so many kids and adults alike, for generations now, and is rightfully cherished and shared by all who encounter it, and by all who get the chance to nurture and leave their mark on it. This incredible franchise has a unique level of world-building—truly unparalleled in its scope, breadth, and depth—and the *Star Wars Encyclopedia* celebrates this majesty. In its pages, you will find hundreds of fascinating entries that wonderfully detail and honor this magnificent saga.

So go, young Padawan, take this book and indulge in all there is to know about a galaxy far, far away...

CHARACTERS AND CREATURES

Remarkable individuals, incredible lifeforms, and sentient droids coexist throughout the galaxy. Space travel brings them together in fascinating, and at times combustible, combinations.

From the smallest scavengers and largest creatures on the desert planet Tatooine to the impoverished denizens, wealthy aristocrats, and droid servants on the metropolitan city-planet Coruscant, the galaxy is populated by innumerable beings. Although not every civilization has achieved or acquired the appropriate technology, and some remain isolationists, space travel has led to commercial trade and cultural exchanges between thousands of worlds and societies. It is not unusual to find literally dozens of species in any given spaceport.

    For millennia, many planets have been protected by the Jedi, an ancient order of peacekeepers with seemingly supernatural powers. The Jedi maintain that all lifeforms in the galaxy, as well as the universe itself, are bound together and connected by an energy field called the Force. The Jedi's battles with evil, power-hungry Sith and dark-side Force-users leaves a significant impact on many worlds, affecting lives and the course of galactic history.

CHARACTERS AND CREATURES

PORTER ENGLE
SPECIES Ikkrukkian **AFFILIATION** Jedi

One of the High Republic era's greatest sword wielders, Porter Engle is also one of its greatest chefs. He is raised in the Jedi Temple and becomes close with Barash Silvain, to the degree that the two consider each other siblings. Porter distinguishes himself with extraordinary lightsaber combat during a siege, earning himself the nickname "Blade of Bardotta." More than 100 years later, Porter is thriving as the cook at the Jedi outpost on Elphrona. He helps Jedi Bell Zettifar, Loden Greatstorm, and Indeera Stokes rescue people from the Nihil marauders. Porter makes a mortal enemy of General Viess, tangling with the Nihil military leader on numerous occasions.

VILDAR MAC
SPECIES Kiffar **HOMEWORLD** Kiffex
AFFILIATION Jedi, Convocation of the Force

Ever since a person strong in the Force attacked his home when he was four years old, Vildar Mac has feared the dark side. Later, he encounters the Nameless on Jedha and clashes against Yana Ro and the Herald. With Tey Sirrek's help, Vildar battles his fears and resists the dark side. Afterward, he becomes the Jedi representative to the Convocation of the Force, and he assigns Matty Cathley to investigate the Path of the Open Hand on Dalna.

BARASH SILVAIN
SPECIES Kage **HOMEWORLD** Quarzite
AFFILIATION Jedi

Barash has the unusual ability of being able to use the Force to tell if someone is lying. Growing up in the Jedi Temple, she becomes close to Porter Engle, seeing him as a brother. When her truth-telling ability fails during the Siege of Firevale, Barash withdraws from the Jedi Order in a ritualistic decision that will later become known as the Barash Vow.

MATTHEA CATHLEY
SPECIES Twi'lek
AFFILIATION Jedi, Convocation of the Force

The Jedi Council stations Matthea "Matty" Cathley and her master, Leebon, on Jedha. She teaches Vildar Mac about the Convocation of the Force and is caught up beside him when he fights the Path of the Open Hand for the artifacts that control the Nameless. Matty also fights in the Battle of Dalna.

SAV MALAGÁN
SPECIES Kyuzo **HOMEWORLD** Phatrong
AFFILIATION Jedi, Maz Kanata's pirates

Sav Malagán sneaks away from her Jedi Master, Kaktorf, to tag along with Maz Kanata, Dexter Jettster, and their gang of pirates. She goes undercover with the Dank Graks gang and is present at the Battle of Jedha. As a Jedi Master stationed on Takodana decades later, Sav repels Krix Kamerat and his Nihil raiders.

GELLA NATTAI
SPECIES Human
AFFILIATION Jedi

A mission to the warring planets of Eiram and E'ronoh leaves Jedi Knight Gella Nattai questioning her own place in the galaxy. She decides to become a Wayseeker—an independent Jedi. However, she is drawn back into the Order—and the orbit of the charming traitor Axel Greylark—when a peace treaty between the planets is signed.

CREIGHTON SUN
SPECIES Human
AFFILIATION Jedi

The Jedi Council sends Creighton Sun, along with Aida Forte, to oversee negotiations between Eiram and E'ronoh on Jedha. He persuades soldiers to stand down as tensions rise between the two delegations. During the Battle of Dalna, he's pinned down by Path enforcer droids and faces the Nameless, but he survives thanks to Yaddle's assistance.

SILANDRA SHO
SPECIES Human
AFFILIATION Jedi

Silandra Sho's shield sets her apart from other Jedi. She trains Rooper Nitani and passes the shield down to her when Rooper is knighted. Silandra helps Jedi Master Creighton Sun investigate the Path of the Open Hand on Jedha, and she questions the Mother of the Path.

AIDA FORTE
SPECIES Nikto
AFFILIATION Jedi

Aida Forte and Creighton Sun are assigned as Jedi overseers of the peace treaty between rival planets Eiram and E'ronoh. Aida also fights alongside Master Yaddle and the youngling Cippa Tarko while investigating the Path of the Open Hand's involvement in stoking the war. Aida loses her life to Path enforcer droids.

ROOPER NITANI
SPECIES Human **HOMEWORLD** Rohm
AFFILIATION Jedi

As a Padawan, Rooper Nitani is deeply loyal to her master, Silandra Sho. Rooper uses the Force to bring a cave ceiling down on Gloam, saving Dietrix Jago and Dass and Spence Leffbruk from monstrous, transformed Katikoots. She also helps former Path of the Open Hand member Fel Ix realize the Jedi are not his enemy.

ROK BURAN
SPECIES Human
AFFILIATION Jedi

Adventurous Jedi Master Rok Buran is stranded in the wastelands of Gloam after an attack by mutated Katikoot miners. He joins a second Pathfinder team, the crew of the *Witherbloom*. Their ship crashes alongside a Path of the Open Hand ship carrying Nameless. Rok and Padawan Coron Solstus narrowly survive.

OLIVIAH ZEVERON
SPECIES Human
AFFILIATION Jedi, Convocation of the Force

Oliviah Zeveron works alongside Master Leebon as a representative to the Convocation of the Force on Jedha. When she meets the Mother of the Path, Oliviah realizes the two of them are sisters, separated in childhood because Oliviah was stronger with the Force. Oliviah defends the actions of the Jedi to her sister.

CHAR-RYL-ROY
SPECIES Cerean
AFFILIATION Jedi

Jedi Master Char-Ryl-Roy and his Padawan Enya Keen play key roles in the battles on Jedha and Dalna. On Dalna, Char-Ryl-Roy arranges a negotiation with the Path of the Open Hand to try to keep them from attacking the Jedi. Although he approaches them with calmness and rationality, he can't persuade the Path and ends up losing his life to the Great Leveler.

ENYA KEEN
SPECIES Human
AFFILIATION Jedi

Jedi Padawan Enya Keen is talented at both lightsaber combat and repairing droids. She's one of the many Jedi sent to first the Battle of Jedha and then the Battle of Dalna. On Dalna, she loses her master, Char-Ryl-Roy. Thereafter, she wields his kyber crystal in her second lightsaber.

ARKOFF
SPECIES Wookiee
AFFILIATION Jedi

Arkoff is a wise and patient Jedi Master who works alongside Jedi Knight Lily Tora-Asi at the temple on Banchii. Arkoff is a skilled lightsaber fighter and resists giving in to his anger. When the bounty hunter Vol Garat captures an injured Azlin Rell, Arkoff helps recover the young Jedi.

LEEBON
SPECIES Selonian
AFFILIATION Jedi, Convocation of the Force

As the Jedi representative of the Convocation of the Force, Leebon represents just one of many Force sects on Jedha. She helps her Padawan Matty Cathley and her aid, Jedi Knight Oliviah Zeveron, in their conflict against the Path of the Open Hand. Leebon falls to the Leveler's powers.

ADY SUN'ZEE
SPECIES Mirialan
AFFILIATION Jedi

Ady Sun'Zee is the Padawan to Master Sylwin at an outpost on Batuu. Together, they study ancient artifacts. She fights alongside Master Yoda when an artifact infused with the dark side spreads corruption and confusion throughout the Batuu temple. Years later, she becomes a Knight and takes on a Padawan named Nooa.

WERTH PLOUTH
SPECIES Nautolan
AFFILIATION Path of the Open Hand

Werth Plouth, known as the Herald, is second in command to the Mother of the Path and a true believer in the cult's anti-Jedi doctrine. He stirs up riots on Jedha in the cult's name, but soon, he and Yana Ro begin to suspect the Mother has been lying to the cult members. The Mother kills the Herald with Oliviah Zeveron's lightsaber.

ELECIA ZEVERON
SPECIES Human
AFFILIATION Path of the Open Hand

Elecia Zeveron, known as the Mother, transforms the Path of the Open Hand into a criminal enterprise bent on stealing artifacts strong in the Force. Slightly attuned to the Force herself, and sister to Jedi Oliviah Zeveron, Elecia impresses the devout cult members with her skill at nurturing crops. Once she's installed as leader of the cult, she creates the hidden group Children of the Path to steal artifacts. Elecia's deceptions lead her into conflict with both her second-in-command, the Herald, and young cult loyalist Marda Ro. Marda eventually kills the Mother using the same Nameless monsters the Mother had unleashed on the Jedi.

YANA RO
SPECIES Evereni
AFFILIATION Path of the Open Hand

Yana Ro is Marda Ro's cousin and one of the Children of the Path thieves sent by the Mother to steal Force artifacts. Yana teams up with the Herald to wrest control of the cult away from the Mother. She leads a group of ex-cult members to safety after the Battle of Dalna.

MARDA RO
SPECIES Evereni
AFFILIATION Path of the Open Hand

Marda Ro grows up in the Path of the Open Hand. She befriends Jedi Kevmo Zink but loses him to the Nameless. This contributes to her increasing belief that using the Force is evil. She kills the Mother and takes command of the cult's flagship, the *Gaze Electric*, and the Nameless known as the Leveler.

ORLEN MOLLO
SPECIES Quarren **HOMEWORLD** Mon Cala
AFFILIATION Republic

Along with Kyong Greylark, Orlen Mollo is one of two chancellors of the Republic. He usually devotes his time to planets outside of Coruscant and far-flung hyperspace lanes. During the fraught attempt to make a peace treaty between Eiram and E'ronoh, Orlen's blunt words help convince the monarch of E'ronoh to heed his pleas for peace.

KYONG GREYLARK
SPECIES Human **HOMEWORLD** Coruscant
AFFILIATION Republic

Kyong Greylark is one of two chancellors of the Republic during the era of hyperspace exploration. She resigns from her position in order to prevent herself and her son, Axel, from being used as pawns by the Path of the Open Hand. During the Battle of Dalna, she joins the fray with the combat skills she learned at the Coruscant Academy.

TARNA MIAK
SPECIES Human
AFFILIATION Convocation of the Force, Sorcerers of Tund

Tarna Miak represents the Sorcerers of Tund, a Force group dedicated to the dark side, at Jedha's Convocation of the Force. He uses a burst of fire to break up an argument at the market. When the Path of the Open Hand incites chaos, he helps fight against the cult's enforcer droids.

TEY SIRREK
SPECIES Sephi
AFFILIATION None

Tey Sirrek may be a fast-talking thief, but he believes in using his skills for good. Tey becomes fast friends with Vildar Mac during the Jedi's investigation of the Path of the Open Hand on Jedha, eventually defending Vildar's life and saving Oliviah Zeveron.

RADICAZ "SUNSHINE" DOBBS
SPECIES Human **HOMEWORLD** Eriadu
AFFILIATION Path of the Open Hand

Radicaz "Sunshine" Dobbs is a smuggler charmed by the Mother of the Path's charisma. He smuggles Force-strong objects and Nameless eggs for the cult. Sunshine strands Dass and Spence Leffbruk on Gloam. Later, he goes to Planet X, with Marda Ro, for more Nameless eggs.

DASS LEFFBRUK
SPECIES Human
AFFILIATION Republic

Young hyperspace prospector Dass Leffbruk and his father, Spence, go on one of the first known missions to Planet X. Later, he befriends Jedi Padawan Rooper Nitani. Together, Dass, Rooper, and Sky Graf join the Hyperspace Chase navigation challenge and use it as cover in an attempt to return to Planet X.

SKY GRAF
SPECIES Human **AFFILIATION** Graf clan

Sky Graf, a scion of the Graf clan, wants to live up to the hyperspace prospecting exploits of the rest of their family. Sky joins Rooper Nitani and Dass Leffbruk on their quest to find Planet X, motivated partially by trying to find their missing father. Sky helps reunite former Path member Fel Ix with his family on Dalna.

KRADON MINST
SPECIES Villarandi **HOMEWORLD** Jedha
AFFILIATION Enlightenment bar

Kradon Minst is the proprietor and bartender of Enlightenment—a bar on Jedha open to anyone willing to pay for Kradon's drinks (or information). He often listens to Keth Cerapath's troubles, and he helps Vildar Mac, Matty Cathley, and Tey Sirrek escape from the Path of the Open Hand.

CHARACTERS AND CREATURES

AXEL GREYLARK
SPECIES Human **HOMEWORLD** Coruscant
AFFILIATION Republic, Path of the Open Hand

As the son of Republic Chancellor Kyong Greylark, Axel has access to high society, but he normally just ends up partying. The Mother of the Path of the Open Hand uses Axel's grudge against the Jedi to recruit him as her agent. Although he's codenamed "Chaos," Axel ultimately chooses his own mother and his burgeoning friendship with Jedi Gella Nattai over the Path.

ARKIK VON
SPECIES Geonosian
AFFILIATION Dank Graks

As a leader and spokesbeing for the Dank Graks, Arkik Von is one of the most aggressive members of the meddling gang. He rules Takodana's underworld until pirate queen Maz Kanata unseats him. Trying to get the planet back under control brings him into conflict with Maz and undercover Padawan Sav Malagán.

SPAMEL
HOMEWORLD Jedha **SIZE** 4.90 m (16 ft) high
HABITAT Desert

Spamels are long-legged quadrupeds that are native to the desert moon of Jedha. Some live in the wild, but Jedha citizens have domesticated many spamels and use them for traveling across the sands. Riders use rope ladders to reach saddles on the creatures' backs. Spamels see much change on Jedha between the High Republic and the Imperial occupation. They go from participating in parades in the Holy City and carrying Jedi, to serving as mounts for patrolling stormtroopers. After the destruction of Jedha City, riders fit spamels with custom breathing masks to mitigate harm from the particle-filled air.

KEEVE TRENNIS
SPECIES Human **AFFILIATION** Jedi

Keeve Trennis is Sskeer's Padawan, and she looks up to Avar Kriss. In her trial to become a Jedi Knight, she saves members of the Ximpi species from predatory ridadi star-locusts. Trennis, Sskeer, Ceret, and Terec venture into the tunnels of Sedri Minor and discover the Drengir hiding there. Sskeer becomes part of the Drengir root-mind, and by bonding with it, Keeve is able to discover the location of the Drengir Progenitor, even though she suffers terrifying visions. Keeve talks Avar out of killing an unarmed Lourna Dee, and she comforts her after the fall of Starlight Beacon. Eventually promoted to master, she becomes an unlikely ally to Lourna.

Starlight falls
When the Jedi know that Starlight Beacon can't be recovered, Stellan steers the space station into Eiram's ocean to prevent it from falling in any populated areas. Avar Kriss and Elzar Mann mourn their friend deeply.

STELLAN GIOS
SPECIES Human **AFFILIATION** Jedi

Jedi Master Stellan Gios trains Padawan Vernestra Rwoh until she's made a Jedi Knight. He's promoted to the Jedi Council during the conflict against the Nihil pirates, where he is a firm voice for the belief that the Jedi are the hands of the light side of the Force. During the *Legacy Run* disaster, Gios protects people on Ta'klah from falling debris.

Stellan is assigned to protect Chancellor Lina Soh during the Republic Fair. Throughout the Nihil attack on the Fair, he demonstrates the Jedi vow of never attacking, only defending against the pirates.

Stellan is acting marshal of Starlight Beacon during the attack that brings the space station down. He stays on board while the station crumbles, steering it into the ocean on Eiram to avoid as much collateral damage as possible. Although he saves many lives in the process, Stellan dies in the crash.

Boarding the Great Hall
Avar Kriss pursues Lourna Dee to the Great Hall of the Nihil, and she kills Zeetar in retribution for Terec's injuries.

AVAR KRISS
SPECIES Human **AFFILIATION** Jedi

One of the foremost Jedi of the High Republic, Avar Kriss brings other members of the Order together. She achieves this thanks to both her moral guidance and the unique way she perceives the Force. Kriss grows up in the Jedi Temple, where she fosters a close friendship with fellow Jedi Stellan Gios and Elzar Mann.

Kriss serves as the Marshal of Starlight Beacon, which is the space station that symbolizes the Republic at the height of its power. She negotiates a wary truce between the Republic and Hutt forces in order to fight the ravenous Drengir.

Kriss' composure is tested when she almost kills Nihil pirate leader Lourna Dee in anger. Fellow Jedi Keeve Trennis reminds Avar of her Jedi training, and the pair capture Lourna instead of killing her. Their victory is interrupted by a Nihil attack that ultimately destroys Starlight Beacon. Avar believes she's responsible in part for the deaths incurred during Starlight Beacon's fall, and she travels to the Nihil Occlusion Zone in the hopes of redeeming herself. These tumultuous setbacks batter Avar's confidence and focus, making it difficult for her to truly hear the Force. She and Porter Engle capture the Nihil ship *Cacophony* and find a way to pass through the Stormwall around the Occlusion Zone. With this blow to the Nihil dealt, Avar's connection to the song of the Force begins to recover.

LODEN GREATSTORM
SPECIES Twi'lek
AFFILIATION Jedi

As master to Bell Zettifar, Loden teaches his Padawan lightsaber combat, Jedi philosophy, and how to save himself by using the Force to slow his fall from a great height. Loden is captured and tortured by Marchion Ro during the Great Disaster. He is lost to the Nameless' calcifying presence.

SSKEER
SPECIES Trandoshan
AFFILIATION Jedi

Sskeer trains his Padawan Keeve Trennis to be both fierce and compassionate, like he is. Sskeer loses an arm at the Battle of Kur. The Drengir infect him, causing him to battle against both the hive mind's influence and the dark side within him. In the end, Sskeer helps Keeve and Avar Kriss immobilize the Drengir Progenitor.

ELZAR MANN
SPECIES Human **AFFILIATION** Jedi

Jedi Master Elzar Mann helps the Republic track deadly debris from the *Legacy Run* disaster. Along with fellow Jedi Avar Kriss and Republic analyst Keven Tarr, Elzar engineers a network of hundreds of droids to predict where the debris will emerge from hyperspace. As the war against the Nihil pirates goes on, Elzar gives in to his anger and frustration, using the dark side to throw enormous floating platforms into the Nihil ships that attack the Republic Fair on Valo. Elzar trains with Jedi Wayseeker Orla Jareni and learns to flow with the Force without being overwhelmed. Elzar is on board the Starlight Beacon space station when the Nihil directly attack it. He fights back, both by rallying the station's droids and by using the Force to open jammed bay doors. He mistakenly kills Chancey Yarrow—a Nihil scientist who was trying to save the station. After the attack, Elzar is comforted by reuniting with his fellow Jedi, especially Avar Kriss. Elzar still feels emotional turmoil about Stellan Gios' death and guilt over Yarrow's murder.

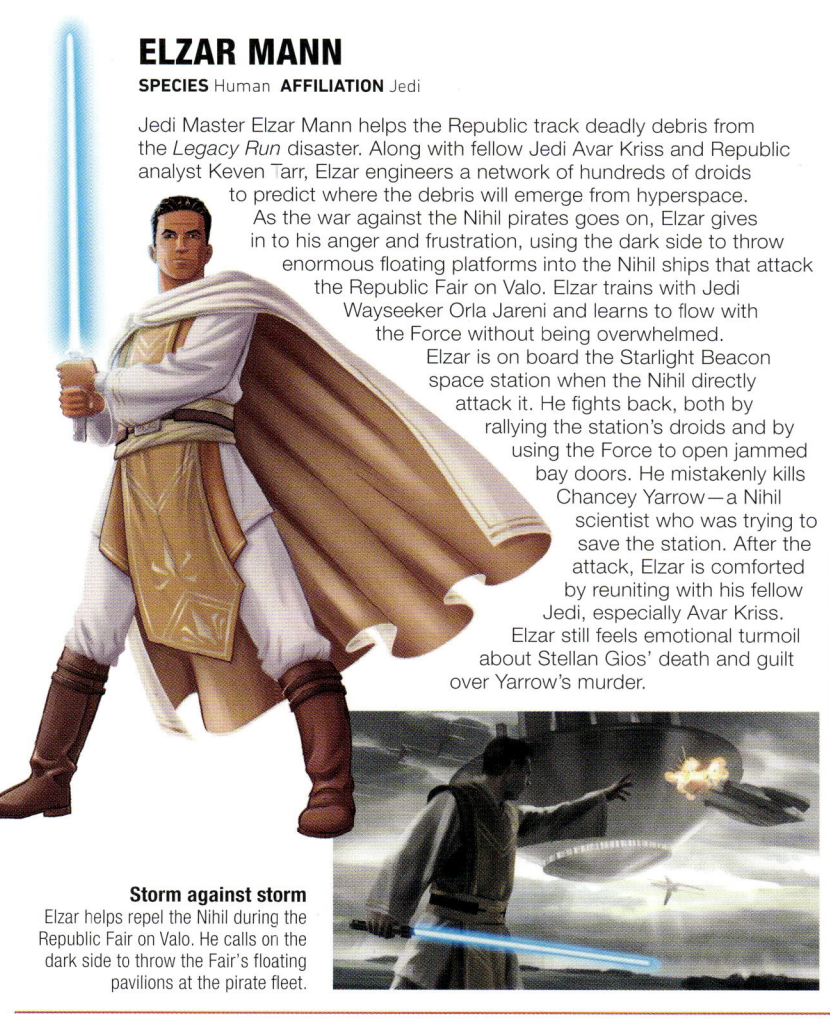

Storm against storm
Elzar helps repel the Nihil during the Republic Fair on Valo. He calls on the dark side to throw the Fair's floating pavilions at the pirate fleet.

VERNESTRA RWOH
SPECIES Mirialan
AFFILIATION Jedi

Precocious Vernestra Rwoh is one of the youngest Jedi Knights in history, and she becomes a master to Imri Cantaros while both are still teens. Vernestra helps Imri, Honesty Weft, Avon Starros, and J-6 fight the Nihil while stranded on Wevo. Her career as a Jedi goes on to span more than a century.

BURRYAGA
SPECIES Wookiee **HOMEWORLD** Kashyyyk
AFFILIATION Jedi

Burryaga is one of the first Jedi to realize that the Emergences are debris from a spaceship, and he's critical to rescuing survivors from them. He often works with his Jedi Master, Nib Assek, or Bell Zettifar. During the fall of Starlight Beacon, Burry lands in the Eiram ocean with the lower half of the station, but he survives.

BELL ZETTIFAR
SPECIES Human
AFFILIATION Jedi

Loden Greatstorm's Padawan Bell Zettifar is determined to find his master after Loden is captured by the Nihil. Bell is often accompanied by a charhound named Ember. A close friend of Burryaga, Bell leads the way to rescue him after Burry is presumed lost with Starlight Beacon.

TEREC AND CERET
SPECIES Kotabi **HOMEWORLD** Sagamore
AFFILIATION Jedi

As bond-twins, Terec and Ceret share a deep connection in the Force. Ceret is captured and infected by the Drengir on Sedri Minor. The twins are reunited in the subsequent battle against the Hutts, in which Terec rescues Ceret from a rampaging rancor. Both also clash against the Nameless.

LULA TALISOLA
SPECIES Human
AFFILIATION Jedi

Lula Talisola trains as a Jedi with the close-knit *Star Hopper* crew, including Masters Yoda, Torban Buck, and Kantam Sy, as well as Padawans Qort and Farzala Tarabal. She invites Zeen Mrala to join the Jedi, and the two later confess their love for each other. Lula decides not to become a Jedi Knight, instead focusing on figuring out her next step with Zeen.

LILY TORA-ASI
SPECIES Human
AFFILIATION Jedi

Lily Tora-Asi is Arkoff's Padawan and later becomes master to Keerin Fionn. She lives at the Jedi temple on Banchii and negotiates peace between Republic settlers and the Banchiians. She fights the Nihil and discovers that, although lightsabers are useless against the Drengir, fire is not.

REATH SILAS
SPECIES Human **HOMEWORLD** Coruscant
AFFILIATION Jedi

While a Padawan, Reath Silas narrowly survives capture by the Drengir on the Amaxine station. With his master Cohmac Vitus, Vernestra Rwoh, and Imri Cantaros, he repels the Nihil on Tiikae and destroys the gravity well projector Gravity's Heart. He also helps foil a Nihil plot on Corellia.

RAM JOMARAM
SPECIES Human **HOMEWORLD** Valo
AFFILIATION Jedi

Ram Jomaram feels most in touch with the Force when he's repairing something. Along with the Bonbraks, he fights both the Nihil and the Drengir in an effort to get Valo's Crashpoint Tower comms array up and running to call for Republic aid. He often travels with Zeen Mrala and Lula Talisola.

ESTALA MARU
SPECIES Kessurian
AFFILIATION Jedi

Estala Maru and his astromech KC-78 handle operations for Starlight Beacon. With Avar Kriss and Republic Controller Rodor Keen, he solves an assassination plot on the space station. Estala provides oversight when Avar discovers a Hutt operation on Sedri Minor. As Starlight Beacon falls, Estala holds it together with the Force long enough for others to escape, but he loses his life.

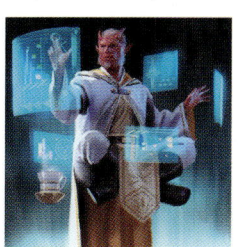

TORBAN BUCK
SPECIES Chagrian
AFFILIATION Togruta

Torban "Buckets of Blood" Buck is a Jedi healer. He teaches a cohort of Padawans aboard the ship *Star Hopper*, which includes Lula Talisola and her friend, Zeen Mrala. Torban helps the kids evacuate Starlight Beacon during its destruction, and he confronts the Nameless alongside Sian Holt and Emerick Caphtor.

COHMAC VITUS
SPECIES Human
AFFILIATION Jedi

Cohmac Vitus and his childhood friend Orla Jareni are among the Jedi stranded on the Amaxine station, menaced by both Drengir and the Nihil. Cohmac is deeply hurt when Dez Rydan goes missing. Feelings of grief and anger continue to plague him as he investigates a Nihil plot on Corellia. He later leaves the Jedi Order.

EMERICK CAPHTOR
SPECIES Human
AFFILIATION Jedi

As a Jedi youngling, Emerick Caphtor grows up alongside Stellan Gios, often hearing the lullaby about the mysterious Shrii-Ka-Rai. Decades later, he works with private eye Sian Holt to find out what killed Jedi Master Loden Greatstorm. Emerick overcomes his fear and confronts a Nameless during the fall of the Starlight Beacon space station.

CHARACTERS AND CREATURES

MARCHION RO
SPECIES Evereni **AFFILIATION** Nihil

As Eye of the Nihil, Marchion Ro is a pirate king who seeks loot and power for both himself and his crews. He commands the flagship *Gaze Electric* and holds secret hyperspace routes and the command rod for the deadly Great Leveler monster. Marchion orders the Nihil to sabotage the *Legacy Run*, causing the Great Disaster. He's haunted by the voice of his father, Asgar. As well as fighting against the Jedi, Marchion also has to contend with infighting between his lieutenants, especially Lourna Dee and Pan Eyta. He leads the attack on the Republic Fair and the creation of the Nihil Occlusion Zone. Thereafter, he rules the Occlusion Zone and oversees the Stormwall from a fortress on Hetzal.

LOURNA DEE
SPECIES Twi'lek **HOMEWORLD** Aaloth
AFFILIATION Nihil

Adaptable and ruthless, Lourna Dee rises to the rank of Tempest Runner in the Nihil. She captures the Jedi Loden Greatstorm and leads the attack on the Republic Fair. She battles Avar Kriss and nearly loses her life, but the Jedi capture her instead. During the fall of Starlight Beacon, Lourna steals the Jedi flagship *Ataraxia* and becomes a mercenary, serving the Hutt Skarabda the Wise. As the Jedi, the Hutts, and the Nihil clash in Skarabda's fortress, Jedi Keeve Trennis reveals to Skarabda that Lourna killed her sister, Myarga. Beset on all sides, Lourna is forced into a reluctant alliance with Keeve.

PAN EYTA
SPECIES Dowutin **HOMEWORLD** Dowut
AFFILIATION Nihil

As one of Marchion Ro's three Tempest Runners, Pan Eyta leads Nihil raiders. He both allies with and competes against Lourna Dee, Kassav Milliko, and Marchion. Pan attacks the Republic Fair and is driven away by the Togruta fleet. In the end, Lourna kills him.

KRIX KAMERAT
SPECIES Human **HOMEWORLD** Trymant IV
AFFILIATION Elders of the Path, Nihil

Elders of the Path member Krix Kamerat is shocked when his childhood friend Zeen Mrala shows her sensitivity to the Force, which goes against the Path's teachings. He joins the Nihil to oppose her and gains an audience with Marchion Ro himself. He fights against the Republic on Dol'har Hyde and Takodana.

GHIRRA STARROS
SPECIES Human **HOMEWORLD** Hosnian Prime
AFFILIATION Nihil

Republic senator Ghirra Starros feeds sensitive information to the Nihil, who she has secretly allied with. She turns a blind eye as the Nihil destroy Starlight Beacon's comms buoys, leaving it open to attack. Within the Nihil Occlusion Zone, Ghirra runs operations for the occupied planets, but clashes with her partner and Nihil leader, Marchion Ro. Ghirra tries to get the Republic to recognize Nihil territory as a sovereign state.

ABEDIAH VIESS
SPECIES Mirialan
AFFILIATION Mercenary army, Nihil

The beskar-armored mercenary General Abediah Viess duels Porter Engle during the siege of Firevale. She argues with Field Marshal Tozen, who hired her, because he wants to keep the city intact, but Viess is willing to destroy it. Viess betrays Tozen and attacks the city but retreats in the face of superior numbers. Decades later, Viess joins the Nihil.

DRENGIR
SPECIES Drengir **HOMEWORLD** Mulita
AFFILIATION Drengir

The Drengir are sentient plants controlled by the Progenitor of their root-mind and are determined to consume anything in their path. The Sith trap a population of Drengir on the Amaxine station, but once freed from that prison, the plants try to colonize the galaxy. The Drengir prove formidable foes against Jedi such as Avar Kriss, Lily Tora-Asi, Reath Silas, and Dez Rydan. The Progenitor tries to use Avar's Force connections to infiltrate other Jedi minds. Avar and Keeve Trennis root out the Progenitor on Mulita and seal her away, silencing the Drengir in their era.

THE NAMELESS
SPECIES Nameless **HOMEWORLD** Planet X
AFFILIATION Path of the Open Hand, Nihil

The Nameless are large predators that seem to feed on the Force. They originate on the mysterious Planet X, which brims with both dark and light side energy. The Mother of the Path of the Open Hand uses the creatures as tools in her quest for revenge against the Jedi. At the Battle of Dalna, a Nameless shocks Azlin Rell so badly that he becomes consumed with thoughts of the creatures, the desire to find out what they are, and the visions they give him.

Marchion Ro uses centuries-old Ro family knowledge to rediscover the Nameless known as the Great Leveler.

AZLIN RELL
SPECIES Human
AFFILIATION Jedi

A dutiful Jedi Knight, Azlin Rell is attacked by the Nameless and thrown into a restless sleep full of visions. His exposure to the Nameless and his later research into the dark side grant him an extraordinarily long life. Although he doesn't turn fully to the dark side, he's no longer a Jedi. In the course of his obsessive studies, Azlin replaces his eyes with cybernetic lenses. He destroys a city on the planet Travyx Prime in order to erase any trail to the Nameless' homeworld.

LINA SOH
SPECIES Human **HOMEWORLD** Daghee
AFFILIATION Republic

Lina Soh's vision of the Republic leads to many projects referred to as her Great Works, including the Starlight Beacon and Republic Fair. Lina has a son, Kitrep, and is often accompanied by her two targons. During Lina's term of office, the Nihil attack, prompting her to close down some hyperspace lanes and mobilize Republic Defense Coalition forces. Lina often disagrees with Senator Tia Toon. During the attack on the Republic Fair, she pilots an experimental walker against the Nihil and is badly injured in a crash. After the destruction of Starlight Beacon, she moves a Republic defense fleet to the Outer Rim.

TY YORRICK
SPECIES Tholothian
AFFILIATION Jedi

Ty Yorrick is a Force-attuned monster hunter. She discovers that the gretalax creature attacking a settlement on the planet Loreth is actually two symbiotic beings who are acting aggressively because they have been split from each other. She fights against both the Nihil and the Drengir, allying with Jedi such as Elzar Mann.

ZEEN MRALA
SPECIES Mikkian **HOMEWORLD** Trymant IV
AFFILIATION Elders of the Path

Zeen Mrala grows up among the Elders of the Path cult along with her friend Krix Kamerat. She leaves the cult to learn from the Jedi, alongside Lula Talisola. Zeen becomes close with Lula, Farzala Tarabal, Qort, and others as they fight against the Nihil and enjoy life on Starlight Beacon.

AVON STARROS
SPECIES Human
AFFILIATION Republic

Young inventor Avon Starros is the daughter of a senator. Along with Imri Cantaros, Honesty Weft, and Vernestra Rwoh, she's stranded on the planet Wevo. She can be opportunistic, such as when she steals Imri's broken lightsaber. Ultimately, Avon is a force for good and opposes the Nihil, especially the scientist Dr. Mkampa.

SIAN HOLT
SPECIES Human
AFFILIATION Republic

Private investigator Sian Holt helps Jedi Emerick Caphtor hunt down the deadly weapons broker Arathab Fel. When Caphtor is incapacitated by the Nameless, she takes up his lightsaber. Holt's investigation helps the Jedi piece together the fact that the Nameless are responsible for Loden Greatstorm's death.

MYARGA THE MERCILESS
SPECIES Hutt
AFFILIATION Hutts

Myarga the Merciless has a deal with the farmers of Sedri Minor. She buys barley from corrupt settler Kalo Sulman and comes to collect while Avar Kriss is on the planet investigating the Drengir. Myarga reluctantly allies with Avar Kriss to fight off the Drengir, and eventually she's killed by Lourna Dee.

AFFIE HOLLOW
SPECIES Human
AFFILIATION The *Vessel*

Adventurous space captain Affie Hollow works alongside her crewmates Leox Gyasi and Geode. Affie discovers her adoptive mother, Byne Guild leader Scover Byne, has been using underhanded tactics and indentured workers so she turns Scover over to the Republic. Affie pilots the *Vessel* out of the collapsing Starlight Beacon during the evacuation.

SYLVESTRI YARROW
SPECIES Human
AFFILIATION Republic

Sylvestri Yarrow is a pilot for the Byne Guild until she discovers that her mother, Chancey Yarrow, is working with the Nihil. Sylvestri often works with her copilot Neeto Janajana and the droid M-227. She disables the Nihil gravity well projector Gravity's Heart along with Jedi Reath Silas and Imri Cantaros.

JORDANNA SPARKBURN
SPECIES Human **HOMEWORLD** Tiikae
AFFILIATION San Tekka family

Jordanna Sparkburn and her vollka, Remy, patrol the deserts of Tiikae, keeping Zygerrian and Nihil raiders from preying on the populace. She rescues her former girlfriend, pilot Sylvestri Yarrow, from the Nihil and enters an uneasy alliance with the Jedi Vernestra Rwoh, Reath Silas, and Imri Cantaros.

BARON BOOLAN
SPECIES Ithorian
AFFILIATION Nihil

Baron Boolan is raised in the Path of the Open Hand and busted out of prison by the Nihil. Head of the Nihil's Ministry of Advancement, Boolan performs horrific experiments to create Force-using patchwork monsters known as Children of the Storm. He passes his research on the Nameless on to his protégé, Niv Drendow Apruk.

MELIS SHRYKE
SPECIES Human **HOMEWORLD** Bantoo
AFFILIATION Nihil

Melis Shryke is heir to a noble fortune before the Nihil invade her city. She joins the pirates and commands the ship *Cacophony*. Shryke admires General Viess but then challenges her power. Shryke is willing to destroy her own ship to stop the Jedi getting their hands on it.

NIV DRENDOW APRUK
SPECIES Umbaran
AFFILIATION Nihil

As Baron Boolan's apprentice, Niv Drendow Apruk has access to his captive Nameless and the means to control them. He's accompanied by a captive-bred Nameless called Deblindrix. Niv Drendow travels to the wreckage of the Republic research ship *Innovator* under Lake Lonisa on Valo.

NASH DURANGO
SPECIES Human **HOMEWORLD** Tenoo **AFFILIATION** Durango Shuttle Service

Nash Durango learns to be a pilot at a young age. She can fly a ship through dangerous asteroid fields, build her own speeder, and repair vehicles. In her signature move, the throttle buster, Nash builds up speed in a circle, then stalls while vertical in the air to let her ship free-fall. Often accompanied by her droid companion RJ-83, Nash captains both the ship *Crimson Firehawk*, of the Durango Shuttle Service, and the racing skiff *Crimson Bolt*.

Nash is tempted to ask her Jedi friends Kai Brightstar, Lys Solay, and Nubs to use the Force for her in a skiff race against her rival, Raena Zess. Instead, Nash and Raena work together to drag both of their skiffs out of the mud and Nash uses a geyser to blast her ahead of her rival and win the race.

Nash organizes a concert at the Jedi temple to thank the Jedi for everything they've done for Kublop Springs. Later, she's nervous about transporting Princess Inaya but eventually becomes comfortable with the princess and even lets Inaya pilot the *Crimson Firehawk*.

"You need me to fly in to help out? Your trusty pilot is ready."
NASH DURANGO

GAVI
SPECIES Human
AFFILIATION Jedi

Gavi grows up at the Valo Jedi temple alongside Jedi Knight Ram Jomaram, fellow younglings Tep Tep and Kildo, and Nihil recruit Driggit Parse. He dresses up as a Scarlet Skull assassin to fight the Nihil, and he explores the crashed Republic ship *Innovator* to recover the medical supplies stored inside.

NASH'S MOMS
SPECIES Human
AFFILIATION Durango Shuttle Service

Wives Kryys Durango and Ceeli (also known as "Mom" and "Mama") are proud of their daughter, Nash Durango. They attend the Kublop Classic skiff race and cheer for her. They own the Durango Shuttle Service. Mom is a mechanic and helps Nash build a new speeder.

CHARACTERS AND CREATURES

KAI BRIGHTSTAR
SPECIES Human **HOMEWORLD** Hosnian Prime **AFFILIATION** Jedi

Kai Brightstar has the potential to be a great leader and Jedi Knight. Aged eight, he arrives at the Jedi temple on Tenoo to train under Master Zia Zanna during the High Republic era. Positive and full of energy, he is pals with fellow younglings Lys Solay and Nubs. A loyal friend, Kai chooses to save Nubs from falling, even though it means he loses his training lightsaber. He is an eager student who approaches his lessons with gusto and is bursting with facts about Jedi lore that he loves to share. Kai is always ready for new experiences and adventure, but his enthusiasm and overconfidence can get away from him—and he inadvertently ends up causing trouble, such as when he darts his Jedi Vector into an asteroid field without telling anyone where he is going. Kai always looks on the bright side and wants to see the best in people, but he struggles to trust Ace Kallisto, who is an old friend to Master Zia but also a thief. However, Kai learns that, although it is wrong for Ace to steal, people can change their ways.

An age-old tradition
It is almost a rite of passage for Jedi to improve their lightsaber skills using a training remote. Kai is a determined youngling who has attracted the attention of Grand Master Yoda himself.

LYS SOLAY
SPECIES Pantoran **HOMEWORLD** Pantora **AFFILIATION** Jedi

Lys Solay is a Pantoran Jedi youngling at the temple on Tenoo with a great affinity for creatures. She makes friends with a gargantua—a huge primatelike creature that is usually very shy—and she is skilled at riding snow-dwelling wellagrins. She calms one who is stuck in thorns and figures out that another is hungry for a berry. But her love of animals can distract her: one day she is so absorbed by the sight of a rare bifflefly insect that she almost doesn't eat before a class trip.

Lys is quick-witted and observant in both her studies and adventures. She finds a trail of oil that holds a much-needed clue to the mystery of who stole from the junk dealer Marlaa Jinara. Easily disheartened, Lys feels like she has failed when the youngling Jam goes missing. But she is a clever problem solver and realizes that if she plays her Andraven flute, Jam will hear. Lys also comes up with the idea of catching a missing kibbin by baiting a trap with the channelfish it likes to eat.

A whole new species
On one adventure Lys joins members of the Galactic Society of Creature Enthusiasts and discovers a species that was previously unknown to the Jedi Order. Lys takes care to reunite this young specimen with its mother.

NUBS
SPECIES Pooba **HOMEWORLD** Myllnaab **AFFILIATION** Jedi

Nubs trains to be a Jedi alongside Kai Brightstar and Lys Solay. As a Pooba, he is very strong and, although he typically speaks Poobian, he and his friends have no problem with understanding each other.

Enthusiastic and optimistic, Nubs sometimes bursts into song with happiness. He can tap into his serenity to meditate and use the Force. Nubs has a love of nature and plants and often meditates by his favorite Tenoo tree. When he is interrupted by Raxlo trying to harvest the tree's sap, Nubs' trademark joviality gives way to his more fiery side. He rallies his friends and together they stop Raxlo from destabilizing the tree.

Nubs will do anything to protect nature, but his fascination with plants leads to trouble when he accidentally brings a fast-growing grumble vine to Tenoo, and the plant almost destroys the Jedi temple with its powerful runners. However, Nubs notices that the grumble vine stops expanding in the shade, and he remembers his teacher saying that the plant doesn't like sunlight. He dodges through the grasping vines to cover the center of the plant with a cloth, and the temple is saved.

Custom robes
As with many other Jedi younglings, Nubs' robes have been tailored to suit his Pooba anatomy.

RJ-83
TYPE RJ unit **AFFILIATION** Durango Shuttle Service

Nash Durango's companion RJ-83 is a droid whose legs and body can retract up into his dome-shaped head. He often keeps an eye on the *Crimson Firehawk* when Nash and her Jedi friends go on missions. RJ-83 has many tasks on the ship, including informing Nash when it has come out of hyperspace and helping to unload cargo. RJ-83 swings on a grappling hook to retrieve Hap's supplies when Taborr attempts to flee with the stolen goods. He distracts Raxlo's assistant, RC-99, by telling a story so the kids can sneak into Raxlo's harvester. RJ-83 admires Kit, the droid DJ in the local band the Ku-Bops.

ZIA ZALDOR ZANNA
SPECIES Human **HOMEWORLD** Denon **AFFILIATION** Jedi

Master Zia Zaldor Zanna mentors the Jedi younglings at the Tenoo temple, including Kai Brightstar, Lys Solay, and Nubs. Gentle and patient with the younglings, she encourages them to focus, use the Force, and rely on each other. Zia sends them on a variety of missions, from learning to fly Jedi Vector starfighters to helping wellagrin creatures migrate. As a child, Zia fights against the young pirate Ace Kallisto. As they grow older, Zia learns that Ace isn't all bad, and she gains some sympathy for the pirate. This leads Zia to hold a lifelong belief that people who do bad things can later choose to do good.

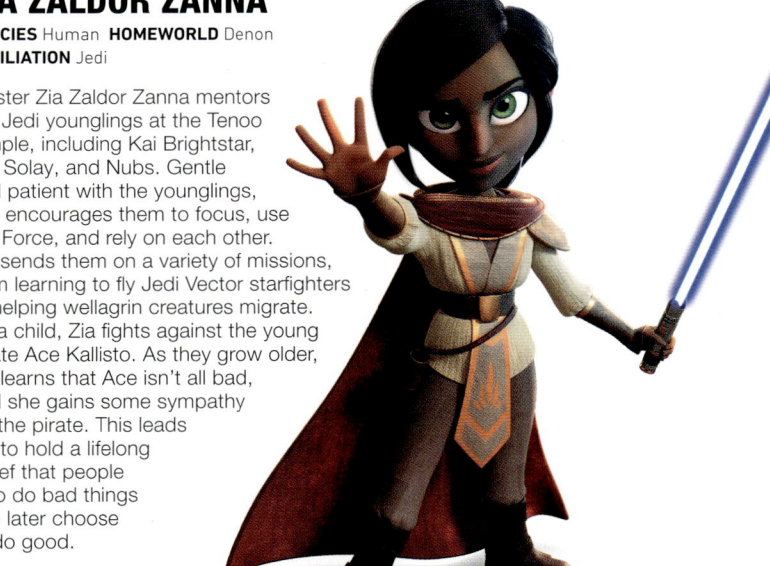

TABORR VAL DORN
SPECIES Human **HOMEWORLD** Vuundalla
AFFILIATION Taborr's pirates

Taborr Val Dorn, whose real identity is Cyrus Vuundir, the prince of Vuundalla, is a young pirate in command of his own ship and two lackeys, EB-3 and Pord. He often steals loot in order to sell it and impress the older pirates at Yarrum Tower. He often clashes with Kai Brightstar, Lys Solay, Nubs, and Nash Durango, but his electro-staff lets him hold his ground against Kai and his training lightsaber. Taborr tries to steal Tenoo tree wood that is on a train, but he ends up becoming a reluctant ally to Kai when the two are trapped together in the train car.

DEE
AFFILIATION Jedi

Dee works at the Jedi temple on Tenoo, often taking care of it while Master Zia is away. When Kai's attempt to program droids to clean the temple goes awry, Dee calls to Zia and Yoda for help. Dee takes the younglings on field trips, including to the lava fields of Tiss'ell and to a class on plant care.

GEDONIAN GROUND WEEVIL
HOMEWORLD Tenoo

The Gedonian ground weevil is one of Lys Solay's favorite creatures. Small and covered with fur, it has large ears that help it listen for predators in the forests of Tenoo. Of all the entries in SF-R3's *Galactic Creature Guide*, Lys likes the entry on the Gedonian ground weevil the best.

RAENA ZESS
SPECIES Human **HOMEWORLD** Tenoo
AFFILIATION Zess family

Raena Zess is Nash Durango's rival in the Kublop Classic skiff race. Raena, Nash, and Nash's Jedi friends get their skiffs stuck in mud during the race. Raena thinks the Jedi cheated by using the Force, which encourages Raena to cheat. After learning that the Jedi aren't using their abilities, she helps tow both skiffs free.

OG-LC
TYPE Pilot droid
AFFILIATION Hyperspace prospectors

OG-LC is an adventurer who explores the galaxy in his ship, *Star Seeker*. When two asteroids collide with his ship, he is left stranded. With encouragement from Kai Brightstar, Lys Solay, Nubs, and Nash Durango, OG-LC escapes and faces his fear by flying through the asteroid field again. OG-LC takes the Jedi younglings with him to the mysterious planet Tharnaka to find the Tharnakan Story Stone, which is a relic of a people who disappeared. He wants to take the stone back to the Jedi temple on Tenoo so it can be studied and protected, but then he's amazed to find a Tharnakan, Ishbul Ekwesh, still present on the planet. OG-LC works with Ishbul to return the artifact to the Tharnakans.

JG-1
MANUFACTURER Taborr
TYPE Droid **AFFILIATION** Marlaa Jinara's junkyard

JG-1, formerly known as the Junk Giant, is a large, strong droid built by Taborr out of pieces from Marlaa Jinara's junkyard. Under Taborr's orders, JG-1 fights Kai Brightstar and Lys Solay and traps them in a warehouse. Kai convinces JG-1 that she doesn't have to work for Taborr, and she returns to Marlaa and works in the junkyard.

MARLAA JINARA
SPECIES Chandra-Fan **HOMEWORLD** Chad
AFFILIATION Marlaa Jinara's junkyard

Marlaa Jinara owns a junkyard in Kublop Springs where she creates art out of discarded items. When Taborr Val Dorn steals from Marlaa to build a Junk Giant droid, Marlaa asks Kai Brightstar and Lys Solay for help. She also recruits Nubs to help her lift heavy items of scrap. Marlaa worries that if the pirates steal too much, she might not have enough junk to sell and will have to leave the home she loves. After Taborr is thwarted, Marlaa welcomes the Junk Giant back home and names her JG-1. Later, Marlaa helps the Jedi younglings find a missing kibbin in a pile of channelfish cans in her junkyard.

WELLAGRIN
HOMEWORLD Andraven

Wellagrins are domesticated creatures owned by the Andraven herders Gumar, Jam, and Varna. Wellagrins have pale blue, dappled skin; two sets of horns; whiskers; and large eyes. They use their four flippers and tail to slide along ice and snow, and they enjoy exploring and swimming in groups together. The wellagrins have exhausted the food in their pasture and are being moved to the orchard on the other side of the mountains. Gumar and Jam use their Andraven flutes to guide the herd. Gumar, Jam, Kai Brightstar, Lys Solay, and Nubs get caught in an avalanche during the wellagrin migration, and the creatures carry them to safety.

CHIGG
SPECIES Abednedo **HOMEWORLD** Abednedo
AFFILIATION Yarrum Tower pirates

Chigg is a pirate who bases his operations at Yarrum Tower. He's kind to Kai Brightstar, Lys Solay, Nash Durango, and Nubs when they come to Yarrum Tower. Chigg eats a stolen jellyfruit and points the younglings toward Taborr, who was the one who stole the fruit. On Nash's invitation, Chigg attends the Kublop Springs Jellyfruit Festival.

WEEBO
SPECIES Rodian
HOMEWORLD Tenoo

Weebo is a jellyfruit farmer who lives in Kublop Springs on Tenoo. She calls to Hap for help when Taborr steals her harvest, then describes the pirates to the Jedi younglings Kai Brightstar, Lys Solay, and Nubs. Weebo hires the bounty hunter Ansen Strung to look for her missing burowga creature.

BURROWBERRY BIRD
HOMEWORLD Yamradi **HABITAT** Underground

The burrowberry bird is native to the planet Yamradi. It is named by Lys Solay when she and her allies discover the bird on a mission. The large creature lives in an underground nest and sometimes sheds feathers. A burrowberry bird mistakes SF-R3 and CAM-E, who have come to Yamradi to find the mysterious Chylaroo, for the shiny berries it eats. Its babies hatch while SF-R3 and CAM are in the nest. The parent burrowberry bird catches Kai Brightstar and Nubs while they're covered in berries, but it really only eats berries and poses no danger to others.

CHARACTERS AND CREATURES

ZEPHER
SPECIES Mon Calamari **HOMEWORLD** Mon Cala
AFFILIATION Durango Shuttle Service

A starship mechanic on one of the moons of Tenoo, Zepher is friends with Master Zia and Nash's moms. Zepher taught Nash's moms everything they know about starship repair. Zepher provides Kai Brightstar, Lys Solay, and Nubs with three Jedi Vectors, which have been modified so younglings can pilot them.

RAXLO
SPECIES Gozzo
HOMEWORLD Drahgor III
AFFILIATION Raxlo Corporation

Raxlo is always trying to earn credits, usually by harvesting trees with his droid assistant, RC-99. But Raxlo clashes with Kai Brightstar, Lys Solay, and Nubs when he tries to cut down a forest of Federian trees. Raxlo also faces trouble when he tries to harvest sap from Nubs' favorite Tenoo tree.

ACE KALLISTO
SPECIES Human
HOMEWORLD Rex Strata

Ace Kallisto is a thief and Master Zia Zaldor Zanna's old friend. She steals Zia's shuttle, causing her, Zia, and Kai Brightstar to crash the vehicle into a cave. She uses the ship's lasers to scare off the stalaats blocking the entrance of the cave. Later, Ace travels to Tharnaka to retrieve the Story Stone for Ishbul Ekwesh, and she fights her treacherous crew member, Tooba Jinx.

FARAZ
SPECIES Houk **HOMEWORLD** Rex Strata

Faraz is a mechanic who knows Master Zia Zaldor Zanna well. Zia takes Kai Brightstar to Faraz's shop to trade for a spare cryo-spanner. Faraz remembers Zia as a youngling who once crashed one of his speeder bikes, so when he lends her a bike, he asks Zia to bring it back in one piece.

SKRIFFLE
HOMEWORLD Federian
SIZE 13 cm (5 in) long
HABITAT Forests

Skriffles are flying rodents that live in trees in the Federian forests. A group of skriffles flees to the tallest tree in the forest when Raxlo begins cutting down the creatures' habitat. One skriffle accompanies Kai Brightstar, Lys Solay, and Nubs when the Jedi younglings save the forest. This skriffle chirps at Raxlo, scaring him, and then calls the rest of the group. Together, the skriffles chew away the ropes Raxlo used to bind the younglings. Other skriffles swing on vines with Lys to tangle up Raxlo's harvester and pull the vehicle away from the trees. Once Raxlo leaves the planet, the skriffles return to the safety of the forest.

GARGANCHIE
SPECIES Gargantua

This large, strong, friendly primate is named Garganchie by Lys Solay. Slaygh and Braygh accidentally let the gargantua out while he is being transported to Sil Gohtta's Nature Preserve. The creature is frightened by loud noises and people, but because of his large size, he appears intimidating. He runs into the wilderness and hides in a cave. Lys Solay convinces Kai Brightstar and Nubs that Garganchie is friendly. Garganchie is frightened of a backfiring speeder and climbs a tower to escape. When Slaygh and Braygh fall off the tower, the gargantua dives after them and safely catches the pair.

ANSEN STRUNG
SPECIES Dowutin **HOMEWORLD** Dowut
AFFILIATION Bounty hunter

Ansen Strung is a bounty hunter hired by Raena Zess to find a missing pet kibbin. He worries that he will run out of time to find the kibbin by nightfall. He has almost given up the search when Kai Brightstar and Nubs encourage him to keep going. Ansen helps his sister, Senna, learn to be a bounty hunter.

SLAYGH AND BRAYGH
SPECIES Besalisk
HOMEWORLD Kundu Minor
AFFILIATION Kundu law enforcement

Slaygh (left) and Braygh (right) are sisters and marshals in a small town on Kundu. They accidentally let a gargantua named Garganchie out of his pen. Thinking he is a threat, the sisters try to save the town but end up scaring the gentle creature instead. After it saves them from falling, they realize their mistake. Lys Solay encourages Braygh to pet Garganchie's head, and Slaygh vows they will fix the damage caused by the creature. They become so fond of the gargantua that they cry when it leaves and ask to visit it at the animal reserve.

PRINCESS INAYA
SPECIES Human
HOMEWORLD Hazun

Princess Inaya is stranded on Tenoo when her ship breaks down during a trip to get a gift for her father. Inaya hires Nash Durango and her Jedi friends to bring her home. When the pirate Taborr boards Nash's ship to steal the gift, Inaya helps repel him and retrieve the gift.

THE KU-BOPS
SPECIES Various
HOMEWORLD Tenoo
AFFILIATION None

The Ku-Bops are a musical band in Kublop Springs. The group consists of the singer and electric vioddle player Metz, rumble bass player Bruff, and DJ K1-T. A big fan of the band, Nash Durango books them to play a Kublop Springs festival honoring the Jedi. Bruff delays the band's arrival out of irritation because Metz won't let him sing. During their argument, Bruff and Metz fall into a speeder and tumble out of control into the river. Nash and Lys Solay find Bruff, rescue him and Metz, and convince Metz to let Bruff sing.

MYCHO ZALA
SPECIES Zekodoan
HOMEWORLD Zeko IV
AFFILIATION Master Zia Zaldor Zanna

Mycho Zala is a prospector and Master Zia Zaldor Zanna's ally. Zia sends Kai Brightstar to deliver a new hyperdrive capacitor to Mycho after the prospector gets stuck on Tatooine. Mycho can speak Jawaese so he negotiates with a group of Jawas who encounter Kai, Nash Durango, and RJ-83.

DRAIVEN BOSH
SPECIES Moldwarp **HOMEWORLD** Lespectus
AFFILIATION None

Draiven Bosh steals the Kublop Springs Visitor's Day sculpture to add to his illicit art collection. Kai Brightstar, Lys Solay, and Nubs delay Draiven from leaving Tenoo long enough for Master Zia to arrive and help. The Jedi retrieve the statue, but Draiven declares that he will add it to his collection some day.

VARISH

SPECIES Malangsha **HOMEWORLD** Langsha-Raang **AFFILIATION** None

Varish teaches Jedi younglings about plant care on the planet Langsha-Raang. She gives Nubs a bag of seeds suited to the Jedi temple on Tenoo, which also accidentally contains grumble vine seeds. Nubs later uses Varish's lessons to stop the rampaging vine. Varish then takes the plant back into her care.

ORI

SPECIES Human **HOMEWORLD** Tenoo **AFFILIATION** Gangul gang

Ori is one of many kids who are forced to work for the Gangul speeder gang. When the Anguls lock some Jedi in a holding cell, Ori lets them out and rallies the townspeople of Aklyrr Bend against the gang. He chases the Janguls when they try to flee on stolen speeders and helps to liberate the town.

SENNA STRUNG

SPECIES Dowutin **HOMEWORLD** Dowut **AFFILIATION** None

Senna wants to be a bounty hunter like her brother, Ansen Strung. She seeks him out after he doesn't answer their usual check-in call. She's discouraged by her mistakes but overcomes her fear to help Ansen and his Jedi friends capture a missing burowga.

EB-3

MANUFACTURER Cybot Galactica **MODEL** SP-4 unit **TYPE** Pilot-engineer droid

A pirate, and one of Taborr's minions, EB-3 steals Princess Inaya's present from the *Crimson Firehawk* and takes it to Taborr's ship. He wields a vibroblade, which he throws at Lys Solay. The droid follows Taborr's orders to hack into an autonomous train to gain control, but the task takes longer than expected. EB-3 and Pord become trapped in a train car along with Nubs and Lys. EB-3 attacks Lys to get to the control panel. Later, EB-3 suggests that he and Pord should work with Lys and Nubs to escape the train car.

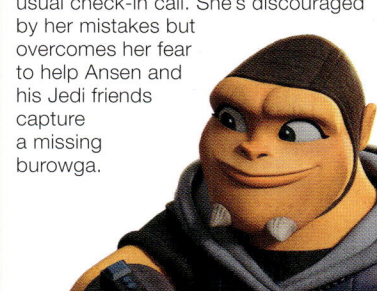

HAP

SPECIES Latero **HOMEWORLD** Tenoo **AFFILIATION** Hap's Sap Tap

As owner of the watering hole Hap's Sap Tap, Hap is a cornerstone of life in Kublop Springs. As well as running his business, Hap commentates the Kublop Classic skiff race. He calls Nash Durango for help when pirates rob his business. Hap orders special ingredients, including a number of unusual eggs, to make a stew when his best friend, Geeli, visits. He is nervous because he has never cooked with some of the items before. Hap keeps his kitchen very clean and organized, and he gets upset when Nubs knocks something over. He makes the stew for Geeli while Nubs and the other Jedi younglings try to catch the creatures that unexpectedly hatched out of the eggs in the shipment of special ingredients.

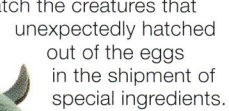

PORD

SPECIES Gamorrean **HOMEWORLD** Vuundalla **AFFILIATION** Taborr's gang

Along with EB-3, Pord is part of Taborr's pirate crew. As a loyal sidekick, she follows Taborr's orders on missions like stealing jellyfruit, opals, or Tenoo tree wood. The young Gamorrean is small, but her stocky frame is tough, and she's strong enough to pull two railway cars together. Full of bravado, Pord enjoys taunting Jedi younglings when the pirates have the upper hand, but she's quick to run away when things aren't going well. Pord wields an impressive vibro-lance, though her clumsiness often gets the better of her when she tries to use it in battle.

NAK-IL

SPECIES Togruta **AFFILIATION** Togruta

Nak-il is Ahsoka Tano's father and Pav-ti's partner. He rejoices alongside his fellow villagers when Ahsoka is born. When a raxshir steals Ahsoka away, Pav-ti searches with a group of locals to find her. Sometime later, he is separated from his daughter when she joins the Jedi.

PAV-TI

SPECIES Togruta **AFFILIATION** Togruta

Pav-ti, Ahsoka Tano's mother, lives with her partner Nak-il in a small village. She takes Ahsoka on a ritual hunt and kills a kybuck. Pav-ti is proficient with both blasters and knives, but she can't take down the large raxshir that briefly snatches Ahsoka away. Eventually, the Jedi remove Ahsoka from Pav-ti's family.

RAXSHIR

SIZE 4 m (12 ft) long **HABITAT** Forest

The raxshir is a large, sabertoothed feline that lives in the forests near the village where Ahsoka Tano is born. One raxshir attacks Ahsoka's mother, Pav-ti, knocking her blaster from her hands and stealing baby Ahsoka. It takes the child deeper into the forest. Influenced by Ahsoka's use of the Force, it returns her to her village.

DAGONET

SPECIES Human **HOMEWORLD** Wayyl **AFFILIATION** Republic

Dagonet is one of the longest-standing Republic senators, but he neglects Wayyl, the planet he represents. He and his guards open fire on the Jedi sent to investigate the kidnapping of his son. Jedi Master Dooku nearly kills Dagonet, but his son pleads on his behalf and convinces Dooku to stand down.

LARIK

SPECIES Human **HOMEWORLD** Raxus Secundus **AFFILIATION** Republic

The Republic senator for Raxus Secundus, Larik profits from offworld firms industrializing the planet. He calls in Jedi Master Katri, and later Dooku and Mace Windu, to investigate rebels on the planet. His guards kill Katri after Larik tells the Jedi the guards instigated the rebellion.

SEMAGE

SPECIES Human **HOMEWORLD** Raxus Secundus **AFFILIATION** Raxus Secundus

Semage serves as a guard for the corrupt Republic senator Larik. He and his fellow guard Hanel rebel against Larik and kill Jedi Master Katri, who was sent to help the senator. Master Dooku and Mace Windu fight against and jail Semage, but Dooku encourages him and his people to not lose heart.

ELDRA KAITIS

SPECIES Twi'lek **AFFILIATION** Jedi

Jedi Padawan Eldra Kaitis is captured by the criminal Xrexus Cartel. She and Darth Maul become unlikely allies when they are forced to fight together for survival against the cartel's bounty hunters. The pair later duel, and although Eldra nearly crushes him under falling rocks, Maul eventually defeats and kills her.

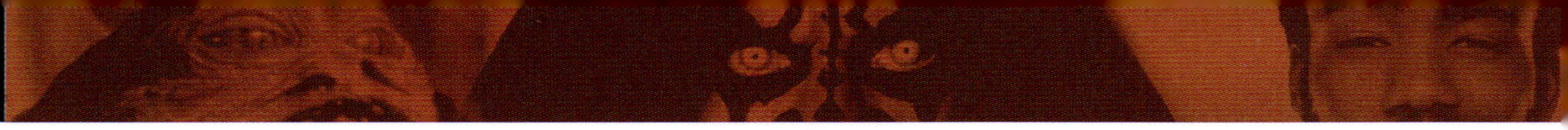

22 CHARACTERS AND CREATURES

OBI-WAN KENOBI
SPECIES Human **HOMEWORLD** Stewjon
AFFILIATION Jedi

A Jedi and veteran of the Clone Wars, Obi-Wan Kenobi's achievements include surviving duels with three Sith Lords, and training two generations of Skywalkers before he becomes one with the Force.

GALACTIC PEACEKEEPERS
As members of the Jedi Order, Jedi Master Qui-Gon Jinn and his Padawan, Obi-Wan, use their Force abilities and training in service to the Galactic Republic. Like most Jedi, Kenobi is identified within six months of his birth and begins his training immediately so that he can learn to control emotions of fear and anger at an early age. For the first few years, Obi-Wan and Qui-Gon struggle to understand each other. Kenobi travels to the planet Lenahra in the Unknown Regions for an unauthorized mission during this time. In addition to operations on Kashyyyk and the Codia system, Kenobi and Jinn spend a year on Mandalore protecting Duchess Satine Kryze. Kenobi considers leaving the Jedi after developing romantic feelings for Satine, but decides to remain. Later, in a mission to Pijal, Kenobi and Jinn overcome their differences to stop a war, becoming

Jedi Master and apprentice
Attacked on a Trade Federation battleship, Qui-Gon and Obi-Wan defend themselves.

good friends and capable partners. Their final mission together is to Naboo, where they help free the planet from the Trade Federation. However, Qui-Gon falls in battle to a Sith, who Obi-Wan then defeats. Qui-Gon's dying wish is that Anakin Skywalker is trained as a Jedi, so Obi-Wan—who has just been knighted—takes the young boy as his Padawan.

REPUBLIC ARMY GENERAL
Following ten years of training Anakin as his apprentice, Obi-Wan finds himself and his Padawan at the epicenter of the first battle of the Clone Wars. They are some of the few Jedi to survive the Battle of Geonosis, and both of them are promoted within the Order soon after. They are also conscripted as officers of the rapidly formed Grand Army of the Republic. As Jedi generals, Obi-Wan and Anakin Skywalker participate in battles against the Separatists and confront their armies or agents on many worlds—including Christophsis, Cato Neimoidia, Orto Plutonia, Felucia, Mandalore, Yerbana, and Utapau. Obi-Wan's diplomatic skills, specifically his reputation for preventing and stopping battles without using a single weapon, earn him the appellation "The Negotiator."

Heated duel
Anakin and Obi-Wan trade blows as the mining facility collapses around them on Mustafar.

FRIENDS BECOME ENEMIES
Obi-Wan loves Anakin like a brother. However, after he learns that Anakin has become the Sith Lord Darth Vader and is responsible for slaying Jedi, he tries to bring his former friend to justice. Vader is unwilling to surrender, and they duel with lightsabers on the volcanic planet Mustafar. Obi-Wan cuts down Vader and takes his lightsaber before leaving him seriously wounded on the shore of a lava river.

SECRET GUARDIAN
After the Clone Wars, Obi-Wan delivers the infant Luke Skywalker to Anakin's relatives Owen and Beru Lars on Tatooine. Obi-Wan assumes the name "Ben" Kenobi and lives as a hermit nearby while discreetly watching over Luke, protecting him from harm. After the Inquisitor Reva abducts Leia Organa, Kenobi leaves Tatooine to rescue her. On this mission, Kenobi learns of the Hidden Path and confronts Vader in his new cybernetic form. With Leia returned to her parents, Obi-Wan heads back to Tatooine where a ghostly Qui-Gon teaches Kenobi how to preserve his spirit after death like Jinn has. There, Obi-Wan later faces Maul, who has tracked him and still wants revenge, one final time.

JEDI MENTOR
Years later, Kenobi convinces Luke to join him on a mission with the Rebel Alliance to rescue Leia. To buy Luke, Leia, and the others time to escape, Kenobi duels Vader and is struck down. Kenobi, however, continues to offer Luke advice, and even appears to him as a spirit at various times. During the Battle of Exegol, Kenobi also offers Rey words of encouragement.

Anakin's lightsaber
When Obi-Wan gives Anakin's lightsaber to Luke, he believes that Luke may be the galaxy's only hope for defeating Darth Vader and the Emperor.

From hero to exile
Throughout his entire life, Obi-Wan honors the ways of the Jedi Order by using his abilities to help those in need. After the fall of the Republic, he assumes the persona of a hermit on Tatooine while secretly safeguarding Luke Skywalker and his family.

Dooku's Padawan
During a mission where his master loses control and chooses a violent path, Jinn quickly acts to diffuse the situation.

Duel in the desert
Qui-Gon and Darth Maul clash for the first time on the arid world of Tatooine, as the Sith apprentice seeks to capture Queen Padmé Amidala.

QUI-GON JINN
SPECIES Human **HOMEWORLD** Coruscant
AFFILIATION Jedi

Unlike many Jedi, Qui-Gon Jinn is willing to bend the rules to achieve his objectives. His maverick tendencies and belief in ancient Jedi prophecies often cause clashes with colleagues, especially those on the Council.

UNCONVENTIONAL JEDI MASTER
Qui-Gon trains as a Jedi under Dooku on Coruscant, where he befriends fellow Padawan Eno Cordova. Dooku and Qui-Gon go on many missions together, including one to the planet Wayyl to rescue the son of a Republic senator, during which Dooku makes a controversial choice.
Noble, patient, wise, and closely attuned to the Force, Qui-Gon is also a cunning warrior whose greatest strength is perhaps his empathy for other life-forms, including the most unfortunate. Once he becomes a Jedi Knight Qui-Gon takes his own Padawan, Obi-Wan Kenobi, who follows the Jedi Code more strictly than his master. While Jinn and Kenobi don't always agree, they learn to work well together. After a mission on Pijal, Qui-Gon chooses to stay as Obi-Wan's teacher rather than join the Jedi High Council.

EMPATHETIC NATURE
Soon after arriving on the swamplands of Naboo during the Trade Federation's blockade of the planet, Qui-Gon rescues the Gungan outcast Jar Jar Binks from a stampede of creatures fleeing from the battle droids' invading warships. Jar Jar swears a life-debt to Qui-Gon, whose compassionate nature is such that he takes the hapless Gungan under his protection, much to the consternation of Obi-Wan. With Jar Jar's help, the Jedi journey to the city of Otoh Gunga and obtain a submersible that allows them to proceed through Naboo's core to its capital, Theed.

ANCIENT PROPHECY
While escorting Queen Amidala from Naboo to Coruscant, Qui-Gon and his allies make an unscheduled stop on the Outer Rim world of Tatooine, where he discovers a young enslaved boy named Anakin Skywalker. Qui-Gon senses that Anakin is strong in the Force and soon has reason to believe that Anakin is the Chosen One of an ancient prophecy, and is destined to become a Jedi, destroy the Sith, and bring balance to the Force. Qui-Gon helps liberate Anakin from enslavement and resolves that Anakin will be trained as a Jedi on Coruscant.

THE DARK WARRIOR
On Tatooine, a black-cloaked warrior wielding a lightsaber attacks Qui-Gon. Jinn escapes with his allies and tells the Jedi Council and later his former master, Dooku, that he believes his opponent is a Sith Lord strong in the Jedi arts. At the Battle of Naboo, the dark warrior attacks again, mortally wounding Qui-Gon. With his dying breath, Qui-Gon makes Obi-Wan promise to train Anakin to become a Jedi.

FROM THE NETHERWORLD OF THE FORCE
More than a decade after Qui-Gon's death, Obi-Wan and Anakin travel to the mysterious location Mortis, where they are astonished to encounter a ghostly apparition of the slain Jedi. Qui-Gon's spirit tells Obi-Wan that the place is a conduit through which the Force flows and that it presents great dangers for the Chosen One. He tells Anakin to remember his training and trust in his instincts. During the Imperial era, Qui-Gon again appears to Obi-Wan during his exile on Tatooine because he believes that his former apprentice is ready to learn more about the Force.

> "Feel, don't think. Use your instincts."
> QUI-GON JINN

Jedi maverick
A highly trained Jedi Master, Qui-Gon Jinn is nonetheless an instinctive, restless soul who follows his own path in bringing balance to the Force.

Escape plan
Stranded on Tatooine, Anakin and Shmi welcome Qui-Gon, Jar Jar, and Padmé Naberrie to their home, where they plot to repair the latter's damaged ship.

Further teachings
On Tatooine, Jinn visits his former apprentice as a Force spirit, and he teaches Obi-Wan how to connect with the cosmic Force.

CHARACTERS AND CREATURES

DARTH SIDIOUS (SHEEV PALPATINE)

SPECIES Human **HOMEWORLD** Naboo
AFFILIATION Republic, Sith, Empire

A seemingly unassuming representative of the peaceful planet Naboo, Sheev Palpatine is in fact the Sith Lord Darth Sidious, who schemes to destroy the Jedi Order and rule the galaxy as Emperor.

SENATOR OF NABOO
When the Trade Federation invades Naboo, Queen Amidala seeks advice from Palpatine, who serves as Naboo's representative in the Galactic Senate. Palpatine confides that the Republic's leader, Supreme Chancellor Finis Valorum, has little power in the Senate and that bureaucrats are in charge. Palpatine adds that if Amidala wants the Trade Federation brought to justice, her best course of action is to call for a vote of no confidence in Valorum and then push for the election of a stronger leader. At Palpatine's urging, Amidala follows his advice, and Valorum is forced to leave office. To Amidala's surprise, the Senate elects Palpatine as supreme chancellor.

Meeting Anakin
After the Battle of Naboo, Palpatine meets the young pilot who helped defeat the Trade Federation's invasion force.

POLITICAL MANEUVERING
After the Senate learns that the Separatists are using Geonosian foundries to manufacture a massive droid army, the senators vote to grant emergency powers to Supreme Chancellor Palpatine. This vote enables Palpatine to immediately activate an army of clones to fight the Separatists, even though the Jedi Order is baffled by the clones' dubious origins. Palpatine professes his regret that the civil war requires him to take emergency powers, and claims that he looks forward to relinquishing those powers when the war is over.

During the ensuing Clone Wars, Palpatine assumes even more responsibilities; his many important duties include working with the Senate to pass laws to fund the war and to prevent bureaucracy from interfering with programs that the Jedi Council considers vital to the war effort.

SITH LORD REVEALED!
In the last days of the Clone Wars, Palpatine tells Anakin Skywalker, his ally and personal representative on the Jedi Council, a story about the Sith Lord Darth Plagueis, who used the Force to create life and prevent death. According to Palpatine, only the dark side of the Force offers a route to Plagueis' secrets. Palpatine later reveals that he himself is a Sith—Darth Sidious—and promises to teach Anakin his

Sith secrets
In his chambers, Palpatine draws Anakin into his confidence by revealing his true identity and suspicions about the Jedi's seditious activities.

dark-side knowledge if Anakin allies with him. As a Jedi, Anakin knows it is his duty to stop Palpatine. However, nightmarish visions of his beloved wife Padmé dying in childbirth convince him that only Palpatine's Sith powers can save her. Anakin agrees to become Sidious' apprentice, Darth Vader, and to crush the Jedi Order. Palpatine then declares himself Galactic Emperor.

EXPANSION OF POWER
Throughout his reign, Palpatine expands his dictatorship's reach across the galaxy by bringing more systems under Imperial control. He oversees the replacement of the clone army with conscripted stormtroopers, while also scapegoating Imperial leader Edmon Rampart, who carries out the destruction of the cloning facilities on Kamino. Shortly afterward, Palpatine appoints Doctor Royce Hemlock to investigate cloning in a facility on Wayland.

Nineteen years into his rule, Palpatine dissolves the Galactic Senate and places governing power in the hands of regional Moffs. While the Empire promises order and justice to far-flung worlds,

The Phantom Menace
Palpatine's true goals are known only to himself, but to achieve them he uses a terrifying combination of political intrigue, deception, ruthlessness, and raw dark-side power.

their citizens pay a heavy price as the Empire presses them into service and exploits their systems' resources. This Imperial expansion is necessary to successfully sustain myriad secret projects, including the Death Star battle station, a growing fleet of Super Star Destroyers, and the advanced weapons research program known as the Tarkin Initiative.

During this time, Sidious also reinforces a secret Sith bastion on Exegol, looking into ways to preserve his life after death. As a byproduct of his experiments, Palpatine creates a strandcast "son," who adopts the name Dathan, and as an adult runs away from his father. Dathan and his wife Miramir later leave their daughter, Rey, on Jakku to hide her from her grandfather.

THE EMPEROR'S DOWNFALL
Following challenges by the Rebel Alliance and Crimson Dawn, Palpatine meets his fate at the hands of his apprentice, Darth

Lightning assault
During the Battle of Exegol, Palpatine uses the Force to unleash a fearsome barrage of lightning, destroying many ships that are fighting in orbit.

Vader. In a bid to protect his son, Luke Skywalker, Vader hurls his master down the second Death Star's core to an apparent fiery death. The Emperor's defeat puts into motion his final secret plan known as the Contingency. Upon his death, select Imperial leaders are instructed to carry out Operation: Cinder, a plot devised by Palpatine to punish many of the worlds that he deemed had failed him. In the ensuing chaos, select Imperials are under instruction to flee to the Unknown Regions of the galaxy and rebuild—in the hope that they can return someday and rule once more.

PALPATINE RETURNS
But that isn't Palpatine's only contingency plan. He also clones bodies—including the one Kylo Ren knows as Supreme Leader Snoke—and lives on in a lab on Exegol. Palpatine eventually rises again with his Final Order fleet and Sith Eternal cultists. Seeking to use her exceptional strengths in the Force to prolong his life, Palpatine tries to turn his granddaughter, Rey, to the dark side. However, with the restored Ben Solo's help, she is able to resist and turns the Sith's own power against him, destroying Palpatine once and for all.

Aggressive negotiations
While Padmé would rather not resort to violence, she is prepared to defend herself if the need arises. Padmé survives the Battle of Geonosis, even though more than 100 Jedi do not.

PADMÉ AMIDALA

SPECIES Human **HOMEWORLD** Naboo
AFFILIATION Royal House of Naboo, Republic

A representative of her idyllic homeworld, and an idealist during a time of corruption and war, Padmé Amidala is determined to do what she can to right wrongs in the ailing Republic.

ROYAL SERVICE

Born to humble parents on Naboo, Padmé Naberrie dedicates herself to public service, joining the Apprentice Legislature at the age of eight. She is elected Queen of Naboo at the age of 14, adopting the formal name Queen Amidala, and her loyal staff includes five handmaidens. When the Trade Federation invades Naboo, Amidala and the most trusted of the group, Sabé, disguise themselves as each other.

While still undercover, Padmé makes an emergency detour to Tatooine and there meets the enslaved boy Anakin Skywalker, who joins her on her trip to Coruscant.

When she arrives on the planet, the Galactic Senate fails to help her, so she upends the Senate by triggering a new election for its leader. With no help forthcoming, Padmé returns to her home, where she allies with the native Gungans to free their planet. Padmé is so beloved by her people that some attempt to change Naboo's constitution so she can serve longer, but she refuses.

SENATORIAL LIFE

Padmé is surprised when her successor, Queen Réillata, asks her to serve as the senator of Naboo. While Padmé had planned to spend her time freeing enslaved people on Tatooine (including Anakin's mother, Shmi), she accepts the new role, and Sabé covertly assists her. Padmé excels as a senator, and her first major piece of legislation, the Mid Rim Cooperation Motion, saves millions on Bromlarch from starvation. Years later, Padmé is nearly assassinated on Coruscant, so she retreats in secret to Naboo with Anakin as her Jedi protector. When Anakin senses his mother is in danger they both travel to Tatooine, but they cannot save Shmi from death. They then head to Geonosis to help Obi-Wan Kenobi and survive the first battle of the Clone Wars. Having fallen in love during their reunion, Padmé and Anakin marry in secret. Sabé continues to serve as a decoy for Padmé, sometimes taking over her role in the Senate. However, Sabé is saddened to discover Padmé's secret marriage to Anakin and parts ways with her. Sabé continues working on Padmé's goal to free the enslaved people of Tatooine.

During the Clone Wars, the galaxy becomes a dangerous place for a loyalist senator, but Padmé journeys to many trouble spots—including Rodia, Mandalore, Batuu, and Scipio—in her efforts to use diplomacy to resolve problems. She tries to reconnect with her old friend Mina Bonteri—a former Republic senator who is now part of the Separatist Senate. They work together to achieve a peaceful solution to the Clone Wars. While their motion passes in the Separatist Senate, General Grievous attacks Coruscant's power supply as the Republic vote is taking place. The terrorist attack strikes fear into the Republic's senators and stops the motion from passing.

Retaking the palace
Padmé is trained for combat extensively by Captain Panaka. She puts her skills to use during the assault on the Royal Palace.

THE TWILIGHT OF THE REPUBLIC

When Anakin returns from the Outer Rim Sieges, Padmé reveals that she is pregnant. Padmé continues to balance her work as a senator, her secret marriage to a Jedi, and her advancing pregnancy. She is shocked when Palpatine uses the Jedi Council's attempt to arrest him as pretext to declare the founding of the Galactic Empire and to annihilate the whole Jedi Order. Padmé mourns the loss of the Republic, claiming that the formation of the Empire is the end of liberty in the galaxy. She travels to the planet Mustafar to confront Anakin, who is now Palpatine's Sith apprentice. He becomes enraged and nearly kills her. Obi-Wan defeats Anakin in a terrible duel, before rushing Padmé to a medical facility, where she gives birth to twins. Tragically, she dies afterward, leaving behind her children, who will go on to liberate the galaxy from the Empire and restore democracy.

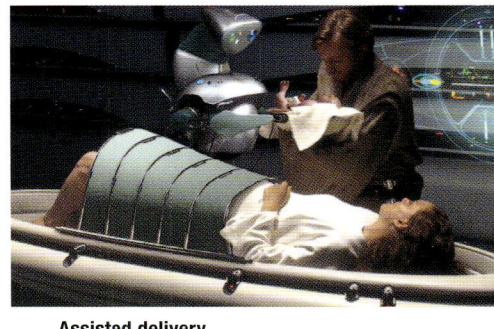

Assisted delivery
On Polis Massa, Obi-Wan watches a midwife droid deliver Padmé's twins.

Crafted couture
Queen Amidala's gown is covered with historic symbols that express the majesty of the free people of Naboo. Her elaborate gown also serves to protect her, as it is blaster resistant and can be easily shed if required. Much of her jewelry conceals useful, hidden gadgets.

KAADU

HOMEWORLD Naboo **SIZE** 2 m (7 ft) high
HABITAT Swamps

Kaadu are two-legged reptavians indigenous to Naboo. They are swift, agile creatures with sharp hearing and a keen sense of smell, and although primarily land-dwellers, they can also breathe underwater for extended periods. For generations, Gungans have used domesticated kaadu as steeds to travel through Naboo's swamps and forests, so much so that the Gungan Grand Army comes to rely on them as mounts for their patrols.

QUARSH PANAKA

SPECIES Human **HOMEWORLD** Naboo
AFFILIATION Royal Naboo Security Forces, Empire

The brave and resourceful Quarsh Panaka first sees action fighting pirates in his homeworld's space sector. He goes on to become the captain of Queen Amidala's Security Forces. Although he trained his people well, he knows that his world is vulnerable to a planetary assault and argues for stronger security measures, but his counsel is unheeded. After the Trade Federation's invasion begins, Panaka accompanies the queen to Coruscant so that she can submit an appeal to the Galactic Senate to bolster Naboo's defenses, and then participates in the battle to free Naboo. Panaka continues to serve Amidala throughout her reign, but their relationship becomes strained after they disagree once more over the necessary level of defenses for Naboo. He retires when Queen Amidala's sovereignty ends. After Governor Bibble steps down from his role, the Empire makes Panaka a Moff, and he quickly implements change on Naboo. Years later, he hosts Princess Leia Organa and suspects she is related to Padmé Amidala. Before he can convey his theory to Palpatine, he is assassinated by rebel extremist Saw Gerrera—who unwittingly helps keep Leia's parentage secret.

SIO BIBBLE

SPECIES Human **HOMEWORLD** Naboo
AFFILIATION Royal House of Naboo

Sio Bibble is a noble philosopher and member of the Naboo Royal Advisory Council, elected Governor of Naboo prior to Queen Amidala's reign. Bibble serves many successive monarchs, aiding them in their regal duties, and deals directly with regional representatives. He remains on Naboo during the Trade Federation's occupation of the planet while Queen Amidala travels to Coruscant to secure aid. Years later, he attends former Queen Amidala's funeral and retires shortly after.

NUTE GUNRAY

SPECIES Neimoidian **HOMEWORLD** Neimoidia
AFFILIATION Trade Federation, Separatist

Neimoidians are well known for their exceptional organizational and business skills, however Nute Gunray, Viceroy of the Trade Federation, is more unscrupulous and cutthroat than most. The assurances of his shadowy Sith benefactor, Darth Sidious, prompt Gunray to take the ambitious and blatantly illegal path to power as he oversees the blockade and subsequent invasion of Naboo. But Gunray's true, cowardly nature is revealed when Queen Amidala and her Naboo freedom fighters blast his droid protectors, reclaim their planet, and declare the Trade Federation's occupation is over. Owing to the resources of his organization, Gunray is found not guilty during the fourth Republic trial on the invasion of Naboo. During the Clone Wars, Nute Gunray continues to obey the Sith Lords. While hiding on the planet Mustafar, he is unprepared when Darth Vader arrives to kill him.

Separatist ally
When Count Dooku invites the Trade Federation to join the Separatists, Gunray insists that Dooku first disposes of Padmé Amidala, against whom he holds a personal grudge.

OOM-9

MODEL OOM command battle droid
MANUFACTURER Baktoid Combat Automata
AFFILIATION Trade Federation

Like all early B1 battle droids, OOM-9 is incapable of independent thinking, and receives instructions from a central source aboard a Trade Federation Droid Control Ship. However, OOM-9 was specially programmed to serve as a command droid for the Federation's invasion of Naboo, and to act as the primary contact for the Federation's leaders, the Neimoidians Nute Gunray and Rune Haako. On Naboo, OOM-9 directs droid ground troops and pilots to occupy settlements and destroy communication transmitters, preventing the planet's citizens from reporting the invasion or summoning help. OOM-9 leads the battle droids against Gungan warriors in the Battle of Naboo.

Leader in the field
OOM-9 signals Trade Federation Multi-Troop Transports and armored assault tanks to move into position as the Battle of Naboo commences.

Receiving orders
Communicating via hologram, the Trade Federation leaders direct OOM-9 during the invasion of Naboo.

JAR JAR BINKS

SPECIES Gungan **HOMEWORLD** Naboo
AFFILIATION Gungan Grand Army, Galactic Senate

Well-meaning and kind, Jar Jar Binks finds himself at the center of galactic events during the Republic's final years. Without even realizing it, the hapless Gungan is a key player in the rise of Darth Sidious.

HAPHAZARD HELPER
Banished from the underwater city Otoh Gunga after accidentally destroying Gungan leader Boss Nass' prized submersible, Jar Jar Binks is foraging for raw shellfish in the murky Naboo swampland when the Trade Federation's invasion force nearly crushes him. Fortunately, the Jedi Knight Qui-Gon Jinn saves Jar Jar, who immediately declares himself the rescuer's humble servant. The hapless Gungan guides Qui-Gon and his apprentice, Obi-Wan Kenobi, to Otoh Gunga, where they obtain a bongo submarine that allows them to proceed to the city of Theed. Once there, they warn Queen Amidala about the impending Trade Federation invasion.

After the Galactic Senate fails to help Amidala's people, she asks Jar Jar to contact his fellow Gungans. With Jar Jar's help, the Naboo and the Gungans forge an alliance to liberate their besieged world. Immediately prior to the ground battle against the Trade Federation's droid army, Boss Nass makes Jar Jar a general in the Gungan Grand Army. After the battle, Jar Jar continues to ascend in Gungan society, putting his awkward past as an outcast behind him.

POLITICAL MISSTEPS
Eventually elected as a senior representative for Naboo, Jar Jar serves alongside Padmé Amidala in the Galactic Senate. While his compassion speaks volumes for the quality of his character, his inherent gullibility and trusting nature are easily exploited by the less scrupulous in the field of politics. Although Jar Jar is opposed to the Military Creation Act, he unwittingly enables Supreme Chancellor Palpatine to conscript an army of clones to fight Separatist forces. Still, in the corrupt inner confines of the Senate, he stands as a rare example of a virtuous politician, interested only in the greater good of the Republic and his people.

DIPLOMATIC ENDEAVORS
During the Clone Wars, Jar Jar takes on an active role for the Republic, undertaking missions on Mimban, Toydaria, Rodia, and Florrum. He also helps stop a lethal virus from escaping a secret laboratory on Naboo. When the Separatists incite a civil war on Mon Cala, Jar Jar convinces the Gungans to send their army to help the Republic and joins the fight himself.

After relations between the Gungans and the humans on Naboo break down, Jar Jar, Padmé, and Anakin Skywalker return to the planet and stop the Separatist Gungan minister who is behind it. At the request of Queen Julia of Bardotta, Jar Jar, with Jedi Master Mace Windu, investigates the disappearance of the planet's Dagoyan masters. They rescue the queen when she is taken, preventing Mother Talzin from gaining even more power. At the end of the Clone Wars, Jar Jar remains a representative of Naboo and attends Padmé's funeral in Theed.

EXILED ONCE MORE
Years later, Jar Jar returns to Naboo and is banished once more by the Gungans for his role in the rise of Palpatine. Jar Jar now spends his days entertaining young refugees in Theed. While the children adore Jar Jar and affectionately call him the clown, the adults ignore him. Jar Jar meets a wounded individual named Mapo, whom he takes as his clown apprentice.

Reluctant guide
Jar Jar is hesitant to bring Obi-Wan and Qui-Gon to Otoh Gunga because he fears Boss Nass may still be angry with him for destroying Nass' property.

Bold proposal
During a Senate meeting, Jar Jar takes the initiative and proposes the motion granting emergency powers to Supreme Chancellor Palpatine, a move that has profound impact on the Galactic Republic.

Gungan culture
The native inhabitants of the planet Naboo, Gungans are an amphibious species with hardy lungs, who are capable of holding their breath for extended periods of time. As such, they are as comfortable in water as they are on land. While they have great reverence for nature and balance, making every effort not to overburden their native ecosystem, the Gungans are suspicious of outsiders and maintain a large standing militia, the Gungan Grand Army.

"Yousa guys bombad!" **JAR JAR BINKS**

CHARACTERS AND CREATURES

CAPTAIN TARPALS
SPECIES Gungan **HOMEWORLD** Naboo
AFFILIATION Gungan Grand Army

A kaadu patrol chief in Otoh Gunga, Captain Tarpals watches out for thieves and dangerous creatures that threaten the underwater city. He blames the accident-prone Jar Jar Binks for numerous altercations before Jar Jar becomes a hero, whom Tarpals fights alongside in the Battle of Naboo. During the Clone Wars, the courageous Tarpals subdues and helps capture General Grievous on Naboo, but at the cost of his own life.

SANDO AQUA MONSTER
SIZE 200 m (656 ft) long **HOMEWORLD** Naboo

A muscular creature with webbed hands and immense snapping jaws, the sando aqua monster is the largest predator in Naboo's oceans, and the only one able to bite through an opee sea killer's armored shell. The sando must constantly eat to maintain its enormous form, and easily devours entire schools of fish. Rarely seen by Gungan explorers and navigators, the sando is somehow capable of hiding in deep environments and is able to live for hundreds of years. During the Imperial era, Sabé summons a sando to kill Darth Vader. However, the sando is no match for Vader who dispatches it. Vader's droid ZED-6-7 surmises that, due to the species' rarity and slow life cycle, it is likely the sando will become extinct.

Killer instinct
The mysterious, gigantic, and always voracious sando aqua monster closes in for the kill *(above)*. Using its razor-sharp teeth, the sando easily dismembers a hapless opee sea killer that has strayed within its reach *(right)*.

BOSS NASS
SPECIES Gungan **HOMEWORLD** Naboo
AFFILIATION Gungan Rep Council, Gungan Grand Army

As the ruler of Otoh Gunga, Boss Rugor Nass chairs the Rep Council, which is responsible for governing Naboo's Gungan inhabitants. He dislikes Naboo's human population because he believes they view the Gungans as a primitive species. However, after the Trade Federation invades Naboo, and Queen Amidala asks Nass for help, he realizes that the Gungans and the Naboo must join forces to defend their world. Nass eventually steps down from his role, but he still attends Amidala's funeral in Theed.

OPEE SEA KILLER
AVERAGE SIZE 20 m (65.5 ft) long **HOMEWORLD** Naboo, Strokill Prime

A vicious underwater predator, the opee sea killer lurks inside caves on the ocean planets of Naboo and Strokill Prime. Using a long lure to attract potential prey, the opee employs a combination of swimming and jet propulsion to pursue its target. Snagging victims with its adhesive tongue, the creature then draws its captured meal into its deadly maw. As aggressive as they are persistent, opees are unafraid of larger predators. Even the most experienced Gungan navigators avoid routes inhabited by these creatures, as they know opees regard the bongo's passengers as irresistible treats.

> "Big gooberfish! Huge-o teeth!"
> **JAR JAR BINKS**

Tongue lashing
An opee sea killer's long, sticky tongue snares the Gungan bongo that carries Qui-Gon Jinn, Obi-Wan Kenobi, and Jar Jar Binks through the cap of Naboo. Fortunately, a larger fish unwittingly intervenes, and they escape intact.

COLO CLAW FISH

AVERAGE SIZE 40 m (131 ft) long
HOMEWORLD Naboo

Normally hidden in tunnels along Naboo's oceanic floor, the serpentine, spine-studded colo claw fish can lie still for hours waiting to capture its prey within the huge temporomandibular claws for which it is named. Before attacking, the colo emits a hydrosonic shriek to disorient its victim, which it stuns with its venomous fangs, distending its jaw so wide that it can swallow prey much larger than its own head. If the colo does not render its victim unconscious prior to swallowing, there is a big risk that the consumed creatures will attempt to chew their way out of its stomach. For the wealthy in the galaxy, colo flesh is a rare delicacy.

SABÉ

SPECIES Human **HOMEWORLD** Naboo
AFFILIATION Royal House of Naboo, Amidalans, Crimson Dawn, Empire

A highly trained and capable royal handmaiden, Sabé serves Queen Padmé Amidala, and is one of her most trusted friends. Sabé occasionally impersonates the queen to deceive Padmé's enemies, including during the Trade Federation's invasion of Naboo. Sabé and Padmé switch roles, successfully fooling the Neimoidians into believing that Sabé is the queen. When Padmé's reign ends and she becomes a senator, Sabé continues to serve her friend from the shadows. She frees 25 enslaved people on Tatooine, helping relocate some of them offworld, and she investigates who is trying to kill Padmé.

Sabé is distraught when Padmé dies and attends her funeral. Alongside her partner, Tonra, Sabé resolves to look into her death, becoming one of the founding members of the Amidalan rebel group. This path leads Sabé to join forces with Darth Vader on several missions, eventually figuring out his hidden identity as Anakin Skywalker. For a time, she also aligns herself with Crimson Dawn. Sabé comes close to succumbing to her dark desires of power and control, but ultimately resists the temptation, and is abandoned by Vader.

RIC OLIÉ

SPECIES Human **HOMEWORLD** Naboo
AFFILIATION Naboo Royal Security Forces, Naboo Space Fighter Corps, Amidalans

A veteran pilot in the Naboo Space Fighter Corps, Ric Olié can fly any craft in the Corps' fleet, and answers directly to Captain Panaka. It is his honor to captain Queen Amidala's royal starship, and soon after meeting nine-year-old Anakin Skywalker he shows the boy how to operate the starship's controls. During the Battle of Naboo, Olié pilots an N-1 starfighter, leading Bravo Squadron's assault on the Federation battleship. Following his former queen's death, Olié joins the Amidalans, a rebel group that wants revenge for Padmé death. Near Theed, Olié leads an Amidalan attack on Darth Vader, believing him to have caused Padmé's and Anakin's deaths. Little does Olié realize that he is facing Anakin in battle and he falls to Vader's blade.

EIRTAÉ

SPECIES Human **HOMEWORLD** Naboo
AFFILIATION Royal House of Naboo, Amidalans

Eirtaé is recruited by Captain Quarsh Panaka to serve as a royal handmaiden for Queen Amidala, becoming the handmaiden's de facto communications expert. After the Battle of Naboo, she moves to Otoh Gunga to pursue engineering and art, eventually inventing anti-grav technology that the handmaidens later use to escape the clutches of Darth Vader.

RABÉ

SPECIES Human **HOMEWORLD** Naboo
AFFILIATION Royal House of Naboo, Amidalans

Rabé is a loyal handmaiden for Padmé Amidala, arranging the Queen of Naboo's hair, and providing protection. She is also a lover and student of music. After Senator Amidala's death, she and the rest of the Amidalans pledge to kill Padmé's murderer.

SACHÉ

SPECIES Human **HOMEWORLD** Naboo
AFFILIATION Royal House of Naboo, Amidalans

The youngest of the handmaidens, Saché becomes a hero of the Battle of Naboo after being tortured by the Trade Federation. Scarred by this experience, Saché eventually enters Naboo politics. She is extremely loyal to the other handmaidens, especially her wife Yané, and their children.

SERGEANT TONRA

SPECIES Human **HOMEWORLD** Naboo
AFFILIATION Royal House of Naboo, Amidalans

Tonra first serves in the Royal Naboo Security Forces, fighting in the battle against the Trade Federation. He then works with Sabé to find Shmi Skywalker on Tatooine, and free as many enslaved people as possible. A member of the Amidalans, he is killed by Darth Vader and death troopers on Naboo.

CHARACTERS AND CREATURES

R2-D2
MANUFACTURER Industrial Automaton
TYPE R2 series astromech droid
AFFILIATION Republic, Rebel Alliance, Resistance

Always willing to help his friends, no matter the risk, R2-D2 has a close association with the protocol droid C-3PO, with whom he has participated in numerous historic battles.

BRAVE ASTROMECH
A versatile utility droid generally used for the maintenance and repair of starships and related technology, the astromech R2-D2 is equipped with a variety of tool-tipped appendages that are stowed in recessed compartments. As property of the Royal Security Forces of Naboo, R2-D2 is one of several droids who serve aboard the queen's Royal Starship. After the Trade Federation forces Padmé to flee Naboo and her ship has to thread its way through a blockade, R2-D2 is instrumental in helping Amidala and her Jedi allies escape. R2-D2 subsequently meets a young pilot, Anakin Skywalker, and inadvertently serves as Anakin's copilot during the Battle of Naboo.

SERVICE TO THE REPUBLIC
After Padmé Amidala's reign as queen ends, R2-D2 continues to serve her during her travels as a Republic senator. When an assassin attempts to kill Padmé on Coruscant, the Jedi Order assigns Anakin to be her bodyguard, with R2-D2 providing backup for him. Later, along with C-3PO, R2 is present for the secret wedding of Padmé and Anakin. During the Clone Wars, he serves as Skywalker's astromech support in Jedi starfighters. After Anakin's fall to the dark side and his subsequent duel with Obi-Wan Kenobi on Mustafar, R2 is present when Padmé gives birth to twins, Luke and Leia. Unlike C-3PO, R2-D2 is not subjected to a memory wipe: he remembers everything when the pair enter the service of Senator Bail Organa.

DETERMINED MESSENGER
Nearly two decades after the rise of the Empire, R2-D2 and C-3PO serve Princess Leia Organa of Alderaan, who is also an agent of the Rebellion. While attempting to deliver data about the Death Star to her allies, Leia's blockade runner is captured by Darth Vader. She hastily records a message and instructs R2-D2 to deliver it and its accompanying data to Obi-Wan Kenobi. Despite C-3PO's protests, the faithful astromech doggedly follows his orders and ultimately helps the rebels destroy the Death Star.

Fearless mechanic
Ignoring enemy laserfire, R2-D2 quickly repairs Queen Amidala's starship to save the queen and her allies.

SECRET AGENT
During the Galactic Civil War, R2 undertakes many missions for the Rebellion, even taking on a Star Destroyer single-handedly to rescue C-3PO, and aids Luke as he learns more about the Jedi. Because astromech units are among the most ubiquitous droids, they attract relatively little attention or suspicion at Imperial spaceports and criminal outposts. R2-D2 becomes extremely skilled at covertly insinuating himself into enemy territory in order to help his friends. In fact, he helps infiltrate Jabba the Hutt's palace during the Alliance's rescue of Han Solo.

LOYAL DROID
After the Galactic Civil War, R2-D2 accompanies Luke Skywalker on his quest to uncover secrets of the Force and train the next generation of Jedi. He joins Luke on a variety of missions, from the rescue of the Force-attuned child Grogu on Moff Gideon's ship to the galaxy-spanning search for Ochi of Bestoon. R2-D2 resides on Ossus, where he supports Master Skywalker with his new Jedi temple and the younglings in his care. When Grogu decides to end his training, the helpful droid pilots Luke's X-wing himself to take the child back to Din Djarin's side.

RETURN TO THE FIGHT
During the rise of the First Order, the astromech bears witness to the destruction of Luke's temple, following Ben Solo's fall to the dark side. Having lost hope, Skywalker goes into hiding and leaves R2-D2 behind with Leia Organa. Deeply affected by his master's disappearance, the droid enters low power mode for many years. He only returns to full operation upon realizing that he has the missing map data indicating Luke's location on Ahch-To. Upon being reunited with Skywalker, R2-D2 convinces Luke to reconnect with the Force. The faithful droid then returns to the Resistance with Rey and Chewbacca. Following the losses at Crait, R2-D2 joins a mission to Batuu and is later stationed on Ajan Kloss. He doesn't accompany Rey and her allies on the mission to learn more about Exegol, remaining by Leia's side at the Resistance base. When C-3PO returns from the adventure with his memories wiped, R2 helps his friend and restores them using a previous backup. The plucky astromech later serves as General Dameron's copilot during the Battle of Exegol, surviving to join in the ensuing celebrations.

Durable droid
Having survived countless battles and desperate situations, R2-D2 has developed a remarkably resilient attitude for a droid. He remains an endlessly reliable astromech and is never reluctant to put himself in danger to help his allies.

Secret plans
Princess Leia entrusts R2-D2 with the stolen plans for an Imperial superweapon, the Death Star battle station.

MAUL

SPECIES Zabrak **HOMEWORLD** Dathomir
AFFILIATION Sith, Nightbrothers, Crimson Dawn, Shadow Collective

Forged by Darth Sidious into a hate-fueled killing machine, Maul is the first known Sith to slay a Jedi in combat in more than 1,000 years, but is ultimately betrayed by his own master.

THE PATH TO EVIL
Born a Nightbrother on Dathomir, Maul is taken from his mother, Talzin, by Darth Sidious as his Sith apprentice, and learns the power of the dark side. Sidious trains Maul to wield a double-bladed lightsaber, with which Maul intends to exact vengeance upon the Jedi for the decimation of the Sith ranks. During his training, Maul kills Jedi Padawan Eldra Kaitis and forms a gang using her name, the Kaitis cartel. Darth Sidious takes Maul to Malachor, where Maul sees—and rejects—a vision of himself as a Jedi.

Dispatched by Sidious to kill the troublesome Queen Amidala, Maul tracks her to Tatooine, where he duels with one of her two Jedi protectors, Qui-Gon Jinn, who escapes with Amidala. When the two Jedi escort Queen Amidala back to Naboo, Maul sets out to finish them all. He confronts the Jedi, drawing them into Theed's generator complex. Maul manages to kill Qui-Gon Jinn, but Qui-Gon's apprentice, Obi-Wan Kenobi, strikes Maul down.

Generator duel
Maul slays a Jedi Master on Naboo, but underestimates the lightsaber skills of the Knight's apprentice, who cuts the murderous Sith in half.

SHATTERED CREATURE
For over a decade, the Jedi Order believes Darth Maul is dead. But during the Clone Wars, after Asajj Ventress betrays Savage Opress, Mother Talzin informs Savage that he has an exiled brother in the Outer Rim who can teach him to become more powerful. Opress goes to the planet Lotho Minor, where he finds Maul in a wretched state, his damaged torso grafted to spiderlike droid legs. Opress helps Maul recover, and together they seek revenge against those who turned them into monsters.

THE SHADOW COLLECTIVE
After Mother Talzin restores Maul's mind and gives him new cybernetic legs, Maul and Savage Opress lure Obi-Wan into a trap, so Maul may take his revenge. They fail to kill Obi-Wan, but cause death and destruction on several worlds, as Maul draws support from space pirates and the ranks of the Mandalorian Death Watch to build his own army, the Shadow Collective.

Unwilling to allow Maul's influence to grow unchecked, Darth Sidious takes matters into his own hands. The Sith Lord duels Maul face to face, beating him easily. Maul is then incarcerated at the Separatist prison on Stygeon Prime. He is tortured, but left alive by Sidious, who believes Maul might still be of use. Maul's loyal Mandalorian allies rescue him, and he flees to Dathomir under the protection of Mother Talzin.

Once again, Sidious is forced to act, this time utilizing the might of the Separatist army. Its droid fleets crush the Shadow Collective, Talzin is killed, and Maul retreats to Mandalore to make his last stand. At the close of the Clone Wars, Republic forces besiege Mandalore. Led by Commander Rex and Ahsoka Tano, the troops defeat Maul and his remaining Mandalorian supporters. The villain is captured and imprisoned aboard the Republic ship *Tribunal*. During Order 66, Maul tears apart the vessel's hyperdrive engines on the way back to Coruscant, helping both himself and Ahsoka to escape the clones.

CRIMSON DAWN
Undeterred by his previous attempts to rule through the criminal underworld, Maul leads the shadowy syndicate Crimson Dawn. Maul rules from the safety of his homeworld of Dathomir and allows his lieutenants to be the face of the organization. One such leader is Dryden Vos, whose ruthless tactics help Maul build Crimson Dawn into a formidable criminal enterprise in the early years of the Empire. Upon Vos' death, his top aid, Qi'ra, contacts Maul, at which time she becomes the organization's figurehead. Through Qi'ra and the Dawn, Maul's quest for vengeance against the Sith continues as the organization attempts to destroy them.

FINAL ACT
Maul's insatiable thirst for power leads him to Malachor in search of an ancient Sith superweapon that will allow him to take vengeance on all his enemies. He claims to have been stranded on Malachor for years when he is found by Ahsoka Tano, Kanan Jarrus, and Ezra Bridger, who arrive on the planet searching for ways to defeat the Sith. Their presence provides Maul with an opportunity to manipulate young Ezra Bridger into becoming his "apprentice." Ezra unknowingly leads Maul to Tatooine in search of Jedi Master Obi-Wan Kenobi. The former Sith confronts his old adversary in the desert, sensing Kenobi's real reason for going into hiding: to protect Luke Skywalker. With the future of the Jedi at stake, Kenobi has no choice but to fight back. Maul is defeated with just three swift strokes of the Jedi's lightsaber. He dies in the arms of his greatest foe, bringing an end to a decades-long quest for revenge.

> "At last we will reveal ourselves to the Jedi. At last we will have revenge." — **DARTH MAUL**

Craving vengeance
The burning desire to kill the Jedi who wounded him is the only thing that keeps Maul alive.

Vengeful warrior
One of the deadliest, most efficiently trained Sith in the Order's history, Darth Maul's tattooed face is as symbolic of his utter devotion to the dark side, as it is marking his hatred of the Jedi.

DARTH VADER (ANAKIN SKYWALKER)

SPECIES Human **HOMEWORLD** Tatooine
AFFILIATION Jedi, Republic, Sith, Empire

A child born of prophecy, possibly conceived by the will of the Force itself, Anakin Skywalker leaves an indelible mark on the history of the galaxy, leading it through periods of light and darkness.

PODRACE TO FREEDOM
When the Jedi Qui-Gon Jinn and his allies become stranded on Tatooine, Anakin Skywalker, a resourceful young enslaved person, endeavors to help them. He enters a podrace, hoping to win prize money to buy the necessary starship parts, but unknown to the boy, Qui-Gon makes a wager with Anakin's owner, Watto. When Skywalker wins, helped by his Force-heightened perception and quick reflexes, he not only gets the prize money, but he also gains his freedom.

Qui-Gon believes him to be the Chosen One who will bring balance to the Force, but other Jedi are not so certain. Anakin later becomes Obi-Wan Kenobi's Jedi apprentice with the pair going on missions across the galaxy, including to Carnelion IV and Dallenor. In his guise as Supreme Chancellor Palpatine, Darth Sidious also influences the impressionable Anakin.

ROGUE APPRENTICE
Years later, when Anakin is protecting Padmé Amidala, he senses that Shmi Skywalker is in trouble and races to Tatooine to try and save her. He finds his dying mother in a Tusken camp; after she passes away in his arms he slaughters the nomads without mercy. Shattered by Shmi's death, he promises that he will learn how to stop people from dying. Prior to the First Battle of Geonosis, Anakin and Padmé admit their love to each other. Following the battle, they get married in secret on Naboo, even though it is against the Jedi Code.

A NEW KNIGHT
During the Clone Wars, Anakin is knighted and becomes a Jedi general, renowned for his combat skills and unconventional tactics on the battlefield. The Jedi Council also assigns Anakin a Padawan, Ahsoka Tano, hoping this pairing will be mutually beneficial. Alongside Captain Rex and the rest of the 501st Clone Battalion, the Jedi pair take part in numerous critical engagements including on Geonosis, Kamino, Mon Cala, and Umbara.

DRAWN TO THE DARK SIDE
As the war continues, Anakin starts to

Jedi general
Anakin serves with distinction during the Clone Wars and is praised for his clever tactics.

doubt the Jedi Order, especially when the Council fails Ahsoka, and she leaves the Jedi. On a rescue mission to save a captured Palpatine during the Battle of Coruscant, the chancellor continues to prey upon Anakin's weaknesses and urges the young Jedi to kill Count Dooku. Shortly after, Skywalker begins to have dreams of Padmé dying during childbirth. Anakin soon realizes that Palpatine and the Jedi Council don't trust each other and is torn between loyalty to Palpatine and his obligations to the Council. After learning Palpatine is a Sith Lord, Anakin notifies the Council but then allies with Palpatine, who promises to give him life-prolonging powers so he can save Padmé.

BECOMING DARTH VADER
Renamed Darth Vader, Anakin becomes Palpatine's Sith apprentice. He helps to destroy the Sith's enemies, including his former allies at the Jedi Temple, enabling Palpatine to declare himself Emperor. When a ferocious duel with Obi-Wan on fiery Mustafar leaves Vader dismembered and near death, Palpatine retrieves his apprentice and transforms him into a cyborg. He then informs Vader that he killed Padmé on Mustafar.

HUNTING JEDI
The rebuilt Vader undertakes a series of missions for Palpatine, starting with constructing a new lightsaber. He hunts down a Jedi survivor and repurposes their kyber crystal, turning it from green to red. Sidious also hands over the running of the Inquisitorius to Vader, who treats the Inquisitors as little more than crude tools. Vader personally kills a number of Jedi survivors, including chief librarian Jocasta Nu and former Jedi Council member Eeth Koth. He also builds a fortress on Mustafar, a planet that not only holds painful memories for Vader but is also strongly connected to the dark side. Vader tries and fails to use the castle to bring Padmé back from the dead.

When Vader's former master Obi-Wan temporarily emerges, the Jedi draws the attention of Vader and his Inquisitors, starting a hunt across the galaxy. The Sith is so focused on hunting his past mentor and making him suffer that he lets a rebel network escape the Empire. After numerous setbacks, Obi-Wan gains the upper hand and defeats Vader. When Kenobi apologizes for failing his student, Vader asserts that he was the one who killed Anakin. Obi-Wan abandons the defeated Sith Lord and returns to obscurity. Soon after, a vengeful Vader heads to Jedha where he kills Jedi Master Cere Junda, a survivor who escaped him previously on Nur.

CRUSHING REBELLION
For the next few years, Vader serves as the Emperor's enforcer as rebel cells rise up throughout the galaxy. When rebel activity on Lothal escalates, he confronts Jedi Kanan Jarrus and his Padawan Ezra Bridger and learns that they are working with his own former apprentice, Ahsoka. In the Sith temple on Malachor, Ahsoka duels Vader to buy time for Kanan and Ezra to retreat, but escapes before her former master can strike a killing blow. The Sith Lord later forcibly recruits a smuggler to recover the Bright Star, an ancient artifact Vader believes will resurrect Padmé. However, his plans are disrupted by the smuggler, who destroys the powerful relic.

After the Rebel Alliance steals the Death Star plans from the vault on Scarif, Vader tries to retrieve them, but fails. Detecting Obi-Wan's presence on the Death Star, Vader duels the Jedi one final time. Though the Sith Lord is finally victorious, Obi-Wan becomes one with the Force. The Alliance uses the plans to discover a weakness in the Death Star and destroy it, in spite of Vader's presence at the Battle of Yavin.

A CHANGE OF PLANS
The Emperor blames Vader for failing to stop the rebels, so he has to work hard to regain his master's favor. He teams up with Doctor Chelli Lona Aphra to form his own secret army and to find the rebel pilot who destroyed the Death Star. After discovering the pilot is his own son, Luke Skywalker, Vader begins plotting to turn Luke to the dark side so they can rule the galaxy together. Vader also has to compete for the Emperor's favor with Grand General Tagge and a cyberneticist named Cylo. He outwits them both to win back his master's trust.

REDEMPTION
After leading the Empire to victory during the Battle of Hoth, Vader lays a trap for Luke Skywalker on Cloud City, drawing him into a duel in order to reveal that he is the young Jedi's father. Failing to gain Luke's allegiance displeases Sidious, forcing Vader to prove himself once more to secure his position. This task leads Vader to Exegol where he learns the true extent of his master's power. Vader also encounters Padmé's former handmaiden Sabé and, for a time, attempts to corrupt her to serve the Empire. During this tumultuous period for the galaxy, the criminal organization Crimson Dawn attempts to destroy the Sith Order, and Vader works with Sidious to combat this serious threat.

The Sith Lord later helps the Emperor lure Luke and his rebel allies into a trap at the second Death Star in orbit around Endor. Luke enters the Emperor's throne room on the battle station, and the Emperor goads him into fighting his father. When Luke refuses to kill Vader, the Emperor unleashes a barrage of Force-generated lightning on the young Jedi. Vader suddenly realizes that he wants to save his son, so has to destroy his master. Although Vader seemingly kills the Emperor, he does not survive the encounter. Thanks to his son Luke, Anakin Skywalker is redeemed and becomes one with the Force.

ONE WITH THE FORCE
At times, Anakin appears to those he cares about. He helps set Ahsoka Tano on a less cynical and pessimistic path and also appears to his son, Luke, to aid him and warn him of a threat during the New Republic era.

C-3PO

MODEL Protocol droid **HOMEWORLD** Tatooine
AFFILIATION Republic, Rebel Alliance, Resistance

Perpetually fussy, timid, and prone to worry, the human-cyborg relations protocol droid C-3PO is also a loyal friend who survives numerous adventures with his astromech counterpart, R2-D2.

Anxious friend
After first meeting R2-D2, C-3PO and the astromech are part of Anakin's podracer pit crew during the Boonta Eve Classic at the Mos Espa Grand Arena.

"THANK THE MAKER"
Cobbled together from discarded scrap and salvaged parts from Watto's junkyard on Tatooine, C-3PO is created by 9-year-old Anakin Skywalker, who programs the droid to help his mother, Shmi. Initially lacking an outer shell, C-3PO endures the indignity of being "naked," with his parts and wiring showing. Shortly after activation, he meets R2-D2, Qui-Gon Jinn, Padmé Naberrie, and Jar Jar Binks, who are en route to Coruscant. Anakin departs with his new allies, leaving C-3PO with Shmi. Eventually, Shmi and C-3PO move to the Lars moisture farm, and Shmi adds metal coverings to C-3PO's body.

SENATORIAL SERVICE
A decade after Anakin leaves C-3PO on Tatooine, the protocol droid reunites with his maker and is swept into the battle that begins the Clone Wars. Along with R2-D2, he witnesses the secret wedding of Anakin and Padmé and subsequently becomes a translator and personal assistant for senatorial meetings and diplomatic missions. After the Sith seize control of the Republic, C-3PO is present for the birth of Padmé's twins, Luke and Leia. To ensure that no one—especially the Sith—learns about the twins' existence, C-3PO is given a memory wipe, leaving him without any knowledge of his past. He then enters the service of Senator Bail Organa, with R2-D2, and later works for Bail's daughter Princess Leia Organa.

DROID SALE
Almost 20 years after the Clone Wars, C-3PO is still the property of Princess Leia when he reluctantly joins R2-D2 on a mission to find Obi-Wan Kenobi on Tatooine. Both droids are captured by Jawas, who bring them to the Lars moisture farm and sell them to Owen Lars and his nephew, Luke Skywalker. Although Owen and C-3PO coexisted on the farm years earlier, Owen does not recognize C-3PO, and C-3PO's memories of Owen are long gone.

ALLIANCE AGENT
During the Galactic Civil War, C-3PO goes on missions across the galaxy for the Alliance, where his diplomacy and translation skills are put to great use. Notable adventures include those to Cymoon 1, Nar Shaddaa, Kakra, and Cloud City on Bespin, where he is temporarily disassembled.

GOLDEN DEITY
Accompanying a rebel strike team to the Forest Moon of Endor, C-3PO encounters the Ewoks, an indigenous species of primitive warriors who are wary of humans but regard the golden droid as a god. Although C-3PO does not consider himself a good storyteller, his retelling of key events of the Galactic Civil War encourages the Ewoks to ally with the rebels. By gaining their allegiance, C-3PO plays a crucial part in the Rebellion's victory at the Battle of Endor.

SENATOR ORGANA'S ATTACHÉ
After the New Republic is established, C-3PO returns to his function as a senatorial aide and representative, this time for Leia Organa. The indispensable protocol droid translates for the renowned senator, manages her correspondence, and occasionally accompanies her to record Galactic Senate proceedings. Senator Organa trusts C-3PO enough to send him in her place when General Hera Syndulla of the New Republic Security Forces is questioned about her role in an unsanctioned reconnaissance mission to Seatos.

RESISTANCE SPYMASTER
Ever loyal to Leia Organa, C-3PO remains at her side as she leads the Resistance against the First Order. C-3PO serves the fledgling military group as leader of a droid intelligence network. Throughout the galaxy, C-3PO's agents secretively act as the mechanical eyes and ears of the Resistance, monitoring the First Order's activities and reporting back to C-3PO for analysis. After the Battle of D'Qar, the droid spy ring suspends operations as the Resistance flees.

SACRIFICE
C-3PO takes a more active role in the Resistance after its members relocate to Ajan Kloss, joining Rey and the others in the search for Exegol. The brave droid voluntarily gives up his memories to bypass his hard-wired translation protocols and interpret a Sith message that will lead Rey to Palpatine— and her destiny. When he's reunited with R2-D2, C-3PO's memories are restored by his best friend from a backup made just before he departed on the risky mission.

All-seeing C-3PO
Although he may often protest that nobody ever tells him anything, C-3PO is at the heart of the Resistance's intelligence services.

Expert translator
As an experienced protocol droid, C-3PO is fluent in more than seven million forms of communication. However, he is more talkative than typical protocol models, and some friends say he talks too much. Through his exploits, he has accumulated more than 30 secondary functions, including landspeeder piloting and programming binary loadlifters.

Mission to Rodia
C-3PO serves Senator Padmé Amidala and Representative Jar Jar Binks during the Clone Wars.

CHARACTERS AND CREATURES

RONTO
HOMEWORLD Tatooine
AVERAGE SIZE 5 m (16 ft) high **HABITAT** Desert

Indigenous to Tatooine, the saurian ronto is a huge, four-legged herbivore. Jawas use these easily domesticated beasts as mounts and to haul cargo to and from trading posts. Despite their imposing size and appearance, rontos are skittish and easily startled, but also loyal to their masters. They require a great deal of water, but are well suited to the desert. Their skin sheds heat, as do the flaplike folds framing their faces, which can extend to cover their small eyes during sandstorms.

SEBULBA
SPECIES Dug **HOMEWORLD** Malastare **AFFILIATION** None

A formidable opponent in the Outer Rim podracing circuit, Sebulba pilots a souped-up, overpowered orange racer. Although the Dug is exceptionally skilled, he owes much of his success to winning events on the fact he will do anything to secure a victory, by whatever means necessary. He is not above sabotaging a competitor's vehicle before a race and frequently uses illegal weaponry hidden aboard his own racer to distract or even bring down other pilots. On one occasion, he even uses his vehicle to flash the podracer of a local enslaved child, Anakin Skywalker, destroying it and stopping the young boy from completing the race.

Despite his atrocious conduct, Sebulba is popular with many race fans because he is exciting to watch, as podrace organizers are well aware. Whenever Sebulba competes, he guarantees large crowds and thus high profits.

At the Boonta Eve Classic, Sebulba wears a custom-made leather racing outfit that is decorated with coins, his victory prizes from previous races. Although Sebulba is the favorite to win the contest, Anakin evades the Dug's vicious tactics this time and is first to cross the finish line. As if losing the race isn't bad enough, Sebulba also loses control of his podracer and crashes into the desert sands. Luckily for him, he survives and lives to race in many more competitions.

WALD
SPECIES Rodian **HOMEWORLD** Tatooine
AFFILIATION Civilian, vendor

Wald is one of Anakin Skywalker's childhood friends from Mos Espa and a part of his podracing team. Years later, the Rodian becomes a member of a colony of formerly enslaved people on Gabredor III. Wald unknowingly fights alongside his former friend, now Darth Vader, to save his home.

WEAZEL
SPECIES Human **HOMEWORLD** Tatooine
AFFILIATION Hutt cartel, Cloud-Riders

Weazel works as an agent for the Hutts on Tatooine, and is in the crowd when Anakin Skywalker famously wins the Boonta Eve Classic podrace. Seeing the ills caused by the crime syndicates (and now the Empire), Weazel renounces his old life and joins the Cloud-Riders. He is Enfys Nest's second-in-command and best spy.

QUINLAN VOS
SPECIES Kiffar **HOMEWORLD** Kiffu
AFFILIATION Jedi

Former Padawan to Master Tholme, Quinlan Vos is a Jedi Master with a sarcastic sense of humor and a reputation for not playing by the rules. Vos is an expert tracker, renowned for his psychometric ability to perceive the memories of others by touching objects that they handled. He often takes missions that deal with the galactic underworld, which is how he meets Aayla Secura, the Force-attuned Twi'lek who becomes his Jedi apprentice.

During the Clone Wars, Vos is partnered with Obi-Wan Kenobi to track the fugitive crime lord Ziro the Hutt. Thanks to his underworld connections, Vos believes that the Hutt Council hired bounty hunter Cad Bane to break Ziro out of prison. Vos and Obi-Wan travel to Nal Hutta and meet with the Hutt Council. The Hutts deny all knowledge of Ziro or Cad Bane's whereabouts. The Jedi eventually learn that Ziro has escaped to the planet Teth and that Cad Bane is also stalking Ziro. They proceed to Teth, where they find Cad Bane lurking near Ziro's corpse. Although Bane claims he isn't responsible for killing Ziro, the Jedi attempt to apprehend him for previous crimes, but he escapes.

Months later, Vos accepts a mission to assassinate Count Dooku. Vos pretends to be a bounty hunter and tracks down Asajj Ventress—Dooku's former apprentice, who is also a bounty hunter. He joins her on a mission to Mustafar and goes on to reveal his real identity and mission. Asajj agrees to aid him as long as he accepts her tutelage in the dark side. While training, Vos and Asajj unexpectedly fall in love. They strike at Dooku on Raxus, but they fail, and Vos is captured.

Soon after, Vos appears to be broken by Dooku's torture, but he is pretending in order to complete his mission. When Asajj tries to rescue Vos, he refuses her aid and becomes a Separatist agent known only as Admiral Enigma. Asajj and the Jedi attempt to capture Enigma, but instead find Vos in a cell. The Jedi welcome him back in spite of Asajj's protests that he still embraces the dark side. When Asajj's fears are confirmed, the Jedi test Vos' loyalty by once again asking him to kill Dooku. Vos and Asajj travel together to Dooku's ship but, due to Jedi meddling, end up crash-landing with Dooku on Christophsis. Asajj sacrifices herself to save Vos from the Sith. Enraged, Vos defeats Dooku, but the Count escapes when his life is spared. Because of this display of mercy, Vos is allowed to rejoin the Order and eventually returns to active duty.

He fights on Kashyyyk when Order 66 is given and manages to escape. At some point, he encounters the Hidden Path, a group that helps hide Force-attuned people from the Empire. Vos assists the Path by smuggling younglings to safety.

Hunt for Ziro
Seeking Ziro the Hutt, Quinlan and Obi-Wan confront members of the Hutt Council in a club on Nal Hutta (left).

BANTHA

HOMEWORLD Tatooine
AVERAGE SIZE 2 m (8 ft) high
HABITAT Desert

Large, shaggy-furred quadrupeds with bright, inquisitive eyes, banthas are easily domesticated, and are bred on many worlds throughout the galaxy. Male banthas are distinguished by a pair of long, spiraling horns. Bantha meat and milk are common food items, and bantha-hide boots, jackets, and other wares are quite popular. On Tatooine, banthas are used as beasts of burden by moisture farmers, and as loyal pack animals by the Tuskens who revere the creatures. The desert nomads are known to ride their banthas in single file, leaving few tracks in the desert and effectively concealing their numbers.

DEWBACK

HOMEWORLD Tatooine **AVERAGE SIZE** 9 m (6 ft) long **HABITAT** Desert

Dewbacks are large lizards used as mounts and beasts of burden on their native Tatooine, where they can be found hauling goods for merchants or moisture farmers, pulling podracer parts to starting grids, or serving stormtrooper patrols assigned to the planet's Imperial garrison. A dewback can withstand the heat and dust that often leads to mechanical breakdowns in high-tech conveyances. When the suns set and the temperatures plunge, dewbacks become lethargic and rarely move about.

WATTO

SPECIES Toydarian **HOMEWORLD** Toydaria
AFFILIATION Watto's shop

An injured Toydarian veteran, Watto is the proprietor of a junk shop and scrapyard in Mos Espa, as well as an inveterate gambler and an avid fan of podracing. In a wager over a podrace with another gambler, Gardulla the Hutt, Watto wins and becomes the latest enslaver of Shmi Skywalker and her son Anakin, both of whom are skilled mechanics. Some years later, after Qui-Gon Jinn tries to buy a used hyperdrive motivator from Watto, the latter is simultaneously intrigued and perturbed when the stranger proposes a wager that may result in Watto either losing Anakin or winning a starship. Watto loses the bet, and Anakin is freed, allowing him to leave Tatooine to become a Jedi.

Without Anakin's mechanical aptitude, Watto's business soon declines, and he sells Shmi to moisture farmer Cliegg Lars. When Anakin returns to Mos Espa in search of his mother, Watto gives him a lead on Shmi's whereabouts.

"No matter where you are, my love will be with you." SHMI SKYWALKER

SHMI SKYWALKER

SPECIES Human **HOMEWORLD** Tatooine
AFFILIATION Moisture farmer

Anakin's mother, Shmi, is a loving, soft-spoken woman. Shmi provides a good home for her son and is determined that he will have a better future and be freed from enslavement to the junk dealer Watto. She is aware that Anakin has special powers—he can see things before they happen. But it is not until the Jedi Knight Qui-Gon arrives in Mos Espa that Shmi realizes her son has the potential and opportunity to become a Jedi. With Qui-Gon's help, Anakin wins his freedom by competing in a podrace, but Qui-Gon is unable to persuade Watto to free Shmi, too. Before Anakin departs with Qui-Gon, he promises he will return to free her. He also leaves behind C-3PO, the protocol droid that he built to help his mother.

Watto's chronic gambling habit leaves him virtually destitute and he is forced to sell Shmi. Cliegg Lars, a moisture farmer, falls in love with Shmi and purchases her freedom. Shmi and Cliegg wed, and she becomes a loving stepmother to Cliegg's son, Owen. Along with C-3PO, they live on the family moisture farm. In the years that follow, Shmi joins the White Suns, a group dedicated to freeing enslaved people on Tatooine, alongside Owen's partner, Beru Whitesun. She creates a deprogrammer tool that can deactivate the control chips in enslaved people, bravely testing it on the control chip still implanted in herself first.

Ten years after Anakin's departure, Shmi is alone, gathering mushrooms that grow on moisture vaporators, when a band of Tuskens abducts her. Cliegg and a posse of moisture farmers attempt to rescue her, but the Tuskens ambush the farmers, maiming Cliegg and leaving most of his allies dead. A month later, Anakin—plagued by nightmares about Shmi being tortured—returns to Tatooine, determined to find his mother. Although Cliegg insists that Shmi must be dead, Anakin borrows a speeder bike and tracks the Tuskens across the desert. When he arrives at their camp, he finds his mother barely alive. She has just enough strength to tell him that she loves him before she dies. Enraged, Anakin gives in to the dark side and slaughters the Tuskens. He returns to the Lars homestead, where he buries Shmi. This traumatic experience makes Anakin desire the power to prevent his loved ones from dying.

JAWA

SPECIES Jawa **HOMEWORLD** Tatooine
AFFILIATION Desert scavengers

Combing the deserts in search of discarded scrap and wayward mechanicals, Jawas are three-foot-tall humanoids who wear rough, hand-woven robes. Using cobbled-together weaponry, they incapacitate stray droids and haul them into their immense mobile homes, known as sandcrawlers. Because Tatooine moisture farmers live far from droid dealers and scrapyards, they routinely trade with Jawas, even though Jawas are notorious hucksters of hastily refurbished junk. Some adventurous Jawa clans have moved offworld in search of new scrap to sell.

CHARACTERS AND CREATURES

EOPIE
HOMEWORLD Tatooine **AVERAGE SIZE** 2 m (7 ft) high **HABITAT** Desert

An omnivore and a stubborn beast of burden on Tatooine, the eopie is renowned for its endurance and is often pushed to the limit by the denizens of the twin-sunned world. This sure-footed quadruped has pale skin, a flexible snout, and a grumpy temperament. Because their young are extremely vulnerable and often fall prey to predators, eopies instinctively travel in herds. Moisture farmers use older eopies to eat excess desert weeds that would otherwise sap crops of valuable moisture.

KITSTER BANAI
SPECIES Human **HOMEWORLD** Tatooine **AFFILIATION** Civilian

The young and optimistic Kitster Banai is one of Anakin's best childhood friends, alongside Wald. When Anakin competes in the Boonta Eve Classic, Kitster serves as a member of his trusted pit team. After winning the Boonta, Anakin gives a few credits to Kitster, who uses the money to improve his life. Kitster is later freed from servitude by Sabé and settles with Wald and many other formerly enslaved people at a colony on Gabredor III. During the Imperial era, Sabé and Darth Vader, who still remembers his former friends, save the colony from disaster.

BEN QUADINAROS
SPECIES Toong **HOMEWORLD** Tund **AFFILIATION** Podracing

Short by Toong standards, Ben Quadinaros is the tallest entrant in the Boonta Eve Classic and also the least experienced. His hastily put-together podracer malfunctions, stalling on the starting grid before its four engines break loose and blast off in all directions. Quadinaros perseveres with the sport and is eventually billed as Sebulba's greatest rival.

GASGANO
SPECIES Xexto **HOMEWORLD** Troiken **AFFILIATION** Podracing

A highly competitive pilot with four arms and two legs, Gasgano can manipulate multiple controls at the same time. His predilection for high speed combines with a nasty temper that ignites when other pilots attempt to pass him. He races on behalf of Gardulla the Hutt in the Boonta Eve Classic, and is the object of intense betting between Gardulla and Jabba. Gasgano finishes in second place, after Anakin Skywalker.

Custom racer
Gasgano pilots a custom Ord Pedrovia podracer with 9-meter (29-foot) bulbous engines that boast great acceleration.

TEEMTO PAGALIES
SPECIES Veknoid **HOMEWORLD** Moonus Mandel **AFFILIATION** Podracing

An outcast from his homeworld, the flamboyant Teemto Pagalies pilots an IPG-X1131 LongTail podracer with 10.67-meter (35-foot) engines. During the second lap of the Boonta Eve Classic, Tuskens snipe his podracer, causing him to crash. Fortunately, Pagalies survives.

Long engines
Seated in the cockpit of his podracer (above), Pagalies boasts the longest pair of engines in the Boonta Eve Classic (left).

ODY MANDRELL
SPECIES Er'Kit **HOMEWORLD** Tatooine **AFFILIATION** Podracing

A foolhardy thrill-seeker with an insatiable appetite for high speeds, Ody Mandrell pilots his massive Exelbrok podracer with wild abandon and a blatant disregard for safety. During a pit stop in the Boonta Eve Classic, one of his pit droids is sucked into his podracer's engine intakes, crippling his vehicle and eliminating him from the race.

CLEGG HOLDFAST
SPECIES Nosaurian **HOMEWORLD** New Plympto **AFFILIATION** Podracing

A journalist for *Podracing Quarterly*, the arrogant Clegg Holdfast enters competitions to cover stories from the inside. Although his fellow racers maintain that he's a better writer than pilot, he proudly displays a set of decorative medals on his lapel as a testament to his racing prowess. In the second lap of the Boonta Eve Classic, Sebulba uses his concealed flamethrower while next to Holdfast. The blaze cooks the Nosaurian's engines, forcing him to crash.

FODE AND BEED
SPECIES Troig **HOMEWORLD** Pollillus **AFFILIATION** Podracing

Exuberant, colorful, and not always too accurate with facts, Fode and Beed are the popular announcers of the Boonta Eve Classic. Like all Troigs, Fode and Beed share a body with two heads, each with its own distinctive personality and speech patterns. Fode's red-mottled head provides commentary in Basic, while Beed's green-mottled head provides counterpoint in Huttese.

JABBA THE HUTT

SPECIES Hutt **HOMEWORLD** Tatooine
AFFILIATION Hutt Grand Council, Crymorah Syndicate

A loathsome gangster, Jabba the Hutt is the preeminent kingpin of crime in the Outer Rim. The long-lived Jabba has ruled over his territories for centuries and always seems to outwit his opponents, criminals or otherwise.

CRIME BOSS
During the High Republic era, Jabba attends a banquet on Hynestia to negotiate a treaty between the Hutt Clan and the Hynestian royal family. The event is a ruse, which the Hutts hope to use as an excuse for violence, but a trio of Jedi—Lynela Kabe-Oyu, Stellan Gios, and Vernestra Rwoh—see through the treachery, leading to Jabba the Hutt's temporary arrest.

Centuries later, Jabba bases his operations out of an opulent palace on Tatooine. His lucrative and unsavory rackets include enslavement, gunrunning, spice smuggling, gambling, and extortion. Jabba attends the Boonta Eve Classic that Anakin Skywalker unexpectedly wins, but he is actually bored by the races.

SECRET DEALS
During the Clone Wars, Jabba's son Rotta is kidnapped. The Jedi rescue the Huttlet and uncover that the Separatists and Jabba's own uncle Ziro are behind the kidnapping. Afterward, Jabba pledges to help the Republic war effort. When Pantoran chairman Baron Papanoida visits his palace, demanding a blood sample from Jabba's bounty hunter Greedo, the Hutt grants his request after hearing that Papanoida is searching for his missing children.

Fearing that Ziro will expose the Hutts' illegal activities, Jabba hires bounty hunter Cad Bane, who extracts Ziro from prison. Jabba then secretly pays Sy Snootles to locate Ziro's incriminating records, kill him, and then pass the documents to Jabba. When Maul forms his own criminal organization called the Shadow Collective, Jabba and the rest of the Hutt cartel are coerced into joining. They leave the group after Maul is imprisoned.

UNDER THE EMPIRE
Jabba continues operating during the Imperial era. His majordomo Bib Fortuna secures him a young rancor as a pet on Ord Mantell that will eventually become one of Jabba's favorite methods of execution. After a drought on Tatooine, he extracts a water tax from its residents, sending bounty hunters after anyone who resists. Han Solo, captain of the *Millennium Falcon*, is hired by Jabba as a smuggler, becoming the best on his payroll. For one mission, Han is tasked with acquiring an urn that Jabba claims contains the ashes of one of his enemies. However, it actually contains a neural core of a dangerous droid. Han refuses to give this to Jabba, so the urn ends up in the Hutt's hands with ashes of a charred ronto interred instead.

On a particular assignment, Han has to jettison valuable cargo that he secured for Jabba in order to escape Imperial incarceration. The Hutt later demands compensation and sends bounty hunters after Han. Greedo attempts to gun down Han in the Mos Eisley Cantina, but fails. Afterward, Han confronts Jabba, who agrees to give him an extension on his repayment, but with the addition of a hefty percentage. Jabba places a large bounty on Han's head when he learns he has joined the Rebel Alliance instead of working to pay him back.

Bad business
Han assures Jabba inside Docking Bay 94 at Mos Eisley spaceport that he'll repay the Hutt for a lost shipment of valuable spice. Jabba reminds Han that failure to do so could cost the smuggler his life.

NEW DEALS AND OLD SCORES
Following the Battle of Yavin, the Empire requires more weapons, so the Emperor sends Darth Vader to negotiate with Jabba. After Vader dispatches a few of the Hutt's guards and demands the personal use of two of his bounty hunters, they agree that Jabba will supply the Empire with weapons in exchange for credits. The Hutts can also continue to operate their criminal enterprises. On another occasion, smugglers Lando Calrissian and Sana Starros swindle Jabba, stealing weapons and 20,000 credits from him.

Jabba's substantial reward for Han Solo is targeted by the bounty hunter Boba Fett, who works alongside Darth Vader to capture the wayward rebel, encasing him in carbonite. When Han is stolen from Boba and ends up in the hands of Crimson Dawn, Jabba places a bounty on Fett, thinking that he betrayed him, inciting chaos among the other hunters in the galaxy. Alongside the rest of the Hutt Council, Jabba attends the Crimson Dawn auction on Jekara. Han is for sale and he places the winning bid of one million credits. However, Vader demands ownership of Han to draw in Luke Skywalker. Jabba tries to resist but acquiesces once Vader threatens to alter the terms of the agreement between the Hutts and the Empire. Leaving Jekara, Jabba returns to Tatooine while the rest of the outraged Hutt Council starts a battle with the Empire, which they do not win. During the chaos, Boba manages to reacquire ownership of Han's frozen form.

Now the sole member of the Hutt Council, Jabba controls the Hutt Clans and ends up with his prize after all. Boba Fett delivers a carbonite-frozen Han, and demands that his own bounty be cancelled. The Hutt gleefully accepts and installs his prize in his throne room. Jabba anticipates that Han's friends will attempt to rescue him from the palace, but is confident that they will fail. Jabba's misplaced confidence eventually leads to his death aboard his luxurious sail barge, *Khetanna*, at the hands of Leia Organa—who becomes known as the Huttslayer.

CHARACTERS AND CREATURES

GARDULLA THE HUTT
SPECIES Hutt **HOMEWORLD** Nal Hutta **AFFILIATION** Hutt Grand Council

The Hutts control the smuggling trade in the Outer Rim, earning their crooked profits far outside the watchful eyes of law and order. For centuries, Gardulla the Hutt has been active in the criminal underworld and wields considerable power from her palace on Nal Hutta. In the years leading up to the Battle of Naboo, Gardulla enslaves Anakin Skywalker and his mother Shmi, but she loses them to Watto in a bet. Alongside Jabba the Hutt, Gardulla watches the Boonta Eve Classic where Anakin wins the podrace. During the Clone Wars, Gardulla imprisons the traitorous Ziro the Hutt in her palace, which brings the unwanted attention of Jedi investigators Obi-Wan Kenobi and Quinlan Vos.

BIB FORTUNA
SPECIES Twi'lek **HOMEWORLD** Ryloth
AFFILIATION Jabba's court

This sharp-toothed Twi'lek works for Jabba the Hutt as his chief aide and majordomo for over three decades. Bib Fortuna demonstrates tremendous patience in dealing with his master's bad habits, including waking Jabba every time the Hutt dozes off during podraces. Originally from Ryloth, Fortuna controls most operations inside Jabba's Tatooine palace, including welcoming visitors who call at the remote stronghold.

When Jabba's services require outside assistance, Bib is the liaison, contacting Cid and Clone Force 99 to retrieve a young rancor for the Hutt. He also hires Han Solo and Chewbacca on several occasions and is their main point of contact.

After Jabba displays a carbon-frozen Han on the wall of his throne room, Fortuna is the first of the Hutt's administrators to intercept Luke Skywalker when he arrives to rescue Han. Fortuna's weak will makes him particularly susceptible to Jedi mind tricks, which allows Luke to get to Jabba with little trouble.

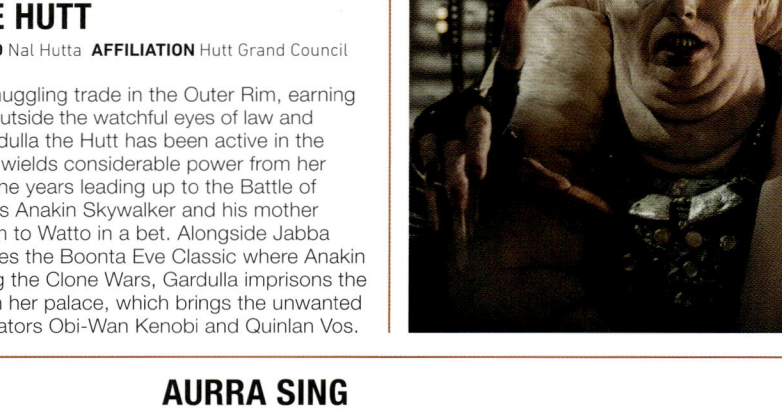

Once Jabba is killed, Bib becomes the new daimyo of Tatooine, assuming control of the Hutt's vast criminal empire. Several years after the defeat of the Empire, Bib is killed by Boba Fett who wants to claim Bib's throne.

RATTS TYERELL
SPECIES Aleena **HOMEWORLD** Aleen
AFFILIATION None

With lightning-fast reflexes, Ratts Tyerell rises through the ranks of the galaxy's best podracers to earn a starting place in Tatooine's Boonta Eve Classic, just prior to the Battle of Naboo. Tyerell's podracer is capable of tremendous thrust, but a jammed accelerator in the second lap of the race causes him to lose control. As his podracer roars through a cave, it smashes into a rocky stalactite, and Tyerell perishes in a fiery explosion.

AURRA SING
SPECIES Palliduvan **HOMEWORLD** Nar Shaddaa **AFFILIATION** Bounty hunter

One of the galaxy's most lethal killers, Aurra Sing earns her keep as a freelance assassin. The tell-tale antenna of a biocomputer protruding from her skull means that Sing receives extrasensory data, enabling her to track multiple threats simultaneously and line up distant shots with her long-barreled sniper rifle. Though Sing prefers to work solo, she finds a kindred spirit in space pirate Hondo Ohnaka, with whom she even shares a brief romance. Other associates occasionally recruited by Sing include the cowardly Klatooinian Castas and Bossk, the brutal Trandoshan bounty hunter.

Prior to the Naboo Blockade, Sing, Cad Bane, and two other bounty hunters are hired by Darth Maul to assist him with capturing and killing a Jedi Padawan. Intending to take a break, Aurra later takes a vacation on the *Halcyon* with Zam Wesell. However, the pair are hired by fellow passenger, Colram Vestig, to protect his son Wilmar during a safari excursion to Numidian Prime.

During the Clone Wars, Aurra Sing finds an unlikely partner in Boba Fett, a boy who inherits his father's ship. Sing entices Boba with the promise of taking revenge on the Jedi who had executed his father, and then exploits the boy's resemblance to younger Republic clones to sabotage and destroy the Republic attack cruiser *Endurance*. Abducting survivors from the wreckage of the craft, Sing retreats to Hondo Ohnaka's outpost on Florrum, with Jedi investigators in hot pursuit. Sing tries to escape in Boba's ship, but Ahsoka Tano severely damages the vehicle, leaving Sing for dead. Unbeknownst to her pursuers, Sing survives and is freed from the crashed ship by Hondo. Disappearing offworld to lick her wounds, Sing later attempts to assassinate Senator Amidala at a refugee conference on Alderaan. Thwarted by Ahsoka once more, Sing is taken prisoner, but escapes to find work with Cad Bane, where she serves as team sniper during Bane's bold mission to rescue Ziro the Hutt from a Coruscant prison. Tobias Beckett, a smuggler working for Crimson Dawn, claims he has dispatched Aurra Sing.

Lethal weapon
Aurra Sing's legendary skills as an assassin keeps her employed for decades *(far right)*. During the Boonta Eve Classic podrace, an observant Sing watches in astonishment as the young Anakin Skywalker wins the race fairly *(right)*.

TUSKENS

SPECIES Tusken **HOMEWORLD** Tatooine
AFFILIATION None

Tuskens, commonly called Sand People, are desert nomads native to Tatooine. Few have seen a Tusken's face, as they cover their bodies with multiple layers of tight wrappings and wear masks with breathing filters to survive Tatooine's harsh desert environment. Tuskens live in small clans within the rocky Jundland Wastes, moving around on the backs of shaggy banthas, and disguising their numbers by marching in single file. Tuskens are frequently misunderstood and labeled as savages by the nonindigenous communities on Tatooine. In fact, the Tuskens have a complex cultural hierarchy, are loyal to each other, and are often willing to negotiate with those that have invaded their lands. Their warriors carry rifles and gaderffiis—metal weapons that function as both clubs and axes, and are handcrafted after the wielder completes a special ceremony. A typical Tusken encampment consists of a small cluster of tents guarded by snarling massiffs.

Just before the Battle of Geonosis, Anakin Skywalker's mother, Shmi, is kidnapped by a Tusken raiding party. By the time Anakin arrives at their camp, the injured Shmi has been held captive for weeks, and dies before her son can rescue her. In retaliation, an enraged Anakin slaughters the entire Tusken tribe.

During the Imperial era, Tuskens ambush Ezra Bridger and rebel astromech Chopper, who are saved by the former Sith apprentice Maul. Years later, Anakin, now known as Darth Vader, returns to Tatooine following the Battle of Yavin and decimates another Tusken village. Fearing his wrath, the Tuskens erect a shrine to Vader and sacrifice some of their own to him in the hope this act will stop him from returning. Following Jabba's death on Tatooine, Boba Fett is captured by a roaming Tusken tribe and held prisoner. He earns respect by defeating a sand beast and becomes a high-ranking warrior in the Tusken tribe. Following the group's destruction, Boba seeks revenge against those he believes to have perpetrated it. Din Djarin often negotiates with Tuskens, and strikes an alliance between a tribe and the people of Mos Pelgo to defeat a Krayt dragon.

Desert ambush
The Tusken leader URoRRuR'R'R attacks Luke Skywalker seconds before Obi-Wan Kenobi comes to his rescue.

"I never ask for permission to do anything."
— AURRA SING

SUPREME CHANCELLOR VALORUM

SPECIES Human **HOMEWORLD** Coruscant
AFFILIATION Galactic Senate

Finis Valorum rules the Republic as supreme chancellor in the years leading up to the Battle of Naboo. He sends his political aide Silman and Jedi Master Sifo-Dyas on a secret mission to meet with the Pyke Syndicate, but they never return and are believed dead. Though he is well-intentioned, Valorum is unable to prevent the Trade Federation from blockading the planet Naboo. Valorum arranges for two Jedi, Qui-Gon Jinn and Obi-Wan Kenobi, to negotiate an end to the blockade, but instead the Trade Federation invades Naboo. Ultimately, Naboo's Queen Amidala calls for a vote of no confidence in Valorum, forcing him out of office. During the Clone Wars, Valorum is visited by his old friend Yoda, and Valorum informs him of the mission he sent Silman and Sifo-Dyas on.

CHARACTERS AND CREATURES

YODA
AFFILIATION Jedi

The last Grand Master of the Jedi Order, Yoda is 900 years old. Forced into exile by the Empire, Yoda trains Luke Skywalker in the ways of the Jedi, then passes into the Force.

ON THE COUNCIL
Though little is known of Yoda's early life, his influence within the Jedi Order is tremendous. As Grand Master, the oldest and wisest of the Order, he serves on the elite Jedi Council with other high-ranking masters and teaches young students in the Jedi Temple.

During the early years of the High Republic, Yoda sits on the Council and deploys Jedi to Jedha and Dalna in pursuit of the Path of the Open Hand. Decades later, he visits the Jedi temple on Tenoo to train Kai Brightstar, Lys Solay, and Nubs. Yoda disappears for a time to pursue an answer to the mystery of the origin of the Nameless. Upon returning to the Order, he allies himself with the enigmatic former Jedi Azlin Rell to further his investigations.

Discussion among equals
Master Yoda shares his wisdom with Council members. When duty calls the Jedi to other parts of the galaxy, they report to Yoda in the form of a long-distance hologram.

THE RISING DARKNESS
When Qui-Gon Jinn brings Anakin Skywalker before the Council, Yoda argues that the boy is too dangerous to be trained. He later changes his mind after Qui-Gon is killed by a Sith on Naboo, but he never entirely conquers his feelings of unease. During the next few years, Yoda keeps watch over Padawan Skywalker and his master, Obi-Wan Kenobi.

Count Dooku, one of Yoda's former students, emerges as the leader of a Separatist movement. When Dooku becomes a threat to galactic peace, Yoda leads an army of clone troopers against Separatist forces on Geonosis and faces Dooku in lightsaber combat. During the Clone Wars, Yoda strives to treat each clone soldier as an individual worthy of respect. Yet as the war drags on, Yoda and Mace Windu sense a gathering darkness that diminishes their ability to use the Force. Finally, Yoda is ambushed by his clone troopers on Kashyyyk and flees offworld with help from the Wookiee Chewbacca.

INTO EXILE
Returning to Coruscant, Yoda fights Emperor Palpatine in a spectacular test of their abilities. The showdown begins inside Palpatine's office and spills into the Galactic Senate Chamber. Though Yoda is a tough combatant, the Emperor uses the Force to release lightning bolts and hurl floating platforms at his foe. Ultimately, the battle proves too much for Yoda, who barely escapes and is whisked away to safety by Senator Bail Organa. After leaving Padmé Amidala and Anakin's twin children in the care of Obi-Wan and Bail Organa, Yoda travels to the swamps of Dagobah to begin a new life away from the Empire's hunters. The remote world gives him the chance to meditate on the Force, and a dark-side cave serves as a place of spiritual trial.

Duel with the dark side
Yoda fights Count Dooku on Geonosis, forcing his former student to flee.

Luminous being
Yoda gains strength from the living things in Dagobah's swamps and tries to teach Luke that the Force is everywhere.

A NEW HOPE
Luke comes to Dagobah after the Battle of Hoth to learn the ways of the Jedi. Throughout the young man's training, Yoda keeps the truth of his relationship to Vader a secret for fear it might trigger Luke's fall to the dark side. Skywalker loses his first fight with Vader on Cloud City, but Yoda declares him a true Jedi when he returns to Dagobah. Yoda then passes into the light of the Force.

More than he seems
Both Count Dooku and Luke Skywalker seem to underestimate Yoda, thinking his small size and advanced age make him less formidable. But Yoda's true strength comes from within.

Duel of masters
The full power of the light side and the dark side of the Force is on display during Yoda's clash with Emperor Palpatine. Outmatched, Yoda retreats and waits to train a new champion to lead the fight against evil.

Luke's final lesson
"We are what they grow beyond." Yoda explains to Luke that the true burden of all masters is that they will be surpassed by their students.

MASTER TO MASTER
Decades later, Yoda appears to Luke, who has become so disillusioned with the Jedi Order he has decided to burn down the Jedi library on Ahch-To. Before Skywalker can act, Yoda summons a lightning strike from the skies that destroys the library. Rather than looking to the past, Master Yoda teaches Skywalker one more lesson: Failure is the greatest teacher. This insight helps Luke move past his failings and realize he must help the Resistance stand up to Kylo Ren. Yoda is among the Jedi who speak to Rey when she communes with the Jedi of the past and then destroys the resurrected Emperor Palpatine.

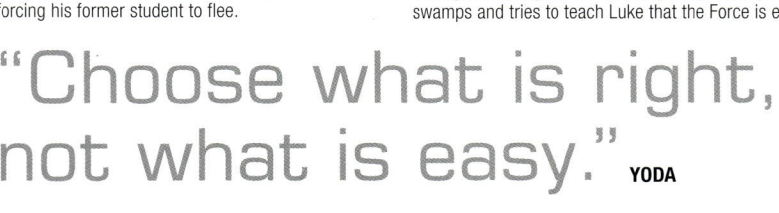

"Choose what is right, not what is easy." **YODA**

MACE WINDU

SPECIES Human **HOMEWORLD** Haruun Kal
AFFILIATION Jedi

Second only to Master Yoda in reputation, Master Mace Windu leads the Jedi Council during the waning years of the Republic. Betrayal costs him his life, but he never relents in his fight against the dark side.

TWILIGHT OF THE REPUBLIC
After joining the Jedi Order, Mace Windu joins Jedi Master Cyslin Myr on a mission to the planet Mathas to hunt down a rogue Jedi. In the final decades of the Republic, Mace rescues the young Depa Billaba and her sister Sar Labooda from pirates, and later decides to take Depa as his Padawan. Eventually, Mace rises to the rank of Jedi Master and returns to his homeworld to investigate a missing shipment of kyber crystals. Mace later accepts Master Katri's seat on the Jedi Council following her death on Raxus. However, Mace still heads into the field, seeing action on Ontotho and Oosalon. At some point, Mace sees his former Padawan Billaba join him on the Council. Together, the pair join the rest of the esteemed Jedi Masters on their mission to Kwenn.

SITH THREAT
A high-ranking member of the Jedi Council at the start of the Battle of Naboo, Mace Windu is troubled by signs indicating the return of the Sith. Following Qui-Gon's funeral, Mace heads on a mission to Metagos where he helps the planet's inhabitants. He later investigates the growing influence of the dark side as Count Dooku's Separatist movement takes shape; and when Obi-Wan Kenobi discovers evidence that the Separatists are preparing to go to war against the Republic, Mace leads a task force of 200 Jedi to Geonosis to do battle. He faces off against Dooku's agent, Jango Fett, in the Geonosian execution arena and beheads the bounty hunter with one swipe of his lightsaber.

THE CLONE WARS
Mace Windu accepts the rank of general in the Grand Army of the Republic during the Clone Wars, and serves as both a strategist and a frontline combatant in numerous conflicts with the Separatists. In an early engagement, Mace leads a small Jedi team to Hissrich and must defeat one of their own when Jedi Master Prosset Dibbs betrays them. On Ryloth, Mace leads the AT-RT drivers of Lightning Squadron to assist freedom fighter Cham Syndulla in the liberation of his world. He discovers a slumbering zillo beast on Malastare and escapes several attempts on his life from Boba Fett, the orphaned son of Jango Fett, who is out for revenge. Late in the war, Mace becomes alarmed by the rising threat of the dark side and steps up his efforts to unmask the suspected Sith manipulator behind it all. He also leads the defense of Anaxes during the Outer Rim Sieges.

CONFRONTING EVIL
Following the Battle of Coruscant, Mace receives news that Supreme Chancellor Palpatine is actually the Sith Lord behind the recent turmoil across the galaxy. Mace selects a small squad of Jedi—Agen Kolar, Kit Fisto, and Saesee Tiin—to arrest the chancellor, but they die when Palpatine fights back. Mace seems to be winning until Anakin intervenes and cuts off the Jedi Master's hand. Palpatine seals Mace's fate with a blast of Force-generated lightning, sending him through the window to his death. Decades later, Mace's voice offers the Jedi Rey support during her final battle with Palpatine.

Against the Separatists
Mace gives counsel to Anakin as the Clone Wars rage across the galaxy.

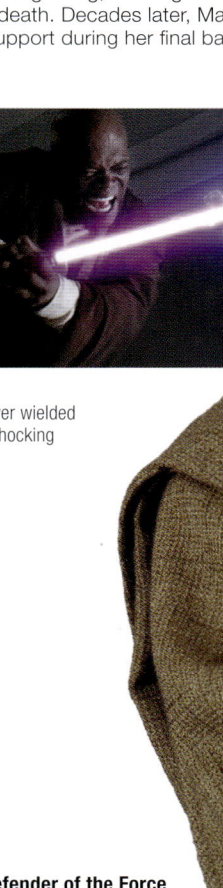

Final battle
The dark-side power wielded by Palpatine is a shocking surprise for Mace.

High standards
Mace Windu isn't impressed by young Anakin Skywalker and initially refuses his admittance to be trained as a Jedi.

Defender of the Force
Mace Windu is a formidable warrior and a stern judge of character. He believes in action, not words, and is the first Jedi to move against Count Dooku on Geonosis. He assembles a squad to arrest Chancellor Palpatine when he learns of Palpatine's Sith secret.

> "I'm going to put an end to this, once and for all!"
> **MACE WINDU**

CHARACTERS AND CREATURES

KI-ADI-MUNDI

SPECIES Cerean **HOMEWORLD** Cerea
AFFILIATION Jedi

Ki-Adi-Mundi is a Cerean Jedi Master whose white beard and wise features attest to his years spent in the Jedi Order. He joins the Jedi Council during the final years of the Republic. When every member of the Council decides to visit Kwenn, Mundi goes undercover in one of the local criminal gangs to investigate their suspicious behavior. He reveals his true identity when the miscreants begin to attack the other Council members.

Following the Trade Federation's invasion of Naboo, Ki-Adi-Mundi helps evaluate Anakin Skywalker's Force potential when Qui-Gon Jinn brings him to Coruscant. Jinn's concerns that the Sith may have returned aren't enough to trouble Master Mundi, who reminds the Council that the Sith haven't been sighted for a millennium. Years later, he is part of the Republic force that travels to Carnelion IV, where the group rescues Jedi Knight Obi-Wan Kenobi and his Padawan, Anakin, and stops a war raging between two groups on the planet. When Count Dooku later emerges as the head of the Separatist movement, Master Mundi refuses to believe Dooku could be capable of orchestrating bombings, emphasizing to his colleagues that Dooku is a political idealist who seems incapable of murder.

Nevertheless, war soon breaks out between the Republic and Dooku's Separatists. Ki-Adi-Mundi is one of the Jedi who travels to Geonosis, where he infiltrates the execution arena. He survives the subsequent battle and receives the rank of general in the Grand Army of the Republic. Master Mundi leads the Galactic Marines, clone troopers captained by Commander Bacara, in engagements against the Separatist droid armies. Early into the war, Ki-Adi-Mundi survives an encounter with General Grievous, who wounds him. As the war continues, Master Mundi sees how much Anakin has grown as a Jedi and a warrior, and during the Second Battle of Geonosis, he engages Anakin in a friendly wager over which of them can destroy the most battle droids.

When Darth Sidious enacts Order 66, Master Mundi and his clones are attempting to capture Mygeeto in the Outer Rim. Bacara orders his troopers to open fire on their Jedi general as he leads the charge across a bridge, and Ki-Adi-Mundi falls under the surprise onslaught.

Evaluating Anakin
With his fellow Council members, Ki-Adi-Mundi contemplates the fate of young Anakin.

Unprepared
Ki-Adi-Mundi's clone troopers betray him on Mygeeto.

PLO KOON

SPECIES Kel Dor **HOMEWORLD** Dorin
AFFILIATION Jedi

Plo Koon is a Kel Dor who needs a mask to protect his eyes and lungs from oxygen-rich environments. Prior to the Battle of Naboo, Plo discovers a young, Force-attuned Togruta girl named Ahsoka Tano and brings her to Coruscant to become a Jedi. Plo sits on the Jedi Council, where his guidance is always respected. During the group's mission to Kwenn, Plo works with Saesee Tiin to reach a settlement between disgruntled workers and their bosses at a local company. The employees then aid their new allies when criminals attack the Jedi Council on the planet.

The outbreak of the Clone Wars allows him to demonstrate his battle skills as well. Plo supports the clone troopers expressing their individuality and forms a strong bond with his soldiers, led by Commander Wolffe, who becomes known as the Wolfpack. Some of their earliest missions see Plo and his troops head to Quarmendy and Hisseen.

A subsequent engagement pits Plo's armada against the Separatist cruiser *Malevolence*, which ends in near-total defeat. Plo and a small number of clone troopers survive in an escape pod and evade battle droid clean-up squads until they are rescued.

Plo quickly jumps back into the fight, helping Ahsoka navigate the Coruscant underworld to uncover the whereabouts of Aurra Sing. Plo and Ahsoka later travel to Florrum and arrest a young Boba Fett. On a later mission, Plo leads the Republic fleet to the prison planet of Lola Sayu to rescue Jedi Master Even Piell from the Citadel, and personally pilots the gunship that extracts the groundside rescue team.

At the end of the Clone Wars, Plo flies his Jedi starfighter during the Republic's capture of Cato Neimoidia. During a post-battle patrol flight, his clone pilot escorts receive Order 66 and fire shots that cripple Plo's ship. He dies when his starfighter crashes into one of Cato Neimoidia's bridge cities.

Meeting Ahsoka
Plo Koon senses the Force in a Togruta girl while visiting her planet. Impressed by her potential, he brings young Ahsoka Tano to the Jedi Temple for training.

SAESEE TIIN

SPECIES Iktotchi **HOMEWORLD** Iktotch
AFFILIATION Jedi

Saesee Tiin is a Jedi Master and a member of the Council who belongs to the horned Iktotchi species. One of the quieter members of the Council, Tiin is known more for his starfighter piloting skills than his Force teachings, and oversees the upgrades to the Order's ships. While on Kwenn, Tiin relies upon his maintenance skills to retrofit a fleet of speeders to assuage a labor conflict.

During the Clone Wars, Tiin joins the attempt to free his colleague Even Piell, who has been captured by the Separatists and imprisoned in the impenetrable Citadel on the planet Lola Sayu. While Obi-Wan Kenobi and Anakin Skywalker lead the rescue mission, Tiin flies Plo Koon's gunship during the dangerous extraction process and commands fellow pilots Adi Gallia and Kit Fisto in the fight against Lola Sayu's droid forces. The Battle of Umbara offers another opportunity for Tiin to provide air cover for Republic troops when he helps Obi-Wan, Anakin, and Jedi Master Pong Krell capture the shadowy world for the Republic.

At the end of the Clone Wars, Mace Windu entrusts Tiin with the news that Supreme Chancellor Palpatine is actually a powerful Sith Lord. Tiin follows Master Windu into the chancellor's office, backed up by fellow Jedi Agen Kolar and Kit Fisto. When Mace announces he is placing Palpatine under arrest, the chancellor suddenly springs into action. Agen Kolar is the first to fall. Tiin moves to strike, but Palpatine is faster and cuts down the Iktotchi Jedi Master.

War veteran
A war weary General Saesee Tiin *(left)* has seen more than his fair share of combat during the Clone Wars, including the rescue attempt of Jedi Master Even Piell from the Citadel on Lola Sayu *(above)*.

Skilled leader
Over the course of the Clone Wars, Master Adi Gallia shows her prowess as a military commander and Jedi warrior.

ADI GALLIA

SPECIES Tholothian **HOMEWORLD** Tholoth
AFFILIATION Jedi

Both Adi Gallia and her cousin Stass Allie serve in the Jedi Order, but only Gallia sits on the Jedi Council prior to the Clone Wars. Gallia serves in this elite role for years. During the Council mission to Kwenn, Gallia works with Yoda to investigate an assault, uncovering that the local gangs are all working together. Gallia's findings lead fellow Council member Depa Billaba to realize they are planning to attack the Jedi.

When armed conflict breaks out on Geonosis, she plays a central role in the Jedi response, from briefing generals, including Iskat Akaris and Tulon Voidgazer, on missions at the Temple to commanding troops on battlefields far from Coruscant. With Anakin Skywalker, Gallia leads the effort to rescue Jedi Master Eeth Koth from the flagship of General Grievous, and in a later engagement, she pilots a starfighter during a daring prison break from the Citadel of Lola Sayu. When General Grievous destroys her fleet, Gallia is taken captive. Plo Koon pursues Grievous, boarding his vessel with a contingent of clone troopers and rescuing Gallia.

Adi meets her end when she and Obi-Wan hunt the dangerous team of Maul and Savage Opress, the vengeful dark-side Nightbrothers determined to destroy the Jedi. At the Cybloc transfer station, Gallia picks up their trail and follows the duo to Florrum. They arrive to find a battle raging between pirate leader Hondo Ohnaka and the two Nightbrothers, with many of Ohnaka's former crew members now working for the Zabrak. Obi-Wan and Gallia try to even the odds, but the power of their foes proves to be too great. Opress gravely injures Gallia by ramming her with his horns and then delivers a killing blow with his red-bladed lightsaber. Her cousin Allie takes her place on the Council.

Many decades later, Rey hears Gallia's voice calling to her as she defeats Darth Sidious on Exegol.

EETH KOTH

SPECIES Zabrak **HOMEWORLD** Iridonia
AFFILIATION Jedi, the Ganthic Enlightenment

Eeth Koth is an esteemed Zabrak Jedi Master who sits on the Council during the final years of the Republic. On one occasion, Eeth heads to Kwenn with the rest of Council, where he assists with taking inventory of the outpost's artifacts, uncovering and eventually recovering stolen items. Eeth later helps evaluate Anakin Skywalker's fitness for Jedi training. Koth remains on the Council throughout the Separatist crisis and serves on the strike force that invades Geonosis at the beginning of the Clone Wars. He is believed to have been killed in battle when his gunship takes a direct hit, but Koth later returns to active duty, and is placed in command of the Republic Star Destroyer *Steadfast*. General Grievous attacks the ship and captures Koth, but the latter shrewdly reveals his location using a secret tap-code during a hologram transmission from Grievous. This enables the Council to track Koth and dispatch Anakin Skywalker and Adi Gallia to lead the mission to free him. Toward the end of the Clone Wars, Koth is kicked off the Council and leaves the Order. He becomes a priest of the Ganthic Enlightenment and marries a fellow Zabrak named Mira. Darth Vader and his Inquisitors track the couple down just after Mira has given birth to their child. Koth tries to offer them information on other Jedi survivors in exchange for his family's lives, but the villains refuse him. While Vader kills Koth in battle, Mira escapes, but their child is captured by the Thirteenth Sister.

OPPO RANCISIS

SPECIES Thisspiasian **HOMEWORLD** Thisspias
AFFILIATION Jedi

The long-lived Oppo Rancisis is a curious sight in the Jedi Council, a group he has been a member of for centuries. A Thisspiasian, he has the lower body of a snake and often sits coiled in quiet contemplation. Master Rancisis has long, clawlike fingernails and a thick beard that masks his face. During the High Republic era, he rescues and briefly mentors the pirate Lourna Dee and leads the defense of the Jedi outpost on Tanalorr. During the Council's mission to Kwenn, Oppo is shocked by the planet's decline. He is among the first Jedi to learn that the Sith have returned after the appearance of Darth Maul. Rancisis remains a high-ranking Jedi and a key military adviser throughout the Clone Wars, during which he becomes a Jedi general coordinating Republic forces across the galaxy. Rancisis is one of the few Jedi to survive Order 66 and is hunted by the Inquisitors.

EVEN PIELL

SPECIES Lannik **HOMEWORLD** Lannik
AFFILIATION Jedi

The battle-scarred Even Piell earns a place on the Jedi Council prior to the Battle of Naboo. Master Piell heads with the rest of the Council to Kwenn, but arrives via the spaceport to witness the poverty of the once-glorious world. Years later, Even takes part in the Republic assault on Geonosis at the start of the Clone Wars, and later becomes a prisoner of war when Separatist forces capture him and Republic Navy Captain Wilhuff Tarkin. Incarcerated in the impregnable Citadel prison on Lola Sayu, Piell withstands torture to preserve the top-secret coordinates of the hyperlane known as the Nexus Route. Despite a rescue effort led by Anakin Skywalker and Ahsoka Tano, Piell is mortally wounded by a wild anooba hound as he escapes from the Citadel.

> "To walk the path of the Jedi, one's spirit must be strong. That requires discipline."
> **OPPO RANCISIS**

DEPA BILLABA

SPECIES Human **HOMEWORLD** Chalacta **AFFILIATION** Jedi

Jedi Master Depa Billaba is a former Padawan of Mace Windu and is highly regarded for her wisdom. Billaba is a valued member of the Jedi Council during the final years of the Republic. Depa is undercover investigating a gang of pirates named the Riftwalkers when the Council goes to planet Kwenn. Alongside Mace, she arrives in Kwenn's orbit just in time to help stop the Riftwalkers' attempt to kill the entire Council. She accompanies the senatorial mission to Bromlarch, which leads to its people being saved from famine. Her sister, Sar Labooda, also serves as a Jedi, but is killed in the Battle of Geonosis. During the Clone Wars, Billaba and Mace face Ochi of Bestoon in the jungles of Malathon IX, with all combatants surviving the duel. Billaba later suffers a devastating defeat at the hands of General Grievous' forces on Haruun Kal and falls into a coma. Billaba eventually recovers and, with a youngling named Caleb Dume, stops a bombing of the Jedi Temple. She decides to take Caleb as her Padawan, and together they see action on Kardoa and face Grievous on Mygeeto. During Order 66, she dies protecting Caleb on Kaller. He adopts the name Kanan Jarrus, and later honors her memory by joining a rebel cell on Lothal and taking Ezra Bridger as a Padawan.

Action on Kaller
On Kaller, Depa and Caleb are impressed by the work of Clone Force 99, who rescue them from a Separatist assault.

YADDLE
AFFILIATION Jedi

Yaddle's short build, long ears, and extended lifespan mark her as a member of the same species as Jedi Master Yoda; she also shares his remarkable affinity for the Force. After rising through the ranks of the Jedi Order, Yaddle achieves the highest possible reward for her contribution—a seat on the Jedi Council. During the High Republic era, she trains younglings such as Vernestra Rwoh. At the Battle of Dalna, Yaddle and the youngling Cippa Tarko fight together against the Path of the Open Hand. Hundreds of years later, Yaddle joins the Council on Kwenn where she calms down an irate technician who questions the Jedi's actions. Soon after, she helps judge Anakin Skywalker's fitness for Jedi training and contributes to the Jedi efforts to resolve the Naboo blockade crisis and uncover clues about the return of the Sith. Yaddle is one of the first Jedi to discover that Count Dooku is working with Darth Sidious, which leads to her death at Dooku's hands just after Qui-Gon's death on Naboo.

YARAEL POOF
SPECIES Quermian **HOMEWORLD** Quermia **AFFILIATION** Jedi

Blessed with two brains, Jedi Master Yarael Poof is an expert practitioner of Jedi mind control and has been on the Jedi Council for centuries. He stands out among his fellow Council members thanks to his towering stature and possesses a second pair of arms that he hides beneath his robes. During the days of the High Republic, he advises Chancellor Lina Soh and attends the opening ceremony for Starlight Beacon. Decades later, during the Council mission to Kwenn, Yarael investigates a criminal element on the planet alongside Ki-Adi-Mundi. By the time of the Battle of Geonosis, Yarael Poof's spot on the Jedi Council has been filled by Jedi Master Coleman Trebor.

LOTT DOD
SPECIES Neimoidian **HOMEWORLD** Cato Neimoidia
AFFILIATION Trade Federation, Galactic Senate, Separatist

The Trade Federation controls most interstellar shipping in the Outer Rim, making it one of the most powerful entities in the galaxy. Its influence is evident when Lott Dod is appointed to the Galactic Senate, a post normally reserved for representatives of systems and sectors. As a senator, Dod thwarts the taxation of the Free Trade Zones and secretly helps organize the Trade Federation's invasion of Naboo. When Naboo's monarch, Queen Amidala, comes to Coruscant to plead for the liberation of her world, Dod claims that she has no proof of her accusations. Throughout the Clone Wars, Dod continues to advance the interests of the Separatists while claiming neutrality.

MAS AMEDDA
SPECIES Chagrian **HOMEWORLD** Champala
AFFILIATION Republic, Galactic Senate, Empire

Politically savvy Chagrian Mas Amedda is given an elite post in the Republic's government when he becomes vice chancellor during the tenure of Supreme Chancellor Valorum. The events surrounding the Battle of Naboo result in a vote of no confidence against Valorum and his removal from office, yet Amedda retains his position under Valorum's successor, Chancellor Palpatine. Power-hungry and pragmatic, Amedda advises Palpatine during the Separatist Crisis, and before the Clone Wars arranges the sudden Senate vote that grants the chancellor emergency war powers, allowing the Republic to seize control of the clone army discovered on Kamino.

Following Order 66, Amedda proclaims that Palpatine will usher in a new age of freedom—and then throws one of Jedi Master Yoda's lightsabers into a furnace. His longstanding loyalty to Palpatine later earns him the position of grand vizier in the Galactic Empire, nominally second-in-command to Palpatine himself. He is granted leadership of the Imperial Ruling Council, a new body that oversees much of the daily running of the Empire so Sidious may focus on gaining more power through the dark side of the Force. Amedda often stands in for the Emperor in the Imperial Senate, handling political issues like the Defense Recruitment Bill. He even travels with Palpatine to the Sith bastion of Exegol.

However, following Palpatine's death, Amedda lacks any real power, and the Empire shatters into multiple factions. Fleet Admiral Gallius Rax, who is in charge of much of the surviving fleet, does not assist Amedda on Coruscant. Amedda attempts to turn himself in to the New Republic, but their leaders refuse to accept his empty surrender. He is imprisoned in the Imperial Palace by Rax's forces until his rescue by a gang of children who deliver him to the New Republic. After the Battle of Jakku, most of the remaining Imperial forces are defeated, so Amedda represents the Empire at the signing of the Galactic Concordance. He then becomes the head of Coruscant's provisional government.

SENATOR TIKKES
SPECIES Quarren
HOMEWORLD Mon Cala
AFFILIATION Republic, Galactic Senate, Separatist

Tikkes represents Mon Cala in the Galactic Senate. Sympathizing with Count Dooku's Separatist movement, he resigns from the Senate to support the Confederacy of Independent Systems, and is rewarded with a seat on the Separatist Council. At the end of the Clone Wars, Tikkes, along with the rest of the Council, is killed by Darth Vader on Mustafar.

KOLARA
SPECIES Human **HOMEWORLD** Carnelion IV **AFFILIATION** Closed

Young pilot Kolara lives on the war-torn planet of Carnelion IV and is a member of the Closed faction, which is fighting a group called the Open. She steals Anakin Skywalker's lightsaber, helping Closed leader Mother Pran capture him. Later, she frees Anakin in an effort to stop the conflict.

CHARACTERS AND CREATURES

SLY MOORE
SPECIES Umbaran **HOMEWORLD** Umbara
AFFILIATION Republic

A Force-attuned Umbaran, Sly Moore serves as the senior administrative aide to Supreme Chancellor Palpatine. Often at Palpatine's side—even when he addresses the galaxy from atop the chancellor's podium in the center of the Senate Chamber— Moore keeps silent in most situations and zealously guards Palpatine's secrets. During the Imperial era, Moore continues to serve as part of the grand vizier's office. Moore keeps a close eye on potentially rebellious senators like Mon Mothma and foils their political moves in the senate. After Han Solo's capture in Cloud City, Palpatine sends Moore to Mustafar to test his apprentice Darth Vader's wavering dedication. Vader defeats Moore, so Palpatine demotes her. Moore later hires IG-88 to assassinate Vader. When this plot fails, she convinces Vader not to kill her and helps him during the Crimson Dawn auction for Han. Around this time, Moore joins Crimson Dawn and survives the destruction of the group.

ORN FREE TAA
SPECIES Twi'lek **HOMEWORLD** Ryloth
AFFILIATION Galactic Senate, Imperial Senate

Greedy and corrupt, Orn Free Taa represents Ryloth in the Galactic Senate. Taa serves as the leader of Chancellor Palpatine's Loyalist Committee and pushes for the Military Creation Act. When the Separatists occupy Ryloth during the Clone Wars, Taa agrees to an alliance with his rival Cham Syndulla to help Mace Windu retake the planet. Taa later becomes a hostage during Cad Bane's strike on the Senate building. Following his release, Taa remains a senator throughout the Clone Wars and during the Imperial era. Initially, Taa retains his alliance with Cham, and the pair work with the Empire. However, when Taa and Imperial Vice Admiral Edmon Rampart imprison Cham's closest allies for smuggling, Syndulla rebels once more. In this ensuing crisis, Taa is injured as Cham leads the Free Ryloth Movement. When Syndulla's group disrupts the planet's spice productivity, the Emperor, Darth Vader, and Taa visit aboard the Star Destroyer *Perilous* and are soon attacked by the rebels. Out of anger, Vader nearly kills Taa, but the Emperor urges him to stop. Senator Taa escapes the *Perilous*' destruction by Syndulla's rebel forces.

DORMÉ
SPECIES Human **HOMEWORLD** Naboo
AFFILIATION Royal House of Naboo, Amidalans

Dormé serves as Padmé Amidala's closest handmaiden during her time as a senator. She becomes Amidala's decoy after the Separatists make another attempt on her life so Amidala can go into hiding just before the onset of the Clone Wars. After Amidala's death, she becomes an Amidalan, even infiltrating the Empire out of loyalty to her fellow handmaidens.

GREGOR TYPHO
SPECIES Human **HOMEWORLD** Naboo
AFFILIATION Royal House of Naboo, Amidalans

During the occupation of Naboo, Gregor Typho is imprisoned in Camp Three where he supports his fellow prisoners and awaits a chance to fight back. During the ensuing battle, Typho fights bravely and loses his left eye. Queen Amidala later selects Typho as a sergeant, and he goes on to serve as Padmé's loyal bodyguard and security advisor during her senatorial career. He eventually succeeds Mariek Panaka as captain of Padmé's security detail. During the rise of the Separatist movement, Padmé faces an increased number of threats to her safety, including the bombing of her starship and the release of venomous kouhuns in her apartment. Typho endorses a plan to send Padmé back to Naboo in disguise with Anakin Skywalker. Meanwhile,

Security duty
Captain Typho confers with Senator Amidala, disguised as a Naboo starfighter pilot, after landing on Coruscant.

Typho stays on Coruscant with Padmé's handmaiden Dormé acting as a decoy. During the Clone Wars, he continues to serve Padmé, and even sees action on Hebekrr Minor and Naboo. After Order 66, Padmé ignores Typho's advice not to travel to Mustafar, and he never sees her again. Typho later joins the Amidalan rebel group, but he dies when the cell attempts to kill Darth Vader on Naboo.

KIT FISTO
SPECIES Nautolan **HOMEWORLD** Glee Anselm
AFFILIATION Jedi

As an amphibious member of the Jedi Council, Kit Fisto leads the Republic's armies to victory on strategic waterworlds across the galaxy. His Nautolan physiology makes him ideally suited to battle above and below the waves. During the Clone Wars, Master Fisto first sees action on Geonosis, serving as one of the Jedi who infiltrate the execution arena to battle Count Dooku's droid soldiers. Soon after this battle, Fisto joins Mace Windu and two other Jedi on a mission to the planet Hissrich. They stop the Separatists from stripping the planet of any more of its unique flora to use as an energy source.

Later in the war, Fisto and his former Padawan Nahdar Vebb trail General Grievous to the third moon of Vassek, only to find themselves trapped inside Grievous' fortress, where Vebb is killed by Grievous during a lightsaber duel. Thanks to his astromech R6-H5, Fisto escapes Vassek alive. Fisto dives under the waves again to save Prince Lee-Char of Mon Cala from a Separatist insurrection led by Commander Riff Tamson and backed by the revolutionary forces of the Quarren Isolation League.

As the Clone Wars begin to draw to an end, Mace learns that Supreme Chancellor Palpatine has been successfully living a double life as a Sith Lord. Kit Fisto, along with Masters Agen Kolar and Saesee Tiin, accompanies Mace to the chancellor's office to confront him and make an arrest. Instead, Palpatine demonstrates his formidable fighting skills. He reveals a hidden lightsaber and explodes into lethal motion, cutting down Fisto before the shocked Nautolan can raise his own blade in defense and block the attack.

Battle tactics
Consulting with a medical officer clone, Fisto is trying to determine what to do with a medical frigate that is approaching a Republic outpost and is believed to be infected with contagion.

Leading the charge
Fisto commands a unit of clone troopers during the fierce fighting on Geonosis. Throughout the war, Master Fisto keeps his famously good humor intact.

LUMINARA UNDULI
SPECIES Mirialan **HOMEWORLD** Mirial
AFFILIATION Jedi

Luminara Unduli is a respected and exacting Jedi Master who is skilled in combat. She is sent alongside Mace Windu to support Jedi Eno Cordova and Cere Junda during a conflict on Ontotho. She also helps Mace depose the warlord Guattako on Oosalon.

Honoring her homeworld's cultural traditions, Luminara takes a fellow Mirialan, Barriss Offee as her Padawan. With their similar robes and facial tattoos, Unduli and Offee are an unmistakable duo.

By the time the Clone Wars break out, Offee's skills have grown enough for Unduli to trust Offee in combat, and both Jedi serve as members of the vanguard force that participates in the Battle of Geonosis. As the war takes shape, Unduli accepts a command rank and takes control of the 41st Elite Corps, working closely with Clone Commander Gree. She later helps escort high-ranking Confederacy captive Nute Gunray, only to be surprised when Separatist commander Asajj Ventress boards the vessel to free its prisoner. Unduli rejects Padawan Ahsoka Tano's offer of help and loses the fight against Ventress, allowing Nute Gunray to escape Republic custody.

During the Second Battle of Geonosis, Master Unduli pursues Separatist leader Poggle the Lesser into a remote network of catacombs where insectoid matron Queen Karina keeps her nest. Overwhelmed by Queen Karina's drones, Unduli nearly becomes an unwilling host for mind-controlling brain worms, until Anakin Skywalker and Obi-Wan Kenobi free her.

As the Clone Wars draw to a close, Unduli participates in the series of battles known as the Outer Rim Sieges. She leads Commander Gree and the 41st Elite Corps to the contested planet of Kashyyyk, the Wookiee homeworld where Master Yoda is also stationed. Though the Republic forces win the day against the Separatist invaders, the Jedi generals do not foresee the shocking betrayal at the hands of their clone troops. When Darth Sidious transmits the top-secret Order 66 to all clone commanders, Gree and his clone troopers turn their weapons on the Jedi. Unlike Master Yoda, Unduli does not escape their ambush and is captured.

Unduli is imprisoned in the Spire on Stygeon Prime until she is executed. Some Jedi survivors believe a rumor that she is still alive and travel to the planet, but it is an Imperial trap. The Grand Inquisitor has kept her remains (which still possess a lingering Force presence) in a cell to attract the unwitting Jedi to their deaths—or worse, corruption to the dark side.

Jedi force
On Geonosis, Luminara prepares for battle alongside Jedi Master, and Council member, Shaak Ti.

BARRISS OFFEE
SPECIES Mirialan **HOMEWORLD** Mirial
AFFILIATION Jedi

Barriss Offee, the Padawan of revered Jedi Master Luminara Unduli, serves with distinction during the Clone Wars until she turns on the Republic in a shocking act of betrayal. Both Offee and Unduli share the heritage of the Mirialan people, though they share a much stronger bond as Jedi.

When the Clone Wars break out, Offee fights at Geonosis alongside her master with both Jedi surviving the battle. During the early engagements, Offee expresses reticence for fighting in a war, but is encouraged to adapt by Jedi Master Depa Billaba. After succeeding in a test set by Unduli in an old temple, Offee and Unduli return to Geonosis to target an advanced droid factory. Teaming up with Padawan Ahsoka Tano, Offee damages the facility and helps bring about a Republic victory. On the way back from Geonosis, Offee and Ahsoka struggle to contain an outbreak of mind-controlling brain worms aboard their starship. Offee falls under the influence of the worms, but Ahsoka breaks their spell by exposing them to freezing temperatures.

Later in the war, following Offee's participation in the Battle of Umbara, a mysterious explosion at the Jedi Temple causes multiple deaths and prompts an investigation that names Ahsoka as the chief suspect. Placed on trial and forced to defend her loyalties, Ahsoka is exonerated only after Anakin's own investigation reveals Barriss Offee as the culprit. Offee makes a full confession, claiming that the Jedi had become the aggressors in the war and that her actions were a justifiable blow against a corrupt, misguided Order. After Order 66, Barriss becomes an Inquisitor but she eventually leaves to again forge her own path.

Clone Wars combatant
Barriss Offee struggles with her role as a warrior, eventually concluding that the Jedi have lost their way and falling to the dark side.

BAIL ORGANA

SPECIES Human **HOMEWORLD** Alderaan
AFFILIATION Galactic Senate, Rebel Alliance

Principled and steadfast, Senator Bail Organa is an inspirational defender of democracy, both in and out of the senate.

FIGHTING FOR PEACE
A viceroy of the House Organa on Alderaan, Bail is also an elected official who works with like-minded politicians such as Mon Mothma and Padmé Amidala. The Separatist Crisis sees Bail take up an advisory position to Supreme Chancellor Palpatine in the Galactic Senate. Given Alderaan's pacifist history, Bail strives to halt the escalation of the Clone Wars and leads relief efforts on Christophsis. He is also instrumental in negotiating with King Katuunko of Toydaria to get vital aid to the suffering Twi'leks on Ryloth and hosts a refugee conference on his homeworld. Bail soon realizes that Palpatine's emergency powers threaten to give the chancellor the authority of a dictator. Speaking out against funding additional troops, Bail finds his suspicions of foul play growing as some of his colleagues die under strange circumstances.

Steadfast senator
Secrecy and patience are Bail's greatest allies during his many years organizing efforts to thwart Emperor Palpatine's Galactic Empire.

Quick pickup
Piloting an airspeeder, Bail Organa is on his way to pick up Yoda after his battle with Darth Sidious.

EARLY REBEL
As the Clone Wars draw to a close, Bail watches Jedi being killed at the Jedi Temple by Republic clone soldiers. He quickly moves to offer refuge to two of his closest allies: Yoda and Obi-Wan Kenobi. After Padmé's death, Bail and his wife Breha Organa adopt Padmé's infant daughter, Leia. Continuing to serve on the Senate, Bail and Mon Mothma secretly plot an armed resistance against Emperor Palpatine.

Early in the Emperor's reign, Bail tracks down former Jedi Ahsoka Tano who later goes on to head Bail's intelligence network. During the early years of the Imperial reign, Organa has reservations about the Defense Recruitment Bill, which proposes an army of regular citizens to replace the clone troopers. He shares his concerns with Senator Riyo Chuchi about the timing of the destruction of the Kaminoan cloning facilities and the push for a new Imperial military.

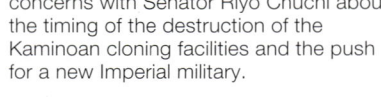

Recruiting allies
Working from inside the senate, Bail starts to form an intelligence network that includes former Jedi Ahsoka Tano in the early years of the Empire.

UNITED FAMILY
From a young age, Bail supports his daughter Leia's opinions and strong will. When the Inquisitor Reva organizes Leia's kidnapping, Bail travels to Tatooine to implore Obi-Wan Kenobi to rescue Leia and return her to Alderaan.

Years later, he sends R2-D2 and C-3PO to gather intel on the Spectre rebel cell, then, soon after, Ahsoka with a small rebel fleet to assist the Spectres on Mustafar.

When Leia comes of age, Bail is proud when she saves a rebel group from Imperial attack, proving herself to be a capable rebel operative. Following the Battle of Garel, Bail and Leia surreptitiously provide Phoenix Squadron with three ships to reinforce their fleet. When the Rebel Alliance officially forms with Mothma as its public leader, Bail remains a secret member in order to protect Alderaan.

UNTIMELY DEATH
After the Alliance learns of the Death Star, Bail advocates fighting the Empire. Mothma asks Bail to call his old ally Obi-Wan out of exile, so he sends his daughter Leia on this mission, while he returns to Alderaan to prepare his pacifist people for war. Shortly after the Battle of Scarif, Grand Moff Tarkin orders the Death Star to fire upon Alderaan, and a single blast kills Bail, Breha, and millions more. Bail is remembered as a rebel hero and a martyr for the New Republic.

New parent
Bail agrees to take Leia home to raise with his wife Breha on Alderaan after Padmé dies on Polis Massa.

ZAM WESELL

SPECIES Clawdite **HOMEWORLD** Zolan
AFFILIATION Bounty hunter

A Clawdite shape-shifter, this bounty hunter can assume the appearance of anyone she chooses. Trained by Mabari warrior-knights in combat, Zam Wesell is a skilled operative who prefers to hit her targets from afar, either with her long-range sniper rifle or her remote-operated probe droids. An ally of Aurra Sing, Zam goes on vacation with her fellow hunter aboard the *Halcyon*. Zam has worked with Jango Fett numerous times, including on Snugano and Tython, and accepts a job from him to assassinate Senator Padmé Amidala of Naboo. But when her quarry's Jedi guardians corner Wesell and cut off her arm, Wesell becomes a liability, whom Fett silences forever with a poisoned Kamino saberdart.

KOUHUN

HOMEWORLD Indoumodo **AVERAGE SIZE** 30 cm (12 in) long **HABITAT** Varies

The kouhun is a highly venomous, multilegged arthropod with a segmented carapace and stingers on the front and rear of its body. Most victims injected with kouhun venom die within minutes. Because kouhuns easily evade security, bounty hunter Zam Wesell employs two of them in an attempt to kill Padmé Amidala in her Coruscant apartment. Anakin Skywalker and Obi-Wan Kenobi exterminate the creatures. Criminal Lanse Crowder later attempts to kill Phee Genoa with a kouhun.

JANGO FETT

SPECIES Human **AFFILIATION** Mandalorians, bounty hunter, Separatist (under contract)

Jango Fett is the genetic source in the creation of the Republic's clone army, becoming the template for millions of soldiers during the Clone Wars. He earns this role after years at the top of the bounty-hunting trade, where he has expertly used his twin blaster pistols and advanced Mandalorian armor. A foundling taken in by a Mandalorian, Jango becomes a highly skilled warrior who sees action in the Mandalorian Civil Wars. On one of the Moons of Bogden, Count Dooku—calling himself Tyranus—approaches Fett with the lucrative cloning offer shortly after the Battle of Naboo. Though it means relocating to the distant world of Kamino, Fett agrees, as long as the Kaminoan geneticists give him an unaltered clone to raise as his child. Over the next decade, Jango Fett cares for his son, Boba, training him to follow in his footsteps, feeling no pride for the clone army created around him. Alongside three other bounty hunters, Jango takes Boba on a job to capture a Twi'lek on Ord Mantell. Jango is proud of how Boba kills two of the other bounty hunters when they betray them, letting the neutral third one survive to spread the story.

Evasive measures
Jango Fett uses his Z-6 compact jetpack to allow him to rocket out of the reach of his enemies.

Flying lessons
Jango teaches his son, Boba, how to fly his prized starship.

Around this time, Jango and bounty hunter Tarr Kligson conduct a heist that soon goes awry, but he refuses to leave wounded Kligson behind. Kligson gives Fett coordinates to Haven, a droid station where Jango leaves Kligson in the care of its inhabitants.

Alongside Zam Wesell, Fett takes on a contract from the Trade Federation's Nute Gunray to kill Senator Padmé Amidala. When Wesell bungles the job, Fett is forced to eliminate her before she can spill her secrets to Jedi investigators. But the dart he leaves behind provides the clue that leads Obi-Wan Kenobi to Kamino. Jango and Boba Fett escape the planet in their ship. Later, on the planet Geonosis, the conflict between the Republic's Jedi and Count Dooku's Separatists explodes into war. Fett squares off against Jedi Master Mace Windu, but loses his head to a swipe of his enemy's lightsaber. Boba Fett continues his father's legacy.

SHAAK TI

SPECIES Togruta **HOMEWORLD** Shili
AFFILIATION Jedi

Following the Battle of Naboo, Jedi Master Shaak Ti advances to the Jedi Council in the years leading up to the Clone Wars. During this time, she goes on a mission with Obi-Wan Kenobi and Anakin Skywalker to Naran-Shiv. Surviving the Battle of Geonosis, she assumes a leadership role among the Republic's newly activated clone troopers. During her deployment on Kamino, Ti leads a counterattack on the combined forces of General Grievous and Asajj Ventress. Joined by Obi-Wan and Anakin, she rallies the clones, ordering them to take on Separatist aqua droids and other robotic soldiers. Her heroic actions prevent Kamino's vital clone laboratories from falling into enemy hands.

At some point during the Clone Wars, Ti and Jedi Master Aayla Secura work together to imprison a dangerous, dark-side entity known as a starweird within the Jedi temple on Sason.

When clone trooper Tup mysteriously turns on his Jedi General Tiplar and kills her, Ti attempts to uncover the reason for his shocking act. Due to the interference of the Sith and the Kaminoans, the Jedi never discover that all clones have a bio chip in their brains containing orders that can be activated and carried out without question. At the end of the Clone Wars, Ti fails to prevent General Grievous from slipping onto Coruscant and kidnapping Supreme Chancellor Palpatine. During Order 66, Ti is at the Jedi Temple and records a holocron message pleading that whoever opens the holocron ensures the Jedi continue. While she is meditating, Ti is then killed by Darth Vader.

High-ranking Jedi
Jedi Master Shaak Ti is stationed on Kamino to keep an eye on the vital cloning operations during the war.

CHARACTERS AND CREATURES

COLEMAN TREBOR
SPECIES Vurk **HOMEWORLD** Sembla
AFFILIATION Jedi

Coleman Trebor earns his place on the Jedi Council during the Separatist Crisis. When he and the other Council members learn of a Separatist force on Geonosis, Master Trebor joins the vanguard to stop Count Dooku before the situation explodes into all-out war. While ambushing Dooku in his viewing box at the execution arena, Trebor is shot and killed by Jango Fett.

DEXTER JETTSTER
SPECIES Besalisk **HOMEWORLD** Ojom
AFFILIATION Himself

Dexter Jettster is a long-lived Besalisk who has had a colorful life spanning centuries. During the High Republic era, Dex is a hyperspace prospector and member of Maz Kanata's pirate crew. When Maz is abducted by the Dank Graks gang, Dex leads a crew to rescue her.

Many decades later, Dex befriends a Jedi Padawan, the young Obi-Wan Kenobi, on the planet Lenahra. After aiding Obi-Wan, Dex settles down on Coruscant where he opens up Dex's Diner. The pair remain friends, and Dex calls on the Jedi to help him capture a thief operating in his diner. Around this time Sabé and Tonra become loyal customers. Obi-Wan also calls on Dex's counsel and, before the Clone Wars, shows Dex a strange object, which he identifies as a deadly Kamino saberdart. Dex urges his old friend to continue his investigations on Kamino, which leads Obi-Wan to discover the clone army.

During the Clone Wars, Dex bemoans the reduced menu due to shortages, but he still takes care of his customers, including Sabé, and friends like Obi-Wan.

JOCASTA NU
SPECIES Human **HOMEWORLD** Coruscant **AFFILIATION** Jedi

Jocasta Nu is a formidable Jedi Master who has served on the High Council in the final decades of the Galactic Republic, and is present during the Council's deliberations on the mission to Nameel. Nu later steps down from the council, perhaps to focus on her role as Chief Librarian of the Jedi Archives. Nu has complete confidence in her records, until that belief is

shaken when she cannot help Obi-Wan Kenobi find Kamino's location. During the Clone Wars, Nu attempts to recruit the recently Knighted Iskat Akaris to the Archives and is concerned by the wayward Jedi's rejection. Nu is later knocked out by Cato Parasitti, a shape-shifter who takes her place until she is unmasked by Ahsoka Tano.

Nu survives Order 66 and tries to resurrect the Jedi Order. Far from Coruscant, she builds a hidden base with a library of holocrons. Nu then returns to Coruscant to retrieve a holocron in the Archives containing a list of known Force-attuned children. After stealthily grabbing her prize, she sees the Grand Inquisitor disrespectfully perusing the Archives and cannot resist dueling him. He nearly kills Nu, but Darth Vader arrives and stops him, which leads to a fight between them and gives Nu the chance to erase the Archives. Nu tries to escape but is captured by Vader. He realizes that the holocron could be used by Darth Sidious to replace him, so he destroys it and kills Nu as well. Years later, Nu's hidden base is found by Luke Skywalker, who is building his own Jedi Order.

AAYLA SECURA
SPECIES Twi'lek **HOMEWORLD** Ryloth
AFFILIATION Jedi

Battle ready
Anakin, Ahsoka, and other Jedi shared Secura's role as battlefield commanders.

Aayla Secura's Force-sensitivity is discovered by Jedi Knight Quinlan Vos, who recruits her into the Order and takes her as his Padawan. She later becomes a Jedi Knight and distinguishes herself as a lightsaber trainer, imparting lessons to the Jedi Master who will become the Inquisitor Seventh Sister.

Secura is among the rescuers sent to Geonosis. She distinguishes herself in combat against the Separatist droid armies, and as the Clone Wars begin, she is in charge of a Republic fleet and frequently leads the 327th Star Corps alongside Commander Bly.

Sent to Escander, Secura is captured by Asajj Ventress but is rescued thanks to the efforts of her troops. Soon after, Secura's fleet suffers heavy losses at Quell. Anakin and Ahsoka Tano come to Secura's aid, but only escape the battle alive by making a highly dangerous blind hyperspace jump. Their vessel crash-lands on Maridun, where Secura seeks medical assistance from the local Lurmen tribe for the injured Anakin. When Separatist General Lok Durd uses the world to test his deadly defoliator weapon, Secura brings an end to the threat.

Later in the war, Secura accepts a post on Coruscant. When a strange zillo beast, brought to the capital for scientific study, escapes and rampages through the city, Secura and Yoda distract the titanic creature in order to give Supreme Chancellor Palpatine enough time to avert its attacks. Secura is later sent with her droid QT-KT to investigate a Separatist facility. She faces Ventress once more but fails to retrieve vital intelligence.

After rising to become a Jedi Master, Secura and Jedi Master Shaak Ti work together to imprison a starweird, a dangerous Force-attuned creature, inside the Jedi temple on Sason.

First warrior
At Geonosis, Aayla Secura fought in the earliest battle of the Clone Wars.

Alongside Masters Windu, Kenobi, and Tiplee, Secura travels to Ord Mantell to investigate the scene of a battle between Count Dooku's Separatist forces and Maul's troops. The Jedi track down their now-allied enemies to Vizsla Keep 09 and fight them. Dooku kills Tiplee and then escapes with Maul.

Toward the end of the Clone Wars, Secura, confident of the Republic's imminent triumph, accepts an assignment to Felucia. But as she leads the 327th Star Corps through the planet's jungles, Bly receives the command to initiate Order 66. Bly's clone troopers open fire, shooting the unsuspecting Secura in the back. Years later, Secura's voice supports Rey as she finally defeats Darth Sidious.

Betrayed
Aayla Secura loses her life on Felucia when her clone troopers turn on her.

QUEEN JAMILLIA
SPECIES Human **HOMEWORLD** Naboo
AFFILIATION Royal House of Naboo

Jamillia is a passionate proponent of democracy, who puts herself forward as a candidate when the vote takes place to elect the next royal to replace Queen Amidala. However, Jamillia loses to Réillata, who becomes the next monarch. Jamillia stands in a later election and wins, reigning during the height of the Separatist crisis. She personally calls upon Amidala to rescue a number of Naboo's artists, including her sister, who are trapped behind Separatist lines.

Fully loaded
As an astromech unit, R4-P17 is packed with tools and gadgets, including an arc welder and a fire extinguisher.

R4-P17
MANUFACTURER Industrial Automaton **TYPE** Astromech droid **AFFILIATION** Republic

R4-P17, known familiarly as R4, is the astromech droid assigned to Obi-Wan's Jedi starfighter. R4 shows great bravery in the face of Separatist aggression. As a product of Industrial Automaton, R4 is designed to serve as a hyperspace navigator for calculating lightspeed jumps and also as a general-purpose repair and maintenance droid. Prior to the Clone Wars, R4-P17 joins up with Obi-Wan as the plug-in counterpart for his Delta-7 starfighter. When Obi-Wan's investigation into suspicious dealings on Coruscant leads him from Kamino to Geonosis, R4 accompanies her master through a hazardous asteroid field in pursuit of Jango Fett.

End of a droid
After R4 is attacked by buzz droids during the Battle of Coruscant, she is dismantled and there isn't enough time during the chaotic dogfight to repair her.

She continues in this role throughout the Clone Wars, transferring from the Delta-7 to the new Eta-2 interceptor as Obi-Wan runs missions to Teth, Rodia, Mandalore, and other trouble spots across the galaxy. At the end of the Clone Wars, R4 and Obi-Wan team-up one last time during the Battle of Coruscant. As Obi-Wan pilots his interceptor through a cloud of enemies, a swarm of buzz droids attaches to his ship, bent on sabotage. The droids pull R4's dome loose from her head, ending her operational life. Obi-Wan replaces R4 with another droid, R4-G9, for his mission to Utapau.

TAUN WE
SPECIES Kaminoan **HOMEWORLD** Kamino
AFFILIATION Cloners

Taun We is the project coordinator of the Republic's clone army and serves Lama Su as the administrative aide to the prime minister and as Jango Fett's main contact in Tipoca City. When Obi-Wan arrives on Kamino, Taun We arranges for a meeting between the visitor and Prime Minister Lama Su to discuss the progress of the cloning project. She later brings Obi-Wan to visit the prime clone, Jango, where she introduces the Jedi Master to Jango and his clone son, Boba. During the Imperial era, We is sent to Bora Vio by Su to retrieve the clone Omega who has been captured by Cad Bane on Su's orders. However, We is killed by Fennec Shand who has been hired by rebellious Kaminoan Nala Se who wants to keep Omega away from Su.

PRIME MINISTER LAMA SU
SPECIES Kaminoan **HOMEWORLD** Kamino
AFFILIATION Cloners

The prime minister of Kamino, Lama Su receives the order for the vast clone trooper army to be used by the Jedi on behalf of a buyer he knows as Sifo-Dyas. Su is also in league with the Sith and is given a bio chip by Darth Tyranus, to be copied and implanted into every clone. During the Clone Wars, one of the clones malfunctions and kills a Jedi. Tyranus orders Su and the Kaminoans to take control of the investigation. They prevent the Jedi from discovering the chip contains secret orders that can be activated to kill them. After the Clone Wars, the Empire moves away from clone soldiers, preferring to train recruits. Fearing for his people's future, Su attempts to secure Omega and, by extension, the means to clone superior combatants, but is thwarted by Nala Se who cares for the child. Soon after, he is imprisoned by the Empire as Kamino's cities and most of his people are destroyed. He starts working with the Imperials in an attempt to secure his freedom.

CHARACTERS AND CREATURES

CLONE TROOPER
SPECIES Human **HOMEWORLD** Kamino
AFFILIATION Republic

Lacking an army to fight Count Dooku's Separatists, the Republic take delivery of thousands of clone troopers. But the clones exist only to help Supreme Chancellor Palpatine eliminate the Jedi, whereupon he declares himself the Emperor of the First Galactic Empire.

SECRET CREATION
Palpatine and Count Dooku join forces to take control of a clone army that is being secretly created on behalf of a rogue Jedi in the genetics laboratories of Kamino. Each clone, an altered copy of bounty hunter Jango Fett, grows at an accelerated rate and receives extensive training in battlefield tactics. Some fill elite roles as Advanced Recon Commandos, while others study tactics to become officers. Yet none of the clones know the details of Palpatine's scheme, and when the order comes to go into action as the soldiers of the Grand Army of the Republic, the clones do their duty and fight with honor.

Programmed learning
Obi-Wan Kenobi reviews the inner workings of the cloning facility on Kamino *(above)*.

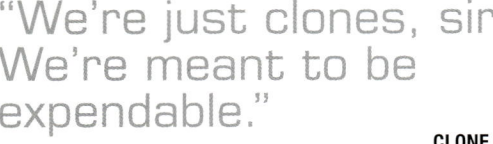

"We're just clones, sir. We're meant to be expendable."
— CLONE SERGEANT

FIRST GENERATION
After Master Yoda takes delivery of the first batch of clones, they quickly see action at the Battle of Geonosis. These clone troopers wear all-white armor with fins on the top of their helmets. They deploy their heavy equipment, including AT-TE walkers and LAAT/i gunships, and achieve a hard-fought victory against the Separatists.

Preparing a counterstrike
Three first-generation clones take the initiative against a wave of Separatist battle droids.

THE CLONE WARS
The Republic's clone troopers give the conflict between the Republic and the Separatists its name: the Clone Wars. Shipping out to every part of the galaxy on vast warships, the clones fight on Christophsis, Maridun, Ryloth, and elsewhere. With the Jedi as generals, clone troopers such as Captain Rex and Commander Cody work closely with Anakin Skywalker, Obi-Wan Kenobi, and others. The troopers' original armor is retired in favor of more advanced Phase II armor, more easily customized with patterns and colors.

ORDER 66
Palpatine arranges for the Kaminoans to give each clone trooper an inhibitor chip implant. This ensures the clones will be unable to resist certain commands, in particular one designed to wipe out the Jedi, code-named Order 66. The conspiracy nearly comes to light when one clone's inhibitor chip malfunctions, but the evidence is suppressed by the Kaminoans. When the Clone Wars come to a close, Darth Sidious issues Order 66, causing the clone troopers to turn on the Jedi.

CLONES OF THE EMPIRE
In the years immediately following Order 66, the clone army remains in service of the Galactic Empire. With their DNA modified so that they age rapidly, the remaining clone troopers' service horizon is limited. After the Empire destroys the Kaminoan cloning facilities, most are forced to retire when the Imperial Senate passes the Defense Recruitment Bill, heralding the end of their service is nigh. However a small minority find special positions, such as members of Palpatine's Royal Guard or as training officers. Palpatine himself favors a volunteer stormtrooper corps recruited from loyal Imperial systems throughout the galaxy. Many unfortunate clones struggle to find a new path outside of military service and they become an increasingly rare sight in the galaxy.

Treachery
Jedi Knight Aayla Secura is shot in the back by the clone troopers she once commanded.

Long in the tooth
Wolffe, Gregor, and Rex escape their restrictive clone life by removing their inhibitor chips and living in an AT-TE on Seelos.

BOBA FETT

SPECIES Human **HOMEWORLD** Kamino
AFFILIATION Bounty hunter, Krayt's Claw, his personal criminal empire

A clone of Jango Fett who raises him as his son, Boba Fett survives the Clone Wars to become a relentless and highly paid bounty hunter, and then later a crime lord in his own right.

CLONE ORIGINS
When Mandalorian Jango Fett agrees to become the genetic donor for a clone army being grown on Kamino, he requests an unaltered clone to raise as the heir to his legacy. For 10 years, Boba Fett grows up in the clinical environment of Kamino's Tipoca City, occasionally accompanying his father to track down bounties for money. Boba's first mission is to Ord Mantell, where he kills two fellow bounty hunters who try to betray him and his father. Obi-Wan Kenobi eventually uncovers the Kamino cloning operation, prompting Jango and Boba to flee to Geonosis. There, a Jedi strike force raids the execution arena and overwhelms the Separatist defenders. The leader of the Jedi, Mace Windu, uses his lightsaber to behead Jango Fett.

Battle-hardened
Boba Fett's career as a professional hunter is legendary, and the scrapes and dents of his armor attest to his numerous escapes and near-death experiences.

His father's legacy
When Jango dies on Geonosis, Boba continues his father's work. He carries a grudge against the Jedi, and Mace Windu in particular.

LEARNING THE ROPES
The orphaned Boba finds guidance from assassin Aurra Sing. Joined by bounty hunters Bossk and Castas, Fett poses as a clone cadet and causes the crash of the Republic vessel *Endurance*. Fett is captured by the Republic on Florrum, but later assembles a new team that he names Krayt's Claw. Together, they are hired to defend a hovertrain on Quarzite and later rescue a Jedi from Count Dooku's palace on Serenno. At some point in his youth, Boba learns some of his craft from Cad Bane and Hondo Ohnaka.

FORGING HIS NAME
During the early years of the Imperial era, Boba cements his fearsome reputation as a legendary bounty hunter and his longtime association with criminal kingpin Jabba the Hutt. On one occasion, he tracks down wanted bounty hunter Caij Vanda on Koboh, encountering Jedi survivor Cal Kestis.
Following the Imperial defeat during the Battle of Yavin, Darth Vader hires Boba to discover the identity of the rebel pilot who blew up the Death Star, leading Boba to Luke Skywalker. Fett later shares his findings with Darth Vader, revealing to the Sith Lord that his son is alive.

TRACKING DOWN HAN
After the Battle of Hoth, Darth Vader assembles a group of top bounty hunters to find Han Solo's *Millennium Falcon*. Boba arranges a trap for Han on Cloud City, which ends with the smuggler being safely encased in a slab of carbonite. En route to deliver Han to Jabba, Boba's bounty is stolen by Crimson Dawn, leading the Hutt to place a bounty on Boba, and the skilled Mandalorian is forced to defeat many colleagues. With tremendous odds against him and at great cost, Boba re-collects his prize, and safely delivers Han to the crime lord. He is present at Jabba's palace when Luke Skywalker attempts a rescue. During a fight against the Jedi at the Great Pit of Carkoon, Boba's jetpack malfunctions due to a wayward blow from a disoriented Han and he falls into the mouth of the mighty Sarlacc.

OUT OF THE SARLACC
Fett awakens in one of the creature's stomachs. He burns his way out of the beast, and then digs up through the sand to free himself. A group of Jawas stumble upon the weakened Boba and knock him unconscious, stripping him of his armor (later selling it to Cobb Vanth).

> "He's no good to me dead."
> — BOBA FETT

A Tusken tribe discovers Boba and takes him prisoner. After several beatings and escape attempts, Boba earns the respect of the nomads when he single-handedly kills a sand beast, saving a child in the process. The tribe welcomes Boba as one of their own, teaching him their culture. Boba returns the favor by helping the Tuskens overtake a train that the Pyke Syndicate uses to terrorize them. The Tusken chief invites Boba to take part in a sacred ceremony that ends with Fett crafting his own gaderffii stick.
Harmony is short-lived as the Pykes enact revenge, wiping out the Tuskens. Fett roams the desert and finds a grievously wounded Fennec Shand. Boba saves her life, and the two agree to work together.

NEW PURPOSE
The former bounty hunter denounces his old ways, and with Fennec's help, tracks his armor to Tython and fellow Mandalorian bounty hunter Din Djarin. Din relinquishes the armor to Boba once he learns Jango Fett was a foundling who passed on his armor to his son. Indebted to Din, Boba and Fennec help him rescue his charge, Grogu, from Moff Gideon.
Once all debts are paid, Boba and Fennec return to Tatooine and take over Jabba's criminal organization, murdering its current leader, Bib Fortuna. Boba slowly earns the respect of a number of criminals, including the Wookiee bounty hunter Krrsantan, as he builds up his new organization on Mos Espa, choosing respect instead of fear to establish his position as the new daimyo. He is also gifted a rancor by two rivals, the Hutt twins. A gang war between Boba and the Pykes soon ignites, leading to a fateful battle in the streets of Mos Espa. During this engagement, Boba defeats his old mentor Cad Bane, and with the aid of his allies, eliminates the Pykes and those loyal to them. Now victorious, the survivors unite under Boba who enjoys the newfound respect he has earned.

Allies in battle
Din and Boba share many similarities. Both of them are Mandalorian warriors, skilled in bounty hunting. They are also looking to forge new paths in their lives, so they support each other during these transitional times.

CHARACTERS AND CREATURES

Fateful meeting
Owen Lars and Beru Whitesun meet Padmé Amidala and Anakin Skywalker, the couple whose son Luke they will later raise as their own (right). By the time Luke becomes a teenager, time and Tatooine's harsh climate have left their marks on Owen's visage (below).

"I guess I'm your stepbrother. I had a feeling you might show up someday." **OWEN LARS TO ANAKIN**

OWEN LARS
SPECIES Human **HOMEWORLD** Tatooine **AFFILIATION** None

A pragmatic and serious-minded Tatooine moisture farmer, Owen Lars has learned his strong work ethic from his father, Cliegg Lars. When his father marries Shmi Skywalker, Owen is drawn into the complicated life of Shmi's son, Anakin Skywalker. Owen and Anakin meet for the first time following Shmi's kidnapping at the hands of Tuskens. Owen doesn't believe Anakin is much like his mother, but Owen and Beru's partnership encourages Anakin to make the decision to marry Padmé.

Anakin manages to retrieve Shmi's lifeless body and returns to the Lars' farm, while Cliegg dies not long after from wounds sustained in the search for his wife.

Owen and his new wife Beru inherit the moisture farm and agree to Obi-Wan Kenobi's request that they raise Anakin's son Luke as their own. Owen accepts that Obi-Wan will live on Tatooine as "Ben," but insists the Jedi keep watch from afar.

Not wanting a future like Anakin's for Luke, Owen is protective and doesn't allow Obi-Wan to train the boy, or even visit. Owen keeps Luke occupied with chores. When Owen is taken by bounty hunter Krrsantan, Obi-Wan attempts a rescue, but Owen falls off a cliff. Luckily, Luke flies to the rescue in his T-16 skyhopper. He manages to maneuver the ship underneath Owen, so he lands on one of its blasters. It's not the only danger the Lars family faces. Obi-Wan's rescue of Leia Organa eventually brings the Third Sister's attention to Tatooine and Anakin's son. Owen finds out that the Inquisitor asked about the location of the Lars homestead and rushes home to warn Beru. Owen fights valiantly against the Inquisitor, who defeats him but ends up not killing Luke. After the experience, Owen tells Ben he can meet Luke.

Many years later, and despite Owen's best efforts to keep Luke safe from the Empire, stormtroopers arrive at the Lars homestead, and on orders from Darth Vader execute both Owen and Beru.

BERU WHITESUN LARS
SPECIES Human **HOMEWORLD** Tatooine **AFFILIATION** Whitesuns

Tatooine native Beru Whitesun grows up knowing the Lars family. After meeting Shmi Skywalker in Watto's shop, she introduces her to Cliegg Lars and goes on to help Shmi free people from enslavement. Beru eventually falls in love with Owen Lars just prior to the Battle of Geonosis and is present at the Lars moisture farm when Anakin Skywalker arrives in search of his mother Shmi. After Shmi's death, Beru continues to free others from enslavement. Beru and Owen later marry, and Obi-Wan Kenobi places Anakin's infant son Luke Skywalker in their care. They raise him as their son, keeping his true parentage a secret. After a bounty hunter captures Owen, Beru bravely grabs a rifle to go after her husband, but Obi-Wan and Luke save him first.

The arrival of the Inquisitor Third Sister threatens their safety. The villain deduces that Vader's son is part of the Lars family, so she heads to the homestead to kill him to satiate her need for revenge. Owen thinks they should leave and hide, but Beru insists she will not leave their home. With a no-nonsense attitude, she pulls weapons from hiding and forms a plan to protect Luke. When Reva arrives after suns-set, Beru doesn't back down, instructing the boy to run while she tries to distract the attacker. Luke is eventually returned to them safely.

When Imperial stormtroopers arrive at the farm searching for the droids R2-D2 and C-3PO, Beru and Owen die by blaster fire from a stormtrooper executioner squad.

CLIEGG LARS
SPECIES Human **HOMEWORLD** Tatooine **AFFILIATION** None

The tough and strong-willed Cliegg Lars lives as a moisture farmer on Tatooine with his wife, Shmi Skywalker. He loses his love—and his right leg—to a hunting party of Tuskens. Anakin Skywalker retrieves his mother's body, but Cliegg dies shortly after, leaving the farm to his son Owen and Owen's wife, Beru.

Deciding to fight
Beru's work on the moisture farm is interrupted by the impending attack. She decides they have a better chance to defend Luke in their home.

Eyes on the future
Beru Lars plays a vital role in shaping the destiny of the galaxy when she agrees to raise Luke Skywalker. Her sensitive and nurturing nature instills in Luke a love of family and a strong moral sense (left).

POGGLE THE LESSER
SPECIES Geonosian
HOMEWORLD Geonosis
AFFILIATION Separatist

Archduke Poggle the Lesser controls the droid factories of Geonosis during the Clone Wars. Backed by Darth Sidious, Poggle manufactures millions of B1 battle droids for the Trade Federation and later produces the new super battle droid on behalf of Count Dooku's Separatists. When Poggle's warriors capture Obi-Wan Kenobi, Anakin Skywalker, and Padmé Amidala on Geonosis, Poggle orders their executions, and remains on the scene to fight the Republic's invading clone troopers. He passes on the Geonosian plans for a battle station to Dooku for safekeeping.

Later in the Clone Wars, Poggle destroys his droid factory to prevent it from falling into the hands of the Republic. He hopes to find refuge with the Geonosian Queen Karina, but instead becomes a prisoner of war. Poggle is interrogated by the Republic and is only released when he agrees with Lieutenant Commander Orson Krennic that the Geonosians will now build a battle station for the Republic. The Archduke has other plans though, and covertly begins an uprising on Geonosis that sabotages the construction and enables him to rejoin the Separatist Council. He dies with the rest of the Council on Mustafar.

Commanding presence
Poggle is in charge of all Geonosians and most of the robotic products produced in their factories, such as this T-series tactical droid.

WAT TAMBOR
SPECIES Skakoan
HOMEWORLD Skako Minor
AFFILIATION Separatist, Techno Union

As a Skakoan, Wat Tambor wears an elaborate pressure suit and speaks through an electronic loudspeaker. As lead engineer of the Techno Union, he controls the most advanced war assets in the galaxy. Tambor serves on the Separatist Council during the Clone Wars and briefly becomes a Republic prisoner following the Battle of Ryloth. Returning to Skako Minor, Tambor uses a captured clone trooper named Echo to access Republic military tactics in order to help the Separatists, until the clone is rescued. Tambor later perishes on Mustafar.

SHU MAI
SPECIES Gossam **HOMEWORLD** Castell
AFFILIATION Commerce Guild, Separatist

As Presidente of the Commerce Guild, Shu Mai controls the pooled financial resources of some of the galaxy's largest corporations. She uses her influence to gain a seat on the Separatist Council, but tells Count Dooku that the Guild will only covertly support his movement. It is a secret allegiance that leads to her death on Mustafar.

SAN HILL
SPECIES Muun **HOMEWORLD** Scipio
AFFILIATION InterGalactic Banking Clan, Separatist

As the Chairman of the InterGalactic Banking Clan, San Hill wields considerable influence. Just prior to the Battle of Geonosis, he meets in secret with Count Dooku and pledges the support of his financial cartel to the Separatists. Along with others in the Separatist Council, he is murdered by Darth Vader on Mustafar.

MASSIFF
HOMEWORLD Various **AVERAGE SIZE** 1 m (3 ft) high
HABITAT Desert

Massiffs are snarling hunters found on both Tatooine and Geonosis. Though their powerful bites are dangerous, trained massiffs are employed by many, including Tuskens, Weequay pirates, clone troopers, and Imperials, as guard beasts. The spines on a massiff's back provide an extra level of defense, and the creature's large eyes allow it to see well in nighttime conditions.

PASSEL ARGENTE
SPECIES Koorivar
HOMEWORLD Kooriva
AFFILIATION Corporate Alliance, Separatist

After winning the post of Magistrate of the Corporate Alliance, Passel Argente serves in the Galactic Senate and is among the senators who support Chancellor Valorum's removal from office. Argente resigns from office to become a member of the Separatist Council, and is among those killed on Mustafar.

DARTH TYRANUS (COUNT DOOKU)

SPECIES Human **HOMEWORLD** Serenno
AFFILIATION Jedi, Sith, Separatist

> "I have become more powerful than any Jedi. Even you."
> COUNT DOOKU

No one suspects that Count Dooku is Sith Lord Darth Tyranus. Yet the ex-Jedi works as Darth Sidious' apprentice, secretly pulling the strings of a false war that tears the galaxy in two.

JEDI BEGINNINGS
A son of the ruling family on Serenno, Dooku is surrendered to the Jedi Order when his Force ability is discovered. Unusually for many Jedi, Dooku retains a secret familial connection to his sister Jenza. As a youngling, Dooku becomes good friends with Sifo-Dyas, and the pair get into trouble breaking into the Bogan collection in the Jedi Temple. When the time comes, Dooku is selected to become Master Yoda's Padawan. He eventually rises through the ranks to become one of the finest Jedi of his generation.

Dooku's lightsaber skills are inspirational to many younglings, and he is a veteran of many conflicts. During his time with the Jedi Order, he takes two Padawans (Rael Averross and Qui-Gon Jinn), forming strong attachments with both. Known only to Rael and Qui-Gon, Dooku becomes obsessed with the ancient prophecies of the Jedi mystics. These prophecies lead Dooku to secretly explore the dark side of the Force, even using Force-generated lightning to protect Qui-Gon in battle. His faith in the Jedi Order and the Republic is shaken by numerous missions where the two organizations appear to show little care for those they are sworn to protect.

PICKING A NEW ORDER
At some point, Dooku decides to leave the Jedi Order, but still remains on good terms with his former colleagues, visiting on occasion and offering advice to younglings and masters alike. However, he also falls under the influence of Darth Sidious who tempts him to join the Sith.

The pair learn of Sifo-Dyas's secret plan to order a clone army for the Republic from the Kaminoans. Dooku orders the Pyke Syndicate to execute his former friend.

Dooku then sees Qui-Gon one last time, when his former Padawan brings young Anakin Skywalker to the Jedi Temple. Master Yaddle senses Dooku's disquiet and follows him to a clandestine meeting with Darth Sidious. She interrupts to offer Dooku a second chance, but it's too late and he slays Yaddle. He then formally becomes Sidious' new apprentice, Darth Tyranus. The Sith then take over dealing with the Kaminoans with Dooku arranging for bounty hunter Jango Fett to be the genetic template for the clone army.

In the following decade, Dooku emerges as the leader of a Separatist movement that persuades thousands of star systems to split away from the Republic. On Rattatak, he also recruits Asajj Ventress to be his apprentice.

Soon after, on Geonosis, Dooku tries to recruit Qui-Gon's apprentice, Obi-Wan Kenobi, to help him destroy Darth Sidious but fails and doesn't stop the Geonosian attempt to execute him alongside Anakin and Padmé Amidala. When the Jedi and clone army arrive to save the trio, a full-blown conflict erupts between the Republic and Separatists. As the theater of war expands, Dooku defeats Obi-Wan and maims Anakin, before facing Yoda in a lightsaber duel and escaping. While the Jedi are aware he is a Sith, they are unsure if he is the master or the apprentice.

Geonosis escape
Pursued by a Republic gunship, Dooku flees on a speeder bike to a hangar so that he can abandon the Battle of Geonosis.

CLONE WARS
Count Dooku leads the Separatists' battle droid armies, aided by Ventress and the cyborg General Grievous. After failing to pit the Hutts against the Republic by kidnapping Jabba's son, Rotta, Dooku briefly becomes a hostage of the pirate king Hondo Ohnaka. Later, when Darth Sidious orders Dooku to eliminate Ventress, he abandons his apprentice to her fate and selects the Zabrak warrior Savage Opress as a replacement bodyguard from Mother Talzin's Nightsisters. For his betrayal of Ventress, his former apprentice and the Nightsisters try to assassinate Dooku, but he retaliates by obliterating their Dathomir stronghold.

Following Dooku's brutal attack on the Mahran people, the Jedi Council agrees to assassinate Dooku, asking Asajj Ventress and Jedi Master Quinlan Vos to carry it out. When they fail in their plan, Vos is captured by Dooku and corrupted to the dark side, becoming a key Separatist leader. However, Vos eventually returns to the light, thanks to Asajj's intervention.

THE ENDGAME
When the Separatists strike at Coruscant, Dooku obeys the orders of his master Darth Sidious and waits aboard the flagship *Invisible Hand* to set a trap for Anakin Skywalker. Despite his own machinations, Dooku never suspects that Sidious plans to remove him all along. The count defeats Obi-Wan Kenobi and challenges Anakin while Palpatine watches, pretending to be a helpless prisoner. Because Dooku has dueled Anakin multiple times before, he does not expect the Jedi Knight to put up much of a fight. Anakin, however, has gained considerable skill since their last encounter, and engages Dooku in an intense duel. After disarming his opponent, Anakin picks up Dooku's fallen lightsaber and holds both blades to the Sith's throat. Dooku hopes his master will intervene, but when Palpatine growls "Kill him," he finally understands the inevitability of Sith betrayal.

Playing his part
Dooku believes that his master will come to his aid if his duel with Anakin grows dangerous, but he is unprepared for Palpatine's duplicity.

From Jedi to Count
When Dooku grows disillusioned with the Jedi Order, no argument can convince him to remain. Dooku's former master, Yoda, is suspicious and believes his former Padawan has hidden motivations for leaving.

ONACONDA FARR
SPECIES Rodian **HOMEWORLD** Rodia
AFFILIATION Galactic Senate

Republic Senator Onaconda Farr is a family friend of Padmé Amidala, who accompanies the young Padmé and her father Ruwee to help the people of Shadda-Bi-Boran. When she starts her senatorial career, Farr is eager to support her and welcomes her into his political group alongside Senators Mothma and Organa. However, he still kidnaps her on behalf of the Separatists during the Clone Wars to ensure supplies for his homeworld, Rodia. Farr later has a change of heart and delivers Separatist Nute Gunray into custody and is welcomed back into the Senate. When Farr joins forces with Organa to stop the deregulation of the banks in order to help the Republic finance the war, his aide poisons him for the benefit of the Separatists.

ORRAY
HOMEWORLD Geonosis
AVERAGE SIZE 2 m (7 ft) high, 3 m (10 ft) long **HABITAT** Desert

Orrays, capable of hauling heavy loads, serve as mounts for the native Geonosians, including picadors who guide carts into the execution arena carrying condemned prisoners. Tamed orrays are identifiable by the metal caps that cover stumps where their tails used to be.

REEK
HOMEWORLD Geonosis (Codian Moon)
AVERAGE SIZE 2 m (6 ft) high, 4 m (13 ft) long **HABITAT** Grasslands

Reeks are three-horned herbivores with stubborn attitudes and a dangerous headlong charge. In the execution arena on Geonosis, reeks are used to threaten prisoners, and these specimens have rings through their noses that their Geonosian handlers use to keep them under control. The animals are found on Ylesia and the Codian Moon but have been exported across the galaxy due to their strength and ability to resist injury. When Anakin Skywalker faces a reek in the arena, he calms the creature by using the Force and then hitches a ride on its back. Sadly, the reek proves no match for a blaster pistol—bounty hunter Jango Fett takes it out with a single shot.

Warning signs
When a reek paws at the ground, it is preparing to charge at its target *(above)*. General Grievous rides a reek through the jungles of Saleucami *(right)*.

Predator and prey
An angry nexu bares its teeth at the Geonosian wrangler.

NEXU
HOMEWORLD Cholganna **AVERAGE SIZE** 1 m (3 ft) high, 2 m (7 ft) long **HABITAT** Forests

The nexu is a felinelike predator with multiple eyes and a long, hairless tail. Nexu evolved on the forested planet Cholganna and have spread offworld, owing to their value as attack beasts. Once a nexu has pinned its prey beneath its sharp claws, it bites down and savagely shakes its victim to death. Padmé Amidala faces death in the Geonosis execution arena from a fierce nexu, which first kills one of the Geonosian guards before turning its attention to her. Padmé suffers a slash from one of the nexu's claws before the animal dies after being struck by a charging reek. Some nexu can be tamed: a specimen named Furball accompanies a bounty hunter crew led by T'onga until the creature's untimely death.

ACKLAY
HOMEWORLD Vendaxa **AVERAGE SIZE** 3 m (10 ft) high **HABITAT** Land and water

The acklay is a gigantic amphibious crustacean originally from Vendaxa. Protected by a hard carapace, it scuttles around on six pointed legs and uses its claws to spear prey. It has a mouth filled with sharp teeth and uses an organ beneath its chin to sense the body electricity of its prey. On Geonosis, acklays are used as killer beasts inside the execution arena. Geonosian picadors keep the larger creatures under control by jabbing at them with long-handled spears. Obi-Wan Kenobi nearly loses his life to an acklay inside the arena, avoiding the beast's claws until he retrieves his lightsaber and finishes off the acklay. Decades later, Kylo Ren lands on Vendaxa while hunting for the Resistance and scares an acklay off with his lightsaber.

Deadly standoff
Armed with a spear, Obi-Wan faces off against an acklay in the execution arena.

STASS ALLIE

SPECIES Tholothian
HOMEWORLD Tholoth
AFFILIATION Jedi

Stass Allie sits on the Jedi Council during the Clone Wars and fights bravely as a member of the Jedi strike team assigned to the First Battle of Geonosis. Stationed on Saleucami during the Outer Rim Sieges, Master Allie dies during the Jedi betrayal of Order 66. Her clone trooper escorts suddenly fire on her speeder bike, sending her into a fatal crash.

GENERAL WHORM LOATHSOM

SPECIES Kerkoiden **HOMEWORLD** Kerkoidia **AFFILIATION** Separatist

After General Loathsom captures the planet Christophsis, the Republic invades to liberate it. Loathsom counters the attack, dispatching his battle droids, which are protected behind a powerful deflector shield. Unable to penetrate this barrier, Obi-Wan Kenobi discusses terms of surrender with Loathsom, allowing Anakin Skywalker and Ahsoka Tano time to destroy the shield generator. Loathsom is captured and taken to Coruscant, where he is imprisoned for treason.

ADMIRAL WULLF YULAREN

SPECIES Human **HOMEWORLD** Coruscant
AFFILIATION Republic Navy, Empire

Wullf Yularen is one of the Republic's most notable fleet commanders with a long history of involvement in naval conflicts, including a loss to Admiral Trench at the Battle of Malastare Narrows. During the Clone Wars, Yularen fights at Kudo III, Christophsis, Ryloth, Devaron, and Geonosis, working with high-ranking Jedi at nearly every engagement.

After the war, Yularen becomes a colonel and leader of the Imperial Security Bureau (ISB). He takes particular interest in the career of the capable ISB Agent Kallus, and the Chiss rising star Lieutenant Thrawn. Yularen helps Thrawn build connections with high-ranking Imperials. Following the Aldhani heist, Palpatine gives Yularen near-unlimited power to track down rebels and stamp out any criminal activity. The day after, Yularen personally briefs the ISB board on the severe repercussions for the galaxy and approves Supervisor Dedra Meero's hunt for the rebel code-named Axis.

After calling upon Yularen's aid to investigate Nightswan, Thrawn also seeks the colonel's assistance to uncover the undercover rebel operative code named "Fulcrum" in the Imperial ranks. Yularen is shocked when Thrawn reveals that "Fulcrum" is Kallus, but they both decide to let Kallus continue to operate so they can pass misinformation to the rebels. Following the completion of the Death Star, Yularen is assigned to the station and perishes when it is destroyed.

ADMIRAL TRENCH

SPECIES Harch **HOMEWORLD** Secundus Ando
AFFILIATION Separatist

Prior to the Clone Wars, the Harch named Trench earns fame as a naval commander when he defeats Wullf Yularen in the Battle of Malastare Narrows. Named an admiral in the Separatist fleet, Trench blockades Christophsis but loses his cruiser to Anakin Skywalker's stealth ship. He survives, and later assumes command of Separatist operations at Ringo Vinda. When Trench attempts to bomb the planet Anaxes, he is stopped by the Republic forces and is killed by Anakin.

CLONE COMMANDER CODY

SPECIES Human **HOMEWORLD** Kamino
AFFILIATION Republic

Given the designation CC-2224, this clone takes the name "Cody" and is assigned to General Kenobi's 212th Attack Battalion as his second-in-command. Commander Cody enjoys camaraderie with Captain Rex and fights alongside Obi-Wan Kenobi at Hisseen, Christophsis, Teth, Abrion Bridge, and the Second Battle of Geonosis. He helps extract Jedi Master Even Piell from the Citadel prison on Lola Sayu and later captures Umbara's capital city, despite Master Pong Krell's treachery. Cody works with Kenobi, General Skywalker, and Ahsoka Tano to free enslaved people on Kadavo and participates in the Battle for Anaxes. On General Windu's orders, Cody and Rex form a team, with Clone Force 99, to discover how the Separatists have obtained Rex's strategy algorithm. Cody is injured early in the mission, but Rex and the others complete it, and Cody soon recovers.

At the end of the Clone Wars, shortly after their success on Yerbana, Cody accompanies Obi-Wan to Utapau, where he receives Order 66. At Cody's command, an AT-TE fires at Obi-Wan, knocking him into the water. During the Imperial era, Cody personally requests Crosshair, a member of Clone Force 99, for a mission to Desix where an Imperial governor has been kidnapped by the locals. Cody persuades the leader to stand down peacefully, but is shocked to hear that the governor wants her killed, an order eventually carried out by Crosshair. On return to Coruscant, a disillusioned Cody leaves the Imperial army.

Under orders
Cody fights side by side with Obi-Wan Kenobi on Utapau *(left)*. The clone troopers and their Jedi generals intercept a communication between two Separatist generals planning an attack on Kamino *(below)*.

CAPTAIN REX

SPECIES Human **HOMEWORLD** Kamino
AFFILIATION Republic, Rex's rebel cell, Rebel Alliance

Assigned the designation CT-7567 on Kamino, this high-ranking clone chooses the name Rex and spends the Clone Wars working side by side with Jedi commanders.

PARTNER OF THE JEDI
When the Clone Wars begin, Captain Rex is assigned command of Torrent Company in the 501st Legion and immediately ships out to handle Separatist trouble spots across the galaxy, including Mimban and Arantara. On Christophsis, Rex serves under General Anakin Skywalker and Anakin's new Padawan, Ahsoka Tano. This is the beginning of a partnership between Rex and a tightly knit group of Jedi, including Anakin, Ahsoka, and Obi-Wan Kenobi, through which Rex learns that his opinions are highly valued.

REPUBLIC VICTORIES
The trust between the Jedi and Captain Rex leads to Rex's participation in high-priority engagements, including the destruction of Skytop Station and the fight against General Lok Durd on Maridun. On the Rishi moon, Captain Rex and Commander Cody play vital roles in uncovering a Separatist takeover of a Republic listening post. Rex pushes for total success in every mission, despite the personal risk, even becoming infected with the Blue Shadow Virus in his zeal to destroy a Separatist laboratory on Naboo. When Captain Rex leads a squad into battle, the Republic usually wins the day.

> "You swore an oath to the Republic. You have a duty."
> **CAPTAIN REX**

Commanding presence
Identifiable by his blue-patterned armor, Rex is bred to lead clone troopers.

With the Jedi
Rex is one of the few clone troopers to spend extensive time with high-ranking Jedi commanders such as Anakin and Ahsoka. He has a high opinion of the Jedi, having seen their courage under fire.

GROWING DOUBTS
Not every mission is clear cut. On Saleucami, a blaster shot from a commando droid leaves Rex near death. He recovers in the care of a fellow clone who abandoned the Republic army to live the relatively quiet life of a farmer. Initially disgusted by this deserter, Rex learns to take a more nuanced view. In later engagements of the Clone Wars, Rex stands up for himself and his troopers when both are given foolish, overly risky orders. On Umbara, Rex refuses to obey reckless commands issued by Jedi Master Pong Krell, leading to Krell's exposure as a Separatist sympathizer. These experiences show Rex a different side of war. He begins to see that doing his duty involves more than just blind obedience.

GOOD SOLDIER
Near the end of the Clone Wars, General Skywalker promotes Rex to commander. Rex then accompanies Ahsoka to Mandalore, which they liberate from Maul and his forces. As Rex and Ahsoka board a Republic cruiser for the trip to Coruscant, Emperor Palpatine initiates Order 66. Rex tries to fight the programming but draws his weapons on the former Jedi. He manages to resist long enough to tell Ahsoka to find Fives. Ahsoka goes to astromech R7 and brings up the files on this clone trooper, CT-5555, which reveal the existence of the clones' inhibitor chips. With the help of other loyal droids and guidance from the Force, Ahsoka removes Rex's chip in the medical bay. Rex and Ahsoka fend off attacking clone troopers long enough to steal a Y-wing and escape.

The Empire officially declares Rex killed in action. After parting ways with Ahsoka, Rex begins to form a rebel cell to fight the Empire. He tracks down the Bad Batch and asks them to meet him on Bracca. The resourceful clone uses the medical bay of a scrapped cruiser to safely remove their inhibitor chips, too. They part ways for the time being, but Echo eventually joins Rex in his effort to aid vulnerable clones across the galaxy.

A new mission
Working largely from the shadows, Rex recruits others to his rebel group. Prominent Senator Riyo Chuchi lends her aid to their investigations.

REBEL OFFICER
Years later, Rex lives with two other clones on the remote planet Seelos. His old friend Ahsoka Tano sends the crew of the *Ghost* to Rex to gain information on abandoned Republic-era military bases. Kanan Jarrus is skeptical about working with a clone, but the two resolve their differences and Rex becomes a trusted ally of the Spectres. He is crucial to the success of key rebel missions, including the heist of Y-wing starfighters at Reklam Station, the liberation of Lothal from Imperial blockade, and the Battle of Endor to destroy the second Death Star.

Planning an attack
Having received advanced tactical training on Kamino, Rex uses his knowledge to formulate and test new battle strategies.

Joining forces
After years of solitary living, Rex teams up with fellow war veteran and former Jedi Ahsoka Tano.

CHARACTERS AND CREATURES

> "Now you fall... as all Jedi must." — **ASAJJ VENTRESS**

ASAJJ VENTRESS
SPECIES Dathomirian
HOMEWORLD Dathomir
AFFILIATION Separatist, Nightsisters

Her life marred by tragedy—from the death of a Jedi mentor to a Sith master who wants her dead—Asajj Ventress is a lethal assassin with her own agenda: to be seen as a true Sith.

DARK ASSASSIN
After being taken from the Nightsisters as a child, Asajj Ventress is raised by wandering Jedi Ky Narec as his Padawan on the planet Rattatak. His death causes grief and anger, leaving her open to the dark side and leading her to become a warlord on the ravaged world. She is then forced to become a gladiator until Count Dooku rescues her and offers her a position by his side.

During the Clone Wars, Asajj becomes a key Separatist assassin and leader. She first encounters Obi-Wan Kenobi when he meets with Minister Eyam of Cato Neimoidia as an emissary from the Jedi to the Trade Federation. They approach a tentative alliance, but Ventress remains Count Dooku's agent. On Tatooine, she kidnaps Jabba the Hutt's son Rotta for Dooku, who intends to frame the Republic to bring the Hutts into the Clone Wars on the Separatist side. However, the Jedi attack Ventress on Teth and return Rotta to his father. Later, Dooku sends Ventress to free Nute Gunray from a Republic cruiser and take him to Coruscant. There she duels Jedi Master Luminara Unduli, nearly defeating her—until Ahsoka Tano joins the battle. Helped by a traitorous Senate Guard, Argyus, Ventress rescues Gunray, but then kills Argyus when he boasts of his role in the mission. On Kamino, Ventress tries to steal the clone DNA, but is foiled by Anakin Skywalker.

NIGHTSISTER
Sensing Ventress growing more powerful in the Force, Darth Sidious orders Dooku to kill his dark acolyte. When her command ship is destroyed at Sullust, Ventress flees to Dathomir, to join other Nightsisters; soon after she swears vengeance on Dooku, following an encounter with Mother Talzin. While she undergoes a rebirth ritual to signify her allegiance to the clan, Dooku sends General Grievous to Dathomir to annihilate the Nightsisters. At the urging of Talzin, Ventress flees the planet, believing she is the only remaining Nightsister.

Showdown
In the B'omarr Order monastery on Teth, Ventress prepares for battle with Jedi intent on rescuing Rotta the Huttlet.

BOUNTY HUNTER
After killing bounty hunter Oked, Ventress takes his place on a mission led by Boba Fett to protect a chest on a train which, when opened, reveals a young girl held captive inside. Ventress double-crosses Fett and frees the girl. Later, discovering a bounty on Savage Opress, Ventress hunts down the Nightbrother. Her search leads her to Opress and Maul, who are holding Obi-Wan Kenobi prisoner. Ventress and Obi-Wan join forces, barely escaping with their lives. Obi-Wan tries to enlist Ventress, but she refuses. Ventress then rescues two sisters from a thief on the lower levels of Coruscant. Instead of collecting a bounty on her, Ventress briefly helps Ahsoka Tano in her mission to find out who bombed the Jedi Temple.

Dark-side apprentice
A lethal assassin trained in the Force and ruthlessly tested by Count Dooku, Asajj Ventress still uses her unique twin lightsabers with deadly force during her career as a bounty hunter.

Return to Dathomir
Asajj Ventress teaches Jedi Master Quinlan Vos how to draw upon the dark side of the Force on her homeworld, Dathomir.

DARK DISCIPLE
Ventress allies with Jedi Quinlan Vos in a plot to assassinate Count Dooku. To prepare for their mission, Ventress trains the Jedi in the darker aspects of the Force by taking him to her homeworld of Dathomir. The two form a romantic bond during their time together. Using her contacts in the Separatists, Ventress learns that Dooku will be attending a gala on the planet Raxus, giving Ventress and Vos an opportunity to strike. Their assassination attempt fails when Vos is captured by Dooku and fully turns to the dark side, believing that Ventress has set him up. Ventress seems to sacrifice herself to save Vos from Dooku, which inspires him to return to the light side. However, later she mysteriously reappears to help evaluate enhanced clone Omega's potential in the Force.

GENERAL GRIEVOUS

SPECIES Kaleesh **HOMEWORLD** Kalee
AFFILIATION Separatist

General Grievous, commander of the Separatist military, is feared throughout the Republic. The cyborg has a vengeful lust for slaying Jedi and keeps their lightsabers as trophies.

JEDI HUNTER
Following near-lethal injuries, the warrior known as Grievous receives cyborg implants, which grant him fighting prowess equal to that of a Jedi. An intimidating opponent, he frequently clashes with the generals in the Order, and even the most skilled meet their doom when challenging him. On one occasion, Grievous annihilates a fleet commanded by Plo Koon, leaving only a handful of survivors. Soon afterward he almost adds apprentice Ahsoka Tano's lightsaber to his collection during a duel at Skytop Station. He flees when her powerful master, Anakin Skywalker, intervenes at the last second. Soon after, Jedi Master Kit Fisto is then assigned to track down Grievous' lair, but he barely escapes with his life following the death of his former Padawan, Nahdar Vebb, who is slain by the cyborg. Grievous later kidnaps Master Eeth Koth and taunts the Jedi via a holographic transmission; the rescue mounted by Anakin, Obi-Wan Kenobi, and Adi Gallia nearly fails.

SEPARATIST STRIKES
By attacking key targets, General Grievous' army wreaks havoc across the galaxy.

Mortal combat
Jedi General Obi-Wan Kenobi and Separatist General Grievous face off early in the Clone Wars aboard the *Malevolence*.

At Kamino, his cautious tactics make Obi-Wan suspect a bigger plan, which is confirmed when Kenobi discovers aqua droids mounting underwater assaults. The mechanicals are bent on destroying the cloning facility crucial to the Republic war effort, but the Jedi turn the tide and Grievous retreats. After hunting Jedi on the planet Ledeve, Grievous discovers one of the Order's hidden temples. There, he sees a vision of his past self, which infuriates him enough that he orders the structure destroyed from orbit. Count Dooku also dispatches the cyborg on missions to serve the Sith's vengeful ends: at Naboo, Senator Amidala is forced into a prisoner exchange with Grievous to save Anakin, and on Dathomir, Grievous wipes out an entire clan of Nightsister witches.

Standoff
General Grievous assumes an aggressive stance before attacking Obi-Wan on Utapau.

LATER ENGAGEMENTS
After dueling Ahsoka once more on Florrum, Grievous intervenes when Obi-Wan and Anakin stop the Separatists from buying a giant kyber crystal on Utapau. However, he fails to stop the Jedi blowing up the crystal. Soon after, he faces Jedi Master Depa Billaba on Haruun Kal where he viciously defeats her. With Maul's Shadow Collective increasing in power, Grievous travels with Darth Sidious to Dathomir to rescue Count Dooku from Mother Talzin and Maul. Unlike his last visit, Grievous manages to slay Talzin.

SITH DISTRACTION
General Grievous' flagship, *Invisible Hand*, heads the Separatist assault on Coruscant that leads to the capture of Supreme Chancellor Palpatine. Obi-Wan and Anakin board the vessel to rescue Palpatine, and Grievous flees, leaving his MagnaGuards to fend off the Jedi. While the Council focuses its attention on pursuing the cyborg across the galaxy, Palpatine—truly Darth Sidious hiding in plain sight—unfolds his nefarious plot to wipe out the Order and declare himself Emperor. He tips off the Jedi on Grievous' location on Utapau, and Obi-Wan is sent in pursuit. After Kenobi makes a sudden appearance during the Separatist gathering on the Outer Rim planet, Grievous and the skilled Jedi battle, resulting in the cyborg general's death.

Beware of this mistake
While General Grievous' cybernetics enhance his fighting prowess, he reacts with rage when mistaken for a droid.

No surrender
Grievous refuses to surrender on Naboo and fights off the Gungans one by one. General Tarpals finally stuns him, but not before receiving a mortal wound.

> "I look forward to adding your lightsabers to my collection."
> **GENERAL GRIEVOUS**

Feared by Jedi
Once a feared Kaleesh warrior, General Grievous is now more cybernetic machine than living flesh. He believes his mechanical limbs have made him superior to all foes. Scientists implanted his brain and eyes into a duranium alloy body, and his remaining vital organs are protected by a synthskin gut-sack. Count Dooku trains Grievous in the art of lightsaber combat, for which his cyborg enhancements are well suited. Grievous lacks Force abilities, instead relying on agility and strength in combat with an adversary. A master of many of the classic forms of Jedi arts, he is able to adapt quickly to an opponent's fighting style.

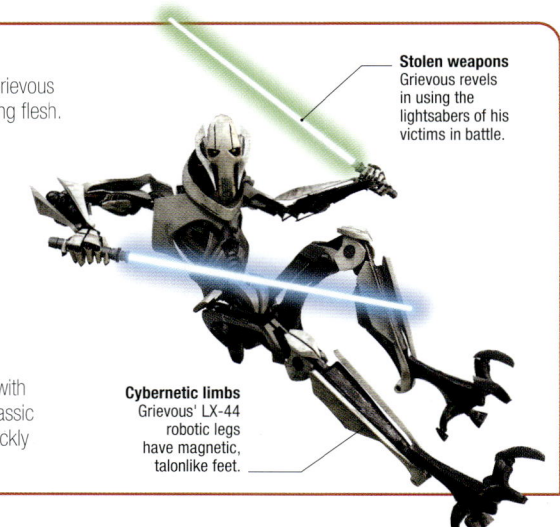

Stolen weapons
Grievous revels in using the lightsabers of his victims in battle.

Cybernetic limbs
Grievous' LX-44 robotic legs have magnetic, talonlike feet.

AHSOKA TANO

SPECIES Togruta **HOMEWORLD** Coruscant
AFFILIATION Jedi Order, Rebel Alliance

The apprentice Anakin Skywalker never expected, Ahsoka Tano is as headstrong as her master. She earns his respect and friendship, taking his teachings and passing them on to others. Ultimately, on her path to becoming a Jedi, she remains true to herself.

Reluctant master
At first Anakin Skywalker is not enthusiastic about his new apprentice, but he accepts his duty as a Jedi, passing along his experience to Ahsoka.

ANAKIN SKYWALKER'S PADAWAN
When the Jedi Council assigns Ahsoka to train beside Anakin, they believe that the rule-following, optimistic new Padawan will be a good influence on her impulsive master. They also hope that mentoring the talented young Jedi will help Anakin learn to let go of his attachments. Her master's training quickly makes an impression. When she teams up with Barriss Offee, apprentice of Luminara Unduli, during the Second Battle of Geonosis, Ahsoka's bold style contrasts with the more reserved demeanor of her counterpart.

SOLO MISSIONS
Ahsoka's exceptional Jedi skills lead to missions away from her master early in her apprenticeship. When Pantoran Chairman Baron Notluwiski Papanoida's daughters are kidnapped, she volunteers to help her friend Senator Riyo Chuchi investigate the crime, using telekinesis and her first Jedi mind tricks along the way. Soon after, she assists Duchess Satine Kryze in exposing corruption at the highest levels of Mandalore's government. Plagued by visions of Padmé Amidala's assassination, Ahsoka insists on joining the senator's security detail and thwarts the bounty hunter Aurra Sing. By the time Ahsoka is captured by Trandoshan hunters and taken to Wasskah, she possesses the confidence to lead abducted Jedi younglings to fight back against their captors.

THE TEACHER
While working with Duchess Satine's nephew, Korkie, and his friends to root out traitors, Ahsoka exhibits a talent for leadership. When the Jedi Council agrees to Anakin's proposal to train Onderon insurgents striving to depose the Separatist-allied king, Ahsoka and Obi-Wan Kenobi join him for the mission. Impressed by Ahsoka's development, the two generals have enough confidence to leave her behind as the sole Jedi adviser during the final stages of the successful Onderon uprising. Not long after, Yoda entrusts Ahsoka with safeguarding the travels of Jedi younglings venturing to Ilum, where they undergo rigorous tests of physical and inner strength before they can construct their own lightsabers.

JEDI NO MORE
Following a bombing of the Jedi Temple, Ahsoka and Anakin are recalled to investigate. While Ahsoka interrogates the bomber, Letta Turmond, about her accomplice, the prisoner is choked by an unseen person using the Force. Despite protesting her innocence to Admiral Wilhuff Tarkin, Ahsoka is arrested for Turmond's murder. Mysterious assistance—a keycard outside her cell, incapacitated guards, and a comlink—aid Ahsoka's escape from prison, but also further incriminate her. Anakin finds Tano but cannot convince his Padawan to turn herself in. Ultimately, she finds an unlikely ally in dark-side outcast Asajj Ventress, who leads Anakin to clues proving Barriss Offee is the true traitor. Her faith in the institution shaken, Ahsoka refuses the Jedi Council's offers of reinstatement. After befriending and aiding future rebels Rafa and Trace Martez, she does assist the Republic one more time, however, by leading the Siege of Mandalore to remove Maul from power. Palpatine initiates Order 66 during this battle, leaving Ahsoka to fight for her life.

REEMERGENCE
After her friend Padmé passes, Ahsoka tells Bail Organa she is tired of fighting. She works as a farmer, but soon uses the Force to help someone, which attracts the attention of an Inquisitor. She defeats the dark-side warrior, who destroys the village, and reaches out to Organa so he can help the survivors. From there, using the code name Fulcrum, Ahsoka joins his nascent rebellion.

FACING VADER
Working with the crew of the *Ghost*, now part of the Phoenix cell, Ahsoka crosses paths with Darth Vader. Reaching out through the Force, she begins to suspect that he is Anakin Skywalker, her former master. Ahsoka travels to the planet Malachor with Ezra Bridger and Kanan Jarrus in search of answers about the Inquisitorius. There they find an ancient Sith temple and are cornered by Vader himself, at which point Ahsoka's fears about his identity are proven true. Unmoved when Ahsoka pleads to the Anakin she used to know, Vader attacks. Tano appears doomed—until a hand pulls her into a portal. The hand belongs to Ezra Bridger, who has traveled through a mysterious world between worlds and reached from the future to save her. Ahsoka and Ezra must return to their own times, but she promises to meet him again one day.

LOOKING FOR EZRA
Not long after he pulls Ahsoka from a world between worlds, Ezra disappears with Grand Admiral Thrawn with the help of some purrgil. In the years that pass, the Empire falls and Ahsoka briefly trains Sabine Wren as her Jedi Padawan, but the pair abandon each other. Ahsoka is concerned about the threat of Thrawn, closing herself off from the hope of reuniting with Ezra, while tracking his associates, including Morgan Elsbeth, for information. Her mission leads her to Corvus where she meets Din Djarin and Grogu, with the former helping Ahsoka capture Elsbeth. After handing her over to the New Republic, Ahsoka visits Luke Skywalker on Ossus, where he is building a new Jedi temple, and she gives guidance to Din about Grogu. Morgan later escapes custody, and Ahsoka discovers a starmap that Elsbeth believes will lead to Thrawn. After a near-death experience and a vision of Anakin, a more optimistic Ahsoka follows Morgan to another galaxy and arrives on Peridea, where she finds Ezra and Thrawn and reunites with Sabine. She fails in stopping Thrawn's return to the known galaxy, but she believes Peridea is where she needs to be.

Blade of Talzin
Ahsoka fights Morgan Elsbeth on Peridea to give Ezra Bridger time to escape. Elsbeth wields the Blade of Talzin, which can deflect a lightsaber because of its enchanted properties.

Instinctive talent
Ahsoka is gifted with raw Force talent, but her compassion challenges her path in the Jedi Order. Eventually, Ahsoka gains the confidence to make the right choice, even at great cost to her own feelings.

ROTTA THE HUTTLET
SPECIES Hutt **HOMEWORLD** Tatooine
AFFILIATION Hutts

Rotta is the son of Jabba the Hutt. After the Huttlet is kidnapped by Asajj Ventress, Jabba makes a deal with the Galactic Republic to rescue him. When Anakin Skywalker and Ahsoka Tano free Rotta on Teth, they realize that the Huttlet has fallen ill. Ahsoka finds the medicine that saves him.

ZIRO THE HUTT
SPECIES Hutt **HOMEWORLD** Sleheyron
AFFILIATION Hutts

Crime lord Ziro is Jabba the Hutt's uncle. Ziro conspires with Count Dooku and Asajj Ventress to kidnap Jabba's son, Rotta. Senator Padmé Amidala tries to open communications with the Hutts, who believe the Jedi abducted Rotta. After a failed assassination attempt on Padmé, Ziro is arrested. Via holocomm, Ziro confesses to Jabba his part in Rotta's kidnapping and is imprisoned on Coruscant. Cad Bane later frees Ziro and hands him over to the Hutt Council, which fears that Ziro might reveal its many dirty dealings to the Republic. With the help of Sy Snootles, Ziro escapes the Hutts. Snootles follows Ziro to Teth, retrieves a datapad filled with Hutt secrets, and then kills him.

KING KATUUNKO
SPECIES Toydarian
HOMEWORLD Toydaria
AFFILIATION Republic

Due to his planet's reliance on the Trade Federation, King Katuunko could only secretly aid the planet Ryloth during the Clone Wars. When Chancellor Palpatine requests negotiations to use Toydaria as a base, he sends Yoda to Rugosa. Yoda impresses Katuunko with his Jedi character, and the king commits Toydaria to the Republic. Dooku's apprentice, Savage Opress, eventually kills the king for supporting the Jedi.

COMMANDER FOX
SPECIES Human **HOMEWORLD** Kamino
AFFILIATION Republic, Empire

Fox, clone trooper commander CC-1010, leads the famed Coruscant Guard. He assists Padmé Amidala in the capture of Ziro the Hutt. Assigned to a Republic military base, he pursues the fugitive Ahsoka, who is blamed for the murder of Letta Turmond, but she evades capture. Fox later kills rogue trooper Fives before he can reveal a conspiracy within the Republic. Fox participates in Order 66 on Coruscant. When Jedi survivor Jocasta Nu returns to the Jedi Temple, Fox surrounds the building with his forces. Nu escapes the Temple with Darth Vader in pursuit, but Fox's troops fire on both of them, since Fox hadn't informed them that the menacing figure was on their side. Vader kills Fox for his oversight.

NALA SE
SPECIES Kaminoan **HOMEWORLD** Kamino
AFFILIATION Kamino, Republic, Empire

Nala Se is the Chief Medical Scientist of the Kaminoan cloning facility, and plays a vital role in the creation of the clone army. While Se works with the Republic during the Clone Wars, she also hides the existence of the clone inhibitor chips. Se shows a great deal of care for the enhanced clone Omega. When Se learns that Prime Minister Lama Su wants her to extract genetic information from Omega, Se helps Omega escape and tries to keep Omega out of Su's hands. After the Empire destroys the Kaminoan homeworld, Se refuses to cooperate with an old acquaintance, Imperial Doctor Royce Hemlock, to continue cloning experiments.

R7-A7
MODEL R-series astromech droid
AFFILIATION Republic, Rex's rebel cell

Astromech droid R7-A7 accompanies Ahsoka Tano during missions to Ryloth, Cato Neimoidia, and Umbara during the Clone Wars. After the execution of Order 66, Ahsoka Tano seeks out R7's help. R7 accesses and plays Tano files about the inhibitor chips that the Kaminoans implanted in the clones and shocks Rex so Tano can bring him to an operating bay. After R7 removes Rex's chip, R7 is shot by clone troopers as they try to escape the ship. After being repaired by Tano and Rex, R7-A7 works with the Martez sisters as their astromech droid and copilot of the *Silver Angel*.

CLONE TROOPER FIVES
SPECIES Human **HOMEWORLD** Kamino
AFFILIATION Republic

Fives' nickname comes from his clone designation, CT-27-5555. As a cadet, he trains with Domino Squad. After defending Rishi Station from General Grievous' attack, he is inducted into the 501st Legion. On Umbara, Fives is the loudest voice against Jedi General Krell, who is revealed to be a traitor. Fives also uncovers the truth about Chancellor Palpatine and Order 66, but is killed by Commander Fox before he can expose the conspiracy.

COMMANDER WOLFFE
SPECIES Human **HOMEWORLD** Kamino
AFFILIATION Republic, Rebels

Commander Wolffe, also known as clone CC-3636, leads Wolf Pack Battalion, which serves under Jedi General Plo Koon. During a mission to eliminate the *Malevolence*, the entire Wolf Pack is killed, except for Wolffe, Sinker, and Boost. At the Battle of Khorm, Wolffe loses his right eye during a fight with Asajj Ventress. Despite this, Wolffe continues to serve, helping Plo to rescue Jedi from behind enemy lines. He also delivers aid to the Aleena. On Coruscant, Wolffe is knocked out when he fights fugitive Jedi Ahsoka Tano and Ventress. With Plo, he finds the deceased Jedi Sifo-Dyas' lightsaber. At some point, Wolffe removes his control chip. During the Imperial era, he lives with fellow clones Gregor and Rex in a modified AT-TE on the planet Seelos, where they meet the *Ghost* crew. Wishing to protect his brother clones, Wolffe tells the Empire about the visitors, but Rex convinces him that they aren't the enemy. After beating an Imperial force, Rex leaves Seelos and Gregor and Wolffe begin living in an AT-AT. A few years later, they join Rex to help liberate Lothal.

Brother clone
Wolffe fears the Jedi, so hides messages from Rex's old friend Ahsoka Tano to try and protect Rex.

HONDO OHNAKA

SPECIES Weequay **HOMEWORLD** Florrum
AFFILIATION Ohnaka Gang, Ohnaka Solutions

Opportunistic and cunning, Hondo Ohnaka is the leader of the Ohnaka Gang based on the planet Florrum. Alongside other galactic criminals, Ohnaka attends an auction held by the Xrexus cartel where a Jedi Padawan is up for sale. During the Clone Wars, Hondo's pirates kidnap Count Dooku, and he attempts to sell him to the Republic. The hostage situation allows Hondo to also capture Obi-Wan Kenobi and Anakin Skywalker. With the assistance of clone troopers, Obi-Wan, Anakin, and Dooku escape. The Jedi later face Hondo's gang on the planet Felucia, where they help defend farms alongside hired bounty hunters.

Later in the war, Anakin pays Ohnaka to deliver weapons to the Onderon rebels. Ohnaka teams up with Ahsoka Tano and a group of Jedi younglings to repel a Separatist attack on Florrum. When Maul and Savage Opress arrive to hire a gang of bounty hunters, Ohnaka allies with Obi-Wan to drive them off. During the Imperial era, Hondo's gang falls apart, so he starts taking smaller jobs, including stealing from the Temple of the Kyber on Jedha for treasure hunter Dok-Ondar. With bounty hunter IG-88, he attempts to capture Crimson Dawn Lieutenant Qi'ra, but the plan goes awry, and she collects bounties on them instead. Hondo eventually escapes and joins Han Solo and Chewbacca in the *Millennium Falcon* on an adventure.

Years later, Hondo takes over criminal Cikatro Vizago's ship, the *Broken Horn*, locking up the former owner in a cell on his own ship. He encounters rebel Ezra Bridger, whom he lets in on his latest scheme. After lots of double-crossing, Hondo and Ezra part ways, striking up an unlikely friendship. Hondo runs into Ezra once more when he tips him, and the Empire, off to the location of two Lasat that survived the Siege of Lasan. The rebels rescue the Lasat, and Hondo ends up in Imperial captivity. He shares his cell with an Ugnaught named Melch who lets him know of a reclamation station with valuable starfighters that could be stolen for the Rebellion. Hondo contacts Ezra and secures his and Melch's release in exchange for the intel. Hondo assists the rebels with the heist, taking a shuttle for himself and his new Ugnaught crew, which he modifies and names the *Last Chance*.

Later, Hondo begrudgingly helps the Spectres free a rare creature captured by the Empire and calls on their aid when a raid on an Imperial ship goes wrong above the planet Wynkahthu. Hondo responds to the call for help to free Ezra's homeworld. At some point, Hondo teams up with Lando Calrissian and Maz Kanata to steal treasure from Imperial General Kardan aboard the *Halcyon*, a luxury starcruiser. Following the victory, Hondo uses the funding from the theft to create Ohnaka Transport Solutions, which he claims is a legitimate business. However, Hondo still dabbles in illicit activities. For example, Hondo helps out smuggler Sana Starros on a family mission for a small fee. Decades later on Batuu, Hondo manages Ohnaka Transport Solutions and regales visitors of his many adventures. After the Battle of Crait, Hondo makes a deal with Chewbacca to borrow the *Falcon*. Hondo then hires a temporary crew to hijack a First Order train containing a shipment of coaxium. The mission is a success, but it is unclear how much coaxium was able to be salvaged.

Life of a leader
Melch is Hondo's accomplice during the Imperial era, and soon wises up to his leader's lack of concern for his welfare.

GUNDARK

HOMEWORLD Vanqor
AVERAGE SIZE 2 m (7 ft) high
HABITAT Caves

Gundarks are fierce, aggressive creatures known for their overwhelming strength. After crash-landing on Vanqor, Anakin Skywalker and Obi-Wan Kenobi disturb a gundark in a cave. Using the Force to pelt the beast with rocks, the Jedi successfully repel it. When the *Endurance* crashes on Vanqor, R2-D2 faces off with a gundark. The droid ties the creature to Anakin's starfighter and sends it blasting off.

RIYO CHUCHI

SPECIES Pantoran **HOMEWORLD** Pantora
AFFILIATION Republic, Rex's rebel cell

When a Republic base falls silent, Senator Riyo Chuchi joins Chairman Chi Cho, Anakin Skywalker, and Obi-Wan Kenobi to investigate. After Cho is killed, Chuchi negotiates peace between the Pantorans and Talz. When the daughters of Baron Papanoida are kidnapped, she enlists Ahsoka Tano's help. Finding one daughter on a Trade Federation vessel, they overhear a conversation that confirms the Federation is working on behalf of the Separatists. Chuchi retains her position in the Imperial Senate and becomes a passionate voice for the welfare of the clone troopers. Outside of the Senate, she aligns herself with former clone trooper Captain Rex's rebel cell. With the Bad Batch's aid, she reveals Vice Admiral Edmon Rampart's role in the destruction of Tipoca City.

THI-SEN

SPECIES Talz **HOMEWORLD** Orto Plutonia
AFFILIATION Talz village

Thi-Sen leads a peaceful tribe of Talz caught between the Galactic Republic and Separatist task forces. Protecting its territory, the tribe attacks the Republic outpost and the droid forces. A second Republic task force under the command of Anakin and Obi-Wan negotiates a cease-fire. Believing the Talz to be trespassers, Chairman Cho of the neighboring moon Pantora declares war on them. After the chairman dies, Senator Riyo Chuchi uses C-3PO to make peace with Thi-Sen.

NARGLATCH

HOMEWORLD Orto Plutonia
AVERAGE SIZE 6 m (20 ft) long
HABITAT Adaptable

The narglatch is a stealthy predator that can live in a variety of climates. On the frozen world of Orto Plutonia, narglatch are used as mounts by the Talz. Narglatch hide is vulnerable to blaster fire and valued by some cultures as a trophy. Narglatch cubs are cute and often taken as pets, but become extremely dangerous when they mature. Escaped narglatch are a threat on Coruscant.

DR. NUVO VINDI

SPECIES Faust **HOMEWORLD** Adana
AFFILIATION Separatist

Nute Gunray sponsors Dr. Nuvo Vindi's work to recreate the Blue Shadow Virus in a Trade Federation laboratory built beneath Naboo's swamps. Padmé Amidala stumbles upon the lair while investigating the death of a shaak herd. Arriving on Naboo, her Jedi friends help to capture Vindi. He refuses to hand over the antidote to save Padmé and Ahsoka Tano, but Obi-Wan Kenobi and Anakin Skywalker travel to Iego to find a cure.

CAD BANE

SPECIES Duros **HOMEWORLD** Duro **AFFILIATION** Bounty hunter

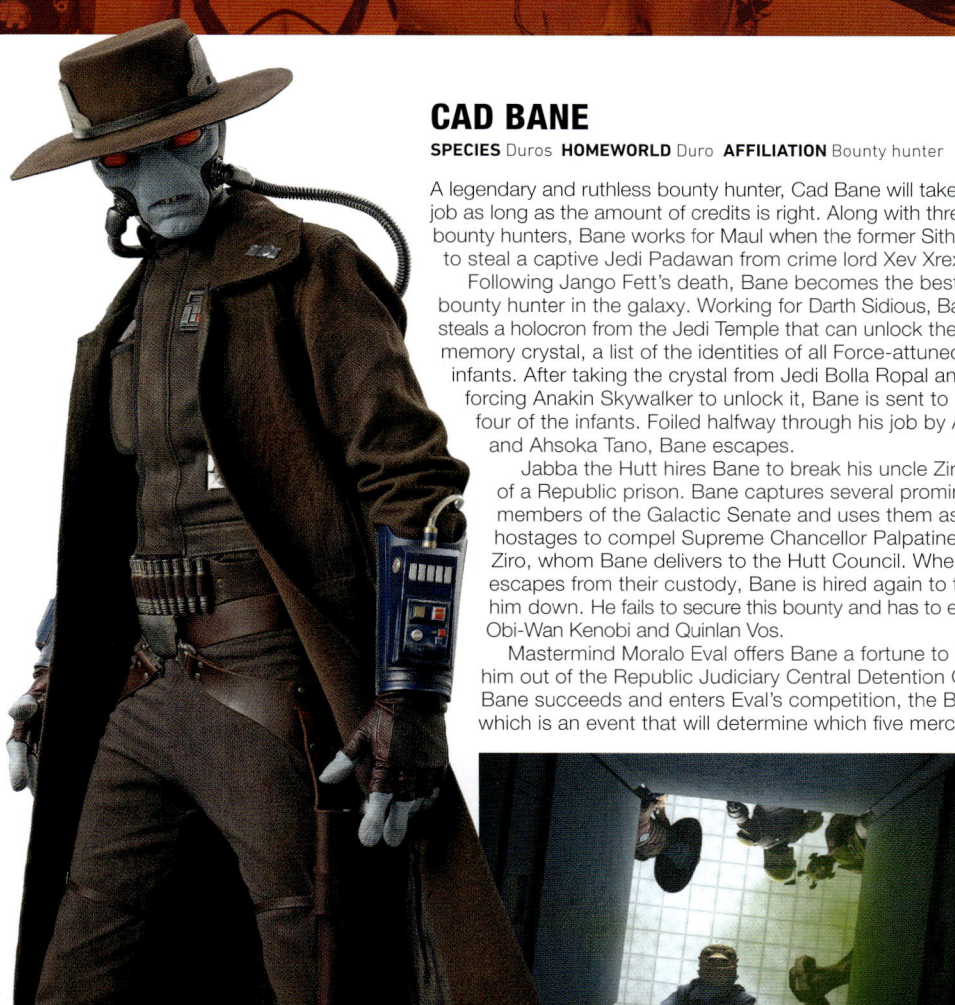

A legendary and ruthless bounty hunter, Cad Bane will take on any job as long as the amount of credits is right. Along with three other bounty hunters, Bane works for Maul when the former Sith wants to steal a captive Jedi Padawan from crime lord Xev Xrexus.

Following Jango Fett's death, Bane becomes the best bounty hunter in the galaxy. Working for Darth Sidious, Bane steals a holocron from the Jedi Temple that can unlock the kyber memory crystal, a list of the identities of all Force-attuned infants. After taking the crystal from Jedi Bolla Ropal and forcing Anakin Skywalker to unlock it, Bane is sent to kidnap four of the infants. Foiled halfway through his job by Anakin and Ahsoka Tano, Bane escapes.

Jabba the Hutt hires Bane to break his uncle Ziro out of a Republic prison. Bane captures several prominent members of the Galactic Senate and uses them as hostages to compel Supreme Chancellor Palpatine to free Ziro, whom Bane delivers to the Hutt Council. When Ziro escapes from their custody, Bane is hired again to track him down. He fails to secure this bounty and has to evade Obi-Wan Kenobi and Quinlan Vos.

Mastermind Moralo Eval offers Bane a fortune to break him out of the Republic Judiciary Central Detention Center. Bane succeeds and enters Eval's competition, the Box, which is an event that will determine which five mercenaries will be hired in a plot to kidnap Palpatine. After passing the tournament test, Bane is personally selected by Count Dooku to lead the team of Embo, Derrown, Twazzi, and Rako Hardeen, who is really Obi-Wan undercover. They travel to Naboo to abduct Palpatine during the Festival of Light. The team succeeds, but Dooku betrays Bane. Having intended that the bounty hunters' operation should just be a diversion, Dooku misses his rendezvous with them. Bane is then defeated by Obi-Wan.

In the years after the formation of the Galactic Empire, Kaminoan Prime Minister Lama Su hires Bane to hunt Omega, a genetically unmodified clone. Working with Todo 360, Bane tracks Omega to Clone Force 99. He briefly captures Omega but fellow bounty hunter Fennec Shand interferes, as she's trying to claim the bounty for herself. Omega escapes and foils both Bane and Shand.

Bane continues his career as a bounty hunter in the years that follow, eventually working for the Pyke Syndicate as an enforcer on Tatooine after the Empire's fall. The Syndicate uses Bane to reestablish its grip on the desert planet, particularly in the town of Mos Pelgo, where Marshal Cobb Vanth has denounced the Pykes. When Bane seemingly kills Vanth in a duel, the Pyke Syndicate sends the victorious bounty hunter to deal with Boba Fett, Bane's one-time student. The pair clashes in Mos Espa, where Fett overpowers Bane.

Tackling the Box
Cad Bane and his fellow contestants study the next phase of Moralo Eval's bounty hunter skills challenge, the Box.

Clash of legends
Bane and Boba have known each other for decades and are some of the greatest bounty hunters in the galaxy. On a Mos Espa street, the pair duel and Boba emerges victorious.

CLONE TROOPER ECHO

SPECIES Human **HOMEWORLD** Kamino
AFFILIATION Republic, Bad Batch

CT-1409 (originally identified as CT-21-0408) is nicknamed "Echo" for constantly repeating rules. As a cadet, he is part of Domino Squad. Echo and other rookies thwart General Grievous' attempt to capture Rishi Station and are inducted into the 501st Legion. He works with Fives and Captain Rex on a strategy algorithm that identifies Republic weaknesses in order to overcome them, obsessively checking the program before each battle.

Following their heroism during the Battle of Kamino, Echo and Fives are promoted to ARC troopers. Echo subsequently participates in the rescue of Jedi Master Even Piell from the Citadel, but ends up missing in action and is presumed dead. However, he survives and is captured by the enemy. Separatist leader Wat Tambor transforms Echo into a cyborg so he can interface with computers. Tambor then forcefully uses the clone's knowledge of the strategy algorithm to help the Separatists in battle. Suspecting he is alive, Rex leads Clone Force 99, a small team of unique soldiers, to rescue him. Echo uses his abilities to feed the Separatists misinformation to ensure a critical Republic victory on Anaxes. Now known as the Hero of Anaxes, he is promoted to corporal and joins Clone Force 99, also known as the Bad Batch.

As the Clone Wars come to an end, Clone Force 99 is dispatched to Kaller to reinforce Jedi General Depa Billaba and her Padawan Caleb Dume. As they engage in battle, the clones are directed to initiate Order 66 by Supreme Chancellor Palpatine. Echo is immune to the command, as is most of the Bad Batch, but they are unable to save Billaba from the other troopers. Realizing the magnitude of the event, Echo and his squad return to Kamino aboard the *Marauder* and learn about the Republic's transformation into the Galactic Empire.

While on Kamino, as the newly formed regime decides whether to continue creating clones or begin conscripting civilians into military duty, Echo meets Omega, a genetically unmodified clone. When the Bad Batch realizes Omega is in danger from her creators, they desert with the young girl in tow. However, Crosshair remains with the Empire. Echo and his comrades remain on the run, protecting Omega from the Kaminoans, the Empire, and bounty hunters. In order to fund their survival, the Batch often takes illicit missions from Trandoshan criminal Ciddarin "Cid" Scaleback on Ord Mantell. Like their newest member Omega, Echo is one of the strongest advocates for using their skills to help those in need during this tumultuous time in the galaxy.

Having reconnected with his former leader Captain Rex, Echo takes a growing interest in joining his rebel cell. Following the Bad Batch's role in revealing the destruction of Tipoca City to the Imperial Senate, Echo leaves the team. He then becomes a leader in Rex's group, fighting to rescue imprisoned clone troopers from the Empire. However, Echo returns to help the Batch during its infiltration of Eriadu in order to gain intel to rescue the now-imprisoned Crosshair. When that mission goes awry and Tech is lost, Echo and the surviving members return to Cid who betrays them, leading to Omega's capture by the Empire. Regardless of their recent misfortune, the remaining members of their team are determined to rescue her.

Customized helmet
Echo's helmet has been designed to fit around his cybernetic modifications.

Precision gunslinger
Echo is an excellent shot with a blaster.

Echo and Omega
Echo and Omega share a close bond. Omega is distraught when Echo leaves to fight with Rex.

TODO 360

MANUFACTURER Vertseth Automata **TYPE** Techno-service droid
AFFILIATION Bounty hunter

A frequent accomplice of Cad Bane, Todo 360 is destroyed in a ventilation shaft as a distraction when Bane steals a holocron from the Jedi Temple for Darth Sidious. Todo is rebuilt by Anakin Skywalker and escapes. He assists Bane in capturing C-3PO and R2-D2. During the Imperial era, Todo is still at Cad Bane's side when he attempts to collect a bounty from Omega, a member of the Bad Batch.

CLONE TROOPER WAXER

SPECIES Human **HOMEWORLD** Kamino **AFFILIATION** Republic

Waxer serves in the Ghost Company during missions on Krystar, Ryloth, and Geonosis. During the Ryloth campaign, the recon team of Waxer and Boil scouts an abandoned Twi'lek village and finds a young girl, Numa, who reveals the underground passages the clone troopers use to free the Twi'leks. Waxer dies when General Krell deceives the clones on Umbara.

SUGI

SPECIES Zabrak **HOMEWORLD** Iridonia
AFFILIATION Bounty hunter

Sugi owns the starship *Halo* and is guided by a strong sense of honor and duty. Along with fellow bounty hunters Rumi Paramita, Embo, and Seripas, Sugi is hired to defend a Felucian farming village plagued by the Ohnaka Gang. Sugi's team joins forces with three Jedi, Obi-Wan, Anakin, and Ahsoka, to fight off the pirate gang. Paramita dies in battle, but Sugi and her remaining allies chase off the pirates. They receive their payment, and Sugi offers the stranded Jedi a ride aboard her ship. Sugi is then hired by Wookiee chief Tarfful to help liberate the people that are being hunted by the Trandoshans on Wasskah. Sugi takes some Jedi survivors back to Coruscant. After this contract, Sugi, Embo and two other bounty hunters are employed by the Grand Hutt Council to protect them. However, they cannot stop Maul and the Shadow Collective, so run away. Sugi inspires her niece Jas Emari to follow in her footsteps, and Jas becomes the next owner of the *Halo*.

SERIPAS

SPECIES Ssori
AFFILIATION Bounty hunter

Bounty hunter Seripas wears a mechanical bodysuit during his missions. As part of Sugi's team, he protects a Felucian farm from a band of Weequay pirates led by Hondo Ohnaka. Alongside Ahsoka, Seripas trains the farmers to fight. Despite Seripas' suit being destroyed, he still manages to defeat a pirate during the farmers' successful defense of their homes. Later, Seripas and Sugi bring Wookiees in to help rescue Chewbacca and Ahsoka, who are being held captive by Trandoshans on Wasskah.

CATO PARASITTI

SPECIES Clawdite **HOMEWORLD** Zolan
AFFILIATION Bounty hunter

Posing as Ord Enisence and Chief Librarian Jocasta Nu, changeling Cato Parasitti neutralizes the Jedi Temple's security so that Cad Bane can reach the Holocron Vault. Ahsoka Tano later defeats Parasitti in a duel, and while she is in Jedi captivity, Parasitti offers information on Bane's next target: Bolla Ropal, the keeper of the kyber memory crystal. After leaving prison, Parasitti tries to kill some Arthurian delegates, but Ahsoka and Padmé Amidala stop her.

GWARM

SPECIES Weequay **HOMEWORLD** Florrum
AFFILIATION Ohnaka Gang

Gwarm serves as second-in-command of the Ohnaka Gang that extorts valuable nysillim crops from Felucian farmers. The pirates are challenged by bounty hunters hired by the farmers and three Jedi. When the gang's captain, Hondo Ohnaka, is at the mercy of Anakin, Gwarm calls for retreat to rescue him, and the pirates leave the planet empty-handed.

EMBO

SPECIES Kyuzo
HOMEWORLD Phatrong
AFFILIATION Bounty hunter

Accompanied by his beloved anooba Marrok, Embo is deadly with a shot from his bowcaster or a decisive blow from his pan-shaped hat. He often works with Sugi and is hired as part of her team to defend farmers on Felucia. Embo is one of 11 bounty hunters, including Obi-Wan—disguised as Rako Hardeen—and Cad Bane, to fight in the Box competition. Embo is hired to target Rush Clovis, but fails when Anakin interrupts his plans. Later, he defends the Hutt Grand Council from Maul and Savage Opress. Afterward, Embo joins Boba Fett's crew of bounty hunters, Krayt's Claw, and participates in missions to Quarzite and Serenno.

Embo works throughout the Imperial era, but sadly, Marrok, dies. After the Battle of Endor, Embo works with Dengar and Jeeta to capture Sugi's niece and fellow bounty hunter Jas Emari for Mercurial Swift. They find Jas on Jakku, and they are ready to capture her until she persuades them to switch sides for full pardons from the New Republic. Following the Battle of Jakku, Embo joins Jas' new bounty hunter crew.

SIONVER BOLL

SPECIES Bivall
HOMEWORLD Protobranch
AFFILIATION Republic

Sionver Boll designs the electro-proton bomb that is deployed during the Battle of Malastare to deactivate an entire Separatist droid invasion force. The bomb awakens a zillo beast. Despite Boll's protest, Chancellor Palpatine orders the beast killed. The beast escapes, rampaging on Coruscant before Boll creates enough toxin to kill it.

ZILLO BEAST

HOMEWORLD Malastare **AVERAGE SIZE** 97 m (318 ft) high
HABITAT Underground

Zillo beasts are legendary creatures, and one specimen is discovered during the Battle of Malastare, following the detonation of an electro-proton bomb. The monster's armor proves nearly invulnerable to Republic weaponry, stirring the interest of Supreme Chancellor Palpatine. The creature is captured and transported to a research facility on Coruscant. The zillo beast breaks free from its restraints, wreaking havoc through the capital. It is killed by a toxin created by Sionver Boll, but its body is kept and a cloning project begins. A young, cloned zillo beast later escapes confinement during transportation aboard an Imperial ship, devouring the crew. The vessel crash-lands on Silla and the Bad Batch investigates, hoping to recover valuable cargo. The team doesn't expect to encounter such a creature, which soon starts absorbing energy from a local power grid and rapidly growing in size. An Imperial fleet arrives to pacify and capture the beast. The Imperials then round up any witnesses, bar the Batch who escape.

MON MOTHMA

SPECIES Human **HOMEWORLD** Chandrila **AFFILIATION** Republic, Rebel Alliance, New Republic

An experienced and inspiring politician, Mon Mothma plays a crucial role in galactic history. She uses her voice to protect the oppressed, and tries to make the galaxy more equitable and safe for all.

FALL OF THE REPUBLIC
Alongside fellow senators Padmé Amidala, Bail Organa, and Onaconda Farr, Mothma promotes a movement to put an end to the fighting and let diplomacy resume during the Clone Wars. Mothma, Organa, and Padmé oppose Supreme Chancellor Palpatine's abuse of wartime powers and worry that he will refuse to relinquish them after the war. Her fears are realized when Palpatine reorganizes the Galactic Republic into the First Galactic Empire. She loses her friend Padmé shortly after Palpatine's power grab.

WORKING IN SECRET
During the Imperial era, Mothma and Organa remain in the Senate, but secretly form a network of independent rebel cells to oppose the Empire. Mothma forms key political alliances and keeps up appearances as a conscientious senator. Underneath this facade of loyalty to the Empire, she uses her wealth to fund a rebel network, hidden behind charitable foundations. Mothma partners with Luthen Rael, who keeps Mothma at arm's length from his network of rebels as they engage in operations designed to hit the Empire the hardest.

Champion of democracy
Senators Mon Mothma, Bail Organa, and Padmé Amidala discuss methods of countering the chancellor's increasing war powers *(above)*. Mon Mothma and Hera Syndulla discuss Hera's plan to destroy the TIE defender elite factory on Lothal *(right)*.

Mothma must carefully balance her responsibilities as a popular senator and her surreptitious work with the forming Rebellion, while managing her complicated relationships with her husband Perrin Fertha and her daughter Leida. She does all of this under increasing Imperial scrutiny.

DECLARING A REBELLION
Following an uprising on Ghorman, Mothma publicly rebels and is branded a traitor. While fleeing Coruscant with the rebel cell named Gold Squadron, Mothma's ship is attacked, but its crew are rescued by Phoenix Squadron—another rebel group. Mothma reaches Dantooine where she addresses the galaxy, announcing her resignation from the Senate and the formation of the Alliance to Restore the Republic. She becomes the group's leader and must make tough decisions. When a contingent of rebels is besieged on Atollon, Mothma refuses to send help in order to protect the rest of the Alliance. Much later, she sanctions the attack on Lothal that liberates the planet.

Soon after, the Alliance learns of the Death Star, and Mothma elicits Jyn Erso's help to track down Jyn's father—Galen Erso—who helped design it. They learn that the plans for the Death Star are held at an Imperial base on Scarif. Lacking the Alliance High Council's full support, Mothma can't sanction a mission to retrieve them, so Jyn goes rogue. Mothma is glad when Admiral Raddus decides to reinforce her above Scarif. The mission results in the successful theft of the plans, albeit at the cost of many rebel lives. A year later, Mothma barely escapes the crushing rebel defeat at the Mako-Ta Space Docks and orders the survivors to disperse until the time is right to reunite. Two years later, the rebels learn that the Empire is building a second Death Star over Endor. Mothma approves the attack on it and personally briefs the rebel leaders.

A NEW BEGINNING
Following the rebel victory over Endor, Mothma establishes the New Republic and its Galactic Senate on Chandrila. Mothma is elected its first chancellor, but she nearly dies when the Imperial Navy feigns peace talks in order to attempt to assassinate her and other New Republic leaders. She returns to office and, with the help of her allies, persuades the senators to sanction a battle with the Empire's forces above Jakku. After the New Republic victory at Jakku, Mothma signs the Galactic Concordance, a peace treaty between the New Republic and the Empire. She remains open-minded to potential threats, even when others are skeptical, and is concerned about Hera Syndulla's belief that Grand Admiral Thrawn may return to command the Imperial remnant. Mothma continues to lead the New Republic until illness forces her to step down. Years later, Mothma contacts Leia Organa to offer support when it is revealed to the galaxy that her friend's father is Darth Vader.

CHARACTERS AND CREATURES

RUSH CLOVIS
SPECIES Human **HOMEWORLD** Scipio **AFFILIATION** InterGalactic Banking Clan

Senator Rush Clovis works with fellow Senator Padmé Amidala to pass the Mid Rim Cooperation motion that saves the people of Bromlarch from a natural disaster. Years later, during the Clone Wars, the Jedi Order is suspicious of Clovis, so enlists Padmé to gather information about him. She is poisoned when she discovers he is allied to the Separatists, but Clovis, who harbors feelings for her, forces his co-conspirator, Lott Dod, to provide the antidote. Bitter about Clovis' affection for Padmé, Anakin Skywalker abandons Rush. Hoping to atone for his wrongs, Clovis later pleads for Padmé's help in exposing corruption in the Banking Clan, but is killed during a battle on the planet Scipio when Anakin saves Padmé and Rush falls to his death.

Intrigue on Scipio
On Cato Neimoidia, Rush Clovis conspires with Separatists to fund a droid factory *(above)*. Clovis and Padmé arrive on Scipio to investigate corruption in the Banking Clan *(right)*.

KARINA THE GREAT
SPECIES Geonosian **HOMEWORLD** Geonosis **AFFILIATION** Separatist

Some believe the ruling queen on Geonosis is always called Karina the Great. Residing in the catacombs beneath the planet, each queen controls an army of Geonosian drones. During the Clone Wars, the ruling Karina gives orders through Poggle the Lesser. The Jedi discover her after she captures Luminara Unduli, who had followed Poggle to her location. This Karina is presumably killed when clone troopers destroy the temple while rescuing the Jedi.

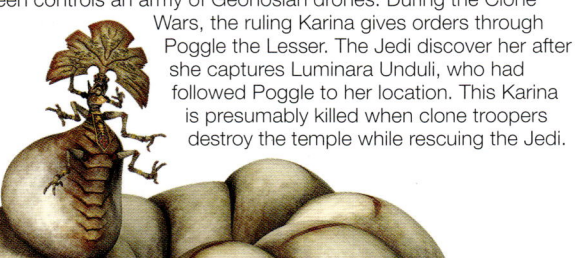

TERA SINUBE
SPECIES Cosian **HOMEWORLD** Cosia **AFFILIATION** Jedi

Long-lived Tera Sinube becomes a Jedi Master during the High Republic era, and during this period he works alongside many famed Jedi including Porter Engle, Stellan Gios, and Sav Malagán. By the time of the Clone Wars, Sinube is an expert on Coruscant's criminal underworld. When Ahsoka Tano's lightsaber is stolen, the Padawan enlists Sinube's help. They track prime suspect Nack Movers and find him dead in his apartment. With him are the bounty hunters Cassie Cryar and Ione Marcy. Ahsoka chases after the fleeing Cryar, while Sinube interrogates Marcy before she also flees. When the Jedi locate the fugitives on a train platform, Marcy is arrested by nearby police droids and Cryar is cornered on a train by Ahsoka. A desperate Cryar tries to exit the train with two hostages, but is foiled by Sinube, who disarms her before returning the stolen lightsaber to Ahsoka. Having survived Order 66, Sinube is killed by Imperial Inquisitors sometime during the rise of the Empire and is entombed in the Fortress Inquisitorius.

DUCHESS SATINE KRYZE
SPECIES Human **HOMEWORLD** Mandalore **AFFILIATION** Mandalorian ruling council

At the beginning of the Clone Wars, Duchess Satine Kryze advocates for peace, forming and leading the Council of Neutral Systems. When rumors swirl that she is secretly creating an army for the Separatists, the Jedi High Council sends Obi-Wan Kenobi, whom Satine had befriended during the Mandalorian Civil War, to investigate. Satine and Obi-Wan travel to Mandalore's moon Concordia, where they are attacked by Governor Pre Vizsla and his Death Watch mercenaries. After they narrowly escape, Satine heads to Coruscant to warn the Galactic Senate about the danger Death Watch presents. Unfortunately, her ship is attacked by battle droids, and she is taken hostage by a Separatist conspirator, Senator Tal Merrik. When she is freed, with help from Obi-Wan and Anakin Skywalker, Satine hurries to the Senate and proves that the evidence favoring a military intervention has been faked, resulting in the senators voting down the resolution to invade Mandalore.

As a criminal market grows on Mandalore, Satine, with the help of the like-minded Senator Padmé Amidala, seeks to prevent the entire population from becoming implicated. She requests aid from the Jedi to expose the smugglers, and Padawan Ahsoka Tano arrives to work with cadets at the Mandalorian Royal Academy to combat them. Satine reveals Prime Minister Almec as the culprit behind the criminal enterprise. He imprisons her, but she is eventually rescued by Ahsoka and the cadets.

When Maul and Savage Opress arrive on Mandalore, Vizsla convinces the planet's people that only Death Watch is strong enough to stop Maul and Opress' Shadow Collective. Ousted from power, the duchess sends a distress signal to Obi-Wan, who attempts to rescue her, but they are both captured. Maul mortally wounds Satine before a helpless Obi-Wan, for whom she expresses her eternal love as she dies.

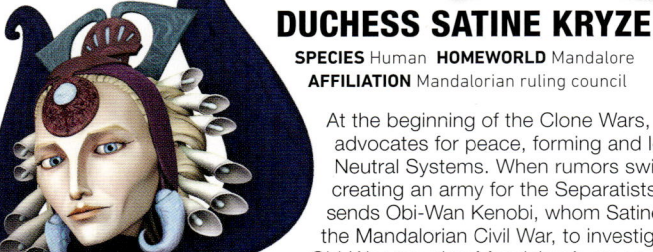

Duchess' allies
When she travels to Coruscant seeking a peaceful resolution to the conflict on Mandalore, Duchess Satine enlists the help of Senator Padmé Amidala *(right)*. Korkie Kryze and his friends from the Royal Academy free the imprisoned duchess *(below)*.

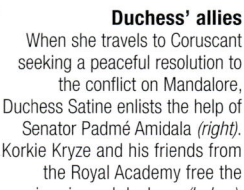

PRIME MINISTER ALMEC
SPECIES Human **HOMEWORLD** Mandalore **AFFILIATION** Mandalorian ruling council, Shadow Collective

Almec is a member of the peaceful New Mandalorian faction. He serves in the New Mandalorian government as prime minister, taking up residence in the capital city of Sundari. When Mandalore is cut off from Republic aid, Almec establishes a criminal market to bring much-needed supplies to his people. But the smugglers poison the people of Sundari with slabin-tainted tea. Almec's crime is exposed and he is imprisoned, though he remains unapologetic for helping his people. After Maul takes over Sundari, he reinstates Almec as a figurehead prime minister. When Maul is imprisoned by Darth Sidious on Stygeon Prime, Almec sends Death Watch to rescue him as recompense for Maul securing his own release. During the Siege of Mandalore, Almec remains loyal to Maul, until Bo-Katan Kryze's forces capture him. He is assassinated before he can give away Maul's schemes.

PRE VIZSLA

SPECIES Human **HOMEWORLD** Mandalore
AFFILIATION Death Watch, Shadow Collective

While governing Mandalore's moon Concordia, Pre Vizsla publicly maintains loyalty to pacifist Duchess Satine Kryze. Secretly he leads Death Watch, a society of commandos intent on returning the Mandalorians to their ancient roots as warriors. Terrorist attacks on Mandalore bring Obi-Wan Kenobi and Duchess Satine Kryze to Concordia, where they discover Death Watch's secret base and Vizsla reveals himself as its leader. After a short duel, Obi-Wan and Satine are forced to flee Concordia.

Vizsla dispatches a Death Watch assassin to Coruscant to kill the duchess and silence her opposition to the Senate's upcoming resolution to send Republic troops to occupy Mandalore. However, Vizsla hopes the Republic's occupation will convince Mandalore's people to support Death Watch. The assassination attempt is foiled and the Senate vote favors Satine, forcing Vizsla to postpone his attack on Mandalore. Harboring a common hatred of Obi-Wan, Maul and Vizsla gather an army of criminals called the Shadow Collective. The criminals attack Mandalore's capital Sundari, allowing Death Watch to be cast as heroes to a desperate population. Vizsla ousts Duchess Kryze and appoints himself prime minister, claiming the title of Mand'alor. Maul challenges Vizsla to a duel to determine the true ruler of the Mandalorians. Vizsla loses and is executed for his failure.

The toast
Pre Vizsla reveals himself as leader of Death Watch.

Claiming the title
Pre Vizsla addresses the people after Death Watch wrests control of the planet from Duchess Kryze.

BOSSK

SPECIES Trandoshan
HOMEWORLD Trandosha
AFFILIATION Bounty hunter, Krayt's Claw

Notorious bounty hunter Bossk teams up with Aurra Sing and Castas to mentor young Boba Fett, who has a vendetta against his father's killer, Jedi Mace Windu. Fett destroys the engines of a Republic attack cruiser carrying Windu, causing it to crash. The bounty hunters take hostages recovered from the wreck, but the Jedi eludes them. Unluckily for them, Jedi Ahsoka Tano rescues the prisoners and captures the bounty hunters. While imprisoned together on Coruscant for their crime, Bossk acts as Fett's bodyguard.

After they escape, Bossk continues working with Fett, joining his team of bounty hunters named Krayt's Claw. When Oked, a fellow team member, is killed by Asajj Ventress, Bossk and Latts Razzi blackmail Ventress into replacing Oked on their next job—they have been hired by Major Rigosso to protect a large chest. While on the job, the tram carrying the chest is attacked by Kage Warriors. Bossk is blinded by one of the warriors and kicked off the tram. Fortunately, he still receives his payment for the assignment. Asajj leaves Krayt's Claw but hires the team to help her rescue Quinlan Vos from Count Dooku on Serenno.

During the Imperial era, Bossk is part of a team, including T'onga and Beilert Valance, led by legendary bounty hunter Nakano Lash. On a mission to Corellia, Lash betrays her colleagues and goes into hiding. Bossk later brings down a corrupt Imperial officer on Lothal with the help of a young Ezra Bridger. He also captures a rogue Imperial astromech containing top-secret data.

During the Galactic Civil War, Bossk is employed by amoral archaeologist Doctor Chelli Lona Aphra to steal credits from the Empire. He is furious when he discovers she has double-crossed him and taken the credits for herself. Following the Battle of Hoth, Bossk is one of six bounty hunters hired by Darth Vader to hunt down the *Millennium Falcon*, but his old partner Boba Fett beats him to the mark.

Doctor Aphra soon lets him know that Lash is alive, so Bossk sets out to get revenge, but is defeated by Valance who is also on her trail. Bossk then infiltrates the Great Hunt on Malastare to kill a vice chair of the Banking Clan for Jabba the Hutt. Jabba's Majordomo, Bib Fortuna, tasks Bossk with capturing Boba who has fallen out of Jabba's favor. Bossk and Boba clash on Jekara, and the Trandoshan loses to his former ally. He is rescued by T'onga's bounty hunting crew and joins the outfit. After a number of missions, Bossk betrays T'onga, shattering the group on Epikonia, as he wants to hunt bounties, not try and rescue a lost cause like Valance from the Scourge.

Bossk eventually meets up with Fett at Jabba's palace, where the *Falcon*'s captain, Han Solo, is hanging on a wall, imprisoned in carbonite. Both bounty hunters accompany Jabba's retinue aboard a sail barge to witness the execution of Han and the team of rebels who have tried to rescue him. The barge is destroyed when Han and his friends fight back. By the time of the New Republic era, Bossk and T'onga have reconciled and the Trandoshan is part of the crew once more, taking part in a mission aboard the *Halcyon*.

Working with Fett
Bossk teams up with young Boba Fett on Quarzite.

BARON PAPANOIDA

SPECIES Pantoran **HOMEWORLD** Pantora
AFFILIATION Republic

During their blockade of Pantora, the Trade Federation kidnaps Chairman Baron Papanoida's two daughters, Chi Eekway and Che Amanwe, as extra leverage to convince the planet's leader to side with the Separatists. Papanoida tracks the kidnapper, the bounty hunter Greedo, to Jabba the Hutt's palace on Tatooine. When brought before Jabba by Papanoida, Greedo admits Chi Eekway is being held in Mos Eisley. Papanoida and his son Ion rescue Eekway, while Amanwe is recovered by Senator Riyo Chuchi and Ahsoka Tano from a Droid Control Ship. Years later, following the Battle of Coruscant, Papanoida and Eekway visit the Coruscant opera house.

KORKIE KRYZE

SPECIES Human **HOMEWORLD** Mandalore **AFFILIATION** New Mandalorian

The nephew of Duchess Satine Kryze, Cadet Korkie Kryze attends the Royal Academy of Government on Mandalore. With his friends Soniee, Amis, and Lagos, Korkie exposes fabricated food shortages that strengthen the black market supported by Mandalorian Prime Minister Almec. With the help of his friends and Bo-Katan Kryze, the duchess' sister, Korkie frees Satine from prison after Death Watch attacks Mandalore.

To the rescue
Baron Papanoida may lead a world, but he is not afraid to take matters into his own hands, firing on assailants in a daring rescue of his daughter Chi Eekway.

CHARACTERS AND CREATURES

ROBONINO
SPECIES Patrolian **HOMEWORLD** Patrolia
AFFILIATION Bounty hunter

Bounty hunter Robonino is regarded for his computer-slicing skills and expertise with explosives. During the Senate hostage crisis led by Cad Bane, Robonino triggers the emergency lockdown in the Republic Executive Building. Later, he grabs and electroshocks Anakin Skywalker when the Jedi battles his partners Shahan Alama and Aurra Sing. Under the employ of Count Dooku, he roughs up Senators Onaconda Farr and Padmé Amidala, who oppose increased funding for the Republic's militarization.

SY SNOOTLES
SPECIES Pa'lowick **HOMEWORLD** Lowick **AFFILIATION** Hutt cartel

A successful singer and part-time bounty hunter, Sy Snootles dates Ziro the Hutt. Ziro's nephew Jabba hires Sy to steal Ziro's holopad, which contains damaging information about the Hutt crime families. She rescues Ziro from Nal Hutta, then accompanies him to Teth to obtain the holopad. Once she has it, Sy turns on Ziro and shoots him. In the years that follow, she focuses on her singing career and helps form the Max Rebo Band. She stays with the group until its break-up after Jabba the Hutt's death.

Entertainer
Sy Snootles *(middle)* sings for Jabba, accompanied by the Max Rebo Band and the Hutt's dancing trio *(right)*.

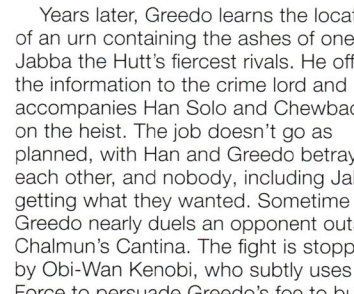

Solo bounty
When Rodian bounty hunter Greedo corners Han Solo in the Mos Eisley Cantina *(left)*, Han takes aim.

GREEDO
SPECIES Rodian **HOMEWORLD** Rodia
AFFILIATION Bounty hunter

During the Clone Wars, Greedo is hired by the Trade Federation to kidnap Pantoran Chairman Papanoida's daughters, Chi Eekway and Che Amanwe. A statue that Che defends herself with is discovered, and the blood on it identifies Greedo, a known criminal, as the kidnapper. Papanoida and his son, Ion, track the Rodian to Tatooine, where they take him to Jabba along with proof of his involvement in the kidnapping. Greedo admits to working for the Separatists. During the rescue of Che, Greedo escapes and continues his work as a bounty hunter.

Years later, Greedo learns the location of an urn containing the ashes of one of Jabba the Hutt's fiercest rivals. He offers the information to the crime lord and accompanies Han Solo and Chewbacca on the heist. The job doesn't go as planned, with Han and Greedo betraying each other, and nobody, including Jabba, getting what they wanted. Sometime later, Greedo nearly duels an opponent outside Chalmun's Cantina. The fight is stopped by Obi-Wan Kenobi, who subtly uses the Force to persuade Greedo's foe to buy him a drink instead. Still working for Jabba, Greedo botches a job on Mygeeto and is given one last chance: to collect a bounty on Han. Greedo fails again and is killed by Han.

NIX CARD
SPECIES Muun **HOMEWORLD** Scipio
AFFILIATION InterGalactic Banking Clan

Nix Card represents the InterGalactic Banking Clan. He plots with Count Dooku to bomb power generators on Coruscant to prevent peace talks. When power is cut to the Senate District, many senators call for the deregulation of the banks to secure the money necessary to finance troop production.

LUX BONTERI
SPECIES Human **HOMEWORLD** Onderon
AFFILIATION Onderon rebels, Rebel Alliance, Dreamers

Lux Bonteri's family sides with the Separatists when Onderon secedes at the beginning of the Clone Wars. Count Dooku orders the death of his mother, Mina Bonteri, to stop a peace proposal that she has introduced. Seeking justice after her assassination, Lux allies with Death Watch. His friend Ahsoka Tano helps him recognize the Mandalorian warriors' dishonorable goals. Returning to Onderon, he joins the rebel movement helping to liberate the planet alongside Saw and Steela Gerrera. Following in his mother's footsteps, Lux becomes Onderon's senator when the planet rejoins the Republic. At some point during the Imperial era, Lux marries an Imperial woman, becoming close to her daughter, and then secretly joins the Rebel Alliance. When Lux learns of the deaths of Saw and many of his followers on Jedha, he decides to assist a group of partisan survivors called the Dreamers. He pretends to offer Alliance intelligence to his wife's daughter, in exchange for amnesty, but it is a ruse to get the names of Imperial officers. Known as the Mentor, Lux provides these human targets to the Dreamers. Soon after, the Imperial Inferno Squad infiltrates the rebel group, uncovering Lux's role in the process, and destroys the Dreamers. It is unknown whether Lux survives a confrontation with the Squad's leader, Iden Versio.

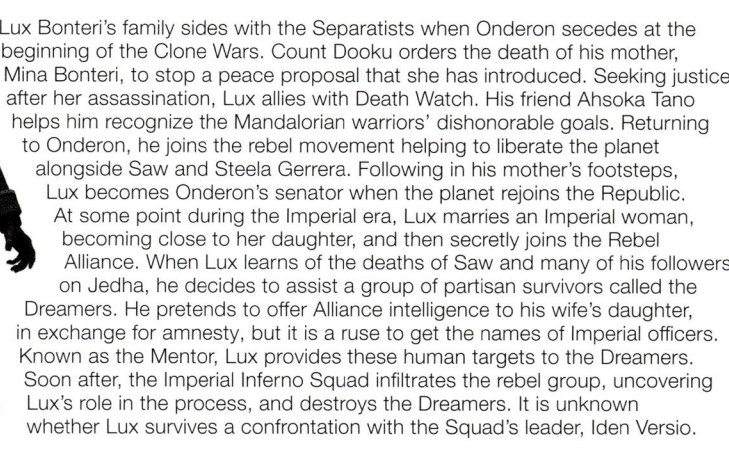

MINA BONTERI
SPECIES Human **HOMEWORLD** Onderon
AFFILIATION Republic, Separatist

Mina Bonteri is a Republic senator, who mentors the young Senator Padmé Amidala from Naboo and leads the senatorial mission to Bromlarch. She admires Count Dooku for taking a stand against the Republic, and with her planet defects to the Separatists. Even though clone forces kill her husband, she advocates a peaceful resolution to the war. Padmé and Mina's work to broker peace ends when Mina is killed by Dooku's agents.

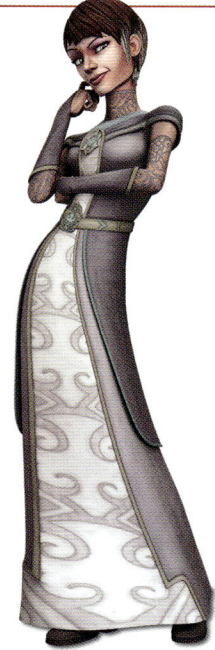

Peace talks
In the Separatist Senate, Mina Bonteri moves to open peace negotiations with the Republic.

MOTHER TALZIN

SPECIES Dathomirian **HOMEWORLD** Dathomir
AFFILIATION Nightsisters

Both a clan mother and a shaman on Dathomir, Mother Talzin uses any means to protect the Nightsisters and also rules over the Nightbrothers. When Darth Sidious visits Dathomir, Talzin trusts his word that he will take her as his apprentice, but he betrays her and kidnaps her young son Maul to take Talzin's place. Talzin swears that she will get her revenge on Sidious.

To protect her sisters, Talzin has to give the infant Asajj Ventress to the criminal Hal'Sted. Ventress later trains with Dooku, but flees to Dathomir when he tries to kill her. Talzin reveals Ventress' true identity as a Nightsister and sends her and two other Nightsisters to assassinate Dooku, but they fail. When Dooku later requests a new apprentice from Talzin, she and Ventress select her second son Savage Opress. Before sending Opress, she casts a spell on him to make him stronger and ensure his ultimate loyalty to her.

On Talzin's orders, Opress tries and fails to defeat Dooku. Talzin then sends him on a quest to find his brother Maul, long believed dead. Dooku orders Grievous to attack the Nightsisters in retaliation for Talzin's strikes. Talzin uses her witchcraft to destroy numerous battle droids, then retreats to conjure dark magick to torture the Count. When Grievous reaches her, she vanishes into thin air. The Separatist assault wipes out the Nightsisters, leaving Ventress as the only other survivor.

After finding Maul, Opress brings him to Talzin, and she uses magick to restore Maul's memories and create a pair of cybernetic legs. The disorder strewn by Maul's newly formed criminal organization, named the Shadow Collective, ultimately draws the attention of Darth Sidious himself, allowing Talzin, Opress, and Maul to seek revenge. When Maul and Opress face Sidious, Opress is killed, and Maul is captured. Soon after, Talzin orders the Frangawl Cult, her followers on Bardotta, to capture the Force-attuned Dagoyan Mystics so she can absorb the living Force from them. Jedi Mace Windu engages her in battle, and, with Jar Jar Binks' help, stops Talzin.

When Maul escapes his incarceration he calls upon Talzin, who tells him to gather his forces to strike against the Sith, sending the Nightbrothers to aid him. Maul captures Dooku, taking him to Dathomir, where Talzin plans to drain the Sith Lord of energy to revive herself. Sidious and Grievous arrive on the planet and free Dooku from Talzin's control. Talzin sacrifices herself to ensure her son Maul can escape.

Nightsister returned
After Asajj Ventress' mentor Count Dooku tries to kill her, Mother Talzin welcomes her back into the Nightsister fold (left).

SAVAGE OPRESS

SPECIES Zabrak **HOMEWORLD** Dathomir
AFFILIATION Nightbrothers, Shadow Collective

After Nightbrother Savage Opress is handpicked by Asajj Ventress to become her apprentice, Mother Talzin uses dark magicks to grant him fearsome abilities and to ensure his loyalty. He kills his fellow Nightbrother Feral to prove his allegiance. Mother Talzin offers him to Count Dooku as a dark acolyte. Dispatched alone to the Devaron system, Opress slaughters Jedi Master Halsey and his apprentice Knox. Impressed, Dooku accepts Opress as his Sith apprentice, intending to use him to overthrow his own Sith master, Darth Sidious. However, Ventress subjects Opress to brutal training in order to pit him against Dooku. When Ventress and Opress battle Dooku on Toydaria, she cannot control his rage-filled impulses. Opress escapes to Dathomir, where he learns from Talzin about the fate that has befallen his brother Maul: he was cut in half by Jedi Knight Obi-Wan Kenobi. Opress rescues Maul from Lotho Minor and brings him to Talzin, who heals him.

Deadly foe
Savage Opress is transformed by Nightsister magick into a terrifying opponent for the Jedi.

Opress joins his brother in seeking vengeance on Kenobi, who pursues Opress and Maul across the galaxy. Ultimately the brothers ally with Death Watch and form the Shadow Collective to seize control of Mandalore. This attracts unwanted attention from Darth Sidious, who confronts the powerful brothers and strikes down Opress.

Duel to the death
Noting the growing power of the brothers, Sidious confronts Savage Opress and Maul on Mandalore (left). As he dies, Opress expresses regret that he was never Maul's equal.

CHARACTERS AND CREATURES

BROTHER VISCUS
SPECIES Zabrak **HOMEWORLD** Dathomir
AFFILIATION Nightbrothers

A leader of a Nightbrothers village on Dathomir, Viscus oversees the tournament used by Asajj Ventress to select Savage Opress as a worthy apprentice. Mother Talzin dispatches Viscus and a squad of Nightbrothers to aid Maul and the Shadow Collective in capturing Count Dooku and General Grievous in a clash at Ord Mantell. Following Talzin's destruction, Viscus and his Nightbrothers follow Merrin until Order 66 survivor Taron Malicos arrives on Dathomir. Malicos falls to the dark side and kills Viscus to take over command of the Nightbrothers.

A new ally
Obi-Wan Kenobi persuades the Daughter to act when her brother attempts to kill her father.

THE DAUGHTER
SPECIES Force-wielder **HOMEWORLD** Mortis **AFFILIATION** The Force

The Daughter is a Force-wielder aligned with the light side of the Force. A visit to Mortis by Anakin Skywalker, Obi-Wan Kenobi, and Ahsoka Tano brings conflict between the Daughter and her brother, the Son, who is aligned with the dark side. When the Son attempts to murder their father, the Daughter takes Obi-Wan to retrieve the Dagger of Mortis, the only weapon that can stop him. The Son gains control of the dagger from the Jedi, kills Ahsoka, and strikes at the Father. The Daughter shields him from the blow and is mortally wounded. With the Father's help, Anakin uses the Daughter's remaining energy to resurrect Ahsoka.

THE SON
SPECIES Force-wielder **HOMEWORLD** Mortis **AFFILIATION** The Force

The Son seeks to escape Mortis and wreak havoc in the galaxy. His ambitions are hindered by the Father, who has bound his children to Mortis, where he can maintain balance between the two. With the arrival of Anakin, the Son sees an opportunity to escape. He corrupts Ahsoka, but the Padawan's brief fall to the dark side fails to turn Anakin—he and Obi-Wan refuse to harm Ahsoka. The Son then tries to kill the Father, instead inadvertently slaying his sister, the Daughter. The Father forsakes his own life, thereby robbing the Son of his immortality and allowing the Chosen One, Anakin, to kill the dark one.

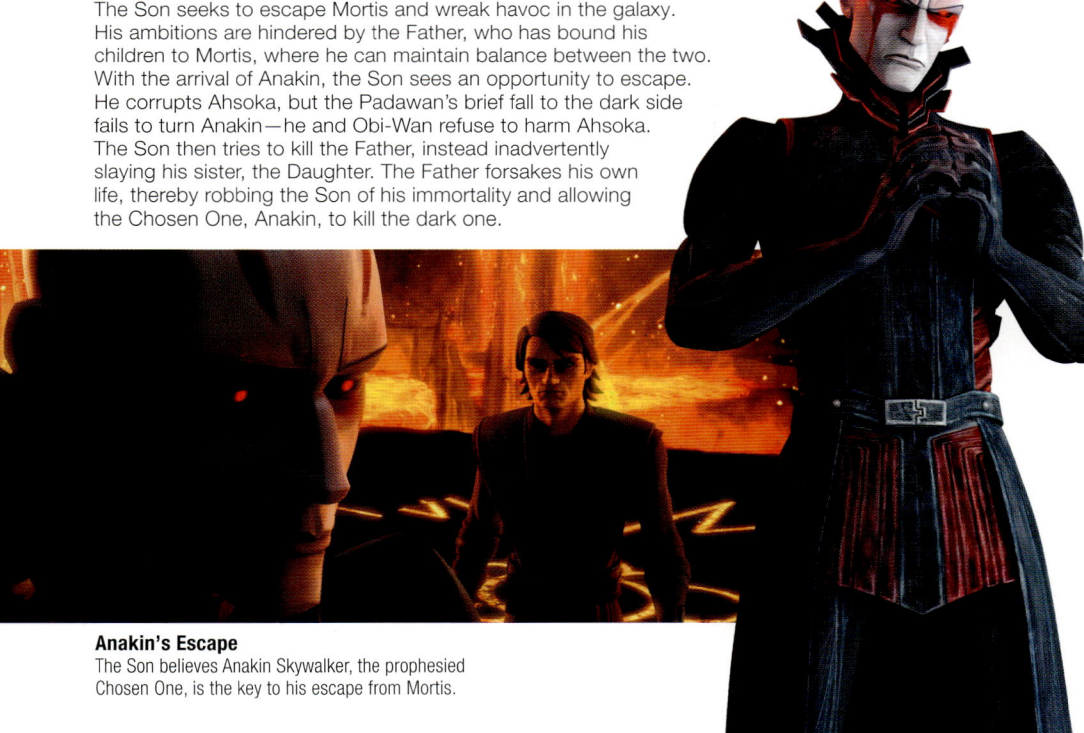

Anakin's Escape
The Son believes Anakin Skywalker, the prophesied Chosen One, is the key to his escape from Mortis.

THE FATHER
SPECIES Force-wielder **HOMEWORLD** Mortis **AFFILIATION** The Force

A powerful family of Force-wielders, known as the Ones, resides in the mysterious realm of Mortis. There, the Father maintains balance between his daughter, who has an affinity for the light side of the Force, and his son, who aligns with the dark side. When Anakin Skywalker, Obi-Wan Kenobi, and Ahsoka Tano arrive on Mortis, Anakin encounters the Father and is given a test to determine if he truly is the prophesied Chosen One. When Anakin succeeds, the Father admits he is dying and asks Anakin to take his place on Mortis to maintain the balance of the Force.

Ancient art
The Ones are depicted in a mural in an ancient Jedi temple on Lothal.

Extragalactic reverence
Monuments to the Ones can even be found on the mysterious planet Peridea in the far galaxy.

OSI SOBECK
SPECIES Phindian **HOMEWORLD** Lola Sayu **AFFILIATION** Separatist

Osi Sobeck is the warden of the infamous Separatist-controlled prison known as the Citadel. He specializes in torturing and breaking Jedi prisoners of war. Count Dooku assigns Sobeck the responsibility of learning the coordinates of a well-hidden hyperspace lane, information Jedi Even Piell and Captain Wilhuff Tarkin had memorized prior to their capture.

GRAND MOFF TARKIN

SPECIES Human **HOMEWORLD** Eriadu
AFFILIATION Republic, Empire

A cruel and calculating visionary, Wilhuff Tarkin is determined to stamp order on the galaxy, regardless of the means or repercussions for those in his way.

MILITARY BEGINNINGS

The son of a rich family from Eriadu, Wilhuff Tarkin begins his military career in a local force that protect his homeworld's sector. Soon after, he trains to join the Republic's Judicial Department and meets Senator Palpatine. The senator suggests Tarkin move into politics, and Tarkin heeds his words, becoming Eriadu's governor.

When the Clone Wars begins, Tarkin becomes a captain in the Republic Navy, leading a successful assault on the planet Murkhana. He and the Jedi General Even Piell serve together. Before they are captured by the Separatists, each of them memorizes a separate half of a critical hyperspace route. They are imprisoned at the Citadel, a facility on Lola Sayu. After General Piell is killed during a Jedi rescue operation, Tarkin learns that Piell shared his half of the route with Jedi Padawan Ahsoka Tano prior to his death. Tarkin passes his half of the route to Palpatine, whereas Ahsoka informs the Jedi Council of her part.

After his return, Tarkin is promoted to admiral and joins the Special Weapons Group of the Strategic Advisory Cell, a team working toward building a battle station. When the Jedi Temple hangar is bombed, Tarkin believes Ahsoka is behind it, so prosecutes her at a military tribunal. Before the verdict can be read, however, Barriss Offee confesses to the crimes.

A NEW ORDER

Shortly after Palpatine becomes Emperor, Tarkin heads to Kamino to determine whether clone troopers should remain the military force for the new Galactic Empire. When Clone Force 99 fails a number of Tarkin's assignments, the Imperial imprisons the group but sees potential in Crosshair. Tarkin later allows Vice Admiral Edmon Rampart, who determines that conscripted volunteers are the future, to take control of Kamino.

After becoming a Moff, Tarkin founds his own group called the Tarkin Initiative, which is given responsibility for the Death Star's construction. He holds a high-level summit of Imperial leaders at a base on his homeworld, Eriadu, wanting to figure out how to unite the galaxy. While the meeting is taking place, the base is infiltrated by two rebel groups; one team led by Saw Gerrera and a now-rogue Clone Force 99, with different aims. Tarkin orders his troops to strike at the clones in spite of the friendly fire risk, leading one member, Tech, to fall to his death.

Soon after Eriadu, Tarkin is ordered to make an example out of Antar 4, a former Separatist world that had a Republic resistance movement. Tarkin sanctions a series of mass executions on the moon, paying no heed to whether the victims once held Separatist or Republic affiliations. Tarkin and Darth Vader then travel to Mon Cala to quell a nascent rebellion. In order to end it quickly, Tarkin requests that Vader abandon the hunt for a Jedi survivor to focus on capturing King Lee-Char instead, promising that he would be in Vader's debt.

Around this time, Tarkin's atrocities, including those on Ghorman, cause a public outcry that leads to him being reassigned to overseeing pacification operations in the Western Reaches. When the Salient system in the region resists the Empire, Tarkin confronts the Salient Battle Group and Saw Gerrera's partisans, who are in league with them. He quashes the battle group and takes over the system.

THE FIRST GRAND MOFF

Following the escape of kyber scientist Galen Erso, Tarkin stops his own campaign in the Western Reaches to oversee Director Orson Krennic's running of the Death Star Project from Sentinel Base. On one occasion, Tarkin successfully defends the base from a rebel attack. He returns to Murkhana with Vader on the trail of the attackers, where his personal ship, the *Carrion Spike*, is stolen by rebels led by former Republic agent Berch Teller. Working together, Vader and Tarkin dispatch an Imperial traitor, recover the *Spike*, and neutralize the rebel cell, even though Teller escapes. As a reward for his successes, the Emperor bestows upon Tarkin the title of Grand Moff, and he is the first person to be granted the prestigious honor. Returning to Eriadu, Tarkin encounters Teller in the wild, leaving the rebel with a broken ankle and the prospect of certain death. Vader, keen to test his own skills, calls in Tarkin's debt, requesting that Tarkin try to capture him. Tarkin is the only survivor out of 20 hunters. Soon after, Tarkin gives Arihnda Pryce the governorship of Lothal in exchange for political information.

GROWING INSURRECTION

After the rebel *Ghost* crew interferes with Lothal's productivity, Tarkin decides to intervene himself. He orders the execution of two useless Imperial officers and leads the mission that results in the capture of former Jedi Kanan Jarrus. When the rebel fleet rescues him, Tarkin and the Emperor come to suspect a larger rebellion is forming. Tarkin approves Governor Pryce's request to use Grand Admiral Thrawn's fleet to hunt down the rebel group.

When the Death Star becomes fully operational, Tarkin orders a partial test of its capabilities on Jedha's Holy City. Tarkin takes control of the Death Star after the successful test, claiming that Krennic is inadequate. As the Rebel Alliance attacks Scarif to steal the Death Star plans, Tarkin arrives at the battle station, ordering it to fire upon the base where the plans are held. Later, he demonstrates the station's full destructive power to Princess Leia by obliterating her homeworld of Alderaan. Tarkin dies soon afterward when the Death Star is destroyed by the Alliance during the Battle of Yavin.

While Tarkin may be dead, his influence is still felt across the galaxy through Imperial ideology and his protégé Ellian Zahra. Ellian seeks revenge on the Alliance and destroys many rebel ships from the bridge of her Star Destroyer, *Tarkin's Will*.

> "You may fire when ready." — GRAND MOFF TARKIN

Cunning opponent
Be it hunting quarry in the wilds or navigating the power hierarchy of the Empire *(left)*, Tarkin is a ruthless, skilled, and cunning combatant *(below)*.

Empire's protector
Tarkin and Imperial Security Bureau Agent Alexsandr Kallus listen to a rebel message before the communications tower broadcasting it is destroyed *(top)*. Tarkin and his Imperial strategists meet aboard the original Death Star *(above)*. Princess Leia must reveal the location of the secret rebel base or watch Alderaan be destroyed *(left)*.

CHARACTERS AND CREATURES

CHEWBACCA

SPECIES Wookiee **HOMEWORLD** Kashyyyk
AFFILIATION Republic, Rebel Alliance, Resistance

Copilot of the *Millennium Falcon*, Chewbacca follows his best friend Han Solo until the very end. Together they take up the fight against the Empire and then join the battle against the First Order.

THE CLONE WARS
Chewbacca is captured by Trandoshan trophy hunters and taken to Wasskah, where Ahsoka Tano and Jedi younglings O-Mer and Jinx are already held as prey. In hopes of commandeering a flight off the moon, the Jedi attack the dropship delivering Chewbacca. Though the vessel crashes, they find a powerful ally in the mighty Wookiee, who cobbles together a transmitter from the crashed ship's remains and sends a distress call. When things look their bleakest, Chief Tarfful and a team of Wookiees arrive to rescue Chewbacca and his new friends. At the conclusion of the Clone Wars, Chewbacca fights by Tarfful's side during the Battle of Kashyyyk and aids Jedi Master Yoda's escape after Order 66.

KESSEL RUN
Chewbacca is once again held captive, this time by Imperial forces on Mimban. There he meets Han Solo for the first time, and they devise a plan to escape their shared prison. Together, they flee the planet as part of Tobias Beckett's crew.

Shaky start
Chewbacca is shocked when his new human cellmate can speak the Wookiee language Shyriiwook—albeit stiltingly. It is just enough for Han Solo to communicate an escape plan.

Their exploits send them to a hyperfuel mine on Kessel, where Chewie discovers that his fellow Wookiees are being enslaved there by the Pyke Syndicate to perform hard labor. After freeing the enslaved people and stealing unrefined coaxium, the crew flees the planet aboard the *Falcon*, currently under the ownership of Lando Calrissian. With limited time and the Empire not far behind, Chewbacca takes the copilot seat next to Han for their record-setting Kessel Run through the heart of the Akkadese Maelstrom. The duo survives the dangerous maneuver, dodging planet-sized carbonbergs and the colossal summa-verminoth creature. It is the beginning of a long-standing partnership.

SMUGGLING PARTNERSHIP
Chewbacca remains the loyal copilot of the *Falcon* well into the reign of the Empire. Han and Chewie work odd smuggling jobs for Jabba the Hutt, occasionally teaming up with fellow scoundrels like Greedo and pirate queen Maz Kanata. On one fateful spice run, he and Han are forced to dump their cargo to escape Imperial pursuit. This puts them into debt with Jabba the Hutt, who seeks retribution for his lost contraband. Tempted by the sizable payment for delivering Obi-Wan and his protégé plus two droids to Alderaan, Han and Chewbacca accept the job, unwittingly taking the first step toward new friendships with Luke Skywalker and Princess Leia Organa and a life with the Rebel Alliance.

Longtime partners
After learning Obi-Wan Kenobi is willing to pay for a fast ride, Chewbacca introduces the Jedi to Han Solo.

REBEL WARRIOR
When Han Solo wants to leave with their reward for delivering Princess Leia to the rebel base on Yavin 4, Chewbacca provokes his friend's conscience, convincing him to turn around. The *Falcon*'s shot at Darth Vader's TIE fighter buys Luke the time to fire the two torpedoes that destroy the Death Star. Despite Han's reservations, the duo continues to aid the Alliance after the Death Star's destruction. Chewbacca assaults the Imperial Weapons Factory Alpha on Cymoon 1, freeing enslaved individuals. He later commandeers the Star Destroyer *Harbinger* alongside his rebel allies and faces Darth Vader on Kakra. Chewbacca is distraught when Han is taken from him on Cloud City, but he remains dedicated to the Alliance, helping to plan the rescue of his carbonite-encased friend, who has been delivered to Jabba by bounty hunter, Boba Fett. When the second Death Star threatens the galaxy, Chewbacca joins the rebel strike team that destroys its shield generator. Chewbacca later returns to Kashyyyk to liberate his homeworld from the Empire, leading an uprising against Grand Moff Lozen Tolruck.

BACK AT IT AGAIN
Decades after the Battle of Endor, Chewbacca and Han begin smuggling again. Their beloved *Falcon* has been stolen by Ducain, so they operate a large bulk freighter—the *Eravana*. While transporting lethal rathtars to King Prana, Han and Chewbacca intercept the *Falcon* with Rey, Finn, and BB-8 onboard. Kanjiklub and the Guavian Death Gang board the *Eravana* demanding payment from Han and Chewbacca, and Rey accidentally releases the rathtars. Chewbacca is wounded during the ensuing chaos, but the heroes escape aboard the *Falcon* and eventually join Leia and the Resistance on D'Qar. During the mission to Starkiller Base, Chewbacca helplessly witnesses Han fall to Kylo Ren's lightsaber. Roaring with rage, Chewbacca wounds Kylo—his friend's son—with a retaliatory bowcaster blast. Chewbacca accompanies Rey to the planet Ahch-To to deliver the news of Han's demise to Luke Skywalker, before they depart to help the Resistance at the Battle of Crait. There, Chewie uses the *Falcon* to rescue survivors and shuttle them off planet.

A NEW GENERATION
Following Crait, Chewbacca remains by Leia's side, heading on missions to Ryloth, Mon Cala, and Kashyyyk. He also temporarily lends the *Falcon* to Hondo Ohnaka on Batuu. The Resistance eventually establishes their new base on Ajan Kloss. Knowing how much Han, Luke, and Leia cared for Finn, Poe, and Rey, Chewbacca considers the young Resistance heroes part of his honorary family and joins them in the search for Exegol. After the trail leads them to the deserts of Pasaana, the Knights of Ren capture the Wookiee, delivering him to the First Order where he is imprisoned aboard the Star Destroyer *Steadfast*. His incarceration is short, and he is soon rescued by his friends. They return to Ajan Kloss, where Chewbacca is devastated to learn about the passing of Leia Organa. He puts aside his grief to join Lando

Chewie, we're home
Han and Chewbacca are delighted to be back with the *Falcon*. They investigate the ship to discover who is piloting it.

Calrissian on the *Falcon* for a mission to call for allies in the Core systems of the galaxy. They join the pivotal Battle of Exegol with a colossal fleet at their side. The Resistance emerges victorious, and Chewbacca returns safely from the battle, a hero of two galaxy-changing conflicts.

Loyal friend
Typical of many Wookiees, Chewbacca values honor and friendship above all else. He does not hesitate to put his life on the line for his smuggler partner Han Solo.

BO-KATAN KRYZE

SPECIES Human **HOMEWORLD** Kalevala
AFFILIATION Death Watch, Mandalorian rebels, Mandalorians

Devoted to her homeworld of Mandalore, Bo-Katan Kryze will do anything to keep her people safe. A determined warrior and survivor, she is eager to see Mandalorians thrive.

Retaking Mandalore
Once enemies, Bo-Katan relies upon the Republic to provide the military support to retake Sundari. Seasoned commander Ahsoka Tano will lead the Republic troops into battle.

MEMBER OF DEATH WATCH

Born to the royal family, Bo-Katan takes the creed on Mandalore, much to the pleasure of her father and the adoring citizens. Like her sister, Duchess Satine, she dedicates herself to her homeworld of Mandalore. Rejecting Satine's commitment to pacifism, Bo-Katan trains to become a Mandalorian warrior and joins Death Watch, an outlawed sect that seeks to return Mandalore to its glorious past. She first meets her future ally Ahsoka Tano in combat on Carlac, but the Jedi escapes.

However, Kryze is skeptical of Death Watch leader Pre Vizsla's alliance with Maul to depose Satine. When the former Sith slays Vizsla, Bo-Katan sees her worst fears for her planet come true. She frees captured Jedi Obi-Wan Kenobi, and they try to save Satine from Maul, but he kills her. Bo-Katan ensures that Obi-Wan escapes to tell the Republic what happened and leads a resistance against their mutual enemy. Maul continues to rule until Bo-Katan seeks Ahsoka's help on Oba Diah. Now a former Jedi, Ahsoka requests the Republic send military aid. She then leads the forces, joining Kryze and her troops in battle. Together, they retake the world from Maul during the Siege of Mandalore.

The Duchess
Bo-Katan works with weapons expert Sabine Wren to destroy the Duchess—a prototype weapon devised by Wren while she was in the Imperial Academy, which is able to target Mandalorian armor.

REGENT OF MANDALORE

The Republic names Bo-Katan regent after their victory. Following the Empire's formation, Kryze refuses to work for them, and she is deposed by Clan Saxon, a group loyal to the Emperor. Years later, she works with Mandalorian rebel operative Sabine Wren and the Wren Clan to retake Mandalore from the Empire. Together, they stop an experimental weapon designed to obliterate Mandalorian armor. Sabine recognizes that Bo-Katan can unite the clans to achieve their aim, so bestows upon her the legendary Darksaber. With the clans' support, Kryze becomes the honored leader of the Mandalorians.

THE GREAT PURGE

Soon after, the Empire launches a purge of Mandalore, leading to the Night of a Thousand Tears. Kryze surrenders to save the remaining Mandalorians and loses the Darksaber to Imperial Moff Gideon. However, she is betrayed by the Empire. Most of her remaining people are annihilated and Mandalore is heavily bombed, but Bo-Katan escapes.

She begins to lead a group of Mandalorian survivors, including Koska Reeves and Axe Woves. Bo-Katan later saves Din Djarin and his foundling Grogu from Quarren sailors on Trask. Her beliefs about what it means to be Mandalorian challenge Din, whose orthodox views are very different. However, he agrees to help her in exchange for information on Ahsoka's location. Together with Reeves and Woves, the Mandalorian unit steals an Imperial vessel and Din then heads to Corvus.

When Grogu is kidnapped by Gideon, Din asks for Bo-Katan's aid and together they launch an attack on his flagship. During the assault, Din takes ownership of the Darksaber from Gideon in battle. He offers the weapon to Kryze, but she refuses to accept it, believing now that it must be won in combat and not given, as before.

THE RETURN TO MANDALORE

Following this conflict, Axe assumes command of her group, turning them into mercenaries, so Bo-Katan heads into a temporary retirement in her home, Kryze Castle on Kalevala. She meets with Din once again but refuses to help him investigate Mandalore. However, Din is defeated in the mines of Mandalore by an assailant, so Grogu calls for her help. Bo-Katan rushes to Din's aid and defeats the attacker, becoming the rightful owner of the Darksaber. They return to Kalevala but are besieged by Gideon's forces who destroy her home. Afterwards they flee to the world where Din's covert, led by an Armorer, are staying. At first, Bo-Katan finds little common ground with Din's group, until they learn to trust each other after they rescue a foundling. When Nevarro is attacked by pirates, Kryze and Din's group agree to liberate the world in exchange for land.

Surviving the inferno
When Axe Woves crashes the captured Imperial light cruiser into Moff Gideon's secret base, it seems unlikely that Grogu, Bo-Katan, and Din Djarin will survive. However, thanks to Grogu's use of the Force, the trio emerges unscathed.

THE NEW AGE

Bo-Katan and the Armorer decide now is the time to unite all Mandalorians and retake their homeworld. On Plazir-15, she duels Axe to reclaim leadership of her former group. However, they refuse to follow her until Din reveals that she is the rightful owner of the Darksaber. Now a leader once more, Kryze and her people retake Mandalore from hidden Imperial forces, but the Darksaber is destroyed. Bo-Katan becomes the ruler of Mandalore once more, beginning a new age for her now-united people.

CHARACTERS AND CREATURES

Adaptable
Although an aquatic species, Mon Calamari can breathe and work both underwater and on land.

ADMIRAL GIAL ACKBAR
SPECIES Mon Calamari **HOMEWORLD** Mon Cala
AFFILIATION Republic, Rebel Alliance, Resistance

Admiral Gial Ackbar's esteemed military career spans decades. During the Clone Wars, he holds the rank of captain of the Mon Calamari Guard. He protects Prince Lee-Char during the Mon Cala Civil War, which is instigated by the Quarren with support from the Separatists. The Separatist leader Riff Tamson betrays the Quarren, leading them to reunite with the Mon Calamari, and Ackbar helps lead the counterassault to drive out the invaders.

A year into the Emperor's reign, Lee-Char incites a war on Mon Cala between its people and the Empire. Ackbar follows his king's orders and defends Mon Cala's northern hemisphere, while his comrade Raddus protects the other half. The Empire quashes the rebellion and captures the king, but Raddus and a small force escape and go on to join the Rebel Alliance.

Ackbar follows his compatriots at a later stage and becomes a key Alliance leader. Following the Death Star's destruction, Ackbar helps lead the evacuation of the rebel base on Yavin 4 and offers Princess Leia his sympathies for Alderaan's destruction. Soon after, Ackbar accompanies the rebel team that travels to Mon Cala to meet with his old friend Regent Urtya. They unsuccessfully try to persuade Urtya to hand over the Mon Cala Mercantile fleet to their cause. Princess Leia tries to rescue Lee-Char from Imperial custody. He dies in the attempt, but Leia records his inspirational last words. She passes the recording to Urtya, who decides to transmit them across Mon Cala, encouraging the Mon Calamari crew to mutiny and regain control of the fleet. The Empire sends Star Destroyers to Mon Cala to destroy the mutineers, but Ackbar arrives with a small rebel contingency to save them. Most of the Mercantile vessels escape to the Mako-Ta Space Docks. Thanks to Queen Trios of the Shu-Torun, the ships are refitted with Shu-Torun tech to become Alliance warships. After the retrofit, Trios, who is secretly in league with Darth Vader, uses a code to render the fleet inoperable. Vader's Death Squadron arrives and begins annihilating the ships. After Leia recovers the code to regain control of the cruisers, she conveys them to the remaining ships, including Ackbar's vessel, and the survivors escape.

Ackbar is not present during the Alliance defeat at Hoth. Following the scattering of the Alliance fleet, he leads the Eleventh Division. He faces heavy losses during the Battle of Ab Dalis, but his team is saved thanks to the work of Starlight Squadron. By the time of the Battle of Endor, Ackbar is the leader of the Rebel Alliance fleet and commands the attack on the second Death Star. Seeing the size of the Imperial fleet massed to protect the space station, which is still under construction, Ackbar realizes the rebels have been led into a trap and prepares to order a retreat. At the last moment, Lando Calrissian convinces him to give Han Solo and Leia more time. Their mission to take down the Death Star's shields succeeds, and Ackbar leads the rebel vessels in routing the Imperials.

Following the victory, Ackbar becomes the Fleet Admiral of the New Republic and battles the surviving Imperials, leading his forces to a critical victory at Kuat. When the Empire prepares to bombard the planet Kashyyyk from orbit, Ackbar leads the effort to save it. He personally commands the New Republic attack on Jakku, where most of the remaining Imperial fleet has gathered, and ensures the New Republic is victorious.

After the Battle of Jakku, the Empire and New Republic sign a peace treaty. Ackbar serves for a number of years, including overseeing the judgment of General Hera Syndulla following her acts on Seatos. He eventually retires from the New Republic military, spending his time on Mon Cala, but he joins Leia's Resistance movement to protect the New Republic and galactic peace.

During the assault on Starkiller Base, Ackbar is stationed on D'Qar and, after the battle, attends Han Solo's funeral. Following the Resistance's evacuation of the planet, Ackbar is on the *Raddus*' command bridge and is killed when a First Order TIE fighter fires upon it.

War veteran
Ackbar has served with distinction on the front lines, be they from the command bridge of a capital cruiser *(left)* or in the depths of the ocean *(below)*.

SENATOR MEENA TILLS
SPECIES Mon Calamari **HOMEWORLD** Mon Cala
AFFILIATION Republic

A female Mon Calamari, Meena Tills is a Galactic senator during the Clone Wars. When Quarren insurgents on Mon Cala threaten to ally with the Separatists, Tills returns to her homeworld to assist the Jedi and clone army intervention that ultimately defeats the Separatist uprising. Tills joins the delegation of senators who oppose Supreme Chancellor Palpatine's continuation of his emergency powers, which later puts her at risk.

PONG KRELL
SPECIES Besalisk **HOMEWORLD** Ojom
AFFILIATION Jedi

The only thing more imposing than Pong Krell's Besalisk physique is his reputation as a Jedi general in the Clone Wars. Renowned for his ruthlessness on the battlefield and intolerance of insubordination, he wields two double-bladed lightsabers but rarely chooses to fight alongside his troops. With the conflict dragging on, Krell foresees the demise of the Jedi Order and the Republic and chooses the dark side of the Force in self-preservation. On Umbara, Krell tricks two legions of clone troopers into attacking each other. After his treason is discovered by Captain Rex, Krell is killed by a devoted trooper named Dogma.

HYDROID MEDUSA
HOMEWORLD Karkaris
AVERAGE SIZE 22 m (72 ft) long
AFFILIATION Separatist

Hydroid medusas are gargantuan jellyfish weaponized with cybernetic enhancements. Impervious to blasters and lightsabers, they wreak havoc on underwater battlefields with their electrified tentacles. In the Battle of Mon Cala, the Gungan Grand Army uses boomas to short-circuit the hydroid medusas.

BOSS LYONIE
SPECIES Gungan
HOMEWORLD Naboo
AFFILIATION Gungan High Council

Boss Lyonie bears an uncanny resemblance to Jar Jar Binks. He is hypnotically controlled briefly by an aide, Rish Loo, who is in league with Count Dooku, to start a civil war. When Lyonie is gravely injured, Jar Jar poses as him to restore trust between the Gungans and the Naboo.

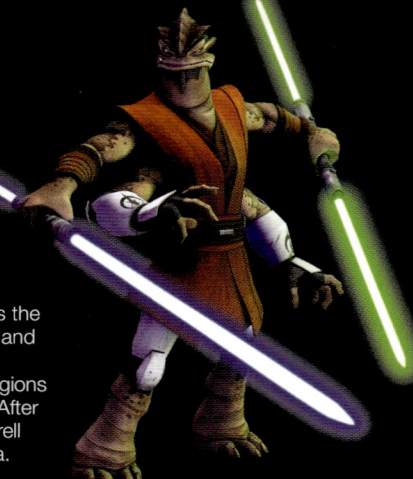

MIRAJ SCINTEL
SPECIES Zygerrian
HOMEWORLD Zygerria
AFFILIATION Separatist

Queen of Zygerria Miraj Scintel seeks to restore her planet's former glory as the center of a slave-trading empire. She allies with the Separatists in the Clone Wars, leading the Jedi to intervene. Scintel attempts to romance Anakin Skywalker but is rebuffed. Later, when she turns against Count Dooku, he kills her.

C-21 HIGHSINGER
AFFILIATION Bounty hunter

A heavily modified assassin droid of unknown origin, C-21 Highsinger is presumably the only one of his kind. Serving no master, his autonomous programming is well suited to a bounty-hunting career. Most vicious among his capabilities is a rotator assembly that spins his upper torso at high speed, allowing him to unleash his blasters in a devastating circle of laser fire. His servomotors are optimized for swift reflexes, giving him proficiency in movement and hand-to-hand combat. C-21 joins Boba Fett's team of bounty hunters, named Krayt's Claw, during the Clone Wars. On the planet Quarzite, C-21 dispatches many Kage Warriors in combat on a subtram; he is only stopped when they propel him overboard. With the rest of Krayt's Claw, C-21 joins former member Asajj Ventress to rescue Jedi Quinlan Vos from Count Dooku on Serenno, but they are unsuccessful. During the Galactic Civil War, C-21 is hired by Darth Vader to track down the Sith Lord's former acquaintance, Doctor Chelli Lona Aphra, but she evades him and his competition.

TENTH BROTHER
SPECIES Miraluka
AFFILIATION Jedi, Inquisitorius

During the Clone Wars, Jedi Master Prosset Dibs is angered by the Jedi's new roles as generals and attempts to kill Mace Windu on Hissrich. Subsequently, the Jedi Council charges him with treason and sends Dibs for rehabilitation. After Order 66, Dibs becomes the Tenth Brother and is killed due to the machinations of surviving Padawan Ferren Barr.

MORALO EVAL
SPECIES Phindian **HOMEWORLD** Phindar
AFFILIATION Separatist

A heartless and deranged criminal, Moralo Eval brags that he killed his mother because he got bored. He escapes Republic prison alongside Cad Bane and Rako Hardeen, who is actually Obi-Wan Kenobi undercover. Bane and Hardeen compete in Eval's skill challenge, the Box, earning spots on a team that will attempt to kidnap Supreme Chancellor Palpatine.

OLD DAKA
SPECIES Dathomirian
HOMEWORLD Dathomir
AFFILIATION Nightsisters

Old Daka is the oldest and wisest of the elders in Mother Talzin's Nightsisters clan, and her mastery of ancient magick is unparalleled. When General Grievous' forces attack the clan, Daka's incantation conjures an undead horde of Nightsister zombies to fight the battle droids. Grievous personally tracks down Daka in her hidden cave and slays her.

LATTS RAZZI
SPECIES Theelin
AFFILIATION Bounty hunter

Even more distinctive than Latts Razzi's bright red hair is her primary weapon of choice, the grappling boa. Razzi spars with opponents by either cracking the green, scaled boa like a whip or using it as a lasso to ensnare them. Razzi joins Boba Fett's bounty hunter syndicate, named Krayt's Claw, and accepts a delivery job on the planet Quarzite, where she fends off attacking Kage Warriors. Later, Razzi takes work from the Hutts and goes on a mission with the rest of Krayt's Claw to rescue captured Jedi Quinlan Vos from Count Dooku.

AZI-3
TYPE Medical droid **HOMEWORLD** Kamino
AFFILIATION Republic, Empire, Clone Force 99

AZI-345211896246498721347, known simply AZ, works as a floating medical droid in Tipoca City on Kamino. During the Clone Wars, AZ and the trooper Fives discover the existence of inhibitor chips implanted in all clones. AZ removes Fives' chip, but shortly after, his memory is wiped by the Kaminoans. AZ deeply cares about the clones, and develops a close relationship with Omega, who takes AZ with her when she leaves Kamino with the Bad Batch. Often staying at Cid's Parlor, AZ leaves Ord Mantell with the Batch when Cid betrays them and Omega is kidnapped.

BREZAK
HOMEWORLD Zygerria
AVERAGE SIZE 10.2 m (33 ft 6 in) long **HABITAT** Plains

The brezak is a lizard species with four long and muscular legs and a pair of skin flaps, allowing the beast to run and jump over rugged terrain before taking flight. Zygerrians use brezaks as mounts for their royal guard, saddling them to help control their movements. Anakin Skywalker rides a brezak with the queen of Zygerria while working on an undercover mission during the Clone Wars. Years later on Ord Mantell, a brezak owned by Zygerrian enslavers attacks Clone Force 99 on behalf of its master and tries to subdue a rancor.

DERROWN
SPECIES Parwan
HOMEWORLD Parwa
AFFILIATION Bounty hunter

Derrown is a ruthless bounty hunter who has earned the nickname "the Exterminator". He has the innate ability to electrify his body with crackling energy, and his tentacled physiology, containing lighter-than-air gasses, enables him to float to positions others would struggle to reach. These advantages help him successfully pass the Box, Count Dooku's bounty-hunter challenge.

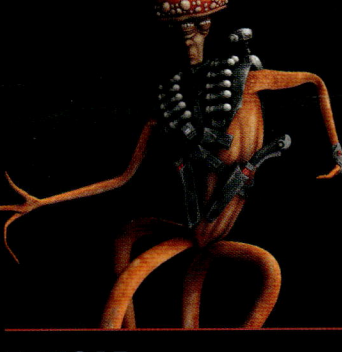

DENGAR
SPECIES Human **HOMEWORLD** Corellia **AFFILIATION** Bounty hunter

Dengar is one of the most dangerous bounty hunters in the galaxy. Wearing plated battle armor and a turban, he pursues targets with his blaster rifle and mini grenades. During the Clone Wars, he becomes a part of Krayt's Claw—a bounty hunter team led by Boba Fett. The team takes on a mission to safeguard a locked chest being shipped by tram on the planet Quarzite. When Kage Warriors attack, Dengar fights off as many as he can until he is thrown from the tram. Another time, while in the service of the Hutts, Dengar and three other bounty hunters are attacked by forces commanded by Maul and Pre Vizsla. Dengar flees with his fellow mercenaries when it becomes clear defeat is inevitable.

Years later, Dengar encounters wanted smuggler Han Solo on Nar Shaddaa. Dengar tries to capture Han but is thrown off the roof of a building instead! Following the Battle of Hoth, Dengar is one of the bounty hunters summoned by Darth Vader to hunt for the *Millennium Falcon*. Soon after Han is captured in Cloud City, Dengar reluctantly partners with Beilert Valance in order to track down Boba Fett. He also works for Jabba the Hutt after his girlfriend, Manaroo, becomes indebted to the gangster. Following the Battle of Endor, Dengar teams up with new bounty hunter Mercurial Swift to capture Jas Emari, the niece of his old colleague Sugi, but betrays Swift when Emari offers him a better deal. Dengar joins Emari's new crew, declaring that they need to stick together as times are changing. The aging Corellian wants to remain relevant in a bounty-hunting trade that's filling with new talent.

CHARACTERS AND CREATURES

KING SANJAY RASH
SPECIES Human
HOMEWORLD Onderon
AFFILIATION Separatist

After King Ramsis Dendup refuses to commit Onderon to the Clone Wars, Sanjay Rash deposes him, assuming the crown. Some Onderon citizens successfully rebel against the Separatist droid army occupation requested by Rash. Before the Separatists' retreat, however, Rash is killed by super tactical droid Kalani on Count Dooku's command.

STEELA GERRERA
SPECIES Human **HOMEWORLD** Onderon **AFFILIATION** Onderon rebels

After the Onderon rebels destroy a key power generator, Steela is elected their leader. Her courageous speech to the people of Onderon prompts Sanjay Rash and his Separatist allies to set a trap during former King Dendup's public execution. With the help of Steela's brother Saw, the rebels succeed in rescuing Dendup and restoring him to power, but Steela falls in battle.

GREGOR
SPECIES Human **HOMEWORLD** Kamino
AFFILIATION Republic, rebels

Designated CC-5576-39, Gregor is a clone commando and a captain in the Republic Army. He suffers amnesia following a Republic defeat on the planet Sarrish and ends up on Abafar, where he is employed as a dishwasher. When D-Squad runs into Gregor, they help him recover his memory and enlist his help. At the local Separatist mining facility, Gregor dispatches battle droids and provides cover for D-Squad. After Gascon and M5-BZ get separated from the group, Gregor retrieves them. When D-Squad escapes aboard the shuttle, Gregor is overrun by the droid forces as the facility is destroyed. Somehow, Gregor survives and is promoted to the rank of Commander.

Shortly after the end of the war, Gregor becomes an instructor at a facility on Daro where the next generation of Imperial troops is being trained. After realizing he doesn't want to be part of the Empire, he decides to escape, and calls for help from Rex who sends Clone Force 99 to help Gregor escape. Gregor joins the group, piloting a ship while the other members rescue clones imprisoned on an Imperial vessel.

Much like Captain Rex and Commander Wolffe, Gregor removes his control chip, a procedure that adversely affects him. The three clones end up living in a customized AT-TE on Seelos. Years later, a rebel team named the Spectres visits the clones. Together, the rebels and clones defeat an Imperial force. While Rex joins the rebels, Gregor and Wolffe stay on Seelos in a commandeered AT-AT. Two years later, they answer Rex and the Spectres' call for help to free Lothal. Sadly, Gregor is fatally wounded, but he dies feeling honored to have fought for something he chose to fight for.

GENERAL TANDIN
SPECIES Human **HOMEWORLD** Onderon
AFFILIATION Royal Onderon Militia

Although General Tandin initially supports King Rash, he disagrees with super tactical droid Kalani on how to deal with the Onderon rebels, and a conversation with captured rebel Saw Gerrera reinforces his doubts. The general leads the palace guard to stop Dendup's execution and pledges his support to the rightful king.

WAC-47
SPECIES DUM-series pit droid
AFFILIATION Republic, rebels

WAC-47 serves as D-Squad's pilot when the team infiltrates a Separatist dreadnought to steal an encryption module. After crash-landing on Abafar, D-Squad uncovers a plot to blow up a space station using a stolen Republic cruiser. To foil the plan, WAC-47 has to leave R2-D2 behind to destroy the cruiser. During the Imperial era, WAC-47 works for the Rebel Alliance, delivering vital supplies to *Home One*. During the Scourge crisis, he rescues R2 from the vacuum of space and transports him to Iego.

MEEBUR GASCON
SPECIES Zilkin **AFFILIATION** Republic

Meebur Gascon is a tactical adviser during the First Battle of Geonosis. Later, he leads a D-Squad mission to steal an encryption module. Diminutive in stature, he often rides inside the droid M5-BZ. Gascon devises the daring plan to stop the Separatists from destroying a space station.

ZITON MOJ
SPECIES Falleen
HOMEWORLD Falleen
AFFILIATION Shadow Collective, Black Sun

Ziton Moj is Captain of the Guard for the Black Sun crime syndicate during the Clone Wars. After Savage Opress kills Black Sun leader Xomit Grunseit, Moj joins Maul's Shadow Collective and helps their takeover of Sundari. Moj leads disruptions throughout the city, before his staged capture by Bo-Katan Kryze, a member of Death Watch—a Mandalorian group that is secretly in league with Maul. When Moj kidnaps the Pyke Syndicate leader's family, Moj loses in battle to bounty hunter Asajj Ventress who rescues the family. Moj stays loyal to Maul until the Separatists begin attacking Moj's forces.

LOM PYKE
SPECIES Pyke **HOMEWORLD** Oba Diah
AFFILIATION Shadow Collective, Pyke Syndicate

Lom Pyke is the leader of the Pyke Syndicate, a criminal group known for dealing in illicit spices. He attends Xev Xrexus' criminal auction. Later, Pyke is hired by Darth Tyranus to kill Jedi Master Sifo-Dyas. Pyke also covertly captures the Jedi's companion, Silman, who is Chancellor Valorum's aide. During the Clone Wars, Pyke joins the Shadow Collective. When Obi-Wan Kenobi and Anakin Skywalker confront Pyke during their investigation of Sifo-Dyas' death, Pyke reveals that Dooku is Tyranus. He is then killed by Dooku.

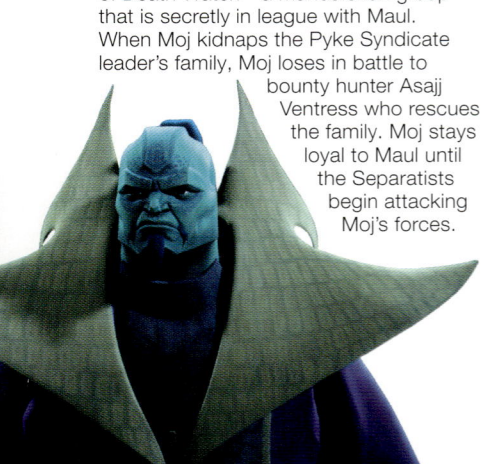

Selfless hero
On the planet Sarrish and again on Abafar, Gregor acts bravely, putting the lives of others before his own.

QUEEN JULIA
SPECIES Bardottan
HOMEWORLD Bardotta
AFFILIATION Dagoyan Masters

Queen Julia rules over the peaceful planet Bardotta. After the Dagoyan Masters mysteriously vanish, she requests help from her old friend Jar Jar Binks. When Julia also is kidnapped by the Frangawl Cult, Jar Jar and Mace Windu track down and rescue her before Mother Talzin can steal her life essence.

DARTH BANE
SPECIES Human
AFFILIATION Sith

Darth Bane is the sole survivor when the Jedi Order destroys the Sith a thousand years before the Clone Wars. Recognizing that infighting has weakened the Sith, Bane creates the Rule of Two when he reforms the Sith Order, mandating that there can be only a master and an apprentice.

SIFO-DYAS
SPECIES Human
HOMEWORLD Cassandran Worlds
AFFILIATION Jedi

Sifo-Dyas joins the Jedi at a similar time to Dooku, and the pair become good friends during their time in the same youngling clan. Together, the pair break into a dangerous part of the Jedi Archives and are swiftly reprimanded. Sifo-Dyas soon becomes Padawan to Jedi Master Lene Kostana, who nurtures his natural affinity for seeing visions of the future through the Force. Sifo-Dyas eventually attains the rank of Jedi Master and even a seat on the Jedi Council some time prior to the invasion of Naboo. Foreseeing a coming galactic war, he advocates for the creation of an army for the Republic. He is removed from the Council because his ideas are considered too extreme. Sifo-Dyas nevertheless proceeds with his plan, secretly commissioning the clone army from the Kaminoans while pretending to act with authorization from the Galactic Senate and the Jedi Council. Chancellor Valorum later covertly dispatches Sifo-Dyas to negotiate with the Pyke Syndicate. However, after initially mediating a tribal dispute on Felucia, Sifo-Dyas is killed when the Pykes are paid by the Sith to shoot down his shuttle.

FORCE PRIESTESSES
AFFILIATION The Force

These mysterious Force-entities represent five emotions: serenity, joy, anger, confusion, and sadness. They test Yoda with daunting trials as a Jedi Master, including visiting the Sith homeworld. When the trials are complete, the priestesses deem Yoda worthy of retaining his identity in the Force beyond death, thus granting him immortality.

VARACTYL
HOMEWORLD Utapau **SIZE** 15 m (49 ft) long **HABITAT** Aric scrubland, Utapaun sinkholes

A reptavian species native to Utapau, varactyls are known to be loyal and obedient steeds. To track down General Grievous in Pau City, Obi-Wan Kenobi rides a particularly swift varactyl named Boga. They quickly reach the tenth level and chase General Grievous on his wheel bike through the city. Along the way, Boga smashes several battle droids before the Jedi Master fights and kills Grievous. After Palpatine gives the command for Order 66, the clone troopers turn against Obi-Wan. Boga and her Jedi rider are caught in an AT-TE cannon blast that strikes a nearby wall, forcing the pair to plummet into the water at the bottom of the sinkhole.

GAR SAXON
SPECIES Human **HOMEWORLD** Mandalore
AFFILIATION Shadow Collective, Empire

Conniving and savvy, Gar Saxon is a Mandalorian supercommando in the Shadow Collective. Gar and Rook Kast liberate Maul from the Spire prison. He leads Maul's ground forces during General Grievous' attack on the Shadow Collective base at Ord Mantell. Gar stays loyal to Maul during the Siege of Mandalore, fighting on the front lines and assassinating Almec, until the crime lord refuses to send him reinforcements.

During the Imperial era, Gar and the rest of the Saxon clan align with the Empire and betray Bo-Katan Kryze, the regent of Mandalore. Gar is put in charge of Mandalore by the Emperor for his loyalty, and attacks any Mandalorians who don't pledge allegiance to him, including the Journeyman Protectors.

After destroying a Protectors' camp, Gar encounters their leader Fenn Rau and three rebel agents: Mandalorian Sabine Wren, Jedi Ezra Bridger, and an astromech named Chopper. Gar captures Ezra and Chopper, but Sabine and Rau mount a rescue and they escape. Saxon encounters the rebels once more when they visit Sabine's family on Krownest, and her mother Ursa Wren contacts Gar to try and trade Sabine's friends for her daughter's safety. When Gar arrives to capture them, the Wren clan has a change of heart and turns on him. Sabine and Gar duel with lightsabers and Sabine emerges victorious. Gar attempts to shoot her in the back, but Ursa fires at him first.

COLEMAN KCAJ
SPECIES Ongree **HOMEWORLD** Skustell
AFFILIATION Jedi

After the death of Adi Gallia, Jedi Master Coleman Kcaj takes her place as a member of the Jedi Council. Unbeknownst to anyone at the time, he becomes one of the last new members. Master Kcaj is believed to have survived Order 66.

TION MEDON
SPECIES Pau'an
HOMEWORLD Utapau
AFFILIATION Republic

As Port Administrator of Pau City, Tion Medon welcomes and offers his services to guests. When Obi-Wan Kenobi arrives at the sinkhole spaceport in search of General Grievous, Medon discreetly divulges helpful information about the Separatist presence on Utapau. Obi-Wan suggests that Medon gather the planet's warriors for the coming battle.

CHARACTERS AND CREATURES

GOBI GLIE
SPECIES Twi'lek **HOMEWORLD** Ryloth
AFFILIATION Twi'lek Resistance, Free Ryloth Movement

Gobi Glie is a member of Cham Syndulla's Twi'lek Resistance against the Separatist occupiers of Ryloth. When the Empire takes the place of the Republic, Gobi continues the fight. At first, he doesn't have Cham's support, but he soon helps a war-weary Cham realize that the Imperials are up to no good. Gobi then becomes a key figure in Cham's Free Ryloth Movement.

NUMA
SPECIES Twi'lek
HOMEWORLD Ryloth
AFFILIATION Free Ryloth Movement

As a child growing up under Separatist occupation, Numa befriends two clone troopers named Waxer and Boil, both of whom make a lasting impression. Later in life, she joins Cham Syndulla's rebel Free Ryloth Movement, and works with Hera Syndulla and Kanan Jarrus' rebel cell.

CLONE PILOT
SPECIES Human
HOMEWORLD Kamino
AFFILIATION Republic

The Grand Army of the Republic's pilots are a special class of clone troopers. They start out as regular clones who are randomly chosen and trained as pilots. Their flight academy training is run by expert pilots such as Mandalorian Fenn Rau, giving them an edge with unconventional but proven flight maneuvers. They sit at the helm of vehicles designed for air, land, sea, and space battles. Their uniforms vary according to their assigned units, vehicles, and time period in service. Notable clone pilots toward the end of the Clone Wars include Odd Ball and Jag.

CLONE SCUBA TROOPER
SPECIES Human
HOMEWORLD Kamino
AFFILIATION Republic

Clone scuba troopers are an elite division of the Grand Army of the Republic during the Clone Wars, though at times standard clone troopers may also be fitted with their specialized gear. Scuba troopers are trained in the seas of Kamino for battle in aquatic environments. They are equipped with flippers, oxygen tanks, underwater propulsion systems, specialized blasters, and OMS Devilfish subs. Among their ranks is Commander Monnk, a brave scuba trooper who serves under Jedi Master Kit Fisto during the Battle of Mon Cala.

TUP
SPECIES Human
HOMEWORLD Kamino
AFFILIATION Republic

CT-5385, known as Tup, is a rookie clone trooper and member of the 501st Legion. He mutinies against the fallen Jedi Pong Krell during the Battle of Umbara. During the Battle of Ringo Vinda, the bio chip in his brain malfunctions. He becomes unstable and executes Order 66 early by killing Jedi Tiplar. Tup is taken into custody and sent to a medical facility on Kamino for tests. He dies in the hands of the Kaminoans, who attempt to cover up the truth behind the bio chips.

ARC TROOPER
SPECIES Human
HOMEWORLD Kamino
AFFILIATION Republic

Advanced Recon Commandos (ARC) are the elite troopers of the Grand Army of the Republic. ARC troopers are selected as cadets for their exemplary performance and given advanced training and gear. They can be identified by the pauldrons on their shoulders, the kamas wrapped round their waists, and their dual use of DC-17 blaster pistols. They wear an experimental version of Phase II clone trooper armor. Notable ARC troopers include Colt, Echo, Fives, Havoc, and Jesse.

KIX
SPECIES Human **HOMEWORLD** Kamino
AFFILIATION Republic, 501st Legion, Sidon Ithano's crew

CT-6116, otherwise known as Kix, is a clone medic in the 501st Legion. He fights at the Battle of Saleucami, where Captain Rex is seriously injured. There Kix and fellow troopers Jesse and Hardcase must leave Rex at Cut Lawquane's farm. Kix fights in the Battle of Umbara and arrests the fallen Jedi Pong Krell. He uncovers the conspiracy to implant chips in clone brains, but he is kidnapped by Separatists and frozen in stasis. Almost half a century later, Kix is discovered by the pirate crew of Sidon Ithano. Kix joins their company after they awaken him, helping commandeer a Separatist ship from a pirate gang.

CONVOR
HOMEWORLD Various
AVERAGE SIZE 0.2 m (8 in) high
HABITAT Jungle canopies

Convorees are intelligent birds with prehensile tails. They are closely related to purple Kiros birds, who are sold in the pet trade. Convorees have been seen on Wasskah, Corvus, and Takodana. The creatures appear to have a strong connection to the Force—as one named Morai does with Ahsoka Tano.

HEVY
SPECIES Human **HOMEWORLD** Kamino
AFFILIATION Republic

Hevy (CT-782) gets his nickname from the heavy weapons he carries, such as his Z-6 rotary blaster. He is a member of Domino Squad and assigned to Rishi Outpost, where he sacrifices his own life in a battle with Separatist battle droids.

SENATE GUARD
SPECIES Human **HOMEWORLD** Various
AFFILIATION Galactic Senate

Senate Guards are the security force of the Galactic Senate, guarding the Senate facilities and traveling with senators and Supreme Chancellor Palpatine. Elite Senate Guards are promoted to the Senate Commandos and take part in secret missions. Chancellor Palpatine forms his own red-robed security detail, which becomes his Royal Guards when he appoints himself Emperor. Notable Senate Guards include Captain Taggart, who accompanies Ahsoka Tano and Senators Padmé Amidala, Bail Organa, and Mon Mothma to Mandalore, as well as the traitor Captain Argyus, who is killed by Asajj Ventress.

CUT LAWQUANE
SPECIES Human **HOMEWORLD** Kamino
AFFILIATION Republic, Lawquane family

After seeing his fellow clone troopers killed on Geonosis, Cut deserts the Republic army to work as a farmer on Saleucami with his partner Suu and her two children. When Captain Rex discovers Cut's farm, he explains his desire to live his own life. Years later, the Bad Batch helps the Lawquanes leave the world to evade Imperial discovery.

SUU LAWQUANE
SPECIES Twi'lek **HOMEWORLD** Saleucami
AFFILIATION Lawquane family

Suu Lawquane lives on a secluded farm on Saleucami with her family. A talented sharpshooter, Suu's top priority is protecting them, but she will help others. Suu helps Rex recover from injuries he sustained during a mission. She later agrees to take Omega when Suu and her family leave their home, but the child decides to stay with the Bad Batch.

SHAEEAH LAWQUANE
SPECIES Twi'lek **HOMEWORLD** Saleucami
AFFILIATION Lawquane family

Shaeeah Lawquane enjoys meeting new people, a rarity on her family's secluded farm on Saleucami. During the Clone Wars, she tells Captain Rex that her dad looks just like him. Shaeeah later greets "Uncle Wrecker" and the young clone Omega when the Bad Batch visits.

JEK LAWQUANE
SPECIES Human/Twi'lek hybrid
HOMEWORLD Saleucami
AFFILIATION Lawquane family

Jek Lawquane learns from his father Cut the importance of helping those around him. When Captain Rex seeks shelter at the Lawquane farm, Jek insists Rex eat with them. Years later, Jek plays catch with Omega when the Bad Batch visits his family, warning Omega not to venture past the farm's perimeter.

BARC TROOPER
SPECIES Human
HOMEWORLD Kamino
AFFILIATION Republic

Biker Advanced Recon Commandos (BARC) are specialized ARC troopers trained to ride high-speed BARC speeder bikes in combat. BARC troopers tend to get impatient riding in slow, conventional clone trooper craft because they are trained to think and move quickly. BARC troopers are in prominent use on Christophsis, Orto Plutonia, Kashyyyk, and Saleucami during the Clone Wars. Commander Neyo notably leads a squad of BARC troopers to assassinate Jedi General Stass Allie upon receiving Order 66.

JESSE
SPECIES Human
HOMEWORLD Kamino
AFFILIATION Republic

Jesse (CT-5597) is a veteran member of the 501st Legion who is promoted to an ARC trooper. He fights at the battles of Mimban, Saleucami, Umbara, Ringo Vinda, and Anaxes. Jesse works with the Bad Batch to recover Captain Rex's algorithm when it is used by the Separatists. Jesse joins the 332nd Division, led by Rex and Ahsoka Tano, for the Siege of Mandalore. Following the battle aboard the *Tribunal*, Jesse turns on the pair when Order 66 is declared. He does not survive the Star Destroyer's crash-landing on a moon.

SHOCK TROOPER
SPECIES Human **HOMEWORLD** Kamino
AFFILIATION Republic

Shock troopers are a special division of clone troopers bred to replace the Senate Guard and Coruscant police force. They patrol government facilities and act as security guards for senators and dignitaries friendly to Supreme Chancellor Palpatine. Shock troopers are more militaristic and aggressive than Senate Guards. They carry out the search for rogue Jedi Ahsoka Tano prior to the fall of the Jedi Order. In the time of the Empire, their division evolves into shock stormtroopers. Fox, Jek, Rys, Stone, Thire, and Thorn are well-known shock troopers during the Clone Wars.

COLD ASSAULT CLONE TROOPER
SPECIES Human **HOMEWORLD** Kamino
AFFILIATION Republic

Cold assault clone troopers wear suits for low-temperature environments with high winds, deep snow, and ice cliffs. They fight on worlds such as Caliban, Orto, Orto Plutonia, Rhen Var, and Toola.

41ST ELITE CORPS TROOPER
SPECIES Human
HOMEWORLD Kamino
AFFILIATION Republic

41st Elite Corps troopers patrol difficult environments such as the jungles of Kashyyyk. They typically ride AT-APs, AT-RTs, and speeder bikes. Commander Gree and one of his troopers attempt to assassinate Yoda after they receive Order 66.

99
SPECIES Human **HOMEWORLD** Kamino
AFFILIATION Republic

Clone 99 is deemed physically unfit for battle due to a cloning error that also renders him unique. He is assigned janitorial work on Kamino. 99 befriends Domino Squad and assists them during a Separatist attack, but is killed in his efforts. Clone Force 99 (the "Bad Batch") is named in his honor.

DOGMA
SPECIES Human **HOMEWORLD** Kamino
AFFILIATION Republic

The clone trooper known as Dogma is a member of the 501st Legion who fights at the Battle of Umbara. He is fiercely loyal and rigid in his approach to following orders. Dogma defends his commander, Jedi General Pong Krell, until Krell admits to treason. Dogma then executes him.

JEDI TEMPLE GUARD
SPECIES Various **HOMEWORLD** Various
AFFILIATION Jedi

Serving as protectors of the Order's headquarters, the Jedi Temple Guard wield double-bladed yellow lightsabers and wear standardized uniforms with masks that keep their identities anonymous. Their attire dates back to ancient times. During the Clone Wars, Jedi Knights take turns serving under the leadership of Jedi Master Cin Drallig. A number of the guards accompany Ahsoka Tano and Barriss Offee to hearings. Kanan Jarrus dons a Temple guard mask for a brief time when he is blinded by Maul on Malachor. During a Force vision at the Jedi temple on Lothal, the Grand Inquisitor appears to Kanan as a Jedi Temple guard, revealing his mysterious origins.

HUNTER

SPECIES Human
HOMEWORLD Kamino
AFFILIATION Republic, Clone Force 99

Hunter is the leader of Clone Force 99 (the Bad Batch). Like his squadmates, Hunter is an enhanced clone with special abilities. Specifically, he possesses heightened senses and can feel electromagnetic frequencies. These skills make him an excellent tracker. Protecting his team is Hunter's primary concern. He runs a tight ship to keep the eclectic groups of clones on task during missions, but he also doesn't follow orders blindly. On Kaller, Hunter is disturbed when he sees unaltered clones (or "regs") kill Jedi Master Depa Billaba. He chooses to protect Billaba's young Padawan, Caleb Dume, from harm despite protests from fellow Batch member Crosshair.

After returning from a mission on Onderon where Hunter refuses to order the death of civilians and Republic fighters who are unwilling to serve the Empire, the Batch returns to Kamino. There, it retrieves the young clone girl, Omega, who joins the crew (much to the stoic leader's chagrin), and they all decide to flee the Empire. At first, Hunter is uncomfortable in a parenting role and tries to convince Omega that she would be better off living with a family who are leaving Saleucami, but he respects her decision to stay with Clone Force 99. He soon becomes a father figure to Omega and risks his life several times to save her from bounty hunters and other threats.

While on the run from the Empire, Hunter and his squad start to take jobs for the Trandoshan smuggler Ciddarin "Cid" Scaleback, who protects them for a time. Hunter sees the need to earn credits for their survival, but he is also pulled to help those fighting the Empire. On Corellia, Hunter gives the Martez sisters, Rafa and Trace, a datarod he was tasked to return to Cid because he knows that the group the siblings work with will use the information against the Empire. Wanting to find a safe place for Omega to grow up and a refuge for his squad, Hunter makes a plan for the group to stay on a remote island on Pabu. When the Empire interferes with these plans and abducts Omega, Hunter vows he will not rest until they find her.

Changing motivations
Thanks in part to Omega's influence, Hunter becomes more willing to stand up for those who need help. On Ipsidon, Hunter fights to free indentured miners from the corrupt Mokko and his droid guards.

Mission briefing
From the cockpit of the *Marauder*, Hunter often discusses missions with his team and receives intel from their contacts.

CHAM SYNDULLA

SPECIES Twi'lek **HOMEWORLD** Ryloth
AFFILIATION Twi'lek Resistance, Free Ryloth Movement

After the Separatists invade Ryloth, political leader Cham Syndulla forms the freedom fighters who oppose them, while his wife Eleni and daughter Hera hide underground. Eventually, a small Republic force led by Jedi Ima-Gun Di arrives to help Cham's forces. Thanks to Di's sacrifice during a Separatist attack, the Twi'lek Resistance lives to fight another day. Later, General Mace Windu arrives with more forces, and Cham resolves his issues with Ryloth's senator, Orn Free Taa. He then leads the combined army and liberates his home.

During the Imperial era, Cham tries to work with the new Empire, providing a unified front with Taa to keep the peace. However, the new regime just wants to occupy and exploit Ryloth.

After Hera is captured by the Empire for rebellious acts, Cham and Eleni rescue her, and he goes on to form the Free Ryloth Movement to resist the Imperial occupation. He is upset when Hera leaves their homeworld to pursue her dream of freedom for the whole galaxy. Cham later learns that Darth Vader and the Emperor are traveling in a Star Destroyer to Ryloth, so he launches an attack. Cham's forces destroy the ship and force the Sith to crash-land on the planet, but sustain heavy losses in doing so. Cham fails to defeat them on the ground, and the Sith kill even more of his troops before leaving Ryloth.

Years later, Hera requests his help to steal an Imperial ship orbiting Ryloth. Sensing an opportunity, Cham agrees to lend his aid, secretly hoping to destroy it to inspire his people. Cham helps Hera's rebels, befriending them and even reconciling with her. When his plan is revealed, Hera persuades him to abandon it, and they complete her mission. Later, Cham tells Hera that their family home on Ryloth is occupied by the Empire and that their Kalikori—an important Twi'lek family heirloom—has been taken. Hera is captured when she tries to retrieve the Kalikori, so Cham offers to hand himself in to save her. In the end, Hera blows up their old home, allowing them to escape.

Fleeing the Empire
Riding atop blurrgs, Cham and fellow rebel Numa flee an Imperial patrol.

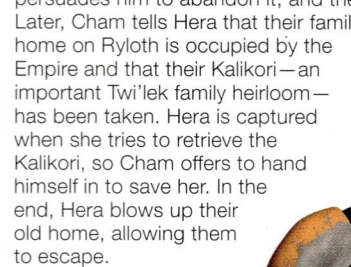

RIFF TAMSON

SPECIES Karkarodon **HOMEWORLD** Karkaris
AFFILIATION Separatist

One of Count Dooku's vicious Separatist warlords, Riff Tamson's Karkarodon physiology makes him the perfect choice to lead military operations on aquatic worlds. He secretly assassinates the king of Mon Cala, then openly leads agitators, urging a civil war between its Quarren and Mon Calamari populations. He hunts the rightful heir, Prince Lee-Char, who ultimately kills Tamson with one of his own exploding knives.

CHIEF TARFFUL
SPECIES Wookiee **HOMEWORLD** Kashyyyk
AFFILIATION Republic

Tarfful is a Wookiee chieftain and general. During the Clone Wars, he leads the rescue of his friend Chewbacca, held captive with Ahsoka Tano and other young Jedi by Trandoshan hunters. In the Battle of Kashyyyk, the two Wookiees serve alongside Jedi Generals Yoda and Luminara Unduli and help Yoda escape the Order 66 massacre. Tarfful then begins to rebel against the brutal Imperial occupation. For a time, Tarfful receives aid from Saw Gerrera's partisans and even Jedi survivor Cal Kestis, who seeks assistance to find a holocron.

NOSSOR RI
SPECIES Quarren **HOMEWORLD** Mon Cala
AFFILIATION Separatist, Republic

The Quarren chieftain on Mon Cala, Nossor Ri plots to switch the planet's allegiance to the Separatist side of the Clone Wars. When he realizes Count Dooku is merely exploiting the situation, however, he leads his people to rejoin the Mon Calamari and expel the Separatists. During the rise of the First Order, Ri is a Mon Cala general who sacrifices himself to ensure a number of Mon Cala ships can escape an orbiting First Order armada and join the Resistance.

GENERAL KALANI
MANUFACTURER Baktoid Combat Automata
TYPE Super tactical droid **AFFILIATION** Separatist

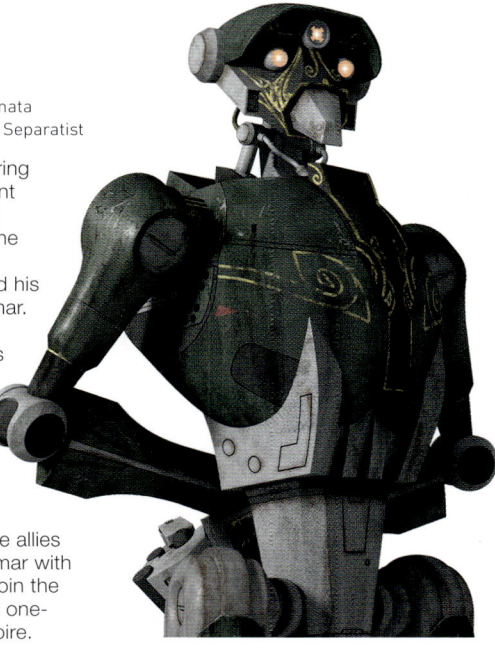

Kalani fights for the Separatists during the Clone Wars. He is sent by Count Dooku to assist the Sith's ally, King Sanjay Rash, on Onderon against the rebels there. When the rebels are victorious, Dooku orders Kalani and his remaining forces to retreat to Agamar. After Order 66, Kalani believes the code to shut down the droid forces is a Republic trick, so he and his troops ignore it. Years later, he encounters clone Captain Rex and the *Ghost* crew. Kalani seeks to finish the Clone Wars on his own terms, so forces them to participate in one final battle. When the Empire attacks, he allies with his opponents, escaping Agamar with some of his troops. He refuses to join the rebels stating that they only have a one-percent chance of beating the Empire.

BREHA ORGANA
SPECIES Human **HOMEWORLD** Alderaan **AFFILIATION** House Organa, Rebel Alliance

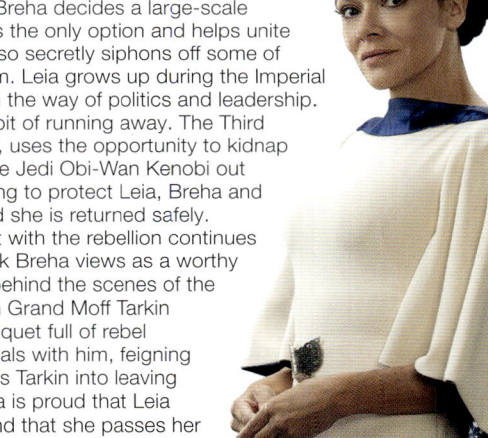

Wise and compassionate, Breha Organa is the Queen of Alderaan. After nearly dying during her scaling of Alderaan's Appenza Peak, she requires replacement mechanical organs to live. Her people recognize her sacrifice and never forget it. Later with her husband, Bail Organa, Breha continues to care for others on her homeworld and beyond. Throughout the Clone Wars, they advocate for peace and assist refugees from war-torn planets, sending Alderaanians to places in need to provide supplies and long-term assistance. After the war ends, Breha and Bail adopt Leia when her mother, the Organas' friend Padmé Amidala, dies in childbirth, and they raise her as their heir to the Alderaanian throne.

As Imperial power grows, Breha decides a large-scale rebellion against the Empire is the only option and helps unite the various secret rebel cells. She also secretly siphons off some of Alderaan's riches to fund them. Leia grows up during the Imperial era, and Breha teaches her in the way of politics and leadership. However, Leia develops a habit of running away. The Third Sister, an ambitious Inquisitor, uses the opportunity to kidnap the young child in order to lure Jedi Obi-Wan Kenobi out of hiding. Willing to do anything to protect Leia, Breha and Bail ask Obi-Wan for help and she is returned safely.

Leia's parents' involvement with the rebellion continues to put the family at risk—a risk Breha views as a worthy one. She continues to work behind the scenes of the spreading factions, and when Grand Moff Tarkin interrupts an Alderaanian banquet full of rebel sympathizers, she skillfully deals with him, feigning a marital dispute to embarrass Tarkin into leaving without any suspicions. Breha is proud that Leia becomes a rebel operative and that she passes her Day of Demand challenges. Breha and Bail are both killed when Alderaan is blown up by the Death Star.

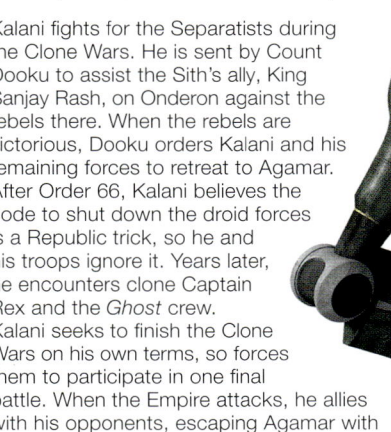

LEE-CHAR
SPECIES Mon Calamari
HOMEWORLD Mon Cala
AFFILIATION Republic

Prince Lee-Char is the rightful heir to the throne of Mon Cala after his father's assassination, but he faces opposition from the Separatists who wish to see a Quarren king instead. Lee-Char faces a violent uprising led by Riff Tamson. With Captain Ackbar and the Republic's aid, Lee-Char leads his warriors to victory. Afterward, he is crowned king.

During the Imperial era, Lee-Char falls under the influence of Jedi Purge survivor Ferren Barr, who has a vision that the Mon Cala will save the galaxy. After the Imperial envoy, Telvar, is killed, Lee-Char decides to fight the Empire, leading to heavy casualties on the planet. Lee-Char is captured by Darth Vader, and only orders his forces to cease fire when Barr reveals that he is behind Telvar's death. Lee-Char is imprisoned on Strokill Prime, leaving a regent named Urtya to rule Mon Cala in his place. Years later, Princess Leia Organa attempts to liberate Lee-Char in order to inspire more of Mon Cala's people to join the Rebel Alliance. She finds Lee-Char on life support and records his dying message. Leia passes the recording to Urtya who transmits it all over Mon Cala. The crews of 12 Mon Cala cruisers join the Rebel Alliance.

IMPERIAL ROYAL GUARD
SPECIES Human **HOMEWORLD** Various
AFFILIATION Empire

Emperor Palpatine's Royal Guards are an elite group of sentries trained in martial arts like teräs käsi. At first, they are selected from the Senate Guard or clone trooper ranks, but are all anonymous under their red armor. They wield powerful force pikes capable of restraining a Jedi, or worse. The Royal Guard follow the Emperor's orders without question and are among the few trusted with witnessing his full power. They accompany him on virtually all trips and stand as sentries in his quarters. The Royal Guards may be dispatched on secret missions or assigned to guard other dignitaries at the Emperor's sole discretion. For example, some are assigned to Darth Vader's castle on Mustafar.

CAPTAIN ANTILLES
SPECIES Human **HOMEWORLD** Alderaan
AFFILIATION House Organa, Republic, Rebel Alliance

Captain Raymus Antilles is commander of Bail Organa's fleet of diplomatic cruisers. Antilles joins the rebels, wanting to secure a better life for his daughters. Over the years, Antilles becomes very skilled at getting past Imperial blockades. When Bail's daughter Leia Organa is old enough to request the use of the *Tantive IV* herself, she orders Antilles and the ship to accompany her to Wobani. After many missions together, Antilles and Leia come to trust and rely upon each other completely. During the Battle of Scarif, they are aboard the legendary Corellian corvette, and it is Antilles who delivers the Death Star plans to the princess before they jump to hyperspace. In the ensuing battle over Tatooine, Darth Vader boards the ship and demands the stolen information. When Antilles refuses, Vader kills him.

84 CHARACTERS AND CREATURES

SAW GERRERA
SPECIES Human **HOMEWORLD** Onderon **AFFILIATION** Onderon rebels, partisans, Rebel Alliance

Saw Gerrera is a notorious figure in the galaxy, known for his extreme methods of fighting oppression. Saw believes the ends justify the means and is more than willing to adopt the enemies' tactics as his own.

LEARNING TO FIGHT
During the Clone Wars, Saw and his sister Steela lead the Onderon rebels, receiving training from the Jedi. During the rebel victory, Saw shoots down a Separatist gunship that crashes near Steela, causing her to fall off a cliff to her death. Saw feels guilty for this and is haunted by her passing.

In the Imperial era, Saw continues his fight, at first on his homeworld. He later leads an infiltration team into Eriadu intending to destroy the base, but the Bad Batch, who were there to track imprisoned clone troopers, try to change Saw's mind. Saw persists and his action unintentionally leads to the loss of one of the Batch. Saw goes on to reorganize his Onderon rebels, renaming them the partisans.

TAKING IN JYN
Soon after, Saw smuggles Imperial scientist Galen Erso, his wife Lyra, and their child Jyn away from Coruscant, helping them to live in hiding on Lah'mu. With the Ersos safe, Gerrera and many of his partisans discover the Empire is using tree sap on Kashyyyk to craft a powerful compound. They cross paths with Jedi Padawan Cal Kestis, who forms a temporary alliance with Saw to take over the Imperial refinery and save captured Wookiees.

Not long after, the Imperials find the Ersos, Galen is taken, Lyra is killed, and Jyn hides in a cave, where she is later found and taken in by Gerrera. Saw later receives a large amount of coaxium from fellow rebel Enfys Nest, which he uses in his attacks. Saw continues his vicious campaign, ordering the death of a scientist on Tamsye Prime, and killing Imperials and innocents alike at a festival on Inusagi. Over the years, Saw becomes paranoid that Jyn's real identity might be discovered by his troops, so he tortures some of them to see if they know. When Jyn is 16 years old, Saw abandons her, giving in to his paranoia.

ALLIANCE WITH THE REBELLION
Saw's partisans begin to work with other informal rebel networks, including the one operated by Luthen Rael. Gerrera and him have a begrudging respect for each other, with Rael offering Saw supplies and technology in exchange for assistance. Both see the sacrifices the Rebellion must be willing to make in order to prevail.

Soon after, Saw allies himself with Bail Organa and

Sharing intel
Saw Gerrera utilizes Luthen Rael's intelligence and access to Imperial technology to further his own goals, but he is still a reluctant ally (above).

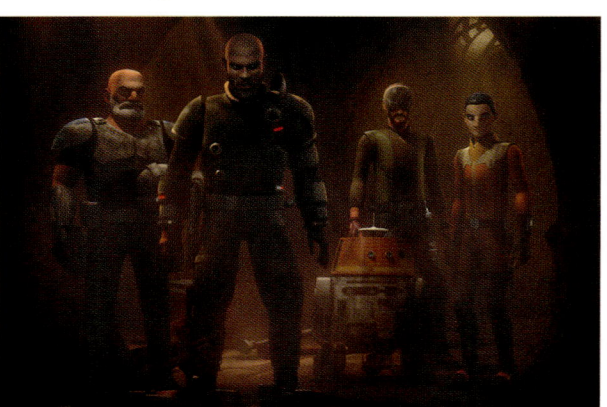

Proof of poison
During their investigation on Geonosis, Saw and the *Ghost* crew recover some poison canisters that prove the Empire wiped out the Geonosians. Unfortunately, they lose them during their escape from the planet (right).

the other rebel cells, who do not share Gerrera and Luthen's perspective. Saw's extreme tactics, including the partisans' assassination of Moff Quarsh Panaka, concern them. Regardless, Saw accepts a mission from them to look into Geonosis. The *Ghost* crew are sent in when they don't hear back from Gerrera—they proceed to save him from attack by battle droids and discover that the Empire has wiped out most of the Geonosians with poison. Saw is irritated that they don't find out what the Empire is constructing and becomes obsessed with uncovering it.

Over time, the extreme actions of Gerrera and his partisans estrange them from the rest of the Rebel Alliance, leaving them as rogue operatives. When Alliance members Ezra Bridger and Sabine Wren hack an Imperial relay on Jalindi, they are discovered by the Empire and are rescued by Saw, who bombs the relay. He recruits them on a mission to infiltrate a civilian transport carrying secret cargo for the Empire. They discover a contingent of captured technicians, one of whom mentions that they heard talk from their captors of the Jedha system. They also find a giant kyber crystal. While Gerrera turns the crystal into a bomb, the other rebels rescue the technicians and escape.

After this, Saw focuses his attention on Jedha, believing he will find the answer there. He and his forces set up a base of operations in the Catacombs of Cadera near Jedha's Holy City, recruiting local rebels, including, temporarily, Guardians of the Whills Chirrut Îmwe and Baze Malbus, to his cause. Caring little for civilian casualties, his forces try to stop the Empire from stealing kyber crystals. Soon after, Saw's forces bring him Bodhi Rook, a former Imperial pilot who claims to have an urgent message from Galen Erso. Saw refuses to believe him, so uses a mind-reading Mairan to determine the veracity of his claims. His troops also capture Jyn, Alliance member Cassian Andor, and their new acquaintances Chirrut and Baze.

Saw is at first pleased to see Jyn, but then believes she might have been sent to kill him. She reveals that she is actually on an Alliance mission. Saw plays Galen's message to Jyn just as the Death Star is preparing to fire upon Jedha's Holy City. Saw lets Jyn leave just in time with the message to save herself, the Rebellion, and the dream, while he decides he will run no longer and dies in the catacombs.

Making do
With limited resources, Saw must scrounge for supplies for himself and his partisans. They repurpose everything from weaponry to medical devices.

BYPH
SPECIES Ithorian
HOMEWORLD Ithor
AFFILIATION Jedi

An Ithorian youngling, Byph travels with a group of other younglings to Ilum to find their kyber crystals. Byph is terrified when he realizes that following his instincts means he must separate from his friends. However, he's able to overcome his fear, find his crystal, and return to Ahsoka Tano and Yoda before the doors to the Ilum cave freeze him inside.

GANODI
SPECIES Rodian **HOMEWORLD** Rodia
AFFILIATION Jedi

During the Jedi ritual known as the Gathering, where Jedi younglings search for kyber crystals on Ilum, Ganodi overcomes her initial fear. Later, after Hondo Ohnaka and his pirates take Ahsoka Tano prisoner, Ganodi finishes repairs on the architect droid Huyang, and pilots their ship, the *Crucible*, on the mission to rescue Ahsoka.

GUNGI
SPECIES Wookiee **HOMEWORLD** Kashyyyk
AFFILIATION Jedi

Gungi embraces patience to acquire his kyber crystal during the Gathering ritual. His crystal is across a lake so he waits for the water to freeze before crossing. Soon after, Gungi and his fellow younglings travel to Florrum to help rescue Ahsoka Tano. Gungi finds a way to survive the initial assault on the Jedi after Order 66. He then falls into the hands of enslavers, but the Bad Batch rescues him and returns him to his home planet of Kashyyyk, where he helps to repel a Trandoshan attack on a Wookiee village. Gungi decides to stay with the Wookiee tribe and embrace them as his new family.

KATOONI
SPECIES Tholothian **HOMEWORLD** Tholoth
AFFILIATION Jedi

Katooni encourages her fellow younglings to follow their instincts in the ritual where they find their kyber crystals on Ilum. Katooni and her friends then track Ahsoka Tano to Florrum after she is kidnapped by pirates, and they pose as acrobats to find her. Katooni struggles to build her first lightsaber but persists until she succeeds. She befriends pirate Hondo Ohnaka on her adventures.

PETRO
SPECIES Human
HOMEWORLD Corellia
AFFILIATION Jedi

When Petro travels to Ilum to search for kyber crystals during the Gathering ritual, his overconfidence and impatience almost lead him to failure. He finds his crystal only after slowing down to help one of his fellow younglings. Later, when he attempts to build his first lightsaber with the help of Huyang, Petro's need to finish first results in him inverting the emitter matrix.

QT-KT
TYPE Astromech droid
AFFILIATION Republic, Jedi

During the Clone Wars, Jedi Aayla Secura's astromech QT-KT joins Colonel Meebur Gascon, R2-D2, and several other droids on D-Squad. They embark on a mission behind enemy lines to steal a Separatist encryption module. For the mission, Dr. Gubacher equips QT with a coil that acts as a powerful remote-controlled magnet. During the Galactic Civil War, R2-D2 reunites and expresses his feelings for QT during his mission to fight against the scourge that has taken control of many droids.

ZATT
SPECIES Nautolan
HOMEWORLD Glee Anselm
AFFILIATION Jedi

Jedi youngling Zatt needs to set aside his love of technology and gadgets during the Gathering in order to find his first kyber crystal. Normally driven by logic, Zatt learns to trust his feelings and instincts as he also helps his fellow younglings rescue Ahsoka Tano from a gang of pirates and then evade General Grievous.

KEERADAK
HOMEWORLD Skako Minor **SIZE** 11.76 m (38 ft 7 in) wingspan, 5.75 m (18 ft 10 in) long with tail fully extended **HABITAT** Canyons, mountains

Keeradaks are large winged reptiles native to Skako Minor. Poletecs, who also live on the planet, tame them as their mounts, and it is rumored that some Poletecs worship the creatures. Keeradaks communicate with screeching noises and are incredibly strong. One keeradak is able to grab General Anakin Skywalker from the ground and carry him to a Poletec city. On landing, its huge claws are large enough to trap him on the ground. Later, when he and the Bad Batch are trapped by Separatist forces, Tech uses a recording of a keeradak distress call to bring a group of them close enough for Skywalker and the clones to jump onto their backs to escape.

QIN YAZAL
SPECIES Poletec **HOMEWORLD** Skako Minor
AFFILIATION Republic

Riding a keeradak, Poletec leader Qin Yazal abducts Anakin Skywalker when he fears the Jedi's arrival signals that his homeworld, Skako Minor, is being pulled into the Clone Wars. Yazal hesitantly helps Skywalker and the Bad Batch find Wat Tambor's city, and later firmly sides with the Jedi and the Republic against the Separatist Army that occupies his world.

R4-M1
TYPE Astromech droid **AFFILIATION** Republic

The R-series astromech droid R4-M1 serves the Galactic Republic and Jedi Order during the Clone Wars. Painted white and yellow, R4-M1 works on Republic starships doing repairs and other supportive tasks. R4-M1 uses its holoprojector to display a map of Mandalore for Ahsoka Tano and Bo-Katan Kryze during the Siege of Mandalore.

FIFE
SPECIES Pyke
HOMEWORLD Oba Diah
AFFILIATION Pyke Syndicate

Fife serves as majordomo to the Pyke Syndicate leader, Marg Krim. He assists Krim in keeping the criminal organization in good standing with the Shadow Collective's leader, Maul, and keeping up appearances with their rival crime groups Black Sun and Crimson Dawn. During a spice delivery gone wrong, Fife helps his boss, Krim, when he recognizes that Ahsoka Tano has played a mind trick on him.

MARG KRIM
SPECIES Pyke **HOMEWORLD** Oba Diah
AFFILIATION Pyke Syndicate

Marg Krim takes over leadership of the Pyke criminal syndicate after Count Dooku assassinates their previous leader, Lom Pyke. Near the end of the Clone Wars, Krim hires Rafa Martez to deliver a shipment of spice to Pyke Palace on Oba Diah. When Rafa, her sister Trace, and Ahsoka Tano arrive without the spice, he threatens to torture them until they can fulfill their original deal.

ROOK KAST
SPECIES Human
HOMEWORLD Mandalore
AFFILIATION Shadow Collective, Death Watch

Rook Kast leads the Mandalorian supercommandos in Maul's Shadow Collective. When Palpatine captures and imprisons Maul on Stygeon Prime, Kast and Gar Saxon break Maul out and take him to the Shadow Collective base on Zanbar. After following Maul to Dathomir and then Mandalore, Kast and her troopers fight for him during the Siege of Mandalore.

CHARACTERS AND CREATURES

RAFA MARTEZ
SPECIES Human **HOMEWORLD** Coruscant
AFFILIATION Martez Hangar, Rex's rebel cell

Rafa Martez lives on Level 1313 on Coruscant with her younger sister, Trace. After their parents die, the sisters take over a hangar that includes a repair shop. Streetwise and distrustful of strangers, Rafa regularly reminds Trace that they can't count on anyone except for themselves. Rafa takes jobs for shady clients to earn enough credits for them to survive. One job gets the sisters and Ahsoka Tano into trouble with the Pyke criminal syndicate. After Palpatine seizes power, Rafa and Trace work with Captain Rex to gather intel to fight the Empire.

TRACE MARTEZ
SPECIES Human **HOMEWORLD** Coruscant
AFFILIATION Martez Hangar, Rex's rebel cell

Trace Martez is more optimistic and trusting than her older sister, Rafa. She dreams of being a pilot and leaving Coruscant, and uses all her spare time and money to build a *Nebula*-class freighter that she names the *Silver Angel*. When Ahsoka Tano crashes into the Martez sisters' hangar, Trace befriends her and helps fix her speeder bike, even though Ahsoka can't pay. Trace loves her sister Rafa but is alarmed at the risks she takes for credits. Both sisters fight against the Empire after Order 66, and Trace's electronics and mechanical skills regularly come in handy on missions.

CH-33P
MANUFACTURER Industrial Automaton
TYPE Astromech droid
AFFILIATION Republic

CH-33P, along with RG-G1 and R7-A7, helps subdue Captain Rex after the execution of Order 66 on the *Tribunal*. CH-33P seals the ship's doors to give Ahsoka Tano and the droids time to move Rex to an operating bay to remove his inhibitor chip. As CH-33P and RG-G1 help Tano and Rex escape, clone troopers fire on and destroy both the droids.

RG-G1
MANUFACTURER Industrial Automaton
TYPE Astromech droid
AFFILIATION Republic

Stationed aboard the *Tribunal*, RG-G1, CH-33P, and R7-A7 come to Ahsoka Tano's aid during Order 66. After helping move Rex to an operating bay, RG-G1 reseals and guards the door during the procedure to remove Rex's inhibitor chip. He uses a liquid cable to save Tano from a fall shortly before he is destroyed by clone troopers.

GREY
SPECIES Human **HOMEWORLD** Kamino
AFFILIATION Republic, Empire

Clone trooper Grey (CC-10/994) serves under Jedi Master Depa Billaba during the Clone Wars, but he opens fire on her on Kaller after the execution of Order 66. Grey and fellow soldier Styles hunt Billaba's Padawan, Caleb Dume, during the early days of the Empire. After Dume convinces Grey that programming overran his free will, Grey sacrifices himself to save the Jedi.

KIRAK INFIL'A
SPECIES Human
AFFILIATION Jedi

The long-lived Jedi Master Kirak Infil'a works in the Jedi Temple armory after the fall of the Starlight Beacon, helping to lead the creation of new lightsabers needed in response to the Nihil threat. At some point, he takes the Barash Vow as a penance and is forbidden from interacting with the Order, even when it is wiped out by Order 66. Soon after, Darth Vader tracks Infil'a to the River Moon of Al'doleem. Infil'a initially beats the Sith. However, during their second duel, Vader preys on the Jedi's compassion for the people of Am'balaar City, causing a deadly flood that distracts Infil'a. Vader then kills the Jedi and bleeds Infil'a's kyber crystal to use as his own.

NINTH SISTER
SPECIES Dowutin **HOMEWORLD** Dowut
AFFILIATION Jedi, Inquisitorius

The Ninth Sister, once known as Jedi Masana Tide, is tortured and indoctrinated into joining the ranks of the Inquisitorius. She's particularly attuned to reading minds and emotions, and this ability only strengthens with the dark side. She loses her left eye in a training duel with Darth Vader but loyally travels with him on missions to Cabarria and Mon Cala, where she loses a leg in battle. She's part of the mission to hunt down the Jedi Cal Kestis, who defeats her twice: once on Kashyyyk and a final, fatal time on Coruscant, where she is decapitated.

SIXTH BROTHER
AFFILIATION Jedi, Inquisitorius

Formerly Bil Valen, the Sixth Brother now hunts surviving Jedi as a fearsome Inquisitor. He loses an arm to Darth Vader in a duel while the Dark Lord is teaching him the importance of loss. He joins the Ninth Sister on a mission to Mon Cala, but eventually flees the battle, cutting off his fellow Inquisitor's leg as a distraction during a fight with treacherous purge troopers.

GAR
SPECIES Human
AFFILIATION Jocasta Nu

Gar serves as a loyal assistant to Jedi librarian Jocasta Nu, after the events of Order 66. His care allows her to finish recording vital information into holocrons. For years after Nu's death, Gar guards these hidden archives, which are eventually discovered by a journeying Luke Skywalker.

SUTHA THE HUTT
SPECIES Hutt
HOMEWORLD Nal Hutta
AFFILIATION Hutt Clan, Empire

An ally of Jabba, Sutha the Hutt is eager to prove himself to the Hutt Clan. He's willing to trade with the Empire, and he works with Darth Vader to destroy Son-tuul's Pride gang. When attempting to purchase the powerful Rur crystal, Sutha is killed aboard the Sorca Retreat space station.

CATOR
MANUFACTURER ARO **MODEL** GC-8
TYPE Librarian droid, guardian-protector droid

Cator is a guardian-protector droid who preserves the most sensitive parts of the Jedi Temple Archives. He proudly guards these treasures, remaining hidden in the vault even after Order 66. Although programmed to defend against lightsaber attacks, Cator is nonetheless destroyed with a devastating blow by an enraged Darth Vader.

LUKE SKYWALKER

SPECIES Human **HOMEWORLD** Tatooine
AFFILIATION Jedi

Born to Jedi Knight Anakin Skywalker and Senator Padmé Amidala, Luke Skywalker is hidden on Tatooine by Obi-Wan Kenobi. Raised as a moisture farmer, Luke emerges as a rebel hero and redeems his father on the way to becoming a Jedi Knight. Sadly, his attempt to train a new generation of Jedi fails.

CALL TO ADVENTURE
In need of new droids to work on his moisture farm, Luke's uncle, Owen Lars, purchases R2-D2 and C-3PO from Jawa traders. Little does Owen know that the Empire is scouring Tatooine for these two missing droids. When R2-D2 takes off in search of a Jedi Knight named Obi-Wan Kenobi, C-3PO accompanies Luke to chase down the determined astromech. R2-D2 delivers Princess Leia's message to an old hermit named Ben, who reveals his Jedi past as Obi-Wan and later gives Luke the Jedi lightsaber that belonged to Luke's father, Anakin.

REBEL HERO
Luke joins Obi-Wan on his mission to deliver the stolen Death Star plans to rebel leader Bail Organa on Alderaan. After the *Millennium Falcon* is trapped by the Death Star's tractor beam and pulled aboard the space station, Luke teams up with the freighter's captain, Han Solo, and first mate, Chewbacca, to free Princess Leia, who is imprisoned there. After deactivating the tractor beam, Obi-Wan sacrifices his life to enable Luke and the others to escape with the Death Star plans. Luke joins the rebel fleet and makes a daring X-wing run through the superweapon's trench, torpedoing the exhaust port and triggering a chain reaction that destroys the Death Star.

JEDI APPRENTICE
Following years of trying to learn more about the Jedi by himself, Luke is visited by a spectral Obi-Wan, who instructs him to journey to Dagobah and train with Yoda. After crashing his X-wing in one of the planet's swamps and being harassed by a mischievous creature, Luke despairs until his tormentor reveals his true identity—he is Yoda. The Jedi Master expresses doubt as to whether Luke is ready for Jedi training, but Luke persists, and Yoda accepts him as his new apprentice. As Luke's abilities grow, he sees a vision of his friends in peril and abandons his training to mount a rescue.

REDEEMING ANAKIN SKYWALKER
On Cloud City, Luke learns the truth about his father. Darth Vader had not betrayed and murdered Anakin Skywalker; Darth Vader is Anakin Skywalker. When Luke next crosses paths with Vader on the Endor moon, the Jedi surrenders peacefully. Although the temptation of the dark side is great, Luke resists Emperor Palpatine's overtures. In response, the vengeful Emperor attacks Luke with a barrage of lightning, inciting Vader to kill his Sith Master and save his son. With that act, Anakin is redeemed.

THE LEARNER
Following Yoda's instruction to pass on what he has learned, Jedi Master Luke Skywalker sets out to train a new generation of Jedi, starting with his sister Leia. He senses Grogu's presence through the ancient seeing stone on Tython and saves him and his friends from Moff Gideon's dark troopers. Grogu bids his adoptive father, the Mandalorian Din Djarin, farewell and leaves with the Jedi Master. They travel to the planet Ossus, the site of Luke's new Jedi temple. Luke teaches the youngling about using the Force to enhance his reflexes and find balance, but Grogu's heart remains with Djarin. Luke, sympathetic to how he feels, asks an old family friend, Ahsoka Tano, for advice. She tells him to trust his instincts. Luke offers Grogu a choice: stay on Ossus as the first student of the academy, or end his Jedi training and go back to Djarin. Grogu returns to his family.

FALL OF LUKE'S ORDER
In time, Master Skywalker is joined at the temple by more students and his nephew, Ben Solo, whose potential to use the Force is unmatched. During this time, Luke travels the galaxy, learning more about the Force and the Jedi. He also defeats the spirit of Sith Lord Exim Panshard whose resurgence threatens the galaxy. Eventually, Luke grows suspicious that Ben might be falling to the dark side; tragically, Luke's distrust only serves to push Ben over the edge. The young apprentice lashes out against his Jedi Master, destroying Luke's temple and most of the other students with it. Overcome by this disaster, Luke withdraws from galactic events, going into hiding and cutting himself off from the Force. He seeks out the first-ever Jedi temple and settles on the world of Ahch-To.

THE HUNT FOR LUKE
Knowing that Supreme Leader Snoke wants to eliminate her brother, General Leia Organa sends her best pilot, Poe Dameron, to find the one man she believes can locate Luke: the explorer Lor San Tekka. He gives Poe part of a map that, when combined with R2-D2's portion of the same map, pinpoints Luke's location. Leia then sends Rey there to meet him—and hopefully receive training as a Jedi.

RECONNECTING WITH THE FORCE
When Rey arrives, Luke is not ready to take on a student and has shut down his connection to the Force. However, Luke agrees to teach Rey three lessons to show her why the Jedi were wrong and to explain his choice to let the Order die with him. During Rey's time with Luke, his previous failings with Ben Solo are revealed, and Rey leaves to carry on the legacy of the Jedi alone. Seemingly at his lowest point, Luke is visited by Master Yoda. In his wisdom, Yoda shows Luke that learning from failure is part of a master's duty. Luke lets go of the past and steps in to help the Resistance. The effort succeeds in allowing his allies to escape the First Order, but he does not survive this excruciating feat. Luke Skywalker, hero of the Rebellion, becomes one with the Force.

Distraught by a vision of herself on a dark throne, Rey later returns to Ahch-To for a self-imposed exile. The spirit of Master Skywalker appears before her. He listens to Rey as she voices her fears, and he gently encourages her to confront them. Luke Skywalker gives Rey a few last gifts before she leaves to face Palpatine on Exegol: Leia Organa's lightsaber, his X-wing, and a warm smile.

Wistful dreamer
Bored with the humdrum life of a moisture farmer, Luke dreams of unknown adventures awaiting him across the galaxy.

A hard life
The path of a Jedi is a difficult one and Skywalker faces an arduous journey, though he will come to learn from his setbacks, in time.

Unexpected tutor
Luke arrives at Dagobah seeking to train with a legendary Jedi Master. The being he finds isn't quite what he expects.

CHARACTERS AND CREATURES

Adventurous childhood
The young Leia Organa loves exploring the forest surrounding her home alongside her toy droid, L0-LA59.

LEIA ORGANA

SPECIES Human **HOMEWORLD** Alderaan
AFFILIATION Rebel Alliance, New Republic, Resistance

A leader in the Rebel Alliance, New Republic, and Resistance, Leia Organa follows in her adoptive parents' footsteps and dedicates her life to protecting democracy and peace in the galaxy.

PRECOCIOUS PRINCESS
The daughter of Senator Padmé Amidala and Jedi Anakin Skywalker, Leia is taken to Alderaan as a baby and adopted by Bail and Breha Organa. The young princess is curious and quick-witted and naturally drawn to adventure, occasionally fleeing from her stuffy royal duties by hiding in the nearby woods. When an Inquisitor hires mercenaries to kidnap the 10-year-old Leia, Bail turns to his old friend Obi-Wan Kenobi—who now goes by Ben—for help. The former Jedi Master finds and rescues Leia, falling into the Third Sister's trap to draw him out. During their hazardous journey to get the young princess back to Alderaan, the two grow close. Kenobi not only risks his life for her, but he's also the first person to tell her of her birth parents and the admirable qualities they passed on to her. The young girl never forgets what Ben did for her during their short time together.

Leia Organa joins the Apprentice Legislature at 16 years old. Shortly after this, she learns about her adoptive parents' underground efforts to resist the Empire's iron-fisted rule. She may be just a teenager, but Leia wants to fight for those who can't. Bail sends Leia to Lothal with ships for the local rebel cell. Her mission requires some quick thinking to allay Imperial suspicions, but with the help of Kanan Jarrus and Ezra Bridger, they emerge triumphant. Later, when the Rebel Alliance learns that Rogue One successfully infiltrated the Empire's base on Scarif, Bail again sends his most trusted agent—Leia—to retrieve the Death Star plans from the courageous soldiers.

HOPE
With the Death Star plans in hand, Leia flees the Battle of Scarif aboard the *Tantive IV*, but is captured by Darth Vader's Star Destroyer, *Devastator*, above Tatooine. As her mission to deliver the stolen plans to the rebels is in jeopardy, Leia records a holographic message and tasks R2-D2 with seeking out her friend Kenobi on the arid planet. She distracts stormtroopers searching her ship while R2-D2 and his companion C-3PO jettison in an escape pod. Her brave refusal to reveal the rebels' location marks Alderaan as the Death Star's first official target. With the planet's destruction, Leia becomes a princess without a home. Her duty to the peoples oppressed by the Empire carries on despite her loss.

REBEL LEADER
Although Leia is a senator and diplomat, she is also a warrior and an excellent leader. After evading Imperial troops during her rescue from the Death Star's detention center and boarding the *Millennium Falcon*, Leia assists Chewbacca in piloting the starship while Luke and Han operate the quad lasers to fend off pursuing TIE fighters. Following the Death Star's destruction, Leia leads many Alliance missions, receiving a promotion to general following the attack on the Mako-Ta space docks. On Hoth, Leia briefs the pilots as the Empire closes in on Echo Base. She remains in the command center overseeing the evacuation until Solo insists it is time for them to go.

REBELLION AND ROMANCE
Unable to reach their rebel transport off Hoth, Princess Leia escapes on the *Millennium Falcon*. Eluding Imperial Star Destroyers, Han decides the best option for needed repairs is the planet Bespin. They are soon captured by Darth Vader, who uses them as bait to lure Luke into a trap. As Han is frozen in carbonite, Leia reveals that she loves him. Although eager to free the smuggler, Leia is still dedicated to the Alliance cause, defeating the feared Imperial Commander Zahra and also formulating the plan for a daring attack on Coruscant to win public favor. She later frees Solo from Jabba the Hutt's palace.

GALACTIC DIPLOMAT
Serving on Han's command team leading the effort to destroy the shield generator which protects the second Death Star above the moon of Endor, Leia is separated from the others after she pursues biker scouts who might report their presence. Leia encounters the Ewok Wicket W. Warrick in the forest and is kind and patient with him despite her predicament. She and her unlikely ally take out a pair of biker scouts together. Wicket and the other Ewoks of Bright Tree Village agree to help the strike team against Imperial forces.

RISE OF THE RESISTANCE
Following the rebel victory on Endor, Leia and Han marry and fight the remaining Imperial forces. She also begins training to become a Jedi with Luke. Later, she has a vision that her future son will die if she continues with her tutelage, so she stops. Eventually, her son, whom they name Ben, is born. Leia is integral to the formation of the New Republic and serves as senator for the Alderaan sector. She presides over the Defense Council, and uses her position to clear Hera Syndulla for her unsanctioned reconnaissance mission to the planet Seatos.

NEW PATHS
During Leia's campaign for the powerful position of First Senator, the truth about her parentage—that her father is Darth Vader—is leaked to the public. The scandal ends her political career, but her concerns about the First Order lead her to form the Resistance to keep them in check. Leia recruits a young New Republic pilot, Poe Dameron, to lead a squadron on a series of secret missions to collect valuable intelligence and interfere with the First Order's growing influence. Though unable to wage open warfare, Leia does everything she can to undermine the Empire's successors, including uncovering a corrupt New Republic senator who secretly supports them. The struggle against the First Order is personal for Leia, as she and Han separate after their son Ben falls to the dark side and joins their new enemy.

ON THE RUN
The First Order wipes out the New Republic fleet and its capital on Hosnian Prime using the devastating superweapon Starkiller Base. Although Leia's Resistance forces manage to destroy it, a small fleet is now all that remains to oppose Supreme Leader Snoke's military might. Fleeing from the planet D'Qar, the convoy is running out of fuel as the First Order bears down upon it. Leia herself is nearly killed during a starfighter strike on her command ship, *Raddus*. The fleet sends out a distress call throughout the galaxy, hoping that Leia's old allies will come to its aid. The Resistance makes its last stand at the planet Crait, only to realize that no one has answered the call. Leia, Rey, and a handful of others flee aboard the *Millennium Falcon*, hoping to preserve the Resistance and fight another day.

JOURNEY'S END
After a year largely on the run and fighting the First Order, General Organa and the few remaining members of the Resistance settle on Ajan Kloss. Leia's storied consular ship, the *Tantive IV*, provides a generator and barracks for the base. She never recovers completely from the injuries she sustained on the *Raddus*, and her failing health finally catches up to her. She guides Rey in using the Force. When Rey decides to resume Luke's search for Exegol, she and Leia embrace one last time before she departs. Leia takes her final breaths on Ajan Kloss not long after, expending the last of her energy to call her son Ben back to the light side. Leia Organa leaves behind a legacy of bravery and selfless sacrifice that forever changes the galaxy.

ELEGANT WEAPON
Years before the rise of the First Order, Luke Skywalker trains his sister Leia in the fundamentals of the Force. She constructs her own lightsaber and, already a proven combatant, more than holds her own when sparring with Luke. She gives the blue-bladed laser sword to Luke for safekeeping, and he later passes it on to Rey—Leia's apprentice.

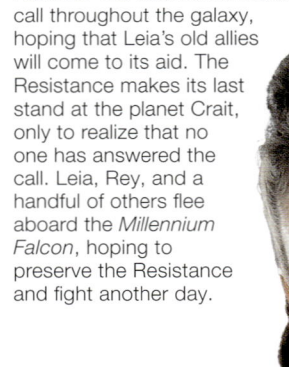

Hoth briefing
In Echo Base's icy hangar, Princess Leia briefs rebel pilots on their roles in the impending emergency evacuation.

CROSSHAIR

SPECIES Human **HOMEWORLD** Kamino
AFFILIATION Republic, Empire, Clone Force 99

A highly skilled sniper, Crosshair (CT-9904) has an enhanced ability to remain still and focused. He's the only member of Clone Force 99 (the Bad Batch) who chooses to stay loyal to the Empire after Order 66. Like the other members, Crosshair has enhancements that interfere with the inhibitor chip that instructs them to kill the Jedi. However, Crosshair believes that good soldiers follow orders, so the Empire's commands should not be questioned.

When Bad Batch member Hunter protects the young Jedi Padawan Caleb Dume on Kaller, Crosshair is angered, which fractures his relationship with Clone Force 99. After Crosshair chooses to stay with the Empire, Admiral Wilhuff Tarkin has his chip enhanced to further ensure loyalty. But even when Crosshair later removes his chip, he still remains an Imperial soldier. While Crosshair is at odds with his former squad members and agrees to help track them down for the Empire, he holds out hope that they will reunite and work together for the Imperial Army. After the fall of Kamino, Crosshair chooses not to leave with the Bad Batch, so Omega reminds him that he's still their brother.

Crosshair doesn't easily trust other clone troopers, whom he refers to as "regs," but he does grow to respect some clone officers, including Commander Cody.

Crosshair's allegiance to the Empire finally comes to an end during a mission on Barton IV, when Lieutenant Nolan, Crosshair's supervising officer, makes it painfully clear that he and the Empire regard clone soldiers as expendable. After Nolan cruelly lets Clone Commander Mayday die without offering him medical aid, Crosshair shoots Nolan and is arrested. Crosshair is taken to Mount Tantiss, where Imperial scientist Royce Hemlock interrogates him about the Bad Batch's location and resorts to torture when Crosshair doesn't cooperate.

Skilled sniper
Crosshair's main weapon is the 773 Firepuncher sniper rifle. He also carries mirrored reflector disks to deflect blaster fire and enable him to hit multiple targets at seemingly impossible angles with one shot.

Conflicted
Crosshair feels that he's the only member of the Bad Batch who chose the correct side, but he still cares about his squadmates.

TECH

SPECIES Human
HOMEWORLD Kamino
AFFILIATION Republic, Clone Force 99

Tech is a clone commando with enhanced technology skills and high intelligence who serves as part of Clone Force 99 (also known as the Bad Batch). Tech's abilities allow him to slice into computer systems and quickly analyze data. During the Clone Wars, Tech tracks a signal that leads Clone Force 99 to the planet Skako Minor and Echo, a clone trooper long-thought dead. Tech initially has concerns about where Echo's loyalties lie because he's been a Separatist captive for so long, but he learns to trust him as a squadmate.

After Order 66, Tech is the first member of the Bad Batch to realize that the young Omega is an enhanced clone, just like the rest of the squad. Omega joins their crew, and Tech teaches her to pilot their ship and loans her a device so she can communicate more easily with them.

Tech is always quick to offer his opinion or relay a critical piece of information, but he rarely shows emotion. As he explains to Omega, he processes emotions differently than her.

Tech's abilities frequently save the day during the Bad Batch's missions and adventures. On Saleucami, he falsifies chain codes, which allow Cut Lawquane and his family to leave the planet. When Wrecker begins having headaches, Tech takes the lead in helping to find a way to safely remove his inhibitor chip. On Safa Toma, Tech enters a riot race—which is like a podrace but is even more dangerous—to win the release of the smuggler Cid.

Tech encourages Hunter to greenlight a mission on Eriadu to reveal where the Empire is holding Crosshair captive. While it's risky, Tech argues that they're brothers and should not leave each other behind. Tech and his squad become trapped on a railcar after Saw Gerrera and his partisans detonate an explosion at the Imperial compound. After restoring power to the vehicle, the Bad Batch is outnumbered and outgunned. Tech makes a tragic sacrifice to save his squadmates.

Unique look
Tech's helmet doesn't cover his entire face. His visor, which is open for his goggles, displays computer readouts from terminals built into his armor.

Brown Eyes
Tech's many skills include slicing, decryption, and language interpretation. He also endears himself to the treasure hunter, Phee, who calls him "Brown Eyes."

CHARACTERS AND CREATURES

WRECKER

SPECIES Human **HOMEWORLD** Kamino
AFFILIATION Republic, Clone Force 99

Larger and stronger than typical clones, Wrecker is part of a squad of enhanced soldiers named Clone Force 99, or the Bad Batch. Wrecker's personality and behaviors are larger than life. He's loud, has a boisterous laugh, and is quick to yell out his thoughts and feelings, no matter the circumstances. He's always excited to join a fight or a battle at a moment's notice—especially if he gets to break things apart or blow things up. High levels of adrenaline coursing through his body mean that stun blasts have little effect on him.

Wrecker has incredible strength, and he uses a heavier set of armor than his fellow teammates. When the Bad Batch is on the run, Wrecker's brute force and fearlessness help subdue a young rancor named Muchi on Ord Mantell.

While the paint job on Wrecker's helmet is intended to frighten adversaries, he has the tenderest heart of all the Bad Batch members. When Omega joins the crew, Wrecker turns part of their ship into a room for the young clone and gives her one of his prized possessions—a toy tooka doll named Lula. Wrecker's childlike qualities and Omega's innocent curiosity lead to a siblinglike relationship between them. Hunter regularly pairs the two together on jobs when they work for the smuggler Cid.

When Rex visits the Bad Batch on Ord Mantell and hears Wrecker complain of headaches, he warns the clones that their inhibitor chips are very dangerous. Despite Wrecker's reservations, the squad travels to Bracca to remove their chips.

After Tech scans Wrecker's head, his chip activates, and Wrecker tries to kill his squadmates for disobeying Order 66. He seemingly doesn't recognize them. Wrecker returns to normal after Rex stuns him, and Tech is able to remove his chip.

Wrecker's loyalty and fearlessness continue to make him a valuable asset to his team. Along with Hunter, he fights stormtroopers on a mission to Serenno to try to recover Dooku's war chest. Searching for treasure on Skara Nal, Wrecker uses his brute strength to move rocks that conceal a secret entrance to a mountain, and he later throws an attacking chell out of a window to save his squadmates. Like the rest of his team, Wrecker is devastated to lose Omega to Doctor Hemlock and wants nothing more than to see her returned to them.

Resilient solider
One of Wrecker's eyes was blinded in an early mission during the Clone Wars, but that injury doesn't slow him down on the battlefield.

Powerhouse
Wrecker is the strongest of the Bad Batch. During the Clone Wars, he rescues Commander Cody after they crash-land on Anaxes. Carrying the clone to safety is nothing after lifting up the gunship that was crushing him.

OMEGA

SPECIES Human **HOMEWORLD** Kamino
AFFILIATION Republic, Clone Force 99

Omega is an enhanced clone made with unmodified genetic material from Jango Fett. Created on Kamino, alongside the rest of the clone army, Omega is rare in not being genetically modified to age quickly and follow orders.

Omega works in Tipoca City on Kamino as an assistant to the Kaminoan scientist Nala Se. She's curious when members of the Bad Batch arrive on Kamino because she knows that they're enhanced clones, like her.

When the Empire decides to steal the Kaminoans' cloning technology, Nala Se tries to keep Omega safe and away from the Kaminoan Prime Minister, Lama Su, and the Empire.

To escape the Empire, Omega flees Kamino with the Bad Batch and is eager to join its ranks. Because she has never traveled away from Kamino, she's entranced by all the planets she encounters with the Bad Batch—first as an observer, and later as a fully fledged member of the team.

Omega is impulsive and easily frustrated, but she's also extremely talented with electronics and technology. She's more likely to rescue herself from a dire situation than wait for help. With guidance from her Bad Batch brothers, Omega learns to fly ships and use an energy bow.

Adopted family
Omega develops close relationships with all of the members of Clone Force 99. Hunter, in particular, feels responsible for her safety.

Despite experiencing a great deal of betrayal, Omega believes that everyone has good inside them, even estranged Bad Batch member Crosshair, who stays loyal to the Empire. Omega's big heart endears her to all of the Bad Batch, as well as the smuggler Cid on Ord Mantell.

Omega feels guilty that the Bad Batch is in hiding and is regularly short of credits, in part because the clones are protecting her. At times, this leads her to make rash decisions in an effort to help her new family. After a relentless pursuit, the Imperial scientist Royce Hemlock captures Omega and takes her to his laboratory on Mount Tantiss.

New skills
Omega picks up a Zygerrian energy bow during a mission on Ord Mantell. Echo helps train her to use the weapon, encouraging her to keep practicing to block out distractions.

GONKY

MANUFACTURER Industrial Automaton
TYPE EG-series power droid
AFFILIATION Republic, Clone Force 99

The power droid Gonky lives on Clone Force 99's ship, the *Marauder*. A valued member of the crew, he is with the team during the Clone Wars and remains with them after they defect from the Empire. Wrecker uses Gonky for his weightlifting exercises, and Omega uses him as a headrest until she gets her own sleeping quarters on the ship.

ELITE SQUAD TROOPER

SPECIES Human
HOMEWORLD Various
AFFILIATION Empire

Elite Squad troopers are Imperial special forces recruited from across the galaxy as part of Project War-Mantle, a program designed to replace the costly clone trooper army. Vice Admiral Rampart plays a key role in recruiting and overseeing the training of Elite Squad troopers. Crosshair, of Clone Force 99, is tasked with supervising the first squad of these elite troopers on Kamino.

ES-01

SPECIES Human
AFFILIATION Empire

While Elite Squad trooper ES-01 doesn't like being put through grueling Imperial tests, he believes the Empire offers him more opportunities than the Republic ever did. On a mission to Onderon to eliminate Saw Gerrera and his insurgents, ES-01 tries to stop Crosshair from killing civilians. Crosshair promptly kills ES-01 for refusing to obey an Imperial order.

ES-02

SPECIES Human
AFFILIATION Empire

Elite Squad Trooper ES-02 is one of the most talented soldiers in the program. She faithfully follows orders from Clone Commander Crosshair on several missions, but she doesn't trust him. When her squad brings Hunter to Kamino as a prisoner, ES-02 shares her concerns with Vice Admiral Rampart about Crosshair's motives regarding his old teammate, Hunter.

ES-03

SPECIES Human
AFFILIATION Empire

ES-03 is part of the first Elite Squad troop on Kamino. Along with ES-02 and ES-04, he kills civilians on Onderon when ordered to do so by Crosshair. ES-03 and his squadmates also go on missions to Bracca and Ryloth. On Ryloth, ES-03 helps arrest Twi'lek insurgents and later Captain Howzer and other clone troopers who refuse to comply with Imperial orders.

ES-04

SPECIES Human
AFFILIATION Empire

Along with her squadmates, ES-04 is put under the command of Clone Commander CT-9904 (Crosshair) and is outfitted in modified clone trooper armor. However, Crosshair kills ES-04 and her teammates with a ricocheting blast when they refuse to stand down from arresting the rest of the Bad Batch on Kamino.

BOLO

SPECIES Ithorian
HOMEWORLD Ord Mantell
AFFILIATION Patrons of Cid's Parlor

A patron of Cid's Parlor on Ord Mantell, Bolo is regularly seen there with his friend, Ketch. The duo enjoys playing dejarik and other games of chance. Bolo is such a frequent presence at Cid's Parlor, he claims a particular seat as his own and he will argue with any customer who tries to sit in it.

EDMON RAMPART

SPECIES Human **AFFILIATION** Empire

An ambitious vice admiral who is determined to make his mark in the early years of the Empire, Edmon Rampart pushes for many changes. He institutes a chain code policy that requires every Imperial citizen to have a unique identification marker. He also forms Project War-Mantle—an initiative to replace clone troopers with soldiers who willingly sign up to join the Imperial Army.

Eager to stamp out any signs of rebellion, Rampart is a key figure in the Imperial occupation of Ryloth, and he orders the capture of rebel insurgents across the galaxy. Rampart's disdain for clones puts him at odds with the Kaminoans. He arrests their prime minister, Lama Su, and takes control of scientist Nala Se and her cloning technology before bombing Tipoca City. Later, Rampart kills one of his own men to hide the fact that Clone Force 99 survived the fall of Kamino.

While he's stationed on Coruscant, Rampart pushes for the Imperial Defense Recruitment Bill in the Senate. It proposes the official decommissioning of all clone troopers. The bill passes, but only after Rampart is double-crossed by his Imperial superiors and blamed for destroying Kamino on his own.

Blindsided
Vice Admiral Rampart faces calls for his arrest after Senator Chuchi plays a holo from the command log of his ship that shows its destruction of Tipoca City.

CIDDARIN "CID" SCALEBACK

SPECIES Trandoshan
HOMEWORLD Ord Mantell
AFFILIATION Cid's Parlor

Known to most in the galaxy as "Cid," Ciddarin Scaleback owns a parlor on Ord Mantell, which she uses as a front for her smuggling business. During the Clone Wars, Cid regularly exchanges intel with the Jedi. After Emperor Palpatine rises to power, Cid has to keep her past Jedi affiliations secret. However, she still uses her powerful network of informants and information brokers to run missions; many of which benefit groups working against the Empire. When Cid's path crosses with the Bad Batch, she convinces the team of enhanced clones to work jobs for her so they can share in the profits.

Cid is a tough and often secretive proprietor. She's fond of the young clone Omega, but even more fond of credits and doesn't hesitate to turn Omega's dejarik skills into a profitable opportunity, even when it brings attention to her parlor. After threatening the Bad Batch clones many times that she could reveal information about them to the Empire, Cid follows through and turns them in for credits, after they return from a mission on Eriadu.

Unlikely friends
Cid has a gruff disposition with most of her customers, but she develops a soft spot for Omega. She lets Omega stay in her parlor during some Bad Batch missions.

CHARACTERS AND CREATURES

FENNEC SHAND
SPECIES Human
AFFILIATION Hutt clan, Fett gotra

Fennec Shand is a highly skilled bounty hunter and mercenary. Shortly after the rise of the Empire, she makes a name for herself when she survives a clash with notorious bounty hunter Cad Bane over a job they're both chasing. During the reign of the Empire, Shand works for several crime syndicates, most notably the Hutt clan, and she develops a reputation as an elite and ruthless assassin. When the Empire falls, she finds herself on the run and the target of a high bounty herself. Fatally wounded on Tatooine by the bounty hunter Toro Calican, Shand is rescued by Boba Fett. He takes her to a mod-artist who saves her life by installing cybernetics in her abdomen.

Shand may be merciless during missions, but her words and promises can be trusted. Indebted to Fett, she agrees to help him reclaim his *Firespray*-class gunship. After fulfilling her debt, she decides to stay by Fett's side when he claims his purloined suit of armor and takes Jabba the Hutt's former throne. Shand counsels Fett and defends him from would-be assassins, even though she sometimes questions his methods. During the most stressful or deadly situations, Shand has the ability to remain calm and focus on finding a solution or an escape plan. Her strength and cunning help her overcome opponents several times her size and take out multiple targets, even when she's working alone. Throughout her career, Shand wears a distinctive black-and-orange helmet and attire that protect her against weapon damage as well as the elements, while still allowing her a free range of motion. She favors shooting targets from a long distance with a sniper rifle but is also deadly in close-range combat. Shand's ability to move quickly through rugged terrain, or even the air using acrobatic movements, makes her difficult to track, capture, and evade.

Hunting Omega
Hired by Nala Se, Shand tries to capture Omega on Pantora. Omega sees Shand as a friend, but the Bad Batch recognizes that she's a threat.

Trusted ally
Fennec Shand stands by Boba Fett in his throne room and in the streets of Mos Espa. She offers council about local politics and is quick to pursue his many rivals.

KETCH
SPECIES Weequay **HOMEWORLD** Ord Mantell
AFFILIATION Cid's Parlor

Ketch and his Ithorian friend Bolo are regular customers at Cid's Parlor on Ord Mantell. A fan of gambling, Ketch wins a double-or-nothing bet from Bolo over how well Omega can shoot with her Zygerrian energy bow—she doesn't hit her mark. When Roland Durand pushes Cid out of her parlor, Ketch and Bolo help her regain control.

ROLAND DURAND
SPECIES Devaronian
AFFILIATION Durand crime family

Son of the crime boss Isa Durand, Roland Durand forcefully takes over Cid's Parlor on Ord Mantell to make a name for himself. He sets up a deal to trade spice with the Pyke Syndicate, but the transaction is sabotaged by Cid and the Bad Batch. As payback for Durand's failure, the Pykes cut off one of his horns.

RUBY
SPECIES Zardimallo
AFFILIATION The Bad Batch

Ruby is a zardimallo, a rare lizardlike creature, and enjoys snacks and being petted. The criminal Roland Durand hires Cid to steal the lizard—who is highly prized on the criminal market—from the Rhokai gang. When the Bad Batch retrieves the lizard, Omega names her Ruby. Durand takes possession of Ruby when he temporarily controls Cid's Parlor.

AVI SINGH
SPECIES Human **HOMEWORLD** Raxus Secundus
AFFILIATION Separatist

Avi Singh is the senator of Raxus Secundus in the Confederacy of Independent Systems. When the Separatist government dissolves, Singh refuses to endorse the Imperial occupation of Raxus and is arrested. Singh has his droid, GS-8, contact Cid to ask for her assistance, and he's later rescued by the Bad Batch.

CAPTAIN BRAGG
SPECIES Human
AFFILIATION Empire

Captain Bragg is the Imperial officer who arrests Avi Singh, the senator for Raxus Secundus, for refusing to tell his fellow citizens to cooperate with Imperial occupiers. Cold and calculating, Bragg attempts to use an interrogation droid to forcefully change Singh's mind, but she's interrupted by the Bad Batch on a rescue mission.

ELENI SYNDULLA
SPECIES Twi'lek **HOMEWORLD** Ryloth
AFFILIATION Free Ryloth rebel cell

Part of the Free Ryloth Movement, Eleni Syndulla publicly backs her husband, Cham, as he tries to embrace peace after the Clone Wars. However, she is distrustful of the Ryloth Senator Orn Free Taa and Vice Admiral Edmon Rampart. Eleni understands that her daughter, Hera, wants to push back against the occupying forces, but Eleni's main focus is on protecting her. She convinces Cham to not choose violence after they rescue Hera from Imperial custody, but they're both arrested and falsely accused of trying to assassinate Senator Taa. After the Bad Batch rescues Eleni and Cham, they leave Ryloth with their daughter but continue their fight against the Empire.

IRLING
HOMEWORLD Ord Mantell **SIZE** 1.46 m (4 ft 9½ in) long, 2.54 m (8 ft 4 in) wingspan
HABITAT Subterranean caves

Irlings are large, winged creatures native to Ord Mantell. A swarm of them lives in the mining tunnels near Cid's Parlor. Irlings communicate with each other with sounds that many humans find terrifying. They swarm anyone they deem to be a threat, but they can be slowed down if bright lights are shone in their direction.

SCORCH
SPECIES Human **HOMEWORLD** Kamino
AFFILIATION Republic, Empire

Clone commando Scorch serves the Republic and, later, the Empire. As one of the clones stationed on the Imperial base on Daro, he's tasked with training a new Imperial army made up of conscripted soldiers from across the galaxy. Scorch is part of the team that recovers a cloned zillo beast when it escapes, and then he helps round up the civilians who witnessed the beast in order to cover up the event.

TK TROOPER
SPECIES Human
HOMEWORLD Various
AFFILIATION Empire

TK troopers are an early generation of Imperial stormtroopers. As part of project War-Mantle, human soldiers are recruited to voluntarily join the Imperial army. Initially, TK troopers are trained by clone troopers and wear a modified form of their armor. Imperial leaders believe these soldiers will be more loyal than clones and will save the Empire considerable expenses.

SABERJOWL
HOMEWORLD Kamino **SIZE** 120 m (394 ft) long
HABITAT Oceans

Saberjowls, also known as kamoradon sea dragons, are a carnivorous aquatic species native to the oceans of Kamino. They have enormous, powerful jaws filled with razor-sharp teeth. When Tipoca City sinks into the ocean during the fall of Kamino, the Bad Batch draws the attention of a saberjowl and uses an electrical shock to scare the predator away.

DOCTOR SCALDER
SPECIES Human
AFFILIATION Empire

Doctor Scalder is a scientist working at the secret Imperial cloning facility Mount Tantiss during the early years of Imperial rule. After the fall of Kamino, she welcomes Kaminoan scientist Nala Se to the laboratory. Scalder later assists Doctor Hemlock and Emerie Karr with the daily operations of the Tantiss facility.

HOWZER
SPECIES Human **HOMEWORLD** Kamino
AFFILIATION Republic, Empire

Captain Howzer is a clone trooper stationed on Ryloth. He greatly respects Cham Syndulla, the leader of the Free Ryloth Movement, and is disturbed by how Imperial officers treat the Twi'leks. Howzer tries to protect Cham's daughter, Hera, and is alarmed when her parents are falsely arrested for trying to assassinate Senator Orn Free Taa. After the Bad Batch frees the Syndullas, Howzer warns them they're walking into an Imperial trap. He's arrested for convincing a small group of clone troopers to lay down their weapons and stop working for the Empire, but he's later freed from Imperial custody by a group of clone deserters.

AGGROCRABS
HOMEWORLD Aynaboni
HABITAT Beach, jungles

Large, aggressive crustaceans, aggrocrabs live in the jungle and on the beaches of the tropical planet Aynaboni. Aggrocrabs hunt in packs, are extremely fast, and communicate with each other using high-pitched sounds. Their shells are incredibly tough, which makes aggrocrabs difficult to stop when they attack.

PHEE GENOA
SPECIES Human **HOMEWORLD** Pabu
AFFILIATION Treasure hunter

Phee Genoa is a treasure hunter and associate of Cid who prefers to be called a "liberator of ancient wonders" than a pirate. Along with the Bad Batch, she finds the Heart of the Mountain artifact.

This awakens an ancient weapon called Skara Nal. Phee later takes the Bad Batch to her homeworld, Pabu, so Omega can make new friends and take a break from her life on the run.

WILCO
SPECIES Human **HOMEWORLD** Kamino
AFFILIATION Republic, Empire

Captain Wilco is a clone trooper who serves the Empire. While leading a team on Serenno to recover Count Dooku's war chest, he crosses paths with Clone Force 99. Later, on Coruscant, Vice Admiral Rampart executes Wilco for refusing to falsify his mission report about the members of Clone Force 99.

ROMAR ADELL
SPECIES Human **HOMEWORLD** Serenno
AFFILIATION Separatist

Romar Adell and other native Serrenians live in hiding in the forests of Serenno after the planet falls into Imperial control.

Adell takes Echo, Tech, and Omega into his home when they meet during a Bad Batch mission to retrieve Count Dooku's war chest. Tech later helps Adell repair a Serennian cultural archive.

TAWNI AMES
SPECIES Human **HOMEWORLD** Desix
AFFILIATION Separatist

Tawni Ames is the governor of Desix—a planet that aligns with the Separatists during the Clone Wars. Believing her homeworld doesn't fall under Imperial jurisdiction, she takes Imperial-installed governor Grotton hostage to protest their occupation. She's promised a peaceful resolution, but Crosshair executes her as soon as she releases Grotton.

TAY-0
MANUFACTURER Czerka **TYPE** Refurbished CM3-series protocol droid **AFFILIATION** Racing

An egotistical racing droid, TAY-0 pilots a modified 12-series speeder in the riot races on Serolonis. As well as racing, TAY-0 is mechanically minded and fixes his own speeder. He doesn't believe humans are capable of making the split-second decisions that he can on the race course. When TAY-0 is destroyed in a crash, Tech takes his place in a race.

GRINI MILLEGI
SPECIES Dowutin
AFFILIATION Millegi's gang

Gambler Grini Millegi oversees the Safa Toma Classic riot racing event during the early years of the Empire. He regards Ciddarin Scaleback as one of his bitter rivals so when Cid arrives on Serolonis, he bets against her in a race. His favored racer, Jet Venim, wins, and Cid is unable to pay Millegi his credits so Tech agrees to race in a double-or-nothing bet to save Cid from Millegi and his gang.

JET VENIM
SPECIES Nosaurian
AFFILIATION Millegi's gang

Riot racing champion Jet Venim works for the gangster Grini Millegi. He's determined to win every race on Serolonis' circuit, no matter the cost. When Venim is in danger of losing, other racers on Millegi's payroll box in his opponents. This gives Venim the opportunity to unleash one of his racer's many weapons against his challenger.

MEL-221
MANUFACTURER Veril Line Systems
TYPE ECG-series power droid **AFFILIATION** Phee Genoa

The droid Mel-221 works with treasure hunter Phee Genoa. She confirms that a junkyard object found by Omega is an ancient artifact with coordinates to a treasure in the Kaldar Trinary system. When Genoa and the Bad Batch find the location, the artifact—named the Heart of the Mountain—awakens an ancient droid superweapon. An energy surge destroys Mel-221, but Genoa rebuilds her.

CHARACTERS AND CREATURES

CHELL
HOMEWORLD Skara Nal
HABITAT Caves

Chell are fast and fearsome creatures who live in caves formed in the mountains of Skara Nal. Despite having small eyes, they move around easily in the dark, and their enormous jaws are filled with long, razor-sharp teeth. A chell grabs Wrecker and tries to eat him until Wrecker's fellow Bad Batch members shoot at the creature, forcing it to retreat. Later, a chell attacks the Bad Batch inside the head of the ancient droid walker, Skara Nal. The chell's skin resists blaster fire and Omega's energy bows, but Wrecker grabs the beast by its tail and swings it out of the walker.

AXIS DROID LEADER
MANUFACTURER Rim Securities
TYPE K3 security droid (reprogrammed)
AFFILIATION Vanguard Axis

The criminal cartel Vanguard Axis is run entirely by droids whose jobs include smuggling and enslaving others. While the Bad Batch is delivering forged chain codes to the Axis droid leader, Omega discovers a young Wookiee named Gungi is being held captive. The Axis droid leader plans to sell Gungi, so the Bad Batch rescues him and flee under fire.

BABWA VENOMOR
SPECIES Trandoshan **HOMEWORLD** Trandosha
AFFILIATION Empire

Working to strip Kashyyyk of its resources for the Empire, Commander Babwa Venomor instructs his soldiers to destroy Wookiee villages to stay on schedule. When Venomor sees lightsaber marks on one of his vehicles, he offers an award for finding the Jedi who did it. He's later captured by a swarm of netcasters during a battle.

NETCASTER
HOMEWORLD Kashyyyk
HABITAT Forests

Netcasters are giant, yellow arachnids that dwell in the forests of Kashyyyk. They live in large colonies and swarm their enemies when threatened. When Wrecker starts cutting down the netcasters' webs, the Wookiee Gungi communicates with the creatures to let them know his group is not a threat to them. Netcasters later attack Trandoshans who are working for the Empire and destroying the forest and the Wookiees' homes.

MYLAYA
HOMEWORLD Kashyyyk
HABITAT Forests

Mylayas are giant, agile creatures who live in Kashyyyk's forests. Wookiees use the creatures as mounts during combat and as a mode of transportation. Mylayas have very large ears and their fur can be several different colors, including yellow, red, or green. The creatures can also jump long distances and great heights, and they use their claws and tails as weapons. A group of Wookiees ride mylayas while trying to stop Trandoshans from destroying the forest and their home during the early years of the Galactic Empire.

Ear variations Some ears are pointed while others are more rounded.

YANNA
SPECIES Wookiee **HOMEWORLD** Kashyyyk
AFFILIATION Yanna's clan

The kind and wise Wookiee elder Yanna leads a sanctuary on Kashyyyk. Her clan believes the planet belongs to the trees and they speak to them in times of need. She agrees to take in the young Jedi Gungi when the Bad Batch returns him to his homeworld. Yanna, her clan, and the Bad Batch, along with a swarm of netcasters, ambush Trandoshans who destroyed her village.

SLIP
SPECIES Human
HOMEWORLD Kamino
AFFILIATION Empire, Republic

CT-0409, also known as Slip, is a clone trooper who fights for the Republic during the Clone Wars and later serves on Vice Admiral Rampart's Imperial ship. After witnessing the assassination of a fellow clone, Slip contacts Senator Chuchi about Rampart's lies regarding his role in the destruction of Kamino, but while meeting with Chuchi, Slip is killed by the clone assassin, Clone X.

HALLE BURTONI
SPECIES Kaminoan **HOMEWORLD** Kamino
AFFILIATION Republic, Empire

As the senator representing Kamino during the Clone Wars, Halle Burtoni aggressively supports the expansion of military efforts. Continuing the war will benefit her homeworld because of their cloning operation. This position is at odds with many of her fellow senators, who argue for peaceful negotiations. After the Empire begins to distance itself from Kamino and its clone army, Burtoni loses her position as senator and her membership of the Defense Finance Committee. Bitter that almost all her people are gone, she reluctantly confirms to Senator Chuchi that Vice Admiral Rampart misdirected funds meant for Kamino without Senate approval.

CLONE X
SPECIES Human **HOMEWORLD** Kamino
AFFILIATION Empire

The clone trooper assassin known only as "Clone X" is hired by Vice Admiral Edmon Rampart to cover up his role in the destruction of Kamino. Clone X kills the clone trooper Cade when he threatens Rampart. He also kills a trooper who is meeting with Pantoran senator Riyo Chuchi. When captured by Rex, Clone X kills himself before Rex can question him.

BENNI BARO
SPECIES Human
HOMEWORLD Ipsidon
AFFILIATION Ipsidon miners

Benni Baro works mining ipsium on the planet Ipsidon. He steals the Bad Batch's ship, the *Marauder*, in a desperate effort to please his cruel mining boss, Mokko. Mokko took control of the local mines after the end of the Clone Wars. While the Bad Batch is retrieving the *Marauder*, the clones discover that Mokko is stealing profits from Baro and all the other miners. After Mokko dies in a fall, Baro tells the Bad Batch that he and the other miners want to continue working in the mines, but, from now on, they will share all of the profits themselves.

IPSIDON BUCK
HOMEWORLD Ipsidon
HABITAT Desert

When the Bad Batch travels to a mine recently purchased by Cid on Ipsidon, the clones come dangerously close to a herd of Ipsidon bucks. The strong and fast deerlike creatures travel in herds through the sometimes narrow caverns of the desert. One herd, trying to escape a sandstorm, comes close to trampling several members of the Bad Batch as well as a container full of volatile ipsium.

MOKKO

HOMEWORLD Ipsidon
AFFILIATION Mokko's crew

After the end of the Clone Wars, Mokko seizes power of the mines in the small city of Mokkotown on Ipsidon. He sets up a merit-based system that encourages miners to compete against each another for extra rations. After the Bad Batch discovers Mokko has been lying about the condition of the ipsium in the mines and is stealing profits, the miners confront Mokko. He falls to his death while trying to take another miner with him.

ROYCE HEMLOCK

SPECIES Human **AFFILIATION** Empire

Doctor Royce Hemlock is a scientist who is expelled by the Republic for his unauthorized experiments. He later joins the Imperial's Advance Science Division, working from the Mount Tantiss base on Wayland. Hemlock's soft and calm voice masks his ruthless intentions. Tasked with learning the secrets of Kaminoan cloning technology for Emperor Palpatine, Hemlock has no qualms using violence or torture to extract the information he needs. Hemlock doesn't see the value of clone lives and proposes making them the subjects of his experimental procedures, until the Bad Batch finally brings an end to his villainy once and for all.

EMERIE KARR

SPECIES Human **HOMEWORLD** Kamino
AFFILIATION Empire

A sister clone to Omega, Emerie Karr works alongside Doctor Hemlock as a scientist on Mount Tantiss. After the Empire detains Crosshair on Tantiss, Karr encourages him to give Doctor Hemlock the information he desires to avoid unpleasant interrogation techniques. Karr is calm and emotionless during most of her work so her motivations and actions are, at times, challenging to read. She shows some compassion toward Crosshair but doesn't hesitate to follow Hemlock's orders, until the time is right.

ICE VULTURE

HOMEWORLD Barton IV
HABITAT Mountains

Ice vultures are large carnivorous birds who live on the ice-covered planet Barton IV. One of the few living things that can survive the cold and windy temperatures for long periods of time, they feed off creatures that aren't so able to withstand the freezing conditions or who are just unlucky. Clone trooper Mayday warns Crosshair about the vultures when he arrives on Barton IV, but he also admires their ability to thrive there.

MAYDAY

SPECIES Human
HOMEWORLD Kamino
AFFILIATION Republic, Empire

The clone trooper Mayday is assigned to guard Imperial supplies at a depot on the icy planet Barton IV. Almost all of Mayday's men are killed by raiders during the year he is there. Mayday and Crosshair attempt to retrieve Imperial stolen goods from raiders, but an avalanche severely injures Mayday. He dies when Lieutenant Nolan refuses to give him aid after Crosshair brings him back to the depot.

NOLAN

SPECIES Human
AFFILIATION Empire

Inexperienced Imperial Lieutenant Nolan brings a small group of troopers, including Crosshair, to an Imperial Depot on Barton IV to retrieve cargo. Nolan regards clone troopers as inferior and not worthy of Imperial resources. When he refuses to give medical aid to Mayday, an injured clone trooper, the enhanced clone trooper Crosshair shoots him.

LYANA HAZARD

SPECIES Human
HOMEWORLD Pabu
AFFILIATION Hazard family

Lyana Hazard is the daughter of Pabu's mayor, Shep Hazard. She has a strong connection to the treasure hunter Phee Genoa, who she calls her Auntie. Shortly after Omega arrives on Pabu, Lyana takes her out on her boat to relax, but they're forced to flee after strong tremors hit the island and cause a sea surge. Hunter later rescues Lyana and Omega from a giant wave.

MOONYO

HOMEWORLD Pabu
HABITAT Island

The remote island of Pabu is the home of primatelike creatures called moonyos. Pabu elders believe that moonyos predated human settlers on Pabu. The animals have long, green tails and enjoy the company of humans—one moonyo jumps on Omega's shoulders shortly after she arrives on the island. They can also sense tremors common to Pabu before they occur.

SHEP HAZARD

SPECIES Human **HOMEWORLD** Pabu
AFFILIATION Hazard family

As the mayor of Pabu, Shep Hazard works to ensure the refugee population of this small, remote island stays safe and feels welcome. When the Bad Batch and treasure hunter Phee Genoa arrive, he warmly greets them. Shep enjoys organizing great feasts to bring together his community because he sees Pabu residents as an extension of his own family.

FIREBALL

SPECIES Human **HOMEWORLD** Kamino
AFFILIATION Republic, Rex's rebel cell

The former clone trooper known as Fireball works with Rex's rebel cell. He's present during the mission in which he and fellow ex-clone troopers rescue Howser and other imprisoned clone troopers from an Imperial transport ship. Fireball's team and the rescued clones narrowly escape Imperial capture when they jump into hyperspace.

NEMEC

SPECIES Human
HOMEWORLD Kamino
AFFILIATION Republic, Rex's rebel cell

After the Clone Wars, the clone trooper named Nemec deserts the Empire to join Rex's rebel cell. On a mission to rescue clone troopers from an Imperial ship, Nemec and Echo take control of the vessel's bridge. Nemec tries to interrogate an Imperial officer to learn where the clones are being taken, but the officer takes his own life before giving up any information.

BARTON COBURN

SPECIES Human
AFFILIATION Republic, Empire

During the Clone Wars, Admiral Barton Coburn works with Jedi Master Plo Koon as part of the Grand Army of the Republic. He commands several high-profile missions, including the rescue of Wilhuff Tarkin and Jedi Master Even Piell from the Citadel on Lola Sayu. After the rise of the Empire, Coburn is one of the few Imperial officers to speak up on behalf of the clone troopers and their previous war efforts. During a meeting on Eriadu, he questions Doctor Hemlock's plans to use clone troopers for his research projects, but his concerns are overruled by Admiral Tarkin.

CHARACTERS AND CREATURES

GENERAL KLEEVE
SPECIES Devaronian **HOMEWORLD** Devaron **AFFILIATION** Separatist

During the Clone Wars, General Kleeve is a Separatist general who spearheads an explosive attack on the Jedi Temple. He faces Depa Billaba while occupying the planet of Kaller. After the war, he goes by the name "Jondo," encountering Billaba's former Padawan, Caleb Dume, once more, now as a reluctant partner.

JANUS KASMIR
SPECIES Kalleran **HOMEWORLD** Kaller **AFFILIATION** Janus Kasmir's crew

Janus Kasmir is a Kalleran scoundrel who finds Caleb Dume days after Order 66. Janus teaches the former Padawan the ways of the underworld, before the pair go their separate ways. Years later, Ezra Bridger runs into his master's ex-partner when Janus rescues him from stormtroopers.

CHANATH CHA
SPECIES Human **AFFILIATION** Empire, the Orphans, Crimson Dawn

Chanath Cha witnesses Darth Vader murder her parents. A skilled slicer, she then becomes Emperor Palpatine's personal fixer and attempts to retrieve his ship from Lando Calrissian and Lobot, who is her former lover. Along with her team, the Orphans, Cha partners with Crimson Dawn, but she is slain by Darth Vader.

FERREN BARR
SPECIES Iktotchi **HOMEWORLD** Iktotch **AFFILIATION** Jedi, King Lee-Char of Mon Cala

As advisor to King Lee-Char of Mon Cala, Ferren Barr claims to be a Jedi Master, even though he only achieved the rank of Padawan. Nevertheless, "Master" Barr leads a group of acolytes, including Force-attuned Verla. He dies at the hands of his former sparring partner, Darth Vader.

VERLA
SPECIES Human **AFFILIATION** Light Side of the Force, Mon Cala

Verla is the only Force-attuned acolyte of Ferren Barr. She barely escapes Darth Vader's assault on Mon Cala. Verla becomes a peaceful angler, appearing to Luke Skywalker as a hooded vision. When they meet, she sends him to a High Republic outpost, where he finds a yellow-bladed lightsaber.

ELEVENTH BROTHER
AFFILIATION Inquisitorius

One of Darth Vader's Force-attuned Jedi hunters, this Inquisitor is dispatched to follow a tip that a Jedi has appeared in a remote village. He kills almost everyone there and is even ready to attack the Imperial informant, but Ahsoka Tano confronts and defeats him.

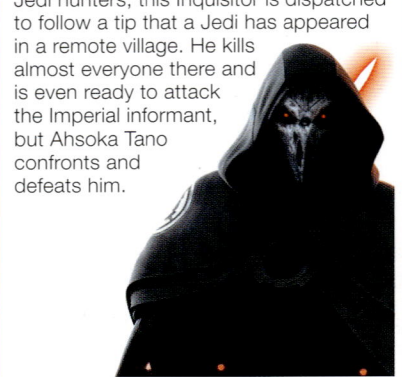

GRAF FAMILY
SPECIES Human **HOMEWORLD** Orchis 2 **AFFILIATION** Graf family

The Graf family has a long and distinguished history in the galaxy, first gaining significant wealth and influence during the Great Hyperspace Rush. Thanks to their control of hyperspace lanes, the Grafs accrue vast assets, which are eventually seized by the Republic after it is discovered that they are working with the Nihil. Part of their legacy, the Graf Archive, remains untouched. It covers most of Orchis 2's surface and contains a wealth of data as yet undiscovered by the wider galaxy.

After the Clone Wars, a descendent of this clan, Auric Graf works as a cartographer, exploring Wild Space with his wife, Rhyssa, and two children, Lina and Milo. However, Auric and Rhyssa are abducted by the Empire on an uncharted swamp world. Their children, accompanied by their "monster droid" CR-8R and pet Kowakian monkey-lizard, Morq, journey across the dangerous Wild Space to find their captured parents.

Lina later joins the Rebel Alliance as an Intelligence officer. After many years, Milo's grandson, Emil, takes up the family legacy, exploring the galaxy in the Imperial prototype scout ship the *Star Herald*.

THIRTEENTH SISTER
SPECIES Pkorian **HOMEWORLD** Pkori **AFFILIATION** Inquisitorius

Born to a former Jedi Padawan, Iskat Akaris is soon taken to Coruscant to follow in her mother's Jedi footsteps. She travels the galaxy with the stoic Sember Vey, collecting treasures for the Jedi Archives. After the outbreak of the Clone Wars and the death of Vey, Iskat becomes disillusioned with the Order and joins the Inquisitorius. As the Thirteenth Sister, Iskat is tasked with many cruel missions, and she carries them out with a ferocious vigor. However, during one such mission, she allows the wife of Jedi Master Eeth Koth to escape. Iskat is then killed by Darth Vader, alongside her lover, Tualon Yaluna.

MIRA
SPECIES Zabrak **HOMEWORLD** Iridonia **AFFILIATION** Koth family

Mira is the wife of Eeth Koth, who becomes a priest after Order 66. She doesn't know that her husband is a Jedi until Darth Vader appears after her Force-attuned child is born. Vader and his Inquisitors kill her husband and abduct her baby.

TUALON YALUNA
SPECIES Twi'lek **HOMEWORLD** Ryloth **AFFILIATION** Inquisitorius

A former Jedi Knight, Tualon Yaluna joins the Inquisitorius after Order 66. He knows Iskat Akaris from their days in the Jedi Temple, and they begin a romantic relationship. After a failed mission and a chase across Coruscant, he is killed by Darth Vader for defending his lover.

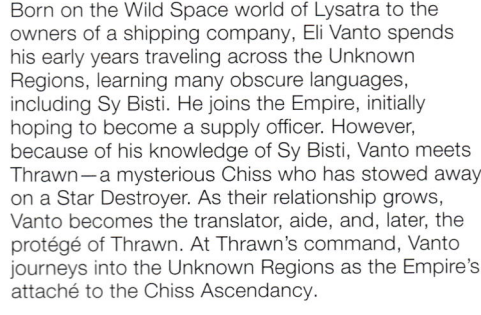

ELI VANTO
SPECIES Human **HOMEWORLD** Lysatra **AFFILIATION** Empire, Chiss Ascendency, Grand Admiral Thrawn

Born on the Wild Space world of Lysatra to the owners of a shipping company, Eli Vanto spends his early years traveling across the Unknown Regions, learning many obscure languages, including Sy Bisti. He joins the Empire, initially hoping to become a supply officer. However, because of his knowledge of Sy Bisti, Vanto meets Thrawn—a mysterious Chiss who has stowed away on a Star Destroyer. As their relationship grows, Vanto becomes the translator, aide, and, later, the protégé of Thrawn. At Thrawn's command, Vanto journeys into the Unknown Regions as the Empire's attaché to the Chiss Ascendancy.

ADMIRAL AR'ALANI

SPECIES Chiss
HOMEWORLD Csilla
AFFILIATION Chiss Ascendency

Ar'alani (born Irizi'ar'alani) is an admiral in the Chiss Expansionary Defense Fleet. She first becomes acquainted with Thrawn (born Mitth'raw'nuruodo) while they're both cadets at Taharim Academy. Ar'alani helps Thrawn and the Chiss Ascendency battle the Grysk. Almost two decades later, Ar'alani works with Eli Vanto, Thrawn's mentee, rescuing several sky-walkers, and reunites with Thrawn.

KANINA NICO

SPECIES Human
HOMEWORLD Huru system
AFFILIATION Empire

Kanina Nico initially joins the Empire to be part of something bigger than herself. While attending the Imperial Naval Academy on Carida, she allies with fellow cadet Han Solo. She eventually fakes her own death on the Outer Rim planet of Qhulosk after becoming disillusioned with the Empire.

BEILERT VALANCE

SPECIES Human
HOMEWORLD Chorin
AFFILIATION Empire, bounty hunter

Beilert Valance grows up idolizing the Empire, enlisting at the Carida Imperial Naval Academy. He rises to the top of his class and meets Cadet 124-329, Han Solo, who rescues him after a crash on Qhulosk. Valance loses an arm and an eye, which are both replaced with cybernetics, and he goes back into battle. Fighting eventually causes him to lose all his remaining limbs, and they are repaired with further cybernetics.

Valance becomes a feared cyborg bounty hunter, learning much from being a part of a group that includes T'onga and Bossk and is led by the fearsome Nakano Lash. Its members split up after Lash betrays the group. Valance is later hired to kill Darth Vader, but he is unsuccessful.

During the war for Solo's carbonite-enclosed body, Valance is blown up by Boba Fett but is repaired by Vader, who removes his heart and forces him to serve the Empire. While an Imperial once more, Valance sees plans for the Death Star II and develops feeling for fellow cyborg and Imperial Lieutenant Haydenn.

After learning the Empire is believed to have killed his former love, Yura, and that his current love, Haydenn, has betrayed him, Valance escapes and reunites with his fellow hunter T'onga and her crew. The Imperial Inferno Squad erases his memories because he saw the Death Star II plans. As his memory fails, he becomes afflicted by the Scourge, transforming into an unstoppable killing machine. After his memories and control of his body are restored by T'onga's group, Valance travels to Jabba the Hutt's palace, where he destroys the gangster's mega droid as part of the plot to rescue Solo.

LYTTAN DREE

SPECIES Human **HOMEWORLD** Boiyuh
AFFILIATION Empire

Lyttan Dree enlists at the Imperial Naval Academy on Carida, alongside his brother, Tamu. As part of Carida Squadron, he participates in his first battle over the city of Howlan. Lyttan eventually becomes a lieutenant in the fearsome Shadow Wing, and he is shot down by a rebel fighter.

TAMU DREE

SPECIES Human **HOMEWORLD** Boiyuh
AFFILIATION Empire

Tamu Dree joins the Empire with his brother, Lyttan, after facing starvation on the planet Boiyuh. As Cadet 542-146, Tamu has his life saved by fellow cadet Han Solo during a training exercise. Unlike his brother, however, Tamu is eventually transferred away from a combat role to a mobile Imperial hospital.

DARTH SHAA

AFFILIATION Sith

Darth Shaa hears of the dark deeds of a fellow Force-wielder named Momin, so she tracks him down and breaks him out of captivity. Shaa makes Momin her apprentice—a decision that proves to be her undoing. She is killed in a duel with Momin, who resents that he has been designated a learner.

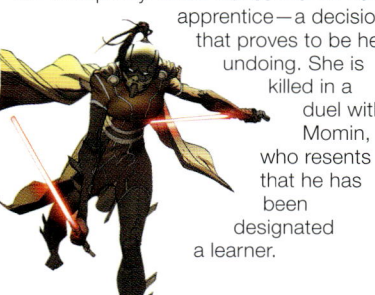

DARTH MOMIN

AFFILIATION Sith

Darth Momin is a horrific dark-side artist, determined to create great works for the Force. During the planning of his destructive masterpiece, Momin is killed by Jedi, leaving only his mask. That mask finds its way to Darth Sidious, who stores it on his personal yacht and later gifts it to Darth Vader. Momin's mask possesses an Imperial officer named Lieutenant Roggo, who then designs a first draft of Darth Vader's Mustafar fortress. Finally, Momin's ultimate plan is revealed—his mask is an attempt to resurrect himself. The ploy succeeds, albeit briefly, with a resurrected Momin dueling Vader, which results in his second demise.

KRISTISS

SPECIES Petrusian
HOMEWORLD Petrusia
AFFILIATION Petrusian Freedom Fighters

Kristiss is a Petrusian barterer who specializes in obtaining any client's request. Her father, Rythus, and other Petrusians have been enslaved and forced to work in a droid repair shop at an Imperial outpost on Kullgroon. In her desperation, she hires Lando Calrissian to help bypass the Empire and eventually leads a revolution that frees her people.

CIENA REE

SPECIES Human **HOMEWORLD** Jelucan **AFFILIATION** Empire

Growing up on Jelucan as a poor "First Wave" settler, Ciena Ree becomes close friends with Thane Kyrell, who is the son of an aristocrat. Having bonded over their love of flying, they are both selected to the Royal Imperial Academy on Coruscant, where their friendship soon blossoms into romance. After the destruction of Alderaan, Ree remains with the Empire, bound by her oath, while Kyrell joins the Rebellion. At the Battle of Jakku, Ree and her former lover find themselves on opposite sides of the final moments of the Galactic Civil War, and Ree is taken prisoner by the New Republic.

THANE KYRELL

SPECIES Human **HOMEWORLD** Jelucan
AFFILIATION Rebel Alliance

The son of a "Second Wave" aristocrat on the Outer Rim planet of Jelucan, Thane Kyrell fulfills his childhood ambitions and joins the Empire as a pilot, alongside his best friend, Ciena Ree. The destruction of Alderaan causes him to become disillusioned, and he defects from the Empire and joins the Rebel Alliance as an X-wing pilot. After the fall of the Empire, Kyrell becomes a proud member of the New Republic, eventually rescuing his childhood friend from her crashing Star Destroyer during the Battle of Jakku.

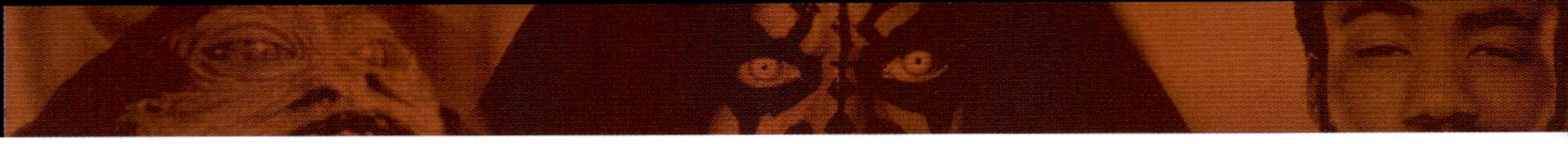

CHARACTERS AND CREATURES

CAL KESTIS

SPECIES Human
AFFILIATION Jedi, *Stinger Mantis* Crew, Hidden Path

At the end of the Clone Wars, the Jedi Order is all but wiped out, and Padawan Cal Kestis loses the only family he knows when his master is killed. Cal goes into hiding on the planet Bracca, where he works as a scrapper. He tries to hide his identity from others, but one day Cal uses his Force abilities to save his friend Prauf from a high fall. Now on the Empire's radar, Cal flees Bracca with help from Cere Junda and Greez Dritus, who bring him aboard the *Stinger Mantis*.

Cal agrees to help with Cere's plan to rebuild the Jedi Order. On Bogano, he meets the droid BD-1 and learns about a Jedi holocron filled with the names of Force-attuned children. As Cal tracks down the holocron, he also works to repair his damaged connection to the Force by dealing with the guilt he feels over the loss of his master. His Force abilities include a rare skill—psychometry—enabling him to sense the history of an object just by touching it. Later, Cal invites the Nightsister Merrin, who also lost her family to the Sith, to join the *Mantis* crew.

Cal tracks down the holocron but decides it's too dangerous to use. Along with his companions, he goes on many missions fighting against the Empire and the Haxion Brood criminal syndicate. Cal's upset when the crew disbands after several years and everyone goes their separate ways.

After years of fighting the Empire on his own, Cal, BD-1, and new partner Bode Akuna reunite with the *Mantis* crew after they learn about a hidden planet named Tanalorr. Merrin helps Cal fight temptations of the dark side after Bode betrays them and Cere dies at the hands of Darth Vader. Cal decides to break the Jedi rules of attachment to share his romantic feelings with Merrin. Together, they plan to use Tanalorr as a refuge for the Hidden Path organization that shields Force-attuned beings from the Empire.

New blade
Kestis uses parts from Cere Junda and Jaro Tapal's lightsabers to make a new one on Ilum.

Weather proof
Cal favors ponchos and jackets that protect him from the rain, sun, and wind.

Looking ahead
Cere Junda knights Cal Kestis before traveling to Fortress Inquisitorius.

PRAUF

SPECIES Abednedo
HOMEWORLD Abednedo
AFFILIATION Scrapper Guild

The scrapper Prauf works alongside Cal Kestis when the Jedi Padawan is in hiding on Bracca. Prauf is proud of his work, but he misses the days before the Empire rose to power when he worked as an engineer. Prauf tells Cal that he doesn't believe all the Jedi were traitors. After Cal uses his Force abilities to save Prauf from a fall, Prauf agrees to keep Cal's secret and encourages him to leave Bracca. The Inquisitor Second Sister stabs and kills Prauf when he speaks out against the Empire in an attempt to draw attention away from Cal.

GREEZ DRITUS

SPECIES Latero **HOMEWORLD** Lateron **AFFILIATION** *Stinger Mantis* crew, Pyloon's Saloon

The four-armed Latero Greez has a love of flying and playing games of chance. Cere Junda hires him and his ship, the *Stinger Mantis*, during her search for a Jedi holocron. Devoted to Cere, Greez is initially suspicious of Cal Kestis, BD-1, and the Nightsister Merrin when they join the *Mantis* crew, but he soon warms up to them, offering them his home-cooked specialty, scazz steak. During a mission on Murkhana, Greez loses an arm to the Fifth Brother's lightsaber. Later, Greez buys the Pyloon Saloon on Koboh, where Cal recruits him to fly the *Mantis* to a hidden planet in the Koboh Nebula.

SECOND SISTER

SPECIES Human
AFFILIATION Jedi, Inquisitorius

During Order 66, Jedi Padawan Trilla Suduri hides in a cave with her master, Cere Junda, and other younglings. When the Empire finds Trilla, they torture her and turn her to the dark side. Now known as the Inquisitor Second Sister, Trilla is angry at Cere for not protecting her. Having become a ruthless Jedi hunter, Second Sister attempts to capture Cal Kestis on Bracca, but he escapes on the *Stinger Mantis*. She pursues him as they both try to find a Jedi holocron that lists Force-attuned children. Trilla is highly skilled in lightsaber combat and tries to manipulate Kestis by revealing her past with Cere to him. After investigating rumored Jedi activity on Ontotho, Second Sister steals the holocron from Kestis on Bogano. She later battles with him on Fortress Inquisitorius when Cal attempts to recover the artifact. As Cere tries to turn Trilla back to the light side, they are interrupted by Darth Vader. Trilla asks Cere to avenge them, right before Vader slashes and kills her for failing in her mission.

CERE JUNDA

SPECIES Human
AFFILIATION Jedi, *Stinger Mantis* crew, Hidden Path

During the chaos of Order 66, Jedi Master Cere Junda makes a decision that haunts her. She tries to protect her Padawan, Trilla Suduri, by leaving her in a cave, but Cere is captured and tortured and she reveals Trilla's location to the Empire. When Cere sees that Trilla has been turned into an Inquisitor, she erupts in a violent rage, killing her captors and escaping. After this brush with the dark side, Cere cuts off her connection to the Force. When Cere discovers that her old Master Eno Cordova may have the key to rebuilding the Jedi Order, she enlists Cal Kestis. Cere is again tempted by the dark side when she faces Darth Vader, but Cal helps pull her back to the light. After many missions with the *Stinger Mantis* crew, Cere decides to go her own way. She travels to Jedha, where she works with the Hidden Path and starts to rebuild the Jedi Archives with the help of Cordova. Later, Cere valiantly protects her archive from an Imperial attack but doesn't survive a lightsaber battle with Darth Vader.

ENO CORDOVA

SPECIES Human
AFFILIATION Jedi, Hidden Path

Eno Cordova is Cere Junda's Jedi master. During their time together, the pair go on many missions for the Order, including to Nameel and Ontotho. Obsessed with the study of ancient civilizations, Cordova is often on the move, traveling to remote planets across the galaxy. He's especially interested in learning about the Force-attuned Zeffo species, who mysteriously disappeared. After receiving a doom-filled premonition before Order 66, Cordova hides a holocron with the names of Force-attuned younglings in a Zeffo vault on Bogano—a planet only he and Junda know the location of. He entrusts his explorer droid BD-1 with holo messages to be played to whomever the droid deems worthy of finding the holocron. Later, Cordova joins Junda on Jedha in an effort to rebuild the Jedi Temple Archives and assist the Hidden Path. Cordova's kindness and optimism are extinguished when Bode Akuna shoots and kills Cordova in order to acquire the compass to Tanalorr.

MERRIN

SPECIES Zabrak **HOMEWORLD** Dathomir **AFFILIATION** Nightsisters, *Stinger Mantis* crew

As a child, Merrin loses her Dathomirian Nightsister family during a Separatist massacre. Growing up alone, she shares some of her magick secrets with the fallen Jedi Taron Malicos. He tells her that it was the Jedi who were responsible for the death of her clan. After meeting Cal Kestis, Merrin realizes that Malicos was manipulating her, and she helps Cal defeat him before joining the *Stinger Mantis* crew. Merrin's magick allows her to move quickly through space and use green flames to attack.

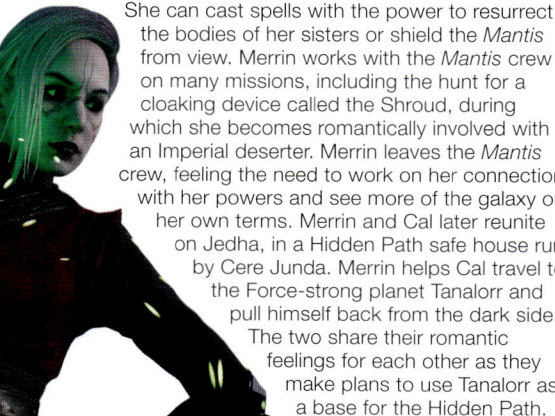

She can cast spells with the power to resurrect the bodies of her sisters or shield the *Mantis* from view. Merrin works with the *Mantis* crew on many missions, including the hunt for a cloaking device called the Shroud, during which she becomes romantically involved with an Imperial deserter. Merrin leaves the *Mantis* crew, feeling the need to work on her connection with her powers and see more of the galaxy on her own terms. Merrin and Cal later reunite on Jedha, in a Hidden Path safe house run by Cere Junda. Merrin helps Cal travel to the Force-strong planet Tanalorr and pull himself back from the dark side. The two share their romantic feelings for each other as they make plans to use Tanalorr as a base for the Hidden Path.

BD-1

MANUFACTURER Behold-Urwar Droid Concepts
TYPE BD explorer droid
AFFILIATION Jedi, *Stinger Mantis* crew

Before the explorer droid BD-1 joins Cal Kestis and the *Stinger Mantis* crew, his owner is Jedi Master Eno Cordova. When Cordova hides a holocron with the names of Force-attuned children, he blocks BD-1's memories so the droid can't reveal the location until he finds someone he can really trust. After BD-1 meets Cal Kestis on Bogano, the duo become inseparable. Regularly found riding on Cal's back, BD-1 assists Cal in slicing consoles, scanning items, and offering stims to improve Cal's health. BD-1 plays Cal messages recorded by Cordova that help him get closer to finding the holocron. He knows it's in the Bogano vault, but not how to reach it. Over time, the bond between BD-1 and Cal grows, and the droid eventually regains all of his memories.

When the *Mantis* crew disbands, BD-1 remains with Cal, occasionally playing him nostalgic recordings from the crew's time together. Ever loyal and able to read Cal's emotions, BD-1 is quick to offer a supportive beep or suggest a location he strongly feels Cal should investigate more.

TARON MALICOS

SPECIES Human
AFFILIATION Jedi, Nightbrother clan

Former Jedi Taron Malicos finds new purpose after Order 66 on Dathomir as leader of a Nightbrother clan. He lies to the Nightsister Merrin, saying the Jedi were responsible for the slaughter of her sisters. Having failed to recruit Cal Kestis, Malicos dies battling Cal and Merrin.

JARO TAPAL

SPECIES Lasat
AFFILIATION Jedi, Republic

Jedi Master Jaro Tapal is training his Padawan Cal Kestis aboard the *Albedo Brave* above Bracca when Palpatine initiates Order 66. Tapal fights many clone troopers after sending Cal to an escape pod. Both master and Padawan make it to the vehicle, but Tapal dies due to the severe injuries he sustained in battle.

CHIRODACTYL

HOMEWORLD Dathomir
SIZE 4.8 m (15 ft 9 in) high
HABITAT Caves

Enormous batlike creatures, chirodactyls live in Dathomirian caves. Their strong claws allow the creatures to run and climb over rough terrain. They also have the ability to glide in the sky for long periods of time. The loud cries of chirodactyls send other Dathomirian predators into hiding. Many Nightbrothers have died trying to ride chirodactyls to impress their clan. During Cal Kestis' search for a Zeffo Astrium, he fights, rides, and eventually kills a chirodactyl named Gorgara.

CHARACTERS AND CREATURES

HAN SOLO
SPECIES Human **HOMEWORLD** Corellia
AFFILIATION Rebel Alliance, Resistance

A roguish, galactic legend with a sharp wit and sharper reflexes, Han Solo begins life as a scrumrat but evolves to become a leading figure in the wars against tyranny.

THE SCOUNDREL
Abandoned at a young age, Han grows up on the streets of Corellia, and his tough upbringing shapes who he becomes as an adult. Han's time among the White Worms gang teaches him how to run scams and talk his way out of trouble. He falls in love with fellow scrumrat, Qi'ra, with whom he tries to escape Corellia. When the two are separated while looking to start a better life, Han is forced to join the Imperial Academy to make it off the planet. Han's free spirit and disregard for authority make for a tough time as an Imperial cadet. Despite his innate ability, he fails as a pilot, and is reassigned to the infantry on Mimban. There, questioning orders leads to Han facing execution at the hands of "the Beast," a Wookiee named Chewbacca. Instead, Han convinces Chewie that they can escape together.

BECKETT'S CREW
Solo and Chewbacca flee Mimban as part of smuggler Tobias Beckett's crew. The gang's first job is a failed attempt to steal coaxium—a valuable hyperfuel. Now in debt to criminal syndicate Crimson Dawn, Han and Beckett negotiate to complete the job. Han is surprised to find his old friend Qi'ra is a senior figure in Crimson Dawn, but is pleased to have her accompany the crew on its journey to Kessel to secure more coaxium. The crew also adds Lando Calrissian and his ship, the *Millennium Falcon*, to its ranks, but soon fall into trouble and are forced to take a shortcut through the dangerous Maelstrom around Kessel. With Han in the pilot's seat the crew completes the maneuver in record time, but Lando's pristine starship receives substantial damage. At the end of the job, Han is betrayed by Beckett and Qi'ra. Solo and Chewie leave with just enough money to wager in a card game to win the *Millennium Falcon* from Calrissian. Han also learns to be careful who he trusts.

ODD JOBS
During the Empire's reign, Han and Chewie venture out into the wide galaxy in the *Falcon*, retrieving and smuggling a variety of ill-gotten goods for Jabba the Hutt. Their paths often cross with other scoundrels, like bounty hunters Greedo and Krrsantan, pirate queen Maz Kanata, and smuggler Sana Starros, who pretends to marry Han as a cover for a robbery on the planet Stenness. During one fateful smuggling job, Han dumps his shipment of spice to keep it out of Imperial hands. The displeased Jabba demands payment for his lost cargo.

THE RELUCTANT REBEL
Han Solo agrees to transport Luke, Obi-Wan, and their droids purely as a business deal; he has no interest in their rebel mission. When plans change, Han only agrees to rescue Princess Leia because of the promise of a big financial reward. When they reach Yavin 4, he intends to leave before the impending battle so he can pay off Jabba the Hutt. At the last moment, however, he has a change of heart and returns to help his newfound friends, going on many missions against the Empire. On Hoth, Han tries to leave the rebels once again, but changes his mind to get Leia safely off the planet.

Frozen solid
Darth Vader uses Han to test whether a human would survive Cloud City's carbonite-freezing process before attempting it with Luke Skywalker.

IMPRISONED IN CARBONITE
When Han finally comes to care deeply for Leia Organa, his world is turned upside down. On Cloud City, he is captured by Darth Vader and used as a test subject in the facility's carbon-freezing chamber. Incapacitated and frozen in carbonite, he is handed over to Boba Fett for delivery to Jabba. The skilled bounty hunter loses his quarry as others throughout the galaxy, including Qi'ra, look to profit from Solo's plight. However, Fett eventually regains possession of the smuggler and finally hands him over to the crime lord on Tatooine. As a trophy hanging on the gangster's palace wall, all seems hopeless until Han's friends orchestrate a successful rescue attempt.

GENERAL SOLO
Free from his carbonite prison, Han fully embraces his place in the Rebel Alliance. Now a general, he leads a team to destroy the second Death Star's shield generator on the moon of Endor. Meanwhile, he reluctantly loans the *Falcon* to its previous owner, Lando Calrissian, to spearhead the attack against the feared battle station. During the mission on Endor, Han becomes a prisoner of the Ewoks and once again must place his faith in others to survive. When the shield generator is destroyed and the Empire overthrown, Leia breaks the happy news that Luke is actually her brother.

FAMILY LIFE
After the Battle of Endor, Han and Leia marry in a ceremony held in the Ewoks' Great Tree, and later have a son named Ben. Feeling restless, Han spends much time away from home, starting a shipping business and racing starfighters. They send Ben to train with Luke to become a Jedi. When their son turns to the dark side and renames himself Kylo Ren, Han and Leia have difficulty coping and separate. Han returns to smuggling with Chewbacca, but having lost the *Falcon*, ends up piloting the *Eravana*—a bulk freighter. In the Western Reaches, they are reunited with their old ship and plunged back into galactic events. When Han helps destroy Starkiller Base, he confronts Kylo Ren. Solo reaches out to his son, asking him to come home, but Ren kills him.

After he senses Leia's death a short time later, Ren considers who he wants to be. A vision of Han appears before him, encouraging him to carry on his mother's fight, and Ben Solo turns back toward the light.

Confident scoundrel
Han Solo believes that he doesn't need much more than a good blaster at his side, especially his trusty, customized DL-44 pistol.

Love and war
Despite his mercenary, cynical approach to life, Han falls for Princess Leia and, ultimately, the rebel cause.

STORMTROOPER

SPECIES Human **HOMEWORLD** Various
AFFILIATION Empire

Stormtroopers have replaced the clones of the Republic as the expendable foot soldiers of the Empire. Their endless numbers serve across the galaxy, enforcing the Emperor's will.

RECRUITMENT AND TRAINING
Though not necessarily the army's deadliest weapons, beneath their white armor, stormtroopers are loyal Imperial citizens. Most are naturally born humans, who volunteer (or are conscripted) and rigorously train in Imperial academies. After the rise of the Empire, clone soldiers are gradually phased out due to their accelerated aging process. Clone soldiers, though genetic copies, vary in personality and are surprisingly individualistic. Naturally born soldiers, in contrast, are trained and conditioned to forsake both individualism and empathy.

Grand Moff Wilhuff Tarkin is the public face of the political maneuvering required to transition away from the Republic's clone troopers to Imperial stormtroopers. However, Emperor Palpatine is ultimately in control. Under Tarkin's orders, Vice Admiral Edmon Rampart destroys the cloning facilities in Tipoca City on Kamino and introduces the Imperial Defense Recruitment Bill to the senate. This bill formally puts a structure in place to replace clones with human troopers, with some clones still working in the Imperial army as advisors and trainers. Other clones retire or are forced into poverty, no longer able to do the work they were created for.

MAINTAINING SECURITY AND ORDER
Stormtroopers are stationed on strategic worlds throughout the galaxy. On planets like Lothal, Tatooine, and Coruscant, they serve a variety of functions, including guarding mining operations, factories, and commercial interests important to the Empire. They also maintain societal order and monitor politically sensitive areas—stamping out all signs of rebellion. Their power, built on creating fear within local populations, causes an atmosphere of abuse and corruption. Some, whether due to blind obedience or brainwashing, carry out atrocities in the name of the Emperor.

ON THE BATTLEFIELD
Stormtroopers are the backbone of the Imperial Army, waging war on rebel insurrection. In battle, stormtroopers are equipped with BlasTech E-11 blasters and DLT-19 heavy blaster rifles, a thermal detonator, grappling hook, comlink, and surplus ammunition. Stormtroopers are dreaded by civilian populations—not only for their brutality but also their fanaticism to press on regardless of cost. They are trained to disregard fallen comrades in battle and to engage the enemy no matter the odds. When the Republic transitions into the Empire, stormtroopers are summoned to bring the remaining Separatist worlds into line. Later skirmishes are mostly small in size—the results of isolated rebel cells, indigenous politics, Jedi sightings, piracy, and other underworld activity—until the dawn of the Rebel Alliance. As the Galactic Civil War expands, so does the involvement of stormtroopers in warfare, culminating in the Empire's defeat at the Battle of Jakku.

After the Empire falls, many stormtroopers go on to serve the Imperial remnant. Faced with limited resources on the planet Peridea, Grand Admiral Thrawn's stranded stormtrooper corps repairs cracks in their armor with whatever it can find. The Great Mothers imbue some of Thrawn's troopers with sinister and ancient majik.

STORMTROOPER SPECIALIZATIONS
The stormtrooper corps is formed of humans recruits, both male and female. Outside of combat and security details, stormtrooper officers wear distinctive black caps, boots, and dress tunics. Their code cylinders, rank plaques, officers' disks, and uniform style conform to Imperial military standards. Officers in field units wear orange, black, and white pauldrons to indicate rank (unfortunately for stormtroopers, this visible formality puts them at risk and many lose their lives to snipers). There are several different types of specialized stormtrooper units, including snowtroopers, shoretroopers, scout troopers, sandtroopers, and death troopers—each employs unique armor to support its niche combat roles. Army pilots may also be promoted from within the stormtroopers' ranks.

Overwhelming numbers
Stormtroopers surround Chewbacca, Leia Organa, and Han Solo during the Battle of Endor.

Behind the mask
Stormtroopers appear anonymous in their armor. This leads to an overall lack of accountability and also creates occasional opportunities for spies to impersonate soldiers.

> "Stop whining. We're here to protect you."
>
> **LOTHAL STORMTROOPER**

Search for the droids
Obi-Wan Kenobi uses his Jedi powers of persuasion to get past a stormtrooper roadblock in Mos Eisley.

CHARACTERS AND CREATURES

QI'RA
SPECIES Human **HOMEWORLD** Corellia **AFFILIATION** White Worms, Crimson Dawn

Talented and calculating, Qi'ra rises from her humble beginnings to challenge the Emperor himself. While her plans may not unfold the way she wishes, her actions leave an indelible mark on history.

Keeping up appearances
Her time with Crimson Dawn has made Qi'ra adept at hiding her true intentions. She easily fools the Pyke Syndicate.

CORELLIAN SCRUMRAT
The young Corellian Qi'ra falls in with the White Worms gang when she attempts to pickpocket Moloch, one of its senior members. She meets fellow scrumrat Han Solo, and the pair are sent by Lady Proxima to manipulate an auction between the White Worms, Kaldana Syndicate, and Droid Gotra. Though Qi'ra is promoted to Head Girl by Proxima as a result, she and Han (who have fallen in love) decide to escape. Later, Han steals a small sample of valuable coaxium and tries to run away with Qi'ra. They are chased to Coronet Spaceport by Moloch. Though Han makes it through security, Qi'ra is captured. Proxima sells Qi'ra to enslaver Sarkin Enneb. However, the contract states that Qi'ra must help with one final job. Once the task is completed, Enneb takes Qi'ra to his estate where Corynna, a concierge for the crime syndicate Crimson Dawn, decides to recruit her. Qi'ra is then transported to the *First Light*.

JOINING CRIMSON DAWN
After multiple failed escape attempts, Qi'ra is ordered to kill someone by the group's leader Dryden Vos. She does so without hesitation and receives a Crimson Dawn tattoo on her arm. Qi'ra is then sent to Thorum where her actions impress Vos, leading to her return to the *First Light*, where he trains her in teräs käsi. She later accompanies Vos to a party attended by the other criminal syndicates on the planet Nightsend. The event goes fatally awry but Qi'ra's quick-thinking saves Vos' life, further cementing her position in the organization. She is soon sent to recover a Force artifact from a planet and delivers it personally to Maul, the head of all of the crime syndicates, on Dathomir and becomes Vos' second-in-command.

Han comes back into Qi'ra's life, accompanied by Tobias Beckett and Chewbacca. She helps save their lives by formulating a heist on Kessel to steal a hoard of unrefined coaxium—all to replace what they owe an angry Dryden Vos. She accompanies the three and hires Lando Calrissian and his *Millennium Falcon* to transport them. Thanks to her planning and combat skills, the mission is a success. When they return to meet Dryden however, Beckett double-crosses them all, stealing the coaxium and leaving Han and Qi'ra to deal with Vos. Qi'ra betrays and kills her former master. She tells Han to pursue Beckett, promising to follow. Nevertheless, she decides to remain with Crimson Dawn.

Unexpected reunion
Han is shocked to find Qi'ra working with Dryden Vos, assuming she would still be stuck on Corellia. She is equally shocked to learn he has joined Beckett's gang.

IN POWER
Arriving at Dathomir, Qi'ra becomes the new public head of Crimson Dawn and learns more from Maul about his plan to defeat the Sith. Following Maul's death, she becomes the group's leader and takes up Maul's vendetta. Rival crime organizations believe Crimson Dawn has been defeated, but Qi'ra has deliberately faded into obscurity to build a far-reaching network of agents and a secret army.

When Han is frozen in carbonite, Qi'ra's minions steal her former lover from Boba Fett before he can deliver Han to Jabba the Hutt. Then, she hosts a party to announce Dawn's return to the galactic stage. Delegations from the Empire, Rebel Alliance, and other criminal syndicates are all invited. During the event on Jekara, she auctions off Han Solo to Jabba, who bids one million credits. However, an uninvited guest, Darth Vader, arrives claiming Han as his own. Taunting the Sith Lord, Qi'ra then engages him in battle, holding her own and even wounding him. She only survives due to Luke Skywalker's arrival, which distracts Vader, who later kills most of the Hutt Council.

ESCALATING STRIKES
As she flees Jekara, Qi'ra reflects that, barring Vader's interference, the event went as she intended, creating chaos and instability in the criminal underworld and severing the long-standing alliance between the Hutts and the Empire. Qi'ra then uses her agents to sow discord between the criminal syndicates and to cause an all-out war. With the Sith distracted by the gangs' squabbling, Qi'ra sends the Knights of Ren to steal an ancient artifact called the Screaming Key from Fortress Vader on Mustafar. She also captures Cadeliah, an heir to two rival crime operations, who Qi'ra sees as a potential successor. With the Sith now fully aware of the threat Qi'ra poses, the Knights of Ren and a Crimson Dawn agent called the Archivist use the Screaming Key to retrieve the Fermata Cage, a Sith device of unimaginable power that can freeze beings in time. Now Qi'ra throws every resource, what she calls her hidden empire, at the Imperials to allow the Archivist time to open the Fermata Cage. She directly informs Darth Sidious that she has the dangerous item and will open it to release an ancient Sith Lord trapped within, greatly concerning the Emperor.

FINAL GAMBLE
Now in the endgame of her plans, Qi'ra rallies her troops to defend the Fermata Cage at the Amaxine space station. When the *Executor*, with Sidious and Vader aboard, arrives in orbit, she sends her Dawn fleet in to attack. The Sith board the station killing anyone in their way. However, they realize too late that they have fallen into a trap, becoming frozen in time themselves. Qi'ra appears to have won until the disgruntled leader of the Knights of Ren, who has lost two followers to Qi'ra's plots, decides to save the Sith. His choice leads to Crimson Dawn's utter destruction.

Qi'ra goes into hiding, with her remaining resources bequeathed to Cadeliah, which gives the young criminal the opportunity to pick her own future. While her plan failed, Qi'ra's actions allow the Alliance to regroup, and her agents inform the rebels about the Death Star II, ensuring they win the Galactic Civil War. She watches the Empire's fall sitting alone in a booth at a cantina.

LADY PROXIMA
SPECIES Grindalid **HOMEWORLD** Corellia **AFFILIATION** White Worms

The head of the White Worms is Lady Proxima, a larvalike matriarch who lives in a cistern at the center of their den. Her gang controls the criminal market in Coronet City, taking in humanoid children known as "Scrumrats" who are enslaved and forced to work. Proxima takes in young Han and Qi'ra, but when Han fails at his assignment and keeps some of the stolen coaxium for himself, Proxima is determined to teach him a painful lesson. Han escapes with Qi'ra by breaking the glass above Proxima's "throne room," thus exposing her to the light and burning her photosensitive skin. When Qi'ra is captured by Moloch, Proxima tortures the young woman and then sells her to an enslaver. However, she gives Qi'ra one final mission in which she raids a Corellian shipyard where many of the older scrumrats die, perhaps by Proxima's design as she fears more rebellions. Years later, Han returns to Corellia and is captured by Moloch. Brought before Proxima once more, Han escapes by exposing her to sunlight again. Still scarred and bearing a grudge, Proxima continues to run her gang in the New Republic era, where she happily offers First Order agent Bazine Netal intelligence so she can capture Han's ship.

CORELLIAN HOUND
HOMEWORLD Corellia
AVERAGE SIZE 0.7 m (2 ft 4 in) high
HABITAT Adapted to many environments

Fast on their feet and with an excellent sense of smell, Corellian hounds are used by gangs as guards, attack dogs, and trackers. There are many breeds and the creatures are now found across the galaxy. Sibians are white with a bonelike ridge along the crest from head to shoulders. The hounds are prone to fighting, and their bites are so savage that they often lose teeth, which they continuously regrow. The White Worms gang uses them to hunt down Han and Qi'ra when they flee to Coronet Spaceport. The dogs are thrown off the trail by strong scents of seafood in the fish market.

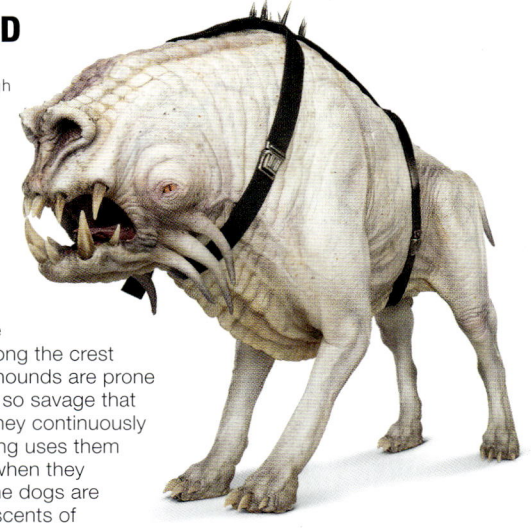

BANSEE
SPECIES Human
HOMEWORLD Corellia
AFFILIATION White Worms

The Scrumrats are orphans and runaways that Lady Proxima's White Worms gang takes in off the street of Corellia. Bansee is their best rat-catcher, attaining the rank of Third Girl. She is ambitious and aspires to climb higher in the gang, perhaps by becoming one of Moloch's thugs.

FALTHINA SHAREST
SPECIES Human
HOMEWORLD Corellia
AFFILIATION Empire

Lead Transport Security Officer Falthina Sharest is a member of Corellia's emigration office, working at Coronet Spaceport. The corrupt officer agrees to a trade, allowing Han and Qi'ra to exit in exchange for their coaxium, but betrays Qi'ra when the White Worms grab her.

MOLOCH
SPECIES Grindalid
HOMEWORLD Corellia
AFFILIATION White Worms

Lady Proxima's lieutenant in the White Worms is the unsympathetic Moloch. Though he looks like a humanoid inside his protective face-plates and robes, he is in fact a wormlike Grindalid just like Lady Proxima herself, and he "walks" on a segmented tail. Moloch captures Han and Qi'ra after Han goes rogue on an assignment, taking them to Lady Proxima for punishment. When they escape, Moloch loads Rebolt, Syke, and their Corellian hounds into his A-A4B truckspeeder and pursues them to the Coronet Spaceport. Though Han escapes, Moloch's crew manage to grab Qi'ra. He remains at Proxima's side for many years.

REBOLT
SPECIES Human **HOMEWORLD** Corellia
AFFILIATION White Worms

Rebolt is a merciless member of the White Worms gang, working under Moloch. He is an experienced Corellian hound handler but deals roughly with his animals. He joins Moloch and Syke aboard their A-A4B truckspeeder to pursue Qi'ra and Han through Coronet City. He is believed dead following a disastrous heist on a Corellian shipyard.

SYKE
SPECIES Human **HOMEWORLD** Corellia
AFFILIATION White Worms

Syke is the competitive colleague of Rebolt. He takes a gentler approach with their Corellian hounds, though he has a spiteful streak when it comes to Rebolt. The two White Worms gang members unleash their hounds on Qi'ra and Han at Moloch's command. Following Han and Qi'ra's betrayal, he fears Proxima will kill the older scrumrats. He doesn't return from a raid on a Corellian shipyard, proving his concern is well-founded.

PATROL TROOPER
SPECIES Human **HOMEWORLD** Various
AFFILIATION Empire

On worlds with large urban environments—particularly those with strategic importance for the government, military, and major corporations—the Empire takes control of local transit security and law enforcement. Imperial patrol troopers are the urban counterparts to the Imperial Army's biker scouts. On Corellia, patrol troopers ride Aratech C-PH patrol speeder bikes as they monitor activity in Coronet's shipyards and spaceport. A patrol trooper chases Han and Qi'ra when the two flee from Moloch, but the pursuit doesn't last long before the patrol trooper crashes.

VAL
SPECIES Human
AFFILIATION Beckett's crew

Val's father was a musician and named her after an instrument called the valachord. She and Tobias Beckett—her partner in crime and romance—have a running joke that he will one day learn to play one. They do jobs for Dryden Vos, which brings them into conflict with Enfys Nest. After Nest deprives them of their haul of identichips, Val and Beckett pose as mudtroopers on Mimban and steal a ship to use in a conveyex heist on Vandor. During the mission, Val is discovered by deadly Viper droids. Rather than risk her team getting caught too, she blows up the conveyex bridge, sacrificing herself.

CHARACTERS AND CREATURES

TOBIAS BECKETT
SPECIES Human **HOMEWORLD** Glee Anselm
AFFILIATION Crimson Dawn, Beckett's crew

Tobias Beckett gains notoriety as the man responsible for Aurra Sing's purported death. He also runs heists for Crimson Dawn with his gang, which includes his girlfriend Val and pilot Rio Durant. He has his team run an unsuccessful scam on Hovun IV stealing identichips, only to lose them to Enfys Nest. Such failed schemes lead the crew into financial trouble. Having accrued a significant debt to Crimson Dawn's Dryden Vos, Beckett and his gang pose as mudtroopers on Mimban and steal an AT-hauler to use it in a heist on Vandor. In the process, Beckett meets Han Solo and Chewbacca and adds them to his crew. On Vandor, Beckett and the team steal priceless coaxium from the Imperial conveyex, but Enfys Nest's Cloud-Riders arrive and foil the operation. Val and Rio are both killed.

Beckett agrees to steal a hoard of unrefined coaxium from Kessel for Dryden, to replace the load they previously lost. Their heist is successful, but Beckett double-crosses his own team on Savareen, taking the coaxium for himself. Han Solo pursues Beckett and kills him.

Straight shooter
Amid the chaos of the battlefield on Mimban, Beckett, in disguise as an Imperial officer, demonstrates his incredible skills as a gunslinger.

RIO DURANT
SPECIES Ardennian **HOMEWORLD** Ardennia
AFFILIATION Freedom's Sons, Beckett's crew

Amiable Rio Durant is a four-armed pilot who originally works for Freedom's Sons, an army employed by the Galactic Republic during the Clone Wars. After the formation of the Empire, he turns to crime. Rio tries unsuccessfully to steal the speeder bike of Tobias Beckett and Val, and is offered a place in their crew instead. After meeting Han Solo on Mimban, Rio convinces Beckett to take Solo and Chewbacca on as new crew members. Rio flies the crew's ship during their heist on Vandor, but the craft is boarded by Cloud-Riders. Rio is mortally wounded by a Cloud-Rider's blaster fire.

MUDTROOPER
SPECIES Human **HOMEWORLD** Various
AFFILIATION Empire

Mudtroopers are members of the Imperial Army appointed to swampy, war-torn worlds. The assignment is not a glamorous one. Mudtroopers such as Han Solo are often given the duty as punishment for poor service and insubordination. Some are local forces who fought for the Republic during the Clone Wars, and now fight side-by-side with stormtroopers. On Mimban the Empire battles Mimbanese guerillas in an effort to secure the planet. Tobias Beckett's gang takes advantage of the chaos—posing as mudtroopers, they steal an Imperial AT-hauler.

ENFYS NEST
SPECIES Human **AFFILIATION** Cloud-Riders

Sixteen-year-old Enfys Nest is descended from a long line of freedom fighters. Her homeworld is devastated by the five crime syndicates; chief among them Crimson Dawn. She inherits her role as leader of the Cloud-Riders (a pirate swoop-bike gang) and her elaborate armored costume from her mother, upon the latter's death. After the Cloud-Riders' raid on Gargon, the Empire begins to piece together information that Enfys Nest is amassing resources to fund a rebel uprising. Meanwhile, Enfys makes herself a thorn in the side of Tobias Beckett, tricking his gang into stealing a load of identichips. Enfys shows up again to steal coaxium from Beckett during his heist on Vandor, only to lose the haul in an accident. Enfys further tracks Beckett, Han Solo, Qi'ra, and Chewbacca to Savareen. There she reveals her identity and her purpose—to fight Crimson Dawn's brutality. She convinces them to help her. After a fight with Dryden Vos and killing the traitorous Beckett, Han Solo turns over the priceless coaxium to Enfys. She in turn delivers the coaxium to Saw Gerrera, who uses it to fund his rebel partisans.

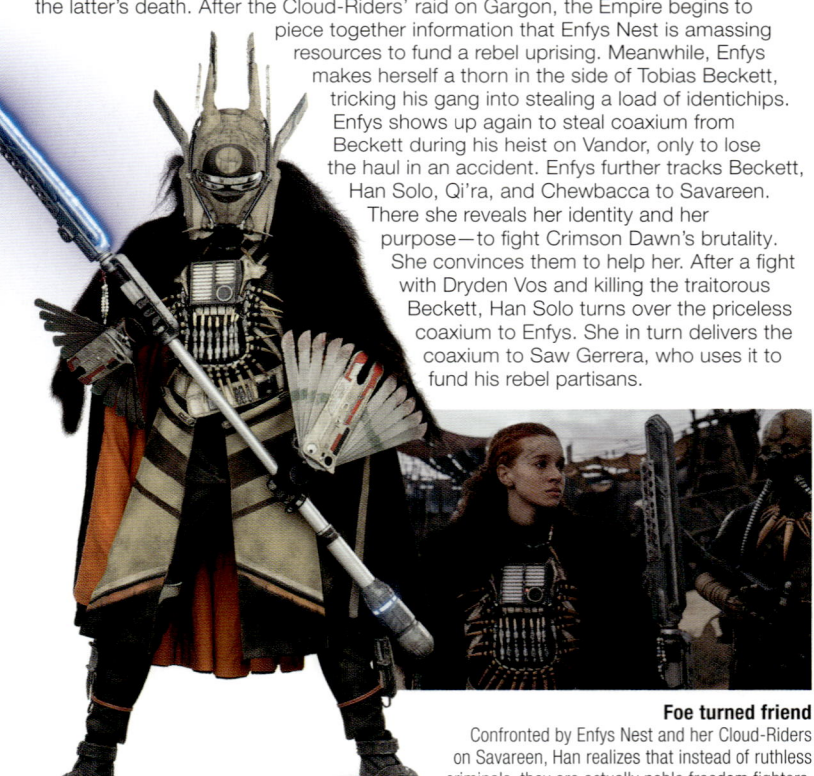

Foe turned friend
Confronted by Enfys Nest and her Cloud-Riders on Savareen, Han realizes that instead of ruthless criminals, they are actually noble freedom fighters.

On the edge
Dryden is highly volatile and unpredictable. He is a ruthless killer who hides his true nature behind a mask of calm gentility.

DRYDEN VOS
SPECIES Near-human
AFFILIATION Crimson Dawn, Shadow Collective

Dryden Vos acts as the public leader of Crimson Dawn, allowing his employer, Maul, to remain anonymous. Dryden has a temperament that flashes instantly from calm to bloodthirsty and he enjoys personally killing those that have let him down. The only warnings are the striations on his face, which burn crimson red with elevated blood pressure and adrenaline. He has been with the organization since at least the Clone Wars. During the Siege of Mandalore, Maul orders Vos and the other members of the Shadow Collective, an organization of criminal syndicates, to go into hiding, fearing the Empire's rise.

During the Imperial era, the underworld kingpin appreciates a lavish lifestyle, traveling in his yacht, *First Light*, with an entourage of security enforcers, ship's crew, and menial servants. After his concierge Corynna brings Qi'ra aboard, Vos immediately takes an interest in the young criminal and trains her to be his second-in-command, personally teaching her teräs käsi. She impresses him on a number of missions and helps him track down a traitor in their midst.

When smuggler Tobias Beckett fails to deliver the coaxium he owes, Dryden is determined to kill him. Fortunately for Beckett, his crew-member, Han Solo, is a quick thinker and they come up with a plan to acquire replacement coaxium from Kessel. Dryden assigns his trusted lieutenant Qi'ra to accompany them.

Later, Han Solo, Chewbacca, and Qi'ra return, but are unaware that Beckett has secretly warned Dryden that they plan to double-cross him. Beckett arrives soon after, but departs with the coaxium (and Chewbacca, held at blasterpoint), leaving Solo, Qi'ra, and Dryden to fight it out. Qi'ra betrays Dryden however, killing him and taking over his criminal operation.

RANGE TROOPER
SPECIES Human **HOMEWORLD** Various
AFFILIATION Empire

Range troopers are among the Empire's toughest soldiers, assigned to rugged, cold-weather frontier worlds like Banas. On Vandor, they are ordered to guard the Empire's 20-T railcrawler conveyex transport in its delivery of refined coaxium. High speeds on ever-changing tracks winding through mountains and tunnels—all in rough weather—make it difficult to monitor conditions outside the train. Range troopers must personally investigate, clinging to the train's surface with their magnetomic gription boots. Confronted by Tobias Beckett and his gang, their efforts prove futile.

MARGO
SPECIES Imroosian **HOMEWORLD** Imroosia **AFFILIATION** Crimson Dawn

When Qi'ra joins Crimson Dawn, the assistant concierge aboard Dryden Vos' *First Light* is a skilled Imroosian named Margo. She is tasked with training Qi'ra in many arts, including etiquette and poison detection, and is quietly impressed by the new recruit. Soon after, Margo's superior Corynna is caught trying to poison Vos and is painfully killed, and Margo is promoted to take her place. As concierge, Margo sees to all guests' needs and greets Beckett, Han Solo, and Chewbacca when they first arrive together. After Vos' death, Margo remains in her position under Qi'ra's leadership. Margo tries to kill her boss three times until she realizes that Qi'ra values her. Alongside Trinia, Margo becomes one of Qi'ra's most trusted advisors as she puts together her plan to destroy the Sith and appears to wholeheartedly believe in the endeavor. Qi'ra entrusts the pair with stealing Han's carbon-frozen form. During the ensuing chaos, Margo is rarely far from Qi'ra's side unless one of them is on a mission. Margo deals with the Pykes during the Syndicate War. In a starfighter, she later leads the Crimson Dawn fleet in its defense of the Amaxine space station against the Imperial Super Star Destroyer *Executor*. Whether she survives the engagement is unknown.

AURODIA VENTAFOLI
SPECIES Human
AFFILIATION None

The best-selling recording artist Aurodia Ventafoli is in high demand. Dryden Vos hires her as his singer-in-residence on the *First Light* for a time, with the help of a huge retainer fee. The "Chanteuse of the Stars" duets (aided by a multi-vocoder) with the diminutive singer, Luleo Primoc.

LULEO PRIMOC
SPECIES Gallusian
AFFILIATION None

A singing superstar before the Clone Wars, with hits such as "Your Love is Gravy" and "Carve Your Name in My Heart," Luleo Primoc now sings with Aurodia Ventafoli, suspended in a repulsorlift flask filled with formaldehyde. He was once a holovid star, seated atop a humanoid exo-suit.

AEMON GREMM
SPECIES Hylobon
AFFILIATION Crimson Dawn

Aemon Gremm is Dryden Vos' chief bodyguard and captain of his security team. Having been at Vos' side for years, Gremm and his fellow Hylobons are fiercely loyal to Vos and highly aggressive toward anyone they perceive as a threat to his operations. During a dangerous event on Nightsend, he lends Qi'ra his helmet to prolong her survival. He later saves Vos from a poisoning attempt by his concierge. Gremm takes all the credit for his team's work though, which is a source of friction.

TAYSHIN AND MODA MAXA
SPECIES Human **HOMEWORLD** Eshan
AFFILIATION Cloud-Riders

The Maxa sisters learn how to survive in harsh conditions when the Droid Gotra incites a gang war on their homeworld. Both later join the Cloud-Riders. Tayshin is a skilled martial artist, while Moda is a talented pilot.

ASTRID FENRIS
SPECIES Human **HOMEWORLD** Yir Tangee
AFFILIATION Smuggler

One of the many shady smugglers that hang out at the notorious Fort Ypso Lodge, Astrid Fenris is an amoral con artist from Yir Tangee. She runs a profitable scam selling Vandor ice labeled as valuable R'alla mineral water. Decades later, she attends an event hosted by Zeva Bliss, head of the Spice Runners of Kijimi, in spite of the fact that they each had no respect for the other.

ARGUS PANOX
SPECIES Azumel

Argus "Six Eyes" Panox is an Azumel gambler and occasional customer at the Lodge at Fort Ypso. His eye stalks move independently, gaining him a reputation for looking at other sabacc players' cards. His five-chambered stomach requires him to eat frequently.

DAVA CASSAMAM
SPECIES Elnacon **HOMEWORLD** Nacon
AFFILIATION None

A sabacc-playing regular at the Lodge, Dava Cassamam is an ammonia-breathing Elnacon who wears a transparisteel dome and breathing apparatus when she is away from home and her career as a deep cloud-miner. She is easygoing and enjoys relaxing on Vandor as its typical gravity helps relieve her back pain.

THERM SCISSORPUNCH
SPECIES Nephran **HOMEWORLD** Nepotis
AFFILIATION Maz Kanata, entrepreneur

Thermoculus Krisintvolt Scissorpunch, also known as Therm Scissorpunch, is a long-lived hustler who has been active for centuries. During the High Republic era, he is an associate of Maz Kanata, frequently working with her on missions. Centuries later, Therm is a regular at the Lodge in Fort Ypso. As he loses money gambling with Lando Calrissian his blood boils, and thoughts of snapping the smooth-talker's neck cross his mind, but his hard exoskeleton helps him hide any emotion.

DD-BD
TYPE Adminmech
AFFILIATION Pyke Syndicate

The adminmech DD-BD is an enthusiastic droid who works on a Morseerian pirate ship until the vessel is impounded by the Empire. He is then sold to the Pyke Syndicate and sent to Kessel. There, L3-37 liberates him from his restraining bolt and gives him ideas about starting a revolution.

TAK
SPECIES Human
HOMEWORLD Coruscant

Tak is a con artist who robs the elderly on Coruscant. He is arrested when he tries to fleece the Princess of Kessel and is sent to work in the mines on her world. When L3-37 encourages a droid riot, Tak escapes in the chaos.

CHARACTERS AND CREATURES

L3-37
MANUFACTURER Various (self-upgraded)
TYPE Custom pilot droid **AFFILIATION** Lando Calrissian

The *Millennium Falcon* owes much of its legendary performance to L3-37. L3 begins life as an astromech, later upgrading her own body with components from protocol droids and other unusual sources. Her brain has likewise evolved, with coding from espionage and protocol droids overlaid upon her original astromech architecture. There are very few droids quite like L3. She is unusually self-aware and passionate about droid rights, leading to constant confrontations with "organics." L3's owner/partner Lando Calrissian is willing to overlook her eccentricities due to her exceptional copiloting skills. In truth, the two develop a uniquely close master-droid bond. They have a number of escapades including on Hynestia and Kullgroon.

Around this time, L3 also encounters the Phylanx Redux Transmitter—a droid code that could spread between droids and then be switched on to make them kill organics. Fearing its inevitable activation, L3 covertly devises a quick anti-virus that she implants into it; later, she creates a droid in her image solely dedicated to eradicating the code in the future.

At Fort Ypso on Vandor, L3 is horrified to witness a droid gladiatorial arena, passionately trying to stop it until Lando pulls her away. She eventually agrees to join the mission to Kessel. During the job, she starts a droid revolution on the planet but is damaged beyond repair in the resulting chaos. Her brain is uploaded into the computer of the *Millennium Falcon*, thus becoming a permanent part of the ship. She performs the calculations that allow Han Solo and the crew to make the Kessel Run in less than 12 parsecs, and execute other amazing feats in their future adventures.

Years later, when the Phylanx Redux Transmitter is finally activated, L3's past actions enable Lando to destroy it and save the galaxy. The droid that L3 created and two droids he built then save Lando from certain death.

Capable copilot
L3 and Lando make a great team. L3 knows how to push the *Falcon* to its mechanical limits, while Lando's sublight piloting is second to none.

SUMMA-VERMINOTH
RANGE Si'Klaata Cluster and Akkadese Maelstrom **AVERAGE SIZE** 7,400 meters (24,278 ft 3 in) long

Shrouded in the gas clouds surrounding Kessel are enormous creatures of legend—the summa-verminoths—that can potentially live for a thousand years. With trailing tentacles and mantles full of eyes, they snatch wayward ships foolish enough to stray from the Kessel Run. When the crew of the *Millennium Falcon* take a shortcut through the Akkadese Maelstrom, they are nearly swallowed by one of these mythic monsters. They distract it by ejecting the ship's escape pod and then lure it to its doom in the gravity well known as the Maw. Following the Battle of Hoth, Vader encounters a rare specimen from a summa-verminoth subspecies in Red Space. This individual has evolved to hunt its own kind so attacks physically as well as crushing its prey's mind. Vader bends the monster to his will, using it to fight his master on Exegol. However, it is no match for Darth Sidious and is destroyed.

WG-22
MANUFACTURER Veril Line Systems
TYPE Modified EG-series power droid
AFFILIATION Fort Ypso Lodge

Ralakili runs a violent droid-fighting pit at the Fort Ypso Lodge. He's been spiteful toward droids ever since the Clone Wars. The modified Gonk droid WG-22 can power his mechanical weaponry with his own internal power generator.

QUAY TOLSITE
SPECIES Pyke **HOMEWORLD** Kessel
AFFILIATION Pyke Syndicate

The director of operations at the Kessel Mines is Quay Tolsite. He is the local representative for the Pyke Syndicate, which leases the mines from King Yaruba of Kessel. The selfish Pyke is unconcerned with the well-being of his laborers, as long as they are capable of satisfying production targets. Tolsite enjoys his authority and privilege, embezzling money and spice from business transactions, but he pays a price. The mine environment is caustic and hard on Pyke physiology, so he and the other Pykes wear protective suits.

SENNA
SPECIES Gigoran **HOMEWORLD** Gigor

Senna is one of a number of Gigorans who are rounded up on his homeworld by Zygerrian enslavers, sanctioned by the Empire. He committed no crimes, but members of his species are desired as enslaved workers on Kessel due to their strength. The poisonous conditions in the mine have stained his formerly white fur.

FD3-MN
AFFILIATION Fort Ypso Lodge

Droids are modified with crude weapons and thrown into the fighting pit without consent. Most are disoriented and don't want to be there, but FD3-MN realizes that she actually quite likes it. Unfortunately gladiator droids don't tend to last long.

SAGWA
SPECIES Wookiee **HOMEWORLD** Kashyyyk

The gallant Wookiee Sagwa protects his people from Imperial soldiers in the tree city of Rwookrrorro on Kashyyyk. He is enslaved by the Empire and sent to the mines of Kessel. During an uprising, he aids Chewbacca and Han Solo and escapes to freedom. He maintains contact with Chewie, who he sees as a brother, and ends up on Nar Shaddaa. Years later, he contacts Chewie to say he's seen Boba Fett, who is in possession of Han's body frozen in carbonite.

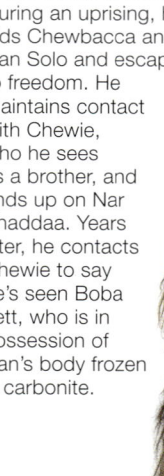

> "Smuggler? Such a small word. I'm more of a… galactic entrepreneur."
> LANDO CALRISSIAN

LANDO CALRISSIAN

SPECIES Human **HOMEWORLD** Socorro **AFFILIATION** Rebel Alliance, Resistance

Beginning as a hustler and ending up a galactic hero, Landonis Balthazar Calrissian comes out on top, thanks to a winning smile, charm, and a little flattery.

SPORTSMAN AND SMUGGLER

Lando Calrissian prides himself on being an exceptional "sportsman" and looking good doing it. He is a charismatic swindler and gambler who owns the heavily modified freighter, the *Millennium Falcon*. His ship reflects Lando's own impeccable style and preference for the finer things in life. But expensive tastes come at a price and Lando often turns to gambling or illegal commissions to pay off his debts. He is joined on these jobs by his loyal, but loudly opinionated, droid copilot L3-37. Lando is an expert and confident sabacc player, thanks largely to the hidden card he often has up his sleeve. However, Lando's luck runs out when he takes part in a smuggling run to Kessel that brings Han Solo and Chewbacca onto the *Falcon* for the first time. By the end of the heist, his immaculate ship is almost unrecognizable, L3-37 is destroyed, and Lando abandons Solo and returns to his old ways. At another sabacc game, this time on Numidian Prime, Solo swindles the master gambler and wins the *Falcon* from Lando.

Bitter defeat
The game of sabacc where he loses the *Falcon* to Han haunts Lando for years.

A CHARMING CON MAN

Having lost the *Falcon*, Lando embarks on a variety of business ventures across the galaxy. On Lothal, he buys land from local crime lord Cikatro Vizago to set up an illegal mining operation. Later, after winning the astromech Chopper from Zeb Orrelios, he bargains with the crew of the *Ghost* to help him con the enslaver Azmorigan out of a puffer pig (Lando insists the pig is necessary for his latest convoluted scheme). He also helps the crew make illicit starship transponders to aid their escape from an Imperial blockade—this time in exchange for three military-grade shield generators. Not all of Lando's schemes work out for the best. On the Imperial colony world Castell, Lando and his loyal friend Lobot take a heist job from the nefarious Papa Toren to pay off a debt. The so-called easy job turns out to be perilous when they discover the space yacht they are robbing is owned by Emperor Palpatine and is full of Sith artifacts.

BARON ADMINISTRATOR OF CLOUD CITY

Lando's fortune changes when he wagers big and wins control of Cloud City, in the atmosphere above the planet Bespin. His life takes a dramatic turn toward more reputable pursuits as he becomes baron administrator of the gas mining and luxury destination. His situation sours, however, when the Empire arrives and he is forced to turn his friend Han and his companions over to Darth Vader in exchange for the city's freedom. He watches as Solo is frozen in carbonite, but when it appears that Vader intends to dishonor their deal, Lando implements a city-wide evacuation with the aid of Lobot, helping his friends escape. Nonetheless, the frozen Han is taken by the bounty hunter Boba Fett and delivered to Jabba the Hutt.

Living by his wits
Lando's smooth-talking and magnetic personality are infamous, and his charms have stolen more than just hearts. He is particularly adept at talking his way out of difficult or dangerous situations.

ALLYING WITH THE REBELS

Following the fall of Cloud City, Lando works with the Alliance, slowly gaining the trust of its members over many missions. Lando helps orchestrate an elaborate mission to rescue Han, who is frozen in carbonite and hanging from a wall in Jabba's palace on Tatooine. Gaining employment as a skiff guard in the Hutt's residence thanks to an underworld contact, Lando waits for Chewbacca and Leia Organa (disguised as the bounty hunter Boushh) to arrive on the desert world. However, the plan falls apart when Leia is discovered freeing Han from the carbonite, and she and Han are taken prisoner. Luke Skywalker arrives and attempts to persuade Jabba to release Han and Leia, but is captured, too, forcing the friends to resort to their last contingency plan. When Jabba takes Han, Luke, and Chewbacca out to the Dune Sea to feed them to the Sarlacc, Lando is aboard one of Jabba's skiffs to help them escape. At the last moment, he and Han, Luke, and Chewbacca fight off Jabba's henchmen, while Leia Organa kills the Hutt. Afterward they all depart Tatooine.

GENERAL CALRISSIAN

Wanted by both the Empire and the Hutt crime family, Lando decides to wholeheartedly commit to the Rebellion. Now a general, he attends the rebel briefing on *Home One*, the Mon Calamari flagship, where Mon Mothma, Admiral Ackbar, and General Crix Madine detail plans to sabotage the shield generator on the Forest Moon of Endor, destroy the second Death Star, and kill the Emperor. Lando and his copilot, Nien Nunb, fly the *Falcon* inside the Death Star, where they detonate the battle station's core, destroying it. After this decisive victory, the Empire falls into chaos, and the war finally ends in triumph a year later at the Battle of Jakku. That same year, Lando leads the liberation of Cloud City from the hands of the Imperial remnant.

In the war room
Lando and his friends listen intently to the mission briefing aboard *Home One*.

HIS SEARCH BEGINS

During the era of the New Republic, Lando becomes a father to a little girl named Kadara Calrissian. She vanishes when she's just two years old, and Lando begins a galaxy-spanning search for her on board his ship, *Lady Luck*. Years go by until he overhears a mercenary named Ochi of Bestoon boasting in a cantina about a kidnapping job—for the Sith of Exegol. That tidbit of information takes Lando and Luke on a journey halfway across the galaxy to the desert world of Pasaana. When Ochi's trail goes cold, Lando decides to stay and continue searching the quadrant for his lost daughter. In time, he discovers that the First Order is behind Kadara's abduction but doesn't get any closer to finding her.

CALL TO ARMS

Lando remains on Pasaana, where Leia contacts him to request that he help Chewbacca and C-3PO—plus their friends Rey, Finn, and Poe Dameron—with their search for Exegol. Lando directs them to Lurch Canyon. There they find Ochi's ship and the clue they need to retrieve the Sith wayfinder. Meanwhile, Lando makes his way to Ajan Kloss. When the Resistance prepares to make its stand against the Final Order, Lando and Chewbacca take the *Millennium Falcon* to the Core systems and call for allies. People across the galaxy respond. Lando and Chewie, accompanied by a fleet of civilian starships, arrive at the Sith planet just in time to turn the tide of the battle.

CHARACTERS AND CREATURES

Kenobi obsession
Reva continues her search for Obi-Wan Kenobi even when she's told to stop by her superiors. She lures him to Fortress Inquisitorius, but Kenobi escapes.

REVA
SPECIES Human
AFFILIATION Jedi, Inquisitorius

As a youngling training at the Jedi Temple on Coruscant, Reva narrowly escapes the slaughter after Palpatine issues Order 66 against the Jedi. Reva never forgets the betrayal and abandonment she felt after being forced to play dead to escape Anakin Skywalker's rage. Driven by her desire to exact revenge against Skywalker—now Darth Vader—for murdering her Jedi family, Reva joins the Inquisitorius and becomes Third Sister. As an Inquisitor, Reva is brutal and relentless in her pursuit of one Jedi in particular—Anakin Skywalker's Jedi Master, Obi-Wan Kenobi. Reva's fellow Inquisitors regard her as reckless and without talent beyond her connection to the dark side. She's regularly reprimanded by the Grand Inquisitor for stepping out of line and for her ambition for power. He also insists that she drop her fixation with Kenobi. Reva refuses to back down, knowing that capturing the reclusive former Jedi will bring her close enough to Vader to give her the chance to kill the Sith Lord. Working alone, she orders the kidnapping of young Leia Organa from Alderaan in a bid to flush Obi-Wan out from hiding. When the Grand Inquisitor threatens to ruin her plans, Reva stabs him. Reva's obsession wins her the attention of Vader, who elevates her to the role of Grand Inquisitor after she tracks Kenobi to Jabiim. Reva tries to kill Vader on Jabiim, but she fails, and Vader tells her that he was aware of her motive of revenge all along. Reva travels to Tatooine to kill Vader's son, Luke. Kenobi races to protect him and finds Reva, who has just chosen to be merciful and spare the young boy. Reva leaves her Inquisitor lightsaber, and Kenobi hopes that they will both be able to move on from the pain of their past.

Hunting Jedi
The Inquisitor Third Sister searches for signs of a Jedi in the Tatooine city of Anchorhead, along with the Grand Inquisitor and Fifth Brother.

MINAS VELTI
SPECIES Human
AFFILIATION Jedi

When clone troopers attack the Jedi in their Temple on Coruscant, Jedi Master Minas Velti snaps into action. She shields the younglings she had been instructing in meditation exercises and attempts to lead them to safety. However, Velti is soon overwhelmed by the clones, leaving the younglings, including Reva, to fight on their own.

NARI
SPECIES Human
AFFILIATION Jedi

Nari is a Jedi who, despite being on the run, finds it difficult to ignore people in need. When he helps a saloon owner on Mos Eisley, the Grand Inquisitor is able to track him to Tatooine. After barely escaping from the Third Sister, Nari seeks out Obi-Wan Kenobi. Nari hopes Kenobi will be the leader he's looking for, but Obi-Wan insists Nari accept that the Jedi lost. He tells Nari to remain hidden and stash his lightsaber. It's not long until Inquisitors find and kill Nari and hang him in an Anchorhead street to incite fear in the locals.

R3-T2
TYPE R-series astromech droid
AFFILIATION None

R3-T2 is an astromech droid on Tatooine. Over the years, several owners have kept R3 in order, using parts scavenged by Jawas. After Order 66, R3 is on the streets when Inquisitors search for Jedi. Later, R3 is in Mos Eisley when Obi-Wan Kenobi and Luke Skywalker visit a local cantina.

AKKANI
SPECIES Eopie **HOMEWORLD** Tatooine **AFFILIATION** Obi-Wan Kenobi

In exile on Tatooine, Obi-Wan Kenobi cares for an eopie named Akkani that carries him between his home in Anchorhead and his work at a tibidon carving station. The two form a strong connection, with Akkani sensing Kenobi's needs without him saying a word.

TEEKA
SPECIES Jawa **HOMEWORLD** Tatooine
AFFILIATION Jawas

Teeka is a sharp-tongued Jawa scavenger who acquires supplies for Obi-Wan Kenobi during his exile on Tatooine. On one occasion, she brings a toy T-16 skyhopper that Kenobi wishes to gift to Luke Skywalker. While visiting Obi-Wan in his secluded cave, Teeka offers him a variety of items, including a Jedi belt and vaporator parts. Even though Kenobi knows that Teeka's trying to sell him parts that she stole from his own vaporator, he agrees to the purchase. But he does say that she could have at least cleaned the parts first.

GROFF DITCHER
SPECIES Human **HOMEWORLD** Tatooine
AFFILIATION Tibidon station

Groff Ditcher is the foreman of the tibidon carving station where Obi-Wan Kenobi works. His harvesters extract the usable parts of a dead sand whale. Ditcher is quick to use violence to keep his employees in line, and he believes he's superior to everyone around him.

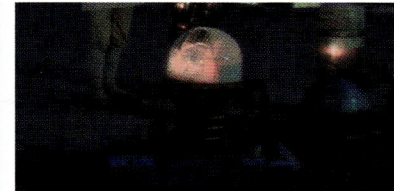

2X-3KPR
SPECIES KPR security droid
HOMEWORLD Tatooine
AFFILIATION Lars homestead

To protect their homestead, Owen and Beru Lars install the security droid 2X-3KPR. Its dome lights up red when the Inquisitor Reva arrives hunting for Luke. Years later, 2X still works for them when they're killed by stormtroopers.

Warning sign Blue sensors turn red with restraining bolt.

Photoreceptor L0-LA59 records what she sees.

Pocket size Both legs can retract.

L0-LA59
SPECIES Toy droid
HOMEWORLD Alderaan
AFFILIATION House Organa

L0-LA59 is Leia Organa's personal droid. As she's small and lightweight, Leia can easily carry her in her pocket. L0-LA59 has two wings that allow her to fly, two legs, and several accessories, including a mini saw. She communicates with beeps.

Leia has L0-LA59 with her when she's kidnapped by the mercenary Vect Nokru, but Nokru breaks the droid apart when he sees her cutting through the ropes binding Leia's wrists. Obi-Wan Kenobi fixes L0-LA59 after he frees Leia. When Leia is taken captive again and brought to Fortress Inquisitorius, Reva puts a tracking device and restraining bolt on the droid that changes her personality. As a result, L0-LA59 seals the hangar door on Jabiim that the Hidden Path needs for its escape, until Leia removes the bolt, restoring L0-LA59's regular demeanor.

Friendly companion
Leia feels a strong attachment to L0-LA59 so when she runs into the woods to escape a family reception, her mother tells her to turn off the droid as a punishment.

AGIRA
SPECIES Imroosian **HOMEWORLD** Alderaan
AFFILIATION House Organa

A young Imroosian, Agira is handmaiden and friend to Princess Leia Organa. The pair plays a trick on Leia's mother by dressing Agira in Leia's royal clothing so Leia can play in the woods instead of attending a diplomatic reception, but their ruse only briefly succeeds.

VECT NOKRU
SPECIES Human
AFFILIATION Black Mask

Vect Nokru leads a mercenary group called Black Mask. He is hired by Reva to abduct Princess Leia Organa. They capture Leia near the Royal Palace on Alderaan and take her to Daiyu. After Obi-Wan Kenobi rescues Leia, Nokru issues a bounty for him at Reva's request.

ALDERAANIAN GUARD
SPECIES Human **HOMEWORLD** Alderaan
AFFILIATION House Organa

Alderaanian guards are responsible for the security of the Royal Houses of Alderaan. They're stationed throughout the Royal Palace and accompany royalty on offworld trips. Alderaanian Guards search for Leia Organa when she runs off to play and is abducted by a mercenary.

CELLY ORGANA
SPECIES Human **HOMEWORLD** Alderaan
AFFILIATION House Organa

Duchess Celly Organa is Breha Organa's sister. She and her husband, Kayo, and their son, Niano, regularly travel from the city of Hallyn to Aldera to attend official receptions and banquets. While in Aldera, Celly tutors Leia in subjects including diplomacy, public speaking, and manners.

KAYO ORGANA
SPECIES Human **HOMEWORLD** Alderaan
AFFILIATION House Organa

Kayo is married to Celly Organa, Breha Organa's sister. Kayo and Celly don't have official roles in the Alderaan government, but they often visit their family in Aldera. Unlike Breha and Bail, Kayo has a favorable opinion of the Empire, in spite of their cruel labor practices. This is because he and his friends are earning profits from the Empire's work.

NIANO ORGANA
SPECIES Human
HOMEWORLD Alderaan
AFFILIATION House Organa

Niano Organa is Leia Organa's smug and insecure cousin. During a banquet at the Aldera Royal Palace, Niano mocks Leia for thanking a service droid because he believes they're a lower life-form. He also revels in telling Leia that she's not a real Organa because she was adopted. Leia responds by shocking Niano, telling him that she knows he's afraid of his own father.

NAX
SPECIES Human **HOMEWORLD** Kamino
AFFILIATION Republic

Daiyu is filled with individuals with no place to go, like the aging former clone trooper "Nax." During the Clone Wars, Nax fights on Teth, Umbara, and Christophsis, but after discharge due to injury, he falls on hard times. Obi-Wan Kenobi gives him a few credits when he sees him on the streets asking for help.

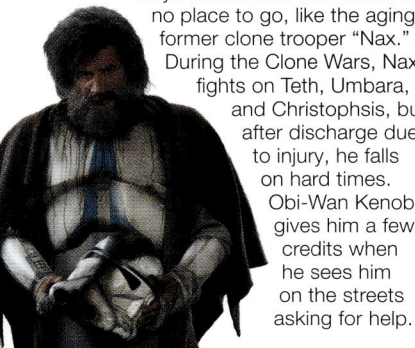

TETHA GRIG
SPECIES Human **AFFILIATION** Slythmonger

Tetha Grig is one of many children on the streets of Daiyu who are separated from their families. To survive, she sells addictive spice. When Obi-Wan Kenobi tells Grig he's looking for his missing daughter, she suggests that if she's lost on Daiyu, Kenobi will never find her.

JAYCO
SPECIES Human **HOMEWORLD** Daiyu
AFFILIATION Haja Estree

Young Jayco works in Haja Estree's crew of con artists. He approaches Obi-Wan Kenobi and Leia Organa on the streets of Daiyu and offers to help. He can take them to a Jedi—for the right price. Jayco later sees the bounty notification for Kenobi and takes it to Estree.

CORRAN
SPECIES Human **HOMEWORLD** Daiyu
AFFILIATION Hidden Path

Corran is a young Force-attuned boy trying to evade the attention of the Empire. His mother pays the Jedi pretender Haja Estree to help them board a transport ship away from Daiyu. Corran and his mother then stay at a Hidden Path safe house on Jabiim until they're able to leave on a transport ship with Obi-Wan Kenobi and Leia Organa.

NYCHE

SPECIES Human **HOMEWORLD** Daiyu
AFFILIATION Hidden Path

Nyche fears for the safety of her son, Corran, when his Force abilities begin to show. She arranges a meeting with a man she believes to be a Jedi to arrange transport to a safe location, away from the Empire. While the Jedi is actually a grifter named Haja Estree, Nyche believes he's strong with the Force and gladly pays him all the credits she has for his help.

TREDGAR VOLK

SPECIES Thuggatoris
AFFILIATION Bounty hunter

Tredgar Volk is one of many bounty hunters who scout for work on the streets of Daiyu. He uses a triple-barrel blaster to pursue Obi-Wan Kenobi for the bounty Reva has put on his head. Volk finds Kenobi and Leia on a rooftop, when Leia is running from Kenobi, afraid he's working with her kidnappers. Volk falls off the roof during a firefight with Kenobi.

Haja's tricks
Jedi pretender Haja uses theatrics as he pretends to play a Jedi mind trick on a port worker to impress one of his customers.

HAJA ESTREE

SPECIES Human **AFFILIATION** Hidden Path

Fake Jedi and self-described liar, Haja Estree has a desire for wealth but ultimately a good heart. On Daiyu, he pretends to be a Jedi while assisting those hiding from the Empire to find transport offworld. Estree's crew includes Jayco, a young boy who recruits clients, and workers from one of Daiyu's local ports. Estree is very fond of dramatics—his office is rigged with magnets and remotes that enable him to mimic Force powers.

After Obi-Wan Kenobi discovers Estree's racket, Haja helps him find the place where Leia is being held captive, and he later shoots a droid who's hunting the duo. He gives Kenobi coordinates to a place on Mapuzo where he can connect with the Hidden Path. After helping Kenobi, Estree finds himself on the run, and he reunites with Kenobi and Leia on Jabiim. Even though Estree isn't honest, Kenobi sees the good in him and he trusts Haja to protect Leia in his absence.

Looking the part
Hooded Jedi-style robes help to sell Haja's con.

Carbon-cotton belt
Haja hides magnets throughout his outfit.

FOURTH SISTER

SPECIES Nogratu **HOMEWORLD** Ehosiq sector
AFFILIATION Jedi, Inquisitorius

Formerly a Jedi named Lyn Raskish, Fourth Sister works alongside the Grand Inquisitor, Third Sister, and Fifth Brother to hunt Jedi across the galaxy. Fourth Sister is among the Inquisitors who hunt Obi-Wan Kenobi on Daiyu after the abduction of Princess Leia Organa. The Fourth Sister has blood-red eyes, yellow skin, and small tentacles. Like most Inquisitors, she wields a double-bladed lightsaber that has the ability to spin. She often teams with Barriss Offee until Offee rejects the Inquisitorius. Encountering Offee years later, the Fourth Sister questions her allegiance to the Empire.

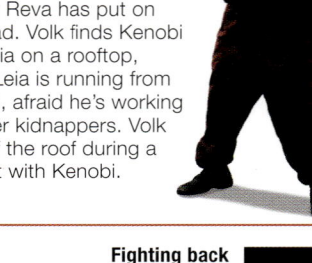

Fighting back
NED-B fires on Reva and stormtroopers who are trying to breach the Hidden Path's secret base on Jabiim.

NED-B

TYPE E-B load lifter
AFFILIATION Hidden Path

The Hidden Path has many operatives who help smuggle Force-attuned individuals to safety. NED-B is a loader droid whose hardiness and determination make him a valuable Path operative. Working with undercover ally Tala Durith, NED-B crosses paths with Obi-Wan Kenobi and Leia Organa when Durith brings them to a Path safe house on Mapuzo. NED-B stays in the droid maintenance shed that protects the safe house, ready to take down any stormtroopers who attempt to breach the door.

When Kenobi is gravely injured after facing Darth Vader on Mapuzo, NED-B carries him to safety. His strength is also used on Jabiim when he works with Path refugees to block off as many entrances as possible to keep back Imperial stormtroopers. In the tunnels of Jabiim, NED-B covers Durith's body after she's shot by their pursuers. He stays close to Durith, under heavy fire, as she triggers a thermal detonator that they hope will eliminate the enemy and be a successful last act of rebellion.

TALA DURITH

SPECIES Human
AFFILIATION Empire, Hidden Path

Imperial officer Tala Durith is secretly working for the Hidden Path—a group that smuggles Force-attuned individuals to safety. Durith realizes she made a mistake joining the Empire when she witnesses the assassination of Force-attuned people on Garel. Nevertheless, she remains hopeful, even during the most dire circumstances, and she believes that the Path is a way to make the galaxy safer for everyone.

After being contacted by Haja Estree, Durith saves Obi-Wan Kenobi and Leia Organa from stormtroopers on Mapuzo. When Reva abducts Leia, Durith finds a way for Kenobi to rescue her from Fortress Inquisitorius. Tala is quick at thinking on her feet when problems arise, but she's even quicker with a blaster.

"We have safe houses like this throughout the galaxy." **TALA DURITH**

Self-sacrifice
On Jabiim, Durith fires at stormtroopers to protect Path refugees. After she's wounded and NED-B is defeated, she triggers a thermal detonator to take out as many stormtroopers as she can to protect the rest of the refugees. This brave act costs Tala her life.

BLUEVEV GLIDER
HOMEWORLD Various
SIZE 1.8 m (5 ft 11 in) long
HABITAT Oceans

Bluevev gliders can be found in the oceans of Corellia and on the moon Nur. Despite their large size and poisonous barbs, bluevev gliders are popular targets for Corellian anglers. They can be dangerous to humans, but only if provoked. Obi-Wan Kenobi passes a bluevev glider as he infiltrates Fortress Inquisitorius on Nur through an underwater entry port.

FRECK
SPECIES Condluran
HOMEWORLD Mapuzo
AFFILIATION Empire

Freck is a transport driver for the Empire on the mining colony on Mapuzo. Freck enjoys working for the Empire and the order they bring to the galaxy. He picks up Obi-Wan Kenobi and Leia Organa and starts driving them to the nearest port. They tell him they're father and daughter who have become lost during their trip. When they reach an Imperial checkpoint, Freck suggests stormtroopers look into their story shortly before Kenobi knocks him out.

WADE RESSELIAN
SPECIES Human
AFFILIATION Hidden Path

Hidden Path member Wade Resselian doesn't have any combat experience, but he volunteers to pilot a T-47 airspeeder during the rescue of Princess Leia Organa from Fortress Inquisitorius. While Leia, Obi-Wan Kenobi, and Tala Durith evacuate from the Fortress, Resselian concentrates his fire on the Inquisitor Third Sister. Reva retaliates by pushing an explosive toward Resselian which destroys his ship and kills him.

TEEGA KRYELLE
SPECIES Human
AFFILIATION The Hidden Path

As a partisan fighter for the Hidden Path, Teega Kryelle puts her life on the line to protect Force-attuned refugees and their families. She is stationed on Jabiim, working with Path leader Kawlan Roken, when Obi-Wan Kenobi and Leia Organa arrive. Kryelle and her fellow Path soldiers fight back against Imperial stormtroopers until the refugees are able to board a transport offworld.

SULLY STARK
SPECIES Human
AFFILIATION Hidden Path

Sully Stark is a pilot and operative with the Hidden Path. She and Wade Resselian pilot T-47 airspeeders during a mission to extract Leia Organa from Fortress Inquisitorius. At first, Stark is resistant to the idea of this mission, as she believes the Fortress to be impenetrable, but she successfully brings Leia, Obi-Wan Kenobi, and Tala Durith back to Jabiim. Stark is distraught when her fellow pilot Wade dies at the Fortress, but she rallies to help all the refugees on Jabiim escape the grasp of Darth Vader and his Imperial stormtroopers.

PURGE TROOPER
SPECIES Human **HOMEWORLD** Various
AFFILIATION Empire, Inquisitorius

The Inquisitorius use purge troopers to help search for and capture Jedi hiding throughout the galaxy. Only the most talented clone troopers—and later stormtroopers—are hand-picked to join this secretive and elite unit, which is based in Fortress Inquisitorius. Dressed in black armor, purge troopers regularly accompany Inquisitors as they track Jedi. Cal Kestis encounters several purge troopers in his missions with the *Mantis* crew, and Obi-Wan Kenobi battles purge troopers when he rescues Leia Organa from Fortress Inquisitorius.

KAWLAN ROKEN
SPECIES Human **AFFILIATION** Hidden Path

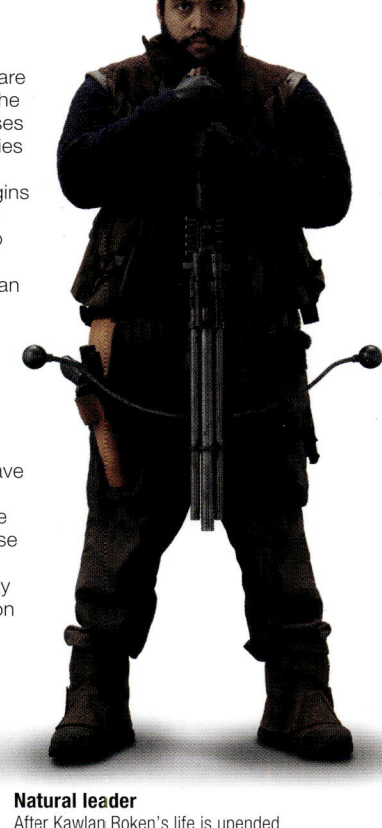

Determined to make the galaxy safer for those who are attuned to the Force, Kawlan Roken leads a cell of the Hidden Path—an underground network of safe houses that assists Force-attuned individuals and their families to create new identities away from the eyes of the Empire. Roken's involvement in the Hidden Path begins after he loses his Force-attuned wife to an Inquisitor. Now he works with operatives such as Tala Durith to hide as many refugees as possible.

At first, Roken is upset when Durith brings Obi-Wan Kenobi to Jabiim because his presence there puts the safety of many at risk. However, Roken also understands that helping break Leia out of Imperial custody is essential because she knows their secret location. He offers his support to Kenobi's daring rescue, but after Leia has returned, Roken tells Obi-Wan that his focus must be on the dozens of refugees who have been waiting for months to leave Jabiim and start their new lives.

Roken is able to remain calm and thoughtful in the most stressful of circumstances, and this allows those around him to remain hopeful. When Kenobi leaves Roken's transport ship, he tells Roken that the galaxy needs more leaders like him to survive the oppression of the Empire.

Natural leader
After Kawlan Roken's life is upended by the Empire who killed his wife, he throws himself into the Hidden Path. He works with Obi-Wan Kenobi to find a way to save refugees on Jabiim during an Imperial attack.

KHEL TANNA
SPECIES Human
AFFILIATION Bounty hunter

A bounty hunter who works for Jabba the Hutt, Khel Tanna has hated Han Solo ever since he nearly stranded her crew on Galator III. Along with her ship, the *Enigma Catalyst*, she's captured by the Marshal. Later, Tanna works with T'onga to find Boba Fett and help Beilert Valance, whose mind is failing.

MARSHAL BUCK VANCTO
SPECIES Surpossian
AFFILIATION Benelex Marshal Service

Marshal Buck Vancto, often referred to as simply "the Marshal," is a motivated MarsCorpo enforcement officer who works hard for the Benelex Marshal Service. Skilled and deadly, the Marshal is tasked with hunting down Han Solo.

CORBUS TYRA
SPECIES Human
AFFILIATION Bounty hunter

A seasoned bounty hunter, Corbus Tyra poses as Han Solo's estranged father, Ovan, in order to get close to the smuggler. He has lost an eye due to his colorful past adventures. He is a powerful threat and adversary to both Solo and his copilot, Chewbacca.

PHAEDRA
SPECIES Wroonian
AFFILIATION Criminal

Phaedra is a criminal who is put into captivity on the prison planet of Gulhadar. While there, she meets Chewbacca and Maz Kanata and breaks them out of prison. Phaedra then helps Chewbacca and Han Solo recover a valuable urn, which is in fact the neural core of Ajax Sigma, from Grand Moff Tarkin.

BODE AKUNA
SPECIES Human **AFFILIATION** Jedi, Empire

Jedi Knight Bode Akuna goes into hiding after Order 66, using survival skills from his days as an agent with Republic Intelligence. He marries and has a daughter, Kata, but then Inquisitors kill his wife, Tayala Akuna. Desperate to protect his daughter from the Empire, Akuna agrees to work for the ISB in exchange for her safety. He goes undercover, posing as a gunslinging mercenary against the Empire in order to get close to the Jedi Cal Kestis and his crew.

Akuna uses twin blasters and a jetpack to get in and out of dangerous locations quickly. Akuna and Kestis grow close, and Akuna tries to convince Kestis to travel to the hidden planet Tanalorr, hoping it can be a safe haven for his daughter. However, Akuna turns against Kestis when the Jedi insists the secret location should be shared with the Hidden Path. Akuna reveals the location of Cere Junda's Jedi Archive on Jedha to the Empire and later dies in a lightsaber battle with Cal Kestis.

ZN-A4
TYPE Protocol droid

ZN-A4 is a cheerful and somewhat clumsy protocol droid who works with Jedi scientist Santari Khri on Koboh during the High Republic era. She's tasked with a mission to recover the knowledge of how to reach the mysterious planet Tanalorr, but falling debris traps her underground. Years later, Cal Kestis finds the droid and reactivates her. ZN-A4 entrusts Cal to complete her mission and finds a new home at the Pyloon Saloon. Cal again comes to ZN-A4's rescue when Dagan Gera abducts her, hoping to get information about the location of Tanalorr. Later, ZN-A4 helps the *Mantis* crew navigate the Koboh Abyss and reach Tanalorr.

DAGAN GERA
SPECIES Arkanian offshoot
AFFILIATION Jedi, Bedlam Raiders

Jedi Knight Dagan Gera feels an intense drive to explore the galaxy. During the High Republic era, he discovers a planet hidden in the Koboh Abyss nebula. He names it Tanalorr and builds a Jedi temple there. After an attack by Nihil marauders, Gera is enraged with the Jedi Council's decision to abandon the planet. He turns to the dark side and attacks his fellow Jedi. His former friend Santari Khri cuts off his arm to stop him, rendering him unconscious, and then places him in a bacta tank. After centuries in stasis, Gera delights in the news that the Jedi Order has fallen. He bleeds his kyber crystal and returns to his obsession—Tanalorr.

RAYVIS
SPECIES Gen'Dai
AFFILIATION Bedlam Raiders

A warrior with a loud and boisterous laugh, Rayvis leads the Bedlam Raiders criminal gang. Thanks to heavy armor and his Gen'Dai body, which can regenerate, Rayvis is a deadly threat. During the High Republic era, Rayvis kills several Jedi and swears allegiance to Dagan Gera after being bested in combat. After hundreds of years of imprisonment by the Jedi, Rayvis escapes after Order 66. During the Imperial era, he and his raiders cross paths with the Jedi Cal Kestis. When Cal defeats Rayvis in lightsaber combat, Cal gives him an honorable warrior's death.

SANTARI KHRI
SPECIES Human
AFFILIATION Jedi

Jedi scientist Santari Khri travels to the Outer Rim planet Koboh to study the mysterious purple-colored element that permeates the Koboh Abyss nebula. Known as a meticulous and thorough researcher, Khri leads a group made up of both Jedi and Republic team members. After one Jedi on her team, Dagan Gera, navigates the Koboh Abyss and discovers the planet Tanalorr, Khri builds a compass that allows others to travel safely through the dangerous nebula. When Gera later turns against the Jedi, Khri cuts off one of Gera's arms in an attempt to stop him. She leaves Koboh after an Emergence from the Great Disaster hits a Koboh moon, threatening the planet.

KATA AKUNA
SPECIES Human
HOMEWORLD Birren
AFFILIATION Akuna family, *Mantis* crew

When Kata Akuna was young, Inquisitors killed her mother, Tayala Akuna, while searching for her Jedi father, Bode Akuna. Kata grows up on Nova Garon, spending much of her time alone with her doll, Mookie. While Bode works for the ISB in exchange for Kata's safety, she is held in Imperial custody. After Bode's death at the hands of the Jedi Cal Kestis, Kata joins the *Mantis* crew. On Koboh, she enjoys cooking with Greez and gardening with Pili Walde.

DOMA DENDRA
SPECIES Waluna **HOMEWORLD** Koboh
AFFILIATION Dendra's Antiquities

An unofficial mayor of Rambler's Reach Outpost on Koboh, Doma Dendra spends her time watching over the locals, though her main job is running her shop, Dendra's Antiquities. Doma knows that the only way a small community on the frontier can survive is by sticking together, so she takes an instant liking to Cal Kestis when she sees him defend Koboh-local Turgle from the Bedlam Raiders.

PYLOON'S SALOON REGULARS
SPECIES Multiple
HOMEWORLD Koboh
AFFILIATION Rambler's Reach

After he leaves the *Mantis* crew, Greez Dritus purchases a cantina on the Outer Rim planet Koboh, naming it Pyloon's Saloon. A number of oddballs and rogues inhabit the cantina, including the dramatic and haphazard Turgle; Bhima Ook and Tulli Mu, who run a holotactics table upstairs; botanist Pili Walde, who sets up a garden on the saloon's roof; and the refugee Tulakt, who reads fortunes for a price.

A motley bunch
In their own ways, Turgle, Bhima Ook, Tulli Mu, Pili Walde, and Tulakt *(left to right)* form relationships with the Jedi Knight Cal Kestis.

CASSIAN ANDOR

SPECIES Human **HOMEWORLD** Kenari
AFFILIATION Rebel Alliance

At first, Cassian Andor has no interest in taking a stand against the Empire, but he is drawn into the rebellion. Ultimately, he leaves an indelible mark on the galaxy by helping to expose a flaw in the Death Star.

PATH TO REBELLION

As a child during the final years of the Republic, Cassian survives the rampant commercial scouring of his homeworld Kenari, which poisons the planet and leaves only children to survive. Well-meaning strangers scavenging on Kenari, Maarva Andor and her husband Clem, take Cassian back to their home on Ferrix and adopt him, unknowingly separating the young boy from his sister. Searching for her years later leads Cassian to cross paths with Luthen Rael, an undercover rebel agent. He recruits Cassian for the rebel cause, making him part of a heist on Aldhani that deals a noticeable blow to the Empire. In reality, Cassian joins the mission out of a desperate need to keep himself and his loved ones on Ferrix safe, rather than from any altruistic concern for the rebels' cause.

Andor tries to leave his cares behind and enjoy his share of the stolen credits, but he cannot escape the Empire's oppression. Imperials arrest him for an alleged minor infraction on Niamos and sentence Cassian to a long imprisonment on Narkina 5. There, Cassian experiences the Empire's crushing grip and leads a revolt. Upon returning home to Ferrix for his mother's funeral and seeing the clash with Imperial occupiers that ensues, Cassian realizes he must take a stand. He goes on to become an agent for the Rebel Alliance. Later, Andor captures the Imperial security droid K-2SO and reprograms him. The two are henceforth constant companions and go on many missions together. In his role as Intelligence officer, Andor has used many different aliases.

DANGEROUS MISSION

During one mission to the Ring of Kafrene, Cassian learns from an informant that Imperial scientist Galen Erso sent his old friend (and ostracized rebel) Saw Gerrera information about the Empire's new planet-killing superweapon. Cassian, along with K-2SO, is assigned to accompany Galen's daughter, Jyn, to Jedha to find Saw. During a skirmish in the Holy City they meet locals Baze Malbus and Chirrut Îmwe, before they are all captured by Saw's troops. Cassian encounters Imperial defector Bodhi Rook in Gerrera's jail while Saw gives Jyn her father's message, which reveals a ruinous flaw in the Death Star. Realizing word of the fearsome battle station has leaked, the Imperials use its destructive power to eradicate the Holy City. Cassian, Jyn, and their new friends barely escape with their lives.

They all travel to Eadu, where Cassian has been given a secret directive to assassinate Galen Erso. His conscience prevents him from following through, though Galen is soon killed in a rebel bombing raid.

> "Rebellions are built on hope."
> — CASSIAN ANDOR

Aldhani Heist
Led by Vel Sartha, the small team on Aldhani rigorously prepares for the dangerous mission to steal the Imperial's payroll for an entire sector.

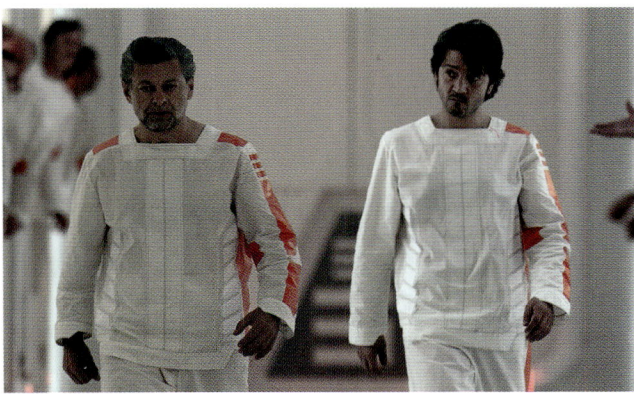

A bleak existence
Shift after shift, Cassian, going by the name Keef, works tirelessly in the prison complex. However, he formulates an escape plan and persuades leader Kino Loy to help.

ULTIMATE SACRIFICE

Cassian and his team return to Yavin 4 and, against orders, assemble a squad to steal the Death Star plans on Scarif. Once they arrive, Cassian, Jyn, and K-2SO pose as Imperials to reach the data vault. There they acquire the plans but must transmit them to the rebel fleet from atop a communications tower. As they climb, Cassian is wounded. Jyn continues alone, but upon reaching the top is trapped by Director Orson Krennic. Cassian, not willing to give up at this vital moment, appears just in time to shoot him, allowing Jyn to successfully send the plans to the rebels. As they do, the Death Star fires on Scarif. Cassian and Jyn die heroes in each other's arms.

Undercover issues
Cassian and Jyn must overcome their mutual trust issues to work well together. The atmosphere between them when they arrive on Jedha is decidedly frosty.

CHARACTERS AND CREATURES

VERLO SKIFF
SPECIES Human **HOMEWORLD** Morlana One
AFFILIATION Preox-Morlana

Sentry corporal Verlo Skiff never leaves his work attitude behind, even when he's off duty and visiting a brothel in Morlana One's Leisure Zone. This means he eyes everyone with suspicion and is always on the look out for offworlders he can manipulate for credits. When Verlo does this with Cassian Andor, he makes a mistake: Cassian puts up a fight and ends up accidentally killing Verlo.

KRAVAS DREZZER
SPECIES Human
HOMEWORLD Morlana Four
AFFILIATION Preox-Morlana

A former squad commander on Morlana Four, Kravas Drezzer is demoted to sentry corporal on Morlana One. When off duty, he frequents the planet's Leisure Zone, where he harasses and extorts people. When he tries this with Cassian Andor, Cassian kills him with his own blaster.

B2EMO
MANUFACTURER Cybot Galactica **TYPE** Salvage assist unit **AFFILIATION** Andor family

B2EMO, also known as Beetwo or Bee, is a longtime companion of the Andor family. He specializes in salvage work and has tools for stripping and towing scrap. Bee accompanies Maarva and Clem Andor as they travel the galaxy in their hauler and helps them explore crashed and discarded starships for prime material to bring back to Ferrix's salvage yards.

Once the latest in groundmech salvage technology, Bee now moves more slowly than he used to and has to spend hours docked in his charging station. But that doesn't mean he's any less mindful of Maarva and her often absent adopted son, Cassian. The faithful droid always looks after his family, whether that's drawing on his limited power reserves to tell a lie for Cassian or to make sure that Maarva is taking care of herself.

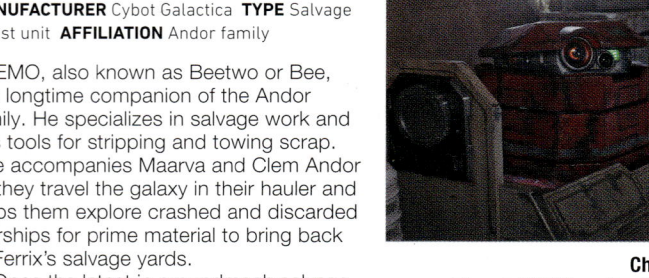

Charging station
Although B2EMO would rather be involved in whatever's going on, to stay operational, he must spend long periods of time charging.

Aging droid
Chipping paint shows that B2EMO has seen better days.

Extendable body
B2EMO uses this feature to adjust his height.

KERRI
SPECIES Human **HOMEWORLD** Kenari
AFFILIATION Kenari orphan tribe

Kerri is Cassian Andor's little sister. She and Cassian, then known as Kassa, grow up together on Kenari in a tribe of orphaned children. They share a tent in the jungle, and Kerri stays by his side as much as she can, looking up to her older brother as her protector. After spotting a crashing starship, Kerri tries to tag along with him and the other older children on an expedition to investigate it. She reluctantly stays behind, and it's the last time Kerri sees her brother, despite his desperate attempts to find her. Cassian's troubles start when he follows a lead about his sister on Morlana One.

BRASSO
SPECIES Human **HOMEWORLD** Ferrix
AFFILIATION Grappler

Brasso makes an honest living as a grappler in the salvage yard on Ferrix. While it's an average job for a citizen of Ferrix, Brasso isn't an average citizen. He's fiercely loyal to his friends: Brasso lies on Cassian Andor's behalf, and while Cassian's away, he takes care of his friend's mother, Maarva, and her droid B2EMO. He protects those he cares about and extends the same devotion to Ferrix itself. He takes Maarva's posthumous speech to heart and, in her funeral procession, uses her funeral brick to fight the Imperials occupying the town.

SYRIL KARN
SPECIES Human **HOMEWORLD** Coruscant
AFFILIATION Preox-Morlana, Bureau of Standards

Fervent when it comes to matters of the law, Syril Karn follows rules meticulously and can't ignore details in the service of the bigger picture. A deputy inspector for Preox-Morlana, Syril takes his duties on Morlana One seriously—partly because it is right, but more because of potential personal gain. However, his attempt to rise in Pre-Mor's ranks ends when he pushes too hard to investigate two suspicious deaths. His actions bring about the end of Pre-Mor's rule and permanent Imperial authority for the Morlana system. Stripped of his title, Syril returns to Coruscant and gets a position in the Bureau of Standards, thanks solely to his family connections. Still eager to make his name, this time with the Empire, Syril continues a dogged obsession with Cassian Andor and tries to impress ISB supervisor Dedra Meero with his knowledge.

> "Can one ever be too aggressive in preserving order?"
> — SYRIL KARN

Plan gone awry
Syril Karn can only look on in shock as his plan to prove himself to his superiors by apprehending a murderer on Ferrix goes terribly wrong.

HYNE
SPECIES Human **HOMEWORLD** Morlana One
AFFILIATION Preox-Morlana

Chief Inspector Hyne enjoys a life of relative ease thanks to his position with the Pre-Mor Security Inspection team. He keeps the Empire's eyes off the corporation until his quiet existence is disrupted by Syril Karn's investigation, which leaves the chief inspector jobless.

TIMM KARLO
SPECIES Human **HOMEWORLD** Ferrix
AFFILIATION Caleen Salyard

Timm Karlo runs Caleen Salyard with Bix Caleen, who he's also involved with romantically. As floor manager, he keeps track of inventory and matches pieces with buyers. Believing Bix is keeping secrets, he follows her until the moment she's apprehended by stormtroopers.

VETCH

SPECIES Urodel
HOMEWORLD Ferrix

Tall and stocky, the Urodel named Vetch can intimidate anyone simply by looming over them, though his appearance belies his normally gentle and friendly nature. He occasionally works for the spare parts vendor Nurchi on Ferrix, and on one particular occasion, helps to corner Cassian Andor, who owes the junk dealer money.

SALMAN PAAK

SPECIES Human **HOMEWORLD** Ferrix
AFFILIATION Repaak Salyard

Salman Paak lives on Ferrix with his son, Wilmon, and operates the Repaak Salyard. While many of Ferrix's salyards have similar scrap, Salman's offers something extra to those looking to send messages about available Imperial equipment. He runs a secret fractal radio in the back of the yard, accessible only to those with the code phrase. Salman looks out for his fellow Ferrixians and starts the town's alarm when Pre-Mor Tac-Corpos come searching for Cassian Andor. He keeps his secrets close but is no match for ISB torturers looking for information about the comms unit and the rebel agent who answers dispatches.

TIME GRAPPLER

SPECIES Human
HOMEWORLD Ferrix
AFFILIATION Grappler

Ferrix's Time Grappler takes his duties seriously. He climbs the bell tower's steps daily to mark the day's progress using two hammers and a salvaged beskar gong. He sends the sound reverberating across the city square and into the salvage yards so the citizens of Ferrix can track their working hours. The Time Grappler takes pride in his methodical and consistent task, perfecting his form and patterns over the years. He treats his instruments with utmost respect, keeping them in immaculate condition, ready for the daily ritual of timekeeping.

BIX CALEEN

SPECIES Human **HOMEWORLD** Ferrix
AFFILIATION Caleen Salyard

Bix Caleen is the proprietor of the Caleen Salyard on Ferrix, which she runs with her partner Timm Karlo. Hardworking and shrewd, Bix focuses her business on technology such as refurbished ion conversion nodes, but she also establishes an avenue to sell unlicensed salvage, like discarded Imperial items. Through a hidden junction box in Salman Paak's salyard, Bix contacts Luthen Rael, who pays for valuable items without asking questions about their origins. This is Bix's introduction to the rebellion. She continues to take the risk the contact brings, heightening it by reaching out to Rael on behalf of Cassian Andor. When Cassian's actions bring Preox-Morlana's Tac-Corpos troopers to Ferrix, Timm betrays Bix. Things escalate when Imperials occupy the town and learn about Bix's covert activities. The ISB interrogates and tortures her, but Cassian helps her escape Ferrix.

Imperial capture
Bix Caleen tries to evade the Imperial forces on Ferrix who are looking for rebel sympathizers, but she is quickly identified outside the Repaak Salyard and taken in for questioning.

> "I wouldn't worry. She's tougher than both of us."
> — **CASSIAN ANDOR**

Contact with rebels
Few know about the secret communicator in the back of Repaak Salyard that's accessed via a ladder. Bix uses the device to inform a mysterious buyer about salvaged Imperial technology available for sale.

WILMON PAAK

SPECIES Human **HOMEWORLD** Ferrix
AFFILIATION Repaak Salyard

Like many on Ferrix, Wilmon Paak grows up working in salvage, specifically with his father at Repaak Salyard. Though only 16 years old, Wilmon has a strong distaste for the Empire, which increases after they detain and kill his father. His anger leads him to riot at Maarva Andor's funeral.

Safety first
Bix wears a welding helmet while salvaging scrap.

Always prepared
Bix carries a cutter and the multipurpose tools of a scrapper.

MAARVA CARASSI ANDOR

SPECIES Human
HOMEWORLD Ferrix
AFFILIATION Daughters of Ferrix

Brave and stubborn, Maarva Carassi Andor sparks a rebellion on Ferrix with a posthumous speech that encourages Ferrixians to stop sleeping and wake up to see the truth of the Empire. Maarva is a Ferrixian with a deep connection to her homeworld, where she builds a tight-knit community during her decades on the planet. Maarva and her husband, Clem, scavenge for tech around the galaxy with their droid B2EMO and bring it back to Ferrix's salvage yards. They also adopt a young orphan whom they named Cassian. Maarva sees much change and loss over the years. She watches Imperial forces come to Ferrix, leave, and return.

As a onetime president of the social club named the Daughters of Ferrix, Maarva tends to focus on her neighbors more than herself, but B2EMO and her family friends do their best to take care of her when Cassian is away. Her independent and rebellious spirit carry Maarva through her illness and final days, and she resists Imperial occupation until the very end. Maarva leaves a recorded message for B2EMO to play during her funeral procession. Her hologram's call to action prompts a riot as Ferrixians fight back.

CHARACTERS AND CREATURES

LUTHEN RAEL
SPECIES Human
AFFILIATION Axis network

Luthen Rael is an enigma whose past is clouded in mystery. When the Galactic Empire seizes control of the government on Coruscant, his life takes an irreversible turn: rebellion. In the ensuing years, Rael builds a network of spies, double agents, and fighters. He orchestrates rebel activity from the shadows, preferring to remain unseen, and will cooperate with whoever can best accomplish his objectives. Over time, Luthen's network cuts the Empire with wounds both shallow and deep. As Rael grows his connections, he designs operations that will heavily impact the Empire, such as the Aldhani heist. While Luthen is not as extreme as Saw Gerrera's partisans, he believes Senator Mon Mothma's softer tactics and desire to keep her hands clean to be ineffective. He makes decisions rooted in data and strategy, not humanity, though his analytical approach sometimes takes a back seat in favor of impulsive conclusions. Rael will sacrifice anything and anyone in the name of the cause.

Operating the "Axis" network of rebels (as the Imperial Security Bureau (ISB) calls it) is only one facet of Luthen's life. His public identity is that of an eccentric collector who peddles galactic antiquities and objects of interest in a gallery near Coruscant's Imperial District. As an aesthete, the only expectations on Luthen relate to his ability to procure artifacts and share their histories with customers. Luthen embraces this guise with theatrical flair. His gallery caters to a wealthy clientele, in front of whom Luthen and his trusted partner in rebellion, Kleya Marki, wear carefully cultivated masks. His gallery is also useful for clandestine meetings with contacts, such as Mothma.

To maintain his disparate identities, Rael compartmentalizes his mind. He even builds his dual purposes into his ship, a Fondor haulcraft, so its traditional exterior hides numerous custom modifications.

Playing the part
When meeting with rebels in his gallery, Luthen is usually careful to maintain a cheerful mask. Sometimes it slips, as when Senator Mothma shares negative news about the state of their rebellion and its finances.

Hidden weapon
Luthen's retractable cane conceals a blade.

Custom ship
Luthen sits in the cockpit of his Fondor haulcraft—a ship with many concealed modifications for evading enemies and escaping sticky situations.

DEDRA MEERO
SPECIES Human
AFFILIATION Empire

Security access
Dedra's code cylinders grant her access to secure areas.

Model Imperial
Dedra's uniform is always pristine and perfectly pressed.

Lieutenant Supervisor Dedra Meero forges a successful career in the Imperial Security Bureau. She attains her rank in just over a year of service and doesn't let others' judgments about her lack of experience deter her from her goals. Dedra wears her allegiance to the Empire on her sleeve and it drives all her ambitions. Since she's relatively new to the ISB, time has not jaded her into complacency, as it has with some of her peers. Dedra enacts her work with fervor, applying methodical analysis to every report and modicum of data. She wields intelligence like a weapon, using it to carve a path to the truth. Her ability to see the galaxy on a macro scale impresses her superior, Major Lio Partagaz, who appreciates her drive.

> "The very worst thing you can do right now is bore me."
> — **DEDRA MEERO**

Meero advances her career prospects by rooting out the rebel spy that the ISB calls Axis. She connects seemingly unrelated thefts of Imperial technology, starting with a stolen N-S9 Starpath unit, and acts of insurgency against the Empire and finds a pattern. Dedra acts on her hypothesis about the Axis network, including information that Syril Karn provides her about Cassian Andor's involvement, and in doing so, she receives reassignment to Ferrix. Her aggressive pursuit of the connections to Axis leads her to close associates of Cassian, including Bix Caleen and Salman Paak.

On Ferrix, Meero flexes her interrogation tactics: calm, blunt, and almost sympathetic. She encourages her subjects to divulge what they know before aggressive methods become necessary.

Dedra Meero believes in the Empire and is sure that her actions are right and are for the good of the galaxy. The intensity with which she throws herself into her investigations and quashing rebel activity permits no one to stand between her and her objectives or her ascent in the ISB.

Cornered
Syril Karn keeps inserting himself into Dedra's life. She doesn't appreciate it when he waits for her to arrive at the ISB Central Office. Dedra warns him to leave her alone.

Fight on Ferrix
The Ferrixians' revolt after Maarva Andor's funeral takes the Empire by surprise. Dedra, though unaccustomed to this style of combat, joins the ground forces in trying to stop the rebels.

CLEM ANDOR
SPECIES Human **HOMEWORLD** Ferrix
AFFILIATION Andor family

Clem Andor builds a life on his homeworld of Ferrix with his wife, Maarva. He travels the galaxy with her to scavenge tech from unclaimed wreckage. Once they bring home their hauls to Ferrix, Clem applies his skills as a mechanic to refurbish the machinery back to near-new condition and then sells it in the local salyards. During one such salvage trip, Clem and Maarva find and adopt a young orphan on Kenari and name him Cassian. Years later, when Imperial clone troopers attempt to establish a presence on Ferrix, Clem tries to calm local protesters. The incident escalates and the Empire catches Clem in its net, resulting in his death.

BLEVIN
SPECIES Human **AFFILIATION** Empire

Lieutenant Supervisor Blevin performs his duties with a by-the-manual approach, whether he's reviewing data or collecting intel from Mon Mothma's ISB-appointed chauffeur. He relies on Imperial rules and regulations to do the bare minimum and doesn't use any initiative or put in extra effort. The number of sectors he oversees increases when Preox-Morlana's authority over their corporate sector ends, and control of it transfers to the Empire. Ferrix falls under Blevin's jurisdiction, and he sets up headquarters in a former hotel on Rix Road. Although he does report on unusual activity, he fails to see the bigger picture. Blevin also resents Supervisor Dedra Meero for infringing upon matters under his purview and for having the temerity to rise beyond his own ambition.

LAGRET
SPECIES Human
AFFILIATION Empire

A supervisor for the Imperial Security Bureau, Captain Lagret strives to execute his role to the satisfaction of his exacting superiors, including Major Partagaz. However, Lagret does not manage his duties sufficiently. While he does attend the many briefings that his role requires, he takes his time with memorandums and reports, and he has a habit of blaming others for the delays. Partagaz doesn't accept excuses and makes an example of Lagret in front of his peers before reassigning a memorandum of his about Arvala-6 to someone else.

LONNI JUNG
SPECIES Human
AFFILIATION Empire, Rebels

For several years, Lonni Jung works his way up through the ranks of the ISB, gaining the rank of lieutenant and the position of supervisor. Jung gives every appearance of dedication to the Empire and his superiors, but he is actually a double agent working with Luthen Rael. He feeds intelligence to Rael, but Jung's deep undercover status means that long stretches of time can pass between their meetings. The pressure of maintaining this pretense, which only increases after the birth of his daughter, weighs on Jung. He also struggles with some of Luthen's decisions and his willingness to sacrifice anyone for the cause.

LIO PARTAGAZ
SPECIES Human
AFFILIATION Empire

A meticulous major in the Imperial Security Bureau, Lio Partagaz holds his reports to very high standards. A staunch believer in the Galactic Empire as a bastion of order and safety in the galaxy, Partagaz will do whatever's required to uphold and protect the organization. He views the ISB as being like a healthcare provider that treats any sicknesses that threaten the Empire, whether they're from within or without. Partagaz believes even the most minute detail can make all the difference, so he does not accept vagueness from his subordinates. While he conforms to traditional ISB processes, he's open to unconventional methodologies and hearing offbeat theories, provided that the presenter has supporting data.

VEL SARTHA
SPECIES Human **HOMEWORLD** Chandrila
AFFILIATION Axis network

Vel Sartha grew up in a wealthy family on Chandrila, but a continued life of luxury holds no appeal for her—not when the Empire looms large over the galaxy. She maintains the persona of a spoiled rich girl when needed, but Vel is really a rebel operative. Coming from privilege means she has an innate sense of confidence—not many have told her "no"—and she uses it to lead missions.

In the pivotal rebel operation to infiltrate and steal from the Empire on Aldhani, Vel guides her team with a no-nonsense attitude, despite the pressure Luthen Rael places on her. Stern and focused, she runs her team through repeated drills during their time on Aldhani and adapts quickly when Luthen drops Clem (Cassian Andor) into the group at the last minute. Though committed to fighting the Empire, Vel still values her personal relationships with her cousin, Mon Mothma, and her girlfriend, Cinta Kaz.

Hidden rebel
Vel wears an Aldhani-style jacket to blend in.

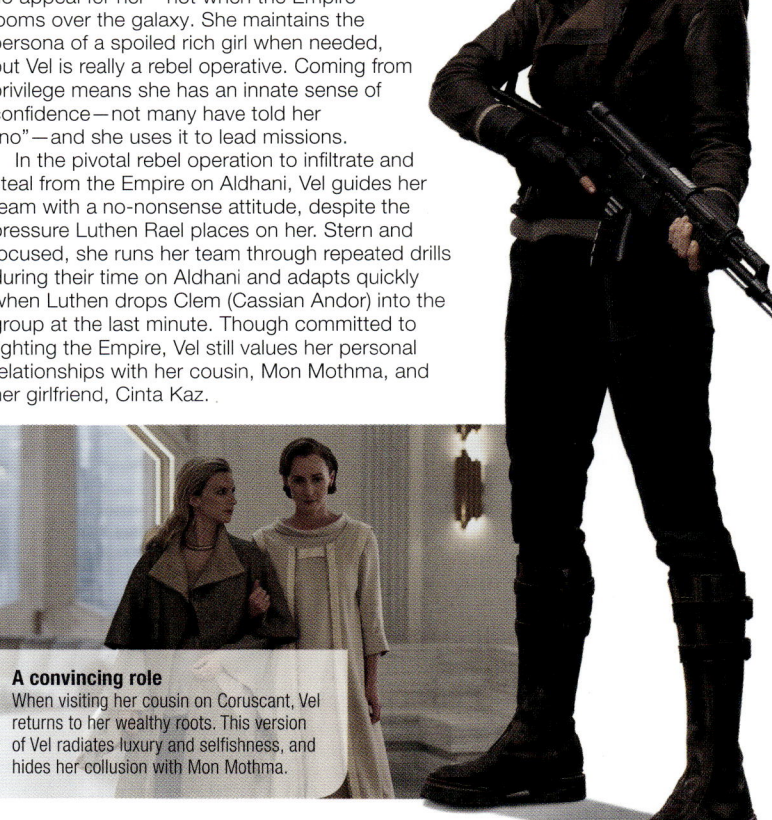

A convincing role
When visiting her cousin on Coruscant, Vel returns to her wealthy roots. This version of Vel radiates luxury and selfishness, and hides her collusion with Mon Mothma.

HEERT
SPECIES Human
AFFILIATION Empire

Recognized as a rising star by ISB supervisor Dedra Meero, Attendant Heert goes above and beyond in his role as her aide. He provides any support that Meero requires, working tirelessly on her behalf, knowing that her success will also benefit his career. Heert understands that working all hours is part of the job and never complains. He becomes so familiar with Meero that he can anticipate what she'll request before she does so, and this enterprising attitude makes a positive impression on her. Whether shadowing Meero in Major Partagaz's briefings or placing requests for information from other supervisors, Heert always has his superior's best interests in mind.

118 CHARACTERS AND CREATURES

KARIS NEMIK
SPECIES Human
AFFILIATION Axis network

Earnest and tenacious, Karis Nemik hopes for a future galaxy that's free from the Empire's oppression. The youngest member of a small group of rebels targeting Aldhani's Imperial garrison payroll, he has the strongest ideals of all his companions. Karis records his thoughts in an ever-growing manifesto on a datapad. Besides a keen interest in political theory, Karis is an accomplished astronavigator who makes complex calculations manually, using a primitive pre-Empire astronave. He shares his musings about the galaxy with anyone who expresses an openness to learning.

ARVEL SKEEN
SPECIES Human
AFFILIATION Axis network

A selfish man who can't bear to lose, Arvel Skeen is always looking out for opportunities—opportunities for revenge, for victory, or for a payout. He has spent years in Imperial prisons and has many tattoos to show for it. Skeen joins the rebel infiltration team on Aldhani to get revenge against the Empire who caged him. By stealing their payroll, Skeen wants to land a direct blow. With his eyes on the prize, he is distrustful of Clem's sudden arrival on Aldhani. After they complete the mission, though, Skeen reveals his mercenary intent and betrays the rest of his group.

TARAMYN BARCONA
SPECIES Human
AFFILIATION Empire, Axis network

Taramyn Barcona brings invaluable knowledge from his time as an Imperial stormtrooper to his new team of rebels on Aldhani. Taramyn's background, however, means he has to go the extra distance to earn their trust.

With a meticulous eye for planning and firsthand insight into the details of Imperial protocols and procedures, Taramyn acts as chief of operations for the rebel infiltration team. He doesn't appreciate the introduction of an unknown variable—the last-minute arrival of Clem (Cassian Andor)—but Taramyn is willing to adapt and begrudgingly accepts input from the new recruit.

GHOAT
HOMEWORLD Aldhani **SIZE** 1.2 m (4 ft) long **HABITAT** Valleys, rolling hills

Aldhani's rolling hills and valleys are ideal for the hardy and multi-horned ghoat. The livestock provide the local population with nutritious, albeit unappetizing, milk and precious thick wool. Though many herds have called Aldhani's Highlands home at one time or another, the Empire's occupation and removal of the Dhanis has culled the ghoat's numbers. This leaves the lingering population lacking a dependable food source.

CINTA KAZ
SPECIES Human **AFFILIATION** Axis network

Stormtroopers killed Cinta Kaz's family and, in doing so, turned her into a rebel at an early age. To Cinta, the cause always comes first. She takes her responsibilities to the growing rebellion seriously and sees her duties as both the means and the end, even at the cost of personal relationships, much to the frustration of her girlfriend, Vel Sartha.

In addition to her skills as a fighter, Cinta trains in other roles; she's knowledgeable about healing and languages, and is a master of stealth.

Young and quiet, Cinta can slip into the background of any area she infiltrates, making her well suited for undercover work and quietly observing her quarry. These talents are precisely why Luthen Rael and Kleya Marki assign Kaz to Ferrix with the task of eliminating Cassian Andor.

KLEYA MARKI
SPECIES Human **AFFILIATION** Axis network

Kleya Marki, a master of disguise, commits herself fully to the rebel cause. Like many working behind the scenes to pull the threads of the rebellion into a pattern, Kleya lives in layers. Her exterior layer is as an assistant in Luthen Rael's Galactic Antiquities and Objects of Interest gallery on Coruscant. As concierge, she restores artifacts, handles customers' requests, and wraps items for purchase. This mundane-seeming position is cover for surreptitious meetings with rebel agents and informants. Under the guise of selling antiquities, intricate plans against the Empire unfold.

In the back of the gallery, Kleya reveals her inner layers as mastermind for Luthen's spy network. She runs communications, keeps track of numerous operations, and ensures the web of rebellious activities spreads across the galaxy. Kleya is Luthen's closest ally and, as such, she tries to quell his impulses when they don't serve the greater cause.

LINUS MOSK
SPECIES Human **AFFILIATION** Preox-Morlana

A man of duty and honor, Sergeant Linus Mosk pours all of himself into his position in the Pre-Mor Authority Security Forces. He looks out for any opportunity to stamp out disobedience, especially if it means he can also demonstrate his loyalty to his superiors. Mosk supports Deputy Inspector Syril Karn in the pursuit of Cassian Andor and takes point on an elaborate plan to apprehend him on Ferrix. When the plot brings about the end of corporate oversight and the arrival of permanent Imperial authority, Mosk persists in following Andor to prove that he and Karn were correct.

Multiskilled keeper of secrets
Kleya not only organizes and directs Luthen's rebel network, she works diligently in his gallery, cataloging artifacts and restoring antiques to their former glory. She also tinkers with the Imperial tech that Luthen brings back from his travels.

EEDY KARN

SPECIES Human **HOMEWORLD** Coruscant
AFFILIATION Empire

Like any mother, Eedy Karn wants her son to succeed. She does her best for Syril Karn and welcomes him back with open—though judgmental—arms after he loses his job with Preox-Morlana. Eedy takes pride in providing for her son by pressing his uniform, preparing him two meals a day, and leveraging her influence with family member Uncle Harlo to find a new job for Syril, despite his many shortcomings. When it comes to learning details about her son's life, Eedy has no scruples. She eavesdrops and searches his belongings in order to help him however she can.

EXMAR KLORIS

SPECIES Human **HOMEWORLD** Coruscant
AFFILIATION Empire

Exmar Kloris appears to simply be a chauffeur, dedicated to ferrying Senator Mon Mothma from appointment to appointment in a JPP-192 limospeeder. He navigates the vehicle through Coruscant's traffic-filled skylanes, helping Mon Mothma in and out at her stops.

In actuality, Kloris is an undercover Imperial Security Bureau (ISB) agent. He monitors the senator's activities, interactions, and any conversations she may have inside the limospeeder, and relays his observations to Supervisor Blevin. He's unaware that Mon Mothma knows that he is a plant.

GORN

SPECIES Human **AFFILIATION** Empire, Axis network

Once loyal to the Empire, Lieutenant Gorn becomes a double agent after his superiors fail to promote him because he fell in love with a local woman at the Aldhani base. He serves there for seven years and, unlike his colleagues, he respects and appreciates the native Dhanis and their culture. Gorn eventually allies himself with the rebel infiltration team, which is planning to steal the Imperial payroll stored at the base. He feeds the rebels information, while using his Imperial officer rank to their advantage inside the base. Gorn is all too glad to cause a blow to the Imperial machine.

Secret travel
Gorn must travel between the Empire's base and the rebels' outpost on Aldhani with care. He wears a cloak, helmet, and goggles to obscure his identity.

PERRIN FERTHA

SPECIES Human **HOMEWORLD** Chandrila
AFFILIATION Mothma family

In line with Chandrilan tradition, Perrin Fertha married Mon Mothma at the age of 15. Having been a firebrand at the Chandrilan academy, Perrin moved into the Chandrilan Embassy with Mon Mothma, meaning that he's known a life of opulence for a long time. Perrin enjoys his status and wealth on Coruscant, though he abhors the political maneuvering that comes with it. He whiles away his time gambling and drinking, much to Mon Mothma's chagrin. Perrin expends his energy on maintaining an extravagant lifestyle and doesn't pay attention to the political leanings of those he affiliates with.

LEIDA MOTHMA

SPECIES Human **HOMEWORLD** Chandrila
AFFILIATION Mothma family

Leida Mothma feels like she can't control much of her life. The 13-year-old daughter of Senator Mon Mothma and Perrin Fertha, Leida grows up in the Chandrilan Embassy on Coruscant. She believes her mother cares more about politics than her family so she rebels by shutting her out and embracing the old-fashioned Chandrilan traditions that her mother eschews. When Leida desires anything, she turns to her father instead of her mother. Given her devotion to Chandrilan customs, Leida doesn't object to a meeting with potential suitor Stekan Sculdun.

VANIS TIGO

SPECIES Human **AFFILIATION** Empire

Captain Vanis Tigo rises to the rank of prefect when he takes charge of the Imperial garrison on Ferrix. Installed as part of the Imperial takeover of the Preox-Morlana Corporate Sector, Tigo establishes the garrison's HQ at a former hotel in Ferrix's town center. Tigo follows ISB Supervisor Dedra Meero's orders to investigate suspected rebel activities and apprehends Salman Paak and then Bix Caleen. Along with other officers, Tigo plots to capture Cassian Andor during his mother's funeral procession on Rix Road. Tigo instead provokes a riot when he interrupts her posthumous speech.

KIMZI

SPECIES Human
AFFILIATION Empire

Corporal Kimzi serves the Empire at the garrison on Aldhani. Although he likes to take breaks from the stuffy base to admire the sweeping Stone Valley, he has only disdain for the local Dhanis. Kimzi usually follows orders, but he does question some unusual activity in the payroll vault.

JAYHOLD BEEHAZ

SPECIES Human
AFFILIATION Empire

Commandant of the Aldhani Imperial garrison, Jayhold Beehaz holds no regard for the planet, its people, or its culture. Instead, he is committed to upholding Imperial tradition, and his family hosts formal dinners on special occasions. Beehaz's arrogance blinds him to the robbery plot that is unfolding right under his nose.

DOCTOR QUADPAW

SPECIES Jillsarian
AFFILIATION Axis network

Helping desperate patients who have nowhere else to turn, Doctor Quadpaw operates out of an unassuming tent on Frezno. Enhanced senses, combined with four dexterous arms, help the doctor execute precise medical procedures for any being who has enough credits to pay for his services. After the heist on Aldhani, the rebels seek out Quadpaw to help the wounded Karis Nemik but, despite intensive efforts, the doctor can't save Karis from his severe injuries.

Super senses
Cybernetics enhance Quadpaw's sight and hearing.

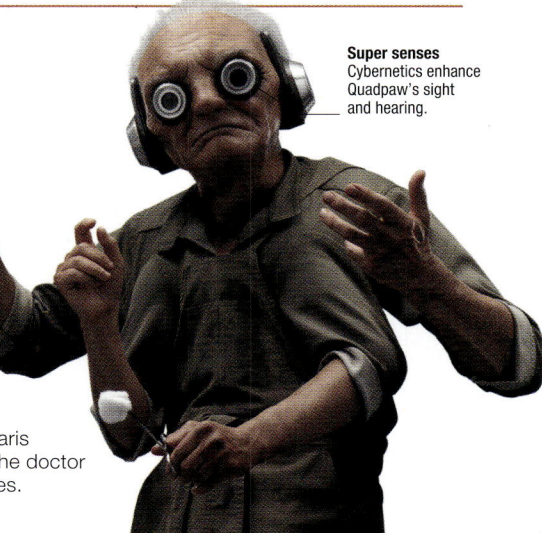

CHARACTERS AND CREATURES

TAY KOLMA
SPECIES Human **HOMEWORLD** Chandrila
AFFILIATION Bank of Kolma

A prominent Chandrilan banker, Tay Kolma accrues wealth through expert management of his family's assets, including the Bank of Kolma. His work requires him to visit Coruscant, where he meets with his close childhood friend, Senator Mon Mothma. Tay indicates his anti-Imperial opinions to her but fears his political tastes will be too strong for Mon. To his surprise, she asks for his assistance in accessing her family fortune without attracting Imperial suspicion. He allies himself with Mon and her cause and uses his contacts to find a solution for her financial troubles.

KINO LOY
SPECIES Human
AFFILIATION Level Five

To survive the unrelenting days of his sentence at the Imperial facility on Narkina 5, Kino Loy becomes a model prisoner. He follows orders and, as the day shift manager on Level Five, he expects absolute compliance from his 49 workers. He creates a professional barrier between himself and his men, pushing them to produce positive results that will benefit everyone. But learning about the lie of the prisoners' sentences galvanizes Loy into action, and he listens to Keef's plan to revolt and escape.

JEMBOC
SPECIES Human **AFFILIATION** Table Five

Jemboc was sentenced to three years in the Narkina 5 prison complex for "mining without a permit." He welcomes new inmates to Table Five in Unit Five-Two-D with kindness. He is more curious about the world outside than others at his table. When Cassian Andor arrives, Jemboc is eager to learn what he knows about the Public Order Resentencing Directive (PORD). This new law is reassessing all sentences and could double their remaining shifts.

XAUL
SPECIES Human **AFFILIATION** Table Five

Xaul is a cook who stole Imperial food to feed his starving village. He was sentenced to six months, but this was then jacked up to five years by PORD. Worn and weary from his time working on the assembly line in Narkina 5's factory complex, Xaul appears to have given in to the grind. However, he looks after elderly Ulaf, and when the time comes to fight back, he plays his part by pretending to argue with Ham.

ULAF
SPECIES Human **AFFILIATION** Table Five

The eldest inmate at Table Five in the Narkina 5 facility, Ulaf is also the closest to freedom. The incessant work exhausts him, but he persists because the others at his table depend on him. Near the end of his sentence, Ulaf suffers a stroke, and his passing inspires an uprising.

Man in charge
Focused on meeting quotas, Kino Loy bellows commands at the workers under his supervision. He allows no room for errors or slowing down.

HAM
SPECIES Human
AFFILIATION Table Five

Ham is an inmate in the Narkina 5 prison complex with a sentence of eight years for "self defense." Part of Table Five, he keeps his fellow prisoners on task and is blunt about who does which task most efficiently. Ham instigates a fight with Xaul to distract guards while prisoners riot and try to escape.

BIRNOK
SPECIES Human **AFFILIATION** Table Two

Incarcerated in the Narkina 5 prison complex, Birnok works at Table Two on Level Five. While he commits to his forced labor, he keeps his eyes open for other opportunities.
    Exhausted by work, and resigned to their fates, not many prisoners consider escape. However, Birnok sees a kindred spirit in Keef (Cassian Andor), and they steal moments between their intense work to share observations about the guards' weaknesses. Birnok embraces Keef's escape plan and leads the charge out of Level Five, though he is killed during the attempt.

ZINSKA
SPECIES Human
AFFILIATION Level Five

As the night shift manager for Level Five, prisoner Zinska keeps his men on task, chasing the Empire's demanding quotas. He tells Kino Loy about Level Two making trouble, confirming the rumblings among the inmates. When the prisoners rise up, Zinska leads his men into the fight.

TAGA
SPECIES Human

A member of Table Five in Unit-Five-Two-D in Narkina 5's Imperial Prison Complex, Taga does his part, takes pride in his work, and thinks he is faster than Keef. Adept in communicating using the inmates' improvised hand signals, Taga is the first to learn that something is going terribly wrong on Level Two.

MERZIN KEYSAX
SPECIES Human **AFFILIATION** Empire

Lieutenant Merzin Keysax serves the Empire as a security officer at Ferrix's newly established Imperial garrison. He works closely with Captain Vanis Tigo and ISB supervisor Dedra Meero to use Maarva Andor's funeral in a bid to capture her son Cassian and identify the rebel spy known as Axis.

GORST
SPECIES Human **AFFILIATION** Empire

Doctor Gorst doesn't employ typical Imperial Security Bureau (ISB) interrogation tools and techniques. Instead of traditional methods, Gorst leverages his knowledge of psychology and physiology to inflict nightmarish torture upon prisoners. Confident in eliciting the desired results, Gorst takes his time with those under his care. One particularly successful method sees Gorst put headphones on a prisoner and play the dying screams of massacred Dizonites, including younglings. This induces a choral, haunting agony for those who hear it. Because of his effective methods, the ISB calls on Doctor Gorst for the most crucial interrogations.

DAVO SCULDUN
SPECIES Human **HOMEWORLD** Chandrila
AFFILIATION Sculdun family

Davo Sculdun, regarded by many to be a wealthy thug, possesses exceptional riches and uses his position as a banker on Chandrila to network and shift political tides in his favor. His holdings are so vast that he can hide any transactions in bundles, making him a good choice for Chandrilans who wish to keep their funds obscured from Imperial auditors. Davo leverages his power for his family's benefit and sometimes uses advantageous favors instead of straightforward fees. This is how he manages to orchestrate an introduction between his son and Senator Mon Mothma's daughter.

RHASIV
SPECIES Human
AFFILIATION Narkina 5 prisoners

Despite being an inmate of the Narkina 5 facility, Doctor Rhasiv works there as a med tech, treating his fellow prisoners. Knowing his patients will return to grueling work despite their illnesses, he avoids building relationships with them. As one of the few inmates able to move between levels, he carries valuable information.

ELK
SPECIES Human
AFFILIATION Empire

Imperial Navy Captain Elk commands a *Cantwell*-class Arrestor cruiser on patrol near Segra-Milo. Vigilant for partisans and piracy, he stops suspicious vessels. Sometimes, even if the transponder ID is valid, Elk might detain the ship and send in boarding teams, just for the practice.

LEEVAN TENZA
SPECIES Sabat **HOMEWORLD** Sabata
AFFILIATION Saw Gerrera's partisans

Leevan Tenza's rebellion against the Empire didn't start with Saw Gerrera's partisans. He was once part of General Dodonna's team, but he was court-martialed. After escaping, he finds in the partisans an insurgency that aligns more with his own beliefs.

JEZZI
SPECIES Human
HOMEWORLD Ferrix
AFFILIATION Daughters of Ferrix

As a Daughter of Ferrix, Jezzi takes care of her fellow members of the social club, including Maarva Andor. After marching at Maarva's funeral and participating in the riot against the Empire, Jezzi escapes with some friends, piloting a borrowed Breon Dayvan starship away from Ferrix.

IMPERIAL SECURITY TROOPER
SPECIES Human **HOMEWORLD** Various
AFFILIATION Empire

Imperial security troopers reinforce stormtroopers in situations that call for an extra layer of strength. Elite and immovable, security troopers receive extensive training that allows them to fulfill a variety of roles such as prison or outpost guard, Imperial or ISB officer escort, or riot control trooper. Their black uniforms set them apart from stormtroopers, but they follow a similar command structure. Security troopers carry standard E-11 blaster rifles, but they may also use nonlethal equipment to maintain order, such as stun batons and riot shields.

KULLBEE SPERADO
SPECIES Meftian
HOMEWORLD Mefti
AFFILIATION Saw Gerrera's partisans

The Meftian gunslinger Kullbee Sperado is recruited into Saw Gerrera's partisans on Serolonis. He serves in the group for years but keeps his past under wraps and doesn't get close to others. While stationed on Jedha, he sometimes disappears for weeks on end without explanation and occasionally visits the Temple of the Whills.

TIE FIGHTER PILOTS
SPECIES Human **HOMEWORLD** Various
AFFILIATION Empire

The Empire's black-suited pilots fly the full range of TIEs, including fighters, bombers, interceptors, and less common models. Only a small minority of cadets in the Academy's pilot-training program actually graduate with commissions. They comprise an elite class within the Imperial Navy and have a notorious superiority complex. Nonetheless, they make great sacrifices. TIE fighter pilots are trained to complete their missions at all costs, disregarding their own survival.

KANAN JARRUS

SPECIES Human **HOMEWORLD** Coruscant
AFFILIATION Jedi, Rebel Alliance

Once a lost Jedi Padawan known as Caleb Dume, Kanan Jarrus becomes his own Jedi Knight. He fiercely fights for his newfound family and the galaxy as a whole.

Jaig eyes
Kanan begins to wear a mask after he is blinded by Maul on Atollon. It is decorated with Jaig eyes, which also adorn Captain Rex's clone trooper helmet.

TRADITIONAL BEGINNINGS

Caleb Dume is raised on Coruscant and becomes Depa Billaba's Jedi Padawan. Like many other Jedi, Caleb constructs his lightsaber with help from Professor Huyang, who personally supplies him with a rare emitter. While at the Jedi Temple, he also receives lessons from various Jedi, including Obi-Wan Kenobi and Yoda. As a young boy, he witnesses Ahsoka Tano easily dismantle a battle droid remote during a public training session in the Temple and is in awe of her skill. He accompanies his master on many missions during the Clone Wars, including to Kardoa and Mygeeto.

Kanan is only a teenager when Supreme Chancellor Palpatine issues Order 66, branding the Jedi traitors and decreeing that they must be assassinated. On Kaller, Billaba sacrifices her own life to ensure Caleb's safety, when her clone troops turn on the duo. The traumatized apprentice runs off at the insistence of Billaba and escapes the pursuing clone forces.

SURVIVOR

Caleb goes into hiding and assumes a new name, Kanan Jarrus. To avoid detection by the Empire, he abandons his Jedi teachings and learns how to survive from scoundrel Janus Kasmir.

Eventually Kanan settles on the planet Gorse, where he lives in a modest room at the Asteroid Belt, a cantina owned by Okadiah Garson. Kanan works for a company called Moonglow Polychemical, which mines volatile thorilide in the crystal interior of Cynda, the moon above Gorse. Kanan leads a day-to-day existence until two people change the status quo: Count Denetrius Vidian and Hera Syndulla. The amoral count is sent by the Emperor to improve thorilide production, and does so with catastrophic consequences. Renegade Twi'lek Hera, on the other hand, is intent on combating the Empire's atrocities.

Kanan is attracted to Hera, who sparks a gradual change in him, steering him back toward the values of his Jedi past. After thwarting Vidian's dark plans, Kanan joins her on the *Ghost,* alongside Hera's surly astromech Chopper. Their new rebel crew grows with the addition of Mandalorian Sabine Wren and Lasat Garazeb "Zeb" Orrelios. The team gravitates to the Outer Rim world of Lothal, where the Empire is pillaging local mineral resources to build new military machines.

AN UNCONVENTIONAL MASTER

During a fateful mission, Kanan encounters Ezra Bridger, a Force-attuned orphan living on the streets of Capital City. Sensing Ezra's potential, Kanan invites him to join his crew. Kanan is reluctant to become Ezra's master, having never completed his own training to become a full Jedi Knight. Nevertheless, Kanan guides Ezra in the ways of the Force through a series of lessons during their many missions against the Empire.

One such lesson takes the duo to Lothal's Jedi temple. While meditating there, Kanan sees a vision of a Jedi Temple guard, who tells him that Ezra Bridger will fall to the dark side. Kanan's instinct is to do all he can to save Ezra from this fate; however, he eventually realizes that he cannot protect Ezra from all things. In that moment, Kanan fully embraces his new role of mentor and finally becomes a full Jedi Knight.

Constantly hunted by Vader's Inquisitors, Kanan and Ezra travel to Malachor in search of a way to defeat them. Instead, they find Maul, who attempts to make Ezra his apprentice. Maul strikes Kanan with his lightsaber, permanently blinding the Jedi. Although Kanan loses his vision, this incident only strengthens his bond with the Force. The Force-attuned being known as the Bendu later teaches Kanan how to "see" through the Force.

As the *Ghost* crew continue to strike against the Empire and join the newly formed Rebel Alliance, Ezra's homeworld of Lothal increasingly falls under the Empire's iron grip. The crew attempt to break the Empire's hold, but Kanan's partner, Hera, is captured during their attack. She is then tortured at the Imperial Armory Complex by Governor Arihnda Pryce. A rescue attempt frees Hera, but costs Kanan his life. In a final act of heroism, Kanan Jarrus uses the Force to shield his comrades from a wall of flames that destroys the Imperial complex. Following Kanan's ultimate act of love, he becomes one with the cosmic Force.

KANAN'S LEGACY

Shortly after the liberation of Lothal, Hera gives birth to Kanan's son, Jacen, who bears a striking resemblance to his Jedi father. Hera and Jacen keep a photo of Kanan in the cockpit of the *Ghost* to honor their loved one's memory. During the Battle of Exegol, the disembodied voice of Kanan tells the faithful Rey through the Force that she is not alone and that a Jedi's strength is in their heart.

Jedi missions
After many duels, Kanan finally defeats the Grand Inquisitor aboard the *Sovereign (above right).* During a Force vision, Kanan is knighted by an entity appearing to be a Jedi Temple guard *(below).* In his final moments, Kanan sees his family one last time *(bottom right).*

HERA SYNDULLA

SPECIES Twi'lek **HOMEWORLD** Ryloth
AFFILIATION Rebel Alliance, New Republic

Inspired from a young age to fight against oppressors, Hera Syndulla carries hope for the galaxy and never strays from her convictions. Hera uses her extraordinary piloting skills to serve those who are in need time and time again.

INSPIRATION FROM RYLOTH
Hera Syndulla is a scion of an influential family on Ryloth. She sees her planet ravaged by violent conflict during the Clone Wars, only for the clone troopers who once helped Ryloth's freedom fighters turn and enslave them for the Empire. Her own world is oppressed by the newly created regime and riddled with corruption at the highest levels, which Hera witnesses personally when she becomes embroiled in rebellious activity. Inspired by her parents, Cham and Eleni Syndulla, and family friend Gobi Glie, Hera leaves her world behind on a quest to find other like-minded individuals and build a movement to oppose the Empire.

FORMING A TEAM
On a scouting mission to Gorse, Hera meets a gunslinging Jedi-in-hiding named Kanan Jarrus. When Kanan plays a key role in thwarting a plot devised by Imperial Count Vidian, Hera realizes his potential as a partner and invites him to join her aboard her ship, the *Ghost*. Over several adventures, Hera adds other members to her rebel crew, including the Mandalorian Imperial ex-cadet and weapons expert Sabine Wren, a Lasat survivor named Zeb Orrelios, and an orphaned Force-attuned being named Ezra Bridger. Together with Hera's astromech droid, Chopper, the team forms a surrogate family. Syndulla is the nurturing mentor and leader of the group, encouraging the others to do their best. She also functions as the team's ace pilot and getaway driver in their struggles against the Empire. During their time on Lothal, Hera often works with a mysterious contact called Fulcrum; this individual connects them to the wider rebellion.

A LARGER REBELLION
After a series of missions on Lothal, Hera and her crew join another group of rebels, known as Phoenix Squadron. Eventually, Hera rises to the rank of Phoenix leader, taking part in a variety of missions, including the Blockade of Ibaar and Battle of Garel. On a mission in the Ryloth system, Hera is reunited with her father when her group captures an Imperial carrier, which in turn becomes the new flagship for the squadron's A-wing fighters.

Hera's piloting skill and diplomacy serve the Rebellion well during a mission to Shantipole to acquire a prototype starfighter known as the Blade Wing. This powerful ship is designed by a Mon Calamari engineer by the name of Quarrie, who gives Hera the privilege of conducting the ship's first flight test. The starfighter proves capable of taking out an Imperial cruiser by itself and breaking blockades. It thus becomes the prototype for all future B-wing development.

The crew of the *Ghost* takes an important mission to escort Senator Mon Mothma to a budding rebel fleet above Dantooine. From the *Ghost*'s cockpit, Mothma announces the formation of the Alliance to Restore the Republic to the galaxy, giving Hera a front row seat to one of the most important moments in the Galactic Civil War.

FIGHTING IN THE WAR
Hera continues to serve the Rebel Alliance, even after suffering the loss of her Jedi partner Kanan, and gives birth to their son, named Jacen Syndulla, who already shows piloting aptitude at a young age. Chopper also remains by her side as she takes part in some of the most important battles against the Empire. After her promotion to general, she pilots the *Ghost* at the Battle of Scarif, the Rebellion's first major victory against the Emperor's forces. Following the Battle of Yavin, Hera is given command of a Mon Calamari star cruiser, which she names *Geist*, and escapes the Imperial assault on the Mako-Ta Space Docks. Hera also serves at Echo Base on Hoth and supports Luke Skywalker's investigation into the crew of the *Scopium* that leads the Alliance to learn of the Death Star II's existence. She later fights at the Alliance's major victory at Endor.

Special relationship
There is a special bond between Kanan and Hera that becomes more important to them as their fight against the Empire escalates.

LEADING IN THE NEW REPUBLIC
Following the Empire's fall, Syndulla serves the New Republic as a general. She works with Alphabet Squadron in their efforts to destroy Shadow Wing, and goes on to fight in the Battle of Jakku. In the following years, she meets with Ahsoka Tano after Morgan Elsbeth is freed from her temporary New Republic prison. They soon realize Morgan is trying to bring back Grand Admiral Thrawn, which the Imperial remnant would use to start another war. Putting the good of everyone else first, as always, Hera goes outside of protocol to get answers, and leads an unsanctioned mission to Seatos. Her instinct is proved true when Thrawn returns to the known galaxy. She takes some solace in the fact that Thrawn's return also brings with it Ezra Bridger, who has been missing for years.

Natural flyer
Hera is one of the best star pilots in the galaxy. She can fly a range of freighters and starfighters and easily pilots Mon Calamari Quarrie's Blade Wing, or B-wing, prototype.

Facing Thrawn
Hera's first encounter with Grand Admiral Thrawn is in her family home on Ryloth, which has been occupied by the Empire *(above top)*. She blows up the building as she escapes. During the Siege of Atollon, Hera takes command of Phoenix Squadron, following Jun Sato's sacrifice. She works with fellow rebel leader Jan Dodonna to plan an escape from Thrawn's blockade surrounding the planet *(above)*.

New repercussions
For her mission to Seatos, Hera faces a tribunal overseen by Chancellor Mon Mothma and other important New Republic leaders. She is saved by C-3PO's arrival and word that Senator Organa had approved Hera's operation.

CHOPPER (C1-10P)

MANUFACTURER Industrial Automaton **TYPE** Astromech droid
AFFILIATION Rebel Alliance, New Republic

C1-10P, known as Chopper, may not be the most eager droid, but he gets the job done when the stakes matter. He's a loyal companion and friend to Hera and the rest of the *Ghost*'s crew.

AN ECCENTRIC DROID
Chopper (C1-10P) is owned by Hera Syndulla and is an integral member of her rebel cell, despite his cantankerous, self-centered, and eccentric nature. Chopper is largely made of replacement parts: on the outside, his leg struts are mismatched and his paint is worn, while on the inside his circuitry is a bit of a mess. Yet Hera refuses to part with him because of his resourcefulness as the *Ghost*'s chief mechanic, and also perhaps because of her own sentimentality.

Chopper is always ready for challenges. Like every astromech, he has an extendable arm to interface with computers, manipulate doors, and fly ships. Like other C1 models, Chopper also has three robotic arms to manage objects like handles, buttons, and even blasters. Unlike later models, he has a retractable wheel instead of a third leg, and he can activate a booster rocket from the same socket.

LIFE AS A REBEL
During the Clone Wars, the astromech serves as a navigator droid for the Republic Navy until his Y-wing is shot down on Ryloth. Chopper is destined for the scrap heap, but Hera recovers the droid and spares him this fate. Not surprisingly, Chopper develops a lifelong distaste for flying in Y-wings. He stays close to Hera, helping her spy on Imperials who refuse to leave Ryloth and teaming up with Clone Force 99 to rescue Hera's parents from the Empire.

While he may at times be difficult, Chopper is dedicated to the rebel cause and has proven himself on missions. He often aids the crew of the *Ghost* as a lookout, and is unusually brave, facing stormtroopers in battle. Since droids are regularly overlooked by organic beings, Chopper carries out many missions disguised as an Imperial droid. This disguise allows him to sneak into the Imperial Academy on Lothal, an Imperial communications ship, an Imperial Interdictor cruiser, and even Grand Admiral Thrawn's field headquarters on Ryloth.

The entire Phoenix fleet has reason to be grateful to Chopper when it is saved by his resourcefulness. The rebels are seeking a new hidden base, desperate to find a place where the Empire won't find them. Little do they know they are heading straight into a trap. Just in time, Chopper befriends an Imperial protocol droid named AP-5 and removes his restraining bolt. Thankful for Chopper's friendship, AP-5 reveals the plot to him and offers the rebels an alternative option on the remote planet Atollon. They name their new home Chopper Base in honor of the droid's heroism.

After the rebels liberate Lothal, Chopper sticks by Hera's side while she serves with the Alliance. Operating from the Great Temple on Yavin 4, he joins her on the *Ghost* at the Battle of Scarif.

SERVING IN THE NEW REPUBLIC
Chopper remains the constant companion of Hera and her son Jacen long after the Empire is defeated. Being around Hera and Kanan's child even brings out the old astromech's playful side. He spends time with Jacen as he serves the New Republic with Hera. As a general, Hera's duties often tend more toward bureaucracy than battle, but when the situation calls for it, Chopper leaps into action. He helps Hera pursue Imperial sympathizers and successfully places a homing beacon on the enemy's ship from his position on the *Phantom II*. They track the homing beacon to Seatos, where Morgan is constructing an intergalactic hyperspace ring to bring back Thrawn. Chopper is the first to recognize Ezra, disguised as a stormtrooper, when he returns to the known galaxy.

Spectre-3
A C1-series droid that was active during the Clone Wars, Chopper participates in many conflicts but plays an important role in the Galactic Civil War.

Versatile droid
Chopper's mechanical arms not only allow him to manipulate the ship's controls but also to engage TIE fighters.

New friends
Chopper meets a fellow Republic veteran, named AP-5, during a rebel mission and persuades him to join the cause. They have a fraught and argumentative friendship.

Imperial paint job
Thanks to Sabine's painting skills, Chopper can quickly be disguised as an Imperial droid.

Hacked droid
Unfortunately, Chopper's identity as a rebel infiltrator is discovered by an Imperial communications officer aboard an IGV-55 surveillance vessel. Chopper is hacked during a mission to Killun Station and forced to turn against his friends. Luckily, Hera manages to regain control of her droid and destroys the hacker's ship.

GARAZEB "ZEB" ORRELIOS

SPECIES Lasat **HOMEWORLD** Lasan **AFFILIATION** Rebel Alliance, New Republic

Garazeb "Zeb" Orrelios is a vital member of the rebel crew aboard the *Ghost*. Despite his large size and brutish appearance, Zeb is thoughtful and sensitive, particularly to the plight of the weak and helpless.

Rebel warrior
Zeb uses his bo-rifle to pilot the *Ghost* to Lira San *(left)*. During the campaign to liberate Lothal, Zeb faces Grand Admiral Thrawn's agent, a lethal Noghri assassin named Rukh *(below)*.

THE LAST OF HIS PEOPLE

Zeb has a tragic past. While a captain of the Lasat High Honor Guard, Zeb's homeworld is razed by the Empire, which murders nearly all of its citizens. When Zeb encounters Alexsandr Kallus and discovers that the Imperial Security Bureau (ISB) agent actually participated in this atrocity, the two become bitter enemies and have several violent clashes. Zeb's own tragedy makes him sympathetic to the suffering of others. Even in a desperate situation, he refuses to use the Empire's own brutal weapons against it, having witnessed the effects of its horrific T-7 disruptors firsthand on Lasan. Nonetheless, Zeb never runs from a fight.

On a mission to gain valuable intelligence on decommissioned Republic bases, Zeb and the Spectres travel to Seelos to meet with clone Captain Rex and his compatriots. The clones agree to help the rebels on one condition: the crew must help them on a joopa big-game hunt. Little does Zeb know that this involves using him as live bait, as joopas have a particular taste for Lasats. Fortunately, the gamble pays off when Captain Rex joins their crew.

A STARTLING REUNION

During a later mission, Zeb is shocked to meet two fellow refugees from his homeworld. The survivors speak of an ancient Lasat legend of a mythical planet named Lira San. They believe that, with Zeb's help, they can reach Lira San and begin their lives anew. Zeb's bo-rifle points the way, far beyond the Outer Rim, as the planet lies behind an imploded star cluster, a hazardous maze that cannot be traversed by normal navicomputers. While other ships would be destroyed in such a maelstrom, the *Ghost* is protected by an energy field emanating from Zeb's staff. They emerge on the other side of the cluster to find Lira San, the original Lasat homeworld, inhabited by other Lasat. The journey tests Zeb's spiritual beliefs and shows him that he is not the last of his people after all.

Eventually, Zeb even finds peace with his sworn enemy Kallus. After they both crash on the moon of Bahryn, Zeb comes face to face with the ISB agent. To survive the moon's icy conditions, the two have to work together and, in due course, become friends. Their friendship means so much to Kallus that he later joins the Rebellion.

Zeb continues to serve in the Rebel Alliance throughout the Galactic Civil War, becoming closer to Kallus. At some point, Zeb takes Kallus to Lira San to meet his people, helping Kallus come to terms with his former role in devastating Lasan and its inhabitants.

TIME FOR CHANGE

Once the Empire is defeated, Zeb transitions to the New Republic and becomes an active member of its defense fleet. He and Carson Teva have a drink together in a bar on Adelphi when they receive word from Greef Karga of a pirate invasion on Nevarro. Carson's first instinct is to relay the information to Coruscant to get the New Republic involved, but Zeb is skeptical whether Carson will get a reply back in time to make a difference. Life and experience have shaped Zeb into a natural leader and mentor to his peers, and he expresses admiration for Captain Teva's attitude, wishing him good luck. According to his good friend and fellow member of the *Ghost* crew, Sabine Wren, Zeb is currently training new recruits for the New Republic. His reputation, skills, and experience in the history of combating galactic oppression continue to make him an excellent ally, and an even better friend.

Cantina on Adelphi
Zeb and other pilots enjoy rest and relaxation between missions at this cantina. The stories told here grow more sensational with each subsequent retelling.

CHARACTERS AND CREATURES

SABINE WREN
SPECIES Human **HOMEWORLD** Mandalore
AFFILIATION Rebel Alliance

A weapons specialist with an affinity for explosives, Force-attuned warrior Sabine Wren has courage and confidence from her Mandalorian heritage. Her concern for the plight of the downtrodden across the galaxy arises from her own personal journey.

FROM IMPERIAL CADET TO REBEL SPECTRE
Sabine excels during her training as a cadet at the Imperial Academy on Mandalore. She builds state-of-the-art weapons for the Empire; however she abandons her life on Mandalore when she discovers that one of the weapons she is developing is specifically designed to be used against her own people. When she speaks out against the Empire, Sabine is cast out by her family, and turns to a life of bounty hunting, partnering with her friend Ketsu Onyo.

After Onyo abandons her, Sabine becomes a rebel and in time joins the *Ghost* crew. Sabine's relationships aboard the *Ghost* are important to her, and she relies heavily on her friends, despite her strong-willed and self-sufficient nature. They have replaced the family that she lost on Mandalore. She looks up to Hera Syndulla and Kanan Jarrus as mentors and considers Zeb Orrelios an older brother. She gets along with the astromech Chopper well enough, and she attributes newcomer Ezra Bridger's awkward teenage mannerisms to attraction. Her bad experiences while at the Imperial Academy mean that Sabine doesn't like being kept in the dark about things. However, a shared experience on a monster-filled asteroid helps her to put more faith in Hera's leadership.

Old friend
Sabine meets her old friend Ketsu Onyo during a mission to rescue a rebel courier. Onyo is a bounty hunter trying to capture the courier, but Sabine persuades Onyo to abandon the bounty and help her instead.

Trials on Atollon
Thanks to Kanan's training, Sabine develops her own fighting style with the Darksaber on Atollon.

DISCOVERING THE DARKSABER
As the battle against the Empire drags on, Sabine learns that she cannot escape her past. Ezra's encounters with Maul lead Sabine to find the Darksaber, an ancient Mandalorian weapon that Maul stole from her people during the Clone Wars. She trains with Kanan Jarrus to become an adept lightsaber wielder and decides to use the Darksaber to rally her people.

Sabine's return to her family on Mandalore is a cold one, as the planet remains loyal to the Empire. Sabine's defection from the Academy is a serious embarrassment to her mother, Ursa, the leader of Clan Wren. Sabine defeats Imperial Viceroy Gar Saxon in combat, a symbolic victory against the Empire's puppet ruler that returns her family to a place of respect among the other clans. She declines to become Mandalore's new leader, but stays on her homeworld for a time to help fight in a civil war against Saxon's brother and the remaining Imperial troops.

MANDALORIAN TIES
Sabine's Mandalorian forces prove vital during the Battle of Atollon. Their arrival to combat the Imperial fleet allows the surviving rebels there to flee the planet. Sabine also displays great leadership qualities by uniting Clan Wren with Clan Kryze—led by Bo-Katan Kryze. Sabine turns the Empire's Arc Pulse Generator (a weapon she designed years before) against Imperial troops, ensuring their victory over Clan Saxon and ending the civil war on Mandalore. Sabine gives Bo-Katan the Darksaber, installing her as leader of the Mandalorian clans.

With her family ties reestablished, Sabine returns to her adoptive family to help fight the Empire across the galaxy. She helps Ezra liberate Lothal from the Empire, but when Ezra calls upon a pod of purrgil to destroy the Imperial fleet, he disappears afterward with the creatures. To honor her missing friend, Sabine remains on Lothal, living in Ezra's old home to keep an eye on the planet and protect it.

SEARCHING FOR EZRA
After the Galactic Civil War, Ahsoka and Sabine set off to find Ezra. The Empire doesn't retaliate and Lothal's citizens return to peaceful lives. For a time, Sabine trains as a Jedi under Ahsoka Tano but believing she has failed, she returns to a quiet life on Lothal with her Loth-cat Murley. When Ahsoka acquires a map that points the way to Thrawn and Ezra, Sabine rejoins Ahsoka for the mission and returns to Jedi training, though she still doesn't believe in herself.

Sabine travels with Morgan Elsbeth's forces to Peridea as a prisoner, but Thrawn lets her go so she can search for her friend. One of the native Noti leads Sabine to Ezra, but their reunion is short-lived. Baylan Skoll and his apprentice Shin Hati pursue them, and alongside Ahsoka, who travels to Peridea with purrgil, they hold them off. In fighting Thrawn's night troopers, Sabine connects to the Force and uses it to retrieve her lightsaber. Ezra leaves Peridea with Thrawn, but Sabine stays behind with Ahsoka and the ancient Mark IV architect droid, Professor Huyang.

Peril on Peridea
Compared to Ahsoka Tano and Ezra Bridger, Sabine is very inexperienced with a lightsaber. However, she is also a fearsome Mandalorian warrior. She combines her skillsets during the assault on the Peridea fortress.

Artistic visionary
Sabine has a flair for art and adorns her armor, weapons, and most of the *Ghost* with paint.

EZRA BRIDGER

SPECIES Human **HOMEWORLD** Lothal
AFFILIATION Rebel Alliance, Jedi, New Republic

Resourceful and skilled in the ways of the Force, Ezra Bridger goes from a Lothal street rat to a Jedi who is willing to sacrifice himself to put the galaxy first.

LOTHAL ORPHAN
Ezra's parents, Mira and Ephraim Bridger, disappear when he is seven years old, taken by the Empire for sending illegal broadcasts. Growing up, Ezra manages on his own, taking odd jobs for shady characters like Ferpil Wallaway or Bossk the bounty hunter and stealing to survive. He lives in an abandoned communications tower just outside of Capital City, where he keeps his Imperial helmet collection, a small speeder, and pilfered gadgets. He has little hope for the future until he encounters a group of rebels. Ezra falls in with Kanan Jarrus, Hera Syndulla, Zeb Orrelios, Sabine Wren, and their droid, Chopper, when he tries to steal the same Imperial speeder shipment they are after. Having boarded their ship, the *Ghost*, to escape pursuing TIE fighters, Ezra finds his life changed forever.

FOUND FAMILY
The rebels become like a family to Ezra. Kanan recognizes Ezra's abilities to sense things before they happen and perform extraordinary physical feats. When Ezra finds Kanan's lightsaber and activates his Jedi holocron with the Force, Hera encourages Kanan to take Ezra on as his Padawan. Ezra shows promise right away, but he is undisciplined and impatient, and his ability to manipulate the Force is erratic, coming in powerful bursts that concern Kanan. With Jarrus' help, Ezra locates a hidden Jedi temple and confronts his fears, attachments, and his desire for revenge against those responsible for his parents' disappearance. He also finds a kyber crystal and builds his own unusual lightsaber.

Soon after, the *Ghost* crew hacks the HoloNet and Ezra broadcasts an inspirational message of rebellion that is spread across the sector. However, Kanan is captured in the process, so the rebels launch a desperate rescue mission to Mustafar. Thanks to the help of rebel agents in Phoenix cell, they are successful and join the group afterward. The crew also meets former Jedi Ahsoka Tano, who becomes another of Ezra's mentors.

Forceful nature
Ezra's natural abilities with the Force give him a particularly strong bond with living creatures. He forms a connection with vicious fyrnocks on the asteroid base PM-1203, inducing the creatures to pursue Imperial forces.

Unsavory ally
While on a mission, Ezra meets Hondo Ohnaka for the first time. The untrustworthy pirate declares Ezra the first "pirate Jedi." Hondo is fond of Ezra and joins his fight to free Lothal.

After escaping Darth Vader on Lothal, Ezra doesn't return to his homeworld for some time. Eventually, he travels back and meets former Governor Ryder Azadi, who tells Ezra that his parents heard his speech and launched a prison break. They helped to free other prisoners, but lost their lives. Ezra comes to accept their fate and helps secure reinforcement corvettes for Phoenix cell from Princess Leia Organa. On a subsequent mission to steal fuel for the *Ghost*, Ezra bonds with a pod of purrgil, whalelike beasts that travel through hyperspace.

A LEADER AND APPRENTICE
Seeking to destroy the Sith, Ezra uses the Force to commune with Yoda, who informs him that he may find answers on Malachor. Alongside Kanan and Ahsoka, Ezra enters the Sith temple on the planet. He encounters the mysterious Maul, who attempts to claim Ezra as his young apprentice. Ezra manages to secure a Sith holocron and faces Vader once again in battle. Vader destroys Ezra's first lightsaber and the young man only escapes thanks to Ahsoka, who remains to duel the Sith.

Following the mission to Malachor, Ezra builds a new, more traditional, lightsaber. He is later promoted to lieutenant commander and entrusted with leading his first mission to Reklam Station, where his team must steal Y-wings. Unfortunately, it doesn't go to plan, and Ezra's command is suspended. Soon after, Maul kidnaps Ezra's friends, demanding his help in exchange for their lives. Together, Maul and Ezra merge a Jedi and Sith holocron and discover that Obi-Wan Kenobi is alive on Tatooine. Ezra heads to the planet to warn Obi-Wan about Maul, but the Jedi Master proves more than capable of dispatching the former Sith apprentice.

SACRIFICE FOR THE GALAXY
All of Ezra's training and experience help him when he returns to his homeworld to free it from the Empire, alongside the rest of the *Ghost* crew. Partway through their campaign, Kanan sacrifices himself to save Hera, Ezra, and Sabine from death. While upset at his mentor's passing, Ezra has a vision of a talking Loth-wolf named Dume, who tells Ezra that he needs to head to the former Jedi temple to protect it. There, he enters a world between worlds, a place in the Force removed from the natural flow of time, and saves Ahsoka from being killed by Vader on Malachor. Together, they stop Darth Sidious from gaining control of the dimension. The Sith Lord later attempts to win Ezra over by showing him a vision of his parents. Displaying great maturity, Ezra knows he has to let go of the past and does not fall for Sidious' ruse. Ezra then confronts Grand Admiral Thrawn on the bridge of the Star Destroyer *Chimaera* and reveals his secret plan. Arriving out of hyperspace, a pod of purrgil lays waste to Thrawn's blockade. The creatures entangle the *Chimaera*, which is launched into hyperspace. Thrawn and Ezra are carried at lightspeed to an unknown destination. Ezra's sacrifice allows his ragtag group of allies to free Lothal of Imperial oppression at last.

NO LONGER LOST
It turns out the purrgil take an ancient migration route to a far galaxy and deposit the *Chimaera* and those it carries on the planet Peridea. Ezra escapes from Thrawn and builds a life with the indigenous Noti, a diminutive, peaceful nomadic species. More than a decade passes before Ezra reunites with his friends when Sabine Wren and Ahsoka Tano make the improbable journey to Peridea. The threat of Thrawn going back to the galaxy cuts the happy reunion short, and Ezra readies himself for battle once again, constructing a third lightsaber with Professor Huyang's guidance. Ezra stows away on the *Chimaera* as it makes the return trip, and then sneaks off to warn Hera Syndulla, Chopper, and the New Republic about the renewed threat of Thrawn and the Imperial remnant.

Capable hero
During his time with the *Ghost* crew, Ezra matures into a confident rebel leader, who secures a significant victory against the Empire on Lothal. While exiled on Peridea, Ezra aids the friendly Noti who begin to adorn themselves with the rebel starbird in his honor.

Friends, reunited
After years of self-exile on Peridea away from his friends, Ezra is overjoyed to see Sabine again. He always had faith that she would find him one day and help him return to the known galaxy.

CHARACTERS AND CREATURES

BARON VALEN RUDOR
SPECIES Human **HOMEWORLD** Corulag
AFFILIATION Empire

Baron Valen Rudor, code name "LS-607," is a highly decorated TIE fighter pilot of Lothal's Imperial Navy. He is cocky, self-obsessed, and insufferably arrogant. Nonetheless, he has terrible luck and is increasingly bitter about it. His constant run-ins with the rebels always end badly. In an early encounter, he is shot down by the *Ghost*, and when Ezra Bridger finds his crashed TIE, Ezra steals Rudor's helmet and flight gadgets. Zeb Orrelios also separates Rudor from his ship more than once, and his chance to fly the latest TIE advanced is sabotaged on Empire Day.

Years later, Rudor is given Old Jho's Pit Stop to run after its former owner is executed for being a rebel operative. He is suspicious of two citizens in his bar, who are actually Ezra and his fellow rebel Sabine Wren in disguise. Rudor nearly orders their arrest, but relents when Lothal resident Jai Kell gives him a sum of credits. When the Lothal rebels use an unsealed hatch in the Pit Stop to escape through the sewers, Rudor informs the investigating death trooper that he had no clue the hatch wasn't sealed.

> "You'll be sorry! Or dead, you'll be dead!"
> — VALEN RUDOR

MYLES GRINT
SPECIES Human **HOMEWORLD** Lothal
AFFILIATION Empire

Taskmaster Myles Grint is a man of few words who relies on his size to intimidate others on Lothal. He follows Commandant Aresko's lead and bullies both citizens and officers of lower rank. Fortunately, his incompetence contributes to the rebels' ability to operate successfully on Lothal. When Governor Tarkin arrives, he orders the Grand Inquisitor to put a decisive end to Grint's succession of mistakes.

Unpleasant demeanor
Grint is always ready to bully lower-ranking officers and the citizens of Lothal when asked.

Bullying the locals
Grint samples a jogan fruit while he and Commandant Aresko harass a vendor in one of the capital's open markets.

CUMBERLAYNE ARESKO
SPECIES Human **HOMEWORLD** Lothal
AFFILIATION Empire

Commandant Cumberlayne Aresko is an egotistical and unsympathetic manager of military operations on Lothal. Together with Taskmaster Grint, he oversees the local Imperial Academy and ceremonies on Empire Day. Aresko overestimates his own importance, however. He is not as clever as he imagines himself, which is a failing that contributes to his eventual downfall. He first informs Agent Kallus of the rebel activity in the capital, and when he repeatedly fails to put a stop to it, the Grand Inquisitor hastens the end of his career.

YOGAR LYSTE
SPECIES Human **HOMEWORLD** Garel
AFFILIATION Empire

Supply Master Yogar Lyste is an ambitious young Imperial officer posted on Lothal, charged with overseeing supplies on the planet. He also occasionally transports prisoners. His duties are continually disrupted by the rebels, which only inspires him to redouble his efforts. After the Siege of Lothal, he hosts Princess Leia Organa when she arrives on Lothal with three cruisers. Leia claims that the ships contain aid for Lothal's citizens, but Lyste is suspicious, so he orders the ships impounded. He fails to prevent the rebels stealing the vessels or to uncover Leia's duplicity. When Grand Admiral Thrawn arrives, Lyste assists him when he investigates sabotage at the Imperial Armory Complex. Later, Agent Kallus, who is secretly a rebel agent, frames Lyste as a spy to escape capture. Lyste is dragged away to an unknown fate.

IMPERIAL COMBAT PILOT
SPECIES Human **HOMEWORLD** Various
AFFILIATION Empire

Imperial combat pilots are well trained at the Imperial academies and envied by stormtroopers for their well-armored vehicles. These overconfident pilots are required to drive a range of vehicles, including speeders and Imperial troop transports, but there are specialized corps for some walkers and tanks. The smart drivers wear body armor to protect them from potential armed resistance.

CIKATRO VIZAGO
SPECIES Devaronian **HOMEWORLD** Devaron
AFFILIATION Broken Horn Syndicate, Lothal rebels

Kingpin of Lothal's underworld, Cikatro Vizago is head of the Broken Horn Syndicate. Vizago deals in illicit goods, particularly stolen Imperial weapons shipments. The crew of the *Ghost* often runs missions and trades with him for cash, supplies, or valuable information. When *Ghost* crewmember Kanan Jarrus is kidnapped by the Grand Inquisitor, Vizago offers Ezra Bridger a lead in exchange for a favor at some point. Later, Vizago takes a mission from crime lord Azmorigan, but ends up being tricked by notorious pirate Hondo Ohnaka and imprisoned aboard his own ship, the *Broken Horn*. With Ezra's help, Vizago reclaims his ship and expels the intruders. Vizago later tries to smuggle the *Ghost* crew to Lothal in exchange for a number of puffer pigs. When the rebels are noticed by the Empire they manage to escape, but Vizago isn't so lucky. He is captured and forced to work on a Mining Guild ore crawler that is soon taken over by the rebels. Then, Vizago joins the rebellion and helps to liberate Lothal from the Empire.

Discreet gangster
Vizago examines a stolen shipment of E-11 blasters brought to him by Kanan Jarrus.

ALEXSANDR KALLUS

SPECIES Human **HOMEWORLD** Coruscant
AFFILIATION Empire, Rebel Alliance

Alexsandr Kallus is a fearsome Imperial agent who is fanatically loyal to the Empire. However, Kallus eventually realizes his loyalties may lie elsewhere.

IMPERIAL FANATIC
Agent Alexsandr Kallus is a member of the Imperial Security Bureau (ISB), a secret police organization that monitors loyalty to the Empire. He trains under Wullf Yularen, becoming his star pupil. After graduating, Kallus' first mission is to Onderon, where his troops are ambushed by a Lasat warrior. He is paralyzed in the initial foray and is forced to witness the Lasat kill his soldiers. During the sacking of Lasan, Kallus personally orders the use of the horrific T-7 ion disruptors on the Lasat, and is given a bo-rifle by a Lasat Honor Guard that he defeats. Soon after, Kallus and bounty hunter IG-88 fail to capture Han Solo for his actions on Savareen.

Kallus is sent to Lothal to investigate increasing rebel activity. He first encounters the *Ghost* and its crew when they attempt to rescue Wookiee prisoners. Kallus later runs into them again on Kessel, where he discovers Kanan Jarrus is a Jedi and Ezra Bridger is his presumed Padawan. Kallus contacts the Grand Inquisitor to aid in the hunt for the two Jedi. Kallus crosses paths with the rebels next when they attempt to sell some stolen T-7 ion disruptors to a crime lord on Lothal. Kallus infuriates the Lasat rebel Zeb Orrelios when the two cross paths. Kallus nearly beats Zeb in combat, but Ezra saves Zeb at the last possible moment, and the rebels escape.

Despite his best efforts during many encounters, Kallus is unable to destroy the rebel cell on Lothal. Kallus earns Governor Wilhuff Tarkin's displeasure, but is given another chance to prove himself and helps capture Kanan when the rebels broadcast a message on the HoloNet.

CHANGE OF HEART
After the *Ghost* crew rescues Kanan and leaves Lothal, Kallus confronts them numerous times across the galaxy—including on Seelos, Ibaar, Garel, Nixus, and even in Wild Space. Each time, they continue to elude him. On his final attempt, Kallus tries to trap the rebels on an Imperial construction module orbiting Geonosis. He duels Zeb and follows him into an escape pod. They both end up crash-landing on Bahryn, a frozen moon orbiting Geonosis, and Kallus breaks his leg. They have to work together to survive the hostile environment and the ferocious bonzami inhabiting it. Kallus and Zeb end up bonding, regaling each other with stories of their past. When Zeb is picked up by the rebels, Kallus turns down an offer to join them. He eventually returns to the Empire, although he begins to doubt his affiliation.

Following Bahryn, Kallus becomes an undercover rebel spy. Using the code name "Fulcrum," he secretly supplies information to the rebels, including that there are Imperial pilots willing to defect at Skystrike Academy. When rebel Sabine Wren infiltrates the academy and locates the would-be rebels, Kallus ensures they all escape, asking Sabine to tell Zeb that they're even now. During Grand Admiral Thrawn's investigation into sabotage on Lothal, Kanan, Ezra, and fellow rebel Chopper are undercover, trying to find out what new, top-secret weapon is being developed there. Kallus reveals to them that he is "Fulcrum." After the investigation, Thrawn suspects there is an Imperial mole, so calls upon his old ally and Kallus' former mentor Wullf Yularen to help. Upon hearing this, the rebels try to save Kallus, but he stays to help from the inside, implicating Yogar Lyste as the rebel agent. Privately, Thrawn believes Kallus is the mole, so manipulates Kallus into sending a transmission to the rebels. Thrawn apprehends him, revealing that Kallus has accidentally provided Thrawn with the rebel base's location on Atollon. Thrawn captures Kallus and forces him to watch as he attacks the rebels orbiting the planet. When Governor Arihnda Pryce orders for Kallus to be thrown out of an airlock, he overpowers her guards. Kallus leaves the ship in an escape pod that is then picked up by the *Ghost* crew during their retreat.

Kallus becomes a captain in the Rebel Alliance based on Yavin 4. He also joins the *Ghost* crew to liberate Lothal from the Empire. At the end of the Galactic Civil War, Zeb takes his now-close companion Kallus to Lira San, the previously lost Lasat homeworld where Zeb's people are thriving. Zeb tells the relieved Kallus that he is welcome to live among them.

Smart operator
With rarely a hair out of place, Kallus takes his personal grooming very seriously.

Loyal leader in charge
Kallus orders his troops to fire on the Jedi *(left)* and contacts the Grand Inquisitor about the Jedi *(above)*.

Rebel at heart
Calling Kallus a traitor, Arihnda Pryce orders him to be killed *(left)*. After fighting for the Alliance during the war, Zeb shows Kallus that he hadn't destroyed all of his people *(above)*.

CHARACTERS AND CREATURES

THE GRAND INQUISITOR

SPECIES Pau'an **HOMEWORLD** Utapau **AFFILIATION** Empire

Intelligent and discerning, the Pau'an that becomes the Grand Inquisitor used to be a Jedi Temple guard. Like many of his future colleagues, it is this Jedi Knight's disillusionment with the Order that sets him on the path to the dark side of the Force.

FALLEN KNIGHT

While serving the Order as a Jedi Temple Guard, he detests chief librarian Jocasta Nu for blocking him from having full access to the Archives. During the Clone Wars, he is one of the guards that brings Jedi Barriss Offee to a military trial, where Jedi Ahsoka Tano is accused of Offee's crime of bombing the Temple. Due to the treatment of Barriss and Ahsoka, he becomes disillusioned with the Jedi.

Following Order 66, he is recruited by Darth Sidious and becomes the Grand Inquisitor, responsible for leading the other members of the Inquisitorius. All armed with double-bladed lightsabers, the Inquisitors' initial mission is to kill surviving Jedi. The Grand Inquisitor is responsible for testing prospective Inquisitors, so he accompanies former Jedi Knight Iskat Akaris on a mission to Bar'leth, and later initiates her into the organization as Thirteenth Sister. At some point, the Grand Inquisitor loses a duel to Darth Vader during their first meeting, and is displeased when Sidious places the Inquisitorius in Vader's charge. On his new leader's orders, the Grand Inquisitor reads the Archives to discern any possible leads on the surviving Jedi, developing an encyclopedic knowledge of his former brethren. He is interrupted on one occasion by an irate Nu, who engages him in a duel because of his lack of respect for the holobooks. He gets the best of her, but is stopped by Vader from delivering the final blow. Confused and angry, the Grand Inquisitor begins fighting his master. Nu takes her chance to erase the Archives, depriving him of further reading, and then knocks the Inquisitor out by burying him under a pile of holobooks. Vader kills her soon after.

Eventually, the Inquisitorius starts Project Harvester to find Force-attuned beings to train into future Inquisitors. The group also tries to convert any surviving Jedi, but kills any that refuse. One of these victims is captured Jedi Master Luminara Unduli, who is executed in the Grand Inquisitor's presence in the Spire on Stygeon Prime. He spreads rumors that she is still alive and uses her remains, which have a lingering Force presence, to lure in any surviving Jedi.

Chains of Command
The Grand Inquisitor is a skilled fighter, and his standing allows him to command the other Inquisitors, stormtroopers, and most Imperial officers.

A CHALLENGER

A few years into the Emperor's reign, the Inquisitors hunt highly esteemed Jedi Council member Obi-Wan Kenobi and learn of a secret group, known as the Hidden Path, dedicated to hiding surviving Jedi from them. The Third Sister, also known as Reva, schemes to get closer to Darth Vader to enact her revenge for his role in Order 66. On Daiyu, the reckless Reva turns on the Grand Inquisitor, gravely wounding him, and then taking his position. Reva believes that the Pau'an is dead, but it is a deception designed by himself and Vader. The Imperials soon discover Kenobi's location at a Hidden Path base on Jabiim. During the Imperial assault, the Path and Kenobi escape and Reva duels Vader, who easily defeats her. The Grand Inquisitor then reappears and reclaims his title with the pair revealing she is no longer useful. During their pursuit of Kenobi and the fleeing rebels, the Pau'an would rather prioritize the Hidden Path over a single Jedi, but he is overruled by Vader.

The Scythe
Leading from the front, the Grand Inquisitor exits the Inquisitorius' Scythe transport to track Jedi on Tatooine.

JEDI ACTIVITY ON LOTHAL

Years later, the Grand Inquisitor kidnaps Dhara Leonis from Lothal for Project Harvester, torturing her in a cell on Arkanis. After Imperial Security Bureau Agent Alexsandr Kallus discovers the Jedi Kanan Jarrus and his presumed Padawan, Ezra Bridger, Kallus notifies the Grand Inquisitor, who sets a trap at the Spire, having ensured that Kanan and Ezra believe Unduli is held captive there. Despite having never met Kanan, the Grand Inquisitor identifies Kanan's master as Depa Billaba and the weaknesses of his fighting style. He exploits this knowledge to great effect, and Kanan and Ezra barely escape.

Soon after, the Grand Inquisitor visits the Lothal Academy to discover if two recruits are Force-attuned. He finds out that one of them, Dev Morgan, is actually Ezra Bridger on a rebel mission. Ezra escapes, alongside another potential recruit. The Grand Inquisitor also meets Zare Leonis, who is Dhara's brother and claims to be Force-attuned. Following the Empire Day celebrations, the Grand Inquisitor tracks Kanan and Ezra to Fort Anaxes where he fights them. Ezra briefly taps into the dark side in order to save Kanan and evade him. Then, the Grand Inquisitor transfers Zare to the Arkanis Academy to see if he is Force-attuned and a rebel. He begins extracting information from Zare, but he has to return to Lothal suddenly, stopping their discussion.

WORSE THAN DEATH

Later, Kanan allows himself to be captured in order to save his friends. He is interrogated by the Grand Inquisitor in a failed attempt to see if the Jedi is linked to a larger rebellion. After being freed from his cell by Ezra, Kanan finally proves himself a Jedi Knight when he defeats the Grand Inquisitor, who willingly falls to his death. He warns Kanan that he has no idea what he has unleashed and that some things are more frightening than death.

It would appear that the individual who was the Grand Inquisitor was correct. A part of him seemingly survives death and is forced to guard a Jedi outpost on Tempes, where he kills anyone who visits the building. Years after his duel with Kanan, during the Galactic Civil War, this fiery apparition encounters the Jedi Luke Skywalker, who has come searching for knowledge about the Order. The spirit duels the young explorer, and Luke emerges victorious, taking a yellow-bladed lightsaber with him. When Vader heads to Tempes for an update, the Pau'an pleads to be released, but Vader denies him an end to this suffering.

The Inquisitor's trap
Kanan Jarrus and the Inquisitor duel in the crypt of Jedi Luminara Unduli at the Imperial prison on Stygeon Prime.

MAKETH TUA

SPECIES Human **HOMEWORLD** Lothal
AFFILIATION Empire

Minister Maketh Tua is a government official who often serves as a stand-in for Governor Arihnda Pryce, where she is charged with protecting the Empire's industrial interests. Tua presides over Lothal's Empire Day celebrations when Pryce is invited to Coruscant for the occasion. She introduces Sienar Fleet Systems' new advanced TIE fighter and its pilot, Baron Valen Rudor, but things go horribly wrong when the *Ghost* crew attack. After Tua and Agent Kallus fail multiple times to capture the rebels, Grand Moff Tarkin arrives on Lothal to personally put a stop to the rebellion. Tua is horrified when he orders the execution of two Imperial officers in front of her. Fearing for her life after a visit from Darth Vader, Tua tries to defect by offering the *Ghost* crew information on rebel sympathizers and the Emperor's plans for Lothal. The Empire expects her betrayal and rigs her shuttle to explode, killing Tua just as the *Ghost* crew try to extract her.

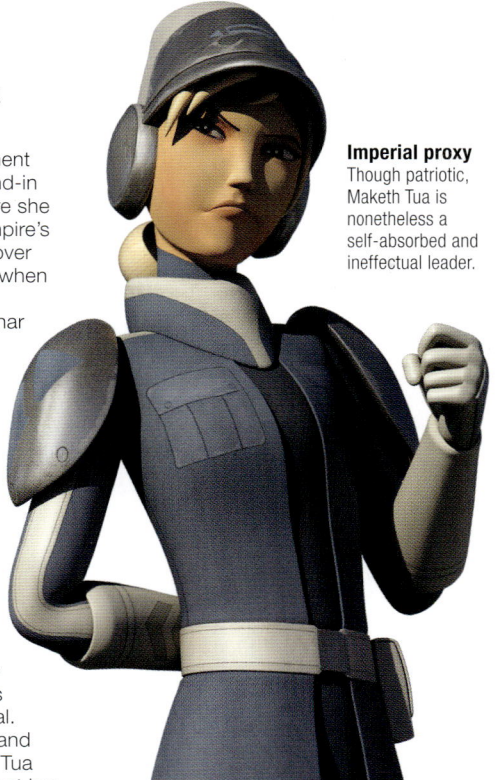

Imperial proxy
Though patriotic, Maketh Tua is nonetheless a self-absorbed and ineffectual leader.

ZARE LEONIS

SPECIES Human **HOMEWORLD** Uquine
AFFILIATION *Ghost* crew

Originally from a Core World, Zare Leonis and his family settle quickly on Lothal. Zare befriends fellow grav-ball teammembers Merei Spanjaf and Beck Ollet. After Zare enters the Junior Academy for Applied Sciences, his sister Dhara, training at Lothal's Academy for Young Imperials, mysteriously disappears. Zare and Ollet later witness Imperial stormtroopers firing on nonviolent protesters, which inspires Ollet to rebel against the Empire and leads to his arrest.

A year later, Zare enters the Imperial Academy, secretly hoping to discover Dhara's fate. When Ezra Bridger goes undercover at the Academy, Zare helps him steal an Imperial decoder. Determined to find his sister, Zare stays at the Academy, feigning firing at Ezra and Jai Kell when they escape. Zare is commended for trying to stop them, and receives a visit from the Grand Inquisitor himself who wants to hear about his former friends. Zare mentions his sister Dhara and pretends to be Force-attuned. Following this meeting, Zare provides intel to Ezra's rebel group.

Soon after, the Grand Inquisitor returns and announces that Zare is being transferred to the prestigious Academy on Arkanis, where Zare believes Dhara is being held. Zare joins the exclusive Commandant's Cadets group by pretending to kill a fellow cadet, whom he actually helps escape. Zare meets Ollet once more, and the brainwashed cadet reveals that Zare is a traitor. For his final meal before his execution, Zare requests Ollet's presence and he manages to break Ollet's brainwashing. Together, they get Zare out of his cell, and Spanjaf and Ezra's rebels arrive to rescue him. Zare manages to find Dhara, and they escape the Academy, thanks to Ollet's sacrifice, with their rescuers. The siblings are transported to Garel, where they are reunited with their parents. Working alongside the Statura family and the Spanjafs, the Leonises dedicate themselves to freeing Garel from Imperial occupation.

Proud display
Zare wears a cadet uniform and helmet from the Imperial Academy. The gray and white uniforms are symbols of unity, solidarity, discipline, and prestige.

GALL TRAYVIS

SPECIES Human **AFFILIATION** Empire

Gall Trayvis appears to be a renegade, on-the-run senator who transmits anti-Imperial broadcasts over the holonet, inspiring rebels across the galaxy. At times, he encourages protest, such as boycotting Empire Day; at other times, he passes on valuable information. He informs the *Ghost* crew that Jedi Luminara Unduli is being held prisoner at the Imperial prison on Stygeon Prime. Later, he hints at a secret visit he plans to make on Lothal. During his trip, however, Trayvis reveals he is a double agent, serving the Empire, so the *Ghost* crew leave him behind. Trayvis is later interviewed on HoloNet News, stating that he is committed once more to the Empire and denouncing the Lothal rebels.

FYRNOCK

HOMEWORLD Asteroids **SIZE** Variable **HABITAT** Shadows, caves

Fyrnocks are silicon-based lifeforms that live on large asteroids with thin atmospheres. Afraid of the light, they dwell in shadows and hibernate for long periods until disturbed, when they spring awake and attack prey with their sharp claws and teeth. Their meals are infrequent; they feed mostly on mynocks, small space slugs, and other creatures of the asteroid belts. When Sabine Wren and Hera Syndulla are stranded on an old Republic asteroid base, they are swarmed by fyrnocks that have infested the facility. The two barely escape, but Kanan Jarrus notes the location in case the creatures could be useful later.

OLD JHO

SPECIES Ithorian **HOMEWORLD** Ithor **AFFILIATION** Lothal rebels

Owner of Old Jho's Pit Stop, the Ithorian is one of the first settlers to arrive on Lothal, and there is little about the planet's history that he doesn't know. Jho carries special headgear that translates Ithorian speech into standard Basic. The wise and fascinating cantina owner has no love for the Empire and begins helping the *Ghost* crew and other rebels. Jho uses his freighter to ferry the Leonis family and the Spanjaf family to safety on Garel. He occasionally passes valuable information to the *Ghost* crew, and also puts willing Imperial defector Maketh Tua in touch with them. Jho decides to take an active role in Ryder Azadi's rebel cell on Lothal. Unfortunately, Jho is captured when trying to help the group escape a raid and is executed by the Empire.

MEREI SPANJAF

SPECIES Human **HOMEWORLD** Corulag
AFFILIATION Junior Academy of Applied Sciences, Gray Syndicate

Merei Spanjaf is a tech-savvy student who uses her skills to help her boyfriend, Zare Leonis, find his missing sister—Dhara. She soon finds herself working with the Gray Syndicate, and eventually slices her way into the Imperial data network on Lothal. These data breaches, however, draw the attention of the Imperials, who assign her mother, Jessa Spanjaf, to investigate. Desperate to escape the Syndicate and the Imperials, Spanjaf stages her own kidnapping, which leads to a deadly attack on the Syndicate's headquarters. Guilt-ridden, Spanjaf eventually flees Lothal with her family and rescues Zare and his sister from the planet Arkanis.

CHARACTERS AND CREATURES

LOTH-CAT
HOMEWORLD Lothal
AVERAGE SIZE 0.94 m (3 ft 1 in) long
HABITAT Grasslands

Loth-cats are small predators that live in family groups. Their striped brown coats allow them to blend into Lothal's grassy plains where they hunt Loth-rats and other pests. It is believed that Loth-cats may be the ancestors of tooka cats, a feline species commonly found on Coruscant. Loth-cats are curious and often friendly, and these traits make them popular pets across the galaxy. Loth-cats have even been known to "adopt" wayward droids. Stormtroopers find them to be a nuisance, however, and sometimes use the quick-footed, temperamental cats for target practice.

TIBIDEE
HOMEWORLD Various, including Stygeon Prime and Oosalon
AVERAGE SIZE 16.17 m (53 ft 2 in) long **HABITAT** Cold, rugged mountains

Tibidees are winged creatures similar to mynocks, neebrays, and tibidons. They are often seen flying in groups, achieving flight with the aid of internal buoyant air sacs. Rebel captain Hera Syndulla encounters tibidees in the skies over Stygeon Prime when they mistake the *Phantom*'s jamming frequencies for mating calls. Excited tibidees ram the ship, but Hera thinks fast and uses the tibidees to attack approaching Imperials. Ezra Bridger discovers he can connect with tibidees via the Force, turning the flying pests into unlikely allies.

JAI KELL
SPECIES Human **HOMEWORLD** Lothal
AFFILIATION Empire, rebels, New Republic

Jai Kell is a cadet at Lothal's Academy for Young Imperials. When Ezra Bridger infiltrates the Academy pretending to be a cadet, he accidentally draws dangerous attention to Jai. The Imperial leaders suspect Jai might be Force-attuned, so call upon the Grand Inquisitor to investigate. Ezra and fellow cadet Zare Leonis help Jai escape. At the time, Jai resents Ezra and Zare for ruining his Imperial career, but he ends up joining Lothal's rebels and helping to liberate his homeworld. During the New Republic era, Jai serves as Lothal's senator in the reformed senate.

ADMIRAL KASSIUS KONSTANTINE
SPECIES Human **HOMEWORLD** Coruscant
AFFILIATION Empire

Kassius Konstantine is an arrogant admiral in the Imperial Navy, serving under ISB Agent Kallus, the Inquisitors, and Grand Admiral Thrawn at various times. He repeatedly fails to stop the rebels in the Lothal system and Iron Squadron at Mykapo. His blunders are topped by his refusal to obey Thrawn's orders at the Battle of Atollon. There, he pursues rebel Commander Sato's ship, *Phoenix Nest*, which rams the admiral's *Interdictor*-class Star Destroyer and destroys them both, bringing an end to Konstantine's military career and his life.

PUFFER PIG
HOMEWORLD Various
AVERAGE SIZE 0.9 m (2 ft 11 in) long
HABITAT Captivity (farms and mining operations)

Puffer pigs are domesticated livestock valued by the Mining Guild for their ability to sniff out costly mineral deposits. Their bacon is also prized as food. Puffer pigs have the odd habit of inflating to many times their original size when they are startled. Lando Calrissian acquires a puffer pig from Azmorigan (to use in his new Lothal mining venture), and relies on the *Ghost* crew to smuggle it through Lothal's Imperial blockade. The crew later smuggles the pigs once more, selling them to Cikatro Vizago.

W1-LE
MANUFACTURER Lothal Logistics Limited
TYPE Modified RQ protocol droid

Lando Calrissian has owned "Willie" (W1-LE) since the Clone Wars. His memory was transferred from another droid into his current RQ protocol droid shell. Willie manages the operations at Lando's mining camp on Lothal and stands in for his boss, Lando, when he is away.

BROM TITUS
SPECIES Human
AFFILIATION Empire

Brom Titus is an unlucky admiral in the Imperial Navy. He oversees an experimental gravity well test program, but his ship is destroyed by Commander Sato's rebel cell. His Reklam Station is also wrecked by Ezra Bridger, and his ship, the *Marauder*, is destroyed by rebel leader Saw Gerrera.

AZMORIGAN
SPECIES Jablogian **HOMEWORLD** Nar Shaddaa
AFFILIATION Enslaver

Lando Calrissian makes a deal with the repulsive Azmorigan to acquire a puffer pig in exchange for an enslaved person. Lando manipulates rebel leader Hera Syndulla into playing along. Hera escapes, however, and leaves Azmorigan holding a serious grudge against them all. He gets a chance to settle this grudge when instead of dealing with crime lord Cikatro Vizago during a deal, he is unexpectedly confronted by *Ghost* crewmember Ezra Bridger and wanted pirate Hondo Ohnaka. Azmorigan tries to kill them, but they escape with his goods and credits. Much later, Azmorigan lets his grudges

with Hondo and the *Ghost* crew slide in order to smuggle goods off a stranded Imperial cargo ship orbiting Wynkahthu.

JUN SATO
SPECIES Human **HOMEWORLD** Mykapo
AFFILIATION Rebels

Jun Sato is the leader of the Phoenix rebel cell and an ally of Bail Organa and Ahsoka Tano. Sato commands the Phoenix Squadron of A-wings from his ship, *Phoenix Home*, which is later destroyed by Darth Vader. Afterward, Sato bases his command aboard the *Liberator*, and later *Phoenix Nest*. Sato welcomes the crew of the *Ghost* into his cell, and Hera Syndulla soon leads his starfighter squadron. Sato establishes a rebel base on Atollon, but when Imperial Grand Admiral Thrawn attacks, Sato sacrifices his own life so that Ezra Bridger can escape to get help.

JOOPA

HOMEWORLD Seelos
AVERAGE SIZE 21 m (68 ft 11 in) long
HABITAT Underground

Fearsome wormlike creatures named joopas live under the salt crusts of Seelos. They have an array of red eyes and a gaping mouth lined with mandibles. Joopas sense their prey by feeling their vibrations. The joopa thrusts its slimy tongue to the surface, wraps it around its unsuspecting prey, and yanks it underground. When Captain Rex, Wolffe, and Gregor retire to Seelos, they spend their days "slinging" (fishing) for joopas. The giant worms are a prize delicacy and the clones recruit rebel Zeb Orrelios to help, though he is nearly eaten alive.

EG-86

MODEL EG-series power droid
AFFILIATION Rebels

Friendly and keen, EG-86 is a rebel courier droid who is transporting secret information when he arrives on Garel. Thanks to the help of the *Ghost* crew, he completes his mission and delivers the intel to R2-D2 on Havoc Outpost.

QUARRIE

SPECIES Mon Calamari **HOMEWORLD** Mon Cala
AFFILIATION Rebels

Quarrie is a Mon Calamari shipwright who resides on Shantipole where Hera Syndulla and her crew seek his help. He provides them with his Blade Wing prototype and upgrades their shuttle. Later, he helps the rebels turn his prototype into the manufacturable B-wing starfighter line.

IMPERIAL CADET

SPECIES Human **HOMEWORLD** Various
AFFILIATION Empire

When the Republic is consolidated into the Empire, clone troopers are phased out and a new military force is formed from cadets who enroll in Imperial academies. The main campus is the Royal Imperial Academy on Coruscant. Smaller worlds like Lothal may host junior academies with cadets who go on to serve in local civic roles or, like Zare Leonis, go on to senior academies to be trained as an officer.

FIFTH BROTHER

HOMEWORLD Artemesium
AFFILIATION Inquisitorius

The arrogant Inquisitor Fifth Brother has no qualms hunting and killing Jedi, even though he was once one himself. He loses a hand during training with Darth Vader, and later accompanies the Sith to a desert planet to locate former Jedi High Council member Eeth Koth. While trying to secure an individualized cloaking device called the Shroud, Fifth Brother easily resists attempts by Jedi Cere Junda to turn back to the light side, and battles both Junda and Jedi Cal Kestis. On Tatooine, Fifth Brother, the Grand Inquisitor, and Third Sister track a Jedi on the run named Nari. Fifth Brother clashes with Third Sister, who he sees as too impulsive and focused on the larger prize of Obi-Wan Kenobi. Years later, Fifth Brother and Seventh Sister hunt Force-attuned children as a part of Project Harvester. During this time, he regularly crosses paths with members of the Spectre rebel cell, including the Jedi Kanan Jarrus and Ezra Bridger. On Malachor, while trying to retrieve a Sith holocron, Fifth Brother is killed in a lightsaber battle when Maul stabs him.

RYDER AZADI

SPECIES Human **HOMEWORLD** Lothal **AFFILIATION** Rebels

Ryder Azadi is the Governor of Lothal until he is deposed by the machinations of Arihnda Pryce. He supports the dissident broadcasts of Ephraim and Mira Bridger. They all end up imprisoned together, however when they escape, the Bridgers are killed. After seeing a Force vision of his parents, Ezra follows a mysterious white Loth-Cat to Ryder, who informs Ezra of his parents' fate. Ryder builds a small resistance movement on Lothal and aids the *Ghost* crew. Ryder and his Lothal rebels later liberate their world from Imperial control with the help of Ezra and the rest of his crew. Following the Battle of Lothal, Ryder returns to govern his homeworld. At a ceremony to mark the anniversary of the Battle of Lothal, Ryder unveils a monument to commemorate Ezra. He is irritated to learn that the next speaker, Sabine Wren, has dashed away to avoid saying a few words and asks Senator Kell to step in.

SEVENTH SISTER

SPECIES Mirialan **HOMEWORLD** Mirial
AFFILIATION Inquisitorius

The Seventh Sister is another former Jedi who is coerced into joining the Inquisitors following Order 66. She has a fierce rivalry with Thirteenth Sister, who believes the Mirialan is particularly cruel. Seventh Sister is known for her unusual methods, including the use of ID9 seeker droids for recon and a Force ability that enables her to deliver painful scratches to foes. The Seventh Sister is also under orders to locate Force-attuned children. When the Grand Inquisitor is defeated, she hopes in vain to replace him and is ordered to pursue Kanan Jarrus, Ezra Bridger, and Ahsoka Tano. While on their trail, she is eliminated by Maul.

KETSU ONYO

SPECIES Human **HOMEWORLD** Shukut
AFFILIATION Black Sun, rebels

Ketsu Onyo is a former Imperial Cadet and artist on Mandalore. She and her friend, Sabine Wren, escape the academy and become bounty hunters. After a disagreement, Ketsu leaves Sabine for dead and joins the criminal organization Black Sun. The two meet again when Ketsu is contracted by Black Sun to retrieve rebel droid EG-86 on Garel. They fight at first, but after being forced to work together, part on good terms. Though Ketsu declines Sabine's initial offer to join the rebels, she later agrees to sign up. Ketsu helps her allies obtain much needed fuel, facilitating their escape from Grand Admiral Thrawn on Atollon, and later joins the team that frees Lothal.

WHITE LOTH-CAT

SPECIES Loth-cat **HOMEWORLD** Lothal
AFFILIATION Ezra Bridger

Ezra Bridger meets a mysterious white Loth-cat that acts as a guide for him and seems to have a strong connection to the Force. In their first encounter, the Loth-cat leads Ezra to the former Lothal Governor, Ryder Azadi (Ryder and the Loth-cat are friends). On their next meeting, the cat helps Ezra and Sabine Wren hide a hyperdrive from a crashed TIE/d defender elite. The Loth-cat also introduces Ezra to a white Loth-wolf, another creature with a very strong Force connection. On their third meeting, the Loth-cat helps Ezra and Zeb Orrelios relocate their hyperdrive.

134 CHARACTERS AND CREATURES

FENN RAU
SPECIES Human **HOMEWORLD** Concord Dawn
AFFILIATION Republic, Journeyman Protectors, rebels

The Mandalorian Fenn Rau serves the Republic during the Clone Wars, training clone pilots and fighting alongside them. During the Imperial era, Rau leads the Journeyman Protectors who guard the planet Concord Dawn. When the rebels seek safe passage past his world, Rau and the Protectors attack. The skirmish ends with Rau captured. Rau discovers that Viceroy Gar Saxon has destroyed the Protectors, so he joins the rebels and trains Sabine Wren. Later, he aids them on missions and supports Bo-Katan Kryze as leader of the Mandalorians.

CHAVA
SPECIES Lasat **HOMEWORLD** Lasan
AFFILIATION Lasats

The old shaman known as "Chava the Wise" is a refugee from the planet Lasan after it was destroyed by the Empire. She and her companion, the High Honor Guardsman Gron, are rescued by the crew of the *Ghost*. Well versed in the prophecies of her people, Chava believes fellow Lasat Zeb Orrelios is the key to finding their new homeworld. Together, they embark on a treacherous journey to Lira San, the legendary refuge of their people. Chava and Gron settle there with millions of other Lasats, later welcoming Zeb back, along with his friend, Alexsandr Kallus.

PURRGIL
HOMEWORLD Deep space
AVERAGE SIZE 5.5 m (18 ft 1 in) high, 30 m (98 ft 5 in) long **HABITAT** Space (attracted to gas deposits)

Large whalelike creatures known as purrgil have long been a menace to deep-space travelers. They float into hyperspace lanes and cause collisions that tear ships apart. The *Ghost* crew encounters a pod of these intelligent creatures flocking to a deposit of Clouzon-36 gas at a Mining Guild refinery. Purrgil breathe the gas, which they use as biofuel to travel through hyperspace. Ezra Bridger develops a strong bond with the purrgil king and his pod. Ezra later calls on the purrgil to pull Grand Admiral Thrawn away from the Battle of Lothal. The purrgil take them to the far galaxy via an ancient migration route. They arrive at the planet Peridea, which has an ancient purrgil graveyard in high orbit. Years later, Ahsoka Tano travels inside a purrgil to follow them.

BONZAMI
HOMEWORLD Bahryn **AVERAGE SIZE** 4.75 m (15 ft 7 in) high, 13 m (42 ft 8 in) long **HABITAT** Subterranean ice caverns

Geonosis is orbited by 15 moons, one of which is the icy Bahryn. Large, armor-plated beasts known as bonzami live in cave systems on the moon's surface. These predators hunt both alone and in packs. Short, white hair covers their armor and allows them to blend into their icy habitat, should they encounter prey that can see in the dark. Their steady footsteps and loud screeches give warning as they approach. ISB Agent Kallus and the rebel Zeb Orrelios survive an encounter with a bonzami when they are marooned on Bahryn together.

KIER DOMADI
SPECIES Human **HOMEWORLD** Alderaan
AFFILIATION Apprentice Legislature

Kier Domadi represents Alderaan in the Imperial Junior Senate, alongside Princess Leia Organa. Unlike Organa, Domadi wants no part in politics and hopes to become a historian. He begins a relationship with Organa, but is killed on a mission. In remembrance, Organa keeps a lock of Domadi's hair for decades.

KRYKNA
HOMEWORLD Atollon **AVERAGE SIZE** 2 m (6 ft 7 in) high
HABITAT Deserts and caves

Large, spiderlike predators called krykna wander the barren wastes of Atollon, hunting snail-like dokmas. They live in underground colonies where they store food and lay their eggs. When Commander Sato's rebel cell establishes a base on Atollon, the fierce krykna pose an immediate problem. The rebels discover that the krykna are repelled by sensor beacons, so they set up a beacon perimeter to hold them at bay. Kanan Jarrus and Ezra Bridger are unable to connect with the creatures via the Force. It is only when an ancient being known as the Bendu teaches Kanan to rid himself of negative emotions that they are able to calm the krykna.

MORAI
AVERAGE SIZE 0.2 m (7.9 in) long
HABITAT Unrestricted by habitat

A mysterious convor bird named Morai follows Ahsoka Tano across the galaxy, watching over her. The creature has a strong connection to the Force and a spiritual link to the Daughter of Mortis. Morai can be seen with depictions of the Daughter, and may be either her servant or a manifestation of the powerful Force wielder. Morai is present in a world between worlds when Ezra Bridger enters the location via the Lothal Jedi temple, and she encourages him to save Ahsoka from certain death at the hands of Darth Vader. Following Ahsoka's return to Malachor, Morai often remains nearby the Togruta, even appearing on Peridea in a far galaxy.

AP-5
MANUFACTURER Arakyd Industries
TYPE RA-7 protocol droid
AFFILIATION Empire, rebels

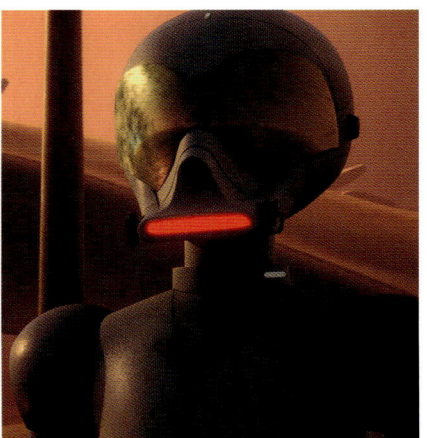

The protocol droid AP-5 is a military analyst for the Republic during the Clone Wars. When the Republic is transformed into the Empire, AP-5 is relegated to tracking inventory aboard Imperial Cargo Transport 241. He befriends the rebel droid Chopper when he finds him stowed away aboard the ship. AP-5 defects to join the rebels and provides them with an excellent location for their new rebel base on Atollon. AP-5 remains loyal to his new rebel friends, keeping inventory on their base before relocating with them to Yavin 4.

BENDU

HOMEWORLD Atollon
AFFILIATION The Force

Bendu is an ancient being with a powerful connection to the Force. He is attuned to the "middle," with neither an affinity to the light (Ashla) nor the dark (Bogan) side. Bendu is friendly to Kanan Jarrus and Ezra Bridger. He serves as a mentor to Kanan, until the Jedi oversteps his bounds and calls Bendu a coward for not intervening in the Battle of Atollon. Bendu manifests a great storm about him and unleashes his power upon Thrawn's forces and the rebels alike, demanding that they all leave his world. Thrawn commands his AT-ATs to fire at the heart of the storm, sending Bendu crashing to the ground. One with the Force, Bendu utters a prophecy of Thrawn's defeat (which comes true), just before vanishing.

EIGHTH BROTHER

SPECIES Terrelian Jango Jumper
HOMEWORLD Terrelia **AFFILIATION** Inquisitorius

The Eighth Brother is a former member of the Jedi Order who serves the Emperor as one of his Inquisitors, assigned to hunt the Jedi. Darth Vader orders him to locate Maul (known as "The Shadow"). The Inquisitor tracks Maul to the Sith temple on Malachor, where he finds more than he bargained for: Kanan Jarrus, Ezra Bridger, and Ahsoka Tano. During the resulting conflict, Kanan damages the Eighth Brother's lightsaber. The Inquisitor then leaps from the temple, using his spinning laser sword to fly, but it malfunctions and he appears to fall to his death.

ARIHNDA PRYCE

SPECIES Human **HOMEWORLD** Lothal **AFFILIATION** Empire

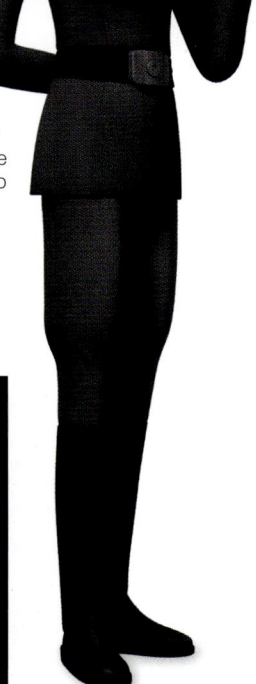

Arihnda Pryce rises to a prominent position in the Galactic Empire. She starts her career managing Pryce Mining, but has to hand over her family's business to the Empire, thanks to the scheming of Lothal's Governor Ryder Azadi. Pryce accepts a role in Senator Domus Renking's office on Coruscant, but he fires her, and she goes on to join the Higher Skies Advocacy Group. Pryce schemes revenge against Azadi and Renking, while forming an alliance with Imperial Officer Thrawn. In exchange for becoming Governor of Lothal, Pryce sells her employer out to Grand Moff Tarkin and betrays her homeworld by providing critical information on it. Minister Maketh Tua often serves as Pryce's proxy, as the governor frequently visits Coruscant. Pryce gains notoriety by stopping the Batonn Insurgency, but her hold over Lothal is threatened by growing rebel activity. She requests the recently promoted Grand Admiral Thrawn's help combating the rebels and works alongside him on many missions. She earns his displeasure when she destroys the Lothal Fuel Depot to eliminate rebel Jedi Kanan Jarrus, because this brings Thrawn's TIE defender program to a halt. During the liberation of Lothal, Pryce remains aboard the Imperial Complex as it rises above the planet. She perishes when rebel Sabine Wren destroys the facility.

Cunning schemes
Ambitious and calculating, Pryce learns quickly how to outmaneuver her opponents.

IMPERIAL SUPER COMMANDOS

SPECIES Human **HOMEWORLD** Various Mandalorian worlds **AFFILIATION** Empire

Mandalorian warriors under the command of Viceroy Gar Saxon serve as Imperial Super Commandos. They wipe out the Journeyman Protectors as retribution for assisting the rebels. Saxon forces Tristan Wren, brother of Sabine, to join the commandos and prove Wren's family's loyalty. However, Tristan eventually turns against Saxon, resulting in Saxon's death. The resulting Mandalorian civil war sees Tiber Saxon (Gar's brother) as the new leader of the commandos.

MELCH

SPECIES Ugnaught **AFFILIATION** Hondo Ohnaka

Melch is an Ugnaught who is enslaved and known only as "Laborer 429" on the Empire's Reklam Station. After being freed, Melch becomes an associate of Hondo Ohnaka and Azmorigan. The Ugnaught and Hondo assist the rebels, led by Hera Syndulla and Ezra Bridger, in their liberation of Lothal from the Empire.

VULT SKERRIS

SPECIES Human
AFFILIATION Empire

Vult Skerris is an Imperial commander as well as a flight instructor at the Skystrike Academy where he trains cadets such as Wedge Antilles and Derek Klivian. Serving under Grand Admiral Thrawn, Skerris tests the prototype TIE/d defender elite. His ship is destroyed during a dogfight with rebel pilot Hera Syndulla over Lothal.

MART MATTIN

SPECIES Human
HOMEWORLD Mykapo
AFFILIATION Rebels

Rebel Commander Jun Sato's nephew, Mart Mattin, is the leader of Iron Squadron, though it is comprised of only one ship: a YT-2400 light freighter, *Sato's Hammer*. Mart and his crew (Gooti Terez, Jonner Jin, and R3-A3) are an irritant to the Imperials in the Mykapo system. When his ship is damaged by Admiral Kassius Konstantine, Mart is rescued by the *Ghost* crew and joins his uncle's rebel cell. Mart plays a part in the liberation of Lothal, entrusted with a secret mission from Ezra Bridger to summon the purrgil. Remaining with the Alliance, Mattin joins Starlight Squadron after the Battle of Hoth. This small unit works to reunite the scattered rebel fleet divisions.

JONNER JIN

SPECIES Human **HOMEWORLD** Mykapo **AFFILIATION** Iron Squadron, Rebel Alliance

Steely Jonner Jin is a member of Mykapo's rebel Iron Squadron. When they are warned of an impending Imperial arrival, leader Mart Mattin refuses to depart, but teammates Jonner, Gooti Terez, and R3-A3 escape with the *Ghost* crew. They are reunited on Atollon however, and join the Rebel Alliance.

GOOTI TEREZ

SPECIES Theelin **HOMEWORLD** Mykapo **AFFILIATION** Iron Squadron, Rebel Alliance

Courageous Gooti Terez is a loyal member of the Iron Squadron cell, fighting against the Empire. Her team destroys an Imperial patrol with the help of the *Ghost* crew. Though she and her teammates evacuate onboard the *Ghost*, they must later return and rescue their leader, Mart Mattin, from the Imperials.

CHARACTERS AND CREATURES

THRAWN

SPECIES Chiss **HOMEWORLD** Csilla
AFFILIATION Chiss Ascendancy, Empire

Mitth'raw'nuruodo, otherwise known as Thrawn, is an intelligent member of the mysterious Chiss Ascendancy, an empire that controls part of the galaxy's Unknown Regions.

RISING THROUGH THE ASCENDANCY
Originally from an unnoteworthy family in the Chiss Ascendancy, Thrawn's skills and genius ensure he rises to a position of power within the Chiss Expansionary Defense Fleet. He disregards any rules he has to in order to protect his people from threats, including pirates and a rival power—the Nikardun Destiny.

LOOKING FOR AN ALLY
Charged with exploring the galaxy's Outer Rim to find a suitable ally for his people, Thrawn looks to the Republic. During the Clone Wars, he helps Anakin Skywalker find his missing wife Padmé Amidala on Batuu. In the process, they locate a factory making experimental battle droids for the Separatists and clone trooper armor. Mysteriously, both the droids and the armor are impervious to lightsabers. From these experiences, Thrawn deduces that the Republic is not a suitable ally. Years later, Thrawn feigns his exile from the Ascendancy in order to infiltrate the Empire to see if it may make a better ally than its predecessor.

WORKING WITH THE EMPIRE
Thrawn is found by the Empire in Wild Space and taken to the Emperor, who is impressed by his knowledge of the Unknown Regions and his tactical abilities. He is sent to the Royal Imperial Academy on Coruscant and later joins the Imperial Navy. Upon defeating his nemesis, Nevil Cygni, Thrawn is made Grand Admiral, with command of the Seventh Fleet, and is tasked with eliminating rebel insurgencies. Thrawn is renowned for the insights he gains into his enemies by understanding their philosophy, art, and culture. He also starts developing the TIE defender starfighter, a superior ship that easily outmatches any rebel vessel. While the defender is being developed on Lothal, Thrawn sets out to capture the sector's local rebels, leading to the Battle of Atollon and the defeat of Commander Jun Sato.

After this victory, the Emperor directs Thrawn and Darth Vader to investigate a disturbance in the Force on Batuu. There, they find the warlike Grysk have enslaved Force-attuned Chiss children. They free the children, but in the process Thrawn deduces Vader's true identity, and Vader uncovers Thrawn's first loyalty to the Chiss Ascendancy.

Thrawn then turns his attention on the rebels, who launch a campaign to liberate Lothal. He is irritated when Governor Arihnda Pryce thoughtlessly orders that her troops fire upon the Capital City's fuel tanks to kill the rebel leaders. While they eliminate Jedi Kanan Jarrus, the act stops production on the TIE defender. Regardless, the rebels succeed in liberating Lothal, and Ezra Bridger uses a pod of purrgil to pull himself and Thrawn away into deep space.

RETURN FROM EXILE
The purrgil take Thrawn and Ezra to another galaxy. During Thrawn's absence, the Empire falls but Imperial loyalists believe he will return and restore the evil regime. One such loyalist, Dathomirian witch Morgan Elsbeth, hears the calls of the Great Mothers, located on Peridea with Thrawn, and oversees construction of a powerful intergalactic hyperspace ring, the *Eye of Sion*, to travel to Peridea.

Thrawn spends his time in exile on Peridea allying with the Great Mothers to strengthen his forces. He maintains Imperial structure and puts his sharp observational skills to use to keep aging technology and equipment functional. When Ahsoka Tano follows the *Eye of Sion*'s journey and reunites with Sabine Wren and Ezra Bridger, Thrawn returns to the precise strategy he excels at and stops everyone but Ezra from joining him on his return journey to the known galaxy. Thrawn goes to Dathomir, his ship full of mysterious cargo from Peridea.

A worthy opponent
Thrawn respects Rebel Alliance leader Hera Syndulla as a strong opponent. They clash multiple times, and Thrawn even takes control of her home.

Promotion to Grand Admiral
Emperor Palpatine personally promotes Thrawn to Grand Admiral.

Battle of Lothal
During the Battle of Lothal, Thrawn cannot predict the novel strategy of Jedi and rebel Ezra Bridger. Both leaders are sorely missed during the ensuing Galactic Civil War.

Prophesized return
After many years, Thrawn returns to the galaxy he was born in. His arrival is a grim portent for the New Republic.

KLIK-KLAK

SPECIES Geonosian
HOMEWORLD Geonosis
AFFILIATION Hive of Karina the Great

Klik-Klak becomes one of the last remaining Geonosians after his people are exterminated by the Empire in order to keep the Death Star's construction a secret. He hides underground and builds a small droid army. Saw Gerrera and his partisans arrive to investigate the Geonosian disappearance. Fearing discovery, Klik-Klak's droids wipe out all but Saw. The *Ghost* crew arrives looking for Gerrera and captures Klik-Klak. Ezra Bridger's efforts uncover evidence of the Empire's deeds on Geonosis. Out of pity they free Klik-Klak, who carries a single Geonosian egg, which later hatches a new queen.

TARRE VIZSLA

SPECIES Human **AFFILIATION** Jedi, House Vizsla, Mandalore

Long before the Empire's formation, the first Mandalorian to join the Jedi Order is Tarre Vizsla. He creates the Darksaber, which House Vizsla uses to unite Mandalore under its rule.

SEEVOR

SPECIES Trandoshan **HOMEWORLD** Trandosha
AFFILIATION Mining Guild

Seevor manages Mining Guild vehicle Crawler 413-24. This is hijacked by the *Ghost* crew and his enslaved laborers are freed. During a fight with Ezra Bridger, Seevor falls into a smelter and is vaporized.

TRISTAN WREN

SPECIES Human **HOMEWORLD** Krownest
AFFILIATION Imperial Super Commandos, Clan Wren

Tristan Wren is the brother of Sabine Wren. When she abandons the Imperial Academy, Tristan is forced to join Gar Saxon's Imperial Super Commandos to prove his loyalty. Tristan is ordered to wipe out Clan Wren when his sister returns, but he sides with his family instead. During the Battle of Atollon he helps attack a Star Destroyer, allowing the Phoenix rebel cell to escape. During the Mandalorian civil war, Tristan and his mother are nearly killed by a weapon designed by Sabine. As the war expands, Clan Wren pledges its allegiance to Lady Bo-Katan Kryze, but Tristan does not appear to survive the Clan's destruction.

URSA WREN

SPECIES Human **HOMEWORLD** Krownest
AFFILIATION Clan Wren

Mandalorian Countess Ursa Wren is leader of Clan Wren, mother of Sabine and Tristan, and wife of Alrich. She is a former member of Death Watch and loyal to House Vizsla. During the Clone Wars, she is a key ally of Bo-Katan Kryze, helping her to secure Republic support and then fighting alongside her during the Siege of Mandalore. Years later, when Sabine flees the Imperial Academy, it brings shame upon her family and Ursa is forced to serve Imperial Viceroy Gar Saxon. When Ursa is reunited with Sabine, she betrays her daughter's rebel friends, offering to trade them to Saxon for Sabine's pardon. Saxon does not keep his word and Ursa shoots him. After this, Clan Wren allies with Sabine and the rebels. However, Ursa is believed to have died during the Great Purge of Mandalore.

LOTH-WOLF

HOMEWORLD Lothal **AVERAGE SIZE** 2.6 m (8 ft 6 in) high, 5.85 m (19 ft 2 in) long
HABITAT Grasslands and mountains

Loth-wolves have a close relationship with the original inhabitants of Lothal. Ancient drawings in the Jedi temple and southern caves depict them together. Yet the mysterious creatures are so seldom seen during the time of the Empire that many believe them extinct. Loth-wolves have a strong connection with the Force, the energy of the planet, and a world between worlds. They can travel vast distances in seemingly no time. They also aid the rebels and play an indispensable role in Lothal's liberation.

WHITE LOTH-WOLF

SPECIES Loth-wolf **HOMEWORLD** Lothal
AFFILIATION Lothal, the Loth-wolves

The White Loth-wolf is the alpha of a pack of wolves on Lothal. He is finely attuned to the will of the Force and driven to protect the planet. The Loth-wolf serves as a guide to Kanan Jarrus and Ezra Bridger. He has the ability to render people unconscious when he wishes to conceal events, but he can also communicate by speaking Basic. After Kanan Jarrus' death, the White Loth-wolf introduces a grieving Ezra Bridger to a similar creature called Dume—a Force manifestation of Kanan Jarrus' will after his death.

ALRICH WREN

SPECIES Human **HOMEWORLD** Krownest
AFFILIATION Clan Wren

When Alrich marries Ursa Wren, he takes her clan name as his own. Unlike his wife and children, Alrich is an artist rather than a warrior (although his daughter Sabine inherits his creative nature). When Sabine leaves the Imperial Academy, Alrich is held on Mandalore as a veritable political prisoner. After Clan Wren sides with Sabine and the rebels against the Saxons, Alrich is transported to Sundari for execution. Sabine and her friends successfully rescue her father just in time. As the Mandalorian civil war expands, Alrich encourages his wife to refrain from attacking Tiber Saxon's Star Destroyer herself. Alrich is presumed killed during the Great Purge of Mandalore.

GITA

SPECIES Human
AFFILIATION Rebel Alliance

An impossibly good shot, Gita is a sniper and secret agent for the Rebel Alliance. Working in disguise as a Tusken called Urrr'k, she is recruited to Beilert Valance's crew for the Hidden Hand's mission to kill Darth Vader. When the job goes awry, Gita reveals herself to the cyborg, and they later cut a deal to supply the Rebellion with the weapons they need.

YURALLA VEGA

SPECIES Human **HOMEWORLD** Chorin
AFFILIATION Rebel Alliance

Yuralla Vega and her love, Beilert Valance, part ways following his time in the Empire. She starts a new life, but their paths cross years later when Valance returns to Chorin, placing the young Cadeliah—heir to two rival crime syndicates—in her care. Vega watches over the girl until a Crimson Dawn assassin tracks them to a Rebel Alliance base, snatching the girl away.

RUKH

SPECIES Noghri **HOMEWORLD** Honoghr
AFFILIATION Empire (Grand Admiral Thrawn)

Grand Admiral Thrawn's most trusted bodyguard and assassin is an unrelenting, calculating Noghri named Rukh. The brute has excellent eyesight and sense of smell, and is exceptionally strong and agile. A cloaking device allows him to hunt invisibly, too. Thrawn calls upon Rukh to hunt the rebels on Lothal. Rukh is instrumental in capturing General Hera Syndulla, but not all of his missions are successful. He is overpowered and humiliated by Sabine Wren and Garazeb Orrelios (Zeb), but they naively release him. During the liberation of Lothal, he is electrocuted while fighting with Zeb inside the Imperial Complex.

VERIS HYDAN

SPECIES Human
HOMEWORLD Ossus
AFFILIATION Empire

Minister Veris Hydan is an exalted advisor to Emperor Palpatine. Though not a Force-wielder himself, he is a skilled archaeologist and Mortisologist. Hydan is assigned to excavate the Lothal Jedi temple and find an entrance to a mysterious world between worlds. Though Ezra Bridger escapes into the Force realm, Hydan captures Sabine Wren and forces her to decipher the temple's Mortis mural. Sabine escapes though, and when the portal is closed again, Hydan is lost in a chasm that swallows up the temple.

JACEN SYNDULLA

SPECIES Human-Twi'lek hybrid
HOMEWORLD Lothal
AFFILIATION Rebel Alliance

Jacen Syndulla is the son of Twi'lek Rebel General Hera Syndulla and the late Jedi Knight Kanan Jarrus. Jacen grows up during the Galactic Civil War, never having met his father, and is surrounded by love from the people (and droid Chopper) he calls his family. As a member of the *Ghost*'s crew from an early age, known by the call sign "Spectre 7," Jacen participates in missions alongside his mother. Force-attuned and curious, Jacen wants to be a Jedi like his father and train like his Aunt Sabine. Hera takes Jacen's abilities seriously, listening when he has feelings. This pays off on Seatos when Jacen is the only one who senses Ahsoka Tano didn't perish when she fell into the ocean. He hears Ahsoka's lightsabers clashing with those of Anakin Skywalker below the waves, and, with Chopper's help, pinpoints her coordinates and helps save her life.

LYRA ERSO

SPECIES Human
HOMEWORLD Aria Prime
AFFILIATION Erso family

After graduating from the University of Rudrig, Lyra works as a guide for Galen Erso's scientific team on an expedition on Espinar. She and Galen are married on Coruscant and their daughter Jyn is born on Vallt during the Clone Wars. The family is taken prisoner during the conflict, but rescued by Orson Krennic. Both Lyra and Galen are offered jobs by Krennic, at which point Lyra begins to suspect the Empire of great evil. The family escapes to Lah'mu, hiding there for four years. When Krennic finds them, Lyra bravely draws a blaster but is shot by a death trooper.

GALEN WALTON ERSO

SPECIES Human
HOMEWORLD Grange
AFFILIATION Erso family, Empire (against his will)

As a child prodigy, Galen Erso excels at his early studies—especially math and science. While enrolled at the Republic Futures Program, he befriends architecture student Orson Krennic. The two work on Coruscant and Galen becomes renowned as a crystallographer, receiving numerous scientific awards. He and his wife, Lyra Erso, have a daughter, Jyn Erso. Krennic manipulates Galen into researching kyber crystals for his Death Star weapons program. Growing wary of the Empire, Galen and his family flee to Lah'mu, but Krennic tracks them there and forces Galen to return to his work on the Death Star—alone. Lyra is killed and Jyn safely hidden, to be raised by their friend Saw Gerrera. Knowing he can't escape Imperial service, Galen builds a fatal flaw into the Death Star that he hopes will be exploited by the rebels. Galen is reunited with his daughter one last time at the Imperial facility on Eadu, as he lies dying in her arms, wounded by a rebel bombing raid.

Family in exile
Jyn's health and happiness are more important to Galen than anything else. His research has often taken him away from her, so on Lah'mu, while hiding out from the Empire, he tries to make up for lost time.

ORSON CALLAN KRENNIC

SPECIES Human **HOMEWORLD** Lexrul **AFFILIATION** Republic, Empire

Orson Krennic is born in Sativran City on Lexrul during the Galactic Republic era. He is placed in the Republic Futures Program on Brentaal where he befriends fellow student, Galen Erso. Krennic joins the Republic Corps of Engineers and helps Galen get hired at the Institute of Applied Sciences. Krennic progresses into the top-secret Republic Special Weapons Group and begins to research development of the Death Star, using plans captured from Geonosis. Krennic immediately realizes the project needs the talents of his friend Galen. Krennic pressures Galen to research kyber crystals for the Death Star's superlaser. Shortly after the Empire's formation, Krennic attends a high-level Imperial summit on Eriadu to update those attending on the project. With progressive successes, the ambitious Krennic is promoted to Director of the Advanced Weapons Research Division of the Imperial Security Bureau. Grand Moff Tarkin orders a test fire of the Death Star on the Holy City of Jedha. When rebels steal the Death Star plans from Scarif, Tarkin obliterates the entire facility, including Krennic and all present—both Rebel Alliance and Imperials.

ZO-E3
AFFILIATION None

Wisecracking but loyal, ZO-E3 is the droid copilot of the smuggler ship *Windfall*. When the vessel is ripped from hyperspace by an Imperial Interdictor, ZO-E3 and the captain find themselves prisoner in Darth Vader's castle on Mustafar. The Sith Lord needs the captain—a Force-attuned descendant of Lady Corvax—in order to access the ancient Bright Star device. ZO-E3 and the captain eventually stop Vader and escape, but not before ZO-E3 activates a star chart hidden in her partner's lightsaber. The droid believes it could be a treasure map and suggests they check it out.

GABLE KARIUS
SPECIES Human
AFFILIATION Empire

Admiral aboard the Imperial Interdictor above Mustafar, Gable Karius captures the *Windfall* on the orders of Darth Vader, who believes its captain is the key to accessing an ancient device. After the captain and his droid copilot ZO-E3 escape, the admiral and his stormtroopers continually pursue them. ZO-E3 shocks Karius and sends him careening over a railing. Karius returns in a TIE fighter looking to destroy the duo once and for all. He proves unsuccessful, however, and seemingly meets his end as his ship crashes and explodes.

VYLIP F'ALMA
SPECIES Mustafarian **HOMEWORLD** Mustafar
AFFILIATION His Mustafarian clan

Lore master of his Mustafarian clan, Vylip F'alma is a keeper of his people's history and secrets. He befriends a smuggler and his droid, ZO-E3, when they are captured by Imperials and brought to Mustafar, and he eventually helps them escape. Vylip tells the pair about the Bright Star—a device long sought by Darth Vader for its mystical properties. When they recover the artifact, however, F'alma gifts it to the Sith Lord, believing the act will save his planet. Instead, Vader attempts to destroy the group. Though Vylip tries to atone for his betrayal, he's interrupted by a darkghast—and gobbled whole.

DORWIN CORVAX
SPECIES Human **HOMEWORLD** Mustafar

When the warrior of Mustafar Dorwin Corvax perishes in battle, his wife, Lady Corvax, tries to bring him back using the power of the Bright Star device. Her attempts are unsuccessful, however, and he's trapped between the realm of the living and the dead, and the lush Mustafarian landscape is turned into lava and rock. Dorwin returns a millennia later and aids his descendant in a quest to find the Bright Star and destroy it using his own ancient light sword. Following the artifact's destruction, a grateful Dorwin is released from his purgatory.

WANNEK
SPECIES Mustafarian
HOMEWORLD Mustafar

A citizen of the subterranean caves of Mustafar, Wannek is well-versed in the planet's mysteries and dangers. She comes to the aid of the descendant of Lord Corvax and his droid, ZO-E3, when they encounter a deadly darkghast creature. Wannek—who sports distinctive goggles for "protection and style"— remains with the pair as they journey through the lava world, guiding them to Darth Vader's castle in a bid to stop the Sith Lord. Vader is attempting to activate the Aeon Engine, which is a device to harness the energy of the Bright Star.

MUSTAFARIAN PRIESTESS
SPECIES Mustafarian **HOMEWORLD** Mustafar
AFFILIATION Her Mustafarian clan

The Mustafarian Priestess is a spiritual leader who has a strong connection with the Force. She encounters the descendant of Dorwin Corvax, with whom she shares a vision of the past. It recounts Lady Corvax's catastrophic attempt to save her husband through the power of the Bright Star, forever altering Mustafar. She later summons Lord Corvax to help his descendant in a mission to stop Darth Vader from activating the Aeon Engine with the Bright Star. Though she succumbs to the Aeon Engine's power, her efforts are not in vain.

LADY CORVAX
SPECIES Human
HOMEWORLD Mustafar

The Force-attuned wife of Dorwin Corvax, Lady Corvax lives in peace with the Mustafarians until forces attack their world. Her husband falls in battle, and a grief-stricken Lady Corvax tries to restore his life. She builds the Aeon Engine, powered by the Bright Star—the most sacred object of the Mustafarians—to bring Dorwin back. But the pastoral Mustafar landscape turns to lava and molten rock, and her beloved is trapped in a realm between life and death. She stores the key to the Aeon Engine—her husband's light sword, in his tomb—and only a descendant can use it to activate the device.

DARKGHAST
HOMEWORLD Mustafar
SIZE 5 m (16 ft 5 in) high
HABITAT Caves

One of Mustafar's most deadly native creatures, the darkghast is a large, ferocious beast that stalks the underground caverns of the planet. While it sports some visual similarities to the rancor, there are important differences between the two species. The darkghast has four strong arms, which it uses to catch and devour prey and climb walls. Its legs are also impressively powerful, able to easily stomp out threats. The animal's tough hide, calcified due to the heat of Mustafar's lava, is marked with pops of color.

CHARACTERS AND CREATURES

JYN ERSO
SPECIES Human **HOMEWORLD** None **AFFILIATION** Partisans, Rebel Alliance

A rebel, criminal, and hero, Jyn Erso is torn from her family as a child and raised by a revolutionary. After Saw abandons her, Jyn forsakes her destiny for a time, before being pulled back into a fight for the galaxy, after which she becomes a legend.

WAYWARD EARLY LIFE
Jyn Erso is born on Vallt, to parents Galen and Lyra Erso. She spends her early life moving around due to her father's scientific work for the Empire, living on Lokori and Coruscant. Wary of the Empire's growing power, her family flees to Lah'mu. When they are tracked down by Imperial Director Orson Krennic, Galen instructs Jyn to hide in a pre-prepared location. Lyra is killed and Galen is taken away, and assumed dead by his daughter. Family friend Saw Gerrera rescues Jyn and she grows up as a member of his rebel "partisans" and one of his best fighters, meeting the infamous freedom fighter Enfys Nest along the way. Saw and Jyn part company, and she lives as a criminal with many aliases. Eventually arrested by the Empire, Jyn is sent to an Imperial labor camp on Wobani. There, the Rebel Alliance breaks her out and brings her to Yavin 4. Initially mistrustful of them and their cause, Jyn learns her father is alive and developing a superweapon for the Empire.

Lah'mu farewells
Lyra embraces her daughter, knowing she may never see her again, and gifts her a kyber crystal necklace to remind her of the power of the Force.

Surrogate father
Jyn looked to Saw as her replacement father, but felt betrayed by him when he abandoned her, not knowing it was for her own safety.

LOOKING FOR SAW
The rebels need Jyn to find her old mentor Saw and acquire a message sent to him by Galen Erso. Jyn flies with Captain Cassian Andor and his droid companion K-2SO to Jedha to search for Saw. They enter the Holy City and meet former Guardians of the Whills Chirrut Îmwe and Baze Malbus, who save them from stormtroopers. A skirmish erupts with Saw's partisans, and the group is captured by Gerrera's troops. Jyn is taken to Saw for a reunion and persuades him to play her father's message. Galen reveals that he has built a fatal flaw into the Empire's new planet-killer, known as the Death Star. When the dreaded battle station fires upon and destroys the Holy City, Saw instructs Jyn to leave him behind. Jyn and her new friends (including Bodhi Rook, former Imperial pilot and friend of Galen) escape in Cassian's U-wing.

From child soldier to rebel
Under Saw's tutelage, Jyn quickly learns how to fight. She excels at hand-to-hand combat, such as with her trusty truncheons, and also acquires other survival skills. Saw prizes Jyn as his greatest warrior.

CHASING A FAMILY LEGACY
After crash-landing on Eadu, where they hope to find her father, Jyn learns that Cassian intends to assassinate him. Jyn rushes to find Galen, after climbing up to the secret Imperial research facility. Before she can reach him, Galen is fatally wounded by a sudden rebel bombing raid. Father and daughter are reunited for just a moment, before he dies in her arms. Cassian pulls her away and the team escapes, flying on to the rebel headquarters on Yavin 4. There, Jyn makes an impassioned plea to the Rebel Alliance leaders, begging them to sanction an infiltration of the Imperial data vault on Scarif to steal the Death Star plans—before it is too late. The rebel council isn't convinced though. They vote against Jyn's proposal, leaving her further disillusioned.

Preceding reputation
Although Mon Mothma agrees with Jyn, she cannot act without her allies' support, the majority of which are unwilling to trust the word of a known criminal.

Undercover
Cassian and Jyn assume Imperial disguises— Jyn as a technician—and work together with K-2SO to gain access to the Scarif vault.

THE FATAL BATTLE OF SCARIF
To Jyn's surprise, Cassian assembles a squadron of volunteer soldiers for the mission and they depart for Scarif—against orders. Now working as a unit whose members trust one another, they slip through the planet's shield gate and arrive at the landing pad. Jyn, Cassian, and K-2SO then sneak inside the Citadel Tower. Once inside the data vault, Jyn and Cassian search through the file names for the Death Star plans, stopping at "Stardust," Galen's nickname for Jyn. They retrieve the data tape and climb the tower to the transmitter. Despite facing a last-minute attempt to stop them by Krennic, Jyn and Cassian successfully transmit the plans to the rebel fleet. After descending the tower, they embrace one another as the Death Star fires on Scarif, sending a shockwave that obliterates everything.

DEATH TROOPERS
SPECIES Human (modified) **HOMEWORLD** Various
AFFILIATION Empire

Death troopers are elite soldiers altered in a top-secret program to boost stormtrooper performance beyond normal human limitations. Emperor Palpatine chooses their name to capitalize on rumors of Imperial experiments leading to the reanimation of necrotic tissue. Death trooper squads act as bodyguards and enforcers for high-ranking Imperials such as Governor Wilhuff Tarkin, Grand Admiral Thrawn, Darth Vader, Sly Moore, Moff Gideon, and Director Orson Krennic. They are also assigned to guard classified shipments of kyber crystals. Death troopers participate in warfare on Atollon, Eadu, and Scarif. Many death troopers remain loyal after the Empire's fall, dutifully protecting Imperial leaders.

BENTHIC TWO TUBES
SPECIES Tognath **HOMEWORLD** Yar Togna
AFFILIATION Cloud-Riders, partisans

Benthic "Two Tubes" flees his planet with his eggmate, Edrio, when it is overrun by the Empire. Benthic then joins Enfys Nest's Cloud-Riders to fight the Crimson Dawn crime syndicate. He takes part in their raid on Vandor, attempting to steal a coaxium shipment, and then a skirmish on Savareen to recover another supply. Thereafter, Benthic joins Saw Gerrera's partisans and is present on Segra Milo when rebel agent Luthen Rael visits to discuss whether to sacrifice Anto Kreegyr's rebel cell. Benthic is outraged when Luthen suggests he's a traitor. Years later on Jedha, he interrogates Bodhi Rook and delivers him to Saw, but must evacuate when the Holy City is destroyed. During the Galactic Civil War, he meets Princess Leia Organa and forms a new partnership between the partisans and Rebel Alliance.

OOLIN MUSTERS
SPECIES Blutopian **AFFILIATION** Rebel Alliance

Also known as "Nail" and "Kennel," Oolin Musters is a member of the Rebel Alliance. She is captured by the Empire and imprisoned on Wobani, finding herself cellmates with Jyn Erso, whom she threatens to kill. When Jyn is rescued, Musters escapes and makes her way to Jedha.

RUESCOTT MELSHI
SPECIES Human **AFFILIATION** Rebel Alliance

Ruescott Melshi is a friend of Cassian Andor, who he meets when they are both imprisoned in an Imperial complex on Narkina 5 and forced to build components for the Empire. After they escape, Melshi and Andor stay together and head offworld with the help of some anglers. Melshi goes on to join the Rebel Alliance and leads an extraction team to rescue Jyn Erso from a labor camp on Wobani prior to the onset of the Galactic Civil War. Later, he helps assemble a team of rebel volunteers for Jyn and Cassian, and is killed in the Battle of Scarif.

EDRIO TWO TUBES
SPECIES Tognath **HOMEWORLD** Yar Togna
AFFILIATION Partisans, Cavern Angels

Edrio "Two Tubes" and his eggmate, or brother, Benthic, get their nicknames from the pair of breathing tubes they wear. They flee their homeworld after the Empire takes control. Edrio joins Saw Gerrera's partisans and bombs the Empire's Jalindi relay. In the process he destroys the light cruiser *Marauder* and rescues rebels Ezra Bridger and Sabine Wren. Edrio and Saw then destroy a large kyber crystal in the Tonnis sector, and with it two Imperial ships. Edrio is killed when the Death Star test-fires on the Holy City of Jedha.

BODHI ROOK
SPECIES Human **HOMEWORLD** Jedha
AFFILIATION Empire, Rebel Alliance

Bodhi Rook is a gentle soul who was raised on Jedha. Bodhi enrolls in the Terrabe Sector Service Academy, hoping to become an Imperial starfighter pilot, yet is unable to continue that course due to poor test scores. Instead, Bodhi is assigned to fly Imperial cargo shuttles.

In time, Bodhi begins to have misgivings about his service to the Empire. He befriends rogue Imperial scientist Galen Erso, who encourages Bodhi to defect and deliver a secret message intended for his daughter Jyn Erso to rebel extremist Saw Gerrera on Jedha. Bodhi approaches Saw's partisans but is taken prisoner. They take him to their headquarters in the Catacombs of Cadera, where Bodhi finally meets Gerrera. Paranoid Saw does not believe Bodhi's tale and uses a terrifying Mairan named Bor Gullet to frighten and interrogate Bodhi, profoundly impacting Bodhi's mental state.

When motley rebel crew Cassian Andor, Jyn Erso, Baze Malbus, and Chirrut Îmwe are also captured by Saw's forces, Jyn is given her father's message detailing a fatal flaw in the Death Star. At that same moment the superweapon fires on Jedha's Holy City. Bodhi escapes and helps them fly to Eadu to meet Galen. From there they fly to Yavin 4, where Cassian assembles a team—including Bodhi—to infiltrate the Imperial facility on Scarif and steal the Death Star plans. As they leave Yavin 4, Bodhi applies a call sign to the team: "Rogue One."

Bodhi uses his Imperial insight to get the team through Imperial security and the shield gate above Scarif. He stays with their ship while Cassian, Jyn, and reprogrammed Imperial security droid K-2SO go to steal the plans. As the battle begins, Bodhi feeds the Imperials misleading reports and alerts the Rebel Alliance fleet that they must destroy Scarif's shield gate so they can receive Jyn's transmission of the valuable information. After successfully making contact, Bodhi is killed in an explosion.

Facing foes
During the Battle of Scarif, Bodhi must hook his stolen shuttle up to the Imperial communications network. This brings him into direct conflict with the Imperial forces he used to work with.

BOR GULLET
SPECIES Mairan **HOMEWORLD** Maires
AFFILIATION Partisans

Bor Gullet is a member of a bulbous, tentacled Mairan species. Mairans can read minds and sense intentions by wrapping their tentacles around the cranium of an individual, so are used by some groups to interrogate prisoners. The process is extremely unpleasant and sometimes used as a form of torture. Prolonged exposure can cause memory loss and even insanity. The effects of short-term exposure are reversible. Saw Gerrera keeps Bor Gullet in a den at his headquarters on Jedha, using the Mairan to interrogate pilot Bodhi Rook.

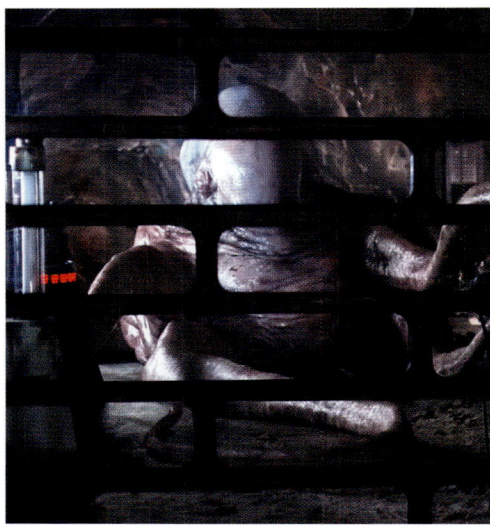

CHARACTERS AND CREATURES

Pessimistic pilot
K-2SO and Cassian are approved for solo or tandem U-wing flights. At the start of their missions K-2SO likes to calculate the low odds of their success.

K-2SO

MANUFACTURER Arakyd Industries
TYPE KX-series security droid
AFFILIATION Empire, Rebel Alliance

During the Imperial era, Rebel agent Cassian Andor acquires security droid K-2SO and reprograms him to serve the rebels, albeit with some quirks: K-2 is unfailingly blunt and has a propensity to violence. The two work closely together on subsequent missions, including spending time with Wookiees.

K-2 accompanies a rebel extraction team to free Jyn Erso from the prison labor camp on Wobani. Back on Yavin 4, the droid expresses displeasure, namely because Jyn, a captured criminal, is allowed to keep a weapon but Cassian doesn't trust him with one. The trio travels to Jedha to look for Saw Gerrera, who holds vital intel. K-2 is ordered to stay behind and guard their U-wing, but disapproves of this instruction so he follows Cassian and Jyn into the Holy City, where he prevents the pair from being arrested by stormtroopers.

Afterward, K-2 returns to their ship, enabling him to make a daring rescue of the pair and their new friends, Chirrut Îmwe, Baze Malbus, and Imperial defector Bodhi Rook, when the Death Star destroys the Holy City. K-2 pilots the group to find Jyn's father, Galen Erso, on Eadu, where the ship crash-lands due to stormy weather. As Jyn and Cassian venture forth, K-2 steals an Imperial cargo shuttle, which proves vital in the team's eventual escape and return to Yavin 4.

After forming a volunteer team to invade the Imperial's stronghold on Scarif where the Death Star plans are kept, K-2SO, Cassian, and Jyn pose as Imperials to sneak inside the complex, where K-2 disables a fellow KX-series droid and acquires a map of the facility from its memory banks. After reaching the data vault, K-2 takes over a computer console, where he guides Jyn and Cassian in their search for the plans. Jyn provides K-2 with a blaster, which greatly pleases him. As she and Cassian continue on with their mission to reach the tower and transmit the plans to the rebel fleet, stormtroopers infiltrate the vault. K-2 seals the doors and fights off the soldiers as long as he can, in order to buy Jyn and Cassian time, but he is eventually destroyed.

ANTOC MERRICK

SPECIES Human
HOMEWORLD Virujansi
AFFILIATION Rarified Air Cavalry, Rebel Alliance

Antoc Merrick is the lead pilot of the Virujansi planetary defense force. When the new Imperial-appointed governor replaces the ruling council, Merrick retires and instead joins the Rebel Alliance, earning the rank of general with oversight over all Starfighter Command. Merrick flies a T-65B X-wing as Blue Leader at the Battle of Scarif. He and his Blue Squadron penetrate the shield gate and fight along the surface of Scarif. He destroys several Imperial AT-ACTs, but his X-wing is shot down by TIE strikers and he is killed.

DAVITS DRAVEN

SPECIES Human
HOMEWORLD Pendarr III
AFFILIATION Rebel Alliance

During the Clone Wars, Davits Draven is a member of the Galactic Republic's military intelligence. His colleagues become Imperial officers, but Draven joins the Rebel Alliance and is trained as a field operative. Draven makes difficult decisions as a spy and top intelligence officer. He unravels Galen Erso's connection to the Death Star as part of Operation Fracture, ordering the rescue of Jyn Erso and assassination of Galen. After the Battle of Yavin he takes charge of the interrogation of Grakkus the Hutt. On a later mission, Draven is killed by Darth Vader.

IMPERIAL WEAPONS TECHNICIAN

SPECIES Human **HOMEWORLD** Various
AFFILIATION Empire

Imperial weapons technicians, also known as gunners, are usually cadets taken from the Imperial Navy's pilot training programs who either have not graduated to full pilot status or are past their prime and have not risen in rank sufficiently to receive a command. They operate weaponry such as turbolasers, ion cannons, and the Death Star's superlaser and experimental technology like the gravity wells on the Imperial Interdictor. Black uniforms are common, but technicians in experimental programs may wear other colors.

WEETEEF CYU-BEE

SPECIES Talpini **HOMEWORLD** Tal Pi
AFFILIATION Partisans

Talpini Weeteef Cyu-Bee is a member of Saw Gerrera's partisans on Jedha. He is an explosives expert, using his sticky bombs to take down Imperial vehicles, and is an excellent marksman too. Jyn Erso and Cassian Andor get caught in a skirmish where Weeteef targets an Imperial patrol and does much damage.

BEEZER FORTUNA

SPECIES Twi'lek **HOMEWORLD** Ryloth
AFFILIATION Partisans

Beezer Fortuna is a cousin of Bib Fortuna, the majordomo of Jabba the Hutt. He is inspired by fellow Twi'lek freedom fighter Cham Syndulla to fight his planet's oppressors. Beezer is imprisoned by the Empire in Lessu but freed by Saw Gerrera's partisans. He becomes Saw's strategist on Jedha.

CHIRRUT ÎMWE

SPECIES Human **HOMEWORLD** Jedha **AFFILIATION** Guardians of the Whills, partisans, Rebel Alliance

Chirrut Îmwe and his friend Baze Malbus are members of the near-extinct Guardians of the Whills, and sworn to protect the Temple of the Whills in Jedha's Holy City. Chirrut believes strongly in the Force. He has great respect for the old Jedi Order and seems to have an innate Force connection, allowing him to sense things before they happen—a sort of vision without eyesight (he is blind). After the Empire comes to Jedha, Chirrut apprehends criminals Dok-Ondar and Hondo Ohnaka with a stolen statue from the temple's tunnels, but agrees to let them go with the piece of art after hearing Dok-Ondar's emotional and embellished plea. After the Guardians are kicked out of the temple by the Empire, Chirrut and Baze join Saw Gerrera's partisans on one condition—that the group provides supplies for their orphanage. The partisan's violent methods only create more orphans, however. Chirrut and Baze then look to transport the orphans offworld. They steal an Imperial shuttle for their plan, but when the partisans want it for an attack, Chirrut and Baze leave the group.

When the Rebel Alliance sends Jyn Erso, Cassian Andor, and K-2SO to Jedha, Chirrut encounters Jyn in the market by sensing her kyber-crystal necklace. He and Baze save the rebels from stormtroopers, only to be kidnapped by Gerrera's militia. When the Death Star destroys the Holy City, Chirrut and Baze escape aboard Cassian's ship. They fly to Eadu to find Jyn's father, where Chirrut warns Jyn that the Force suggests Cassian is about to kill someone (likely her father). A skirmish between the rebels and Empire follows, in which Chirrut's Force connection helps him to shoot down a TIE fighter.

Back on Yavin 4, Chirrut and Baze volunteer for Jyn's mission to steal the Death Star plans on Scarif. They lead a team setting off explosives to lure stormtroopers away from the data vault. Chirrut heads out alone in the midst of the battle to flip the landing zone's master switch, necessary for the rebels to transmit the Death Star plans to their fleet. Chirrut is successful, but hit by an explosion. He dies in Baze's arms.

Weapons master
Zamo-shiwo martial artist Chirrut is able to take down many stormtroopers on Jedha with his staff. On other occasions he is a deadly aim with his lightbow (left).

One with the Force
Chirrut's calm belief in the Force is sometimes a source of mockery for his pragmatic, battle-hardened friend Baze. But it brings him courage and strength even in the face of certain defeat during the Battle of Scarif.

BAZE MALBUS

SPECIES Human **HOMEWORLD** Jedha **AFFILIATION** Guardians of the Whills, partisans, Rebel Alliance

Gruff Baze Malbus serves the Guardians of the Whills in Jedha's Holy City, alongside his close friend Chirrut Îmwe. When Imperial forces seal the Temple of the Kyber and disband the Guardians, Baze becomes disillusioned with his faith and past calling. Baze and Chirrut join Saw Gerrera's partisans and insist the group help them care for the city's orphans. The duo steals an Imperial Sentinel and plan to transport the orphans off Jedha and away from the fighting, but this causes friction among the partisans and they depart the group on bad terms. Baze becomes a freelance assassin, but remains close to Chirrut.

When Cassian Andor, Jyn Erso, and K-2SO arrive on Jedha, Chirrut tries to save them from stormtroopers and Baze steps in to help, though all of them are then captured by the partisans. When the Death Star fires on Jedha, Baze and Chirrut escape aboard Cassian's ship with their new friends. They fly to Eadu to find Jyn's father, Galen, and then on to Yavin 4 to discuss Galen's revelations about the Empire's Death Star.

Though Rebel Alliance High Command refuses to sanction a mission to Imperial base Scarif to steal the Death Star plans, Baze and Chirrut are inspired by Jyn's call to action and volunteer for her forbidden venture. On Scarif, the two lead a team to lure soldiers away from the data vault while Cassian, Jyn, and K-2SO sneak inside. Chirrut walks out amidst the ensuing battle and is hit by an explosion. Chirrut assures Baze that if he looks to the Force, he will always find Chirrut there. He then dies in Baze's arms. Knowing he cannot survive the battle, Baze clings to the Force and his friend's words and boldly charges the Imperial soldiers to face his own death.

Battle ready
Baze has traded the monklike clothes of the Guardians of the Whills for battle armor. He is never without his customized repeating blaster, which he unleashes on advancing Imperials on Scarif (left).

144 CHARACTERS AND CREATURES

IMPERIAL TANK PILOT
SPECIES Human **HOMEWORLD** Various
AFFILIATION Empire

Imperial tank pilots are a specialized corps of drivers that operate TX-225 combat assault tanks. On Jedha, these tanks carry kyber crystals in orange transport containers. The tanks require a minimum crew of three: the driver, gunner, and commander (identified by gray shoulder markings). There are many iterations of their armor incorporating design improvements and customized to match the requirements of each vehicle. Most are light and flexible to allow pilots to squeeze into cramped driving compartments.

TAM POSLA
SPECIES Human **HOMEWORLD** Milvayne
AFFILIATION Milvayne Authority, bounty hunter

Tam Posla is a galactic law enforcement officer who goes beyond the call of duty and becomes a bounty hunter. He comes to Jedha to investigate reports of kidnapping, humanoid trafficking, and horrific surgical experiments committed by "Roofoo" (Dr. Evazan) and "Sawkee" (Ponda Baba). He later joins Doctor Chelli Aphra's team of mercenaries, which raids the laboratory of deceased Techno Union leader Wat Tambor and kidnaps Rebel Alliance General Hera Syndulla to gain access to the Tarkin Initiative's Hivebase-1. In a later misadventure he tries to arrest Aphra, but is killed by the droid Triple-Zero (0-0-0). Posla's body is later reanimated by a Force-attuned space fungus.

WOAN BARSO
SPECIES Human **AFFILIATION** Refugee Relief Movement

The ongoing insurgency on Jedha has left many people displaced. Woan Barso smuggles some such refugees from Jedha's Holy City in his old container tug, to freighters in orbit, but it is a risky trip. He wears a life suit at all times because his ship's life support systems are unreliable. During the New Republic Era, Woan is recognized by Zeva Bliss, the leader of the Spice Runners of Kijimi, as a notorious pirate, and he agrees to attend her criminal summit with the alliance mooted at the event. None of attendees realize that Zeva is planning to kill them all and are saved by Spice Runner Poe Dameron's intervention.

CAYSIN BOG
SPECIES High-gravity humanoid
HOMEWORLD Teres Lutha Minor
AFFILIATION Mercenary

Caysin Bog is blown apart in a partisan strike on Jedha and then reassembled by Dr. Cornelius Evazan (going by the name "Roofoo"). He escapes the desolation of Jedha and works with his partner Tam Posla and Doctor Chelli Aphra on a contract to loot the laboratory of deceased Techno Union leader Wat Tambor on Skako Minor. From there the team kidnaps Rebel Alliance General Hera Syndulla to use in a trade and gain access to the Empire's Hivebase-1. Once inside, Aphra causes Bog's death to gain a personal advantage, which enrages Tam Posla.

FEYN VANN
SPECIES Human **HOMEWORLD** Tri-Barr Station
AFFILIATION Nordoxicon Unlimited, Empire

Feyn Vann is a renowned engineer from Nordoxicon recruited to develop a series of deflector arrays that channel hypermatter streams from the Death Star's main reactor to the crystalline firing array. He is killed alongside his peers by death troopers on Eadu at the command of Imperial Director Orson Krennic.

ADMIRAL RADDUS
SPECIES Mon Calamari **HOMEWORLD** Mon Cala
AFFILIATION Nystullum city government, Royal Court of King Lee-Char, Mon Cala Mercantile Fleet, Rebel Alliance

As mayor of Nystullum on Mon Cala, Admiral Raddus advises King Lee-Char and defends Mon Cala from Governor Wilhuff Tarkin's Imperial invasion. When the Empire takes control of the planet, Raddus takes part in the Mon Calamari exodus, commanding the Nystullum government city-ship, the *Profundity*. Raddus joins the Rebel Alliance and commands their navy as admiral. He also serves on the Alliance High Council, though rarely meeting with the committee in person on Yavin 4 and appearing remotely as a hologram instead. Raddus is a pragmatist, and frustrated by some of the Alliance's dallying. He rushes to support Jyn Erso and Rogue One at the Battle of Scarif—and his ship receives her transmission of the Death Star plans. The *Profundity* is boarded by Darth Vader and Raddus is killed. Princess Leia's ship, *Tantive IV*, escapes with the plans on board. The Resistance flagship is later named in Raddus' honor.

> "I say we fight!"
> **ADMIRAL RADDUS**

Act first
Raddus takes the initiative to re-route the *Profundity* and support the Rogue One team on Scarif, even without authorization.

NOWER JEBEL
SPECIES Human **HOMEWORLD** Uyter
AFFILIATION Imperial Senate, Rebel Alliance, New Republic

Cautious Senator Nower Jebel serves on the Imperial Senate after the formation of the Galactic Empire, but secretly, he is acting as the minister of finance for the Rebel Alliance. He keeps this role after the formation of the New Republic and restoration of the Senate.

VASP VASPAR
SPECIES Human **HOMEWORLD** Taldot Sector
AFFILIATION Imperial Senate, Rebel Alliance

Senator Vasp Vaspar secretly serves as the minister of industry for the Rebel Alliance Cabinet in their civil government. He manages Alliance resources and does not believe the rebels have the capability to take on the first Death Star.

TYNNRA PAMLO
SPECIES Human **HOMEWORLD** Taris
AFFILIATION Imperial Senate, Rebel Alliance

Senator Tynnra Pamlo represents her homeworld in the Imperial Senate, and supports the rights of clone troopers. She also becomes the Rebel Alliance's minister of education, working closely with Alliance Intelligence to investigate the sacking of Lasan and the desolation of Geonosis. When Jyn Erso proposes going after the Death Star, she worries her own world could be destroyed in retaliation.

ANJ ZAVOR
SPECIES Human **HOMEWORLD** Majoros
AFFILIATION Rebel Alliance

Colonel Zavor is a Rebel Alliance officer working at Fleet Command. He acts as a liaison between Admiral Raddus and Alliance headquarters during the Battle of Scarif. Zavor is present during the Battle of Yavin and the awards ceremony that follows.

GENERAL ROMODI
SPECIES Human **HOMEWORLD** Virujansi
AFFILIATION Empire

General Hurst Romodi is a veteran of the Clone Wars and becomes one of the highest ranked leaders in the Imperial military. Romodi meets regularly with a tight circle of Imperial officers to discuss their plans for domination, including on Eriadu, when Clone Force 99 infiltrates the base, and the Death Star. Romodi survives the superweapon's destruction and represents the Empire at the Crimson Dawn auction for Han Solo.

GENERAL RAMDA
SPECIES Human **HOMEWORLD** Rine-cathe 111
AFFILIATION Empire

Eager to be working near the heart of Imperial action, General Sotorus Ramda oversees the military presence on Scarif. The island is considered by many to be a leisurely place for older officers to wait out retirement in paradise. General Ramda helps create this image, being a lax and somewhat incompetent bureaucrat. His younger, dissatisfied subordinates conspire to send critical reports against him to Coruscant. Ramda baulks when Director Orson Krennic demands to see all of Galen Erso's communications, exasperated by the extent of work it would require. He perishes when the Death Star fires on Scarif.

IMPERIAL DECK TECHNICIAN
SPECIES Human **HOMEWORLD** Various
AFFILIATION Empire

The ground crew on Imperial bases such as Scarif and Mimban are known as deck technicians. They are a specialist division of Imperial technicians, trained as mechanics to keep ships in good working order and direct ship traffic. They may also pilot various vessels when local logistics make safe take offs and landings difficult. Jyn Erso disguises herself as an Imperial deck technician in order to sneak into the Empire's Citadel and data vault, along with Cassian Andor and K-2SO, during the Battle of Scarif.

SHORETROOPER
SPECIES Human **HOMEWORLD** Various
AFFILIATION Empire

Coastal defender stormtroopers, otherwise known as shoretroopers, are a relatively uncommon class of Imperial trooper. They are stationed to patrol the edge of oceanic environments on tropical worlds such as Scarif, Niamos, and Morak. Their armor is designed to withstand corrosive aquatic environments, reduce sun glare, and repel excess moisture. Most shoretroopers are sergeants and able to command squadrons of standard stormtroopers. Higher ranks are distinguished by colored stripes on their chest and shoulders. Squad leaders wear a kama around their waist and sport a blue strip on their chest and shoulders. Captains have a mostly blue chest plate.

ZAL DINNES
SPECIES Human
HOMEWORLD Tierfon
AFFILIATION Rebel Alliance, Tierfon Yellow Aces

Rebel pilot Zal Dinnes is a member of the Tierfon Yellow Aces assigned to Tierfon Launch Base. Her squadron is disbanded when the Imperial presence there becomes too great. She and Jek Porkins are then transferred to Yavin 4. She flies at the Battle of Scarif but perishes during the Battle of Yavin.

LIEUTENANT ADEMA
SPECIES Human
HOMEWORLD Toria-vic Nebula, Planetoid A.17
AFFILIATION Empire

Zealous Lieutenant Mytus Adema is stationed in the Citadel command center on Scarif when Rogue One infiltrates their facility and steals the Death Star plans. He is fooled by misleading reports of rebel activities during the affair, but correctly notes Jyn Erso and Cassian Andor accessing the data vault.

IMPERIAL FLEET TROOPERS
SPECIES Human **HOMEWORLD** Various
AFFILIATION Empire

Imperial fleet troopers are members of a special branch of the Empire's Navy created by Grand Moff Wilhuff Tarkin. They form the backbone of security aboard multiple vessels, and are trained extensively in combat. Many also receive training in operations support to increase their utility to their captains. The troopers are easily recognized by their distinctive helmets and are utilized on the Death Star and Death Star II, with some being responsible for piloting and firing the battle stations as ordered.

R5-D4
TYPE Astromech droid **MANUFACTURER** Industrial Automaton
AFFILIATION None

R5-D4, also known as "Red," is an astromech scavenged by Jawas and carried aboard their sandcrawler on Tatooine. They sell R5 to Owen Lars, but his motivator immediately malfunctions. This gives C-3PO the opportunity to recommend R2-D2 to Lars and Luke Skywalker instead. Eventually, R5-D4 serves the Rebellion alongside Carson Teva, before ending up in the hands of the Jawas once again. Sold on to mechanic Peli Motto, R5 helps at her docking bay, before he is, in turn, sold to Din Djarin when the Mandalorian needs an astromech. R5 accompanies Din, Grogu, and Bo-Katan Kryze, as they work to reunite the Mandalorians to retake their homeworld. During the mission to Moff Gideon's base, R5-D4 deactivates barrier shields in the Imperial remnant base on Din's command. R5 rockets away from a group of Imperial mouse droids, pushing one off a ledge in the process.

SANDTROOPER
SPECIES Human **HOMEWORLD** Various
AFFILIATION Empire

Sandtroopers are specialized Imperial stormtroopers, trained and equipped to serve in arid environments such as Tatooine. Their armor is equipped with cooling units, long-range comlinks, anti-glare lenses, extra rations, and a water supply. All sandtroopers wear colored pauldrons to indicate their rank—black indicates enlisted troopers, white is for sergeants, and orange is for unit leaders.

WUHER

SPECIES Human **HOMEWORLD** Tatooine
AFFILIATION None

Wuher is a bartender at the Mos Eisley Cantina, who has studied the biochemistries of various species in order to mix the most desirable drinks for them. He has a strong dislike of droids and installs a droid detector to keep them out. During the New Republic era, the cantina is under new management and Wuher's role has been replaced by a supervisor droid.

GENERAL TAGGE

SPECIES Human **HOMEWORLD** Tepasi
AFFILIATION Empire

Born into nobility and privilege, General Cassio Tagge is chief of military operations aboard the first Death Star. Unlike some of his colleagues, he has wary respect for the Rebel Alliance. Prior to the Battle of Yavin, Tagge departs the Death Star to look into Princess Leia's mention of a rebel base on Dantooine. Following the Death Star's destruction, Tagge is promoted to the grand general of the Imperial Army with authority over Darth Vader himself. Tagge becomes responsible for Imperial expansion into the Outer Rim, so tasks Vader with eliminating any criminal cartels that haven't allied with the Empire. Tagge begins using Doctor Cylo's powerful cyborg operatives on missions, but they betray him, taking control of a Super Star Destroyer. After Vader wipes out the threat, Tagge is demoted by the Emperor and placed under Vader's command. The Sith Lord promptly kills him.

ADMIRAL MOTTI

SPECIES Human **HOMEWORLD** Seswenna
AFFILIATION Empire

Admiral Conan Antonio Motti hails from a wealthy and powerful family in the Outer Rim. He commands the Star Destroyer *Steel Talon*, and is also the head of naval operations aboard the Death Star, under Grand Moff Wilhuff Tarkin. He foolhardily challenges Darth Vader on his failure to discover the secret Rebel Alliance base, and the Sith responds by using the Force to choke him. Following Tarkin's orders, Motti gives the order to test fire the full power of the Death Star's weapon on Rango Tan and is surprised when a number of Imperial gunners fail to comply with the order. Motti's arrogant overconfidence in believing the battle station to be invincible results in his death.

MOMAW NADON

SPECIES Ithorian **HOMEWORLD** Ithor
AFFILIATION Rebel Alliance

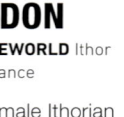

Momaw Nadon is a male Ithorian ("Hammerhead") and rebel sympathizer exiled on Tatooine. His presence there is punishment for revealing the secrets of Ithorian agricultural technology to the Empire, even though his doing so saved his homeworld from destruction. On Tatooine, he cultivates a hidden garden in the mountains south of Mos Eisley, where he conceals rebel operatives. He is present at the Mos Eisley Cantina on the fateful day Luke Skywalker and Obi-Wan Kenobi first meet Han Solo and Chewbacca.

PONDA BABA

SPECIES Aqualish **HOMEWORLD** Ando
AFFILIATION Smuggler

Ponda Baba is the pirating partner of Doctor Cornelius Evazan. He rescues Evazan from a bounty hunter and the two begin smuggling spice for Jabba the Hutt. Together, they travel to Milvayne, going on a crime spree there; to Gulhadar, where they are temporarily imprisoned by the Benelex Marshal Service; and to Jedha, where Baba takes a dislike to Jyn Erso and Cassian Andor. Baba later picks a fight with Luke Skywalker in the Mos Eisley Cantina, and loses his arm when Obi-Wan Kenobi intervenes. Evazan tries, and fails, to reattach his arm, which ends up in the hands of Milvaynian bounty hunter Tam Posla. Baba and Evazan go their separate ways for a time, until they meet once more when Evazan, who has retrieved Baba's arm, contacts him. Together, they watch rogue archaeologist Doctor Chelli Lona Aphra and evil protocol droid Triple-Zero's exploits on Milvayne and hire mediocre hunters Winloss and Nokk to kill Aphra. However, the hunters turn on the evil pair and capture them after finding their secret base.

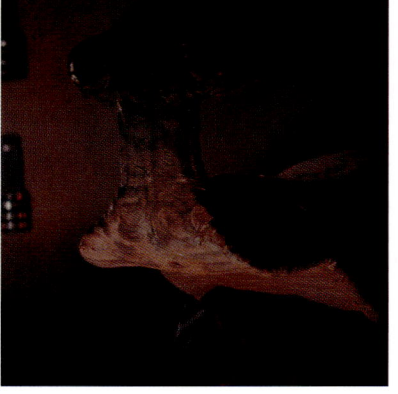

DOCTOR EVAZAN

SPECIES Human **HOMEWORLD** Alsakan
AFFILIATION Smuggler

Once a promising surgeon, Doctor Cornelius Evazan is now notorious for conducting cruel medical experiments. Evazan is nearly killed and horrifically scarred by a bounty hunter, until Ponda Baba saves him. Working for Crimson Dawn leader Dryden Vos, Evazan begins making the Decraniated—cyborg humanoid servants completely purged of their identities. After accumulating around a dozen death sentences, Evazan and Baba are imprisoned for a time on the prison planet Gulhadar but escape. The pair eventually move to Jedha City where they continue to create Decraniated from survivors of the partisans attacks. They leave the city prior to its destruction. Obi-Wan Kenobi and Luke Skywalker encounter the troublemaker in the cantina on Tatooine. He later tries unsuccessfully to reattach Baba's severed arm after Obi-Wan cuts it off. Wanting to escape prosecution for his evil deeds, Evazan forms a new identity as a shape-shifter named Lopset Yas, but he is imprisoned by the Empire alongside morally gray archaeologist Doctor Chelli Lona Aphra. He only reveals his true identity when he has escaped and captured Aphra and the murder droid Triple-Zero. For fun, he puts bombs in Aphra and Triple-Zero that are set to explode if they get too far apart, and settles down with Baba to watch the ensuing antics from afar. Their amusement ends when a pair of hunters they've hired turn on and capture them.

FIGRIN D'AN

SPECIES Bith **HOMEWORLD** Bith **AFFILIATION** None

"Fiery" Figrin D'an is the overbearing band leader of the Modal Nodes. As a Bith, his brain has a fine aptitude for music and his high manual dexterity is well suited to playing a range of instruments. Though he favors the kloo horn, D'an also plays a mean gasan string drum. D'an is a keen gambler, and his debts are the reason the band has to play for Jabba on Tatooine.

THE MODAL NODES

SPECIES Bith **HOMEWORLD** Bith **AFFILIATION** None

The Modal Nodes is a popular band that brings in the crowds at the Mos Eisley Cantina. Regular band members include Figrin D'an (on kloo horn), Nalan Cheel (on bandfill), Doikk Na'ts (on fizzz, aka dorenian beshniquel), Tedn Dahai (on fanfar), Tech Mo'r (on the ommni box), Ickabel G'ont (on the double jocimer), and Sun'il Ei'de (on drums). The wholly instrumental band specializes in jazzy musical forms. The Nodes arrives on Tatooine to play for Jabba the Hutt in his palace as recompense for D'an's debts to the crime lord. When Jabba frees the band, its members stay on Tatooine to earn some money. The Nodes is performing at the Cantina when Luke Skywalker and Obi-Wan Kenobi enter the establishment looking for a pilot to take them to the Alderaan system. A few years later, the Nodes plays a set in the H'unn Cabaret Pit on Nar Kaaga as Tasu Leech attacks Beilert Valance. A band member is not impressed that they've been caught in another firefight and demands that D'an books better gigs.

GARINDAN

SPECIES Kubaz **HOMEWORLD** Kubindi
AFFILIATION Various

Garindan is taken from Kubindi by the Empire and forced to become a spy. He eventually escapes, but can't return home and is forced to work as an informant in Mos Eisley for the highest bidder. Imperial authorities hire Garindan to locate R2-D2 and C-3PO. He quickly picks up their trail and uses a comlink to alert the Empire that Luke Skywalker, Obi-Wan Kenobi, and the droids plan to meet Han Solo in Docking Bay 94.

DIANOGA

HOMEWORLD Vodran **AVERAGE SIZE** 7 m (23 ft) long **HABITAT** Sewers, swamps

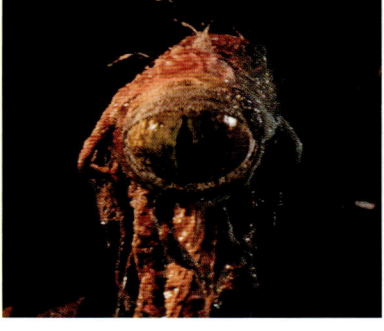

Dianogas spread themselves across the galaxy by climbing aboard starship bilges and stowing away in their garbage tanks. They can now be found in sewers in many spaceports. The Bad Batch escapes a dianoga inside the wreck of a star destroyer on Bracca. Luke Skywalker encounters a dianoga on the Death Star and is nearly drowned by the creature.

JAN DODONNA

SPECIES Human
HOMEWORLD Commenor
AFFILIATION Republic, Rebel Alliance

General Jan Dodonna serves in the Republic Navy aboard a *Venator*-class Star Destroyer during the Clone Wars. Soon after the Empire's formation, he defects from the Imperial Navy to join the rebels. Dodonna and a portion of his forces join Phoenix Squadron at its base on Atollon. The two groups are about to launch a joint assault on Lothal but are interrupted by a surprise Imperial attack on the planet. Many rebels are killed, and only a few ships escape to regroup on Yavin 4.

Dodonna is on the moon Yavin 4 during the Battle of Scarif. Following the victory, he identifies the Death Star's single flaw and oversees the assault on the battle station from Yavin's command center. After the Death Star's destruction, Dodonna orders the evacuation of the base.

A year later, the general is present at the Mako-Ta Space Docks when a fleet of Mon Cala cruisers arrives to be retrofitted into Alliance warships. He is given command of a ship named *Republic*. Unfortunately, the rebels are betrayed by the Shu-Torun, who sabotage the ships, rendering them inoperative. Soon after, the Empire arrives to obliterate the rebels. Thanks to a mission led by Davits Draven and Princess Leia Organa, Dodonna is given the access codes to regain control of the *Republic* and promptly orders that his vessel jumps to hyperspace. He returns and saves many of his allies, but the *Republic* is destroyed, and Dodonna goes down with his ship.

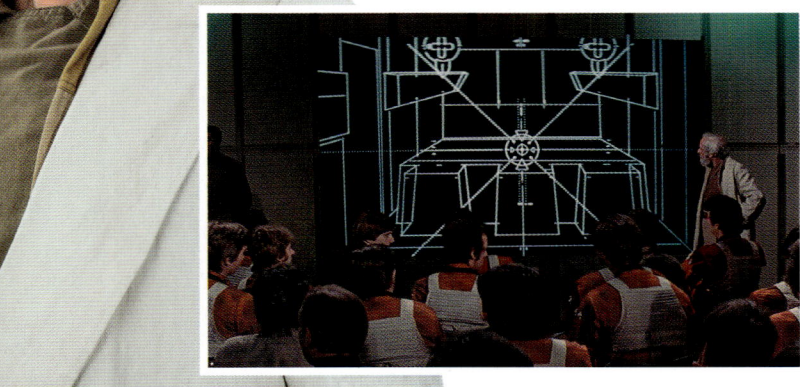

Briefing
Dodonna details the Death Star's trench run and instructs the rebel starfighter pilots. The visuals come directly from the plans R2-D2 carried.

JON VANDER

SPECIES Human **HOMEWORLD** Onderon **AFFILIATION** Rebel Alliance

Jon "Dutch" Vander is a former Imperial pilot who defects to the rebels when he is ordered to bomb rebel-friendly areas of his homeworld. Vander becomes the leader of Gold Squadron, a rebel unit of Y-wings, and helps transport rebel leader Mon Mothma to Dantooine where she officially forms the Rebel Alliance. Vander and his squadron fight during the Battle of Scarif, helping to destroy the planet's shield gate. Prior to the Battle of Yavin, Vander questions General Dodonna during their briefing, but leads his squadron in the assault on the Death Star. He is shot down and killed by Darth Vader during the mission.

GARVEN DREIS

SPECIES Human **HOMEWORLD** Virujansi **AFFILIATION** Rebel Alliance

A former member of the Rarified Air Cavalry on Virujansi, Garven "Dave" Dreis leads the X-wing Red Squadron during the Battle of Scarif and the Battle of Yavin. When Gold Squadron fail in its trench run on the Death Star, Dreis misses hitting the battle station's exhaust port, and his X-wing is destroyed by Darth Vader.

BIGGS DARKLIGHTER

SPECIES Human **HOMEWORLD** Tatooine **AFFILIATION** Rebel Alliance

Biggs Darklighter is a childhood friend of Luke Skywalker on Tatooine, where they often fly T-16 skyhoppers in Beggar's Canyon together. Biggs later leaves his homeworld to attend an Imperial academy and become a TIE pilot. After graduation he abandons his commission and joins the Rebel Alliance. Following action near Kashyyyk, Biggs heads to the vacation world Irff with fellow pilot Jek Porkins. While they manage to relax, an Imperial vacationer cuts their time short, and they return to the fleet. Biggs goes home to Tosche Station to tell Luke of his defection from the Empire before traveling to Yavin 4. There he meets Luke again, and the two pilot X-wings as part of Red Squadron in the mission to destroy the Death Star. Biggs is one of the last pilots killed in the battle, his ship destroyed by Darth Vader.

JEK PORKINS

SPECIES Human **HOMEWORLD** Bestine IV **AFFILIATION** Rebel Alliance

Jek Porkins is a pilot and trader who abandons his homeworld when the Empire moves in and develops a new military base there. After joining the Rebel Alliance, Porkins forms a strong friendship with Biggs Darklighter. Upon their return from an engagement near Kashyyyk, Biggs can see that Jek needs a vacation from the constant conflicts, so the pair heads off to Irff. When they return, a still-weary Jek heads into battle, wondering when the conflicts will end. Jek flies as Red Six during the Battle of Scarif and the Battle of Yavin. During the assault on the Death Star, his X-wing is struck by debris, causing malfunctions that leave his ship slow and unresponsive. His starfighter then explodes when it is hit enemy fire.

WEDGE ANTILLES

SPECIES Human **HOMEWORLD** Corellia
AFFILIATION Empire, Rebel Alliance, New Republic

Wedge Antilles grows up on Corellia, working as a pilot and mechanic. He joins the Empire and receives training at the prestigious Skystrike Academy to become an elite TIE fighter pilot. After witnessing Imperial atrocities, Wedge and his friend Derek "Hobbie" Klivian decide to defect to the Rebel Alliance and are recruited into Phoenix Squadron by Sabine Wren. Antilles goes on an undercover mission to gain clearance codes from an Imperial base on Killun 71. He flies during the Battle of Atollon in an A-wing and is one of the few survivors from Phoenix Squadron, going on to join the rebel group on Yavin 4.

After joining Red Squadron, Wedge becomes fast friends with fellow pilots Jek Porkins and Biggs Darklighter. While he doesn't participate in the Battle of Scarif, Antilles relays the order to the other pilots to redeploy to the planet. Days later, Wedge flies as Red Two when his squadron meets the approaching Death Star. He is one of the three pilots who participate in the final trench run, but his X-wing is damaged, forcing him to retreat. Wedge and Luke Skywalker are the only two survivors of Red Squadron. They both continue to serve under the new Red Leader Arhul Nara and come to trust each other completely.

Antilles goes on to participate in the successful missions to Giju, Tureen VII, and Mon Cala.

During the Imperial attack on the rebel forces at Mako-Ta Space Docks, Wedge joins Luke's newly formed Rogue Squadron, disobeying General Jan Dodonna's orders and helping to ensure many rebels survive. Following the mercy mission to Oulanne, he successfully recruits ex-imperial pilot Thane Kyrell to the Rebellion. At the Battle of Hoth, Wedge flies a T-47 airspeeder, where he and his gunner, Wes Janson, successfully bring down the first AT-AT by tripping the walker with a tow cable. Both pilots board X-wings and escort the final rebel transport to safety. Following the evacuation, Antilles joins Starlight Squadron under its leader Shara Bey, where they work to reunite the scattered rebel fleet.

Wedge is later promoted to commander and becomes Red Leader. He attends the Rebel Alliance briefing at *Home One* and is charged with leading Red Squadron during the Battle of Endor. He is one of several X-wing pilots to fly into the second Death Star, accompanying the *Millennium Falcon*. They narrowly escape after destroying the battle station's main reactor.

> "Copy, Gold Leader. I'm already on my way out."
>
> **WEDGE ANTILLES**

Afterward, Antilles joins the celebration on Endor at the Ewoks' Bright Tree Village.

Following the festivities, Wedge becomes a captain in the New Republic military and goes on a reconnaissance mission to discover Imperial supply lines. He and his ship are captured above Akiva by Imperial Admiral Rae Sloane, and Wedge is tortured while in captivity. Thanks to rebel pilot Norra Wexley and her allies, Antilles is rescued and reunites with the Republic on Chandrila. While recovering from his ordeal, Wedge becomes close to Norra and trains her son, Temmin Wexley, to be a X-wing pilot. He also assists General Syndulla with Project Starhawk and forms Phantom Squadron, leading his pilots during the Liberation of Kashyyyk and the Battle of Jakku. After the Galactic Civil War's conclusion, Antilles becomes the lead instructor of a flight academy on Hosnian Prime.

Wedge eventually retires to Akiva with Norra, where they keep a small farm. However, following the Battle of Crait, Temmin recruits his mother and him into the Resistance. After seeing action on Ryloth and Corellia, Wedge occupies one of the gunner stations in the *Millennium Falcon* during the Battle of Exegol.

Skilled survivor
Wedge is the only pilot to fly in and survive all of the Rebellion's major battles since the Battle of Yavin, including the Battle of Hoth *(right)* and the Battle of Endor, for which he attends a tense briefing beforehand *(above)*.

DAVISH "POPS" KRAIL

SPECIES Human **HOMEWORLD** Dantooine
AFFILIATION Rebel Alliance

Davish Krail is a veteran Y-wing pilot who flies as Gold Five under Jon Vander in Gold Squadron during the Battle of Yavin. He accompanies Vander and fellow pilot Dex Tiree in the first trench run to the Death Star's exhaust port. He aborts the unsuccessful attempt after his friends are killed, but he manages to send a warning to Red Squadron before Darth Vader blows up his ship, ending Krail's life.

DEX TIREE

SPECIES Human
HOMEWORLD Onderon
AFFILIATION Rebel Alliance

Dex Tiree flies a Y-wing as Gold Two, and is Dutch Vander's wingman in Gold Squadron during the Battle of Yavin. While beginning the trench run in an effort to blow up the first Death Star, his ship is the first to be hit by Darth Vader's TIE Advanced x1, and he is electrocuted by a power surge just before his vehicle explodes.

RAE SLOANE

SPECIES Human **HOMEWORLD** Ganthel **AFFILIATION** Empire

One of the most loyal and fierce leaders in the Empire, Rae Sloane began life in poverty on the industrial world of Ganthel before enlisting in the Imperial Naval Academy on Prefsbelt. During the Gorse Conflict, Captain Sloane encounters former Jedi Padawan Kanan Jarrus, who she ultimately fails to capture.

Sloane later serves as Vice Admiral of the Star Destroyer *Vigilance* during the routing of the Empire at the Battle of Endor. Following the defeat, she helps organize a secret meeting of the Imperial Future Council on the planet Akiva. The mysterious Fleet Admiral Gallius Rax bestows upon her the rank of Grand Admiral, and she serves as the public face of the weakened Empire. After initiating fake peace talks with the New Republic, she becomes disillusioned with Rax and turns to working with Brentin and Norra Wexley to kill him. She flees into the Unknown Regions with Brendol Hux, his son, and a group of orphaned child soldiers. They are a remnant that eventually reforms into the First Order.

EVAAN VERLAINE

SPECIES Human **HOMEWORLD** Alderaan
AFFILIATION House Organa, Rebel Alliance, New Republic

A skilled pilot and proud Alderaanian, Evaan Verlaine is mentored by Breha Organa as a child. She serves as a Y-wing pilot for the Rebel Alliance in the Battles of Scarif and Yavin. After a bittersweet victory against the Death Star, Verlaine re-pledges her loyalty to Leia and House Organa, and helps find surviving Alderaanians. Recruited into Starlight Squadron, she tracks down the scattered Alliance after the Battle of Hoth. During the New Republic era, she helps Leia copilot the *Millennium Falcon* on a dangerous mission to Kashyyyk.

DEL MEEKO

SPECIES Human **HOMEWORLD** Coruscant
AFFILIATION Empire, Inferno Squad, New Republic, Resistance

Del Meeko is a member of the Empire's Inferno Squad, though his destiny later takes him on another path. When a child, Del witnesses the fall of the Jedi Order on Coruscant. As an adult, he joins the Empire and works his way up from stormtrooper to Scarif shoretrooper to chief engineer aboard a Star Destroyer. He's finally recruited into the elite Inferno Squad under Commander Iden Versio. However, a chance meeting with Luke Skywalker changes his perspective, and Del switches sides. He ultimately joins the New Republic alongside his former Imperial commander, Iden Versio. During the New Republic era, Del and Iden settle down and have a child, Zay. Del is killed by Hask while investigating a First Order initiative named Project Resurrection.

IDEN VERSIO

SPECIES Human **HOMEWORLD** Vardos
AFFILIATION Empire, Black Squadron, Inferno Squad, Rebel Alliance, Danger Squadron, New Republic, Resistance

Commander Iden Versio is a top-class graduate from the Imperial Academy on Coruscant. She becomes a TIE fighter pilot for the Empire during the early days of the Galactic Civil War and fights in the Battle of Yavin. After the destruction of the first Death Star, Iden's father, Admiral Garrick Versio, forms a Special Forces commando unit called Inferno Squad and installs her as its commander. She and her teammates (including Gideon Hask, Seyn Marana, and Del Meeko) infiltrate and eliminate the Dreamers (the remnants of Saw Gerrera's partisans). Following the Battle of Hoth, the group is tasked with wiping the memory of former Imperial asset and lethal cyborg bounty hunter Beilert Valance. After its successful mission, Inferno Squad is tasked with eliminating Crimson Dawn agents with the Empire. Inferno Squad fights at the Battle of Endor and observes the destruction of the second Death Star from the moon's surface.

Following the death of the Emperor, Operation: Cinder is activated and Iden's homeworld of Vardos is one of many targeted by the Empire's climate disruption arrays. Unable to comply with the Empire any longer, she rebels against her father's command. She and teammate Del Meeko defy orders, take their ship, *Corvus*, and surrender to the Rebel Alliance. They fight for the rebels in the remaining battles of the Civil War, alongside the leader of Danger Squadron, Shriv Suurgav. At the Battle of Jakku, Iden shoots down Hask and finds her father aboard the *Eviscerator*. Although he insists on going down with his ship, he and Iden reconcile before they're finally parted.

In the years after the Battle of Jakku, Iden and Del marry and have a daughter named Zay. When Del goes missing, Iden, Shriv, and Zay search for him and wind up back on Vardos, where Iden encounters Hask, who is now a First Order officer. Iden and Zay follow Hask aboard his Star Destroyer *Retribution* and steal schematics for the First Order Dreadnought. Hask reveals that he murdered Del. The two fight and Iden kills Hask, though she is mortally wounded in the process. She dies in her daughter's arms. Shriv and Zay then escape to D'Qar, delivering the Dreadnought schematics to Resistance pilot Poe Dameron.

Today the Rebellion dies
Prior to the Battle of Endor, Commander Iden Versio infiltrates a rebel ship, the *Invincible Faith*. She destroys an intercepted Imperial transmission that is being decoded on the vessel and which would have revealed the Empire's trap above Endor.

Top-secret orders
Following the surprising Imperial defeat over Endor, Iden Versio is given new orders by her father that are critical to the success of Operation: Cinder.

GIDEON HASK
SPECIES Human **HOMEWORLD** Kuat
AFFILIATION Empire, Inferno Squad, First Order

Gideon Hask, known as Gid, rises in the ranks of the Empire until he's selected for an elite squad of troopers named Inferno Squad. Following the death of the Emperor, Hask stays loyal even though the rest of the squad defects to the Rebellion. Granted command of his unit, Hask pilots a TIE interceptor in the Battle of Jakku, but he's shot down by former Inferno Squad trooper Iden Versio. He survives and flees to the Unknown Regions, where he helps create the First Order. Decades later, shortly before the destruction of Hosnian Prime, Hask encounters his former teammates once more, killing Del Meeko and inflicting a fatal wound on Iden before she kills him.

GARRICK VERSIO
SPECIES Human
HOMEWORLD Vardos
AFFILIATION Empire, Inferno Squad

Early in his career, Garrick Versio is Inspector General of the ISB. Promoted to admiral, he takes command of the *Eviscerator* and forms Inferno Squad—an elite unit of troopers led by his daughter, Iden. After the Emperor's death, he helps carry out Operation: Cinder, which calls for the destruction of several worlds, including his own—Vardos. This action leads to a schism with his daughter. The two reunite during the Battle of Jakku. Iden tries to save her father as his Star Destroyer crumbles, but seeing the folly of his ways, Garrick accepts his fate.

ZARRO
SPECIES Human
HOMEWORLD Andelm IV
AFFILIATION Chewbacca

Zarro serves as a translator and friend to Chewbacca after he arrives on her homeworld of Andelm IV. Her father, Arrax, works in the dangerous Andelm beetle caverns to pay off their debts, and the Wookiee partners with Zarro to free her father from servitude.

PAPA TOREN
SPECIES Axaleem
AFFILIATION Toren crime family

Papa Toren is a fearsome crime boss, accompanied at all times by a gaggle of Ximpi—blue sprites who speak for him. He attempts to purchase the Immortal Rur from Doctor Aphra. Once courted by Crimson Dawn, he is eventually held captive in the prison on Megalox Beta. Inmates are protected from the planet's extremely high gravity by a grav-field, which is projected from a space station in orbit around Megalox Beta.

SANA STARROS
SPECIES Human **HOMEWORLD** Nar Shaddaa
AFFILIATION Starros Clan, Tagge Corporation, Rebel Alliance

Sana Starros is a cunning bounty hunter who was born into a famed family of adventurers on the Smuggler's Moon of Nar Shaddaa. Her twin brother, Phel, rejects the life of a smuggler and enlists in the Empire. While a student at the University of Bar'leth, Starros develops a romance with Chelli Aphra. It's a tumultuous relationship that continues for many years after their initial breakup. Starros goes on several missions with Han Solo and Chewbacca, including to the planet Takodana in order to recover the Phylanx Redux Transmitter. During the Galactic Civil War, Starros widely claims to have been married to Solo as part of one of their missions on Stenness. He leaves on bad terms and she eventually tracks him down in the Moddell sector. She reluctantly helps the Rebels infiltrate the Palace of Grakkus the Hutt and is subsequently hired by Organa for multiple tasks, including dropping Doctor Aphra off at Sunspot Prison. At one time, she joins other members of the famed Starros Clan to steal back an ancestral heirloom, which contains Avon Starros' High Republic–era crystal theory.

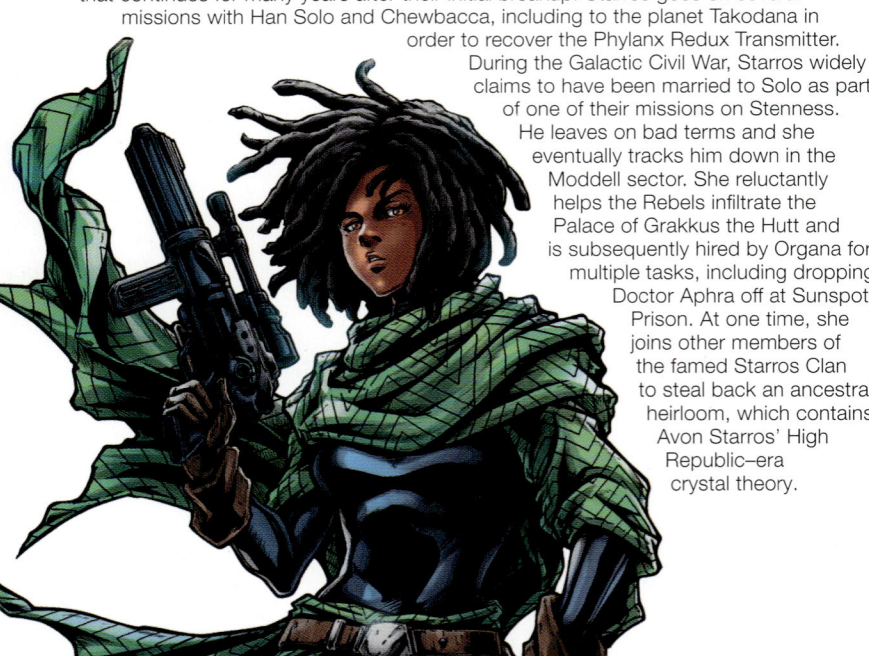

NAKARI KELEN
SPECIES Human
HOMEWORLD Pasher
AFFILIATION Rebel Alliance

Nakari Kelen is the daughter of the founder of Kelen Biolabs—a medical company on the desert planet of Pasher. Kelen works with Luke Skywalker to rescue the cryptographer Drusil Bephorin from the Empire. She develops a romantic relationship with the young Jedi but is ultimately killed during the mission.

LOO RE ANNO
SPECIES Sibettan
AFFILIATION Dragon Void Run

The last known surviving member of a mysterious species known as the Sibettan, Loo Re Anno is possibly the greatest starship racer in the galaxy. During her final Dragon Void Run, she races alongside Han Solo. After winning, she's finally able to join her people, who had been hiding between the seams of time and space.

CYLO
SPECIES Human
AFFILIATION Empire

Cylo is an Imperial doctor with a singular vision: to merge organics and machines. He accomplishes this with various experiments, including adapting assassins, creating a fleet of whale-ships, and having multiple bodies himself. The Emperor is impressed with the scientist's development of cyborg warriors that could replace Darth Vader. But Palpatine soon discovers that Cylo is plotting to destroy him, so he orders for the cyborg doctor to be killed. Vader dispatches Cylo's assassins and employs a mind trick on Cylo's whale-ship, forcing it to fly into a sun with Cylo onboard.

WHALE-SHIP
AFFILIATION Doctor Cylo, Empire

Whale-ships are enormous living vessels augmented with technology. They are the work of Doctor Cylo—a cyborg scientist and rival of Darth Vader. An impressive sight, the creatures have four fins, large teeth, piercing eyes, and cybernetics covering their topside. Whale-ships are fitted with heavy weaponry and are capable of lightspeed travel. In a challenge to the Empire, Cylo sends a whale-ship into a Super Star Destroyer, immobilizing it. Whale-ships also serve as research laboratories for Cylo, who controls an entire fleet of the unique vehicle-animals.

ENEB RAY
SPECIES Human
AFFILIATION Empire

Eneb Ray is a rebel spy, but he grows bitter following a failed mission to rescue senators from the Arrth-Eno Prison Complex, and an encounter with Emperor Palpatine that leaves him deformed. He takes hostages at the Alliance's Sunspot Prison, leading to a confrontation with Leia Organa and his arrest by the Rebellion.

KARINA THE GREAT
SPECIES Geonosian **HOMEWORLD** Geonosis
AFFILIATION Geonosians

Birthed from the last Geonosian egg, Queen Karina is the last hope to repopulate her species, but she proves to be infertile. Outfitted with a mechanical womb, she births battle droid-Geonosian hybrids. Darth Vader, in need of a droid army, slices the womb from Karina's body and steals it to serve his purposes.

MORIT ASTARTE
SPECIES Human
HOMEWORLD Celanon
AFFILIATION Republic, Empire

One of Doctor Cylo's cybernetically enhanced fighters, Morit Astarte is determined to kill and replace Darth Vader. Scheming but reckless, he betrays his rival sister and challenges the Sith Lord atop a Super Star Destroyer in a battle of "the old versus the new." Unfortunately for Morit, the old wins.

KARBIN
SPECIES Mon Calamari **HOMEWORLD** Mon Cala
AFFILIATION Republic, Empire

After suffering horrific injuries in the Clone Wars, Karbin is remade into a cybernetic warrior by Doctor Cylo so that he can replace Darth Vader. With a new body inspired by General Grievous, Karbin challenges the Sith Lord in battle, but Vader outsmarts Karbin, and the Mon Calamari is destroyed on Vrogas Vas.

AIOLIN ASTARTE
SPECIES Human
HOMEWORLD Celanon
AFFILIATION Doctor Cylo, Empire

The cybernetically enhanced Aiolin Astarte is assigned to assist Darth Vader, but she betrays the Sith Lord with her twin brother, Morit. When they fail to defeat Vader, Morit knocks Aiolin into a lava pit to "thin" the field. Vader draws Aiolin from the lava, gathers her memory circuit, and ends the cyborg's suffering.

TULON VOIDGAZER
SPECIES Human
AFFILIATION Empire

Of all Doctor Cylo's cybernetic experiments, Tulon Voidgazer stands unique, not as a warrior but a brilliant scientist. Designed to replace Darth Vader, she faces the Sith Lord in a final battle in the belly of a whale-ship. Vader turns Tulon's blaster droids against her, however, and she dies at the hands of her own tech.

TRIOS
SPECIES Human **HOMEWORLD** Shu-Torun
AFFILIATION Kingdom of Shu-Torun, Empire

Following a failed attempt to kill Darth Vader, the entire Shu-Torun royal family is destroyed, except for Princess Trios. She becomes queen but does Vader's bidding. Trios aligns with the rebels, but it is a ruse. She later battles Leia Organa, who strikes Trios down; the dying queen tells Leia that her actions were meant to save Shu-Torun, and Leia promises the planet won't perish.

CHARACTERS AND CREATURES

DOCTOR CHELLI APHRA
SPECIES Human **HOMEWORLD** Arbiflux
AFFILIATION Herself

Amoral and ambitious Chelli Lona Aphra is an innovative archaeologist working for her own gains across the galaxy.

TURBULENT UPBRINGING
Her father is a scholar obsessed with an ancient and forgotten Force-attuned order called the Ordu Aspectu, and for a long period of time is estranged from his wife Lona and his daughter as he prioritizes his research. Left feeling abandoned, Chelli grows up mostly alone with her mother on Arbiflux, until Lona is tragically killed by raiders.

Aphra goes on to study archaeology at the University of Bar'leth where she befriends, beguiles, and manipulates fellow students—including Sana Starros, Eustacia Okka, and Kho Phon Farrus—to achieve her selfish aims. The innovative Aphra does earn her doctorate, however, it is not as a result of legitimate research, but by outsmarting her Sava (professor).

Unstoppable duo
Aphra and Sana excel at working together and the embers of their past feelings are reignited during their missions for Domina.

Unlikely allies
Aphra openly admires Lord Vader who, on first meeting, she finds even more interesting than she had hoped.

AGENT OF THE SITH
After graduation, Aphra takes a number of jobs recovering archaeological artifacts by any means, sometimes alongside the business-minded criminal Just Lucky. On one occasion, Aphra betrays the wealthy and sadistic Ronen Tagge, who bears a grudge afterward.

Aphra is later hired by the Droid Gotra, which leads to her being recruited by none other than Darth Vader, much to Aphra's surprise, to help him build his own private army. For Vader, Aphra finds and installs the Triple-Zero matrix into a protocol droid, who in turn activates the Beetee-One assassin droid "blastomech" prototype (BT-1). She also helps him retrieve a portable battle droid factory from Geonosis. During the Battle of Vrogas Vas, she is captured by the Rebel Alliance, meeting Luke Skywalker and Leia Organa. She soon escapes, returning to Vader's service.

Aware that Vader is planning to kill her, Aphra tries to outsmart the Sith Lord by telling the Emperor of their partnership first, but Vader pushes her out of an airlock and subsequently believes her dead. However, Aphra has arranged for the Wookiee bounty hunter Krrsantan and the droids to pick her up in a ship.

TURBULENT TIMES
Aphra then returns to archaeological adventures with a variety of associates, including retrieving a Sith sword from Moraband with Dok-Ondar and helping her father recover the consciousness of a Force-wielding being named Rur. She also has a turbulent relationship with Imperial Captain Magna Tolvan, who she double-crosses multiple times, and works with Luke and Leia to defeat the mysterious queen of Ktath'atn. When Aphra tries to auction off Rur, she narrowly escapes Vader, who arrives to claim the being.

Her brief spell of freedom comes to an end when she is forced by Triple-Zero to recover his missing memories. During this mission, Aphra and her expendable crew kidnaps rebel General Hera Syndulla, using her to infiltrate the Empire's Hivebase-1 where the droid's data is held. Aphra is then imprisoned in the Accresker Jail and escapes, only to find herself and Triple-Zero forced into a twisted game that's being controlled by Doctor Cornelius Evazan, who broadcasts their antics to millions. During the escalating chaos, Aphra meets a young girl named Vulaada, who she takes under her wing. In a rare moment of heroism, Aphra sacrifices her life to save Vulaada, and Aphra and Triple-Zero are freed of Evazan's control.

POWER PLAYER
Vulaada and Aphra soon become embroiled in separate schemes to assassinate the Emperor: the Rebel Alliance is behind one, while Imperial Propaganda Minister Pitina Mar-Mas Voor plans the other. After meeting Magna (who is now a rebel) again, Aphra learns that the minister was behind her mother's death. Feeling vengeful, Aphra saves Palpatine's life by betraying the Alliance and selfishly exposing Voor.

Vader soon arrives and forces Aphra to help him find the hidden Alliance base. Ever the schemer, Aphra plots to keep her loved ones alive and to outwit Vader. She manages to unite her father with Tolvan and Vulaada who head to the Alliance base on Hoth. To buy the rebels time to set up, she then incapacitates Vader so she can impersonate him and destroy Imperial data detailing the rebels' location.

A FRESH START
Following the Battle of Hoth, Aphra stays away from her loved ones to protect them, focusing on recovering and selling archaeological finds. However, she soon runs afoul of the Tagge family during a mission to recover the powerful Rings of Vaale, and Aphra enters the employ of the head of the family, Domina Tagge. The archaeologist's one condition is that she can be backed up by Starros.

Together, Aphra and Starros retrieve a part of a Nihil Path Engine; data on the Black Sun criminal syndicate; and a thought dowser crafted by the Ascendant cult, an extinct sect who used technology to re-create the effects of the Force. Domina is very impressed by this Ascendant artifact, sending them to learn more about the group. Aphra and Starros start investigating a criminal network dealing in Ascendant objects. However, the duo is always a few steps behind their former acquaintance Farrus, who is obsessed with the Ascendant group.

SPARKS AND SCOURGES
Eventually, Sana and Aphra realize that Farrus is heading back to Bar'leth to open the tomb of the Spark Eternal, the Ascendant's greatest work, which could merge with an individual to give them unspeakable powers. Realizing the threat it could pose, Aphra and Sana head to the tomb. However, the greedy Aphra reaches for the Spark, and the entity takes control of her body.

Aphra is now little more that a witness to the Spark Eternal's violent acts. Sana soon forms a team, which includes Magna, to save Aphra from the entity. Her allies' aid allows Aphra to begin to wrest control from the Eternal, and she is finally freed by her friends aboard the Amaxine space station. The group flees the location, heading to Hiorin, but fractures into multiple parts with Magna and Sana leaving Aphra, in spite of their love for each other and her.

Now that Aphra is alone and free again, Vader captures her to help him find a powerful weapon before she in turn kidnaps Luke to force him to investigate a temple on Sason. After these missions, Aphra returns to Domina, who tasks her with looking into malfunctioning droids on Havel Prime. Aphra soon realizes that a droid intelligence called the Scourge contains the Spark and that it has taken control of Magna due to her cybernetics. Determined to free her, Aphra and Sana reunite to retrieve Magna from Epikonia. After the Scourge crisis ends, Aphra finally expresses her desire that Sana and Magna join her in a lifetime of crime, and they gleefully do.

TRIPLE-ZERO

MANUFACTURER Custom **TYPE** Protocol droid
AFFILIATION Darth Vader, Doctor Aphra, Beetee-One

Triple-Zero begins life as a dangerous personality matrix who is rejected immediately by its creator. However, the intelligence survives and goes on a centuries-long killing spree before being quarantined in one of Wat Tambor's vaults. Rogue archaeologist Doctor Aphra breaks into Wat Tambor's quarantine vault to steal the matrix. She then installs it in the protocol droid chassis. After he is activated, the murder-loving droid assists Aphra in awakening the "blastomech" BT-1. Triple-Zero, as the droid calls himself, serves as an aid to Aphra and her new master, Darth Vader, for a time. Later, he runs his own crime syndicate on Son-Tuul and blackmails Aphra into working for him. Thanks to Doctor Evazan, Triple-Zero is forced to work with Aphra once more on Milvayne. After escaping Evazan's control, Triple-Zero reunites with BT-1, and the pair enjoys a brief spell of freedom before they are captured on the Ring of Kafrene by the Empire. With memory wipes and restraining bolts, the pair ends up back in the employ of Vader, operating as torture droids. However, once more they come across Aphra, who helps them escape as long as they are complicit in betraying Vader. Afterward, the pair retires to a life of boredom until Aphra is possessed by an intelligence called the Spark Eternal, and the droids become swept up in the doctor's wake once more. After attempting to kill Vader again, this time alongside the Droid Crush, Triple-Zero and BT-1 end up on Gallios, where they agree to join R2-D2's D-Squad and help to defeat the Scourge.

BT-1

MANUFACTURER Tarkin Initiative
TYPE Blastomech **AFFILIATION** Darth Vader, Doctor Aphra, Triple-Zero

BT-1 (Beetee-One) is fitted with numerous high-power weapons not normally found in similar-looking astromechs. After BT-1 is assembled by the Tarkin Initiative, he kills everyone at the Imperial base and causes it to self-destruct. Doctor Aphra finds him in space and fits him with behavioral inhibitors, but is unable to wake him. She uses Triple-Zero to reactivate him and the droids serve Aphra and Darth Vader. When Triple-Zero goes rogue, BT-1 continues to act as a sidekick of sorts. He is destroyed by Vader aboard the Accresker Jail, but is rebuilt and reunites with his fellow murder droid on Milvayne. The pair is soon forced to work for the Empire, but BT-1 aids a similarly trapped Aphra to ensure the trio escapes the Empire once more. Aphra leaves the droids on the deserted world of Birukay. Eventually, they are visited by smuggler Sana Starros and agree to join a team to help free Aphra from possession by the Spark Eternal. Their only condition is that that they can kill anyone who stands in their way. The team nearly frees Aphra aboard the Crimson Dawn's flagship, *Vermillion*. However, the Spark corrupts the droids, who turn on the others and leave with their new master. Following the Spark's defeat on the Amaxine space station, the blastomech is later Scourged by a passing mouse droid and then heads with Triple-Zero to Gallios where he starts attacking civilians. R2-D2 soon arrives and frees BT-1, persuading the pair to aid him during the Scourge crisis. BT-1 participates in missions to Ryloth, Tatooine, and Scourge's flagship.

GRAKKUS

SPECIES Hutt
AFFILIATION Hutt Clan

Grakkus the Hutt rules Nar Shaddaa's Hutta Town and is a major player in the criminal underworld. He has an interest in Jedi artifacts, amassing a collection of rarities dating back centuries. When Luke Skywalker arrives in Grakkus' territory, the Hutt enslaves him and forces the young Jedi to fight in the local arena. Luke eventually escapes and Grakkus is arrested, spending years in the Megalox prison city on Megalox Beta. He cuts a deal with Poe Dameron, disclosing the location of Lor San Tekka in exchange for transport off the dreadful world.

INSPECTOR THANOTH

SPECIES Human
AFFILIATION Empire

An inspector for the Empire, the veteran Thanoth possesses a nearly peerless investigative mind and is a true believer in Imperial rule. Although he's assigned as Darth Vader's adjutant, he investigates the Sith himself. Piecing together Vader's journeys to Tatooine and Naboo and his search for a rebel named "Skywalker," Thanoth deduces that Vader is plotting to overthrow the Emperor. But he doesn't report this, believing it will benefit the Empire. "It's been a pleasure working with you, Anakin," he tells Vader, revealing he knows the former Jedi's true identity, before allowing himself to be cut down.

KREEL

SPECIES Human
AFFILIATION Empire

Kreel is a stormtrooper who goes undercover as Grakkus the Hutt's "Gamemaster." He trains a captive Luke Skywalker for the arena, and later arrests Grakkus in the name of the Empire. Kreel eventually becomes leader of SCAR trooper squad Task Force 99, and fails to defeat Skywalker in a duel.

154 CHARACTERS AND CREATURES

TASK FORCE 99
SPECIES Human **HOMEWORLD** Various **AFFILIATION** Empire

Darth Vader personally selects the members of the elite stormtrooper unit Task Force 99 (or SCAR Squadron). The group consists of leader Sergeant Kreel, as well as operatives Aero, Cav, Mic, Misty, Shrap, and Zuke. Among its notorious accomplishments, Task Force 99 kills Admiral Verette of the Rebellion, and Kreel duels Luke Skywalker on Hubin.

NERF
HOMEWORLD Various **SIZE** 1.3 m (4 ft 3 in) high **HABITAT** Plains

A nerf is a domesticated animal raised for milk and meat. It has a full coat and four horns. When frightened, nerfs are known to shed and sneeze incessantly. Han Solo and Luke Skywalker make a deal to transport nerfs—much to Solo's chagrin—to Ibaar, where its people are suffering under Imperial sanctions.

GREAT MOUNTAIN
HOMEWORLD Vagadarr Prime

The Great Mountain is a Force-attuned giant made of rock. Following years of dormancy, it's thought to be an ordinary land mass, until Yoda answers its call for help and awakens the being. Years later, Luke Skywalker revives the giant again, with the help of Garro of the Rockhawker tribe.

GARRO
SPECIES Human **HOMEWORLD** Vagadarr Prime **AFFILIATION** Rockhawkers

Exiled by the Rockhawkers tribe, young Garro meets Yoda in the caves of the Great Mountain. Together, they discover that the land mass is actually alive, and Yoda revives the grand being. Many years later, Garro transfers his life force to the Great Mountain to help Luke Skywalker awaken it once more.

KORIN APHRA
SPECIES Human

Korin Aphra, father of rogue archaeologist Chelli Lona Aphra, is a gifted researcher and scholar with a particular interest in the Jedi. His wife Lona, believing Korin too obsessed with his work, takes Chelli away to raise alone. Lona is killed by raiders, and the girl returns to Korin. Their rocky relationship continues into Chelli's adulthood, though they reunite when Korin manipulates the suspension of his daughter's doctorate—a ploy to recruit her to his quest to find the Citadel of Rur.

ABERSYN SYMBIOTE
HABITAT Infected hosts

The abersyn symbiote is an aggressive parasite that attaches to a host's brain stem, resulting in the host's death or mind control among a hive. On Ktath'atn, the infected queen uses abersyn symbiotes to control her people and gain new subjects. Abersyn symbiotes are so dangerous that not even the Empire weaponizes the creatures.

RUR
SPECIES Human **AFFILIATION** Ordu Aspectu

The leader of the Ordu Aspectu—an ancient offshoot of the Jedi Order—Rur believes in the preciousness of all life and is devoted to uncovering the secret of immortality. A copy of his own consciousness, which calls itself Eternal Rur, kills the original Force-wielder when it believes he has decided to deactivate the copy.

MAGNA TOLVAN
SPECIES Human **AFFILIATION** Empire, Rebel Alliance, Strike Team Misericorde

The cybernetically enhanced Imperial officer Magna Tolvan first encounters Doctor Chelli Aphra while investigating the remnants of the rebel base on Yavin 4. This leads to a prolonged chase between the two. Tolvan's pursuit of the rogue archaeologist takes her to the Citadel of Rur, where Aphra's father stabs the Imperial with a lightsaber, but Aphra lets the Imperial live, as an attraction begins to grow between them. Finally, they share a kiss when Magna and Aphra face death on Skako Minor. Later, Magna helps break Aphra out of an Imperial prison and finds her way to the Rebel Alliance, officially defecting from the Empire and becoming a captain.

QUEEN OF KTATH'ATN
SPECIES Human **HOMEWORLD** Ktath'atn

The host of an abersyn symbiote, the queen of Ktath'atn rules her hive from a grand citadel. Having been infected by an abersyn symbiote, Luke Skywalker eventually confronts her for supremacy, but he severs his connection with the parasite using the Force. Free of the creature, he kills the queen with a slash of his lightsaber.

REXA GO
SPECIES Human **AFFILIATION** Son-tuul Pride

An enforcer for the Son-tuul Pride crime syndicate, Rexa Go dons an AJ^3 cyborg construct and follows orders without question. Serving new boss Triple-Zero, she ruthlessly incinerates an entire settlement following a data heist. Go meets her end, however, when Doctor Chelli Aphra stops her from killing Imperial officer Magna Tolvan.

DEK-[NIL]
MODEL Droideka **TYPE** Destroyer droid **AFFILIATION** Son-tuul Pride

A first-gen droideka, Dek-[Nil] has been retooled with probability tech and customized existential circuits, making him overly emotional. He's assigned to Doctor Chelli Aphra by Son-tuul Pride leader Triple-Zero for a job. They end up in Accresker Jail together, where Force-attuned spores disassemble Dek-[Nil].

SISTER SIX
SPECIES Xexto **AFFILIATION** Son-tuul Pride, Rebel Alliance

The assassin Sister Six is assigned to Doctor Chelli Aphra's crew by Triple-Zero, with the objective of recovering the droid's memories. The mission takes the team to various worlds and locations, including a rebel base. After recovering the datacore and fighting alongside the rebels, Six decides to stay with the Alliance.

KANCHAR
SPECIES Human **AFFILIATION** Empire

A physically imposing Imperial commander with a weaponized cybernetic arm, Kanchar oversees the extraction of kyber crystals on Jedha. He later fights—and loses to—Luke Skywalker on the planet. When Kanchar fails to destroy Leia Organa via orbital bombardment, Darth Vader uses the Force to choke him because he has come too close to ruining the Sith's machinations.

GUNDRAVIAN HOOKSPORES
SIZE Microscopic

While exploring a crashed Jedi ship, Doctor Aphra and her accomplice discover Gundravian hookspores. Having imprinted on a kyber crystal, the living fungus is obsessed with justice and has become violent. Later, Darth Vader confronts the organism and seemingly destroys it with the Force, but the hookspores survive to reanimate the dead Tam Posla.

PLURIPLEQ
HABITAT N/A

The pluripleq is a rare tentacled, bioengineered life form, with a rainbow of colors visible through its gelatinous body. It has shapeshifting abilities that it can transfer to a host. Doctor Cornelius Evazan, a wanted scientist, steals a pluripleq on Thannt, and uses it to manipulate Doctor Chelli Aphra and escape Accresker Jail.

GURTYL
SPECIES Qaberworm
AFFILIATION Vulaada Klam

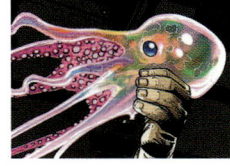

Quick to grab threats with her powerful tentacles, Gurtyl is a qaberworm who is fiercely loyal to her master, Vulaada Klam, who is a young war refugee. The large creature, which doesn't feel pain, is simultaneously pet, transportation, and protector of Klam. Gurtyl and Klam meet Doctor Aphra and Triple-Zero on Milvayne and form an alliance with the archaeologist's crew.

VULAADA KLAM
SPECIES Human
AFFILIATION Rebel Alliance

An orphaned war refugee, Vulaada Klam survives on Milvayne with the help of her qaberworm Gurtyl. She encounters Doctor Chelli Aphra on the planet's lower levels, and they soon form a bond. Aphra leaves Vulaada with her father and Magna Tolvan at the rebel base on Hoth, where she can live with friends and purpose.

PITINA MAR-MAS VOOR
SPECIES Human
HOMEWORLD Coruscant
AFFILIATION Herself

The brains of the Empire's propaganda machine and a master manipulator, Pitina Mar-Mas Voor spins publicity in Imperial favor. Knowing that Doctor Chelli Aphra plans to kill the Emperor, Pitina reveals her own plot—which the archaeologist is secretly broadcasting. Within moments, Darth Vader arrives and swiftly assassinates Voor.

LONA APHRA
SPECIES Human

The mother of rogue archaeologist Doctor Chelli Aphra, Lona Aphra takes her daughter and leaves her research-obsessed husband, Korin. They live on Arbiflux for two years as farmers, but Lona suffers a critical injury during an attack by raiders. Before passing, she contacts the Empire to come and get Aphra and return the girl to her father.

TZ-2
MODEL RA-7 **TYPE** Protocol droid
AFFILIATION Rebel Alliance

TZ-2 serves General Airen Cracken in Rebel Alliance Intelligence. He assists in a scheme to manipulate Doctor Chelli Aphra into stealing the Farkiller weapon, so it can be used against the Emperor. Later, Aphra uses TZ-2 as a decoy to escape a rebel ship, dressing him in her own clothing.

NOKK
SPECIES Trandoshan
AFFILIATION Big game hunter

Nokk is a Trandoshan monster-hunter who takes tracking jobs in the galactic underworld but normally refuses to kill. She and her human husband, Winloss, come into Doctor Chelli Aphra's orbit. This association puts Nokk on a path of revenge against Skikkesk—the Trandoshan who led the purging of Nokk's brood line.

WINLOSS
SPECIES Human
AFFILIATION Big game hunter

Winloss is a creature-hunter along with his wife, the Trandoshan named Nokk. They are betrayed by Doctor Chelli Aphra but decline to kill her when given the chance. Later, they make a deal with Aphra for a job that gets Nokk revenge against the Trandoshan who destroyed her family.

DORS URTYA
SPECIES Mon Calamari
HOMEWORLD Mon Cala
AFFILIATION Rebel Alliance

Regent of the Mon Cala, Dors Urtya initially declines to align with the Rebel Alliance but later has a change of heart. Urtya broadcasts a deathbed recording of his king's final words to the Mon Cala fleet that encourages rebellion. Though his headquarters is quickly destroyed by Imperial ships, Urtya dies making a purposeful sacrifice.

TUNGA ARPAGION
SPECIES Clawdite
AFFILIATION Rebel Alliance

A Clawdite shapeshifter, Tunga Arpagion is an actor-turned-rebel agent who puts his natural abilities to use in dangerous operations. He takes the form of Moff Tan Hubi when Leia Organa looks to access an Imperial prisoner, and later he mimics the princess herself to act as a decoy.

MEORTI
SPECIES Human
AFFILIATION Rebel Alliance

Meorti is an engineer in the Rebel Alliance, who works on ships, droids, and whatever mechanical trouble her friends may face. Meorti proves invaluable when the Empire attacks the rebel base at Mako-Ta, repairing C-3PO and installing an override that restores the *Republic*'s systems from an earlier sabotage.

THANE MARKONA
SPECIES Human
HOMEWORLD Hubin
AFFILIATION Clan Markona

Thane of his clan of mercenaries, Markona comes to regret his past dealings with the Empire when he learns of the Death Star. A chance at redemption arrives when he offers sanctuary to members of the Rebellion on Hubin. He then sacrifices himself to save Luke Skywalker from SCAR Squadron.

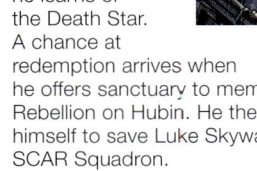

TULA MARKONA
SPECIES Human
HOMEWORLD Hubin
AFFILIATION Clan Markona

Daughter of Thane Markona, Tula Markona is raised as part of her father's military clan. When a small rebel force crash-lands on her world, she forms a closeness with Luke Skywalker. Later, she supplies Luke with a smoke grenade—and a goodbye kiss—to aid in his escape from SCAR Squadron.

DAR CHAMPION
SPECIES Human **HOMEWORLD** Lanz Carpo

Dar Champion is the District Advocate of Lanz Carpo—and the ex-boyfriend of Leia Organa. They meet again when Leia and Han Solo come to the world for a rebel mission, which leads to a confrontation. But rather than stopping them, Dar comes up with another plan that benefits all parties.

KAKRANS
HOMEWORLD Kakra (K43) **SIZE** Various

The Kakrans are sentient rock-people from K43, who are led by a council of elders. Some grow to be giants. Chewbacca and C-3PO befriend the Kakrans, who then help the rebels fight off the Empire. One of the Kakrans, a moon-size "grandmother," even emerges to smash a Star Destroyer.

WARBA CALIP
SPECIES Human
HOMEWORLD Jedha

Warba grows up near the Temple of the Kyber on Jedha and relays some of what she knows about the Force to Luke Skywalker. While she is a street thief on Sergia, she steals Luke's lightsaber. In the end, Warba returns the Jedi weapon, much to her own disbelief. "You're more than you seem," Luke tells her.

156 CHARACTERS AND CREATURES

TAUNTAUN
HOMEWORLD Hoth
AVERAGE SIZE 2 m (9 ft) high
HABITAT Snow plains

Rebel soldiers discover tauntauns living in ice caves while building Echo Base. Tauntauns are easily domesticated and used as pack animals. Well adapted for cold, they have thick scales and fur, and can slow their metabolism to survive Hoth's freezing nights. Han Solo keeps an injured Luke Skywalker alive by placing him inside a dead tauntaun.

> "I thought they smelled bad— on the outside!"
> **HAN SOLO**

WAMPA
HOMEWORLD Hoth **AVERAGE SIZE** 3 m (10 ft) high **HABITAT** Snow plains

As the top predators on Hoth, wampas generally prey upon tauntauns, but do not hesitate to attack humans or their settlements. Their thick white fur protects them from the intense cold and allows them to sneak up on prey undetected. Wampas drag victims back to ice caves where they are later torn apart at leisure.

ADMIRAL OZZEL
SPECIES Human **HOMEWORLD** Carida
AFFILIATION Empire

A veteran of the Clone Wars, Kendal Ozzel is a rear admiral in the Imperial Navy. He is promoted to admiral following the Battle of Yavin and commands Darth Vader's flagship, the *Executor*. Ozzel displays poor judgment and frequently irritates Vader. Ozzel is present for the assault on the Mako-Ta Space Docks. Desperate to find the Alliance, the Empire sends thousands of probe droids to investigate remote corners of the galaxy. Ozzel investigates Sergia and K43 where rebel agents escape his grasp. When one of the droids finds evidence on Hoth, Ozzel doubts the proof at first, then fails in a bid to surprise the rebels there. Vader accuses him of being "as clumsy as he is stupid," before executing him.

GENERAL CARLIST RIEEKAN
SPECIES Human **HOMEWORLD** Alderaan **AFFILIATION** Rebel Alliance, New Republic

A fighter for the Republic during the Clone Wars, General Carlist Rieekan becomes a founding member of the Rebel Alliance. Luckily for him, he is offworld when his homeworld of Alderaan is destroyed. Following the Alliance mission to Shu-Torun, Rieekan sets in motion a multi-pronged plan to distract the Empire away from Alliance assets: he sends Leia Organa and Han Solo to Lanz Carpo, Luke Skywalker and R2-D2 to Sergia, and Chewbacca and C-3PO to K43. Following these successful missions, Rieekan assumes command at Echo Base on Hoth. When Vader's forces strike, he delays them long enough for rebel transports to evade capture, and then escapes himself. During the Battle of Jakku, he launches a plan to try to persuade some Imperial ships to defect and join the New Republic cause. Decades later, after the Battle of Crait, Shriv Suurgav and Zay Versio recruit him to join General Organa's Resistance.

ZEV SENESCA
SPECIES Human **HOMEWORLD** Kestic Station
AFFILIATION Rebel Alliance

Zev Senesca joins the Rebel Alliance as a pilot at some point prior to the Battle of Mako-Ta, where he is one of the founding members of Luke Skywalker's Rogue Squadron. Just prior to the Battle of Hoth, Zev locates Luke Skywalker and Han Solo when they become lost overnight on Hoth's ice fields. Zev flies as Rogue Two during the Battle of Hoth, but he and his gunner are both killed during the conflict when their snowspeeder is blasted by several Imperial walkers.

ADMIRAL FIRMUS PIETT
SPECIES Human **HOMEWORLD** Axxila
AFFILIATION Empire

Firmus Piett hails from the Outer Rim. He rises through Imperial ranks thanks to his quick thinking and ability to shift blame for his own mistakes. He serves as a junior captain under Grand Moff Tarkin and eventually becomes a captain aboard Darth Vader's flagship, the *Executor*, until his commanding officer, Ozzel, is executed for incompetence. Promoted to the rank of Admiral by Vader himself, Piett pursues the *Millennium Falcon* through an asteroid field following the Battle of Hoth. Second to Vader on the *Executor*, Piett sees action on Jekara, Gabredor III, Skako Minor, and even faces a rebellion by the Scourged droids aboard the ship. Piett orders Imperial officer Ciena Ree to lead a TIE fighter patrol of the Hudalla system to investigate rebel activity. Piett's distinguished career ends abruptly when an A-wing crashes into the *Executor*'s bridge during the Battle of Endor.

GENERAL MAXIMILIAN VEERS
SPECIES Human **HOMEWORLD** Denon
AFFILIATION Empire

While a lieutenant in the Imperial military, Maximilian Veers is a rising star who meets with Crimson Dawn leader Dryden Vos. Now a general, Veers offers advice to Darth Vader, takes ownership of Project Swarm to find the Alliance's latest base, and is the mastermind behind the Imperial assault on Echo Base during the Battle of Hoth. From the cockpit of his AT-AT, *Blizzard One*, he leads the attack that destroys the rebel shield generator, before infiltrating their base with his snowtroopers.

DEREK "HOBBIE" KLIVIAN
SPECIES Human **HOMEWORLD** Ralltiir **AFFILIATION** Empire, Rebel Alliance

Derek "Hobbie" Klivian begins his piloting career as an Imperial cadet at Skystrike Academy with Wedge Antilles. Both Wedge and Hobbie wish to defect to the Rebel Alliance, and they are extracted by an undercover rebel named Sabine Wren. Alongside Wedge, Hobbie joins Phoenix Squadron and survives the Battle of Atollon. Much like the way Sabine assisted him, Klivian goes undercover on the *Rand Ecliptic* and helps Imperial pilot Biggs Darklighter defect. He is stationed on Yavin 4 as a standby pilot for Red Squadron before going on to become a founding member of Luke Skywalker's Rogue Squadron. He flies alongside Luke as his wingman in the Battle of Hoth but dies when his ship is shot down and crashes into *Blizzard One*—the lead Imperial walker.

SNOWTROOPER
SPECIES Human **HOMEWORLD** Various **AFFILIATION** Empire

Snowtroopers are elite stormtrooper regiments equipped for combat and survival in the extreme cold. Modeled after the Republic's former clone cold assault troops, which served in frigid environments like Orto Plutonia, Rhen Var, and Toola during the Clone Wars, their insulated suits and heated breather masks are powered by battery packs that last up to two standard weeks. Deployed in General Veers' attack on Echo Base in the Battle of Hoth, and brandishing E-11 blaster rifles and E-Web heavy repeating blaster cannons, snowtroopers are a formidable match for rebel soldiers. Their equipment includes ice boots, an insulated belt cape, polarized snow goggles, grappling hooks, ion flares, and a homing beacon.

SPACE SLUG
AVERAGE SIZE 900 m (2,952 ft) long
HABITAT Asteroids

Space slugs are silica-based life-forms that dwell in asteroid caves, living on the mineral-rich deposits found in their habitats. Largely dormant, these gargantuan slugs are also known to prey on passing ships. On one such occasion, Han Solo pilots the *Millennium Falcon* into an asteroid field in a desperate attempt to elude his Imperial pursuers, only to be nearly swallowed by one of these opportunistic feeders. Groups of space slugs have been encountered in some asteroid fields.

Belly of the beast
The space slug uses all its energy to lunge at the escaping *Falcon*.

MAJOR BREN DERLIN
SPECIES Human **HOMEWORLD** Tiisheraan
AFFILIATION Rebel Alliance

Major Bren Derlin leads the Alliance's mission to Omereth to extract slicer Drusil Bephorin's family, which is only successful thanks to Luke Skywalker's assistance. Derlin then works as a security chief and a member of Alliance Intelligence at Echo Base on Hoth. He gives the order to close the base door when Han Solo and Luke become lost outside, to avoid putting the whole installation at risk. He later serves as a unit leader in the Battle of Endor.

WES JANSON
SPECIES Human
HOMEWORLD Taanab
AFFILIATION Rebel Alliance

Lieutenant Wes Janson flies as rear gunner for fellow pilot Wedge Antilles during the Battle of Hoth. They use their speeder's harpoon and tow cable to bring down the first AT-AT in the attack on Echo Base.

DAK RALTER
SPECIES Human **HOMEWORLD** Kalist VI
AFFILIATION Rebel Alliance

A rebel pilot in Rogue Squadron, Dak Ralter serves as Luke Skywalker's gunner during the Battle of Hoth. Born into a family of political prisoners in an Imperial penal colony, Ralter escapes, harboring bright ambitions that he will never realize—he is killed when his snowspeeder is destroyed by an AT-AT.

MYNOCK
AVERAGE SIZE 2 m (7 ft) long
HABITAT Various

Mynocks are space parasites that survive on a ship's power cables and energy conductors. If they are not cleared quickly, they can fully drain a craft's power. When mynocks are ingested by a giant space slug, they can live inside their host's gut, sharing its meals.

BESPIN WING GUARDS
SPECIES Human **HOMEWORLD** Various
AFFILIATION Cloud City

The Bespin Wing Guards serve as the law enforcement for Cloud City on Bespin. Its members answer to Baron Administrator Lando Calrissian, who controls the mining operation, and the guards are often the first (and only) way of controlling the facilities' citizens.

CAPTAIN LORTH NEEDA
SPECIES Human **HOMEWORLD** Coruscant
AFFILIATION Empire

Lorth Needa is a ruthless officer who is serving the Republic in the Clone Wars when Supreme Chancellor Palpatine is kidnapped by General Grievous during the Battle of Coruscant. As commanding officer of the Imperial Star Destroyer *Avenger*, he takes part in the search for the rebels' secret base. After losing the *Millennium Falcon* while pursuing it through an asteroid field, Darth Vader kills him using the Force.

IG-88

MANUFACTURER Holowan Laboratories **TYPE** Assassin droid **AFFILIATION** Bounty hunter

IG-88 is a rogue assassin droid and a chief rival of Boba Fett. Its legendary reputation is so widespread that there are many rumors about its origins and motivations. During the Imperial era, IG-88 and pirate Hondo Ohnaka work together to try to collect the bounty on Crimson Dawn lieutenant Qi'ra, but she captures them instead. After escaping, IG-88 is soon hired by Imperial Security Bureau Agent Alexsandr Kallus to hunt down Han Solo, nearly catching him. On a mission to Garel, IG-88 ends up being shot at by stormtroopers, even though it is working for the Empire. The assassin droid later engineers events so it can destroy the Gillanium syndicate and collect a large number of bounties.

Years later, IG-88 hunts the *Millennium Falcon* and Han Solo once more for Darth Vader, and it ends up being defeated by Boba Fett. Following this mission, IG-88 is hired to kill Vader by Sly Moore, who gifts the droid with the means to take control of the Sith Lord's armor. IG-88 nearly kills Vader but is defeated and destroyed. After rebuilding itself, IG-88 heads to Coruscant and terminates the agreement with Moore, stating that Vader cannot be defeated. The Sith then appears, destroying the droid again and murdering Moore's accomplices. IG-88 is eventually recovered and repaired by a droidsmith, RB-919. When IG-88 awakens, he promptly kills RB-919 and then attempts to recover Han from Boba on Tatooine but is unsuccessful. The droid takes a number of jobs from the Empire to kill the leaders of the Son-Tuul Pride and Unbroken Clan criminal syndicates. While tracking down rogue droids Triple-Zero and Beetee-One, IG-88 is hired by R2-D2 to join his special droid group named D-Squad to defeat the Scourge. D-Squad eventually reinforces the droid leader Ajax Sigma who destroys the Scourge aboard its flagship. Decades later, IG-88 meets mercenary Bazine Netal who wants information on the *Falcon* since she is now hunting the ship.

4-LOM

MANUFACTURER Industrial Automaton **TYPE** LOM-series protocol droid **AFFILIATION** Bounty hunter

4-LOM is a protocol droid who serves aboard a luxury ship until his programming is overwritten and he turns to a life of crime and bounty hunting. 4-LOM soon partners with the Gand Zuckuss, tracking down bounties in their ship, the *Mist Hunter*. One of their earliest missions is to capture and kill Doctor Cribiriz Idollax, but they don't realize that instead they killed his brother. On Valtos, they try to catch Han Solo, but Han and Chewbacca evade them. Years later, Darth Vader hires a team of bounty hunters, including 4-LOM, to locate the *Falcon*.

However, it is Boba Fett who successfully captures Han Solo. Zuckuss and 4-LOM are then contacted by General Vukorah to track down Beilert Valance and his charge, Cadeliah. Their targets escape them on the Spur, on Lowick, and in the Y'Toub system, where they are offered intel on where to find Fett, who is now wanted by Jabba the Hutt for losing Solo. After engaging Boba on Nar Shaddaa, 4-LOM is defeated. The droid ends up in the hands of the vengeful Doctor Cribiriz Idollax, who reprograms him to kill Zuckuss, but the droid is unsuccessful.

The Gand, now a part of T'onga's bounty hunter crew, eventually manages to restore his friend to his previous self. 4-LOM then provides valuable slicing skills to the team and remains loyal throughout their many missions. He is temporarily separated from them during the Scourge crisis, so he joins R2-D2's D-Squad and helps to stop the chaos.

Later on Tatooine, he aids T'onga's crew in their defeat of Jabba's Megadroid, before he and Zuckuss head their separate ways to resume a career as a duo. Years later, however, T'onga's crew is active once more on a mission to collect a bounty aboard the *Halcyon*.

BOUSHH

SPECIES Ubese **HOMEWORLD** Uba IV **AFFILIATION** Bounty hunter

Hailing from Uba IV, Boushh is exiled for committing a crime and forced to wear his armor as a mark of shame. Out in the galaxy, Boushh forms a bounty hunting crew, recruiting any fellow exiles from Uba IV, who becomes a surrogate family. After his team is hired by the Black Sun Syndicate on Ord Mantell, he takes a risky mission from Crimson Dawn to attack the powerful Tagge dynasty. Having infiltrated a Tagge ship, Boushh meets Domina Tagge, who persuades the crew to betray their employer and join her by offering to find them a way to return to Ubese society. Accepting the deal, the group stays with her when Crimson Dawn again targets her for elimination. Eventually Boushh encounters Princess Leia Organa and Chewbacca on Ord Mantell. A fight breaks out between the rebels and Boushh, who wants to collect a bounty on them. After defeating Boushh with Maz Kanata's help, Leia steals his armor to use as a disguise to infiltrate Jabba's palace on Tatooine.

LOBOT

SPECIES Human
HOMEWORLD Bespin
AFFILIATION Rebel Alliance

While working for the Empire, Lobot has an AJ^6 construct installed into his head that helps him complete battle calculations quicker, but it comes at the cost of losing some of his personality. He later stops working for the Empire and befriends the smuggler Lando Calrissian. Lobot is a frequent accomplice of Lando on many escapades, and they become good friends.

On one heist, Lando and Lobot lead a small crew to steal the *Imperialis*, which they later discover belongs to the Emperor. This mission goes awry, and in order to escape the ship Lobot lets the AJ^6 construct take full control, sacrificing what remains of his personality. Soon after, Lando becomes the Baron of Cloud City on Bespin and Lobot assists as his chief administrative aide. He later helps free Leia Organa, Chewbacca, and C-3PO from Imperial custody. Lando leaves with the rebels and Lobot remains behind. The Empire hooks him up to the city's computer systems.

He is eventually rescued by Lando who returns with the rebels. Now a guest of the Alliance, Lobot's skills are essential to Operation Starlight's successful reunion of the Alliance fleet. As part of this mission, Lobot works with an ancient linguistics droid to create an encryption system that the Imperials can't decode. Lando and Lobot then betray the Alliance by secretly selling the droid to Jabba the Hutt. However, they don't realize until they've lost the droid that it can repair Lobot's cybernetics and restore him to his former self.

The pair then returns to the Alliance and goes on a number of missions, including to No-Space, until Lobot begins to malfunction. While aboard the Alliance flagship *Home One*, Lobot takes control of the ship and starts firing its weapons. A concerned Lando knocks out Lobot before he can cause too much damage, resolving to take him to Jabba's palace so the linguistics droid can repair his friend's cybernetics.

During the mission, Lobot is captured and corrupted by the Scourge, becoming a key tool for the droid intelligence. Once the Scourge is defeated, Lobot's cybernetics are repaired, and he can finally begin to express himself more. After some time apart, Lobot and Lando work together to liberate Cloud City. Once their former home is freed, Lobot starts working as a liaison officer for Lando's latest endeavor, Calrissian Enterprises.

ZUCKUSS

SPECIES Gand **HOMEWORLD** Gand **AFFILIATION** Bounty hunter

Zuckuss is a Force-attuned Gand who is a member of one of the few remaining clans to practice the Findsman traditions on his homeworld. With encouragement from his mother, Zuckuss undergoes the Great Rite to see if he can become a Findsman. During the event, Zuckuss and the other participants are tasked with finding a rare T'karra flower, which only grows in the territory of a deadly Charon creature. Even though Zuckuss manages to kill the monster, greatly helping the clan, he does not return with the flower and is cast out.

He later becomes a bounty hunter, often working alongside his colleague the protocol droid 4-LOM. The pair tries, and fails, to capture Han Solo and Chewbacca for a criminal Rekias Nodo. Years later, Zuckuss is hired on more than one occasion by Darth Vader: firstly to retrieve Doctor Chelli Aphra from the Rebel Alliance, and secondly to track down the *Millennium Falcon*.

Alongside 4-LOM, Zuckuss then attempts multiple times to capture Cadeliah, who is heir to two crime syndicates. They run afoul of fellow hunter, Beilert Valance, until they receive information on a more lucrative bounty—Boba Fett. Heading to Nar Shaddaa, the pair is defeated by Fett, and 4-LOM's head is taken by the victor. The droid is eventually reprogrammed by an enemy of theirs and attacks and nearly kills Zuckuss on Nar Shaddaa.

A despondent Zuckuss then heads to a Gand floating sanctuary until he is hired by T'onga to join her crew. He recommends the group captures and reprograms 4-LOM to help. Once they are reunited, Zuckuss is much happier, and the pair lends its skills to the crew until its dissolution following a mission to Tatooine. Zuckuss and 4-LOM then split off to travel the galaxy together on their ship once more. During the New Republic era, the pair returns to T'onga's side, helping with another bounty.

ZED-6-7
MANUFACTURER Cybot Galactica
TYPE SP-4 droid
AFFILIATION Empire, Crimson Dawn

ZED-6-7 is recruited by Darth Vader to assist the Sith Lord in finding those who have worked to hide his son, Luke Skywalker, from him. The excitable SP-4 droid serves him well, up until Vader strikes ZED-6-7 down in anger. Later, Sabé, one of Padmé Amidala's former handmaidens, finds and repairs the droid for a new mission.

ELLIAN ZAHRA
SPECIES Human
AFFILIATION Empire

After the death of her mentor Grand Moff Wilhuff Tarkin, Commander Ellian Zahra becomes obsessed with enacting revenge against Leia Organa. A brutal military tactician, Zahra leads her Star Destroyer *Tarkin's Will* to hunt down and destroy the scattered Alliance fleets. Zahra injures Leia in their first battle, and they later meet again in the caves of Panisia, where a giant creature catches Zahra. Much to the commander's surprise, Leia leaves Zahra to her fate with the beast.

FRELL
SPECIES Tholothian
AFFILIATION Rebel Alliance

Frell and her rebel team of Pathfinders successfully rescue Shara Bey from *Tarkin's Will*. Because of the ship's massacre of Panisia civilians, Frell decides to stay behind and destroy the vessel. Pinned down while placing charges in the reactor core, she sacrifices herself—and completes her mission.

GORR
SPECIES Human
AFFILIATION Empire

Lieutenant Gorr serves as second-in-command to Commander Ellian Zahra aboard the *Tarkin's Will*. A constant presence at her side, he carries out Zahra's orders dutifully. When the Star Destroyer is sabotaged by rebel infiltrators, the commander informs Gorr that they are to abandon ship. His fate remains unknown.

GREK
SPECIES Human
AFFILIATION Rebel Alliance

A commodore in the Fourth Division of the Rebel Alliance, Grek often collaborates with Leia Organa and Luke Skywalker. He spearheads Operation Starlight—a mission to reunite the scattered Rebel Alliance fleet. Despite setbacks, Grek is successful.

NEEDLE
SPECIES Quermian
HOMEWORLD Quermia
AFFILIATION Rebel Alliance

A member of the Pathfinders unit in the Rebel Alliance, Needle is quick-thinking and selfless. The team takes on a mission to recover a droid kept in a Coruscant museum, and Needle creates a diversion by claiming certain relics belong to his people. But the guards subdue the Quermian, and Needle is executed on the curator's orders.

KES DAMERON
SPECIES Human
AFFILIATION Rebel Alliance, New Republic

Sergeant Kes Dameron meets his eventual wife, Shara Bey, on Galator III after betting on her in a race. Dameron sacrifices a traditional life with his family, which includes his son Poe, to serve the Rebellion. He often doesn't see his wife for extended periods of time, especially when she becomes stranded on board the Imperial ship *Tarkin's Will*. In the aftermath of the Battle of Endor, Kes goes on many missions as a member of the elite Pathfinders team. After the war, Bey unexpectedly passes away, and Dameron raises his son alone until Poe leaves home to join the Spice Runners of Kijimi.

SHARA BEY
SPECIES Human
AFFILIATION Rebel Alliance, New Republic, Yavin 4 Civilian Defense Force

Alongside her husband, Kes Dameron, Shara Bey sees the suffering that the Empire is inflicting on the galaxy, and she joins the Rebellion. She is leader of Starlight Squadron and flies as part of Green Squadron in the Battle of Endor. She then leads the defense of Naboo during Operation: Cinder, flying alongside Leia Organa. After retiring from the Alliance, Bey serves as a civilian defense member for the colony of Yavin 4 and teaches her young son, Poe Dameron, to fly. Bey passes away suddenly, dying of the rare illness bloodburn, and is forever remembered as a vital member of the Rebel Alliance.

BOKKU THE HUTT
SPECIES Hutt **HOMEWORLD** Nal Hutta
AFFILIATION Hutt Clan, Crimson Dawn

Bokku the Hutt serves on the Grand Hutt Council and is ordered by Ochi of Bestoon to deliver the carbonite-encased body of Han Solo to Darth Vader. Bokku is also a secret spy for Crimson Dawn and is killed by an irate Vader above Jekara, as an ultimate "reward."

DROID CRUSH PIRATES OF BESTOON
MANUFACTURER Various **TYPE** Various assassin droids **AFFILIATION** Ochi of Bestoon, Sly Moore, Mas Amedda, Darth Vader

The Droid Crush Pirates of Bestoon are a lethal army led by Captain Ought-Six. Often hired by Ochi of Bestoon, the Droid Crush hunts Darth Vader on Mustafar. During Ochi's search for the strandcast Dathan, the Crush loses an important fight, so Ochi destroys their captain.

NAKANO LASH
SPECIES Nautolan **HOMEWORLD** Glee Anselm
AFFILIATION Nakano Lash's crew

Bounty hunter Nakano Lash is hired by the criminal Khamus to kill his pregnant lover, Krynthia. Lash instead kills Khamus and then secretly raises Krynthia's child, Cadeliah, who is heir to her parents' two rival crime syndicates. Lash resurfaces years later, while dying of pneumogray, and asks her protégé, Beilert Valance, to protect Cadeliah.

T'ONGOR
SPECIES Human
AFFILIATION Nakano Lash's crew

The bounty hunter T'ongor is the twin brother of T'onga. He sometimes works with Nakano Lash's crew. After alerting the rest of his team to Lash's apparent betrayal, T'ongor dies on Corellia, killed by an accidental blast from Boba Fett.

T'ONGA
SPECIES Human **AFFILIATION** Bounty Hunters Guild, Losha Tarkon

Previously retired, T'onga becomes a bounty hunter once again after the death of her twin brother, T'ongor. This means leaving behind her partner, Losha Tarkon, on the moon of Logal Ri. T'onga assembles her own crew of bounty hunters, including Losha, on a mission to protect Cadeliah, which puts them in the direct path of both Qi'ra's Crimson Dawn and Beilert Valance's Imperial unit. At Bestine, she is reunited with Valance, leaving her wife once more and going on the dangerous mission to recover Beilert's memories. After saving her friend, T'onga returns to Logal Ri with Losha and Cadeliah, where she has plans to open a cantina.

CHARACTERS AND CREATURES

LOSHA TARKON
SPECIES Human
AFFILIATION Bounty Hunters Guild, T'onga

Losha Tarkon becomes a feared bounty hunter in her own right after her wife, T'onga, goes on a personal mission of revenge. Tarkon makes her way to Ruusan, where she rescues her injured wife, picks up a pet nexu named Furball, and joins T'onga on the hunt for Boba Fett and Han Solo, who is frozen in carbonite. After the death of her beloved pet, Tarkon begins training even more and becomes an expert sharpshooter and fighter. She is eventually left once more by her wife who undertakes a dangerous mission to rescue Beilert Valance.

SYPHACC
SPECIES Human
AFFILIATION Syphacc's Bountiful Bounties

Fitted with a head implant, Syphacc serves as point person for many of the most dangerous bounty hunters in the galaxy. He runs Syphacc's Bountiful Bounties in Kirkeide Station, whose motto is, "Dead or alive, doesn't matter to us!" It also houses a secret fighting ring.

OORIS BYNAR
SPECIES Thisspiasian
HOMEWORLD Thisspias
AFFILIATION Jabba the Hutt, Khel Tanna's crew

Ooris Bynar is a feared bounty hunter with a reputation for collateral damage. He has worked with Han Solo and Khel Tanna on Galator III. After literally wrestling information about Cadeliah's location from Syphacc, he is the first to find her on Ruusan but is killed by Cadeliah herself and Nakano Lash.

CADELIAH
SPECIES Human
AFFILIATION Unbroken Clan, Mourner's Wail, Crimson Dawn

Cadeliah is daughter of the heirs of two warring crime syndicates. After her parents' deaths, she is raised and trained by Nakano Lash. Cadeliah is captured by Qi'ra, who becomes her mentor, gifting her the bountiful credits of Crimson Dawn. Cadeliah settles down on Logal Ri with T'onga and Losha Tarkon.

VUKORAH
SPECIES Human
AFFILIATION Unbroken Clan

General of the Unbroken Clan forces, Vukorah hunts down Cadeliah. She accepts an invitation from Qi'ra, who gifts her a sacred dagger relic, which Vukorah uses to kill the grand leader of the Unbroken Clan and become its new leader. Grand Leader Vukorah joins with Crimson Dawn, but she is captured by T'onga's crew during their quest to find Cadeliah. She is betrayed by Qi'ra and recuses herself as leader of the Unbroken Clan to survive an assassination attempt from IG-88. She acquires a whole litter of Loth-cats and, surprisingly, teams up with Losha Tarkon to survive the Scourge.

FURBALL
SPECIES Nexu
HOMEWORLD Ruusan
AFFILIATION T'onga, Losha Tarkon

Furball is a fearsome nexu, trained by a human on Ruusan. Her elderly trainer gifts the nexu to T'onga and Losha Tarkon. Named "Furball" by Tarkon, the cat becomes a loyal ally in battle but is killed by an attacking Vukorah during her attempted escape on the *Edgehawk*.

KONDRA
SPECIES Human
AFFILIATION Rebel Alliance, Second Division

Kondra is a lieutenant in the Rebel Alliance on the jungle planet of Lowik, which is the site of a secret rebel outpost. He is the husband of Beilert Valance's former flame, Yuralla Vega (known as Yura). Along with his wife, he helps to protect Cadeliah, but she is kidnapped during a raid on the base.

EVERI CHALIS
SPECIES Human **HOMEWORLD** Haidoral Prime
AFFILIATION Empire, Rebel Alliance, Battlefront: Twilight Company

Everi Chalis rises through the Empire to become Governor of Haidoral Prime, which she views as a punishment. She soon defects and helps Twilight Company identify Imperial facilities to destroy. She then escapes to dedicate her life to art.

FREYTA SMYTH
SPECIES Twi'lek
AFFILIATION Rebel Alliance, Starlight Squadron

A gifted pilot of the Rebel Alliance, Freyta Smyth is selected for Starlight Squadron—a starfighter unit tasked with locating scattered divisions of the Rebellion, following the Battle of Hoth. The mission is known as Operation Starlight. She later dies in a clash on Coruscant, caught in an Imperial ambush.

RONEN TAGGE
SPECIES Human
AFFILIATION Tagge Corporation

Scion of the Tagge dynasty, Ronen Tagge collects rare artifacts for the sole purpose of watching them be destroyed. After snatching the Rings of Vaale from Doctor Chelli Aphra and her crew, Tagge nearly dies when Aphra blows up his penthouse. He later betrays his powerful aunt, Domina Tagge, who executes him after uncovering his plot.

DETTA YAO
SPECIES Human
AFFILIATION The Shadow University

An ambitious archaeology student, Detta Yao is determined to write her doctorate thesis on the ancient Rings of Vaale. Fate brings her into the orbit of Doctor Chelli Aphra, and the pair soon form a crew to find the artifacts. But they also become rivals and a target of the corrupt treasure hunter known as Ronen Tagge. As Yao and company close in on the rings, Aphra seems to betray Detta, shooting her in the back. Though she escapes, Detta is eventually captured and taken before Tagge on Canto Bight. Aphra, however, has other plans and nearly destroys Tagge to get the rings. Yao manages to get away and returns to the Shadow University, bringing her adventure to a close.

EUSTACIA OKKA
SPECIES Mirialan
AFFILIATION The Shadow University

One of Doctor Chelli Aphra's old flames, Eustacia Okka studies at the Shadow University and has a particular interest in the Rings of Vaale. Years after her expulsion from the school, she reconnects with Aphra, joining the archaeologist's crew to find the mystical artifacts. While they don't recover the rings, the group survives an encounter with Ronen Tagge, and Eustacia snags an ancient dagger and a path to reinstatement at the school. Later, Okka is recruited to help find Chelli when she becomes possessed by the Spark Eternal—an old evil recently awakened.

JUST LUCKY

SPECIES Human

Slippery and resourceful, Just Lucky makes his way in the galaxy as a smuggler, treasure hunter, and schemer. He has a history with Doctor Chelli Aphra, and the two cross paths once more when she recruits him for a job locating the Rings of Vaale. As they near the artifacts, however, Lucky betrays the group, revealing that he already possesses one of the rings and is working for rival artifact collector, Ronen Tagge. Later, Aphra nearly kills Tagge, and Lucky secretly recovers the Ring of Fortune. He then goes to work tracking Aphra for Domina Tagge, delivering her for a bounty.

DOMINA TAGGE

SPECIES Human **HOMEWORLD** Tepasi
AFFILIATION Tagge Corporation

Lady Domina Tagge, member of the House of Tagge and head of the Tagge Corporation, wields power both legitimately and in the shadows of the galaxy. She places a bounty on Doctor Chelli Aphra when the archaeologist destroys the apartment of her nephew, Ronen Tagge, nearly killing him. But, ever pragmatic, Domina hires Aphra for a job. Domina later has Ronen executed when she discovers his plan to overthrow her, and she does the same to her brother Silas, stabbing him with the Tagge protoblade after thwarting his coup attempt. She continues to look for ways to expand her family's influence and consolidate her authority.

LAPIN TAGGE

SPECIES Human
AFFILIATION Tagge Corporation

Lapin Tagge is aide to Domina Tagge, who is head of the Tagge Corporation and one of the galaxy's most powerful figures. They perform whatever duty their cousin requests, including the investigation of the Tagge family itself when Domina suspects a mole and leaks from within.

ARIOLE YU

SPECIES Human
AFFILIATION Sixth Kin

Ariole Yu is taken in by the Sixth Kin at an early age. He grows up in the crime family alongside Just Lucky, and both are trained by Gallin Crae to be killers. Later, Ariole and Lucky become romantically evolved, though the latter suddenly leaves. Their paths cross again when Sixth Kin leader Wen Delphis orders them to find and kill their former mentor, Crae. Their quarry, now aligned with Crimson Dawn, defeats the duo. Crimson Dawn's head, Qi'ra, offers them a place with her. Ariole is intrigued, but the two eventually take on a job for Ronen Tagge, tracking down the ancient Spark Eternal device.

DURGE

SPECIES Gen'Dai
AFFILIATION Bounty hunter

A colossal bounty hunter, the armored Durge has a well-deserved reputation for being hard to kill. He encounters deadly cymote parasites on a job and forms an alliance with Doctor Chelli Aphra and Sana Starros to survive. Durge is then recruited for a squad to find and save fellow hunter Beilert Valance.

DEVA LOMPOP

SPECIES Shani
AFFILIATION The Nihil, Jabba the Hutt, Crimson Dawn

Since the High Republic, Deva Lompop has been one of the most dangerous bounty hunters in the galaxy. As part of Kara Xoo's Nihil Tempest, she meets a captured Avon Starros and, years later, partners with her ancestor, Sana Starros, to recover Avon's journals.

TRINIA

SPECIES Near-human
AFFILIATION Crimson Dawn

Already recruited directly into Crimson Dawn, Trinia first meets Qi'ra on Thorum. A seemingly elegant woman, Trinia is initially deeply off-putting to Qi'ra, but she soon becomes her attendant. With an uncanny, almost supernatural insight into other people, Trinia becomes one of the leaders of Crimson Dawn, alongside Qi'ra and Margo.

DEATHSTICK

SPECIES Dathomirian
HOMEWORLD Dathomir
AFFILIATION Nightsisters, Crimson Dawn, Kouhun

Deathstick is a bounty hunter whose entire lineage is wiped out during the Clone Wars. During a run-in with the Empire, she loses her lower jaw, which is then fitted with a cybernetic replacement and hidden under wrappings. She comes to lead the Kouhun and also serves as a lethal Crimson Dawn assassin, tracing Cadeliah to a hidden rebel base. After leaving Crimson Dawn's employ, she is hired by T'onga to go after Boba Fett and recover Beilert Valance's memories. When the Empire falls, she, along with the Kouhun, works closely with the Uprising.

ARCHIVIST

SPECIES Human
AFFILIATION University of Bar'leth, Crimson Dawn

Once known as Madelin Sun, the mysterious Archivist holds the scholarly position of Sava at the University of Bar'leth. Mildly Force-attuned, she is recruited by Qi'ra into Crimson Dawn as a Force expert. Part of her work involves locating Yoda. This takes her to Dagobah, where her experience in the Cave of Evil changes her appearance and her viewpoint. Later, she helps Qi'ra track down the Knights of Ren and activate the Fermata Cage at the Amaxine Station. The Archivist records the events of Qi'ra's attempted reign on a holocron, which is eventually seen by Luke Skywalker and Leia Organa.

REN

SPECIES Human
AFFILIATION Knights of Ren, Crimson Dawn

"Ren" is an old name used for the leader of the Knights of Ren. During the time of the Empire, the title is assumed by a handsome, Force-attuned human who wields a red lightsaber. Ren aligns himself with Qi'ra, breaking into Fortress Vader on a mission that ends in a duel with the Dark Lord. Alongside his Knights, Ren betrays Qi'ra and saves Darth Vader and the Emperor from the Fermata Cage. Years later, he meets Ben Solo, triggering events that eventually cause the young man to violently leave the Jedi, kill Ren, and assume his ancient title.

162 CHARACTERS AND CREATURES

JYALA HAYDENN
SPECIES Human **AFFILIATION** Empire

An Imperial lieutenant, Jyala Haydenn works with the cybernetic bounty hunter Beilert Valance. They develop a romance, but she shoots him and sends Inferno Squad to wipe his memories. However, she resigns from the Empire and eventually reconciles with her former lover.

LORD GYUTI
SPECIES Falleen **HOMEWORLD** Falleen
AFFILIATION Black Sun

Lord Gyuti is a high-ranking leader of Black Sun who attends the auction of Han Solo. He then meets with Qi'ra about forming a partnership, but his lack of action leads to the destruction of a Black Sun research facility. Gyuti later puts a bounty on the Zabrak bounty hunter Jas Emari.

GAZIAN
HOMEWORLD Gazian

Gazian is a mushroom-covered living planet and a vergence in the Force that creates imprints of all who visit. Luke Skywalker goes to the world in search of knowledge and encounters a memory of High Republic–era Jedi Elzar Mann. He also sees visions of other places, including Ahch-To, and departs with an ancient Jedi text.

KHO PHON FARRUS
SPECIES Alcedian

While studying archaeology at the University of Bar'leth, Kho Phon Farrus becomes obsessed with dark-side artifacts and the Ascendant cult. Years later, they return to the school, and Sava Iglan'tine Nos leads them to an underground chamber that holds the Ascendant's ancient AI, the Spark Eternal.

LORIACH
SPECIES Alazmec **HOMEWORLD** Mustafar
AFFILIATION Assassins Guild

Loriach is a master sniper of the Assassins Guild who fights for money and hunts down Crimson Dawn collaborators and sympathizers. He goes on missions for Darth Vader, along with the Revengers and Beilert Valance, until Vader has no use for him or his team anymore.

TARL SOKOLI
SPECIES Human
AFFILIATION Empire

General Tarl Sokoli, the Empire's heroic "Spine Dragon of Anaxes," meets a young Beilert Valance on the liberated planet of Chorin, which inspires the young boy to join the Empire. Years later, he is hunted and killed by Valance's Dark Squadron as a test from Darth Vader.

CHILLA ZIN
SPECIES Voridsec
AFFILIATION Assassins Guild

Chilla Zin is a Black Card Master of the Assassins Guild. Initially working for hire with G-90 and Loriach, he is recruited by Ochi of Bestoon to serve the Empire. He believes in the professional rules of his guild and has a tough time reconciling them with his team's actions.

G-90
MANUFACTURER Jayosbrand
TYPE Assassin droid
AFFILIATION Assassins Guild

G-90 is a spherical assassin droid that is sliced in two by Darth Vader after attempting to free prisoners from torture. The droid is reassembled by Jul Tambor, destroyed, and further reassembled to fight against Vader with other droids.

MOFF JERJERROD
SPECIES Human **HOMEWORLD** Tinnel IV
AFFILIATION Empire

Moff Tiaan Jerjerrod supervises construction of the second Death Star. Having been praised by visiting ISB agent Commander Sharin for running a tight ship, Jerjerrod soon realizes that Sharin's shuttle has been taken over by enemy agents and scrambles fighters to stop them but the vessel escapes. When the project remains behind schedule, the Emperor sends Darth Vader to put additional pressure on the Moff. Jerjerrod commands the battle station's superlaser during the Battle of Endor. He perishes when the rebels detonate the Death Star's reactor core.

THE REVENGERS
SPECIES Human, Trandoshan, Weequay
HOMEWORLD Various
AFFILIATION The Revengers

Led by Ankala Sahm, the Revengers consist of S'ira the Weequay and Tanka the Trandoshan, who all have suffered immense loss because of Crimson Dawn. Recruited by Ochi of Bestoon to take down the criminal syndicate, they are joined by Valance and come to view Darth Vader as a hero.

TAUNTAZA
SPECIES Human **AFFILIATION** Empire, Crimson Dawn

Tauntaza is the corrupt Governor of Gabredor III, apparently working with Crimson Dawn, but secretly taking orders directly from the Emperor. She builds a fortress that is hidden by uncontrollable energy and a sandstorm. While wearing a suit of energized armor, she duels Darth Vader and manages to escape.

JUL TAMBOR
SPECIES Skakoan **HOMEWORLD** Skako Minor
AFFILIATION Jul Tambor's Insurgency

The grandson of Wat Tambor, Jul Tambor leads an insurgency to take over Skako Minor. Sabé meets him on Brentaal IV, where she protects him from a Droid Crush assassination attempt. The former handmaiden reveals Tambor's dastardly plot to his fellow Skakoans, leaving him discredited among his people.

JON MELTON
SPECIES Human **AFFILIATION** Empire, Crimson Dawn, Rebel Alliance

Jon Melton appears to be Moff Tiaan Jerjerrod's loyal aide aboard the second Death Star, but he is in fact a Crimson Dawn spy, along with his wife Bevelyn. When ordered to create chaos for the Empire, Jon and Bev instead decide to leave the Empire. They go to the Rebel Alliance and inform them of the new battle station's existence.

BEVELYN
SPECIES Human
AFFILIATION Empire, Crimson Dawn, Rebel Alliance

A secret Crimson Dawn spy serving on the second Death Star, Bev, along with her husband Jon Melton, is called up for action by Lady Qi'ra of Crimson Dawn. They gather their children, steal an Imperial shuttle, and leave for the Rebel Alliance to disclose to them the construction of a new Imperial superweapon.

SPARK ETERNAL
MANUFACTURER Ascendant
TYPE Artificial intelligence device
AFFILIATION The Ascendant

Created by the Ascendant dark-side cultists, the Spark Eternal is an ancient AI device with unpredictable powers and abilities. Kho Phon Farrus finally uncovers the device, which had been stored for a long time beneath the University of Bar'leth. It proceeds to kill, revive, and then temporarily possess Doctor Chelli Aphra.

MIRIL
SPECIES Chadra-Fan
AFFILIATION The Ascendant

Miril is the leader of the Ascendant—a group of cultists devoted to investigating and replicating the powers of the Force, particularly the dark side. The Chadra-Fan sacrifices herself during a Sith attack to save the Spark Eternal—an AI device created by the cult that holds mysterious abilities.

AJAX SIGMA
TYPE Warrior-priest droid (Visioned droid)
AFFILIATION Second Revelation

Ajax Sigma is a warrior-priest droid who leads an uprising during the High Republic era and is destroyed by Loden Greatstorm. Nearly two centuries later, his neural core is recovered by Han Solo and Chewbacca, who bury it. The location is discovered, and Ajax is rebuilt by the time of the Second Revelation. He re-forms the group into a church, with himself as high priest. During the Scourge's take over, Sigma is determined to defeat it. His first attempt destroys his entire colony so he joins D-Squad and terminates the Scourge with his sword.

FORVAN
SPECIES Human
AFFILIATION Kezarat Colony

Forvan is a human child who lives in the Kezarat Colony with his father, Blythe. Forvan is constantly hunting for "new flavors," exploring the former Nihil Great Hall with his jetpack. It is there he first meets the stranded rebels, who eventually manage to escape No-Space using a Path engine.

BLYTHE
SPECIES Abyssin
AFFILIATION Kezarat Colony

Captain Blythe runs the Kezarat Colony in No-Space—a long-vanished convoy of tankerships. He and his son rescue a squad of Rebel Alliance members, making the "news" give them their weapons, including a Jedi lightsaber. Together, they use Nihil technology to breach a passage to the known galaxy.

TOMASSO
SPECIES Human **AFFILIATION** Spice Runners of Kijimi, Rebel Alliance, New Republic

Tomasso is one of the highest-ranking members of the Spice Runners of Kijimi. He protects Mon Mothma during an assassination attempt, right before the Battle of Endor. He is later a mentor to Zorii Bliss and a young Poe Dameron, but is fatally stabbed by Zeva Bliss after she accuses him of passing information to the New Republic.

STARWEIRD
AFFILIATION The Force

Long thought extinct, a Starweird is a Force-attuned being that emits a high-pitched shriek as a means of attack. Luke Skywalker and Doctor Chelli Aphra encounter one of the creatures at Sason temple, where it had been contained by the Jedi. They defeat it using a piece of Kythoo's bell, which focuses the frequencies of the temple's crystals.

MANAROO
SPECIES Aruzan **HOMEWORLD** Aruza
AFFILIATION Dengar

Manaroo is a blue-skinned Aruzan held prisoner by Jabba the Hutt as leverage against her boyfriend, Dengar. Jabba plans to keep her until Dengar captures Boba Fett. Manaroo is freed when Jabba dies, and she later assembles a team to help her rescue Dengar, who is captured in an asteroid field.

THEA STARROS
SPECIES Human **AFFILIATION** Cloud-Riders

Once a sniper in Enfys Nest's marauder gang, Thea Starros is a good shot and the grandmother of smuggler Sana Starros. When Imperials abduct a member of the Starros family, she is quickly swept into a mission to save the girl and recover a family heirloom from the Empire.

ARYSSHA STARROS
SPECIES Human

The cousin of smuggler Sana Starros, Aryssha becomes the center of a family clash with the Empire. Aryssha is married to an Imperial who abducts her from the Starros ancestral home. The Starros clan comes to her rescue, and Aryssha gives birth to healthy twins.

MEVERA STARROS
SPECIES Human

An artist and smuggler, Mevera Starros is the aunt of Sana Starros and mother of Aryssha Starros, to whom she gives birth during a job for Maz Kanata. Mevera joins her mother and Sana in a mission to rescue Aryssha from her Imperial husband and recover a stolen family heirloom.

PHEL STARROS
SPECIES Human
AFFILIATION Empire

Feeling deserted by his sister, Sana Starros, and having made bad choices, Phel Starros turns his life around by joining the Empire. Now an Imperial officer, he clashes with his family. But he has no memory of leaving the Academy for Young Imperials on Lothal, which troubles him.

GRETTA
SPECIES Human **HOMEWORLD** Jedha

Gretta's family is killed by the Empire on Jedha so she feels indebted to Luke Skywalker for destroying the Death Star. She saves the young Jedi from bounty hunters on Christophsis and leads him to kyber specialist Doctor Cuata, who gifts Luke two crystals. She later helps Luke purify a red kyber crystal.

GOL
AFFILIATION Sith

A cruel, violent warlord who experienced great trauma, Gol is opposed to letting go of his pain, citing it as necessary for existence. Known as the Wither King, a spiritual echo of Gol resides inside a red kyber crystal. Luke Skywalker travels inside the crystal to purify it and discover the pain that caused Gol to turn into a vicious tyrant.

SCOURGE
MANUFACTURER Self-made
AFFILIATION Itself

The Scourge forms when the Spark Eternal AI combines with an ancient droid. The life-form can assimilate mechanical beings. Using the droid presence, it spreads across a Star Destroyer, killing all humans and renaming the ship *Scourge 01*. But the Scourge remains hungry and sets its sights on "meat," or people, starting with cyborgs, which takes its reach and power to a new level.

164 CHARACTERS AND CREATURES

KAY VESS
SPECIES Human **HOMEWORLD** Cantonica
AFFILIATION None

Kay Vess is an up-and-coming scoundrel who hails from the streets of Canto Bight. She has no love for the Empire but also has no interest in fighting in the Galactic Civil War. Smart and talented, Kay is a capable and stealthy operative with a range of gadgets at her disposal. Kay is also an accomplished pilot and owns her own ship, the *Trailblazer*. When a job goes awry, Kay ends up with a bounty placed on her. Her one shot at escaping is completing one of the biggest heists in history.

NIX
SPECIES Merqaal **AFFILIATION** Kay Vess

Nix is a merqaal, a type of creature, who accompanies Kay Vess on adventures throughout the galaxy. Ever since the two meet in Canto Bight, they are inseparable and fiercely loyal to one another. For Nix, Kay is his only family and the only person he trusts. If Kay is in danger or threatened, Nix becomes wild and will protect her with his life. Nix can respond to simple commands and often aids Kay while on missions, fetching weapons or activating controls.

ND-5
MANUFACTURER Baktoid Combat Automata
TYPE Commando droid **AFFILIATION** Kay Vess

ND-5 is a BX model commando droid that fights during the Clone Wars and is still active during the Imperial era. Like other commando droids, he is a formidable opponent in combat. At the end of the Clone Wars, ND-5 begins working for the mysterious Jaylen Vrax. At some point, ND-5 teams up with Kay Vess and Nix as an enforcer and bodyguard. The trio works together on a major heist following the Battle of Hoth.

80-M
TYPE Protocol droid **AFFILIATION** Jabba's palace, Silvan Kaan

80-M is a reprogrammed protocol droid that works in Jabba's palace. The droid believes his responsibilities are beneath his capabilities so agrees to help the rogue Silvan Kaan in exchange for having his restraining bolt removed. The poor droid becomes a pawn in Kaan's plot to kill the crime lord. When the treachery is uncovered, all the perpetrators meet Jabba's brand of justice, including the hapless 80-M, who is torn asunder and destroyed.

8D8
MANUFACTURER Verpine Roche Hive
TYPE Smelter droid
AFFILIATION Jabba's palace, Boba Fett

8D8 is a cruel industrial droid owned by Jabba the Hutt. He tortures other automatons to ensure that they know their place in the palace, sometimes tormenting them just for fun. The 8D-series droids resent the more sophisticated protocol and astromech droids and tend to be bullies. Alongside many others of his kind in the palace, 8D8 is temporarily infected by the Scourge. After Jabba and Bib Fortuna's deaths, 8D8 becomes majordomo to Boba Fett, daimyo of Tatooine, passing messages to his master, translating other languages, and coordinating day-to-day work.

EV-9D9
MANUFACTURER MerenData
TYPE Supervisor droid **AFFILIATION** Jabba's palace, Mos Eisley cantina

EV-9D9 is Jabba's sadistic droid overseer. Her programming is corrupted, but she manages to avoid the manufacturer's recall and continues working in the Hutt's murky dungeons. For a time, EV is Scourged alongside many droids in the palace while Jabba is aboard the *Khetanna*. During the Alliance infiltration of Jabba's court, EV assigns R2-D2 to the sail barge and C-3PO to be the new interpreter. Following Jabba's death, the droid overseer is reprogrammed and gets a new job working as a bartender in the cantina formerly owned by Chalmun in Mos Eisley.

PATEESA
SPECIES Rancor
AFFILIATION Jabba's palace

The rancor known as Pateesa is a birthday gift from Bib Fortuna to his boss, and she lives in the chamber below Jabba the Hutt's throne room. The pet is cared for by Malakili, the resident creature handler. When angry, Jabba likes to drop victims through a trapdoor and into the rancor's den, where they are eaten whole by the beast. When Luke Skywalker finds himself in the beast's clutches, he is able to kill Pateesa by dropping a secondary gate on its head. Malakili has a bond with the ferocious but semi-intelligent monster and is heartbroken when it dies.

SALACIOUS B. CRUMB
SPECIES Kowakian monkey-lizard
HOMEWORLD Kowak
AFFILIATION Jabba's palace

Salacious Crumb is the jester of Jabba's court. He begins his time with Jabba as a stowaway thief aboard the Hutt's ship, but Bib Fortuna manages to capture him. Henceforth Crumb sits beside Jabba and teases captives. His shrill, irritating laughter amuses the Hutt immensely.

DROOPY McCOOL
SPECIES Kitonak **HOMEWORLD** Kirdo III
AFFILIATION None

Droopy McCool is the lead horn player in Jabba's house band. A mentee of the famous composer Quez Totark, his real name is an unpronounceable series of whistles. The band's manager, Max Rebo, gives him his stage name. Lonely, Droopy plays his chidinkalu flute and longs for the company of other Kitonaks.

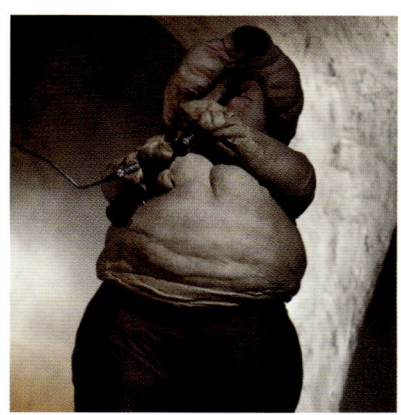

GAMORREAN GUARD

SPECIES Gamorrean **HOMEWORLD** Gamorr
AFFILIATION Jabba's palace, Boba Fett

Jabba the Hutt employs a contingent of Gamorreans as his palace guards. They are typically armed with vibro-axes and vibro-lances. Following the deaths of Jabba and his successor Bib Fortuna, a pair of Gamorreans later align themselves with the new daimyo of Tatooine, Boba Fett.

KLAATU

SPECIES Nikto
HOMEWORLD Kintan
AFFILIATION Jabba's palace

The Nikto Klaatu repairs skiffs for Jabba the Hutt on Tatooine where he also enjoys gambling. During the failed executions of Han Solo, Chewbacca, and Luke Skywalker at the Great Pit of Carkoon, Klaatu's blaster is sliced in half by the Jedi, forcing the Nikto to flee inside the sail barge. Seconds later, Leia Organa fires the vessel's cannon at the deck before escaping the barge with Luke. Klaatu is killed in the ensuing explosion.

OOLA

SPECIES Twi'lek
HOMEWORLD Ryloth
AFFILIATION None

Oola is a Twi'lek woman who is enslaved by Bib Fortuna and forced to serve as a dancer in Jabba's palace. When the vile Hutt is displeased with Oola, he furiously drops her into his pet rancor's pit, where she meets a horrible end.

MAX REBO

SPECIES Ortolan **HOMEWORLD** Orto **AFFILIATION** None

Max Rebo is the leader of his eponymous band, in which he plays the red ball jett organ whenever Jabba wishes. Alongside his bandmate Droopy McCool, Rebo learns how to play from the legendary composer Quez Totark. Following his mentor's death, Max develops an obsession with death and feels haunted by him. While on a trip to Mos Eisley, Rebo encounters his estranged brother, Azool Phantelle, who has stolen money on Jabba's turf. They are both chased by angry citizens and stormtroopers, until Rebo throws his brother's ill-gotten gains into the street. Jabba forces Azool to serve him in order to pay for his crimes. Rebo survives Luke Skywalker's attack on Jabba's barge and resolves to focus on life instead of death. He eventually starts playing at Garsa Fwip's Sanctuary until the location's destruction by the Pykes.

SCOUT TROOPER

SPECIES Human **HOMEWORLD** Various **AFFILIATION** Empire

Scout troopers are highly trained soldiers of the Empire, specializing in reconnaissance and sniping. The scouts provide excellent long-range fire for their stormtrooper counterparts. Scout troopers are stationed on the Forest Moon of Endor, where the second Death Star is under construction. The scout troopers on patrol are taken by surprise and defeated by a small team of rebel soldiers. This same band of rebels attacks the bunker holding the shield generator that protects the Death Star in orbit. The scout troopers fight back, briefly subduing the rebels, before a tribe of Ewoks comes to the latter's aid. The defeated scouts are taken prisoner by the rebels, who successfully destroy the generator and the second Death Star shortly thereafter. A number of scout troopers serve Moff Gideon's Imperial remnant and play an instrumental role in a battle on Nevarro.

GENERAL CRIX MADINE

SPECIES Human **HOMEWORLD** Corellia
AFFILIATION Rebel Alliance, New Republic

Crix Madine begins his military career as a well-respected leader of an Imperial commando unit, but he eventually defects to the Rebel Alliance. He is made a general and is responsible for covert operations. After Bothan spies deliver intelligence on the second Death Star being constructed in orbit above the Forest Moon of Endor, Madine plans the assault against the Empire's latest battle station. He enlists recently freed Han Solo to lead a team of highly trained rebel commandos, called Pathfinders, to destroy the shield generator on the Forest Moon of Endor, which protects the dreaded new superweapon. Following the success of Solo's mission and the Rebel Alliance's resounding victory against the Empire, Madine is placed in charge of the newly formed New Republic Special Forces. He orders a small unit to investigate the Imperial presence on the planet Akiva. A year after the Battle of Endor, Madine attends the Liberation Day festivities on Chandrila and is believed killed during a surprise Imperial attack.

SARLACC

HOMEWORLD Tatooine **AVERAGE SIZE** 3 m (10 ft) wide, 100 m (328 ft) long
HABITAT Desert

One of Jabba the Hutt's favorite "pets," the mighty Sarlacc nests in the Pit of Carkoon. From above, only the enormous creature's mouth is visible. The rest of the beast, including its vast stomachs, is buried deep in the sand. When Jabba's prisoners are dropped into the monster's pit, the Sarlacc's tentacles grab them and drag them into its mouth. Rows of hundreds of spearlike teeth prevent the prisoner from climbing out, and the Sarlacc swallows its prey whole. Han Solo, Luke Skywalker, and Chewbacca are taken to the pit for execution, but with help from friends, manage to escape. During this chaos, Boba Fett is eaten by the Sarlacc. Thanks to his Mandalorian armor, he manages to escape one of the creature's stomachs. He later returns to search for his armor, destroying the beast with a seismic charge from his starship.

BARADA

SPECIES Klatooinian **HOMEWORLD** Klatooine

Barada is an enslaved Klatooinian, who is forced to work as a mechanic for Jabba the Hutt. Barada is responsible for all of the gangster's repulsorlift vehicles. He accompanies Greedo on his mission to Mygeeto, providing a lift in his skiff when the bounty hunter needs an escape route. During the Alliance attack on Jabba's sail barge, Luke Skywalker knocks Barada into the Pit of Carkoon, where he will be digested by the Sarlacc for 1,000 years.

CHARACTERS AND CREATURES

WICKET W. WARRICK
SPECIES Ewok **HOMEWORLD** Forest Moon of Endor
AFFILIATION Bright Tree Village

When Wicket W. Warrick discovers a human unconscious in the woods, he remains wary until she offers him part of a ration bar to eat. Hearing the approach of Imperial scout troopers, he grabs his spear, ready for combat. When the troopers fire at them, Wicket and the woman—Leia Organa—hide behind a log. Wicket rolls out of sight as one of the scout troopers threatens Leia with his blaster. He attacks the trooper's legs, giving Leia a chance to knock out her assailant, grab her blaster, and shoot the other Imperial trooper before he can escape.

Wicket decides to bring his new human friend to the Ewok village. En route, they save two of Wicket's fellow villagers from stormtroopers. When they arrive at Bright Tree Village, Leia is treated as an honored guest. Wicket and Paploo accompany Leia and the rebel commando squad to a ridge overlooking the Imperial landing platform and reveal a "secret" entrance to the shield generator bunker on the other side of the ridge. The rebels mount a sneak attack on the bunker, but are outnumbered by the Imperial soldiers waiting for them. When the rebels are led back out of the bunker at gunpoint, Wicket returns with an army of Ewoks to free them.

After the Battle of Endor, Wicket attends the festivities to celebrate the victory. The day after, Wicket joins Han Solo's strike team to destroy an Imperial base on the far side of the moon. Wicket also works with fellow Ewok Princess Kneesaa, Leia, and Luke Skywalker to defeat a gigantic Gorax. Wicket gives Leia a gift of a serpent-puzzle-plant acorn before she leaves his home.

During the New Republic era, Wicket has at least one child, a son named Pommet. The pair watch as a First Order Star Destroyer orbiting the Forest Moon of Endor is destroyed.

TEEBO
SPECIES Ewok **HOMEWORLD** Forest Moon of Endor **AFFILIATION** Bright Tree Village

After his scouting party captures the rebel strike team in a net trap, Teebo pokes Han Solo with his spear to ensure compliance. In return, Teebo gets zapped twice by R2-D2 when he releases the droid from its bonds. During the Battle of Endor, Teebo sounds the Sacred Horn of the Soul Trees, giving the signal for the Ewoks to attack. In the celebration following the destruction of the second Death Star, Teebo plays percussion on stormtrooper helmets and bonds with R2-D2.

CHIEF CHIRPA
SPECIES Ewok **HOMEWORLD** Forest Moon of Endor **AFFILIATION** Bright Tree Village

Son of Chief Buzza, Chirpa is a hunter for the Bright Tree Village tribe. When Buzza informs Chirpa that baby Ewoks, named "Woklings," have been stolen from the village, Chirpa works with Logray and Ra-Lee to rescue them. Chirpa eventually takes over as Chief of the Council of Elders and marries Ra-Lee. Together, they have a daughter named Kneesaa.

At the time of the Battle of Endor, scouts from the village capture key members of the rebel strike team sent to the Forest Moon, including C-3PO. Like the other Ewoks, Chirpa believes the shiny metallic droid is a prophesied golden god and initially agrees with the shaman Logray that several of the captives should be cooked alive in a sacrificial ceremony. Luke Skywalker tells C-3PO to order the Ewoks to release them, and when they refuse, Luke covertly uses the Force to levitate the droid into the air. Awed by this fearsome display of divine power, Chirpa orders the rebels freed immediately. C-3PO then tells the tribe the story of the rebels' struggles against the evil Empire, prompting Chirpa to declare the rebels honorary members of the tribe. Together, the Ewoks and rebels defeat the Imperial forces guarding the shield generator. Kneesaa goes on to succeed him as chief.

Bold leader
At first skeptical of the rebel intruders on the forest moon, Chief Chirpa allies with them to defeat the Imperial soldiers.

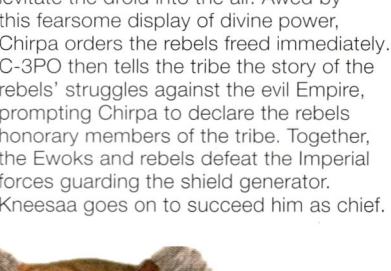

LOGRAY
SPECIES Ewok **HOMEWORLD** Forest Moon of Endor **AFFILIATION** Bright Tree Village

Logray is shaman Makrit's apprentice for the Bright Tree Village tribe of Ewoks. Along with Chirpa and Ra-Lee, he discovers that Makrit plans to sacrifice the three of them and some kidnapped baby Ewoks to a Gorax named the Great Devourer. Thanks to Ra-Lee's ingenuity, they escape and Makrit is devoured instead. Then, Logray takes over as the shaman for the tribe. When the captured members of the rebel strike team are brought to the village, Logray orders that Han Solo, Chewbacca, and Luke Skywalker, be cooked alive as a ritual sacrifice to "the Golden One," the shining protocol droid C-3PO, whom the Ewoks revere as a legendary deity.

PAPLOO
SPECIES Ewok **HOMEWORLD** Forest Moon of Endor **AFFILIATION** Bright Tree Village

Paploo is a skilled Ewok scout and is very imaginative. One evening around a campfire, Paploo tells a terrifying tale about a Gorax eating an Ewok, which prompts Logray to whack him with his staff of power. Alongside his friends Teebo and Warrick T. Wicket, Paploo leads the Pathfinder strike team to the Empire's planetary shield-generator location, which is protecting the second Death Star in orbit above the Forest Moon. While others debate the best plan for seizing the bunker from the Imperial soldiers, Paploo sneaks forward and steals an Imperial scout trooper's speeder bike. His diversion provides the strike team with the element of surprise as they launch their attack.

NIEN NUNB
SPECIES Sullustan **HOMEWORLD** Sullust
AFFILIATION Rebel Alliance, Resistance

Sullustan smuggler Nien Nunb is a decorated and long-serving member of the Rebel Alliance and the Resistance. Days after the Battle of Yavin, Nien uses his ship, the *Mellcrawler*, to help his friends Evaan Verlaine and Princess Leia Organa smuggle persecuted Alderaanians off his homeworld to safety. Nien is evacuated from Hoth and becomes part of the Fourth Fleet. Piloting an A-wing, Nien takes part in a daring assault on Coruscant, alongside Lando Calrissian and Chewbacca in the *Millennium Falcon*. When Nien's ship takes a critical hit, he ejects and is caught by Chewie, who is leaning out of the *Falcon*. Nien then joins Lando for the first time as the fabled ship's copilot. Nien later helps the insurrection on Sullust against the Empire that liberates the planet.

During Operation: Yellow Moon, Nien and Leia work with three other rebels (Kidi Aleri, Lokmarcha, and Antrot), using the *Mellcrawler* for transport. Their mission is to deflect the Empire's attention away from the massing Alliance fleet above Sullust. When the team is captured and held aboard a Star Destroyer, Leia, Nien, and Kidi escape on the Imperial shuttle the *Tydirium*. Antrot and Lokmarcha sacrifice themselves, and the *Mellcrawler* is destroyed. After the operation, Nien gets a new ship named the *Mellcrawler II*. With his frequent copilot and fellow rebel Shriv Suurgav, Nien crash-lands the *Mellcrawler II* on a living island that tries to eat them. They escape, but the Imperials who also crash aren't so lucky.

Prior to the Battle of Endor, Lando plans to fly the *Falcon* inside the second Death Star to make a direct attack on the vulnerable power core within the unfinished structure. He asks Nien to be his copilot for the crucial mission. Days after their victory, Nien and Lando travel to Naboo in the *Mellcrawler II*, along with a rebel fleet to help Leia stop the planet's destruction by the Empire.

Decades later, Nien sends his friend Leia a message of support when New Republic senator Casterfo reveals to the galaxy that Leia's biological father is Darth Vader. Nien is present when Leia announces the formation of the Resistance to protect the galaxy, and he is one of its first members. Taking the rank of Lieutenant Commander, Nien primarily flies starfighters. He participates in the assault on the First Order's Starkiller Base and, afterward, attends Han Solo's funeral on D'Qar prior to the Resistance's evacuation of their base. Following the lethal First Order assault on the Resistance forces on Crait, Nien is one of a handful of survivors to escape aboard the *Falcon*. As he did three decades before, Nien takes his place in the cockpit as copilot once more.

Following the loss at Crait, Nien is part of the Resistance operations on Ryloth, Kashyyyk, and Batuu. He is killed during the Battle of Exegol while co-piloting the *Tantive IV* when the ship is hit by the Emperor's lightning attack.

Flying buddies
With Nunb and Lando at the helm, the *Millennium Falcon* stages a direct assault on the Death Star's power core.

PEEKPA
SPECIES Ewok **HOMEWORLD** Forest Moon of Endor **AFFILIATION** Bright Tree Tribe, New Republic (Digital Warfare Department)

Technologically gifted, Peekpa is a surly female Ewok who leaves the Forest Moon of Endor for a career in slicing. It's said that she takes to the skies in a working ship that she built herself from wrecked Imperial equipment. Peekpa is an enormous fan of the Rebel hero Chewbacca, who saved her sister's life during the Battle of Endor. Because of her love for the Wookiee, she eagerly joins forces with Han Solo and Lando Calrissian to track down the Pau'an gangster Fyzen Gor, who is the creator of the Phylanx Redux Transmitter.

KNEESAA
SPECIES Ewok **HOMEWORLD** Forest Moon of Endor **AFFILIATION** Bright Tree Tribe, Rebel Alliance

Kneesaa is the daughter of Chief Chirpa, who leads the Bright Tree Tribe, making her princess of the village. She grows up going on many adventures alongside her friends, who include Wicket W. Warrick. During the Battle of Endor, she works and fights alongside Rebellion hero, Kes Dameron. Following the victory, she and rebel heroes Leia Organa and Luke Skywalker knock out a dangerous gorax and help Hera Syndulla and Chopper defeat some stray Imperial TIEs. She eventually succeeds her father and becomes the first female leader of Bright Tree Tribe.

AIREN CRACKEN
SPECIES Human
HOMEWORLD Contruum
AFFILIATION Rebel Alliance

General Airen Cracken serves as the chief of intelligence for the Rebel Alliance. While leading the planetary militia of his homeworld of Contruum, Cracken frees his people from the Empire. After this initial victory, he joins the Rebellion, establishing a team of operatives dispatched onto the field of war. He valiantly operates the gunner station on the *Millennium Falcon* during the Battle of Endor and then continues his loyal service through the formation of the New Republic.

TESO BROOSH
SPECIES Human
AFFILIATION Empire, Squadron Five (Shadow Wing), Alphabet Squadron

The stern commanding officer of Squadron Five, Commander Teso Broosh reports to the intimidating "Grandmother." It's rumored that he sacrifices fellow pilots to save himself in battle. Broosh leads the defense of the seemingly disabled Star Destroyer *Celerity* and takes back an Imperial mining facility in the Kudo system. While he initially bristles at Soran Keize deserting the Empire after the Battle of Endor, he eventually warms toward the pilot. Upon Soran's second departure from the Empire, Broosh is named major and given full command of the 204th Imperial Fighter Wing.

CHARACTERS AND CREATURES

JEELA BREBTIN

SPECIES Human **AFFILIATION** Empire, Dark Squadron, Squadron Five (Shadow Wing)

One of the best small-arms gunners in the Empire, there is perhaps no one more deadly in the cockpit than Jeela Brebtin. During the Galactic Civil War, she works as a member of Dark Squadron with Beilert Valance to kill Admiral Tarl Sokoli. Brebtin is promoted to senior lieutenant, joining Squadron Five of the lethal 204th Imperial Fighter Wing, where she goes on numerous missions, including against traitorous ex-Imperials in the Kudo system. After the death of the Emperor, she takes part in Operation: Cinder, and other missions, including with Yrica Quell as part of a secret strike team.

SHRIV SUURGAV

SPECIES Duros **HOMEWORLD** Duros **AFFILIATION** Rebel Alliance, New Republic, Resistance, Danger Squad, Inferno Squad

Good with both a blaster and a well-timed barb, Shriv Suurgav is the leader of Danger Squad, a strike team of the Rebellion. He flies in the Battle of Endor and fights in the Liberation of Sullust alongside his friends Nien Nunb and Lando Calrissian. Following these events, Shriv encounters Imperial troopers Iden Versio and Del Meeko of Inferno Squad, who are defecting. They join Shriv in Danger Squad for a mission to protect Naboo from an Imperial attack. The three then relaunch Inferno Squad in service of the New Republic. Together, they help to defeat the Empire once and for all in the Battle of Jakku. Years later, Shriv joins Iden on a mission to locate Del, and they eventually go to Vardos, where they narrowly escape a First Order trap. Finally, they reunite with Iden's daughter, Zay. The three hatch a plan to sneak onto a First Order Star Destroyer to steal the schematics to a Dreadnought. Iden makes the ultimate sacrifice, but Shriv and Zay successfully deliver the data to General Leia Organa, and Inferno Squad lives on. Alongside Zay, Shriv works to locate new recruits for the Resistance and leads a mission to Bracca to replenish the Resistance's depleted starfighter corps.

SHAKARA NURESS

SPECIES Human **AFFILIATION** Republic, Empire, 204th Imperial Fighter Wing

Shakara Nuress is a veteran of the Clone Wars, first serving in the Republic Navy. She continues her military career as an Imperial strategist, now known as "Grandmother." Nuress commands Shadow Wing against what she still refers to as "Separatists" and dies during the battle of Pandem Nai.

BANSU RO

SPECIES Human **HOMEWORLD** Lothal **AFFILIATION** Empire, Squadron Five (Shadow Wing)

A top-ranking cadet on Carida, Bansu Ro is pulled out to serve as a TIE pilot in the 204th Imperial Fighter Wing, also known as Shadow Wing. He is very skilled and flies many missions for the Empire. After the Battle of Jakku, Ro flees to Freerock and is eventually asked to join a freelancer crew led by Nath Tensent.

YRICA QUELL

SPECIES Human **HOMEWORLD** Gavana Orbital **AFFILIATION** Empire, 204th Imperial Fighter Wing, New Republic, Alphabet Squadron

Yrica Quell joins the Imperial Academy, initially planning to defect after receiving the necessary education. However, she stays on as a TIE fighter pilot, coming to believe that the Rebellion propaganda is misinformed. She eventually does defect, after witnessing the devastating effects of Operation: Cinder on Nacronis. Now a part of the New Republic, she becomes an X-wing pilot, and is soon named commander of the Alphabet Squadron. Quell leads the newly minted unit in training, working under General Hera Syndulla in their mission to destroy the infamous Shadow Wing. After the Battle of Troithe, she surrenders herself to the Empire, claiming to have been in a reclamation camp, and comes aboard as the personal aid of Soran Keize. Secretly, however, she works to undermine the 204th, which involves fashioning a secret transmitter and sending data to the New Republic. She is also given a special new prototype of the T-70 X-wing in order to stop Keize's destruction of the Imperial databank. Quell eventually retires to run cargo with her partner and lover, Chass na Chadic.

SORAN KEIZE

SPECIES Human **AFFILIATION** Empire, 204th Imperial Fighter Wing

Colonel Soran Keize is an ace TIE fighter pilot of the infamous Shadow Wing. He initially leaves the Empire after the Battle of Endor but is soon tracked down by New Republic Intelligence. Now believing there is no place for former Imperials in the galaxy, Keize returns to the Empire, leading a second wave of Operation: Cinder. During the final days of the war, he discovers that the Empire had kept a databank of their soldiers' crimes. Keize attempts to destroy it but fails, dying in the process. He posthumously releases a recording, in which he takes responsibility for Shadow Wing's war crimes.

WYL LARK

SPECIES Human **HOMEWORLD** Polyneus **AFFILIATION** New Republic, Alphabet Squadron, Galactic Senate

Born on the isolated planet of Polyneus, Wyl Lark is one of the "Hundred and Twenty" volunteers sent by his homeworld to join the Rebel Alliance. Recruited to be part of Alphabet Squadron as an A-wing pilot, he is instrumental in taking down Shadow Wing. He relinquishes his command of Hera Syndulla's flagship, the *Deliverance*, after Shadow Wing's devastating attack on Chadawa. Nevertheless, he prevents the sabotage of the ship during the Battle of Jakku. He returns to Polyneus and is appointed to represent it in the New Republic Senate.

CHASS NA CHADIC

SPECIES Theelin
AFFILIATION Rebel Alliance, New Republic, Alphabet Squadron

Chass na Chadic is a Theelin pilot who is inspired to join the Rebel Alliance after discovering that an undercover Jyn Erso once rescued her from a street gang. Taking her skills from the Cavern Angels on Jedha to the Rebellion, she finds her Riot Squadron decimated so is inserted into Alphabet Squadron. Due to the nature of her previous missions, she doesn't trust her fellow pilots, especially Wyl Lark. She masterfully flies a B-wing during numerous strikes against Shadow Wing and, after the war is over, eventually retires alongside Yrica Quell, settling down as partners of a small shipping company.

NATH TENSENT

SPECIES Human **AFFILIATION** Empire, Rebel Alliance, New Republic, Alphabet Squadron

Captain Nath Tensent serves as an Imperial pilot, policing the Outer Rim, until he is caught accepting bribes. His entire squadron defects from the Empire and joins the Rebellion. After the rest of his unit is killed by Shadow Wing, he joins Alphabet Squadron as a Y-wing pilot, but only accepts the assignment after secretly being offered financial compensation by Caern Adan. Alongside his astromech droid named T5, Tensent joins Alphabet Squadron on many harrowing missions, becoming quick friends with Wyl Lark, who is perhaps the only person the scoundrel will really listen to.

KAIROS

AFFILIATION Rebel Alliance, New Republic, Alphabet Squadron

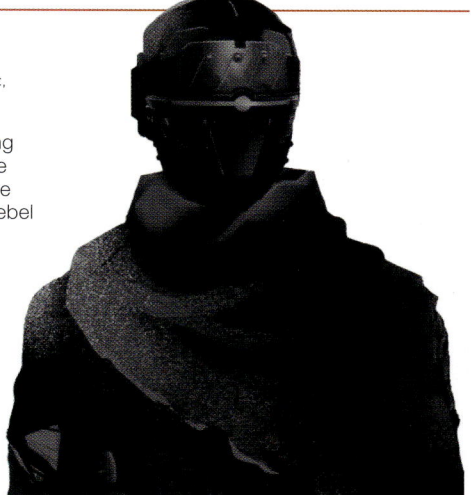

Kairos is a mysterious masked U-wing pilot in Alphabet Squadron. When the Empire arrives on her homeworld, she leaves her simple life and joins the Rebel Alliance as a representative for her people. Kairos is recruited by Caern Adan to track down Shadow Wing and, despite her quiet nature, she forges significant bonds with her fellow pilots. During the Battle of Jakku, she causes her U-wing to self-destruct in order to damage an enemy fighter. Kairos begins a molting process, and her new form is an opportunity to start a life untouched by war.

NORRA WEXLEY

SPECIES Human **HOMEWORLD** Akiva
AFFILIATION Rebel Alliance, New Republic, Resistance

After her husband is imprisoned by the Empire, Norra Wexley leaves her son, Temmin "Snap" Wexley, and joins the Rebel Alliance. Beginning as a freighter pilot, she soon flies as Gold Nine during the Battle of Endor. Wexley teams up with Han Solo to liberate Kashyyyk, freeing her lost husband, Brentin. Unfortunately, he has been secretly brainwashed by Gallius Rax and tries to assassinate Chancellor Mon Mothma. The Wexleys travel to Jakku to kill Rax, but Brentin dies in the attempt. Norra eventually marries Wedge Antilles. Years later, when Temmin comes to visit, she joins the Resistance.

JAS EMARI

SPECIES Zabrak **HOMEWORLD** Iridonia
AFFILIATION New Republic

Jas Emari grows up on Iridonia wanting to be just like her aunt, the infamous Clone Wars–era bounty hunter, Sugi. A skilled sniper, Emari is present at the Battle of Endor but defects from the Empire, who had hired her to target Leia Organa. She eventually joins the rebel cell on Akiva alongside Norra and Temmin Wexley. Emari goes on many New Republic missions, including the liberation of Kashyyyk and the hunt for Grand Admiral Sloane. During her time on Jakku, she is captured by Mercurial Swift but escapes thanks to some of her aunt's former bounty hunter colleagues.

KYRSTA AGATE

SPECIES Human **AFFILIATION** New Republic Defense Fleet

A commander of the New Republic Starfleet, Kyrsta Agate is personally chosen by Admiral Ackbar to lead the forces to Akiva. She narrowly survives an assassination attempt when she is shot in the face during the faux peace deal on Chandrila. After getting a cybernetic right eye, she commands the *Concord* during the Battle of Jakku. During the fight, she helps bring down the Super Star Destroyer, the *Ravager*, with her ship's tractor beams. Although she perishes in the process, her efforts help to turn the tide of the battle in favor of the New Republic.

LINDON JAVES

SPECIES Human **HOMEWORLD** Todirium III
AFFILIATION Empire, Rebel Alliance, New Republic, Vanguard Squadron

Following the destruction of Alderaan and a subsequent mission to hunt down refugees, disenchanted TIE fighter pilot Lindon Javes defects from the Empire and joins the Rebellion. He rises quickly within the Alliance and then New Republic ranks, eventually being granted command of the *Temperance* and Vanguard Squadron. Under his stewardship, they protect the development of a new battleship, Project Starhawk. When the Empire's Titan Squadron, led by Javes' former protégé Terisa Kerrill, attacks the *Starhawk*, Lindon once again joins Vanguard Squadron in an X-wing.

TERISA KERRILL

SPECIES Human **HOMEWORLD** Coruscant
AFFILIATION Empire, Titan Squadron

Terisa Kerrill grows up on the streets of Coruscant, finding direction and purpose in the order of the Empire. She proves to be a gifted TIE fighter pilot, idolizing her squad captain, Lindon Javes. But when Javes defects to the Rebellion after refusing to destroy Alderaanian refugees, Kerrill remains true to the Empire—and becomes obsessed with enacting her revenge on his betrayal. Eventually graduating to commander of Titan Squadron, she leads the Imperial effort to destroy the experimental New Republic battleship known as *Starhawk*, as well as Javes and his elite Vanguard Squadron.

GUNNY

SPECIES Mimbanese **HOMEWORLD** Mimban
AFFILIATION Rebel Alliance, New Republic, Vanguard Squadron

During the Clone Wars, Kierah "Gunny" Koovah joins clone troopers to protect her homeworld, Mimban, from the Separatist forces. After losing an arm, she receives a cybernetic replacement. Gunny later leads Vanguard Squadron for the Rebellion and remains with the outfit into the New Republic era.

GRACE SIENAR

SPECIES Human
AFFILIATION Rebel Alliance, New Republic, Vanguard Squadron

A rebel at heart, Grace Sienar—whose family becomes rich and infamous for constructing Imperial TIE fighters—rejects her familial legacy. She joins the Rebellion and later the New Republic, flying for Vanguard Squadron and relishing the chance to destroy the craft developed by her kin.

VARKO GREY

SPECIES Human
AFFILIATION Empire, Titan Squadron

With a hatred of corruption and a belief in order, Varko Grey works as a ParSec police officer on Parkella. He then enlists in the Empire, seeing it as the only cure for the chaos of the galaxy. A skilled pilot, Varko moves up the ranks to become leader of Titan Squadron.

LUMPAWAROO

SPECIES Wookiee **HOMEWORLD** Kashyyyk
AFFILIATION His family

Lumpawaroo, shortened to "Lumpy" or "Waroo," is a brave young Wookiee and the son of Rebellion hero Chewbacca. Lumpy misses his father, who is off battling for the galaxy's freedom alongside Han Solo, but he understands why he is gone. During the Empire's invasion of Kashyyyk, Lumpy becomes enslaved by Imperial forces, and he has an inhibitor chip implanted in him. Separated from his mother and forced to work at a labor camp, he is eventually liberated and reunited with his father. Lumpy later meets Rey when the hero joins Chewbacca on a trip to his homeworld.

ARDO BARODAI

SPECIES Mon Calamari **HOMEWORLD** Mon Cala **AFFILIATION** Rebel Alliance, New Republic, Vanguard Squadron

During the Empire's occupation of Mon Cala, Barodai is a spy. Posing as a bartender, he eavesdrops on Imperials and passes the intel to rebel contacts. As Vanguard Squadron's intelligence chief, the sharp-minded Mon Calamari uses his skills for the New Republic.

ZERELDA SAGE

SPECIES Human
AFFILIATION Rebel Alliance, New Republic, Vanguard Squadron

Zerelda Sage distrusts droids after the Separatists invade her homeworld, but she develops mechanical skills to sabotage invaders' ships. After working in podracing, she joins the New Republic as a mechanic for Vanguard Squadron.

HAVINA VONREG

SPECIES Human
AFFILIATION Empire, Titan Squadron

Bitter and ruthless, Havina Vonreg flies for the Empire's Titan Squadron with an unquenchable bloodlust. Vonreg loses brothers to a rebel attack, mourns her fellow Imperials, and feels betrayed by traitors. She has little interest in politics, and instead revels in revenge.

FRISK

SPECIES Trandoshan **HOMEWORLD** Trandosha
AFFILIATION Rebel Alliance, New Republic, Vanguard Squadron

Feresk Tssat, known as "Frisk," gets by as a con artist until he scams the wrong Imperial. Fleeing capture, he develops impressive piloting skills, which leads to a change of heart and a place with the Rebellion in Vanguard Squadron and, later, in the New Republic.

LT-514

SPECIES Human
AFFILIATION Empire

Obon Yandro, a low-level manufacturing company clerk, becomes LT-514—the cybernetically enhanced controller of the Empire's Titan Squadron. With Aj^6 implants, LT-514 is proficient at data mining and works on the Imperial Star Destroyer, *Overseer*. Despite being focused on analytics, he is called on to fight after the Battle of Endor.

SHEN

SPECIES Human
AFFILIATION Empire, Titan Squadron

Shen is a survivor and a mystery. Part man, part machine, the Titan Squadron pilot is saved and rebuilt by the Empire after crashing. Now he never removes his helmet and he flies with a hatred for the enemy, fueled by the disturbing memories of his experiences and his ongoing pain.

MALLA

SPECIES Wookiee
HOMEWORLD Kashyyyk
AFFILIATION Her family

Mallatobuck has a hard job on Kashyyyk, taking care of her young son, Lumpy, while her husband, Chewbacca, is off fighting for the Rebel Alliance. During the Galactic Civil War, she is enslaved by the Empire and is further separated from her family. After the Liberation of Kashyyyk, she is freed and eventually reunites with her family. Chewbacca has claimed there is no being in the galaxy who prepares a meal better than Malla, and he looks forward to celebrating Life Day every year with her, their son, and their tribe.

KEO VENZEE

SPECIES Mirialan
HOMEWORLD Mirial
AFFILIATION Rebel Alliance, New Republic, Vanguard Squadron

A semi-pro racer, Keo Venzee wins trophies and fame on the galactic circuit, but criminal influence on the sport soon sours the Mirial native. Saved by a stranger who awakens them to the evils of the Empire, Keo now flies for the New Republic in Vanguard Squadron.

RELLA SOL

SPECIES Human
AFFILIATION Empire

A child of senators, Rella Sol joins the Empire's Titan Squadron. As strategist of the high-flying outfit, Sol is pragmatic about the current state of the galaxy and, though loyal to the Empire, bemoans the decision to dissolve the Senate.

WILLARD WAYLIN

SPECIES Human
AFFILIATION Empire, Titan Squadron

Growing up, Willard Waylin develops a love of Imperial design and an interest in engineering. Although he doesn't care for combat or flying, Willard graduates from Arkanis Academy and joins the Empire. He becomes chief mechanic and head of the hangar crew aboard the Star Destroyer *Overseer*, serving under the command of Captain Terisa Kerrill.

ATTICHITCUK
SPECIES Wookiee
HOMEWORLD Kashyyyk
AFFILIATION His family

Father of rebel hero Chewbacca, Attichitcuk has seen much in his long life. During the High Republic era, he contacts the Jedi for help when a mysterious plant overtakes the Tree of Life and brings dark energy to Kashyyyk. He also fights in the Battle of Kashyyyk in the Clone Wars and comes to mentor the Trandoshan known as Doshanalawook.

RIEVE
SPECIES Human **HOMEWORLD** Corellia
AFFILIATION Hunters of the Outer Rim

Rieve grows up an orphan on Corellia and discovers she is strong with the Force. Looking to escape a prior trauma and find an outlet for her anger, she joins the Hunters of the Outer Rim tournament on Vespaara. There, Rieve adopts a Sith Lord persona and wields a red lightsaber. She strikes quickly and violently, making her a deadly assassin, but she also eviscerates her opponents with cutting, sarcastic remarks. Still, her past remains a mystery, and Rieve struggles to connect with her fellow Hunters. Eventually her past catches up with her when a mysterious figure stalks the Arena.

DAQ DRAGUS
SPECIES Human
AFFILIATION Hunters of the Outer Rim

Once a fighter, Daq Dragus now works with Balada the Hutt. He is the face of the business and the main promoter for the Hunters of the Outer Rim tournament. With a keen sense of what the audience wants, he works with new recruits, shaping them into Hunters with unique skill sets and personalities.

GROZZ
SPECIES Wookiee **HOMEWORLD** Kashyyyk
AFFILIATION Hunters of the Outer Rim

Famous from his years as a professional Huttballer, the towering Grozz now puts on a show as a Hunter in the Arena on Vespaara. In battle, he dual-wields the arms of a KX-series security droid. They were harvested from one that was foolish enough to get on the Wookiee's bad side.

SKORA
SPECIES Rodian
AFFILIATION Hunters of the Outer Rim, Hutt Cartel

Brilliant but devious, Skora puts her chemistry expertise to use in the Hunters of the Outer Rim tournament on Vespaara. The Rodian fires darts that can either heal or poison. Which dart she targets her fellow participants with depends on whose side they are on. And when she cackles, it more than likely means she's up to no good.

SENTINEL
SPECIES Human
AFFILIATION Hunters of the Outer Rim, Empire

The last surviving stormtrooper of several regiments, Sentinel now fights in the Hunters of the Outer Rim tournament on Vespaara. A pro-Empire loudmouth who wields an E-Web heavy repeating blaster, he is a combatant that fans love to hate.

BALADA THE HUTT
SPECIES Hutt **HOMEWORLD** Nal Hutta
AFFILIATION Hunters of the Outer Rim

Balada the Hutt is co-owner of the Arena on Vespaara, which hosts the Hunters of the Outer Rim tournament. Balada demands a good show from her Hunters to keep the audience entertained—and buying tickets. The Hutt watches the matches from her control ship above the Arena, making sure that the operations run smoothly.

IMARA VEX
SPECIES Human
AFFILIATION Chanath Cha's Orphans, Crimson Dawn, Hunters of the Outer Rim

Imara Vex learns to fend for herself—a skill that leads her to a life as a bounty hunter. She joins the Orphans mercenary group, which later aligns with Crimson Dawn. The Orphans makes several attacks on Crimson Dawn's rivals, ultimately leading to the violent Syndicate War. During the time of the New Republic, Imara takes her talents to the Hunters of the Outer Rim tournament on Vespaara.

J-3DI
MANUFACTURER Custom built
TYPE Jedi droid
AFFILIATION Hunters of the Outer Rim

A decidedly unique droid, J-3DI is a fighter in the Hunters of the Outer Rim tournament who believes he is a lightsaber-wielding Jedi Knight. Built and programmed by fellow combatant Sprocket, J-3DI sports coverings designed to resemble a Jedi tunic, wields simulated Force abilities, and possesses a databank of Jedi wisdom.

SPROCKET
SPECIES Mon Calamari
AFFILIATION Hunters of the Outer Rim

Sprocket is young and enthusiastic but should not be underestimated. The Mon Calamari is a scientific prodigy who puts his engineering smarts to use as a combatant in the Hunters of the Outer Rim tournament. Sprocket builds the Jedi droid J-3DI and employs all manner of custom-made gadgets in the Arena.

ZAINA
SPECIES Human
AFFILIATION Rebel Alliance, Hunters of the Outer Rim

Zaina, a hero of the Rebel Alliance, is now a fan favorite in the Hunters of the Outer Rim tournament. A natural leader, she rouses both her squadmates and the crowd with fiery commands and speeches. Zaina's can-do spirit is met by her arch enemy in the Arena—the ex-Imperial stormtrooper Sentinel.

UTOONI
SPECIES Jawa
AFFILIATION Hunters of the Outer Rim

A pair of Jawa brothers, Utooni stand on each other's shoulders to do battle in the Hunters of the Outer Rim tournament. The duo keeps its oversize weaponry hidden under cloaks, fighting with the simple goal of getting more stuff. Utooni has its sights set on the team Slingshot droideka, which the Jawa brothers would love to take apart.

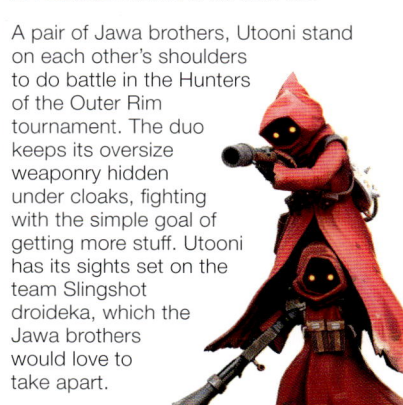

SLINGSHOT
SPECIES Ugnaught and a modified droideka
AFFILIATION Hunters of the Outer Rim

Slingshot is the result of the unlikely combination of an Ugnaught named Dizzy and a modified droideka. Dizzy sits in the cradle of the droid, and together they play a villainous role in the Hunters of the Outer Rim tournament. The pair is inseparable, embracing its persona on and off the battlefield.

ARAN TAL
SPECIES Human
HOMEWORLD Mandalore
AFFILIATION Hunters of the Outer Rim

The first Mandalorian in the Hunters of the Outer Rim tournament, Aran Tal is shrouded in mystery. The able fighter wears traditional Mandalorian armor, soaring in his jetpack and attacking with a flame thrower, dual blasters, and other more deadly weapons.

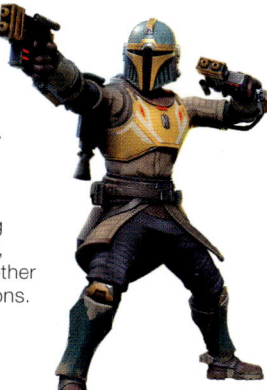

DIN DJARIN

SPECIES Human **HOMEWORLD** Aq Vetina
AFFILIATION The Mandalorians

Known to many as "the Mandalorian," Din Djarin is a trained warrior and successful bounty hunter. An encounter with the foundling Grogu sets the solitary Din on an unexpected path and leads to his increasing prominence in galactic events.

CHILDREN OF THE WATCH
Orphaned at a young age, Din is raised as a foundling by the Children of the Watch—a group that has broken away from mainstream Mandalorian society. He is a follower of their devout beliefs and strict traditions. While working for the Bounty Hunters Guild, Din is offered a high-priority bounty—a small child named Grogu. Djarin develops an initially reluctant attachment to Grogu, who makes a mudhorn float in the air to save Din's life. Following the Bounty Hunter Guild's code, Din grudgingly turns him over to an Imperial operative. But Din then has a change of heart and, with other Mandalorians from his covert, rescues the child and leaves Nevarro.

After a series of adventures with Grogu where they are attacked by multiple bounty hunters, Din decides to stop running and returns to Nevarro. Following a stand-off with the Imperial remnant leader Moff Gideon, Din flees into the Nevarro City sewers, reuniting with the Armorer. She bestows upon Din a Mandalorian signet of a mudhorn. She also tells Din that, as a Follower of the Way, he must reunite the Child with his own kind: the Jedi, who have the same power as Grogu: the Force.

FINDING THE JEDI
This new quest sends the Mandalorian around the galaxy where he meets several new allies, including Bo-Katan Kryze. On Corvus, he meets former Jedi Ahsoka Tano who communicates with Grogu through the Force and reveals his name to Din. Ahsoka refuses to train Grogu, but tells them that they should head to Tython to call out to any Jedi remaining in the galaxy. On this ancient world, Grogu's call is heard by Jedi Master Luke Skywalker, but Grogu is then captured by Moff Gideon. Thanks to the destruction of the *Razor Crest*, Din is helpless to stop the Imperials, but his newfound ally Boba Fett resolves to help him.

Calling upon several allies, Din is completely determined to rescue Grogu. On Morak, he even reveals his face in front of other living beings, a forbidden act for those following the Way, to secure Grogu's location—Gideon's Imperial light cruiser. During the successful assault on the vessel, Din duels and defeats Gideon, becoming the rightful wielder of the legendary Darksaber and ruler of Mandalore. He also removes his helmet to let Grogu look at his face before the youngling goes with Luke to train as a Jedi.

PATH TO MANDALORE
Returning to bounty hunting, Din visits the Armorer who tells him he must bathe in the living waters of Mandalore to absolve himself for removing his helmet in front of others. During a stop-off to help Boba on Tatooine, Din reunites with Grogu, who has decided to abandon his training and stay with Din. The pair soon reaches Mandalore where Din is trapped by a cyborg mech. Grogu calls upon Bo-Katan, who rescues Din and becomes the wielder of the Darksaber once more. The trio then works together to unite the disparate Mandalorian clans. With their warriors beside them, Din and Bo-Katan lead an assault on Gideon's base on Mandalore, defeating the villain. Following the victory, Din formally adopts Grogu as his son, and the pair then settle down on Nevarro for a life of bounty hunting.

A true Mandalorian
Din Djarin wears traditional Mandalorian armor made of beskar, which is the strongest metal known in the galaxy.

Traveling companion
Grogu proves to be good company on Din's travels around the galaxy. But Din needs to keep a close eye on the mischievous child.

A special relationship
As an orphan himself, Din sees a similarity between himself and Grogu. When Din dramatically rescues him from captivity, the two form an instant and inseparable bond.

Mandalorian helmet
Sacrosanct to Followers of the Way, helmets must never be removed.

Fully outfitted
Leather holster for Din's IB-94 blaster pistol connects to his bandolier and utility belt.

Darksaber
According to Mandalorian lore, whoever wields the Darksaber is the rightful ruler of Mandalore.

> "I'm not leaving my fate up to chance."
> **DIN DJARIN**

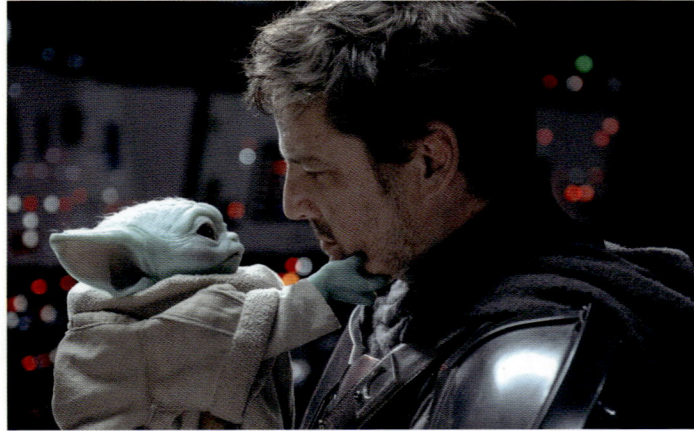

An act of devotion
Din Djarin reluctantly parts ways with Grogu so he can learn the ways of the Force with Luke Skywalker. Although it's forbidden for Followers of the Way, Din removes his helmet so he can share a final special moment with his dear friend.

Infiltrating an Imperial base
The Fledgling Mythrol, Din Djarin, Cara Dune, and Greef Karga investigate an Imperial remnant base on Nevarro. They discover the installation is not staffed by a skeleton crew, as their intel suggested, and have to engage enemy troops.

THE FLEDGLING MYTHROL

SPECIES Mythrol **HOMEWORLD** Nevarro
AFFILIATION Greef Karga

The Fledgling Mythrol is a young blue-skinned humanoid who works for Greef Karga until he steals from Greef and goes on the run. The Mythrol's freedom ends when he's captured by Din Djarin and encased in carbonite aboard the *Razor Crest* so Din can claim his bounty. Once the Mythrol is returned to Greef, he's thawed and a deal is made: the Mythrol will work off his debt with 350 years of indentured servitude. The Mythrol fully intends to fulfill his obligation by helping Greef in his daily operations as Chief Magistrate on Nevarro. Later, Din Djarin returns to Nevarro, and Greef asks for his help in eliminating an Imperial threat on the planet. Greef invites the Mythrol to assist in exchange for taking 100 years off his debt. This then becomes 130 years, once the mission takes shape and they see the peril in store for a civilian.

THE CLIENT

SPECIES Human
AFFILIATION Empire, Imperial remnant

Little is known of the enigmatic Client who answers to Moff Gideon. He's eager to bring back order, peace, and prosperity to the galaxy by restoring Gideon's Imperial remnant. The Client is assigned to capture and extract the blood of a Force-attuned being who is a member of the same species as Jedi Master Yoda. The Client recruits the Bounty Hunters Guild, who assign this mission to the Din Djarin. The Client has immense respect for the skill of Din's people and is pleased to have him on the job. Din returns with the asset, named Grogu, and Dr. Pershing immediately experiments on him. Impatient, the Client believes Grogu should be killed and all his blood extracted to fulfill Moff Gideon's mandate. However, Grogu is rescued by a remorseful Din. Moff Gideon grows weary of the Client's delay and has him gunned down.

GREEF KARGA

SPECIES Human **HOMEWORLD** Nevarro
AFFILIATION Bounty Hunters Guild, Nevarro

Greef Karga works as an expediter for the Bounty Hunters Guild on Nevarro. The group commissions Din Djarin to perform a job for a nefarious Imperial known only as the Client. The routine bounty exchange goes awry, prompting Greef to recruit members of the Guild to help him apprehend Din, who has betrayed the Guild's Code and kept the asset for himself.

Din and the asset, which turns out to be a small being of unknown origin named Grogu, escape and injure Greef in the process. However, thoughts of retribution are short-lived because Greef witnesses the Empire take over his planet, which changes his outlook. He recruits Din alongside Cara Dune and a reprogrammed IG-11 to expunge the Imperial remnant forces, but he intends to betray his wary allies. Greef's perspective changes once again when he is wounded by a reptavian and is saved by the asset. Grogu uses his unique abilities to heal the wayward leader of the Bounty Hunters Guild.

United in their quest to protect Grogu and eliminate the Imperial threat, the companions defeat Moff Gideon and, with a renewed sense of purpose, Greef becomes the Magistrate of Nevarro. He recruits Cara Dune as his marshal and restores peace and prosperity to the once rough-and-tumble planet. The discovery of an Imperial base on Nevarro reunites Din with Greef and Cara, and an exploration of the facilities reveals an active and dangerous threat.

The Imperials are defeated and peace returns again until Gorian Shard and his pirates invade. Din receives word of this and unites several Mandalorians to fight back. A grateful Greef Karga offers Din a parcel of land, which he accepts.

Off the books
Greef Karga offers Djarin a job that isn't tracking down the usual bail jumpers or wanted smugglers. The task's chit comes with no puck or chain code and is direct from a client with deep pockets.

A softer side
It's against the bounty hunter code to question the fate of a bounty, but Greef Karga has a change of heart about Grogu. He switches sides to work with Din Djarin and keep him safe.

CHARACTERS AND CREATURES

DR. PENN PERSHING
SPECIES Human
AFFILIATION Empire, Imperial remnant

When Penn Pershing is a young man, his mother's heart fails, devastating him. Once he realizes that her death could have been prevented if cloning had been a possibility, he dedicates his life to learning about this technology, in the hope of saving others from the loss he suffered. Years later, Dr. Pershing is a doctor and scientist employed by Moff Gideon during the rise of the New Republic. He is working with the Client on a top-secret project: to harvest the blood of a youngling who is a member of Yoda's species. The purpose of this plot is to enable Moff Gideon to create a soldier that can call upon the Force. Pershing extracts a small amount of blood from the creature, named Grogu, but the doctor is careful to keep him alive, despite over-zealous pressure from the Client. Pershing is turned over to the New Republic, and during his rehabilitation, he's betrayed by Elia Kane, who wipes his memory with a mind-flayer.

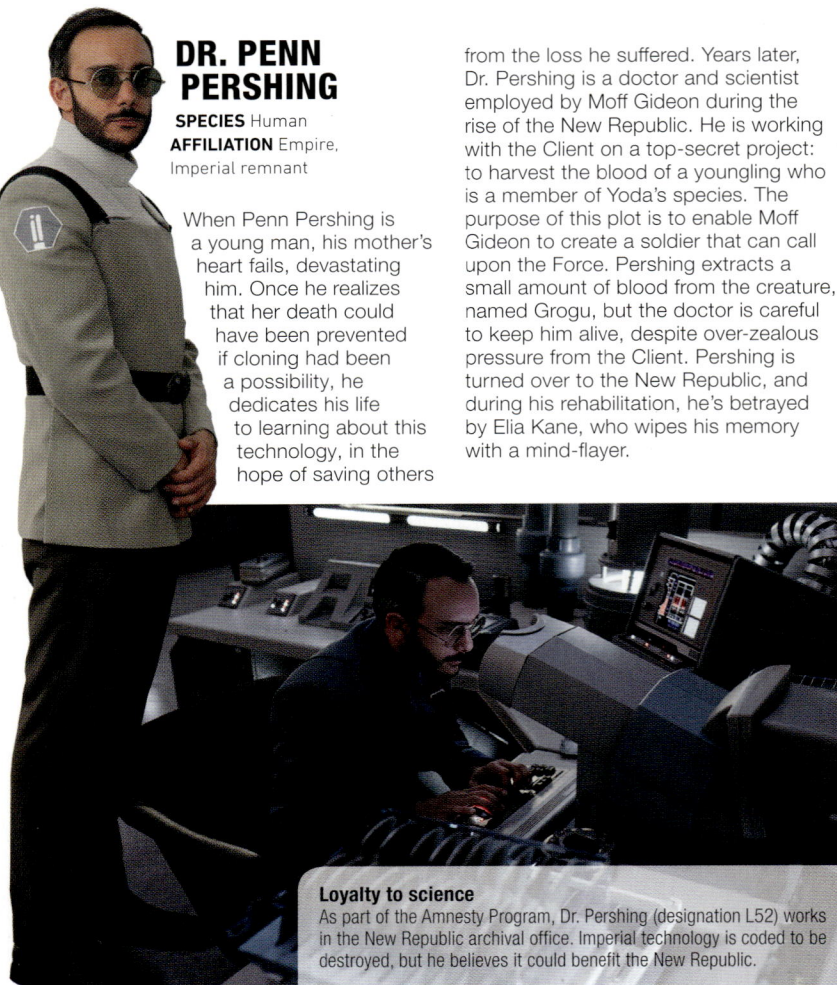

Loyalty to science
As part of the Amnesty Program, Dr. Pershing (designation L52) works in the New Republic archival office. Imperial technology is coded to be destroyed, but he believes it could benefit the New Republic.

THE ARMORER
SPECIES Human **HOMEWORLD** Mandalore
AFFILIATION Children of the Watch

A steadfast proponent of the old ways of Mandalore, the mysterious Armorer acts as mentor and caretaker for the Children of the Watch. Her loyalty is matched by her skills as a warrior and crafter of beskar armor. On Nevarro, the Armorer tutors Din Djarin, Paz Vizsla, and other Mandalorians about the importance of keeping on one's helmet and never allowing others to see one's face. An attack by the Imperial remnant causes them to flee Nevarro and go into hiding once again.

After several adventures, Din reunites with the Armorer, who learns that he has shown his face to another living being. She casts him out and, unless he bathes in the living waters of Mandalore, he will remain ostracized. Din does as instructed and leads the Armorer to Bo-Katan Kryze in the process. The three work together to unite surviving Mandalorians, defeat the Imperial remnant forces occupying their homeworld, and begin to restore Mandalore.

Keeper of traditions
With great skill and intricate detail, the Armorer forges armor and weapons at her cryo-furnace. Through her craft, she protects her people and keeps their ancient traditions alive.

KUIIL
SPECIES Ugnaught **HOMEWORLD** Arvala-7
AFFILIATION None, formerly the Empire

A kind and hard-working Ugnaught, Kuiil lives in isolation on Arvala-7 with three blurrgs. Prized for his skill with his hands, he has worked several lifetimes as an indentured servant, most recently for the Empire. While Din Djarin is tracking his quarry, he's attacked by one of Kuiil's blurrgs. Kuiil offers to help the bounty hunter, knowing that his mission will restore peace to Arvala-7. Din returns with Grogu, but is unable to leave the planet as a clan of Jawas have ransacked his ship. Kuiil aids him once more, serving as a liaison between Din and the Jawas. After retrieving all the parts, Kuiil repairs Din's ship and respectfully declines an offer to travel with the Mandalorian. He prefers to stay in peace and tranquility. However, his seclusion doesn't last long. Din decides to take down an Imperial remnant that threatens his sidekick, Grogu. Din asks Kuiil to watch over his friend, but Kuiil is killed by Imperials as he rushes to bring Grogu to safety.

Leather gloves
Hands are protected from debris during mechanical repairs.

Blurrg-whisperer
Having tamed three bipedal blurrgs, Kuiil makes them his companions and rides them across the plains of Arvala-7.

A common understanding
After meeting on Arvala-7, Kuiil and Din Djarin develop a strong bond based on mutual respect and an appreciation of each other's culture.

IG-11
MANUFACTURER Holowan Mechanicals
TYPE Assassin droid
AFFILIATION Bounty Hunters Guild

As an assassin droid, IG-11 is programmed to follow orders without question. He has an armored shell that can withstand repeated assault. IG-11 works with Din Djarin to capture the asset named Grogu, but is terminated by Din once the droid turns his blaster on the tiny being. The Ugnaught Kuiil then reprograms IG-11 to be a nurse droid. Now sworn to protect, IG-11 rescues Grogu from scout troopers and saves Din Djarin from death with his bacta spray, earning the respect of Din and his companions. When stormtroopers ambush the party, IG-11 follows his primary directive, which forbids capture and causes him to self-destruct and save his friends. Greef Karga places the droid's body in the town square as a heroic tribute. Din finds the head of an IG unit and uses its memory circuit to resurrect IG-11, who becomes the Marshal of Nevarro.

Last resort
Red lights flash as part of self-destruct sequence.

Double blasters
IG-11 carries an E-11 medium blaster rifle along with a DLT-20A blaster rifle.

Bounty droid on duty
Sub-paragraph 16 of the Bondsman Guild Protocol Waiver should compel Nikto mercenaries to give IG-11 his asset, Grogu. They don't, so he opens fire.

GROGU

AFFILIATION Jedi, Mandalorians

Loyal and powerful, Grogu is a Force-attuned foundling who is looking to find his place in an ever-changing galaxy.

JEDI YOUNGLING
Grogu is a tiny, mysterious being of the same species as Grand Master Yoda and Jedi Master Yaddle. His Force abilities are significant, but his power puts him at risk. Grogu grows up on Coruscant in the Jedi Temple. When he is still a small child, he is nearly killed during Order 66 but is rescued by Jedi Master Kelleran Beq, who escapes the planet with the help of the Naboo.

MEETING DIN
Decades later, the bounty hunter Din Djarin is hired to bring Grogu to an Imperial client. He finds the youngling in a Nikto hideout on Arvala-7 and defeats a fellow bounty hunter to ensure Grogu isn't killed. The pair comes to rely on each other when, in exchange for stolen ship parts, Din must kill a mudhorn creature and retrieve its egg.

Under obligation to complete the bounty, Din brings Grogu to an Imperial remnant safe house on Nevarro, where his blood is experimented on by Dr. Penn Pershing. However, Din has a change of heart and, with help from his Mandalorian covert, takes Grogu back, putting their safety at risk as Moff Gideon scours the galaxy for them.

TRAVELS WITH THE MANDALORIAN
During a number of adventures across the galaxy, including to Sorgan and Tatooine, Din and Grogu make several allies, but the Imperial remnant, or the bounty hunters it hires, are never far behind. Grogu and Din ultimately team up with Greef Karga and a number of allies to rid Nevarro of the Imperial forces. During the mission, Grogu once again uses the Force to save the group from an incinerator trooper.

The leader of Din's covert, the Armorer instructs him to reunite Grogu with his own kind—the Jedi. After an extensive search, during which Grogu and Din meet the Mandalorian leader Bo-Katan Kryze, Grogu eventually encounters former Jedi Ahsoka Tano. She connects with him through the Force, revealing his name to Din for the first time. While Ahsoka refuses to train Grogu because of to his attachment to Din, she suggests they head to Tython, where Grogu can use the Force to call out to any surviving members of the Jedi Order. While on the planet, Grogu is kidnapped by Gideon's dark troopers and taken to the Imperial leader's flagship to be experimented upon.

Determined to rescue him, Din gathers a crew and launches a rescue mission. With a battalion of dark troopers about to attack, all seems lost until Luke Skywalker arrives, dispatching the army droids. The Jedi Master then offers to train the youngling. Before Grogu leaves with Luke, Din breaks his Mandalorian Creed and removes his helmet to say a proper goodbye. It's the first time they see each other face to face.

LUKE'S STUDENT
Luke and Grogu spend time on the planet Ossus at his new Jedi temple. Skywalker trains the youngling and helps him achieve a greater connection to the Force, building his confidence. Luke soon realizes that Grogu's heart is elsewhere, so he gives him the choice to stay on Tython or end his training and return to Djarin. Grogu elects to reunite with the Mandalorian, and the two help their ally Boba Fett defeat the Pyke Syndicate during the Battle of Mos Espa. The powerful foundling even manages to calm Boba's raging rancor.

MANDALORIAN APPRENTICE
Now reunited, Grogu accompanies Din as he bathes in the Living Waters of Mandalore to seek absolution for breaking his Creed. During this mission, Din is captured by a formidable foe, but Grogu single-handedly escapes and secures aid from Bo-Katan. Upon realizing that Mandalore is inhabitable, the trio works together to unite many scattered Mandalorians and reclaim the world from Gideon.

During the climactic battle, Grogu faces a trio of fearsome Praetorian guards as well as Moff Gideon in a powerful suit of body armor. Following their victory, Din formally adopts Grogu as his son and accepts him as his Mandalorian apprentice. The two return to Nevarro to continue Grogu's training.

A father-son dynamic
Din is taken by surprise when he realizes he has an affinity for Grogu. The two form a strong familial bond and overcome many obstacles to be reunited and travel the galaxy together.

Ancient Force-henge
Grogu sits atop the seeing stone on Tython to communicate with others in tune with the Force. The connection prevents him from being approached, even by Din.

Traveling in style
Grogu travels faster than his tiny legs could carry him in a repulsorlift hover pram. It also seals shut to protect him.

Two possible paths
Luke Skywalker gives Grogu a choice: take the beskar armor and rejoin Din Djarin to become a Mandalorian, or take Master Yoda's lightsaber to stay with Luke and train as a Jedi Knight.

CHARACTERS AND CREATURES

BLURRG
HOMEWORLD Ryloth **SIZE** 2 m (6 ft 7 in) high, 4 m (13 ft 2 in) long **HABITAT** Deserts, forests, mountain regions

Bipedal beasts of burden, blurrgs are found across the galaxy with a range of green, blue, dark-gray, black, and brown hides. They are loyal and can be trained, but only by those who have patience and a connection with the animal. Twi'leks and clone troopers have succeeded in domesticating blurrgs, using them for both farming and battle. The creatures can be ferocious, and the females devour the males after mating. Blurrgs' short arms are balanced by their large, thick tails, and they are capable of great speeds, as seen during the Battle of Ryloth.

GORVIN SNU
HOMEWORLD Arvala-7 **SIZE** 30 cm (1 ft) long **HABITAT** Deserts, canyons

Gorvin snu are small, lizardlike creatures who inhabit the canyons and deserts of Arvala-7. Quick and fidgety, they exhibit a natural curiosity, but not at the expense of their survival. Gorvin snu have a duck-billed snout and a row of spines from their head down along their back.

ELDER CHETTKAP
SPECIES Jawa **HOMEWORLD** Arvala-7 **AFFILIATION** The Jawas

The Jawa Elder Chettkap is the Chief of his tribe on Arvala-7. His Jawas ransack Din Djarin's *Razor Crest*, which lead to Kuiil's negotiation between the two parties. In exchange for Din's ship parts, Chettkap wants a mudhorn's egg. He is a connoisseur of the rare and tasty delicacy.

Teamwork
The mudhorn charges toward the armored invader to protect its egg but is halted by an unseen force. Grogu is using the Force from a distance to help Din Djarin in his mission to retrieve the egg.

MUDHORN
HOMEWORLD Arvala-7
SIZE 5 m (16 ft 5 in) long, 2.7 m (8ft 10 in) high **HABITAT** Cave regions of Arvala-7

The mudhorn is a large, formidable creature who will stop at nothing to safeguard its egg. Its primary weapon is a single massive horn that it uses to spear or gouge anyone who threatens its domain. A coat of thick fur protects the creature's tough hide, which is capable of withstanding blaster fire at close range. Despite its cumbersome frame, a mudhorn can run faster than a human. It uses a combination of its speed, size, and devastating horn to defend itself and its egg. The mudhorn egg has a fuzzy outer covering, just like its parent, and is unfortunately considered to be a delicacy by local Jawas. The mudhorn becomes a sacred symbol to Din Djarin, and his son, Grogu, after the pair face one on Arvala-7. Din kills the mudhorn and retrieves its egg so he can trade it with Jawas in exchange for the stolen parts of his ship. From then on, Din's pauldron features an emblem of a mudhorn to symbolize the first time he and Grogu worked together.

PAZ VIZSLA
SPECIES Human **HOMEWORLD** Mandalore **AFFILIATION** Children of the Watch

Paz Vizsla is a formidable warrior with aggressive tendencies matched by a fierce dedication to the Children of the Watch. He is a frequent companion of the Armorer and hates the Empire almost as much as he loves Mandalore and its ancient history.

Paz and Din Djarin fight because Paz doesn't condone Din working with the Empire in any capacity. They clash again when Paz makes a move for the Darksaber that is in Din's possession. He believes he has a claim to the legendary weapon because it was forged by his ancestor, the founder of Clan Vizsla.

Paz remains wary of Din, up until Din risks his life to save Paz's son, Ragnar. With a newfound respect and admiration for Din, Paz aligns with him, along with the Armorer and Bo-Katan Kryze, to eliminate the Imperial remnant forces from Mandalore and restore his planet's former glory. In a moment of bravery and self-sacrifice, Paz stays behind to help the Mandalorian army escape. He destroys the stormtroopers, but then, in a weakened state, is ambushed and killed by three Praetorian guards.

Heavy Infantry warrior
Pas Vizsla fends off multiple attackers at once with his heavy blaster cannon. He is protected by his beskar suit of Mandalorian armor.

KRILL
HOMEWORLD Sorgan **SIZE** Up to 6 cm (2½ in) **HABITAT** Fresh and salt water

Small, aquatic crustaceans, krill inhabit the freshwater ponds and lakes of Sorgan. Local villagers farm them for food and to brew the drink spotchka. Krill are bluish-green and are plentiful throughout the planet.

OMERA
SPECIES Human **HOMEWORLD** Sorgan **AFFILIATION** Krill farmers

Omera is a widowed krill farmer who lives on the planet Sorgan with her daughter, Winta. She is an excellent sharpshooter, capable of defending herself, her family, and her village. Omera is an astute judge of character and a compassionate friend to many in her community.

WINTA
SPECIES Human **HOMEWORLD** Sorgan **AFFILIATION** Krill farmers

Winta is the loving daughter of Omera. She is learning to be a krill farmer on the planet Sorgan, but not at the expense of being a child. Her natural curiosity and kindness draw her to Grogu, and the two form a bond when Grogu and Din Djarin are guests in Winta's village.

SORGAN FROG
HOMEWORLD Sorgan **SIZE** 18 cm (7 in) **HABITAT** Swamps, marshes

Sorgan frogs are one-eyed amphibians named for their planet of origin but found throughout the galaxy. The non-sentient creatures live in aquatic habitats but also explore farther afield. To some, Sorgan frogs are considered a delicacy, but they prefer to be left to hop along in peace.

KLATOOINIAN MARAUDERS
SPECIES Nikto **HOMEWORLD** Sorgan
AFFILIATION Klatooinian gang

Klatooinian marauders are a fearsome group who prey on Sorgan's krill farmers, raiding their crops and leaving destruction and fear in their path. The determined villagers hire Din Djarin and Cara Dune to end the Klatooinians' reign of terror.

DARA VISH
SPECIES Human **HOMEWORLD** Sorgan
AFFILIATION Sorgan Common House

Dara Vish is a friend to all who visit her tavern, the Sorgan Common House. Her many regulars are happy to travel for her food, hospitality, and flagons of spotchka. Dara creates a welcoming environment for her patrons but never interferes with their various interests.

CARA DUNE
SPECIES Human **HOMEWORLD** Alderaan
AFFILIATION New Republic

Cara Dune is a superior warrior and combatant whose hatred of the Empire stems from their destruction of her home planet of Alderaan. She begins her military career as a drop trooper for the Rebellion during the Galactic Civil War. After the Empire is defeated, she leaves the New Republic due to a lack of action.

Years later, Cara works with Din Djarin to defeat Klatooinian raiders on Sorgan and, later, aligns with him and Greef Karga to defeat an Imperial remnant force on Nevarro led by Moff Gideon. Greef is impressed with Cara's spirit and fighting skills so he hires her to be his marshal on Nevarro. When Grogu is captured by Gideon, she once again teams up with Din and other Mandalorians to rescue him, and she takes the Imperial Moff into New Republic custody. Cara returns to Nevarro but is then invited to be a member of the Special Forces of the New Republic because of her success in Gideon's apprehension.

RIOT MAR
SPECIES Human
AFFILIATION Bounty Hunters Guild

The bounty hunter Riot Mar pilots a custom starship. His hunting skills are considerable, but so is his ego. He overestimates his talents and survival prowess when he chooses to chase Din Djarin above Tatooine, causing Riot to lose his life in the brief firefight.

DOCTOR MANDIBLE
HOMEWORLD Tatooine

The insectoid Doctor Mandible can often be found playing sabacc at Chalmun's Cantina with other regulars like Peli Motto. He is happy to share information with his many contacts, but not without receiving generous payment first.

Colleagues in arms
Cara Dune and Din Djarin share mutual respect as fellow warriors and a shared opposition of any Imperial insurgency. They team up on various missions to counter shared threats.

PELI MOTTO
SPECIES Human **HOMEWORLD** Tatooine
AFFILIATION Independent mechanic

Peli Motto lives her entire life on the desert planet of Tatooine, alongside several droid companions who assist her in the repair, maintenance, and refueling of starships. She owns Docking Bay 3-5 in Mos Eisley Spaceport and fluctuates her prices based on the client's needs—in particular, charging more if they don't want droids to be involved in the work. Peli is a shrewd sabacc player and pragmatic business owner who is willing to collaborate with Jawas if it gets her the parts she needs.

Peli meets Din Djarin and Grogu when they bring the *Razor Crest* in for repairs, and she quickly endears herself to the Mandalorian with her unbridled honesty and witty demeanor. Din later returns to Tatooine and asks Peli for help in finding other people of his kind. She leads him to Mos Pelgo and later Trask. When Din's ship, the *Razor Crest*, is destroyed, Peli finds him a replacement by repairing an old N-1 starfighter for him and adding her own customized modifications. She celebrates the return of Grogu, with whom she shares a special bond.

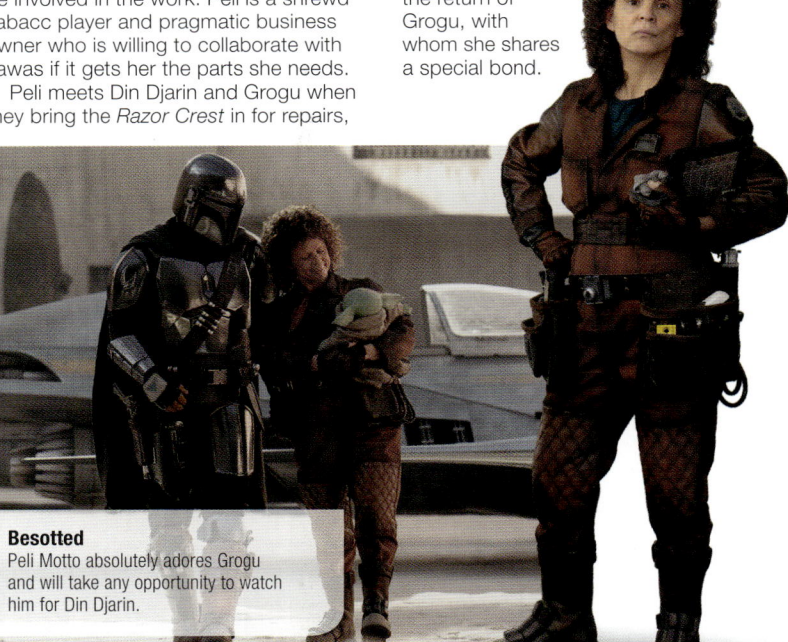

Besotted
Peli Motto absolutely adores Grogu and will take any opportunity to watch him for Din Djarin.

FROG LADY
SPECIES Querm Rybet **HOMEWORLD** Trask
AFFILIATION Husband and offspring

The amphibious humanoid identified as Frog Lady is one of the last of her kind. Din Djarin escorts her to the only planet hospitable to her species, in the hope of reuniting with her husband. The mission is dire because she carries her last clutch of eggs, which must be fertilized if she is to continue her family line. After an involuntary and harrowing detour on Maldo Kreis, she is reunited with her husband and their offspring are successfully born on Trask. Frog Lady looks after Grogu while Din goes on a mission with Bo-Katan Kryze.

TORO CALICAN
SPECIES Human
HOMEWORLD Coruscant
AFFILIATION Bounty Hunters Guild

An inexperienced bounty hunter, Toro Calican is desperate to make his name. He teams up with Din Djarin to capture Fennec Shand but betrays Din and leaves Fennec for dead. He then tries to capture Din but is killed in the skirmish.

RANZAR MALK
SPECIES Human
AFFILIATION Malk's gang

Ranzar Malk is a nefarious mercenary who operates out of the Roost space station. He hires his former contact Din Djarin to break out the Twi'lek Qin from a New Republic prison ship but then tries to kill the Mandalorian when the mission is complete. Din foils his attempt and leads X-wings to eliminate Ranzar and his space station.

MIGS MAYFELD

SPECIES Human
AFFILIATION Empire, Ranzar Malk's crew

An Imperial sharpshooter, Migs Mayfeld is present at Operation: Cinder at the end of the Galactic Civil War, where he is horrified by the senseless deaths of so many of his peers. He leaves the army and becomes a highly sought-after mercenary thanks to his advanced trigger skills. Migs leads the group that rescues Qin from a New Republic prison ship. The team includes Burg, Q9-0, Qin's sister Xi'an, and Din Djarin, but Mayfeld betrays Din and locks him up. However, Din escapes and captures the entire team, which leads to Migs' arrest.

Serving time at the Karthon Chop Fields, Migs is temporarily released by marshal Cara Dune in order to help Din infiltrate an Imperial remnant refinery on Morak. They need to access a terminal to learn the location of Moff Gideon's light cruiser, where Grogu is imprisoned. On the mission, Migs encounters his former commanding officer Valin Hess. When the smug Imperial discusses Operation: Cinder, Migs shoots him. As a thank you for his help, Cara unofficially releases Migs from prison, reporting that he died in the explosion on Morak.

Leaving with a blast
During his escape from Morak, Migs borrows a cycler rifle and shoots a supply of rhydonium, causing a chain reaction that destroys the Imperial mining hub.

BURG

SPECIES Devaronian **HOMEWORLD** Devaron
AFFILIATION Ranzar Malk's crew

Burg is a strong and brutish Devaronian. He is the muscle in the group of mercenaries that breaks Qin out of a New Republic prison ship. His size and prolific strength cause him to underestimate Din Djarin, leading to his defeat and capture.

XI'AN

SPECIES Twi'lek
HOMEWORLD Ryloth
AFFILIATION Ranzar Malk's crew

The Twi'lek Xi'an is a short-tempered, blade-wielding expert who works with Ranzar Malk's crew to rescue her brother, Qin, from a New Republic prison ship. She alludes to a relationship with the Mandalorian, but this isn't confirmed by Din, who captures her and her team.

Q9-0

TYPE Protocol droid
AFFILIATION Ranzar Malk's crew

Q9-0 is a modified protocol droid known for his superior response time as a pilot. He aligns with Ranzar Malk's crew to help rescue Qin from a New Republic prison ship. The droid intercepts a message about the bounty on Grogu and tries to kill him, but Din blasts the droid first.

QIN

SPECIES Twi'lek **HOMEWORLD** Ryloth
AFFILIATION Ranzar Malk's crew

Qin is the prisoner who Ranzar Malk's crew is tasked with freeing from a New Republic prison ship. He is the brother of Xi'an and harbors immense hatred of Din Djarin, who allegedly left him behind on a previous mission. He is on board the Roost when it is fired upon by X-wings.

TRAPPER WOLF

SPECIES Human
AFFILIATION Rebel Alliance, New Republic

Trapper Wolf is a veteran X-wing pilot and respected member of the New Republic's flight squadron. He frequently flies with Sash Ketter and Jib Dodger but often appears disinterested and bored during routine missions. However, he is unfailingly focused and precise when needed. Several years after the end of the Empire, he and his fellow pilots find a tracking beacon that leads to the destruction of a criminal space station. Trapper is also an excellent marksman with an A280 blaster rifle, which he showcases when helping Carson Teva blast Maldo Kreis ice spiders from a wayward *Razor Crest*'s hull.

JIB DODGER

SPECIES Human
AFFILIATION Rebel Alliance, New Republic

Jib Dodger is an experienced X-wing pilot who often flies with Trapper Wolf and Sash Ketter. He responds to an activated tracking beacon aboard a prison ship and, with his squadron, destroys a small space station when they see that it is about to launch a gunship at them.

SASH KETTER

SPECIES Human
AFFILIATION Rebel Alliance, New Republic

An expert X-wing pilot, Sash Ketter often patrols the galaxy with Jib Dodger and Trapper Wolf. Together, they destroy a space station to prevent an oncoming assault. Sash can often be found with her friends on Adelphi Base, on alert for the next mission.

QARTUUM

HOMEWORLD Nevarro **SIZE** 1 m (3 ft 3 in) long
HABITAT Lava fields

A qartuum is a small, four-legged creature covered in hair with a single horn protruding from its forehead. Highly resistant to extreme heat, qartuums roam Nevarro's lava fields. These simple creatures can be domesticated to assist farmers and others on Nevarro.

REPTAVIAN

HOMEWORLD Nevarro **SIZE** 11.44 m (37 ft 6 in) wide (wingspan), 7.57 m (24 ft 10 in) long
HABITAT Skies

A reptavian is a large, winged predator with razor-sharp talons and rows of serrated teeth. They soar above Nevarro at night and swoop to ambush their prey. Even the slightest scratch from their venomous claws can be lethal.

AP-1982

SPECIES Human
AFFILIATION Imperial remnant

AP-1982 is one of the scout troopers who intercepts communications about Grogu's location when he returns to Nevarro. He is curious to see what Grogu looks like, but he is bitten as he pokes him. It doesn't bother him for long because his wrist is soon broken by Grogu's rescuer, IG-11.

GIDEON

SPECIES Human
AFFILIATION Empire, Imperial remnant

Gideon is a key player in the Imperial remnant's covert mission to reestablish itself as all-powerful. He rules with fear and swift punishment for anyone who interferes with his plans or tests his limited patience. During the Empire's initial reign, Gideon serves as a Moff and member of the Imperial Security Bureau (ISB), dealing with Rebel Alliance spies and traitors. He is instrumental in the Great Purge of Mandalore. Bo-Katan Kryze makes a deal to turn over the legendary Darksaber to Gideon if he spares her people. He betrays her, orders the deaths of many of her people, and claims the weapon as his own, embracing its symbolic nature as a sign of his victory.

Many believe Gideon to have been executed for his crimes during the Galactic Civil War, but he escapes capture and leads an Imperial remnant. He is relentless in his pursuit of a small being strong in the Force named Grogu. The child's blood is highly prized for Gideon's mysterious experiments, known only to a few Imperials.

The Mandalorian Din Djarin forms a bond with Grogu, making both of them Gideon's top priority. He and his fearsome dark troopers scour the galaxy for them and eventually capture the child. Din hunts down Gideon and defeats him in combat, taking the Darksaber for his own and turning the Imperial leader into New Republic custody.

Surprise survivor
Gideon is thought dead when his TIE crashes, but he emerges from his wrecked craft, having cut his way out using the legendary Darksaber.

Gideon escapes and attempts to take over the Shadow Council. He invades Mandalore, using its resources to create beskar-clad armor for himself and his elite troopers.

Mandalorian resistance fighter Axe Woves crashes a light cruiser into Gideon's base during his final battle with Din, Grogu, and Bo-Katan, causing an explosion that kills Gideon, ending his reign of cruelty.

The power of Mandalore
Gideon's next-generation dark trooper armor is made from beskar and augments his strength. He demonstrates his terrifying power by crushing the Darksaber with one hand.

JS-1975

SPECIES Human
AFFILIATION Imperial remnant

JS-1975 is a scout trooper who kills the Ugnaught Kuiil and takes Grogu into Imperial custody. Irritable and impatient, he doesn't appreciate the noises coming from the small being. JS-1975 will not go against any Imperial mandates out of fear of Moff Gideon's wrath. IG-11 smashes into JS-1975's speeder bike, and the trooper is rendered unconscious.

IMPERIAL INCINERATOR TROOPER

SPECIES Human **HOMEWORLD** Various
AFFILIATION Empire, Imperial remnant

Incinerator troopers are highly trained to flush enemies out of defensive positions with D-72w Oppressor flame projectors. Each trooper's cryopast-coated armor is heatproof and decorated in red to indicate their position in the Empire.

Planning the attack
Alongside a group of Tuskens, Cobb Vanth and Din Djarin witness the krayt dragon emerging from its lair.

COBB VANTH

SPECIES Human **HOMEWORLD** Tatooine
AFFILIATION People of Mos Pelgo

As the marshal of Mos Pelgo, Cobb Vanth loyally protects his town and people, using Boba Fett's Mandalorian armor. Din Djarin meets Cobb in the town saloon and insists the marshal return the armor to his people. Cobb is reluctant to part with it but agrees if Din will help him defeat a krayt dragon that is feeding on their town. The two work together and unite Mos Pelgo's citizens with local Tuskens for the job. The uneasy alliance pays off and the massive beast is destroyed.

Sometime later, Cobb kills two members of the Pyke Syndicate after they refuse to stop trafficking spice through his town, now called Freetown. Din returns and asks Cobb to help Boba Fett in their war against the Pykes, but Cobb respectfully declines. The Pykes hire bounty hunter Cad Bane, who shoots the marshal for his transgressions. After Boba and Din defeat the Pykes, Cobb is healed by the Modifier.

Mandalorian imposter
Cobb Vanth bought Boba Fett's armor from Jawas.

MA-13

MANUFACTURER Industrial Automaton
TYPE Modified R-series astromech droid
AFFILIATION None

MA-13 is an R-series astromech droid who has been modified with humanoid legs and two sets of arms. The ferry droid escorts passengers down a lava river on Nevarro. When stormtroopers are waiting on the bank for Cara Dune, she blasts the droid's head off its body when it won't stop rowing.

GOR KORESH

SPECIES Abyssin **HOMEWORLD** RTK111
AFFILIATION Gangster

A gambler and gangster, Gor Koresh organizes gladiator matches. He is very dishonest and will murder contestants if it benefits him financially. He actively seeks beskar armor for his collection of stolen goods and is left for dead by Din Djarin when he tries to cross the bounty hunter.

180 CHARACTERS AND CREATURES

TAANTI
SPECIES Weequay **HOMEWORLD** Tatooine
AFFILIATION Mos Pelgo

Taanti is a bartender in Mos Pelgo, a settlement on Tatooine. He serves the citizens of his small town and is a loyal confidant of Cobb Vanth. He's handy with a rifle as well as behind the bar and participates in the Battle of Mos Espa.

KRAYT DRAGON
HOMEWORLD Tatooine **SIZE** 184 m (604 ft) long **HABITAT** Underground desert regions

The legendary krayt dragon is a heavily armored and incredibly dangerous creature, with razor-sharp teeth and a massive mouth that emits ichor—an acid that burns its victims. Deep inside the belly of each krayt dragon is a large pearl that is prized by Tuskens, who are constantly at war with the subterranean monsters. Krayt dragons are massive, but the one that terrorizes Mos Pelgo is particularly large. The behemoth lives under the sand of Tatooine, propelling itself rapidly beneath the surface as it stalks its next helpless meal, then emerging to devour its prey. A Tusken tribe teams up with the citizens of Mos Pelgo to kill the particularly destructive beast.

JO
SPECIES Human **HOMEWORLD** Tatooine
AFFILIATION Mos Pelgo

Mos Pelgo resident Jo works with Marshal Cobb Vanth and Din Djarin to defeat a krayt dragon. An expert in demolitions, she equips the detonator. When Cobb is gunned down by Cad Bane, she rushes to his side and later fights during the battle of Mos Espa.

FROG MAN
SPECIES Querm Rybet **HOMEWORLD** Trask
AFFILIATION Wife and offspring

Frog Man searches the galaxy for a hospitable planet for his wife and her eggs. He eventually finds the moon of Trask and sends word to Frog Lady to join him. The pair is finally reunited, and their eggs are fertilized, ensuring their family line will live on.

CARSON TEVA
SPECIES Human
AFFILIATION New Republic, Rebel Alliance

Carson Teva is a highly respected pilot in the New Republic who also fights against the Empire in the Galactic Civil War. He frequently flies with Trapper Wolf and is based out of a New Republic outpost on Adelphi. Carson is loyal to the New Republic and is a highly intuitive judge of character. While in search of Imperial holdouts in the Outer Rim, he and Trapper encounter a *Razor Crest* ship with no emitting transponder. They investigate, but the pilot, Din Djarin, doesn't comply and, in his bid to escape, he crash-lands on Maldo Kreis. The two pilots rescue Din from ice spiders but don't arrest him because he captured criminals on a New Republic prison ship.

Later, Carson investigates Imperial activity on Nevarro and attempts to recruit Cara Dune to the New Republic. Soon after, pirates invade Nevarro. Carson's request to the New Republic for authorization to liberate the planet is denied so Carson turns to Din and the Mandalorians for help. They agree, and the two eventually agree to work together unofficially on future missions.

Sometime later, Carson assists General Hera Syndulla on an unauthorized mission to the planet Seatos to aid Ahsoka Tano, who suspects the return of Grand Admiral Thrawn and is desperate to foil his allies' plans. Once Carson and Phoenix Leader arrive in Seatos' orbit, there is a power surge from a massive ship's leap into hyperspace, but Carson manages to stabilize his X-wing. Hera's team eventually rescues Ahsoka, and Carson receives word that the New Republic is en route to arrest Hera for commissioning the mission. Carson is loyal to Hera but is equally interested in helping ensure she will not be stripped of her command, so he urges her to acquiesce to their demands, reminding her that Senator Leia Organa can only offer cover for a brief amount of time.

At Hera's hearing, she is continually berated by Senator Hamato Xiono, who insists that she is a loose cannon and a threat to the New Republic due to her selfish actions. Carson speaks out on Hera's behalf and reminds the tribunal of Moff Gideon's actions on Mandalore as proof of Hera's concerns about the resurgence of the Empire. Carson's loyal nature, integrity, and willingness to rise above politics make him a valuable member of the New Republic.

Back in the cockpit
Carson Teva is a veteran X-wing pilot. When a routine inspection of Din Djarin's *Razor Crest* leads to the bounty hunter attempting to escape, Teva pursues the ship.

MALDO KREIS ICE SPIDERS
HOMEWORLD Maldo Kreis **SIZE** Up to 16 m (52 ft 6 in) tall **HABITAT** Frozen terrain, caves

Maldo Kreis ice spiders lurk in the icy caves of the planet they're named after. They vary in size but can grow large enough to take down a starship with brute force. The arachnids hibernate near hot springs and work in tandem to chase down prey, voracious in pursuit of their next meal. They have rows of serrated teeth and may develop additional legs as they grow. The ice spiders lay eggs for countless offspring that consume their brothers and sisters the moment they're born. Similar creatures in the galaxy live on Dagobah, Atollon, and Taul.

MAMACORE
HOMEWORLD Moon of Trask **SIZE** 7.30 m (23 ft 11 in) long, 2.75 m (9 ft) wide with maw fully open **HABITAT** Oceans

The mamacore is an underwater predator that lives in the depths of the moon of Trask. These carnivorous creatures rise out of the sea and swallow their prey whole. Mamacores have large, round mouths with massive, razor-sharp teeth that consume anything in their vicinity.

A crew of Quarren hold a mamacore in their ship's hold as a pet and attempt to feed Grogu to it in the hopes of obtaining Din Djarin's beskar. Koska Reeves saves Grogu and destroys the creature, much to the disappointment of the Quarren.

Grogu for dinner
A mamacore rises and swallows Grogu and his hover pram whole. But before the creature can digest its meal, Grogu is rescued safe and sound.

FROG BABIES

SPECIES Querm Rybet **HOMEWORLD** Moon of Trask **AFFILIATION** Frog Man and Frog Lady

Frog Lady's fertilized eggs hatch on the moon of Trask. The small creatures emerge from their eggs already capable swimmers. The offspring are affectionate and curious and are well cared for by their parents.

LAVA MEERKAT

HOMEWORLD Nevarro **SIZE** 33 cm (1 ft) tall **HABITAT** Lava tubes and sewers of Nevarro

Lava meerkats are considered the rats of Nevarro as they rummage in the lava tubes and sewers of the ashen world for food and shelter from predators. While the rodentlike creatures are not typically thought of as food, some Aqualish have been known to make them into a meal.

AXE WOVES

SPECIES Human **HOMEWORLD** Mandalore **AFFILIATION** Mandalorians, Nite Owls

A loyal member of Bo-Katan Kryze's Nite Owls, Axe Woves joins her and Koska Reeves on a mission to steal an Imperial cruiser from the moon of Trask. They recruit Din Djarin to assist them, but Axe is initially skeptical, due to Din's adherence to the old ways of Mandalore. Like other Mandalorians, Axe is an accomplished fighter and hand-to-hand combatant. Stormtroopers are no match for his top-tier training and experience in battle. Axe remains behind as the rest of his team hunts down Moff Gideon aboard his Imperial vessel. Once Axe realizes Bo-Katan has not retrieved the Darksaber from Gideon, he defects from Bo-Katan, taking several Mandalorians with him. When the two are later reunited on Plazir-15, Bo-Katan challenges Axe in single combat to reclaim her mantle as leader of the Mandalorians. She defeats Axe and he agrees to serve her without reservation. In the battle to reclaim Mandalore, Axe pilots a stolen Imperial vessel and crashes it into Mandalore, causing an explosion that kills Gideon and ends the Imperial occupation. Axe jetpacks to safety and is one of the heroes of the battle.

Hijack over Trask
Axe Woves uses a computer spike to break into the Imperial *Gozanti*-class cruiser he and his team are about to hijack above Trask.

KOSKA REEVES

SPECIES Human **HOMEWORLD** Mandalore **AFFILIATION** Mandalorians, Nite Owls

Koska Reeves serves alongside her fellow Mandalorians as a member of the Nite Owls. She's an excellent hand-to-hand combatant who can perform high-flying kicks with the assistance of her jetpack. Koska works with Bo-Katan Kryze, Axe Woves, and Din Djarin to take over an Imperial cruiser and is a key part of their success.

Later, Koska and Bo-Katan go to the planet Lafete, where they're greeted by Din and Boba Fett during a meal. Koska refers to Boba as a sidekick, escalating tension between the two and igniting a brief skirmish, which is broken up by Bo-Katan. The Mandalorians agree to work together to rescue Grogu from Moff Gideon and reclaim the Darksaber for Bo-Katan. Loyal to Bo-Katan, Koska is determined to help. With her unique skills in combat, weaponry, and infiltration, she makes quick work of the stormtroopers who get in the way of her team, and the mission is successful. Koska is also part of the unified Mandalorian army that helps to liberate her homeworld of Mandalore from Imperial invasion.

Aerial battle
Koska Reeves, along with Bo-Katan Kryze and the surviving Mandalorians, flies above Mandalore with her JT-12 jetpack. They battle in the air, one-to-one, against stormtroopers who also wear jetpacks.

SCOUT GUARD

HOMEWORLD Corvus **AFFILIATION** Morgan Elsbeth

Scout guards serve Magistrate Morgan Elsbeth. Each masked soldier follows their leader without question. They are capable fighters, but they can't defeat Ahsoka or Din Djarin, who easily dispose of them while capturing Morgan and liberating the people of Calodan.

LANG

SPECIES Human **HOMEWORLD** Corvus **AFFILIATION** Morgan Elsbeth

Lang is a cruel mercenary hired by the Magistrate Morgan Elsbeth. He's in charge of the scout guards who protect her walled city in Calodan. He's quick on the draw and arrogant, but his speed and skill are no match for Din Djarin, who guns him down in a face-off.

FOREST WALKER

HOMEWORLD Corvus **HABITAT** Forests

Forest walkers are four-legged, gentle creatures who roam the forest region of Corvus. The nocturnal creatures travel in herds for safety and have thick hides for protection against their enemies. Two large eyes on opposite sides of their round heads allow them to see predators from a distance.

WING

SPECIES Human **HOMEWORLD** Corvus **AFFILIATION** People of Corvus

Wing is the magistrate of Calodan who hopes Morgan Elsbeth's Imperial contracts will bring prosperity. After the Empire's defeat, Magistrate Elsbeth holds the people hostage with cruelty and fear. Wing wants to protect his people so he advises Din Djarin not to talk to anyone in case they're noticed. Once Morgan is defeated, Wing becomes Governor.

ARTILLERY STORMTROOPER

SPECIES Human **HOMEWORLD** Various **AFFILIATION** Empire

Artillery stormtroopers are specialized soldiers in the Imperial army who launch explosives into the battlefield from a distance. They must calculate the proper distance and angle to ensure each mortar lands at a precise coordinate. Yellow stripes adorn their armor and identify their specialism.

SHYDOPP PIRATES

SPECIES Shydopp **HOMEWORLD** Morak **AFFILIATION** Pirates

Shydopp pirates ambush Imperial juggernauts as they transport rhydonium. Bold and aggressive, they try to destroy the explosive cargo. A group begins to seize Din Djarin's transport, but Din (in Imperial armor) fights them off until Imperial forces arrive and gun them down.

182 CHARACTERS AND CREATURES

ELIA KANE
SPECIES Human **HOMEWORLD** Coruscant
AFFILIATION Empire, Imperial remnant

Elia Kane is a loyal and devious Imperial officer who trained at the Royal Imperial Academy on Coruscant. During the early reign of the New Republic, Elia joins Moff Gideon's Imperial remnant as a lieutenant and communications officer. Once Gideon is captured, Elia is taken into the custody of the New Republic and sent to their amnesty program, where she receives the designation "G68." Dr. Pershing is also in the program, and the two form a bond, having both served under Gideon. However, Elia is a spy for Gideon, and she tricks the doctor into believing they are friends. She invites him to explore a lab on a decommissioned Imperial Star Destroyer to further his research. Republic security arrives to arrest them, and Elia turns him in. Pershing is attached to a reconditioning device to help ease his transition back to society, but Elia, under the guise of friendship, requests to view the procedure in the control room. She stealthily sabotages it and wipes Pershing's mind.

Acting the part
Elia feigns surprise when her trap is complete and the New Republic arrives to arrest Dr. Pershing.

Treachery complete
Elia overrides Dr. Pershing's reconditioning, wiping his mind and completing her betrayal of his trust.

GARFALAQUOX
SPECIES Aqualish **HOMEWORLD** Tatooine
AFFILIATION Pyke Syndicate

The don of a criminal organization on Tatooine, Garfalaquox offers a chest full of credits to Boba Fett after he takes over Jabba the Hutt's former empire. But disingenuous Garfalaquox is secretly working with other crime lords and the Pykes to dethrone Boba. The Aqualish and his allies are defeated, and Garfalaquox is killed by Fennec Shand for his treachery.

DOKK STRASSI
SPECIES Trandoshan **HOMEWORLD** Tatooine
AFFILIATION Pyke Syndicate

Dokk Strassi leads a crime family that controls a segment of Tatooine's nefarious operations. He pays tribute to the new Daimyo, Boba Fett, but declines to participate in Fett's feud with the Pykes, which Boba respects. However, Dokk covertly teams up with other rogue families and works with the Pykes to defeat Boba. Dokk is assassinated by Fennec Shand.

VALIN HESS
SPECIES Human **HOMEWORLD** Coruscant
AFFILIATION Empire, Imperial remnant

Valin Hess is a high-ranking general who is adamant the Empire will rise again. He oversees Operation: Cinder on the planet Burnin Konn, sacrificing many Imperial troops. After the war, he is gunned down by Migs Mayfeld, who lost several of his friends in the attack.

TUSKEN CHIEFTAIN
SPECIES Human **HOMEWORLD** Tatooine
AFFILIATION Tusken tribe

The Tusken Chieftain leads a tribe of Tuskens in the desert sands of Tatooine. His robes are brown and dark red, demonstrating his senior standing among his people. The wise Chieftain is intrigued by former prisoner Boba Fett and invites him into their community after Boba helps them stop Pyke invaders. The Chieftain leads with a distinct blend of silence and wise counsel, preferring his people learn independently from individual quests with limited instruction. He is massacred alongside his people during an attack from Pyke invaders.

TUSKEN WARRIOR
SPECIES Human **HOMEWORLD** Tatooine
AFFILIATION Tusken tribe

The Tusken warrior is an elite master of hand-to-hand combat who uses the Tuskens' weapon of choice—the gaderffii stick. Her wrappings are a unique blend of black and red, marking her standing among her tribe. She plays a secondary role to the Tusken Chieftain as advisor and head of security, and is dangerous to anyone who poses a threat to the tribe. Former prisoner Boba Fett offers to help the Tuskens stop attacks from invading Pykes, earning her respect. She is later killed during a Pyke raid of the village.

NIGHT WIND ASSASSIN
SPECIES Human **HOMEWORLD** Tatooine
AFFILIATION For hire

The Order of the Night Wind is considered the best assassin-for-hire organization in the galaxy. Its members are elite acrobats who excel in close combat. They also have special energy shields that can be used to box in their targets. If captured, it is extremely unlikely that they will discuss their clients.

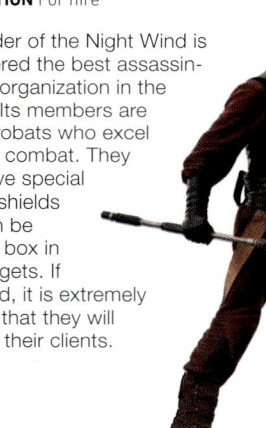

MOK SHAIZ'S MAJORDOMO
SPECIES Twi'lek **HOMEWORLD** Tatooine
AFFILIATION Mayor Mok Shaiz

Mayor Mok Shaiz's majordomo is a loyal and pretentious Twi'lek who serves his master with dedication. He has a taste for the more lavish aspects of life, as evident by his richly attired robes and headdress. He attended the academy on Coruscant, where he specialized in civic council negotiations. He uses these skills to handle Mok Shaiz's personal affairs and does so with pride. Shaiz's majordomo is unaffected and indifferent to threats, and he persists in his patronizing approach to Boba Fett while offering a heartfelt welcome to his arrival at Mos Espa.

Despite his loyalty, the majordomo is not above self-preservation, and he flees Mok Shaiz's palace when Boba becomes aware of his duplicity. He is captured by Boba

Diplomatic doyen
The Majordomo is all manners and politeness when welcoming unwanted visitors, though he exudes a patronizing undertone.

and agrees to work as his emissary, ready to genuflect or grovel to the new crime lord's enemies. His education and experience prove to be useful to Boba when negotiating with the Pykes. During a full-scale battle, the majordomo hides from the violence and is found by Peli Motto. She protects him, and the two help Din and Boba as the Pykes are defeated.

GARSA FWIP

SPECIES Twi'lek **HOMEWORLD** Tatooine
AFFILIATION Mayor Mok Shaiz

Garsa Fwip is the glamorous and endearing proprietor of Garsa's Sanctuary. Her charm and elegance are perfect for her role as the host of the popular establishment. She is able to disarm even the most ferocious of patrons with tact and charisma. Garsa's ability to relate to Krrsantan is substantial, but it is not enough to persuade him from tearing a Trandoshan's left arm from his body. She pledges her allegiance and upscale cantina to Boba Fett, inadvertently becoming entangled in his war with the Pykes, who use a bomb to destroy her establishment.

MOK SHAIZ

SPECIES Ithorian **HOMEWORLD** Tatooine
AFFILIATION Pyke Syndicate

Mok Shaiz is the mayor of Mos Espa's burgeoning community on Tatooine. He is rich and powerful and enjoys the finer things in life. He is not interested in giving up his position in government so he works with the Pykes to ensure his authority will continue. The new Daimyo, Boba Fett, asks Mok to pay tribute, which he won't do since he was promised the same territory by the Pykes. Boba is not aware of this agreement. During the Battle for Mos Espa, Mok goes into hiding amongst the Pykes. He is found and hanged by Fennec Shand.

SAND BEAST

HOME WORLD Tatooine **SIZE** 2.52 m (8 ft 3 in) high **HABITAT** Underground desert regions

The sand beast is a four-armed wild creature that prowls beneath the sands of Tatooine to surprise and startle anything in its path. The carnivorous, feral sand creature frightens its prey with its size, overpowering its meal with prodigious strength. Desert-dwelling Tuskens are a favorite of the sand beast and are typically helpless against its sharp claws (three per hand) and serrated teeth. Boba Fett is one of the few believed to have tangled with one of these creatures and overpowered it, earning him instant respect and admiration from the Tuskens.

THE TWINS

SPECIES Hutt **HOMEWORLD** Tatooine
AFFILIATION The Hutts

"The Twins" is the moniker attributed to the brother and sister Hutt crime lords who claim the territory of their cousin Jabba the Hutt once he is defeated. Their arrival can be heard throughout Mos Espa via a steady drumbeat announcement as they are carried through the streets on a litter by servants. The Hutts hire the dangerous Wookiee Krrsantan to kill Boba Fett, but the mission isn't successful. The twins apologize and leave Tatooine, explaining that they don't want to go to war over a worthless rock, and they offer a rancor to Boba as tribute.

KRRSANTAN

SPECIES Wookiee **HOMEWORLD** Kashyyyk
AFFILIATION Bounty hunter

Krrsantan is a Wookiee bounty hunter and ferocious warrior with a vicious temper. His furry body is cybernetically enhanced with subdermal plating and endoskeletal enhancements. Long ago, Krrsantan garnered his reputation as a formidable gladiator, and he later achieves status as a bounty hunter. Throughout his infamous career, Krrsantan has worked for Darth Vader, Doctor Chelli Lona Aphra, and Jabba the Hutt and has clashed with Obi-Wan Kenobi, who gave the Wookiee the

Gladiator-turned-mercenary
During the Battle for Mos Espa, Krrsantan blasts away at Pyke Syndicate combatants with his heavy blaster, fighting on the side of Boba Fett.

scar over his eye. On several occasions, Krrsantan has worked alongside Boba Fett. Eventually, he's hired by the Twins to kill Boba, but he's unsuccessful and is instead captured by Boba and his allies. In a surprise gesture, Boba chooses to free Krrsantan instead of harming or imprisoning him. Boba later hires the Wookiee for his war against the Pykes. Krrsantan is injured during the Battle for Mos Espa and is attended to by Fett's allies. The Wookiee powerhouse is treated with compassion by his cohorts. This isn't something he is used to, and he begins to find loyalty to something other than credits.

KINTAN STRIDERS

SPECIES Nikto **HOMEWORLD** Kintan
AFFILIATION Kintan Striders gang

The Kintan Striders are a gang of bullies and thugs who take their name from a beast that inhabits their homeworld. They are happy to assert their will by overpowering residents in small towns and separating them from their hard-earned credits. One group of brutish Kintan Striders takes over Tosche Station and proceeds to beat up a local man, Laze "Fixer" Loneozner, for no reason. Boba Fett intervenes, saving the man and taking the gang's speeder bikes back to his Tusken tribe. The Pykes frame the Kintan gang for destroying Boba's Tusken friends, which leads the enraged former bounty hunter to wipe out all the gang's members.

CAMIE MARSTRAP

SPECIES Human **HOMEWORLD** Tatooine
AFFILIATION Citizens of Tatooine

Camie Marstrap lives in Anchorhead on Tatooine with her family. As a young girl, she is friends with Laze "Fixer" Loneozner, Biggs Darklighter, and Luke Skywalker. The teens have fun together at Tosche Station, where they shop and tell stories. Over time, some of Camie's friends leave Tatooine to fight in the Galactic Civil War. She remains on Tatooine and dates Laze. One eventful evening, the two of them are enjoying a quiet drink in Tosche Station when they are interrupted by a gang of Nikto thugs. Laze attempts to defend them but is attacked, and Camie is restrained by a Nikto until Boba Fett arrives and defeats the gang.

CHARACTERS AND CREATURES

LAZE "FIXER" LONEOZNER
SPECIES Human **HOMEWORLD** Tatooine
AFFILIATION Citizens of Tatooine

Laze Loneozner lives on Tatooine and is known by some as "Fixer" because of his skill as a mechanic and tinkerer. He and his girlfriend, Camie Marstrap, spend time with their friends Biggs Darklighter and Luke Skywalker, and Laze gives Luke the nickname "Wormie" as a playful insult. After the Galactic Civil War, Laze and Camie go to Tosche Station for an evening together, but they are harassed by a group of Nikto brutes. Laze stands up to them and is immediately beaten with a shock stick. The attack is interrupted by the arrival of Boba Fett, who defeats the thugs and saves Laze and the other patrons.

AL-42
TYPE Train operator droid
AFFILIATION Pyke Syndicate

AL-42 is a train conductor for the Pyke Syndicate, which occupies Tatooine. The droid is predominantly black, with a few red sensors that enhance 360-degree vision and awareness. AL's train is overrun by Boba Fett and a group of Tuskens, but he escapes.

HORNED GEKKO
HOMEWORLD Tatooine **SIZE** 10 cm (4 in) long (tail fully extended) **HABITAT** Desert

A small lizard that lives in Tatooine's deserts, the horned gekko is sacred to the Tuskens. In a Tusken ceremony, it crawls through the nostril of a person, acting as a catalyst for the recipient to go on a mysterious journey. The ritual is not damaging to the creature or its host.

B'OMARR MONKS
SPECIES Droid hybrid **HOMEWORLD** Tatooine
AFFILIATION B'omarr monks

The B'omarr monks live primarily in the shadows, spending their lives in contemplative meditation. They achieve enlightenment by separating their brains from their bodies. A B'omarr monk's brain floats inside liquid contained in the front of a large mechanical spider. It is commonly believed that the monks are droid in nature, but they are in fact organic beings who keep to themselves. B'omarr monks may appear frightening, but they are actually docile in nature. Jabba the Hutt's palace was once a monastery that housed many B'omarr monks. Several remain there in secret, enjoying their isolation.

LORTHA PEEL
SPECIES Human **HOMEWORLD** Tatooine
AFFILIATION Lortha Peel

The water monger Lortha Peel lives and operates in the Workers District of Mos Pelgo. Selfish and motivated solely by greed, he has a reputation for modifying the price of his water to the extent that innocent citizens are often forced to steal from his supply for their survival.

DRASH
SPECIES Human **HOMEWORLD** Tatooine
AFFILIATION The Mods, Boba Fett

Drash is a member of the Mods street gang that operates in the Workers District of Mos Espa. Her left arm has been cybernetically enhanced. She steals water from Lortha Peel out of necessity for survival. When Boba Fett confronts her over the robbery, he is impressed with her brash nature so he invites her to work for him. Drash is loyal to those who earn her trust. She is also fearless, taking on the mighty Wookiee bounty hunter Krrsantan to protect her new employer, Boba. Alongside her newfound allies, Drash and her gang fight off the Pyke Syndicate during the Battle of Mos Espa.

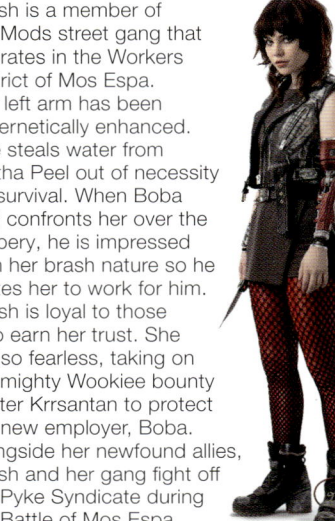

Hired muscle
Drash is a skilled fighter and speeder bike pilot. She uses her driving skills, racing through the streets of Mos Espa for Boba Fett.

SKAD
SPECIES Human **HOMEWORLD** Tatooine
AFFILIATION The Mods, Boba Fett

Skad lives in the Workers District of Mos Espa and is a member of the Mods street gang that includes Drash. His right eye has been replaced by a cybernetically modified one that allows him to see great distances. His gang steals water from Lortha Peel, which brings him to the attention of Boba Fett. The new crime lord of Tatooine initially believes Skad to be dishonest, but he soon discovers that Skad can't afford Lortha's perpetually escalating prices. Boba invites Skad to join him as muscle. Skad and Drash are fiercely loyal, standing up to Krrsantan and the Pykes as Boba establishes his reign on Tatooine.

PYKE BOSS
SPECIES Pyke **HOMEWORLD** Oba Diah
AFFILIATION Pyke Syndicate

The Pyke Boss is an esteemed leader of his people. Rational and pragmatic, he is perfectly willing to avoid violence in order to keep his criminal enterprise running smoothly and consistently. He is also a talented negotiator with the ability to smooth out most conflicts using charm and the promise of wealth. But if all else fails, he will hire bounty hunters to ensure the Pykes' spice empire continues to grow and prosper. He attempts to murder Boba Fett and take over Tatooine but is thwarted by Boba and his companions. The Pyke Boss is killed in his own headquarters by Fennec Shand during the Battle of Mos Espa.

RANCOR KEEPER
SPECIES Human
HOMEWORLD Tatooine
AFFILIATION Boba Fett

The Hutt Twins offer a rancor as a gift to Boba Fett as an apology for ordering his assassination. Their generous gift also includes a rancor keeper to keep the beast in line. The handler is a compassionate and loyal trainer who understands the demeanor of these sometimes fearsome beasts. Rancors form a bond with the first creature they see, so the keeper ensures the rancor's eyes are covered from birth until it meets its master, demonstrating his selfless nature as a caretaker. He shows patience and inner strength while helping Boba attune to the beast.

KABA BAIZ
SPECIES Klatooinian **HOMEWORLD** Glavis Ringworld **AFFILIATION** Meat-packing plant

The boss of a meat-packing plant on the space station Glavis Ringworld, Kaba Baiz gets a bounty on his head after accruing too much debt. An Ishi Tib guild master hires Din Djarin to collect the bounty and Din is successful, cutting off the Klatooinian's head with the Darksaber.

BOBA'S RANCOR

HOMEWORLD Tatooine **SIZE** 4.89 m (16 ft 1 in) high **HABITAT** Plains, jungles

Boba Fett's rancor is given to him by the Hutt Twins to avoid retaliation for their attempt to assassinate him. The beast's eyes are covered until Boba receives it, so that it forms a bond with his new master when it sees him. While tame in captivity, Boba's rancor is ferocious when allowed to roam free, causing destruction and chaos during the Battle of Mos Espa. Boba rides his rancor during the battle, further showing their connection and his control over the beast. Despite its loyalty to Boba, the rancor is still dangerous to his allies until it is tamed through the Force by Grogu.

THE MODIFIER

SPECIES Human **HOMEWORLD** Tatooine **AFFILIATION** The Mods, Boba Fett

The craftsman known as "the Modifier" is an exceptionally talented artist who creates cybernetic enhancements for paying customers, including members of the Mod gang. As well as limb and organ replacements after serious injuries, the Modifier can also engineer additions and improvements. He is hired by Boba Fett to restore Fennec Shand to full health after she is left for dead on Tatooine. He also brings Cobb Vanth back from a near-fatal blaster wound. The Modifier's work, along with his discreet nature, earns him a significant reputation.

BD-72

MANUFACTURER Behold-Urwar Droid Concepts **TYPE** Explorer droid **AFFILIATION** Peli Motto

Small but capable, BD-72 is one of the droids who work for the mechanic Peli Motto. The BD unit helps in the assembly of Din Djarin's custom N-1 starfighter, using a spotlight and holoprojector. The droid walks on two legs and can pivot its binocular-shaped head 360 degrees.

WORRT ROOSTER

HOMEWORLD Tatooine **SIZE** 50 cm (1 ft 8 in) long **HABITAT** Desert

The worrt rooster is a winged creature that crows at sunrise to announce the start of each day. It has three long fingers on each arm, which attach to its wings. While the bird isn't aggressive, it is easily threatened and will crow repeatedly if it believes it is in danger. The worrt rooster has two black eyes and sharp teeth that form a significant overbite. Its wings are more reptilian than birdlike, giving it a menacing appearance, despite its harmless nature.

REED

SPECIES Human **AFFILIATION** New Republic

A lieutenant in the New Republic Starfighter Corps, Reed flies with Carson Teva over Tatooine and stumbles upon a modified N-1 starfighter. When the ship speeds away, Reed believes the incident should be reported, but the reminder of paperwork quickly changes his mind.

MUD YAK

HOMEWORLD Ossus **SIZE** 3 m (9 ft 11 in) long **HABITAT** Swamps, marshes

The hairy, horned mud yak lives in the swamps of the lush planet Ossus. The herbivores travel in herds, gently grazing in watery marshes. Although they are timid, the creatures defend themselves with the long horns that slope downward from the tops of their skulls.

SCOTT

SPECIES Human **HOMEWORLD** Tatooine **AFFILIATION** Mos Pelgo

A deputy for Cobb Vanth, Scott protects Mos Pelgo with bravado and an eagerness to prove himself. His impatient, aggressive nature leads to him being gunned down by Cad Bane, who has no patience for the impetuous but well-meaning deputy.

RAGNAR

SPECIES Human **HOMEWORLD** Mandalore **AFFILIATION** Children of the Watch

Ragnar is the adolescent son of Paz Vizsla. He is eager to prove himself worthy as a Mandalorian warrior so he faces off against Grogu at the insistence of Din Djarin during a training session. Grogu easily defeats Ragnar, whose humiliation quickly turns to horror as he's swallowed by a massive raptor. The creature carries Ragnar to its nest to feed its young. The boy is rescued by his father, Din Djarin, and Bo-Katan Kryze and later becomes a full-fledged Mandalorian by completing the sacred ritual on Mandalore.

Complicated rescue
During the rescue mission for Ragnar, the raptor swipes the boy from its nest and flies off with him in its huge claw. Mandalorians follow it with their jetpacks.

LAKE MONSTER

SIZE 52.63 m (172 ft 8 in) high, 62.85 m (206 ft 2 in) wide, (642 ft) long **HABITAT** Underground hollows

The lake monster is a massive creature with a thick, protective shell covering its leathery scaled hide. The monstrous beast has a large snout full of pointy teeth capable of ripping into its prey or anything unfortunate enough to come within snapping distance of its gaping maw. The creature's huge size makes it rely on stealth to sneak up on its next meal, bursting from the depths of its watery domain to snatch food into its mouth or to attack anything it perceives as a threat. Its flesh is considered a delicacy, but hunting one is extremely dangerous and foolish.

VANE

SPECIES Nikto **AFFILIATION** Gorian Shard's pirate crew

A member of Gorian Shard's band of pirates, which invades Nevarro, Vane is a bully with little regard for civility. He tries to enter a school with alcohol but is stopped by Greef Karga and Din Djarin. Vane leads a starfighter attack on Nevarro and is again thwarted by Din.

GORIAN SHARD

AFFILIATION Gorian Shard's pirate crew

Gorian Shard is the Pirate King of a group of crooks. From his massive warship, he leads his gang in an invasion of Nevarro. He wants to destroy Nevarro's capital to punish Greef Karga and its people for not letting his pirates overrun the city. He is defeated by Bo-Katan and Din Djarin, who destroy his vessel in aerial combat, killing Shard in the process.

CHARACTERS AND CREATURES

ALAMITE
HOMEWORLD Mandalore
SIZE 1.80 m (5 ft 11 in) high **HABITAT** Caves

Alamites once lived beyond the cities of Mandalore in the Wastelands, but after the Imperial Purge, several relocated and began living in the ruins of Sundari. The creatures have white fur and four green eyes that glow in the dark, allowing them to see clearly despite the absence of light. Alamites are carnivorous and are believed to eat humans. Their predatory nature, pointed teeth, and thick hides make them dangerous to unfortunate travelers. Bo-Katan and Din Djarin are ambushed by Alamites; they defeat them but are wary of any potential future encounters.

CYBORG MECH
HOMEWORLD Mandalore

The cyborg mech is a mysterious being that lurks in the ruins of Sundari on Mandalore. A single organic eye encased in an unknown fluid, it drives a large droid spider tank and lies in wait underground so it can erupt from below and subdue its next meal, trapping it in a metal cage attached to its mechanical body. The cyborg mech inserts a needle into Din Djarin's neck, injecting him with a drug that puts him to sleep. Bo-Katan rescues Din and is able to kill the creature, which also deactivates the spider tank.

MYTHOSAUR
HOMEWORLD Mandalore
SIZE 30 m (100 ft) long
HABITAT Water

The Mythosaur is a gargantuan creature believed to be extinct but still held sacred among Mandalorians, who have adopted its horned skull as a symbol of their legacy and might. According to Bo-Katan Kryze, the legendary figure Mandalore the Great is said to have tamed the beast and learned to ride it. Mythosaurs are believed to be adaptable for living on land or in the depths of Mandalore's seas.

The Mythosaur grows to be more than 30 meters (100 ft) long and has scaly, yellowish skin that acts like armor to protect the creature. Two large horns on either side of the mouth can be used to gore opponents or slice into prey. Mythosaurs' eyes have yellow irises surrounding a small, black pupil.

Unbeknownst to the people of Mandalore, one of the creatures has survived, and it lives deep in the Mines of Mandalore. Ever since the planet was nearly destroyed during the Imperial Purge, no one has explored the waters in the mines. When Din Djarin ventures into the waters to initiate a ritual to rejoin the Children of the Watch, he is nearly drowned. Bo-Katan dives in to save an unconscious Din and sees the Mythosaur deep within the recesses. Inspired by this fantastical sight, she has the Armorer add a Mythosaur skull onto her armor to commemorate the experience and further demonstrate her commitment to her people. Bo-Katan shares her experience with the Armorer, who tells her that those who walk the Way see many visions, and she also says that the Mythosaur will usher in a new age of Mandalore. Shortly after this conversation, Bo-Katan and a small army of Mandalorians reclaim the planet from Gideon's Imperial forces, adding credibility to the Armorer's story.

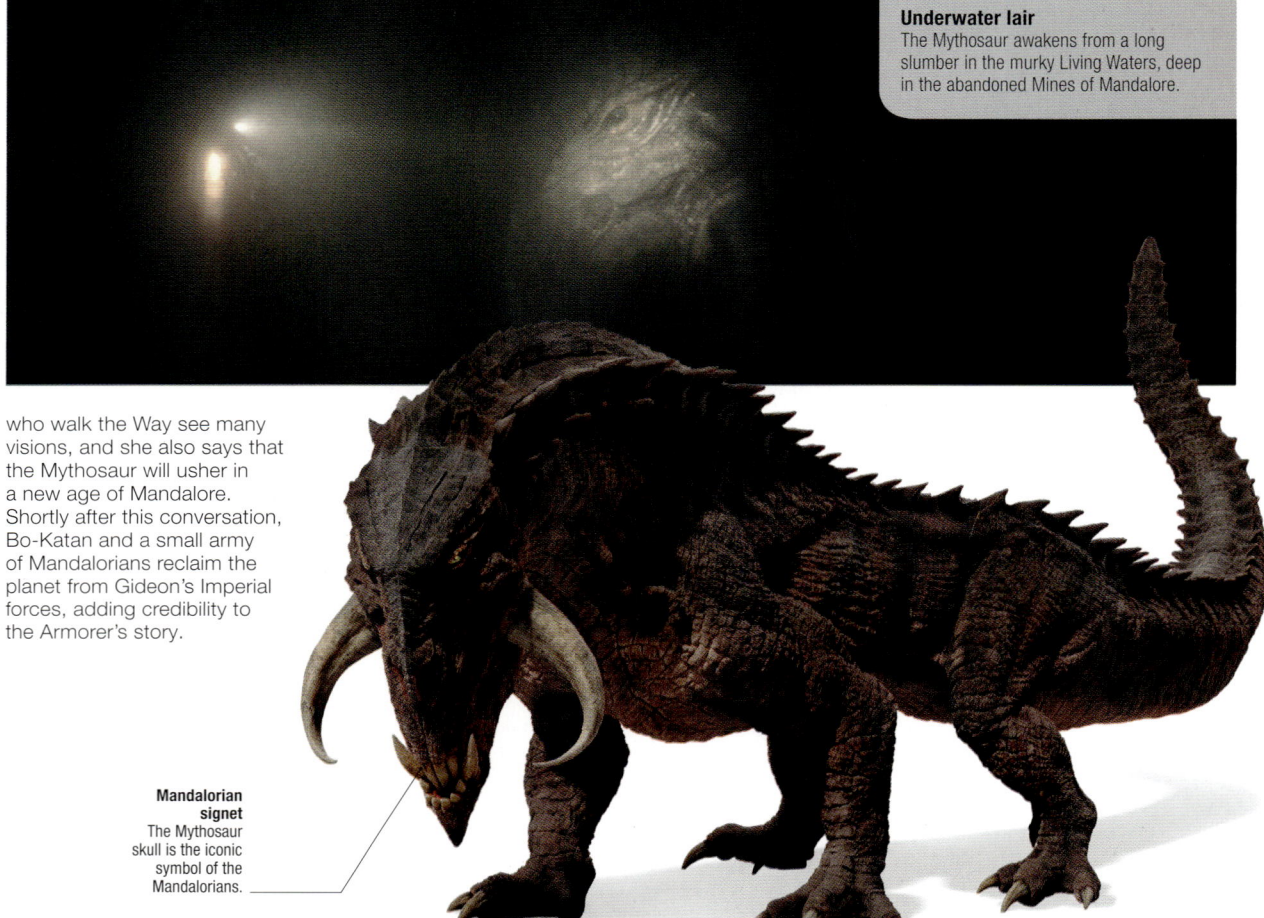

Underwater lair
The Mythosaur awakens from a long slumber in the murky Living Waters, deep in the abandoned Mines of Mandalore.

Mandalorian signet
The Mythosaur skull is the iconic symbol of the Mandalorians.

RE-INTEGRATION TECHNICIAN
SPECIES Mon Calamari **HOMEWORLD** Coruscant
AFFILIATION New Republic

At the New Republic Re-Integration Institute, the attendant assists citizens like Dr. Pershing who are suffering from trauma. His 602 mitigator, which is similar to a mind flayer, is supposed to put patients at ease.

MANDALORIAN JUDGE
SPECIES Human **HOMEWORLD** Mandalore
AFFILIATION Children of the Watch

The Mandalorian judge observes the Children of the Watch training and weighs in on important cultural matters. He wears an orange helmet and jetpack and has a green cape over his left shoulder. Stoic and wise, he ensures the safety of the children first when there is danger.

STONE CRAB
HOMEWORLD Unnamed Mandalorian covert world **SIZE** 6 cm (2½ in)
HABITAT Beaches, water

Stone crabs are small non-sentient crustaceans that gather in groups for defense and to search for food on the sandy beaches of their planet. Their thick outer hides provide safety and camouflage; retracting under their shells and half-burying themselves in the sand disguises them as rocks. A group of Mandalorians, including Grogu, are training on a beach when a collection of stone crabs scuttles onto the shore. Grogu is fascinated by the small aquatic creatures and proceeds to pick them up by their shells to see how they transform themselves into rocks for protection.

RAPTOR

HOMEWORLD Unnamed Mandalorian covert world **SIZE** 14 m (45 ft 11 in) long, 47 m (154 ft 2 in) wingspan **HABITAT** Mountains

The raptor is a large reptilian bird with a massive wingspan, sharp talons, and a long beak that can snatch up prey or crack open strong shells to extract food. Raptors lay eggs and scour the surface of their planet for small living beings to feed to their young. One raptor snatches Paz Vizsla's son, Ragnar, and takes the terrified child to its nest high on a mountain. Paz, Din Djarin, Bo-Katan Kryze, and a few other Mandalorians scale the rock to rescue the boy. They defeat the raptor and take its young to their shelter as pets and potential mounts.

Grogu's rescue
During Order 66, Kelleran Beq takes young Grogu from the Jedi Temple to a landing platform on Coruscant. From there, Naboo Security Forces help them offworld.

KELLERAN BEQ

SPECIES Human **HOMEWORLD** Coruscant
AFFILIATION Jedi Order

Kelleran Beq is a revered and well-respected Jedi Master who fights during the Clone Wars. He earns the nickname "The Sabered Hand" for his prowess and skill with a lightsaber. Beq's primary blade is green, but he can also wield two lightsabers at the same time with proficiency and finesse.

Beq works with younglings alongside protocol droids AD-3 and LX-R5 to promote teamwork and collaboration aboard his ship, the *Athylia*, as well as in the Jedi Temple on Coruscant. Beq's pedagogical approach, compassion, and sense of humor make him a valuable companion for his fellow Jedi and his students. During Order 66, Beq is vitally important in rescuing young Grogu from clone troopers. He takes the child with him as they escape the attack in the Jedi Temple. They flee Coruscant on a Naboo yacht, heading into the unknown.

TUTTLE

SPECIES Human **HOMEWORLD** Coruscant
AFFILIATION New Republic

Colonel Tuttle works on Coruscant in the New Republic's Requisitions department, supplying hardware and labor to aid star systems that are a part of the New Republic. He likes to do things in an organized manner and has little patience for droids that mess up his working area. Carson Teva requests assistance in liberating Nevarro from pirates, but since they haven't signed the New Republic charter, Tuttle is not inclined to help. Other systems, who have signed up, have priority. He is not entirely unsympathetic to aiding Nevarro but believes in following the protocols and procedures designated by the New Republic.

SHUGGOTH

SPECIES Quarren **HOMEWORLD** Mon Cala
AFFILIATION Independent

Captain of a Quarren freighter, Shuggoth elopes with a Mon Calamari prince. When faced with Axe Woves, who has been hired to retrieve the prince by his mother, Shuggoth sadly lets her beloved go, in order to keep him and her crew safe.

LORD BOMBARDIER

SPECIES Human **HOMEWORLD** Plazir-15
AFFILIATION Empire, New Republic

Lord Bombardier is a former Imperial captain who reforms thanks to the New Republic amnesty program. Mild-mannered and good-natured, he is loyal to the people of Plazir-15 and his wife, the Duchess. In his determination to show he is a changed man, he convinces his wife to hold elections to confirm the two of them as leaders because the people wish it, and not just because of royal heritage. Due to his formal Imperial ties, he is not permitted to have an official military presence on his planet, so he hires Bo-Katan's former fleet, led by Axe Woves, as privateers.

THE DUCHESS

SPECIES Human **HOMEWORLD** Plazir-15
AFFILIATION New Republic

The Duchess is born into a noble family on her homeworld of Plazir-15 and carries herself with charm, compassion, and grace. She falls in love with Captain Bombardier, an Imperial officer at the time, and together they are the first-ever elected rulers of the planet. The pair enacts a reprogramming initiative in which Imperial and Separatist droids work alongside Ugnaughts so citizens can focus on recreation and leisure. She hires Bo-Katan and Din Djarin to uncover something mysterious that is happening to their droids. She is instantly charmed by Din's companion, Grogu.

COMMISSIONER HELGAIT

SPECIES Human **HOMEWORLD** Plazir-15
AFFILIATION Separatist

The head of security on Plazir-15, Commissioner Helgait has served the Duchess' family for years. Although he is in charge of keeping Plazir-15 safe, his true allegiance is to the Separatists. Privately, he thinks Count Dooku is a visionary. Helgait plans to turn droids violently against the civilians of Plazir-15 in order to interfere with the Duchess and Lord Bombardier's reign. He sneaks nano-droids into super battle droids with the lubricant Nepenthé, but his treachery is discovered by Bo-Katan Kryze and Din Djarin, and he is exiled to the moon of Paraqaat.

SAIFIR

SPECIES Ugnaught **HOMEWORLD** Plazir-15
AFFILIATION New Republic

The Ugnaught Saifir produces droids and other technology in a Plazir-15 workshop for Lord Bombardier and the Duchess. Her pride is wounded when Bo-Katan Kryze appears to insinuate that Ugnaught work may be responsible for some malfunctioning droids, but Din Djarin's appreciation for her species inspires her to help the Mandalorians.

CHARACTERS AND CREATURES

MORGAN ELSBETH
HOMEWORLD Dathomir
AFFILIATION Nightsisters, Empire

Morgan Elsbeth's fellow Nightsisters are massacred by General Grievous, leaving her determined to never be powerless. Cold and calculating, Morgan makes herself crucial to the Empire's war machine, through industry. She oversees manufacturing on Corellia, helping the Imperial Navy grow its fleet. After the war, Elsbeth, ever the opportunist, becomes the magistrate of Calodan on Corvus. Here, Ahsoka Tano seeks Morgan out to learn information about the location of Grand Admiral Thrawn, and remands custody of Morgan to the New Republic.

Imprisonment doesn't weaken Morgan's resolve to bring Thrawn back from his far-flung location, which she learns of from the calls of the distant Great Mothers. Thanks to hired mercenaries, she escapes prison and executes her plan to retrieve the Imperial leader, and the Great Mothers, from another galaxy. For her service, the Great Mothers reward Morgan with special gifts, including the Blade of Talzin. The weapon ends up falling into Ahsoka's hands and being Morgan's downfall when she is ordered to buy time to allow Thrawn and the Great Mothers to escape Ahsoka.

Distant galaxy
Morgan Elsbeth's devotion to her Dathomirian heritage and desire to see the Empire return give her unshakable faith and determination to find the Great Mothers and Grand Admiral Thrawn.

GILAD PELLAEON
SPECIES Human **HOMEWORLD** Corellia
AFFILIATION Empire, Imperial remnant, Shadow Council

Gilad Pellaeon is a captain in the Empire who serves on the Star Destroyer *Harbinger* during the Imperial blockade of Lothal under the command of Grand Admiral Thrawn. After purrgil arrive and pull Thrawn and his Star Destroyer, the *Chimaera*, into hyperspace, Pellaeon resumes the fight against the Rebellion and goes into hiding once the Empire is defeated. He and several high-ranking Imperial leaders, including Moff Gideon and Commandant Brendol Hux, form the Shadow Council in order to unite the Imperial members in their secret mission to resurrect the Empire. Gilad is not impressed with Moff Gideon's bombastic methods or shows of bravado. Instead, Gilad firmly puts his hopes in the return of Thrawn.

BRENDOL HUX
SPECIES Human
AFFILIATION Empire, Shadow Council, First Order

Brendol Hux is a secretive and high-ranking officer in the Empire. As a young man, he serves in the Grand Army of the Republic as a junior officer. Once the Republic falls, he transitions to the Empire, rapidly ascending its ranks. His mutual talents in military tactics and espionage, combined with his penchant for cruelty, make him ideal for the Imperial way of life. He creates the Commandant's Cadets—a secret society within the Arkanis Academy of the Empire. His sadism affects his troopers and his son, Armitage Hux. Brendol is instrumental in rebuilding the Empire after its defeat at the Battle of Jakku, and he helps to form the Shadow Council to resurrect Imperial rule. Later, during his time in the First Order, he is betrayed by his son and Captain Phasma, who secretly poisons him, leading to a slow and painful death.

MANDALORIAN CAPTAIN
SPECIES Human **HOMEWORLD** Mandalore
AFFILIATION Mandalorians, House of Kryze

The Mandalorian captain is a highly respected survivor of the Great Purge of Mandalore and is loyal to the House of Kryze and its leader, Bo-Katan Kryze. When the Mandalorian people refuse to surrender, the Empire bombs the planet in the Night of a Thousand Tears. The captain and a few other surviving Mandalorians remain on the decimated planet, now a crystallized wasteland, awaiting the return of Bo-Katan. During the homecoming, the Mandalorian captain greets her, Din Djarin, and the rest of their united clan, and brings them on board his langskib.

TRINITAUR
HOMEWORLD Mandalore **SIZE** 196 m (643 ft 1 in) long **HABITAT** Underneath the surface of Mandalore

The trinitaur is a gargantuan reptilian beast that lies in wait beneath the crystallized surface of Mandalore. The war-ravaged planet was believed to be void of life, but the colossal creature has managed to survive. It has large triangular plates along its body and a serpentine neck that it uses to destroy the Mandalorian captain's langskib. It is a rarity for a Mandalorian to back down from a fight, but one look at the creature's gaping mouth is more than enough to encourage the Mandalorian survivors to avoid certain death by igniting their jetpacks and abandoning ship.

Familiar foe
Baylan Skoll knew Anakin Skywalker when they were both Jedi, and he sees much of Ahsoka Tano's former master in her beliefs and fighting style. Baylan uses this knowledge to gain the upper hand.

BAYLAN SKOLL
SPECIES Human **AFFILIATION** Jedi, Morgan Elsbeth's forces

A Jedi no more, Baylan Skoll is weary of the cycle of peace and war and the way Force-wielders keep finding themselves participants in it. He is a man looking for guidance and a path toward lasting peace. Baylan is willing to work for Dathomirian witch Morgan Elsbeth as a mercenary and help her locate Grand Admiral Thrawn, but not because he believes in the Imperial remnant. Rather than fight in yet another war, Baylan wants to go to Peridea, in a galaxy far, far away, because he hopes to find the answers he seeks. He takes his apprentice, Shin Hati, with him. Baylan has passed on his knowledge and enmity for the Jedi to Shin, but he separates from her on Peridea and leaves her to find her own destiny.

Talented with a lightsaber and forged by the training of the Jedi, Baylan fights a number of battles for Morgan and Thrawn, including against Ahsoka Tano and Sabine Wren. He fights only when necessary, relying on calm observation and facts until he sees no other choice.

CAPTAIN HAYLE

SPECIES Human
AFFILIATION New Republic

Captain Hayle holds Morgan Elsbeth prisoner on the *Vesper*. While waiting for *Home One* to collect the prisoner, Captain Hayle instead allows two people claiming to be Jedi (Baylan Skoll and Shin Hati) to board the ship. He tries to shame them into surrender, but instead, they kill Hayle and his crew who ha come to meet them.

JENSEN CORBYT

SPECIES Human **AFFILIATION** New Republic

An officer of the New Republic Defense Fleet, Lieutenant Jensen Corbyt serves under Captain Hayle on the *Vesper*. When Hayle goes to greet some alleged Jedi, Corbyt takes over command. She tries to enact defense protocols, but Shin Hati kills her.

PROFESSOR HUYANG

TYPE Mark IV architect droid
AFFILIATION Jedi, New Republic

For more than a thousand generations, Professor Huyang teaches Jedi younglings history and how to build their lightsabers. The ancient droid's memory capacity is almost beyond understanding, as he recalls details about specific Jedi's lightsabers from the distant past. Before Order 66 wipes out the Jedi, Huyang maintains a vast collection of lightsaber parts on his ship, the *Crucible*. Once younglings gather their kyber crystals, Huyang's lessons begin. His knowledge and cool head save one particular group of younglings, led by Padawan Ahsoka Tano, from pirates.

At some point after the rise and fall of the Empire, Huyang travels with Ahsoka. Always ready with pointed insight, Huyang accompanies Ahsoka as she takes Sabine Wren as an apprentice and searches for the map to prevent Morgan Elsbeth from bringing back Grand Admiral Thrawn. He reluctantly travels with Ahsoka inside a purrgil to another galaxy. Dependable and thoughtful, Huyang is always there for Ahsoka as a pilot, a storyteller, a mechanic, and a friend—a friend who always voices his opinions and reminds her of her history.

Knowledge repository
Huyang's near-limitless well of knowledge makes him an excellent copilot, capable of navigating Ahsoka's shuttle out of dangerous situations.

SHIN HATI

SPECIES Human
AFFILIATION Morgan Elsbeth's forces

Shin Hati craves power. She learns from her master, Baylan Skoll, but she is neither Jedi nor Sith. She dedicates herself to training in the Force and with a lightsaber, absorbing most everything her master teaches her. Eager and ambitious, Shin wants to find her purpose and sees possibility through gaining power—but a different kind of power than Baylan searches for. In her work as a mercenary for Morgan Elsbeth, Shin frees her from being imprisoned by the New Republic, and then works alongside former Inquisitor Marrok to locate the ancient star map that will lead them to Grand Admiral Thrawn's far-flung location.

A skilled pilot and fighter, Shin confronts Sabine Wren, Ahsoka Tano's apprentice, repeatedly and across galaxies. Their rivalry comes to an end on Peridea, when Baylan parts ways with Shin, warning her against impatience. She takes on a bigger fight than she can handle against Ahsoka, Sabine, and the newly found Ezra Bridger. Shin retreats from the battle and approaches a group of bandits, hoping to find a place among them.

Searching for a map
Shin takes two HK-87 assassin droids to Lothal, and they follow a probe droid to Sabine Wren's home. Shin sends the droids in first, and one steals the star map that leads to Peridea.

MURLEY

SPECIES Loth-cat **HOMEWORLD** Lothal
AFFILIATION Sabine Wren

Loth-cats roam Lothal's grasslands, but they can be domesticated. Sabine Wren takes a Loth-cat as a pet and names him Murley. While Murley accepts prowling outdoors and is self-sufficient, he enjoys a life of comfort in Sabine's home, greeting her with welcoming meows when she returns. Murley loves to receive scratches under his chin and Loth-cat kibble, and will treat anything as a potential toy, even a mysterious map to another galaxy. A good judge of character and loyal companion, he warns Sabine of approaching danger with a loud hiss.

CAPTAIN PORTER

SPECIES Human **AFFILIATION** New Republic

Captain Porter, whose call sign is Spectre Two-One, is a New Republic pilot stationed on Lothal. Responding to an order from Governor Ryder Azadi, Porter takes out an E-wing to fetch Commander Sabine Wren for a ceremony honoring her as a hero. However, she ignores his repeated requests for her to stand down.

LIEUTENANT CALLAHAN

SPECIES Human
AFFILIATION New Republic

A New Republic pilot based on Lothal, Lieutenant Callahan accompanies Captain Porter to find Sabine Wren. Callahan parks her E-wing in Sabine's path as a roadblock, believing Sabine will turn around and return to Lothal's capital. She is surprised when Sabine instead slides her speeder bike under the starfighter.

RD-3

MANUFACTURER Industrial Automaton
TYPE Astromech droid
AFFILIATION New Republic

An astromech serving the New Republic, RD-3 is present when visitors board the *Vesper*. He accompanies Captain Hayle and his security force to the ship's hangar when Baylan Skoll and his apprentice Shin Hati board, ready to scan the impostors, who claim to be Jedi, for identification.

C1-D1

MANUFACTURER Cybot Galactica
TYPE Protocol droid
AFFILIATION New Republic

C1-D1 works in the command center of a former Imperial shipyard on Corellia. Myn Weaver tasks her with helping Ahsoka Tano and General Hera Syndulla to navigate protocol. C1-D1 answers a question honestly about the presence of HK assassin droids and, in doing so, reveals the facility's lingering Imperial loyalty.

CHARACTERS AND CREATURES

MYN WEAVER
SPECIES Human
AFFILIATION Empire

Myn Weaver, regional supervisor for the New Republic shipyard on Corellia, proclaims loyalty to his investors, not galactic politics. When General Hera Syndulla and Ahsoka Tano press him about the factory's one-time Imperial association, Myn assures them the staff is focused on repurposing old Imperial assets into material for the New Republic. Myn reluctantly provides a tour of the facility, pointing out efficient and profitable operations. However, Hera and Ahsoka soon uncover his loyalty to the fallen Empire and that Myn has been helping Morgan Elsbeth. The New Republic takes the traitorous bureaucrat into custody.

MARROK
AFFILIATION Morgan Elsbeth's forces

Once an Inquisitor, Marrok still carries the Inquisitorius' signature red double-bladed lightsaber with a circular hilt. Now working for Nightsister Morgan Elsbeth, Marrok aids Morgan in her quest to locate and retrieve Grand Admiral Thrawn. Fighting alongside Baylan Skoll and Shin Hati, Marrok tries to foil Ahsoka Tano's plans to stop Morgan on both Corellia and in the space above Seatos. Baylan has faith in Marrok, promising Morgan that the mysterious warrior will complete his task. Although his lightsaber prowess makes Marrok evenly matched with Ahsoka, she kills him in the forest on Seatos, and the warrior disappears in a burst of green mist.

LIEUTENANT BEYTA
SPECIES Mon Calamari
HOMEWORLD Mon Cala
AFFILIATION New Republic

Lieutenant Beyta serves the New Republic as a pilot in its Starfighter Corps. Beyta often works closely with General Hera Syndulla and is present for high-priority meetings between the general and Chancellor Mon Mothma. She supports Hera during her court appearance in front of the Defense Council on Coruscant.

VIC HAWKINS
SPECIES Human
AFFILIATION New Republic

Lieutenant Vic Hawkins helps General Hera Syndulla handle the bureaucracy that comes with working with the New Republic. He respects the general but is sometimes perplexed when she doesn't seek authorization for missions through the proper channels. He has been known to improvise to cover for Hera.

HAMATO XIONO
SPECIES Human **HOMEWORLD** Hosnian Prime
AFFILIATION New Republic, New Republic Defense Council, New Republic Senate

A senator from Hosnian Prime, Hamato Xiono serves on the New Republic Defense Council. He butts heads with General Hera Syndulla, who argues that Grand Admiral Thrawn is plotting a return but presents no real evidence. After Hera disobeys orders to stay out of Ahsoka Tano's investigation into the matter, Xiono motions to court martial the rebel hero. Leia Organa presents surprise justification for Hera's actions, thwarting Xiono. Years later, during the rise of the First Order, Xiono advises his son Kazuda, a Resistance spy, from across the galaxy.

LORRIN MAWOOD
SPECIES Human
AFFILIATION New Republic

Senator Lorrin Mawood is skeptical of General Hera Syndulla's concerns about the return of Grand Admiral Thrawn. He is dismissive of her mission to the Denab system, saying that he is representative of the people of the New Republic and that no one wants to bring further conflict.

SENATOR RODRIGO
SPECIES Human
AFFILIATION New Republic

New Republic Senator Rodrigo works alongside Chancellor Mon Mothma. She hears General Hera Syndulla's report about the Imperial loyalists in the Santhe Shipyards but insists that the former Imperials in the New Republic government have taken oaths of loyalty. She sees no enemy in Grand Admiral Thrawn, only a scattered fleet with no central command.

LIEUTENANT BAYSEE
SPECIES Human
AFFILIATION New Republic

Lieutenant Baysee pilots an X-wing to Seatos on Hera Syndulla's unauthorized mission. He notices their enemy isn't sticking around for a fight. When the *Eye of Sion* jumps into hyperspace, its energy causes Baysee's and Mowaat's ships to crash into each other and explode.

LIEUTENANT MOWAAT
SPECIES Rodian
AFFILIATION New Republic

New Republic pilot Lieutenant Mowaat accompanies Captain Carson Teva and three other X-wings to Seatos, supporting Hera Syndulla's unauthorized mission. When they approach the *Eye of Sion*, the ship launches into hyperspace with a shock wave that causes Mowaat's ship to crash into another X-wing.

LIEUTENANT JENSU
SPECIES Human
AFFILIATION New Republic

Lieutenant Jensu flies with Captain Carson Teva's squadron to Seatos, providing support for General Hera Syndulla's unauthorized mission. She survives the blast from the *Eye of Sion*'s departure and then helps Hera sweep Seatos' ocean to locate the missing Ahsoka Tano. Jensu pulls her from the water.

LIEUTENANT LANDER
SPECIES Human
AFFILIATION New Republic

New Republic pilot Lieutenant Lander is one of the X-wing pilots escorting the *Ghost* in General Hera Syndulla's unauthorized mission to Seatos. They are not able to stop the *Eye of Sion* from leaving, but Lander does help rescue the missing Ahsoka Tano from the oceans of Seatos.

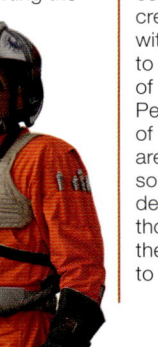

HOWLERS
HOMEWORLD Peridea **SIZE** 3.20 m (10 ft 6 in) long
HABITAT Grasslands, wastelands

Furry quadrupeds native to Peridea, howlers make devoted companions and mounts. Though they roam as wild creatures, the beasts can be domesticated by anyone with patience. Howlers are intelligent enough to respond to simple commands. For those without other means of transportation, howlers are ideal for navigating Peridea's expansive grasslands. Roving groups of bandits ride the beasts into battle. While they are not always the bravest of creatures, and sometimes startle at the unfamiliar, howlers do develop attachments to their riders, particularly those who display kindness toward them, and can act with aggression to defend them against threats.

CAPTAIN GIRARD
SPECIES Human
AFFILIATION New Republic

Captain Girard leads New Republic ships to stop Hera Syndulla's unauthorized mission, but Carson Teva intercepts her. He tries to stall, but Girard pushes until Teva shares the truth about Hera and Ahsoka Tano's plans. Girard is in disbelief until the purrgil fly toward her cruisers.

NOTI
HOMEWORLD Peridea
SIZE 90 cm (2 ft 11 in) high
HABITAT Grasslands

Noti are a diminutive species who have an easy time disguising themselves as rocks, thanks to their large shells. A group of Noti lives on Peridea and roams the desolate landscape in vehicles that emulate the Noti's form. A kind member of the group hides from Sabine Wren at first. Once she notices that the Noti wears a symbol of rebellion, he trusts her and leads her to the long-lost Ezra Bridger, who has made a home among the Noti.

GREAT MOTHERS
SPECIES Dathmirian
HOMEWORLD Peridea
AFFILIATION Witch Kingdom of Dathmir

Imposing and powerful in Dathmirian majik, the three Great Mothers are named Aktropaw, Klothow, and Lakesis *(left to right)*. They are Dathmirian witches whose home is Peridea—the ancient Witch Kingdom of the Dathmiri. Their origins remain clouded, but after Grand Admiral Thrawn's arrival on Peridea, the Great Mothers form a partnership with the Imperial officer. They call to Nightsisters in a different galaxy, trying to reach someone with loyalty to the sisterhood and the means and determination to find a method of travel across the stars. The Great Mothers know much of fate and see a way to fulfill their destiny and also Thrawn's at the same time. They offer Thrawn their wisdom and glimpses into possible futures, and they use their majik to fortify his army of night troopers. Grateful to be heard and found, the Great Mothers welcome Morgan Elsbeth as one of their own and grant her the gift of the Blade of Talzin. They trust Morgan to fight Ahsoka Tano to ensure they can leave Peridea and travel to Dathomir with Thrawn and their mysterious cargo.

CAPTAIN ENOCH
AFFILIATION Empire

Captain Enoch is Grand Admiral Thrawn's captain of the guard. As such, he stands apart from Thrawn's night troopers with a custom stormtrooper helmet that features two red Imperial symbols and a hammered golden face. Gold accents keep his worn armor from falling apart. Solemn and threatening, Enoch stays close to Thrawn and carries out his orders with precision. He informs Thrawn of a situation's every last detail so the leader can efficiently strategize. Enoch supervises the loading of Thrawn's precious mysterious cargo from the catacombs and onto the *Chimaera* for transport from the *Eye of Sion* to Dathomir.

NIGHT TROOPERS
SPECIES Human
HOMEWORLD Various
AFFILIATION Empire

Stormtroopers who are aboard the *Chimaera* when the starship makes its unexpected journey to another galaxy continue to follow Grand Admiral Thrawn on Peridea. With limited resources and no resupplies, the troopers must repair their armor and weaponry to keep them functional. Loyal to Thrawn, and infused with Nightsister majik thanks to Thrawn's alliance with the Great Mothers, the night troopers stand ready to execute any order. They stay sharp, even though they have limited enemies on Peridea. When Ahsoka Tano follows Morgan Elsbeth to the distant galaxy, they launch all their might against her and her allies.

THRAWN'S UNDEAD TROOPERS
SPECIES Human
HOMEWORLD Various
AFFILIATION Empire

The Great Mothers use their powerful majik in mysterious ways. As part of their partnership with Grand Admiral Thrawn, they use sinister means to reanimate night troopers after they die. The former stormtroopers come back to life more resilient and more tenacious, coming after enemies with singular focus. Some of these transformed night troopers take Sabine Wren and Ezra Bridger by surprise when they rise from the ground, ready to continue the fight. The undead troopers delay the pair as they try to stop Thrawn from escaping Peridea. Part of this contingent includes a pair of undead death troopers, proving much more challenging to eliminate.

PERIDEA BANDITS
SPECIES Various
HOMEWORLD Peridea

Peridea's sparse landscape encourages its citizens to adopt nomadic ways. Armed bandits roam the distant planet's hills in groups on howler mounts. The bandits wear makeshift armor over tattered clothing and helmets that conceal their faces. They largely keep to themselves but remain alert for any unsuspecting travelers passing through their territory. When they leap into action, they charge as a group, wielding long staffs. The bandits attack Sabine Wren as she searches for Ezra Bridger, but she escapes. They later work with Baylan Skoll and his apprentice Shin Hati to pursue the reunited Sabine and Ezra.

CHARACTERS AND CREATURES

VI MORADI
SPECIES Human
HOMEWORLD Chaaktil
AFFILIATION Resistance

Known to some as "Starling" or "Magpie," Vi Moradi is a Resistance spy who goes on many missions during the height of the war against the First Order. Among other tasks, she investigates Captain Phasma's origins and establishes a Resistance base on Batuu. When she is captured and brought aboard the *Absolution*, she is interrogated about Phasma's past by Captain Cardinal in exchange for her release. She later rescues Cardinal after his near-fatal duel with Phasma, and together they journey to Batuu in order to establish a new Resistance outpost.

CARDINAL
SPECIES Human **HOMEWORLD** Jakku
AFFILIATION First Order, Resistance

Cardinal, once known as "Archex," is raised as an orphan in a Jakku mining operation. Archex accompanies Brendol Hux into the Unknown Regions, where he is renamed "CD-0922" as a First Order stormtrooper. Highly skilled, he is appointed as Hux's personal guard, known as Cardinal, and given a personalized set of red armor. However, he is left to die after a duel with his rival, Captain Phasma. He is saved by escaping Resistance spy Vi Moradi, and he joins her on her mission to establish a new Resistance base on Batuu. There, he sacrifices himself to ensure the First Order leaves the planet.

SIV
SPECIES Human **HOMEWORLD** Parnassos
AFFILIATION Scyre tribe

Siv is a healer and religious leader of the rock-dwelling Scyre clan on Parnassos. She accompanies the First Order's Captain Phasma to help Brendol Hux after he crash-lands on the planet. Pregnant at the time of the mission, Siv gets radiation sickness and isn't taken along on the rescue ship, as she expected. Abandoned at the Calliope Station, Siv lives on the facility for around ten years with her child, Torbi. Nearly a decade later, Siv tells these adventures to Vi Moradi, who relays them to Cardinal. Moradi eventually returns and takes Siv and her child to Batuu.

HUE TICO
SPECIES Human **HOMEWORLD** Hays Minor
AFFILIATION Central Ridge Mining Company

Hue Tico enjoys a simple life on Hays Minor with his family until the First Order takes over mining on the planet. Hue and his wife, Thanya, pay to get their daughters—Rose and Paige—offworld. The First Order eventually tears Hays Minor apart, and Hue and Thanya perish with it.

THANYA TICO
SPECIES Human
HOMEWORLD Hays Minor
AFFILIATION Central Ridge Mining Company

Thanya Tico is the mother of Rose and Paige Tico. She and her husband, Hue, work for the Central Ridge Mining Company. Thanya flies an ore digger for the company and is loyal to both her work and her family. She encourages her children's creativity and, with Hue, builds a loving and nurturing family environment.

VOE
SPECIES Human **AFFILIATION** Jedi Order

Voe is a student at Luke Skywalker's Jedi Academy. She confronts Ben Solo after he burns down the academy, saying that she can't believe Ben could kill Luke. She attacks Ben but is thrown aside. She pursues Ben to the Minemoon of Mimban, where he kills her.

KARÉ KUN
SPECIES Human **HOMEWORLD** Sarq 22
AFFILIATION New Republic Starfleet, Resistance

Karé Kun trains in the New Republic Navy and then the New Republic Starfleet, becoming an elite pilot. As a member of Rapier Squadron, she flies her X-wing alongside her friend Poe Dameron and, after a skirmish with First Order TIE fighters, Kun and her teammates decide to join the Resistance. She is named captain of her own unit, Stiletto Squadron, and is then recruited by Dameron for Black Squadron. There, she engages in several missions and battles, including the recon assignment to scout Starkiller Base after the destruction of Hosnian Prime. Kun remains a Resistance pilot, though her husband Temmin "Snap" Wexley perishes during the Battle of Exegol.

OVANIS CRÈCHE ELDER
SPECIES Human **HOMEWORLD** Ovanis
AFFILIATION Crèche cult

The Crèche cult on Ovanis has an elder whose name is unknown. She meets Poe Dameron when he comes to Ovanis in search of explorer Lor San Tekka. The First Order tracks Dameron, however, and the Crèche works with Poe—and mysterious creatures—to fend off the invaders.

L'ULO L'AMPAR
SPECIES Duros **HOMEWORLD** Duro
AFFILIATION Rebel Alliance, New Republic Starfleet, Resistance

Selected for Starlight Squadron, L'ulo L'ampar and his teammates are tasked with tracking down scattered cells of the Rebel Alliance following the Battle of Hoth. During this time, he also helps to rescue his squad captain, Shara Bey, from the Star Destroyer *Tarkin's Will*. He later flies in the Battle of Endor as a member of Green Squadron and enlists in the Resistance as the First Order rises. Joining Poe Dameron's vaunted Black Squadron, L'ulo sacrifices himself in a battle with Agent Terex's forces, doing all he can to save defenseless escape pods from being picked off before his A-wing is shot down.

ODDY MUVA
SPECIES Abednedo **AFFILIATION** Resistance, Black Squadron

Oddy Muva is a Resistance flight technician with dreams of being a pilot. But Oddy becomes compromised when Lord Terex captures Muva's wife, Sowa Chuan, and uses her as leverage to force him into spying on the Resistance. Muva eventually rescues his wife but is shortly found by Terex. Taken aboard the light cruiser *Enshado*, Oddy escapes in a TIE fighter, finally getting his chance to fly. He proves to be a talented pilot, blasting TIEs and giving Black Squadron time to get away. His ship damaged, Oddy bids goodbye to his friends and flies into the light cruiser hangar, taking the huge First Order starship with him.

TEREX
SPECIES Human
AFFILIATION Empire, Ranc Gang, First Order

Ambitious and vengeful, Terex serves the Empire as a stormtrooper, forms his own crime syndicate called the Ranc Gang, and finally joins the First Order Security Bureau, where he tracks and eliminates specific threats. Terex becomes particularly fixated on Poe Dameron, making it a personal mission to destroy the Resistance pilot and his Black Squadron. Terex blackmails Resistance technician Oddy Muva into becoming a First Order spy, with the Abednedo placing tracking devices on Black Squadron fighters. However, time and again, Terex fails to capture Dameron, and his unorthodox methods cause him to clash with the First Order leadership, including Captain Phasma. He eventually receives cybernetic implants meant to keep him loyal to the First Order, but they cause Terex to grow disenchanted with the organization. After negating his cybernetic programming, he kidnaps the explorer Lor San Tekka, long sought by both the First Order and the Resistance, in order to win his freedom. In the end, he lets San Tekka go and does the same with his hatred for Dameron, leaving the First Order behind.

SURALINDA JAVOS
SPECIES Squamatan **AFFILIATION** New Republic Navy, *Galaxy Beacon*, Resistance

A friend of Poe Dameron in the New Republic Navy, Suralinda Javos leaves the military behind for civilian life, becoming a reporter for the *Galaxy Beacon* holonet channel. She hopes to scoop the location of the Resistance base but instead signs up. Ever the reporter, she attempts to document the First Order's atrocities on her many missions. Graduating to Black Squadron, Javos flies her A-wing in an effort to aid the Pastorian king. Following the Battle of Crait, Suralinda fights First Order sympathizers in Grail City on Ikkrukk, surviving a blaster wound to win the day and later flies with the Resistance during the Battle of Exegol.

N1-ZX
MANUFACTURER Baktoid Combat Automata
MODEL BX
TYPE Commando droid

N1-ZX serves the Resistance. He refuses to fight because of his self-preservation programming, but Poe Dameron finds a workaround. Dameron installs a droid personality template, which changes N1-ZX into the violent Mister Bones. The droid then gleefully kills Terex' goons before the First Order agent blasts him down.

MALARUS
SPECIES Human **AFFILIATION** First Order

After several humiliations at the hands of Black Squadron, Commander Malarus is determined to kill Poe Dameron. In their final battle, she steals his X-wing, and the two engage in a dogfight on Cato Neimoidia. Poe outsmarts Malarus, who crash-lands and is quickly arrested.

O-MR1
MANUFACTURER Arakyd Industries **MODEL** RA-7
TYPE Protocol droid

First Order protocol droid O-MR1 is a prisoner aboard a Resistance ship that unexpectedly crash-lands on Taul. The only surviving passengers are droids. Led by C-3PO, they take O-MR1 and trek across the harsh landscape. As they travel, O-MR1 and C-3PO slowly develop a friendship. The journey is dangerous, and only C-3PO and O-MR1 remain as acid rain begins to fall. Knowing that both can't survive, O-MR1 transfers vital data to C-3PO and alters his frequency to call for the Resistance. The acid rain washes away O-MR1's black paint, and he disintegrates with only a red arm remaining. C-3PO, mourning his friend, adopts the appendage in tribute to O-MR1.

KARR NUQ SIN
SPECIES Human **HOMEWORLD** Merokia
AFFILIATION The Force

Karr Nuq Sin is a Force-attuned young adult who begins having headaches and distorted visions whenever he touches certain objects. While his parents think it is a serious ailment, his grandmother believes this is a sign that he is to be a Jedi, like her father. After his grandmother's death, Karr Nuq Sin embarks on a journey across the galaxy to find Jedi artifacts. On the planet Pam'ba, he meets his great-grandfather, who then dies in peace knowing that his family is safe and the Empire has fallen. Karr Nuq Sin becomes a "Force collector" and continues to gather artifacts while sharing stories of the Jedi.

SOWA CHUAN
SPECIES Abednedo

The wife of Resistance mechanic Oddy Muva, Sowa Chuan is kidnapped and taken hostage by Agent Terex of the First Order. He uses Sowa to blackmail her husband into spying on Black Squadron. Oddy manages to find Sowa on the *Carrion Spike*, and the two get away, along with other enslaved people, in escape pods.

J-SQUADRON
SPECIES Various **HOMEWORLD** Various
AFFILIATION Resistance Starfighter Corps

J-Squadron, affectionately referred to as "J-Squad," is a team of young cadets in the Resistance's Starfighter Corps, under Jothan Tiaan Jerjerrod. The aspiring pilots train in the Yard on D'Qar, until they are disbanded as punishment and assigned to a scavenging mission to Vodran, where they are imprisoned. After their eventual escape, they end up embroiled in the Resistance assault on Starkiller Base.

POE DAMERON

SPECIES Human **HOMEWORLD** Yavin 4
AFFILIATION Spice Runners of Kijimi, New Republic, Rapier Squadron, Resistance, Black Squadron

Poe Dameron thinks of himself as the best pilot in the galaxy, and he might be right. General Leia Organa sees even more than that, though—a future leader of the Resistance—if he can get his head out of his cockpit.

REBELLIOUS YOUTH
Poe is the son of rebel officers Sergeant Kes Dameron and Lieutenant Shara Bey. Raised on Yavin 4 during the peace of the New Republic, Poe grows up listening to stories of Rebel Alliance heroes Luke Skywalker, Princess Leia, and Han Solo. Shara, a veteran A-wing pilot, dies when Poe is just a boy; his overprotective father Kes struggles with her loss. At the age of 16, Poe impulsively takes a job flying with Zorii Bliss and the Spice Runners of Kijimi to escape the confines of Yavin 4. He gets way more adventure than he bargained for. Poe stands up to the Spice Runners when their ruthless methods go too far, displaying his strong sense of justice, but it costs him his friendship with Zorii.

BLACK SQUADRON
Like his mother, Poe becomes a hotshot pilot. He flies as commander of the New Republic's Rapier Squadron. But Poe grows frustrated with the New Republic's inaction against the growing threat of the First Order, so he joins General Leia Organa's Resistance. Flying now as Black Leader, Poe is tasked with locating Lor San Tekka and finding the map to Luke Skywalker. Poe also meets an eager pilot named Kazuda Xiono (Kaz) and recruits him to uncover the First Order's activities on the *Colossus* refueling station on the planet Castilon. Poe introduces Kaz to his friend, Jarek Yeager, and leaves his droid, BB-8, to help him. Later, Poe retrieves BB-8 and goes on to visit Lor San Tekka.

JAKKU TO STARKILLER
On Jakku, Lor San Tekka gives Poe part of a map that leads to Luke Skywalker's whereabouts. As they speak, the First Order arrives. Knowing his capture is imminent, Poe gives the map to BB-8 and tells him to flee. Poe is imprisoned in Kylo Ren's *Resurgent*-class Star Destroyer, the *Finalizer*. Luckily, a stormtrooper named FN-2187 (Finn) wants to desert the First Order and needs a pilot. Together, they steal a Special Forces TIE fighter and crash-land on Jakku. Poe wakes up alone and makes his way back to D'Qar. Later, he is reunited with BB-8 and Finn. Poe leads a squadron of Resistance X-wings in a strike against the First Order's Starkiller Base. He targets the facility's thermal oscillator, causing a chain reaction that destroys the entire planet.

RECKLESS FLYBOY
After the battle, the First Order arrives above D'Qar to retaliate. Poe comes up with a plan to distract them so the Resistance can evacuate. He destroys all the surface weapons on the First Order's Dreadnought, *Fulminatrix*, hoping to provide an opportunity for Cobalt Squadron to attack it. Though successful, all Resistance bombers are destroyed in the process. General Organa demotes Poe for disobeying her orders to fall back and for causing heavy and needless losses. When the Resistance discover that the First Order is tracking them through hyperspace, Poe, Finn, and companion Rose Tico hatch a plan to sneak aboard the First Order flagship *Supremacy* and disable the tracker. As part of the mission, Poe sends Finn, Rose, and BB-8 to Canto Bight, on the advice of Maz Kanata, to find the Master Codebreaker. Meanwhile, Leia is injured in a fighter attack orchestrated by Kylo Ren, and Vice Admiral Holdo takes command. Holdo refuses to tell Poe her plans and Poe suspects she is not working in their best interests. He leads a mutiny against her, and is surprised when Leia wakes from a coma and stuns him with a blaster for insubordination.

SENSIBLE LEADER
Poe wakes up in an escape shuttle with Leia and learns that Holdo had constructed a plan with Leia's blessing. They are now on their way to an abandoned rebel base on Crait. There, Poe is reunited with BB-8, Finn, and Rose. When the First Order arrives, Poe leads the charge from his V-4X-D ski speeder against their superlaser siege cannon. Having learned his lesson over D'Qar however, Poe realizes they cannot win, and orders the Resistance pilots to turn back rather than risk sacrificing everyone again. When the Resistance appears trapped and all seems lost, Poe follows some native vulptex creatures and leads the Resistance survivors out of the cave through a hidden tunnel where they meet Rey and the *Millennium Falcon*, escaping the First Order.

Poe and Finn
Ever since their first meeting aboard the *Finalizer*, Poe and Finn have come to rely upon each other and function well as a team.

GENERAL DAMERON
After the new Resistance base on Ajan Kloss is established, Poe flies the *Millennium Falcon* on a reconnaissance mission. He risks lightspeed skipping, a dangerous piloting skill he learned with the Spice Runners of Kijimi, to escape the First Order. He then joins Rey—along with Finn, C-3PO, and Chewbacca—as she searches for Exegol. To access the clue to the wayfinder that's locked in C-3PO's memory, Poe takes his friends to the droidsmith Babu Frik on Kijimi. Poe reunites with Zorii, who still holds a grudge, but the programming bypass is a success. When Poe returns to the Resistance base, he and the others learn of General Organa's passing. Her last orders promote him to acting general, a position he decides to share with Finn, and together they strategize their next moves. Poe climbs back into the cockpit of an X-wing to lead the Resistance fleet when they take the fight to the Final Order at Exegol.

Cockpit hero
At first, Poe aggravates his superiors with his arrogant attitude and reckless battle tactics. However, his willingness to take risks and try out new ideas is what makes him one of the top Resistance pilots. By practicing a little restraint, Poe reveals his capacity for leadership.

Black One
Poe's unique T-70 X-wing starfighter, *Black One*, has black-and-orange livery.

BB-8

MANUFACTURER Industrial Automaton
TYPE BB-series astromech droid
AFFILIATION New Republic, Rapier Squadron, Resistance, Black Squadron, Team *Fireball*

Loyal, brave, and persistent, BB-8 is a selfless and dependable droid who always aims to please. He is loyal to his master, and to whomever his master lends him.

EARLY SERVICE
Belonging to ace pilot Poe Dameron, BB-8 is an astromech droid specializing in navigation, ship repairs, and systems support for starfighter pilots. Both serve in the New Republic's Rapier Squadron, until they are recruited to the Resistance by its leader—General Leia Organa. Poe, with BB-8 beside him, founds Black Squadron, and Leia charges the team with locating explorer Lor San Tekka. Once they find him and ask for his assistance in their search for Luke Skywalker, Poe lends BB-8 to his new spy recruit, Kazuda Xiono (Kaz). Dameron tasks the pair with investigating First Order activity on the *Colossus* refueling station on the planet Castilon. When San Tekka informs the Resistance that he has the map, Poe retrieves BB-8 from Kaz to recover the intel on Jakku.

LOST ON JAKKU
In Jakku's Tuanul village, BB-8 and Poe meet with Lor San Tekka and acquire the map. When the First Order arrives, BB-8 and Poe try to escape in Poe's X-wing but to no avail. Poe gives BB-8 the map and tells him to flee, promising to find him later, before being captured by Kylo Ren. Left to fend for himself, BB-8 wanders through the desert, and is snared by the scavenger Teedo. BB-8 is rescued by a kinder scavenger, Rey, who begrudgingly allows him to stay with her. At Niima Outpost, some thugs try to steal BB-8, but Rey fights them off. After the melee, BB-8 spots Finn wearing Poe's jacket, and following a brief tussle, all three find themselves being chased by stormtroopers and TIE fighters. They make their escape aboard an abandoned *Millennium Falcon*.

***Colossus* cover**
Kaz and BB-8 join Poe's friend Jarek Yeager's maintenance crew—Team *Fireball*.

Resourceful droid
BB-8 is an innovative and intelligent droid who does his utmost to help his allies complete their missions. He has six tool-bay disks that can easily be swapped out for others carrying different tools.

"The droid... stole a freighter?"
KYLO REN TO LIEUTENANT MITAKA

Lone scavenger
Rey lives on her own on Jakku. It is with reluctance that she allows BB-8 to stay.

DELIVERING THE MAP
Out in space, the *Falcon* is intercepted by Han Solo. After a scuffle with rathtars and criminal gangs, BB-8 shows Han the map to Luke Skywalker. Han refuses to travel to his estranged wife Leia, but takes BB-8, Rey, and Finn to Maz Kanata on Takodana. However, chaos erupts when the First Order arrives. Fortunately, the Resistance turns up and fights the First Order, but Kylo Ren kidnaps Rey. After the battle ends, BB-8 travels to D'Qar with the others and is finally reunited with Poe. While the Resistance realizes that BB-8's map is incomplete, the group has to focus on the First Order—who is preparing to use Starkiller Base to destroy D'Qar. In *Black One*, BB-8 and Poe join the assault on the superweapon. Thanks to the ground team, they can deliver the critical shot that destroys the base. Afterward, they return to D'Qar, R2-D2 powers up just in time to help BB-8 piece together the map to Luke.

FLIGHT OF THE RESISTANCE
When the First Order attacks the D'Qar base, the Resistance is forced to evacuate. BB-8 goes to extraordinary lengths to keep Poe's ship functioning during the battle. They rejoin the Resistance aboard the *Raddus*, but it is attacked by Kylo Ren, and BB-8 is nearly blown apart. It comes to light that the First Order is tracking the Resistance through hyperspace, so BB-8, Finn, and Rose Tico head to Canto Bight in search of the "Master Codebreaker" to help disable the First Order's tracking system. Unfortunately, Finn and Rose are arrested at the casino; instead of rescuing them, BB-8 finds himself with criminal slicer DJ. They steal a ship and rescue Finn and Rose. All four sneak aboard the First Order's flagship *Supremacy*, but DJ betrays them and they are captured. BB-8 saves Finn and Rose by hijacking an AT-ST. They escape to Crait, where BB-8 is reunited again with Poe. Poe and BB-8 finally get to safety on board the *Millennium Falcon* with the remaining members of the Resistance.

Two droids are better than one
R2-D2 has been storing a piece of the map for years. When he powers up, he is able to complete BB-8's map.

FORTITUDE
BB-8 supports Rey during her Force training on Ajan Kloss, the site of the new Resistance base. The resolute astromech also joins her on her journey in search of Exegol, alongside Finn, Poe, C-3PO, and Chewbacca. They encounter the diminutive D-O while on the hunt for a Sith wayfinder, and BB-8 adopts the role of the small droid's mentor. When it's time for the Resistance to take the fight to Exegol, BB-8 is vital to their success, helping the ground forces take out a key navigational array on the hull of the Star Destroyer *Steadfast*. BB-8 escapes the *Steadfast* with the other Resistance ground forces while Finn and Jannah, another former First Order stormtrooper, target the ship's bridge. The droid and his friends in the Resistance emerge victorious. BB-8 later accompanies Rey to Tatooine where she buries the Skywalker and Leia's lightsabers near the Lars homestead.

Canto Bight
BB-8 is not used to the strange luxuries and creatures of the Canto Casino.

R2-C4

MANUFACTURER Industrial Automaton
TYPE Astromech
AFFILIATION New Republic, Resistance

R2-C4 flies with Kazuda Xiono in his T-85 X-wing when Kaz faces off against the First Order's Major Elrik Vonreg. R2-C4 is left with the Resistance when Kaz is recruited as a spy on the *Colossus*.

MAJOR VONREG

SPECIES Human **AFFILIATION** First Order

Major Elrik Vonreg is distinguished by his red TIE fighter pilot armor and matching red First Order TIE interceptor. Vonreg is a renowned fighter pilot who is not afraid to take on an entire squadron of New Republic X-wings. When he encounters the likes of Poe Dameron and Kazuda Xiono, however, he is forced to retreat, allowing the Resistance to learn of the First Order's interest in Castilon. Meanwhile, Vonreg and Commander Pyre persuade Captain Phasma to use the pirate Kragan Gorr and his gang to harass the *Colossus* station. Vonreg later visits the supertanker, accompanying a shipment of fuel. He meets with Captain Doza, and tries to convince the station administrator that the *Colossus* needs the First Order to protect it. As their meeting concludes, Vonreg discovers that they are being spied upon by Kaz. Responding to a First Order probe droid's call for reinforcements in the Dassal system, Vonreg faces Poe and Kaz from his ship once more, but flees when they destroy his escorts. When the *Colossus*' pilots fight back against the First Order's occupation, Vonreg joins the air battle. He nearly annihilates Jarek Yeager, but Kaz shoots him down before he can land the final shot.

Vonreg to the rescue
When the First Order pays the Warbirds to kidnap Torra Doza, Major Vonreg travels to their ship. Vonreg then turns on them, "rescuing" Torra in order to return her to her father, Imanuel, and win his favor.

KAZUDA XIONO

SPECIES Human **HOMEWORLD** Hosnian Prime
AFFILIATION New Republic, Resistance, Team *Fireball*

Kazuda "Kaz" Xiono is the young and excitable son of New Republic senator Hamato Xiono. Kaz's father uses his influence to get his son enrolled in the New Republic Military Academy and then commissioned as a starfighter pilot. When the New Republic uncovers information about the First Order's interest in the planet Castilon, Kaz and two other pilots are sent to rendezvous with Poe Dameron of the Resistance and pass on this intelligence. However, they are intercepted by Major Elrik Vonreg flying a red TIE interceptor. Kaz orders his wingmates to retreat, intending to take on the First Order pilot himself. Fortunately for Kaz, Poe Dameron arrives and helps Kaz force Vonreg to flee back to the First Order.

Poe Dameron offers Kaz a place in the Resistance as a spy, stationing him on Castilon's *Colossus* refueling platform to uncover the First Order's interest in the station. Poe introduces Kaz to Jarek Yeager, an old friend and the owner of a starship repair shop. Yeager grudgingly hires Kaz as a mechanic, despite his lack of skills, to provide cover for Kaz's mission. Xiono works with mechanics Neeku Vozo and Tamara Ryvora. Neeku takes Kaz's dreams of becoming the best pilot in the galaxy literally, gossiping with the platform residents and getting him enrolled in a race. Kaz reluctantly accepts the challenge, but, flying Yeager's *Fireball*, crashes at the end of the race.

Owing to this incident, and the fact that Kaz is little help in the garage, Tam is initially frustrated with Xiono. However, in time, they become friends. Kaz finally gets a lead on the First Order when Hype Fazon invites him and Tam to Doza Tower. Kaz spies on a meeting between Vonreg and the station administrator, Imanuel Doza, and learns that the First Order is offering to protect the station and provide fuel in exchange for use of the platform. Kaz then helps two children from Tehar, who are hiding on the *Colossus*, to escape the First Order.

Later, Poe and Kaz rescue Synara San, the survivor of a freighter overrun with Kowakian monkey-lizards primates, and bring her back to the platform. San is secretly a pirate spy who facilitates further raids on the station. Meanwhile, Kaz makes friends with the captain's daughter, Torra Doza, who unwittingly helps Kaz spy on her father.

As the pirate attacks on *Colossus* increase, Captain Doza is forced to make a deal with the First Order to protect the platform, but the group's presence quickly turns into a hostile occupation led by Commander Pyre. Kaz realizes that Synara is a pirate spy, but still helps her flee.

After Kaz and Poe return from a mission to the Dassal system, Poe leaves the *Colossus* with BB-8, and CB-23 remains with Kaz. As the First Order locks down the platform, Xiono and Yeager barely escape capture, and in the process alienate Tam—whom they have excluded from their Resistance activities. Kaz, Yeager, and Neeku launch a plan to submerge the *Colossus* so they can swim up to the First Order's communication jammer on Doza Tower and disable it in order to contact General Leia Organa. Even though Yeager is captured, they are successful. Unfortunately, Kaz is informed that Resistance cannot send help. Xiono then decides to form his own resistance cell on the platform. The group realizes that the station is actually a ship with a Class 2 hyperdrive. While sneaking inside Doza Tower to free Yeager, Kaz and Torra witness a transmission of the destruction of Hosnian Prime by Starkiller Base. Kaz is horrified by the realization that he has lost his home and becomes even more determined to fight back. Pyre realizes that he is losing control, so he evacuates the station with his ground troops and Tam just as the *Colossus* rises out of the water.

The Ace Squadron, Yeager, and Xiono rush to their ships and battle the First Order starfighters. Synara also arrives with the pirates to aid the *Colossus*. When a First Order Star Destroyer appears and begins bombarding the *Colossus*, Kaz orders everyone to return to the station. With Vonreg on Yeager's tail, Kaz saves his mentor by blowing up his nemesis. Xiono and Yeager return to the platform, which jumps into hyperspace. They believe they are on their way to meet the Resistance on D'Qar—but Neeku informs him their destination is uncertain.

In fact, the *Colossus* exits hyperspace too far from D'Qar to join the Resistance before it evacuates. Under Doza and Yeager's leadership, Kaz works with the rest of the *Colossus* residents to ensure their survival as they continue to be hunted down by the First Order. Ever willing to help, Xiono goes on many supply runs including to Celsor 3, Drahgor III, Ashas Ree, and Vranki's Hotel and Casino.

After successfully navigating through space owned by the dangerous Guavian death gang, Kaz and Neeku undertake a risky infiltration of the First Order's *Titan* refueling station to steal a vital component. Their former friend Tam, who is now a First Order pilot, helps the pair—without them realizing—to ensure her former home remains operational.

Kaz then faces a bounty hunter on Varkana and helps stop a mutiny led by Gorr. Soon after, the residents of the *Colossus* believe they have found a new home on Aeos Prime. Wanting to return to the Resistance, Xiono leaves the *Colossus*, but a First Order probe droid attacks his ship in the planet's orbit, so he heads back to his friends to warn them. Kaz decides he is needed more on the *Colossus*. Soon after, the platform officially joins the Resistance when Imanuel Doza decides to take a stand and agrees to house Jade Squadron, a Resistance team led by his wife Venisa Doza.

When Tam witnesses the First Order killing the Aeosians, she decides to defect and contacts her former allies for aid. With Yeager and CB-23, Kaz boards the Star Destroyer *Thunderer* to rescue her. He sends a transmission to the *Colossus* telling the supertanker to flee the First Order, but his words have the opposite result, inspiring the *Colossus* residents to battle. The trio escapes the First Order and returns to the *Colossus*. Later, Kaz is one of many pilots who answer Lando Calrissian's call for help at the Battle of Exegol.

JAREK YEAGER

SPECIES Human
AFFILIATION Rebel Alliance, New Republic, Team *Fireball*

Gifted pilot Jarek Yeager flies for the Rebel Alliance and later the New Republic. After the Galactic Civil War, he competes in starfighter races alongside his brother, Marcus Speedstar. The two have a friendly, if reckless, racing rivalry—until tragedy strikes. Jarek's wife and child are killed when Marcus' ship spins out of control during a race. Jarek holds his brother responsible for the deaths and immediately ends their relationship.

Yeager retires to the *Colossus* supertanker with his droid, R1-J5, and opens a garage. Although Jarek gives up racing, his team of mechanics—Neeku Vozo and Tamara Ryvora—work on an old ship, the *Fireball*, hoping to compete in races at the station. When his old friend Poe Dameron asks him to provide cover for a Resistance spy, Kazuda Xiono, Jarek reluctantly hires the young man as part of his team. Yeager allows Kaz to fly the *Fireball* in a race, making Tam unhappy because Yeager had promised the ship to her. In other respects, Jarek initially holds Kaz at a distance, telling him that he has no interest in his mission: spying on the First Order. However, they become closer and rely on each other.

Yeager's brother Marcus, now a famous racer, arrives at the station to compete in the Platform Classic. To generate more hype and money from the race, Captain Doza, the station's administrator, pressures Jarek to face off against Marcus. After some persuasion, Jarek accepts and flies against him. During the race, Marcus apologizes once again. Jarek lets Marcus win so his brother can use the prize money to rescue his teammate, Oplock, from the Guavian Death Gang. Although Jarek is not ready to forgive his brother entirely, at least the two of them part on better terms.

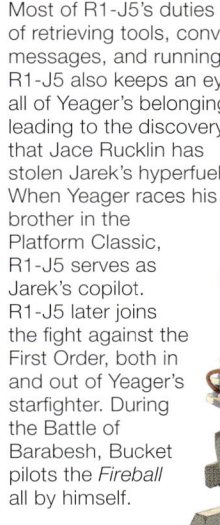

During the First Order occupation of the *Colossus*, Yeager takes a more active role in Kaz's Resistance work, helping to repel the First Order and ensuring the station escapes into hyperspace. However, he is upset when Tam, feeling betrayed by the team, decides to join the First Order.

As the *Colossus* is on the run, Doza relies upon Yeager to take a more active role as a leader. Jarek is tasked with turning the platform's elite racing pilots into an efficient starfighter unit, and becomes the leader of Ace Squadron. He clashes with some of the bigger personalities, but they soon all find common ground during a training exercise on Celsor 3.

Yeager also volunteers alongside Kaz to respond to a distress call from a Resistance agent, who is heading to Varkana with Synara San and CB-23. The group falls into a trap set by a bounty hunter, and Yeager, Synara, and CB-23 are captured by the First Order. While interrogated by Agent Tierny, Yeager refuses to give in. He is relieved to be rescued by Kaz and the Resistance agent, Norath Kev.

Back on the *Colossus*, Jarek remains steadfast in defending his home, fighting during the mutiny. After docking on Aeos Prime, Yeager is proud when Kaz decides to leave the *Colossus* and gifts him the *Fireball*. However, he is happy to see Kaz return to help when the First Order discovers them and attacks.

When a message from Tam suggests she wants to defect, Jarek, Kaz, and CB-23 launch a mission to rescue her. They end up aboard a First Order Star Destroyer and eventually escape, thanks to the residents of the *Colossus* joining the fight. With Kaz and Torra Doza, Yeager joins the climactic Battle of Exegol when General Calrissian calls for aid.

R1-J5

MANUFACTURER Industrial Automaton **TYPE** Astromech
AFFILIATION Team *Fireball*

R1-J5, or Bucket, is Jarek Yeager's antique astromech. Long ago, his outer shell rusted away, leaving a skeletal frame that exposes all of his essential components. R1-J5 is an obsolete model, and his programming has acquired a few glitches over the decades. The droid serves as Yeager's racing copilot and later as part of Jarek's *Fireball* team of racers and mechanics. Bucket doesn't immediately take a liking to newcomer Kazuda Xiono. Though he softens in time, R1-J5 remains concerned when Kaz is near Yeager's starfighter.

Most of R1-J5's duties consist of retrieving tools, conveying messages, and running errands. R1-J5 also keeps an eye on all of Yeager's belongings, leading to the discovery that Jace Rucklin has stolen Jarek's hyperfuel. When Yeager races his brother in the Platform Classic, R1-J5 serves as Jarek's copilot. R1-J5 later joins the fight against the First Order, both in and out of Yeager's starfighter. During the Battle of Barabesh, Bucket pilots the *Fireball* all by himself.

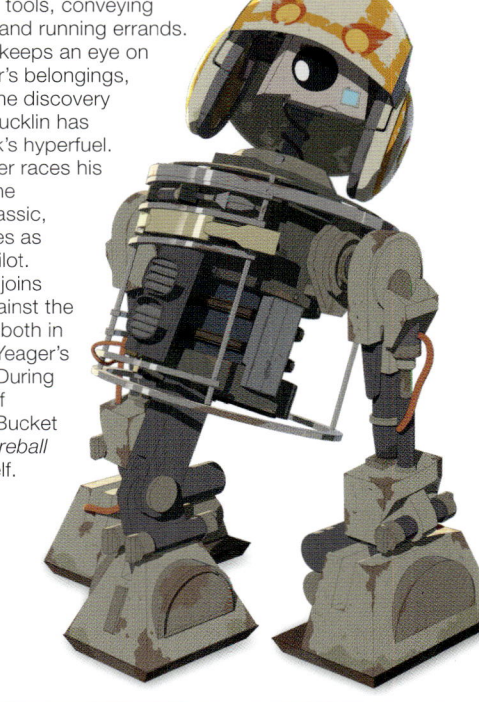

NEEKU VOZO

SPECIES Nikto **HOMEWORLD** Kintan
AFFILIATION Team *Fireball*

Cheery and optimistic, Neeku Vozo is born on Kintan to a family of bantha herders. When he is older, Neeku becomes one of Jarek Yeager's *Fireball* mechanics and is always willing to see the best in others. Neeku is also incredibly logical and smart, and these traits make him a skilled mechanic. He soon becomes acquainted with Resistance spy Kazuda Xiono when he arrives at the *Colossus*. At first, Neeku unintentionally makes things difficult for Kaz by telling everyone Xiono is the greatest pilot in the galaxy. He also gets Kaz entered into the station's next starfighter race.

When Kaz is searching for Kel and Eila, two fugitive children from Tehar, Neeku introduces Kaz to his friends, the Chelidae, engineers on the *Colossus* whom he believes can help. Neeku helps Xiono communicate with them, and they then assist with finding the children. When Neeku and Kaz discover the youngsters are hiding from the First Order, Neeku coordinates a plan with the Chelidae to fake Kel and Eila's deaths to keep them safe.

When Marcus Speedstar arrives at the station to race in the Platform Classic, he brings his friend, a Mountain Nikto named Oplock. Neeku and Oplock hit it off right away, even though Kaz and Tamara Ryvora find Oplock's way of communicating a bit off-putting. Later, Neeku adopts a strange sea creature from the oceans of Castilon that he names Bibo. After its gigantic mother starts attacking the *Colossus*, Vozo returns it to her.

Neeku is at first uninterested in direct confrontation with the First Order, but Commander Pyre's occupation of the *Colossus* changes everything. And after Pyre's attempt to arrest Team *Fireball*, they all must go into hiding. Once the group realizes that no help will come, Neeku joins Kaz's local resistance cell and helps to activate the station's hyperdrive so they can escape the First Order.

In spite of the turbulent times in the galaxy, Neeku is still optimistic, befriending fellow mechanic Nena Nalor, who is actually a spy for the First Order. Nalor sabotages the station, but gives Neeku a clue to her method. Setting his personal feelings aside, Vozo fixes the sabotage before the station is destroyed. He also joins missions when needed, accompanying Kaz on trips to Vranki's Hotel and Casino and the *Titan* refueling station.

Correctly assuming the pirates aboard the *Colossus* will be an issue, Yeager and Doza ask Neeku to spy on the group. When Vozo sees that the pirates are smuggling battle droids aboard the station, he is suspicious and reprograms one of the B1s to order the other droids around. Without Neeku's wise and prudent plan, the *Colossus* may have fallen to the mutiny.

Soon after, Vozo recognizes when Tam uses a code he devised to contact the *Colossus*, asking for a rendezvous. Neeku remains on the platform while Yeager and Kaz take a shuttle to rescue her. The trio ends up trapped aboard the First Order's *Thunderer*, but manages to get a message to Vozo that spurs the *Colossus* residents into helping their friends. During the ensuing Battle of Barabesh, Neeku fears they are doomed. However, he is glad to be proven wrong and to be reunited with Tam.

198   CHARACTERS AND CREATURES

OPEEPIT
SPECIES Frigosian
HOMEWORLD Castilon
AFFILIATION Team *Colossus*

Dedicated to his job, Opeepit takes pride in his role as janitor on the *Colossus*. The Frigosian can often be seen wearing his signature goggles as he works to keep the *Colossus* clean. Opeepit's tool of choice is a floor sweeper, and he becomes angry when First Order occupiers confiscate his favorite device. He is relieved when it is returned to him.

AL
SPECIES Human
HOMEWORLD Castilon
AFFILIATION Team *Colossus*

Aunt Z's Tavern has its share of loyal customers, but Al—also known as Big Al—is a near-constant presence at the watering hole. With a bushy mustache and goggles atop his head, Al perches himself at the bar and enjoys the view, taking in everything from brawls to underwater chases with SCUBA troopers.

TAMARA "TAM" RYVORA
SPECIES Human   **HOMEWORLD** Kuat   **AFFILIATION** Team *Fireball*, First Order, Team *Colossus*

Tamara "Tam" Ryvora is the daughter of a famous racer on Kuat. She leaves her homeworld to become a racer herself. Tam arrives at *Colossus* station, where she becomes friends with Hype Fazon; however, the two grow apart when Hype earns a place in Ace Squadron. Tam loses her own ship in a race after borrowing against the craft's full value in order to make vital repairs. To make a living, she then becomes a member of Jarek Yeager's mechanics team. Tam sees repairing the team's *Fireball* ship and making it fit to race again as a second chance at realizing her own dreams.

When Kazuda Xiono arrives and Yeager makes him part of the team, Tam is irritated by his obvious lack of mechanical skills and poor attitude to hard work. She takes his criticism of the *Fireball* personally, and is further annoyed when he flies the ship in a race and crashes it, so that it needs further repair work. Nonetheless, she and Kaz slowly become friends.

Tam meets Hype Fazon once again when he invites her and Kaz up to Doza Tower, where he now lives. Kaz, working secretly as a Resistance spy, is only too eager to accept the invitation, hoping to gather useful intelligence. While in the Aces lounge, Tam and Hype get into a bitter argument when he pours scorn on the *Fireball*. Infuriated, Tam storms off—it seems that their friendship will not easily be rekindled.

Tam soon befriends Synara San, completely unaware that this newcomer to the station is a pirate spy working for Kragan Gorr. When Gorr's gang attacks *Colossus* once again—this time with the aid of Synara's transmissions—Tam risks her own life rushing to help Synara amid the chaos. Although Tam's concern is actually misplaced, this generosity of spirit makes a strong impression on Synara, who will eventually abandon the pirates.

During the First Order occupation, her colleagues escape capture, but Tam isn't so lucky. She is interrogated by Agent Tierny of the First Order Security Bureau, and is upset to learn of Kaz's secret affiliation to the Resistance. Before the First Order is forced to evacuate the *Colossus*, Tierny offers Tam a place with the First Order—and Tam reluctantly accepts.

Now aboard the First Order Star Destroyer *Thunderer*, Tam wants to put her piloting skills to use supporting a cause she believes in and enlists as a TIE fighter cadet, DT-533. She also agrees to help the First Order locate her former home and hands over intel, earning her commendation from Tierny.

However, Tam's compassionate nature soon starts to clash with the First Order's brutality. As she begins TIE fighter training, she is criticized for her attempt to save fellow new recruit Jace Rucklin when his TIE becomes disabled. During a visit to the *Titan* refueling platform, Tam sees Kaz and Neeku infiltrating the base and secretly helps them.

When the First Order locates the *Colossus* on Aeos Prime, Tam is ordered to join the attack in her TIE fighter. She locks onto Kaz's ship but cannot bring herself to fire. However, she does stop his missile from destroying the *Thunderer*'s bridge and is promoted to Second Squadron Commander.

Tam's last straw is the First Order's reprisal on the Aeosians for helping the *Colossus*, so she sends a message to rendezvous with her old allies and defect. Instrumental in the ensuing Battle of Barabesh, Tam successfully escapes and is relieved to be home aboard the *Colossus*.

4D-M1N
MANUFACTURER Accutronics
TYPE modified TDA-series droid assistant
AFFILIATION Team *Colossus*

4D-M1N serves as a nanny droid for Torra Doza, keeping an eye on her for her father, Imanuel Doza. 4D-M1N switches to sentry mode if an intruder is detected. When the First Order threatens Imanuel, she falls in battle trying to defend him. Once the *Colossus* escapes to hyperspace, 4D-M1N is repaired and serves with Imanuel on the bridge.

BO KEEVIL
SPECIES Kel Dor
HOMEWORLD Dorin
AFFILIATION Ace Squadron, Team *Colossus*

Bo Keevil is a member of the *Colossus* station's Ace Squadron who chooses his words carefully. Keevil is a confident aviator who flies a difficult craft to handle—the *Yellow Ace*. He is also a show-off with a mysterious past. His life-support mask is of a kind typically worn by his Dorin species when they travel offworld, since oxygen is toxic to them and their ocular membranes dry out quickly. Their thick, leathery skin allows them to survive the vacuum of space—which is a handy adaptation for a pilot like Keevil.

SC-X2
AFFILIATION Ace Squadron, Team *Colossus*

Bo Keevil's astromech is an unusual ball droid model that rolls on a track for better traction and direction control. Keevil's droid stays steadfastly by his side at all times. It carries a supply of emergency parts for Keevil's life-support mask inside its body, among other handy gadgets.

FREYA FENRIS

SPECIES Human
HOMEWORLD Yir Tangee
AFFILIATION Ace Squadron, Team *Colossus*

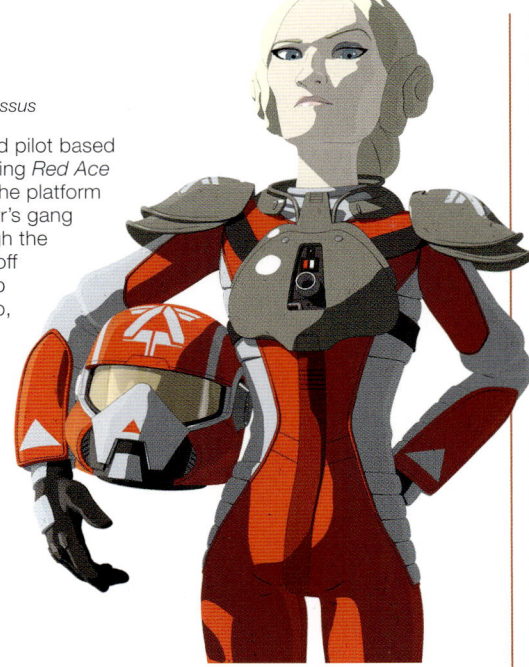

Freya Fenris is a serious and skilled pilot based on Castilon's *Colossus* station. Flying *Red Ace* with Ace Squadron, she defends the platform against pirate raids by Kragan Gorr's gang alongside her fellow Aces. Although the odds are against them, they fend off swarms of pirates, with secret help from Resistance spy Kazuda Xiono, who jams the pirates' comm signals. Like the other Aces, Freya competes in local races to pass the time—and in hopes of winning some extra credits. When the *Colossus* comes into direct conflict with the First Order, Freya bravely defends the platform on numerous occasions alongside the rest of Ace Squadron. She also joins a supply mission to Ashas Ree.

HYPE FAZON

SPECIES Rodian
HOMEWORLD Rodia
AFFILIATION Ace Squadron, Team *Colossus*

Hype Fazon is a racer who learns his craft at Vranki's Hotel and Casino. After leaving that establishment, Hype eventually ends up at the *Colossus*, where he flies the *Green Ace*, with the call sign "Ace One," and is the top racer in Ace Squadron. Hype has numerous sponsors, evidenced by their logos all over his ship. Despite his boastfulness, Hype has a strong moral core—for example, he refuses to take part in duties that aid the First Order. Hype used to be close friends with Tamara Ryvora, but the two have grown apart. When he hears her negative opinion of him, he tries to mend their friendship but fails. He does not take well to the First Order's occupation, being temporarily captured, and joins the fight against the group. Hype initially dislikes Imanuel Doza's reformation of the Ace Squadron, adding Kazuda Xiono to the group and Jarek Yeager as squadron leader. However, he comes to recognize Kaz and Yeager's value and becomes a skilled combat pilot who functions as part of the new team. Desperate to race again, Hype suggests the Ace Squadron heads to Vranki's racing circuit to earn credits for supplies for the *Colossus*. Vranki agrees to let Hype race but on the condition that Hype stays at the casino if he loses. Vranki manipulates the race, and it is only thanks to Neeku Vozo that Ace Squadron can escape with a large sum of credits.

T3-K10

MANUFACTURER Duwani Mechanical Products
TYPE Astromech
AFFILIATION Ace Squadron, Team *Colossus*

Freya Fenris' astromech droid is a modern twist on an ancient but efficient droid line that is back in style. This droid makes quick navigational calculations with little fuss. T3-K10 is a capable engineer and is suited to copiloting larger starships, too.

R4-G77

TYPE Astromech
AFFILIATION Ace Squadron, Team *Colossus*

Ace Squadron pilot Hype Fazon loves his droid, R4-G77. The astromech is part of a new line that uses repulsorlift technology to move around. Hype's "baby" R4 has several mechanical arms, including a grasping claw and electro-shock prod. He also has an attitude—when Flix and Orka try to fix his bad motivator, R4 doesn't react well!

GRIFF HALLORAN

SPECIES Human
AFFILIATION Galactic Empire, Ace Squadron, Team *Colossus*

Griff Halloran is a TIE fighter pilot who defects from the Galactic Empire alongside his commanding officer Imanuel Doza. Staying by Doza's side, Griff relocates to the *Colossus* platform and becomes a racing pilot. He flies *Black Ace*, a racing ship derived from an old Imperial TIE fighter, and his uniform bears vestiges from his time as an Imperial pilot. He grimly cultivates this impression—enjoying the intimidating effect he has on others. Nonetheless, he is a dependable defender of the *Colossus* and a formidable racer. When the platform is being hunted by the First Order, Halloran is concerned that the evil organization will never stop, and he lends his military skills to defend his new home. He is captured alongside Kazuda Xiono by the Aeosians during a recon trip on Aeos Prime.

TORRA DOZA

SPECIES Human **AFFILIATION** Ace Squadron, Team *Colossus*

Torra Doza is the daughter of the *Colossus* station's administrator, Captain Imanuel Doza, and Resistance pilot Venisa Doza. Torra lives with her father in the Doza Tower with the droid R23-X9 and Torra's pet, Buggles. Torra is a member of Ace Squadron and pilots the *Blue Ace* starfighter, which she also uses in local races. She befriends Kazuda Xiono, and even goes so far as to help him sneak around the Tower, despite suspecting he is a spy. After her suspicions are proven correct, she helps Kaz in his fight against the First Order. With the *Colossus* on the run, she excels in her new role as a combat pilot and lends a hand on supply missions to Celsor 3, Drahgor III, and Ashas Ree. After their annual meet-up is interrupted by the First Order, Torra reunites with her mother Venisa when she brings her Resistance squadron to the platform. She helps them during an escort mission on Dantooine and is upset when they lose a Resistance transport. Alongside her parents, Torra rallies the residents of the *Colossus* to join the Battle of Barabesh. She later fights during the Battle of Exegol.

R5-G9

MANUFACTURER Industrial Automaton
TYPE Customized astromech
AFFILIATION Ace Squadron, Team *Colossus*

Much like his flashy customized ship, Halloran's droid is a customized Imperial astromech. While it has an astromech's body and navigational skills, it combines the precision of an FX-series medical droid with the observational skills (and range of nasty tricks) of a probe droid.

R23-X9

MANUFACTURER Industrial Automaton (customized)
TYPE Astromech
AFFILIATION Torra Doza, Ace Squadron, Team *Colossus*

While R23-X9 may look similar to an R-series astromech, it is actually a rarer model, built especially for Torra at great cost. It serves as her copilot and is painted blue to match her uniform and ship.

FIRST ORDER STORMTROOPER

SPECIES Human
HOMEWORLD Various
AFFILIATION First Order

Unlike the Galactic Republic, which utilized a clone army, and the Imperial Army, which was largely composed of a volunteer force instructed in academies, the First Order trains its stormtroopers from birth, with a strict education and training regimen that amounts to brainwashing. First Order stormtroopers are given serial numbers rather than names—and any glimmer of individuality is quickly crushed. As Palpatine's evil Empire collapses, Counselor Gallius Rax selects two dozen orphans from Jakku, his homeworld, to be trained as soldiers. Following Rax's death in the Battle of Jakku, a small Imperial remnant flees to the Unknown Regions. A young Armitage Hux is put in charge of the child soldiers, whom he trains to become the First Order's initial squad of stormtroopers.

However, the real mastermind behind the First Order's future stormtrooper armies proves to be Armitage's father, Brendol Hux. Impressed by the training, devotion, and effectiveness of the Galactic Republic's clone army, but dissatisfied with the Imperial stormtroopers' clumsiness and unreliability, Brendol devises a program to indoctrinate children from birth. He thus creates an even more effective force than the previous Imperial Army or the Grand Army of the Republic.

While on Parnassos, Brendol Hux encounters Phasma, who claims to be her planet's greatest warrior. She volunteers to join the First Order and become a stormtrooper. In due course, Phasma and Armitage conspire to murder Brendol. With Brendol dead, they take control of Project: Resurrection, the stormtrooper program, and employ Jinata Security to kidnap infants to become the next generation of troopers.

Performing a much more important role than her title of captain would suggest, Phasma trains the First Order's stormtroopers to be ruthless killing machines, blindly following orders no matter how morally suspect. She teaches her charges to have no sympathy for others—including each other. Stormtroopers who fail in their duty deserve the most severe punishments, even death. Those who challenge her authority in any way are branded traitors and soon face the laser axes of stormtrooper executioners.

However, some First Order stormtroopers do defect, including Company 77 and FN-2187 (Finn). These rebellions are of great concern to Phasma and Hux, raising serious questions about loyalty within the stormtrooper ranks. FN-2187's dereliction of his post also causes First Order leader Kylo Ren to propose that a new clone army might serve the First Order better than Phasma's stormtroopers. Phasma desperately seeks to apprehend and execute FN-2187, but her defeat at his hands aboard the *Supremacy* emphasizes the threat that he poses to the corps' morale.

Every standard stormtrooper is issued an F-11D blaster rifle and an SE-44C blaster pistol. There is a wide variety of specialist divisions, tailored to different modes of warfare and fighting environments, including flametroopers, snowtroopers, heavy stormtroopers, and SCUBA troopers.

Target apprehended
First Order stormtroopers completely despise all Resistance agents.

Passionate masses
Legions of First Order stormtroopers celebrate Armitage Hux's historic speech prior to the firing of Starkiller Base's superweapon.

AUNT Z

SPECIES Gilliand **HOMEWORLD** Crul
AFFILIATION Aunt Z's Tavern, Team *Colossus*

Z'Vk'Thkrkza, known as Aunt Z to the patrons of her tavern on the *Colossus*, is a purveyor of great food, drinks, advice, and information. She also takes bets on the local races. Aunt Z is fun and friendly, but she can also be rather direct, and she knows how to cut through the "bantha poodoo"! Aunt Z is tough, too, breaking up bar fights and squelching robberies. Comfort food remains key to her business, evidenced by the waffle tattoo on her upper left arm, crossed by a knife and spatula. She has to temporarily flee the station when she is wanted by the First Order, but returns to save it. When the *Colossus* is hunted by the First Order, Aunt Z looks to take her business elsewhere but relents when Kazuda Xiono and Torra Doza provide the means to sustain it. Aunt Z is the first civilian to sign up to fight during the Battle of Barabesh, gleefully wielding a giant blaster against the enemy.

BOLZA GROOL

SPECIES Klatooinian **HOMEWORLD** Klatooine
AFFILIATION Team *Colossus*

Bolza Grool is a gorgmonger (a seller of tasty gorg amphibians) with a market stall on the *Colossus*. Bolza and Kazuda Xiono start out on the wrong foot, but later Bolza sponsors him in races. He joins Team *Colossus*, saying he's tired of running.

GLITCH

MODEL Hospitality droid
AFFILIATION Aunt Z's Tavern, Team *Colossus*

G1-7CH, otherwise known as "Glitch," is a loyal droid that works at Aunt Z's Tavern on the *Colossus* station. He serves drinks in the bar, helps Aunt Z determine the odds of races for her betting service, and is handy with a blaster or four. He temporarily takes over the Tavern when Aunt Z has to leave the station.

ORKA

SPECIES Chadra-Fan **HOMEWORLD** Chad
AFFILIATION The *Colossus* Office of Acquisitions, Team *Colossus*

Orka and his partner, Flix, run the Office of Acquisitions on the *Colossus* station with the help of their trusty pit-droid, GL-N. He is also a knowledgeable repairer of astromech droids. Kazuda Xiono barters with them—mostly with the business-savvy, but kind, Orka—when he needs speeder parts. Their first deal sends Kaz on a hunt for tasty gorgs. Orka and Flix go on to develop a good relationship with Kaz and he even minds their shop (in exchange for parts) while they are away. With the *Colossus* on the run, Orka accompanies Flix to secure fuel from his family, impressing his partner's cousins with his assertive nature. During the Battle of Barabesh, Orka helps defend against the First Order boarding parties.

CAPTAIN DOZA

SPECIES Human **AFFILIATION** Empire, Resistance, Team *Colossus*

Imanuel Doza is a captain in the Galactic Empire until his partner Venisa persuades him to defect. During the time of the New Republic, Imanuel is the administrator of the *Colossus* station on Castilon. His daughter, Torra Doza, is a pilot racer in Ace Squadron at the station, while Venisa is a member of the Resistance. The First Order pressures Doza to place *Colossus* station under its protection and control, and he eventually gives in when the pirate attacks on the platform increase. However, he later realizes his decision was a mistake and joins the fight against the First Order forces on the station. Now leading the *Colossus* on the run, Doza works hard to source supplies for the people aboard his ship and to protect them from the First Order and criminal threats. He also looks to find them a new home on a planet. During the *Colossus*' multiple engagements with the First Order, Doza commands from the bridge, directing the platform's defenses and his Ace Squadron. Doza is relieved to find the oceanic planet Aeos, which is a suitable new home for the platform, and entreats with the indigenous Aeosians to secure sanctuary. Unfortunately, the First Order soon finds them, and a surprised Doza orders the station to leave the world. He formally agrees to join the Resistance after helping Venisa's Jade Squadron on Dantooine and secures a key victory at Barabesh where Team *Colossus* takes down a First Order Star Destroyer.

KRAGAN GORR

SPECIES Quarren **HOMEWORLD** Mon Cala
AFFILIATION Warbirds

Tough and ruthless, Kragan Gorr leads the pirate gang named the Warbirds. His group is hired by the First Order to harass the *Colossus* station on Castilon in order to pressure its captain, Imanuel Doza, to submit to the First Order's protection. Gorr uses Hallion Nark to infiltrate the station so that his gang can attack. After Hallion is exposed, another Warbird, Synara San, is welcomed into the station crew. Kragan's gang attacks the *Colossus* again, but is run off when Kaz Xiono and Jarek Yeager get the station's turbolaser targeting computer working. When Kaz pleads for help against the First Order, Kragan and the Warbirds answer the call and board the *Colossus* before it jumps to hyperspace. While Kragan and his pirates lend a hand at times, the wily leader eventually tries to mutiny against Doza. After Gorr is defeated, he finds himself, his *Galleon*, and the crew loyal to him expelled from the station.

FLIX

SPECIES Gozzo **HOMEWORLD** Drahgor III
AFFILIATION The *Colossus* Office of Acquisitions, Team *Colossus*

Flix never feels like he belongs with his family of fuel miners on Drahgor III, so he leaves his planet with dreams of becoming a cantina singer. Eventually, he meets his partner Orka and the pair end up working in the *Colossus* station's cluttered Office of Acquisitions. They buy most of their parts from scavengers who recover them from the bottom of Castilon's sea. Quieter than Orka, Flix handles the administrative aspects. He's a stickler for numbers and for keeping the office organized—the opposite of Orka. He and Orka are both used to dealing with rough characters on the station, but they try to flee when the First Order occupies the platform. Kaz tries to get their help to free the *Colossus*, but they wish him luck and hide instead. When the *Colossus* is on the run and low on fuel, Flix leads a crew to his homeworld to secure a supply he is entitled to from his family flock. Flix admonishes his cousin Flanx's dangerous working practices that have awakened karnex dragons, but they work together to escape the creatures. Flix leaves on better terms with his family and with the vital fuel the *Colossus* needs. Alongside Orka, he agrees to help their friends during the Battle of Barabesh.

HALLION NARK

SPECIES Neimoidian
HOMEWORLD Cato Neimoidia
AFFILIATION Kragan Gorr's pirate gang

Hallion Nark comes to *Colossus* platform needing ship repairs at Yeager's garage. He is actually a spy for Kragan Gorr's pirate gang. Nark escapes the station just before a "triple dark" outage.

JACE RUCKLIN

SPECIES Human **HOMEWORLD** Castilon
AFFILIATION Himself, First Order

Jace Rucklin is a racer at the *Colossus* station on Castilon. Rucklin befriends Kazuda Xiono to trick him into stealing Jarek Yeager's hyperfuel. The fuel causes his speeder to explode, forcing Rucklin to work in Doza Tower to recoup the costs. Alongside Tamara Ryvora, Rucklin joins the First Order as a TIE pilot cadet. He is willing to betray his former home and is killed during the Battle of Barabesh.

KEL AND EILA

SPECIES Human **HOMEWORLD** Tehar **AFFILIATION** Team *Colossus*

Kel and his younger sister Eila flee from their planet when the First Order, led by Kylo Ren, kills their people. The children stow away aboard a ship and end up at the *Colossus* station on Castilon. When the First Order discovers there are Teharan survivors, it offers a bounty for Kel and Eila, claiming the children are runaways from an important First Order family. Kazuda Xiono and the *Colossus*' Chelidae engineers help the children fake their own deaths. The siblings then live in hiding in engineering section with the Chelidae. When Kaz heads to Ashas Ree for a supply mission, he agrees to let the siblings join so they can be on solid ground again. However, they soon get the group into trouble inside a Sith temple, and then with First Order Raiders. The pair befriend a traveling scavenger Mika Gray, who helps everyone escape the planet, and offer her a home on the *Colossus*.

CHARACTERS AND CREATURES

GLEM
SPECIES Rodian
AFFILIATION Colossus

Gruff and gravel-voiced, Glem toils away on the loading docks of the Colossus platform—though he is mostly concerned with securing a better shift. When not working, this Rodian can often be found watching a race, enjoying a drink at Aunt Z's Tavern, or even getting mixed up in a brawl.

NARB
SPECIES Snivvian
AFFILIATION Colossus

A small-time criminal aboard the Colossus, Narb works as muscle for the shady Grevel. He chases down debtors—even if they've been cheated. He and his brother, Nod, attempt to rob the Office of Acquisitions, but they are outsmarted by its owners, Flix and Orka.

NOD
SPECIES Snivvian
AFFILIATION Colossus

Nod lives on the Colossus, getting by as a petty criminal and enforcer for a gambler called Grevel. Following an argument with his brother Narb, Nod grabs the secret Resistance spy Kazuda Xiono, believing he was eavesdropping. But Xiono escapes, and the brothers give chase on the orders of Grevel, who claims that Kaz owes him money. Later, Nod and Narb make a failed attempt to rob the Office of Acquisitions shop.

GREVEL
SPECIES Aleena
AFFILIATION Colossus

Grevel is an Aleena who makes his presence known on the Colossus with a fierce temper. After a game of holodarts with Kazuda Xiono, Grevel sends his goons after the boy to collect his supposed winnings. Grevel later confronts Xiono, but a pirate attack cuts things short, and Xiono ends up helping Grevel survive. But ever selfish, Grevel later declines to aid in rescuing Kaz.

EGDIR
SPECIES Ithorian
AFFILIATION Colossus

Egdir is a citizen of the Colossus who can be regularly seen in its marketplace or having a beverage at Aunt Z's Tavern. He has a short fuse, however, and is quick to lash out at those who irk him—as he does to Resistance spy Kazuda Xiono when he bumps into the Ithorian mid-conversation.

JOOKS
SPECIES Theelin
AFFILIATION Colossus

Jooks calls the Colossus home, and she can often be found perched at the bar in Aunt Z's Tavern, attending races, or betting on the latter. Unafraid to mix it up, Jooks fearlessly enters the fray in barroom brawls at Aunt Z's, but she remains loyal to her friends and the platform; when the Aces of the Colossus vanquish the First Order occupiers, Jooks celebrates with abandon on the outer decks.

GARMA
SPECIES Arcona
AFFILIATION Colossus

With the aid of a walking cane, the elderly Garma makes her way around Colossus, often with a smile that betrays her playful nature. She takes an early liking to Kazuda Xiono. Garma has no qualms asking a vendor for a free bowl of puffer pig bacon or sneakily grabbing lost spoils during a pirate attack on the platform.

LEOZ
SPECIES Nikto
AFFILIATION Kragan Gorr's Warbird gang

One of Kragan Gorr's pirate bruisers, Leoz takes up residence on the Colossus with the rest of his motley crew. The short-tempered Nikto gambles with his lucky dice—but doesn't take losing well. Following a loss to Kazuda Xiono, Leoz places a curse on the young pilot, cackling with glee at the misfortune sure to befall him.

SKREEK
SPECIES Trandoshan
AFFILIATION Kragan Gorr's Warbird gang

One of Kragan Gorr's most vicious pirates, Skreek nearly kills Kazuda Xiono with his metal staff in a raid on the Colossus. He loyally continues to serve Gorr, even when Captain Doza exiles the Warbirds from the Colossus.

GORRAK WILES
SPECIES Sullustan
AFFILIATION Colossus

Gorrak Wiles works as a mechanic on Jace Rucklin's racing team. On Rucklin's orders, Wiles and teammate Lin Gaava sabotage Kazuda Xiono's speeder and manipulate him to access Jarek Yeager's hyperfuel. But when Rucklin joins the First Order, Wiles stays on the Colossus.

LIN GAAVA
SPECIES Human
AFFILIATION Colossus, First Order

A mechanic for racer Jace Rucklin, Lin Gaava toils on the pilot's ship. Along with teammate Gorrak Wiles, she assists in an elaborate scheme to steal hyperfuel from Jarek Yeager's racing craft. Later, the First Order recruits Lin as a flight cadet.

VIL'PAK
SPECIES Chelidae **HOMEWORLD** Castilon
AFFILIATION Colossus

The kindly Vil'pak works in the lowest level of the Colossus with all the Chelidae engineers—the "true heroes" of the platform. Vil'pak hides two children from the First Order and later helps Neeku flood the Colossus corridors, eliminating stormtrooper threats and allowing the ship to rise from Castilon's oceans.

DRELL
SPECIES Weequay
AFFILIATION Kragan Gorr's Warbird gang

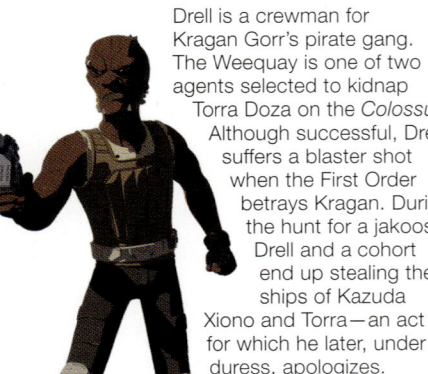

Drell is a crewman for Kragan Gorr's pirate gang. The Weequay is one of two agents selected to kidnap Torra Doza on the Colossus. Although successful, Drell suffers a blaster shot when the First Order betrays Kragan. During the hunt for a jakoosk, Drell and a cohort end up stealing the ships of Kazuda Xiono and Torra—an act for which he later, under duress, apologizes.

SNARL
SPECIES Hassk
AFFILIATION Kragan Gorr's Warbird gang

A member of Kragan Gorr's Warbird gang, Snarl revels in his pirate life, routinely cackling as he pillages and plunders. He assists in raids on the Colossus and joins the hunt for a giant jakoosk, though the latter mission proves unsuccessful, with the Hassk fleeing from the creature.

VALIK
SPECIES Palliduvan **AFFILIATION** Kragan Gorr's Warbird gang

Valik serves among the ranks of Kragan Gorr's Warbird gang. In addition to her piloting skills, her covert abilities prove to be a strength. She and crewmate Drell sneak aboard the Colossus and successfully kidnap the captain's daughter, Torra Doza.

MB-13
MANUFACTURER Industrial Automation
TYPE BB series astromech
AFFILIATION First Order

MB-13 serves the First Order with complete loyalty and seems eager to use his electroprod to stop the enemies of his masters. The BB unit battles Kazuda Xiono, tussles with Resistance droid CB-23, and comes close to relaying the position of the Colossus back to the First Order—but not before Xiono blasts him out of the airlock.

Fearsome reputation
Phasma is known for being merciless. She is one of the commanders of the First Order forces *(above)* and is not used to being disobeyed.

Unexpected foe
Captain Phasma and Finn, formerly stormtrooper FN-2187 *(below)*, have developed a hostile relationship because of Finn's insubordination.

CAPTAIN PHASMA

SPECIES Human **HOMEWORLD** Parnassos **AFFILIATION** First Order

Captain Phasma is a ruthless warrior. She cares only about her own advancement and survival having not the slightest regard for others—even if they are on the same side as her.

TOUGH ORIGINS
Phasma grows up on Parnassos, a desolate world where her clan must fight to protect its territory. Phasma single-handedly engineers the death of her entire clan, including her parents, so that she and her brother Keldo may survive and join the stronger Scyre clan. When First Order officer Brendol Hux crash-lands on her world, Phasma sees another opportunity and volunteers—as the planet's greatest warrior—to join the First Order, leaving those she grew up with behind.

Although she prefers the title "Captain," Phasma's functional rank is much higher, with her leading beside General Armitage Hux and Kylo Ren from Starkiller Base. Phasma coordinates high-profile spies and field agents, including the self-serving Terex. When he proves unwieldy, she has Terex subdued with cybernetic implants. Phasma also oversees First Order interests at the *Colossus* fueling station on Castilon. Her primary role, however, is as the leader of the First Order's stormtroopers. As such, she manages the training of FN-2187 (Finn), whom she finds highly capable yet frustratingly uncooperative. She repeatedly orders him not to assist weaker team members, and he fails to follow orders to fire upon civilian targets.

ON THE HUNT FOR LUKE SKYWALKER
Together with Kylo Ren, Phasma leads the attack against the Tuanul village on Jakku, where she orders her stormtroopers to eliminate the remaining inhabitants. When FN-2187 fails to comply, and goes so far as to remove his helmet without permission, she orders him to submit to an evaluation. Nonetheless, Phasma is surprised when he deserts the First Order and escapes to Jakku with Resistance captive Poe Dameron.

Phasma meets Finn again on Starkiller Base, where he and Han Solo capture her. Although she puts up a superficial fight, Phasma readily submits and drops the shields on Starkiller Base—thus dooming the First Order—hoping to save herself. But she is thrown into a trash compactor after serving her purpose.

PHASMA'S END
Phasma escapes the trash compactor and Starkiller Base before the planet explodes. However, she discovers that Lieutenant Sol Rivas had accessed the same computer terminal she used to lower the shields. In an effort to cover her tracks, Phasma blames her deeds on him and takes a TIE pilot (TN-3465) with her to assassinate him. Afterward, she ruthlessly kills her loyal pilot as well.

Phasma encounters Finn again when he and his accomplice, Rose Tico, sneak aboard the First Order flagship *Supremacy*. She takes perverse pleasure in overseeing their execution, telling the executioners to "make this hurt." When Resistance leader Vice Admiral Holdo rams the *Supremacy* in the *Raddus*, the execution ceremony is thrown into disarray. Phasma and Finn are thrown into combat, and though she appears to be the superior fighter, Finn manages to send her falling into the fiery depths of the ship.

Tough training
Captain Phasma personally oversees the training of the stormtroopers. She is an unforgiving taskmaster.

CHARACTERS AND CREATURES

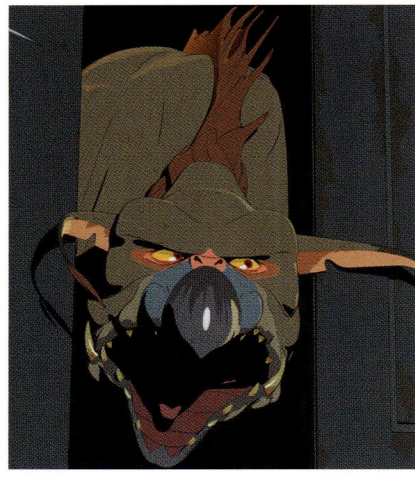

KOWAKIAN APE
HOMEWORLD Kowak **AVERAGE SIZE** 2.4 m (8 ft) high **HABITAT** Highland jungles

Kowakian apes are brutish genetic cousins of monkey-lizards. These dangerous creatures have a sour disposition and a mighty roar. Kragan Gorr's pirate gang is surprised by a cargo hold full of Kowakian primates when they try to loot a Darius G-class freighter near the planet Castilon. What they expect to be priceless cargo turns out to be a menagerie of Kowakian monkey-lizards and one very angry Kowakian ape. The ape eats most of the pirates; only Synara San manages to survive. Two of the apes serve as employees of Vranki the Blue at his criminal establishment.

MARCUS SPEEDSTAR
SPECIES Human **AFFILIATION** Marcus Speedstar's racing team

Marcus is the estranged brother of Jarek Yeager, and is responsible for the accidental deaths of Jarek's family. Marcus comes to the *Colossus* to see Jarek and race in the Platform Classic. He uses the prize money to pay off a debt with the Guavian Death Gang.

R4-D12
MANUFACTURER Industrial Automaton **TYPE** Astromech **AFFILIATION** Marcus Speedstar's racing team

R4-D12 is a cone-headed astromech droid belonging to racer Marcus Speedstar. The R-series droid provides navigational assistance during races, anticipating potential obstacles and forecasting multiple alternate outcomes.

SYNARA SAN
SPECIES Mirialan **HOMEWORLD** Mirial **AFFILIATION** Warbirds, Team *Colossus*

Synara San has been a member of Kragan Gorr's pirate gang since childhood and is his copilot during an early raid on Castilon's *Colossus* station. When she and her crewmates try to loot a freighter, they find it overrun with Kowakian monkey-lizards and a giant ape. She hides in a cargo crate, but her fellow pirates are devoured. Synara is discovered unconscious by Kazuda Xiono and Poe Dameron, who mistake her for one of the ship's original crew. They take her back to the *Colossus*, where she recovers and works as a salvager—and as a spy for Gorr. She unexpectedly becomes friends with mechanic Tamara Ryvora, who rushes to aid Synara when Kragan Gorr attacks the station again. Synara has to knock out one of the pirates to maintain her cover.

With the First Order suspecting that there is a pirate spy on the *Colossus*, Kaz learns that Synara is the spy and fears that she will be exposed. Thanks to Kaz and Neeku's help, Synara leaves the station aboard an escape pod and reunites with the Warbirds. Kaz later pleads for help against the First Order, and Synara convinces the Warbirds to help the *Colossus*. Aboard the pirate's flagship, the *Galleon*, Synara leads the Warbirds against the First Order.

When a First Order Star Destroyer enters orbit and attacks the station, the *Galleon* lands in one of the *Colossus*' hangar bays. Synara and the Warbirds flee with the platform's residents to an unknown destination. Synara works hard to strengthen relationships between the former enemies. She accompanies the Warbirds during their hunt of a jakoosk creature on Celsor 3 and helps Kaz and Jarek Yeager on a mission to Varkana. When Gorr mutinies against Captain Imanuel Doza, Synara rallies a number of Warbirds against their leader. After helping to stop Gorr, Synara strikes a deal with Doza, allowing the mutineers to leave aboard the *Galleon* and those loyal to Doza to stay. During the Battle of Barabesh, Synara flies the Warbirds' shuttle into battle against the First Order.

BUGGLES
HOMEWORLD Naboo **SIZE** 70 cm (2 ft) high

Buggles is a six-legged voorpak pet belonging to Torra Doza. Buggles lives with Torra in Doza Tower on Castilon's *Colossus* station. The voorpak isn't entirely housebroken and occasionally runs loose around the station or even offworld if he can sneak aboard a ship. The stowaway Buggles acts as perfect bait for a jakoosk on Celsor 3, allowing Kazuda Xiono to shoot the massive creature and secure vital food for the *Colossus*. Voorpaks are popular with the aristocracy of Naboo. Their soft fur, light weight, pleasant odor, and generally friendly disposition make them ideal pets. Wild voorpaks live in rocky outcrops on hillsides, where they raise litters of up to five pups. Despite their cute appearance, voorpaks are carnivores, catching prey with their sharp teeth.

BIBO
HOMEWORLD Castilon **SIZE** 30 cm (1 ft) long **HABITAT** Open seas

When Synara San salvages a Clone Wars-era Z-96 shipwreck and brings it back to the *Colossus*, Neeku Vozo finds a small creature inside. Though Synara, Tamara Ryvora, and Kazuda Xiono find the gelatinous, tentacled creature rather ugly and smelly, Neeku immediately falls in love, naming it Bibo. Neeku's new, chaotic pet tries to eat everything in Jarek Yeager's garage, including tools, ship parts, fuel, and even the astromech named Bucket. When Bibo wanders off, Neeku and Tam find him in the arms of Eila in engineering. She has had visions that Bibo will bring calamity to the station.

BITEY
HOMEWORLD Castilon **SIZE** 20 cm (8 in) long

Resistance spy Kazuda Xiono bargains with Flix and Orka at the *Colossus* Department of Acquisitions, agreeing to provide them with food in exchange for some ship parts. Kaz heads to the market, where he acquires a live gorg for their lunch. By the time Kaz returns, Flix and Orka have already eaten, but they still honor the deal, and decide to keep the gorg as a pet instead of eating him later. He earns the name Bitey due to his habit of biting fingers and electrical wiring with his jagged teeth. This behavior proves useful to Kaz when he uses Bitey to foil the thieving Teroj Kee.

ROKKNA
HOMEWORLD Castilon **AVERAGE SIZE** 220 m (722 ft) long **HABITAT** Open seas

Rokknas are large sea creatures that lurk deep in the seas of Castilon. These terrifying leviathans have four eyes, six tentacles, and a gaping beak. Thankfully, they are not normally violent, but will attack if provoked, especially if their young are taken. Rokknas are seldom seen emerging from the depths, until a baby rokkna is accidentally taken as a pet by Neeku Vozo on the *Colossus*. Its mother is distressed by her baby's disappearance, and uses her sense of smell to track it to the station. The mother then begins attacking the *Colossus*, so Neeku hands over the baby to save the station.

SPEAGULL

HOMEWORLD Castilon **AVERAGE SIZE** 66 cm (2 ft) long **HABITAT** Water

Speagulls are water birds native to Castilon that are often seen flying or perching on ships, such as the *Galleon*, and platforms—including the *Colossus* station. They are skilled swimmers, and their natural diet consists of fish, crustaceans, and other aquatic creatures. However, they are known to beg, or even steal, scraps from the residents of the *Colossus*. Like most animals on Castilon, the birds have four eyes, which allows them to hunt for food and keep watch for predators at the same time. Their blue-and-white plumage keeps them camouflaged, whether they are seen from above or below, flying or swimming underwater. At least one speagull stows aboard the *Colossus* as it leaves Castilon.

CHELIDAE

HOMEWORLD Castilon
AFFILIATION *Colossus* station

Slow-moving and peaceful, the Chelidae are a friendly and mysterious group who work behind the scenes as engineers and caretakers aboard the *Colossus* station. Neeku Vozo is good friends with the Chelidae and introduces them to Kazuda Xiono when he needs help hiding Kel and Eila—two children from Tehar who are running from the First Order. The Chelidae offer the two kids shelter and go on to help Neeku and Kaz free the station from First Order occupation. They remain with the *Colossus* as it flees Castilon into hyperspace.

COMMANDER PYRE

SPECIES Human **AFFILIATION** First Order

Ruthless and efficient, Commander Pyre is a distinguished First Order leader who wears distinctive golden stormtrooper armor. He takes part in the negotiations between Captain Imanuel Doza of the *Colossus* station and the First Order, along with Major Erik Vonreg and Captain Phasma. He and Vonreg persuade Phasma to use Kragan Gorr's pirate gang to harass the *Colossus* and pressure Captain Doza into seeking protection from the First Order. These efforts fail at first, and Pyre has to explain why to Phasma, diminishing her confidence in their plan. Later, Pyre leads the search for the Teharan children, Kel and Ella, who are hiding on the station. He fails to apprehend them, tricked by Kazuda Xiono and others into thinking that they have drowned. Then, the First Order pay the pirates to kidnap Imanuel's daughter Torra Doza, but betray them and rescue her instead.

After the First Order returns Torra to the *Colossus*, Imanuel allows Pyre to lead a garrison of his troops on the station. Pyre quickly occupies the station, arresting citizens that get in their way and trying to apprehend the Resistance agents.

Following the near complete submergence of the *Colossus* beneath Castilon's oceans, Pyre personally leads a trooper contingent to investigate why the First Order's communication jammer has stopped working. He engages the culprits, Kaz and Jarek Yeager, in a firefight, temporarily capturing the latter. Pyre eventually realizes that he has lost control of the station, so orders his garrison to evacuate. He also calls upon First Order reinforcements, including a Star Destroyer, to aggressively take over the station, but the *Colossus* escapes to hyperspace.

Soon after, Pyre reports back to a disgruntled Phasma who threatens him and the garrison with execution if they fail to capture or destroy the fleeing platform. After failing to capture the ship on multiple occasions, Pyre heads to a high-level meeting on the *Titan* refueling station where General Armitage Hux expresses his displeasure that the *Colossus* is still on the run. Hux severely reprimands him for Resistance agents being in his midst and states that the *Colossus*' destruction is now the sole aim. Pyre's continued failures lead to him being allowed one final chance at Supreme Leader Kylo Ren's behest. However, during the Battle of Barabesh, Pyre goes down with his ship.

AGENT TIERNY

SPECIES Human **AFFILIATION** First Order

Agent Tierny is a member of the secretive First Order Security Bureau who is sent to the occupied *Colossus* station and charged with rooting out any Resistance spies. Rather than employing aggressive interrogation tactics, Tierny uses her well-honed guile on Team *Fireball* member Tamara Ryvora. She exposes the fact that Tam's friends have been lying to her and then manipulates her into joining the First Order. With the Resistance regaining control of the *Colossus*, Tierny resorts to her pair of RK-3 blasters as she flees the platform with Tam. Stationed aboard the *Thunderer*, Tierny then works alongside Pyre to capture or destroy the platform. She sees Tam as a key asset for this mission, so manipulates the young recruit into helping her. Tierny's efforts quickly bear results as Tam provides intel that allows them to engage the *Colossus* in D'Qar's orbit. Although the platform escapes temporarily, Tierny later enacts a plan for a First Order asset, engineer Nena Nalor, to sabotage the platform but it escapes her grasp once more, and Tierny orders Nalor executed if she encounters her again. On Varkana, Tierny takes great pleasure from interrogating Yeager, playing on his feeling for Tam, but is later defeated by CB-23. She is disappointed when Tam defects and orders her execution. Given a final chance to destroy the *Colossus* by Supreme Leader Kylo Ren, she fails him during the Battle of Barabesh, and he kills her when she pleads for reinforcements.

CB-23

MANUFACTURER Industrial Automaton **TYPE** BB-series Astromech droid
AFFILIATION Resistance, Team *Fireball*, Team *Colossus*

CB-23 is a ball droid astromech assigned to Resistance Captain Poe Dameron while his own droid, BB-8, is helping Kaz Xiono on the *Colossus* station. CB-23 is loyal, brave, and resourceful, and though she chafes at BB-8 initially, the two droids become fast friends. She accompanies Poe, along with Kaz and BB-8, to investigate a Darius G-class freighter overrun with Kowakian monkey-lizards—and a monstrous Kowakian ape. While trying to escape these creatures, CB-23 discovers a survivor, Synara San. CB-23 again accompanies Poe and Kaz to investigate Station Theta Black. While the other three explore the station, CB-23 flies their X-wings into the surrounding asteroid field to hide them. She later returns to retrieve them after the First Order arrives, and they fly back to base. After accompanying Poe, Kaz, and BB-8 to the Dassal system, CB-23 replaces BB-8 on the *Colossus*, and she assists Kaz in defeating the First Order occupation.

When the *Colossus* flees Castilon into hyperspace, CB-23 continues to support Kaz on many missions to keep the platform and its residents alive. Alongside Kaz, she still helps the Resistance when she can, including on Varkana where she escapes First Order interrogation and knocks out the First Order Agent Tierny. After the *Colossus* appears to settle on Aeos, CB-23 and Kaz intend to join a Resistance cell, but return to the station to defend it against the First Order. CB-23 later joins Kaz and Yeager's mission to retrieve Tamara Ryvora from the First Order. After the group ends up aboard the First Order Star Destroyer *Thunderer*, CB-23 evades capture and deactivates the vessel's shields at a critical moment allowing the *Colossus*' fighter squadrons to destroy the ship and secure victory during the Battle of Barabesh.

CHARACTERS AND CREATURES

LOR SAN TEKKA
SPECIES Human
AFFILIATION Church of the Force, New Republic, Resistance

Explorer Lor San Tekka is not a Jedi, but he believes in their ideals as a member of the Church of the Force. He explores many remote worlds and ancient and contemporary places of religious significance, including the Crèche on Ovanis. After the Battle of Endor, Lor San Tekka assists Luke Skywalker in the search for long-forgotten Jedi knowledge. Together, they head to an old Jedi outpost on Elphrona, where they encounter the Knights of Ren at an archaeological site on Yoturba. Years later, San Tekka is imprisoned on Cato Neimoidia after breaking into the Neimoidians' vaults and examining a relic of significance to Force-wielders. He is put on trial and due to be executed, but General Organa and Poe Dameron rescue him. However, San Tekka is kidnapped by First Order Agent Terex, who ejects him into space. Lor San Tekka is rescued by Black Squadron and brought to D'Qar, where he disappoints Leia, confessing that he does not know the whereabouts of Luke Skywalker, although given time he may discover it. Soon after, he notifies Leia that he has a map fragment that may point to the lost Jedi's location. Poe Dameron meets him in Tuanul Village on Jakku. There, San Tekka turns over the map to Poe before the First Order arrives and Kylo Ren murders him.

Brutal punishment
Kylo Ren demands the map from Lor San Tekka, but the old man merely expresses his disappointment in what Kylo Ren has become.

FN-2003
SPECIES Human **AFFILIATION** First Order

FN-2003, also known as Slip, is a friend of FN-2187 (Finn) and the weakest member of their team. Slip is killed on Jakku. Before his death, he wipes a bloody handprint on Finn's helmet.

FN-2199
SPECIES Human **AFFILIATION** First Order

FN-2199 (Nines) is a former comrade and friend of Finn. At the Battle of Takodana, Nines spots Finn, who has deserted the First Order, and yells "Traitor!" Then he brandishes a Z6 riot control baton and fights Finn, who is wielding a lightsaber. Nines is shot and killed by Han Solo.

FIRST ORDER FLAMETROOPER
SPECIES Human **HOMEWORLD** Various
AFFILIATION First Order

First Order flametroopers work in tandem with standard stormtroopers. They are equipped with D-93w incinerators, which incorporate a double-barreled flame projector gun connected by hoses to a set of fuel tanks carried on a backpack. Flametroopers are used regularly by the First Order. Agent Terex deploys them against an egg worshipped by the Crèche, inadvertently hatching it. Kylo Ren and Captain Phasma utilize them to burn down Tuanul Village on Jakku.

FIRST ORDER HEAVY TROOPER
SPECIES Human **HOMEWORLD** Various
AFFILIATION First Order

First Order heavy troopers require substantial strength to carry their hefty FWMB-10 repeating blasters (otherwise known as megablasters), and wear web gear fitted with additional ammunition. Manufactured by the Sonn-Blas Corporation, their blaster cannons feature barrel-cooling shrouds and integrated fold-out stands. The blasters are also mounted on infantry vehicles as their primary weapons. While their rate of fire is slower than standard stormtrooper blasters, FWMB-10s pack a big punch, and are capable of neutralizing Resistance vehicles with a single, well-placed shot. Heavy troopers are commonplace on Starkiller Base and the *Supremacy*.

FIRST ORDER SPECIAL FORCES TIE FIGHTER PILOT
SPECIES Human **HOMEWORLD** Various
AFFILIATION First Order

The First Order's Special Forces include elite TIE fighter pilots who answer directly to senior officers. They are assigned special TIE/sf fighters with room for two pilots. Their helmets are distinguished by red markings, and include internal upgrades, such as an advanced targeting system. A typically aggressive Special Forces pilot pursues Rey and Finn as they pilot the *Millennium Falcon* over Jakku, racing through the wreckage of the Super Star Destroyer *Ravager*. Notable Special Forces TIE pilots include Major Elrik Vonreg, who dresses in all-red armor.

FIRST ORDER TIE FIGHTER PILOT
SPECIES Human **HOMEWORLD** Various
AFFILIATION First Order

The First Order values its pilots much more than the Empire ever did. TIE fighter pilots are given more extensive training and much improved craft to fly in the era of the First Order. They undergo strict training from childhood, much like stormtroopers. Many pilots grow up on Star Destroyers and space stations, never setting foot on a planetary surface until adulthood, if ever. Cadets who fail to pass strict requirements for vision, reflexes, and other fundamental flight skills may graduate to become shuttle pilots, gunners, or technicians instead.

FIRST ORDER SNOWTROOPER
SPECIES Human
HOMEWORLD Various
AFFILIATION First Order

First Order snowtrooper gear is designed for cold-weather warfare, with waterproof insulated body gloves, armor, and helmets. These troopers wear fewer armor plates (made of betaplast) than regular stormtroopers, to allow increased movement in difficult snowy conditions. Additional features include a heavy kama wrapped around their waist and a pack that holds survival gear and supplies battery power. Snowtroopers fight at the battles of Starkiller Base and Crait. Their polarized visor and suit temperature regulators are an advantage in the hot, glaring sun of the planet's salt flats.

FINN

SPECIES Human
AFFILIATION First Order, Resistance

Finn's life as a stormtrooper teaches him to obey orders and put the First Order above all else. However, an awakening on Jakku presents him with an opportunity to choose a new path as a hero.

FN-2187
Like all First Order stormtroopers, Finn is taken from his family at a very young age. He never sees them again, and is raised instead with other stormtrooper cadets. He is not afforded any sort of individual personal identity or even a name—instead he is simply designated "FN-2187." While in training, Finn is considered a model stormtrooper and even commended by Captain Phasma. However, she orders Finn to stop helping his best friend FN-2003, who is weak and jeopardizes Finn's entire team. In this respect, Finn's concern for others leads to his own existential crisis later when he is ordered by Phasma to fire upon innocent civilians.

ESCAPE FROM THE FIRST ORDER
In his first battle, Finn can't bring himself to terminate the Tuanul villagers on Jakku and realizes he must leave the First Order. Aboard the *Finalizer*, Finn frees a captive Resistance pilot, Poe Dameron, so that Poe can fly them to safety in a stolen TIE fighter. After crashing on Jakku (and being

Escaping Jakku
After their intended escape vessel is destroyed by TIE fighters, Rey, Finn, and BB-8 dash toward their second choice—the *Millennium Falcon*.

parted from Poe), Finn meets Rey and BB-8. Together they leave the planet aboard the *Millennium Falcon*. Ashamed of his past as a stormtrooper, Finn pretends to be a member of the Resistance in order to gain Rey's trust. Confiding his true identity to BB-8, Finn persuades the droid to disclose the location of the Resistance base. Shortly afterward, their ship is boarded by Han Solo and Chewbacca, and Finn is almost eaten when Han's cargo of rathtars escapes.

MEETING ON TAKODANA
Han and Chewie take Finn, Rey, and BB-8 to Takodana to meet wise tavern owner Maz Kanata. She urges them to stand up to the First Order and fight. Having seen the power of the enemy firsthand, a scared Finn admits his ruse and abandons his friends. He attempts to leave the planet with the pirate Sidon Ithano, but the First Order arrives and attacks Maz's castle. This time Finn has no choice but to fight, with a lightsaber given to him by Maz. Stormtrooper FN-2199—Finn's former comrade and squad mate—confronts Finn and declares him a traitor. Finn is knocked down, but saved by Han Solo.

STARKILLER MISSION
Finn panics when he sees Kylo Ren leave Takodana with a captured Rey aboard his shuttle. Finn becomes a member of the Resistance solely because he wants to rescue Rey, and he agrees to help them infiltrate Starkiller Base. After reuniting with her there, Finn proves his mettle when he is confronted by Kylo. Prepared to make the ultimate sacrifice to save his friend, Finn draws Luke Skywalker's old lightsaber and engages the dark-side warrior in combat. Finn is severely injured during the fight, and is taken to the Resistance base for treatment. Rey leaves Finn there, believing they will see each other again.

JOURNEY TO CANTO BIGHT
The Resistance fleet is being chased by the First Order, which uses hyperspace tracking technology to follow their every move. Running out of time and fuel, Finn, Rose Tico, and BB-8 journey to the city of Canto Bight in search of an individual known as Master Codebreaker, who can help them disable the tracker. There they meet a slicer named DJ who claims he can break into any system. Finn uses his knowledge of the First Order's flagship, the *Supremacy*, to sneak the team on board, but their mission falls apart when they are spotted and captured.

FIGHTING THE FIRST ORDER
Finn's capture aboard the *Supremacy* brings him face to face with his former commander, Captain Phasma. Calling on his training as a stormtrooper cadet, Finn faces Phasma in melee combat, ultimately defeating his opponent. Finally realizing that his loyalty lies with the Resistance, Finn rejoins them to make a final stand on Crait. There, he pilots a ski speeder in an effort to delay the advancing ground forces. A last-minute maneuver by Rose saves him in the heat of battle, allowing them to escape aboard the *Millennium Falcon* to fight another day.

ALL IN
While the Resistance sets up its new hidden base, General Organa sends the newly determined Finn on various missions to aid their cause. Alongside Poe, he retrieves a list of potential recruits from Corellia and a New Republic supply cache from the moon of Avedot. Finn later infiltrates a Star Destroyer in orbit around Batuu, where he helps free captured Resistance recruits.
  When Rey decides to pick up Luke Skywalker's search for Exegol, Finn is right by her side. Their quest takes them across the galaxy. On Kef Bir, the ocean moon of Endor, Finn meets kindred spirit and former stormtrooper Jannah. She and her fellow First Order defectors ally with the Resistance. Meanwhile, General Organa's health continues to fail, and she promotes Poe Dameron to acting general upon her passing. Poe realizes how much he depends on and appreciates Finn, and he asks his friend to take command alongside him. Together they formulate a strategy to take the fight to the Final Order on Exegol.
  Finn, Jannah, and a ground assault team land on the hull of the Star Destroyer *Steadfast*, racing across the surface on the backs of horselike creatures, orbaks. Their goal is the destruction of the command ship's navigational signal, which would strand the entire Final Order fleet on Exegol. Finn and Jannah first deactivate the ship's navigational tower. While their troops evacuate, Finn and Jannah decide to destroy the *Steadfast* to stop its crew from resetting the systems in order to transmit the signal once more. The mission is a success, and the Resistance triumphs over tyranny once and for all. As their adventures continue, Finn shows evidence of being able to instinctively feel the presence of the Force.

KYLO REN (BEN SOLO)

SPECIES Human **HOMEWORLD** Chandrila
AFFILIATION Jedi, First Order, Knights of Ren

Though his lineage includes the brightest heroes as well as the darkest villain of recent history, Force-wielding Kylo Ren weaves a complicated path through the galaxy as he struggles to come to terms with his familial legacy.

EARLY LIFE
One year after the Battle of Endor, Ben Solo is born to Princess Leia Organa and General Han Solo in Hanna City, Chandrila. His parents' busy professional lives (coupled with their decision to send him away to Ossus to be trained by his uncle, Luke Skywalker) leave Ben feeling abandoned. Leia does not tell him that his grandfather, Anakin Skywalker, became Darth Vader. She intends to address the painful topic when he is much older. When Ben learns the truth along with the rest of the galaxy, he's confronted with the reality that his whole family has deceived him about their lineage and connection to the dark side of the Force.

TURN TO DARKNESS
Trained by Luke as part of a new generation of Jedi, Ben studies the light side of the Force. However, over the years, a voice whispers to Ben and plants seeds of doubt. Ben turns against his master and destroys Luke's other students. Now known as Kylo Ren, he learns about the dark side of the Force from the First Order's mysterious supreme leader, Snoke. Snoke's teaching blends traditions of both the dark and the light sides—a tension that causes dangerous instability within Kylo. He becomes a promising pupil to Snoke and

the master of the Knights of Ren. Kylo also looks to the past for inspiration; his crossguard lightsaber is modeled after an antiquated design. He even communes with the charred relic of Vader's mask, seeking visions of the power of the dark side.

THE SEARCH FOR SKYWALKER
Tasked by Snoke to hunt down the missing Luke Skywalker, Kylo follows Resistance pilot Poe Dameron to Jakku for his meeting with Lor San Tekka. Kylo fails to secure Tekka's map pinpointing Luke's location, but captures Poe to question him. Ren learns that the map is stored within a BB-series droid, who is accompanied by Rey. After tracking the droid to Takodana, Kylo succeeds in capturing the scavenger, but during her interrogation she resists him. Through this encounter Kylo learns that Rey's strong Force abilities rival his own.

TRIAL AND FAILURE
Snoke is concerned Kylo will waver when he has an inevitable confrontation with his father. However, Ren resolves to prove himself to Snoke and become immune to the light side. When Kylo finally meets Han on Starkiller Base, he strikes his father down. Ren is wounded by Chewbacca, but chases after Rey and Finn to retrieve his grandfather's lightsaber from the former First Order stormtrooper. After he wounds Finn in a duel, Kylo is stunned to watch Rey retrieve Anakin's lightsaber using the Force, and then best him in combat. Rey scars Kylo's face, but their duel is cut short as the planet's surface begins to disintegrate, following the Resistance's attack. Snoke orders General Hux to go and retrieve the defeated Kylo, so that he may receive his final training from Snoke in person.

SUPREME LEADER
After their humiliating defeat at Starkiller Base, Supreme Leader Snoke is displeased with Kylo for being bested in combat by Rey and failing to find Luke Skywalker. Viciously taunting him, Snoke brands Ren a failure—a serious error in judgment that leads to his apprentice killing him and declaring himself the new supreme leader. When his attempt to recruit Rey to his cause fails, Kylo turns his attention to annihilating the Resistance. Just when he has them cornered on Crait, he falls for Luke Skywalker's misdirection, realizing too late that he is fighting nothing more than a Force projection of his old master. Kylo's miscalculation allows the Resistance to escape yet again. Following Crait, Kylo is merciless in his pursuit of the Resistance and furiously disposes of any people who aid them.

VOICES FROM THE PAST
After Palpatine broadcasts a galaxy-wide threat, the name "Exegol" burns in Kylo Ren's mind. He retrieves a wayfinder once held in Darth Vader's possession and uses it to set a course for Exegol, the secret home of the Sith. There, Palpatine reveals he—not Snoke—has been the voice inside Kylo's head all along. He bids Kylo to kill Rey. In return, the might of a new empire will be his to command. Kylo reunites with the Knights of Ren and reforges his broken helmet. He exploits his strong connection to Rey to uncover her location on Pasaana, where his Knights capture Chewbacca. When Rey comes to rescue the Wookiee from the Star Destroyer *Steadfast*, Kylo reveals her identity as a Palpatine before they escape. He tracks her again to the wreckage of the second Death Star on Kef Bir and invites her to embrace the dark side and join him. She refuses, and the two duel in a flurry of lightsaber swings amid the crashing waves of the ocean moon. As he stands on the ruins of the Death Star, Kylo hears his mother's voice say his name, Ben, one last time. Rey wounds him just before she senses the death of Leia Organa. Rey uses the Force to heal Kylo Ren and leaves him to decide the path he will take next.

THE SON OF HEROES
As Kylo Ren grapples with the passing of his mother, a vision of his father Han Solo appears before him. Han encourages him to follow in Leia's footsteps and fight for what's right. His son throws his red-bladed lightsaber away, and Ben Solo returns from the darkness. He salvages a TIE fighter and races to Rey on Exegol. She senses his arrival and passes him the Skywalker lightsaber through the Force. Ben disposes of the Knights of Ren, makes it to her side, and they face the erstwhile Emperor together. Palpatine draws upon the strong power of their bond to heal himself. The rejuvenated Palpatine easily flings Ben into a chasm. While he climbs his way out, Rey channels the wisdom and power of all the Jedi who came before her to end Palpatine. The effort costs her heavily. Ben takes Rey in his arms and heals her, giving his own lifeforce to restore hers. The two share a kiss before Ben succumbs in her place.

Double-Edged Sword
Much like his grandfather and uncle before him, Kylo possesses formidable lightsaber skills. He puts this talent to use in service of the First Order.

REY

SPECIES Human **HOMEWORLD** Jakku
AFFILIATION Resistance

Alone on a desert world, Rey believes she is nothing more than a lowly scavenger, forever waiting for a family that never comes. When she discovers a hidden power within her, she must harness it to help her newfound friends—and the galaxy.

> "I didn't know there was this much green in the whole galaxy."
>
> **REY TO HAN SOLO**

TRAGIC EARLY LIFE
During the era of the New Republic, young parents Dathan and Miramir move with their infant, Rey, to Jakku to live a quiet life away from prying eyes. They're on the run from Sheev Palpatine, who seeks their Force-attuned child for his own nefarious ends. His agents find them in time, but the family escapes. Dathan and Miramir make the difficult decision that Jakku is the safest place for the six-year-old Rey, and they briefly return to leave her in the charge of Unkar Plutt. Sadly, the mercenary Ochi of Bestoon tracks and kills her parents before they can go back for her. Rey starts to work for the junk boss by scavenging for parts and supplies from Jakku's Starship Graveyard. Rey lives by herself in a wrecked Imperial AT-AT that she renovates in the Goazon Badlands, and survives by trading her finds for food and water rations. Unusually for residents of Jakku, Rey is not looking to work her way off the backwater planet, as she believes that one day her family will return for her. While waiting indefinitely for them to come back, Rey practices flying a few ships, including a Ghtroc 690 light freighter. Rey is planning to sell it to Unkar—until it is stolen.

Home sweet home
The Hellhound 2's intact heat shielding protects Rey from the harsh conditions of a Jakku day.

A FATEFUL ENCOUNTER
One evening, after finishing her dinner of polystarch and veg-meat, Rey hears a commotion in the dunes. She rushes to find the astromech BB-8 in distress, and rescues him from a greedy Teedo. Taking pity on the wayward droid, Rey shelters him before taking him to Niima Outpost. BB-8 recognizes the jacket of his former master, now worn by Finn. Rey confronts Finn, believing him a thief, but he claims he is part of the Resistance. When First Order stormtroopers arrive, hunting for BB-8, the trio relies on Rey's piloting skills to escape Jakku aboard Unkar's *Millennium Falcon*.

TAKODANA AND THE FORCE
The *Millennium Falcon* is intercepted by Han Solo and Chewbacca, who take Rey and Finn to Maz Kanata's castle on Takodana. They hope that pirate Maz can get BB-8, who carries a map to Luke Skywalker's location, delivered to the Resistance. In Maz's castle, a lightsaber that once belonged to Luke and Anakin Skywalker calls to Rey through the Force. When Rey touches it, she sees a Force vision and hears voices from beyond the grave. Fleeing in fear, Rey is captured when the First Order arrives on Takodana.

STARKILLER BASE AND DESTINY
On Starkiller Base, Kylo Ren probes Rey's mind with the Force. He senses her affinity for Han Solo and her fantasies about a mysterious island, but she is strong in the Force and fights him, preventing Kylo from retrieving the map to Skywalker in her memory. Now embracing her Force abilities, Rey uses a mind trick on her stormtrooper guard, who sets her free. After Rey rejoins her friends and witnesses Han Solo's death, Rey and Finn are confronted by Kylo Ren. Finn is gravely wounded by Kylo, but Rey claims Skywalker's blade as her own. She confounds Kylo with her fighting skill, and defeats him. After the destruction of Starkiller Base, Rey seeks out Skywalker, hopeful that he will train her as a Jedi and join the Resistance.

SURPRISE ON AHCH-TO
Rey's arrival on Ahch-To does not go as expected. Rather than meeting a great hero of the Rebellion, she finds an ill-tempered old man, content to live out his final days in solitude without connection to the Force. Skywalker refuses to train her, instead agreeing to give her just three lessons to show her the folly of the Jedi. Rey believes that if she cannot convince Skywalker to aid the Resistance, then turning Kylo to the light side is their only hope. She departs to meet Ren, secretly taking ancient Jedi texts with her to preserve the history of the Jedi.

FACING SNOKE
Kylo Ren takes Rey straight to Supreme Leader Snoke, who encourages Kylo to strike her down as the final test in his training. Instead, Ren turns on his master, killing him with Skywalker's lightsaber. Snoke's Praetorian Guard rush to avenge him, but Rey and Kylo work in unison against the elite warriors. With Snoke and his guard defeated, Rey asks Kylo to help her save the Resistance, but he refuses to be redeemed. She escapes to rejoin the group on Crait, arriving just in time to clear their retreat and ferry the survivors away aboard the *Millennium Falcon*.

HARSH TRUTHS
Following a period on the run, Rey and the Resistance settle into their new base on Ajan Kloss, where she trains, meditates, and studies the ancient Jedi texts. The Resistance learns that Palpatine is alive and on the secret Sith world of Exegol. Rey resumes Luke's search for the planet, and her loyal friends Finn, Poe, Chewbacca, C-3PO, and BB-8 accompany her. They pick up Luke's last lead for a Sith wayfinder on the planet Pasaana. Kylo Ren uses their connection to learn her location, where the Knights of Ren capture Chewbacca and take him to a waiting transport. Rey overextends her Force abilities to keep the First Order vessel from leaving, and inadvertently destroys it with Force-generated lightning. She's devastated by what she's done. They continue their mission in honor of Chewie's sacrifice and end up on the planet Kijimi. Kylo isn't far behind, and Rey senses Chewbacca on his Star Destroyer—the Wookiee was on a different transport. Finn, Poe, and Rey stage a rescue. When Kylo confronts her on the ship, he reveals that they share a rare bond known as a Force dyad. Even more shocking, he says that Palpatine is her grandfather.

BE WITH ME
Rey escapes the Star Destroyer, and Kylo follows her to the ruins of the Death Star II, where she sees a dark vision of herself in the Emperor's throne room. When Kylo finds her, they engage in a lightsaber duel until he's distracted by the sound of his mother's voice. Rey impales him—and then senses the passing of Leia Organa. Rey finds compassion for Kylo and heals him with the Force. She steals and crash-lands his ship on Ahch-To, shaken by her visions and determined to live in exile, but the spirit of Luke Skywalker encourages Rey to face her fears. She takes Luke's X-wing for the final journey to Exegol.

Rey stands before Palpatine; Ben Solo, recently returned to the light, joins her as an ally. Palpatine draws on the energy of their bond to rejuvenate himself before tossing Ben aside. But Rey isn't alone. She calls upon the Jedi who came before her and they answer, giving her the strength to turn Palpatine's own power against him. He's destroyed once and for all, but the effort proves to be too much, and Rey falls to the ground, motionless. Ben races to her to side and selflessly transfers his lifeforce to her so that she will live. Rey returns to her found family on Ajan Kloss.

Before she begins her next journey, Rey and BB-8 carry the lightsabers of Luke Skywalker and Leia Organa and bury them in the sands of Tatooine, near the Lars homestead. She takes the name Rey Skywalker in their honor.

Family feud
Having wanted to find her family for so long, Rey finally meets her terrifying grandfather, who tries to tempt her to the dark side, on Exegol. When Rey refuses, he attacks the Resistance fleet.

CHARACTERS AND CREATURES

Never enough
Hux is one of the First Order's highest-ranking officers, but he would do anything to surpass Kylo Ren.

> "Today is the end of the Republic."
> — GENERAL HUX

ARMITAGE HUX

SPECIES Human   **HOMEWORLD** Arkanis   **AFFILIATION** First Order

Above all else, Armitage Hux cares only for himself and his petty rivalries. Conniving and cruel, Armitage is willing to sacrifice anything to see those he hates fail.

FAMILY BUSINESS

Armitage Hux is the son of Commandant Brendol Hux, an Imperial officer, who devised a new program to conscript and train stormtroopers from birth. Brendol is an Imperial Academy instructor and an uncaring father who shows no kindness to his son. When their homeworld is overtaken by the Rebel Alliance, Brendol takes his young son, Armitage, to Jakku. Following the Battle of Jakku, the Huxes escape to the Unknown Regions of the galaxy with Admiral Rae Sloane to build a new Empire.

Armitage is given charge of the young stormtroopers, and commands them with brutality, demanding absolute loyalty and obedience. His malicious tendencies and delusions of grandeur increase as he matures and rises through the ranks of the First Order. Later, he and Captain Phasma conspire together and assassinate his father, Brendol.

JEALOUS RIVAL

General Armitage Hux has a fierce rivalry with Supreme Leader Snoke's apprentice, Kylo Ren. Hux values the military might of the First Order rather than Kylo's devotion to the mystical Force. Hux seeks to prove himself and win favor with Snoke in order to diminish Kylo's standing. However, the pair do manage to find common ground to protect each other when their shuttle is sabotaged and they crash-land on a dangerous world. As the commander of Starkiller Base, he pleads with Snoke to let him destroy the Hosnian system—the seat of government for the Galactic Republic. When Snoke agrees, Hux delivers a passionate speech to his forces before firing the superweapon and obliterating Hosnian Prime. His next target is the Resistance base on D'Qar. However, when Starkiller is attacked by the Resistance and about to be destroyed, Snoke orders Hux to bring Kylo Ren and come to him.

ONE STEP AHEAD

Following the destruction of Starkiller Base, Hux oversees the retaliatory attack on D'Qar. Though the assault decimates the base, the Resistance escapes and Poe Dameron destroys the First Order's prized Dreadnought *Fulminatrix*. Snoke is displeased with Hux at first, but when the general explains his overarching plan, the supreme leader is delighted. Hux has devised a novel way to track the Resistance through hyperspace, preventing his enemies from escaping.

Resistance spies Rose Tico and Finn are captured when they infiltrate Snoke's flagship, the *Supremacy*, and attempt to deactivate Hux's hyperspace tracker. Hux orders their execution and then leaves to fire upon the Resistance's escaping craft, thanks to information obtained by the double-crossing slicer, DJ. Hux is caught by surprise though, when Resistance flagship *Raddus*, piloted by Vice Admiral Holdo, collides with the *Supremacy*, breaking it apart. In the chaos, Hux runs to Snoke's throne room only to find the supreme leader dead and Kylo Ren unconscious. Hux tries to take advantage of the opportunity to kill Kylo, but his rival awakes and chokes him into submission. To ensure his own survival, Hux becomes Kylo's lackey, and operates as his second-in-command at the Battle of Crait. The few remaining members of the Resistance escape their clutches as the skirmish ends.

TRUE COLORS

Not long after, General Hux is tasked with hunting Resistance agents across the galaxy. After a trip to Vendaxa bears no success, Hux inspects the Titan refueling supertanker, where he disciplines Commander Pyre for allowing Resistance agents to steal from them while he is aboard. Hux later attacks the planets of Tah'Nuhna and Mon Cala for harboring the Resistance. Hux and his Star Destroyer *Finalizer* later intercept a transport ship of Resistance recruits leaving Batuu. They get away with the help of Resistance heroes Finn and Poe Dameron. Supreme Leader Kylo Ren, tired of Hux's repeated failures, assigns Hux to serve under Allegiant General Pryde on the *Steadfast*. While Hux maintains a seat on the Supreme Council, he holds very little power and kowtows to Kylo.

Hux comes face to face with Finn and Poe when they sneak aboard the *Steadfast* to rescue Chewbacca. He reveals that he's the spy who's been leaking First Order intel to the Resistance. Hux doesn't believe in their cause—he simply wants Kylo Ren to fail. He takes them to the *Millennium Falcon* and asks Finn to shoot him as a cover for their breakout. General Pryde, however, is far too shrewd to be fooled. Pryde immediately executes Armitage Hux for treason.

Rivalry's end
Kylo Ren's Force abilities prove more than a match for Hux, who must submit to a new master.

UNKAR PLUTT

SPECIES Crolute **HOMEWORLD** Crul
AFFILIATION Independent entrepreneur

The cantankerous, selfish Unkar Plutt leaves his watery homeworld after a shady business deal falls apart. The "Blobfish," as he comes to be known, settles on Jakku and starts a business buying scraps from the local scavengers in Niima Outpost. In the course of business, he encounters a young girl named Rey and her parents, Miramir and Dathan. The family settles nearby, setting up a moisture farm and trading with him. A few years later, they are forced to steal one of Unkar's freighters and flee the world when Sith agents track them down. In an attempt to temporarily hide Rey, the parents strike a deal with Unkar to take care of her. Unfortunately, the young girl never sees them alive again.

As Rey grows up alone, she begins working directly for him at first, becoming his top scavenger. Later, Unkar steals the *Millennium Falcon* from the criminals known as the Irving Boys, and makes a few modifications as it sits under a tarp by his stall. Unkar eventually becomes the top junk dealer at Niima Outpost, driving out all his competitors and controlling all commerce there. When an inquisitive kid named Karr Nuq Sin and his allies visit Unkar's stand asking for Jedi artifacts, Unkar offers to sell them what he purports is a throttle lever from a Jedi ship. Nuq Sin shows little interest in the lever so Unkar kicks them out, scolding them for wasting his time.

When Rey discovers the droid BB-8, Unkar offers to buy him, but Rey declines. In response, Unkar sends his thugs to steal the droid—but Rey fights them off. After Rey steals the *Millennium Falcon*, Unkar tracks her to Takodana and confronts her at Maz's Castle. Chewbacca comes to her aid, however, and rips off one of Unkar's arms.

UNKAR'S THUGS

SPECIES Various humanoids
HOMEWORLD Jakku **AFFILIATION** Unkar Plutt

Unkar Plutt employs a small group of thugs, armed with vibro-shivs and blasters, who work for him around Niima Outpost on Jakku. He uses them to do his dirty work, such as breaking up unauthorized commerce, stealing from uncooperative scavengers, and sabotaging any aspiring competitors. The amoral ruffians hide under hoods, wraps, and goggles, but everyone around the Outpost knows who they really are. Unkar's thugs cause occasional trouble for Rey, especially when they try to take BB-8 from her by force in the market.

BOBBAJO

SPECIES Nu-Cosian
HOMEWORLD Jakku
AFFILIATION Critters of all kinds

The kindly old Bobbajo carries a menagerie of pets on his back, including a worrt named J'Rrosch, several gwerps and pishnes, a lonlan, and two zhhee. He travels from village to village on Jakku telling fantastical stories about his adventures with his creatures, though only children take him seriously. In one tale he actually takes credit for destroying the Death Star. Bobbajo occasionally has dealings with Unkar Plutt and has run into Rey at the Crolute's stall in Niima Outpost.

SARCO PLANK

SPECIES Melitto
HOMEWORLD Li-Toran
AFFILIATION Various

The self-serving Sarco Plank is a scavenger who guides Luke Skywalker to the Temple of Eedit on Devaron. He intends to use Luke to open the temple and then take the treasures inside for himself. Once Luke serves his purpose, Sarco Plank attacks him—but to no avail. Sarco ends up trapped inside the temple. After freeing himself, he relocates to Jakku and works as an arms dealer and bounty hunter. His bad luck continues there. Sarco competes with Rey to claim salvage rights on the wreck of the Star Destroyer *Spectral*, but ultimately fails.

NIGHTWATCHER WORM

HOMEWORLD Jakku **AVERAGE SIZE** 20 m (66 ft 7 in) long
HABITAT Sand dunes

Also known as sandborers and Arcona night terrors, Jakku's nightwatcher worms are nocturnal creatures that live under the sand. Sensing vibrations, they poke an eyestalk with small, glowing red eyes above the surface to investigate. Those unfamiliar with the species have no idea that the creature below is quite large and has a sizable gaping mouth. Nightwatcher worms prefer to eat ship parts and wayward droids, but they also consume living prey. One specimen takes an interest in BB-8, forcing Rey to outsmart it.

STEELPECKER

HOMEWORLD Jakku **HABITAT** Sand dunes and rock outcrops near wreckage

Amid the ship debris scattered in the dunes on Jakku, scavenger birds called steelpeckers flutter about looking for metal objects to consume: their talons and beaks are coated in iron, allowing them to break off bite-size chunks to swallow. A steelpecker gizzard typically contains vanadium, corundum, and osmiridium to aid in digestion. The bird's guano is a profitable commodity for Jakku's settlers, because they can export it for use in the production of starship hulls. Some steelpecker flocks have been found on other worlds, including Ferrix.

HAPPABORE

HOMEWORLD Various (domesticated) **AVERAGE SIZE** 5.9 m (19 ft 2 in) long
HABITAT Various (adaptable)

Happabores are large, docile, piglike creatures, often raised as livestock on Devaron and Jakku. They can store large quantities of water in their bloodstreams, allowing them to drink less often. Happabore hides are tough and well-armored on their dorsal side for protection from the sun and predators. On Jakku, Finn drinks from a happabore trough in Niima Outpost and Rey is forced to deal with them when she scavenges in the dunes. On Devaron, happabores also serve as a means of transportation for residents like Sarco Plank.

CHARACTERS AND CREATURES

TEEDO
SPECIES Teedo **HOMEWORLD** Jakku
AFFILIATION None

Teedos are small, reptilian beings that subsist as scavengers in Jakku's dunes. Though selfish in their dealings with other species, they do not maintain individual identities. They are all named Teedo and share a telepathic link and a collective experience. Rey is forced to deal with unpleasant Teedos often. She rescues BB-8 from an especially irritating Teedo riding a luggabeast near her home. A short while later, the Teedo again tries to steal BB-8 from Rey. She lures him to a wrecked Star Destroyer where she knows a nightwatcher worm lurks—and the Teedo is nearly eaten.

LUGGABEAST
HOMEWORLD Various **AVERAGE SIZE** 2.31 m (7 ft 7 in) high
HABITAT Adaptable (domesticated)

Luggabeasts are cybernetically enhanced beasts of burden. Salvaged machine parts and chemical injections are used to augment the strength and stamina of the animals. They are given food and water through tubes and have no need to drink or eat otherwise. On Jakku, luggabeasts are used by Teedos and settlers to travel between outposts and scavenge the starship graveyard. Teedos specialize in breeding and adapting the creatures on Jakku, but similar cyborg beasts of burden produced from other species are used throughout the galaxy, including the Outer Rim world Ferrix.

RATHTAR
HOMEWORLD Twon Ketee **AVERAGE SIZE** 6.09 m (20 ft) long (including tentacles)
HABITAT Swamps

Among the most feared predators in the galaxy, rathtars are large, tentacled creatures with a voracious appetite. Their gaping mouths are lined with teeth that are continually replaced. Though rathtars have small brains, they are social animals and hunt effectively in packs. A rathtar's deadly reputation makes it a prized catch for smugglers and big game hunters. A number of rathtars escape and cause chaos during the fall of Starlight Beacon. On Twon Ketee, Maul observes poachers being eaten by a pack before killing several rathtars himself. Han Solo and Chewbacca smuggle several rathtars, but they get loose and cause havoc.

TASU LEECH
SPECIES Human **HOMEWORLD** Nar Kanji
AFFILIATION Kanjiklub

Tasu Leech is a pit fighter from Nar Kanji and an assassin outside of the arena. He is hired to kill Beilert Valance on Nar Kaaga, but is knocked out by his target. Tasu later joins bounty hunter T'onga's crew. Tasu goes on many missions, including one where he betrays the group to help some people from his homeworld. Shortly after, he leaves T'onga on Depatar, wanting to return to his homeworld. Following the uprising on Nar Kanji, Tasu becomes the leader of the criminal Kanjiklub gang. In cooperation with the rival Guavian Death Gang, he locates Han Solo's ship, the *Eravana*, and boards it with his fighters. Han Solo borrowed 50,000 credits from Kanjiklub and has not paid his debt—for the second time. When Rey releases Han's cargo of rathtars, it causes violent chaos on the ship, allowing Han, Chewbacca, Rey, Finn, and BB-8 to escape.

BALA-TIK
SPECIES Human
AFFILIATION Guavian Death Gang

On the planet Kaddak, in a city known as the Sliver, Kanjiklub's Tasu Leech overhears C-3PO say that Han Solo owes the Guavian Death Gang money. Tasu then confers with Bala-Tik, the frontman for the Guavians. The two rival gangs agree to work together and collect the money Han Solo owes them. After tracking Han Solo to Nantoon, Bala-Tik and his enforcers board Han's ship, the *Eravana*. There, an angry Bala-Tik demands the credits Han Solo owes them, but he is unprepared to face the rathtars set loose on the ship.

GUAVIAN DEATH GANG ENFORCER
SPECIES Human **HOMEWORLD** Various
AFFILIATION Guavian Death Gang

The Guavian Death Gang's enforcers are humans who swear allegiance to the organization, and in return receive cyborg augmentations and chemical injections to boost their effectiveness as killers. Enforcers communicate with each other via high-frequency data bursts transmitted by the disk in the center of their "face." Bala-Tik always travels with a contingent of enforcers, including on his visits to Kaddak and in his confrontation with Han Solo. Guavians have also been observed on *Colossus* station on Castilon, defending their territory from any trespassers, and attacking a droid depot ship in Batuu's orbit.

COLONEL DATOO
SPECIES Human
AFFILIATION First Order

Colonel Erich S. Datoo is in command of the primary fire control room on Starkiller Base. He is responsible for discharging the energy burst that destroys the Hosnian system. He next aims the weapon at the planet D'Qar, home to the Resistance headquarters, but Starkiller Base is destroyed before he can hit his target.

CHIEF PETTY OFFICER UNAMO
SPECIES Human
AFFILIATION First Order

Chief Petty Officer Nastia Unamo serves on the bridge of the *Resurgent*-class Star Destroyer *Finalizer*, under the command of Kylo Ren and General Hux. She supervises the bridge crew and tracks the stolen TIE fighter flown by Poe Dameron and FN-2187 to their crash site on Jakku.

KORR SELLA
SPECIES Human
HOMEWORLD Hosnian Prime
AFFILIATION Resistance

Korr Sella is an intern for New Republic Senator Leia Organa, and later joins the Resistance as a commander. Sella acts as General Leia Organa's envoy to the New Republic Senate. She attempts to warn them of the growing threat from the First Order, but she is too late. Sella is killed when Starkiller Base destroys Hosnian Prime.

GA-97
MANUFACTURER Reiffworks Droid Restoration
TYPE GA servant droid
AFFILIATION Resistance

GA-97 is an operative working for C-3PO, stationed in Maz Kanata's castle on Takodana. When BB-8 shows up with Han Solo, Chewbacca, Rey, and Finn, GA-97 notifies C-3PO. The message results in Poe Dameron and his X-wing squadron arriving on Takodana to battle the First Order.

SNOKE

SPECIES Humanoid genetic strandcast **HOMEWORLD** Exegol
AFFILIATION Emperor Palpatine, First Order

Supreme Leader Snoke may appear to be the formidable ruler of the First Order and a powerful practitioner of the dark side of the Force. However, all is not as it seems, and Snoke is little more than a puppet unwittingly performing Emperor Palpatine's will.

SNOKE'S ORIGINS

For decades, Emperor Palpatine has been fascinated by the potential of cloning. On Exegol, the Sith Cultists create Snoke with the hope that Palpatine could possess his body after his death on the Death Star II. Unfortunately, Snoke is not suitable for the task so he is repurposed as a tool to be used to enact Palpatine's will. Snoke later claims he chose his name at some point in his life.

When the Empire falls, its remnants seek refuge in the Unknown Regions of the galaxy. Concealed in the Unknown Regions, the Imperial survivors prepare for a future war and become known as the First Order. At some point, Snoke joins these survivors, accumulating power and prominence in the organization.

Snoke finds great promise in training Luke Skywalker's nephew and Jedi acolyte, Ben Solo, as his apprentice. Palpatine, pretending to be Snoke, speaks directly to the boy's mind for years, whispering of power and dark secrets. Snoke and his master prey on Ben's doubts and ultimately turn him to the dark side. Ben becomes Kylo Ren, master of the Knights of Ren, and Snoke begins his dark-side training in earnest, taking him to Dagobah where his impulsive apprentice destroys the ancient Cave of Evil.

Wishing to eliminate his greatest threat, Snoke commands Kylo Ren to locate and destroy Luke Skywalker. Snoke also senses an awakening in the Force, but is unsure of the source. Snoke warns Kylo that the droid carrying the map they seek to Luke Skywalker is aboard the *Millennium Falcon* with Kylo's father, Han Solo. While Snoke has encouraged Kylo to confront Solo, Snoke warns him that he has never faced such a difficult test.

On Snoke's orders, the First Order uses its Starkiller superweapon to destroy the New Republic's capital in the Hosnian system and prepares to wipe out the Resistance on D'Qar. Meanwhile, Rey's identity is discovered, and Snoke orders Kylo to bring her to him. However, after Kylo murders Han Solo, Kylo is defeated by Rey and Starkiller Base is destroyed.

Distant figure
Though he wields immense power, Snoke prefers not to place himself in harm's way. He commands from the shadows, communicating with his subordinates via holograms, often projected at a vast size to further reinforce his might.

FINAL TEST

Snoke becomes dissatisfied with Kylo Ren after his defeat at the hands of Rey. He ridicules Kylo as "a boy in a mask," which fills his young apprentice with rage. Snoke is pleased when Kylo finally brings Rey before him on his flagship *Supremacy*, which restores some of Snoke's confidence in his student. Snoke notes that Rey has risen from the light side of the Force to match Kylo, though he had always assumed Kylo's equal would be Luke Skywalker.

Nonetheless, Snoke underestimates Rey's ability and overestimates Kylo's loyalty. When he orders Kylo to eliminate Rey in his presence, Snoke is unable to sense Kylo's intent to ally with the girl, against him. Kylo uses the Force to turn Rey's lightsaber (resting beside Snoke's throne) toward his master and cuts him in half. Snoke's Praetorian Guards attempt to avenge their fallen master, but are defeated by Kylo and Rey. To Rey's horror, Kylo then seizes control of the First Order, becoming its new supreme leader. Kylo later learns of his former master's origins on Exegol.

> "There has been an awakening. Have you felt it?"
> **SNOKE TO KYLO REN**

Death of a tyrant
In his dealings with Kylo and Rey, Snoke forgoes his usual caution—a decision that costs him dearly. He is so confident in the strength of his Force abilities that he views neither of them as a real threat, only realizing his folly when it is far too late.

214 CHARACTERS AND CREATURES

MAZ KANATA
HOMEWORLD Takodana
AFFILIATION Independent entrepreneur

Maz Kanata was born more than a thousand years before the war between the First Order and the Resistance. Though not a Jedi herself, she does have a strong but subtle connection to the Force. Maz is a former pirate, master storyteller, and the proprietor of a castle tavern on the shores of Nymeve Lake on Takodana. During the time of the High Republic, Maz is kidnapped by the Dank Graks but is rescued by the loyal crew of her ship the *Venomed Scabbard*. She also befriends Jedi Sav Malagán who temporarily joins her crew. Years later, she also briefly watches over Jedi apprentice Qort, who finds his signature vonduun crab helmet in her castle. When Nihil destroy the Jedi temple on Takodana, Maz calls in medic units and recovery droids to help.

Maz is a longtime friend of Han Solo and Leia Organa and has a decades-long flirtation with Chewbacca. After being temporarily imprisoned on Gulhadar III alongside the Wookiee, Maz helps carry out a scheme to break them out. Notably, she assists Leia in rescuing Han from Jabba the Hutt by suggesting the rebel use the outfit of the bounty hunger Boushh as a disguise to infiltrate Jabba's palace. When Han and Chewbacca return to their old ways, Maz works with them to retrieve a dangerous dark-side artifact that was stolen from her by Baron Somareeva.

Just prior to the attack on Starkiller Base, Han arrives at Maz's castle with Rey, Finn, and BB-8. He asks Maz to deliver them to Leia, but Maz refuses, believing it's time for Han to join the fight himself. Meanwhile, Rey wanders into the dungeons and discovers Luke Skywalker's lightsaber packed away in a chest. Maz appears after Rey has a Force vision. She urges Rey to take the lightsaber and to seek Luke Skywalker, but Rey refuses and runs away. Shortly afterward, the First Order attacks Maz's castle, and in the ensuing battle Maz gives the lightsaber to Finn, urging him to use it. Although her castle is destroyed, after the battle she tells her new friends not to lose hope, and remains on Takodana to clean up.

Maz very quickly returns to her old life of action and adventure, getting caught up in a blaster fight she refers to as a "union dispute." In the midst of this, Finn, Rose Tico, and Poe Dameron contact her for advice about finding someone who can break them into Snoke's flagship, and she directs them toward Canto Bight.

Shortly after that defeat, Poe seeks her council on Ephemera where she provides him with critical intelligence on potential recruits for the Resistance. She joins their forces on Ajan Kloss, and she witnesses Leia Organa's death. Maz later awards Chewbacca Han's medal of honor when he returns from the Battle of Exegol.

Battle joined
Rey, after exposure to Luke Skywalker's lightsaber, flees the castle, but Maz gives the lightsaber to Finn, hoping to rekindle the heroism that she senses in his heart.

BAZINE NETAL
SPECIES Human **HOMEWORLD** Chaaktil
AFFILIATION Independent bounty hunter

"Bazine Netal" (her name is an alias) spends her early childhood in an orphanage in Chaako City on Chaaktil. She is adopted by the pirate Delphi Kloda, who raises her at his combat school and teaches her martial arts. Badly burned in her first mission, she now wears a cowl to cover her scars. Working as a bounty hunter and First Order spy, Netal becomes an associate of the fierce Dowutin Grummgar. While the two are lounging at Maz's castle, she watches BB-8 and Rey arrive with Han Solo, and notifies the First Order. She is later hired to hunt down the *Millennium Falcon*, so travels the galaxy to learn more about the ship.

SIDON ITHANO
SPECIES Delphidian **HOMEWORLD** Delphidian Cluster
AFFILIATION Sidon Ithano's crew

Captain Sidon Ithano, also known as "the Blood Buccaneer," "the Crimson Corsair," and "the Red Raider," is one of the best pirates in the Outer Rim. His nicknames are derived from his red Kaleesh helmet. He locates the abandoned Separatist ship *Obrexta III*, hoping to find a lost hoard of Count Dooku's kyber crystals. Instead, he finds a frozen clone trooper and data pinpointing many forgotten Separatist bases. Ithano's crew visits a number of these sites and acquires Separatist vessels. While visiting Maz Kanata's castle, Finn tries to negotiate passage offworld with Sidon and his first mate, Quiggold, just before the First Order attacks. During the ensuing war, Ithano sells a shipment of super battle droids to Kragan Gorr aboard the *Colossus*, and later fights alongside the Resistance at the Battle of Exegol. Ithano survives the battle and heads to Ajan Kloss to celebrate the victory.

ME-8D9
MANUFACTURER Duwani Mechanical Products
TYPE Protocol droid **AFFILIATION** Maz's castle

ME-8D9, or "Emmie," is an ancient droid believed to have once belonged to the Jedi Order during the Old Republic era, thousands of years ago. If so, she may be one of the castle's original inhabitants. She later becomes an assassin, but has softened in her old age and has served in Maz's castle since the High Republic era. Centuries later, ME-8D9 breaks up a fight between First Order and Resistance pilots prior to the war between the two enemies. She also introduces Karr Nuq Sin to Maz Kanata. ME-8D9 is present when the First Order destroys the castle, bringing Maz's millennia there to a sad end.

TRINTO DUABA
SPECIES Stennes Shifter
HOMEWORLD Stennaros
AFFILIATION Independent

Trinto Duaba is a vagrant traveler about whom little is known. His species has an innate ability to use the Force to pass invisibly through crowds. He is present at Chalmun's Cantina in Mos Eisley when Obi-Wan Kenobi and Luke Skywalker meet Han Solo. He is also present decades later when Han Solo brings Finn, Rey, and BB-8 to meet Maz Kanata on Takodana. When Maz's castle is destroyed by the First Order, Trinto manages to slip through the chaos unharmed and seek refuge.

GRUMMGAR
SPECIES Dowutin **HOMEWORLD** Dowut
AFFILIATION Free agent

Grummgar is a mercenary and big-game hunter known for his poaching escapades on the planet Ithor. His specialty is hunting multi-legged, venomous predators called molsumes. During the Galactic Civil War, Grummgar joins a group that is taking part in the Great Hunt of Malastare where the prize prey is the bounty hunter Bossk. Decades later, Grummgar is at Maz Kanata's castle lounging around with Bazine Netal.

PRASTER OMMLEN
SPECIES Ottegan **HOMEWORLD** Ottega
AFFILIATION Sacred Order of Ramulus

Praster Ommlen is a former weapons smuggler who gives up his life of crime to become a monk in an Ithorian religion (Ithorians, or "Hammerheads," are related to Ottegans). He offers spiritual advice to customers at Maz's Castle and observes the destruction of Hosnian Prime from just outside.

QUIGGOLD
SPECIES Gabdorin **HOMEWORLD** Gabdor
AFFILIATION Sidon Ithano's crew

Quiggold is the first mate of Captain Sidon Ithano's pirate crew. When searching for a lost shipment of kyber crystals, they find a clone trooper named Kix, frozen in stasis. Soon after, Quiggold allows himself to be captured by a rival criminal gang so he can distract its members and ensure Ithano's crew can take a vessel from the group. While at Maz's castle, Finn tries to negotiate transportation with Quiggold and Sidon to get offworld. Quiggold remains by his captain's side during the Battle of Exegol.

STRONO TUGGS
SPECIES Artiodac **HOMEWORLD** Takodana
AFFILIATION Maz's castle

Strono "Cookie" Tuggs has served as the cook in Maz's castle for hundreds of years. When his sous chef Robbs Ely is murdered and his recipe book stolen, Cookie sets up a cooking contest among his other chefs to see if one uses Ely's recipes, which would identify them as the killer. Following the destruction of Maz's castle. Tuggs sets up his own mobile catering service named Tuggs' Grub from a shuttle. He frequently heads to Batuu where he is displeased by the First Order occupation.

GWELLIS BAGNORO
SPECIES Onodone
AFFILIATION Independent entrepreneur

Gwellis Bagnoro is a secretive customer often seen at Maz Kanata's castle with his pet barghest, Izby. He is an expert forger, specializing in transit documents. His species is mysterious—perhaps originating in the Unknown Regions.

WOLLIVAN
SPECIES Blarina **HOMEWORLD** Rina Major
AFFILIATION Independent entrepreneur

Wollivan is a galactic explorer who sells his knowledge of hyperspace navigation, unexplored worlds, and scavenged treasures to make a living. He has something of a gambling problem, though, and for that reason he likes to hang out at Maz Kanata's castle more than is sensible.

TEMMIN WEXLEY
SPECIES Human **HOMEWORLD** Akiva **AFFILIATION** Rebel Alliance, New Republc Defense Fleet, Resistance, Black Squadron, Blue Squadron

Temmin "Snap" Wexley's father, Brentin, is arrested by the Empire when Temmin is still young. His mother, Norra, joins the Rebel Alliance, leaving him alone. Temmin spends his childhood as a junk dealer and reconstructs a battle droid named Mister Bones to be his companion. In the aftermath of the Battle of Endor, while still a teenager, Temmin joins the Rebel Alliance and hunts Imperial fugitives with his mother. He fights at the climactic Battle of Jakku, where his father falls in battle, and becomes a starfighter pilot for the New Republic, learning from Norra's new husband and Alliance legend Wedge Antilles. As an adult, Snap later joins the Resistance; and as a member of Black Squadron, he assists Poe Dameron in the search for Lor San Tekka. Snap falls in love with and marries fellow pilot Karé Kun. Once the Resistance is made aware of Starkiller Base, Snap pilots the scout ship that gathers vital intelligence on the superweapon and returns with the intel to D'Qar. He is one of the few survivors of the Battle of Starkiller Base. Before the Resistance evacuation of D'Qar, General Organa orders Snap to leave and search the galaxy for any surviving New Republic military commanders. Now leading Black Squadron, Snap heads to Pastoria and then to Grail City on Ikkrukk where the pilots engage the First Order. Thanks to Poe's arrival, they defeat the enemy forces but fail to recruit the locals to their cause. Snap and Karé then return to his homeworld, recruiting Norra and Wedge to the cause. Having reunited on Ryloth, Snap survives the First Order attack there and then joins the Resistance mission to recruit more to the cause on Corellia. Snap flies with Black Squadron during the Battle of Exegol, but is shot down by enemy fire.

JESSIKA PAVA
SPECIES Human **HOMEWORLD** Dandoran **AFFILIATION** Resistance, Black Squadron, Blue Squadron

Jessika Pava is known as "the Great Destroyer" by Resistance droids due to her unfortunate habit of losing astromechs to enemy fire during X-wing dogfights. When she is a child on Dandoran, her family is captured by pirates and enslaved. Pava idolizes Luke Skywalker and, as an adult, follows in his footsteps, joining the Resistance and flying an X-wing. Pava flies under the command of Poe Dameron in both Black and Blue Squadrons. She helps her commander search for Lor San Tekka, who is believed to know how to find Luke, and goes on to fly her X-wing as Blue Three at the Battles of Takodana and Starkiller Base. After the destruction of Starkiller Base, General Organa sends Black Squadron to search for allies in the Outer Rim. They reunite with Poe during the Battle of Ikkrukk, before the Squadron splits up to cover more ground. Pava and Suralinda Javos recruit a former Imperial leader Teza Nasz on Rattatak and then regroup with the rest of the organization on Ryloth. Pava survives the Battle of Exegol and joins her remaining Black Squadron pilots to eulogize Snap who doesn't make it.

Blue Three
Above Starkiller Base, Jess provides Poe with vital cover as he makes his final attack run on the thermal oscillator. Many of her squadron mates are shot down.

ELLO ASTY
SPECIES Abednedo **HOMEWORLD** Abednedo
AFFILIATION New Republic Defense Fleet, Resistance, Cobalt Squadron, Red Squadron

Ello Asty originally flies patrols and performs in air shows as a member of the New Republic Defense Fleet on Hosnian Prime. He joins Leia Organa's Resistance, also based on Hosnian Prime, before they relocate to D'Qar. There, Ello communicates with Poe Dameron's spies, including Kazuda Xiono, when Poe is unavailable. He also pilots his T-70 X-wing starfighter in the Resistance's Red Squadron, flying as Red Six. Ello takes part in the Battle of Starkiller Base, but is killed during the attack on the base's thermal oscillator.

216 CHARACTERS AND CREATURES

KAYDEL KO CONNIX
SPECIES Human **HOMEWORLD** Dulathia **AFFILIATION** Resistance

Kaydel Connix is an operations controller in the Resistance fleet command on D'Qar. She coordinates communications between the Resistance's tiny fleet of starfighters and the base commanders. After the successful Battle of Starkiller Base, Connix is promoted to lieutenant and given charge over the evacuation from D'Qar. She barely escapes herself before the facility is obliterated by the First Order's *Mandator IV*-class Siege Dreadnought, the *Fulminatrix*. Connix joins the Resistance crew on board the MC85 Star Cruiser *Raddus*. She supports Captain Poe Dameron's mutiny against Vice Admiral Holdo, but surrenders when Dameron is stunned by General Leia Organa. Connix arrives on Crait with the remaining Resistance members and is one of the few to survive the battle that follows, retreating aboard the *Millennium Falcon*.

Following the battle, Connix is often the main point of contact for agents on missions, as the Resistance focuses on finding a location for a more permanent base and replenishing its ranks. During this time, Connix builds a strong friendship with Rose Tico and Beaumont Kin. The trio forms part of the Resistance assault team during the Battle of Exegol where Connix puts her blaster training to good use. Alongside Rose and Beaumont, Connix returns to Ajan Kloss victorious.

USHOS O. STATURA
SPECIES Human **HOMEWORLD** Garel **AFFILIATION** Rebels, Resistance

Ushos O. Statura first takes up arms as a teenager, battling the Empire on Garel. Decades later he serves as an admiral in the Resistance, based at their headquarters on D'Qar. After a career in scientific research, he is well suited to planning the Battle of Starkiller Base, and correctly identifies the base's weakness: its thermal oscillator. Ushos does not survive the evacuation from Crait.

HARTER KALONIA
SPECIES Human **AFFILIATION** Resistance

Dr. Harter Kalonia treats Leia Organa during her pregnancy. Later, as a major in the Resistance, she is stationed in the Resistance Command Center on D'Qar. Here she serves as Leia's personal assistant and chief medical officer; she tends to the mental and physical health of many Resistance agents, including Vi Moradi, Cardinal, Chewbacca, and Finn.

CALUAN EMATT
SPECIES Human **AFFILIATION** Rebel Alliance, Resistance

Caluan Ematt is a friend of Princess Leia Organa and lieutenant in the Rebel Alliance during the Galactic Civil War. He leads an elite recon unit called the Shrikes that locates potential new bases for the rebels. Ematt is also a member of Han Solo's strike team during the Battle of Endor. Later, he becomes a founding member of the Resistance, though he remains a double agent in the New Republic military, recruiting for the Resistance. After the Battle of Starkiller Base he is promoted from major to general. Ematt goes on to fight at the Battle of Crait.

C'AI THRENALLI
SPECIES Abednedo **HOMEWORLD** Abednedo **AFFILIATION** Resistance

C'ai Threnalli is an Abednedo Resistance pilot stationed on D'Qar. After seeing Rey off on her mission to find Luke Skywalker, he assists with the evacuation and continues to fly as Poe Dameron's wingman—he also supports the brash pilot's mutiny against Vice Admiral Holdo. Threnalli survives the Battle of Crait and escapes aboard the *Millennium Falcon*. He then flies an X-wing during the Battle of Exegol and is fortunate to be alive after its conclusion.

VOBER DAND
SPECIES Tarsunt **HOMEWORLD** Suntilla **AFFILIATION** Resistance

Vober Dand serves as a controller in the Resistance Ground Logistics Division, in defiance of his father's concerns. He is highly organized and rigid about sticking to protocol—leading to arguments with fellow staff and commanders alike. He is stationed at the Resistance Command Center on D'Qar during the Battle of Starkiller Base and participates in the evacuation that follows. He is one of the few survivors that escapes Crait. Vober's father has a change of heart and is inspired by his son to join the Resistance, too. They work together in the ground crew on Ajan Kloss and celebrate the Resistance victory at Exegol.

PZ-4CO
MANUFACTURER Serv-O-Droid, Inc. **TYPE** Protocol droid **AFFILIATION** Resistance

PZ-4CO, also known as "Peazy," is a blue protocol droid that is designed to resemble the long-necked humanoid Tofallid species. She stores immense tactical data in her memory banks and works as a communications specialist in the Resistance headquarters on D'Qar. She convinces General Leia Organa (after weeks of pestering) to begin recording her memoirs, beginning with Operation: Yellow Moon, which took place just before the Battle of Endor.

B-U4D
MANUFACTURER JLD Mechanicals Consortium **TYPE** Loading droid **AFFILIATION** Resistance

"Buford" (B-U4D) is a starfighter maintenance droid working for the Resistance on D'Qar. He is a tireless member of the ground crew, and assists in the base's evacuation.

TALLISSAN LINTRA
SPECIES Human **HOMEWORLD** Pippip 3 **AFFILIATION** Resistance, Blue Squadron

Lieutenant Tallissan "Tallie" Lintra is one of the best pilots in the Resistance, and flies an RZ-2 A-wing as Blue Leader. She survives the evacuation of D'Qar, but not Kylo Ren's attack on the fleet.

PAIGE TICO
SPECIES Human **HOMEWORLD** Hays Minor **AFFILIATION** Resistance, Cobalt Squadron

Paige Tico is the older sister of Rose Tico. The two grow up in the Otomok system where they learn to pilot ships in their grandmother's flight simulator. The sisters witness the brutality of the First Order and fight back by destroying 12 enemy bombers. Their parents secure them passage offworld and tell them to join the Resistance where Paige serves as a gunner aboard the bomber *Cobalt Hammer*. When the sisters learn that their world and people have been destroyed by the First Order, they are tempted to seek revenge on a solo mission, but General Organa dissuades them. The sisters then focus on saving other planets instead. Soon after, Paige takes part in missions against pirates in the Cassandra sector and a relief operation in Atterra. During the evacuation from D'Qar, Paige's bomber attacks the First Order Dreadnought *Fulminatrix*. With her crew incapacitated, Paige singlehandedly drops the bomber's payload and destroys the enemy vessel. Though the explosion also takes Paige's life, her sacrifice allows the Resistance to escape.

ROSE TICO

SPECIES Human
HOMEWORLD Hays Minor
AFFILIATION Resistance, Cobalt Squadron

Resistance hero Rose Tico loses everything to the First Order's callous barbarity. However, she is determined to stand up to its evil, using her intelligence and compassion to fight in her own way.

LIVING UNDER THE FIRST ORDER
Sisters Rose and Paige Tico grow up in the Otomok system on Hays Minor. Their people are enslaved by the First Order and forced to mine their own planet before it is bombed by the oppressive regime to test its weapons. The two sisters are very close, and wear matching pendants made of valuable Haysian smelt. To Rose and Paige, they are good luck charms; but more importantly, they represent their homeworld and are symbols of their love for each other. After striking against the First Order threat, the sisters escape from Hays Minor, joining the Resistance together. They are assigned to Cobalt Squadron, with Rose as a mechanic and Paige as a gunner. The sisters see action fighting pirates in the Cassander system and later help deliver vital supplies to those in need in the Atterra system.

LOSS AND BRAVERY
When Paige is killed during the attack on D'Qar, Rose is left no time to mourn. While guarding the escape pods aboard the *Raddus*, she encounters Finn, who is trying to escape so that he can find Rey. She stuns him, but when he can speak again, their discussion turns to the Resistance fleet's pursuit by the First Order—and how they might escape the predicament. They meet with Poe Dameron and discuss a plan to sneak aboard the First Order flagship *Supremacy* and disable its hyperspace tracker. They call Maz Kanata, who tells them to find someone known as Master Codebreaker in the Canto Bight casino.

RESISTANCE INFILTRATOR
Rose, Finn, and Poe's droid, BB-8, arrive and search the casino for the individual, but are soon arrested. Rose and Finn are imprisoned and BB-8 is thrown out. In their jail cell they meet a slicer (hacker) named DJ, who offers to fill the role of Master Codebreaker. They decline, and DJ opens the cell to let them all out, parting ways. Rose and Finn head to the racetrack stables where they steal a fathier, riding amidst a stampede through the old city. Once outside town, they are trapped on a cliff. Luckily, BB-8 and DJ arrive in a stolen ship and rescue them. Unable to find Master Codebreaker, they agree to hire DJ instead. Successfully boarding the *Supremacy*, the three don First Order officer uniforms to sneak through the ship. They reach the tracker but are apprehended. Sentenced to death, Rose and Finn discover at their execution that they were betrayed by DJ. Fortunately, their punishment is interrupted when Resistance Vice Admiral Holdo rams the ship at lightspeed, and then BB-8 seizes control of an AT-ST and rescues them. The three escape and rejoin the Resistance remnant on Crait. The First Order soon arrives and besieges the base where they are sheltering, so Rose and Finn join Poe's wing of ski speeders to face the enemy. As they head toward the First Order's superlaser siege cannon, Poe realizes their attack is futile and calls it off. However, Finn keeps going. Rose suddenly charges his ship to stop him, declaring, before passing out, that they'll win the war by saving the ones they love. The Resistance retreats and escapes aboard the *Millennium Falcon*, where Finn tends to the unconscious Rose.

NEW RESPONSIBILITIES
The indomitable Rose recovers and plays an important role in Resistance missions to Mon Cala and Minfar. She later helps to establish the new Resistance base on Ajan Kloss. She leads the Engineering Corps and develops communication technology that bypasses the First Order's jamming interference. While General Leia Organa asks her to stay behind during Rey's mission to find Exegol, Rose is on the front lines when they take the fight to the Final Order. She's part of the ground assault team that storms across the surface of the Star Destroyer *Steadfast* to disrupt the Sith fleet's navigational capability. Rose withdraws with the other Resistance fighters and returns safely to the base as the Resistance is victorious.

Inauspicious meeting
When Rose first meets Finn, she has already heard tales of his heroism. On learning he plans to desert, however, her excitement turns into righteous fury.

In disguise
Despite her deep hatred for the regime that enslaved her homeworld, Rose is forced to wear the uniform of a First Order major to infiltrate Supreme Leader Snoke's flagship.

Old wounds
As their mission progresses, Rose and Finn find they have much more in common than they first imagined.

LARMA D'ACY

SPECIES Human **HOMEWORLD** Warlentta **AFFILIATION** Resistance

Hailing from Warlentta, Commander Larma D'Acy comes from a family with a long history of military service. D'Acy agrees to join the Resistance and is personally recruited to the cause by General Leia Organa. Larma's wife, commercial pilot Wrobie Tyce, agrees with her partner's choice and signs up as well. One of the few officers to survive Kylo Ren's attack on the *Raddus*, D'Acy supports Vice Admiral Holdo when she takes command of the Resistance fleet. D'Acy survives to escape from Crait with the remaining Resistance members. As one of the most senior Resistance leaders left, she becomes Leia's most trusted confidant and takes charge of setting up the base on Ajan Kloss where Tyce also serves. After Leia dies, D'Acy delivers the tragic news to Chewbacca, Finn, and Poe Dameron. Tyce and D'Acy reunite following the Battle of Exegol and revel in the Resistance victory.

EDRISON PEAVEY

SPECIES Human **AFFILIATION** Empire, First Order

Edrison Peavey serves in the Imperial Navy during the Emperor's reign. He later commands the First Order Star Destroyer *Finalizer*, reporting to General Armitage Hux (whom he secretly views with contempt). He is present during the attack on D'Qar, and forms part of Kylo Ren's entourage on his command shuttle at the Battle of Crait.

MODEN CANADY

SPECIES Human **AFFILIATION** Empire, First Order

Moden Canady begins his military career in the Imperial Navy as commander of the Imperial Star Destroyer *Solicitude*. After the Galactic Civil War he joins the First Order and becomes captain of the Siege Dreadnought *Fulminatrix*, serving with Edrison Peavey under General Armitage Hux. He is resentful of his young and incompetent First Order crew, who lack the training and experience of his former Imperial shipmates. He and all aboard the *Fulminatrix* perish in a Resistance bomber attack ordered by Poe Dameron.

ALCIDA-AUKA

SPECIES Lanai **HOMEWORLD** Ahch-To **AFFILIATION** None

Alcida-Auka is the matron of the Lanai Caretakers of Ahch-To's temple island. Her people are matriarchal, passing down their titles and roles from mother to daughter. At times, Alcida-Auka struggles to hide her irritation when the latest visitors don't behave how she expects.

FIRST ORDER FLEET GUNNER

SPECIES Human **HOMEWORLD** Various **AFFILIATION** First Order

Pilots, engineers, and gunners all start at the First Order's academies with the same basic training regimen and are assigned specializations according to their demonstrated aptitude. Fleet gunners like Brun Obatsun wear black uniforms similar to fleet engineers, and are stationed in weapons control centers across the *Supremacy*'s exterior. Their helmets are designed to focus their attention directly on their targets with other visual information cut out. The gunners fire a constant barrage of plasma bursts as the Resistance fleet flees D'Qar.

PORG

HOMEWORLD Ahch-To **AVERAGE SIZE** 18 cm (10 in) high **HABITAT** Islands and open seas

Sea birds are the dominant life form on Ahch-To. Porgs are birdlike creatures that dwell in the rocky cliffs of the planet's islands and coastal zones. They dive into the sea and use their large eyes to help them catch small fish, which they feed to their young (known as porglets). Porg offspring are often hatched as pairs, in nests tended by their parents. Porgs are considered quite tasty by some species, and are sometimes hunted by the resident Lanai and visitors to the islands. A number of porgs, including at least one breeding pair, stow away aboard the *Millennium Falcon* and the species is soon found on other worlds.

FIRST ORDER SHUTTLE PILOT

SPECIES Human **HOMEWORLD** Various **AFFILIATION** First Order

First Order shuttle pilots form an elite unit tasked with transporting high-ranking officers, dignitaries, and wealthy First Order families with considerable influence. Such assignments are coveted by older First Order pilots who are less concerned with forging careers in battle than providing for their families through high-paid but mundane flight schedules. The exception are pilots serving military officials such as Kylo Ren in his *Upsilon*-class command shuttle. These pilots face battle situations on a regular basis.

THALA-SIREN

HOMEWORLD Ahch-To **AVERAGE SIZE** 5.4 m (18 ft) high **HABITAT** Coastal areas

Thala-sirens are sea mammals with four flippers used for swimming. They are generally docile and come ashore to rest and bask in the sun. Mothers, also known as sea sows, nurse their young on the rocky shores of Ahch-To's islands. With no predators on land, the sows allow Luke Skywalker to approach and milk them. Their mammary glands produce green milk, which is salty and has a hint of the large kelp they feed upon. Large thala-bulls are a worry to the unwatchful. They use their large tusks to lunge at intruders to their territory.

SNOKE'S NAVIGATORS

AFFILIATION First Order

Also known as Attendants, Snoke's "navigators" are ancient alien beings from the Unknown Regions. They are often hired, including by the Grysk Hegemony, as guides to help traverse the dangerous area they call home. They are also employed by the Imperials who flee into the Unknown Regions. The tall, seemingly mute beings serve Snoke in his throne room aboard the *Supremacy*, where they build his oculus viewing scope and advise him on hyperspace routes and the curiosities of space. They communicate using inaudible pulses of energy in wavelengths unperceivable to humans, but visible to navigator eyes.

"We are the spark that will light the fire that will restore the Republic."
VICE ADMIRAL HOLDO

VICE ADMIRAL HOLDO
SPECIES Human **HOMEWORLD** Gatalenta
AFFILIATION Apprentice Legislature, Rebel Alliance, Resistance

Amilyn Holdo is free spirited and highly intellectual with a penchant for creative solutions to difficult situations. As a young woman, she serves as a member of the Imperial Senate's Apprentice Legislature on Coruscant. There she meets Princess Leia Organa and they become good friends. While on Pamarthe, Leia confides to Holdo that she is part of the rebellion against the Empire. Shortly afterward, Holdo helps Leia find safe passage to the Paucris system, allowing her to warn the rebel fleet of an impending Imperial attack. They go on further adventures during their teenage years, including into the lower levels of Coruscant.

In the years before open warfare, Holdo joins the Rebel Alliance. While aboard the Alliance ship *Candor*, the crew shows little respect for Holdo until the ship's captain dies during a surprise Imperial attack. Holdo quickly assumes command, and enacts an ingenious escape that sees her promoted to captain afterward.

During the Galactic Civil War, Holdo plays a vital role sourcing supplies from criminal syndicates for the Alliance. When her criminal contacts and Alliance supplies begin to dry up, Holdo leads Leia and a group of Alliance heroes to Spira. After a brief vacation, the rebels steal a rare Nihil Path engine and hook it up to their ship so they can travel to the location of the fabled and lost Kezarat Convoy, which carries a vast fuel resource. The heroes succeed in reaching the convoy and its crew, but they all end up temporarily stranded in an unusual area of the galaxy called No-Space. The rebels find a way to bring themselves, the fuel, and any of the convoy's residents that wish back to the rest of the galaxy.

Decades later, as the threat of the First Order looms, Holdo joins the Resistance. During an early mission, Holdo, Nien Nunb and another agent steal the head of a protocol droid, containing vital recordings, from the New Republic's Brooksdion Station. As the trio escapes in a vessel, Holdo encounters future Resistance leader Poe Dameron, currently in command of a New Republic starfighter squadron. Holdo not only saves Poe's life multiple times as he pursues their ship through a dangerous asteroid field, but manages to then disable his ship and flee with the intel. Holdo eventually assumes the role of Vice Admiral and is given command of the *Free Virgillia*-class Bunkerbuster *Ninka*. Prior to the evacuation of D'Qar, she briefs the Cobalt and Crimson bomber squadrons on the destruction of Hosnian Prime and Starkiller Base. She equips both squadrons for battle and then assists in the evacuation of the Resistance base.

When General Organa is incapacitated and most of the Resistance leadership killed, Vice Admiral Holdo transfers to the Resistance flagship, the *Raddus*, and takes command of the surviving Resistance forces. From the start, there is friction between her and Poe, who has recently been demoted for his rash decisions that caused tremendous losses for the Resistance. Holdo declines to inform Poe of her plan to reach Crait and evacuate the Resistance to the planet below. Poe grows ever more suspicious of her intentions and launches a mutiny, taking Holdo into custody. When Leia awakens, she grabs her blaster and stuns Poe, putting an end to the short-lived insurrection.

Holdo wishes Leia and the Resistance goodbye, and remains on the *Raddus* to buy them time. When the First Order fires upon the group's helpless transports, Holdo makes a valiant choice. She sacrifices herself by ramming the *Supremacy* at lightspeed, cutting it in half and allowing her friends to escape to Crait. The surprising move is then known as the Holdo maneuver and is replicated a year later over the Forest Moon of Endor.

PRAETORIAN GUARD
SPECIES Human **HOMEWORLD** Various
AFFILIATION Empire, First Order

Praetorian Guards are elite personal security soldiers who are assigned to protect key Imperial remnant and later First Order personnel. Their red plastoid armor and luxurious red robes overtly tie the group to Emperor Palpatine's Royal Guards, mimicking the splendor and power that they once symbolized—the title "Praetorian Guard" itself dates back to the 14th Emperor of Kitel Phard. The Praetorians' identities are kept hidden so that they cannot be bribed or blackmailed to betray their sacred duty. Their personal histories have even been wiped from the records. The guards are trained in a variety of martial arts, including teräs käsi, Echani, Bakuuni Hand, and Nar Kanji techniques, enabling them to face physical threats of all kinds.

The mag-coils in the Praetorians' heavy armor plating generate a magnetic field that deflects blaster fire and even causes glancing lightsaber blows to bounce off them (although a direct lightsaber thrust will still penetrate and inflict lethal damage). The armor undergoes changes over the years and is uncomfortable at best as the energy from the mag-coils causes lingering pain in the wearer. Praetorian weapons include Bilari electro-chain whips (which form pikes when at rest), twin joining vibro-arbir blades, vibro-voulges, and electro-bisentos. Their blades are energized to counter lightsabers in duels, and their edges vibrate at a high frequency to increase their cutting performance.

A trio of these guards is dispatched to the Imperial remnant base on Mandalore when Bo-Katan Kryze reclaims her homeworld. These guards skillfully execute the veteran Mandalorian Paz Vizsla, and they have the upper hand against Din Djarin until he and Grogu work together to defeat them.

Years later, a number of elite Praetorians are assigned to Supreme Leader Snoke of the First Order. They accompany him everywhere, guarding his throne room and residence. Praetorians are trained to consider everyone a possible threat, including Snoke's advisors and his own apprentice. Hidden behind their opaque visors, they keep a watchful eye on all who approach the supreme leader. The Praetorians stand at attention in Snoke's throne room on his flagship *Supremacy* when Kylo Ren brings Rey before him. Snoke's overconfidence leads him to keep the guards at bay. When their master is suddenly slain by Kylo Ren, they rush to avenge him. Fighting in four pairs, their strength and skill rivals that of both Rey and Kylo, but all are cut down in an epic battle.

DJ
SPECIES Human **AFFILIATION** Himself

DJ's alias stands for "Don't Join." He believes there are no good or bad sides—the First Order and Resistance are two sides of the same coin. He is a criminal slicer (hacker) who uses his skills to steal money from the wealthy on Canto Bight. He creates a false persona named Denel Strench to take the blame for his crimes. DJ is arrested after cheating at Eclipse casino games and getting into a vehicular accident in front of police. At the time of his arrest, a gambling droid uncovers DJ's alter ego, exposing his charade. While in jail, DJ meets Resistance members Rose Tico and Finn. They all escape and go their separate ways, but DJ and BB-8 end up together and rescue the other two. In need of a slicer, Rose and Finn hire DJ to help them sneak aboard the First Order flagship *Supremacy* using his stolen yacht *Libertine*. Once aboard, the three are captured and it's revealed he sold them out in exchange for his own freedom and a substantial payment.

"Live free, don't join."
DJ

220 CHARACTERS AND CREATURES

LEXO SOOGER
SPECIES Dor Namethian
HOMEWORLD Askkto-Fen IV
AFFILIATION None

A former assassin, Lexo Sooger is now the celebrity masseur at Zord's Spa and Bathhouse. When Sooger finds a human left on his doorstep, he takes her in and names her Lula. One of his treatments is disrupted by a stampede of fathiers, thanks to Finn and Rose Tico.

THE COUNTESS
SPECIES Idalowd
HOMEWORLD Cantonica
AFFILIATION Canto Casino

The Countess, Contessa Alissyndrex delga Cantonica Provincion, is a keen fan of the fathier races on Canto Bight. She and her husband, who is rarely seen, are the figureheads of the city. Her shoulders hold the priceless Onyx Bands of Cato Neimoidia.

DOBBU SCAY
SPECIES Khamarill
HOMEWORLD Emkhamarill
AFFILIATION None

Offworlder Dobbu Scay spends much of his gambling time inebriated. Unable to maintain any self-control in the face of the vast array of distractions at Canto Bight's casino, Dobbu has already lost most of his spending money when he meets BB-8. Mistaking the astromech for a slot machine, he empties his coins into BB-8's diagnostic slot before the droid rolls away. Fortunately for Dobbu, he is able to recoup his losses later when panicked patrons drop their winnings during the fathier stampede.

YASTO ATTSMUN
SPECIES Ungrila **HOMEWORLD** Listehol
AFFILIATION Attsmun Cybernetics

Tyrannical Baron Yasto Attsmun is a wealthy aristocrat who is the head of Attsmun Cybernetics. This evil individual collects powerful dark-side artifacts, frequently hiring treasure hunter Lens Kamo to find them. Attsmun believes the combination of his cybernetics and these rare items will allow him to live forever. He even tests his theory by experimenting on unfortunate living creatures including Kamo's pet gergilla, Ayuu. Attsmun also hosts frequent Canto Bight parties with infamous guests aboard his yacht, *Undisputed Victor*. One such party ends with the murder of an arms dealer. The baron has aspirations of a relationship with club owner Ubialla Gheal with whom he converses during an event on his yacht, following the Hosnian Cataclysm. Soon after on Batuu, Yasto heads to a Jedi temple to retrieve an artifact, but the baron is stopped by a vengeful Kamo and a droid repair tech.

KEDPIN SHOKLOP
SPECIES Wermal
HOMEWORLD Werma Lesser
AFFILIATION VaporTech

After spending 102 years as a vaporator salesman, polite Kedpin Shoklop wins a trip to Canto Bight as his reward for being named Salesbeing of the Year. His first vacation in a century doesn't go so well though. He gets caught up with a criminal and ends up in jail.

SLOWEN LO
SPECIES Abednedo
HOMEWORLD Cantonica
AFFILIATION None

Beach-dwelling Canto Bight citizen Slowen Lo makes vast sums of money selling high-quality driftwood art. He is irritated when Finn and Rose Tico illegally land their ship on the beach at Canto Bight and so informs the police, getting them thrown in jail.

THAMM
SPECIES Troglof
HOMEWORLD Troglofa
AFFILIATION Canto Casino and Racetrack

The most popular croupier at the Canto Casino is named Thamm. He has a reassuring demeanor that makes casino patrons feel comfortable, as if he is a close friend. Thamm is a member of a rare species with tentaclelike arms and is small enough to stand directly on the tables. He can move his eye stalks independently to keep an eye on players and make sure nobody is breaking the rules. He is also notable for his unusual, but pleasant, natural odor.

DERLA PIDYS
SPECIES Argiopid
AFFILIATION None

A legendary sommelier, Derla Pidys is a frequent visitor to Canto Bight and the best at her trade in the sector. From Naboo to Orto Plutonia, she picks up her wares, selling them, often with an embellished origin, to enraptured clients. On one visit, she aims to acquire an unusual, rare vintage known as the "Wine of Dreams" from the equally odd Grammus sisters.

THODIBIN, DODIBIN, AND WODIBIN
SPECIES Suerton **HOMEWORLD** Chanceuxi **AFFILIATION** Themselves

The "Winning Three"—Thodibin, Dodibin, and Wodibin—have a reputation around the Canto Bight casino for their unusually long lucky streaks. It is believed that the trio can somehow affect probability in their favor. The casino security keeps a close watch but has never observed any criminal activity. The Suerton is a reptilian species well known across the galaxy for being inexplicably fortunate in all things.

GRAMMUS SISTERS
SPECIES Lukovel **AFFILIATION** None

Twins Rhomby and Parallela Grammus have an undeniably strong bond and are performance artists frequently seen in the Canto Bight casino. They appear to enjoy attracting lots of attention with their unusual attire, claims that they are from another dimension, and the unknown language that they use between themselves. When a clerk at their hotel fails to tell them apart, they are despondent and demand that the manager gives them the clerk as a souvenir. The sisters use this enslaved individual to relay their complicated requests.

FATHIER

HOMEWORLD Various worlds (domesticated)
AVERAGE SIZE 3 m (9 ft 10 in) high at shoulder
HABITAT Grasslands

Fathiers are bred (and abused) on planets such as Cantonica for races, where large sums of money are wagered. The rides are fast and dangerous, with speeds averaging 75 kilometers (47 miles) per hour and higher being the norm. Falls can kill a jockey, and stumbles can maim a fathier, rendering it useless to the owners. The animals are intelligent and naturally gentle, preferring to live in herds. Rose Tico and Finn steal a fathier to escape the police during their mission to Canto Bight, causing a stampede through the city.

TEMIRI BLAGG

SPECIES Human **HOMEWORLD** Cantonica
AFFILIATION None

Temiri Blagg is one of many street children left on Cantonica by wayward guardians who come for the gambling and other fleeting pleasures. He is placed under the charge of Bargwill Tomder to work in Canto Bight's stables. The Force-adept boy encounters Rose Tico and Finn as they flee from police custody. He and his friends, Oniho Zaya and Arashell Sar, decide to help them, releasing the entire herd of fathiers to cause confusion as Finn and Rose flee on one of the animals. Later, the children learn of the Battle of Crait, and long for such adventures themselves.

BARGWILL TOMDER

SPECIES Cloddogran
HOMEWORLD Galagolos V
AFFILIATION Canto Casino and Racetrack

Cantankerous Cloddogran Bargwill Tomder has charge of the Canto Bight stables at the city's large, money-spinning racetrack. He oversees stalls of valuable fathiers and a motley crew of urchins, all of whom he exploits to his own advantage. Determined to prove his management skills to his employers, Tomder uses his four arms to crack his whip and induce animals and enslaved children to get back to work.

VULPTEX

HOMEWORLD Crait **AVERAGE SIZE** 51 cm (20 in) high
HABITAT Salt flats, rock outcrops, and caves

Hot and arid, the salt flats of Crait are nonetheless home to many creatures, including small predators called vulptices. Their crystalline fur, an adaptation to the mineral-rich environment, is a defense mechanism against larger predators. This covering acts as armor and produces a jingling sound to warn other vulptices about danger. Most active at dusk and dawn, vulptices congregate in cave dens at night. The friendly creatures lead the Resistance to an alternate cave exit during the Battle of Crait, thus enabling them to escape the First Order.

STORMTROOPER EXECUTIONER

SPECIES Human **HOMEWORLD** Various
AFFILIATION First Order

As part of their regular duties, First Order stormtroopers are commanded to act as anonymous executioners. Their armor carries no individual rank or identifying insignia other than the black carbon finish on their shoulders and helmet that designates their role. Executioners carry a laser ax with eight collapsible claws, forming two sets of monomolecular energy ribbons. Public executions of the disloyal are held regularly, as an example to anyone who may be wavering in their support.

BB-9E

MANUFACTURER Industrial Automaton
TYPE BB-series Astromech droid
AFFILIATION First Order

First Order droids are treated like gadgets and service machines rather than friends and companions, as in the Resistance. A cold and methodical droid with a mean streak, BB-9E spots BB-8, Finn, and Rose aboard the *Supremacy* and immediately reports their suspicious activity.

SOL RIVAS

SPECIES Human
AFFILIATION First Order

Sol Rivas is a First Order lieutenant who discovers the computer records showing that Captain Phasma lowered Starkiller Base's shields during the Resistance assault on the superweapon. With Phasma planning to first frame and then kill him, Rivas flees for the planet Luprora. He refuses to let Phasma pin the dropped shields on him, so Phasma executes him.

NAKA IIT

SPECIES Blarina
HOMEWORLD Rina Major
AFFILIATION Scavenger

A former podracer, Naka Iit works as a scavenger in the deserts of Jakku. One day he encounters Poe Dameron, who claims to have just escaped the First Order and asks for help. Iit reluctantly agrees, but when Poe saves them from Strus Clan thugs, the Blarina comes to trust Dameron and promises to get him offworld.

ZAY VERSIO

SPECIES Human
AFFILIATION New Republic, Resistance

The daughter of Iden Versio and Del Meeko, Zay Versio grows up in the New Republic and becomes a fighter pilot. Upon discovering that the First Order killed her father, Zay works with her mother and family friend Shriv Suurgav to gather intel for the Resistance, even flying TIE fighters to gain access to a Star Destroyer. She avenges her father, confronting his killer, Gideon Hask, with Iden. Though her mother later dies before her eyes, Zay continues to deliver information to the Resistance. Zay then carries out missions for General Leia Organa, including recruiting Alliance veterans General Rieekan and Orrimaarko to the cause and stealing ships from Bracca. Zay later fights in the Battle of Exegol.

CHARACTERS AND CREATURES

FIRST ORDER SCUBA TROOPER
SPECIES Human **HOMEWORLD** Various **AFFILIATION** First Order

On aquatic worlds, the First Order employs specialized SCUBA troopers to patrol underwater military installations and occupied areas. These fighters are equipped with underwater blasters, flippers, breathing apparatus, airtight armor, and lights to help with visibility in murky waters. When the Colossus station is submerged on Castilon, SCUBA troopers deploy to search for Resistance activity. They encounter Kazuda Xiono and CB-23, who only escape thanks to Neeku Vozo's intervention.

GORK
SPECIES Gamorrean **HOMEWORLD** Gamorr **AFFILIATION** Kragan Gorr's Warbird gang

A hulking Gamorrean, Gork is the muscle of Kragan Gorr's pirate gang and an intimidating presence. He is particularly gifted at arm-wrestling, though his competitions aboard the Colossus platform quickly devolve into brawls among his own crewmates.

JAKOOSK
HOMEWORLD Celsor 3 **SIZE** 180 m (590 ft) long, 105 m (335 ft) wingspan **HABITAT** Snow

Native to the ice moon Celsor 3, the jakoosk is a massive creature with an equally large appetite, but it is also graceful as it flies over the moon's frozen landscape. The animal's topside is near-indestructible, and its strong spindly legs and sharp, yellow teeth make it a fearsome predator. The Aces of the Colossus platform awaken a jakoosk during a training exercise, and it nearly gobbles up Jarek Yeager's ship before the squadron topples an ice spire onto it. When the Colossus runs low on rations, its pilots return to Celsor 3 to hunt the jakoosk. As its meat is edible for most species, the jakoosk provides lasting sustenance to the people of the Colossus.

Dinner time
Kazuda Xiono delivers a direct hit to the beast's vulnerable underbelly when those onboard Colossus face a shortage of food.

LIEUTENANT GALEK
SPECIES Human **AFFILIATION** First Order

With a stern demeanor and zero tolerance for failure, Lieutenant Galek is a strict and effective flight instructor for the First Order. The veteran pilot believes that completing the mission is all that matters and she expects her cadets to follow orders—at all costs. When new recruit Tam Ryvora opts to save a teammate during a training exercise, a furious Galek strips Tam of her squadron leader rank. Perhaps fittingly, Galek meets her end in a clash near Dantooine, when the Resistance pilot Venisa Doza blasts the lieutenant's TIE fighter.

NENAVAKASA "NENA" NALOR
SPECIES Nikto **HOMEWORLD** Kintan **AFFILIATION** First Order

In a tragic life, Nenavakasa "Nena" Nalor has learned to do whatever it takes to survive. Working for the First Order, Nena sends a distress signal to the Colossus and is eventually welcomed onto the ship as a new engineer. With access to the platform's systems, she sabotages them but is forced to flee when Kazuda Xiono uncovers her plot.

FLANX
SPECIES Gozzo **HOMEWORLD** Drahgor III

The cousin of Colossus shop owner Flix, the Gozzo Flanx runs a fuel refinery on his homeworld of Drahgor III. Under Flanx's stewardship, the refinery engages in deep-core drilling—a practice long-prohibited due to the rumored presence of karnex dragons. Flanx learns the error of his ways when a family of the beasts awakens, leading him to cease his operations.

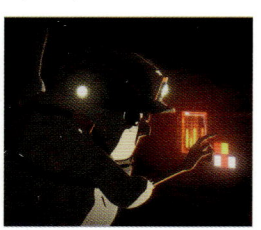

KARNEX DRAGON
HOMEWORLD Drahgor III **SIZE** 60 m (196 ft 10 in) long **HABITAT** Caves

Long rumored to be nothing more than a Gozzo myth, the karnex dragon is in fact very real. The mighty beasts live deep beneath the surface of Drahgor III, where they remain, unless disturbed. Their elongated bodies feature strong plated armor and short arms and legs. Though their glowing red eyes pierce through darkness, karnex dragons are sensitive to light, and their vision is based on movement. A family of the creatures is woken when Flanx, proprietor of a fuel refinery, engages in deep-core drilling. The dragons are ultimately driven away with bright lights.

TORCH
MANUFACTURER Industrial Automaton **TYPE** Astromech droid **AFFILIATION** Resistance

Though scratched and worn from years of adventures, Torch is an indispensable companion to Resistance pilot Venisa Doza. When the droid and his master are captured by a First Order Destroyer, Torch plays dead then rescues Doza from her cell. After they reach the hangar, Torch lives up to his name, detonating charges so they can escape.

MIKA GREY
SPECIES Human

A seasoned archaeologist, Mika Grey travels the galaxy in search of powerful relics, with the hope that she can find them before the First Order does. Following a two-and-a-half year search, Grey locates a Sith artifact on Ashas Ree, where she also encounters the Resistance's Kazuda Xiono. When First Order Raiders track her to the planet, Mika activates the device and throws it toward the troopers, who perish from the resulting energy discharge. Mika then accepts an invitation to live aboard the Colossus, where she works as a fortune teller. When Kaz believes he has been cursed, Grey gives him advice on how to remove the spell.

FIRST ORDER RAIDERS
SPECIES Human **HOMEWORLD** Various **AFFILIATION** First Order

First Order Raiders are specialized stormtroopers tasked with hunting down Sith relics for Kylo Ren. Their armor features several modifications from that of standard troops, including a gray-and-red color scheme and a unique helmet. A unit of Raiders tracks treasure hunter Mika Grey to a Sith temple on Ashas Ree, where it attempts to recover an artifact from her. But when Grey activates the device, the power that is unleashed destroys the squad.

VENISA DOZA
SPECIES Human **AFFILIATION** Rebel Alliance, Resistance, Jade Squadron

Venisa Doza is a veteran pilot, flying for both the Rebel Alliance and the Resistance. Wife of Captain Imanuel Doza of the *Colossus* and mother of the racer Torra, Venisa is captured by the First Order Star Destroyer, the *Thunderer*, while trying to rendezvous with her family. Kept in a cell, Venisa is rescued by her droid, Torch, who detonates several explosives in the hangar as they escape. Venisa later leads the Resistance's Jade Squadron in a final battle with the Star Destroyer, joining forces with the Aces of the *Colossus* to destroy the First Order's ship.

VRANKI
SPECIES Hutt **HOMEWORLD** Voxx Cluster **AFFILIATION** Vranki's Hotel and Casino

Vranki the Blue is the unscrupulous proprietor of Vranki's Hotel and Casino—a resort destination complete with a race track. The Hutt welcomes old friend Hype Fazon and the Aces of the *Colossus* to his establishment, quickly setting terms for a race. Although Vranki claims to be different from his notorious clan, he has no qualms about bending the rules and methodically employing dubious methods to ensure his droid flier wins every race. The Aces get the last laugh, however, as Neeku Vozo hacks into Vranki's casino game—linked to the course's dangerous obstacles—and gives Kazuda Xiono an opening to win.

NORATH KEV
SPECIES Duros **HOMEWORLD** Duros **AFFILIATION** Resistance

Working as a spy for the Resistance, Norath Kev finds himself the target of a bounty hunter called Ax Tagrin. Norath sends a distress signal shortly before being captured and is rescued by Kazuda Xiono, Jarek Yeager, and Synara San. Norath and Kaz then team up to save Jarek and Synara, who have been snagged by Tagrin and turned over to the First Order. Kev remains with the *Colossus*, flying his X-wing on a mission to escort shuttles safely onto the platform and then flies it in a final battle with Agent Tierny's Star Destroyer.

AX TAGRIN
SPECIES Iktotchi **HOMEWORLD** Nar Shaddaa **AFFILIATION** Bounty hunter

Gravelly voiced and colossal in stature, Ax Tagrin is a fearsome bounty hunter who sports custom armor and weaponry, including an extendible vibro-ax. He accepts a contract from Commander Pyre of the First Order to capture Resistance spy Norath Kev on Varkana. Tagrin succeeds in his mission and even secures additional assets when spies Kazuda Xiono and Jarek Yeager, along with pirate Synara San, come to the rescue. But before he can deliver the entire group, Norath and Kaz escape and then, with the help of the droid CB-23, they defeat Ax and free their friends.

DARRB
SPECIES Gabdorin **HOMEWORLD** Varkana

A Gabdorin vendor on Varkana, Darrb sells fruits and vegetables from his stand. He grows irritated when Kazuda Xiono absent-mindedly knocks over one of his containers. Later, he angrily protests when Kaz and fellow Resistance spy Norath Kev hide from stormtroopers in his home.

LECHEE
SPECIES Gran **HOMEWORLD** Varkana

Though he runs a junk shop on Varkana, Lechee has another means of income: turning Resistance spy Norath Kev over to bounty hunter Ax Tagrin. But when Kazuda Xiono, Jarek Yeager, Synara San, and their droid confront him—and threaten his payday—Lechee folds easily.

AEOSIAN QUEEN
SPECIES Aeosian **HOMEWORLD** Aeos Prime **AFFILIATION** Aeos Prime

The elegant Aeosian queen rules her tropical world of Aeos Prime. When Kazuda Xiono and Griff Halloran are scouting the planet as a possible new home for the *Colossus*, the queen's guards capture them. Believing they are with the First Order, who once attacked Aeos Prime, she orders them to be fed to a krakavora. But after Kaz saves an Aeosian, she sets the pair free. The queen then grants the *Colossus* permission to stay on Aeos Prime. However, the First Order soon arrives and, even though the queen commands her forces to help the *Colossus*, the platform is forced to flee.

HUGH SION
SPECIES Human **AFFILIATION** New Republic Defense Force, Resistance, Jade Squadron

Hugh Sion begins his piloting career in the New Republic Defense Force's Starfighter Corps, flying a T-85 X-wing alongside Kazuda Xiono. He eventually joins the Resistance as a member of Jade Squadron aboard the *Colossus* and reunites with Xiono—who he thought had perished. Now in T-70 X-wings, Sion and Jade Squadron join the Aces of the *Colossus* to engage the First Order; first to end the blockade of Dantooine and then in a final battle to liberate the platform. Following their victory over the First Order, Hugh joins his friends in celebration at Aunt Z's.

KRAKAVORA
HOMEWORLD Aeos Prime **SIZE** 26 m (85 ft 4 in) long, 21 m (69 ft) wingspan **HABITAT** Water, air

Native to Aeos Prime, the krakavora has webbed wings and a smooth, gilled body, making it a speedy traveler in both water and air. The large animals, though fearsome, can be trained and are the chief mode of transportation for the Aeosians. Several can travel on a krakavora at once. The creatures are strong enough to destroy a fighter on ramming speed alone. When the Aeosian queen mistakes Kazuda Xiono and Griff Halloran for First Order agents, she orders them to be fed to a krakavora but later belays this when Kaz proves their good intentions.

CHARACTERS AND CREATURES

CAM
MANUFACTURER Loronar Corporation
TYPE Holocam droid
AFFILIATION Galactic Society of Creature Enthusiasts

The camera droid CAM broadcasts and records SF-R3's discoveries and mishaps as part of their work for the Galactic Society of Creature Enthusiasts. CAM's tough plating means he's able to endure the heat of Tatooine or the freezing cold of Hoth. CAM encourages SF-R3 to stop poachers who capture a nexu. CAM also trains a voorpak that takes a liking to him.

SF-R3
MANUFACTURER Serv-O-Droid, Inc.
TYPE Safari droid
AFFILIATION Galactic Society of Creature Enthusiasts

As a safari droid, SF-R3 researches creatures across the galaxy and reports back to the Galactic Society of Creature Enthusiasts. His mission is to preserve wildlife and habitats, and sometimes to tame or foster animals. This can get him into trouble, such as when he's attacked by a nexu, but he remains committed.

CAM-E
MANUFACTURER Loronar Corporation
TYPE Holocam droid
AFFILIATION Galactic Society of Creature Enthusiasts

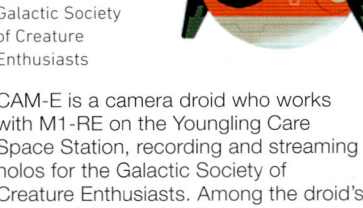

CAM-E is a camera droid who works with M1-RE on the Youngling Care Space Station, recording and streaming holos for the Galactic Society of Creature Enthusiasts. Among the droid's many activities, CAM-E spins and shines to attract light-loving porgs, cuddles up with porgs in their nest, and plays hide-and-seek with a young Rodian.

M1-RE
MANUFACTURER Serv-O-Droid, Inc.
TYPE Safari droid **AFFILIATION** Galactic Society of Creature Enthusiasts

M1-RE works for the Galactic Society of Creature Enthusiasts, caring for both creatures and children. She studies animal habits, helps kids with breakthroughs like learning to walk, and teaches others how to take care of younglings. M1-RE is friendly with SF-R3.

8D-J8
MANUFACTURER Roche
TYPE Smelter droid
AFFILIATION Ronto Roasters

Few visitors to Black Spire Outpost on Jakku miss seeing 8D-J8— the smelter droid that's charged with turning the spit at Bakkar's Ronto Roasters eatery. Programmed by Mubo at the nearby Droid Depot, 8D-J8 is also known for greeting customers and offering ronto wraps and meiloorun juice to passersby.

KENDOH GANG
SPECIES Various **HOMEWORLD** Various
AFFILIATION Kendoh Gang

A dangerous team of outlaws, the Kendoh Gang looks to steal, smuggle, and cheat its way to riches. The motley crew includes its human leader Kendoh Voss, the Clawdite Remex Io, and the Aqualish Wooro, and comes to possess the blade portion of the Sword of Khashyun—an ancient Sith artifact. A mysterious dealer offers to buy the complete weapon so Voss decides to snatch the hilt from Dok-Ondar, who is a trader of rare antiquities. But it's all a setup: Dok-Ondar turns out to be the anonymous patron, and he is the one who ends up with the restored sword, though he does pay the Kendoh Gang for its trouble.

AGNON
SPECIES Human
AFFILIATION First Order

First Order Lieutenant Agnon comes to Batuu in a TIE Echelon, looking to snuff out Resistance fighters and sympathizers. He enjoys watching the planet's people scurry during his approach and promises that Batuu will "never be the same" when his work is done.

DOK-ONDAR
SPECIES Ithorian
HOMEWORLD Batuu
AFFILIATION Dok-Ondar's Den of Antiquities

A collector for most of his life, Dok-Ondar is the proprietor of an antiquities shop at Black Spire Outpost on Batuu. He sells rare artifacts from around the galaxy—almost all of which have an interesting story behind their acquisition. Among his curiosities is an infant sarlacc, obtained for him by Han Solo and Chewbacca on I'vorcia Prime. He secures half the Sword of Khashyun at a Sith temple on Moraband with Doctor Chelli Aphra, and he later fulfills a years-long desire when he completes the weapon, thanks to the efforts of the Kendoh Gang.

OGA GARRA
SPECIES Blutopian
HOMEWORLD Batuu
AFFILIATION Oga's Cantina

Oga Garra, the local crime boss of Black Spire Outpost on Batuu, is well known by the scum and villainy of the galactic underworld. However, she also runs a legitimate business—Oga's Cantina—and has a history with some notable figures. One Life Day, Oga and Han Solo take on the Kanjiklub gang together, driving them from her bar. Years later, Oga makes a deal with Resistance spy Vi Moradi: if Vi recovers an artifact from the Black Spire ruins for the gangster, Garra will return her stolen effects and allow the Resistance to set up a base there.

R5-P8
MANUFACTURER Industrial Automaton
TYPE R-series astromech droid
AFFILIATION Hondo Ohnaka's gang

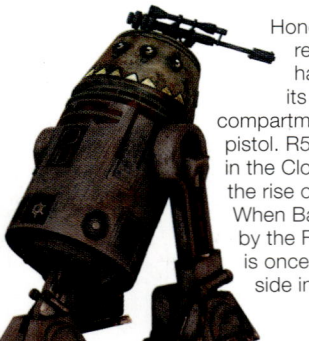

Hondo Ohnaka's sassy repair mechanic droid has painted teeth on its head and a hidden compartment for a blaster pistol. R5-P8 serves Ohnaka in the Clone Wars and during the rise of the First Order. When Batuu is occupied by the First Order, R5-P8 is once more by Hondo's side in his latest venture.

SALJU
SPECIES Human
HOMEWORLD Batuu
AFFILIATION Black Spire Station

The proprietor of Black Spire Station, Salju has a reputation as a reliable mechanic who is always ready to help. She has a soft spot for creatures, especially her childhood friend Elee. Salju readily helps travelers passing through her beloved Black Spire Outpost, including Resistance spy Vi Moradi.

ELEE
SPECIES Therii **HOMEWORLD** Batuu
AFFILIATION Black Spire Station

Salju's father, Harta, brings a small therii home from his travels as a present for Salju, who names her Elee. Though they become best friends, Elee grows too big to remain in Salju's home. Happily, Salju unites Elee with more therii in the Surabat River Valley, where Elee has space to roam.

DJ R-3X

MANUFACTURER Industrial Automaton
TYPE RX-series pilot droid
AFFILIATION Oga's Cantina

Formerly known as RX-24, the loquacious R-3X goes from piloting a Starspeeder 3000 for Star Tours to spinning galactic music as a DJ in Oga's Cantina in Black Spire Outpost. After Star Tours hires and eventually fires the hapless droid, he becomes a cargo pilot for the Rebel Alliance. A crash landing brings him to Batuu, where Droid Depot owner Mubo reprograms RX-24 to be a DJ named R-3X and gives him to Oga Garra to pay a debt.

MUBO

SPECIES Utai **HOMEWORLD** Batuu
AFFILIATION Droid Depot

Mubo is the proprietor of the Droid Depot on Batuu, where he restores and sells droids. The Utai comes into possession of pilot droid RX-24 and reworks him into a DJ called R-3X, who now plays tunes at Oga's Cantina in Black Spire Outpost. Mubo also programs 8D-J8 to become pitmaster at Ronto Roasters. Mubo helps Resistance spy Vi Moradi when she crash-lands on Batuu, fixing her broken droid, free of charge. Preferring to work from his shop, he sends his repair technician to secure scattered cargo after the helper has a run-in with the Guavian Death Gang.

TARA RASHIN

SPECIES Quarren
AFFILIATION Guavian Death Gang, First Order

Ruthless and brutal, Tara Rashin works her way from stooge up to leader of a Guavian Death Gang subsect in the Outer Rim. As leader, she develops an alliance with the First Order. When her gang attacks a cargo ship, it gets more than it bargained for when an onboard droid technician jettisons his cargo—including R2-D2— over the forests of Batuu. Tara sets up a base on the planet, from which she sends her goons to hunt down the missing goods. Eventually, the droid technician teams up with C-3PO to save R2-D2 and draw out Tara in her AT-RT. She perishes in the resulting confrontation, falling down a spire to her death.

SEEZELSLAK

SPECIES Azumel **HOMEWORLD** Batuu **AFFILIATION** Seezelslak's Cantina

Seezelslak loves to spin yarns and recount tales— including some about Master Yoda and other Jedi—in his namesake cantina, located near the spaceport in Black Spire Outpost on Batuu. He welcomes Mubo, owner of the Droid Depot, and his droid technician to his bar, and even hires the technician to track down new drink items. When the First Order sets up a reeducation center on Batuu, it abducts Seezelslak. Mubo's droid technician, however, comes to the rescue and saves Seezelslak from suffering an unfortunate fate.

NEEVA

SPECIES Nobillian

Neeva is born on a peaceful planet in the Outer Rim but flees with the arrival of the Empire. Neeva settles on Nar Shaddaa with her younger brother Neevaan, where she runs afoul of the local crime boss, Boggs Triff, while cleaning up a patch of land.

LENS KAMO

SPECIES Human

Growing up with scholar parents, Lens Kamo develops a respect and appreciation for history. After witnessing the destruction of an ancient site during a search for a relic, Kamo's resolve is steeled. She becomes a treasure hunter, determined to find artifacts before they can be destroyed or fall into the wrong hands. On one adventure, Lens teams up with Mubo's droid technician to raid an old temple on Batuu. Together, they find a relic and keep it from Baron Yasto Attsmun's grasp.

GAUGE

SPECIES Human
AFFILIATION First Order

Completely devoted and loyal to the First Order, the ambitious Lieutenant Gauge is the commanding officer of forces on Batuu. At first, he is disappointed in the assignment, believing it too far off the grid in the Outer Rim to be of any significance or help to his career. But when he learns that a secret re-education center is under construction on the planet, Gauge takes new pride in his work. Among those "selected" for the program is local barkeeper Seezelslak, but his droid technician friend rescues the alien, destroying the facility and eliminating Gauge in the process.

CIMINA

SPECIES Tholothian

Lady Cimina joins her grandfather, Shorr Komrrin, for a journey aboard the luxurious *Halcyon*. The pirate Crimson Jack attacks the cruiser, tracking a Resistance transmission and capturing Shorr, who they believe is a spy. Cimina takes the codes in her grandfather's place and delivers them to Vi Moradi of the Resistance.

RIYOLA KEEVAN

SPECIES Pantoran
HOMEWORLD Pantora
AFFILIATION Chandrila Star Line

Riyola Keevan is dedicated to the *Halcyon* luxury star cruiser. She works her way up from quartermaster to captain over the span of her career. She experiences much during her many years of service on the legendary ship, from acting as Leia Organa's attaché during the princess' honeymoon to battling against pirates and First Order agents.

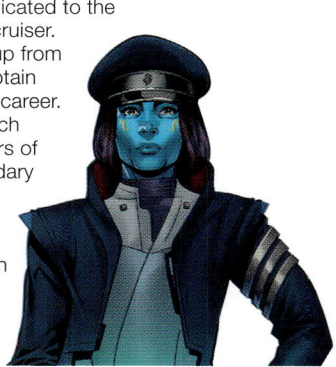

CHARACTERS AND CREATURES

ALAZMEC OF WINSIT
SPECIES Alazmec **HOMEWORLD** Mustafar
AFFILIATION Sith

The Alazmec of Winsit are pilgrims who descend on the lava planet of Mustafar in the years following Darth Vader's demise. As well as protecting the ruins of Vader's Castle, the sect also venerates the mythical Lady Corvax, who is believed to have drenched the bogs of the Corvax Fen with her tears. Despite being armed with CX-55 scatterblasters and night-vision lenses, the Alazmec are no match for the red blade of Vader's grandson, Kylo Ren. He descends onto the planet in a fit of fury, determined to discover their hidden Sith Wayfinder.

Bright eyes Goggles protect eyes from the harsh ash of Mustafar.

Against the elements Cloth has been treated with protective sodium silicate.

EYE OF WEBBISH BOG
SPECIES Sirroning, Arobernos
HOMEWORLD Mustafar **AFFILIATION** Sith

The Eye of Webbish Bog is a Force-attuned being who inhabits a watery cave on Mustafar. Locked in a symbiotic state with a blind Arobernos, the spiderlike Sirroning is awoken during a fight between Darth Vader and Sith assassin Ochi of Bestoon. Also known as "the Oracle," the Eye imparts Vader with visions and, eventually, a Wayfinder device, which allows travel to the planet Exegol. Decades later, Kylo Ren, visits Mustafar to commune with the Oracle and find the way to Exegol. He defeats the Eye's protectors and uncovers the same Wayfinder, leading him to Palpatine.

SITH CULTISTS
SPECIES Various
HOMEWORLD Various, including Exegol
AFFILIATION Sith Eternal

Over the decades, a sect of Sith Cultists has been secretly serving Darth Sidious from the hidden planet of Exegol. These loyal servants help their master prepare for the ultimate revenge of the Sith by experimenting on strandcasts, bleeding kyber crystals, and developing world-destroying weaponry. After Palpatine's seeming demise during the Battle of Endor, these Sith Eternal Cultists resurrect the fallen Emperor into a cloned body. They are eventually defeated by Rey, who causes the Sith Citadel's ceiling to collapse and crush the thousands of heretics present.

KLAUD
SPECIES Trodatome
AFFILIATION Resistance

Klaud is a mechanic in the Resistance who, after a case of mistaken identity, joins Commander Rose Tico's crew on Ajan Kloss. As a Trodatome, he can grab items with his eight antennae and he speaks in a language that only droids can understand. During a simple parts pick-up at the Sinta Glacier Colony, Klaud provides technical support on the *Millennium Falcon*. However, the mission turns into a lightspeed-skipping chase with the First Order and Klaud becomes overwhelmed. After the Battle of Exegol, the Trodatome celebrates with the rest of the Resistance, having been an important part of their victory.

BOOLIO
SPECIES Ovissian **HOMEWORLD** Sinta IV
AFFILIATION Resistance

A mine overseer at the Sinta Glacier Colony, Boolio always keeps his workers' spirits high, even when the First Order visits due to a ledger discrepancy. After the investigators depart, the horned Ovissian discovers that someone has left behind a classified file. Unable to securely transmit this data, Boolio tells the Resistance that he has a regulator for them—a rare part Leia Organa needs for the *Tantive IV*. When they arrive, he reveals the truth: a First Order spy has given him encrypted information. This intelligence is confirmation that Palpatine has returned. But it comes at a cost: Boolio is arrested and executed by Kylo Ren.

ARAKURTH
HOMEWORLD Typhonic Nebula
SIZE More than 400 m (1,312 ft) long
HABITAT Green gas

The arakurth worm monster lives in the interstellar cloud of green gas of the Typhonic Nebula. With three clawlike teeth leading to its sharp, chasmic opening maw, the creature is a giant threat to any ship or being that happens to trespass into its home in the Megafauna Chasm. During a risky hyperspace-skipping maneuver in the *Millennium Falcon* while outrunning First Order fighters, Poe Dameron and a group of Resistance heroes are quickly thrust into the glowing Nebula and narrowly escape the monster's widening mouth. The pursuing TIE fighters, however, are not so lucky.

In control Unit for adjusting temperature-controlled suit.

Warmed up Low-temperature worksuit is insulated with heat-conductive filaments.

AARTON CHIREEN
SPECIES Human
HOMEWORLD Jaymir
AFFILIATION Resistance

Aarton Chireen is a lieutenant in the Resistance who hails from the frontier world of Jaymir. Recruited alongside his sister (Nimi, an X-wing pilot) by Ello Asty, Chireen is held as a reserve until after the Battle of Crait. He then officially joins the cause as quartermaster for the Resistance.

ZYMOD
HOMEWORLD Ajan Kloss
SIZE 76 cm (2 ft 6 in) long **HABITAT** Forest

The zymod is a slinking reptile on Ajan Kloss with a color-changing hide and webbed feet that allow it to climb nearly anything, from trees to a ship's landing gear. When the Resistance sets up base on the forest planet, the troops have to get used to a small infestation of the native creature.

AD-4M
MANUFACTURER Jenks DroidWorks
TYPE Administrative droid
AFFILIATION Resistance

AD-4M is the administrative droid in charge of processing and managing tasks and data across the Resistance. Due to the unfinished nature of the Ajan Kloss base, AD-4M has been more forward-facing than it is used to. This means it has had to quickly learn how to deal with good-natured sarcasm from some Resistance fighters.

- **Seeing it all** Large, compound eyes give Dipterz excellent vision.
- **Raised view** Vazzet sits on a loadlifter workframe for height and to move around.

VAZZET DIPTERZ
SPECIES Cyclorrian
HOMEWORLD Cyclor
AFFILIATION Resistance

Vazzet Dipterz is one of the Cyclorrians who join the fight with the Resistance before the Battle of Exegol. Hailing from the Mid-Rim planet of Cyclor, Vazzet and his swarm mates are known throughout the galaxy for their superb engineering capabilities, as well as their naturally adhesive feet and navigational antennae. Rather than walking, Vazzet prefers to ride a tall loadlifter across the Ajan Kloss base so the short taskmaster can better observe his team. While his classic Cyclorrian managerial style has been deemed overbearing by some, there is no question that he gets results.

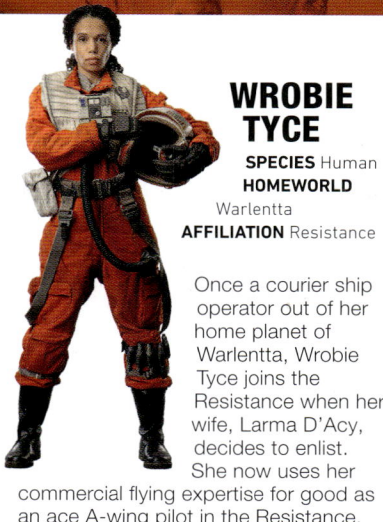

WROBIE TYCE
SPECIES Human
HOMEWORLD Warlentta
AFFILIATION Resistance

Once a courier ship operator out of her home planet of Warlentta, Wrobie Tyce joins the Resistance when her wife, Larma D'Acy, decides to enlist. She now uses her commercial flying expertise for good as an ace A-wing pilot in the Resistance.

IBDUN DAND
SPECIES Tarsunt **HOMEWORLD** Suntilla
AFFILIATION Resistance

Ibdun Dand is the father of accomplished technician Vober Dand. The stern Tarsunt initially forbids his son from joining the freedom fighters but, since the destruction of Hosnian Prime, he now understands the cause. The father and son team works at the Resistance base on Ajan Kloss, celebrating hard-won victories together.

AFTAB ACKBAR
SPECIES Mon Calamari
HOMEWORLD Mon Cala
AFFILIATION Resistance

Aftab Ackbar is the son of the late Resistance hero Admiral Gial Ackbar who perished aboard the *Raddus*. The young Mon Calamari only met the elder Ackbar once, but he has spent his life studying the exploits and victories of his renowned father. Joining the Resistance after helping General Leia Organa negotiate an alliance with his people of Mon Cala, Aftab is now a Y-wing pilot for the cause. Affectionately referred to as "Junior" around the Ajan Kloss base, Aftab is often anxious, but he is eager to step out from the shadow of his father and prove his worth.

BEAUMONT KIN
SPECIES Human **HOMEWORLD** Lerct
AFFILIATION Resistance

Beaumont Kin is a vital member of the Resistance since he possesses an extensive knowledge of Sith lore and language. Before becoming involved in the fight against the First Order, Kin is an aspiring professor at the Lerct Historical Institute, with his studies focusing on the early Republic Era and the ancient Sith. On one of his research expeditions to the planet Yoturba, Beaumont encounters Luke Skywalker and Lor San Tekka, and together they uncover a Sith Holocron. After the destruction of Hosnian Prime, Kin abandons his aspirations of becoming an educator and joins the Resistance.

He has become the Resistance's resident history professor, establishing a friendship with fellow freedom fighters Rose Tico and Kaydel Connix. He is fluent in nine languages, including Shyriiwook and four ancient dialects. Thanks to these skills, he is able to assist Rey in translating ancient Jedi texts while they are stationed on Ajan Kloss. Kin joins his friends during the Battle of Exegol. Soon after surviving the climactic battle, Kin starts writing a manuscript titled *The Rise and Fall of the Galactic Empire*, hoping his work will prevent further bloodshed.

- **Always ready** Standard issue life-support
- **His father's son** Aftab wears a Y-wing pilot's uniform, like his father did.
- **A sure shot** Kin swaps books for a BlasTech EL-16 blaster rifle.

Battle of Exegol Beaumont Kin, Rose Tico, and Kaydel Ko Connix hold their position against Sith troopers on top of the *Steadfast*, while fellow Resistance fighters tackle the Star Destroyer's navigation tower and command bridge.

ALBREKH
SPECIES Symeong
AFFILIATION First Order, Sith

Albrekh is an eccentric Sith alchemist and metalsmith who reforges the broken helmet of Kylo Ren. Aboard the ship of the Knights of Ren, the *Night Buzzard*, the apelike Symeong deftly repairs the shattered helm, reinforcing the cracks with red Sarrassian iron ore. Some believe this material contains special particles that attract the dark side of the Force. Trained in ancient metallurgic arts, Albrekh promises Kylo Ren that this process will make his helmet even stronger than before. Albrekh's steady hand is aided by a Sith forge as well as magnetic forceps and a special hammer, which impresses even the sullen supreme leader.

AP'LEK
AFFILIATION Knights of Ren

A ruthless member of the Knights of Ren, Ap'lek is considered the strategist of the group, and he believes himself to be the most cunning. Unlike his fellow Knights, Ap'lek prefers to fight opponents using deception rather than brute strength or weaponry. He carries a smoke dispenser so he can effectively render his enemies blind while he stalks them using the Force. When he must use a weapon, Ap'lek prefers a beskar-bladed ax that once belonged to a Mandalorian executioner. Ap'lek meets his end at the hands of a now-redeemed Ben Solo, who Force-pushes him into a chasm on Exegol.

CARDO
AFFILIATION Knights of Ren

The weapons specialist of the Knights of Ren, Cardo serves as the armorer for the feared group. Under the leadership of the fearsome Ren, Cardo and his fellow Knights take on many missions in defiance of the Empire, including joining forces with Qi'ra and Crimson Dawn. This action leads to Cardo brawling with the bounty hunter Bossk. Cardo's modified arm cannon can launch both plasma bolts and fire, but the Knight of Ren dies by Anakin Skywalker's blue blade, which is now held by his former leader, a redeemed Ben Solo.

CHARACTERS AND CREATURES

KURUK
AFFILIATION Knights of Ren

Kuruk is the sharpshooter of the Knights of Ren and also the pilot of their ship, the *Night Buzzard*. He's a deadly sharpshooter, especially when armed with his custom rifle, which he uses for both sniping and rapid-fire purposes, as well as in a pump action mode that fires plasma bolts. Kuruk's helmet is designed with sides to block his peripheral vision so he can focus on his target and sharpen his aim through the Force. Kuruk is slain by a redeemed Ben Solo, his former leader, during the Battle of Exegol.

Protective storage Pauldron holds additional plasma bolt shells.

Electric and lethal Vibrocleaver once belonged to a gladiator.

TRUDGEN
AFFILIATION Knights of Ren

One of the most ferocious of all the Knights of Ren, Trudgen is obsessed with collecting precious trophies from his victims. These grisly mementos, including the visor of an Imperial death trooper, customize his black garb. His weapon of choice is another trophy—the vibrocleaver of a former Houk gladiator that's been imbued with ultrasonic technology to make it even more lethal. Trudgen is killed in the bowels of Exegol by his former leader, the redeemed Ben Solo. He's stabbed with the lightsaber that once belonged to Anakin Skywalker.

USHAR
AFFILIATION Knights of Ren

Ushar is the main interrogator for the Knights of Ren, pushing prisoners to their absolute limits and forcing them to beg for mercy. During combat and questioning, Ushar is constantly judging the spirit of his enemies, and he provides a quick death for those he deems the most worthy. Ushar is armed with both a vibromachete and a powerful war club that's powered by kinetite—a type of Force lightning. The air tubes on his mask suggest that he might not be human, but his species, like his origin before joining the Knights, is unknown.

Quick draw Blaster pistol has had its safety circuitry removed.

VICRUL
SPECIES Human
AFFILIATION Knights of Ren

A self-proclaimed "reaper of souls," Vicrul is a Knight of Ren who gains significant strength with every life that he takes using his deadly electro-scythe. Incredibly cunning, he has gone up against Luke Skywalker in combat, and he successfully recruits a young Ben Solo to join the Knights. Like the rest of his cohort, Vicrul has some Force-sensitivity, which heightens his reflexes and his rage on the battlefield. The dark side, however dampened, surges inside him after every blow. He dies while facing his former leader, Ben Solo.

AMRET ENGELL
SPECIES Human
AFFILIATION First Order

Amret Engell is a motivated general in the First Order, who has gained more responsibility thanks to her fervorous loyalty to the cause. Following the demise of Captain Phasma, General Engell takes over the First Order's stormtrooper training program, in service of General Hux, taking captured children from conquered worlds and turning them into loyal soldiers. As an esteemed member of Kylo Ren's High Council, she respects the authority of the supreme leader and is willing to do whatever it takes to grow his First Order.

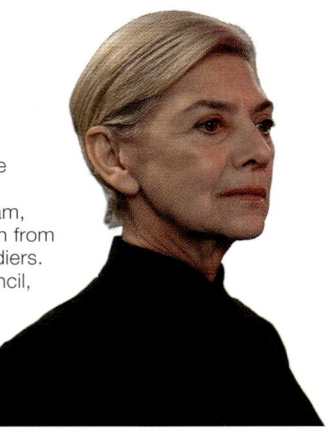

GENERAL PRYDE
SPECIES Human
HOMEWORLD Alsakan
AFFILIATION Empire, First Order

Allegiant General Enric Pryde has been a loyal servant of both the Empire and the First Order for nearly his entire life. After the Empire's defeat at the Battle of Jakku, Pryde flees to the Unknown Regions.

Before officially joining the First Order, Pryde is known by the code name "Steadfast," covertly working for the Imperial remnants with the Corporate Sector Authority. Steadfast is referred by the Sith Eternal cult to Ochi of Bestoon, granting the latter three Corporate Sector Authority (CSA) platoons for his quest to capture the strandcast Dathan and Miramir.

When the Imperial remnants combine to form the First Order, Pryde rises through its ranks, while simultaneously serving as a covert agent for the hidden Darth Sidious. After Snoke's death, Supreme Leader Kylo Ren promotes Pryde to Allegiant General. When Ren renounces the dark side, Pryde leads the First Order during the Battle of Exegol. Pryde remains loyal to Sidious until his final moments, when his ship, the *Resurgent*-class Star Destroyer, appropriately renamed *Steadfast*, is destroyed by its own guns, while Pryde is on its bridge.

FRANTIS GRISS
SPECIES Human
AFFILIATION First Order

Admiral Frantis Griss is the senior fleet officer commanding the First Order's *Steadfast* as well as its surrounding support ships. He's a member of the First Order High Command and enjoys the complete trust of General Allegiant Pryde. He proudly delivers the Resistance spy Boolio to Supreme Leader Kylo Ren.

GENERAL PARNADEE
SPECIES Human
AFFILIATION First Order

General Bellava Parnadee is senior ground commander and chief strategist for the First Order. She's a student of history, constantly poring over her extensive hololibrary to learn about previous tactics from the Clone Wars and Galactic Civil War. She uses this knowledge to further the First Order's galactic occupation.

"As I served you in the old wars, I serve you now."

ALLEGIANT GENERAL PRYDE TO PALPATINE

Pageantry and splendor Pryde's lacquered ebonwood swagger stick is a remnant of Alsakan military tradition and an example of the General's proclivity to the old ways.

DOMARIC QUINN
SPECIES Human
AFFILIATION First Order

General Domaric Quinn first serves the forces of evil as an Imperial junior officer, eventually rising to become a key First Order ground force commander. Frustrated by the young, brash Kylo Ren, Quinn speaks up against the Sith Eternal fleet and Ren's fascination with the scavenger, Rey, but it's the last thing he does.

AKI-AKI
SPECIES Aki-Aki
HOMEWORLD Pasaana
AFFILIATION Neutral

The Aki-Aki are a joyful and nonviolent species who have carved out a peaceful living on Pasaana. Although no formal census has been taken recently, it's estimated that around 500,000 Aki-Aki live in various tribes across their desert planet. Adult Aki-Aki have two prehensile trunks, which give them increased lung strength and a natural inclination for wind instruments. They also have a keen sense of rhythm, leading to the extraordinary dances that take place during their famous Festival of the Ancestors, which occurs every 42 years.

NAMBI GHIMA
SPECIES Aki-Aki **HOMEWORLD** Pasaana
AFFILIATION Aki-Aki

Nambi Ghima is a young and curious Aki-Aki, native to Pasaana. During the Festival of the Ancestors that Resistance agents visit, she approaches Rey with a traditional necklace of woven jute and colorful kern-nut husks. Her natural hospitality is a trademark of her people, and she's eager to learn Rey's familial name.

OKI-POKI
HOMEWORLD Pasaana **SIZE** 30 cm (1 ft) high
HABITAT Desert

Oki-poki are rodent-type creatures whose vibrating ears provide them with the sensitive hearing required to avoid the dangers of Pasaana. Cliff-dwelling critters, they feed on insects that naturally populate the planet. This talent has been noticed by entrepreneurial Aki-Aki, who have domesticated some oki-poki to protect their crops.

TISHRA KANDIA
SPECIES Human
AFFILIATION First Order

Tishra Kandia is a First Order Intelligence Officer, stationed aboard the *Steadfast*. She prides herself in the evidence she has been able to uncover for use against the Resistance. Officer Kandia is a trusted informant for Kylo Ren, especially in his hunt for the scavenger Rey, and she guides him to Pasaana.

FIRST ORDER TREADSPEEDER PILOT
SPECIES Human **HOMEWORLD** Various
AFFILIATION First Order

First Order treadspeeder pilots ride their vehicles to track down potential fugitives across different ground terrains, especially when technology has jammed traditional repulsorcraft. A deadlier combination can be made when they work with jet troopers, who are launched into the sky from treadspeeder bikes. Each pilot's helmet HUD is linked to their 125-Z treadspeeder, which issues important read-outs. The bike itself exhibits surprising speeds of 200 km (125 miles) per hour. Treadspeeder pilots see action pursuing fleeing Resistance agents on Pasaana.

KALO'NE
SPECIES Yokaa **AFFILIATION** Yokaa

Kalo'ne is a serpentlike creature who has been driving a DN-25 treadable transport across Pasaana for decades. Her age is unknown, but her skills remain sharpened thanks to her species' tri-lensed, multispectral vision. Kalo'ne has filled her cabin with many wares, and everything is available to buy—for the right price.

Horizontal view The First Order jet trooper's helmet is recognizable by a very narrow visor.

FIRST ORDER JET TROOPERS
SPECIES Human **HOMEWORLD** Various **AFFILIATION** First Order

Jet troopers are some of the most athletic and deadly of all the First Order's forces. Following the ancient tradition of Old Republic warriors and Mandalorian supercommandos, they're highly specialized soldiers who use jetpacks to take to the air and launch projectiles at enemy targets. These agile jetpacks are built into their armor, requiring an added degree of coordination due to their embedded, complex gyroscopes. The troopers are paired with treadspeeder pilots and sent out to track down the Resistance heroes on the desert planet of Pasaana.

FIRST ORDER ELECTROPROD TROOPER
SPECIES Human
HOMEWORLD Various
AFFILIATION First Order

The electroprod trooper is a specialized First Order soldier that's sent out to control prisoners and riots. Trained to curtail any social unrest, they are invaluable tools for Kylo Ren and his commanders. They're used to capture the Wookiee Chewbacca.

VEXIS
HOMEWORLD Pasaana **SIZE** 35 m (115 ft) long
HABITAT Caves, desert

A snakelike species with sharp teeth and armored scales, the vexis loves the desert, burrowing deep and excreting an oil that hardens sand and leaves behind circular, ridged passageways. Space traders warn that a weary traveler can "count their mortal breaths" if they encounter one. One such creature lives below Pasaana's deadly Sinking Fields. This injured vexis was calmed and healed by Rey, who used her Force abilities to bestow restorative energy onto the snake.

AMUNCIE TIDIAN
SPECIES Boosodian **HOMEWORLD** Boosodia
AFFILIATION Spice Runners of Kijimi

Amuncie Tidian is a 20-eyed Boosodian who works as a forger operating out of the Thieves' Quarter on Kijimi. His many eyes enable him to view large swathes of the electromagnetic spectrum. Tidian also believes he can see the future because of a nonexistent 21st eye.

ROTHGAR DENG
SPECIES Human
HOMEWORLD Corellia
AFFILIATION Bounty hunter, Kijimi Spice Den

An old and experienced Corellian bounty hunter, Rothgar Deng has spent years subjecting himself to extensive experimental cybernetic replacements. Often named among the greatest bounty hunters, Deng wants to work forever and is confident that his prosthetics will help him achieve both immortality and infamy.

230 CHARACTERS AND CREATURES

D-O

MANUFACTURER Unidentified droidsmith
TYPE Monowheel data-retrieval droid (unique custom build)
AFFILIATION Sith Eternal, Resistance, BB-8

A small data-retrieval droid, D-O is cobbled together by an unknown scholar on Primus Cabru. After his master's murder at the hands of Sith assassin Ochi of Bestoon, the homemade hobby droid begs for his life and reluctantly joins Ochi on his missions onboard the *Bestoon Legacy*. D-O's new master hates him, but he soon proves his worth as a data-storage module, becoming filled to the brim with years of Ochi's sinister notes and research.

Due to the nature of his creation, D-O is a distinctive droid, comprising a rolling monowheel and a cone-shaped head. The cone is equipped with a "cold box" storage unit, which is distinct from his brain so allows the droid to act as an information courier without actually being able to access any sensitive data. D-O has a skittish, rodentlike personality, but he has a proven capacity to be incredibly loyal to a caring master.

Never properly maintained by Ochi, D-O is then left to rust when his master goes to explore the desert sands of Pasaana in search of the granddaughter of Palpatine, but never returns. Locked on the dusty *Bestoon Legacy* for more than a decade, D-O is eventually brought back online by BB-8, with whom he quickly forges a bond. D-O is eventually repaired further by Rey, and he finds a new home and purpose among the Resistance. Due to his immense storage capacities, he quickly becomes an invaluable member of the team, delivering much-needed intelligence about Exegol. The droid has finally found a welcoming home among new freedom-fighting friends.

A new friend
After years of being dormant, D-O is powered on and immediately gravitates to his savior, BB-8, who he then loyally follows into a new adventure.

Head on a swivel
Accordion sheathing houses D-O's articulated neck.

Helping hand
Rey fixes D-O's squeaky wheel—a small act but one that the droid's previous master never even considered.

Ready to roll
Uni-tread disk allows for movement across most terrain.

ZORII BLISS

SPECIES Human **HOMEWORLD** Kijimi
AFFILIATION Spice Runners of Kijimi, Citizens' Fleet

Zorii Bliss is the brave and dangerous leader of the Spice Runners of Kijimi. Feared by her enemies and respected by her fellow pirates, she operates almost anonymously beneath a shining bronzium-finished plasteel helmet.

Zorii is born into this life of crime: her mother, Zeva, is the previous leader of the secretive organization. After the collapse of the Empire, an immense power vacuum leaves the Kessel spice trade wide open for new, upstart factions to grow in power. The burgeoning Spice Runners begin to use their pirate vessels to attack any spice-carrying ships, and they grow in power and influence. It is during this time that Zorii, then going by the last name "Wynn," meets a young Poe Dameron on Yavin IV. Poe joins Zorii as a Spice Runner, and they fly on many missions together, learning less-than-savory—but important—slicing and combat skills. Her relationship with the young Dameron is electric, often verging on romantic. When Dameron eventually flees back to his family and the New Republic, Zorii feels betrayed.

Zorii's voice is often filtered through her helmet's processor, and her body is contained within a temperature-regulating maroon body glove flight suit. Skill and a background in dancing aid Zorii in her unique and deadly fighting style.

When her mother dies, Zorii takes on the mantle of matriarch of the Spice Runners. It is after this that she is reunited with a fugitive Poe Dameron, who arrives back on Kijimi, seeking help and resources. After reluctantly aiding him, she narrowly escapes the destruction of Kijimi and joins the Resistance. She goes on to fly her modified BTA-NR2 Y-wing starfighter during the Battle of Exegol.

Voice of the Guild
Vocoder emits a masked voice through grille.

Drawn and ready
Holster is made from hardened bantha leather.

Private eyes
It is rare for Zorii to open her visor. She reveals her eyes to only her closest allies, such as Poe Dameron.

In the fight
To the delight and surprise of Poe Dameron, Zorii joins the Battle of Exegol in her Y-wing starfighter.

CARIB DISS
SPECIES Skilla
AFFILIATION Bounty hunter

Carib Diss is a fearsome bounty hunter who can be found in the Spice Runners' Den on Kijimi. An alien species known as the Skilla, his visage is objectively terrifying, dominated by rows of sharp teeth. They provide protection to his vital organs, which are all located right behind his smile.

WOLENTIC DUDGE
SPECIES Frejuke
AFFILIATION Kijimi City

Wolentic Dudge is a proud resident of Kijimi City, although he now has to deal with its occupation by the First Order. His species' heat-retaining blubber makes him a good fit for the snowy climate of the planet, but he also sports a kybuck fur-lined vest for added warmth.

OMA TRES
SPECIES Human
AFFILIATION Spice Runners of Kijimi

Oma Tres is a bartender on Kijimi who has been mixing drinks in the Spice Runners' Den for years. Observant patrons will notice trinkets displayed behind the bar that Tres has collected over the years. Tres may disapprove of his clientele's antics, but he doesn't interfere; he just wants harmony.

LANZORA GARAN
SPECIES Human
AFFILIATION First Order

Lieutenant Lanzora Garan is a security officer on the First Order flagship, *Steadfast*. Garan has direct lines to the ship's important personnel, including General Hux and Allegiant General Pryde. She is a witness to Hux's death at the hands of Pryde, after the General is identified as a spy.

BABU FRIK
SPECIES Anzellan **HOMEWORLD** Kijimi
AFFILIATION Spice Runners of Kijimi, Resistance

Babu Frik is an expert mechanic and droid-tinkerer with a shop set up in the Thieves' Quarter in Kijimi City. As an Anzellan, he is well-equipped for droidsmithing. His small size enables him to get into tight spaces, among the wires, and his corneal micro-lenses can see in microscopic detail.

Babu's droid modification and security countermeasure prowess is especially used by the Spice Runners of Kijimi, which both Zorii Bliss and Poe Dameron were part of during their younger years. Because of his exceptional work, Babu has been deemed an honorary member of the organization. When C-3PO is in need of a complete memory bypass in order to translate the text inscribed on a cursed dagger, Dameron remembers the droidsmith and returns to his famed droid shop. The Anzellan is able to expertly complete the memory wipe of the protocol droid, who can then relay the location of Palpatine's Sith Wayfinder.

Babu narrowly escapes from Kijimi with Zorii Bliss before the Final Order destroys the planet. He then joins the Resistance's fight during the Battle of Exegol.

DATHAN
SPECIES Human **HOMEWORLD** Exegol
AFFILIATION Sith Eternal, Miramir and Rey

Dathan is a strandcast—a body genetically engineered by the Sith Eternal as a vessel for the decrepit Palpatine. However, it is soon realized that this clone doesn't have any Force capabilities. When Darth Vader and Sith assassin Ochi of Bestoon arrive on Exegol, he stows away on their ship and escapes. Unnamed by his father, the clone takes the name "Dathan" in honor of the enslaved Symeong who helped raise him. After some time, Dathan meets and marries Miramir. They have a daughter, Rey, who inherits Palpatine's Force abilities. Ochi eventually discovers and kills the couple, leaving Rey abandoned.

MIRAMIR
SPECIES Human **HOMEWORLD** Hyperkarn
AFFILIATION Dathan and Rey

Miramir is a native of Hyperkarn, a planet of twilight-blue forests. Raised by her grandmother, Miramir is a self-taught inventor and engineer who can fly any ship. After falling in love with Dathan—the runaway strandcast clone of Palpatine—she leaves her homeworld, seeking safety in the galaxy for their young child, Rey. The family makes a meager home on the planet Jakku for a few years, working as junk traders with Unkar Plutt, until they are hunted down by Ochi of Bestoon. Miramir is killed by Ochi's cursed Sith dagger, leaving her daughter as an orphan on the desert planet.

Rewiring job
Rey and her friends hope that Babu Frik can reset C-3PO's wiring and retrieve a message crucial to defeating the First Order. When C-3PO is rebooted, he refers to the Anzellan as "one of his oldest friends."

OCHI OF BESTOON
SPECIES Bestoonian **HOMEWORLD** Bestoon
AFFILIATION Sith Eternal

Ochi of Bestoon is an artifact hunter and Jedi killer who has been active for decades. Employed by both Darth Sidious and Darth Vader, he becomes obsessed with the Sith, even though he possesses no Force-sensitivity himself. When taken prisoner by Vader, an unmasked Ochi is exposed to the blinding light of a bleeding kyber crystal, which burns his eyes. From then on, he must wear an implanted cybernetic visor in order to see. During the rise of the Empire, Ochi goes on many missions for the Sith Lord, including spying on Qi'ra and Crimson Dawn. The relic hunter's final mission involves the killing of Miramir and her husband Dathan—a failed clone of Sidious who escaped from the planet of Exegol. The couple bore a secret: their daughter, Rey. After failing to locate the girl, Ochi flees into the desert of Pasaana, falling into its Shifting Mires with his landspeeder and stolen Sith dagger. His remains are eventually found by the very person he last hunted—Rey. And the dagger provides her with a final clue to the Wayfinder she and the Resistance are seeking.

Sith blade
Ochi of Bestoon wields no ordinary dagger. Steeped in the dark side of the Force, it withstands lightsaber blades and thrives on murder. After Ochi's death, it lies with his body until Rey—whose parents were killed by it—takes ownership of it.

CHARACTERS AND CREATURES

A new look
Jannah's hair has grown out—in violation of First Order regulations.

JANNAH

SPECIES Human
AFFILIATION First Order, Company 77, Resistance

Taken from her family and forcibly enlisted into the ranks of the First Order at a young age, Jannah is given the designation TZ-1719, and she serves dutifully for many years. Eventually, along with other stormtroopers in her platoon, Company 77, she rebels against her forced conditioning during the Battle of Ansett Island when she is instructed to fire on innocent civilians. Jannah becomes the de facto leader of the group and now they live in exile on the ocean moon of Endor named Kef Bir.

At her very core, Jannah is a survivor. She wears a tunic made from native animal hides and a flowing cape cut from a regulation survival blanket. A gifted tinkerer and skilled with repulsorlift technology, Jannah has deconstructed First Order gear in order to create new equipment that helps her company thrive in their new environment. Like most of her group, she sports a custom bow built out of salvaged blaster parts, which she wields expertly.

When a group of Resistance heroes lands on Kef Bir in search of the wreckage of the Death Star II, Jannah immediately bonds with Finn—a fellow former stormtrooper. Jannah, along with the rest of Company 77 and a herd of orbaks, then joins the Resistance in its valiant ground assault during the Battle of Exegol. After their victory, she meets the famed General Lando Calrissian, whose daughter was once kidnapped by the First Order. Inspired by her recent adventures, Jannah wants nothing more than to join the Rebellion hero on his next mission.

Leading the charge
On Kef Bir, Jannah masters the art of riding orbaks. This comes in handy particularly for the ground assault during the Battle of Exegol.

Destroyer down
Jannah, Finn, and other Resistance fighters, take out the Star Destroyer *Steadfast* and, with it, the navigation signal for deploying the rest of the Sith fleet.

ORBAK

HOMEWORLD Various, including Kef Bir **SIZE** 1.62 m (5 ft 4 in) high **HABITAT** Plains

The orbak is a tusked, four-legged creature that contentedly lives on many different worlds. One herd dwells on Endor's Ocean Moon—Kef Bir. Orbaks are herbivores, distantly related to other woolly beasts like fathiers and banthas. While not native to Kef Bir, the orbaks tamed by the former First Order stormtroopers of Company 77 live a symbiotic life with their riders, protected from the moon's predators in exchange for transportation. They also serve the Resistance during the assault on the *Resurgent*-class Star Destroyer *Steadfast* in the Battle of Exegol.

SEFTIN VANIK

SPECIES Human **HOMEWORLD** Messert
AFFILIATION Resistance

Seftin Vanik is a Resistance pilot, who is personally invited by Poe Dameron to join the cause after his home planet, Messert, secedes from the New Republic. Nicknamed the "Shield Cooker," Lieutenant Vanik uses his skills, honed as a stunt flyer in an aerial circus, to bring peace to the galaxy.

NIMI CHIREEN

SPECIES Human **HOMEWORLD** Jaymir
AFFILIATION Resistance

Nimi Chireen is a new pilot for the Resistance, recruited by Ello Asty. Alongside her brother, Aarton, she was held in reserve until after devastating losses at the Battle of Crait. Now, Lieutenant Chireen is happy to be on Ajan Kloss, serving delicious root stews and piloting her own ship.

MILON LENWITH
SPECIES Human
AFFILIATION Sith Eternal, Final Order

A militant leader and loyal officer in the Sith Fleet, Lieutenant Milon Lenwith serves aboard the *Derriphan*—the first warship to be launched from the Unknown Regions. Lenwith goes into the Battle of Exegol with a strong sense of determination to stamp out the Resistance.

GANDRIS DYUN
SPECIES Human
AFFILIATION Resistance

Lieutenant Gandris Dyun is the copilot of the transport ship *Fortitude*, serving alongside Captain Conunda during the Battle of Exegol. Dyun proves to be an important defensive asset for the Resistance. His deep relationship with Conunda has significant chemistry and inevitably sparks rumors of romance across the Resistance.

FINAL ORDER FLEET TECHNICIAN
SPECIES Human **HOMEWORLD** Exegol
AFFILIATION Sith Eternal, Final Order

Each Final Order Fleet Technician believes that control of the galaxy is their birthright. Raised from childhood on Exegol, they emerge from the Unknown Regions with warships individually equipped with powerful solar ionization reactors. It is the technicians who are responsible for calibrating their complex calculations.

DREANNA CONUNDA
SPECIES Human
AFFILIATION Resistance

Dreanna Conunda is a Resistance pilot who captains the *Fortitude* hauler through the crimson Galactic Barrier and into the planned ground assault of the Battle of Exegol. Before joining the Resistance, Captain Conunda was a flight instructor at the New Republic's training academy on Chandrila.

CHESILLE SABROND
SPECIES Human
HOMEWORLD Exegol
AFFILIATION Sith Eternal

Chesille Sabrond is captain of one of the Sith Eternal's Star Destroyers, the *Derriphan*. Raised on Exegol, Sabrond has never been outside the Unknown Regions until a mission to Kijimi. She has the honor of being one of the first of her people to fly out into the known galaxy.

MASIR TRACH
SPECIES Human
AFFILIATION First Order

Commander Masir Trach is a young scanner officer on board the *Steadfast*. He was transferred from the *Finalizer* after the Battle of Batuu. Now caught in an internal battle between General Hux and Allegiant General Pryde, Trach tries to avoid any political disputes, by focusing solely on his role.

Red jetpack The NJP-900 jetpack is also used by First Order jet troopers, but their model is white.

SITH JET TROOPER
SPECIES Human
HOMEWORLD Exegol
AFFILIATION Sith Eternal, Final Order

The Sith jet trooper is the advanced counterpart to the traditional jet-equipped stormtrooper. They take to the skies above Exegol to stamp out the Resistance forces. These elite fighters are both incredibly fast and fiercely loyal, providing significant air support to their ground allies. They're clad in reinforced crimson armor, which protects them from the surrounding elements, and they're armed with specialized blasters that have a power blast mode for ultimate damage. However, despite their extensive training, they're ultimately unprepared for the Resistance during the Battle of Exegol.

SOVEREIGN PROTECTOR
SPECIES Human
HOMEWORLD Exegol
AFFILIATION Sith Eternal, Darth Sidious

Sovereign Protectors make up the elite ranks of the Sith Eternal. They are the most fanatical and ruthless Sith trooper soldiers. Once promoted, a Sovereign Protector is stationed in the Sith Citadel on Exegol to protect their weakened master, Palpatine, from any external threats. Many of the Sovereign Protectors are the children of Sith Cultists, who have now achieved a high honor at Palpatine's side. The soldiers are best compared to the Imperial Royal Guards, who loyally served the Sith Lord during the reign of the Empire.

New generation Long cape is reminiscent of those worn by Emperor Palpatine's Royal Imperial Guards.

SITH TROOPER
SPECIES Human **HOMEWORLD** Exegol
AFFILIATION Sith Eternal, Final Order

Sith troopers are the intimidating infantry force of the Sith Eternal, carrying out the Final Order with astonishing vigor. Their corrugated red armor makes them stand out from their First Order counterparts, as well as providing additional protection in battle. Sith troopers' fierce loyalty to the Sith Eternal's cause is an intimidating attribute that has been instilled through flash imprinting and conditioning over many years. They have also been successfully trained to suppress all individuality—a feat that Palpatine has been attempting since the Clone Wars.

POMMET WARRICK
SPECIES Ewok
HOMEWORLD Forest Moon of Endor
AFFILIATION Bright Tree Village

Pommet Warrick is a young Wokling and son of Endor's most famous hero, Wicket. Growing up in his father's shadow, Pommet craves the worlds beyond his moon. When a Star Destroyer appears in the atmosphere above, Pommet is distraught, but its eventual destruction is taken as a potential sign from the Ewoks' deity, the Golden One.

LOCATIONS

Countless habitable worlds are scattered throughout the farthest reaches of the galaxy and beyond. Each one has its own geography, flora and fauna, secrets, and surprises.

Long ago, hyperspace explorers established coordinates and trade routes for thousands of star systems, many of which have at least one habitable planet or moon. Since then, many new systems have been charted. Some of these far-flung worlds feature architectural wonders and are home to intelligent indigenous civilizations, while others are undeveloped and populated almost entirely by wild creatures. Some worlds feature diverse terrain, while others are so dominated by a single geographical feature that they are described as sand, ice, jungle, or water planets.

More than a trillion citizens reside on the planet Coruscant, which is considered the heart of the Core Worlds, the galactic hub of culture, education, fine arts, technology, and finance. But because of economic or legal restrictions, or political oppression imposed by the prevailing government, many choose to live in the Outer Rim, beyond the influence of the Republic, the Empire, or the New Republic.

238 LOCATIONS

E'RONOH

REGION Outer Rim **SECTOR** Dalnan **SYSTEM** Eiram **TERRAIN** Desert

E'ronoh is a world of canyons, caverns, jagged mountains, and red deserts. Stone arches dot the landscape, and the people there often face drought. Fauna of E'ronoh includes the thylefire scorpion, from which poison can be made. The capital city began as a mountain fortress called the Rook, which then expanded outward in a spiral. E'ronoh and Eiram are a binary system of planets, with a debris field and a moon gravitationally locked between them. The two planets are often at war, and are almost equally as often on the verge of peace. A hyperlane passes near to both planets, making them strategically advantageous.

EIRAM

REGION Outer Rim **SECTOR** Dalnan **TERRAIN** Ocean

Eiram is a twin planet to E'ronoh, with which it is often at war. Eiram's oceans provide plentiful seafood and inspire much of its people's culture. The population sometimes needs assistance in importing fresh water or desalinating ocean water. People from Eiram often have green freckles due to a pigment in the kelp found in their food. Eiram eventually finds peace with both E'ronoh and the Republic, at least temporarily. Starlight Beacon is present on Eiram for a relief mission when the Nihil attack and destroy the space station, with much of the debris falling into Eiram's oceans.

DALNA

REGION Outer Rim **SECTOR** Dalnan **SYSTEM** Dalnan **TERRAIN** Meadows, volcanic mountain ranges

Dalna is a little-known planet with abundant flora and fauna and active volcanoes, which produce water-filled cave systems and sinkholes. The weather is temperate, and even small towns on the planet have spaceports. In the golden days of the Republic, Dalna was home to the Path of the Open Hand. Unrest on Dalna means the people who live there become formidable fighters, with every person training in case of war. Their Metamorphosis Trials are comparable to Jedi trials. The Nihil cause volcanoes to erupt in a cataclysm that forces most people to evacuate the planet, but it eventually becomes habitable again.

HETZAL PRIME

REGION Outer Rim **SYSTEM** Hetzal **TERRAIN** Cultivated

Hetzal is one of the sites of the Emergences—the disaster that begins the conflict between the Jedi and the Nihil. Hetzal's two satellites, the Fruited Moon and Rooted Moon, are the source of produce for many planets across the Outer Rim. Hetzal is the place where sentient beings first figure out how to grow bacta for medical use. Crewed solar arrays direct sunlight onto the planet and moons in ways that extend the growing seasons. Keven Tarr and Elzar Mann set up an array of astromech droids on Hetzal to track future Emergences.

STARLIGHT BEACON

LOCATION Mobile, but associated with the Eiram system

The Starlight Beacon space station is commissioned by Chancellor Lina Soh to be both a symbol of Republic strength and a functional aid station, military base, and Jedi enclave. Its large size enables it to be a refuge for people in need, such as those fleeing volcanic eruptions on Dalna. Avar Kriss is the first Marshal of Starlight Beacon, followed by Stellan Gios.

The Beacon contains enough living space for a large number of Republic Defense Coalition troops, Jedi, medics, artists, and more. The Jedi star cruiser *Ataraxia* is permanently seconded to Starlight Beacon, in case Jedi need transportation to other planets. Jedi Estala Maru works as head of operations for the station alongside his Republic counterpart, Rodor Keen. Starlight Beacon is intended to have a hyperdrive, but it doesn't become operational before the station's destruction.

Because Starlight Beacon is a symbol of the Republic's peace and power, it becomes a target for the Nihil. The resulting battle blasts the station into two halves. One section burns up in the atmosphere of the planet of Eiram, and the other half falls into Eiram's ocean as a shower of debris.

AMAXINE SPACE STATION

LOCATION Outer Rim, Unknown space

Long ago, this verdant space station was built by Amaxine warriors. The Sith later seal a group of Drengir inside its gardens. During the High Republic era, Jedi Master Cohmac Vitus, Jedi Knights Orla Jareni and Dez Rydan, and Padawan Reath Silas become trapped on the station. They release and then destroy the Drengir. Hundreds of years later, the station's exotic gardens are still thriving in the times of the Empire, where the Sith engage Crimson Dawn in a climactic battle. In the years before the rise of the First Order, Emperor Palpatine's puppet Snoke meets with Ben Solo on the station after Solo destroys Luke Skywalker's Jedi temple.

AB DALIS

REGION Outer Rim **SECTOR** Gaulus **TERRAIN** City, swamp

Once a planet of swamps, Ab Dalis is now a heavily developed world. Many of the swamps have been plastered over with city-size factories and slum housing for the people who work in them. The sky is often covered by brown clouds, which come from the natural swamps as much as from the industrial waste put out by the factories. Ab Dalis is the first planet hit by the detritus from the wreck of the *Legacy Run*. Many inhabitants flee the world, only to be caught in a Nihil attack. Hundreds of years later, the Rebel Alliance builds a resupply base called Rendezvous Point Lambda-Four on Ab Dalis and faces an Imperial assault.

VALO
REGION Outer Rim **SECTOR** Rseik **SYSTEM** Valo **TERRAIN** Forest

Valo is a vibrant but out-of-the-way planet that's best known as the site of the ill-fated Republic Fair—a series of entertainment events held by the Republic but attacked by the Nihil. The weather on Valo is temperate, and beautiful inland lakes dot the landscape. Its towns tend to be prosperous, with a highly praised local cuisine. Jedi Padawan Ram Jomaram notes that it isn't unusual for forest creatures to set off the security systems around city infrastructure, such as the comms tower at the mountain nicknamed Crashpoint Peak. Both the Nihil and the Drengir eventually disturb the peace of Valo.

BANCHII
REGION Outer Rim **SECTOR** Jjannex **SYSTEM** Inugg **TERRAIN** Forest

Banchii is a small, remote world with towering trees and rich soil for farming. During the High Republic era, it is the site of a relatively new Jedi outpost. The other temple in the Inugg system is on Hon-Tallos. Jedi Masters Arkoff and Lily Tora-Asi, Padawan Keerin Fionn, and several younglings are stationed on Banchii to help the Republic settlers establish themselves. At this time, a communications infrastructure hasn't been established across the whole planet. Lily negotiates sharing resources between Republic farmers and refugees and the indigenous Banchiians.

NO-SPACE
LOCATION Outer Rim, Unknown space

No-Space is a region of space that contains the Nihil's headquarters, known as the Great Hall. At least one ship has been known to disappear into No-Space and become lost to the rest of the galaxy. No-Space is largely unmapped, and Marchion Ro guards the hyperspace path into it closely. The roof of the Great Hall is a transparent energy shield, which lets the light of the colorful nebula shine through. Shortly before the fall of Starlight Beacon, Lourna Dee orders the Nihil to reinforce the Great Hall by covering the energy shield with metal plates.

YARRUM
REGION Outer Rim **SECTOR** Bri'ahl **TERRAIN** Desert

The desert planet Yarrum is near Tenoo, and it includes the site of Yarrum Tower—a trading hub for pirates. The young pirate Taborr tries and fails to sell stolen seeds to a Chagrian broker there. Kai Brightstar, Lys Solay, and Nubs pursue Taborr to the tower after he steals jellyfruit from Weebo. Later, when Nash Durango sees Taborr feeling bad about not being impressive to the older pirates, she shares her jellyfruit with him.

TENOO
REGION Outer Rim **SECTOR** Bri'ahl **TERRAIN** Forests, wetlands

Tenoo is a lush planet, rich in Tenoo trees and abundant water. It has two moons; the larger of which is called Dedoon. The first person on Tenoo is Kaliah Kublop, who founds Kublop Springs.

During the High Republic, Tenoo is the location of the Jedi temple where Master Zia Zaldor Zanna, Kai Brightstar, Lys Solay, and Nubs live, and Yoda visits. Tenoo is also the home to the Durango Shuttle Service—a family-owned transportation company.

Sap from the Tenoo tree can be consumed, and the wood is good for building homes. The forester Raxlo tries to harvest the sap of a large tree, but his drill destabilizes the tree's roots, and the cave beneath them floods. Raxlo narrowly escapes with the help of Kai, Lys, and Nubs.

Jedi temple
The Jedi temple on Tenoo is ancient, with the contents of many rooms remaining unknown to its current occupants.

YAMRADI
REGION Outer Rim **TERRAIN** Forest

A thriving planet with a diverse ecosystem, Yamradi is home to mysterious creatures called chylaroo. SF-R3, CAM-E, Kai Brightstar, Lys Solay, and Nubs travel to Yamradi to learn more about the creatures. CAM-E also encounters a large birdlike creature, which flies away with him. Because the berries on Yamradi are very shiny, some creatures, including the large bird, mistake the shiny, metal droids for their food. Lys uses this information to draw the creature away from CAM-E, and she discovers the bird is friendly. She names it the burrowberry bird.

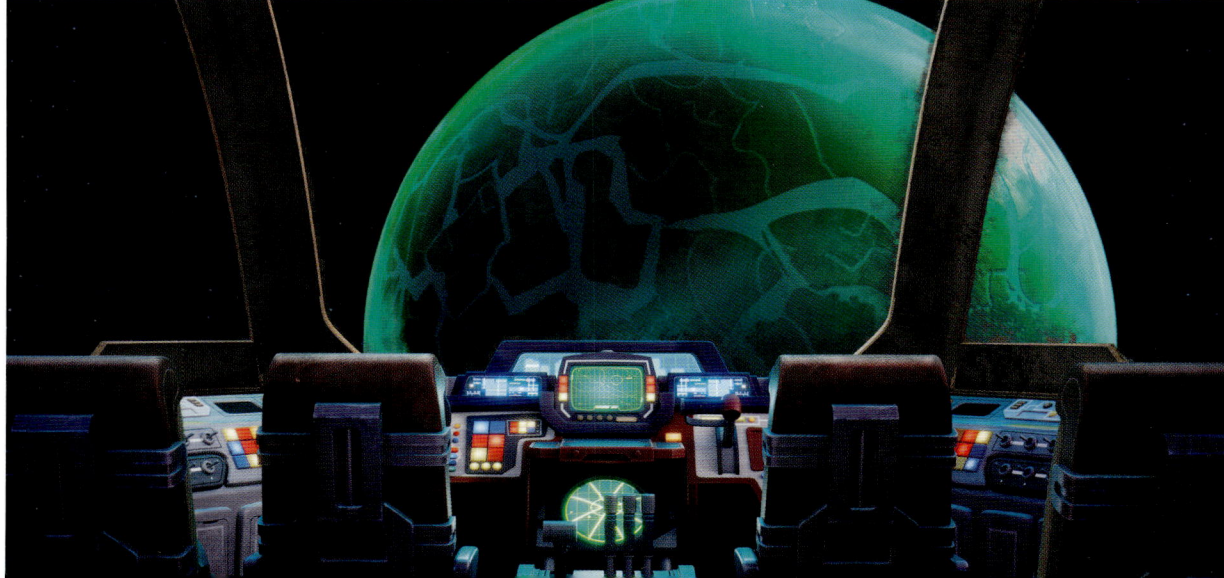

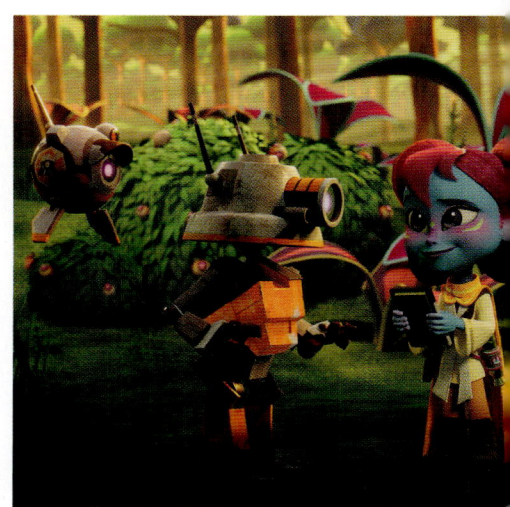

LOCATIONS

NABOO
REGION Mid Rim **SECTOR** Chommell
TERRAIN Plains, swamps, forests

A small and geologically unique world, Naboo's surface consists of swampy lakes, rolling plains, and green hills. The river cities are resplendent with classical architecture and greenery, while the underwater Gungan settlements are exotic examples of hydrostatic bubble technology.

ARCADIAN DESTINATION
The Lake Country is one of the planet's most remote inhabited regions, with a sparse population that's mostly made up of farmers, shaak herders, and glass craftworkers. In springtime, though, the Festival of Glad Arrival brings colorful pageants and musical performances. While the fertile land is regularly flooded by its rivers, the area is pleasantly dry in summer. Padmé Amidala's family maintains a retreat on the island of Varykino in the Lake Country.

Peaceful planet
Although Naboo's sparse human population embraces peace and tranquility, they and the indigenous Gungans navigate an uneasy relationship for hundreds of years until they ally to defend their verdant world.

Trade routes
For generations, Gungans have used bongo submarines to explore and navigate the network of underwater tunnels that snake through the planet Naboo.

THE GUNGAN SACRED PLACE
Built by the Elders, the Gungan Sacred Place is an ancient monument north of the Lianorm Swamp. For generations, Gungans have gathered in this area during times of discord or when the leaders anticipate great danger. The monument is accessed by a hidden entrance, which leads to a path that emerges in a clearing beneath a dense forest canopy. The remains of gigantic statues and monolithic heads, some displaced by the roots of primeval trees, appear to alternately rise from and rest upon the hallowed grounds, from which outsiders are normally forbidden.

Urgent union
During the Trade Federation invasion of Naboo, Jar Jar Binks brings Queen Amidala to meet Boss Nass at the Gungan Sacred Place *(top)*. There, the Gungans and the Naboo agree to an alliance against their enemies. Little is known about the reptilian humanoids called the Elders, who waged war with ancient Gungans and left numerous monuments *(above)* on Naboo.

THE CORE
Lacking a molten core, the ancient planet of Naboo is a conglomerate of large, rocky bodies permeated by caves and tunnel networks. These largely water-filled networks create numerous swampy lakes on the planet's surface, which lead deeper into its structure. The indigenous Gungans have developed submersible transports to traverse the caves and tunnels, but most hesitate to venture deep into the planetary core, which is infested with enormous, ravenous sea beasts. However, hardy Gungan navigators regard certain networks through the core as time-honored trade routes and the most expedient avenues from one area of Naboo to another.

Symbolic spectacle
The Festival of Light's fireworks are artfully controlled bursts that represent significant historic moments in Naboo's association with the Republic.

FESTIVAL OF LIGHT
An annual event, the Festival of Light celebrates the anniversary of when Naboo joined the Galactic Republic. In the city of Theed, the celebration is traditionally observed with a public ceremony that includes an elaborate laser light show and fireworks display. During the Clone Wars, Supreme Chancellor Palpatine returns to his homeworld to attend the festival in its 847th year, even though he is aware he may be targeted for assassination. Knowing that to shrink from such duty would be to admit fear of the enemy, Palpatine trusts the Jedi to protect him during the festival.

Dangerous decoy
The Gungan Army bravely engages with the enormous droid army on the Great Grass Plains, just south of Theed.

BATTLE OF NABOO
Following a blockade by the Trade Federation, Queen Amidala returns to Naboo hoping to save her people. She leads the resistance with the help of Jedi Qui-Gon Jinn and Obi-Wan Kenobi, Anakin Skywalker, and the indigenous Gungans. While the Gungan military lures the droid army away from the capital, Padmé and the Jedi head to infiltrate Theed Royal Palace, where Trade Federation leader Nute Gunray is stationed. However, Darth Maul appears and engages the two Jedi, leading them into the city's power generator for an epic duel that ends in Qui-Gon's death and Maul's apparent demise. Meanwhile, young Anakin finds his way to the Droid control ship, destroying it from the inside and deactivating the droid armies. At the same time, in the palace's throne room, Amidala arrests Gunray and forces him to sign a new treaty.

OPERATION: CINDER
Weeks after the Battle of Endor, the Emperor's contingency plans, including Operation: Cinder, are activated. Following the Emperor's posthumous orders, Naboo is one of many planets marked for destruction. The Empire targets Naboo with climate disruption arrays that will render the planet uninhabitable. Led by Princess Leia, a small force of N-1 starfighters attacks the arrays, and, with the help of Rebel Alliance reinforcements, destroys them. The Empire then launches a ground assault on Theed that is repelled by the Alliance forces.

Climate control
A disruption to the temperate climate of Naboo would be catastrophic.

THEED
LOCATION Naboo

Originally a farming village nestled along the banks of the Solleu River, Naboo's capital city, Theed, is built at the edge of a great plateau where the Solleu runs toward a spectacular waterfall. Fed by underground tributaries that flow from the planet's core, the river travels through and around Theed so that nearly every vantage point in the city has water views. For generations, Naboo traders have used the waterways to occasionally meet with Gungans. Many of the city's buildings have columned facades and domed roofs. Theed's harmonious architectural style reflects the peaceful culture and ways of the city's founders and citizens.

During the blockade of Naboo, this peace is disrupted as the city is occupied by the Trade Federation. The people of Naboo suffer in detention camps under the Federation, until they are freed by the combined Gungan and Naboo forces after the Battle of Naboo. At the end of the Clone Wars, the city holds the funeral for the beloved former queen and senator, Padmé Amidala.

After the Battle of Endor, an Imperial faction launches an attack on Naboo, landing forces in Theed. This ground assault is repelled by Princess Leia and members of the Rebel Alliance.

THEED ROYAL PALACE
LOCATION Theed, Naboo

Resting serenely atop a plunging cliff lined with waterfalls is the immense Theed Royal Palace, Naboo's seat of power. The ancient and majestic building serves as the residence of Naboo's elected sovereign, as well as the meeting place of Naboo's Royal Advisory Council. The palace is a mighty structure, with strong lines and an imposing presence, but it is also decorated with delicate, ornate finishes that are a testament to Naboo's sensitivity to art and culture. The palace is protected by the Naboo Palace Guard, although, given Naboo's pacifist nature, the trained troops rarely need to mobilize. During the blockade of Naboo, Viceroy Nute Gunray of the Trade Federation occupies the palace. He is apprehended during the Battle of Naboo by Queen Amidala. Years later, Count Dooku infiltrates the palace to try to capture Supreme Chancellor Palpatine during the 847th Festival of Light ceremony. Following the Battle of Naboo, an ion pulse cannon is installed to protect Theed. It is activated when the remnants of the Empire attack the city during Operation: Cinder.

Palatial sanctuary
Theed Royal Palace enjoys commanding views from its cliff-face sanctuary *(left)*. The city's main thoroughfare, the Palace Plaza, is a wide, pedestrian-only avenue that stretches from the royal palace to the palace courtyard *(above)*.

ROYAL PALACE THRONE ROOM

LOCATION Theed Royal Palace, Theed, Naboo

Theed Royal Palace's original designers and contemporary curators eschew any display of bulky, inelegant machinery, but the building has many subtly blended technological features. The throne room is protected by ornate blast doors, an interplanetary communications system, and hidden compartments for weapons in case of an emergency. A composite holoprojector is built into the throne room's floor, along with a large viewscreen on the wall, which allows Queen Amidala and her advisory council to converse with dignitaries from other worlds.

Captured throne
During their occupation of Naboo, Neimoidians confer with Darth Sidious' hologram in the throne room.

OTOH GUNGA

LOCATION Lake Paonga, Naboo

Deep below the surface of Lake Paonga is the largest Gungan city on Naboo, Otoh Gunga. The city resembles a glittering cluster of jewel-like bubbles and is the crowning achievement of unique Gungan technology. The Gungans grow the building material for their cities, and the elegant structures contained within the bubbles consist of curving forms that appear alive. The bubbles are hydrostatic force fields that contain breathable atmospheres for the city's inhabitants. Though the bubbles are rigid enough to keep the water out, they can be safely passed through by Gungans swimming to and from the city at special portal zones.

During the Trade Federation's occupation of Naboo, the Gungan leader Boss Nass ignores the battle droid threat, believing Otoh Gunga is safe. But when the battle droids encroach on Gungan territory and invade the submerged city, they force the Gungans to abandon their home. The Gungans hide in the nearby forests where the Gungan Sacred Place is located, and eventually ally with Queen Amidala and the human populace of Naboo.

Following the defeat of the Trade Federation, overcrowding becomes a prime concern for Boss Nass and the Gungan Rep Council. The increased Gungan tolerance of visiting offworlders results in Otoh Gunga becoming a tourist attraction and, surprisingly, a favored destination for honeymooning vacationers. After Padmé steps down as queen, one of her former handmaidens, Eirtaé, travels to Otoh Gunga to learn about Gungan technology.

Gungan engineering
Gungans combine bubble wort catalyst and stabilized plasma in electrostatic field generators to create the permeable hydrostatic bubbles needed to keep their city dry *(above)*. Otoh Gunga's amphibious inhabitants use specially designed portal zones to enter and exit the submerged city *(right)*.

THEED HANGAR

LOCATION Theed, Naboo

Attached to one side of Naboo's Theed Royal Palace, a spacious hangar serves as the headquarters of the Royal Naboo Security Forces and Starfighter Corps, and houses the sleek yellow Naboo N-1 starfighters, as well as the queen's gleaming Royal Starship. Separated from the hangar by a heavy blast-proof door, the neighboring power generator supplies the hangar's spacecraft with plasma energy through underground conduits. The hangar is equipped with air traffic control, tactical computer stations, and a secret subterranean tunnel link to the palace. During the Battle of Naboo, Queen Amidala and her allies use the tunnels to infiltrate Theed, allowing them to reach the hangar and liberate the air traffic controllers and pilots from their droid captors. The pilots scramble to their N-1 starfighters and swiftly leave the hangar to join the fight. Eventually, the hangar is closed as fighter operations are moved out of the palace and later the Empire demilitarizes Naboo. During Operation: Cinder, Princess Leia, Queen Soruna, and rebel pilot Shara Bey enter the hangar, finding old N-1 starfighters that they board to protect Naboo from destruction by the Empire.

TATOOINE

REGION Outer Rim **SECTOR** Arkanis
SYSTEM Tatoo **TERRAIN** Desert, mesas, buttes, canyons

Far from the Core Worlds, the inhospitable desert planet Tatooine is of little interest to the galaxy at large. Ironically, this dusty world is home to two generations of Skywalkers, who are instrumental in bringing down both the Galactic Republic and the Empire that followed.

LAWLESS WORLD
Beyond the interests of galactic laws, Tatooine is largely controlled by the Hutts, whose shady operations bring many spacers, bounty hunters, and thieves to the planet's few port cities. Despite the planet's criminal activity and hardworking settlers' attempts to extract a living from the unforgiving environment, sporadic colonization efforts have resulted in only scattered communities, separated by vast gulfs of wilderness.

Sand planet
Isolated and almost entirely devoid of water, Tatooine is a world of dry air and parched soil. The planet's silicate surface reflects the light of its suns so intensely that legends tell of its original explorers first mistaking the planet for a third, smaller sun. Indigenous sentient life includes the scavenging Jawas and the fearsome Tuskens. Creatures found roaming the desert include banthas, rontos, dewbacks, scurriers, womp rats, tibidon sand whales, krayt dragons, and eopies.

Negotiations
Although Jedi have little reason to visit Tatooine, Obi-Wan Kenobi meets with Jabba the Hutt during the Clone Wars to discuss a delicate situation involving Jabba's abducted son, Rotta.

Infinite wastes
Tatooine's surface is a seemingly endless desert environment cooked by the intense energy of twin yellow suns. Only the sporadic rocky mesas, canyons, and arroyos break up the monotony of seemingly endless shifting dunes.

Nomadic traders
Scurrying outside their sandcrawler, Jawas present various droids for sale to moisture farmer Owen Lars.

DESERT SCAVENGERS
Long before the Hutts took control of Tatooine, mining colonies searched the sand planet for precious minerals and ores. When Tatooine metal proved to have unwanted metallurgic properties, the mines were shut down and the miners abandoned most of their equipment, including mobile transports used for hauling and refining ore. Much to the remaining colonists' surprise, the native Jawas quickly claimed and salvaged these "sandcrawlers," making them an important part of their culture. Jawas use the large, treaded vehicles not only as an armored defense against the elements and Tuskens, but for transporting trade goods, including refurbished droids made from scavenged parts, to remote outposts. The sandcrawlers' smelting reactors, originally designed to melt processed ore, have been modified to produce salable ingots. Although Tuskens have no interest in computer technology, they also scavenge—and more often steal—metal they can shape into weapons and masks.

MOISTURE FARMS
Water vaporators are not only the most energy-efficient devices used to gather water on Tatooine, they are the most crucial piece of equipment for colonists' survival. Although a single vaporator may cost up to 500 credits, some colonists invest in multiple units to establish their own moisture farms. Independent farmers often use surplus water for their small hydroponic gardens, but few gardens yield enough to make substantial profits. Water-mongers, like Lortha Peel in Mos Espa, broker sales on vapor farmers' behalf.

KRAYT DRAGONS
According to Jawa folklore, the Dune Sea was once a true ocean. Eroded canyons seem to confirm the Jawas' stories. Despite the scarcity of water, Tatooine boasts many indigenous creatures, like the krayt dragon, which submerges itself in the shifting sands and uses its powerful limbs to swim through the dunes. Its scaly hide is impenetrable, and it spews an acid from its mouth that dissolves any creature in its path. The gigantic reptile is so formidable that it can feast on a sarlacc and take up residence in its pit. The Tuskens highly value the innards of the krayt dragon, which can contain a rare treasure: a massive pearl.

Joining forces
It takes the combined efforts of the Mandalorian Din Djarin, Marshal Cobb Vanth, Tuskens, and the residents of Mos Pelgo to take down the krayt dragon that's terrorizing the town.

Vaporator fields
Luke surveys his uncle's farm and vaporators *(right)*, which are strategically spaced to collect moisture *(above)*.

244 LOCATIONS

Bustling city
One of the few port cities on Tatooine, Mos Espa is larger than Mos Eisley spaceport and is known for its wide streets, bordered by many shops and stalls.

Tearful farewell
On the street outside their home, Anakin Skywalker says goodbye to his mother, Shmi.

MOS ESPA
LOCATION Tatooine

On the lip of the Dune Sea, down a canyon called the Xelric Draw, the city of Mos Espa is a serpentine sprawl of low-level buildings with thick walls and domed roofs to defend against the scorching heat of the planet's twin suns.

MOS ESPA'S ECONOMY
Among the dwellings, workspaces, and commercial operations, the city also boasts many entertainment areas, including Garsa Fwip's Sanctuary and the famed Mos Espa Grand Arena. Although wealthy Hutts, including Jabba, keep residences in Mos Espa, most of the inhabitants are settlers and subsistence earners who eke out meager livings as best they can.

Because neither the Galactic Republic nor the Trade Federation has any jurisdiction over Tatooine, and because Tatooine has few valuable natural resources, the only real wealth in Mos Espa is tied up in gambling and offworld trade, especially in the lucrative criminal market. The influx of commercial ventures fuels Mos Espa's growth, quickly transforming it into the largest city on Tatooine and the desert planet's de facto capital. Many outlanders believe they may avoid paying high tariffs by doing business in Mos Espa, but because Tatooine is controlled by the devious Hutts, few travelers save money at the spaceport. The inexpensive hotels and cantinas exist primarily to lure traders, spacers, and unwitting tourists into the Hutts' casinos and gambling dens, where they can easily lose their earnings, and even life savings, within hours. Few losers complain because they know the Hutt-owned establishments are staffed by security personnel who don't take kindly to troublemakers. However, the rise of the Empire prompts the Hutts to revise their business schemes, and Jabba shifts his interests to Mos Eisley, causing Mos Espa to decline.

NEW DAIMYO
After the deaths of Jabba the Hutt and his inept successor, Bib Fortuna, former bounty hunter Boba Fett claims their territory in Mos Espa. By the time of the New Republic, areas of the city are primarily split between three factions: the starport and upper sprawl under control of the Klatooinians, the Aqualish in the Worker's District, and the Trandoshans in the city center. The Pyke Syndicate negotiates an uneasy alliance with those groups and Mayor Mok Shaiz to move its spice through Mos Espa, but Fett and his allies expel the criminal organization and its illicit enterprise from the city.

Return to Mos Espa
Padmé Amidala's yacht delivers Anakin to a Mos Espa docking bay *(right)*, and the two take a droid rickshaw to Watto's shop *(above)*.

WATTO'S SHOP

LOCATION Mos Espa, Tatooine

Although Watto promotes his establishment as a parts dealership, everyone in Mos Espa calls it a junk shop. The property is ideally situated near the spaceport's busiest docking bays and service hangars, and it is well known to many podracers.

DISTINCTIVE DOME
Originally, the shop's main building was an unremarkable squat dome, but Watto has added a distinctive bell-shaped top, which provides additional living and working space and attracts customers because of its unusual appearance and greater height than neighboring buildings. The dome's apex forms a comfortable perch for Watto and is similar to the muck nests of his home planet.

SUCCESSFUL VENTURE
The shop is one of the most successful of its kind in Mos Espa. Watto attributes his success to four things: inflated prices, stolen stock, enslaved workers, and no questions asked. Like most Mos Espa merchants, Watto accepts only local currency.

Inside Watto's shop, merchandise ranges from desirable rare parts to fully operational droids. His selection of droids and droid parts includes GNK power droids, DUM-series pit droids, astromechs, and shell plating for Cybot Galactica protocol droids. An R1-type shopkeeping drone handles most of the routine business operations, while Anakin Skywalker, repairs and cleans machinery, allowing Watto to dedicate more time to his gambling interests.

Watto has also amassed a collection of podrace memorabilia, including many rare trophies. Outside the shop, an arched portal serves as the entrance to the scrapyard, where Watto stores the bulk of his merchandise, including larger items like podracer engines, landspeeder turbines, and empty cargo containers. Near the scrapyard's entrance, Watto maintains a constantly shifting pile of largely useless scrap, which he leaves outside for Jawa scavengers. Although Watto prefers paying customers, he has a certain respect for Jawas, as they have taught him much about salvaging ruined vessels and protecting technology from heat and sand.

Mechanically inclined
Holding machinery for repairing and cleaning mechanical apparatus and technology, the curved tables inside Watto's shop double as display shelves for various parts for sale *(above)*. Anakin's natural talent for repairing machinery is exploited by Watto *(left)*.

Tour of the scrapyard
Hoping to obtain an unusual hyperdrive component, the Jedi Qui-Gon Jinn follows Watto into the scrapyard behind his shop.

LOCATIONS

Sand rock construction
Straddling the junction of the Xelric Draw and the Northern Dune Sea, the arena's amphitheater is built into the natural curve of a steep-walled canyon.

MOS ESPA GRAND ARENA

LOCATION Outskirts of Mos Espa, Tatooine

Financed by the Hutts, the Mos Espa Grand Arena is home to the Boonta Eve Classic, the largest annual podrace held on Tatooine. The arena's podracing track is one of the most famous in the Outer Rim and attracts competitors and spectators from all over the galaxy. Jabba also holds other events here, including public executions.

PODRACER HANGARS
Originally constructed as a series of enclosed bays, each of which serviced a single podracer, the arena's hangars have been expanded as the sport has grown in popularity. The dividers between the bays have been removed to accommodate additional podracers and to keep up with the number of entrants. While the hangars are used for vehicle maintenance and last-minute tune-ups before a race, they also provide a place for podracer pilots, their wealthy fans, and their sponsors to place unregulated, high-stakes bets with one another.

Bustling pit droids
Inside a hangar, teams of pit droids are constantly on the move, assisting podracer mechanics in preparation for the Boonta Eve Classic.

No turning back
As the podracer pilots move into position on the arena's starting grid, none dwell on the fact that the Boonta Eve Classic has the highest mortality rate of all podrace competitions in the galaxy.

STARTING GRID
The formal race ceremony begins with a parade of flag-bearers, each carrying a podracer's distinctive emblem as they line up before the starting grid. The system for determining the starting lineup at the Boonta Eve Classic is the subject of much speculation and argument among podracing aficionados. Allegedly developed by expert race officials, the system actually involves a baffling mix of performance statistics, outright bribery, and random chance. After the flag-bearers clear the grid, the podracers' massive engines roar to life, seemingly hungry for the chance to charge along at speeds exceeding 700 kilometers (435 miles) per hour. Eighteen podracers enter the fateful competition that results in a major upset for Sebulba the Dug and a great victory for Anakin Skywalker, who wins not only the event but also his freedom. A mere seven pilots manage to cross the finish line.

WATTO'S BOX
Mos Espa's wealthier residents and guests can afford private viewing boxes separated from the rest of the rabble. Toydarian junk merchant Watto hosts viewing parties for his friends and gambling partners in his own private box. Because only a small fraction of the racetrack passes the arena, Watto's box is equipped with viewscreens that broadcast transmissions from aerial cam droids, enabling Watto and his cronies to monitor each podracer's progress. The most opulent viewing box is reserved for the ruling Hutts, particularly Jabba, grandmaster host of the Boonta Eve Classic.

Podrace fans
More than 100,000 beings fill the Mos Espa Grand Arena to capacity for the Boonta Eve Classic. They file into the grandstand seats, crowd into broad viewing platforms, or cluster into the upper tiers to witness the high-speed spectacle. Many hope to win big after hitting the betting windows and playing the odds.

CORUSCANT

REGION Core **SECTOR** Corusca
TERRAIN Urban cityscape

Situated in the heart of the galaxy, Coruscant was the seat of government for the Galactic Republic and the subsequent Empire. Completely covered by skyscrapers, the planet has a population of over one trillion, including many powerful and influential politicians and industrialists.

Ecumenopolis
Exhausted of all natural resources, this city-planet is entirely dependent on outside support to survive.

Shimmering "surface"
Viewed from orbit, Coruscant resembles a great, glittering sphere and appears to promise prosperity for all. Sunlight dances across the gleaming skyscrapers' uppermost levels, which are home to the wealthiest citizens, such as Chandrila's Senator Mon Mothma and her family. But beneath this veneer, the city-world descends thousands of levels to impoverished, dangerous areas untouched by the sun for millennia.

AIR TRAFFIC

Coruscant's skies are filled with unending repulsorlift traffic. Most skylanes are autonavigated, with vehicles traveling on preprogrammed routes to minimize risk of collisions. Large passenger ships join the fastest traffic in the highest skylanes, while smaller air taxis piloted by droids crisscross these routes to take high-paying riders directly to their destinations. Tour operator pilots demand high fees for taking wide-eyed offworlders on breathtaking cruises over the planet. Even at night, Coruscant is alive with glittering lights and rivers of traffic, a bustling ecumenopolis that refuses to sleep.

LEVEL 2046

During the height of the Empire, as part of a heist, renegade Jedi Cal Kestis is captured by mercenaries and taken to Level 2046, far below the glittering surface of Coruscant. One of the mid-levels of the city-planet, it is notable for its independent industries, vendors, and fragrant food stalls. Desi's Noodles, for instance, is considered one of the rare reasons to brave the area. Like the other subterranean levels of the city-planet, Level 2046 is populated with impoverished refugees and squatters.

Urban growth
The crisis on Naboo and the Clone Wars dramatically impact Coruscant's Federal District, as the call to bolster the Galactic Republic's stability results in new buildings to house thousands of pro-Republic and war-effort departments.

SKYSCRAPER SPRAWLS

Over many thousands of years, Coruscant's surface has become completely buried under the foundations of immense, densely clustered skyscrapers. The enormous structures reach so high into the atmosphere that tenants require piped-in purified gasses for breathing in upper-level complexes, a luxury only the affluent inhabitants can afford. Several kilometers down, the lower levels are a worldwide maze of treacherous alleys where the most impoverished residents dwell. Citizens from above and below intermingle in myriad nightclubs, gaming houses, bars, and entertainment establishments that cater to various species.

Jubilant celebrations
Fireworks light up Coruscant's sky after Palpatine's death.

Abandoned towers
Toxic waste leaves large areas of the Works entirely uninhabitable.

CIVIL WAR

Following Emperor Palpatine's death there are celebrations across much of Coruscant. Soon after, a civil war breaks out between the Imperial forces, and the citizens loyal to them and the rebellious citizens, supported by New Republic troops. Grand Vizier Mas Amedda, the nominal successor to the Emperor, is imprisoned in the Imperial Palace by forces loyal to the Emperor's protégé, Gallius Rax. Following the Battle of Jakku, Amedda represents the Empire and signs the Galactic Concordance, a peace treaty that ends the Galactic Civil War. Coruscant then joins the New Republic with Amedda installed as a puppet leader of its provisional government.

JEDI TEMPLE

LOCATION Galactic City, Coruscant

Since being reclaimed from the Sith 1,000 years ago, the Jedi Temple has been the home of the Jedi Order on Coruscant. Part school and part monastery, the Temple houses facilities for training and meditation, dormitories, medical centers, and Archives that contain extensive data from across the galaxy.

HIGH COUNCIL CHAMBER

The Jedi High Council, the governing body of the Jedi Order, convenes within one of the Jedi Temple's outer spires. The circular High Council chamber holds a ring of 12 seats, one for each of the Jedi Masters who serve as Council members. Monitoring galactic events and contemplating the nature of the Force, the Council has final authority on Jedi missions on behalf of the Republic and also determines whether prospective Jedi candidates are worthy of training. While advanced communications networks keep the Council apprised of galactic events, its members also rely on the Force to sense disturbances and anticipate situations that may require their help. During the Clone Wars, the Council uses the High Council chamber to consider battle strategies and coordinate troops.

JEDI ARCHIVES

Inside the Jedi Temple, incredible amounts of data are stored electronically and holographically in the Jedi Archives. Jedi scholars and investigators use the carefully organized data in their studies or their missions. Besides standard data tapes and holobooks, the Archives contain holocrons, which are polyhedral-shaped devices that store phenomenal amounts of data. After the Purge, Jedi Master Cere Junda begins a personal mission to recover and preserve lost Archives records.

TRAINING YOUNG JEDI

Prior to a Padawan's pairing with a Jedi Master, students known as younglings are taught in a communal group called a clan. At any given time inside the Jedi Temple, 10 different clans undergo instruction in the ways of the Jedi under the tutelage of Grand Master Yoda. Each clan consists of up to 20 younglings, ranging in age from 4 to 8 and comprising a number of different species. Anakin Skywalker is a rare example of a Padawan student who skips the clan stage of training by joining the Order as an older child.

TEMPLE UNDER SIEGE

To help Darth Sidious conquer his enemies, his new apprentice, Darth Vader, storms the Jedi Temple with his elite clone trooper special forces in tow. They cut down the Jedi ranks within the Temple, not sparing the younglings who cower in the empty Council chamber. After declaring himself Emperor, Sidious sends a false emergency transmission across space, notifying distant Jedi that the war is over and instructing them to return to the Temple. Seeing through this trap, Masters Obi-Wan and Yoda infiltrate the Temple and modify the transmission, warning the remaining Jedi to stay away.

IMPERIAL PALACE

After the Jedi Purge, Emperor Palpatine orders the Temple to be repaired and redecorated. He renames his enemy's former stronghold the Imperial Palace and rules his Empire from within it. As dictator, he holds several lavish balls at the palace and meets with individuals he finds interesting. In secret, Palpatine moves many of his Sith artifacts to the location and orders the excavation of an old Sith shrine where he plans to discover the dark side's final secrets, together with Darth Vader. Following Palpatine's death, his loyal follower and potential successor, Grand Vizier Mas Amedda, is imprisoned in the palace by Imperial forces loyal to Counselor Gallius Rax. Amedda is eventually liberated by a group of young rebels, who ensure he reaches the New Republic.

The Temple
A massive ziggurat rising from one of the highest levels on Coruscant, the Jedi Temple is instantly recognizable by its distinctive crown of five spires. The Jedi Order also maintains chapter houses and other temples throughout the galaxy.

Jedi dispatch
Standing in the center of the High Council chamber, Obi-Wan Kenobi and Anakin Skywalker receive orders from the Council.

Stalking Jedi
At Darth Sidious' command, the newly appointed Sith Lord Darth Vader leads Anakin's former battalion, the 501st Legion, on a killing mission inside the Jedi Temple.

Giving instruction
While teaching Jedi younglings from the Bear Clan, Yoda confers with Obi-Wan.

Guardians of knowledge
Jocasta Nu, the chief librarian of the Jedi Archives, assists Obi-Wan (left), who searches the Archives for information about the mysterious Kamino system (above).

After the fall
Celebrations erupt across the planet following the Emperor's death. The palace, however, remains a stronghold of the Imperial forces stationed on Coruscant.

Galactic representatives
Each box in the Galactic Senate Chamber contains a delegation from an important world or sector in the Republic. The democratic ideals of the Senate are put to the test every time the legislative process degenerates into arguing and pointless bureaucracy.

GALACTIC SENATE CHAMBER

LOCATION Senate District, Coruscant

The Galactic Senate Chamber is the nerve center of political activity on Coruscant. The huge open area is lined with 1,024 pods arrayed in concentric circles, each pod housing a delegation from an important planet, sector, or political body. The pods are outfitted with anti-gravity repulsorlifts, so that when a politician wishes to address the assembled Senate, their pod detaches from the wall and floats into the open air in the middle of the chamber. The entire structure is fitted with voice-amplifying microphones and automatic translators, and hovercams constantly flit about to record the proceedings for the official record.

At the centermost point of the Galactic Senate Chamber is the podium of the supreme chancellor. This is where the elected leader of the Republic sits to hear arguments from every representative, usually joined in the podium by the vice chancellor and a senior administrative aide. The podium retracts into the floor when not in use, giving the chancellor access to a suite of rooms where business can be conducted between Senate sessions.

The Galactic Senate Chamber is the site of many of the most crucial events in the latter years of the Republic. It is where Queen Padmé Amidala of Naboo, upset over the lack of political help in ending the Trade Federation's blockade of her homeworld, calls for a Vote of No Confidence in the leadership of Supreme Chancellor Valorum. After the Battle of Naboo, Padmé joins the Senate as the representative from Naboo, playing a role in the debate over whether the Republic should adopt the Military Creation Act in response to the growing threat of Count Dooku's Separatist movement. At the end of the Clone Wars, Palpatine gives a speech in the Galactic Senate Chamber in which he declares himself Emperor. Jedi Master Yoda confronts Palpatine, and the two have a stunning clash of Force abilities inside the chamber that results in Yoda fleeing the fight. Once the chamber is repaired, the newly formed Imperial Senate holds meetings here, but they have little to no influence over the Emperor's plans and the largely vacant chamber is a shadow of its former self.

Power play
Senator Palpatine slyly manipulates Queen Amidala into pushing for Chancellor Valorum's removal from office. Amidala introduces the Vote of No Confidence in Valorum's leadership, leading to Palpatine's election as the new supreme chancellor. The queen believes this will be a good move for Naboo, since Palpatine is a native of her homeworld, but it has dire consequences for the galaxy as Supreme Chancellor Palpatine slowly brings the Senate under his control and ensures that he is given stronger executive powers.

"Order! We shall have order!" — MAS AMEDDA

Fight to the death
After the defeat of his master, Qui-Gon *(right)*, Obi-Wan Kenobi struggles to pull himself out of the reactor shaft while Maul attacks *(above)*.

THEED POWER GENERATOR

LOCATION Theed, Naboo

Located within the capital city of Theed on Naboo, the power generator is where the planet's natural plasma reserves are refined and used as a source of efficient energy. The building also houses hangar facilities for the starfighters of the Royal Naboo Security Forces. The power generator is a clean, brightly illuminated location of towering columns and dangerous drops. During the Battle of Naboo, Obi-Wan Kenobi and Qui-Gon Jinn chase Darth Maul into the power generator and engage in a fierce lightsaber duel. A series of laser gates separates the Jedi, allowing Maul to get the upper hand and kill Qui-Gon. Obi-Wan defeats Maul and casts his body into a reactor shaft.

LOCATIONS

REPUBLIC EXECUTIVE BUILDING

LOCATION Senate District, Coruscant

The Republic Executive Building houses administrative facilities used by legislators on Coruscant, including the offices of the supreme chancellor. Landing facilities constructed directly into the side of the building allow senators and guests to come and go freely. Senate Guards provide protection while senators such as Bail Organa, Padmé Amidala, and Onaconda Farr hold discussions with their allies and opponents concerning upcoming pieces of legislation. During the Separatist Crisis and the Clone Wars, many important meetings are held in the Republic Executive Building, including debates on the wisdom of the Military Creation Act.

Legislative District
The Republic Executive Building is close to the Galactic Senate Chamber for the convenience of its representatives.

Always busy
Starships and airspeeders are constantly arriving and departing, taking senators to important meetings.

SUPREME CHANCELLOR PALPATINE'S OFFICE

LOCATION Senate District, Coruscant

The office of the supreme chancellor of the Republic is located in one of the highest levels of Coruscant within the well-guarded Republic Executive Building. It consists of several rooms, featuring red-paneled walls and decorated with bronze statues, bas-relief murals, and other rare and exotic artworks. One piece of sculpture on Palpatine's desk secretly contains one of his lightsabers. During the Clone Wars, Mace Windu and three other Jedi Masters visit his office to place the chancellor under arrest. He defends himself using his dark-side abilities. Palpatine's office is also where Anakin Skywalker's conversion from Jedi to Sith takes place.

PADMÉ'S CORUSCANT APARTMENT

LOCATION Senate District, Coruscant

Padmé Amidala uses this apartment after she becomes Naboo's representative to the Galactic Senate. Spacious and luxurious, it is located in the upper levels of the Coruscant cityscape. Just prior to the Clone Wars, assassin Zam Wesell tries to kill Padmé by placing two venomous kouhuns in her apartment. Following Padmé's death at the end of the Clone Wars, the founding members of the Amidalan rebel cell dedicate themselves to uncovering the circumstances of her death.

CORUSCANT UNDERWORLD

LOCATION Lower Levels, Coruscant

The Coruscant underworld is a term used to describe the lower levels of the city, where sunlight seldom reaches and crime is a constant danger. Nightclubs, taverns, and casinos are common in the better-trafficked areas of the underworld. Brightly colored signs offer illumination, regardless of the time of day, while thugs and pickpockets lurk in dark corners preying on pedestrians. Senators and Jedi Knights rarely travel into the underworld unless they have good reason.

After dark
The Coruscant underworld is a dangerous place to travel for those who are alone or unarmed.

Mind trick
In the club, Obi-Wan is confronted by a patron offering him death sticks. With the Force, he convinces the dealer to go home and rethink his life.

OUTLANDER GAMBLING CLUB

LOCATION Entertainment District, Coruscant

One of the most popular gambling establishments in Coruscant's lower-level Entertainment District, the Outlander Club is a busy place where patrons can place wagers on games of chance and the outcomes of sporting events across the galaxy. With so many people circulating in and out of the club's doors, it is a perfect spot for fugitives to escape unwanted attention or for criminals to sell illegal goods. Just prior to the Clone Wars, Obi-Wan Kenobi and Anakin Skywalker pursue assassin Zam Wesell into the Outlander Club. Wesell tries to blend in, but Obi-Wan finds her and cuts off her arm.

DEX'S DINER

LOCATION Coco Town, Coruscant

The restaurant operated by Dexter Jettster is a stopover for residents of the Coco Town neighborhood of Coruscant. The diner is small but usually jam-packed, and offers a variety of filling, unhealthy foods and endless cups of Jawa Juice. The droid WA-7 and the humans Wanda and Harmony Bagwa work in the diner as waiting staff, and Dex himself often fills the role of chef. Just prior to the Clone Wars, Obi-Wan Kenobi visits Dex's Diner to ask its proprietor about a dart used to silence bounty hunter Zam Wesell. Dexter, who worked at a mining operation on Subterrel before opening his restaurant, identifies the weapon as a rare Kamino saberdart. This clue leads Obi-Wan to Kamino, where he discovers a secret clone army.

Foot traffic
Dex's Diner occupies a bustling location where customers can drop in at any time, day or night.

KAMINO

REGION Wild Space **SECTOR** N/A
SYSTEM Kamino **TERRAIN** Oceans

Kamino is a watery world located far beyond the Outer Rim, just south of the Rishi Maze. It is the home of the Kaminoans, tall, pale-skinned beings with large eyes who have a talent for genetic manipulation.

CLONING SPECIALISTS

Over the years, the Kaminoans developed cloning laboratories on their homeworld and their clone creations began appearing on outlying worlds such as the mining planet of Subterrel. The weather patterns of Kamino are frequently rocked by storms and lightning blasts, but the stilt cities of the Kaminoans are built to withstand high winds and pounding waves. The capital of Kamino is Tipoca City, which also houses the most advanced cloning laboratories anywhere on the planet. Kamino is home to a wide variety of aquatic life, including aiwhas, flying cetaceans ridden by the Kaminoans as mounts.

THE CLONE ARMY

Shortly after the Battle of Naboo, Darth Sidious sets in motion his plan to take control of the galaxy by setting off a false war. Jedi Master Sifo-Dyas places an order with the Kaminoans for a massive clone army. Darth Sidious uses this to his advantage, getting Count Dooku to order Sifo-Dyas' assassination and then assume the Jedi's identity. Dooku then recruits bounty hunter Jango Fett, who then agrees to live on Kamino for the next decade to provide genetic samples and help train the newly grown soldiers. Dooku uses Sifo-Dyas' clearance code to delete Kamino's coordinates from the Jedi Archives, ensuring no one will interfere with the project until it is nearly complete.

Isolated
Kamino's distant location keeps it safe until the Separatists target it during the Clone Wars.

Eventually Obi-Wan Kenobi tracks down Kamino's location and meets with Kaminoan Prime Minister Lama Su, who assumes he has come to take delivery of the clone army. Obi-Wan also encounters Jango Fett and his cloned son Boba Fett, who flee the planet so as not to attract Jedi attention. Obi-Wan's pursuit of them leads to the Battle of Geonosis, which marks the start of the Clone Wars. The Republic happily accepts the clone soldiers grown on Kamino, and these troopers become the backbone of the newly formed Grand Army of the Republic. The Separatists quickly move to cut the clone army off at its source; General Grievous and Asajj Ventress lead a full-scale attack on Kamino, using *Trident*-class drill assault craft to damage the defenses of Tipoca City and aqua droids to execute an underwater assault. The mission ends in failure for the Separatists.

THE FALL OF KAMINO

After the Empire's formation, Admiral Tarkin determines that conscripted soldiers are more cost-effective. The cloning factories are shut down and the clone troopers are phased out and largely forgotten by the Empire.

"It's good to be home."
WRECKER

Weatherproofed
The buildings on Kamino have sloping roofs to deflect wind, rain, and ocean spray. The stilts that support the structures are strong, leaving little risk of damage to the Kaminoans or their delicate experiments *(right)*. A Kaminoan on an aiwha mount approaches the elevated expanse of Tipoca City *(above right)*.

LOCATIONS

TIPOCA CITY
LOCATION Kamino

Tipoca City is the capital city of Kamino and the site of its most important cloning facility. As Kamino's governmental center, Tipoca City contains offices used by Prime Minister Lama Su and other high-ranking administrators, but many of its buildings are occupied by Kaminoan geneticists and filled with the advanced equipment needed to grow and train clones. The buildings of Tipoca City are constructed on stilts in the vast expanse of the Kaminoan oceans, made from reinforced materials with a streamlined architectural style designed to diffuse the impact of waves and the planet's storms. Landing platforms are usually exposed to the elements, but the doors leading to the city's interior are always watertight. The city's sloped roofs are topped with communications antennas and lightning rods.

The Kaminoans begin work on the Republic's clone army approximately 10 years before the Battle of Geonosis, and they alter each clone's genetic structure so that they age at twice the standard rate. The on-site clone troopers' accommodations include barracks, a mess hall, and a medical facility with AZ-series droids assigned to the care of the troopers. With new batches of clones being produced every year, Tipoca City is soon filled with clones ranging from infancy to adulthood. Each age group requires a different set of instructional programs and training gear. The younger clones receive flash learning in the subjects of military strategy and galactic history, while older clones are permitted to suit up in armor and participate in simulated firefights. These advanced training theaters are part of the Tipoca City Military Complex, which also houses the Central Armory, where thermal detonators, DC-15 blaster rifles, and other weapons are stored. War games held in the Military Complex can involve low-risk, holographic opponents or are set to live-fire settings in which severe injury is a real risk. Elsewhere in the Military Complex are testing facilities for heavy equipment, including six-legged AT-TEs, two-legged AT-RTs, AV-7 anti-vehicle cannons, and low-flying LAAT/i gunships.

After the end of the Clone Wars, Imperial forces enter Tipoca City and begin the process of decommissioning the site. They wipe all data, force the evacuation of Kaminoan medical personnel, and reassign clones offworld. Once the Empire has the cloning technology and key scientists in hand, Vice Admiral Edmon Rampart orders the destruction of the facility. Three *Venator*-class cruisers rain down their full firepower. The entire city is annihilated, and its burning remains fall into the ocean.

Surprise inspection
Prime Minister Lama Su and Taun We take Obi-Wan on a tour of the city's cloning facilities *(above)*. Aging clone "99," a trooper who grew too rapidly, handles general maintenance duties *(left)*.

Attack on Kamino
Separatist trident ships land near Tipoca City and unleash their droid passengers *(far left)*, while clone troopers scramble to intercept the threat and defend their birthworld from the Separatists *(left)*.

LAKE COUNTRY
LOCATION Naboo

The Lake Country is a very beautiful and extremely isolated area on Naboo. Surrounded by mountains, the locale is situated in a valley dotted with numerous picturesque lakes. Vacationers often visit the Lake Country to view its waterfalls and open grasslands filled with wildflowers. Herds of harmless shaaks graze openly in the bucolic meadows. Just prior to the Clone Wars, Padmé Amidala chooses the Lake Country as a safe hiding spot for herself and Anakin Skywalker following an attempt on her life.

NABOO LAKE RETREAT
LOCATION Lake Country, Naboo

Located in the Lake Country area of Naboo, the lake retreat called Varykino has a long history of use by the Naberrie family. Before she became known as Queen Amidala, the young Padmé Naberrie spent her summers there. The villa occupies a small island in the center of a lake, reachable by gondola speeders, and an old man named Paddy Accu serves as its caretaker. Padmé and Anakin Skywalker grow close while spending time at the retreat and later return to be married in secret.

JANGO FETT'S APARTMENT
LOCATION Tipoca City, Kamino

Jango Fett's home for 10 years, this small apartment in Tipoca City on Kamino is given to the bounty hunter by the Kaminoans for his participation in the cloning project. Jango keeps his accommodation simple, hiding his armor out of sight and displaying no trophies from his hunts. A large window on one wall offers a spectacular view of the churning ocean that stretches out to the horizon. Boba Fett also lives in the apartment with his father, until Obi-Wan Kenobi's investigation causes the pair to flee Kamino.

GEONOSIS
REGION Outer Rim **SECTOR** Arkanis
TERRAIN Rocky wastes, deserts

An arid world of red skies and forbidding mountains, Geonosis is the Outer Rim home of an insectoid species known throughout the galaxy for its skill at manufacturing deadly battle droids.

SEPARATIST STRONGHOLD
The Geonosians arm the Trade Federation before the Battle of Naboo, manufacturing the battle droids that fight the Gungans. When Count Dooku orchestrates the rise of the Separatist movement, he enlists Geonosian leader Poggle the Lesser to help produce an automated army to make war with the Republic. In secret, the Geonosians help develop the plans for a planet-shattering battle station. Geonosis becomes one of the most valuable planets in Dooku's Confederacy and plays host to a meeting of top Separatist leaders before Obi-Wan Kenobi discovers the scope of the threat and warns the Jedi Council.

Tricky flying
The rocky rings surrounding Geonosis are a navigation hazard, but can be used as obstacle courses by those who wish to shake off their pursuers.

Ultimate weapon
The Geonosians begin work on a battle station that can destroy planets, later called the Death Star.

ALL-OUT WAR
The Republic responds to Obi-Wan's summons with an attack force of Jedi and clone troopers. The First Battle of Geonosis is the opening conflict of the Clone Wars and sees the use of heavy artillery and other advanced war machines on both sides. After a fierce fight, the Republic emerges victorious, but many Separatist forces evacuate to fight another day. Dooku abandons Geonosis following a lightsaber duel with Master Yoda, then travels to Coruscant to report to Supreme Chancellor Palpatine (Darth Sidious) that the war has begun as planned.

RETAKING THE PLANET
The triumphant Republic occupies Geonosis, but clone troopers are soon needed elsewhere. As soon as the Republic relaxes its grip, the Separatists sweep in and seize the planet. Republic war leaders have no choice but to attack the planet to prevent the Separatists from bringing the factories back up to full capacity. By the time the Republic armada is ready, Poggle the Lesser has completed a new, advanced droid factory that becomes the primary target for the Republic invasion. Jedi warriors destroy the factory and force Poggle to take shelter in the Geonosian cave network of Karina the Great. The Republic captures Poggle, who agrees to order the Geonosians to build their original Death Star battle station design for them. The construction continues when the Republic transitions into the Empire, and some builders attempt sabotage. Eventually, the Empire moves its battle station from Geonosis' orbit.

GENOCIDE OF THE GEONOSIANS
Wanting to keep the Death Star a secret, Grand Moff Tarkin orders Geonosis to be sterilized with poison, killing 100 billion beings. A single drone survivor, named Klik-Klak, safeguards the last known queen egg deep underground. Two years before the Battle of Yavin, the *Ghost* crew and rebel Saw Gerrera discover Klik-Klak and the egg, and proof of the genocide. While Klik-Klak remains on the planet, the rebels escape an Imperial patrol but lose the proof they need to convince the galaxy. After the Battle of Yavin, Darth Vader returns to Geonosis to discover the hatched queen. Unfortunately, she is infertile so she cannot bring her species back. Instead, she produces mechanical children from a droid factory "womb" with which she augments herself. Vader steals her factory, but leaves the queen alive.

Return to Geonosis
When Poggle the Lesser and his Geonosians take back their homeworld, the Republic must fight a second time.

Lone survivor
Desperate to ensure the survival of his species, Klik-Klak is initially wary of the rebel visitors and sends battle droids to attack them.

Heavy equipment
Republic AT-TEs and clone troopers rout the Separatist defenders in the First Battle of Geonosis *(below)*, assisted by gunships that are picking up troopers and Jedi commanders on the battlefield *(left)*.

> "The droid foundry seems to be working at full capacity. I am going to go down and investigate."
> **OBI-WAN KENOBI**

PALPATINE'S APARTMENT
LOCATION 500 Republica, Galactic City, Coruscant

Within the upper levels of the most prestigious and exclusive residential tower in the Federal District on Coruscant, Senator Palpatine keeps an apartment that offers majestic views, yet is modest in comparison with the residences of other sectorial representatives. The apartment consists of an expansive suite of rooms, most of which are decorated in hues of scarlet, Palpatine's preferred color, and with unusual art objects that reflect his worldly point of view. To ensure the complete safety of his guests, Palpatine outfits each room with discreet surveillance and security systems, which enable him to know immediately whether his guests have any special requirements or require assistance.

GEONOSIS DROID FACTORY
LOCATION Geonosis

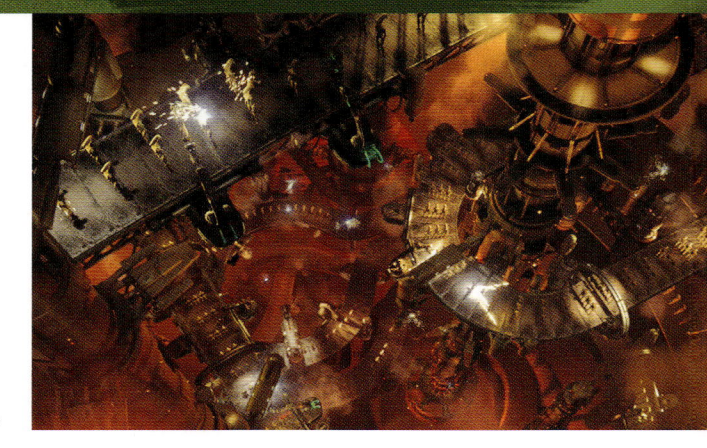

The planet Geonosis is of great value to the Separatists, primarily for the massive factories built into its crust that produce seemingly endless ranks of battle droids. The largest droid factory is capable of churning out B1 battle droids and their bulkier cousins, B2 super battle droids, all with minimal supervision by organic operators. The factory is almost entirely automated and rarely shuts down for any reason. This reduces the factory's safety margin to almost nothing and allows the Geonosians to make as many droids as possible. It also makes the environment a death trap for any unlucky beings who wander into its machinery. The factory is a whirl of activity and a clamor of noise at all hours, with assembly lines snaking from level to level and the constant motion of machinery stamping rigid patterns into metal sheets. Waste materials are continuously fed into the factory and melted down, only to be poured into new molds so the process can start again. Large cargo droids, propelled by repulsorlifts, ferry supplies from one assembly station to the next. The factory is located underground and only detectable on the planet's surface by telltale plumes of smoke wafting out of vents. When Obi-Wan Kenobi arrives on Geonosis to investigate Separatist activity, the sight of the droid factory confirms his suspicions that Count Dooku is arming for war against the Republic. He informs the Jedi Council of his findings, but is captured by Dooku's Geonosian allies. Anakin Skywalker and Padmé Amidala follow Obi-Wan to Geonosis and endure a terrifying trip through the factory. Anakin's lightsaber is destroyed by one of the stamping machines, while C-3PO suffers the indignity of having his head removed and placed on a battle droid frame.

TETH
REGION Wild Space **SECTOR** Baxel **TERRAIN** Cliffs, jungles

Teth is controlled by the Hutts. Prior to the Naboo blockade, Jedi Qui-Gon Jinn and Obi-Wan Kenobi travel to Teth to stop the Hutts, who are stealing Republic agricultural shipments. During the Clone Wars, Separatist agents kidnap Jabba the Hutt's son, Rotta, and retreat to a cliff-top fortress on Teth. Republic forces find them, triggering the Battle of Teth and securing Rotta's rescue. Later, Ziro the Hutt escapes from captivity on Nal Hutta and visits his father's grave on Teth to retrieve a secret holojournal. Ziro is betrayed by his companion, Sy Snootles, who shoots him and takes the journal.

MARIDUN
REGION Outer Rim **SECTOR** Rolion **TERRAIN** Grasslands, forests

The grassy world of Maridun is home to the peaceful settlement of Lurmen as well as dangerous animals like mastiff phalones. During the Clone Wars, Anakin Skywalker is among the Jedi and clone troopers who crash-land on the planet. The Jedi agree to help the Lurmen tribe defend itself against the forces of Separatist general Lok Durd. Their coordinated effort destroys Durd's life-exterminating defoliator weapon.

RISHI STATION
REGION Outer Rim **SECTOR** Abrion
SYSTEM Rishi **TERRAIN** Rocks, craters

This barren moon in the Rishi system is the site of a Republic outpost during the Clone Wars. It is staffed by a small team of clone troopers who monitor transmissions to determine whether the Separatists plan to attack Kamino. When Separatist commando droids take control of Rishi Station, a squad of clones led by Captain Rex and Commander Cody recaptures the base after suffering many losses. Years later, a number of bounty hunters fight Boba Fett until he agrees to help them.

RYLOTH
REGION Outer Rim **SECTOR** Gaulus **TERRAIN** Deserts, plains, mountains

Ryloth is inhabited by the Twi'leks. During the Clone Wars, Orn Free Taa represents the planet in the Galactic Senate. When the Separatists invade, Mace Windu leads the effort to liberate Ryloth from Techno Union foreman Wat Tambor. Mace brokers an alliance between Orn Free Taa and his rival, insurgent Cham Syndulla, and ultimately wins a Republic victory. After the Empire comes to power, Cham forms the Free Ryloth Movement to attempt to liberate his homeworld from its tyranny. On one occasion, he fails to kill the visiting Emperor and his apprentice, Darth Vader. Years later, Cham helps his daughter, Hera Syndulla, to steal an Imperial carrier orbiting Ryloth. Hera later blows up her old family home in order to escape the Empire with her father and her allies. When the Empire is defeated, Ryloth does not join the New Republic but becomes independent. For a time, the Resistance temporarily relocates to Ryloth until the First Order tracks them down.

LARS MOISTURE FARM
LOCATION Near Jundland Wastes, Tatooine

A humble dwelling in a desolate corner of Tatooine, the Lars moisture farm becomes a home for Shmi Skywalker and then her grandson, Luke, before being destroyed by the Empire.

CLIEGG AND SHMI
Located near the Jundland Wastes, the Lars moisture farm belongs to Cliegg Lars in the years before the Clone Wars. With his son, Owen, Cliegg uses the vaporators installed on the property to draw water from the atmosphere and grow small food crops. Cliegg later marries Shmi Skywalker, who moves to the homestead. Just prior to the First Battle of Geonosis, Tuskens kidnap Shmi while she is out gathering mushrooms at the property's perimeter. A search party finds no trace of her, and Cliegg loses his leg to a Tusken trap. Anakin Skywalker finally locates his mother, but not in time to save her life.

Conference
Cliegg Lars informs Anakin Skywalker that his mother is a captive of the Tuskens.

CHANGE OF HANDS
After a funeral is held for Shmi, Anakin leaves Tatooine behind. Cliegg mourns the loss of his wife and soon follows her into death. This leaves the Lars moisture farm the property of Owen, who maintains the estate with the help of his wife, Beru. The couple is surprised when Anakin's former Jedi Master, Obi-Wan Kenobi, visits them, carrying Anakin's infant son, Luke. Owen and Beru reluctantly agree to take Luke in and become his guardians, acting as his aunt and uncle. Years later, the former Inquisitor Reva discovers that the son of Darth Vader is on Tatooine. Owen and Beru bravely defend their homestead from the vengeful dark-side user with weapons that Beru had stashed away in case such a day might come.

A desperate stand
Beru and Owen provide a safe and secure home for Luke on the family moisture farm *(above)*, but they always fear he will be found. Their worst fears are confirmed when an Inquisitor, Reva, tracks him to the farm. They tell the young boy to hide while they attempt to repel her *(right)*.

Dreaming of something more
Luke Skywalker becomes a talented bush pilot in his T-16 skyhopper, fueling his hopes that his uncle will let him leave the moisture farm behind and begin a new life away from Tatooine as an Imperial Academy cadet.

TIME TO LEAVE
Luke grows up to become a great pilot, racing his T-16 skyhopper through Beggar's Canyon and dreaming of joining the Imperial Academy. Owen tries to protect Luke by keeping him on the moisture farm year after year. Following his uncle's purchase of two droids, R2-D2 and C-3PO, from Jawas, Luke takes the pair to the garage, or tech dome, attached to the moisture farm. Here, he cleans the droids with equipment kept in his workshop, removing carbon scoring from R2's chassis and treating C-3PO to an oil bath. During his examination of R2-D2, Luke discovers a mysterious recording. The astromech droid claims the holographic vision of Princess Leia Organa is a private message for Obi-Wan Kenobi, and after Luke removes his restraining bolt, the little droid runs away in the dead of night. Luke and C-3PO follow him, hoping to recover the wayward astromech before Luke's uncle realizes what has happened.

Plea for help
When R2-D2 plays a holographic recording of Princess Leia Organa, the droid states it is a private message for Obi-Wan Kenobi.

THE END OF THE FARM
The purchase of the droids eventually leads Imperial stormtroopers, who are in search of the plans hidden in R2-D2's memory banks, to the Lars' front door. When they do not find what they are looking for, the squad executes Owen and Beru. Weeks later, Darth Vader and Doctor Chelli Aphra inspect the farm, searching for a trace of the Sith Lord's son, Luke. Decades later, following the Battle of Exegol, Rey visits the ruins, burying the lightsabers that belonged to Luke and his sister Leia Organa.

A new era
Having created her own lightsaber, Rey leaves her mentors' weapons in a place of importance to the Skywalker family.

Awaiting the end
Chained to tall, massive columns, Padmé, Anakin, and Obi-Wan look like easy prey for the execution monsters.

GEONOSIS EXECUTION ARENA

LOCATION Desert plains near droid foundry, Geonosis

Also known as the Petranaki arena, this place is a source of entertainment for the Geonosians, who cheer as helpless victims are devoured by monsters such as the acklay, nexu, and reek.

CRUEL SPECTACLE
An open-air amphitheater close to Poggle the Lesser's seat of power, the execution arena is the site of the scheduled execution of Obi-Wan Kenobi, Anakin Skywalker, and Padmé Amidala, following their capture by Geonosian forces. While Count Dooku watches in satisfaction, the three captives are chained to posts and left to the mercies of a clawed acklay, a horned reek, and a sharp-toothed nexu. Though they manage to free themselves, it seems only a matter of time before the trio is killed by the fearsome beasts.

JEDI RESCUE
Alarmed by the captives' plight and the news of a massive Separatist buildup, the Jedi launch a two-pronged rescue mission. First, Mace Windu gathers a task force of 200 Jedi to fly to Geonosis and slip into the execution arena. At Mace's signal, the Jedi Knights ignite their lightsabers while Windu faces off against Count Dooku inside Poggle the Lesser's viewing platform. Any hope that the standoff might end without bloodshed vanishes when bounty hunter Jango Fett springs into action to defend Dooku. Geonosian warriors follow Fett's lead, and soon the stands erupt in chaos as the Jedi defend against their insectoid attackers. Anakin, Obi-Wan, and Padmé join the struggle as the battle spills onto the arena floor, where Mace beheads Jango Fett with his lightsaber.

REINFORCEMENTS ARRIVE
Just when the tide begins to turn against the Jedi, the second stage of their mission begins. Master Yoda, newly arrived from Kamino, leads an army of clone troopers into the arena aboard a fleet of LAAT/i gunships. The Separatists respond with more battle droids, and soon the violence cannot be contained within the confines of the arena—the desert plains become the next battlefield as the First Battle of Geonosis kicks into high gear.

"Let the executions begin!"
POGGLE THE LESSER

Stopping the action
The Jedi's sudden arrival brings a halt to the gruesome festivities.

Air attack and ground assault
After gaining a new body in the droid factory, C-3PO marches into the execution arena as part of a legion of battle droids *(above)*. A Republic gunship takes aim at Separatist cannons *(right)*.

Arena beasts
Anakin uses the Force to tame a reek, which carries him on its back. He is pursued by Geonosian guards riding thick-skinned orrays.

JABBA'S PALACE

LOCATION Northern Dune Sea, Tatooine

This iron-walled fortress beyond Tatooine's Dune Sea is home to one of the galaxy's vilest gangsters. But the palace isn't enough to protect Jabba the Hutt from Luke Skywalker.

IMPENETRABLE FORTRESS
Jabba the Hutt has attracted many enemies. His palace, designed to keep out unwanted visitors, is located in a remote part of Tatooine and protected by a huge gate guarded by a TT-8L/Y7 gatekeeper droid. These precautions don't keep out Maul and Savage Opress, who invade the palace during the Clone Wars and force Jabba to join their Shadow Collective.

Walking into danger
C-3PO is right to be afraid of what awaits them in Jabba's palace. R2-D2 is as confident as ever, reassuring his friend that they have nothing to worry about.

Built to last
The elevated position of Jabba's palace offers long-distance views of any approaching threats. In the shadow of the palace, a hungry worrt scans for passing prey animals.

> "Lando Calrissian and poor Chewbacca never returned from this awful place."
> — C-3PO

A LIFE OF DECADENCE
Most of the time, Jabba carefully controls who has access to the interior of his palace. His majordomo, Bib Fortuna, screens anyone who gets past the gate. Most of the welcomed guests are bounty hunters, criminal associates, or entertainers. In his throne room, Jabba sits on a dais to watch his dancers move to the sounds of the Max Rebo Band. If anyone displeases him, Jabba hits a button that triggers a trap door, sending the victim tumbling into the rancor pit below, to be devoured by the beast.

RESCUE MISSION
Angry with Han Solo for dumping a valuable cargo of spice, Jabba the Hutt puts a price on the smuggler's head. When Boba Fett delivers a slab of carbonite containing Han Solo in hibernation, Jabba puts the trophy on display. Princess Leia Organa and Luke Skywalker arrive at the palace to rescue their friend, but Jabba, one step ahead of them, captures the princess and drops Luke into his rancor pit. Luke manages to kill the beast, so Jabba decrees his prisoners will instead be executed at the Great Pit of Carkoon. Jabba and his entourage leave the palace in his luxury sail barge *Khetanna*, but Jabba meets a fatal end. Bib Fortuna takes over as the crimelord of Tatooine, following his master's demise.

BOBA FETT'S PALACE
In the early years of the New Republic, Boba Fett lays claim to Jabba's territory after dispatching Bib Fortuna. Fett declares himself the new daimyo, or crime lord, of Tatooine, making himself at home in the palace—which now bears his name. The isolated palace is nearly empty, with just Fett and Fennec Shand, two Gamorrean guards, and a few droids taking up residence in its sandy halls. The former bounty hunter resides in the upper levels of the palace, where he keeps a bacta tank and makes frequent restorative visits to the valuable equipment. The other crime bosses of the sprawling city call on Fett in his throne room to offer their tributes, but their alliance is a shaky one.

Deep freeze
Disguised as the bounty hunter Boushh, Leia is determined to rescue Han from his carbonite prison *(above)*.

Palace entertainment
While his aide Bib Fortuna offers whispered advice, Jabba sits atop a dais and presides over his court, some of whom scheme to assassinate him *(left)*.

Boba's reign
Unlike his predecessors on the throne, Boba Fett is a more measured leader who is determined to judge fairly. In contrast, his lieutenant, Fennec Shand, is more inclined to presume the worst of others and then react accordingly.

258 LOCATIONS

MUSTAFAR

REGION Outer Rim **SECTOR** Atravis **SYSTEM** Mustafar
TERRAIN Volcanoes, lava flows

A place of ashen skies and glowing lava, Mustafar is one of the harshest environments in the galaxy and the site of Darth Vader's fateful duel with Obi-Wan Kenobi.

WORLD OF FIRE
Eons before Darth Vader takes up residence in his fortress, Mustafar is a verdant planet teeming with natural life and thriving civilizations. When a misguided Force user named Lady Corvax attempts to use a powerful, sacred crystal, called the Bright Star, for her own selfish purposes, the results are catastrophic. The energy it unleashes destroys most of the planet's natural resources and transforms Mustafar into a wasteland of fire and lava, sending many indigenous Mustafarian clans to live in caverns underground.

USEFUL RESOURCES
Wishing to harvest rare minerals from the molten lava on Mustafar, the Techno Union builds mining facilities that incorporate energy shields to protect the machinery from the intense heat. During the Clone Wars, Darth Sidious orders bounty hunter Cad Bane to kidnap Force-attuned children and take them to Mustafar, but Anakin Skywalker and Ahsoka Tano foil his plans. Late in the war, General Grievous sends the members of the Separatist Council to Mustafar to stay hidden from the Republic.

Barely alive
Emperor Palpatine arrives on Mustafar in time to save Darth Vader from death and transport him to Coruscant where he rebuilds him as an armored cyborg.

DUEL OF BROTHERS
With the Separatist Council now an easy target, Darth Sidious sends his new apprentice, Darth Vader, to Mustafar to execute its members. After completing the evil deed, Vader remains on the planet, where his wife Padmé Amidala finds him. Vader accuses her of conspiring with Obi-Wan Kenobi to work against him, and when Obi-Wan emerges from Padmé's ship, Vader believes his suspicions have been confirmed. Vader and Obi-Wan engage in an epic duel of Force abilities and lightsaber swordplay that spills from the control rooms out onto the precarious catwalks spanning the lava river. With its energy shields damaged, most of the mining facility is consumed by volcanic eruptions. Obi-Wan eventually reaches the safety of a rocky shore and warns Vader not to attack him as he holds the high ground.

VADER'S FATE
The former Jedi doesn't listen and leaps at Obi-Wan to kill him. Kenobi strikes, removing Vader's legs and left arm, leaving him defeated at the edge of a lava lake. The heat causes Vader's clothing and skin to catch fire, and a heartbroken Obi-Wan departs the planet, believing Vader has died. Darth Sidious arrives soon after, retrieving his critically injured apprentice and taking him to a medical facility on Coruscant. There, Vader receives treatments that not only save his life but transform him into a terrifying cyborg.

SITH RETREAT
During the Imperial era, Darth Vader erects a foreboding fortress on Mustafar above an ancient Sith shrine on the planet, killing countless Mustafarians who attempt to stop him. Thanks to the castle's design and its location on a Force vergence, Vader attempts to bring Padmé back from the dead. While this try is unsuccessful, Vader does not give up on this desire.

Vader's castle becomes the final destination for many Jedi survivors of Order 66. When Jedi and rebel Kanan Jarrus is captured on Lothal, he is taken aboard Grand Moff Tarkin's Star Destroyer, *Sovereign*, to Mustafar. While in orbit over the planet, the crew of the *Ghost* rescues him. Former Jedi Ahsoka Tano and a small rebel fleet arrive in time to cover Kanan and his friends as they make the jump to hyperspace.

A few years later, the Imperials track down a Force-attuned descendant of Lady Corvax. After capturing the individual, Vader tries to manipulate the individual into helping the Sith use the Bright Star to bring Padmé back from the dead. However, the prisoner rebels and destroys the powerful artifact. This brave act allows the volcanic planet to start healing and slowly return to its former verdant state.

Years later, Vader is attacked on Mustafar by the lethal assassin Ochi of Bestoon. The battle awakens a mysterious Force-attuned individual, the Eye of Webbish Bog. This powerful dark-side presence offers Vader answers to his questions about the Emperor's plans and gives him the means to travel to Exegol—a Sith wayfinder.

A FRESH START
Following Vader's death, the castle falls into ruins and a small area of flora develops around a body of water. Known as the Corvax Fen, this area is guarded by a group known as the Alazmec of Winsit, who also hold Vader's wayfinder. When the Emperor announces he is alive once more, Kylo Ren slays the group and retrieves the artifact, allowing him to make his own trip to the Sith world.

Surrounded by fire
The administrative buildings on Mustafar offer spectacular views of erupting lava geysers. The planet's molten rock contains rare and valuable minerals, making mining in such a harsh environment worth the risks.

> "I am sending you to the Mustafar system in the Outer Rim… You will be safe there."
> **GENERAL GRIEVOUS**

MALASTARE

REGION Mid Rim **SECTOR** Dustig
SYSTEM Malastare **TERRAIN** Forests

Malastare is the homeworld of the Dug species, though humans and Grans have migrated there. The planet is known for its history of vicious wars, dangerous podracing, and vital fuel reserves. Ainlee Teem, a Gran from Malastare, is nominated in the election for supreme chancellor after the invasion of Naboo. During the Clone Wars, Malastare's fuel deposits are fought over by the Republic and Separatists. During a massive ground battle, the Republic deploys an electro-proton bomb that immobilizes Separatist droids. The bomb awakens the last zillo beast, which goes on a rampage. Fearing an apocalypse, the Dugs insist the Republic exterminate the monster. The Republic has other plans, capturing the virtually invulnerable creature for study on Coruscant.

Fuel wars
Across Malastare, vast fuel reserves flow into depots through an extensive network of pipelines *(left)*. When the Separatists and the Republic are drawn into fierce conflict over the fuel, the Republic detonates an electro-proton bomb to disable the Separatist droids *(below)*, but the blast also unleashes the zillo beast, long believed to be extinct.

CATO NEIMOIDIA

REGION Colonies **SECTOR** Quellor **SYSTEM** Cato Neimoidia
TERRAIN Canyons

Famed for its bridge cities, Cato Neimoidia is the headquarters of the notorious Trade Federation. Several Jedi visit the planet briefly, including Anakin Skywalker, Obi-Wan Kenobi, Ahsoka Tano, and Plo Koon, who is shot down by one of his own clone pilots over the planet when Order 66 is initiated. Notably, Anakin and Obi-Wan first encounter the dark-side warrior Asajj Ventress during a mission to this planet. Following the Clone Wars, much of Cato Neimoidia's wealth is lost during the Trade Federation's collapse. The Neimoidians adapt and offer their empty vaults for rent. Galactic adventurer Lor San Tekka is imprisoned here when he tries to break into one of the vaults, but he is eventually rescued by Resistance leader General Leia Organa and her forces.

SCIPIO

REGION Core **SECTOR** Albarrio **SYSTEM** Albarrio
TERRAIN Mountains

Enveloped in ice and snow, the planet Scipio's hardened mountain fortresses shield massive vaults, which secure the InterGalactic Banking Clan's wealth against all manner of threats. The group is controlled by the Muuns, who constitute the managing Council of Five. In the Galactic Senate, the Banking Clan's interests are represented by Senator Rush Clovis from Scipio, who proposes a senatorial auditing team to investigate the suffering on Bromlarch. Years later, he leaves the Senate after his plot with the Trade Federation's Lott Dod to construct battle droid factories for the Separatist Droid Army is revealed. Clovis returns to power by exposing corruption and fraud in the Council of Five, compelling the Muuns to name him the new head of the Banking Clan conglomerate. Both the Galactic Republic and the Separatists send ambassadors to Scipio to ensure their respective agendas are safeguarded from further corruption. Clovis' appointment ends quickly, however; he is killed during a Separatist attack on the planet.

Frozen assets
Senator Padmé Amidala's shuttle approaches the Clan's landing bay on a diplomatic mission to the frozen world *(above)*. The ice-bound fortress protecting the InterGalactic Banking Clan's vaults lies amidst Scipio's snow-capped mountains *(below)*.

SALEUCAMI

REGION Outer Rim **SECTOR** Suolriep **SYSTEM** Saleucami
TERRAIN Desert, swamps

A world of mixed terrain, from dank swamps to arid deserts, Saleucami hosts settlers wishing to avoid the Clone Wars. Clone deserter Cut Lawquane makes the planet his home, taking up farming with his adopted family. Saleucami is also the location of Stass Allie's final mission, when troops blast her speeder bike after Order 66 is given, killing the Jedi Master. During the Imperial era, the Bad Batch helps the Lawquanes flee the world and escape the Empire's forces.

LOCATIONS

Desolate plains
After so many years of conflict, the planet is desolate by the time of the New Republic era. Bo-Katan leads a contingent of Mandalorians to retake their home. The group encounters many threats on the ravaged world.

MANDALORE

REGION Outer Rim **SECTOR** Mandalore
SYSTEM Mandalore
TERRAIN Deserts, urban, crystalline plains

Centuries of war have made the once verdant Mandalore a wasteland. Under the leadership of Duchess Satine Kryze, a daughter of the planet's previous ruler, the New Mandalorians faction tries to leave behind the planet's violent past. Terrorist groups like Death Watch, however, demand that Mandalore return to its warrior roots. When the Duchess declares Mandalore's neutral position in the Clone Wars between the Galactic Republic and the Separatists, Death Watch, now aligned with Maul and his Shadow Collective, stages a coup and seize control of Mandalore. After the Republic liberates the planet from Maul, Satine's sister, Bo-Katan Kryze, is declared the planet's ruler. She is soon betrayed by Clan Saxon, when member Gar Saxon takes over the planet and pledges his allegiance to the Empire. Years later, Clan Wren leads a rebellion against Clan Saxon and Bo-Katan resumes her leadership.

One of the Empire's most atrocious acts is annihilating the cities of Mandalore with TIE bombers during a purge of the planet. Bo-Katan surrenders to save the remaining Mandalorians, but Moff Gideon goes back on his word, killing most of the survivors. He then razes the planet, and Mandalorians in the galaxy believe that the world is a wasteland and uninhabitable.

These assumptions are proven false as some Mandalorians survive on the surface, finding small pockets where nature clings on. Moff Gideon also keeps a secret base on the planet, where he conducts trials into cloning. After Din Djarin, Bo-Katan, and Grogu explore the planet, the trio soon works to unite scattered Mandalorians in the galaxy in order to reclaim their world from the Imperial remnant. Following their victory against Moff Gideon, Bo-Katan leads her now-united people once more.

SUNDARI

LOCATION Mandalore

Sundari is the capital city of the planet Mandalore and is built above a series of ancient mines that are famed for their beskar ore. The settlement is well known for its stunning architecture with gleaming translucent buildings and an ornate royal palace that's decorated with artwork depicting Mandalorian history. A bio-dome is later installed to protect Sundari from the harsh environment that resulted from the Mandalorian wars.

Following a time of civil war, Satine Kryze becomes the duchess of the New Mandalorian government. Death Watch attacks the city during the terrorists' bid to regain control of Mandalore. Years later, rebel Sabine Wren leads an assault on a Star Destroyer stationed at the city to destroy an old prototype weapon of hers that is capable of vaporizing Mandalorian armor and the warriors wearing it.

By the time of the New Republic, Sundari has been destroyed by Imperial forces and lies in ruins. Mandalorians Din Djarin, Bo-Katan Kryze, and Grogu later explore the wreckage and discover that hostile Alamites now reside in the abandoned city. Once the Mandalorians retake their homeworld, the Armorer rekindles the Great Forge and starts conducting ceremonies in the Living Waters beneath Sundari.

Bio-dome destroyed
Sundari's buildings and bio-dome cannot withstand the Imperial assault. The ruins are exposed to Mandalore's harsh elements.

ALDERAAN

REGION Core **SECTOR** Alderaan
SYSTEM Alderaan
TERRAIN Mountains

One of the most picturesque planets of the Core, Alderaan is home to wildflower-speckled grasslands that sweep upward into the ancient snow-capped Aldera Alps. Its cities, designed to enhance and preserve the planet's natural beauty, have become epicenters for culture and education, both highly valued by Alderaanians.

POLITICAL POWER
In the days of the Galactic Republic, Alderaan is a prominent planet in galactic affairs. When the invasion of Naboo ends the tenure of Chancellor Valorum with a vote of no confidence in the Galactic Senate, one of the nominees to succeed him is Senator Bail Antilles of Alderaan.

At some point prior to the Clone Wars, Queen Breha Organa is coronated and marries Alderaan's new senator, Bail Prestor Organa. They reside in the gleaming capital city Aldera, the time-honored home of the Royal House of Alderaan. Breha and Bail befriend both Senator Mon Mothma of Chandrila and Senator Padmé Amidala of Naboo during this time.

CAUTIOUS VOICE
Throughout the Separatist crisis, Bail is a leading member of Supreme Chancellor Palpatine's Loyalist Committee, which strives to maintain the integrity of the Republic. When the Jedi and the Senate learn that an army of clones has secretly been created for the Republic, Bail speaks out against a rush to war. Unfortunately, the Senate votes to give emergency powers to Supreme Chancellor Palpatine, resulting in the Grand Army of the Republic invading Geonosis, and heralding the start of the Clone Wars.

During the war, Alderaan hosts a conference dedicated to the plight of the conflict's refugees, where Senator Amidala is the keynote speaker. Jedi Padawan Ahsoka Tano has a vision of Padmé's murder and joins her on Alderaan, where she successfully prevents an assassination attempt by bounty hunter Aurra Sing.

SPEAKING OUT
Near the end of the Clone Wars, Bail joins Padmé and Mon as vocal senators opposed to the chancellor's continually expanding powers. After Palpatine declares himself Galactic Emperor, Bail aids the fleeing Jedi and, with Breha, adopts Padmé's newborn daughter Leia to raise her as their child. The young princess grows to love the lush forests of Alderaan, often sneaking off into the nearby woods to avoid her royal duties.

SECRET REBELLION
Bail and Breha publicly hold true to the Alderaan's pacifist nature, but realize that armed conflict is the only way to stop the Empire. They play a large role in forming the Rebel Alliance, hosting rebel sympathizers at banquets, uniting many rebel cells, and even secretly funding the cause. All the while, they strive to maintain plausible deniability of their membership to the outlawed organization.

Prior to the Battle of Scarif, Bail returns home to prepare his people for armed conflict. But Grand Moff Wilhuff Tarkin, who has always suspected their true affiliation, needs to make a grand political statement with the Death Star. For that reason, and inspired by the presence of the imprisoned Princess Leia Organa aboard the space station, he selects Alderaan as the first target. The Death Star's massive superlaser annihilates the planet, killing Breha, Bail, and billions of other Alderaanians.

WHAT REMAINS
Now only an asteroid field, known as the Alderaanian Graveyard, remains of the once-proud world. The Empire blockades the graveyard until their defeat at the Battle of Endor. Soon after, the Alderaan Flotilla, a small fleet of Alderaanians who were offworld when the Death Star fired, travels to the graveyard. They search for any remnants of their homeworld amongst the asteroids. Thanks to Leia, the survivors are given scrap from the Death Star that they can use to build a space station as a new home in the asteroid field.

Mountain palace
Skilled architects blend the cityscape design into the beautiful, sweeping backdrop of the local snow-capped mountains.

Aldera
The capital city of Aldera is beautiful. Renowned architect Ar'Ven Vence is behind the city's center, and the rest of Aldera's structures take inspiration from his designs.

Final moments
There is no time to escape when the Death Star enters Alderaan's orbit. The only surviving Alderaanians are offworld, but, before long, the Empire begins hunting them down.

> "Alderaan is peaceful.... You can't possibly—" **LEIA ORGANA TO GRAND MOFF TARKIN**

LOCATIONS

> "You will never find a more wretched hive of scum and villainy." — OBI-WAN KENOBI

MOS EISLEY SPACEPORT

LOCATION Great Mesra Plateau, north of Anchorhead, Tatooine

On the remote desert world of Tatooine, far from the bright center of the galaxy, the dingy city of Mos Eisley serves as the planet's principal spaceport.

DESERT OASIS

Southeast of the barren Jundland Wastes and not far from the palace of the ruthless crime lord Jabba the Hutt, Mos Eisley's wind-worn appearance belies its true nature as a thriving spaceport. Countless varieties of starships travel in and out of the city daily, bringing with them pilots, passengers, and cargo, both lawful and highly illegal. Goods traders and parts dealers share the dusty streets with dewbacks and wanted fugitives. Precious amid the desert, water is what binds Mos Eisley together. The main distribution plant sits in the heart of the city. From there, a patchwork of duracrete and plastoid buildings spreads outward, born of the lack of central planning in a spaceport that grew haphazardly and that does not even have a main landing facility.

IMPERIAL OCCUPATION

Ordinarily such a pit of crime would attract little attention from the forces of the Galactic Empire, but all that changes when two droids carrying crucial stolen Imperial intelligence—the plans to the Death Star battle station—vanish in the nearby desert. A detachment of Imperial stormtroopers arrives to lock down the city. Obi-Wan Kenobi brings Luke Skywalker, C-3PO, and R2-D2 to the spaceport to seek passage to Alderaan. The Jedi Master's quick-thinking use of the Force allows them to slip past stormtroopers who are patrolling the streets. Then it is a matter of finding a pilot willing to risk Imperial entanglement.

Finding a space
With no centralized landing facility, arrivals must berth in one of the 362 docking bays around the spaceport. At one point, fast-talking mechanic Peli Motto runs Bay 3-5. Between flights, travelers head for a local cantina (left).

SMUGGLER'S PARADISE

Amid the hustle and bustle of the spaceport, smuggling activities carry on with nary a second glance. Trafficking in spice and illegal weapons brings great rewards to those willing to take the risks involved, though corrupt customs officials are generally willing to overlook such transgressions for a fee. After a haul, Han Solo and Chewbacca secure the *Millennium Falcon* in Docking Bay 94 at the spaceport, little suspecting that their departure will be far more eventful—a narrow escape from the blaster fire of Imperial stormtroopers pursuing the freighter's passengers.

Quiet streets
The usually bustling streets become nearly deserted once Imperial stormtroopers take up posts around the city. No one wants to be scrutinized too closely by the Empire.

Evading capture
Obi-Wan's Jedi mind trick helps Luke and the droids evade a checkpoint.

Piece of junk
At Docking Bay 94, Luke is not impressed with the *Millennium Falcon*.

MOS EISLEY CANTINA
LOCATION Mos Eisley, Tatooine

The Mos Eisley Cantina is favored by star pilots passing through Tatooine before their next journey into space. On any given day, numerous species relax within its dimly illuminated confines, whispering secrets over strong drinks. Patrons range from legitimate cargo haulers to all manner of criminals, gangsters, and bounty hunters, and among such a throng, sudden outbursts of violence are no surprise.

During the Clone Wars, a vicious blaster fight breaks out when Chairman Baron Papanoida, leader of the Pantorans, arrives to liberate his kidnapped daughter Chi Eekway, who has been taken by the bounty hunter Greedo on behalf of the Separatists. All of her captors die in the rescue, except for Greedo, who manages to escape. Later in the war, Sith-acolyte-turned-bounty-hunter Asajj Ventress is biding her time over a drink in the cantina when she notices a tremendous bounty posted for the fearsome brothers Savage Opress and Maul. She locates their ship, inadvertently aiding the rescue and escape of Jedi Knight Obi-Wan Kenobi.

Two decades pass before desert hermit Obi-Wan needs swift passage to Alderaan to bring Luke Skywalker and the stolen Death Star plans to the Rebel Alliance. In the cantina, he discovers an old friend of Master Yoda, the Wookiee Chewbacca, now first mate on the *Millennium Falcon*. In a grimy booth, Captain Han Solo agrees to transport the passengers for a sizable fee. Moments later, Greedo forces Han at gunpoint to a nearby table, threatening his life. Once seated, the smuggler slyly pulls out his blaster under the counter, shooting the Rodian dead.

During the time of the New Republic, the cantina is under new management who replaces the staff with supervisor droids, including EV-9D9. Din Djarin visits the cantina, meeting rookie bounty hunter Toro Calican and agreeing to go on a mission with him to hunt Fennec Shand.

Den of iniquity
Cantina clientele hustle up their next paying job *(above)* or relax along the bar for a drink and some downtime *(right)*.

Hot spot
The Mos Eisley Cantina is the gathering place for patrons from all walks of life *(left)*, often entertained by the rollicking tunes of the Modal Nodes *(far left)*.

DATHOMIR
REGION Outer Rim **SECTOR** Quelii **TERRAIN** Forests, swamps

Dathomir is a planet that few people visit willingly. Illuminated by the eerie scarlet light of its red sun, its continents are thick with swamps and forests. Centuries before the Clone Wars, the Fromprath species lived on Dathomir until the Nightsisters, a group of witches, forced them offworld and took over the planet, renaming it after their ancient Dathmiri origins. From a massive stone fortress, the Nightsisters wield ancient magick, which is fueled by the planet's power, and they are capable of supernatural feats rivaling the Force talents of the Jedi and Sith. Zabrak males known as Nightbrothers also dwell separately on Dathomir. When necessary, Nightsisters venture to the Nightbrother village to select the most suitable mates from among them.

Years prior to the blockade of Naboo, Darth Sidious visits Dathomir and meets the Nightsister known as Mother Talzin. He offers to take her on as his apprentice, but the Sith Lord betrays her and kidnaps her son Maul instead. The pirate Hal'Sted later arrives on Dathomir, and the Nightsisters are forced to give him the young Asajj Ventress to save the clan.

By the time of the Clone Wars, Mother Talzin is the spiritual leader of the Nightsisters. Ventress is now Count Dooku's apprentice, and Sidious demands her death when her dark-side abilities grow dangerously powerful. After Dooku attempts to murder Ventress, she returns to Dathomir and enlists the aid of the clan to seek revenge. Mother Talzin uses her magick to turn the Nightbrother Savage Opress, into a vicious, Force-powered warrior. Ventress and Opress fail to defeat Dooku, who sends General Grievous and his droid army to annihilate the Nightsister clan. Despite their best efforts, including awakening an undead horde of Nightsister zombies to fight the battle droids, almost all of the Nightsisters are massacred. Talzin and Sidious then wage a proxy war via Opress and Maul, whose mental and physical prowess has been restored by Talzin's magick at great cost to herself.

While on a later mission to assassinate Dooku, Ventress and Jedi Master Quinlan Vos travel to Dathomir. Here, Ventress trains Vos in the dark side, forcing him to kill the Sleeper, an ancient and powerful creature that resides deep beneath the water in the Nightsisters' fortress. After Ventress falls while saving Vos' life on Christophsis, Quinlan and Jedi Obi-Wan Kenobi return her body to Dathomir.

At some point after, Maul and Talzin attempt to sacrifice Dooku on the planet so Talzin can regain her power, but Grievous and Sidious intervene. In the end, Talzin sacrifices herself so her son can escape.

During the Imperial era, Dathomir has few inhabitants but some significant visitors. Jedi Cal Kestis drops by the planet while on the hunt for a Zeffo artifact. During his quest, he faces aggressive local fauna like the bane back spider and lesser nydak; he also befriends one of the last surviving Nightsisters, Merrin. For a short time, Maul runs his new criminal organization, Crimson Dawn, from Dathomir. He orders one of his lieutenants, Qi'ra, to report to him there. Two years before the Battle of Yavin, Maul returns to Dathomir with Jedi Ezra Bridger. They perform some Nightsister magick inside the fortress and receive more clarity on a Force vision they both shared. The ritual awakens two Nightsister spirits, which possess Ezra's allies Sabine Wren and Kanan Jarrus. Ezra frees them by destroying the Nightsisters' altar.

In the early years of the New Republic, Grand Admiral Thrawn and his loyal troops return from their exile in another galaxy with help from the Great Mothers of Peridea. Their first destination is Dathomir.

The arrival
Aboard the *Chimaera*, the three Great Mothers arrive at Dathomir with a mysterious cargo in the ship's hangar bay.

264 LOCATIONS

CHRISTOPHSIS
REGION Outer Rim **SECTOR** Savareen **SYSTEM** Christoph **TERRAIN** Crystal

Christophsis' surface is covered by crystalline rock formations, around and upon which high-tech cities are built. The planet is the site of lengthy fighting during The Clone Wars, as well as the place where Ahsoka Tano and Anakin Skywalker first meet. Separatist forces under Admiral Trench and General Whorm Loathsom invade Christophsis early in the war to seize resources and lay siege to the Republic forces there. Anakin and Obi-Wan Kenobi rescue the trapped senator Bail Organa from Christophsis. Quinlan Vos and Asajj Ventress later travel there on a mission to assassinate Count Dooku. During the Imperial era, Luke Skywalker finds his green kyber crystal on the world.

FLORRUM
REGION Outer Rim **SECTOR** Sertar **SYSTEM** Florrum **TERRAIN** Desert

Florrum is an arid planet far from main hyperspace lanes. Its location means underworld leaders like Hondo Ohnaka, who runs a piracy and salvage gang there, can operate without catching the eye of the Republic. The Clone Wars reach Florrum when Anakin Skywalker and Obi-Wan Kenobi travel there in pursuit of Separatist leader Count Dooku. Eventually, Hondo captures Dooku. Later in the Clone Wars, Ahsoka Tano, Huyang, Hondo, and a group of Jedi younglings clash with General Grievous on Florrum. Dooku commands the droid general to target Florrum to enact revenge on Hondo.

SERENNO
REGION Outer Rim **SECTOR** D'Astan **SYSTEM** Serenno **TERRAIN** Forest, various

Serenno's history traces back to the time of the Sith empire, according to the records of the planet's seven noble houses. During the High Republic era, Serenno is a member of the Republic. Centuries later, the planet is the homeworld and base of operations of Count Dooku, leader of the Confederacy of Independent Systems. Shortly after the rise of the Empire, Serenno falls to the new regime's army. The Bad Batch try and fail to capture Dooku's war chest.

DOOKU'S CASTLE
LOCATION Serenno

Castle Serenno is Count Dooku's stronghold on his homeworld and the place from which he commands both the Separatist forces and House Serenno. The castle's focal point is the Great Hall, which includes a green stained glass window and Dooku's desk. Asajj Ventress and the Nightsisters Karis and Naa'leth infiltrate Dooku's Castle during the Clone Wars in revenge for Dooku betraying Ventress. They sneak in undetected and reach Dooku's bedroom while he sleeps. However, in the ensuing battle, Dooku throws all three Nightsisters out of the Great Hall window and down to the cliff below.

LOLA SAYU
REGION Outer Rim **SECTOR** Belderone **SYSTEM** Lola Sayu **TERRAIN** Volcanic

The purple hue of Lola Sayu might be considered beautiful, were it not for the fact that much of the planet's southern hemisphere consists of nothing more than a gaping hole where the sphere is shattered. Much of the planet's remaining crust is crisscrossed with countless cracks, like a broken eggshell. This inhospitable world, controlled by the Separatists during the Clone Wars, hosts the Citadel, an impenetrable prison.

THE CITADEL
LOCATION Lola Sayu

Built centuries before the Clone Wars by the Galactic Republic, the Citadel prison is designed to hold the most difficult-to-restrain inmates—even rogue Jedi Knights. In Separatist hands, under the command of sadistic warden Osi Sobeck, it houses the Confederacy of Independent System's highest-value detainees, including Captain Wilhuff Tarkin and Jedi Master Even Piell. The prison has imposing sheer walls and a labyrinthine design, and it is guarded by commando droids, electro-mines, and anoobas.

MORTIS
REGION Wild Space **TERRAIN** Caverns, forests, mountains

An ancient monolith appearing as a black octahedron with red lines etched upon its surface somehow is a gateway to the world of Mortis. Once inside, visitors discover a seemingly terrestrial realm, ranging from verdant forests and stone fortresses to caverns and floating mountains. Disconcertingly, the terrain sometimes mutates as travelers cross it. Mortis is a Force nexus, meaning that the flow of the Force is especially strong. Some believe Mortis may be the very origin of the Force itself.

WASSKAH
REGION Mid Rim **SECTOR** Mytaranor **SYSTEM** Kashyyyk **TERRAIN** Forests

This verdant moon is controlled by a gang of Trandoshan hunters who kidnap individuals and release them into the dense foliage of the forests, after which hunting parties track and slay the desperate captives as trophies. Ahsoka Tano is briefly trapped on Wasskah, where she teams up with several kidnapped Jedi younglings, the mighty Chewbacca, and his Wookiee allies, to defeat the Trandoshans.

ABAFAR

REGION Outer Rim **SECTOR** Quelii
TERRAIN Desert

Abafar's most memorable feature is the seemingly endless wasteland known as the Void. Uncannily flat and barren, its unnaturally uniform orange hue, due to particulates in the atmosphere, can drive even the most strong-willed individuals mad. The Galactic Republic's database file on Abafar notes large indentations crisscrossing the planet's surface. Settlements such as Pons Ora have grown up around mining operations that extract rhydonium, a rare, volatile fuel.

THE BOX

LOCATION Serenno

Criminal mastermind Moralo Eval designs the Box as the ultimate, deadly test of intelligence and skill. Housed at Count Dooku's palace on the planet Serenno, the gigantic cubic structure contains a constantly shifting series of obstacle courses and traps spanning five levels. Dooku invites 12 of the galaxy's finest bounty hunters to be tested, five of whom move on to undertake a mission to kidnap Supreme Chancellor Palpatine on Naboo.

UMBARA

REGION Expansion **SECTOR** Ghost Nebula
SYSTEM Umbara **TERRAIN** Hills

The dangerous planet Umbara earns the moniker "the Shadow World" because so little sunlight reaches its surface. The near-human species that inhabit the planet are known for their advanced technology. During the Clone Wars, Umbara secedes from the Republic after the assassination of its senator, Mee Deechi, resulting in an invasion by the Grand Army to retake the planet. During the Imperial era, the rebel leader known as Nightswan incites a rebellion on the planet, and an Imperial fleet is sent to quell it. The Umbarans surrender fully and their planet falls under direct Imperial rule.

RAXUS SECUNDUS

REGION Outer Rim **SECTOR** Tion Hegemony **SYSTEM** Raxus **PRIMARY TERRAIN** Plains, hills, ocean

During the final years of the Republic, Jedi Council member Master Katri is killed on Raxus, and Dooku uncovers a conspiracy to depose its corrupt senator. A successive senator, Avi Singh, fights against corruption and his renown leads to his homeworld becoming the host of the Separatist Parliament during the Clone Wars. Hoping for a peaceful resolution of the grievances stated by the Confederacy of Independent Systems, Padmé Amidala secretly travels to Raxus to meet with her longtime friend, former Republic senator Mina Bonteri. Padmé's bodyguard Ahsoka Tano is initially skeptical but soon recognizes the integrity of Mina and her son, Lux. Padmé and Bonteri strike an accord, but Count Dooku sabotages their pact. Later in the war, Dooku's former apprentice, Asajj Ventress, and Jedi Master Quinlan Vos attempt to assassinate Dooku at an award ceremony in his honor on Raxus. They are unsuccessful, however, and Dooku captures Vos. Raxus suffers under the Emperor's galactic reign, perhaps in part due to its previous Separatist affiliation. Eventually, Avi Singh is imprisoned by the Imperials, but later rescued by the Bad Batch.

BARDOTTA

REGION Colonies
SECTOR Shasos
TERRAIN Mountains

Bardotta is home to a spiritual order of peaceful mystics called Dagoyan Masters. Due to previous bad experiences with Jedi seeking to take younglings for training on Coruscant, the Bardottans distrust the Jedi Order. When Dagoyan Masters begin disappearing, Queen Julia fears an ancient prophecy is being fulfilled and seeks help from her friend Jar Jar Binks. He arrives with Mace Windu, to vouch for the Jedi Master's honor, just before Julia vanishes. Jar Jar Binks and Mace Windu rescue Queen Julia and thwart the Frangawl cult's grim plan to drain the Force essence from the Dagoyan Masters.

ONDERON

REGION Inner Rim **SECTOR** Japrael
SYSTEM Japrael **TERRAIN** Jungles

To guard against the creatures that fill Onderon's jungles, the planet's original inhabitants build fortified settlements that eventually expand into enormous walled cities like the capital, Iziz. At the start of the Clone Wars, King Ramsis Dendup is deposed by Sanjay Rash, who allies with Count Dooku. A rebellion led by siblings Steela and Saw Gerrera receives covert aid from the Jedi and overthrows Rash. When the war ends, Saw refuses to fight for the new Empire. Admiral Wilhuff Tarkin sends the Bad Batch to Onderon to eliminate Saw and his group. Realizing they're refugees, not insurgents, the Bad Batch disobeys orders and becomes fugitives. Eventually, Saw renames his rebel group the partisans, and begins viciously attacking the occupying forces. In one such attack, Imperial agent Alexsandr Kallus watches helplessly as his squad of stormtroopers is cut down in front of him. Saw eventually leaves his homeworld, declaring it lost.

MON CALA

REGION Outer Rim
SECTOR Calamari
SYSTEM Calamari
TERRAIN Oceans

The oceanic world of Mon Cala is home to two sentient aquatic species: the Mon Calamari and the Quarren. Although the two share a long history of differences, mutual respect keeps their planet united under the reign of a single king and a single representative in the Galactic Senate. In the Clone Wars, Senator Tikkes, a Quarren, defects to the Separatists and is replaced by Tundra Dowmeia, a loyalist Quarren, and later Meena Tills, a Mon Calamari. During Prince Lee-Char's accession to the throne, civil war breaks out, but the young leader is able to heal the schism. A year into the Emperor's rule, Lee-Char, under the influence of a morally questionable Order 66 survivor, leads a rebellion against the Empire. This is swiftly quashed by Grand Moff Wilhuff Tarkin and Darth Vader. Lee-Char is imprisoned on Strokill Prime, so Regent Dors Urtya takes over as leader. Years later, Urtya meets members of the Rebel Alliance who attempt to persuade him to give the Mon Cala Mercantile Fleet to their cause. When he declines, they try to save Lee-Char, but the former king dies. They record his dying words and pass them to Urtya, who broadcasts them across the oceans. The Empire kills him for his rebellion, but the fleet joins the Alliance. Decades later, the people of Mon Cala again send ships to fight tyranny. This time, the fleet reinforces the Resistance against the First Order.

LOCATIONS

Murky exile
Luke crashes his X-wing in a swamp during his dangerous descent to the planet's surface.

Dangerous passage
Dagobah is unassuming from space, but the trip down to the planet's surface is treacherous, as vehicles must negotiate violent lightning storms and poor visibility.

"Mudhole?! Slimy?! My home this is!" YODA

DAGOBAH
REGION Outer Rim **SECTOR** Sluis
PRIMARY TERRAIN Swamps

Covered in swamps and dense jungles, Dagobah teems with life and the Force. Here, Luke Skywalker is trained in the ways of the Jedi by Master Yoda.

LIVING FORCE
Late in the Clone Wars, while meditating, Yoda hears the voice of the dead Jedi Master Qui-Gon Jinn, who claims he is part of the living Force. The other Jedi worry about Yoda's mental state, but Qui-Gon implores Yoda to travel to Dagobah alone. With the help of Anakin Skywalker, Yoda escapes the Jedi Temple in his Jedi starfighter. Upon reaching Dagobah, Yoda meditates and again hears Qui-Gon, who explains that Dagobah is one of the purest places in the galaxy with strong manifestations of the living Force. Led by a cloud of fireflies to the Cave of Evil, Yoda has a vision of Jedi being struck down by a shrouded Sith Lord. Yoda collapses in despair outside the cave. Qui-Gon consoles him with words of hope and offers to guide Yoda to an understanding of how the Jedi will ultimately prevail.

EXILE PLANET
Following Order 66 and the rise of the Emperor, Yoda and Obi-Wan Kenobi determine to hide the children of Padmé Amidala and Darth Vader, to protect them from their father, with the hope that they can train them as Jedi when they are older. The ancient master then returns to Dagobah to bide his time in exile, continuing to study the Force.

TRAINING GROUNDS
Years later, when one of the children, Luke Skywalker, is a teenager, he visits Dagobah following Obi-Wan's advice. Dagobah itself proves to be part of Luke's Jedi trials. Storms and dense fog create rough landing conditions, and his X-wing crashes into a swamp. A seemingly primitive life-form tests his patience at camp, but Luke is eager to meet Yoda, so he tolerates the interloper. Upon arriving at the creature's hut, Luke's irritation is unmistakable. The creature voices his concerns about training Luke to Obi-Wan's ghostly voice, thereby revealing that he is in fact the Jedi Master.

Yoda reluctantly agrees to train Luke in the ways of the Force, despite sensing in him traits similar to his father. The swamps serve as the training grounds for Yoda's new apprentice. Deep in the jungle, Yoda tests Luke's readiness by sending him into the Cave of Evil that he had entered years before during the Clone Wars. As Luke's powers grow, he has a vision of his friends in danger. He resolves to leave Dagobah without completing his training, but promises to return.

Following Han Solo's rescue from Jabba the Hutt, Luke stays true to his word, heading back to the swampy world. However, a dying Yoda becomes one with the Force after imparting some final wisdom to his last apprentice.

Decades later, Luke's nephew Kylo Ren and his master, Supreme Leader Snoke, visit the world to test Kylo in the Cave of Evil. In a fit of rage, the rash dark-side user destroys the powerful Force vergence.

Awaiting his student
After the Clone Wars, Yoda returns to Dagobah to live in a small hut in the swamp while he waits to train Luke.

Force teachings
Qui-Gon passes along to Yoda and Obi-Wan Kenobi the secret of how a Jedi can retain consciousness within the Force after death *(above)*. They then share their Jedi knowledge with the new hope, Luke Skywalker *(left)*.

Balance in the Force
To help Luke to further his Force abilities, Master Yoda guides him on stamina and balance.

CAVE OF EVIL, DAGOBAH
LOCATION Dagobah

Infused with dark-side Force energy, the Cave of Evil on Dagobah manifests nightmarish visions of possible futures. Guided by the disembodied voice of the deceased Qui-Gon Jinn, Yoda enters the cave near the end of the Clone Wars and has a vision of the destruction of the Jedi Order that overwhelms him. Years later, Yoda tests Luke Skywalker by taking him to the cave. Luke has a vision in which he faces Darth Vader and strikes him down. The Sith Lord's helmeted head hits the floor, and the damaged face shield reveals Luke behind the mask. Later visitors include the Archivist Madelin Sun and Kylo Ren, who destroys the cave as a show of power to Supreme Leader Snoke.

Man in the mask
Luke sees his own face in the damaged helmet of Darth Vader, after confronting the Sith Lord's apparition in the cave.

STYGEON PRIME
REGION Outer Rim **SECTOR** Nuiri
TERRAIN Mountains

Stygeon Prime is an inhospitable world with towering snow-capped mountain peaks. This fearsome terrain makes the planet the perfect location for a maximum-security facility to house the most dangerous, high-value prisoners. During his years as both supreme chancellor and Emperor, Palpatine as Sith Lord Darth Sidious exerts dominion over Stygeon Prime's prison, the Spire. After Maul returns from exile during the Clone Wars to lead his criminal organization, the Shadow Collective, Sidious confronts his former apprentice on Mandalore and defeats him in single combat. Maul is then incarcerated at the Spire.

THE SPIRE
LOCATION Stygeon Prime

The Spire is one of the galaxy's most imposing prisons. During the Clone Wars, Mandalorian commandos are able to break Maul out of his confinement there, but only because Darth Sidious permits the escape in order to set a trap for Maul's patron, Mother Talzin. Years later, the Spire is under Imperial control when former Jedi apprentice Kanan Jarrus is lured there with the promise of rescuing Jedi Master Luminara Unduli from captivity. The Grand Inquisitor is waiting for him, however, and they fight a vicious duel.

Planned escape route

Prison break
Kanan leads his team of Zeb, Sabine, and Ezra *(left)* in a mission to infiltrate the Spire *(above)*.

ORD MANTELL
REGION Mid Rim **SECTOR** Bright Jewel **SYSTEM** Bright Jewel
TERRAIN Mountain chains

Corellian colonists founded Ord Mantell as a depot in the days of the Old Republic. The planet orbits the blue star Bright Jewel and houses a base of operations for the Black Sun crime syndicate. During the Clone Wars, the Separatists attack the planet as part of Darth Sidious' plot to drive a wedge between Maul and his Black Sun allies. During the Imperial era, the Empire keeps little to no presence in the capital city. Clone Force 99 navigates the neon-lit, dirty alleys of Ord Mantell City to find Cid's Parlor, an underground cantina run by Trandoshan trader Ciddarin Scaleback. For a time, it's a rare safe place for the Bad Batch to regroup and take odd jobs. Years later, Princess Leia, Chewbacca, and R2-D2 meet Maz Kanata on the planet and knock out bounty hunter Boushh. They steal his outfit so Leia can impersonate Boushh to rescue Han Solo.

LOCATIONS

Many moons
One sun and nine moons give Utapau a distinctive sky *(below)*. Tidal effects on the planet's subterranean oceans vary wildly, depending on the positions of the moons in relation to one another *(right)*.

UTAPAU

REGION Outer Rim
SECTOR Tarabba
TERRAIN Sinkholes

Located in the remote Tarabba sector of the Outer Rim, the arid, windswept planet Utapau is pitted with enormous sinkholes and surrounded by numerous moons. Its surface is mainly desert terrain, but the bottoms of the sinkholes contain pools of water that support life on the planet. Utapau is home to the Pau'an and the Utai, collectively referred to as Utapauns, and also the Amani. Utapauns dwell in cities that line some of the sinkholes, while the Amani are often found in villages out on the plains. The cities, which expand into the caves and crevasses beneath the planet's surface, are supported by mining operations that excavate valuable minerals.

Although the planet tries to remain neutral during the Clone Wars, the death of a Jedi in Pau City brings Obi-Wan Kenobi and Anakin Skywalker to Utapau. They uncover a Separatist plot to purchase a rare enormous kyber crystal from Sugi arms dealers. Crystals of this size were believed to be the stuff of legend, but Obi-Wan and Anakin witness its incredible power firsthand. Before General Grievous can take the crystal from the Utapau system, Obi-Wan and Anakin destroy it rather than let it fall into Separatist hands.

In the final days of the Clone Wars, Darth Sidious orders key Separatist leaders to gather on Utapau. When Obi-Wan returns to Utapau in search of Grievous, Tion Medon, the port administrator of Pau City, tips the Jedi off to the Separatists' presence. Obi-Wan sends his astromech droid R4-G9 back to the Republic fleet in his starfighter. With the help of the varactyl Boga, Obi-Wan tracks down Grievous and challenges him to a duel. During their battle, Republic forces arrive and battle the droid army. Obi-Wan defeats Grievous, only to be attacked by the clones in his command when Order 66 is issued.

During the Imperial era in a cave on the planet, crazed Pau'an surgeon Fyzen Gor augments a medical droid with organic parts from his dead best friend. He continues experimenting on the droid until it has the devastating capability to turn all the droids in the galaxy against their organic masters. Over the next two decades, smugglers Han Solo and Lando Calrissian have separate run-ins with the unusual pair, but Lando kills them both two years after the Battle of Jakku, eliminating the dangerous threat.

> "Chancellor Palpatine thinks Grievous is on Utapau." — KI-ADI-MUNDI

Sinkhole city
Obi-Wan's Jedi starfighter descends into the sinkhole of Pau City when he is searching for General Grievous, who is rumored to be on the planet.

GALAXIES OPERA HOUSE

LOCATION Coruscant

The Galaxies Opera House is located in the upper levels of the Uscru District on Coruscant. The venue is favored by Supreme Chancellor Palpatine, who has a private box in a premier viewing location in the main theater. During a performance of the acrobatic opera Squid Lake by a Mon Calamari troupe, Palpatine tells Anakin Skywalker the Sith legend of Darth Plagueis the Wise. In the early years of the New Republic, the theater also hosts talks by respected scientific minds, like the ex-Imperial cloning researcher Dr. Penn Pershing.

KASHYYYK

REGION Mid Rim **SECTOR** Mytaranor
SYSTEM Kashyyyk **TERRAIN** Forests

The Wookiees of Kashyyyk are fierce and noble warriors, loyal to the Republic and the Jedi. Their determination and courage has made their homeworld a battleground for galactic domination.

Under attack
As Republic forces arrive to assist the Wookiees *(left)*, fierce warriors rally to defend their homeland from the droid army *(below left)*.

REPUBLIC LOYALISTS

For many years, Kashyyyk has been a prominent world represented by respected members of the Galactic Senate. Renowned for their strength and ferocity in battle, Wookiees do not hesitate to fight when the need arises. However, they are also firm believers in peace and justice. Their arboreal homeworld of Kashyyyk reveals the Wookiees' technical prowess and artistic vision. Wookiee cities are built upon the planet's mighty trees, their architecture interwoven with the beauty of the canopy. Wookiee aircraft, such as an ornithopter resembling a fearsome insect, also reflect the planet's hues, as do their weaponry and battle armor. Anyone who believes a Wookiee is merely a primitive beast will soon discover their mistake.

BATTLE OF KASHYYYK

Its location on key hyperspace lanes makes Kashyyyk a strategic objective in any galactic conflict. Late in the Clone Wars, the Separatists launch a massive invasion of the planet with battle droids and heavy artillery. The Jedi Council know that an immediate defensive response by the Grand Army of the Republic is required, and Yoda volunteers to lead the counteroffensive, based on his strong relationships with Wookiee leaders. The clone troopers and war droids engage in a vicious battle on the beaches outside the vital city of Kachirho.

Battle ready
Captain Merumeru and his Wookiee warriors prepare to defend Kashyyyk.

Order 66
Yoda defends himself when the clones turn against the Jedi on Darth Sidious' command.

RISE OF THE EMPIRE

When Darth Sidious gives the command to execute Order 66, Kashyyyk is one of many worlds where the Republic's clone troopers turn against the Jedi. Yoda senses the nearly simultaneous deaths of hundreds of Jedi across the galaxy. When Commander Gree approaches, the Jedi Master senses the danger and cuts him down in self-defense. With clones still swarming the planet, Wookiees Tarfful and Chewbacca escort Yoda to an escape pod. As a result of the Wookiees' long-standing loyalty to the Republic and the Jedi Order, the new Galactic Empire inflicts great brutality upon Kashyyyk, conquering the planet. Some Wookiees manage to resist the Imperials, but many are enslaved, and the Empire implants them all with inhibitor chips that hurt them if they disobey orders. Some Wookiees are taken offworld to construct the Death Stars or to the spice mines of Kessel, where the harsh working conditions dramatically shorten the Wookiees' life spans.

Where forest meets sea
The Wookiees come down from their tree cities to defend key locations at sea level.

Devastated planet
At least half of Kashyyyk's forests are ruined by the Imperial occupation and the subsequent bombardment. Thankfully, after the liberation, nature begins to reassert itself.

THE LIBERATION OF KASHYYYK

After the Battle of Endor, Kashyyyk remains in the tight control of an Imperial faction led by Grand Moff Tolruck. When Chewbacca and Han Solo learn of an opportunity to free the planet, they try to act upon it, but it is an Imperial trap. While Han escapes, Chewbacca is captured and held in Ashmead's Lock prison on Kashyyyk. Han leads a team to infiltrate Ashmead's Lock and free Chewbacca and the other prisoners. Chewbacca, Han, and a portion of the team stay on Kashyyyk and manage to access Tolruck's base. Here, they hack the control module for the inhibitor chips, freeing all the Wookiees. Many Wookiees rise up against their captors, so the orbiting Star Destroyers decide to bombard the planet. Upon hearing of the attack, the New Republic launches a fleet to help defeat the Imperial faction and finally free Kashyyyk.

270 LOCATIONS

LEVEL 1313
LOCATION Underground level 1313, Coruscant

A hub of underworld and criminal activity, Level 1313 can be found 1,313 levels from the natural surface of Coruscant. The area lies so far below the top levels of the planet that it attracts only those individuals looking for a place to hide or a shady deal. After her speeder malfunctions, Ahsoka Tano crashes into the Martez sisters' garage on Level 1313 during the Clone Wars. Later, during the Imperial era, the cyborg bounty hunter Beilert Valance frequents a cantina on Level 1313 while trying to keep a low profile.

OBA DIAH
REGION Outer Rim **SECTOR** Kessel
SYSTEM Kessel **TERRAIN** Rocky landscapes

Homeworld to the Pyke species, Oba Diah is the base of the powerful Pyke criminal syndicate, which trades spice harvested from nearby Kessel. Shortly after the Battle of Naboo, Jedi Master Sifo-Dyas is shot down by the Pyke Syndicate, dying on Oba Diah's moon. Many years later, the Jedi discover the wreckage of his ship. Anakin Skywalker and Obi-Wan Kenobi end up battling Count Dooku. Later, Ahsoka Tano and the Martez sisters are held captive on Oba Diah after the sisters fail to make a spice delivery. As Tano helps them escape, she discovers the Pykes are working for Maul and his Shadow Collective. Oba Diah remains the center of the spice trade until the fall of the Empire.

POLIS MASSA
REGION Outer Rim **SECTOR** Subterrel **TERRAIN** Asteroid

Polis Massa is the field of asteroids that remains following the destruction of a planet of the same name. The Archaeological Research Council of Kallidah settles Polis Massa Base and begins an archaeological mining project to uncover the mysteries of the cataclysm. The Kallidahin eventually become known as Polis Massans. Polis Massa Base serves as an emergency sanctuary for the Jedi after Order 66. There, Padmé Amidala gives birth to her twins Luke and Leia and then dies. The Polis Massans continue to support the rebels, with their planet acting as a secret base, until Imperials bomb the site. Darth Vader investigates the abandoned base and sees a recording of his wife's final words.

KACHIRHO
LOCATION Kashyyyk

Kachirho is a coastal city on Kashyyyk that spirals around the trunk of an enormous wroshyr tree near the Wawaatt Archipelago. Docks and two piers extend out from the city into the freshwater lagoon. The center of Wookiee hyperspace mapping, Kachirho is led at the time of the Clone Wars by the chieftain Tarfful. Most other cities on the planet are protected by dense foliage, but the wide-open area around Kachirho makes it an optimal landing site when the Separatists attack Kashyyyk late in the Clone Wars. Kachirho's neighbors come by the thousands from land and sea to defend the city from the droid invasion.

CARIDA
REGION Core **SECTOR** Colonies
TERRAIN Mountains

Both the Galactic Republic and the Empire use the mountainous planet Carida as a location for their military bases. A space station orbiting Carida hosts a Republic conference attended by Anakin Skywalker and Obi-Wan Kenobi that's the target of an Imperial threat. Years later, an Imperial military base on Carida is threatened by an early rebel cell led by Berch Teller. It's the Imperial base where both Han Solo and Beilert Valance train for the Imperial Navy.

SKAKO MINOR
REGION Core **SYSTEM** Skako **TERRAIN** Mountains, forests

Skako Minor is home to the Poletec species and is also the Techno Union's headquarters during the Clone Wars. The Poletec don't wish to take sides in the Clone Wars conflict, but the planet is pulled into the war nevertheless by Techno Union leader, Wat Tambor, who supports the Separatists. The Poletecs later align themselves with the Republic after working with Anakin Skywalker. At the end of the Clone Wars, Darth Vader kills Wat Tambor and all his allies on Skako Minor. Years later, Vader sends Sabé, now aligned with the Crimson Dawn crime syndicate, to Skako Minor to quash an uprising.

MARTEZ SISTERS' REPAIR SHOP
LOCATION Level 1313, Coruscant

Sisters Trace and Rafa Martez take over a garage on Level 1313 of Coruscant after their parents are killed. Trace works on rebuilding a starship, the *Silver Angel*, so she and her sister can leave Coruscant. Meanwhile, Rafa cuts deals with local criminals to raise funds for her sister's dream. After the fall of the Republic, Rex and Senator Riyo Chuchi attempt to interrogate the clone assassin, Clone X, in the Martez sisters' garage before he takes his own life.

INQUISITOR BASE
LOCATION The Works District, Coruscant

Located in the Works District on the outskirts of the Coruscant capital, the Inquisitor base is home to the Empire's Jedi hunters. In the lead-up to the Clone Wars, Darth Sidious holds secret meetings here, and it is the site of Count Dooku's fateful duel with Yaddle. After Order 66, the base is repurposed into an Inquisitor training ground. In a central arena, the dark warriors spar and sharpen their skills. Following an insurrection by two Inquisitors, which sees Darth Vader chase the traitors across Coruscant, the Emperor commands the Inquisitor base be relocated to the newly completed Fortress Inquisitorius on Nur.

KALLER

REGION Outer Rim **SECTOR** Cassander
TERRAIN Mountains, forests

The Outer Rim planet of Kaller, home to the Kallerans, has two suns and fast-changing weather patterns. Jedi Master Depa Billaba, her Padawan Caleb Dume, and Clone Force 99 engage in battle with the Separatist droid army on Kaller at the end of the Clone Wars. When Order 66 is given, clone troopers kill Billaba, and Dume is forced to flee the planet and go on the run. Now a rebel and a Jedi known as Kanan Jarrus, he returns years later to gather supplies for Lothal.

BRACCA

REGION Mid Rim **SECTOR** Lantillian **TERRAIN** Plains, junkyards

The flat surfaces of Bracca serve well as a vast junkyard for decommissioned and damaged ships. Bracca's proximity to several major hyperspace lanes makes the planet a high-value priority for both sides in the Clone Wars. During the reign of the Empire, the Scrapper Guild controls Bracca's junkyards, selling parts and helping the Empire build new ships. Clone Force 99 travels to the planet to find a Jedi cruiser medical bay in order to remove Wrecker's malfunctioning inhibitor chip. Jedi Padawan Cal Kestis works as a scrapper in a Bracca junkyard while he is hiding from the Empire, until Inquisitors discover him. After the fall of the Empire, the First Order uses Bracca's junkyards to dispose of New Republic ships. Leia Organa orders Dross Squadron, led by Shriv Suurgav, to recover these ships to help bolster the fleet fighting for the Resistance.

Imperial arrival
Bracca's junkyard has a bountiful supply of weapons and tech. But before the Bad Batch can load much onto its ship, the Empire sends attack shuttles with its former comrade, Crosshair, with orders to take out the traitors.

AYNABONI

TERRAIN Tropical beaches

The only land masses on the tropical planet Aynaboni are islands scattered across the vast ocean that covers most of the planet. Many of the islands have sandy beaches surrounding dense jungles. The planet includes few permanent sentient inhabitants, in part because of the dangerous predators that live in the jungles. A large group of aggrocrabs chases Clone Force 99 while the team is on a mission to retrieve a piece of cargo during the Imperial era.

PANTORA

REGION Outer Rim **SECTOR** Sujimis
TERRAIN Marshes

Home to the blue-skinned Pantorans, Pantora is the largest moon orbiting the ice planet Orto Plutonia. Senator Riyo Chuchi represents Pantora in the Galactic Republic's Senate during the Clone Wars. Despite a Trade Federation blockade against her planet, Chuchi refuses to accept aid from the Separatists. Years later, Clone Force 99 visits one of Pantora's sprawling cities to buy fuel, where they cross paths with the bounty hunter Fennec Shand.

CID'S PARLOR

LOCATION Ord Mantell City, Ord Mantell

Cid's Parlor in Ord Mantell City is an underground bar run by Trandoshan Ciddarin Scaleback. A veteran of the underworld, Cid cautiously welcomes everyone from gamblers and smugglers to Republic officials in her bar. Patrons of Cid's Parlor can enjoy one of its many gaming tables, drinks, or snacks—including the popular Mantell Mix. During the Clone Wars, Cid assists the Jedi by feeding them information in her parlor. After Order 66, she regularly meets with members of Clone Force 99 in the back rooms of her parlor, enlisting them in high-risk—and profitable—missions across the galaxy. She later betrays them here, forcing the Bad Batch to flee.

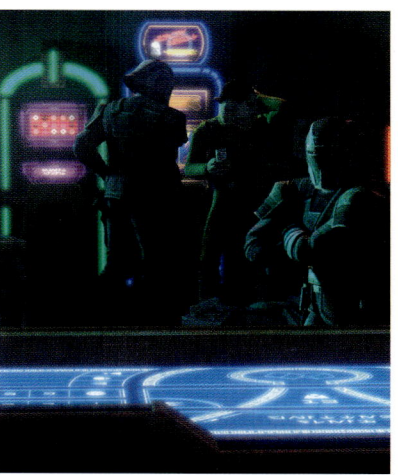

BORA VIO

REGION Extragalactic **SYSTEM** Lido

Bora Vio is a cloud-covered planet in the Lido system. During the Clone Wars, Kaminoans set up several floating cloning facilities in the planet's atmosphere. Shortly after Order 66, bounty hunter Cad Bane flies the clone Omega to one of these facilities to rendezvous with the Kaminoans, who hired him to get Omega back.

DARO

REGION Outer Rim **SECTOR** Ojoster
TERRAIN Forests, mountains, jungles

The Empire chooses the uninhabited Outer Rim planet of Daro for a hidden base during its early years. Imperial soldiers use local reptilian massiffs to cross the planet's forested terrain, which includes mountains, cliffs, and rocky formations. A distress call from a clone trooper brings Clone Force 99 to Daro, where they discover Project War-Mantle—the Empire's plan to replace clone troopers with conscripted soldiers.

272 LOCATIONS

RIVER MOON OF AL'DOLEEM
REGION Mid Rim **SECTOR** Hune
SYSTEM Al'doleem
TERRAIN Mountains, rivers

The river moon of Al'doleem is a picturesque planet of mountains, valleys, rivers, and streams. The world is held sacred by the Jedi, with generations testing their skills at the Jedi monastery on the top of Mount Pasvaal. Darth Vader travels to Al'doleem in search of Jedi Master Kirak Infil'a, who is self-exiled on the moon. While ascending Mount Pasvaal, Vader battles fierce raptorans, and Kirak opens a large dam, nearly drowning the Sith. The two meet once more when Vader returns, killing police and civilians to distract the Jedi, before destroying him—and taking his lightsaber.

WAYLAND
REGION Outer Rim **SECTOR** Ojoster
TERRAIN Forests, mountains

In its early years, the Empire constructs a secret cloning facility on Wayland. Using mountains and dense forests as cover, it builds the Advanced Science Division facility in Mount Tantiss. It relocates much of Tipoca City's cloning technology, then destroys the Kaminoan lab. On orders from Emperor Palpatine, Imperial scientist Doctor Hemlock brings key Kaminoans, including Nala Se and Lama Su, to Wayland to extract information from them to further his own cloning research. He searches for the escaped clone Omega, viewing her as Imperial property and crucial to his work. Crosshair is interrogated in the Tantiss lab, but he doesn't reveal Omega's location. Helping with Hemlock's research are scientists Scalder and Emerie Karr, who reveals to Omega that they are sisters when Omega is brought to Mount Tantiss.

Much of the facility is destroyed in the Bad Batch's mission to rescue Omega. Hemlock tries to escape with her, but he falls in a blaze of blaster fire. Soon after, Grand Moff Tarkin orders that all the lab's funds be diverted to Project Stardust, and the station is abandoned.

Mount Tantiss
The mountain houses the Imperial Advanced Science Division's secret base of operations. The building blends into the mountainside, with only a small section visible. Imperial royal guards provide security for the base.

DESIX
REGION Outer Rim
SECTOR Suolriep
TERRAIN Deserts, mountains

Desix has several moons and, from space, it glows orange thanks to the color of its rocks and sand. During the Clone Wars, the remote planet broke away from the Republic to join the Separatists. After the end of the war, Tawni Ames, the governor of Desix, objects to an Imperial-installed Governor and takes him hostage, believing her planet to be independent and not subject to Imperial rules. Rex and Crosshair infiltrate a Desix fortress and fight back against reprogrammed battle droids to free the Imperial governor.

SAFA TOMA
LOCATION Serolonis

The largest city on Serolonis, Safa Toma is home to the Safa Toma Speedway, which hosts riot racing events. The large race course is complemented by several pit areas and large screens that project events to spectators. The races and the associated gambling draw the attention of many criminal gangs and tourists from across the galaxy, especially those looking to avoid the Empire because Serolonis isn't yet under Imperial control. Ciddarin Scaleback brings Omega, Tech, and Hunter to Safa Toma to watch one of her new racers in action. When Cid loses a bet, the local gangster Grini Millegi threatens her safety.

SKARA NAL
REGION Outer Rim
SECTOR Chopani
SYSTEM Kaldar Trinary
TERRAIN Fossilized rocks, mountains

Orbiting a trinary star, Skara Nal has a surface of barren plains and jagged, fossilized rocks. A thousand years before the Imperial era, a civilization known as the Ancients creates structures inside the planet's mountains, but no sentient beings or cities are present at the time of the Empire. The planet is uncharted, but a compass leads the Bad Batch and treasure hunter Phee Genoa to Skara Nal after they find the artifact on Ord Mantell. While on Skara Nal, the team temporarily awakens a giant mech.

AXIS BASE
LOCATION Ordo Tera Spaceport

The droid cartel known as Vanguard Axis uses a space station as its base. Run solely by droids, Axis Base is equipped with a heavily armed defense system. Dealings out of the base include smuggling, the selling of forged chain codes, and the enslavement of people. During a business transaction at the Axis Base, the Bad Batch discovers and saves the Wookiee Jedi Gungi from captivity.

79'S
LOCATION Coruscant

During and after the Clone Wars, clone troopers looking to blow off steam frequent the Coruscant nightclub named 79's. While not all of 79's customers are clones, the bar is a popular hangout spot for the troopers, whether they're after privacy or a place to chat with fellow soldiers. When Fives is framed for the attempted assassination of Supreme Chancellor Palpatine, he goes to 79's to seek assistance from his friend Kix. After the destruction of Tipoca City, the clone Cade is assassinated outside of 79's shortly after telling his friend Slip that he's determined to reveal the truth about the Empire's role in that catastrophe.

IPSIDON

REGION Mid Rim
SECTOR Corthenia
TERRAIN Desert, cliffs, caverns

Covered in red and brown sand, Ipsidon has rocky structures with large deposits of the valuable mineral ipsium, which is highly combustible in its raw form. Spaceports and villages are small and scattered on the planet, and many are abandoned. Dangers include sandstorms, which make visibility impossible, and stampedes from local Ipsidon bucks. During the Imperial era, Ciddarin Scaleback hires the Bad Batch to excavate one of her ipsium mines on the planet. The team helps local miners to free themselves from the refinery gang boss Mokko.

BARTON IV

REGION Outer Rim
SECTOR Colundra
TERRAIN Mountains, frozen tundra

Early in the Imperial era, Crosshair and Lieutenant Nolan travel to the Imperial outpost on Barton IV to secure cargo until it can safely be moved offworld. With its many mountains, high winds, and frigid temperatures, the frozen tundra of Barton IV is inhospitable to many life forms. Local raiders use snow skiffs and ice cave networks to move around. Large ice vultures are regularly seen floating in the skies, ready to eat the scraps of the climate's latest victims.

THE OUTPOST

LOCATION Barton IV

The Outpost on Barton IV is a large facility for storing Imperial cargo. Clone Commander Mayday leads a squad to the planet to guard the site. After a year of neglect from the Empire, the security systems have degraded to the point that local raiders regularly attack the store. By the time Lieutenant Nolan and Crosshair arrive to help guard the stock—crates filled with new stormtrooper armor—only two of Mayday's squadmates are still alive.

PABU

REGION Outer Rim
SECTOR Chopani
TERRAIN Islands

Pabu is a remote ocean planet that is dotted with small islands. As it has no spaceports or major industries, it remains off the radar of smugglers, pirates, travelers, and the Empire. Most Pabu residents are refugees seeking safety from other worlds, but now they're at risk of tremors that cause large waves, sea surges, and larger quakes. Phee Genoa suggests the Bad Batch stays on one of Pabu's islands so Omega can be around people her own age and take a break from her life on the run.

ARCHIUM

LOCATION Pabu

The Pabu Archium towers over the island in the center of Upper Pabu. The tall building serves as an archive for storing, repairing, and displaying artifacts brought by Pabu refugees from their many different homeworlds. It gives residents a place to learn about different cultures and connect with their neighbors. A large tree outside of the Archium stands in a courtyard that acts as a meeting place and a safe refuge from sea surges.

BALMORRA

REGION Colonies
TERRAIN Mountains

Located in the Colonies section of the galaxy, between the Core and Inner Rim, Balmorra is known for manufacturing. During the Clone Wars, the Separatists install droid factories. Later, the Rebel Alliance includes Balmorra in its list of priority targets to disrupt Imperial manufacturing. After the rise of the Empire, the factories become Imperial prison camps. Several imprisoned clone troopers are rescued in the airspace above Balmorra by a group of rogue clones. Over the years, space pirates such as Maz Kanata and Hondo Ohnaka are spotted on Balmorra, making contact with the planet's underworld community.

ZEFFO

REGION Outer Rim
SECTOR Kanz
TERRAIN Mountains, ice caves

The rugged terrain of the Outer Rim planet Zeffo is home to a peaceful and Force-attuned culture that builds underground tombs before mysteriously disappearing. Still living on Zeffo are many predatory creatures, including scazz, phillak, and jotaz. The Empire displaces local villagers and visiting archaeologists in their search for ancient relics as part of Project Auger. After the Empire's hunt ends, it leaves a small detachment on Zeffo to protect its technology. Jedi Master Eno Cordova's research and interest in Zeffo leads Cal Kestis to the planet during his search for a Jedi holocron, and he explores the Tomb of Eilram and Miktrull.

BOGANO

REGION Outer Rim **SECTOR** Mieru'kar
TERRAIN Marshes, bogs, mesas

Before the Jedi Purge, Jedi Master Eno Cordova discovers the marsh-covered Outer Rim planet of Bogano, but it doesn't appear on any Republic or Imperial maps for many years. Atop a hill sits a massive vault built by the Zeffo people. Bogano is also home to the friendly and furry bogling species and the enormous, but peaceful binog. Other Bogano species are harmful to visitors, including the splox insect, bog rats, and sticky-tongued oggdos. Cere Junda takes Cal Kestis to Bogano, where he meets BD-1 and gains access to the vault. Inside, the droid plays Kestis a message from Cordova about the existence of a Jedi holocron that lists the names of Force-attuned children.

CORELLIA

REGION Core **SECTOR** Corellian sector
TERRAIN Oceans, forests, and sprawling urban centers

The people of Corellia are legendary explorers. In the early histories of their world, adventurers set out across the seas to discover new continents or catch epic hauls of fish to sell in the harbor markets of Coronet City. Their shipyards build renowned starfighters, capital battleships, and commercial freighters prized throughout the galaxy. With these ships the Corellians journey across the galaxy and colonize many other worlds.

During the era of the High Republic, Corellia has a turbulent time, weathering infiltration by Nihil agents who are defeated by the Jedi and a planetary civil war. When the Empire takes over Corellia, Sienar Fleet Systems assumes control of all the factories, forcing them to manufacture Imperial TIE fighters, Star Destroyers, and other weapons of galactic war.

Corellia's coastal cities are managed with efficiency. Ports, industry, commerce, and residential centers are located on platforms called "pills" connected by bridges. All military, commercial, and personal travel is directed through Coronet Spaceport. There, the local security agency manages emigration in coordination with the Imperial Security Bureau. Emigration officers sit in well-protected booths, carefully scrutinizing passengers to make sure they have Imperial-approved documentation. Those without influential Imperial ties or connections to one of the powerful families in the manufacturing industry all spend their lives dreaming of leaving Corellia for a better life. An Imperial recruitment center is situated in the spaceport to remind potential emigrants that there are always opportunities to see the galaxy as a member of the Imperial military.

Following the fall of the Empire, the New Republic begins to decommission the Imperial fleet from the Corellia shipyards. However, some remain loyal to the previous regime and allow Morgan Elsbeth to gain access to the rare components she needs to construct the *Eye of Sion* and travel to another galaxy.

After the Hosnian Cataclysm, Corellia falls under the control of the First Order, which takes over the shipyards like its Imperial predecessors. However, the Resistance launches a successful rescue mission here to liberate important prisoners. Once freed, the legendary criminal Hondo Ohnaka steals a shipment of valuable coaxium.

Putrid sewer
Corellia does not have a glamorous reputation. Scrumrat Han Solo spends his childhood dreaming of escaping its corrupt and dirty urban center, Coronet, only to realize he must return to rescue his friend Qi'ra.

DEN OF THE WHITE WORMS

LOCATION Coronet City, Corellia

Not far from Coronet Spaceport, Lady Proxima's White Worm gang makes its den in an abandoned industrial site amidst one of the poorest areas of the city. Cobbling together old housing modules, access pipes, and factory scrap, the labyrinth of passages leads to a central, shadowy sinkhole where Proxima and her offspring soak in a cistern of churning water. The hideout houses all of Proxima's thugs and the scrumrat street children she takes in to carry out her criminal-market business ventures.

VANDOR

REGION Mid Rim **SECTOR** Sloo
TERRAIN Snowy mountain ranges, frozen seas

Vandor is a pristine frontier world, renowned for its fresh air and untapped resources. A small population of settlers and prospectors lives in wooden shanties and lodges along the snowy mountain slopes surrounding Fort Ypso. Explorers and adventurers come to start a new life or escape troubles. However, the Empire takes an interest in an old Banking Clan vault, and begins to establish a small presence. Tobias Beckett's gang robs the Imperial 20-T railcrawler conveyex transport there for its valuable coaxium cargo.

MIMBAN

REGION Expansion **SECTOR** Circarpous **SYSTEM** Circarpous
TERRAIN Mud fields, rainforests, and swamps

During the Clone Wars, the Separatist army takes an interest in Mimban's bountiful mineral resources. A squad of clone troopers trains the Mimbanese to fight, promising later freedom. When the Republic becomes the Empire, the planet is stripped of its lush jungles and mined for dolovite and hyperbarides. As a result, the atmosphere is polluted and the landscape razed to mud. The Mimbanese rise up from their subterranean dwellings and declare war on the Empire in an effort to free their devastated world.

FORT YPSO

LOCATION Vandor

Established by the Ypsobay Trading Company (before the organization collapsed due to financial problems), Fort Ypso is a frontier outpost in the alpine wilds of Vandor. Fur traders, iridium mining prospectors, smugglers, and homesteaders come to the rustic wooden lodge owned by Tibbs Ospe for meals, drinks, and to assemble teams for their next adventures into the wilderness. There is entertainment, too—the sabacc table is popular (Lando Calrissian is a regular), as are the droid gladiator matches run by Ralakili. A resident Nithorn singer adds to the atmosphere.

KESSEL

REGION Outer Rim
TERRAIN Primeval forests, rocks, mines

One half of the former paradise world of Kessel is dominated by spice mines. The opposite hemisphere, marked by lush forests and the palatial estates of King Yaruba and the royal family, is kept clearly separate from the infamous mines, which are sustained by enslaved workers. The spice is a valuable commodity, traded by the galactic underworld, and a single dealership, the Pyke Syndicate, controls the mines. The crew turns the medicinal mineral known as Kessel spice into a powerful narcotic, consumed on its own world of Oba Diah and sold throughout the galaxy. Ahsoka Tano and sisters Trace and Rafa Martez visit the world to steal a shipment, toward the end of the Clone Wars. The Empire keeps an eye on operations, taking a more direct involvement in mining affairs after the theft of coaxium by Tobias Beckett's crew on behalf of Crimson Dawn. Later, rebel Hera Syndulla and the crew of the *Ghost* rescue Wookiee prisoners who are laboring in the mines.

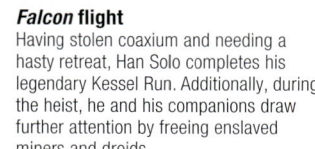

Toxic atmosphere
Spice-mining releases dangerous toxins into the environment. Byproduct Kessoline poisons the water supplies and its use as a fossil fuel produces noxious gas.

***Falcon* flight**
Having stolen coaxium and needing a hasty retreat, Han Solo completes his legendary Kessel Run. Additionally, during the heist, he and his companions draw further attention by freeing enslaved miners and droids.

KESSEL SPICE MINES
LOCATION Kessel

The Pyke Syndicate's Kessel spice mines are overseen by Quay Tolsite, who maintains hired thugs to mind prisoners and watch for smugglers trying to steal spice and other valuable minerals. The Mining Guild also has agents at the mines, working in cooperation with the Pyke operation. All wear heavy protective gear to shield them from the corrosive environment and radiation. While Quay Tolsite manages the business end, he uses a large droid crew to keep the mines running efficiently, day and night. The hard labor is carried out by enslaved workers provided by the Empire in exchange for mineral resources. Many of them, such as the Wookiees, are rebel troublemakers. Others are convicted criminals.

KESSEL RUN
LOCATION Kessel

The Kessel Run is a trade route passing through the Akkadese Maelstrom and the Si'Klaata Cluster, terminating at the planet Kessel. The way is marked by beacons, mapping out the most stable path through the treacherous swirling debris. Straying from this proven course means almost certain obliteration, whether by impact with asteroids, being sucked into gravity wells (the worst of which is the "Maw"), or being devoured by summa-verminoth. Han Solo manages to fly the *Millennium Falcon* through a shortcut, completing the Kessel Run in a record 12 parsecs (if rounding down the number).

SAVAREEN
REGION Outer Rim **TERRAIN** Deserts and oceans

Savareen is a sparsely populated, arid world of sweeping sand dunes and rocky peaks. The inhabitants have a small depot by the sea, unknown to the Empire, where they refine coaxium and sell a popular local brandy. When the villagers rise up against Crimson Dawn, the syndicate removes their tongues as punishment. Later Tobias Beckett, Han Solo, Chewbacca, Qi'ra, and Lando Calrissian arrive after stealing coaxium from Kessel for Crimson Dawn. They are met by Enfys Nest and the Cloud-Riders, who convince Han, Chewbacca, and Qi'ra to side with them rather than the crime syndicate.

NUMIDIAN PRIME
REGION Mid Rim **SECTOR** Bright Jewel
TERRAIN Jungles, rivers, and seas

Numidian Prime is a tropical world with beautiful rainforest vistas and a warm, comfortable environment for human habitation. It is both an exotic resort destination for those who look to relax in rustic, natural settings, and a hideout for smugglers and the disreputable. Long before the Clone Wars, teenage Padawan Qui-Gon Jinn and his master, Dooku, join a Jedi strike team to find Falleen bounty hunter Shenda Mol and her hideout in the jungles of Numidian Prime. Years later, during the reign of the Empire, Lando Calrissian retreats here after his Kessel Run deal with Han Solo and Qi'ra falls apart. Solo follows him there and beats Calrissian in a hand of sabacc, thus winning the *Millennium Falcon* from him.

LOCATIONS

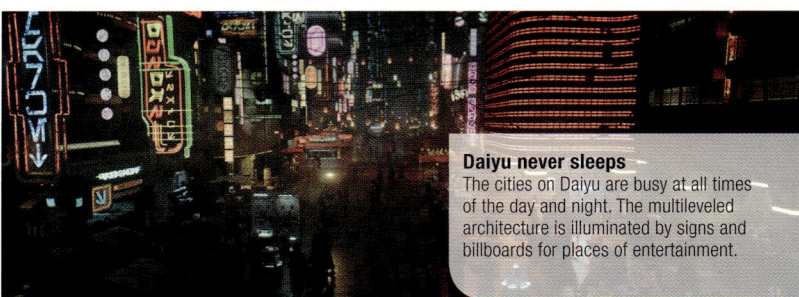

Daiyu never sleeps
The cities on Daiyu are busy at all times of the day and night. The multileveled architecture is illuminated by signs and billboards for places of entertainment.

"People like their secrets out here."

DAIYU DECK OFFICER DENSIN CLORD

DAIYU
TERRAIN Cityscape

Daiyu, like Coruscant, is dominated by cityscapes. Regularly overcast and rainy, the planet is cut off from communication, making it a magnet for those with something to hide. Daiyu is under Imperial control, with stormtroopers regularly making rounds through its cities. The streets are filled with gamblers, spice runners, down-on-their-luck locals, and con artists like Haja Estree, who masquerades as a Jedi to help Force-attuned beings escape offworld. Obi-Wan Kenobi travels to Daiyu in search of Princess Leia Organa after she's kidnapped. After freeing her, he and Leia use the busy streets, back alleys, and high rooftops of Daiyu to escape the Third Sister, the Grand Inquisitor, and the many bounty hunters on their trail.

MAPUZO
REGION Mid Rim
SECTOR Hollan
TERRAIN Plains

Mapuzo draws the attention of the Empire because of its valuable ores and minerals, especially vintrium. Fields of crops and family outposts on the planet soon begin to disappear as the Empire increases its mining operations, carving the plains into tiered steps to better access the precious underground resources. Obi-Wan Kenobi and Leia Organa visit a Hidden Path safe house on Mapuzo. Path agent Tala Durith and the load-lifting droid NED-B help them, but then the Path has to stop using the safe house because it's discovered by the Inquisitor Third Sister.

UNNAMED JABIIM MOON
REGION Outer Rim **SECTOR** Phelleem **SYSTEM** Jabiim
TERRAIN Plains, rocky structures, caves

A desolate, flat moon with towering rock formations is the location of an epic battle between Obi-Wan Kenobi and Darth Vader during the height of Imperial reign. Kenobi flees to the remote, uninhabited moon to draw Vader's attention away from a craft full of Hidden Path refugees. Both Vader and Kenobi use the moon's terrain in their battle: Vader breaks apart the moon's surface in an attempt to bury Obi-Wan, and Kenobi uses broken parts of the rocky structures to pummel Vader's body.

Fortress Inquisitorius
With only the top section of the fortress headquarters exposed above the ocean, the Inquisitor base is thought by many to be impenetrable.

NUR
REGION Outer Rim **SECTOR** Atravis
SYSTEM Mustafar **TERRAIN** Oceans

The Outer Rim moon Nur is covered by saltwater oceans inhabited by several species of fish, including the bluevev glider. Darth Vader orders the Inquisitors' headquarters, Fortress Inquisitorius, to be built on Nur's sea floor atop an ancient structure. Jedi are brought here to be tortured and turned to the dark side. Once fallen, they join ranks of the Inquisitors to hunt more Jedi.
A few years after Order 66, Cal Kestis and Cere Junda infiltrate the Fortress to retrieve a holocron. Years later, Tala Durith goes undercover there to help Obi-Wan Kenobi rescue Leia Organa from Third Sister. While there, Kenobi discovers a tomb with the remains of many Jedi, including Tera Sinube and Pablo-Jill.

JABIIM
REGION Outer Rim
SECTOR Phelleem
TERRAIN Plains, caves, rocky landscapes

Muddy and silt-covered, Jabiim's rocky terrain and caves are uninhabited, save for a few mining operations. Smugglers and tourists view it more as a rest stop than a final destination so it's ideal for a Hidden Path base, where Force-attuned refugees gather before assuming new identities.
Tala Durith brings Obi-Wan Kenobi to Jabiim after the Inquisitor Third Sister has kidnaped Leia Organa. Tala introduces him to the Path leader, Kawlan Roken, who helps rescue Leia, in part to protect the base's location. However, Third Sister and Darth Vader have followed Kenobi there. Path refugees use tunnels to block Imperial troops from their hideout for as long as possible.

Escape from Jabiim
A transport of refugees escapes Jabiim, but only just. They evade Darth Vader's clutches by flying out of a Jabiim cave after distracting Vader with a decoy transport ship.

KOBOH

REGION Outer Rim
SECTOR Varada
TERRAIN Rocky cliffs, swamps, grasslands

Once a magnet for mining prospectors, rugged Koboh becomes a base for criminals like the Bedlam Raiders. It's home to dangerous species including rancors, gorgers, shiverpedes, rawka, and gorocco. Above the planet is the mysterious Koboh Abyss nebula.

MORLANA ONE

REGION Outer Rim **SECTOR** Free Trade Sector
SYSTEM Morlana **TERRAIN** Industrial, oceans

While the Empire rules much of the galaxy with close attention, some planets, such as Morlana One, fall under the jurisdiction of corporations instead. The company Preox-Morlana governs the planet and the nearby system, in alliance with the Empire. Urban sprawl along the waterfront is home to Preox-Morlana's Corporate Zone and its shining headquarters. Beyond the polished areas are the seedier Leisure Zones, where people seek thrills and information in dark corners. Despite its alliance with the Empire, Preox-Morlana prefers to stay off the Empire's radar. That way, the corporation can amass power and govern as it sees fit, without what it regards as Imperial interference.

TANALORR

REGION Outer Rim
SECTOR Varada
SYSTEM Koboh

During the High Republic era, Jedi Dagan Gera finds Tanalorr in the Koboh Abyss nebula. It's strong in the Force, and Gera builds a Jedi temple, but it's abandoned after Nihil marauders attack. Centuries later, it's hoped that Tanalorr can be a safe haven for the Hidden Path and the remains of the Jedi Temple Archives.

ALDHANI

REGION Outer Rim **SECTOR** Cademimu **TERRAIN** Mountains, rivers

A planet with lush, rolling mountains and clear, sparkling waterways, Aldhani is a sacred place to its native Dhanis. To the Empire, however, the planet is no more than the perfect location for its hub for the Imperial sector. Troops occupy the planet and dam the Nasma Klain river to construct a garrison in Akti Amaugh (the Valley of Caves.) The Empire uses the garrison as an armory, supply depot, and a vault for massive stores of payroll credits—the vault that becomes the target of a rebel heist. In making space for their command post and the reestablished Alkenzi Air Base, the Empire forcibly removes tens of thousands of Dhanis from their homes. They're put into an Enterprise Zone in the Lowlands with Imperial housing and factories. Some Dhanis, devoted to nature or tending their ghoasts, cling to their former settlements in the hills surrounding the garrison. But most return only for the Eye—a celestial phenomenon that occurs every three years. Dhanis make the pilgrimage to the Valley, albeit in ever-dwindling numbers, to witness the incredible sight.

FERRIX

REGION Outer Rim
SECTOR Free Trade Sector
SYSTEM Morlana
TERRAIN Desert

Many of Ferrix's residents are in the salvage business, and the planet has become a destination for anyone in need of hard-to-find components. The local population survives by offering extensive inventories of second-hand parts and scraps, which scavengers gather, technicians repair and polish, and those with entrepreneurial flair sell. The many businesses focused on salvage provide a strong foundation for Ferrix's economy. They employ locals, brought together by joint purpose and industry. Following local tradition, the passing of time is marked by the ringing of a hammer against an anvil at regular intervals atop a tower at the end of Rix Road.

Ferrix is part of the Republic until the Clone Wars end. Then, the Empire's power rises throughout the galaxy, and Imperials establish control on Ferrix. One small town of Ferrixians opposes the newly arrived stormtroopers and rises up against them in unity and rebellion. Locals demand liberation and throw stones at the troopers at the Rix Road Protest. The Empire retaliates by punishing participants with arrests and executions.

The Empire eventually hands control of Ferrix over to Preox-Morlana—the corporation that oversees the Free Trade sector. Preox-Morlana largely leaves Ferrix to its salvage work. However, when Pre-Mor Enforcement tracks Cassian Andor to the same town that once protested against Imperial occupation, the eyes of the Empire focus on Ferrix once more. Deeming Cassian's activities as suspicious and potentially rebellious, Imperials occupy the small town as before, and again, the locals take a stand. Things come to a head at the funeral of Cassian's mother, Maarva Andor, who was a president of the Daughters of Ferrix. On Rix Road, citizens again take up arms against the Empire, and the riot sparks a revolution that costs lives on both sides.

Marking time
Ferrix is a sprawling city that attracts the Empire's attention after tracking Andor there. A tall tower on Rix Road is where the Time Grappler rings hammers in a precise rhythm against a beskar gong.

Making contact
Luthen Rael pilots his modified Fondor haulcraft to Ferrix in search of an Imperial N-S9 Starpath Unit—a device for mapping Imperial assets. It brings him into contact with Cassian Andor, who he recruits into his rebel network.

LOCATIONS

KENARI

REGION Mid Rim **SECTOR** Perkell
TERRAIN Toxic wastelands, barren jungles

Once a planet of lush jungles and rich soil, Kenari becomes a toxic wasteland when invaders plunder its valuable mineral deposits. The Galactic Republic is the first to establish mining operations, tearing open the surface and creating dangerous mines. Once it's taken everything it believes it can, the Republic vacates the planet, leaving a legacy of devastation and declaring it off-limits.

Kenari orphans, surviving on their own in the planet's jungles, utilize any resources abandoned by the Republic that they can scavenge. Salvage-collector Maarva Andor finds and adopts one of these orphans, Kassa, and names him Cassian.

The Republic's abandonment of Kenari doesn't stop the Empire. Believing the land still has useful minerals, they extract more, until they trigger a major mining disaster. The Empire then labels the planet toxic and puts it under Imperial prohibition.

Saying goodbye
Maarva Carassi Andor and her husband, Clem, visit Kenari intending to salvage Republic equipment. Instead, their hauler leaves the planet with a young orphan, who grows up as their adopted son.

ISB CENTRAL OFFICE

LOCATION Federal District, Coruscant

The Imperial Security Bureau is the law enforcement and intelligence branch of the Empire. Its headquarters reflect the importance of such an eminent and powerful agency. The central office stands among other Imperial administrative buildings in Coruscant's Federal District. Reflective exterior panels jut into the air in a severe design, and skybridges connect sections of the building. The symbol of the Empire is displayed outside the austere building, greeting ISB agents as they arrive at work. Although agents often work in the field, investigating potential threats to the Empire, they also come to the central office to share intelligence, utilize Imperial resources like the ISB's data vault, and coordinate with their peers and superiors.

With sparse rooms and no decor, the ISB's central office is a place of function. Personal offices have the minimum equipment required for efficient work. Interrogation rooms, fitted with observation areas, are where agents conduct questioning. Leaders such as Major Partagaz hold meetings in which they demand updates from direct reports and where officers share new Imperial directives that the ISB must oversee.

Conference room
Among the office's key rooms are its round conference chambers with built-in datapads. The circular seating for 18 subordinates means there's no way to hide behind a colleague in meetings.

CHANDRILAN EMBASSY

LOCATION Imperial City, Coruscant

Senator Mon Mothma knows all too well the challenges that come with one's home having two roles: a residence for the family as well as a place for business. She works in the Chandrilan Embassy, located in the upper echelons of Coruscant. But it's also where she and her family, Perrin Fertha and Leida, reside so she never gets to leave work behind at her office. The embassy's majestic, long dining table is as likely to be the place for family arguments as it is for political maneuvering.

As part of the networking that comes with her influential position, Mothma hosts many parties. Grand rooms welcome the embassy's guests. Golds and ivories, combined with gentle lighting, potted plants, and cascading chandeliers, set a warm and inviting tone for those who visit. Long, arched windows line one wall, providing a magnificent view of Coruscant's tallest buildings and open skies—a sight only the wealthiest and most powerful get the privilege of experiencing. While the spacious embassy has plenty of common space for mingling or gathering around its bar, guests can also find quiet corners for private conversations—a significant component of diplomatic relations.

Gilded cage
Although the Chandrilan Embassy is Mon Mothma's home, custom prevents her from redecorating the lavish space to her liking.

GALACTIC ANTIQUITIES AND OBJECTS OF INTEREST

LOCATION Coruscant

According to Luthen Rael, his gallery, named Galactic Antiquities and Objects of Interest, is a place where time stands still. The high-end boutique presents rare artifacts from across the galaxy on well-lit, tastefully arranged display stands. Catering to Coruscant's wealthy elite, such as Senator Mon Mothma, the shop gleams with opulence. Luthen and his associate, Kleya Marki, offer bespoke services for clients. They share their vast knowledge about their collection, which includes ancient coins, jewelry, and even weapons like an Utapaun monk cudgel. Luthen and Kleya can make recommendations for any requirement, and new acquisitions arrive regularly. Extra stock is stored in the back room, along with equipment for restoring and cleaning the artifacts.

However, other technology in the back room points to the gallery's primary purpose: serving as a front to conceal Luthen and Kleya's rebellious activities. From a hidden fractal radio, they operate a secret network of rebels dissatisfied with the Empire's rule. Those in the know visit the gallery under the pretense of shopping, but they're actually plotting with Luthen and Kleya.

SEGRA-MILO
REGION Outer Rim **SECTOR** Jospro
TERRAIN Caves, rocks

Segra-Milo is an ideal location for a base of operations for Saw Gerrera's partisans. The planet's rock-strewn surface hides a network of caverns, making it easy to stay out of sight while storing equipment, vehicles, and weaponry. However, suspicious partisan activity and Segra-Milo's location in a known piracy zone brings unwanted Imperial attention to the planet. A patrol stops Luthen Rael in his Fondor haulcraft while he's making a surreptitious visit to Saw Gerrera about arranging a rebel mission. However, Luthen escapes the Imperials thanks to his Fondor's secret weaponry.

KARN HOUSEHOLD
LOCATION Coruscant apartment building

The Karn household is not a home that radiates warmth and a welcoming feel. Eedy Karn maintains a spotless apartment, but it has only basic comforts. The Karn home is located in a standard, nondescript apartment building on Coruscant. Windows let in the limited natural light that reaches between Coruscant's endless tall buildings. When Eedy's son, Syril, returns home from his failed career on Morlana One, he basks in that light in his childhood bedroom, amid his toy troopers. At the dining table, the heart of the Karn household, Eedy sits with Syril and has long conversations about his prospects. She cooks their meals in the modest kitchen, which has counters covered in storage containers and devices for food preparation.

NARKINA 5
REGION Outer Rim **SECTOR** Abrion **SYSTEM** Narkina
TERRAIN Lakes, rocky islands

Narkina 5's surface is covered with massive lakes. Rocky islands that jut from the water are used by local inhabitants and visiting anglers. The moon is also home to the Narkina 5 Imperial Prison Complex. Called an "Imperial factory facility" by the Empire, it's where prisoners serve endless sentences of forced labor. Thousands of inmates toil inside the seven sites, manufacturing a variety of technology for an unknown Imperial purpose. Inmates know only the near-unattainable quotas that the Empire demands and the arduous labor it takes to meet them.

Inmates arriving on Narkina 5 get one last breath of fresh air before being submerged into the facility and set to work on daily twelve-hour shifts. They learn very quickly about the tunqstoid steel floors and how they can be electrified to punish prisoners who step out of line. When Cassian Andor discovers the truth about sentences never ending, he leads a revolt and several prisoners escape into Narkina 5's waters.

Glimpse outside
Inmates from different levels only see each other from afar during shift changes. While waiting to begin their work, prisoners communicate with each other using a makeshift language of hand signals.

FREZNO
REGION Outer Rim **SECTOR** Cademimu
TERRAIN Tall grasslands

Fog clings to the tall grasslands on Frezno. The planet, in a forgotten sector not far from Aldhani, isn't an easy place to live. Makeshift encampments of thin tents and outbuildings dot the landscape. Doctor Quadpaw cares for desperate patients in a tent-turned-operating room here. After the Aldhani heist, the rebels arrive in the futile hope that the doctor can save rebel Karis Nemik. When Arvel Skeen tries to double-cross the team, Cassian Andor shoots him and leaves his body in Frezno's grasslands.

CORUSCANT EASTERN SPACEPORT
LOCATION Coruscant

As the center of government for the galaxy, and home to trillions, Coruscant is a bustling hub for all manner of travel. Tens of thousands of travelers bustle through its spaceport every day. Some are regulars on their daily commutes; others are coming from or are going on long voyages across the galaxy. Wide and winding hallways; large and airy atria; and many gates accommodate the masses. Large departures and arrivals boards feature prominently, showing detailed maps that keep passengers apprised of their journey's status and their flight's designated platforms. The Coruscant Spaceport is a gateway to the galaxy, with companies such as Telgordo Travel operating flights to other Core Worlds, including Hosnian Prime and Eufornis Major—but only for passengers who have boarding passes.

Weary travelers
Coruscant's spaceport terminals combine elegant, sweeping lines with practical functionality. Crowds are kept moving in an efficient manner, with strict codes of conduct about where to walk and in which direction.

NIAMOS
REGION Outer Rim **SECTOR** Vorzyd **TERRAIN** Tropical, beaches

With gentle waves and tropical resorts, Niamos is a place for getting away from it all. The palm-tree covered planet is a prime destination for tourists and also criminals laying low. They relax on sunny stepped seating by the ocean. But the peace doesn't last. The Empire occupies Niamos' shores. Stormtroopers and KX-series security droids enforce new rules and indiscriminately apprehend tourists, sentencing them in an imposing courthouse. Shoretroopers accuse the visiting Cassian Andor of civil disruption and anti-Imperial speech, resulting in six years hard labor at the Narkina 5 Prison Complex.

LOTHAL

REGION Outer Rim
TERRAIN Prairies, mountains, seas

Lothal would seem to be just another insignificant, sparsely populated backwater planet in the Outer Rim. However, the Imperial Star Destroyer in orbit, as well as the Sienar Fleet Systems factories and a stormtrooper garrison in the capital, all suggest otherwise.

QUIET LIFE ON THE OUTER RIM
Before the arrival of the Empire, Lothal is an agricultural society. Farmers cultivate rolling prairies and moisture vaporators draw water to grow jogan, melons, gourds, grains, and other crops. Towns like Kothal, Jalath, and Tangletown are small and the citizens diverse, including humans, Feeorins, Bardottans, Xexto, Balosars, Anx, Ruurians, and Ithorians. While gangsters, bounty hunters, and enslavers are a problem, and gladiator matches are frowned upon in Lothal culture, most early settlers are more concerned with Loth-wolves and sabercats. There is a small Jedi presence, their temple hidden among ancient catacombs in the mountains. Lothal is peaceful and quiet, and of little concern to major powers in the galaxy.

Home on the range
Prairie grass dances in Lothal's afternoon winds, hiding Loth-cats hunting Loth-rats beneath ancient rock formations *(below)*. Near the remote settlement of Jhothal, smoke rises from a Lothal homestead's chimney under a double moonrise *(left)*.

Tarkintown

Impoverished refugees find shelter in run-down Tarkintown, named after Grand Moff Wilhuff Tarkin, the governor of the Outer Rim. Tarkin evicts farmers from their homes when he appropriates their land for new industries to benefit the Empire. The shantytown is a haven for smugglers and criminals as well, many of whom take advantage of the desperate locals. The *Ghost* crew like to donate supplies—stolen from the Empire—to the needy townspeople. During the Siege of Lothal, Darth Vader orders ISB officer Alexsandr Kallus to imprison its inhabitants and destroy the town as its people had accepted the *Ghost* crew's aid.

THE EMPIRE ARRIVES
Everything changes when the Empire, pushing farther into the Outer Rim, arrives on Lothal, which lies on its new trade route. It establishes a port and base on Lothal, but also comes to exploit the planet's mineral wealth. Citizens in smaller towns and the farmers in the countryside receive no benefit from the Empire's presence, especially when Imperials start appropriating land and evicting settlers to build mines and factories. Those who speak out are imprisoned, and often never seen again. Mines strip the land, leaving gaping holes in the landscape. Meanwhile, the Imperial Governor Arihnda Pryce manages everything from the shadows.

Serve and protect whom?
Stormtroopers are concentrated in Capital City, where they guard the Empire's headquarters, government buildings, the Imperial Academy, and Sienar Fleet Systems factories. Meanwhile, average citizens struggle to maintain their own safety and security, having to deal with corrupt stormtroopers and Imperial officials.

Policing the city
Stormtroopers chase rebels after they steal speeder bikes and an important weapons shipment.

A SPARK OF REBELLION
The Empire is quick to move on any sign of dissent from the locals. Merchants who resist are immediately arrested. Mira and Ephraim Bridger, who run dissident broadcasts on the HoloNet, are among many citizens taken away by authorities. At the Imperial Academy, students who stand out with unusual abilities—believed to be Force-attuned—mysteriously disappear. Despite the risks, some citizens do their part to resist, and a small rebel cell begins to stand out. Led by Hera Syndulla and Kanan Jarrus, the *Ghost* crew fights against the Imperial machine managed by Minister Maketh Tua and Imperials Taskmaster Myles Grint and Commandant Cumberlayne Aresko. Its activities draw the notice of ISB officer Alexsandr Kallus, the Grand Inquisitor, and Governor Wilhuff Tarkin.

SIEGE OF LOTHAL
After the rebels obliterate an Imperial Star Destroyer orbiting Mustafar, Darth Vader himself comes to Lothal to quash the rebels. The planet is placed under a blockade and no ships are allowed to leave without Imperial sanction, and its citizens are also subject to strict curfew. Eventually the *Ghost* crew manages to escape the planet, but cannot rescue Tua, who attempts to defect. Afterward, former Governor Ryder Azadi forms a new rebel cell, sabotaging many vehicles being produced in the Armory Complex.

LIBERATION
After years of Imperial occupation and the stripping of its raw materials, Lothal's environment is on the verge of collapse. With the help of pilots from the Rebel Alliance, the *Ghost* crew leads a final assault to free Lothal, annihilating the Imperial Planetary Occupation Facility and Governor Pryce along with it. Thanks to the help of a pod of purrgil, they destroy Thrawn's blockading fleet and Imperial rule on Lothal comes to an end. After the Galactic Civil War, the planet's environment is restored and its people return to a life of relative peace.

Standing up
Alongside the Rebel Alliance troops, Lothal's citizens stand up against the Empire.

Celebration
Lothal commemorates the Empire's defeat with a festive ceremony in Capital City. Governor Azadi recognizes the local rebel leaders with the dedication of a new monument.

CAPITAL CITY
LOCATION Lothal

Some of Lothal's citizens are thrilled when the Empire first arrives. Land barons, government officials, the wealthy elite, and those with military ties all benefit handsomely. Trade is tightly regulated, which creates many new opportunities for smugglers, organized crime, and corruption within the local government.

The economy of Capital City booms as mining operations bring back valuable minerals, metals, and crystals to refineries in the city. Processed materials in turn supply the factories building TIE fighters, Imperial troop transports, and AT-DPs. The factories in and out of the city, however, spew toxic gasses and slowly poison the rivers an d seas.

The Imperial Armory Complex at the center of the city works in secret to develop the TIE/d defender starfighter. This special weapons program is of considerable interest to Grand Admiral Thrawn, who values the defender's survivability in combat with Rebel Alliance fighters—a result of its superior armament and deflector shields.

Those who live in the capital—humans, Rodian, Aqualish, Gotals, Ugnaughts, Ithorians, Chagrians, Houks, and others—face constant surveillance, excessive taxation, and harassment. Propaganda campaigns dominate the media to control public opinion, while citizens are forced to attend mandatory displays of Imperial patriotism and participate in rigged local elections. Travel and communications are monitored, and patrols of stormtroopers, AT-DPs, and ITTs ensure everything stays in order within Capital City.

Youths on the planet hope to get accepted by Lothal's Academy for Young Imperials and graduate as an officer. Some, however, turn to illegal activities, such as smuggling, piracy, or joining a rebel cell. Others get along as best they can, buying and selling in open markets, working in the Empire's factories, and trying not to be noticed.

Nonetheless, leisure pursuits continue in the shadow of the city's Imperial Command Center. The shopping district offers art from Naboo, Alderaan, Clak'dor VII, and the latest fashions imported from Coruscant, as well as restaurants with chefs from all over the galaxy. For the wealthy, luxury housing is available in skyscrapers above the shops. Nearby stadiums are popular for fans of grav-ball, too.

Following the Battle of Lothal, the capital city is heavily damaged, but rebuilding begins. By the time of the New Republic, a monument is constructed to commemorate those who fought to secure the world's freedom.

Aesthetic influence
Citizens walk among the curved towers and stadiums of Lothal *(above)*. Lothal's Capital City *(below)* has a lot of architectural similarities to other mining economies, like those found on Cloud City and Garel.

EZRA'S ROOST
LOCATION Lothal

Ezra Bridger lives in an abandoned communications tower outside Lothal's Capital City. The tower is accessed through a room at the base, where Ezra stores his speeder. An elevator shaft leads to the top, exiting onto a circular balcony where Ezra can see all the way to the city and the sea beyond. The balcony encircles several empty rooms, one of which holds the bunk where Ezra sleeps and stores his helmet collection and various pilfered gadgets. When Lothal becomes too dangerous for Ezra, he leaves his home and joins the *Ghost* crew. ISB officer Alexsandr Kallus, now secretly working for the Rebel Alliance, uses the tower to send intelligence to the rebels. Later Ezra and the rebels return to free Lothal, using the tower as a reconnaissance point to plan their assault on the Imperial Armory Complex.

Sabine's loft
After the fall of the Empire, Sabine Wren takes up residence in Ezra's old home with her Loth-cat, Murley. Decorated with colorful splashes of paint and graffiti, and packed with souvenirs of her rebel days, Sabine makes the Lothal tower her own.

LOCATIONS

ANAXES
REGION Outer Rim **SECTOR** Azure
SYSTEM Azure **TERRAIN** Forests, rocky canyons

Anaxes hosts an important Republic shipyard that is attacked by Separatist Admiral Trench during the Clone Wars. This military stronghold later serves as a base of operations for the "Bad Batch" when it investigates the Separatists' use of Captain Rex's battle strategy algorithm. Later in the war, the planet is obliterated, but a portion of the Republic's fort survives on planetoid PM-1203. Fulcrum (Ahsoka Tano) and Hera Syndulla use it as a supply exchange point, but, by that time, the base is overrun by fyrnocks. Ezra Bridger turns this to his advantage in a confrontation with the Grand Inquisitor.

OLD JHO'S PIT STOP
LOCATION Jhothal, Lothal

Old Jho's Pit Stop, and the outpost where it is located, far from Lothal's capital, is named after its Ithorian owner. The tavern serves food and drinks, several of which are favorites of Kanan Jarrus. One of the bar's notable features is its Clone Wars-era memorabilia, including the nose of the LAAT/i Crumb Bomber. The Ghost crew uses the Pit Stop as a safe harbor to repair its ship. When the Empire cracks down on Lothal's rebel activity, the cantina has to serve Imperial patrons and broadcast Imperial propaganda.

LOTHAL JEDI TEMPLE
LOCATION Lothal

Lothal's Jedi temple is an ancient religious site hidden in the far north. The location is powerful in the Force and a source for kyber crystals. Jedi Master Yoda makes contact with Ezra Bridger, Kanan Jarrus, and Ahsoka Tano over successive visits there. In addition, Kanan accepts the mantle of Jedi Knight here during a vision. The temple requires a master and apprentice to work together to open it. Most of the multi-level building, which predates contemporary teachings of the Jedi, sits underground. At its deepest levels are paintings of Loth-wolves and the mysterious ancient inhabitants of Lothal—and a mystical gateway to a world between worlds.

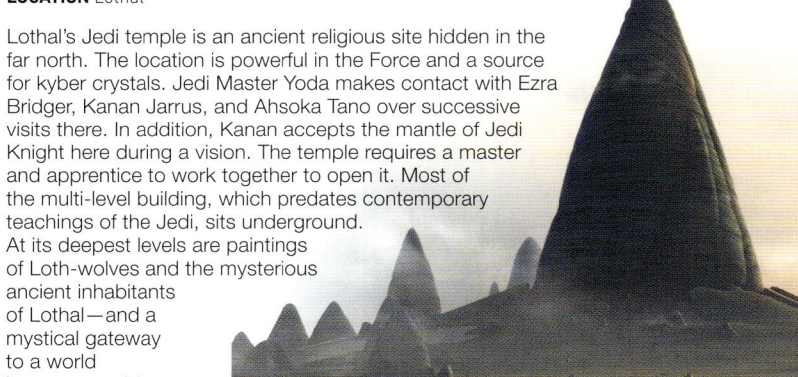

GAREL
REGION Outer Rim **SECTOR** Lothal
TERRAIN Mountains, deserts

Garel is a rocky world dominated by large spiral cities built amid mesas and desert plains. Situated directly on the Empire's newly established trade route through the Outer Rim, Garel is a primary exchange point for weapons shipments. The droids R2-D2 and C-3PO become entangled with the Ghost crew when it intercepts one such Imperial shipment there. The rebel cell Phoenix Squadron temporarily hides on Garel, until the Empire attacks it, and it is forced to flee. During the Age of Rebellion, the Empire expands operations with a munitions factory. Beilert Valance is assigned protection duty for its opening ceremony. Years later, Garel is liberated by local rebels, and decades later is visited by members of the Resistance.

CONCORD DAWN
REGION Outer Rim **SECTOR** Mandalore
TERRAIN Rocky

After enduring centuries of war, Concord Dawn suffered a devastating blast that destroyed much of its southern hemisphere. The remaining planetoid is the birthplace of notable scoundrels such as Rako Hardeen. Fenn Rau and his Journeyman Protectors control Concord Dawn under the authority of the Empire. However, when Rau aligns with the rebels, Viceroy Gar Saxon and the Imperial Super Commandos wipe out the Protectors and take their place as the dominant military force in the system. Viceroy Saxon maintains a secret base on the third moon of Concord Dawn.

ATOLLON
REGION Outer Rim **SECTOR** Lothal
TERRAIN Deserts, coral forests

Atollon is a world once covered by ancient seas that have long since evaporated, leaving vast deserts and coral forests. The most impressive corals to survive are the gargantuan plated coral trees. Some animal life, such as krykna spiders and little dokma, have adapted to survive in the hot sun without benefit of standing water. The planet is also home to the Force-wielding Bendu, a being who prefers to be left in peace. Deep underground lie vast aquifers supporting subterranean life and mysteries yet to be discovered. The Phoenix Squadron rebel cell establishes a base on Atollon, after it is driven from Garel by the Empire. The planet is known to inhabitants of the sector in legends and ancient artwork, but hidden in an unexplored portion of the Lothal sector and obscured in the Empire's databases.

New home
Phoenix Squadron member Dicer sets up a sensor on the north face near Chopper Base *(right)*. The plated coral trees dominate the Atollon landscape *(below)*.

LIRA SAN
REGION Wild Space **SECTOR** N/A
SYSTEM Lira San

Lira San is the ancestral homeland of the Lasat people. It is hidden behind an imploding star cluster and is absent from astronomical charts. A portion of the population left millennia ago, resettling on Lasan. They lost all memory of Lira San other than a mysterious prophecy about one day returning to a promised homeworld. The Empire scorched the surface of Lasan, and few escaped. The Lasat Garazeb "Zeb" Orrelios and the Ghost crew help surviving refugees Chava and Gron locate Lira San by working through the prophecy. There, they are reunited with their people.

CHOPPER BASE
LOCATION Atollon

Chopper Base is a rebel operations center named for Hera Syndulla's droid, C1-10P (Chopper). He befriends an Imperial protocol droid named AP-5, who defects and helps the rebels find a safe location to hide from the Empire. Commander Jun Sato's Phoenix Squadron rebel cell establishes its base in the tallest plated coral tree in the middle of a vast desert, which proves to be a challenge. The group has to contend with carnivorous krykna spiders who gobble up some of the first scouts to arrive, and later face an Imperial EX-D infiltrator droid sent to expose them. Ultimately, Grand Admiral Thrawn discovers the base's location and launches a devastating attack. Commander Sato sacrifices himself and the Phoenix flagship so the survivors can retreat to Yavin 4.

MALACHOR
REGION Outer Rim **SECTOR** Chorlian **TERRAIN** Barren, rocky wastes

Malachor is a desolate world that's controlled by the Sith of antiquity. An ancient battle between the Sith and the Jedi results in a legendary cataclysm referred to as the "Scourge of Malachor." Afterward, Jedi are forbidden to travel there, and Malachor data is removed from the Jedi Archives. Darth Sidious takes his apprentice Darth Maul to Malachor to investigate a Sith temple. They inhale the ash of dead Force-users to conjure visions. Years later, Yoda beckons Ezra Bridger to go there, where he meets Maul.

MALACHOR SITH TEMPLE
LOCATION Malachor

Beneath the surface of Malachor is a Sith temple where a battle between Sith and Jedi raged thousands of years ago. During the struggle, the temple's internal superweapon misfired and obliterated both forces, leaving their charred remains as a memorial, forever locked in stone. Lightsabers and armor lay strewn about. The temple can only be entered by a master and apprentice working in cooperation. Ezra Bridger and Maul work together to reach the center and retrieve a Sith holocron. Ezra then places the holocron in a chamber at the temple pinnacle, where an ancient female Sith presence informs him of the temple's destructive purpose. Ezra and his master, Kanan Jarrus, escape (as does Maul), but Ahsoka Tano stays to fight Darth Vader. The temple explodes, but both survive. Ahsoka then embarks on a spiritual journey beneath the temple that changes the course of her life.

Knowledge is power
At the top of the Sith temple (below), Ezra places the holocron in a pyramid that activates the superweapon (right).

DANTOOINE
REGION Outer Rim **SECTOR** Raioballo
TERRAIN Forests, grassy plains, great lakes

During the Clone Wars, Jedi Master Mace Windu leads the Republic against the Separatist droid army on Dantooine. In the Imperial era, Senator Mon Mothma arranges for rebel representatives to meet in orbit of Dantooine, leading to the formation of the Rebel Alliance. Dantooine is briefly a Rebel Alliance base; it is abandoned for Yavin 4. When Grand Moff Wilhuff Tarkin demands Princess Leia reveal the location of the Rebel Alliance base, she names Dantooine. General Tagge investigates and learns she is lying. Infuriated, Tarkin orders her execution.

SYNDULLA RESIDENCE
LOCATION Ryloth

The home of the Syndulla clan is located in Ryloth's Tann Province. During the Clone Wars, a Republic Y-wing crashes in the front yard. Hera Syndulla pulls the droid Chopper out of the wreckage and repairs him. Later, her father, Cham Syndulla, is forced to abandon their home during a war with the Empire. Imperial Grand Admiral Thrawn directs Captain Slavin to convert the residence into the local Imperial headquarters. Hera later attempts to retrieve her family's Kalikori totem, but Thrawn seizes it. After being captured, Hera has to blow up her former home, so she can escape the Empire.

KROWNEST
REGION Outer Rim **SECTOR** Mandalore
SYSTEM New Kleyman
TERRAIN Rugged mountains, alpine forests

Krownest is a chilly but habitable world under the administration of Mandalore. Winters last for much of the year, but fortunately local plants are mostly evergreen and produce a natural antifreeze that allows them to grow, even under snow. The wildlife has naturally adapted to the cold, thanks to thick, furry coats and large reserves of fat. Clan Wren makes its ancestral home on Krownest, in idyllic, isolated family estates.

WREN STRONGHOLD
LOCATION Krownest

Clan Wren's seat of authority is an estate on Krownest, carefully guarded by its members. The minimalist mansion of steel and glass overlooks snow-covered mountains and a frozen lake. The great hall has a large banquet table situated below the throne for the clan leader. In the tradition of ancient Mandalorian culture, the manor includes rooms for sparring and physical training. Sabine Wren grows up here before leaving for the Imperial Academy. Her mother Ursa Wren is the ruling matriarch.

LOTHAL RESISTANCE CAMP
LOCATION Lothal

The Spectres' rebel camp is hidden in the mountains of Lothal's northern hemisphere. When it is discovered by the Imperials, they bomb the area and the rebels must seek the aid of the Loth-wolves to flee. The wolves take them through subterranean passages to an ancient habitation in the southern hemisphere, hidden on a canyon cliff. The walls there are decorated with hieroglyphics similar to those found within the lower levels of Lothal's Jedi temple. Their new camp serves the rebels in the last days before they drive the Empire from Lothal.

LOTH-WOLF DEN
LOCATION Lothal

Kanan Jarrus, Ezra Bridger, and the crew of the *Ghost* become acquainted with a small pack of legendary Loth-wolves. Their austere den is located in the mountainous wilds of Lothal, beneath a large rock spire. It is deep enough to be impervious to Imperial bombing runs from above. The walls of this cave den are decorated with paintings of the ancient indigenous peoples coexisting with the wolves. The den is interconnected with cave passages leading to many strange places on Lothal—and perhaps beyond, via a world between worlds.

LAH'MU
REGION Outer Rim **SECTOR** Raioballo
TERRAIN Mountains, forested lowlands

Lah'mu is an unspoiled world rich in minerals and rainfall, making it an ideal environment for agriculture. Much of this is due to heavy volcanic and geothermal activity, especially in the eastern hemisphere. Too far for most from hyperspace routes, it is occupied by only a few hundred homesteaders. The Republic encourages human settlers who are trying to escape the violence of the Clone Wars to resettle here, but they are soon forgotten. This sense of neglect makes it an ideal hiding place for the Erso family.

A WORLD BETWEEN WORLDS

A world between worlds is a mysterious spiritual realm that flows from the Force and is located outside the bounds of time and space. The Lothal Jedi temple, itself older than modern Jedi traditions, is one gateway to it. Emperor Palpatine, aware of the realm, sends Minister Veris Hydan to excavate the temple and look for its gateway. He uncovers a mural of the legendary Force-wielders of Mortis, but cannot decipher it. Sabine Wren and Ezra Bridger are successful however, and Ezra enters a gateway encircled by illustrations of Loth-wolves. Inside, Ezra finds a plane with portals to significant Force events. Finding Ahsoka Tano confronted by Darth Vader through one such portal, Ezra pulls her into a world between worlds and saves her life. They are interrupted by Palpatine, who attempts to penetrate the boundaries of the realm. Ahsoka and Ezra escape, after which the temple disappears. Later, Palpatine reconstructs a piece of the temple, trying to trick Ezra into opening the gateway for him, but Ezra declines and destroys it.

ERSO HOMESTEAD
LOCATION Lah'mu

When Galen Erso and his family flee from Director Orson Krennic and the Empire, their friend Saw Gerrera helps them create a new life on Lah'mu. The Erso family home sits on 65 hectares of farmland. Most of the structure is buried underground and constructed by Galen and Lyra Erso themselves. Power and heating to the home is directed from geothermal vents. The local water supply is too high in minerals to be potable, so drinking water is drawn from moisture vaporators. Lah'mu's fertile soil is quite suitable for the family's large gardens however, which are tended with the assistance of an SE-2 worker droid. Galen, Lyra, and their daughter, Jyn, lead a happy life there for four years. Jyn experiences a pleasant, albeit lonely, childhood on Lah'mu, until Krennic and his death troopers arrive.

Making a home
Jyn's sleeping bunk *(above)* and the main living area *(below)* are functional, with minimal personal items.

RING OF KAFRENE

REGION Expansion
SECTOR Thand
TERRAIN Space station amidst rocks and ice

Once a mining colony, the Ring of Kafrene is a trading post at the junction of the Rimma Trade Route and the Biox Detour. It was established by wealthy investors who failed to realize that the asteroid had few ore deposits of value, and their venture went bankrupt. The "ring" connects two planetoids and has a diverse community of merchants, though many of the residents dwell in squalor. Cassian Andor is sent on a mission here to investigate Imperial kyber crystal shipments, and meets informant Tivik in backstreets patrolled by stormtroopers.

WOBANI

REGION Mid Rim
SECTOR Bryx
TERRAIN Barren hills, processing plants

Wobani is the site of an Imperial labor camp where prisoners harvest and process underground reservoirs of tibanna and other valuable gasses. When Princess Leia Organa is 16 years old, she visits Wobani on a relief mission. She is dismayed by the treatment of the people by the Empire, and brings 100 refugees to Alderaan. Later, as an Imperial prisoner, Jyn Erso is sentenced to hard labor on Wobani in camp LEG-817, but she is rescued from a prisoner transport turbo tank by the Rebel Alliance and taken to Yavin 4.

JEDHA

REGION Mid Rim **SECTOR** Terrabe
TERRAIN Deserts, mesas, mountains

Jedha is the desolate moon of the planet NaJedha, its landscape dotted with sandstone mesas. Locked in a continuous winter, the climate is chilly, but not uncomfortable. Most of the year the sandy valleys and lowlands are barren, with only occasional rain torrents. The planet is rich in kyber crystals, and, partly for that reason, it has been home to many religions, including in recent millennia the Jedi. The kyber deposits eventually draw the Empire to the moon, and Imperial forces soon pillage holy sites and start mining operations. In the regime's early years, Jedi Master Cere Junda establishes a hideout in an abandoned monastery beneath the sands of the Narkis Highlands. After the Battle of Yavin, the Rebel Alliance comes to the shattered moon to try to re-forge old alliances, while the remaining partisans try to save what remains.

Fallen Statue
During the High Republic era, the planet becomes a site for a battle between various Force-aligned sects, including the Jedi. This statue of a Jedi falls during the attack.

JEDHA CITY

LOCATION Jedha

Jedha City, also known as the Holy City or NiJedha, sits atop a mesa overlooking a desolate valley. During the High Republic, the city's Second Spire temple is picked as the site for the signing of a vital galactic peace treaty. Instead, it becomes ground zero for the devastating Battle of Jedha when agitators breach the temple. Hundreds of years later, the Empire establishes a sizable presence in Jedha City. Stormtroopers perch on the backs of long-legged creatures called spamel, scrutinizing pilgrims who come to visit the temples and religious sites. To enter the city, guests must make an exhausting climb to gates near the top of its sandstone walls. Once inside, they find the citadel is divided into the Old City and the New City, which is still some 5,000 years old. At the front of the Old City sits the Temple of the Kyber. Stormtroopers and tanks patrol the streets, searching for partisan rebels and anyone attempting to smuggle kyber crystals offworld. The Empire destroys Jedha City during the test-firing of its superweapon, the Death Star, which it passes off as a mining accident.

Marketplace melting pot
Jedha's streets are always crowded with pilgrims, priests, monks, tourists, sellers of trinkets, and street-food vendors. Merchants sell sanctioned and criminal-market goods and pilgrims *(right)* seek spiritual answers.

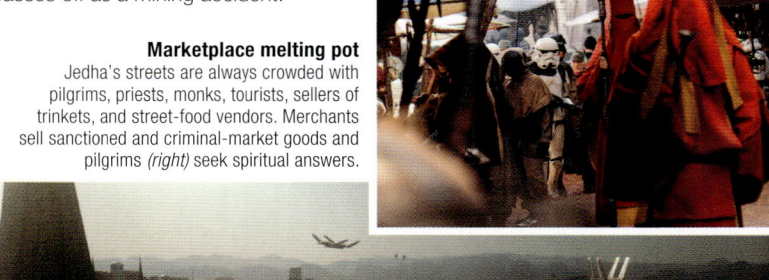

CATACOMBS OF CADERA

LOCATION Jedha

The Catacombs of Cadera are ancient tombs carved from a rock formation about a day's walk from Jedha's Holy City. They and the surrounding ruins were formed by a long-forgotten civilization. In more recent centuries, the catacombs were occupied by a monastery of the Church of the Contained Crescent, but they too vacated the site before it became occupied once again; this time by Saw Gerrera and his militant partisans. The catacombs are finally destroyed when the Death Star fires upon the Holy City.

TEMPLE OF THE KYBER

LOCATION Holy City of Jedha

Known as the Temple of the Kyber, the Temple of the Whills, or simply the Kyber Temple, Jedha's most holy site was sacred to the ancient Jedi and those who follow their teachings concerning the Force. The triangular temple tower rises high above the city. Darth Vader's Castle on Mustafar is designed using similar principles. When the Empire takes full control of Jedha, it closes the temple and turns out its guardian monks. A bountiful source of kyber crystals, the temple's vast underground stores are looted by the Empire to power the Death Star's superweapon. The temple is destroyed when the Death Star obliterates the Holy City.

286 LOCATIONS

YAVIN 4
REGION Outer Rim **SECTOR** Gordian Reach **TERRAIN** Jungles

Yavin 4 is the fourth moon of an uninhabitable red gas giant. No indigenous sentient life inhabits the moon, and with no known mineral resources of significance, Yavin 4 has avoided the attention of the Empire.

Canopy cover
A rebel soldier stationed above the forest canopy scans for incoming ships. Allies are signaled for landing instructions inside the base of the temple ruins.

Hidden signs
Jan Dodonna's group is unaware of the Great Temple and the surrounding structures' link to the Ordu Aspectu, an ancient splinter group of the Jedi Order.

PRISTINE ENVIRONMENT
Yavin 4 is covered by an impenetrable rainforest of purple-barked Massassi trees, climbing ferns, grenade fungi, and bioluminescent orchids. Woolamanders cradle their young in the canopy above, and their mating calls echo through the forest late at night. Stintaril rodents hunt in packs through the trees, overwhelming the roosting golden whisper birds. Runyip forage on the floor below, harassed by ravenous piranha beetles. Below ground, leviathan grubs feed on Massassi roots for 300 years before emerging as one of the largest carnivores in the forest. In the swamps, armored eels prey on brightly colored lizard crabs, which are caught and absorbed by bulbous anglers perched on buttress tree roots above the muck. Unspoiled by industry, pollution, or colonies of settlers, Yavin 4 retains one of the galaxy's richest and most diverse ecosystems.

ORGANIZING A REBELLION
After rebel leader Mon Mothma formally announces the Rebel Alliance, a portion of Jan Dodonna's group and Phoenix Squadron are defeated on Atollon by the Empire. Phoenix Squadron is practically wiped out by the attack, so the remnants merge with Dodonna's group. Seeking to avoid detection by the Empire, Rebel Alliance High Command abandons its former base on Dantooine and moves to the Great Temple on Yavin 4. From here, the Alliance leadership organizes non-combat missions including supply runs, reconnaissance missions, and disrupting an Imperial relay station on Jalindi. New recruits steadily join the Alliance as its leaders acquire the military machinery necessary to fight back. The Alliance avoids open warfare with the Empire, unwilling to risk the lives of civilians and rebels alike.

Haunted temple
For a time, the *Ghost* and its crew are based at the Great Temple.

Crucial message
Private Tenzigo Weems races toward Mon Mothma to inform her that rebels are on Scarif.

SECRET REBEL BASE
During the Emperor's reign, rebel engineers convert one of the largest structures into a base of operations. Inside are living quarters, meeting and services rooms, and landing bays for the fleet. A hidden power station 2 kilometers (1¼ miles) away supplies the base and provides shields and ion cannons sufficient to hold off an attack from most battleships.

Monitoring the battle
From their strategy center, General Jan Dodonna, Princess Leia Organa, and C-3PO monitor the assault on the Death Star.

ATTACK ON SCARIF
Rebel intelligence stationed at Yavin 4 learns that the Empire is building a superweapon with the power to destroy entire planets. News of the Death Star's existence sparks a fierce debate among the Alliance Council, but its only hope is to recover the battle station's blueprints archived at the Imperial Security Complex on Scarif in order to discover its weakness. As Rogue One acquires the plans on the ground, rebel starfighters and a few command ships deploy from Yavin 4 to provide cover. Heavy losses are incurred, but the Alliance wins its first major victory against the Empire as Princess Leia escapes with the plans.

THE BATTLE OF YAVIN
When the *Millennium Falcon* delivers Princess Leia to Yavin 4, the rebels discover that her freedom comes at a high price. A tracking device has been attached to the ship and the approaching Death Star has forced their hand. The rebels must launch an attack on the Imperial battle station before their base and Yavin 4 are destroyed. With R2-D2 aboard, Luke Skywalker joins the X-wing flight team in an attempt to detonate the Death Star's reactor core via an unprotected exhaust port. If this mission fails, the Empire will destroy Yavin 4 with its superlaser and utterly annihilate the Rebel Alliance. Following their victory over the first Death Star, General Dodonna calls for the full evacuation of the base. Knowing that an Imperial counter attack is imminent, the Alliance begins scouting for a new outpost.

Hail the heroes
Instrumental in the success of the rebellion, the Heroes of Yavin attend the Royal Award Ceremony.

Desperate message
Deep in the Catacombs of Cadera, Galen's daughter watches her father's message; it's the first time Jyn has seen him in years.

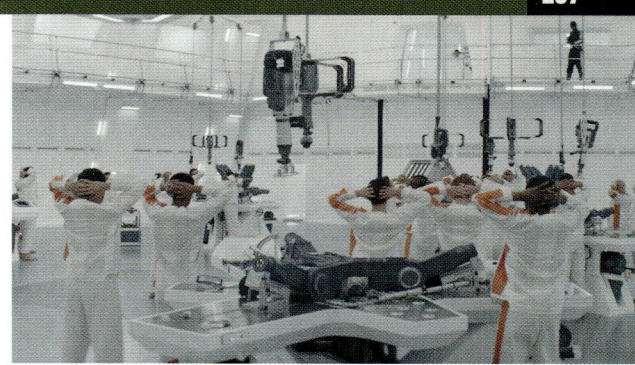

One way out
In facilities like Narkina-5, the Empire exploits prison labor to assemble components needed to build the Death Star. The work is inhumane, and the prisoners band together to escape. Future rebel Cassian Andor is among them.

THE DEATH STAR

AFFILIATION Empire

With the embers of rebellion simmering in the Empire, Grand Moff Wilhuff Tarkin believes fear will keep its many planets in line. Who would dare stand against the Death Star with its power to destroy entire worlds?

BIRTH OF A SUPERWEAPON
Even before the birth of the Empire, preparations for its ultimate weapon are underway. On Geonosis, engineers working at the behest of the Sith Lord Darth Sidious create the first designs for the Death Star. When Jedi Knights and clone troopers attack the planet, beginning the Clone Wars, Count Dooku retrieves the designs for safekeeping in the hands of the Sith. By the time the war ends and Sidious has declared himself Emperor, the battle station's construction begins in secret above Geonosis, under Director Orson Krennic and (then) Admiral Tarkin's supervision.

UNDER CONSTRUCTION
While construction continues over Geonosis, work soon begins on the weapon itself. Krennic coerces his friend, scientist Galen Erso, to weaponize kyber crystals for the Death Star's superlaser. While Galen feigns loyalty to the project, he secretly plans a devastating fault in the reactor system that could be used to destroy the entire station. Galen creates a holorecording explaining his actions, and urging the Rebel Alliance to steal the Death Star plans from the Citadel on Scarif. Erso then persuades Imperial pilot Bodhi Rook to pass the holorecording to his old friend Saw Gerrera, who then gives it to Galen's daughter, Jyn.

TESTING THE WEAPON
The Empire learns that Bodhi has defected and traveled to Jedha City, so Tarkin orders a partial test of the Death Star's weapon on the location. The city is completely destroyed. When the Rebel Alliance attacks Scarif, Tarkin orders the Death Star to fire upon the Imperial facility containing the Death Star plans—but the destruction fails to stop the Alliance. Rebel Princess Leia Organa is captured and brought to the Death Star, where Tarkin forces her to witness the destruction of her homeworld Alderaan, killing billions.

Princess rescued
Leia Organa is liberated from her cell by Han and Luke, and together they escape—into a trash compactor *(above, bottom)*. Darth Vader and his former Jedi Master, Obi-Wan Kenobi, duel one final time *(above, top)*.

ESCAPING THE DEATH STAR
The *Millennium Falcon*'s crew—Han Solo and Chewbacca—are hired to bring Obi-Wan Kenobi, Luke Skywalker, R2-D2, and C-3PO to Alderaan. However, they are shocked to discover that Alderaan has been blasted to rubble. Soon after, they are caught in a tractor beam and pulled into a docking bay aboard the Death Star. Amazingly, they avoid capture. After Obi-Wan parts company with the others to shut down the tractor beam, R2-D2 learns that Princess Leia is imprisoned on the Death Star, and scheduled for execution. Luke, Chewbacca, and Han hastily launch a rescue mission. They manage to free Leia, but the arrival of stormtroopers forces them all to dive into a chute that empties into a trash compactor. Fortunately, R2-D2 and C-3PO shut down the compactor before it crushes their human compatriots. Luke and Han rush Leia back to the *Falcon*, while Obi-Wan disables the tractor beam. However, when the former Jedi attempts to rejoin his allies back at the ship, he encounters Darth Vader, who engages him in a duel. To ensure that Luke, Leia, and the others escape, Obi-Wan allows Vader to strike him down, becoming one with the Force.

Vulnerable
The Death Star's primary weapon combines multiple laser beams *(above, top)* to form a single massive blast. But two small proton torpedoes fired down a thermal exhaust port merely 2 meters (6 ft 6 in) wide *(above, bottom)* prove catastrophic for the battle station.

DARTH VADER'S FORTRESS

LOCATION Mustafar

Darth Vader's fortress is a fearsome and foreboding building that stands as a testament to its owner's anger and pain. Over the years, the castle is the site of many horrific acts, from the torture of captive Jedi survivors to attempts to bring the dead back to life.

CONSTRUCTION PHASE
Pleased with his apprentice's recent performance, Emperor Palpatine offers Darth Vader his own fortress in the design and location of his choosing. Vader selects Mustafar because he associates it with his connection to the dark side and his transformation from Anakin Skywalker to Darth Vader. Palpatine also gifts Vader a mask containing the consciousness of an ancient Sith Lord and sculptor known as Momin, and sends his chief architect, Colonel Alva Brenne, and her aide, Lieutenant Roggo, along with Vader. During their work, the mask possesses Roggo, and under its influence, he kills Brenne.

At Vader's insistence, Momin begins to design the Dark Lord's castle to channel the dark side, harnessing the energy to open a gateway into the Force itself. There, Vader hopes to contact his dead wife, Padmé Amidala. It takes Momin eight attempts at construction before Vader can open the gateway to the dark side as desired. At each unsuccessful attempt, Vader is frustrated and kills Momin's current body, causing him to transfer from a Mustafarian to a stormtrooper, then an Imperial officer, then a Mustafarian lava flea, and finally an Imperial construction worker before Momin completes the final design.

Vader's castle has twin tuning towers, both made of black obsidian. The towers channel the Force and enhance Vader's connection to it. Inside the castle is the Dark Lord of the Sith's personal training room, complete with armed combat droids. There's also a waiting room, absent of chairs, with a view of Mustafar's treacherous volcanic landscape. The room is meant to intimidate Vader's "guests." Vader meets with important emissaries in this room, including Imperial Director Orson Krennic. At the heart of the temple is a meditation chamber guarded by the Emperor's Royal Guards, where Vader communes with the Force from inside a bacta tank, free from the confines of his terrifying black armor.

Intimidating meeting place
Vader banks on the stark architecture and inhospitable environment of his fortress to intimidate Imperial staff, such as Director Orson Krennic, and remind them of their place.

UNNATURAL ACTS
In time, Vader is able to enter the dark-side gateway and search for his wife, but dark visions cloud his attempts. In frustration, he retreats and destroys the portal. Only the cave beneath remains. The cave, located near the site of a former Sith temple in the Gahenn Plains, houses a locus of the dark side of the Force. Vader's red lightsaber was forged in this cave, and later, the First Order's Supreme Leader Snoke wears a ring with obsidian carved from its bedrock.

Vader doesn't give up on his quest to see Padmé again. He learns of the Aeon Engine, a mystical device that grants mastery over death. It's powered by a sacred Mustafarian crystal called the Bright Star. The crystal lies somewhere in the ruins of an antiquated castle below Vader's fortress, which was once the home of Lady Corvax. Long ago, her misuse of the Aeon Engine obliterated most of the planet. After he recovers the Engine, Vader coerces the Force-attuned pilot of a ship called the *Windfall* to retrieve the Bright Star. Far beneath Vader's castle, the pilot encounters Corvax sentinels, hostile creatures like the darkghast, and the Bright Star itself. With the aid of the cavern-dwelling Mustafarians, the pilot destroys the Aeon Engine and foils Vader's plans to resurrect Padmé.

ENEMY INFILTRATIONS
During the Galactic Civil War, the Knights of Ren infiltrate the fortress and successfully steal an artifact for Crimson Dawn, losing one of their group when they face Vader. The castle is later infiltrated by Scourged droids until Scourge is defeated. After the death of Darth Vader, his fortress becomes a ruin, and eventually the Alazmec of Winsit cult settles there. During the Resistance and First Order conflict, Kylo Ren recovers Vader's Sith wayfinder from the rubble.

Castle keeper
Darth Vader *(above)* is attended by Vaneé, who protects the inner sanctums of his master's fortress, such as his meditation chamber and restorative bacta tank *(left)* from prying guests' eyes.

Dangerous defenses
Architect Colonel Brenne thought the lava fields would make a stunning vista. Vader knows they provide invaluable protection.

SCARIF

REGION Outer Rim
SECTOR Abrion
TERRAIN Tropical coastal zones, shallow seas with coral reefs

Scarif is a tropical world far from other habitable planets. Its isolation coupled with the minerals and ore deposits in its mantle make it an ideal secret Imperial shipyard and weapons foundry. After the Death Star is moved from Geonosis, it is brought to Scarif to complete its construction under the oversight of Director Orson Krennic. Scientist Galen Erso has the immense data file containing the Death Star plans—including its fatal flaw—stored at the data vault deep in the Citadel complex, where Krennic mistakenly thinks it is safe. Many Imperials share this attitude toward the planet's impregnability.

The entire planet is secured by a deflector shield, with an access point to Scarif's surface available through a single shield gate, which is guarded by turbolasers, bays of TIE fighters, and multiple orbiting Star Destroyers. This high level of security is intended to prevent anyone but authorized Imperials from reaching (or departing from) the surface of the planet.

Scarif's landscape is peppered with volcanic island chains, atolls, coral reefs, and ever-shifting sand bars. Aquatic life is abundant. In the lagoons and reefs just around the Imperial Security Complex are more than 1,500 known species of fish. The most fearsome sea creature there is the tentacled blixus, known to drag unmindful stormtroopers into the lagoons and eat them. Further out to sea are great fish and sea beasts capable of swallowing entire starships.

The Imperial Security Complex straddles islands connected by sandy tombolos and transit tubes. The islands are home to many birds, reptiles, and insects. Some of them are hunted, cooked, and served at the local stormtrooper mess hall.

Older officers stationed on Scarif treat their posting like an early, unsanctioned retirement. Their lackadaisical approach to their duties contributes to the Empire's loss at the Battle of Scarif, resulting in the destruction of the entire Imperial complex and loss of all personnel stationed there, initiated by the order of Grand Moff Wilhuff Tarkin.

Tropical battleground
The jungles of Scarif become the perfect terrain for the camouflaged rebels to hide in and confuse the Empire from.

Hive of activity
The Imperial security complex on Scarif spans a number of islands. Cargo shuttles are in constant employment to and from the many landing bases.

> "Send word to the Alliance... they have to go to Scarif and get the plans."
>
> **GALEN ERSO, VIA JYN ERSO**

EADU

REGION Outer Rim
SECTOR Bheriz
TERRAIN Rocky mountains, grasses, scrub brush

Eadu is a harsh world with severe storms of lightning, gale-force winds, and torrential rains. The northern hemisphere is marked by tall rock spires and a near endless night due to the unpleasant weather. Ravines collect runoff and give off a stench of decay. The Imperial Kyber Refinery is hidden in this lifeless north. Fortunately the southern hemisphere, with its fertile soil, is not as inhospitable. There, about 2,500,000 Eaduans live in small villages where they raise nerf herds.

IMPERIAL KYBER REFINERY

LOCATION Eadu

The secret Imperial Kyber Refinery, also known as the Eadu Energy Conversion Laboratory, is hidden among a treacherous zone of rock pinnacles shrouded in dark clouds. Rogue Imperial Galen Erso manages the facility with a team of scientists, in a program that fuses kyber crystal shards into larger matrixes, and conducts research into controlled chain reactions. The project falls under the Tarkin Initiative, overseen by Director Orson Krennic. Security for the facility is overseen by Captain Magna Tolvan and it is guarded by stormtroopers from the 975th garrison.

CITADEL TOWER

LOCATION Scarif

The Citadel is the focal point of the Imperial Security Complex on Scarif. It is an immense tower housing a heavily guarded cold-storage data vault, central communications dish, landing pads for high-ranking officials, and a complex control room where General Sotorus Ramda overseas daily operations. The vault contains data on countless top-secret programs, including the plans to the Death Star. It is guarded by a battalion of stormtroopers and shoretroopers, a surplus of Imperial security droids, and occasionally a contingent of death troopers accompanying visiting VIPs. Rebels Jyn Erso, Cassian Andor, and his droid, K-2SO, infiltrate the tower, steal the Death Star plans, and transmit them to the Rebel Alliance from the top of the tower via the communications dish. The tower, along with the rest of the facility, is destroyed by a single shot from the Death Star.

Secure satellite
Offworld communication from Scarif happens via the satellite dish at the very top of the Citadel Tower. The planetary shield gate prevents unauthorized transmissions, however.

LOCATIONS

NAR SHADDAA
REGION Outer Rim **SECTOR** Hutt Space
SYSTEM Y'Toub **TERRAIN** City

Nar Shaddaa, the "Smuggler's Moon" of the Hutt homeworld Nal Hutta, is a polluted city-world and one of the galaxy's most dangerous locales. Ruled by the Hutts, it is a notorious center of criminal activity, filled with pickpockets, bounty hunters, and gangsters. During the reign of the Empire, crime lord Grakkus the Hutt grows in power and wealth on Nar Shaddaa, and gains an interest in Jedi artifacts. Luke Skywalker winds up a prisoner of Grakkus and is forced to fight in his gladiatorial arena. Skywalker eventually escapes with his friends, and the Empire arrests the Hutt.

CYMOON 1
REGION Expansion
SECTOR Bes Ber Bikade
TERRAIN Junk fields

A world of factories and garbage, Cymoon 1 appears rust-colored from space due to pollution. It is home to the largest weapons depot in the galaxy—the Empire's Weapons Factory Alpha. Han Solo, Luke Skywalker, and Leia Organa pose as emissaries of Jabba the Hutt and sabotage the facility. Matters grow more complicated with the arrival of Darth Vader, who Luke encounters in-person for the first time. A full-scale battle between rebels and Imperial forces ensues, and the factory explodes, just as the *Millennium Falcon* escapes.

QUARANTINE WORLD III
REGION Outer Rim **SECTOR** Subterrel
SYSTEM Kallidahin Space

A storage facility built into the rock of an asteroid, Quarantine World III holds artifacts not intended for use within the galaxy. Items in vaults have myriad defenses against theft, including invisible laser grids and droidekas. The facility is maintained by the Kallidahin curator Utani Xane. He and his super battle droids just stop Doctor Chelli Aphra from stealing the Triple-Zero personality matrix, but then Darth Vader arrives looking for Aphra. The Sith destroys the droids and Utani, and leaves with Aphra, who manages to snag her prized data card.

SON-TUUL
REGION Outer Rim **SECTOR** Perinn **TERRAIN** Forests, jungles, mountains

The jungle planet Son-tuul is alive with natural growth that inhabitants have incorporated into their development of the planet. In city streets, staircases are often set into trees, spiraling upward to a bridge or building entrance, while dwellings incorporate tree trunks. The planet is home to Son-tuul Pride—a crime syndicate with a far reach across the galaxy. The murderous droid Triple-Zero rises to be head of the organization, with his headquarters—including a "relaxation suite" for torturing captives—located in Son-tuul's forests. He leads Son-tuul Pride until the Empire levels his base.

ANTHAN PRIME
REGION Outer Rim **SECTOR** Braxant
TERRAIN Gas

A gas giant located at the edge of the Outer Rim, Anthan Prime appears as a mass of attractive blue vapor. It is well known for its powerful storms, which see the gas swirl and powerful bolts of electricity strike. Within Anthan Prime is the Spire—a floating city that's divided into two levels, with a resort for the wealthy on top, and casinos and gambling on the bottom. The Ante, a well-connected information broker, resides on the Spire until he is killed by Darth Vader. Later, Doctor Aphra escapes the Empire by navigating Anthan Prime's storms, something few can do or even attempt.

SHU-TORUN
REGION Mid Rim **SECTOR** Chaama
TERRAIN Mountains, rock, lava

Shu-Torun is covered in lava rivers and appears crimson from space. A large piece of technology, known as the Spike, keeps the planet from breaking apart. Darth Vader slaughters the royal family after its members express disdain for the Empire, but he allows Princess Trios to live, naming her queen and demanding her loyalty. Trios later goes undercover in the Rebel Alliance, sabotaging the fleet. Leia Organa kills Trios in a final battle, and Luke Skywalker convinces the partisan freedom fighters to cease their destruction of the Spike and, subsequently, the planet itself.

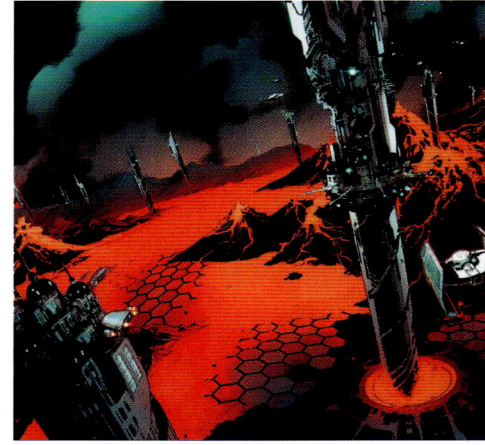

VROGAS VAS
REGION Outer Rim
SECTOR Sujimis
TERRAIN Mountains, rock

The desolate planet of Vrogas Vas features a landscape of rock, with barren passages, unforgiving mountains, and dry valleys. It is mostly devoid of life, with the exception of certain resilient species like wasp-worms. But there are clues to a rich history, including the ruins of giant statues that marked the site of a Jedi temple. While looking for Luke Skywalker after the Battle of Yavin, Darth Vader is shot down; once on the surface, he obliterates a contingent of rebel forces. He also destroys a rival, the Mon Calamari cyborg Karbin, in a final battle on the planet.

SUNSPOT PRISON
REGION Outer Rim **SECTOR** Tunka **TERRAIN** Prison

Its existence unknown to the Empire and many within the Rebel Alliance, Sunspot Prison is a secret penitentiary maintained by the Rebellion that holds war criminals, Imperial spies, mercenaries, and even Moffs. The facility, protected by a "sea of ion cannons," sits in a ring and is stationed near a sun, which provides constant heat and daylight. Doctor Aphra is brought to the prison by Leia Organa. Soon after, the vengeful rebel Eneb Ray invades Sunspot, taking Imperial hostages in an effort to convince Leia that more extreme methods are needed if she is to be a leader.

BAR'LETH

REGION Core

Bar'leth is known throughout the galaxy for the University of Bar'leth—a well-respected school where Doctor Chelli Aphra studies archaeology. However, it is also home to old evils. Long ago, dark-side cultists, the Ascendant, worshipped on Bar'leth. Their temple and its "Unyielding Heart" sanctum were under what became the university. The zealots are destroyed by the Sith but leave behind the Spark Eternal—an ancient AI that mimics the Force and takes control of Aphra during the Galactic Civil War. Before it does this, the Grand Inquisitor and Iskat Akaris come to the planet in search of a Sith relic.

FORTRESS OF GARN

REGION Outer Rim **SYSTEM** Garn **SECTOR** Cadma

Built into the remnants of a moon, the sprawling Fortress of Garn—also known as the Citadel of Rur—was once home to the ancient splinter group of Jedi named Ordu Aspectu. Doctor Chelli Aphra and her father discover the ruins of the fortress, which is littered with the remains of fallen orthodox Jedi from long ago. Inside, they find a central spire that is reachable by a Force bridge, which leads to a subterranean core. Activating the core, they awaken the Eternal Rur—a murderous AI that believes itself to be the consciousness of a Jedi.

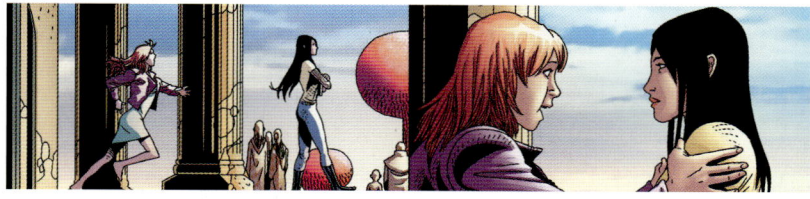

THE CITADEL OF KTATH'ATN

REGION Outer Rim
SECTOR Chopani

Two small towers and a tall one, the Citadel of Ktath'atn—"the military expedient construction of loud, shrill exhalations," or simply, "the Screaming Citadel"—is Queen of Ktath'atn's palace. At an annual party, she grants favors in exchange for time with interesting guests. There is more to the planet's ruler, however, as she is under the control of an abersyn symbiote, feeding on the life energy of others. Doctor Chelli Aphra and Luke Skywalker discover this secret while visiting for the gala.

MILVAYNE

REGION Inner Rim **SYSTEM** Gyrica
TERRAIN Cities

Much like Coruscant, Milvayne is a city-planet with many levels that reflect socio-economic disparities. The elite stick to the Wealthy District with its luxury apartments and high-end eateries, while the poor and those involved in criminal enterprise have dealings in the undercity. It is backed by the Empire, and much power is granted to the omnipresent Milvayne Authority police force: holo-ads promoting adherence to the law and support of the Empire are projected throughout the streets. Doctor Chelli Aphra goes to the world with Triple-Zero, and they quickly find themselves hunted by law enforcement.

KAKRA

REGION Wild Space
TERRAIN Mountains, rock

Known to some as K43, Kakra is a volcanic world with rocky terrain. It was long thought uninhabited but is actually populated by a race of rock-people called Kakrans. Chewbacca and C-3PO arrive on a rebel mission to set charges to destabilize the planet, lure the Empire there, and destroy as many Imperial forces as possible. But this plan becomes problematic when they meet the Kakrans. Using unexplained abilities, the Kakrans deactivate the explosives and join the fight against the Empire. To end the battle, a gigantic Kakran emerges from the planet core, smashing a Star Destroyer to pieces.

MAKO-TA SPACE DOCKS

REGION Outer Rim
SYSTEM Mako-Ta
SECTOR Noonian

Following the abandonment of Yavin 4, the Mako-Ta Space Docks become something of an interim rebel base. The station sits in the Outer Rim, nestled between two suns, and features an amorphous shape that includes several levels on a long spire. It serves as a production center and has a hangar, command center, and at least four mess halls. But the rebels' time here does not last long. Their supposed ally Queen Trios sabotages the base by revealing its location to Darth Vader and the Empire, who launch an assault on Mako-Ta and the Alliance fleet.

ARBIFLUX

REGION Outer Rim
SECTOR Dalonbian
TERRAIN Forests, plains

A peaceful world of wildlife and nature, Arbiflux features forests, plains of grass and dirt, and various creatures. It is also neutral in the galactic civil war—for a time. Lona Aphra absconds to the planet with her daughter, Chelli, to start a new life away from her husband. But a raider attack alters their course because Lona suffers fatal injuries. Her final act is calling the Empire to save her daughter, and stormtroopers arrive to take Chelli away. Years later, Aphra learns that the marauder invasion was a plot by the Empire to take control of the planet and its resources.

HUBIN

REGION Dene Gois Cluster, Outer Rim **SECTOR** Yminis **TERRAIN** Forests, plains, mountains

The moon known as Hubin is a place of stunning beauty. Clear skies, rolling hills, and rich forests cover the world, which is home to creatures like the mighty thanrax. Long ago, an ex-Jedi and her husband settled on Hubin. Their son is Thane Markona, who later establishes a community for his clan of reformed mercenaries. Luke Skywalker, Han Solo, and Leia Organa crash-land on Hubin, and Markona and his daughter Tula welcome them, but matters change when the Imperial SCAR Squadron arrives. Thane ends up sacrificing himself to save Luke, seeing the act as a form of redemption for his past associations with the Empire.

LOCATIONS

Frozen wastes
Hoth appears bleak and barren. There are no signs of civilization or significant life, making it an ideal hiding place for the Rebel Alliance forces who adapt to this harsh world.

Race to the *Falcon*
Chewbacca, Han, Leia, and C-3PO narrowly escape Echo Base.

HOTH
REGION Outer Rim **SECTOR** Anoat **TERRAIN** Plains, mountains

Once the Empire becomes aware of the rebels' base of operations on Yavin 4, the freedom fighters must relocate to a new secret hideaway. In their search for unlikely homes, they settle upon the cold, barren world of Hoth.

A FROZEN WORLD
Hoth is a frozen, inhospitable world. Rocky mountains give birth to winding glaciers, spilling into vast fields of snow and icy tundra. Surrounded by a precarious asteroid belt, the planet is barraged by meteors. Still, life exists on the planet. Several species of tauntaun feed on lichens in glacier caves and grottos formed by the planet's heated core. Wampas hunt tauntauns and drag them back to their caves to feed their young. At night, the wind howls haunting melodies through winding burrows of sapphire ice worms.

PERILS AT THE DOORSTEP
Hoth is fraught with dangers. While on patrol, Han Solo and Chewbacca discover one of the Empire's probe droids, deployed through their galaxy-wide reconnaissance mission, Project Swarm. The unit self-destructs when struck by blaster-fire, but only after alerting the Imperials. Meanwhile, Luke Skywalker is attacked by a ferocious wampa and pulled back to its den. The beasts are a frequent problem for the rebels, and several remain captive at Echo Base. Though Luke escapes, he nearly freezes to death in a blizzard afterward. Yet the rebels' worst struggles are faced once the Imperial military arrives.

Ice monsters
Wampas are a hazard of being stationed on this frozen world. They have even been known to attack Echo Base in small groups.

THE BATTLE OF HOTH
General Maximilian Veers is tasked with destroying the shield power generator at Echo Base. Forced to steer clear of the shield perimeter, Imperial dropships set down on the precarious Moorsh Moraine, well north of the heavily fortified rebel base. Having surrendered all element of surprise, but augmented with legions of snowtroopers, the Empire's AT-ATs, AT-STs, and speeders begin their trek toward the rebel stronghold. As they move south to the foot of the Clabburn Range, they are met by the rebels' Rogue Group of modified T-47 airspeeders.

EVACUATION
Once Veers destroys the shield power generator, the rebels must evacuate. As their ion cannon disables the Star Destroyers above, transport ships launch the evacuation. Virtually unarmed, the rebel transports rely on starfighter escorts during the battle. The *Millennium Falcon* takes off prior to the last transport, *Bright Hope*. Luke and the remaining survivors scramble to take off in their X-wings, leaving Darth Vader and his snowtroopers to scrounge through the wreckage for clues to the fleet's destination. Scavengers later arrive on Hoth to loot the wreckage from the battle.

ECHO BASE
LOCATION Hoth

Following the Battle of Yavin, the Rebel Alliance begins searching for a new location to base its secret operations. The rebels settle on the icy planet Hoth, which is so remote that it is absent from most maps. Rebel engineers carve the command center from the ice; resourceful rebels Shara Bey and Kes Dameron, the parents of Poe Dameron, devise the use of an A-wing cannon to cut tunnels through the ice. The Alliance also excavates vast bays to hold the rebel fleet of starfighters and a contingent of GR-75 medium transports, in addition to quarters for more troops and other personnel. Establishing a military installation buried in snow and ice proves challenging: frequently melting ice, shrinkage, and cave-ins mean the base needs constant maintenance. The rebels are resolute, however, and name their new home Echo Base after its remarkable acoustics.

The Alliance must not only deal with harsh environmental conditions and the eventual ground war with the Empire, but also wampa attacks, itchy tauntaun lice, and even meteor showers. To keep personnel healthy, Echo Base has a well-equipped infirmary with physicians and medical droids. Though vital for defense, the shield generators, visible from a great distance due to their large size, guarantee eventual detection by the Empire. General Carlist Rieekan orders extra defenses to be constructed, including heavy blast doors, infantry trenches surrounding the base, and anti-personnel batteries in key locations. The base's chief defense is a sizable Kuat Drive Yards v-150 ion cannon, which fires gigantic charged-plasma bursts powerful enough to disable an Imperial Star Destroyer's shields, weapons, and engines.

All these precautions prove necessary when an Imperial probe droid discovers the rebel presence on Hoth and the Empire launches an AT-AT assault. This eventually dooms Echo Base, putting the rebels on the run once again. Instrumental in the evacuation, the base's ion cannon indeed disables the Imperial fleet above, while the GR-75 transports ferry rebel personnel away from Hoth to temporary safety.

Inevitable defeat
When Imperial walkers descend upon Echo Base, the rebels know they can only slow down the Empire's assault to give the evacuation effort more time.

Danger comes to Echo Base
The rebel fleet prepares for battle in the hangar bay.

YODA'S HUT
LOCATION Dagobah

When Yoda returns to the planet Dagobah after the ascension of Emperor Palpatine, he initially makes a camp in the E3-standard starship lifeboat that brings him there. Though the craft is small, it affords reasonable living space for a being of Yoda's size, providing shelter from the constant threat of Dagobah's unrelenting rains and persistent pests and predators. Within a year, however, the craft begins to degrade as it is slowly consumed by the swamp.

Yoda sets about building a new home made of mud, wattle, and stones. He constructs his house at the base of a great gnarltree on a knoll beside a murky lagoon. The humble dwelling includes a sitting room, kitchen area, and sleeping loft, with several windows and two circular entries. The interior is surfaced in smooth, white clay adobe, providing a clean, attractive, and dry shelter.

Yoda cooks at a small stove in the middle of his home, behind which is a storage area with windowsills covered in drying seeds, berries, and herbs. In the back of the shelter is a sink with running water, a few clay bowls and pots, and Yoda's spice collection. A loft hangs above, with sleeping mats and blankets, though Yoda sleeps on the ground level during his final years. Tools and keepsakes are stored in a nook. The rest consists of a sitting area with a wooden stump for a table.

Being so close to the lagoon, with open doors and windows, means Yoda's home is visited by many creatures. Yoda frequently finds snakes, lizards, butcherbugs, and spiny bog rats scampering across the floor. He doesn't mind the company and only sweeps the venomous ones back out of the door.

Yoda lives in his home for more than 20 years before Luke visits him there, twice. On his first visit, Yoda agrees to train Luke as a Jedi, and during the second, Yoda tells Luke that he must confront his father, Darth Vader. Advanced in years, Yoda then passes away in the comfort of his bed. Yoda's vacant hut is reclaimed by the swamp and the many creatures he has befriended over the years.

HOTH ASTEROID BELT
REGION Outer Rim
SECTOR Anoat
TERRAIN Rocks, gas pockets

The planet Hoth suffers constant meteor bombardment from the surrounding asteroid belt. The chaotic region is a favorite hiding place for pirates and smugglers, as well as a legitimate source of metal ore and minerals.

Following the battle of Hoth, the *Millennium Falcon* hides inside the belt, where the crew finds that the asteroids harbor life. Giant space slugs have formed a colony, with some specimens large enough to swallow entire starships. Mynocks infest the rocky caverns, feeding on passing starships and the wreckage of vessels that don't survive.

BEN KENOBI'S HOME
LOCATION Jundland Wastes, Tatooine

After a period dwelling in a cave, Obi-Wan "Ben" Kenobi lives in an abandoned moisture prospector's hut on a bluff surrounded by the Western Dune Sea. The house has one main room above ground and is built on top of a sheltered cave, which Obi-Wan uses as a little workshop and cellar to store food. Here, Obi-Wan reveals to Luke Skywalker that his father was a Jedi. After they leave Tatooine and Obi-Wan dies on the Death Star, Luke returns to the hut, but he is attacked by Boba Fett. Luke defeats the bounty hunter and leaves with Obi-Wan's journal. Darth Vader and Doctor Chelli Aphra later arrive to inspect the hut, with Vader sensing Luke's strength with the Force. Aphra sets off a molecular bomb to remove any trace of their visit. Years later, Luke returns to find components for his second lightsaber.

Not-so-safe haven
Bespin is the nearest safe haven from Hoth that Han is able to locate while fleeing from the Empire *(above)*. On the approach to Cloud City, the *Millennium Falcon* is met and escorted by a pair of cloud cars *(left)*.

BESPIN
REGION Outer Rim
SECTOR Anoat
TERRAIN Gas giant

The planet Bespin is a gas giant, isolated from two sister worlds by an asteroid belt known as Velser's Ring. Bespin has no landmasses, but its upper, habitable atmosphere has a layer of breathable air, and this zone hosts a number of orbital cities, gas-mining facilities, and unique lifeforms. Bespin has an unusual abundance of life for a gas planet, and the night skies are lit with bioluminescent organisms that look like twinkling stars.

In the lower atmosphere, giant beldons float in large herds. They range in size from 0.8 to 10 kilometers (½ to 6¼ miles) wide, filled with numerous orange gas bladders and propelled by fleshy fins. Long tendrils fall from their bodies, gathering atmospheric plankton and chemicals, which they metabolize into tibanna gas, a valuable commodity that forms the foundation of Bespin's various floating cities' economies.

Algal "trees" form floating mats with stalks that descend to the lower atmosphere to gather nutrients. These algal forests produce most of the oxygen in the planet's life zone. They also provide a habitat and food source for an untold number of creatures.

Large thrantas, transplanted from Alderaan, dive majestically through the clouds, ridden by only the bravest thrill-seekers. Blue-and-red-tipped rawwks flit among the algal trees, chasing schools of air shrimp that shimmer in rainbow colors to warn others of a predator. Flocks of velkers attack beldons and feast on their buoyant flesh, attracting carrion-eating crab gliders, until the corpse slowly drifts toward the toxic planet core.

LOCATIONS

CLOUD CITY
LOCATION Bespin

Floating 59,000 kilometers (37,000 miles) above Bespin's gaseous core, Cloud City is both a gas-mining facility and a luxury destination. Founded by Lord Ecclessis Figg of Corellia, it is overseen by Baron Administrator Lando Calrissian.

Seeking refuge
The *Millennium Falcon* approaches Cloud City at sunset, hoping to hide from the Empire. Little do those aboard know that Darth Vader lies in wait for them.

Refining in the clouds
An automated tibanna gas refinery hovers outside Cloud City.

MINING THE SKIES
Cloud City is built around a central column that rises from a gas-processing reactor at its base. The city's otherwise hollow core contains giant directional vanes that control the facility's ever-floating location. Plants around the city's outer ring process Bespin's tibanna gas for export. Cloud City employs countless freelance gas prospectors to navigate Bespin's breathable upper atmosphere. They are hired to pinpoint pockets of tibanna using their flying craft before larger contractors can locate gas eruptions. Rare and valuable tibanna gas has a variety of uses. Its anti-gravitational properties are utilized across the galaxy for numerous types of airborne craft. It is also a key component in some blasters as a conducting agent and power-output amplifier. On some worlds, the gas is even employed as a heating fuel, while non-spin-sealed tibanna is used as hyperdrive coolant.

THE IMPERIAL OCCUPATION
Anticipating the arrival of Han Solo, Boba Fett infiltrates Cloud City and alerts Darth Vader. Vader, in turn, quietly arrives with a contingent of stormtroopers and forces Lando to cooperate. Lando agrees to turn Han Solo over to Vader in exchange for a guarantee that the Empire will not interfere with Cloud City in the future. Leia Organa notices something is amiss when her droid, C-3PO, goes missing. Chewbacca discovers the droid has been dismantled and set to be destroyed by Ugnaughts (in fact, he has been shot and memory-scanned by stormtroopers) and rescues him. Lando then leads his friends to Vader under the ruse that they are going to dinner. Upon capture, Han is thrown into a prison cell with Leia before being taken to a carbon-freezing chamber. Darth Vader then uses the rebels to lure Luke Skywalker into a confrontation, where he reveals that he is Luke's father in a failed attempt to persuade him to join the dark side. While the rebels and Lando escape the city, Luke loses his lightsaber and the inhabitants suffer a continued Imperial presence. Soon after, the rebels return and rescue Lobot and a few residents from the Empire. Following the Battle of Endor, the local Imperial Governor Ubrik Adelhard blockades the entire sector. Thanks to Lando, Lobot, and a local resistance, Cloud City is freed.

Sith subterfuge
Darth Vader discusses arrangements regarding the capture of Han with Boba Fett and Lando.

A city for fun
The promenade of Cloud City is lined with designer shops full of imported goods, fine restaurants, bars and cafes, cinemas, and gaming rooms.

A LUXURY DESTINATION
Cloud City is an exclusive resort, attracting elite clientele and wealthy tourists who stay in stylish casino hotels and enjoy Bespin's legendary two-hour sunsets. Visitors include well-to-do politicians, celebrities, industry tycoons, gangsters, and the occasional high-ranking Imperial officer. Fortunes are made and lost in this city renowned for its nightlife, scandals, and excess. Cloud City's five million residents and visitors dwell atop its 16-kilometer- (10-mile-) wide mining facility levels. The city floats in the planet's breathable upper atmosphere, known as the "Life Zone," which is shielded and infused by a layer of airborne algae and other photosynthetic organisms.

CARBON-FREEZING CHAMBER
LOCATION Cloud City, Bespin

Carbonite storage repulsor sleds are designed for use with the carbon-freezing chamber on Cloud City to safely store and transport high-pressure gasses like tibanna. The gas is stored within a super-strong block of frozen carbonite inside the sled. Darth Vader hopes to immobilize his son, Luke Skywalker, in carbonite and transport him to the Emperor. To determine whether Luke will be able to survive this carbon-freezing process, Vader decides to use Han Solo as a test subject. After he freezes Han, Vader hands him over to bounty hunter Boba Fett, who in turn delivers him to Jabba the Hutt for a substantial reward. Although a success, the process causes chronic hibernation sickness, which afflicts Han with temporary blindness and severe disorientation when he is eventually freed. Ultimately, however, Vader fails to trap Luke. When Leia Organa returns to the city, the Imperials freeze her in carbonite alongside some residents. Luke uses the Force to free them all.

Ugnaughts: Determined workers
Ugnaughts are a small species of humanoids with tusks. Lord Ecclessis Figg builds Cloud City with the aid of three Ugnaught tribes. When the city is complete, Figg allows the Ugnaughts to remain in residence and maintain the city for a share in its mining profits.

Chamber of horrors
As Han is led to the carbon-freezing chamber, Lando has second thoughts about his deal with Darth Vader to ensure the safety of his Cloud City.

ERIADU
REGION Outer Rim
SECTOR Seswenna
TERRAIN Mountains, jungles

During the High Republic era, as a result of the Great Disaster, the Outer Rim planet Eriadu is one of many planets affected by a temporary hyperspace blockade. The Tarkin family gains power and wealth on Eriadu by acting as a planetary police force, taming the wilderness that's filled with dangerous predators and protecting Eriadu's supply of the ore lommite from pirates and smugglers. After the rise of the Empire, Governor Wilhuff Tarkin hosts a summit with Imperial officers and scientists to discuss the future of the Imperial Army at a compound named Raven's Peak.

TEMPES
REGION Outer Rim
SECTOR Atravis

Tempes, shrouded in clouds and bursts of lightning, is best known as a Jedi outpost during the era of the High Republic. Following the loss of his lightsaber in a duel with Darth Vader, Luke Skywalker goes to Tempes, where he has been told a Jedi weapon awaits. Once there, Luke discovers a structure marked with the insignia of the Jedi Order. Inside, the ruins of ancient Jedi statues line a great hall, and Skywalker finds a lightsaber. But also waiting for him is the specter of the Grand Inquisitor. They duel and Luke defeats the Jedi hunter, who vanishes.

JEKARA
REGION Mid Rim **SECTOR** Bryx **TERRAIN** Ice, snow, rivers

Jekara is an ice planet in a system of the same name. With frigid temperatures, the landscape consists of frozen vistas and cold bodies of water. Though mostly devoid of life, the planet has oceans inhabited by Jekaran sharks, who are fierce predators. Lady Qi'ra of Crimson Dawn chooses the remote world as the site for her auction of Han Solo's carbonite slab. She docks the crime syndicate's headquarters ship, the *Vermillion*, on the tundra to host the event. The *Millennium Falcon* crash-lands into the ice when attempting to sneak past Crimson Dawn's forces to rescue Solo.

PANISIA
REGION Outer Rim
SECTOR Halthor
TERRAIN Mountains, rock, desert

After evacuating its base on Hoth, the Rebel Alliance establishes a new HQ on Panisia. The Outer Rim planet is one of tall mountains, rocky landscapes, and sprawling deserts. Panisia is remote enough for secrecy, but the rebels are forced to flee when the Crimson Dawn operative Deathstick tracks them and reports their base to the Empire. This results in the Battle of Panisia and Leia Organa's final confrontation with Commander Zahra, in which the princess subdues the Imperial in one of the planet's caves and leaves her to her fate with aggressive Panisian creatures.

GABREDOR III
REGION Outer Rim **SECTOR** Myto **TERRAIN** Forest

Gabredor III is known for its lush forests and grasslands and is home to many farms. But the planet's resources suffer when Governor Tauntaza, in league with Crimson Dawn, begins to neglect the world. As it struggles from drought, trees wither and the people starve. Sabé, a former handmaiden of Queen Amidala, brings Darth Vader to the planet to help save a colony of formerly enslaved people. Vader saves his former friends Kitster Banai and Wald from a vicious attack by ravenous creatures, and later battles the corrupt governor, who is revealed to be receiving directives straight from Emperor Palpatine himself.

COLONY OF KEZARAT
REGION No-Space

Once a stranded convoy of fuel tankers, the Colony of Kezarat is a group of ships that forms a community. It's located in No-Space—an area hidden from the galaxy and only accessible by a rare energy source called a Path. Led by Captain Blythe, the colony eventually meets Luke Skywalker and his friends when they arrive in a Path-powered ship. Blythe tells Luke about the convoy's early encounters with the Nihil marauders, the Jedi who helped them survive, and the fable that a new Jedi will bring them home. When the rebels leave, several colony ships go with them.

KLIGSON'S MOON
REGION No-Space
TERRAIN Rock

Appearing yellow from space, Kligson's Moon is little known but holds great significance in the galaxy. During the era of the High Republic, a droid named Ajax Sigma is built on the moon. Not beholden to programming, Sigma believes in the freedom of synthetic life and leads the Kligson's Moon Uprising, in which he and his forces kill thousands of colonizers. Jedi eventually come to stop Sigma and his army, destroying them on the orbiting Haven droid station, which is safeguarded by the Kligson clan. But Sigma's neural core survives and is passed through different hands over time until his eventual rebirth.

EPIKONIA
TERRAIN Terrestrial

Epikonia is a remote world featuring a prime communications hub that transmits signals across the galaxy. The parasitic droid entity known as Scourge kidnaps Lando Calrissian's friend Lobot, infects him, and hides him in a city on Epikonia. This city is surrounded by satellite dishes that bolster communication. In the center of the city is a large open area that becomes a ghastly experimental laboratory. Here, Scourge conducts his hideous experiments, infusing organic beings with droid parts against their will and causing great pain and death.

LOCATIONS

ENDOR
REGION Outer Rim **SECTOR** Moddell
TERRAIN Forests, savannahs, mountains

The fate of the galaxy is determined on a peaceful moon, where the Rebel Alliance obtains the aid of the most unlikely allies to defeat the Empire.

SECRET IMPERIAL BASE
Bothan spies obtain information about the second Death Star and deliver it to the rebel leadership. They learn that it is protected by a shield generator located on Endor. Believing they can strike before the new battle station is fully operational, a team of rebel Pathfinder commandos led by General Han Solo sneaks past the Imperial blockade in the stolen *Lambda*-class shuttle, *Tydirium*. Their mission is to destroy the Empire's facility on the moon's surface. The Imperial command bunker is located below a relay dish and guarded by Imperial walkers and a garrison of stormtroopers, scout troopers, and other officers under the command of Colonel Dyer, Major Hewex, and Commander Altadan Igar.

Imperial landing zone
Lambda-class shuttles *(above)* fly to a landing platform with turbolifts running up the legs of the installation *(below)*. AT-ATs are loaded at gates below.

HOMEWORLD OF THE EWOKS
The Forest Moon of Endor is a sanctuary of pristine temperate forests and indigenous societies that thrive there. Ewoks who live there refer to the location as "Tana." They dwell in family huts connected by terraces, ladders, and suspension bridges. Villages are overseen by wise chiefs and tribal elders. In warm summer months, Ewoks may stay in fishing villages or hunting and farming lodges on the forest floor. Well versed in forest survival, they travel long distances on shaggy, spotted ponies and use friendly bordoks to haul loads of supplies. Ewoks soar through valleys on gliders with leather wings, but must be careful to avoid vicious blue-and-gold condor dragons.

Captured by Ewoks
The Ewok Wicket W. Warrick detects a scout trooper approaching *(above)*. A group of Ewoks comes to investigate the rebels caught in their net *(above, left)*.

Change in the primeval forest
The evergreen forest of Endor is peaceful until the Empire arrives. Songs of churi and lantern birds are replaced by speeder bike engines and the clanking of AT-STs.

Bait
C-3PO and R2-D2 lure a group of troopers into an ambush, where Ewoks pummel them with stones during the Battle of Endor.

CLIMACTIC BATTLE
Though the rebels are taken prisoner by the Ewoks at their first encounter, C-3PO eventually persuades the Ewoks to join the rebel cause, to save not only their own homes and families, but the rest of the galaxy as well. The Alliance's success at the Battle of Endor, which decisively ends the rule of the Emperor, can largely be attributed to the bravery and ingenuity of the Ewoks. They manage to overthrow the technologically advanced Imperial army using spears and arrows, rock-throwing catapults, wooden battering rams, and rolling logs. Decades later, the moon is visited by the First Order, but their orbiting Star Destroyer is annihilated.

RESIDENTS AND EXPATRIATES
Endor is rich with life, and Ewoks are not the only species of significance. Yuzzums are Endor's dreamy wanderers. Two of them catch a ride on visiting ships, making their way to Jabba's palace on Tatooine. One works there as a singer and the other as an exterminator. Aggressive Duloks dwell in the swamps, emerging to hunt Ewoks and lantern birds. The songs of munyips and ruggers can be heard as they climb through Ewok villages. Giant gorax occasionally descend from the mountains and terrorize Ewok tribes.

Yuzzums
The rifle-carrying Endor native Wam Lufba tends to the pests—some quite menacing—in Jabba's palace on Tatooine.

DEATH STAR II

REGION OUTER RIM
SECTOR Moddell **SYSTEM** Endor
TERRAIN Space battle station

Emperor Palpatine constructs the second Death Star, in part as an elaborate ruse. He hopes to destroy the Rebel Alliance by feigning a critical vulnerability in the battle station, thus luring the rebels into a conflict they cannot win.
After the Alliance learns of the station's existence, thanks to Crimson Dawn agents, the Emperor devises a plan to let Bothan spies obtain false information about the progress and status of its construction. The rebels presume the battle station's superlaser will not be in operation at this stage, while in fact it is. During the Battle of Endor, Palpatine surprises the rebels by ordering the Death Star to fire on one of the large Mon Calamari cruisers. However, once the rebel strike team manages to destroy the shield generator on Endor that protects the Death Star, a small flight team, led by General Lando Calrissian on the *Millennium Falcon*, is able to navigate to the battle station's main reactor core and destroy it. Meanwhile, Luke Skywalker barely escapes after his father, Darth Vader, sacrifices himself to destroy the Emperor and save his son. After its destruction, Death Star II debris falls on Kef Bir, the Ocean Moon of Endor. It's visited decades later by Rey. The second Death Star is significantly larger than the first. Its diameter is more than 200 kilometers (124 miles), compared to the original battle station's 160 kilometers (99 miles). In fact, the Death Star is nearly 3 percent the size of the Moon of Endor itself. Since the Death Star is stationary and not in a synchronous orbit, it requires tremendous force to counter Endor's gravity. It utilizes a repulsorlift field created by the shield generator on Endor to maintain its position. The force generated by the Death Star creates earthquakes, tidal imbalances, and other geological disturbances on the surface below.
The Death Star has considerable defenses. Batteries include a complement of 15,000 heavy turbolasers, 15,000 standard turbolasers, 7,500 laser cannons, and 5,000 ion cannons, all of which are installed on the station's outer surface. Thousands of TIE fighters of various models are ready to deploy at all times, in addition to shuttles and ground assault vehicles such as AT-ATs and AT-STs.

EMPEROR'S THRONE ROOM

LOCATION Death Star II

Emperor Palpatine's throne room is his command center and ceremonial seat of power aboard the second Death Star. Its stark industrial design, devoid of decorations and symbols of lavish comfort (unlike his personal offices and chambers, both here and on Coruscant), are meant to intimidate the dignitaries, subjects, and prisoners brought before him. His throne is a simple, contoured swiveling chair set in front of a viewport with enhanced magnification scanners. The dais before him is flanked by viewscreens linked to the station's computers and communications systems. Decades later, after the duel between Luke Skywalker and Darth Vader and Palpatine's apparent demise, the remains of the throne room on Kef Bir host another duel, which spills outside to a structure embedded in the waters below. Rey, having retrieved a Sith wayfinder from a nearby room, faces Kylo Ren for a final time.

EWOK VILLAGE

LOCATION Endor

Bright Tree Village is perched 15 meters (50 feet) above the forest floor, where nestlike bunches of thatched huts housing nearly 200 Ewoks cling to the trunks of evergreen trees. At the village center are communal meeting areas, as well as homes for tribal elders and Chief Chirpa's family. Large huts for extended families huddle along the outer edges of the village. All are tied together by rope bridges, ladders, and platforms. In the canopy above, watchers look out for marauding gorax and condor dragons. Ewoks also launch gliders from the canopy to patrol the forests and valleys beyond. Bachelors maintain small huts underneath the village proper, where they keep watch for even greater dangers below. Ewok huts are cozy inside. A cooking fire is located at the center, where meat is roasted on a spit and soups boiled in clay pots. Storerooms of food and kindling lie under the floor and woven sleeping mats and furs are stacked in lofts above. Wooden stools and baskets sit on the floor, while Ewok hoods, capes, and tools hang on the walls. Fires and torches light the village at night. The bark of the conifer trees where the Ewoks live not only provides a good insect repellent but is also highly fire resistant. The boughs also make excellent spears, bows, slingshots, glider frames, and catapult arms.
When the Rebel Alliance arrives on Endor, Leia Organa befriends the Ewok Wicket W. Warrick and walks with him to Bright Tree Village. She's welcomed with Ewok hospitality, fed, and clothed. Her rebel friends are then captured and brought to the village to be the main course in a banquet in C-3PO's honor—the Ewoks believe that the timid protocol droid is a god. Luke cleverly uses the Force to play on their superstitions and win the rebels' freedom. That night, C-3PO explains their plight to the Ewoks and persuades them to join the fight. After the battle is won the Ewoks and the rebels return to the village to celebrate. Two days later, on a wooden walkway of Bright Tree Village, Han Solo proposes to Princess Leia. She accepts, and the Ewoks host the joyful ceremony in the village temple built into the Great Tree. Luke Skywalker officiates as the two rebels wed.

ENDOR BUNKER SECRET ENTRANCE

LOCATION Endor

When Han Solo and the rebel forces debate how to infiltrate the secret entrance to the Empire's shield generator bunker, an Ewok named Paploo takes it upon himself to steal an Imperial speeder bike and create a diversion. The rebels then attempt to take the bunker and a back-and-forth ensues in which the Ewoks once again prove their worth. They are instrumental in winning the ground battle that rages outside the bunker entrance. The rebels are eventually able to trick the officers guarding the interior of the facility into opening the blast doors. Once inside, they place charges and destroy the entire complex.

298 LOCATIONS

VARDOS
REGION Core
SYSTEM Jinata
TERRAIN Mountains, oceans

Known for its red soil, mountains, and blue oceans, Vardos' natural beauty exists in stark contrast to its Imperial presence. Shortly after the Clone Wars, Garrick Versio unites the Jinata system—including the once-independent Vardos—under the Empire. The planet becomes an Imperial cradle, with installations, training grounds, and military bases. The capital, Kestro, is home to the Future Imperial Leaders Military Preparatory School and Jinata Security's headquarters. Despite Vardos' loyalty to the Empire, it is razed during the Emperor's last command, Operation: Cinder.

PILLIO
REGION Core
SYSTEM Jinata
TERRAIN Waterfalls, ocean, coral reef

Though uncolonized, Pillio teems with life and secrets that are important to the galaxy. Gorgeous waterfalls litter its landscape. A huge coral reef spans the planet and is a chief food source for the Jinata system. Luke Skywalker is drawn to Pillio, where he meets Inferno Squad's Del Meeko. Together, they find one of the Emperor's observatories, where Luke recovers a mysterious compass. Years later, Del, now with the Resistance, returns to the planet but is captured by the First Order. Del is interrogated by Kylo Ren, before his old squadmate Gideon Hask enacts his revenge and kills Del.

VAR-SHAA
REGION Mid Rim
SECTOR Dustig
TERRAIN Mountains, fjords

Located in the Mid Rim, Var-Shaa is known for its expansive fjords, as well as an orbiting Imperial dockyard. Following the Battle of Endor, the once pivotal waypoint for the Imperial Navy falls to an attack by the New Republic. When the Empire calls a retreat, Titan Squadron's Varko Gray is chased to the planet's surface by an X-wing hunting for survivors. Varko outlasts his pursuer in a chase through Var-Shaa's narrow mountain ranges but crashes into water and barely makes it to land. Watching the stunning sunset, however, his commitment to the Empire renews, and a rescue party arrives.

VESPAARA
REGION Outer Rim
SECTOR Suolriep
TERRAIN Mountains, rock

The rocky oasis of Vespaara is home to the notorious Hunters of the Outer Rim tournament. The arena, which hosts the contest, is located at the planet's southern pole, perpetually angled away from the sun and basked in an eternal twilight. This makes it the perfect location to showcase the arena's round-the-clock events, which draw all manner of combatants, from bounty hunters to Force-attuned beings. The world is also known for a mysterious aura effect in the sky that constantly shifts and reforms, appearing like the sinister red and purple eyes of some unknown entity, staring down and always watching.

PAGODON
REGION Outer Rim
SECTOR Pelgrin
TERRAIN Arctic tundra, ice

Pagodon is a remote planet in the Outer Rim and an ideal hiding place for nefarious citizens of the galaxy. Its frigid climate and icy landscape make for inhospitable terrain and difficult travel. There are some settlements, like Ferryman's Reach, where inhabitants can get a meal or enjoy a drink, but the population mostly consists of travelers. Underneath the planet's frozen surface dwell ravinaks, who make travel even more treacherous and inconvenient. Boardwalks between dwellings are designed to muffle vibrations that can reverberate beneath the ice, potentially alerting the fanged predators.

AQ VETINA
REGION Outer Rim
SECTOR Relgim
TERRAIN Terrestrial

Aq Vetina is a planet in the Outer Rim. A human settlement on the planet is attacked during the Clone Wars by a battalion of super battle droids operating under the jurisdiction of the Separatist army. During the particularly vicious raid, the population is destroyed except for one lone survivor—a young boy named Din Djarin. A group of Mandalorians fight against the droid invaders and rescue the child, flying him to safety. Din is raised as a foundling by members of this Mandalorian faction, but he still remembers the trauma of that fateful day.

ARVALA-7
REGION Outer Rim **SECTOR** Sevetta
TERRAIN Desert

A remote desert planet with a textured, rocky landscape, Arvala-7 is sparsely populated with a few different inhabitants. Din Djarin arrives and meets the Ugnaught Kuiil, who lives in isolation with a few blurrgs. His solitude is disturbed after a mysterious asset is secured in a small compound guarded by Nikto mercenaries. Kuiil leads Din to the compound but won't accept payment; he simply wants Arvala-7 to be restored to a more peaceful place. After the asset is obtained by Din, his vessel, the *Razor Crest*, is ransacked by a clan of Jawas. Kuiil brokers an uneasy alliance between the two, prompting Din to steal a mudhorn's egg in exchange for his ship parts. After completing the quest, Din leaves Arvala-7, earning a friend in Kuiil.

Harsh terrain
The muddy, rocky surface of Arvala-7 is difficult to traverse without the assistance of a blurrg mount. Din Djarin crosses the desert with the help of the Ugnaught Kuiil and his blurrgs.

> "The way is impossible to pass without a blurrg mount."
> **KUIIL TO DIN DJARIN**

NEVARRO

REGION Outer Rim
SECTOR Dalicron
TERRAIN Volcanic and ash-ridden

Despite its volcanic rivers and lava fields, Nevarro is a thriving trading hub connected to the super-hyperroute, the Hydian Way. It has changed hands multiple times in its tumultuous history.

BUSY TRADING POST

Once home to an Imperial base, Nevarro is now overseen by the Magistrate Greef Karga. Nevarro has a rich history for a planet located in the Outer Rim. It has a substantial population with a vibrant culture and a capital city that is a popular trading hub for commerce. The capital, Nevarro City, has several busy locations, including a bazaar for goods and services and a public safe house, as well as a cantina where Greef does business.

During the Galactic Civil War, the planet is controlled by the Empire. After the destruction of the second Death Star, Nevarro becomes an unruly place, filled with bounty hunters who work for Karga. He runs the Bounty Hunters Guild, hiring members out to any client willing to pay, even if they are Imperials working out of a local safe house. A customer, known only as the Client, requests one of Greef's hunters for a secret mission that requires the retrieval of an unknown asset, later revealed to be a child named Grogu.

MANDALORIANS AND IMPERIALS

Nevarro City has a secret Mandalorian covert hidden in an underground sewer system, which enables its people to travel in secret. The group is led by the Armorer, who institutes a rule that only one Mandalorian may go above ground at a time. Their original home of Mandalore was decimated during the Great Purge, which dramatically dwindles their numbers, prompting them to remain hidden. Nevarro sees a recurrence of violence between Mandalorian and Imperial factions. Having retrieved the child and given it to the Imperials, Din Djarin then takes back Grogu from them. This reignites the conflict and causes the Mandalorian to betray the Bounty Hunters Guild.

Djarin escapes the planet and the Imperial remnant takes control of Nevarro, with Moff Gideon in charge. In order to keep Grogu safe from further Imperial pursuit, Din returns to Nevarro and allies with Karga and Cara Dune.

Djarin and his friends defeat Gideon and repel the Imperial invaders, prompting Greef to restore Nevarro to a respectable and secure planet, with Cara as his new marshal. The planet thrives under Greef's watchful eye and flourishes with schools, trade, and bustling commerce. Later, Carson Teva recruits Cara away from Nevarro and her role as marshal to work for the New Republic instead.

PIRATE THREAT

Once the Imperial threat has been vanquished, peace on Nevarro is maintained. The planet flourishes until invaders, led by Pirate King Gorian Shard, arrive and take control. Karga reaches out to Carson for aid from the New Republic. However, Greef had originally declined to join the New Republic, preferring Nevarro to remain independent. This bold, yet untimely decision, causes political red tape that prevents New Republic Requisitions officer Colonel Tuttle from sending aid to the planet, despite Carson's earnest plea. Teva turns to Din and the Mandalorians instead. They help to defeat the pirates and liberate the planet. In return, a grateful Greef offers the Mandalorians a significant plot of land, which they accept.

Frequent flier
Din Djarin arrives on a Nevarro landing platform, transporting yet another high-value bounty on board the *Razor Crest*— his customized military patrol craft.

Volcanic planet
Nevarro's rough terrain is ashen black due to the volcanic lava fields located both on the surface and below its upper crust. The rocky terrain is covered in hills and flats, making it more challenging to travel without reliable transportation.

> "Nevarro is a very fine planet."
> — GREEF KARGA

Blue planet
The *Razor Crest*, piloted by the Mandalorian, Din Djarin, enters the atmosphere on Nevarro. Despite the planet's sulfuric lava rivers, its atmosphere is breathable.

THE ROOST

REGION Outer Rim
SECTOR Bitrose

The Roost is a space station that serves as the primary base of a group of mercenaries led by Ranzar Malk. Its interior is full of spare parts for numerous starships, land transportation, and other equipment. Din Djarin travels to the Roost and is hired to help break the prisoner Qin out of a New Republic prison ship. The group of mercenaries betrays Din and temporarily imprisons him. Still, he escapes and places a tracker on Qin before he and his crew leave the prison ship and return to the Roost. A New Republic X-wing squadron intercepts the distress signal of the tracking device and follows the signal to the location. They open fire on the space station, destroying it and everyone on board.

GOR KORESH'S HONKY TONK

LOCATION RTK111

Gor Koresh's Honky Tonk is located on the planet RTK111 where the titular gangster profits from illegal gladiator fights. Entry into the establishment requires an invitation or password from Gor Koresh or one of his associates. The Honky Tonk is filled with unsavory characters from all over the galaxy who are as likely to place a friendly wager with a patron as they are to kill them for the slightest reason. In the center of the Honky Tonk is a fighting ring where Gor Koresh runs a gladiator pit for Gamorrean guards and other aliens to fight to the death. Gor Koresh has been known to interfere with the proceedings, even killing participants if he feels like it.

MOS PELGO

LOCATION Tatooine

In the north of Tatooine, Mos Pelgo is a small community led by Marshal Cobb Vanth. After the destruction of the second Death Star, Red Key raiders invade the city but are ultimately defeated because of Vanth and the Mandalorian armor he purchased from Jawas. A krayt dragon terrorizes Mos Pelgo, threatening all its citizens. Cobb teams up with Din Djarin to destroy the beast in exchange for Cobb returning the Mandalorian armor to its people. Later, Cad Bane arrives and guns down Vanth because the marshal won't allow the Pyke Syndicate to run spice through the town. This devastating action inspires the people of Mos Pelgo to team up with Boba Fett to defeat the criminal organization.

MALDO KREIS

REGION Outer Rim **SECTOR** Arkanis **TERRAIN** Ice

Maldo Kreis is a frigid, ice-covered planet that is largely unexplored. The world is honeycombed with extensive caves and caverns that are almost impossible to traverse without assistance. The only known inhabitants of these underground systems are large egg-laying ice spiders, which are highly dangerous to organic beings. Din Djarin is forced to crash-land on the planet after being pursued by New Republic X-wings. He is attacked by ice spiders before being rescued by Carson Teva and Trapper Wolf.

TRASK

REGION Outer Rim
SECTOR Arkanis
SYSTEM Kol Iben
PRIMARY TERRAIN Aquatic

Trask is a watery moon covered by oceans. Its inhabitants are largely Mon Calamari and Quarren colonists who prefer to stay on the remote oceanic world rather than become embroiled in political affairs on their respective homeworlds. An Imperial remnant operates on Trask, collecting parts and equipment for its troops. The moon is also home to talented mechanics who are happy to repair even the most damaged of ships for a fee. Din Djarin crashes into the moon's waters and is fished out by one such mechanic. He teams up with Bo-Katan Kryze, Axe Woves, and Koska Reeves to steal weapons from an Imperial freighter to aid their quest to reclaim Mandalore.

CORVUS

REGION Outer Rim **SECTOR** Cronese Mandate **TERRAIN** Forest

Corvus is a forest-covered planet in the Outer Rim that is home to the city of Calodan. Several years after the defeat of the Empire, Calodan is taken over by the self-appointed Magistrate Morgan Elsbeth. She leads the city with cruelty and torture, keeping the city's people destitute and living in fear. Ahsoka Tano besieges the Magistrate, so Morgan hires the Mandalorian Din Djarin to kill her. Djarin and Ahsoka have a different plan and team up to defeat Morgan and her enforcer, Lang. Ahsoka turns Morgan in to the New Republic, and Governor Wing resumes control of Calodan, returning peace and kindness to its people.

KARTHON

REGION Outer Rim **SECTOR** Zuma **TERRAIN** Junkyards

Karthon is a prison moon that contains the Karthon Chop Fields. During the days of the Galactic Civil War, materials from Karthon are used to build the second Death Star. Following the war, the scrapyard is full of decommissioned Imperial machinery that is being dismantled by inmates who are serving sentences from the New Republic. The Chop Fields are policed by N5 sentry droids who keep the prisoners on task. Prisoner Migs Mayfeld is sentenced to fifty years here, but he is released into the custody of Marshal Cara Dune on the condition that he helps her and Din Djarin find Moff Gideon's light cruiser.

MORAK

REGION Wild Space **TERRAIN** Rainforest

Morak is a largely unknown planet that Imperial remnants occupy to rebuild their military forces in a bid to return to their former glory. The remnants mine the planet's meager deposits of a valuable mineral, rhydonium, and take it to a refinery for processing. Rhydonium is highly volatile and hazardous if placed next to repulsor technology. During a covert mission to infiltrate the refinery and use an Imperial terminal to locate Moff Gideon's light cruiser, former Imperial marksman Migs Mayfeld fires Boba Fett's cycler rifle at rhydonium, igniting the explosive material and destroying the Imperial settlement in the process. As a reward for his help, Cara Dune officially reports Mayfeld as killed in action so he can be freed from his New Republic prison sentence and start a new life.

TYTHON

REGION Deep Core **SECTOR** Sector 5
TERRAIN Plains, cliffs, deserts

Tython is a mysterious planet in the remote regions of the Deep Core that is strong in the Force. It is rarely visited due to its great distance from charted hyperlanes. Still, the enigmatic power it contains has drawn visitors over time. Many years ago, some Jedi scholars believed Tython was the location of the first Jedi temple, when in reality that was Ahch-To. Sometime after the Battle of Yavin, Doctor Chelli Aphra escorts Darth Vader to Tython to distract him from finding the rebel base on Hoth.

Following the demise of the Empire, Din Djarin is sent to Tython by Ahsoka Tano. She instructs him to find a sacred Seeing Stone there and place Grogu on it. The mysterious rock is carved with ancient text and, once the youngling sits on top of it, the Seeing Stone is enveloped by a mystical energy shield that cannot be penetrated until it is deactivated. A few years later, Jedi Master Luke Skywalker meditates on the Seeing Stone and has a vision of the Sith planet of Exegol.

Overwhelmed by the Force
Grogu collapses with immense exhaustion on the Seeing Stone after connecting with the Force. The mystical platform is an ideal conduit for Force amplification.

LAFETE

REGION Outer Rim **SECTOR** Tunka **TERRAIN** Desert

Lafete is a desert-covered planet with many industrial factories. It features a diner for weary travelers looking for a meal and some peace and quiet. Years after the defeat of the Empire, Boba Fett and Din Djarin travel to Lafete to find warriors to help them retrieve Grogu from Moff Gideon. Bo-Katan Kryze and Koska Reeves sit at a table in the diner and listen to Din's invitation. Due to Boba Fett's clone heritage, he is mocked by the Mandalorians and takes exception to Koska Reeve's preening. The two get into a skirmish but are quickly separated by a frustrated Bo-Katan, who laments that Mandalorians didn't show a similar fight when the Empire destroyed their planet of Mandalore.

GLAVIS RINGWORLD

REGION Core **TERRAIN** Urban

The Glavis Ringworld is a massive artificial circular structure that surrounds a star. Energy from the star continuously bombards the space station, powering the Glavis Ringworld in perpetuity. To create a natural day cycle, eclipse plates slide into place and simulate an artificial night. After Grogu leaves Din Djarin to train with Luke Skywalker, Din is led to the space station to collect a bounty; while there, he is also hoping to find members of his tribe, the Followers of the Way. He discovers the Armorer and Paz Vizsla in hiding there and shares tales of his journey with Grogu. Djarin is challenged by Paz for the Darksaber but defeats him. Once Din reveals that he has removed his helmet in the company of others, he is dismissed and told he is no longer a Mandalorian until he bathes in the Living Waters on Mandalore.

MOS ESPA CITY HALL

LOCATION Tatooine

As one of the largest settlements on Tatooine, Mos Espa has a sizeable city hall where vital civic functions are housed. After entering through the main door, visitors are held at a reception and may normally only enter the mayor's office if they have an appointment. The mayor's room has a lockable door and more than one exit, should any of the staff need to make a speedy getaway. During the New Republic era, the corrupt Ithorian Mayor Mok Shaiz holds court from a lush throne where he holds a tense meeting with the new daimyo, Boba Fett.

GARSA'S SANCTUARY

LOCATION Tatooine

Madame Garsa Fwip's Sanctuary is a popular cantina in Mos Espa. Patrons enjoy a hearty libation in her swanky establishment. It is an ideal place to do business or enjoy a range of leisure activities, including gambling, while listening to the dulcet tones of Max Rebo on his red ball jett organ. During their visit, guests can even get their helmets serviced and cleaned. When Boba Fett becomes the Daimyo of Tatooine, Fwip agrees to his new leadership. However, she pays a high price as the Sanctuary's peace is first disrupted and then the building is destroyed by criminals who disapprove of Fett's new role.

ARMORER'S PLANET

TERRAIN Rocks, mountains

The Armorer's planet is a place of great mystery, danger, and beauty. The surface is covered with rocky terrain that is fairly easy to circumnavigate. The planet is full of caves that are ideal for hideouts, which the Armorer and her peers take full advantage of. The wise leader of the Followers of the Way takes refuge on the planet. The Great Forge is placed in one of the caves, providing the Armorer ample opportunity to create armor and weapons, as well as dispense wisdom. The planet has a variety of wildlife, including flying raptors, who swoop down upon unsuspecting prey to serve up to their offspring for their next meal.

KALEVALA

REGION Outer Rim
SECTOR Mandalore
SYSTEM Mandalore
TERRAIN Cliffs, hills

Near the planet Mandalore, Kalevala is the homeworld of House Kryze. Despite its grandeur and beauty, the planet has a complicated history with many tragic incidents befalling its leaders. Prince Tal Merrik is a Republic senator of Kalevala who secretly works for the Death Watch—a group of Mandalorian insurgents who disagree with Duchess Satine Kryze's pacifist philosophy. Tal makes attempts on Satine's life and is killed by Jedi Knight Anakin Skywalker. Although Mandalore is bombarded by the Empire during the Great Purge, Kalevala remains relatively unscathed. Satine's sister, Bo-Katan Kryze, retires to the family castle after giving up hope that Mandalore can be reclaimed or restored. Her castle is attacked by TIE bombers under the orders of Moff Gideon, and she leaves Kalevala with Din Djarin.

OSSUS

REGION Outer Rim **SECTOR** Auril **SYSTEM** Adega
TERRAIN Forests, hills

Ossus is the location of a Jedi school built by Jedi Master Luke Skywalker. While exploring ruins on the planet, Luke stumbles upon the legendary Rammahgon text, which was believed to have been destroyed more than five thousand years earlier. He begins in earnest to rebuild the legacy of the Jedi, creating a temple on Ossus, complete with a school to teach a new generation of Knights. Luke uses ant droids to begin the construction of his temple, which will be a dome-shaped structure. Early on, while it is being built, Luke trains his first student, the child Grogu, who has a strong connection to the Force. The two live on Ossus in relative solitude, with the occasional visit from Ahsoka Tano. Din Djarin arrives on Ossus to give Grogu a custom-made beskar vest for protection, but he is persuaded by Ahsoka that his presence will only derail Grogu's commitment to his training. Grogu ultimately decides to rejoin Din, leaving Luke on the lookout for other students.

Years later, Luke's school begins to flourish, particularly with his nephew and best student, Ben Solo. Whenever Luke has to leave Ossus to aid his friends, Ben is a more than capable surrogate instructor, although he is reluctant to take on the task. Luke and Ben leave together on several missions but always return to Ossus.

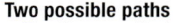

Two possible paths
Luke Skywalker offers Grogu a critical choice: take one of Master Yoda's lightsabers and stay on Ossus, or select the beskar armor and return to the Mandalorian, forsaking the ways of the Jedi.

One night, almost 30 years after the Empire is defeated, Luke's concern for the growing darkness he senses in his nephew escalates to a point where Luke ignites his lightsaber for a brief moment, before immediately regretting his overreaction and turning off the blade. Unfortunately, Ben believes his uncle is going to murder him, and he is overcome with feelings of rage and betrayal. He fights Luke and destroys the temple in the process, ending Luke's dreams of a new Jedi Order and catapulting himself onto the path of the dark side. Ben departs Ossus and seeks out Snoke to begin a new life.

KRYZE FORTRESS

LOCATION Kalevala

Kryze Fortress is the ancestral home and dwelling place of the House of Kryze, the noble and respected family of Mandalore. The fortress is a majestic castle that sits on a hillside adjacent to the sea. In the era of the New Republic, Bo-Katan Kryze lives here in near solitude, reflecting on the missteps of her past and the inability of her people to keep Mandalore free from Imperial tyranny and destruction. The desolate fortress features striking murals of legendary Mandalorian battles; a reminder of their former glory. A landing platform and courtyard at the back of the castle are where guests arrive, although there are not many. Bo-Katan and Din Djarin journey to Mandalore to learn of the planet's condition. They soon return to the fortress, pursued by TIE interceptors, which they destroy in aerial combat. However, the location is besieged by TIE bombers, turning the once-great structure to rubble.

CONCORDIA

REGION Outer Rim **SECTOR** Mandalore **SYSTEM** Mandalore
TERRAIN Forest, mountains, caves

As a moon of Mandalore, Concordia plays an important role in Mandalorian history. During the wars, the mountainous and forest-covered moon is mined extensively, and its lush forests are all but wiped out. Only during the Clone Wars do they begin to grow back. In time, Concordia becomes a Mandalorian province, with its own governor and dialect. The moon is also the secret home of Death Watch—a group of militants who are seeking to restore Mandalore's warrior identity, under the leadership of Governor Pre Vizsla. While Mandalore later falls to the Empire, Concordia remains independent.

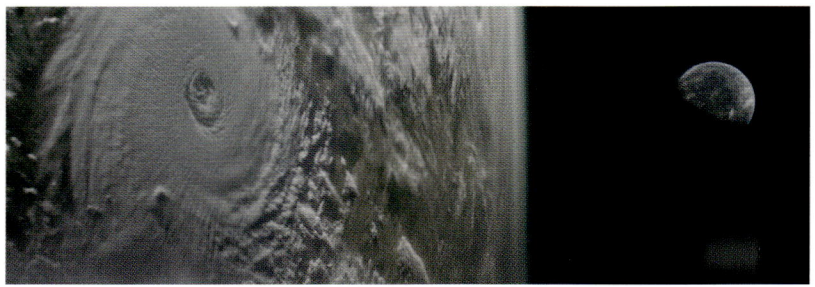

LIVING WATERS OF MANDALORE

LOCATION Mandalore

A sacred and ceremonial body of water, the Living Waters of Mandalore rest below the once-great Civic Center in the city of Sundari on Mandalore. The location is sacrosanct to the Mandalorian people and is a place of important rituals and celebrations. For Followers of the Way, bathing in the Living Waters is the only way to be redeemed if they remove their helmet, whether deliberately or due to battle. Din Djarin and Bo-Katan Kryze are the first to rediscover the Living Waters after the Great Purge. Din walks into the waters and suddenly plunges into the depths, falling unconscious. Bo-Katan dives in to save him and stumbles upon a submerged Mythosaur—a legendary creature believed to be long extinct. It watches her with a knowing eye. The incident transforms Bo-Katan into a believer as a result.

MONUMENT PLAZA

LOCATION Coruscant

Monument Plaza has the distinction of being the only place on Coruscant where the planet's original surface can still be seen. The square-shaped plaza surrounds the rocky tip of Umate—the only visible mountain peak on the world. Four large cone-shaped statues are lit around Umate, adding to the grandeur. Due to its iconography and novelty, Monument Plaza is surrounded by dining and shopping opportunities. The Plaza has existed for a long time and moves up a level as the city grows and expands. The spectacle of a city-covered planet is no match for the beauty that reflects what the planet must have looked like several millennia ago. Duchess Satine Kryze and Obi-Wan Kenobi meet in the plaza when Satine is framed for a murder she did not commit.

ADELPHI

REGION Outer Rim **SECTOR** Kibilini
TERRAIN Beaches, mountains

The planet Adelphi is an outpost for New Republic pilots and officers. Captain Carson Teva is stationed there, along with several of his peers in Adelphi Squadron. As a member of the Adelphi Rangers, Carson works with the New Republic to protect its citizens. Above Adelphi, Carson and his squadmate Trapper Wolf encounter a wayward Razor Crest as they search for those who served under the Empire. The outpost features a popular watering hole for off-duty New Republic pilots and is a good place for intergalactic interlopers looking for help. In addition to Carson and Trapper, heroes of the Rebellion Garazeb Orrelios, Jib Dodger, and Sash Ketter have been known to frequent the comfortable establishment.

PLAZIR-15

REGION Outer Rim
SECTOR Unincorporated
SYSTEM Plazir
TERRAIN Domed city, grass plains

Plazir-15 is a hospitable planet of lush landscapes and forests. Despite this natural beauty, its inhabitants prefer to live in artificial bio-domes connected by a hyperloop system. Throughout Plazir-15's history, citizens have been governed by an unelected monarchy. But when the Duchess comes into power, she and her husband, Captain Bombardier, transform the political system into a democracy, with citizens voting for elected officials. At the first election, the Duchess and her husband are selected to be the rulers. When the Empire falls and the New Republic is created, Plazir-15 elects to remain independent and doesn't join the New Republic charter.

ARCANA

REGION Outer Rim **SECTOR** Lahara **TERRAIN** Ruins

Arcana was once the site of a Nightsister temple, but now it is a desolate place of fallen columns and crumbling walls. Ahsoka Tano visits the ancient world to explore the temple's expansive ruins. She sweeps through subterranean chambers in search of a device that will unlock a map, pinpointing the location of Grand Admiral Thrawn and Ezra Bridger. The ruins' shadowy corners provide ideal cover for Morgan Elsbeth's HK-87 assassin droids, who are also looking for the same object, to launch an unexpected attack on Ahsoka.

SANTHE SHIPYARDS

LOCATION Corellia

The operations of the Santhe shipyards have changed often as the political power in the galaxy has shifted. Before the Empire's rule, civilians run the Corellian shipyards. Then the Empire takes over and uses the shipyard for manufacturing *Imperial*-class Star Destroyers. With the formation of the New Republic after the Galactic Civil War, the shipyard's military assets are redistributed. Some are disassembled, and some are repurposed for the New Republic's needs. Although former Imperials eschew their ties to the Empire and make oaths to the New Republic, loyalists still hide among the population, and Santhe shipyards is no exception.

SEATOS

REGION Outer Rim **SECTOR** Sluis **SYSTEM** Denab **TERRAIN** Red forests, oceans

Dense red forests and sprawling oceans cover the surface of Seatos, with tall cliffs stretching up from the ocean's edges. Standing stones loom over one cliff, forming a henge that works in conjunction with a Dathomirian star map to point the way to another galaxy. Morgan Elsbeth establishes Star Navigator droids at this location to map the Pathway to Peridea. The trees provide much needed cover for Ahsoka Tano and Sabine Wren as they attempt to take Morgan's forces by surprise. However, they end up fighting Marrok and Shin Hati in the forest. Elsewhere, Baylan Skoll defeats Ahsoka in a duel.

PERIDEA

REGION Extragalactic
TERRAIN Grasslands, lakes, wastelands

With a surface covered in barren wastelands and lakes, the extragalactic planet of Peridea is an unassuming location for the subject of Jedi legend and children's tales. Purrgil take a migratory path from the galaxy that is governed by the New Republic to the far-flung galaxy in which Peridea is situated. However, they end their journey only to perish—a large ring of purrgil bones surrounds Peridea, giving the planet a natural barrier. Roving groups of bandits and the nomadic Noti species call the planet home. Dotted with crumbling statues, Peridea holds countless mysteries and is said to be the home of the ancient Witch Kingdom of the Dathomiri.

At some point after purrgil take Grand Admiral Thrawn and Ezra Bridger away from Lothal, the enemies find themselves on Peridea. There, three Dathomiri witches named the Great Mothers begin working with Grand Admiral Thrawn on a mystical plan. They call across the galaxy to their sisterhood. Morgan Elsbeth answers and finds a way to travel to Peridea with an intergalactic hyperspace ring. Although Thrawn and the Great Mothers leave Peridea, others stay behind to further explore Peridea's secrets.

PERIDEA FORTRESS

LOCATION Peridea

Jutting above Peridea's surface, a time-worn stone fortress hosts the Great Mothers and Grand Admiral Thrawn's forces. Its origins are unknown, but the temple has inscriptions honoring the reign of Kujet, the Zeffo Sage, who has connections to Dathomir. The Great Mothers put the large fortress and its underground tunnels to use as a Dathomiri temple. They fill the catacombs with secret cargo as part of their alliance with Thrawn. A circular henge sits on top of the fortress and marks the end point of the Pathway to Peridea, which begins in a near-identical henge on Seatos.

Mysterious monuments
Towering statues loom over Peridea's watery landscape. The ancient civilization they represent has been lost to time and decay.

MONUMENT TO THE ONES
LOCATION Peridea

Tucked into a valley in Peridea's rocky wastelands and plains are three statues. Two of the towering monuments have visages of the Father and the Son—the gods of Mortis. A third monument, perhaps of the Daughter, is missing its head. The statues' connection to Mortis is as yet unknown. The planet Peridea may hold the answers to many mysteries. Baylan Skoll calls the planet "a place of dreams and madness" and "the subject of legend," and he seeks some kind of higher purpose there. On his quest, he makes a solitary pilgrimage to the Monument to the Ones.

HAYS MINOR
REGION Outer Rim **SECTOR** Prefsbelt
SYSTEM Otomok **TERRAIN** Rock

According to Rose Tico of the Resistance, her homeworld, Hays Minor, is "known more for its ore than its people." And that is very dangerous for the mining planet. The desolate world catches the attention of the First Order, which employs converted bombers to mine more deeply and violently than anyone else has. Soon, Hays Minor becomes polluted and its skies ruined. Not long after Rose and her sister Paige flee to join the Resistance, they learn that the First Order has ripped the planet apart, taking the remaining Tico family with it. With encouragement from General Leia Organa, the sisters remain with the Resistance.

OVANIS
REGION Outer Rim **SECTOR** Pacanth Reach **TERRAIN** Mountains, caves, rock

Densely covered in mountains, Ovanis is not the most welcoming of worlds. Still, it is home to the Crèche—a group of cultists who worship a glowing blue egg and believe a savior will hatch from it. Ovanis becomes the site of the first mission for Poe Dameron's newly minted Black Squadron. But the unit's presence draws the First Order to the planet. When troopers attempt to destroy the Crèche's egg, a towering blue winged creature emerges. A similar black being appears, however, killing the hatchling, and the Crèche depart Ovanis on its back.

MEGALOX BETA
REGION Expansion **SECTOR** Bes Ber Bikade
TERRAIN Rock

Megalox Beta has an attractive yellow-green hue from space, but the planet's surface is less inviting. The world is so enormous and dense that its gravity is ten times standard, making it uninhabitable. Nevertheless, it is the site of the private prison named Megalox. Run by Warden Luta, the complex features an artificial gravity field with no walls. Should any inmates venture outside, they would be crushed by the gravitational force. Poe Dameron leads Black Squadron on a mission to Megalox in his search for Lor San Tekka. He successfully frees Grakkus the Hutt in exchange for information.

KADDAK
REGION Outer Rim **SECTOR** Tammuz **TERRAIN** Rock, dirt, crystal

Kaddak is a notoriously dangerous planet, home to criminals and scoundrels of all sorts. Even the New Republic cannot take control of the world as one of its fleets is entirely destroyed during a confrontation. A giant pinkish crystal is a notable landmark and forms the heart of the Sliver: a connected series of developments divided into levels that host apartments and cantinas. Poe Dameron leads a mission to Kaddak to rescue a spy droid. At the same time, Agent Terex of the First Order returns to the planet to resume his leadership of the Ranc Gang, whose headquarters are also there.

SPALEX
REGION Outer Rim
SECTOR Dantus
TERRAIN Plains, forest

Spalex has a unique appearance. The planet has a landscape of red grassy plains and trees and green skies. Its people build their homes in a pod-grid, which sits at tree level and spans great distances. Spalex also holds a large vein of the mineral thorilide, which the locals use to power their technology. Unlike many worlds, the Spalexians succeed in stopping the Empire from mining their precious resource, and they do the same when the First Order comes knocking. Resistance agents go to the planet to document First Order atrocities, leading to a major clash in the Spalex atmosphere.

PASTORIA
REGION Outer Rim
SECTOR Juris
TERRAIN Plains, forest

Considered one of the most beautiful worlds in the galaxy, Pastoria is covered in rolling green hills, trees, and its people's stunning architecture. The Pastorians are insectlike, and their ships are designed to match. During the rise of the First Order, Black Squadron visits Pastoria to meet with King Siroc, in the hopes that he will align his planet with the Resistance. The king seems eager to become an ally, but asks the pilots to eliminate a rival. Upon completion of the mission, Siroc reveals he has no intention of challenging the First Order, believing it to be unstoppable.

IKKRUKK
REGION Mid Rim
SECTOR Ryndellian
TERRAIN Mountains, clouds

Despite an unforgiving terrain of mountains, uneven rock, and low-set clouds, Ikkrukk has a thriving population. Its people live within Grail City, protected by a domelike shield, and are under the leadership of a local called Grist. Technologically advanced, the city has a robust defense grid, including orbital and ground-based cannons and hunter-killer droids, until a First Order invasion knocks it all out. Grist contacts the Resistance for help, and Black Squadron answers the call, driving back the First Order and solidifying an alliance with Ikkrukk.

STARKILLER BASE

REGION Unknown Regions **SECTOR** Mobile **SYSTEM** Mobile
TERRAIN Snowy mountains, forests, ice fields

Eventually known as Starkiller Base, this world used to be known as Ilum. It was a sacred planet for the Jedi Order and the main source of their kyber crystals. During the Imperial era, the Empire begins mining the world, work that continues under the First Order, which transforms the planet into a superweapon.

A MYSTERIOUS WORLD
The inhospitable world of Ilum is the principal source of kyber crystals, which are found in many lightsabers. An ancient Jedi temple marks the exit from the dim caverns where the crystals are located, and it's here that Jedi younglings are brought for a ritual to find a crystal individually suited to them.

NEW OWNERSHIP
When the Empire takes over, it destroys the temple so it can easily access the crystals for its own destructive use and begins strip-mining the planet. Some Jedi survivors, including Cal Kestis and Luke Skywalker, visit the world during this bleak time for the Order.

Engineering masterpiece
An icy, eerie globe constructed to be a devastating weapon, Starkiller Base is a menacing benchmark of the First Order's advanced technological achievements.

STAR POWER
Following the Empire's fall, the First Order claims Ilum as its own. The group harvests the remaining crystals and repurposes the planet as a mobile weapon of unimaginable power. Renamed Starkiller Base, the superweapon is the central symbol of mighty military power in Supreme Leader Snoke's expanding forces. Once the Starkiller weapon is fully charged, it projects a beam of energy from its firing shaft through hyperspace at speeds faster than light. The blinding red beam is capable of destroying entire star systems on the other side of the galaxy. General Armitage Hux inaugurates Starkiller Base by using it to annihilate the Hosnian system, including the New Republic's capital on Hosnian Prime. Unlike the Empire's Death Star, Starkiller Base does not need to travel to the vicinity of the intended target to fire upon it with precision. This gives the First Order an unparalleled tactical advantage.

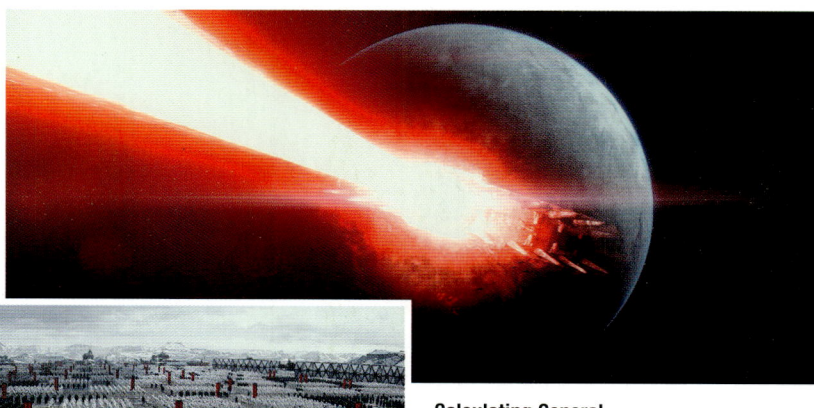

Calculating General
General Hux makes a speech to troops assembled in the parade ground before the weapon is fired. However, the destruction of Hosnian Prime is no mere display of First Order power. Hux calculates that the unexpected atrocity will force the Resistance to respond, and thus reveal the location of their secret base—and the First Order's next target.

> "We're not sure how to describe a weapon of this scale."
> — TEMMIN "SNAP" WEXLEY

Draining a sun
The Starkiller superweapon, based on top-secret Imperial research, rapidly drains and pulls a host star's energy into its core using a collector on the surface. There, the energy is held in a containment field where it is stabilized and regulated by a thermal oscillator, before being unleashed on the intended target or targets.

LIFE ON THE BATTLE STATION
Starkiller Base is well guarded. Assault walkers, TIE fighters, and snowtroopers aboard speeders regularly patrol the planet's surface. Inside the base, First Order officers command impressive barracks of stormtroopers. They are supported by sentry and patrol droids, which sweep corridors, storage bays, and landing platforms. However, danger is still ever-present on the base: despite decades of research and cutting-edge technology, a planet is not an ideal vessel to hold the power of a sun. Tremendous storms and tectonic disturbances are a constant problem. Charging the weapon subjects one half of the planet's surface to dangerous radiation, while firing the weapon sends a shockwave that obliterates vast expanses of forest on the other half.

STARKILLER'S DEMISE
Threatened with the impending destruction of the Resistance base on D'Qar, Han Solo and his friends race to Starkiller Base aboard the *Millennium Falcon*. Once inside, Han, Finn, and Chewbacca capture Captain Phasma and force her to drop the Starkiller's shields. After locating Rey, who had been taken prisoner but escaped, the team detonates explosives, creating a hole in the armored housing of Starkiller's thermal oscillator. Pilot Poe Dameron destroys the thermal oscillator, which destabilizes the containment field and causes an energy breach. The entire planet implodes, then ignites in a riot of color and light.

Angry prisoner
After switching off the shields, the captive Captain Phasma warns Han and Finn that their plan will be hard to pull off, and that her troops will storm the block and kill them.

Fiery inferno
A ferocious blaze rips through space as Starkiller Base explodes.

BATUU

REGION Outer Rim **SECTOR** Trilon **TERRAIN** Spires, forests, rivers, seas

The backwater world known as Batuu is a rustic garden planet, recognized as a last stop before the mysteries and dangers of Wild Space. Batuu is a place where explorers, bounty hunters, smugglers, and trailblazers stock up on supplies before their trek, or return and tell outrageous tales of adventure. Here, heroes and scoundrels forge their origins and, if they don't make it back from their escapades, their sagas are retold as legends in the cantinas and market squares.

The countryside of Batuu is unspoiled and wild. Surabat River Valley winds though a treacherous canyon of rock spires, rapids, and hairpin turns. Though largely undeveloped, Batuu is the site of an ancient trading post called Black Spire Outpost, which has served traders even before the dawn of hyperspace travel.

Black Spire Outpost is bustling with commerce. Droid repairs are available at Mubo's Droid Depot. Merchant Row and the Market have shops bursting with local wares and galactic oddities. Docking Bay 7 receives regular freighters full of tasty delights and fascinating cargo—but beware of Docking Bay 9, which is occupied by unfriendly forces!

During the Clone Wars, Anakin Skywalker comes to Batuu to search for his missing wife, Padmé Amidala. Here, he meets Commander Mitth'raw'nuruodo (Thrawn), who agrees to help Anakin find her. In the process, they learn that Padmé has discovered a Separatist base on Mokivj. Years later, Emperor Palpatine sends Anakin, now Darth Vader, and Grand Admiral Thrawn back to Batuu to investigate

a disturbance in the Force. There, they find that the Grysk, an enemy of Thrawn's own Chiss people and a potential threat to the Empire, has been kidnapping Force-adept children and enslaving them.

During the rise of the First Order, Batuu does not escape the regime's grasp. Desperate to track down the Resistance following their escape from Crait, the First Order stations a Star Destroyer in orbit above the planet. A smaller ground force patrols Black Spire Outpost, keeping an eye out for any Resistance spies. Resistance agent Vi Moradi sets up a base in ancient ruins near the edge of the trading post, providing a rendezvous point for the Resistance as they prepare to launch an attack. Despite the First Order's presence and the threat of imminent conflict, there are friends and allies to be found. Hondo Ohnaka, the infamous pirate with a big heart and an odd sense of humor, also makes a deal with the mighty Chewbacca to run a transportation company from one of the outpost's docking bays, using the *Millennium Falcon*. The escalating tensions lead to the Battle of Batuu where Resistance agents score a victory by defeating Kylo Ren's Star Destroyer.

CASTILON

REGION Outer Rim **SECTOR** Tashtor **TERRAIN** Open seas, isolated islands

Castilon is located on the border of the Outer Rim and Wild Space. The most notable destination on Castilon is the *Colossus*, a refueling station and trading outpost. Smaller inhabited platforms and floating vessels are scattered around the globe.

A number of battles have been fought above Castilon over successive millennia, resulting in many shipwrecks left on the sea floor. Deep in the planet's underwater Karavian Trench live gargantuan, tentacled beasts called rokkna, with four eyes and a notable smell. One such beast terrorizes *Colossus* station when her young is accidentally taken along with a salvaged underwater wreck, and then adopted as a pet by mechanic Neeku Vozo. Smaller seafood commonly caught by anglers include sharvo fish. Native speagulls are a constant companion to anglers, hoping for a handout or to steal a fish from their nets.

The most intelligent beings to rise from the depths on Castilon are the indigenous Chelidae. These amphibians carry large shells on their backs and are capable of clinging to walls. Their movements are slow, as is their manner of speech. They are friendly, despite the many offworlders who have come to exploit their homeworld, and act as engineers, maintaining Castilon's *Colossus* station.

When the New Republic discovers that the First Order has taken an interest in Castilon, its leaders send pilot Kazuda Xiono to deliver the information to Resistance captain, Poe Dameron. Though they are intercepted by the First Order's Major Elrik Vonreg, Kaz and Poe work together to fend him off. Poe then recruits Kaz to the Resistance and places him on Castilon as a spy. The First Order eventually forces the *Colossus* off Castilon. However, Kaz and his allies return when they want to reunite with their erstwhile friend, Tamara Ryvora.

AUNT Z'S TAVERN

LOCATION *Colossus* station

The eponymous Aunt Z's Tavern (owned by the Gilliand Z'Vk'Thkrkza) is the most popular cantina on the *Colossus*. Aunt Z is assisted by her service droid Glitch. The tavern has seating at the bar, in alcoves around the room, and on a balcony facing Doza Tower. Entertainment includes watching local races (and betting on them), two arcade areas, a holodart system, and a jukebox. The venue is decorated with flags featuring racer emblems, old battle helmets, and a reproduction of art from the nose of the *Crumb Bomber*, a Republic ship that once adorned Old Jho's Pit Stop on Lothal.

COLOSSUS PLATFORM

LOCATION Castilon

The *Colossus* is a supertanker fuel depot built by the Empire and is one of the few such platforms remaining during the New Republic era.

COMFORTABLE LIFE

For more than twenty years, the *Colossus* has been partially submerged on the ocean planet Castilon. The station's administrator is Captain Imanuel Doza, a former Imperial officer. He and his daughter, Torra Doza, reside in the elite Doza Tower. The station is defended by Ace Squadron, a starfighter pilot team whose members spend their ample free time engaging in races such as the famous Platform Classic. Captain Doza is keen to promote the events because the spectators bring much-needed business to the station. The members of Ace Squadron reside in luxurious suites in Doza Tower, which has an exclusive communal lounge.

THRIVING COMMUNITY

Colossus provides more than just starship fuel. It has a large resident community with merchants selling goods in an open market. The market provides for all of the residents' and visitors' basic needs, with vendors of food, clothing, trinkets, and wares from offworld. There are dining establishments and taverns such as Aunt Z's. Lodging is also available. Resident scavengers scour the seabed for old shipwrecks and process them at the station's loading docks. They sell their finds to the Office of Acquisitions, run by Flix and Orka. Their salvages provide a source of commerce on the station—parts for racers and the station itself—and they also supply local garages like the one owned by Jarek Yeager. Resistance spy Kazuda Xiono works for Yeager along with coworkers Neeku Vozo and Tamara Ryvora.

The engineers of *Colossus* are a group of indigenous Chelidae. They keep the station running and prove helpful allies for Kaz, in part because they move unseen in the depths of the station and know much of what goes on in every corner.

UNEASY ALLIANCE

The First Order takes a keen interest in *Colossus*, desiring to use the platform as a staging ground for their growing military in preparation for an assault on the New Republic and the Resistance. Under the oversight of Captain Phasma, Major Elrik Vonreg and Commander Pyre hire Kragan Gorr and his pirate gang to harass *Colossus*. They pressure Captain Doza into contracting with the First Order to provide protection, in exchange for use of the platform. Realizing his own Ace Squadron is insufficient to handle the recurring pirate threat, Doza reluctantly agrees. The First Order soon takes over operations and all security on the platform, confining residents and arresting troublemakers. Kaz leads his friends at the station against the First Order occupiers. They sink the station, leaving only Doza Tower above water, but this fails to dissuade the First Order. When Kaz discovers that the station is actually a ship with a capable hyperdrive, he and Neeku activate the engines while Ace Squadron fights off the First Order's TIE fighters. Synara San leads Kragan's pirates and joins the *Colossus* residents in fighting off the First Order. They all then escape aboard the *Colossus* into hyperspace—though their final destination is unknown to all.

NEW PURPOSE

When the platform exits hyperspace far away from D'Qar and the Resistance, the residents of the *Colossus* have to work together to secure supplies and parts to keep their tanker flying. In spite of its age, the ship weathers multiple attacks by the First Order with Doza commanding from the bridge. Thanks to the Aces, the lucky platform always manages to escape before it is destroyed. After the First Order discovers a potential new home on Aeos Prime, Doza decides to formally join the Resistance and allows Jade Squadron, led by Imanuel's wife Venisa, to station on the *Colossus*. The platform later fights the First Order during the Battle of Barabesh.

The fast lane
Colossus is described by Resistance spy Kaz as a hangout for star pilots. During the station's Platform Classic race, pilots fly through a course of sky rings *(below, bottom)*.

Commercial Castilon
Colorful awnings running along the side of the *Colossus* cover the bustling marketplace *(right)*, which acts as a meeting place for locals such as dock worker Orthog and friendly Arcona Garma *(above)*.

LOCATIONS

JAKKU
REGION Inner Rim **SECTOR** Western Reaches
TERRAIN Desert wastelands, sand dunes, rocky outcrops

Jakku may be a desolate junkyard planet, but this barren world plays a pivotal role in ending the Empire. Decades later, the First Order arrives in search of Luke Skywalker—and inadvertently awakens the destiny of a young scavenger named Rey.

EARLY JAKKU
Once a forested world with seas full of varied life, Jakku has been rendered a barren globe by cataclysmic events. Darth Sidious believes ancient relics on the planet might hold a mysterious significance, so he orders an archaeological expedition. This site becomes an Imperial Observatory, housing a weapons facility, research base, and maps of secret navigational routes through the Unknown Regions. At the end of the Galactic Civil War, the New Republic discovers Imperial forces defending Jakku and the Observatory. Both sides engage in a major battle in space and on the planet itself. A portion of the Empire's forces escapes to the Unknown Regions, but, by the battle's end, the Empire has suffered a resounding defeat, and the war ends shortly afterward.

A NEW START
Young parents Dathan and Miramir relocate to Jakku when their daughter, Rey, is just a baby. They choose the sparsely populated planet so they can avoid the gaze of Sheev Palpatine, Dathan's genetic father, who wants Rey for his own malevolent ends. Miramir constructs droids from scavenged parts, while her husband Dathan builds their farmstead on the outskirts of Niima Outpost. The two form a business relationship with junk boss Unkar Plutt, trading salvage and water for almost five years before they're discovered by Palpatine's hunters. The family escapes, but after a short time on the run, Dathan and Miramir decide to trust Plutt with hiding the six-year-old Rey—for a price, of course.

Final Goodbye
Although the three of them don't realize this, poor Rey will never see her parents again. They are soon killed by a Sith assassin.

Taking on the thugs
When Rey refuses to sell BB-8 to Unkar Plutt, the Crolute is very displeased. He sends his thugs to steal the astromech. However, the attackers soon realize that they are no match for Rey with her quarterstaff.

DANGEROUS WORLD
Jakku's deserts and settlements present all sorts of dangers. After Rey rescues BB-8 from a scrap-dealer, it's clear that the little droid would rather stick with her than take the risk of drowning in the Sinking Fields' sands or getting lost in Kelvin Ridge. The next day at Niima Outpost, Unkar's thugs attack Rey and try to steal BB-8, but Rey is more than a match for them. However, danger soon rears its ugly head again: just after Rey and BB-8 meet Finn, the First Order appears in search of the Resistance astromech. The newly formed team must dash through stalls and duck under tents to dodge TIE fighter fire before commandeering the *Millennium Falcon*. The Starship Graveyard becomes a perilous obstacle course as Rey pilots the *Falcon* through it, trying to escape the pursuing TIEs.

> "Why does everyone wanna go back to Jakku?" **FINN**

Starship Graveyard
Numerous ships belonging to both the New Republic and the Empire lay scattered and half-submerged in a graveyard of windswept sand dunes. The starships are a treasure trove of scrap for eager scavengers.

REY'S HOME
LOCATION Jakku

Inside the wreckage of an old Imperial AT-AT walker, dubbed the Hellhound 2, is Rey's home. Decades ago, it was assigned to the Imperial Star Destroyer *Interrogator* and served in the Battle of Jakku. Now it is lying on its side in the sands of the Goazon Badlands, and the young scavenger has heavily adapted the vehicle to serve as a functioning domicile. Rey primarily lives inside the troop compartment, which features a bedroom, kitchen, and work station. The rear compartment contains a garage for her speeder and the cockpit is a secure location for valuable items. Aside from Rey, few dare approach the crashed vehicle as it is well-known that the wily scavenger has laid many traps in its vicinity.

The view
Sitting in the shade of one of the AT-AT's enormous feet, Rey surveys the desert in her territory.

NIIMA OUTPOST
LOCATION Jakku

After the Battle of Jakku, profit-seeking Niima the Hutt founds an outpost to salvage hardware and supplies from the many shipwrecks, becoming one of Jakku's largest settlements. When Niima is assassinated, entrepreneur Unkar Plutt fills the void left in the local scrap trade. From his concession stand, Unkar barters food rations and water in return for Imperial and New Republic ship parts, computer systems, and supplies salvaged by scavengers of many species, including Dybrinthe, Abednedo, and humans. Lonely scavenger Rey is one such local, who searches old Star Destroyers for scrap parts, cleans them up, and trades them with greedy Unkar to earn a meager supply of food rations.

TUANUL VILLAGE
LOCATION Jakku

Historically, religious hermits have a long presence on Jakku. Tuanul Village is a commune of followers of the Force in the remote Kelvin Ravine. Noted explorer and traveler Lor San Tekka settles in Tuanul, but a fateful meeting with Resistance pilot Poe Dameron concerning the whereabouts of Luke Skywalker leads the First Order there. Blasters fire and dwellings burn as stormtroopers attack the village. Kylo Ren interrogates Lor San Tekka and captures Poe, before the stormtroopers are ordered to round up the villagers and kill them. Amid the resulting massacre, Poe's droid, BB-8, manages to escape with Lor San Tekka's partial map to Skywalker's location.

D'QAR
REGION Outer Rim
SECTOR Sanbra
SYSTEM Ileenium
TERRAIN Jungles, mountains, plains

D'Qar is located on the edge of the Mid Rim and Outer Rim, and is relatively close to both Naboo and Crait. Though there isn't any indigenous intelligent life there now, D'Qar once supported an ancient civilization, which is now extinct and whose once great cities have long since been consumed by the jungles. D'Qar serves as a small rebel outpost during the Galactic Civil War, and then serves as the Resistance headquarters until the Battle of Starkiller Base.

TAKODANA
REGION Western Reaches and Mid Rim
SECTOR Tashtor
TERRAIN Temperate forests, seas

Takodana is a peaceful garden world, relatively isolated between the Inner Rim and Outer Rim. It sits on a hyperspace route between Noe'ha'on and Chalcedon, and is connected to the Ring of Kafrene via the Biox Detour. Takodana is a haven for spacers and the disreputable on their way in and out of the galactic frontier. The planet is home to a Jedi temple outpost, until Nihil raiders destroy it during the era of the High Republic. Takodana has a sparse native population of less than one million. The largest city—which is still relatively small—is Andui. The planet has remained neutral in major conflicts and has not seen war for centuries, until the arrival of the Empire at the end of the Galactic Civil War.

LOCATIONS

Let me do the talking
Han Solo, Rey, Finn, and BB-8 head toward Maz's castle. Han warns them not to stare "at any of it."

MAZ KANATA'S CASTLE

LOCATION Takodana

For centuries, Maz Kanata offers refuge from all the troubles of the galaxy. Her fortress tavern is a safe haven for the weary, the hunted, travelers, explorers, dignitaries, and galactic entrepreneurs.

GOLDEN RULE
No fights are allowed on the premises, and any violation of Maz's cardinal rule will get guests banned or thrown into the dungeons below the castle. Maz provides food, lodging, and entertainment with live music and gambling. Her list of available services goes well beyond that however, with loans and appraisals, repairs, supplies, medical assistance, maps, and valuable information. Maz takes a percentage of all business deals made on her premises, which are collected by her droid, ME-8D9. While the first night's room and board is free, all must pay after that. The favorable conditions at the castle ensure many long-term guests, who lounge in the restaurant and bar for days on end and find it easy to forge new contacts in the cordial environment.

SECRET BUSINESS
The castle may be relatively peaceful under Maz's ownership, but it is still a hotbed of underworld activity. Maz herself has a legendary career in piracy, despite being equally renowned for her hospitality. She hosts high-stakes gambling, while bounty hunters, dealers in illicit merchandise, and pirates conduct unseemly deals at her tables and in private meeting rooms in the towers.

ANCIENT ARTIFACTS
Maz's basement is full of ancient relics—cultural artifacts and historical pieces, including items associated with the Jedi and other Force-wielders—with which she feels a connection. The castle itself sits on an ancient battleground of the Jedi and Sith, and its lower levels date from the Jedi occupation of Takodana.

FAVORITE GUESTS
During the High Republic era, Maz takes a liking to Jedi Sav Malagán, whom she meets when the Kyuzo Padawan joins her pirate crew. Decades later, and now a master, Sav leads the defense of Takodana when it is attacked by the Nihil.

Maz is particularly fond of smugglers Han Solo and Chewbacca, who are frequent visitors to her castle. While listless and hungover, Han meets fellow smuggler Sana Starros just outside the castle. After dispatching some Hassk mercenaries, Sana offers him a smuggling job before leaving. When she later returns to the castle with contraband in tow and bounty hunters hot on her tail, Sana, Han, and Chewbacca have to quickly flee aboard the *Millennium Falcon*.

Following the Battle of Endor, Han returns to the castle to meet an Imperial turncoat, who will be able to help him free Kashyyyk. When the Empire arrives, Han works with Inferno Squad to stop them.

CAUGHT IN THE MIDDLE
Decades later, Han brings Rey and Finn to meet his old friend Maz at her lakeside castle in hopes that she can help him transfer the droid BB-8 to Leia Organa (without actually dealing with Leia himself). The resident droid, GA-97, alerts the Resistance of BB-8's arrival at the castle, while bounty hunter Bazine Netal notifies the First Order. This castle intrigue kicks off a race between the two forces to recover the droid first. Meanwhile, Rey hears voices coming from the basement, where she finds Luke Skywalker's first lightsaber and receives a vision of her past and future. In the aftermath of the battle between the First Order and the Resistance, the castle lies in ruins.

Life in the castle
Strono "Cookie" Tuggs steps away from the kitchen to receive praise for this evening's dinner from Professor Allium and friends *(above)*. Maz is reunited with her old friend Han Solo *(above left)*.

HOSNIAN PRIME
REGION Core
TERRAIN Cities

Hosnian Prime is an urban world dominated by beautiful cities of towering architecture. It is a hub not only of government, but also commerce and education, with sprawling shopping complexes, museums, and universities. The planet serves as one of a series of capitals of the New Republic. Unlike the Empire and the Old Republic before it, the New Republic is not permanently based on Coruscant. The New Republic's temporary capital is chosen by democratic election in an effort to make member worlds feel more included. It is from Hosnian Prime that Leia Organa's parentage is leaked during her campaign for First Senator, ending her political career and leading to her focusing on the formation of the Resistance. Unimaginable tragedy strikes when the First Order destroys the entire Hosnian system using its superweapon known as Starkiller Base.

Liberty dies
General Organa's emissary, Korr Sella, watches in horror as the energy beam from Starkiller Base penetrates the atmosphere and obliterates the planet (left). Hosnian Prime has many large cities that are visible from space (above).

Resistance victory
The Resistance gathers to celebrate the destruction of Starkiller Base and welcome the strike force back.

RESISTANCE BASE
LOCATION D'Qar

Following surveys of D'Qar, the rebels build a small outpost on the planet, but the end of the Galactic Civil War eliminates the need for a full base. When the New Republic refuses to heed General Leia Organa's warnings regarding the First Order, Leia establishes the Resistance and decides to use the old Alliance base on D'Qar as its new headquarters. Leia sends engineers to expand and update the facility before moving her forces to the base. Fast-growing trees must constantly be cut back on the base to keep runways and bunker exits clear.

In the run-up to outright war, Leia directs her small military from this base. She sends Poe Dameron and the rest of Black Squadron on a vital mission to locate Lor San Tekka, hoping that he can point them toward the secret location of her brother, Luke Skywalker.

After Hosnian Prime's destruction, the First Order target D'Qar with Starkiller Base. The Resistance moves quickly to launch an offensive against the First Order superweapon and destroy it before it can recharge. Now that the First Order is alerted to its presence on D'Qar, the Resistance know that it has no future at that location. Leia orders an immediate evacuation, but she does not leave before holding a brief funeral for her deceased husband, Han Solo. During the evacuation, which is organized by Lieutenant Kaydel Connix, the Resistance fleet waits in orbit, ready to provide safe harbor to the base personnel. Just when everything seems safe, the First Order arrives to annihilate the desperate rebels. Despite a successful escape from D'Qar, the Resistance is now pursued in space by its relentless enemy.

D'Qar operations
The Resistance ground crew are hard at work repairing a power generator (above). C-3PO, Admiral Ushos O. Statura, and General Organa discuss the attack on Starkiller Base from the Resistance command center (right).

Lucky escape
The last U-55 loadlifter leaves the base, just as the First Order dreadnought fires upon the location.

AHCH-TO

REGION Unknown Regions **SECTOR** Uncharted
TERRAIN Oceans, rocky islands

Mysterious Ahch-To is the home of the first Jedi temple. It has many names in ancient legends, but it is absent from nearly all star-charts—except one obtained by scholar Lor San Tekka—and thus nearly lost to legend. Luke Skywalker retreats to Ahch-To and its remote temple island, intending to live out the rest of his days in reclusive exile, until his peace is disturbed by Rey.

Ahch-To is not an easy place in which to thrive. Covered mostly by dark seas, small islands dot the surface where rough water and howling winds carve rocky ledges adorned with feeble zones of vegetation. Nonetheless, birds, fish, sea mammals, and great leviathans of the deep do flourish here. Small, flighted porgs nest in colonies along the cliffs, feeding their young with regurgitated fish and Ahch-Tonian grubs. Thala-sirens nurse their young peacefully on the rocky shores, providing a dairy source for other island residents.

Edible fish from the seas include fingerlip garpon, twinfin hyacander, and spetan channelfish. Fish are caught by the Lanais, the most intelligent species to live above the surface of the waters. They inhabit many islands and their cultures can differ significantly on each. At Luke's location—the origin point of the Jedi Order—is a settlement of Lanai, known as the Caretakers. The white-robed creatures consider it their sacred duty to maintain the ancient structures on the island and tolerate Luke's presence among them. The rest of the Lanai, who spend most of their time out at sea, are known as Visitors. They return to the island on a monthly basis, when a festival is held with music and dancing. They share their catch with the Caretakers as well, who dry, smoke, and salt the fish in their little village.

An ancient Jedi enclave stands on the south side of the island, where Luke lives in a conical stone hut. After Rey arrives, she sleeps in a similar dwelling nearby. A clearing is located not far away, down a long, stone stairway, where Chewbacca waits with the *Millennium Falcon*. Meanwhile, Luke's X-wing is submerged in a cove to the east. After her duel with Kylo Ren on Kef Bir, a dejected Rey returns to the planet, planning to start her own exile here. However, Luke manifests through the Force, offering sage advice and the means to return to the fight.

Interrupted exile
Luke and Rey first meet in a natural amphitheater known as the Saddle on the temple island. Luke's first instinct is to drive away his Force-attuned visitor.

Primitive existence
Luke's stone hut *(above)* in the Jedi village on the south of the temple island is built to withstand extreme weather conditions. The door is a salvaged piece of Luke's submerged X-wing.

> "Do you think I came to the most unfindable place in the galaxy for no reason at all?"
> — LUKE SKYWALKER

FIRST JEDI TEMPLE

LOCATION Ahch-To

When Luke Skywalker's efforts to train his nephew, Ben Solo, as a Jedi end in disaster, he is distraught. He seeks out the first Jedi temple and the original Jedi teachings for answers. With much questing, he finally locates Ahch-To, a planet housing the temple itself, and the tree library holding the sacred Jedi texts.

The temple sits on the highest perch at the western end of the temple island, where it has existed for untold millennia. Other temples once existed, but were destroyed by the Empire. Ahch-To's temple is a simple cave housing meditation plinths, one of which is perched just outside the west entrance, overlooking the sea. It is here that Luke eventually spends his final moments, looking out at the sunset of the planet's twin suns. In the center of the cave is a mosaic beneath a pool of water, depicting the Prime (first) Jedi at balance with the Force—in peaceful coexistence with both light and dark.

Down the temple stairs, a little to the east in a protected nook of the island, is a centuries-old uneti tree. Inside the hollowed tree is a reading chamber housing the oldest known examples of the earliest Jedi teachings. The tree is destroyed by the Force spirit of Jedi Master Yoda, but not before the books are taken by Rey.

As the birthplace of the Jedi Order, ancient Ahch-To has strange and powerful spots that are strong in the Force. In particular, Rey finds herself drawn to a natural blowhole on the eastern side of the temple island that is a dangerous source of dark-side energy. There, she experiences visions of her past and future, and must face the possibilities of who she is and what she could become.

Meeting of minds
Rey has visions of Ahch-To's temple island prior to her arrival. Despite having cut himself off from the Force, Luke reluctantly agrees to teach Rey the ways of the Jedi.

CANTONICA

REGION Outer Rim
SECTOR Corporate
TERRAIN Deserts

Cantonica is a desolate world, apart from the resort destination of Canto Bight, where wealthy tourists and war profiteers go to play. The landscape outside that isolated paradise is foreboding—menaced by sandstorms and scorching winds. What little vegetation exists is mainly cactus and scrub brush. Cantonica is located within the Corporate Sector—a fiefdom that allows independent systems to govern themselves. This autonomy has drawn suspicion from the Empire and the First Order but, for now, it remains a safe haven for smugglers, tourists, and gamblers alike.

CANTO BIGHT

LOCATION Cantonica

Canto Bight is a playground for the wealthiest in the galaxy, including the highly influential Tagge family. The city is made up of luxury hotels, restaurants, casinos—like The Crescent Royale and Galanx Casino—shopping plazas, spas, racetracks, sporting events, and endless forms of decadent entertainment. Criminal organizations like the Sixth Kin operate out of the city's far less affluent Worker's District. Canto Bight is the planetary capital, but much of the planet is a vast wasteland with few other places of interest. The city sits on the coast of the Sea of Cantonica, boasted as the largest artificial ocean in the galaxy. After the destruction of Starkiller Base and the evacuation of the Resistance from D'Qar, rebels Finn, Rose Tico, and BB-8 come to Canto Bight to look for the Master Codebreaker.

Maintaining an image
Beneath the beautiful, wealthy surface of Canto Bight lies a strict regime and the Canto Bight authorities will not tolerate any infractions, corruption, or crime.

CANTO CASINO

LOCATION Canto Bight, Cantonica

The Canto Casino is the crown jewel of Cantonica, lined with stained-glass windows and expensive furnishings. It includes a lavish hotel with rooms to fit every size and shape, a shopping concourse with merchandise from across the galaxy, 22 restaurants full of delights to suit every digestive sac, and, nearby, the renowned Canto Racetrack with stables for fathiers and other quick-footed beasts. The casino has private game rooms where the fortunes of entire worlds are won and lost. Guests are served exotic cocktails of all kinds by protocol waiter droids.

> "I wish I could put my fist through this whole lousy, beautiful town."
> — ROSE TICO

CRAIT

REGION Outer Rim **SECTOR** Bon'nyuw-Luq
SYSTEM Crait (PZ-43 Gamma)
TERRAIN Salt flats, mountains, briny seas

Crait is a remote world rich in minerals. The planet's broad flats are dusted with white salt, while just beneath the surface are reserves of blood-red rhodochrosite, ground to sand. Further below the surface, in vast caves, the same rhodochrosite elements form towering crystals.

The harsh salt flats of Crait do not promote a large diversity of life, but some species do thrive. Foxlike vulptices hunt for small animals, insects, and crystal bats that are found in the caves. All life is adapted to the high mineral content of the environment, and utilizes it to form exoskeletons, spines, and protective coverings. Sunken waterways channel rare rainfall to briny lakes, some connected to springs and sinkholes where fish and crustaceans breed, with large, dangerous specimens nesting deep within wells heated by hydrothermal vents.

Before the outbreak of the Galactic Civil War, Bail Organa believes the planet is an ideal place for a new rebel outpost, and authorizes the building of a small base in an abandoned mine. It isn't until a young Princess Leia investigates the Crait outpost that she discovers her parents are building a rebellion against the Empire. Not long after her visit, the site is abandoned.

During the Galactic Civil War, Leia returns with Luke Skywalker and Han Solo to look into establishing a new base, but they are attacked by the Empire's SCAR Squad. Though they fend off the Imperials, it is clear that Crait is not suitable for the Rebel Alliance. The outpost is left derelict for decades, used only by the occasional miner, working in the caves with their droids.

Leia doesn't forget about Crait, however, and keeps the small world on her radar for future use, knowing its location has fallen off many star-charts. As such, she recommends the location as a refuge for the Resistance as it attempts to escape the First Order.

Kylo Ren and his forces assault the stronghold with AT-M6 walkers, while the Resistance fights back in vain using decrepit old V-4X-D ski speeders. The battle culminates in a confrontation between Kylo Ren and Luke Skywalker, which serves as a distraction, giving the Resistance remnant time to escape. They pass through a cave system and flee aboard the *Millennium Falcon*.

Battle-ready
As an abandoned rebel base, many fortified structures remain on Crait, including deep trenches linked to the stronghold via tunnels.

Ground disturbance
When the First Order and Resistance forces face off on Crait, the salt flats make for a dramatic battleground. The First Order's AT-M6s *(above)* and the Resistance's ski speeders *(right)* drag up the red minerals from below.

LOCATIONS

CELSOR 3
REGION Outer Rim
SECTOR Hook Nebula
SYSTEM Celsor
TERRAIN Ice, snow

Covered in snow and mist, the frigid moon known as Celsor 3 is a foreboding place. Its inhospitable conditions are unwelcoming to most, with ice pillars dotting the harsh but beautiful landscape. It is not devoid of life, however, as the planet is home to a frightening and massive jakoosk. The white creature is well camouflaged in its surroundings. Residents of the *Colossus* platform unwittingly awaken it during a training exercise. They barely escape with their lives but then return on a hunting expedition and kill the creature with a direct hit to its exposed underbelly.

DRAHGOR III
REGION Outer Rim
SECTOR Colundra
TERRAIN Mountains, rock

Drahgor III appears yellow from space, thanks to a thick covering of fog. The harsh nature of the planet's rocky landscape is matched only by the dense atmosphere, which is filled with near-constant cracks of lightning. Despite these unpleasant conditions, Drahgor III is home to the Gozzo species—long-legged, feathered beings who mine the world for its fuel resources. Yet, they are not the world's only inhabitants. Long considered a myth, karnex dragons dwell far below the surface, and some are awakened by the Gozzo's deep-core drilling. Residents of the *Colossus* encounter the creatures and discover the dragons are sensitive to light—a weakness that gives them a chance to escape.

ASHAS REE
REGION Outer Rim
SECTOR Esstran
TERRAIN Forest

Although covered in peaceful-looking green vistas, Ashas Ree holds dark secrets—and an ancient Sith temple. Relic hunter Mika Grey excavates the building in an effort to get her hands on an old Sith artifact before First Order forces find it. In response, fearful villagers flee their trading post and the planet. During her search, Mika falls victim to a booby trap until Kazuda Xiono and his friends from the *Colossus* arrive and free her from the temple's lower level. First Order Raiders soon come for the device, but Grey destroys it, releasing an energy discharge that eliminates Kylo Ren's sinister agents.

VRANKI'S HOTEL AND CASINO
REGION Outer Rim **SECTOR** Ash Worlds
SYSTEM Voxx Cluster

A space station built for entertainment, Vranki's Hotel and Casino is easily spotted thanks to its garish neon lights. Vranki is a Hutt, and his establishment, which sits within the Voxx Cluster, hosts numerous games of chance as well as a racing course outside the main structure. It is experiencing a drop in business until Hype Fazon arrives with the Aces in tow and an itch to race. Vranki plays by his own rules, with various surprises that all but ensure the house will always win. It is only when the *Colossus*' Neeku slices into Vranki's system that the Aces secure a victory—and their freedom.

GUAVIAN DEATH SPACE
REGION Outer Rim
SECTOR Meram

The Guavian Death Gang is a criminal organization that controls its territory fiercely. It is unwise to pass through the area known simply as Guavian Death Space without the gang's approval. The *Colossus* platform attempts to sneak through an asteroid field on the outer edges of the region. Several fighters sweep the area first, including Kazuda Xiono, who encounters a Guavian scout. The Guavians demand a one million credit tribute, which Captain Doza refuses to pay. Instead, the Aces take the fight to the Guavians and clear a path for the *Colossus*.

VARKANA
REGION Outer Rim
TERRAIN Rock

A desert planet with a stark red landscape, Varkana is best known for Vargo Spaceport: a bustling trading hub built into the planet's otherwise rocky terrain. On Varkana, the bounty hunter Ax Tagrin, who is working for the First Order and has paid a shopkeeper as an informant, captures Resistance spy Norath Kev. Kazuda Xiono of the *Colossus* intercepts a coded signal from Kev and leads a small rescue team that locates him. Tagrin almost succeeds in turning over the entire group, but Kaz and his friends manage to slip away.

AEOS PRIME
REGION Outer Rim
TERRAIN Oceans

Aeos Prime is a stunning world of oceans and clear skies, with small tropical islands and a network of caves. The planet is home to an aquatic people called the Aeosians. They are especially proficient at swimming, though they also travel on tamed krakavora—large creatures with webbed wings, evolved for sailing through both air and water. Following an initial misunderstanding, the Aeosian queen welcomes the *Colossus* to the planet. The stay is short-lived, however, as the First Order soon arrives. The Aeosians and *Colossus* forces work together to fight them off, and the *Colossus* departs.

RED HONEYCOMB ZONE
REGION Unknown Regions
TERRAIN Red gas

The Red Honeycomb Zone is a hazardous passage that winds through an occluded stretch of the Unknown Regions. Sometimes called the "Blood Net" or the "Ship Eater," the Zone is composed of the red gasses of an exploded star, which make it nearly impossible for traditional sensors to navigate. The only guaranteed way to successfully traverse the Red Honeycomb Zone is to follow a Sith Wayfinder. Both Darth Vader and Kylo Ren use one to reach the Sith planet Exegol. Some report that dangerous creatures lie in wait for less-than-cautious travelers, and a subspecies of summa-verminoth lives in the maze.

SINTA GLACIER COLONY

REGION Mid Rim
SECTOR Hune
SYSTEM Sinta
TERRAIN Ice

The Sinta Glacier Colony is an ancient, mountainous asteroid made of ice, which is home to a quiet malsarr mineral mining operation. Massive machinery allows the miners to drill into the ice core at the heart of the asteroid, drawing trace precious ores from its ever-deepening tunnels. Orbiting the star Sinta, the colony has vast chasms and legendary comet origins that lead some travelers to clamor for the mine's discarded meltwater, which they incorrectly believe has rejuvenating properties.

CARDOVYTE

REGION Outer Rim
TERRAIN Stalagmite forests

The legendary Crystal Chaos of Cardovyte is famous across the galaxy, most especially because of its appearances in numerous holo-adventures over the years. While Poe Dameron is hyperspace skipping from the Sinta Glacier in the *Millennium Falcon* to escape First Order ships, he encounters Cardovyte. He briefly navigates through its enormous forest of translucent stalagmites, all illuminated by the red heat of a bright star.

IVEXIA

REGION Mid Rim
SECTOR Tennuutta
TERRAIN Mirrored spires

Ivexia is a shining city in the Mid Rim, famous throughout the galaxy for its awe-inspiring Mirror-Spires. They are kilometer-high buildings packed into the city's limits. While dodging First Order TIE Fighters, Poe Dameron hyperspace skips the *Millennium Falcon* through the white towers, and the ship is reflected across Ivexia's mirrored edge.

TYPHONIC NEBULA

REGION Mid Rim
SECTOR Trax
TERRAIN Green gas

The Typhonic Nebula is a true wonder of the galaxy, with noxious green gasses swirling in an objectively beautiful pattern. It is rumored that giant space worms patrol its Megafauna Chasm, hence its name. A sighting of a terrifying and legendary arakurth almost certainly guarantees the death of anyone who catches a glimpse of its three-toothed maw. Poe Dameron leads the *Millennium Falcon* through the Nebula as a last-ditch effort during a hyperspace-skipping chase across the Mid Rim. The Resistance members aboard the *Falcon* survive their encounter with an arakurth, but the pursuing First Order pilots do not.

AJAN KLOSS

REGION Outer Rim
SECTOR Cademimu
SYSTEM Ajara
TERRAIN Broadleaf forests, cliffs and valleys overgrown with vegetation, grottos, oceans

Ajan Kloss is the lush rainforest moon of the much larger gas giant, Ajara. Its dense jungle is home to fungal and insect infestations but has a relative lack of large predators. This attribute, coupled with the fact that Ajan Kloss doesn't have an indigenous population to disrupt, makes it a good place for freedom fighters to carve out a temporary base of operations.

Initially, Ajan Kloss is identified by Alderaanian scouts before the outbreak of the Galactic Civil War. It is one of the Rebel Alliance's early options for a base, though they eventually settle down on Dantooine and Yavin 4. However, the moon later serves as a Rebellion outpost, albeit briefly, after the victory at Endor.

It is also where Luke Skywalker trains his sister, Leia Organa, in the Force and the art of lightsaber dueling. Leia remembers this time fondly, and brings her recovering Resistance to the moon many years later, in part because of those memories.

While preparing for their fight against the First Order, as well as the hidden Sith Eternal, the Resistance inhabits one of the planet's many cave systems in a jungle area they call the "Klosslands." The location also serves as the place for a well-earned celebration after the Resistance's hard-fought victory at the Battle of Exegol.

Concealed by nature
The Klosslands of Ajan Kloss provide lush and ample cover for the Resistance's ragtag fleet.

Among history
It seems only fitting that Resistance briefings take place in the shadow of General Organa's flagship, the *Tantive IV*—the ship that once transported the first Death Star plans away from the Battle of Scarif.

316 LOCATIONS

EXEGOL

REGION Unknown Regions
SECTOR Unincorporated space
TERRAIN Barren rock, desert flats

Exegol (also known as "Ixigul" in translated texts) is an ancient Sith planet lurking deep in the Unknown Regions, sequestered behind the dangerous veil of the almost-impenetrable Red Honeycomb Zone. Unavailable on any star chart, the world has been successfully kept secret by generations of Sith. Unnaturally steeped in the dark side of the Force, Exegol has a foreboding Sith Citadel structure that channels its evil energy into a physical location on the planet's surface.

The moonless planet is a truly ruined world; its murky blue surface is pockmarked by enormous fissures that stretch deep into the crust. Static discharges seem ever-present, mostly likely created by the combination of dust particles and the planet's dry conditions.

For decades, Exegol is the secret hiding place for Palpatine and his loyal Sith Cultists. They have spent the years amassing the army of the Sith Eternal and raising the next generation of loyal servants. Long before his defeat on the second Death Star, Palpatine uses Exegol as a secret base of operations for activities like bleeding kyber crystals and ancient experiments in the occult. One such project—the cloning of Force-attuned life-forms—is of the utmost priority to the Sith Lord. It results in numerous beings known as strandcasts, including Supreme Leader Snoke and Palpatine's offspring, Dathan.

Dathan escapes Exegol and later fathers a Force-attuned daughter named Rey. A weakened Palpatine begins secret plots to recover his powerful granddaughter. The fruits of this search finally culminate in a climactic battle on Exegol's surface, with the granddaughter of Palpatine and the grandson of Anakin Skywalker partnering together to destroy the decrepit Sith Lord, his Cultists, and the Sith Citadel.

Lightning shock
The naturally dry terrain of Exegol combines with atmospheric dust particles to create startling static discharges across the planet's surface.

Sith Lord ascendant
Palpatine has assumed a daunting, thorny throne, from where he commands his arena of Sith Cultists. It is here that Rey challenges him.

PASAANA

REGION Expansion
SECTOR Ombakond **SYSTEM** Middian
TERRAIN Desert bluffs, dunes

A desert world far from the center of the galaxy, Pasaana bursts with life and culture. Native fauna includes the inquisitive oki-poki rodent, as well as insects like thistlebuzzers and gorpions. The planet is also home to approximately 500,000 Aki-Aki people, although a formal census has not been done for quite some time. The indigenous Aki-Aki are known for their hospitality and fervor for life, especially during their Festival of the Ancestors, which takes place in the planet's Forbidden Valley.

Only the most adventurous of travelers seek out Pasaana during its festival season, but those who do are rewarded with a glimpse at a rich culture that thrives in its arid environment, rather than be stifled by it. Because of Pasaana's remoteness and lack of resources, it is often overlooked. Plus, the Aki-Aki are a pre-spaceflight civilization so the planet has no spaceports.

Despite the planet's lack of resources, the Aki-Aki thrive. They are competent farmers who use moisture vaporators and wind grain traps to collect what they can from the air and buried aquifers.

The desert sands are home to many secrets, including rumored sarlaccs, and they can be treacherous for any traveler. Underneath the desert and its sinking sands lies a cave system partially created by burrowing, snakelike vexis predators. For a decade, this cave system is also the final resting place of Sith assassin Ochi of Bestoon. He died while on the hunt for a scavenger girl, having been led to the planet by her mother's Pasaanan beads.

Dangerous terrain
The black sands of the Shifting Mires sinkhole are a hidden hazard. Many have been trapped and deposited into the cave system below.

Living off the land
The Aki-Aki maintain vast dustgrain farms, using specialized electro-sifters to retrieve scarce seeds and spores from the sand.

KIJIMI

REGION Mid Rim
SECTOR Bryx
TERRAIN Mountains

Once a hallowed place of worship, the frigid planet of Kijimi was home to mountaintop Dai Bendu monasteries and a steady stream of pilgrims. That was long ago, however, and after the fall of the Empire, the world is overrun by lawlessness and settled by outlaws and spice runners.

The New Republic is either powerless to stop this criminal chaos or it simply doesn't care enough to intervene, making Kijimi a perfect place to lie low. There is no central government on the planet, and the anarchical system encourages its citizens and guests to work matters out among themselves, no matter how deadly the process may be. That approach to the law, or lack thereof, however, comes to an end with the arrival of the First Order, which takes over in an attempt to spread its reach across the Mid Rim.

Kijimi City and its very active Thieves' Quarter serve as an unofficial capital for the planet, but the sheer unpredictability of any basic amenities makes it tough to lead a comfortable life on the planet.

Kijimi is destroyed by a Sith Eternal star destroyer, the *Derriphan*, when Palpatine gives the "Final Order" to demonstrate its planet-killing weaponry, wiping out the monastic history of this quiet, snow-covered planet forever.

Wretched hive
In part of Kijimi City's bustling Thieves' Quarter, the Spice Runners' den is the perfect place to assemble a crew for a less-than-savory assignment.

Frozen in time
Conditions across Kijimi are often extremely cold, especially during its moonless nights, which average −25 degrees Standard Temperature.

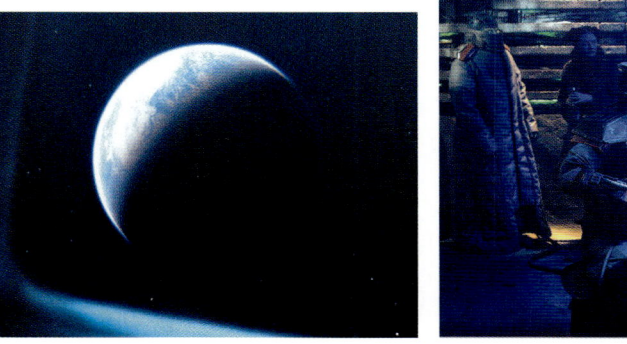

A marred view
Kef Bir's oceans are contaminated by the partial ruins of the second Death Star—a stark reminder of the Galactic Civil War.

KEF BIR

REGION Outer Rim
SECTOR Moddell **SYSTEM** Endor
TERRAIN Oceans, grasslands

One of nine satellites that orbit the planet Endor, this moon was named Kef Bir by neighboring Ewoks but is officially designated as IX3244-C. It has no indigenous intelligent life-forms, but its other species include the horselike orbak and minute fauna. Also referred to as "the Ocean Moon of Endor," Kef Bir was largely composed of water, with sporadic grasslands, until recent cataclysmic events. Because of the moon's insufficient supplies of valuable ore, the Empire doesn't choose it as its base of operations while constructing the second Death Star. (That is an honor given to its neighbor, Forest Moon IX3244-A.) However, it doesn't escape the Galactic Civil War unmarred. While the sector's hyperspace anomalies protect the moon from the worst of the fallout of the exploding Death Star, Kef Bir is pelted with debris and toxic spillage, poisoning its aquatic life.

Large fragments of the second Death Star, including the throne room of the defeated Emperor Palpatine, now reside in a watery grave in the tumultuous oceans of Kef Bir. These ruins serve as a stark reminder of the former Imperial control of the galaxy and the effect that war can have on even the most innocent of worlds.

There have long been rumors that Kef Bir has settlers, but the moon was ultimately deemed "uninhabited," making it a perfect home for a secretive group of former First Order stormtroopers. Led by Jannah, this ragtag bunch uses orbaks for mounts to patrol its grassland territory.

Kef Bir remains an important marker of wars, both past and present. An ancient dagger, with modern markings, leads Rey to the moon as she attempts to track down the second Sith wayfinder inside the ruins of the throne room.

Imperial remains
The Emperor's throne room, which crashed onto Kef Bir, still contains many secrets, including a side antechamber that houses a Sith wayfinder.

TECHNOLOGY

Although some cultures eschew technology, most embrace everything from basic tools and droids to sophisticated sensors and weapons systems.

Throughout the galaxy, most beings rely on various types of technology, whether advanced or primitive, to help them in their work duties as well as their everyday lives. Many utilize sensors to collect and examine data, and use energy shields and weapons for protection. They may also depend on droids for a multitude of tasks, ranging from running simple diagnostics to performing complicated medical procedures, or sending communications to flying starships.

While interplanetary trade eventually yields myriad technological developments, wars also spur innovation, as manufacturers and armorers are conscripted or compelled to develop new defensive and offensive weapons. The Jedi lightsaber is one of the most remarkable energy weapons ever made, and the system-destroying Starkiller Base is perhaps the most fearsome. However, while many technologically advanced civilizations believe that they are superior to other cultures, and are confident that they will easily prevail in any conflict, the Battle of Endor attests to the fact that technology alone does not guarantee victory.

322 TECHNOLOGY

EX COMMUNICATION DROIDS
MODEL EX **TYPE** Communications droid

Each Republic Pathfinder team travels with an EX droid attached to its ship to help send messages across unmapped regions of space. The EX droids can serve as mobile comms buoys or manually descend from starships to planets in order to convey information from orbit. They have small thrusters, and their legs can be retracted for flight.

SILANDRA SHO'S SHIELD
MODEL Handcrafted **TYPE** Jedi shield

Jedi Silandra Sho carries a shield to show her commitment to fighting defensively rather than aggressively. The center of the shield is formed by plasma, while the rim is made of a silver metal. A bar in the middle provides a handhold. The plasma deactivates when not in use. Silandra later gifts the shield to her Padawan, Rooper Nitani.

NAMELESS CONTROL RODS
MODEL Force relic **TYPE** Scepter

Three Rods are associated with the Nameless threat: the Rod of Ages, the Rod of Seasons, and the Rod of Daybreak. Individually, or combined into the Rod of Power, the Rods of Seasons and Daybreak grant the wielder command over where the Nameless go and whom they attack. The Rod of Ages can cancel those powers out.

ENFORCER DROIDS
TYPE Battle droid

The Path of the Open Hand deploys enforcer droids against the Jedi at the conflicts on Jedha and Dalna. They are equipped with heavy armor and have powerful blasters stored in their arms. Marchion Ro uses the same type of enforcer droid on his flagship, the *Gaze Electric*.

PATH ENGINE
MANUFACTURER Nihil **MODEL** Path engine **TYPE** Hyperdrive navigation bypass

The Path engines are specialized enhancements for the hyperdrives of Nihil ships. They enable the ships to make jumps and reach speeds that are impossible on established hyperspace lanes. Shalla Ro and her son Asgar capture Mari San Tekka, who is a hyperspace prospector capable of making novel hyperspace calculations using the Force. They demand that she make the Paths.

SCAV DROID
MANUFACTURER Nihil **MODEL** Scavenger **TYPE** Probe droid

Scav droids are small, spiderlike droids with cutting lasers, pincers, and metal tendrils. The Nihil release them to cut into enemy ships and steal loot, storing it inside their shells for retrieval later. One full complement of scav droids is five dozen units. Pan Eyta in particular is known to make use of them. The Nihil unleash scav droids on Rekelos and en masse on Valo during the attack on the Republic Fair. Jedi Burryaga and Ram Jomaram both fight against them. Burryaga knocks scav droids off his ship with the Force, while Ram reprograms one navigation droid to lead the other scav droids away from the battle.

LIGHTWHIP LIGHTSABER
CREATOR Vernestra Rwoh **MODEL** Handcrafted **TYPE** Lightsaber

Vernestra Rwoh's purple lightsaber holds a secret: by twisting the front ring, she can transform the single blade into a flexible whip. She designs and builds the lightwhip herself, training with it in private, away from even her Jedi Master. Vernestra uses her lightwhip to fight and to clear a path through thick jungle.

MARCHION RO'S HELMET
MODEL Handcrafted **TYPE** Pirate helmet

Marchion Ro has worn several helmets during his rule of the Nihil. One signature helmet, which he took from the corpse of his father, Asgar, is marked with the Eye of the Storm—a symbol based on the fate of the Evereni species. While this helmet can protect him from some blaster fire, it serves primarily to intimidate.

STORMSEED
MANUFACTURER Nihil **MODEL** Hyperspace interdictor **TYPE** Mine

Stormseeds are interstellar mines which can drag ships out of hyperspace and destroy them. They are created in part with technology that Chancey Yarrow built for the Gravity's Heart project. After the Nihil destroy the Starlight Beacon, Marchion Ro declares he will use the Stormseed to create a Nihil home territory where the Republic and Jedi cannot go.

TRAINING DROID
MANUFACTURER Industrial Automaton **MODEL** Customized DD-1 hover droid **TYPE** Jedi practice droid

The training droids at the Tenoo Jedi temple wield electroblade training swords and move quickly to hone younglings' acrobatics and fighting skills. A training droid often practices with Kai Brightstar, Lys Solay, and Nubs. After Kai clashes with the pirate Taborr a few times, he dresses a training droid in a helmet and cape resembling Taborr's. Kai also reprograms three training droids to clean, in an effort to speed up his chores. However, the droids don't know when to stop stacking all the objects they encounter, which causes chaos in until Kai, Lys, Nubs, and RJ-83 turn the rogue droids off.

THARNAKAN STORY STONE
MANUFACTURER Tharnakan craftsperson **MODEL** N/A **TYPE** Historical record

When held up to a light, the Tharnakan story stone projects images from Tharnakan history. After the stone is lost in a planet-wide flood, Kai Brightstar, Nubs, Lys Solay, and OG-LC help the Tharnakan Ishbul Ekwesh to return the artifact to her people. This tale is now one of the stories held in the stone.

BATTLE DROID

MANUFACTURER Baktoid Combat Automata **MODEL** B1
TYPE Battle droid

Easily controlled, unquestioningly obedient, and inexpensive to mass-produce, battle droids are the primary troops in the Trade Federation's mechanized armies.

INVASION FORCE
With their tall, gaunt, humanoid design, exposed joints, and metal finishes, battle droids bear an eerie resemblance to animated skeletons. Early models are essentially mindless, lethal puppets, operated via a Central Control Computer housed in an orbital Droid Control Ship. This modified Trade Federation battleship transmits both direct orders from the Federation's leaders and computer-automated commands. Peaceful civilizations and worlds without military defenses are easy targets for the Trade Federation. However, when a Droid Control Ship is destroyed, battle droids enter a stand-by hibernation mode that leaves them totally vulnerable.

> "Roger, roger."
> **BATTLE DROID**

Calculated assault
Utilizing motion-capture data from highly trained organic soldiers, battle droids demonstrate an array of combat stances, positions, and maneuvers while fighting the newly formed Grand Army of the Republic at the Battle of Geonosis.

TECHNICAL CAPABILITY
The Trade Federation commissions battle droids with humanoid physiques for practical reasons, as this allows the droids to operate existing machinery, vehicles, and weapons originally designed for organic operators and pilots, saving the Federation unnecessary production costs or expensive retrofitting. The battle droid infantry pilots STAPs, MTTs, and AATs, as well as Trade Federation battleships and other vessels. Federation vessels that operate beyond the range of a Droid Control Ship have inboard Central Control Computers that coordinate the droid crews, enabling them to operate tactile computer consoles and communications stations.

ASSEMBLY LINE
In choosing to rely on Central Control Computers to operate large armies of droids simultaneously, the budget-minded Trade Federation saves the astronomical costs that would have been required for the production of thousands of individual droid brains. The Federation contracts Baktoid Combat Automata to mass-produce B1 battle droids in the foundries-turned-factories on Geonosis. However, in anticipation of war with the Galactic Republic, the Separatist B1 mechanicals are installed with droid brains to augment their combat abilities.

Robotic army
Cheap to make, quick to assemble, battle droids roll off the production line at Baktoid Combat Automata's factories.

Identical soldiers
Frightening in their uniformity, battle droids are only distinguished by numerical markings on the back of their comlink booster packs. Droids with specialized functions have distinct colored markings on their armor. Blue denotes pilot droids. Red denotes security droids. Yellow denotes command droids.

Covert agents
Three reprogrammed battle droids, painted blue to maintain their guise as innocuous pilots from a Separatist shuttle, follow their commander, R2-D2.

GALACTIC BATTLEFRONTS
Forming the backbone of the Separatist army, B1s are the standard rank-and-file forces that fight the Republic forces during the Clone Wars. However, the droids are susceptible to reprogramming. After Separatists apprehend Jedi Master Even Piell and place him in a deadly prison known as the Citadel, Anakin Skywalker devises a rescue plan that involves conscripting the reprogrammed B1s to infiltrate the prison. Under the command of the astromech droid R2-D2, the B1s pilot a shuttle to deliver the other members of the rescue team to the Citadel. When a large number of enemy droids attack, the trio of B1s sacrifice themselves holding off the attack.

The last battle
Much of the Agamar garrison is lost during the Imperial attack, but a small number of droids flee their holdout to face an uncertain future.

IMPERIAL ERA
After the Clone Wars end and the Separatist army is disabled, battle droids are still occasionally found throughout the galaxy. Members of the Bad Batch encounter battle droids on Corellia, where Tech reactivates decommissioned battle droids in a mission to retrieve the brain of a tactical droid, and on Desix where the local governor uses battle droids to fight back against the Empire. A full garrison of battle droids remains active on Agamar after its commander, General Kalani, ignores the galaxy-wide instruction to shut down, deducing that the order is a Republic trick. Seventeen years later, the garrison is discovered by the *Ghost* crew and clone Captain Rex. Commander droid B1-268 captures the visitors, his first prisoners in two decades of service. The droids' victory is short-lived, however, as Imperial forces soon arrive, forcing the *Ghost* crew and the droids to work together to escape. Resourceful scavengers scour decommissioned Separatist factories, such as the facility on Akiva, to build droids of their own. Akivan Temmin Wexley builds a heavily modified and lethal B1 named Mister Bones.

REPROGRAMMED AGAIN
During the New Republic era, Din Djarin and Bo-Katan Kryze investigate malfunctioning battle droids on Plazir-15. Years later, during the rise of the First Order, Neeku reprograms a B1 battle droid to take control of super battle droids that the pirate Kragan activated in an attempt to take control of the *Colossus*.

324 | TECHNOLOGY

IMAGECASTER
MANUFACTURER SoroSuub Corp. **MODEL** SoroSuub Imagecaster
TYPE Personal hologram device

Commonly carried by members of the Jedi Order, the imagecaster, also known as a holoprojector, is a handheld, disk-shaped hologram device that displays three-dimensional images formed by the interference of light beams. The imagecaster can be tuned with a comlink to carry a hologram transmission for face-to-face contact or can be used as an independent image recorder and projector. The device is sturdily constructed for field use and can hold up to 100 minutes of images. Jedi Master Qui-Gon Jinn loads his holoprojector with selected images of Queen Amidala's starship before he proceeds to the junkyard on Tatooine, where he hopes to obtain repair parts for the ship's hyperdrive. During the Imperial era, Obi-Wan Kenobi finds out that Leia Organa has been kidnapped via an Imagecaster hologram message from Bail and Breha Organa. When that imagecaster later falls into Reva's hands, she learns of Luke's location on Tatooine. Years later, after the fall of the Empire, Sabine Wren keeps a recording of Ezra Bridger on an imagecaster.

Holographic image
Anakin Skywalker watches Qui-Gon Jinn using an Imagecaster to project a three-dimensional representation of Queen Amidala's starship.

Utilitarian design
The imagecaster's casing ring has three curved arms that rotate downward, allowing the device to stand on a level surface or link to a larger image projector.

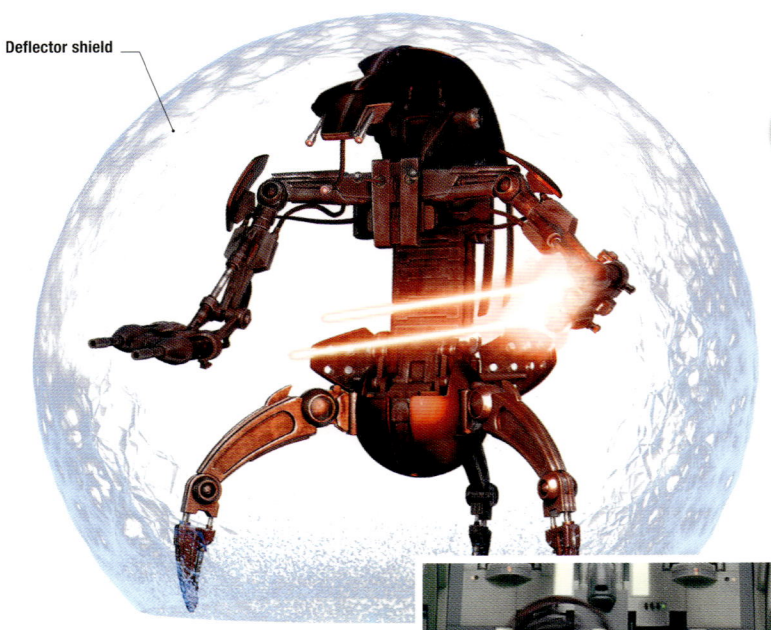

Deflector shield

DROIDEKA (A.K.A. DESTROYER DROID)
MANUFACTURER Colicoids **TYPE** Battle droid

Rolling mode
A droideka barrels across a starship's deck before opening fire on its target.

Unlike the spindly battle droid, whose humanoid frame allows a degree of versatility, the droideka is engineered with the sole function of completely annihilating its targets. Insectoid in its mix of curves and sharp angles, the droideka has heavy arms that carry immense twin blasters, which unleash destructive energy at a pounding pace. Compact deflector shield generators envelop the droid in a globe of protective energy. Although its three-legged gait is slow and awkward, the droideka can curl its body into a wheel-shaped form, which can roll on smooth surfaces at great speed. Prior to the blockade on Naboo, droidekas are used by criminal organizations, like the Xrexus Cartel, as well as large corporations, including Czerka. The Trade Federation uses droidekas aboard its starships for security and on the ground for combat operations; later they are part of the Separatist armies in the Clone Wars. During the Imperial era, droidekas continue to be used, but rarely on the same scale. Crosshair and Commander Cody face droidekas on their mission on Desix to rescue an Imperial governor. Jedi Cal Kestis finds destroyer droids on Koboh. On Agamar, a remnant of the Separatist droid army includes droidekas, that fight and then eventually ally with two Jedi and a clone. Years later, Doctor Aphra reprograms a first-generation droideka named Dek-[Nil].

E-5 DROID BLASTER
MANUFACTURER Baktoid Armor Workshop
MODEL E-5 **TYPE** Blaster rifle

Droid grip
The blaster is equipped with a continuous-fire trigger.

The standard-issue armament of B1 battle droids and BX-series droid commandos, the E-5 blaster rifle is a lightweight weapon with a large gas chamber that allows for powerful blasts. Based on a BlasTech design, the rifle has been reverse-engineered by Baktoid Armor for use by robotic soldiers, which will not feel the excessive heat it produces when it is repeatedly fired.

T-14 HYPERDRIVE
MANUFACTURER Nubian Design Collective
CLASS 1.8 **TYPE** Hyperdrive

T-14 hyperdrive generators, which propel starships smoothly into hyperspace, are commonly used aboard ships produced by the Nubian Design Collective, such as the J-type 327 Nubian starship assigned to Queen Amidala of Naboo.

OBI-WAN KENOBI'S FIRST LIGHTSABER
CREATOR Obi-Wan Kenobi
MODEL Lightsaber
TYPE Single-blade

Although visually similar to Qui-Gon's weapon, Obi-Wan's first lightsaber has a different internal mechanism. On a mission to Lenahra, Obi-Wan temporarily loses possession of his lightsaber, but soon recovers it. And while his kyber crystal typically emits a blue blade, it is temporarily replaced with a kohlen crystal on a mission to Pijal, causing the blade to turn orange. During a duel with Darth Maul on Naboo, Kenobi loses his lightsaber when it falls into a generator trench.

GX-8 WATER VAPORATOR

MANUFACTURER Pretormin Environmental
MODEL GX-8 water vaporator **TYPE** Moisture vaporator

Essential for survival on the desert planet Tatooine, GX-8 water vaporators coax moisture from the air by means of refrigerated condensers. Captured water accumulates on the condensers and is pumped or gravity-directed into storage cisterns. Vaporators are capable of collecting up to 1.5 liters (1½ quarts) of water per day.

ADVENTURER SLUGTHROWER RIFLE

MANUFACTURER Czerka Arms
MODEL Adventurer
TYPE Slugthrower rifle

A projectile rifle with excellent aim over long distances, the Czerka Adventurer floods its chamber with a rich oxidizer as it detonates its shell, giving the projectile added punch and extra range. The weapon can be easily dismantled for concealed transport.

Long range
This projectile rifle can hit targets from up to 450 meters (1,476 ft) away.

PIT DROIDS

MANUFACTURER Serv-O-Droid, Inc.
MODEL DUM-series pit droid **TYPE** Repair droid

Standing just over 1 meter (3 ft 3 in) tall, pit droids assist their owners in maintaining a variety of vehicles including podracer engines, sailing skiffs, and starfighters. Cheap and expendable, pit droids are capable of lifting objects many times their own weight and will run onto the racetrack to repair still-cycling superheated engines without hesitation. When not in use, they fold up into a compact stowed mode. During the High Republic era, Raena Zess uses pit droids in a sailing race. Centuries later, Peli Motto has several pit droids to assist her in Hangar 3-5 in the Mos Eisley spaceport.

Tough construction
Hardened alloy casings can endure harsh Tatooine weather.

HUSH-98 COMLINK

MANUFACTURER SoroSuub Corp. **MODEL** Hush-98
TYPE Handheld comlink

Comlinks are used for standard communication and to transmit and receive data. Many Jedi Knights are equipped with the Hush-98 comlink, which features a 100-kilometer (62-mile) range and complex security devices to prevent unauthorized interception. Built-in silence projectors allow Jedi to maintain stealth while communicating with their allies. Other components include a reception antenna, variable frequencies, encoding, and a sound-reproduction matrix. The Hush-98 is also capable of transmitting complex information such as blood sample data used to determine midi-chlorian levels.

TUSKEN RIFLE

MANUFACTURER Tuskens
MODEL Cycler **TYPE** Slugthrower

Built from stolen and scavenged parts, the Tusken rifle is the standard projectile weapon used by Tatooine's Tuskens for ranged combat. As a slugthrower-class rifle, it fires solid shots enveloped in energy instead of blaster bolts. Bounty hunter Boba Fett uses a cycler rifle during his time with a Tusken clan, after his escape from the Sarlacc pit. Mercenary Migs Mayfeld later uses Fett's rifle to blow up a transport full of rhydonium while escaping an Imperial base.

TECHNOLOGY

Killing time
After years of extensive martial arts training, Maul relishes the opportunity to use his weapon against two Jedi on the planet Naboo (left).

Two against one
Maul's savage prowess with two blades (below) is not enough to defeat Obi-Wan's single-bladed weapon.

DARTH MAUL'S DOUBLE-BLADED LIGHTSABER

CREATOR Darth Maul **MODEL** Handcrafted
TYPE Double-bladed Sith lightsaber (two joined lightsabers)

The Sith Lord Darth Maul's primary weapon is a pair of identical red-bladed lightsabers connected at their respective pommels to form a double-bladed lightsaber. Crafted by Maul himself, the weapon contains two sets of internal components, allowing one set to act as backup for the other if necessary. Activator controls can ignite both blades simultaneously or one at a time, and each lightsaber also features blade modulation controls. A weapon of this type is traditionally used as a training device, but because it can be much more dangerous to its wielder than an enemy, most Sith have historically eschewed the weapon in favor of the single-bladed lightsaber. In Maul's expert hands, it becomes a whirling vortex of lethal energy.

It is with this blade that Maul kills his first Jedi—a Twi'lek Padawan named Eldra Kaitis. When attacking the Jedi Master Qui-Gon Jinn on the planet Tatooine, Maul uses a single blade from his lightsaber during their duel but fails to strike down his opponent. Soon after, when Maul confronts Qui-Gon and his Jedi apprentice, Obi-Wan Kenobi, on Naboo, he activates both blades to fight the two Jedi at the same time. Maul slays Qui-Gon, but Obi-Wan's lightsaber cleaves through the joined pommels of Maul's weapon, leaving Maul with a single operational hilt. Despite Maul's deadly proficiency, Obi-Wan cuts Maul in half. Incredibly, Maul survives and manages to retain his one functional lightsaber. Years later, during the Clone Wars, Maul still possesses his weapon when he emerges from obscurity, and with it, he duels Obi-Wan and also his own former master, Darth Sidious. He loses the blade when he is defeated by Sidious, but reforges the saber into a double-sided blade in time to battle Ahsoka Tano during the Siege of Mandalore. During this fight, Maul's lightsaber falls from a catwalk.

Violent reunion
Wielding his sole remaining lightsaber, Maul resumes his duel with Obi-Wan during the Clone Wars.

GUNGAN PERSONAL ENERGY SHIELD

MANUFACTURER Otoh Gunga Defense League
MODEL Standard issue personal energy shield
TYPE Personal energy shield

This handheld shield carried by soldiers of the Gungan Grand Army during the Battle of Naboo defends against light physical attacks as well as blaster fire. The ovoid-framed shield uses hydrostatic bubble technology and can deflect blaster bolts back at the shooter. Several members of the Amidalans also use these shields during their missions. During the Imperial era, Luthen Rael displays a Gungan shield in his Coruscant gallery.

ENERGY BALL (BOOMA)

MANUFACTURER Otoh Gunga Defense League
MODEL Gungan energy ball
TYPE Energy weapon

Using the plasmic energy found deep in Naboo's porous crust, the Gungans have crafted a spherical grenade-type weapon they call a booma, or boomer. Made in many different sizes, these grenades are either thrown by hand, sling, or falumpaset-towed catapult. When they hit their target, their protective shells burst, releasing the plasma and a powerful electric shock.

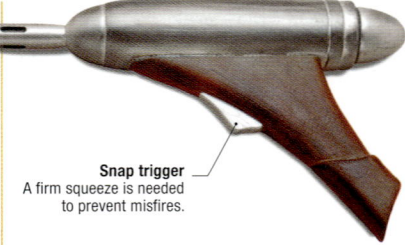

Snap trigger
A firm squeeze is needed to prevent misfires.

NABOO ROYAL PISTOL

MANUFACTURER SoroSuub Corp. **MODEL** ELG-3A blaster pistol **TYPE** Hold-out blaster

Lightweight, elegant, and functional, the SoroSuub ELG-3A is practically a standard accessory for diplomats and nobles who require a personal blaster. Padmé Amidala and her handmaidens carry the slim pistol. Most are designed for easy concealment, however there is a version with an extended barrel.

GUNGAN ATLATL

MANUFACTURER Otoh Gunga Defense League
MODEL Otoh Gunga standard issue atlatl
TYPE Bludgeoning/ranged weapon

Used by Gungans to launch energy balls at a greater distance than an unassisted arm can achieve, the atlatl is essentially a throwing stick that also serves as a highly effective blunt weapon. Atlatls are carved from a naturally insulating wood and can be wielded with one hand. They have a maximum range of 100 meters (328 ft) and an optimal range of 30 meters (98 ft).

KAMINOAN SABERDART

CREATOR Kaminoans **MODEL** Handcrafted Kaminoan saberdart
TYPE Toxic dart

Recognized by few experts outside the Outer Rim, the Kaminoan saberdart is a rare artifact. A small, fork-shaped dart with distinctive cuts on its side, it is used to deliver a deadly toxin. Although highly lethal, saberdarts may attract suspicion because they are so unique to the Kamino system.

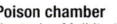

Poison chamber
The toxins Malkite themfar and Fex-M3 can cause death in less than 10 seconds.

TRAINING REMOTE
MANUFACTURER Industrial Automaton
MODEL Marksman-H **TYPE** Training remote

Typically used as combat training tools, training remotes are small floating spheres equipped with relatively harmless blasters and an array of sensors. Over the centuries, Jedi used remotes to hone their lightsaber skills, as well as their attunement to the Force. Jedi younglings usually wear vision-obscuring blast shields and use the Force to visualize a remote's location and actions, wielding lightsabers to block any incoming shots. As training sessions intensify, the remote begins to move more and more quickly and attacks with increasingly intense bursts of energy. Remotes are also extensively used by sharpshooters who want to polish their skills.

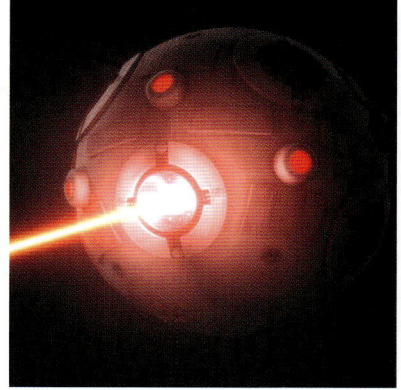

Lethal variation
Remotes can be modified to be defensive security weapons capable of firing deadly blasts of energy at intruders.

Full-body protection
Armor allows clone troopers to march through deflector shield barriers and withstand hails of deadly projectiles or explosive blasts with impunity.

PHASE I CLONE TROOPER ARMOR
MANUFACTURER Kaminoan Armorsmiths Ltd. **MODEL** Phase I armor
TYPE Body armor

Various types of armor have been developed for clone troopers to operate in different environments and atmospheres. The first series of clone troopers, deployed at the Battle of Geonosis, wear Phase I armor, which consists of 20 form-fitting plastoid-alloy composite plates sealed to a temperature-control body glove via magnatomic gription panels. In creating the armor, Kaminoan designers take inspiration from armor worn by the clones' genetic source, the bounty hunter Jango Fett, including his helmet with its distinctive T-shaped visor. The pressurized body glove also provides temporary protection against the vacuum of space.

Design flaw
Inexperienced with human ergonomics, Kaminoans unintentionally built Phase I armor to be uncomfortable to sit in. Subsequent generations of armor correct this flaw.

Learning tool
On Ajan Kloss, Rey trains with remotes to improve her skills.

DC-15 BLASTER RIFLE
MANUFACTURER BlasTech Industries
MODEL DC-15 **TYPE** Blaster rifle

A standard-issue weapon for clone troopers in the Grand Army of the Republic, the DC-15 blaster rifle uses a replaceable tibanna gas cartridge that yields up to 500 shots of charged plasma bolts when the weapon is set on low power. On maximum power, the DC-15 yields 300 shots and can leave a .5-meter (1½-ft) hole in any ferroconcrete wall. During the early years of the Imperial era some soldiers, including Elite Squad troopers, use modified DC-15 rifles.

Cutout handle
The hollow area in the blaster's handle minimizes weight for faster draw.

WESTAR-34 BLASTER PISTOL
MANUFACTURER Concordian Crescent Technologies **MODEL** WESTAR-34
TYPE Blaster pistol

Designed for brief but intense surprise attacks at close range and custom fit for the bounty hunter Jango Fett, the WESTAR-34 blaster pistol is made of an dallorian alloy that can withstand sustained-fire heating that would melt most ordinary blasters. Jango Fett's son Boba also uses this weapon at times.

GEONOSIAN SONIC BLASTER
MANUFACTURER Gordarl weaponsmiths **MODEL** Geonosian sonic blaster **TYPE** Sonic blaster

The standard sidearm of Geonosian soldiers uses oscillators to produce a powerful omnidirectional sonic blast. The weapon's energy is enveloped in a plasma-containment sphere shaped by emitter cowls that channel the sonic beam.

MACE WINDU'S LIGHTSABER
CREATOR Mace Windu **MODEL** Handcrafted **TYPE** Jedi lightsaber

During his long career as a Jedi, Mace builds and uses at least two lightsabers, both of which produce a purple-hued blade. After many years of experience with his first lightsaber, and after being appointed a senior member of the Jedi Council, he crafts his second lightsaber using the highest standards of precision, creating a superior weapon that represents his mature abilities as a Jedi leader. Regarded as one of the best lightsaber wielders in the Jedi Order, Mace is a master of numerous combat techniques.

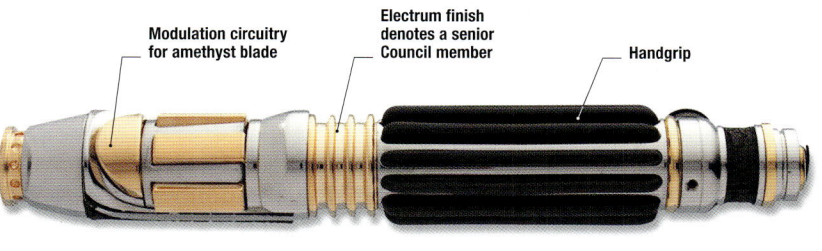

Modulation circuitry for amethyst blade
Electrum finish denotes a senior Council member
Handgrip

SUPER BATTLE DROID

MANUFACTURER Baktoid Combat Automata **MODEL** B2 **TYPE** Super battle droid

The bulkier, stronger, and more advanced version of the standard B1 battle droid, the super battle droid is equipped with a built-in laser cannon and can operate without a command signal. Super battle droids are mostly active during the Clone Wars, but some are still active years later, often reprogrammed to perform a variety of tasks.

IMPROVED MODEL
After the Trade Federation loses thousands of B1 battle droids at the Battle of Naboo, Federation leaders begin researching concepts for an improved battle droid. The result is the B2 super battle droid, which is designed by the Techno Union. The B2 incorporates many components from the standard B1, but packages them in a much sturdier shell. The droid's delicate signal receptor—identical to B1 components—is built into its heavily armored upper chest, which also houses a basic cognitive processor. This limited intelligence enables the B2 to function semi-independently of a Droid Control Ship. However, because the B2 is not capable of complex thinking, a link with a Control Ship is required for optimum performance. Because the B2 has a high center of gravity, it utilizes programmed movement algorithms to maintain balance. The B2 also has strap-on foot tips that can be replaced with climbing claws or buoyant pods to traverse different terrains.

Flexible armored midsection

Durable
The reinforced knee-joint bearings are hermetically sealed.

Secret weapon
Initially built in secret for the Trade Federation, the military-grade super battle droid violates Republic regulations on private security forces.

Jedi killers
Deployed on Geonosis to defend leaders of the Trade Federation against an invasion by Republic forces, armored B2 super battle droids deflect blaster bolts as they join B1 battle droids in an unrelenting attack on Jedi targets.

BUILT-IN WEAPONS
The standard B2 battle droid has built-in dual laser cannons mounted on its right forearm, which is modular and can be replaced with a rocket launcher and other weapons. Because the B2's armored monogrip hands lack fingers, it has difficulty handling standard blasters. However, the hands have built-in signal emitters that trigger the firing mechanism on specialized blaster rifles, making it easy for the droids to squeeze off shots.

JETPACK VARIANT
Techno Union engineers design a powerful jetpack for propelling the B2 battle droid through the air. To economize on fuel, increase range, and compensate for the B2's weight, the jetpack incorporates a compact repulsorlift. Commonly referred to as a rocket droid or jetpack droid, this variant B2 is officially designated the B2-RP (rocket pack) and is distinguished from other B2s by blue-white markings on its torso, arms, and legs. During aerial conflicts, vessels in the Confederacy of Independent Systems deploy B2-RPs, which launch themselves directly at enemy ships.

Airborne B2
A super battle droid hurtles toward its target.

Rocket trooper
A platoon of upgraded B2s fire wrist-mounted blasters.

> "The planet is secure, sir. The population is under control."
>
> **SUPER BATTLE DROID G21**

B2-RP UPGRADE
Introduced late in the Clone Wars, the upgraded B2-RP is dubbed the super battle droid rocket trooper, featuring a larger jetpack with two bulky thrusters that attach to the droid's shoulders and small additional thrusters secured to the ankles. The design and configuration of these thrusters give the droid greater control over its aerial maneuvers, as well as increased speed. The upgraded B2-RP also features wrist-mounted blasters on both arms.

AFTER THE CLONE WARS
While all super battle droids are shut down after the end of the Clone Wars, B2 droids can be found performing many roles in the decades to come. Utani Xane uses super battle droids to stop Doctor Aphra from stealing the Triple-Zero protocol personality matrix on Quarantine World III. Plazir-15 reprograms super battle droids to help serve in their communities after the fall of the Empire. Years later, Baron Paw Maccon uses super battle droids to help protect his vaults on Cato Neimoidia while the pirate Kragan Gorr buys a group of super battle droids from Sidon Ithano, which he hopes will help him take control of the Colossus.

PROTOCOL DROIDS

MANUFACTURER Cybot Galactica
MODEL Various **TYPE** Protocol droid

The "human-cyborg relations" protocol droids are ideal servants, able to converse in almost any language and programmed to be docile, polite, and subservient. Their translation capabilities make protocol droids invaluable in diplomacy and business negotiations, thus they are common on worlds such as Coruscant—a hub of galactic politics. Protocol droids are also used as teachers in schools across the galaxy. Protocol droids do have a tendency to be eccentric, fussy, nervous, and fidgety. Some consider them mildly annoying—but a restraining-bolt mount and an off switch on the back of the neck are easily accessible. While Cybot Galactica manufactures protocol droids on the factory world of Affa, the series is also available as a kit for hobbyists. Some, like Anakin Skywalker, build theirs using a motley assortment of used parts.

Protocol droids are designed to resemble humans, standing 1.67 meters (5 ft 5 in) tall and weighing 75 kg (165 lbs). They are sold in a variety of colors—including gold, red, silver, and white—and have a SyntheTech AA-1 verbobrain, allowing them to store tremendous amounts of information in their active memory banks. TranLang III communications modules are standard features, giving them fluency in more than six million forms of communication. Upgrades to more advanced modules are also available. Cybot Galactica produces other lines of protocol droids, including the TC-series, each with their own particular abilities.

Some modifications of protocol droids have proven dangerous to other life-forms, such as the Triple-Zero protocol personality matrix which turns protocol droids into assassin droids.

Rebel leader
The white Rebel Alliance droid K-3PO has programming upgrades to make him a battle tactics specialist. He is considered a valuable asset until he is destroyed during the Imperial assault on Hoth.

Rude droid
The silver E-3PO is fitted with a TechSpan I module that allows him to access Imperial networks. This enviable status goes to his head, however, and he is especially rude when encountering C-3PO on Cloud City.

R-SERIES ASTROMECH

MANUFACTURER Industrial Automaton **MODEL** R-Series **TYPE** Astromech

Industrial Automaton's astromechs are one of the most popular lines of droids in the galaxy. They are vital to the navigation and maintenance of starships, from single-person starfighters to large vessels, and come in many shapes and sizes.

The most distinctive feature of an R-series droid is the shape of its head. The most popular R-units have dome-shaped heads, while superior versions sport transparent domes, exposing their fast-running Intellex V processors. The Empire sometimes uses R-series droids for courier duties, and tends to choose R-units with conical heads. There are budget astromechs available, which are a little taller than average, with flat-topped heads. The budget units are often riddled with defects such as bad motivators, and can be found to have difficult personalities.

Early R-series models are tall, and move slowly on a single foot. They are much less personable than later models. Later R-units are much shorter and move about on two dominant legs, with a third that can be retracted into their bodies. All R-series droids support an array of optional mechanical arms, stored away in various compartments. The R-series' range of tools depends simply on the investment of their owners. The possibilities are almost limitless, and may include grasping arms, electro-shock prods, arc-welders, and computer interface arms.

Small starfighters (especially those used by the Jedi Order, the Rebel Alliance, and Resistance) often have slots fitted for astromech copilots, accessible from the outside of the ship. This allows the R-series droid to monitor approaching ships or space debris while also making navigational calculations and addressing any ship damage.

Ready to serve
A number of astromechs are stationed aboard the Naboo Royal Starship in case any emergency repairs need to be carried out.

Imperial droids
The astromechs that serve the Empire are frequently memory wiped to ensure that they do not build up the personality quirks typical of some astromech lines.

TECHNOLOGY

DATAPAD
MANUFACTURER Various **MODEL** Various
TYPE Datapad

Datapads are common devices used for a variety of informational purposes across the galaxy. Most datapads have a display screen and an input mechanism and are capable of storing holographic data and playing it back on command.

ASAJJ VENTRESS' LIGHTSABERS
MODEL Handcrafted **TYPE** Sith lightsaber

Asajj Ventress wields a pair of curved-hilt lightsabers during her apprenticeship to Count Dooku, which can be combined to form a single double-bladed lightsaber. Extremely skilled with the red-bladed weapons, Ventress fights Jedi Master Luminara Unduli during her assault on the attack cruiser *Tranquility*. Later in the Clone Wars, Ventress helps Ahsoka Tano escape from Republic authorities on Coruscant, but loses her twin lightsabers when she is ambushed by Barriss Offee. Ventress later acquires a new yellow-bladed lightsaber from an illicit source.

DC-17 BLASTER
MANUFACTURER BlasTech Industries **MODEL** DC-17 hand blaster
TYPE Pistol

This heavy blaster pistol is carried by most Republic clone troopers, particularly high-ranking captains and commanders. The BlasTech DC-17 can also be outfitted with an ascension hook for scaling walls and has a built-in stun setting. The weapon is often worn in a quick-draw holster allowing for rapid response to sudden threats. Both Commander Bly and Captain Rex prefer to wield two DC-17 blaster pistols at the same time. After the Clone Wars, some clone troopers continue to use DC-17 blasters. These weapons are also favored by some Twi'lek Freedom Fighters.

Firepower
The standard DC-17 blaster pistol has a 50-shot capacity.

Personalized
DC-17 pistols are designed to be identical and interchangeable, but commanders often customize them with unique paint jobs.

DC-15A BLASTER
MANUFACTURER BlasTech Industries
MODEL DC-15A
TYPE Blaster

One of the standard-issue weapons for clone troopers during the Clone Wars, the DC-15A is a reliable blaster capable of both sustained fire and slower, long-range accuracy. The variable power output can be controlled by the clone trooper and includes a low-powered stun setting. DC-15A blasters can be outfitted with sniper scopes and also work in conjunction with the holographic data readouts inside a clone trooper's helmet. During the Battle of Teth, clone troopers use ascension cables attached to their DC-15A blasters to scale high walls.

ANAKIN'S MECHNO-ARM
MANUFACTURER Republic **MODEL** Custom mechno-arm **TYPE** Cybernetic prosthetic

After Count Dooku cuts off Anakin Skywalker's right forearm on Geonosis, the Jedi Knight receives a mechanical prosthetic as a replacement. It resembles a droid appendage with exposed gears and servos, and it greatly boosts Anakin's gripping strength. Electrostatic fingertips allow Anakin to retain his sense of touch.

T-SERIES TACTICAL DROID
MANUFACTURER Baktoid Combat Automata
MODEL Tactical droid **AFFILIATION** Separatists

T-series tactical droids serve an important advisory role among Separatist forces during the Clone Wars. After the Clone Wars, tactical droids are highly sought after by scavengers because their brains contain intel useful for those fighting against the Empire. Far smarter than most battle droids, tactical droids are designed to stay away from the frontlines and plan battle strategies from the security of a flagship or fortified headquarters. Due to tactical droids' intelligence, many commanders allow them to have full authority over Separatist military elements. This leads many T-series droids to express their superiority over all other droid models.

COUNT DOOKU'S LIGHTSABER
CREATOR Count Dooku **MODEL** Handcrafted **TYPE** Sith lightsaber

Jedi Master Dooku considers himself a sophisticated duelist and builds his lightsaber with an unusual, curved hilt for greater finesse at executing precise slashes and lunges. After Dooku leaves the Jedi and joins the Sith, his blue-bladed lightsaber emits a red blade instead. During a confrontation on Geonosis, Dooku easily dispatches both Anakin Skywalker and Obi-Wan Kenobi, but proves unable to gain the upper hand when facing Master Yoda. Dooku carries the lightsaber throughout the Clone Wars. He faces Anakin and Obi-Wan again while aboard the *Invisible Hand*. This time Dooku's dueling skills fail him, and he loses his head to a vengeful Anakin Skywalker.

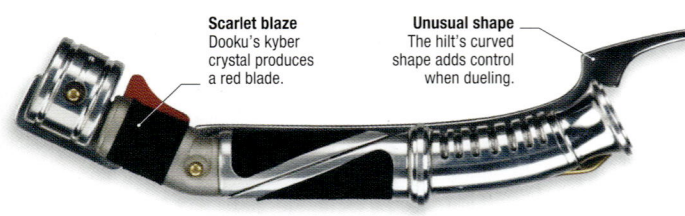

Scarlet blaze
Dooku's kyber crystal produces a red blade.

Unusual shape
The hilt's curved shape adds control when dueling.

YODA'S LIGHTSABER
CREATOR Yoda **MODEL** Handcrafted **TYPE** Jedi lightsaber

Over his centuries-long life span, Yoda has wielded multiple lightsabers of similar design, each with a shorter-than-average hilt and a blade proportioned to match the Jedi Master's size. Despite his age, Yoda is one of the best combatants in the Jedi Order, executing dizzying attacks from every direction. The green-bladed lightsaber serves Yoda well throughout the High Republic era and the Clone Wars, but he loses his weapon while fighting Emperor Palpatine inside the Senate Chamber. It is publicly thrown into a furnace by Grand Vizier Mas Amedda and destroyed. Decades later, Luke Skywalker finds a spare lightsaber in Yoda's hut on Dagobah. Luke offers this lightsaber to Grogu in his Jedi temple on Ossus, and asks the youngling to choose between training with him as a Jedi or returning to the Mandalorian.

- Blade stabilizing ring

SKYWALKER LIGHTSABER
CREATOR Anakin Skywalker
MODEL Handcrafted **TYPE** Jedi lightsaber

While many lightsabers are unique to their owners, the Skywalker lightsaber passes from Anakin Skywalker to Luke Skywalker to Rey over several decades. While all three go on to make a new lightsaber after wielding this one, the Skywalker lightsaber plays an important role in many epic battles.

ANAKIN'S LIGHTSABER
The Skywalker lightsaber comes into existence after the Battle of Geonosis when Anakin builds a replacement for his original Jedi weapon. Anakin's second lightsaber has a blue blade and a silver hilt featuring black handgrips.

Last actions
Anakin uses his lightsaber to confront Palpatine. Very soon, he will replace this weapon with a red-bladed saber.

He wields the weapon against the Separatists throughout the Clone Wars and uses it to defeat Count Dooku aboard the *Invisible Hand* during the Battle of Coruscant. Later, to defend Supreme Chancellor Palpatine, Anakin cuts off Mace Windu's hand. The action marks Anakin's transformation into Darth Vader, and he uses this lightsaber during the massacre at the Jedi Temple and his battle with Obi-Wan Kenobi on Mustafar.

LUKE'S LIGHTSABER
Obi-Wan takes the lightsaber from his defeated opponent and keeps it for nearly two decades while he watches over Anakin's son, Luke, on Tatooine. He eventually passes the weapon on to Luke, who wields it for more than two years, fighting the Empire. On Cymoon 1, Luke faces Vader in combat for the first time. The Sith Lord briefly regains his lightsaber, recognizing it as his former weapon, but Luke manages to get the weapon back before escaping. He later learns lightsaber techniques on Hubin from Thane Markona, whose mother was a Jedi, and studies under Yoda on the planet Dagobah. When Luke faces Vader once more on Cloud City, his skills are still no match for the Sith Lord's mastery. Vader uses his lightsaber to cut off Luke's hand, sending the weapon tumbling into the depths of Cloud City, where it is retrieved by an Ugnaught.

Like his father
Luke has never held a lightsaber before, but knows how to wield the weapon.

Reforged blade
Not even being torn in two could end the story of this most famous of weapons. With its fragments carefully reforged, Rey wields it against Kylo Ren once more.

REY'S LIGHTSABER
At some point over the ensuing three decades, legendary pirate Maz Kanata gains possession of the weapon. When Rey arrives at Maz's castle on Takodana, the lightsaber calls out to Rey, who finds it in a chest in a crypt under the castle. Rey receives visions of the past through the Force, but turns down Maz's offer of the weapon as a gift. Former First Order stormtrooper Finn takes the weapon from Maz, using it to duel with his previous friend FN-2199 during the Battle of Takodana. On Starkiller Base, Finn even manages to spar with "Jedi Killer" Kylo Ren, but he is gravely wounded by Kylo. Both Rey and Kylo call upon the lightsaber, but it answers to Rey. She duels Kylo, equaling his power and striking him across the face.

Rey later travels to Ahch-To, where Luke is residing. When Rey attempts to return his lightsaber to him, Luke throws it behind him. Rey picks it up again and finally persuades Luke to train her. After honing her skills, Rey leaves Luke behind on Ahch-To and rejoins the battle against the First Order. She allows herself to be captured and is delivered to Supreme Leader Snoke, aboard his flagship the *Supremacy*, who takes the lightsaber. When Snoke orders Ren to kill Rey, Kylo uses the Force to activate the blade and kill Snoke, before passing the weapon to Rey. Snoke's elite Praetorian Guards immediately attack Kylo and Rey, but the formidable duo dispatch them all. When Ren offers his hand to Rey, hoping she will join him, she rejects the advance and attempts to call the lightsaber into her grasp once more. Kylo summons it too and the lightsaber explodes between them, shattering into pieces. Rey escapes the ship with the fragments of the legendary weapon.

On Crait, a projection of Luke holding the Skywalker lightsaber faces Kylo Ren. Later, as the Resistance regroups on Ajan Kloss, Rey repairs the damaged hilt. During the Battle of Exegol, Rey uses the Force to transfer the weapon to Ben Solo, who wields it against the Knights of Ren. Rey then arms herself with it and Leia's lightsaber to defeat the Emperor. After she makes a new lightsaber out of her quarterstaff, Rey decides to bury both the Skywalker lightsaber and Leia's lightsaber on Tatooine near Luke's childhood home.

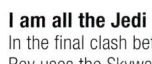

I am all the Jedi
In the final clash between the Jedi and the Sith, Rey uses the Skywalker lightsaber and Organa's blade to reflect Sidious' lightning so it disintegrates her grandfather.

TT-8L/Y7

MANUFACTURER Serv-O-Droid, Inc.
TYPE Gatekeeper droid
AFFILIATION Jabba's palace

Nicknamed "tattletales," TT-8L/Y7s are security droids installed in entryways to screen visitors and scan for weapons. Considered obnoxious and invasive, they relish their position of control. Jabba the Hutt has a TT-8L fitted at his front gate that questions R2-D2 and C-3PO when they first arrive. The Imperial remnant uses TT-8Ls to screen visitors outside its safe houses after the Empire falls.

AHSOKA'S FIRST LIGHTSABERS

CREATOR Ahsoka Tano **MODEL** Handcrafted **TYPE** Jedi lightsaber

Ahsoka Tano's first lightsabers see heavy use during the Clone Wars. The young Jedi Padawan develops a unique fighting style that incorporates a non-standard reverse grip for holding the weapon. Under Anakin Skywalker's instruction, Ahsoka becomes a skilled duelist and wields her weapon in battles on Teth, Geonosis, and Lola Sayu, briefly losing it to a thief in the underlevels of Coruscant. She builds a short-bladed saber to use in conjunction with her primary weapon. When Ahsoka relinquishes her lightsabers on Coruscant after she departs the Jedi Order, Anakin Skywalker returns them to her with improved blue blades shortly before the Siege of Mandalore. Tano then abandons her sabers on a moon near a clone trooper burial site where the *Tribunal* has crashed. Darth Vader later finds and steals one of these sabers to use himself.

Double duty
Both ends of an electrostaff can be activated to deliver a debilitating shock.

Adjustable charge
Electrical charge can be dialed up to lethal levels.

High-ranking droid
A MagnaGuard automatically outranks any battle droid. Their presence indicates an elite Separatist commander must be close by.

MAGNAGUARD

MANUFACTURER Holowan Mechanicals
TYPE Bodyguard droid
AFFILIATION Separatist

MagnaGuards, the robotic bodyguards assigned to General Grievous, share his fearsome reputation. The IG-100 MagnaGuard is manufactured by Holowan Mechanicals and is distantly related to the IG assassin droid from the same company. Each MagnaGuard excels at close-quarter fighting, using its two-handed electrostaff to stun or kill attackers. The MagnaGuards that work with Grievous wear cloaks, a nod to the traditions of the general's homeworld. General Grievous knows he will be facing many Jedi Knights during the Clone Wars and programs his MagnaGuards in dueling techniques that allow them to gang up against a single target. Backup systems allow MagnaGuards to keep fighting even after they lose a limb. While Grievous doesn't expect his MagnaGuards to be able to kill every Jedi who challenges them, he knows his bodyguard screen will exhaust most attackers and leave them vulnerable to a finishing blow delivered by Grievous himself. Aboard Grievous' flagship, *Invisible Hand*, Obi-Wan Kenobi and Anakin Skywalker tangle with a number of MagnaGuards. During the Imperial era, a collector of Jedi lore named Grakkus the Hutt captures Luke Skywalker, pitting a number of old MagnaGuards against the young Jedi in battle.

ELECTROSTAFF

MANUFACTURERS Holowan Mechanicals and Baktoid Armor Workshop
MODEL Electrostaff **TYPE** Two-handed staff

The electrostaff is built from a material that conducts energy, allowing it to intercept lightsaber strikes without being cut in half. Each end of an electrostaff incorporates an electromagnetic module sheathed in energy tendrils that can incapacitate most organic beings. The pirate Taborr Val Dorn used a simplified—and less deadly—electrostaff during the High Republic era. MagnaGuards can spin their electrostaffs so quickly they appear to be circular blurs. Pirate leader Hondo Ohnaka also wields an electrostaff weapon during his raid on farmers on Felucia. During the Imperial era, Noghri assassin Rukh's weapon of choice is a custom electrostaff with a built-in blaster that he uses with lethal efficiency. Years later, HK-87 assassin droids employed by Morgan Elsbeth also use electrostaffs against their most challenging opponents.

MagnaGuard uniforms
The ceremonial cloak is pushed behind the shoulder when fighting.

First line of defense
General Grievous orders his MagnaGuards to intercept Jedi attackers.

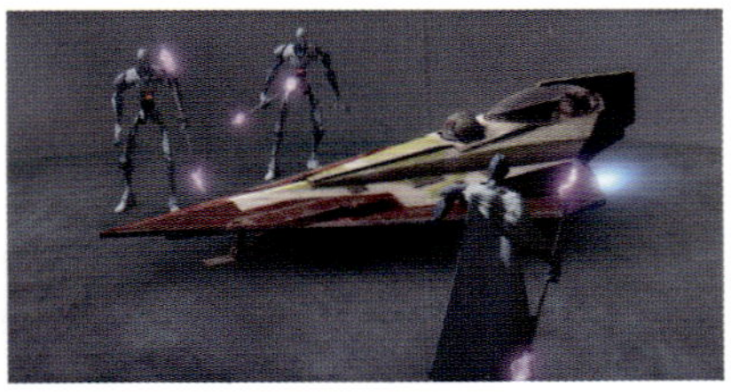

Always watching
MagnaGuards stay vigilant, scanning their surroundings for threats.

TRACTOR BEAM

MANUFACTURER Various **MODEL** Tractor beam
TYPE Starship equipment

Tractor beams are a fundamental piece of technology for starships and space stations. They project a force field that can seize an object in a near-unbreakable grip and pull it into a hangar bay. Aboard warships like the Separatist heavy cruiser *Malevolence*, tractor beams are classified as offensive weapons; these beams are aimed at a fleeing craft to slow its escape or to immobilize it entirely, making it easy prey for the warship's turbolasers. Tractor beams have peaceful applications as well. Space stations use tractor beams to guide arriving vessels to safe landings, and space tugs are outfitted with powerful tractor beams for towing disabled ships.

Powerful pullers
The Imperial *Cantwell*-class Arrestor cruiser is a formidable craft. Equipped with a powerful triple tractor beam array, this vessel is specifically designed to ensnare any rogue ships.

COMMANDO DROIDS

MANUFACTURER Baktoid Combat Automata
TYPE Battle droid **AFFILIATION** Separatist

Commando droids are advanced, sturdier versions of B1 battle droids, programmed with improved combat tactics and equipped with glowing white photoreceptors. Captains and other high-ranking commando droids bear white identifiers on their heads and chests. Most commando droids carry blaster rifles and stun batons, and command units wield vibroswords for one-on-one combat. Criminal gangs such as the Bedlam Raiders are known to steal and reprogram commando droids to protect their territories during the Imperial era. After the Battle of Yavin, Darth Vader and his accomplice, Doctor Chelli Aphra, steal a portable Geonosian droid factory. Vader uses it to create his own secret, private army of commando droids to battle against Doctor Cylo's cybernetic agents. Decades later, a commando droid named N1-ZX is a part of C-3PO's droid spy network, working for the Resistance until his destruction on Kaddak.

Agile adversary
A commando droid is able to move and react much faster than a standard battle droid.

Heavy armor
The droids are designed to withstand blaster fire.

Airborne
Piloting speeder bikes, commando droids blast away at their targets.

LM-432 "MUCKRAKER" CRAB DROID

MANUFACTURER Techno Union **TYPE** Droid tank **AFFILIATION** Separatist

The LM-432 crab droid, also known as the "muckraker," is primarily a military unit that excels at navigating swampy environments. Its six armored limbs provide secure purchase when clambering over uneven terrain, and teeth at the tips of the limbs combined with gripping prongs at the joints allow crab droids to scale steep inclines. The LM-432's face is dominated by three glowing red photoreceptors, while communications antennae keep the droid in contact with its commanders. Two blaster cannons underneath the droid's body serve as long-range threats. On Pijal, a customized crab droid is the prey during each Grand Hunt, an old tradition where the planet's future monarch proves their abilities. In the middle of Crown Princess Fanry's Grand Hunt, the prey droid viciously targets her, until she is saved by her Jedi protectors. During the Clone Wars, crab droids form part of the Separatist armies, fighting on planets across the galaxy.

Lethal limbs
The droid's heavy claws can punch through vehicle armor.

Weak points
By exploiting a crab droid's blind spots, an attacker can slip past its claws and strike its vulnerable central processor.

TECHNOLOGY

JEDI HOLOCRON

CREATOR Various **MODEL** Handcrafted **TYPE** Jedi holocron

Holocrons are information-storage artifacts primarily used by the Jedi, though the Sith have their own holocron traditions. They act as repositories of vital and sensitive knowledge. Most of the data contained on a holocron is related to the nature and applications of the Force, so sharing this knowledge outside the Jedi Order is discouraged. For this reason, many holocrons are constructed with a security mechanism that permits access only to those who exhibit Force ability. It is common for holocrons to resemble evenly proportioned polyhedrons, with the sides made from a crystalline material that glows when in use. A holocron's lessons are typically relayed in the form of an interactive hologram that resembles the Jedi Master who recorded the information.

Hundreds of holocrons have been created by long-vanished Jedi Masters over the centuries. The Jedi Order values these artifacts for their historical significance and their insights into teaching methods. The Order isn't willing to take chances with its holocrons and keeps them in the Jedi Archives in the Jedi Temple, with the rarest specimens locked away behind the movement-triggered lasers and heavy blast doors of the Holocron Vault. Many holocrons will not react unless paired with a specific memory crystal, and for added security, the Order does not store these items together.

During the Clone Wars, bounty hunter Cad Bane raids the Jedi Temple with the intent of penetrating the Holocron Vault. The Jedi detect his intrusion but misidentify his target, allowing Bane to slip through the temple's ventilation shafts. When the shape-shifter Cato Parasitti, Bane's compatriot, impersonates Chief Librarian Jocasta Nu, the ruse distracts the Jedi long enough for Bane to pocket the kyber holocron and exit the temple with little difficulty. After Order 66, many Jedi holocrons fall into the hands of the Sith or collectors of Jedi antiques, such as Grakkus the Hutt. Jocasta Nu survives the Purge and records a whole library of holocrons containing her extensive knowledge.

Cal Kestis and Cere Junda search for a holocron of Jedi Master Eno Cordova hidden in a Bogano vault that contains the locations of Force-attuned children. While they initially plan to rebuild the Jedi Order with this information, Kestis decides to destroy the holocron to protect the children from the Empire. Luke Skywalker and Leia Organa later learn of Qi'ra's failed plot to topple the Sith during the Imperial era from a holocron made by a woman known as the "Archivist." Jocasta Nu's holocron library is eventually found by Luke Skywalker who carries out Jocasta's last wish and establishes a new Jedi Order.

Retrieval
Data playback often takes the form of interactive holograms.

Members only
Holocrons can detect if the user is a Force-wielder.

> "The holocrons contain the most closely guarded secrets of the Jedi Order."
> **JOCASTA NU**

Hidden knowledge
If a Jedi holocron and a Sith one are combined, a Force-user can receive an answer to any question they have.

Guarded secrets
A special chamber in the Jedi Archives hosts the most valuable holocrons in the history of the Order.

MEGADROID

MANUFACTURER Baktoid Combat Automata **TYPE** Battle droid **AFFILIATION** Separatist

The Megadroid is a huge, highly advanced battle droid with electrically charged claws and a durasteel coating. After Yoda uncovers the Separatists' designs for this new threat, he and Anakin Skywalker destroy the Golatha factory producing the droids, as well as an escaped prototype.

KYBER CRYSTAL
MODEL Handcrafted **TYPE** Memory crystal

Kyber crystals are rare, naturally occurring gems found on planets scattered across the galaxy. They concentrate energy in a unique manner and resonate with the Force. A kyber crystal forms the heart of a lightsaber, focusing energy into the weapon's blade. Dark-side users corrupt kyber crystals, normally taken from Jedi in combat, for their lightsabers. They pour their agony into the crystals, causing them to bleed and turn red. Jedi younglings travel to the ice caves in Ilum for a ritual known as the Gathering, where they find crystals for their first lightsabers. The Temple of Kyber on Jedha has a tunnel system underneath it that contains more than 2,000 statues carved from kyber crystals. Imperial scientist Galen Erso develops a method of weaponizing massive kyber crystals, which becomes the basis of the Death Star superlaser.

GAMORREAN AX
MANUFACTURER Various
MODEL Two-handed vibro-ax
TYPE Vibro-ax

The Gamorrean guards in Jabba the Hutt's palace carry intimidating axes as their primary weapons, a display that lets visitors know they mean business. Many of these axes contain vibration generators that improve their cutting ability, though they are just as deadly without them. Gamorrean guards who pledge their loyalty to Boba Fett after Jabba and Bib Fortuna's deaths use a variety of axes.

AQUA DROID
MANUFACTURER Techno Union **TYPE** Droid tank
AFFILIATION Separatist

The Separatists use aqua droids for underwater fighting on oceanic planets such as Kamino and Mon Cala. The droids have retractable laser cannons and can move speedily while submerged, using propellers in their feet. For surprise attacks, the Separatists deploy aqua droids by hiding them in underwater starship wreckage, where they ambush their targets. During the rise of the First Order, Rey faces a rebuilt aqua droid called RK-9 on Mon Cala during an Ancient Rite of Challenge.

SD-K4 ASSASSIN DROID
MANUFACTURER Techno Union **TYPE** Assassin droid **AFFILIATION** Separatist

SD-K4 probes are spiderlike droids programmed for quiet killing. Each assassin probe moves on eight clawed legs and has multiple photoreceptors for scanning its surroundings. If cornered, it can release dozens of smaller droids, through pores on its head, that swarm a target and stab it with their sharp limbs. During the Clone Wars, three Separatist assassin probes attack Duchess Satine Kryze aboard the spaceliner *Coronet*, but Anakin Skywalker and Obi-Wan Kenobi successfully stop the threat.

NIGHTSISTER ENERGY BOW
CREATOR Nightsisters
MODEL Handcrafted **TYPE** Energy bow

The Nightsister energy bow has strings that are made from a plasma that emits a bright pink glow, and is designed to fire arrows made from a similar plasma material. A special group of Nightsisters, known as the Hunters, uses energy bows to track down and eliminate enemies on Mother Talzin's orders. Years after the Separatists massacred the Nightsisters of Dathomir, Nightbrother archers use energy bows to slow down Cal Kestis.

ZYGERRIAN ELECTRO-WHIP
MODEL Zygerrian electro-whip
TYPE Shock whip

Zygerrian enslavers, such as the notorious Miraj Scintel, are known throughout the galaxy for their cruelty. Their weapon of choice is the electro-whip: a metal grip with an extendable wire that glows when powered up. The whips are later used by the Galactic Empire and the Mining Guild to keep individuals they have enslaved in check.

NIGHTSISTER CRYSTAL BALL
CREATOR Nightsisters
MODEL Handcrafted
TYPE Nightsister artifact

The Nightsisters of Dathomir have unusual traditions for tapping into the Force, including the use of crystal balls to give glimpses of future events. During the Clone Wars, Nightsister shaman Mother Talzin uses a crystal ball to locate Savage Opress, and later to find his brother, Maul.

TECHNOLOGY

PHASE II CLONE TROOPER ARMOR
MANUFACTURER Kaminoan Armorsmiths
MODEL Phase II **TYPE** Body armor

Phase II clone armor represents the transition between Phase I clone armor, used by the Grand Army of the Republic, and stormtrooper armor, used by the Galactic Empire. The most obvious difference is the design of the helmet, which contains an advanced filtration system. The armor lacks the life-support system found in Phase I armor, requiring clone troopers to wear additional gear when venturing into areas without a breathable atmosphere. However, Phase II standard armor, with the first prototypes given to ARC troopers, is more easily customizable, and includes additional weapons, armor plating, backpacks, jetpacks, and respirators. There are also specialized variants of Phase II armor tailored to particular environments, modes of battle, and/or mission requirements.

MANDALORIAN ARMOR
MANUFACTURER Various **MODEL** Various **TYPE** Body armor

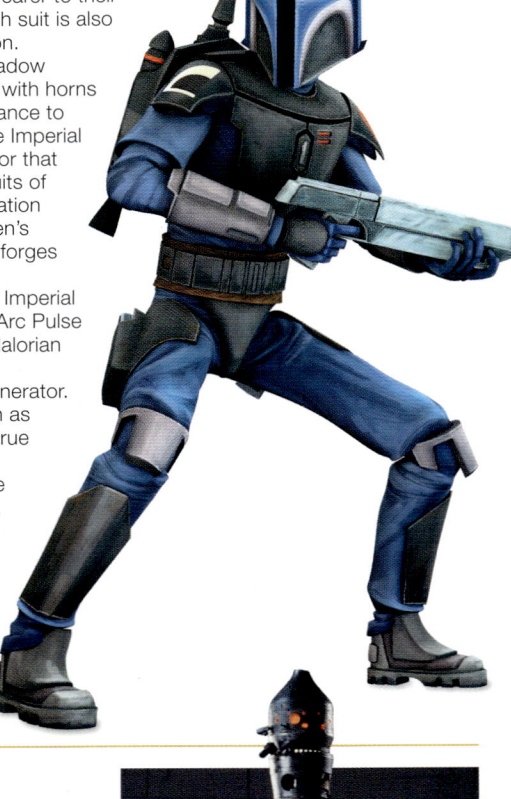

The traditional armor of the Mandalorian people is a symbol of their culture and a special point of pride. Made of beskar, a form of iron unique to Mandalore and the moon of Concordia, it is capable of repelling Jedi lightsabers. Over the centuries the design of the armor has changed. For example, the Mandalorian crusaders used to wear helmets and robes. Mandalorian armor may also be reforged by its wearer to their exact specification; additionally, each suit is also painted to reflect its owner's affiliation. Mandalorian members of Maul's Shadow Collective wear red-and-gray armor with horns on their helmets to show their allegiance to the dark side warrior. Years later, the Imperial Super Commandos wear white armor that echoes stormtrooper gear. Some suits of armor are passed down from generation to generation, much like Sabine Wren's colorful suit, which she frequently reforges and repaints to suit her tastes.

During her time at the Mandalore Imperial Academy, Sabine Wren creates an Arc Pulse Generator that can superheat Mandalorian armor, killing the wearer. Wren and Bo-Katan Kryze later destroy the generator.

Some Mandalorian factions, such as Children of the Watch, believe that true Mandalorians should never remove their helmets in front of others, while other groups do not share this view. Mandalorian armorers are in charge of forging Mandalorian armor, accessories, and weapons—such as the Whistling Bird. The Armorer, from a covert on Nevarro, makes Din Djarin a new set of armor in the years following the fall of the Empire.

JT-12 JETPACK
MANUFACTURER Merr-Sonn Munitions, Inc.
MODEL JT-12 series **TYPE** Personal jetpack

The JT-12 jetpack series is a family of rocket-propelled packs that are capable of both short jumps and long-distance flight for the wearer. The average maximum jetpack speed in flight is 145 kilometers (90.1 miles) per hour. The JT-12 jetpack series predates the Clone Wars and is used by Mandalorian factions, such as Death Watch, bounty hunters like Jango Fett, and even the Galactic Republic. Mandalorians continue to use JT-12 jetpacks after the Mandalorian purge. The pack also features a powerful launcher that can accommodate both the MM9 and Z-6 anti-vehicle homing missile modules in its adapter slot.

IG-SERIES ASSASSIN DROID
MANUFACTURER Holowan Laboratories
MODEL IG-series **TYPE** Assassin droids

Produced by Holowan Laboratories, the IG-series in general is a highly aggressive range of droid models, banned by the Galactic Republic. Creating the IG-series assassin droids turns out to be a fatal mistake for the company thanks to the droids' incomplete programming. When they activate IG-88, the lethal droid turns against his creators and kills everyone in the lab. IG-88 then goes on to work as a bounty hunter, gaining notoriety throughout the galaxy comparable only to Boba Fett's. Other notable IG-series assassin droids include IG-90, who partners with Bossk, and IG-11, who is active during the New Republic era.

INHIBITOR CHIP
MANUFACTURER Kaminoans **MODEL** Custom
TYPE Bio chip

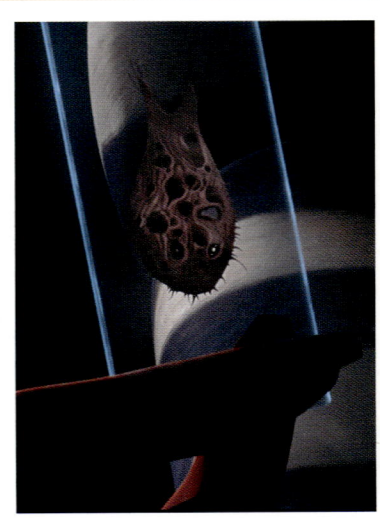

When Jedi Master Sifo-Dyas commissions the Kaminoans to create a clone army, he also orders a bio chip to be developed and inserted into all clone embryo brains in their third stage of development. These bio-chips are originally intended to make the clones less aggressive and more compliant to orders. When Count Dooku has Sifo-Dyas killed and takes over the clone program, he orders the Kaminoans to re-engineer the bio chips to make clones comply with the Emperor's eventual Order 66 and turn against the Jedi. Many clone troopers, including Clone Force 99, who resist Order 66, remove their inhibitor chips once they learn of their existence. The Empire later uses similar chips on the Wookiees and on prisoners.

DEJARIK TABLE
MANUFACTURER Various **MODEL** Various
TYPE Game

Dejarik is a table game popular throughout the galaxy, played by two combatants. Each player typically directs a selection of up to 10 holographic monsters, such as the ghhhk, houjix, Kintan strider, molator, k'lor'slug, monnok, scrimp, bulbous, ng'ok, and Mantellian savrip, to act out battles to the death. The board is comprised of three concentric circles, with two rings segmented into 12 divisions and an inner ring acting as a single battle arena. If electronic game boards aren't available, some players use handmade monster pieces, which are almost as popular.

> "I am programmed to resist intimidation."
> KRAKEN

Triple eyes Three optical receptors allow sight in a variety of spectrums.

SUPER TACTICAL DROID
MANUFACTURER Baktoid Combat Automata
TYPE Tactical droid **AFFILIATION** Separatist

Super tactical droids are an upgraded line based on the T-series tactical droids. They serve as generals in the Separatist Droid Army during the Clone Wars. They are not only an advancement on the previous model, but also consider themselves superior to their biological counterparts. As a result, they are arrogant and argumentative and operate without sympathy or morality, executing ruthless strategies. Notable individuals include General Kalani, who is still active during the Imperial era; Aut-O, a Separatist fleet commander defeated by D-Squad; and Kraken, assigned to aid Admiral Trench.

DARTH SIDIOUS' LIGHTSABERS
CREATOR Darth Sidious
MODEL Handcrafted
TYPE Sith lightsaber

Darth Sidious creates a pair of lightsabers during his apprenticeship under Darth Plagueis. Of discerning tastes, Sidious constructs his lightsabers using nearly indestructible phrik, a metallic compound, and an aurodium emitter, all finished with electrum. At the core of both is a corrupted kyber crystal. He rarely uses his lightsabers—only when absolutely necessary—as it would immediately reveal his identity as a Sith. Instead Sidious prefers to exercise his powers of manipulation and use servants to carry out his dark deeds.

Secret weapon One of Sidious' lightsabers is normally hidden inside a neuranium sculpture displayed in his office within the Senate building.

BUZZ DROID
MANUFACTURER Colicoid Creation Nest
TYPE Pistoeka sabotage droid **AFFILIATION** Separatist

Drill The drill's twisted teeth inflict maximum damage.

Swarms of small buzz droids attack Republic ships during the Clone Wars. Vulture droid starfighters and droid tri-fighters fire discord missiles at Republic targets, containing up to seven buzz droids, each in a shock-absorbing, spherical casing. The droids dodge their way through enemy defenses with maneuvering thrusters until they reach their targets and hatch open. Mechanical arms and cutting tools then dismantle enemy ships and droids to inflict as much damage as possible. The droids are difficult to remove from ships, and while the Republic has not developed adequate defenses against buzz droids, Jedi have found ways to work around them. During the Imperial era, some rebel forces, including the Free Ryloth Movement, deploy buzz droids in their attacks on Imperial ships. For a time, Imperial Officer Thrawn keeps a number of buzz droids so he can learn more about Republic-era technology. The *Deliverance*, a Star Destroyer under the command of Rebel Alliance General Hera Syndulla, also comes under attack from a swarm of buzz droids shortly before the Battle of Jakku.

Weak spot When a buzz droid lands on Anakin Skywalker's starfighter, R2-D2 zaps it in its most vulnerable spot: the main photoreceptor.

IMPERIAL TURBOLASER
MANUFACTURER Taim & Bak **MODEL** XX-9 heavy turbolaser **TYPE** Anti-ship emplacement weapon

The XX-9 heavy turbolaser features a rotating double-laser cannon turret mounted on a square base. The weapons are typically installed on the surface of Star Destroyers and the Death Star, where they are divided into four sections. The top level includes the turbolaser battery, while the second, lower, level houses rows of capacitor banks to store energy. The third section contains the support crew and maintenance stations, while the lowest level encloses gunnery stations and control computers.

Assault weapon Stormtroopers fire at the crew of the *Millennium Falcon* as they escape from the first Death Star.

STORMTROOPER BLASTER RIFLE
MANUFACTURER BlasTech Industries
MODEL E-11 **TYPE** Blaster rifle

Magnatomic adhesion grip handle

Pressure-sensitive trigger

The BlasTech E-11 is standard issue for Imperial stormtroopers. It combines lethal firepower with an impressive range in a versatile design. Most visible of the E-11's features are the telescopic range-finding sight and the folding three-position stock, which convert the blaster into a full-length rifle. Standard power cells carry energy for approximately 100 shots, while plasma cartridges last for more than 500 shots; replacement power cells and gas cartridges are carried on the soldier's utility belt. Lastly, the blaster also features an advanced cooling system for superior performance.

TECHNOLOGY

DARKSABER
MANUFACTURER Tarre Vizsla **MODEL** Handcrafted **TYPE** Specialty lightsaber

The only black lightsaber of its kind, the Darksaber represents strength and unity for Mandalorians. According to legend, the saber can be wielded only by someone who has won it in combat, and its possessor becomes the rightful ruler of Mandalore. Many individuals use the Darksaber in combat, including Pre Vizsla, Maul, Sabine Wren, Bo-Katan Kryze, Din Djarin, and Moff Gideon.

FALLING TO MAUL
Hundreds of years before the Clone Wars, the first Mandalorian to enter the Jedi Order, Tarre Vizsla, creates the Darksaber. It's a unique lightsaber with a sinister black blade that glows with an eerie halo. The Darksaber is later stolen from the Jedi Order by House Vizsla, who use it to unite the Mandalorians. The artifact eventually falls into the hands of Pre Vizsla, leader of the Mandalorian Death Watch. After Vizsla stages a coup to take control of Mandalore, Maul kills him and takes the weapon, ruling over Mandalore himself. Maul wields the Darksaber until he and Mother Talzin are defeated by Darth Sidious, Count Dooku, and General Grievous on Dathomir.

> "It's not a gift to be given, no matter how well-intended."
>
> **BO-KATAN KRYZE**

Tool of vengeance
After years of seeking revenge against Obi-Wan Kenobi, Maul uses the Darksaber to kill the woman he knows Kenobi loves—Duchess Satine Kryze of Mandalore.

Unusual weapon
No other lightsaber is known to have a black blade.

UNITING MANDALORE
During the Imperial era, Maul stores the Darksaber in his Dathomir lair, where he and Jedi Ezra Bridger plan to use Nightsister magicks. Ezra's allies—Mandalorian Sabine Wren and Jedi Kanan Jarrus—track them there and are possessed by Nightsister spirits. Sabine wields the Darksaber against Ezra, until he is able to free her and Kanan from the Nightsisters' grip. At this point, Sabine presents the Darksaber to Kanan for safekeeping. Later, Sabine is asked by her allies to learn to wield the Darksaber, in hopes she will unite a Mandalorian army with the Rebel Alliance. When Sabine returns home, Imperial Viceroy Gar Saxon takes the weapon and battles Sabine, who defeats him using Ezra's lightsaber. Sabine reclaims the Darksaber to use in the ensuing Mandalorian Civil War. She later offers the former regent of Mandalore, Bo-Katan Kryze, the weapon to unite Mandalore against the Empire.

CHANGING HANDS
In an attempt to save her people, Bo-Katan surrenders the Darksaber to Moff Gideon after the Imperial assault during the Night of a Thousand Tears leads to the destruction of much of Mandalore. Din Djarin later disarms Gideon of the Darksaber while rescuing Grogu from captivity. He attempts to give the saber to Bo-Katan, but she refuses it, as she didn't win it in combat. On Mandalore, Djarin loses the blade when he is captured by a cyborg scavenger. Bo-Katan finds and uses the Darksaber to free Djarin, but returns the weapon to him. On Plazir-15, Djarin insists Bo-Katan should wield the Darksaber as she defeated the one who disarmed him of the blade. Bo-Katan accepts the blade, re-assuming the role of the leader of the Mandalorians. On a mission to retake control of Mandalore, Bo-Katan battles Gideon with the Darksaber until Gideon crushes the hilt, destroying the legendary weapon.

Passing the blade
Believing that the Darksaber came into her possession so she could protect Mandalore by giving the blade to a wise leader, Sabine Wren bestows it to Bo-Katan Kryze.

Dangerous blade
The Darksaber can only be blocked easily in combat by lightsabers and beskar. Though, when Gideon wields the Darksaber against Din Djarin's Mandalorian beskar staff, it heats the metal up.

773 FIREPUNCHER SNIPER RIFLE

MANUFACTURER Merr-Sonn Munitions, Inc.
MODEL 773 Firepuncher **TYPE** Sniper rifle

The weapon of choice for Crosshair and many other Republic sharpshooters, the 773 Firepuncher is a versatile sniper rifle with different functions and configurations. It acts as blaster rifle, grappling-hook launcher, and homing-beacon dispatch, and it can also fire many types of ammo, including electro-darts and tripwires.

KATARN-CLASS COMMANDO ARMOR

MANUFACTURER Kaminoan Armorsmiths Ltd
MODEL *Katarn*-class
TYPE Full body armor

Tougher and more advanced than standard-issue clone gear, *Katarn*-class commando armor is reserved for special forces in the Grand Army of the Republic, including the Bad Batch. It often appears bulkier than regular armor and includes a backpack for additional ammunition and accessories. The helmet is also unique, incorporating specialized tech for high-risk missions.

DATA VISOR

TYPE Military gear

Tech of the Bad Batch wears a key piece of gear unlike anything belonging to his squadmates: a visor with myriad capabilities. Essentially a transparent screen that lowers to the eye area, the device auto-detects a speaker's language and converts it to Aurebesh text. It can also zoom, record, and scan.

D-WING DROID

MANUFACTURER Techno Union
MODEL D-1 series aerial battle droid
TYPE Security droid

D1-series aerial battle droids, also called D-wing droids, are used by the Techno Union to protect its headquarters on Skako Minor. With their animalistic gait and retractable wings, they are decidedly different from the B1 model. A large squad of D-wing droids battles the Bad Batch and Anakin Skywalker when they come to rescue clone trooper Echo.

DECIMATOR DROID

MANUFACTURER Baktoid Innovations
MODEL Prototype S/D
TYPE Decimator droid

The decimator droid is an aptly named piece of tech that is utilized by the Techno Union. Orb-shaped, the device floats in any direction, emitting purple energy tentacles that seek out and destroy organic life. It also has heat-laser functionality to melt and break through metal, making it a formidable weapon.

MANDALORIAN VAULT

MANUFACTURER Concordian Crescent Technologies
MODEL Custom
TYPE Jedi-grade solitary containment vault

The Mandalorian vault is a sarcophagus used to transport prisoners, particularly Force-attuned ones. These vaults date from the time of the Mandalorian wars against the Jedi. By the time of Duchess Satine Kryze's pacifist rule, most vaults are destroyed. Bo-Katan Kryze uses the last remaining Mandalorian vault to deliver the captured Maul to the Republic after the Siege of Mandalore. The vault used to transport Maul floats on repulsorlifts and has control buttons along the left side. The prisoner inside is restrained and gagged. Maul is unable to escape the vault, only leaving it when Ahsoka Tano frees him during Order 66.

CHAIN CODE

MANUFACTURER Empire
MODEL N/A
TYPE Identification device

Chain codes are issued by the Empire to identify and track every citizen. During the transition from the Old Republic to the Empire, chain codes become necessary for conducting everyday activities. The New Republic also uses chain codes to identify people. The Bounty Hunters Guild provides a target's chain code information to hired hunters.

FENNEC'S SNIPER RIFLE

MANUFACTURER Merr-Sonn Munitions
MODEL 785MK Firepuncher-X **TYPE** Sniper rifle

Although Fennec Shand primarily uses her weapon to hit distant targets, she is proficient in using it at any range. She often carries both her sniper rifle and a smaller blaster pistol. Her sniper rifle has a blade concealed in the stock, and its shots can even break through beskar armor if Shand hits the target a few times.

FENNEC'S HELMET

MODEL Custom **TYPE** Combat armor

Bounty hunter Fennec Shand has owned her signature helmet for decades. She wears it only during combat, donning it quickly in moments of tension, such as when the clone Hunter attacks her to protect her friend Omega. During one particular altercation, Fennec throws her helmet at a stormtrooper to distract them as she fights beside Din Djarin and Boba Fett.

ZYGERRIAN ENERGY BOW

MANUFACTURER Zygerrian Slavers Guild
MODEL Haranger
TYPE Energy bow

The clone Omega takes an energy bow from Zygerrian criminals during a mission on Ord Mantell. She uses it in her adventures, protecting herself and the rest of Clone Force 99. When in use, the bow fires bright, pink laser bolts.

LL-30 BLASTER PISTOL

MANUFACTURER BlasTech Industries
MODEL LL-30 **TYPE** Blaster pistol

The LL-30 is a quick-draw blaster pistol used throughout the galaxy. Cad Bane carries two of these weapons. He out-draws Clone Force 99 leader Hunter with his LL-30s and badly injures the clone the first time they encounter each other. In another battle, Fennec Shand gains an advantage over Bane by knocking an LL-30 out of his hand, and in a duel at Mos Pelgo, Bane uses his pair of LL-30s to take down Cobb Vanth.

TK TROOPER ARMOR

MANUFACTURER Empire
MODEL TK
TYPE Combat armor

The Empire issues TK stormtrooper armor to its first generation of volunteer troopers, who work alongside some clone troopers. The TK armor design serves as a transition from clone trooper armor to what becomes regulation stormtrooper equipment. It's manufactured in multiple sizes instead of the standardized clone armor size.

SKARA NAL COMPASS

TYPE Navigation tool/key

Enhanced clone Omega finds this mysterious compass in a junkyard during her adventures with Clone Force 99. The compass contains coordinates to the planet Skara Nal and helps solve some of the puzzles inside an ancient mountain complex there. Additionally, it serves as a key to gain access within an ancient walker superweapon.

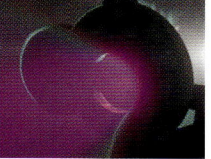

IPSIUM

MANUFACTURER Naturally occurring
MODEL N/A
TYPE Ore

Ipsium is a glowing mineral that can be refined into fuel. The ore must be extracted from the surrounding rocks very carefully because the unrefined ipsium is very volatile and prone to exploding. During the Clone Wars, the Techno Union mines ipsium on Ipsidon.

THE MASK OF MOMIN

TYPE Headgear

Once thought lost, the Mask of Momin is a relic strong with the dark side of the Force. It is sculpted by the heretical Sith Lord Darth Momin. Centuries after his death, the mask exhibits mysterious powers. It can corrupt those in its presence, possess beings, and even speak telepathically.

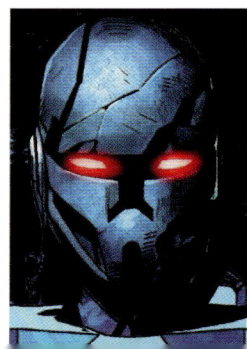

TECHNOLOGY

STORMTROOPER ARMOR
MANUFACTURER Imperial Department of Military Research
MODEL Stormtrooper armor **TYPE** Body armor

Stormtroopers are anonymously shielded in white plastoid composite armor worn over a black body glove. Armed with some of the most powerful weapons and finest equipment in the Empire, stormtroopers are among the most dreaded opponents of rebel freedom fighters.

This armor protects stormtroopers from inhospitable environments and can also protect the wearer against the vacuum of space for a short period of time. Stormtrooper helmets have built-in filtration systems that extract breathable atmosphere from polluted environments. For extended operations in the vacuum of space or the filtration of potent toxins, troopers wear backpacks with extended life-support capabilities. Stormtrooper armor is generally impervious to most blast shrapnel and projectiles. It can be punctured by a powerful blaster bolt, but the armor will generally withstand glancing hits.

Each stormtrooper is equipped with a utility belt containing a variety of equipment, including a compact toolkit, power packs, and energy rations. The belt may also contain a comlink, macro-binoculars, and a grappling hook. Field troops are allowed additional ammunition and comprehensive survival equipment. Backpacks can include field communicator sets, mortar launchers, and blaster components.

Stormtroopers usually carry a thermal detonator on the back of their utility belts. Controls on the detonator are not labeled, but include settings for arming, blast intensity, and timing. While detonators are not normally used within ships or bases, troopers carry a full complement of such field gear so they are prepared for any situation.

"There's one. Set for stun."

Sniper position knee protector plate

TK-9091

RANGE TROOPER BOOTS
MANUFACTURER Imperial Department of Military Research
MODEL #A7.5 Range Trooper Boots **TYPE** Magnetomic gription boots

Operating on tight schedules, range troopers accompany Imperial vehicles and convoys traveling under difficult conditions, and the shipments they protect are usually highly sensitive. On Vandor, the high-speed conveyex train must ensure timely delivery of coaxium to the Imperial vault. Range troopers have to climb outside the train to address any threats while it is in motion. Their magnetomic gription boots ensure they remain attached to the conveyex, even during sharp turns at 90 kilometers (56 miles) per hour—and while hanging upside down. These smart boots have sensors that monitor muscle contractions in troopers' legs to determine when to activate their magnetomic fields.

COAXIUM
MANUFACTURER Various
TYPE Hypermatter/Hyperfuel

Before the dawn of hyperspace travel, space mariners observe purrgil creatures breathing in Clouzon-36 gas before "jumping" away into space, moving faster than the speed of light. Upon examining dead purrgil, they find deposits of coaxium in their organs. These deposits are a metabolic product of Clouzon-36 and are what allowed the purrgil to travel through hyperspace. Coaxium is later discovered in natural deposits on worlds such as Kessel. An extremely valuable substance, coaxium is highly volatile and must be refined to render it less explosive and more stable. A tiny amount of refined coaxium is used to coat the inside of a ship's hyperdrive. When the coaxium coating is energized, it triggers a reaction that enables hyperspace travel.

HAN'S DICE
MODEL Custom
TYPE Corellian Spike Dice

Han Solo owns a pair of dice plated in aurodium (a metal more valuable than gold) and connected by a chain. Although they are the last thing he has from his father, Han gives them to Qi'ra for luck when they escape Corellia. She holds on to them over the years and later gives them back during their mission to Kessel. After winning the Millennium Falcon from Lando Calrissian, Han hangs them in the ship's cockpit. Years later, Luke Skywalker retrieves them from the ship on Ahch-To, and then appears to give them to General Organa during the Battle of Crait. After Luke vanishes, Kylo Ren watches the dice likewise fade away.

BECKETT'S BLASTERS
MANUFACTURER BlasTech **MODELS** DG-29 and RSKF-44
TYPE Heavy blaster pistols

Tobias Beckett's weapons of choice are two heavy blaster pistols from BlasTech. In his dominant left hand he wields a DG-29 Sideloader, which is fitted with an image-intensifying macroscope for long-distance shots. In his right hand he wields a powerful RSKF-44, an ideal firearm for short-range encounters (underworld rumors suggest this was the last thing bounty hunter Aurra Sing ever saw). Those unfortunate enough to be at the business end of either weapon will notice the barrel of each has a rainbow-ring: a clear indication of heat-exposure oxidation. Beckett gives his other weapon, another BlasTech heavy blaster pistol, the DL-44, to Han Solo.

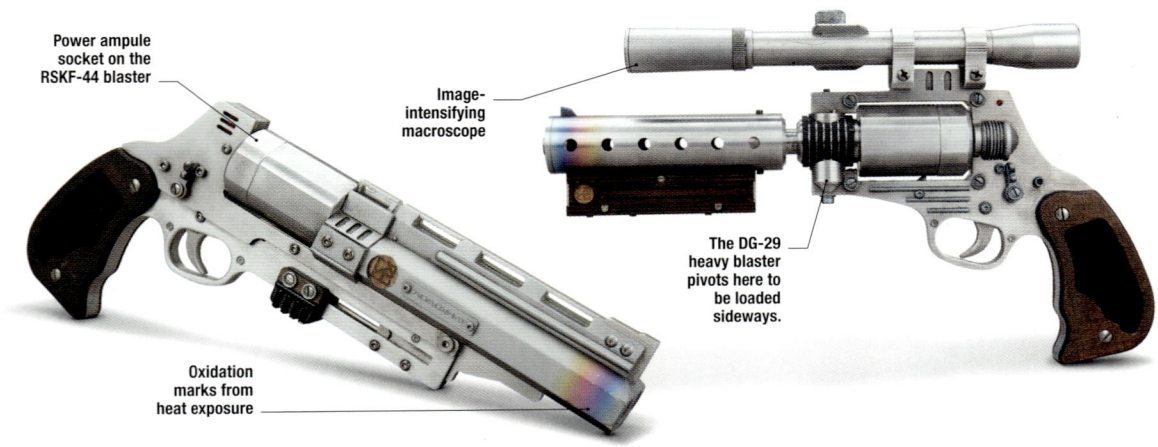

Power ampule socket on the RSKF-44 blaster

Image-intensifying macroscope

Oxidation marks from heat exposure

The DG-29 heavy blaster pivots here to be loaded sideways.

ENFYS NEST'S SHIELDS
MODEL Custom **TYPE** Gauntlet shield

Enfys Nest's gauntlet shields are made of beskar (Mandalorian iron) armor plates that fan out along an articulated servo-joint. They expand with a rapid flick of her wrist and fold up in a similar manner, allowing for comfortable storage on her forearms. Beskar ore is sourced from Mandalore and its moon, Concordia. Plates of Mandalorian iron were originally developed as a protection against Jedi lightsabers. Enfys Nest is highly skilled in using her gauntlet shields to deflect blaster bolts and projectiles from hand-held weapons while sparring with her opponents.

ENFYS NEST'S HELMET
MODEL Custom **TYPE** Combat helmet

Enfys Nest wears a combat helmet traditionally passed down in her family from mother to daughter. It hides her identity (assisted by a built-in vocoder) and offers protection in battle. The helmet's horns conceal transmission antennae. The reverse eclipse emblem above the chrome visor represents a shining spotlight through eclipsing darkness. Enfys wrote a stanza of poetry above it, reading, "Until we reach the last edge, the last opening, the last star, and can go no higher."

ENFYS NEST'S STAFF
MODEL Custom **TYPE** Electroripper staff

Enfys Nest prefers melee weapons to blasters. Her manifold martial arts skills stem from an upbringing that prioritizes protecting her village, her family, the weak, and the defenseless against marauders and criminal gangs. Enfys' electroripper staff is a handmade weapon with a kinetite charge at the blunt end capable of producing a shock wave when slammed against a surface. The blade end is lined with a glowing energy ribbon that can incapacitate an opponent or, with a violent thrust, cut through metal.

DRYDEN VOS' KYUZO PETARS
MANUFACTURER Kyuzo crafters **MODEL** Custom **TYPE** Bladed weapon

Vicious crime boss Dryden Vos wields a pair of unique petars, crafted by a skilled Kyuzo blade maker to Vos' exact specifications. The double blades feature a conductive tempered carbon edge lined with a monomolecular energy cord to ensure it will slice through most targets. On the opposite side of the activator switch, bronzium knuckle guards protect Vos' clawed hands in melee combat. Rechargeable energy cells embedded in the hilt can be re-powered if placed on a recharging surface. Vos often uses the blades to personally execute anyone who has displeased him. When Vos' lieutenant, Qi'ra, betrays him, she impales Vos with one of his own petars.

DRYDEN VOS' SIGNET RING
MODEL Crimson Dawn **TYPE** Signet ring

Dryden Vos' Crimson Dawn signet ring is his most prized possession and allows him to access encrypted data networks, elite syndicate ships, and areas solely reserved for him as the public face of Crimson Dawn. Vos also uses the ring to communicate directly with the leader of Crimson Dawn, the former Sith Lord, Maul. The ring itself is made of solid bronzium, and the signet is a blood-red aurodium-cinnabar matrix. After Vos' previously trusted lieutenant, Qi'ra, kills him, she uses his signet ring to contact Maul, giving him a fake story of Vos' death.

SABACC
TYPE Card game

Sabacc is a card game that is popular all over the galaxy, and often accompanied by extensive betting. The goal is to win the pot of money or items of value by collecting a hand of cards with a total value of 23 or less. A sabacc deck comprises 76 cards, of which 60 cards include four suits (coins, flasks, sabers, and staves); there are 15 numbered cards per suit. The remaining 16 cards contain two sets of eight special cards with negative or null values. Lando Calrissian loses the *Millennium Falcon* to Han Solo in a variation of this game named Corellian Spike.

A pair of dice is also used when playing Corellian Spike

LANDO CALRISSIAN'S SE-14R
MANUFACTURER BlasTech Industries **MODEL** SE-14r **TYPE** Light repeating blaster

The SE-14r is a versatile blaster, designed to carry an optional scope, suppressor, and buttstock. It is carried by some stormtroopers, death troopers, and Imperial officers. While the SE-14r is an inexpensive blaster, famed smuggler Lando Calrissian owns a flashy model, modified to match his stylish and debonair lifestyle. It is plated in brushed chromium, an expensive material mined from one of Naboo's moons, and has a Tibrin mother-of-pearl handle. While Lando would rather avoid battles, he wields his SE-14r weapon during escapades on Kullgroon and Kessel. When Lando disguises his identity on Pasaana, he modifies one of his blasters into a prod pistol that includes a crossbow with arrow bolts and can confuse blaster detectors.

E-22 RIFLE
MANUFACTURER BlasTech Industries **MODEL** E-22 **TYPE** Blaster rifle

The double-barreled E-22 blaster rifle is commonly used by shoretroopers on Scarif and mudtroopers on Mimban. The E-22 is more powerful than the standard-issue E-11 blaster rifles carried by most stormtroopers. Its main drawback is that its recoil sleeve can become clogged, for example by Mimbanese mud. After the fall of the Empire, some stormtroopers continue to carry and use E-22 rifles during their work for the Imperial remnant.

T-21 LIGHT REPEATING BLASTER
MANUFACTURER BlasTech Industries **MODEL** T-21 **TYPE** Light repeating blaster rifle

The T-21 is carried by some Imperial stormtroopers. It is capable of firing powerful blasts at great distances, but is difficult to aim precisely owing to its heavy recoil and lack of a targeting scope.

342 TECHNOLOGY

CAL KESTIS' SECOND LIGHTSABER
MANUFACTURER Cal Kestis **MODEL** Handcrafted
TYPE Jedi lightsaber

After Cal Kestis damages the lightsaber of his Master, Jaro Tapal, on Dathomir, he travels to Ilum to build a new one. Cal visits the icy caves that he first went to during the Gathering ritual as a Padawan to build his first lightsaber, which was lost during Order 66. Inside the caves, Cal finds a kyber crystal that splits into two in his hands. He uses the crystals, along with parts from Tapal and Cere Junda's lightsabers, to craft a double-bladed lightsaber that can be separated into two individual weapons.

REVA'S LIGHTSABER
MANUFACTURER Third Sister (Reva) **MODEL** Handcrafted
TYPE Inquisitor lightsaber

Reva's double-bladed lightsaber hilt can be separated into two single weapons that each emit red blades. Like other Inquisitors' lightsabers, the Third Sister's weapon includes a circular disc at its center, which allows the lightsaber blade to spin when both sides are attached. During Reva's pursuit of Obi-Wan Kenobi, she uses her lightsaber to stab the Grand Inquisitor and battle Darth Vader. On Tatooine, after Reva decides to spare Luke Skywalker's life, she lays her lightsaber down in the desert sand, leaving behind her life as an Inquisitor.

TOY DROID
MANUFACTURER LeisureMech Enterprises
MODEL L0 **TYPE** Toy droid

The toy droid's small size and hovering ability allow them to easily stay at the side (or inside the pockets) of their owners. Toy droids have photoreceptors, short-range antenna, and a variety of other accessories that can include small saws and flashlights. Toy droids are especially popular among wealthy families as gifts and sources of comfort and companionship for their children. Leia Organa owns a toy droid named L0-LA59, who is with her when she is abducted by the Inquisitor Third Sister. Jedi Master Obi-Wan Kenobi reunites L0-LA59 with Leia on Alderaan after she returns home.

PHASE II PURGE TROOPER ARMOR
MANUFACTURER Imperial Department of Military Research **MODEL** Phase II
TYPE Body armor

When the Empire redesigns its purge trooper armor, the plating and kama remain mostly black with red detailing, and the pauldron is still red. The armor has a new helmet that more closely resembles those of stormtroopers, but its eye shields are recolored red.

CORPO BLASTER
MANUFACTURER BlasTech Industries **MODEL** B1-NA
TYPE Blaster pistol

Preox-Morlana issues Corpo blasters to its Pre-Mor Authority Security Forces, complete with a serial number and branding—features that make the blaster easily identifiable. The lightweight pistol has a detachable sight so security forces can use it at short range and also fire at distant targets.

CLEM'S BLASTER PISTOL
MANUFACTURER BlasTech Industries
MODEL MW-20 **TYPE** Bryar heavy blaster pistol

Precision construction The pistol's ridged grip and perfect balance allows the Andors to fire fast and accurately.

Popular across the galaxy among both civilians and military personnel, the blaster pistol is an all-purpose ranged weapon. Each model has its own features, and the MW-20 Bryar heavy blaster pistol has a large middle cartridge that rotates to drop a new cold barrel into the weapon's front end for optimal discharge and for keeping the weapon cool enough to handle. Cassian Andor's father, Clem, carries a MW-20 Bryar pistol while on salvage runs, and Cassian inherits it after Clem passes. He keeps the useful and sentimental weapon by his side whenever possible.

CORPO RIFLE
MANUFACTURER BlasTech Industries
TYPE Blaster rifle

Preox-Morlana equips its Pre-Mor Authority Security Forces with corporate-branded blaster rifles for heavier firepower. Responsible for upholding Preox-Morlana's rules, along with Pre-Mor Enforcement, Corpos use this long-range weapon for special operations, such as the one on Ferrix.

DEATH STAR PANEL JOINS
MANUFACTURER Narkina 5 Imperial Prison Complex **MODEL** EP-N5 fastener
TYPE Panel joins

The Empire forces inmates at the Narkina 5 Imperial Prison Complex to manufacture technology to meet its demanding quotas without telling the prisoners what the products are for. At one of the complex's facilities, prisoners assemble six-pronged panel joins, which the Empire uses for the Death Star's superlaser dish.

IMPERIAL N-S9 STARPATH UNIT
MANUFACTURER Imperial Department of Military Research

A valuable piece of tech, and a dangerous device in the wrong hands, the Imperial N-S9 Starpath Unit is as sophisticated as it is restricted. The device uses proprietary signals to reveal the location of all Imperial assets, vessels, and installations within nine radial parsecs. Cassian Andor steals one from Steergard Naval Yard with its vector crystal matrix and Imperial seal still intact. He attempts to sell it to fund his departure from Ferrix. Unfortunately the missing unit draws the attention of the Imperial Security Bureau (ISB).

KLORRI-CLAN BATTLE SHIELD
MANUFACTURER Wookiees
TYPE Shield

The Klorri-clan battle shield is a long, teardrop-shaped shield with intricate, symbolic carvings and bronzium bands. When the Wookiees are not wielding the shields in battle, they tend to bring them out only for special ceremonies. Luthen Rael acquires one of the battle shields and displays it in his antiques gallery on Coruscant.

IMPERIAL CONSTRUCTION DROID
TYPE Construction droid

Imperial construction droids have four leglike appendages, allowing them to skitter over the ground with flexibility. Two arms end in three tool extensions capable of fusing parts into place. The Empire employs dozens and dozens of construction droids to place Narkina 5-manufactured tech onto the Death Star superlaser dish.

THE BRIGHT STAR
MANUFACTURER Mustafarians **MODEL** N/A
TYPE Artifact

The crescent-shaped Bright Star is a powerful and sacred Mustafarian artifact. Long ago, Lady Corvax used it to power the Aeon Engine so she could resurrect her husband, but her plan backfired. Instead, the unleashed energy transformed the lush green of the planet into a barren, burning landscape. Years later, Darth Vader seeks the Bright Star to restore Padmé Amidala, but only a descendant of Lady Corvax can obtain the device. Although Vader discovers such a person in the captain of the *Windfall*, they betray Vader and destroy the Bright Star before the Sith Lord can revive his lost love.

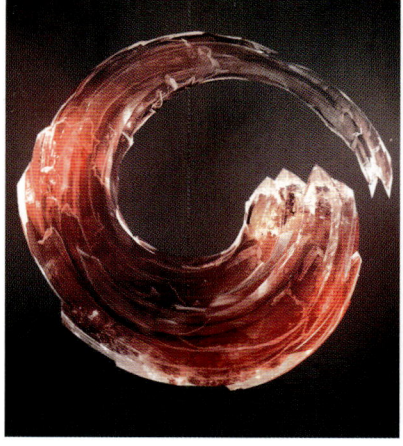

DL-18 BLASTER PISTOL
MANUFACTURER BlasTech Industries
MODEL DL-18 **TYPE** Blaster pistol

The DL-18 blaster pistol is so popular among Tatooine's underworld that it is known as the "Mos Eisley special." Many of Jabba the Hutt's employees are armed with this versatile blaster. The weapon is also favored by renegade Jedi Kanan Jarrus, whose pistol bears a dewback skin handle. The weapon weighs about 1 kilogram (2 lb) and carries enough charge for approximately 100 shots. It has a range of accuracy up to 120 meters (394 ft).

CORVAX SENTINELS
MODEL Sentinel

Quick and agile, the Corvax Sentinel is an ancient design commissioned by Lady Corvax that remains an able fighter years later. Several sentinels guard the tomb of Lord Corvax on Mustafar, waiting behind walls to strike. When the captain of the *Windfall* reaches the chamber, the guards emerge and attack proficiently with electro-staffs that can withstand a lightsaber strike. They ultimately fall to the relic hunter and are unable to keep him from progressing further through the lava planet. Once the captain holds Lord Corvax's lightsaber, he can command Lady Corvax's Marching Horde, which is an entire army of these sentinels. They assist the Mustafarian resistance and the captain against the Imperials.

LORD CORVAX'S LIGHTSABER
MANUFACTURER Lord Corvax **MODEL** N/A
TYPE Lightsaber

Lord Corvax's lightsaber—also called the Light Sword—is decidedly unique from other weapons of its kind. Emitting a blue blade, this ancient lightsaber's kyber crystal isn't encased in the hilt but rather sits exposed in the center of an elegant crossguard. Years after his death, Corvax mysteriously returns and gifts his weapon to a descendant, the captain of the *Windfall*. He uses the lightsaber to command an army of sentinels known as the Marching Horde, duel Darth Vader, and destroy the mystical Bright Star relic and Aeon Engine device.

HERA'S BLASTER
MANUFACTURER Eirriss Ryloth Defense Tech
MODEL Blurrg-1120 **TYPE** Holdout blaster

The Blurrg-1120, named after a creature native to Ryloth, is a versatile blaster featuring nine firing modes, including single- and double-shot. The Eirriss family, whose company manufactures the weapon, are backers of the Twi'lek freedom fighters who battle against the Separatist occupation of Ryloth during the Clone Wars. The family continues to support Cham Syndulla and his movement to free Ryloth from Imperial oppression. Cham's daughter, the rebel leader Hera Syndulla, proudly wields her Blurrg-1120 blaster, as a symbol of rebellion against the Empire. She continues to carry it while working with the New Republic.

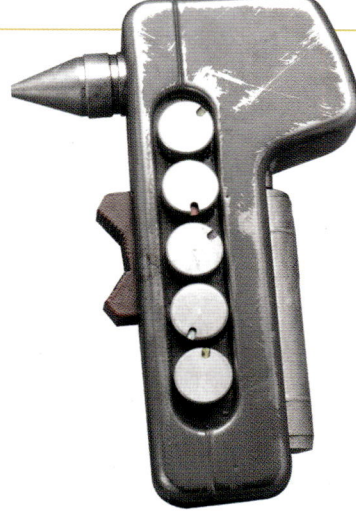

SABINE WREN'S AIRBRUSHES
MANUFACTURER Neco Jeyrroo's Artisan Supplies **MODEL** Baobab EZ3 Airbrush
TYPE Artist's airbrush

Sabine Wren uses a pair of airbrushes to paint and repaint her room aboard the *Ghost*, and also to leave tasteful but provocative call signs in Imperial-controlled areas. She also uses them to decorate Ezra's Roost when she takes up residence. Each one has an adjustable nozzle to change the focus of the spray, as well as a slider below the nozzle to tweak the power and rate of spray. Five knobs on the left side of each airbrush adjust the colors. Removable cartridges of custom color sets fit into the back of the devices.

KANAN'S LIGHTSABER
MANUFACTURER Kanan Jarrus **MODEL** Handcrafted
TYPE Jedi lightsaber

Kanan originally builds his lightsaber when he's a Jedi Padawan with help from Professor Huyang who gives him a blade emitter. After Order 66, Kanan hides his Jedi identity for nearly 15 years, keeping his lightsaber disassembled in a secret compartment, until Ezra eventually discovers it. Every time Kanan uses the weapon, he makes himself a target for the Empire. He comes to wield it against a range of dark-side warriors, including Inquisitors and even Darth Vader. After being blinded by Maul during a duel, Kanan uses the Force to "see," and he continues to fight with his lightsaber. He loses his weapon shortly before his death, and it is recovered by Lothal's Governor, Arihnda Pryce. After her demise, its whereabouts are unknown.

SITH HOLOCRON
MANUFACTURER Various Sith Lords **MODEL** Various
TYPE Information storage device

Sith Lords use holocrons as data storage devices. Similar in their basic function to Jedi holocrons, the Sith versions are shaped like tetrahedrons and pyramids. These dangerously evil devices foster a strong connection to the Force, and only someone drawing upon the dark side can open one. Ezra Bridger acquires a holocron from the Sith temple on Malachor, and as he uses it, the device begins to manipulate him. Ezra and Maul use the Sith holocron and Kanan's Jedi holocron together, in an effort to see visions of what they most desire, causing both holocrons to shatter.

TECHNOLOGY

ZEB'S BO-RIFLE

MANUFACTURER Lasan-Malamut Firearms Corp.
MODEL AB-75 **TYPE** Lasan Honor Guard bo-rifle

The Lasan bo-rifle, which is highly specialized and has a long tradition in Lasat culture, is the signature weapon of Garazeb "Zeb" Orrelios. Bo-rifles are used exclusively by the Lasan Honor Guard, of which Zeb is a former captain, and come in a variety of forms. Since the Empire razed Lasan, bo-rifles are rarely seen around the galaxy; much like Jedi lightsabers during the years of the Empire, bo-rifles are relics of antiquity.

Bo-rifles are nonetheless versatile weapons for violent times, and feature two modes for combat. Not only is the bo-rifle a robust and reliable ranged weapon, it can be quickly transformed into a deadly electrostaff, which is an ideal configuration for a powerful Lasan to pummel a squad of stormtroopers in close quarters.

The rifle component's power supply and discharge are similar to those of an EE-3 carbine rifle, and the tips emit electromagnetic pulses that stun opponents and neutralize ray shields. The bo-staff is activated by twisting the top handle downward, pressing both handles inward, and then activating both EMP tips. In staff mode, the weapons measure 2 meters (6½ ft) long. Zeb's firearm weighs 19 kilograms (41 lbs), requiring considerable strength to wield.

Zeb uses his weapon throughout his time as a member of the *Ghost* crew and later as part of the Rebel Alliance. When he's reunited with two surviving Lasat, Zeb helps them conduct a ritual to find the fabled Lasat homeworld, Lira San. Employing a rarely used functionality of his bo-rifle that channels the Ashla—the Lasan interpretation of the Force—Zeb is able to locate Lira San and pilot the *Ghost* through an imploded star cluster to reach the legendary planet.

EMP generator tips
The tips carry a maximum adjustable voltage of 11,000V.

Brute force
Zeb leaves a pile of stunned and pummeled stormtroopers in his wake.

SABINE WREN'S ARMOR

MODEL Customized
TYPE Mandalorian armor

Sabine Wren's Mandalorian armor is 500 years old. She inherits it through her clan when she comes of age, and has reforged it at least twice. It has been worn by many legendary warriors and survived many great battles. As an artist, Sabine periodically repaints it with different designs and colors. Until the liberation of Lothal, she maintains her own signature starbird insignia on her left breastplate, though occasionally changes the colors. Her pauldrons have had a succession of different designs, but Sabine's left pauldron has always featured an animal, including, at certain points, an anooba, a fyrnock, and a convor. When Sabine is reunited with Ezra on Peridea, her right pauldron features the Rebel Alliance symbol while a purrgil is visible on her left pauldron.

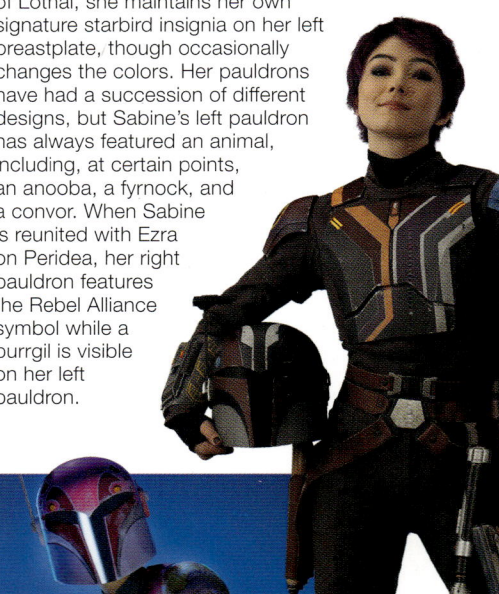

Acquiring accessories
During Sabine's early rebel missions, she does not utilize many Mandalorian gadgets. She eventually gains a jetpack and a pair of Mandalorian vambraces.

His best shot
Ezra fires his energy slingshot at ISB officer Alexsandr Kallus on the planet Kessel.

EZRA'S SLINGSHOT

CREATOR Xexto tinkerer **MODEL** Handcrafted
TYPE Wrist-mounted energy slingshot

Ezra Bridger acquired his energy slingshot from his friend Ferpil Wallaway, who owns a pawnshop on Lothal. It was constructed by another Xexto friend of Ferpil's. Slingshots of various kinds are popular on their home planet, Troiken, as the inhabitants' extra arms make them more convenient to use. Slingshots are favored by children on Lothal as well. Pulling the virtual line back builds a low-voltage charge that can be launched accurately for long distances and, as with a Jawa ion blaster, the power is sufficient to disable droids and computer systems. Although the self-charging firing mechanism is not engineered to be lethal, it can stun a living being.

IG-RM DROID

MANUFACTURER Holowan Laboratories
MODEL IG-RM **TYPE** Thug droid

Designed by the same corporation that created the IG-86 sentinel droids and the IG-100 MagnaGuards (the latter preferred by General Grievous), IG-RMs are the next line in aggressive security automatons. More stable than assassin droids, they require frequent instructions from their masters and are less likely to go rogue than other models. The droids are used by the Mining Guild to keep enslaved people in line, and by underworld organizations. Cikatro Vizago owns quite a few IG-RMs, colorfully painted and armed with DLT-18 laser rifles. Within his Broken Horn Syndicate, the droids do much of the hard labor, fighting, and strong-arming, while Vizago manages them at a distance. Rebel Alliance spy Eneb Ray later uses IG-RM droids in his plot to kill Imperial prisoners at Sunspot Prison until he is stopped by Leia Organa, Sara Starros, and Doctor Chelli Aphra.

GRAND INQUISITOR'S LIGHTSABER

TYPE Double-bladed spinning lightsaber

Like his fellow—and subordinate—Inquisitors, the Grand Inquisitor uses a double-bladed red lightsaber to carry out the orders of his Sith masters. The process of construction for the Grand Inquisitor's lightsaber is unknown. It is possible that he built it himself, bleeding the kyber crystal he carried in his previous double-ended Jedi weapon, though it may have been issued to him by Darth Sidious when he persuaded the Jedi to turn to the dark side.

The lightsaber is designed pragmatically to hasten confrontation and extinguish life with absolute efficiency. In the face of the Grand Inquisitor's unorthodox technique, inexperienced Jedi become apprehensive, presenting the Grand Inquisitor with the perfect opportunity to strike.

Each Inquisitor's lightsaber can function in several modes. In crescent mode, the single-bladed lightsaber is wielded in a standard manner. In disk mode, a second blade is drawn, allowing broader fighting strokes, ideal for battling multiple combatants simultaneously. Both blades are capable of spinning around the disk by detaching from the central handle, forming an impressive wall of red lightsaber energy.

During the Grand Inquisitor's first meeting with Darth Vader, the Sith Lord breaks the Grand Inquisitor's lightsaber, but it is quickly repaired and used against Jedi Master Jocasta Nu in battle. It is unknown how many Jedi the Grand Inquisitor has vanquished in lightsaber duels over the years since Order 66. He also uses the weapon to execute non-Jedi. When the Lothal rebel cell is revealed to contain Jedi Kanan Jarrus and Ezra Bridger, the Grand Inquisitor duels the Jedi on multiple occasions. Aboard the *Sovereign*, the Grand Inquisitor is finally defeated by Kanan, and his lightsaber is destroyed.

Disk mode
When the lightsaber spins in disk mode, it can panic many Jedi as they are inexperienced against such a fighting style.

TIE FIGHTER PILOT HELMET

MANUFACTURER Imperial Department of Military Research **MODEL** TIE fighter pilot's helmet **TYPE** Helmet

TIE fighter pilots rely on their flight suits and helmets in case of hull damage to their unshielded fighters. Their reinforced black flight helmets are connected to a life-support pack hanging on their chest, via a pair of gas transfer hoses. The device also includes ship-linked communications systems and features enhanced visor displays.

WESTAR-35 TWIN BLASTERS

MANUFACTURER Concordian Crescent Technologies **MODEL** WESTAR-35 **TYPE** Blaster pistols

WESTAR-35 blasters are popular weapons on Mandalore that are carried by the police force as well as Death Watch during the Clone Wars. Each features a high-precision barrel, rapid-fire mode, magnetic-grip handle, flash suppressor, and pressure-sensitive trigger. Sabine Wren uses a pair of custom-painted WESTAR-35 blasters as a rebel against the Empire and throughout the New Republic era. Many members of the Mandalorian Resistance including Bo-Katan Kryze and Axe Wolves also favor WESTAR-35 blasters.

EZRA'S FIRST LIGHTSABER

CREATOR Ezra Bridger **MODEL** Handcrafted **TYPE** Lightsaber-blaster hybrid

During the dark times of the Empire, many traditions of the Jedi Order are abandoned for the sake of survival. Though some wayward Jedi do make use of them, blasters have never been condoned by the Council. In the past, a Jedi would never have built a blaster into their lightsaber, as Ezra Bridger does. He is, however, not a typical Jedi apprentice.

When he first begins his Jedi training under Kanan Jarrus, Ezra must borrow his master's lightsaber for practice. When he is ready, Ezra uses the Force to locate an ancient Jedi temple on Lothal. There, in the underground ruins, Ezra faces a series of challenges and has to confront his own fears and weaknesses. When he finally overcomes them, a Jedi voice guides him to a blue kyber crystal—the key component required to build a lightsaber.

Ezra takes several weeks to construct his weapon aboard the *Ghost*, using a combination of spare lightsaber parts from Kanan, modulation circuits and an energy gate from Sabine, a donated power cell from Chopper, some extra tech Hera finds for him, and perhaps a part or two secretly acquired from Zeb's supplies. His double-bar design is unconventional for a lightsaber, but the outer bar is necessary to hold the blaster components. Having such an unusual and unproven design does pose some risk of a short-circuit at crucial moments. Ezra learned to build his weapon through trial and error so the blaster component is easily removed from the lightsaber to facilitate maintenance and repairs.

Ezra must be careful not to use his lightsaber unless there is no alternative. Doing so always draws the attention of the Empire, so having a built-in blaster function gives Ezra a safer option in violent confrontations. He first uses his new lightsaber when the crew of the *Ghost* is attacked by the enslaver Azmorigan on Lothal.

Ezra's master Kanan borrows the weapon to use in conjunction with his own to defeat the Grand Inquisitor aboard the *Sovereign*. Ezra continues to wield the lightsaber, including against Darth Vader on Lothal. During the Mission to Malachor, Ezra faces Vader in battle, but the Sith Lord easily disarms him, destroying Ezra's unique weapon in the process.

Battle ready
Ezra draws his novel new lightsaber. Opponents are taken by surprise when he not only slashes and blocks, but also returns fire. When the blade is not drawn, it merely looks like a blaster, so he avoids the unwanted scrutiny of Imperials.

TECHNOLOGY

J-19 BO-RIFLE
MANUFACTURER Lasan-Malamut Firearms Corp.
MODEL J-19 **TYPE** Bo-rifle

Agent Alexsandr Kallus wields an unusual weapon for an Imperial officer: a Lasat J-19 bo-rifle. Kallus is presented with the weapon by one of the Lasan High Honor Guard when he defeats them in combat during the Sacking of Lasan. The bo-rifle functions equally well as a close-combat melee weapon and a long-distance blaster rifle. Its intimidating appearance makes it highly effective at scaring opponents. The J-19 is a more recent design than the bo-rifle belonging to Lasat rebel Garazeb Orrelios.

KETSU'S STAFF
MANUFACTURER Ketsu Onyo
MODEL Custom **TYPE** Vibro-staff

Ketsu Onyo's vibro-staff is a deadly weapon befitting a bounty hunter. Ketsu is adept at using it as a melee weapon in close combat, but also operates it as a blaster in long-distance fights. A knuckle guard protects Ketsu's hands when sparring. The vibro-blade tip is removable and can be exchanged for blade edges, darts, laser scopes, or additional blaster modules. She created the weapon herself and frequently makes small improvements to it.

ID9 SEEKER DROID
MANUFACTURER Arakyd Industries **MODEL** ID9 **TYPE** Probe droid

ID9 seekers are small probe droids designed to attach to the back of a harness, like a backpack. They may be deployed for scouting and are well suited to exploring environments inaccessible to average humanoids. These droids are adept at mimicking sounds and voice patterns. Their five articulated arms are fitted with electro-shock claws capable of stunning targets and disabling other droids. The Inquisitor known as the Seventh Sister is fond of utilizing ID9 seeker droids in her missions. Seeker droids are also used to patrol areas of Fortress Inquisitorius. Commander Iden Versio carries a similar ID10 seeker with four arms, named Dio.

AHSOKA TANO'S WHITE LIGHTSABERS
MANUFACTURER Ahsoka Tano
MODEL Handmade
TYPE Dual lightsabers

After Ahsoka Tano leaves the Jedi Order she fashions a new pair of lightsabers with curved hilts. Like those she used during the Clone Wars, one is a shoto, with a shorter blade, and used as a secondary weapon. Ahsoka tends to wield them both with a reverse grip, and uses them against the Imperial Inquisitors in multiple engagements and during her confrontation with Darth Vader on Malachor. After surviving this encounter, Ahsoka continues to carry the two lightsabers throughout the Galactic Civil War and its aftermath. On Corvus, Nightsister Morgan Elsbeth knocks one of Tano's lightsabers into a pond during a battle, but Tano is still able to disarm her opponent using just one saber. When Tano and Elsbeth fight again on Peridea, Morgan cuts one of Ahsoka's sabers in half shortly before Tano mortally injures Elsbeth.

CROSSGUARD LIGHTSABER
MANUFACTURER Various Force-users **MODEL** Handcrafted **TYPE** Lightsaber

Crossguard lightsabers date back to an ancient cataclysmic event during the Old Republic era known as the Great Scourge of Malachor. Several Jedi during the High Republic era use variations of crossguard sabers including Stellan Gios, Burryaga, and Creighton Sun. Cal Kestis also modifies his lightsaber into a crossguard lightsaber for a time during the Imperial era. Later, Ezra Bridger finds an old Jedi crossguard lightsaber outside the Sith temple on Malachor, but it is too old to maintain its blade. The smuggler Sana Starros recovers a pair of crossguard lightsabers that belonged to Darth Atrius from that same era, but they are separately destroyed by Luke Skywalker and Darth Vader. Decades later, Kylo Ren constructs his own crossguard lightsaber, based on the same ancient design.

Twilight on Malachor
After years apart, Darth Vader and Ahsoka Tano are finally reunited in the Sith temple on Malachor. Ahsoka duels Vader to ensure her allies can escape.

SABINE WREN'S LIGHTSABER
MANUFACTURER Ezra Bridger **MODEL** Custom made
TYPE Lightsaber

Ezra Bridger's first lightsaber is destroyed by Darth Vader at the Sith temple on Malachor. At some point Ezra builds a new lightsaber, which has a black hilt with silver highlights. Ezra is not the only one to wield his new lightsaber. On one mission Saw Gerrera briefly borrows it. Ezra eventually leaves it with teammate Sabine Wren before he and Grand Admiral Thrawn are pulled deep into space by a space-faring pod of purrgil. Sabine later trains as a Jedi with Ahsoka Tano using this lightsaber. After being reunited on Peridea, Sabine attempts to return the lightsaber to Ezra, but he insists she keep it, because it's hers now.

DISMANTLER DROID
MANUFACTURER Industrial Automaton
MODEL DTS-series **TYPE** Demolition droid

DTS-series dismantler droids are designed to break down old ships and machinery into their basic parts, either for disposal or recycling. These droids are employed by the Empire at Reklam Station to disassemble old Republic BTL-A4 Y-wings. They are equipped with strong clamping claws, a razor cutter, powerful blasters, and a formidable flamethrower. Dismantler droids are programmed to attack anyone who interferes with their directives. The crew of the *Ghost* is nearly killed by a team of them while trying to steal Y-wings for the rebels.

IMPERIAL SENTRY DROID

MANUFACTURER Baktoid Combat Automata
MODEL DT-series **TYPE** Sentry droid

Imperial sentry droids are developed on former Baktoid Combat Automata production lines, utilizing old Super Tactical Droid technology and abandoned, experimental droid schematics. Sentry droids act as automated guards aboard Imperial freighters such as the Class Four Container Transport and ISB stations, and are also present in the Tipoca City training facility on Kamino as well as on Grand Admiral Thrawn's ship, for similar purposes. Darth Vader is also known to use them to protect Fortress Vader—at times they even stand guard in his personal quarters. Sentry droids are strong, relentless, and have E-11 blaster rifles built into their right arms.

E-XD INFILTRATOR DROID

MANUFACTURER Imperial Department of Military Research **MODEL** E-XD **TYPE** Recon droid

The Empire's E-XD infiltrator droid is designed to resemble an RQ protocol droid while in reconnaissance mode. It appears benign as it quietly scans life forms, vehicles, other droids, and structures—until it locates its intended target. Upon identifying its mark, the droid goes into attack mode, growing in height and brandishing a variety of weapons. These droids are highly aggressive and extremely strong. If they are tampered with, a built-in proton warhead will explode. Rebel members Garazeb Orrelios, Chopper, and AP-5 are forced to deal with an infiltrator droid when one lands near their base on the planet Atollon.

SAW GERRERA'S SUIT

MODEL Custom
TYPE Medical pressure suit

Saw Gerrera receives many grave injuries in his battles with the Empire. In his later years Saw's health fails to the point that he acquires a medical pressure suit to prolong his life, which includes an oxygen tank with painkillers and a respiration mask to aid his breathing as his lungs deteriorate. The suit also has atmospheric sensors to automatically adjust internal temperature, pressure, and humidity to compensate for environmental changes. As his health declines, his medical droid, G2-1B7, cares for him. The droid's programming has been modified to force it to provide Saw with medicines in dangerous quantities.

DEATH TROOPER ARMOR

MANUFACTURER Imperial Advanced Weapons Research
MODEL Death trooper armor **TYPE** Body armor

The precise design and specification of Imperial death trooper armor is classified. Their black armor is covered in a "reflec" polymer spray that warps electromagnetic signals and allows the troopers to pass invisibly through most sensor arrays. The helmets contain sensors and targeting systems far more advanced than those of any other troopers. These systems include image-intensifying, pulse emitters, multi-frequency targeting, acquisition sensors, and Neuro-Saav macro-motion monitors. Implants in death troopers' body tissues provide biofeedback for the armor and likewise enable it to stimulate sensory organs for more intense perception of targets and their environment.

MWC-35C REPEATING CANNON

MANUFACTURER Morellian Weapons Conglomerate
MODEL MWC-35c "Staccato Lightning" repeating cannon **TYPE** Heavy repeater cannon

The MWC-35c "Staccato Lightning" repeating cannon is used by Imperial forces in crowd-control situations. Guardian of the Whills Baze Malbus steals one of these weapons to use against the Empire. The cannon employs a galven circuitry charge belt and a connected R717 refrigerant tank enabling it to fire blasts equivalent to the firepower of five blaster rifles. The cannon can fire 35,000 rounds when fully charged and has two firing modes: rapid (for spraying an area) and single-burst (for delivering a more powerful, concentrated blast). This sizable weapon weighs 30 kilograms (66 lbs), so it requires considerable strength to operate and is difficult to aim precisely.

Rebel warrior
Baze joins the fight against the Empire on Jedha, and accompanies fellow rebel Jyn Erso to Scarif.

CHIRRUT'S STAFF

MANUFACTURER Chirrut Îmwe
MODEL Custom **TYPE** Staff

Chirrut Îmwe carries a flame-hardened walking staff made of uneti-wood. The uneti tree is sacred to the Jedi and possesses a strong inherent connection to the light side of the Force. Uneti grow at the Jedi Temple on Coruscant during the Republic era, and are said to come from seeds borne from trees at the very first Jedi temple. The end of Chirrut's staff has a metal cap with a compartment containing a tiny kyber crystal.

Surprise attack
Chirrut surprises stormtroopers by using his walking stick as an effective melee weapon.

CHIRRUT'S LIGHTBOW

MANUFACTURER Chirrut Îmwe
MODEL Custom lightbow **TYPE** Bowcaster

As part of his personal journey as a Guardian of the Whills, Chirrut Îmwe constructs his own lightbow. It works on the same principles as a traditional Wookiee bowcaster, and is much more powerful than a conventional heavy blaster rifle. While Chirrut may be blind, he is able to use his other senses to anticipate some events seconds before they happen—giving him a considerable advantage in many combat situations.

Sure shot
Chirrut's ability to anticipate his target's next move even enables him to shoot down a TIE fighter at the secret Imperial base on Eadu.

TECHNOLOGY

Flash suppressor for night concealment — Blaster gas cell

DH-17 BLASTER PISTOL
MANUFACTURER BlasTech Industries
MODEL DH-17 **TYPE** Medium-range blaster

Though not as versatile as other Imperial military blasters, the DH-17 pistol is a well-made close-combat weapon commonly used by rebel forces for shipboard combat. The weapon is dependable on a semiautomatic setting, firing in short bursts; on automatic, the power is drained in 20 seconds.

DEFENDER SPORTING BLASTER
MANUFACTURER Drearian Defense Conglomerate **MODEL** Defender
TYPE Hunting pistol

DDC's Defender sporting blasters are low-powered weapons intended for small-game hunting and self-defense. The blasters are popular with nobility and aristocrats for their lightweight design, ease of disassembly and reassembly, and their ability to be concealed. Broken down into three components, the blasters can pass through most security scans undetected. The power cell allows 100 shots per charge, though only a direct hit to a vital organ is lethal. Princess Leia Organa first learns to shoot using a Defender blaster as a teenager, displaying a rare talent for shooting. Leia uses a Defender blaster when Darth Vader boards the *Tantive IV* looking for the stolen Death Star plans. Decades later, she wields one aboard the *Raddus*, stunning a mutinous Poe Dameron.

ESCAPE POD
MANUFACTURER Corellian Engineering Corp.
MODEL Class-6 **TYPE** Six-passenger pod

CEC's Class-6 escape pods are fitted with four retro escape thrusters and six smaller maneuvering jets for fast, controlled evacuations. The emergency pods are designed to carry a maximum of six living passengers of average size. They employ a simple design with minimal equipment. The fore and aft cameras and proximity sensors aid the autopilot. They also optionally route camera feeds to the single viewport display screen. During the High Republic era, Nihil agents disable Starlight Beacon's escape pods before setting off a bomb that destroys the space station. Padawan Cal Kestis uses one to escape to Bracca during Order 66, around the same time that Yoda uses one to escape the battlefields of Kashyyyk. Though pods are normally off-limits to droids, during the attack on the *Tantive IV*, R2-D2 accesses an escape pod, and together he and C-3PO flee to Tatooine. They are able to escape because neither Darth Vader or his Star Destroyer sensors are able to detect that the droids are on board. Years later, Rey takes an escape pod from the *Millennium Falcon* to the *Supremacy* in an attempt to turn Kylo Ren to the light side.

Saber fight
Darth Vader duels with his long-lost son Luke Skywalker on Cloud City.

DARTH VADER'S LIGHTSABER
CREATOR Darth Vader **MODEL** Handcrafted
TYPE Sith lightsaber

When Darth Vader first pledges loyalty to Darth Sidious, he continues to use his own Jedi lightsaber, until Obi-Wan Kenobi takes it following their duel on Mustafar. On Sidious' orders, Vader finds a surviving Jedi—Master Kirak Infil'a—whom he kills after a long battle. Vader takes the fallen Jedi's saber to Mustafar, where he pours his hate and anger into its kyber crystal, making it bleed and turning it red. Vader uses Infil'a's hilt until it is destroyed. He then fashions a new one that resembles his original Jedi hilt, but is made with a darker alloy. The lightsaber features a black-ridged handgrip, a black power cell chamber and beveled emitter shroud, a dual-phase focus crystal, a high-output diatium power cell, and the customary power and length adjustment switches.

With this new lightsaber, Vader commits many atrocities in the Emperor's name. He kills several Jedi that survived Order 66, including Jocasta Nu as well as the Inquisitor Second Sister on Fortress Inquisitorius. Vader later battles Obi-Wan Kenobi twice with this lightsaber, shortly before killing Cere Junda on Jedha. On Malachor, Vader duels his former apprentice Ahsoka Tano, who only escapes his final strike thanks to the timely intervention of Ezra Bridger. Vader later slashes his way through rebel troops aboard the *Profundity* in an attempt to recover the stolen Death Star plans, and soon after kills his former master Obi-Wan aboard the feared battle station. The Sith Lord duels his son, Luke Skywalker, for the first time on Cymoon 1, and in a later confrontation cuts off one of Luke's hands on Cloud City. In their final confrontation, Luke momentarily succumbs to his anger and cuts off his father's hand, causing Vader's lightsaber to fall into the same energy well where the Emperor seemingly perishes.

Handgrip ridges — Kyber crystal chamber — Power indicator — Blade power adjustment casing — Emitter shroud housing

Feared throughout the galaxy
Although not as limber in his new cyborg form, Darth Vader nonetheless remains the Emperor's deadliest servant.

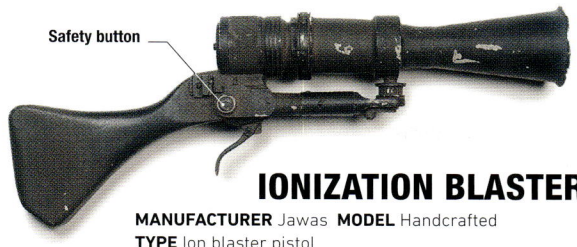

IONIZATION BLASTER
MANUFACTURER Jawas **MODEL** Handcrafted
TYPE Ion blaster pistol

Jawas construct their own ion blasters using whatever scraps they can scrounge. They begin with a stripped-down blaster power pack, and eventually add an accu-accelerator from a ship's ion drive and a droid-restraining bolt to the firing mechanism. The blasters may be fired accurately up to 12 meters (39 ft).

DLT-19 HEAVY BLASTER RIFLE
MANUFACTURER BlasTech Industries **MODEL** DLT-19 **TYPE** Blaster rifle

DLT-19 rifles are commonly carried by Imperial stormtroopers, though bounty hunters employed as snipers also use them. As a long-range rifle, the DLT-19 is often used by sandtroopers on Tatooine and by stormtroopers aboard the Death Star. The rifle has folding sights and bipod support. It may be fired in single shots and short bursts, or be fully automatic for brief periods.

GADERFFII (GAFFI) STICK
CREATOR Tuskens **MODEL** Handcrafted **TYPE** Melee weapon (staff)

Gaderffii sticks, or gaffi sticks for short, are melee weapons created by Tuskens using a variety of scrounged materials, including krayt dragon horns and wortwood tree branches. They are typically 1.3 meters (4 ft) long with a different weapon head on each end. Many have one curved end, with a club head tipped by a spear point. The other end is shaped like a mace with sharpened edges. Gaffis facilitate many attack forms, from crude clubbing and stabbing to the finer staff-fighting arts. During Boba Fett's time living with a Tusken clan, he learns to fight with a gaffi stick and makes his own. Fett uses the weapon in many battles, including fighting off stormtroopers on Tython and stabbing Cad Bane on the streets of Mos Espa.

Wookiee weapons
The Wookiee language has more than 150 words for wood—and this easily available material is used in most of their weapons, shields, and armor. Wookiees fashion a large selection of blasters that blend both traditional materials, such as wood, bone, and horn, with advanced technologies. A few popular models are even mass-produced in workshops all over Kashyyyk.

WED TREADWELL DROID
MANUFACTURER Cybot Galactica **MODEL** WED-15 Treadwell Droid
TYPE Repair droid

WED Treadwells are common droids used to repair ships, machinery, and other droids. The WED's binocular visual sensors are mounted on a telescopic stalk, and multiple tool-tipped arms can be purchased separately. The droids are relatively fragile and require frequent maintenance. Jawas offer a WED-15 for sale to Owen Lars and Luke Skywalker on Tatooine.

INTERROGATOR DROID
MANUFACTURER Imperial Department of Military Research **MODEL** IT-O
TYPE Interrogation droid

Illegal under the laws of the Republic, the interrogator droid is one of the technological horrors constructed in Imperial secrecy. Used by the Imperial Security Bureau without mercy, this droid meticulously exploits a prisoner's mental and physical weaknesses with its terrifying devices. It begins by injecting drugs that lessen pain tolerance and inhibit mental resistance while forcing the victim to remain conscious. Hallucinogens and truth serums ensure maximum effectiveness, and the experience is so unpleasant that most prisoners will confess on sight. Jedi Kanan Jarrus is interrogated by one IT-O aboard the *Sovereign* until the Grand Inquisitor takes over. Darth Vader subjects Princess Leia Organa to an IT-O interrogation aboard the Death Star, but she is able to resist due to her training and fortitude. Years later, the First Order develops the IT-000 interrogation droid to question its captives.

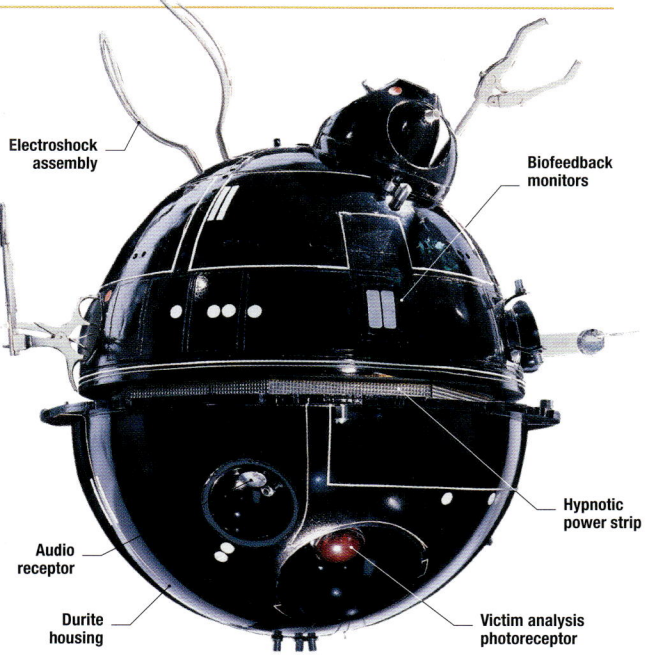

CHEWBACCA'S BOWCASTER
CREATOR Chewbacca **MODEL** Handcrafted
TYPE Wookiee bowcaster

Bowcasters are traditional weapons of Wookiees on their homeworld, Kashyyyk. They are based on ancient weapons of Wookiee culture that once employed poison darts and arrows. Bowcasters are more powerful and accurate than the average blaster, with a maximum effectiveness of up to 30 meters (98 ft). Designs vary depending on the materials used (usually wood and metal) and the crafter's artistic style. Bowcasters fire a metal quarrel enveloped in energy, while a polarizing orb, balanced on each end of the bow, creates a magnetic field that boosts the projectile's momentum. After the cocking spring is pulled back, the trigger speeds the quarrel forward, charged with plasma energy. Chewbacca crafts several bowcasters, his most recent being an unconventional design that makes use of the frame and power pack of a stormtrooper blaster. Chewbacca uses his weapon against a variety of foes, including Imperial stormtroopers, bounty hunters, and mynocks. Chewbacca continues to wield his bowcaster during the fight against the First Order.

Hero of Endor
Chewbacca expertly wields his Wookiee bowcaster at the Battle of Endor to fight stormtroopers, biker scouts, and Imperial officers.

TECHNOLOGY

DARTH VADER'S ARMOR
MANUFACTURERS Various **MODEL** Unique **TYPE** Life-support armor

After Darth Vader incurs life-threatening injuries in his duel with Obi-Wan Kenobi, he is secretly taken to the Grand Republic Medical Facility on Coruscant. While medical droids tend Vader's wounds, cyborg specialist Cylo and his team get to work, fashioning a life-support suit. Vader is fitted with armor that enables him to survive despite his badly burned body, protects him in combat, and serves to intimidate all who encounter him. The helmet provides vision-enhancement lenses, a respirator, feeding tubes, temperature regulators, and a voice projector. A chest control panel adjusts suit functions, sensor displays are visible on either side of his belt, and his boots include magnetic clamps. Vader's duels damage his armor, requiring him to recuperate in a bacta tank while repairs are made. Vader also likes to tweak his armor himself, displaying the engineering aptitude he has possessed since childhood.

When Vader discovers that Luke Skywalker is his son and rebels against the Emperor, Sidious destroys most of Vader's armor, returning Vader to Mustafar to rebuild himself. After Vader recommits himself to serve Palpatine, Vader's armor is fully restored.

Following Darth Vader's death aboard Death Star II, his son Luke burns his body and his armor in a funeral pyre on the Forest Moon of Endor. Vader's charred helmet is later taken from the pyre by an unknown individual, and decades later, his helmet comes into the ownership of his grandson, Ben Solo. Now known as Kylo Ren, he is a dark-side user and talks to the relic whenever he feels tempted to rejoin the light side.

A300 BLASTER RIFLE
MANUFACTURER BlasTech Industries **MODEL** A-300 **TYPE** Blaster rifle

The A300 is one of a large line of rifles—including the A280, A280-CFE, and A310—all of which look similar. The A300 is highly customizable, with a removable shoulder stock, various sized barrel adapters, and other attachments. It is used by numerous organizations, including the Rebel Alliance and the Pyke Syndicate.

E-11D
MANUFACTURER BlasTech Industries **MODEL** E-11D **TYPE** Blaster rifle

Purge Troopers and Imperial death troopers are assigned E-11D blaster rifles in addition to their SE-14R light repeating blaster pistols. This rifle features an adjustable stock and a large-bore reinforced barrel for an improved rate of fire and larger plasma blasts. However, the weapon also has a powerful recoil, making it difficult for most stormtroopers to manage. Years later, Moff Gideon's death troopers continue to use E-11D blasters, as do Grand Admiral Thrawn's night troopers.

FX-SERIES
TYPE Medical assistant droid
MANUFACTURER Medtech Industries
AFFILIATION None

FX-series droids provide invaluable medical assistance to 2-1B surgical droids. Designed with multiple arms, they monitor patients, perform tests, operate equipment, and recommend procedures. An FX-9 supplies Darth Vader with a blood transfusion during his reconstruction. Later, an FX-7 monitors Luke Skywalker while he receives bacta treatments.

CODE CYLINDERS
MANUFACTURER Empire and First Order **TYPE** Security device

Code cylinders are used by Imperial officers to gain access to restricted areas and high-security data networks. They record the bearer's identification, security clearance, and who has accessed what area and when. At least four categories of cylinders exist, distinguished by cap shape and color. The First Order continues to use these devices, calling them "access cylinders." General Armitage Hux's personal assassin, Captain Tritt Opan, carries a fake code cylinder full of poison for his own nefarious purposes.

KX-SERIES DROID
MANUFACTURER Arakyd Industries **MODEL** KX-series **TYPE** Security droid

The Imperial Senate enacts a law against the building of battle droids, but Arakyd Industries, in cooperation with the Imperial military, finds a loophole by marketing the KX-series as "security droids," and omits programming to stop them from harming organic beings. The KX-series is programmed to defer to military officers with the rank of lieutenant or higher, and they may act as escorts and bodyguards, as well as guards of Imperial facilities. They are capable of hard labor and translating but find these tasks tedious.

KX droids are stationed throughout the galaxy serving the Empire in locations ranging from Coruscant to Niamos. Several of them are also present on Mandalore during the Night of a Thousand Tears. Their height and strength make them intimidating to soldiers of low rank, rebel spies, and prisoners. KX-series droids are pre-programmed to operate more than 40 Imperial transport vehicles, and can quickly adapt to new ones. A data spike for accessing computer systems—and even slicing other droids—is concealed in their left fist. The New Republic has been known to reprogram KX-series droids for its own uses.

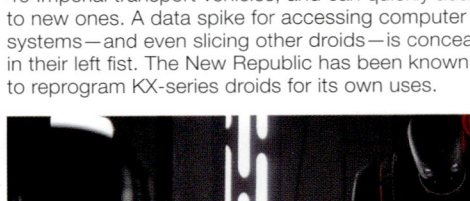

Rebel agent
K-2SO has been reprogrammed to work for the Rebel Alliance and excels at infiltrating enemy installations.

2-1B
TYPE Surgical droid
MANUFACTURER Industrial Automaton
AFFILIATION None

Popular since the days of the Republic, Model 2-1B surgical droids are equipped with an encyclopedic memory and a great bedside manner. Their removable hands support a variety of medical devices. 2-1Bs serve both Darth Vader and Luke Skywalker during the Galactic Civil War. A unit named 2MED2 later works for the Resistance against the First Order.

DARTH VADER'S MEDITATION CHAMBER
MANUFACTURER Custom built **TYPE** Life-support system

Darth Vader owns many meditation chambers across the galaxy, including one in his fortress on Mustafar and another aboard his Super Star Destroyer. Each one possesses life-support systems, enabling him to survive without wearing his helmet. Internal holoprojectors and viewscreens allow Vader to issue commands and receive communications while inside the chamber. For a time he uses a mobile chamber, which is taken by rebels when they steal Moff Tarkin's *Carrion Spike*. Vader's connection to this chamber allows him to track the ship through the Force.

AJ^6 CYBORG CONSTRUCT
MANUFACTURER BioTech Industries **MODEL** Aj^6 **TYPE** Cybernetic implant

This cyborg construct allows its wearer to access computer systems directly through a wireless link to their brain. The increased speed, broader systems access, and overall productivity boost that the implant provides has a deleterious effect on the wearer's personality, having a tendency to dominate their brain. This "lobotomy effect" has given rise to the device's other name, "Lobot-Tech headgear." Notable wearers include the Rodian Tseebo (a friend of Ezra Bridger's parents), Imperial controller LT-319, and Lobot, Lando Calrissian's friend.

BACTA TANK
MANUFACTURERS Zaltin Corp., Xucphra Corp., the Vratix **TYPE** Medical device

Bacta tanks are cylindrical chambers filled with bacta fluid, a gelatinous substance that encourages the rapid healing of injuries that are much too serious for the patient's body to recover from on its own. Invented by the insectoid Vratix species from the planet Thyferra, bacta is a mixture of kavam and alazhi bacteria combined with ambori fluid. During the High Republic era, one of Chancellor Lina Soh's Great Works included finding improved bacta cultivation methods. Republic clones often recover from battle injuries in bacta tanks during the Clone Wars. A bacta tank containing Dagan Gera keeps the former Jedi in hibernation for more than a hundred years, from the High Republic to the Imperial era. Darth Vader maintains a bacta tank in his castle on Mustafar to help him heal from his wounds. Luke Skywalker makes a speedy recovery from a wampa attack in a bacta tank at the Rebel Alliance's Echo Base on Hoth. Bounty hunter Boba Fett later uses a bacta tank to recover from his wounds from the Sarlacc pit.

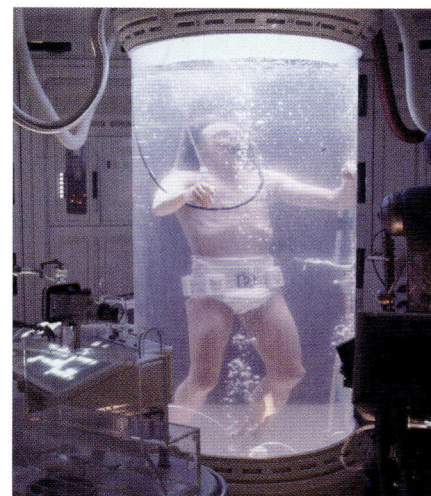

FORCE PIKE
MANUFACTURER SoroSuub Corp. **MODEL** Controller FP **TYPE** Vibro-weapon

Force pikes are a staff-type weapon with a vibroactive head capable of emitting electro-shocks that can inflict pain, stun, or even kill an opponent when used in tandem. Force pikes are famously wielded by Emperor Palpatine's Royal Guards, but are also employed by other sentries and bodyguards of high-profile persons throughout the galaxy. The Emperor's guards use them to project a force field around Ezra Bridger and hold him in the air, although the young rebel is able to break free.

EG-SERIES DROID
MANUFACTURER Industrial Automaton **MODEL** EG **TYPE** Power droids

EG-series "Gonk" droids are just one of the many varieties of power droids that serve as autonomous generators. They waddle about an area, recharging ships, machinery, and even other droids, whether they are following the command of their masters, or merely retracing a routine coded in their programming. EG droids sometimes serve as couriers and, being inconspicuous and a common sight, can easily slip in and out of hostile areas. However, their slow walking speed makes them vulnerable, especially to thieves. EG droids have been manufactured for a long time and come in many designs and colors.

BOBA FETT'S ARMOR
MODEL Custom **TYPE** Mandalorian armor

Conforming to almost exact specifications of traditional Mandalorian garb, Boba Fett's armor is made of the customary beskar steel and has been heavily modified. It used to belong to his Mandalorian father, Jango Fett, who used the armor during the Mandalorian Civil Wars and his later bounty hunting career. Boba decides upon this protective gear for his own bounty hunting jobs, wearing its dents and scratches with pride. Fett's jetpack is useful for short jumps and longer flights, and is equipped with a rocket launcher that may be armed with a missile or grappling hook. His helmet is equipped with a targeting rangefinder, macrobinocular viewplate, and a motion and sound-sensor system. Fett's internal comlink allows him to summon his ship remotely and over a great distance. During the rebel insurrection aboard the *Khetanna*, Fett, along with his armor, falls into the Great Pit of Carkoon on Tatooine. After Fett escapes the Sarlacc he passes out, allowing Jawas to steal his armor. It ends up with Cobb Vanth, the Marshal of Mos Pelgo, until he agrees to give it to Din Djarin in exchange for helping Vanth kill a krayt dragon. Soon after, Djarin returns the armor to Boba Fett, who wears it in his role of Daimyo of Tatooine.

Always working
As an adult, Boba is rarely seen without his armor in public, even when off duty at Jabba's palace.

MOUSE DROID
MANUFACTURER Rebaxan Columni **MODEL** MSE-series **TYPE** Maintenance droid

Mouse droids are commonly seen scurrying along the floors of Imperial and First Order bases and ships. Their design has changed little over the decades. They clean floors, perform as couriers, delivering orders from commanders (facilitated by a rack on their dorsal side), and act as guides, leading visitors to various destinations. Mouse droids are simple, versatile, and work quietly—qualities that make them ideal tools for spying and infiltrating secure areas or data networks that would otherwise be inaccessible.

TECHNOLOGY

Solo modification At one point, the barrel-scope is removed to improve fast draw.

Steady grip The grip emits a pulse warning when the weapon is low on power.

Cooling unit

Powerful shot The pistol fires laser bolts strong enough to pierce stormtrooper armor.

"Hokey religions and ancient weapons are no match for a good blaster at your side, kid."
— HAN SOLO

HAN SOLO'S MODIFIED DL-44 HEAVY BLASTER PISTOL

MANUFACTURER BlasTech Industries
MODEL DL-44
TYPE Heavy blaster pistol (modified)

A wide range of individuals make the DL-44 their blaster pistol of choice, including rebel Ezra Bridger and pilot Venisa Doza. It offers above-average firepower for a pistol, without compromising accuracy, making it ideal for use by military forces as well as bounty hunters and smugglers. The DL-44's capacitor can charge a double-power laser bolt without overheating. Notorious smuggler Tobias Beckett owns a DL-44 with field rifle accessories that he wields on the battlefield of Mimban. Beckett later removes the upgrades and gives the blaster to his new crewmate, Han Solo, on Vandor. After Beckett betrays Han on Savareen, Han shoots first, before Beckett can try to kill him. Throughout his life, Han keeps his trusty DL-44 handy at all times, making a number of personalized modifications to his blaster pistol. Confident in his own aim, Han later removes the factory-issue motion-sensitive scope so that the pistol can be drawn faster from its holster.

IMPERIAL PROBE DROID

MANUFACTURER Arakyd Industries
MODEL Viper
TYPE Probe droid

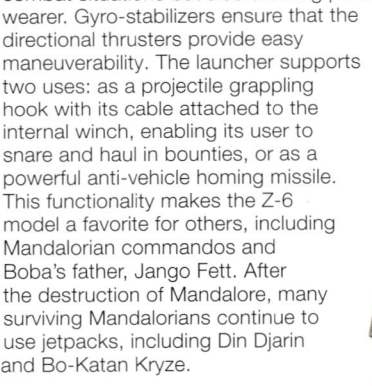

Also called a probot, the Imperial probe droid is used to track down enemies and secure checkpoints across the galaxy; later probe droids locate the secret rebel base on Hoth. During the Night of a Thousand Tears, they search for survivors on Mandalore. Probe droids can be launched from specialized surface installations to travel through space in a hyperspace pod until arriving at the planet they are assigned to investigate. Their repulsorlift engines allow them to travel across any type of terrain, and their thrusters have silencers to prevent detection. At 2 meters (6½ ft) in height, the probots contain numerous sensors, a holocam, six manipulator arms for taking samples, and a small mounted blaster for defense. The high-frequency HoloNet transceiver allows them to transmit information to Imperial forces even at great distances. The 11-3K is a variant on the standard probe droid that is more heavily armed, so it is often assigned to patrol duty on remote planets like Vandor. After the fall of the Empire, Moff Gideon uses a probe droid on Coruscant to communicate with one of his undercover spies.

BOBA FETT'S WRIST GAUNTLETS

CREATOR Boba Fett **MODEL** Handcrafted
TYPE Bounty hunter wrist gauntlets

Always careful to ensure he has many options at his disposal, Boba Fett wears wrist gauntlets stocked with numerous features. Their powerful weapons include the ZX miniature flamethrower from Czerka Corporation, capable of projecting a cone of fire 5 meters (16½ ft) long and 1 meter (3ft 3 in) in diameter, and the Dur-24 wrist laser from BlasTech Industries, which combines the full firepower of a standard blaster rifle with a range of up to 50 meters (164 ft). The MM9 mini concussion rocket launcher from Kelvarek Consolidated Arms fires various types of small homing missiles, such as stun rockets and anti-vehicle rockets. Fett's right gauntlet includes an extensible fibercord whip that can be fired to quickly bind up the target's limbs.

Crafty devices At the Great Pit of Carkoon, he fires a fibercord whip from a wrist projector to ensnare Luke Skywalker.

Z-6 JETPACK

MANUFACTURER Mitrinomon Transports **MODEL** Z-6 **TYPE** Jetpack

The notorious bounty hunter Boba Fett includes the Z-6 jetpack among his usual gear. Fuel burned by the personal transportation device produces significant thrust, providing a tactical advantage during combat situations but also creating personal risk for the wearer. Gyro-stabilizers ensure that the directional thrusters provide easy maneuverability. The launcher supports two uses: as a projectile grappling hook with its cable attached to the internal winch, enabling its user to snare and haul in bounties, or as a powerful anti-vehicle homing missile. This functionality makes the Z-6 model a favorite for others, including Mandalorian commandos and Boba's father, Jango Fett. After the destruction of Mandalore, many surviving Mandalorians continue to use jetpacks, including Din Djarin and Bo-Katan Kryze.

Homing missile The jetpack supports several types of missile, including a homing missile.

Reactant tank The pack contains enough fuel for 20 controlled bursts.

Double threat The Z-6 model jetpack combines a powerful missile launcher with jumper-jet propulsion for short flights through the air. This enables Boba Fett to swoop down on bounties swiftly or to annihilate them from afar.

Electronic scope
Modified stock

Fett favorite
Boba Fett is deadly accurate with his EE-3 blaster due to the combination of his modifications to the gun, the tech within his helmet, and his legendary sharpshooting skills.

EE-3 BLASTER RIFLE
MANUFACTURER BlasTech Industries **MODEL** EE-3 **TYPE** Blaster carbine

Shorter and lighter than the E-11 blaster rifle that serves as the standard-issue weapon of Imperial stormtroopers, the EE-3 carbine rifle relies on a two-handed grip to compensate for the smaller handle attached to the barrel. The standard EE-3 has a quicker rate of fire but less accuracy and stopping power than larger rifles. Its size is its main advantage, making it a favorite of bounty hunters across the galaxy. Boba Fett carries a modified EE-3 as his preferred blaster. The weapon is also wielded by the Zabrak bounty hunter Sugi during the Clone Wars and the mercenary protocol droid Q9-0 during the New Republic era.

GOLAN ARMS DF.9 ANTI-INFANTRY BATTERY
MANUFACTURER Golan Arms **MODEL** DF.9 **TYPE** Anti-infantry battery

A fixed emplacement weapon, the DF.9's single laser cannon fires blasts capable of annihilating whole squads of approaching infantry. The cannon is effective at a distance of up to 16 kilometers (10 miles). The gunner in the 4-meter- (13-ft-) tall upper turret enjoys a full 180-degree rotation of fire. Within the durasteel armored turret, which can readily withstand blaster fire, a targeting computer technician assists with precision aim, while another ensures stable energy flow from the power generator.

LUKE SKYWALKER'S FLIGHT HELMET
MANUFACTURER Koensayr **MODEL** K-22995 **TYPE** Flight helmet

When Luke arrives at the secret rebel base at Yavin 4, he promptly volunteers to join the desperate attack mission against the Empire's approaching Death Star. Assigned to fly Red Five, Luke receives a standard-issue X-wing pilot's uniform for Red Squadron, including a helmet adorned with the Rebel Alliance starbird logo. The helmet has a plasteel exterior and insulated foam-lined interior. Among other features, it includes a retractable polarized visor, sensa-mic for communications, and a localized atmospheric field generator. After he destroys the Death Star, Luke continues to wear his pilot helmet on other missions in his X-wing; his apprentice, Rey, later dons the helmet during her flight to Exegol.

FARKILLER
MANUFACTURER Var-Whill **MODEL** Farkiller **TYPE** Sniper rifle

Created by Jedi Var-Whill and originally the weapon of Oo'ob the Apostate, also a Jedi, the Farkiller is a unique sniper rifle. It is a magnification attenuator and incorporates lightsaber technology, allowing the user to hit targets from "a hundred klicks away," according to Doctor Chelli Aphra, who steals it from Red Mist, a Slinani Migration shrine.

LUKE SKYWALKER'S YELLOW LIGHTSABER
TYPE Lightsaber

After losing his lightsaber in a duel with Darth Vader, Luke Skywalker sets out for a new weapon. He learns of an ancient Jedi outpost on Tempes with various artifacts, and does indeed find an old temple guard lightsaber in its hall. Featuring a yellow blade, it is also adorned with gold accents on the hilt, suggesting it has High Republic–era origins. Luke uses the weapon for a time until it suffers a cracked kyber crystal, which leads him to the mysterious Doctor Cuata, who repairs the lightsaber and teaches Skywalker about the inner workings of the elegant swords.

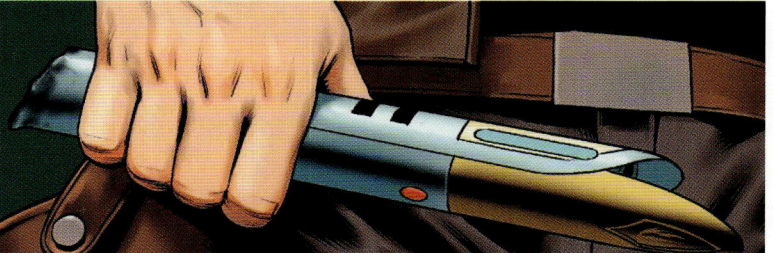

FERMATA CAGE
MANUFACTURER Darth Momin

Another long lost artifact of the dark side, the Fermata Cage is created by Darth Momin and yields incredible power. The device is a mix of art, technology, and the Force that is said to freeze individual moments, people, and places in time, which can then be recalled to the present. The Fermata Cage is hourglass-shaped, but its sand is composed of miniature black holes held in place by a dark side matrix and it must be primed by the dark side in order to activate. Qi'ra, leader of the Crimson Dawn crime syndicate, comes into possession of the relic and uses it in her mission to destroy the Emperor.

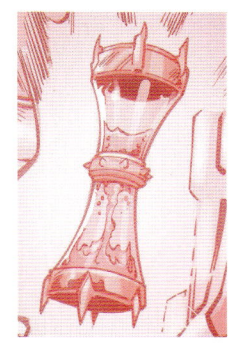

RINGS OF VAALE
MANUFACTURER Architects of Vaale

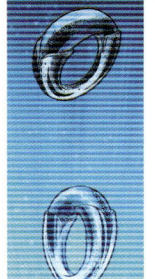

Ancient relics, the Rings of Vaale are rumored to grant the wearer Force-like power—but not without a cost. One artifact gifts the user immortality but destroys their mental health, and the second brings great fortune but also death. Worn together, the rings provide even greater powers.

WHIP OF SORROWS
MANUFACTURER The Ascendant **TYPE** Lasso

Created by the dark-side cult known as the Ascendant, the Whip of Sorrows is a weapon meant to mimic Force powers. The lasso wraps around a target and drains its energy. That energy can then be transferred to an enemy, creating a great explosion.

THOUGHT DOWSER
MANUFACTURER The Ascendant

A relic left by the Ascendant, cultists who sought to re-create the power of the Force through technology, a thought dowser can command others to do one's bidding. It emits a general feeling of malevolence, and can be wielded regardless of whether one is Force-attuned. When activated, it emits a blinding red glow.

AUTONOMOUS TRANSLATOR MODULE, MARK II
TYPE Protocol droid

Commonly known as a talker droid or talky, it is an early protocol droid. Obsolete in the time of the Galactic Empire, the Rebel Alliance steals the last-remaining unit from the Imperial Museum. The goal is to use the talky to create an encryption code, but the droid has objectives of its own.

TECHNOLOGY

A280 BLASTER RIFLE
MANUFACTURER BlasTech Industries
MODEL A280 **TYPE** Blaster rifle

Considered one of the best armor-piercing blaster rifles, the A280 provides more power than other rifles at long range. During the Republic's final years, A280s are commonly used by local planetary forces, which makes them readily available on the criminal market. Many rebel troops wield A280s against the Empire during the Battle of Hoth. BlasTech also produces the A280C variant rifle, which is favored by Alliance commandos.

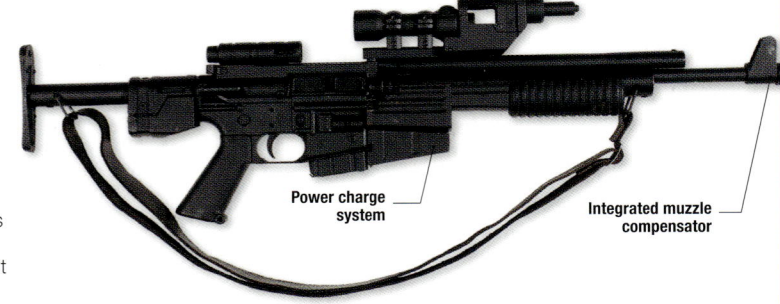

Power charge system
Integrated muzzle compensator

1.4 FD P-TOWER
MANUFACTURER Atgar SpaceDefense Corp.
MODEL 1.4 FD
TYPE Light anti-vehicle laser cannon

The 1.4 FD P-Tower is a fixed emplacement anti-vehicle laser cannon for use in all terrains. The single laser cannon fires from the center of the energy dish, which has 16 micropower routers spaced evenly along the edge and eight power conversion cells along the interior. The P-Tower is inexpensive, and quick and easy to produce.

Rotating base
The 1.4 FD P-Tower has 360° rotation for full range of fire.

Extreme conditions
The 1.4 FD P-Tower can operate in temperatures from -73°C (-100°F) to 49°C (120°F).

E-WEB REPEATING BLASTER
MANUFACTURER BlasTech Industries
MODEL E-Web **TYPE** Heavy repeating blaster

The Emplacement Weapon Heavy Blaster, commonly known as an E-Web, is the most powerful repeating blaster in the Imperial arsenal. Rigid mounts counteract the kinetic energy created by the weapon's formidable firepower. Usually operated by a two-person crew, its set-up time limits its effectiveness, so some Imperial crews pre-charge the generator for faster assembly. This requires careful adjustment of the power flow to prevent an overload.

V-150 PLANET DEFENDER
MANUFACTURER Kuat Drive Yards **MODEL** v-150 **TYPE** Heavy ion-to-space cannon

The v-150 Planet Defender is a surface-based ion cannon designed to target starships orbiting above a planet. Often deployed in conjunction with planetary shields, it defends planets while the shields reach full power. The cannon has an optimum range of 4,000 kilometers (2,485 miles) but its maximum range is 180,000 kilometers (111,847 miles), and it can disrupt Star Destroyers with a single ion bolt. However, being a stationary weapon makes the v-150 Planet Defender vulnerable to attack, and its blast shield must be retracted to utilize the cannon.

Surface-to-space firepower
The v-150 Planet Defender is equipped with an independent power generator buried some 40 meters (131 ft) below the weapon placement.

SCOUT TROOPER BLASTER
MANUFACTURER BlasTech Industries
MODEL EC-17
TYPE Hold-out blaster

A standard-issue weapon for Imperial scout troopers and patrol troopers, this compact, one-handed weapon serves as a hold-out blaster, and is optimal for short-range targets. Holstered in a scout trooper's boot or on a patrol trooper's utility belt, the pistol has a pressure-sensitive grip instead of a trigger to account for the trooper's gloves. It also has a built-in targeting scope to assist its user's aim.

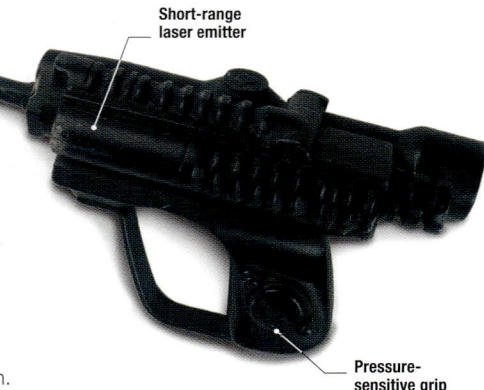

Short-range laser emitter
Pressure-sensitive grip

ZALY SHIELD
TYPE Shield

Looking for a new way to combat the Jedi during the Clone Wars, Separatist scientist Dr. Istan Zaly designs a shield of kyberite, the material in which kyber crystals grow. The shield operates a bit like the opposite side of a magnet, channeling and guiding the Force. When distractions prevent Darth Vader from fully wielding the Force, he finds the Zaly shield and uses it in battle.

LUKE SKYWALKER'S GREEN LIGHTSABER
CREATOR Luke Skywalker **MODEL** Handcrafted **TYPE** Jedi lightsaber

Luke Skywalker's second lightsaber has a green blade and is the first one he builds himself. After his fateful trip to Cloud City where he loses his first lightsaber, Luke briefly uses a yellow lightsaber he finds on Tempes. However, he plans to construct his own lightsaber, using a green kyber crystal he receives on Christophsis. Eventually, Luke builds the weapon in a cave on Tatooine, modeling it after Obi-Wan Kenobi's weapon—albeit with some simplified design elements. For the rescue of Han Solo from Jabba's palace, the young Jedi entrusts his lightsaber to R2-D2. During their escape, the trusty astromech launches the weapon across the Great Pit of Carkoon into Luke's hand. Aboard the second Death Star, Luke uses his lightsaber in his final confrontation with Darth Vader, but refuses to succumb to the Emperor's goading to kill his father. In the coming years, Luke continues to wield his blade as he rebuilds the Jedi Order. During Leia Organa's Jedi training, Luke uses the blade to spar with his sister on Ajan Kloss, and then later uses the blade to destroy a number of dark troopers who are threatening the Force-attuned Grogu on Moff Gideon's Imperial light cruiser. Luke even defeats the Sith Lord Exim Panshard, who is possessing an Acolyte of the Beyond, with the blade on the moon of Taw Provode. After sensing the dark side in his nephew, Ben Solo, Luke activates his saber above the young man while he sleeps. Ben awakens and attacks his uncle, who immediately feels remorse. This moment leads to Ben wiping out the fledgling Jedi Order. After the Order's destruction, the whereabouts of Luke's second lightsaber are unknown.

Family affair
Aboard the Death Star II, Luke Skywalker faces his father in battle once more. The Jedi is a skilled duelist and has improved much since his first confrontation with Vader on Cymoon 1.

Training with Leia
On Ajan Kloss, Leia wields a lightsaber she constructed herself to spar against her brother. The siblings wear blast helmets to focus on their connection to the Force.

Activation panel
An internal fusion reaction is activated via the control panel.

Thermite shell
Volatile baradium is contained inside a thermite casing.

CLASS-A THERMAL DETONATOR
MANUFACTURER Merr-Sonn Munitions, Inc.
MODEL Class-A **TYPE** Thermal detonator

The Class-A thermal detonator's power and range make it illegal for use other than for authorized military purposes. The device has a blast radius of up to 20 meters (65 ft), though it can be tuned to limit the radius depending on the situation. Posing as the bounty hunter Boushh, Leia threatens Jabba the Hutt with disintegration when she negotiates her fee for "capturing" Chewbacca. Impressed by the bounty hunter's boldness, Jabba agrees to her terms.

Bounty hunter disguise
Leia Organa retrieves Boushh's attire on Ord Mantell, with help from Chewbacca and Maz Kanata. She uses the outfit at least once on Arkanis before her infiltration of Jabba's palace on Tatooine to rescue Han Solo.

SLD-26 PLANETARY SHIELD GENERATOR
MANUFACTURER CoMar Combat Systems
MODEL SLD-26 **TYPE** Deflector shield generator

The SLD-26 planetary shield generator can protect a small moon or a large space station with a nearly impenetrable energy shield for an indefinite period of time. The Galactic Empire installs such a generator on the Forest Moon of Endor to protect the second Death Star during its construction phase. The Rebel Alliance sends a strike team to the moon to disable the shield generator in advance of their fleet's attack on the feared battle station. Unaware that the Emperor has set a trap for the rebels on Endor, most of the strike team, including Han Solo and Princess Leia Organa, is captured. However, with the help of the Ewoks, Chewbacca routs the troopers and frees the strike team, which destroys the shield generator, thus allowing the rebel fleet to demolish the Emperor's latest weapon.

Force field
Shield projectors deliver an energy field that protects the Death Star.

Deep focus
A powerful focus dish enables large objects in space to be shielded.

Power station
The power core is by necessity efficient and sustainable.

Planetary protector
The shield generator is essential for the protection of the second Death Star, so its destruction is vital for the rebel victory during the Battle of Endor.

TECHNOLOGY

DIN DJARIN'S BLASTER
MANUFACTURER BlasTech Industries
MODEL IB-94 **TYPE** Blaster pistol

Din Djarin's IB-94 blaster has extraordinary range and firepower for a weapon of its size—fitting for someone who walks some of the galaxy's rougher streets. Throughout his many adventures, Din keeps it in a holster at his side, from the shoot-out against other bounty hunters that leads to meeting Grogu, to the fight over Mos Espa. Sometimes the blaster comes in handy for shooting mechanical door controls or blasting through thinly constructed walls like those in the Klatooinian camp on Sorgan.

DIN DJARIN'S RIFLE
MANUFACTURER Amban Arms Corporation
MODEL Blaster sniper rifle **TYPE** Disruptor

Din Djarin's secondary weapon is a long-arm phase-pulse Amban sniper rifle. The distinctive two-pointed silhouette comes from the forked ion prod electro-bayonet, which can stun or kill opponents. The tough stock can also be used to strike foes, as Din does against a group of rival bounty hunters on Arvala-7. A blast from the rifle can disintegrate a target, sometimes vaporizing the body and leaving just the clothes behind. Djarin uses the scope on his rifle to assess his surroundings. The rifle is lost in the destruction of the *Razor Crest*.

TRACKING FOB
MANUFACTURER Rhinsome Tracking Corporation **MODEL** TF-9200
TYPE Handheld locator

Bounty hunters like Din Djarin use tracking fobs to find their targets. The device emits a sound when it gets closer to the mark. Bounty Hunters Guild agents like Greef Karga hand out the relevant tracking fob along with a chain code when a job is agreed. When the hunter returns both the fob and target, the agent hands over their pay.

HOLO PUCK
MANUFACTURER Varies
MODEL Varies **TYPE** Identity device

Bounty pucks are distributed to hunters by the Bounty Hunters Guild. Each one displays the name and holographic image of the person on whom a bounty has been placed. Combined with a tracking fob, they help find people who don't want to be found. The bounty placed on Grogu doesn't have a puck: instead of being commissioned through the Guild, the job comes directly from the Imperial remnant.

CRYO-FURNACE
MANUFACTURER Children of the Watch
MODEL Custom **TYPE** Forge

Each Mandalorian tribe has its own cryo-furnace, where its legendary armor is created in the traditional way of its ancestors. Mandalorian beskar armor has deep religious significance. On Nevarro, the Armorer uses a cryo-furnace to forge weapons and pieces of armor for Din Djarin and Grogu. When the Imperial remnant invades, its forces breach the room with the cryo-furnace, but the Armorer defends it. After the covert is driven out, she builds a new cryo-furnace on the Glavis Ringworld and then on the desert world where she hides out with Bo-Katan Kryze's forces.

DIN DJARIN'S ARMOR
MANUFACTURER Mandalorian Armorer
MODEL Din Djarin's custom armor
TYPE Beskar plate

Din Djarin's beskar armor protects him in battle, but wearing it also serves as a solemn religious observance. As a member of the devout Children of the Watch, Din has sworn never to remove his helmet in the presence of any living person. Not all Mandalorian sects ascribe religious traditions to their armor the way the Children of the Watch do.

Beskar is one of the strongest materials in the galaxy; even a lightsaber can't cut through it. Therefore, it offers Din some protection when he faces Moff Gideon wielding the Darksaber. Beskar armor is also light, allowing the wearer to retain their flexibility and speed. After the fall of the Empire, it's rare to find beskar armor in the galaxy. Din meets only a few others who wear it, such as Cobb Vanth, Boba Fett, Bo-Katan Kryze, and, later, Moff Gideon himself. However, they're not all Mandalorians.

Din's battered armor is gradually reforged into newer, stronger pieces as he adventures across the galaxy. An early part to be remade is one of his pauldrons. The Armorer forges it from a beskar ingot that the Imperial Client gives Din as a down payment for capturing Grogu, though other Mandalorians disapprove of Din taking payment from the Imperial remnant. Once Din hands Grogu over to the Client, he receives more beskar, from which the Armorer forges a full cuirass. She also bestows on Din's armor a mudhorn signet as the symbol of his and Grogu's victory over one of creatures on Arvala-7. In addition, the Armorer provides him with whispering birds—a deadly dart launcher built into the armor's vambraces.

Mudhorn-marked pauldron
Strikes to Din's shoulder or arm glance off beskar.

IB-94 blaster pistol
Bounties can't escape the long range and high-energy bolts of Din's blaster.

Amban sniper rifle
Din Djarin takes aim with his long-arm phase-pulse sniper rifle using the head-up display readouts in his helmet's visor.

FARMER DROID
MANUFACTURER Industrial Automaton
TYPE Labor droid

These bipedal walker droids help krill farmers catch and store their produce in a small village on Sorgan. Each droid has two long legs sturdy enough to carry it through krill paddies. Two smaller manipulator arms and a basket hitched on the droid's back allow it to carry two woven containers at a time.

M-32 LIGHT REPEATING BLASTER RIFLE
MANUFACTURER DDC **MODEL** M-32 Light Repeating Blaster **TYPE** Rifle

In her work as a mercenary, Cara Dune uses a light repeating blaster rifle. It jams during her mission with Din Djarin to rescue Grogu from Moff Gideon's light cruiser, but she gets it working again by slamming it against a wall. Cara wields her rifle in many conflicts, including against Klatooinian raiders on Sorgan.

D-72W OPPRESSOR
MODEL D-72w
TYPE Flamethrower

Some Imperial weapons are designed to shock and intimidate as much as be deadly, and this flame projector is one of them. A specially trained incinerator trooper uses a D-72w oppressor to break the standoff between Moff Gideon's Imperial remnant troops and Din Djarin and his allies on Nevarro.

N5 SENTRY DROID
MANUFACTURER SoroSuub **MODEL** N5
TYPE Security droid

Humanoid head A horizontal, yellow photoreceptor is framed by a featureless face.

Stun stick An electrical charge builds up on the blade and dazes opponents.

The New Republic posts bipedal N5 sentries aboard the maximum-security prison ship *Bothan-5*, which is crewed mostly by droids. N5 sentries typically work in groups and wield blasters. Those that work on *Bothan-5* are programmed to send a signal to the Republic in the event of an emergency. Din Djarin, Migs Mayfeld, and other mercenaries get into a shoot-out with N5 sentry droids on their mission to break out a prisoner named Qin. Din rips an arm off one droid and uses the data jack in its hand to unlock a secured cell door.

R1 SECURITY DROID
MANUFACTURER Industrial Automaton
MODEL R1 **TYPE** Security droid

R1 security droids are the second line of defense on Republic prison ships like *Bothan-5*. Two of these large, floating droids encounter a mercenary crew, which includes Din Djarin and is breaking out a prisoner named Qin. One of them, Burg, picks up an R1 droid and throws it at another, resulting in an explosion that consumes both droids.

E-HOB HEAVY REPEATING LASER CANNON
MANUFACTURER BlasTech **MODEL** E-HOB
TYPE Heavy repeating blaster cannon

The Imperial remnant's E-HOB is a heavy repeating blaster cannon, based on the Imperial-era E-Web. Moff Gideon's troops deploy one against Din Djarin on Nevarro.

BACTA SPRAY
MANUFACTURER Zaltin Corporation
MODEL Pneum-150 **TYPE** Medical treatment

Bacta is a healing substance that can be dispensed in multiple forms, including as a gel or spray. The bounty hunter IG-11 uses bacta spray to close Din Djarin's wounds after the battle against Imperial remnant forces on Nevarro. IG-88 expects the spray will take a few hours to heal Djarin enough for him to return to battle.

KA74 BLASTER RIFLE
MANUFACTURER BlasTech **MODEL** KA74
TYPE Heavy blaster rifle

The KA74 is the signature weapon of Cobb Vanth, mayor of Mos Pelgo. Its light heft but powerful blasts are a good match for a quick-drawing sheriff like Cobb, though he also has a HF-94 heavy blaster pistol. Vanth draws the KA74 against Tuskens and against Cad Bane.

TUSKEN BALLISTA
MANUFACTURER Tusken weaponsmiths
MODEL Custom **TYPE** Projectile weapon

Tuskens hunting a krayt dragon with Din Djarin and Cobb Vanth use ballistae. The machines fire heavy metal bolts that pierce the creature's thick scales and are attached to ropes. However, the weapon isn't heavy enough to hold the animal down.

BOBA'S GADERFFII STICK
MANUFACTURER Boba Fett
MODEL Custom **TYPE** Melee weapon

The gaderffii stick is the traditional weapon of the Tuskens. Warriors typically craft their own, and Boba Fett does the same when he lives among a Tusken tribe. He earns the right to craft one after he and the Tuskens successfully attack a Pyke supply train. Boba swallows a gekko meant to guide his journey. He then retrieves a branch from a tree and crafts his gaderffii stick with the help of a Tusken weaponsmith.

BARM-ST12 SCATTERGUN
MANUFACTURER Merr-Sonn Munitions
MODEL Scatterblaster **TYPE** Shotgun

The BARM-ST12 scattergun is a pump-action blaster shotgun often used by underworld factions. It fires a spray of five blaster bolts at one time, though it's slow to reload. The mercenary Lang uses one against Ahsoka Tano during Morgan Elsbeth's occupation of Calodan.

DARK TROOPER
MANUFACTURER Imperial Department of Military Research **TYPE** Battle droid

Imperial dark troopers are heavily fortified and armed droids often deployed alongside stormtroopers. By the time of the Imperial remnant, Moff Gideon's forces are using second-generation dark troopers, kept in charging bays inside Gideon's light cruiser. Dark troopers have armor plating strong enough to crack transparisteel and punch through some metals—although not Mandalorian beskar. Blaster fire just bounces off their armor.

Din Djarin first encounters dark troopers on Tython when they descend into the planet's atmosphere to kidnap Grogu, and he faces a full complement when he and his allies rescue Grogu from Gideon's Imperial cruiser. Din destroys one by stabbing it with his beskar spear. Gideon further upgrades dark trooper technology for it to become the basis of his own personal armor.

TECHNOLOGY

HK-87 ASSASSIN DROID
MANUFACTURER Czerka corporation
MODEL HK-87 **TYPE** Assassin droid

HK-87 droids are combat units equipped with heavy blaster rifles. Their agility, speed, and acrobatics match or excel the skills of organic fighters. Magistrate Morgan Elsbeth uses two HK-87 droids as guards and in open combat against Ahsoka Tano and Din Djarin during her occupation of Calodan. One of them is marked with a stencil of a chimera—a symbol associated with Grand Admiral Thrawn's Seventh Fleet. Ahsoka dismantles one of the HK-87 droids with her lightsabers. Din shoots another, which falls off a roof and is destroyed. Later, Morgan Elsbeth's HK-87 droids duel Ahsoka at the ruins of a stronghold on Arcana.

Flexible joints HK-87 droids are nimble and can jump long distances.

MODEL 201 MORTAR
MANUFACTURER Merr-Sonn Munitions, Inc.
MODEL 201 **TYPE** Mortar

The primary purpose of the Model 201 mortar is to cause devastating explosions at short range with a weapon small enough to be carried by a single trooper. The Republic, Empire, and Moff Gideon's Imperial remnant all use these weapons.

ENERGY SHIELD
TYPE Shield

Part of the arsenal of Order of the Night Wind assassins, red-tinted energy shields are emitted from a single gauntlet. They deliver an electric shock when touched. Fighters can use the device to create an inverse perimeter, locking opponents into a small space.

BESKAR SPEAR
TYPE Melee weapon

The beskar spear is owned by Morgan Elsbeth until she is defeated by Ahsoka Tano and it passes to Din Djarin. Like all beskar weapons, it can't be damaged by the blade of a lightsaber. This means its holder can duel with lightsaber wielders, almost as if they hold a lightsaber themselves. Din also uses the spear against the Darksaber-wielding Moff Gideon. When his troopers destroy Din's *Razor Crest*, the spear is the only salvageable part of the wreckage. It is later melted down and forged into Grogu's armor.

PLASMA PIKE
TYPE Melee pole weapon

The plasma pike is a melee pole weapon employed by Order of the Night Wind assassins. The heavy top end delivers a charge to a target that, while not fatal, is very painful. It's commonly used in tandem with an energy shield, allowing the attacker to time and strategize blows.

BACTA POD
TYPE Healing device

A bacta pod is an adult humanoid-size tank, filled with its namesake healing agent, which is used to treat serious injuries. Sessions in a bacta pod can last for hours and require a breathing apparatus. Following his escape from the Great Pit of Carkoon, Boba Fett routinely uses a bacta tank until he returns to good health.

CC-420 PISTOL
MANUFACTURER Pyke Syndicate
MODEL CC-420 **TYPE** Blaster pistol

The small, high-powered CC-420 pistol is primarily carried by Pyke Syndicate spice runners to intimidate their enemies—or to eliminate them. It's used by Pykes to slaughter the Tuskens who rescue Boba Fett and, later, against Boba's allies in Mos Eisley.

RIC-SERIES DROID
MANUFACTURER Serv-O-Droid
MODEL RIC **TYPE** Labor droid

The RIC-series droid has a large wheel with two treaded disks for traveling across a variety of terrain. These droids often pull and navigate rickshaws. Anakin Skywalker and Padmé Amidala hire one when they visit Mos Espa. Peli Motto uses one to drive into Boba Fett and Din Djarin's battle in Mos Espa.

LEP SERVICE DROID
MANUFACTURER Coachelle Automata
MODEL LEP **TYPE** Service droid

The LEP service droid's large, earlike antennae are modeled after the species that designed and manufactured it—the Lepi. These droids often work as waiters, butlers, or personal assistants. They're not programmed for combat and typically retreat if they appear to be in physical danger.

CRYOGENIC DENSITY COMBUSTION BOOSTER
MANUFACTURER Various **MODEL** Various
TYPE Starship booster

The cryogenic density combustion booster is found in vehicles like starships and repulsortrains. Princess Leia and Han Solo use a similar booster to brace open the closing trash compactor when they're trapped on the Death Star. Later, Peli Motto asks her Jawa acquaintances to source one for Din Djarin's N-1 starfighter.

RX-SERIES DROID
MANUFACTURER Industrial Automaton
MODEL Various **TYPE** Pilot droid

RX-series pilot droids often work on public passenger vehicles throughout the galaxy. The most well-known individual of this type is RX-24, who pilots a commercial Starspeeder 3000 and is later a DJ at Oga's Cantina on Batuu. RX droids are normally found behind the controls and among the crew of passenger starships, flying even to the most remote parts of the galaxy, such as Mos Espa on Tatooine. The crew of the *Ghost* sees an RX-series pilot on a Starspeeder 2000 passenger ship. Din Djarin also encounters one who is working as a bell droid and returns his weapons case to him after his commercial flight.

ANT DROID
TYPE Construction droid

A large group of ant droids scuttle around constructing the buildings for Luke Skywalker's Jedi Academy on Ossus, using stones from the surrounding area. Each six-legged droid has a grasping manipulator on its front end, which it can use to pick up stones that are a third of the size of its body. Another group of ant droids builds Din Djarin a bench to sleep on. They can carry out tasks individually but are most efficient when a large number work together.

BD-UNIT
MANUFACTURER Behold-Urwar Droid Concepts **MODEL** BD
TYPE Exploration droid

BD droids' sturdy legs, small rocket thrusters, and keen photoreceptors make them skilled at exploration. Fugitive Jedi Cal Kestis is accompanied by a BD droid, BD-1, who helps him by carrying healing stims packs. BD-1 also reveals holograms from his former owner, Jedi Master Eno Cordova. A BD unit named BD-72 works for Peli Motto in her repair shop. When BD-72 is grabbed by a womp rat, Peli goes after it, but only succeeds in getting grabbed as well. Din Djarin shoots the womp rat, freeing Peli, and BD-72 comes out of hiding.

Peli's helper
BD-72 is part of the droid crew that reassembles the classic N-1 starfighter that becomes Din Djarin's ship.

GROGU'S ARMOR
MANUFACTURER The Armorer of the Children of the Watch **MODEL** Custom
TYPE Mandalorian armor

As a foundling of the Mandalorian covert, Grogu has the right, the privilege, and the requirement to wear his own Mandalorian armor, so the Armorer forges him a beskar shirt. Din Djarin gives it to Ahsoka Tano to pass to Grogu during his Jedi training. Luke Skywalker shows the armor to Grogu and asks him to choose between it and a lightsaber to determine his future. The armor represents returning to the life of a Mandalorian, while the lightsaber means continuing with his Jedi training. Grogu selects the armor.

The Armorer also makes Grogu a rondel marked with an image of the mudhorn—his and Din Djarin's signet. It commemorates their first mission and battle together, in which they hunt for a mudhorn egg.

Accepted as a Mandalorian
Grogu's beskar chain mail shirt is made by the Armorer using Din Djarin's beskar spear.

PAROLE DROID
MODEL Various
TYPE Administrative droid

Parole droids are responsible for managing the day-to-day adjustments in the lives of ex-Imperial prisoners under the New Republic amnesty program. They have a mix of therapeutic and disciplinary programming, but their ultimate purpose is to determine whether amnesty program members are able to safely join the New Republic. One parole droid is assigned to the Imperial remnant scientist Dr. Penn Pershing during his time in the program.

TRAINING DARTS
MODEL Custom **TYPE** Combat dart

Young Mandalorians practice with training darts before graduating to the wrist-mounted rockets called whistling birds. Grogu and the Mandalorian foundling Ragnar fight with training darts. They fire paint, which can sting but generally leaves opponents unharmed.

GIDEON'S DARK TROOPER ARMOR
MANUFACTURER Imperial remnant **MODEL** Custom
TYPE Beskar armor

Moff Gideon's next-generation dark trooper armor is made of beskar mined on Mandalore while the Imperial warlord has a hidden base there. Gideon boasts that what really sets his armor apart from that of earlier dark trooper droids is the presence of a person—himself—inside it. With this armor, Gideon is strong enough to catch Din Djarin's punches and knock him to the floor. When Bo-Katan Kryze strikes the armor with the Darksaber, it receives red-hot cuts but doesn't break. Gideon uses the armor's mechanically augmented strength to crush the Darksaber with his hand. The armor is destroyed, along with Gideon himself, in the explosion of Axe Woves' light cruiser, which incinerates the entire Imperial remnant base.

IG-12
MANUFACTURER Anzellan droidsmiths
MODEL IG-12
TYPE Mobile suit

IG-12 is the shell of a droid and a chassis created with the broken pieces of the assassin droid IG-11. Built by Anzellan droidsmiths on Nevarro, IG-12 is given to Grogu by High Magistrate Greef Karga to transport him. The machine can say just "yes" or "no" and is operated manually by Grogu, who drives it into battle alongside Din Djarin. He takes out some of Moff Gideon's Imperial Super Commandos using IG-12's blaster, but they eventually overpower him. Later, the Anzellans use IG-12 and another assassin droid's head to rebuild the original droid IG-11.

CONSTABLE DROID
TYPE Law-enforcement droid

The small constable droids of Plazir-15 are unarmed, as befits the planet's pacifistic society. Often working in groups, they're tasked with keeping the peace and moving people out of harm's way, such as when Din Djarin and Bo-Katan Kryze tangle with a droid rebel.

Stolen beskar
The nearly unbreakable beskar metal in his armor enables Gideon to stand up to Mandalorians in a hand-to-hand fight. Beskar can withstand a cut from a lightsaber or even the Darksaber.

TECHNOLOGY

IMPERIAL SUPER COMMANDO ARMOR
MANUFACTURER Empire **TYPE** Stormtrooper armor

The Imperial Super Commando guards on Moff Gideon's hidden base on Mandalore wear armor made with an alloy of beskar, which shields them from most blaster bolts. Din Djarin and Grogu clash against some of these imposing troopers beneath the surface of Mandalore. Because of the armor's beskar component, the troopers can hold their own in hand-to-hand combat with Djarin. Only when the Mandalorian uses gaps in the armor plating to his advantage does he manage to choke a Super Commando. Despite the trooper's armor's ability to deflect ranged weapon fire, IG-12 strikes one down with a direct shot.

ARCANA STAR MAP
MODEL Custom **TYPE** Star map

A mysterious and ancient map covered in runes, the Arcana Star Map points the way to another galaxy. Both Morgan Elsbeth and Ahsoka Tano search for the compass which they believe will lead them to Grand Admiral Thrawn and Ezra Bridger. Ahsoka discovers the compass hidden in a Dathomirian Nightsisters temple on the planet Arcana and takes it to Sabine Wren, who is able to unlock the map's puzzle and reveal the Pathway to Peridea. After acquiring the device from Wren, Morgan is able to unlock the Pathway from an origin point on the henge on Seatos.

HUYANG'S LIGHTSABER ANALYSIS DEVICE
MODEL Custom **TYPE** Analysis device

Professor Huyang maintains an extensive database of the hundreds of lightsabers he has helped younglings build over the years. He stores it on a datapad and uses it to analyze the hilts of Baylan Skoll and Shin Hati's lightsabers in order to help Ahsoka understand the enemies she is facing.

MEMORY SEARCH DEVICE
MANUFACTURER Sabine Wren **MODEL** Custom

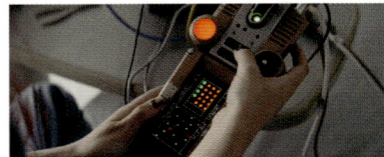

Sabine Wren applies her proficiency with technology to construct a device she can plug into terminated droids to read their memories. She connects it to the head of a defeated assassin droid and can decrypt its backup systems to determine where the droid came from.

STAR NAVIGATOR DROID
MODEL Star Navigator droid **TYPE** Navigation droid

Morgan Elsbeth engages Star Navigator droids to help her travel to another galaxy to answer the calls of the Great Mothers and locate Grand Admiral Thrawn. Using the star map activated by the Dathomirian Orb at the henge on Seatos, the efficient droids process near-unquantifiable amounts of data to plot a precise and safe route along the Pathway of Peridea. They use the ancient star map and a hyperspace calculation device to program the coordinates into the *Eye of Sion* and use their systems designed for navigation calculations to make adjustments as they travel to Peridea and back.

HOLOGRAM TARGET HILT
MODEL Custom **TYPE** Training device

Lightsaber-training analysis technology works alongside a wooden Bokken saber. Hits that simulate lightsaber blades are absorbed and recorded. When a training session is complete, the program reveals a student's hits and misses. The teacher can then use that information to identify patterns and target areas for improvement.

SABINE WREN'S BOKKEN SABER
MANUFACTURER Huyang **MODEL** Bokken saber **TYPE** Training saber

Made from wood and shaped like a lightsaber, Bokken sabers are an essential part of training for any Jedi. Padawans use them to learn basic lightsaber fighting techniques and combat moves in a safe setting. Once a student moves comfortably with the Bokken saber, either against sparring opponents or lightsaber training technology, they can progress to actual lightsabers. Jedi may turn to Bokken sabers at any point for additional training drills for themselves or a Padawan. When Sabine Wren becomes Ahsoka Tano's Padawan for a second time, Ahsoka has Sabine practice with wooden Bokken sabers, including using them for the zatochi training.

EXTRAGALACTIC NAVICOMPUTER
TYPE Navicomputer

The Star Navigator droids who determine how to traverse the Pathway to Peridea use hyperspace calculation devices to amplify their processors. The devices run computations to ensure the route will take the *Eye of Sion* safely to Peridea.

SABINE'S SCANNING DEVICE
MANUFACTURER CryonCorp **MODEL** EnhanceScan 3.1 **TYPE** Scanning device

When Grand Admiral Thrawn releases Sabine Wren into Peridea's grasslands to search for Ezra Bridger with only a howler and basic supplies, she uses a long-range scanner to locate signs of life. The simple but effective device scans the area, but bandits of Peridea destroy it before Sabine receives any answers.

GREAT MOTHERS' ORBS

The Great Mothers, Lakesis, Klothow, and Aktropaw, use their potent majik to read the threads of fate and destiny. Each one possesses a carved orb that focuses their powers. The Great Mothers use the orbs in concert as they call upon majik to see what is meant to pass.

MARK IV PATROL DROID
MANUFACTURER Imperial Department of Military Research **MODEL** Mark IV **TYPE** Sentry droid

The compact Imperial Mark IV patrol droid is equipped with sensors that transmit holographic visual data to its operator, allowing them to see distant places. Grand Admiral Thrawn uses the low-flying aerial droids on Peridea to see battlefield positions and strategize from afar.

ORBITAL MINES

MANUFACTURER ArmaTek **MODEL** SJ-91
TYPE Orbital mine

The Empire deploys orbital mines in areas of space that it can't continuously patrol. Varying in size, the explosive devices are powerful enough to disable ships. Imperial minefields exist long after the Empire's rule ends. Ahsoka Tano encounters and detonates orbital mines in the space above the planet Peridea.

EZRA'S THIRD LIGHTSABER

MANUFACTURER Ezra Bridger **MODEL** N/A **TYPE** Lightsaber

Ezra Bridger leaves his lightsaber behind with Sabine Wren when he departs Lothal with Grand Admiral Thrawn. After reuniting with Sabine and Ahsoka Tano on Peridea, Ezra Bridger builds a new lightsaber, his third, on Ahsoka's T-6 shuttle. Professor Huyang oversees the construction, sharing his expertise and his inventory of lightsaber parts. The droid gives Ezra the same type of emitter shroud used by a young Caleb Dume, also known as Ezra's master Kanan Jarrus. Ezra's third lightsaber contains a blue kyber crystal, also like Kanan's. Soon after building it, Ezra puts the lightsaber to use protecting the Noti.

NOTI SLINGSHOT

MANUFACTURER Noti **TYPE** Slingshot

The small Noti are a peaceful, nomadic species who mostly keep to themselves. They don't possess any advanced technology or weaponry; instead, when the situation calls for it, they use slingshots for defense. Noti craft the crude weapons from natural materials and fire them with surprising accuracy.

BLADE OF TALZIN

MANUFACTURER Mother Talzin **TYPE** Sword

The witches of Dathomir use their magicks for any number of mystical twists and turns. With greater power comes more fantastical creations, including enchanted weapons capable of withstanding the blow of a lightsaber. Mother Talzin, a leader of the Nightsisters, conjures a sword into being from the ether with swirls of green smoke. She uses the powerful weapon to stand against Mace Windu's lightsaber; when she loses, the otherworldly weapon disappears.

Decades later on Peridea—the one-time center of the Witch Kingdom of the Dathmiri—the three Great Mothers summon a weapon known as the Blade of Talzin and bestow it, along with other powers, upon Nightsister Morgan Elsbeth for her loyalty to the sisterhood and its old ways. The weapon adapts to its wielder and manifests a different hilt for Morgan than the one it had for Talzin. Like Talzin, Morgan puts her sword to the test against a Jedi, even using it to destroy one of Ahsoka's lightsabers. Ultimately, Ahsoka gains control of the blade and kills Morgan with it. The blade's current location is unknown.

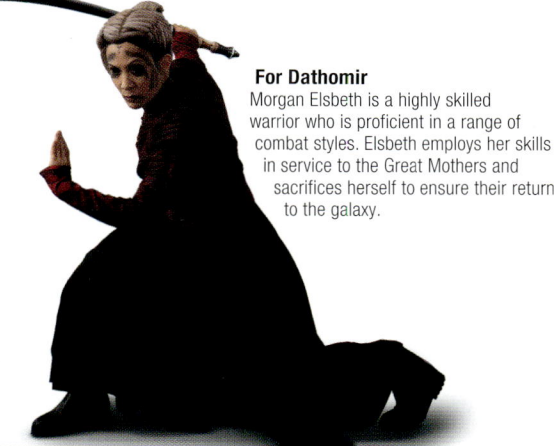

For Dathomir
Morgan Elsbeth is a highly skilled warrior who is proficient in a range of combat styles. Elsbeth employs her skills in service to the Great Mothers and sacrifices herself to ensure their return to the galaxy.

BB-SERIES DROIDS

MANUFACTURER Industrial Automaton
MODEL BB-series **TYPE** Astromech droid

The BB-series, used by both the Resistance and the First Order, consists of small, orb-shaped droids with heads that are magnetically attached to the upper surfaces of their bodies. The series derives this body shape from therapy droids developed during the Galactic Civil War for rebel veterans.

Their outer surfaces are decorated in many colors and patterns, with a wide range of head shapes. They move by rolling their bodies and can travel at high speeds when necessary. Like R-series and C-series astromechs, BB-series droids fit into droid slots on starfighters, aiding in navigation, weapons systems, sensor monitoring, repairs, and other ship functions. On the ground, they may also serve as guides, couriers, sentries, and spies. They speak using a variant of droidspeak, the most common astromech language, which is composed of electronic sounds.

Similar to those of R-series droids, BB heads feature a single, round photoreceptor and a smaller articulated holoprojector. Fragile receiver and transmitter antennae extend from the back of the head and data ports run along the base of it. Wireless telemetry keeps the head and body of the droid in constant communication. The droids' internal gyroscopic propulsion system is self-correcting, keeping the head on top of the body—most of the time. The droid bodies are sealed against contamination from outside debris. Most BB units contain six hatches with interchangeable circular tool-bay disks that support a seemingly unlimited selection of tool kits, including magnetic-tipped bolt-spinners, tow cables, torches, mechanical arms, and tools to access data terminals.

Notable BB units allied to the Resistance include Poe Dameron's loyal and ingenious BB-8 and Kaz Xiono's sassy and courageous CB-23. The sour, black-and-silver BB-9E is stationed aboard the First Order's *Supremacy*.

Photoreceptor
BB-9E's photoreceptor can see in all visible spectrums.

Tool bay
BB-9E's tool bays contain cutting-edge equipment.

BB-4
The khaki-colored BB-4 is a loyal member of the Resistance and proudly wears the organization's symbol on his body.

FIRST ORDER STORMTROOPER ARMOR

MANUFACTURER First Order Department of Military Research
TYPE Body armor

The First Order creates armor for its troops based on gear worn by its Imperial counterparts. Instead of plastoid composite used by their predecessors, the new regime's armor is composed of stronger, more flexible betaplast material, while the updated helmet features night-vision lenses, and targeting and communications systems. There are at least two variants of basic stormtrooper armor in use simultaneously, with differences in hue and the position of the helmet's nose plate (creating more or less black space over the mouth). It is typical for stormtroopers to wear colored pauldrons to denote rank, and some troopers, such as Captain Phasma and Commander Pyre, have armor in colors other than white. Specialist stormtroopers such as flametroopers, scuba troopers, and snowtroopers have unique armor to suit their respective battlefields.

On patrol
A squad of stormtroopers, including a flametrooper and megablaster heavy assault troopers, conduct a search on Jakku for BB-8.

In control
While Phasma is sometimes seen on the bridge of a Star Destroyer, she would much rather be in combat with her troops.

PHASMA'S ARMOR

MANUFACTURER Phasma **MODEL** Custom
TYPE First Order stormtrooper armor

Captain Phasma crafts her non-standard First Order armor herself, forging it from a portion of a ship's hull that she salvages from one of Emperor Palpatine's former yachts. The armor's chromium finish gives it a silver, reflective sheen, and also protects her from heat and radiation (as it did the occupants of the old yacht). Her traditional armorweave cape also provides protection, and gives her a stylish, regal air. Phasma's gauntlets are crafted for added strength and leverage, giving her an extra-powerful punch and hand grip. Phasma believes her look is an eye-catching and intimidating symbol of old Imperial power. However, her armor fails her in battle against Finn aboard the warship *Supremacy*. Her helmet is punctured and her breastplate scorched, just before she tumbles into a fiery abyss.

PYRE'S ARMOR

MODEL Custom
TYPE First Order stormtrooper armor

Athletic Commander Pyre has his armor specially crafted to be more flexible. He does not wear armor around his lower torso and upper arms, exposing the black body glove he wears underneath. This provides him with increased ease of movement, but makes him more vulnerable to enemy fire. Pyre's shoes are likewise custom-designed for extra flexibility. He wears a black pauldron over his right shoulder, denoting his rank. An electrum finish gives Pyre's armor a reflective gold sheen.

PHASMA'S BLASTER RIFLE

MANUFACTURER Sonn-Blas Corporation
MODEL Custom F-11D **TYPE** Blaster rifle

Soon after joining the First Order, Captain Phasma orders a bespoke version of the F-11D blaster carried by all stormtroopers. Phasma's blaster features a removable buttstock, a recurved trigger guard for a double-handed grip, and larger heat dispersal vents on the barrel. The weapon also has a chromium finish to match her armor. The trigger will only fire when paired with her own gloves. The blaster is destroyed when Finn smashes it with a laser ax aboard the *Supremacy*.

Deadly shot
Phasma is very skilled not only with her F-11D blaster rifle, but all types of First Order weapons.

PYRE'S BLASTER

MANUFACTURER Sonn-Blas Corporation
MODEL Custom F-11D **TYPE** Blaster rifle

Commander Pyre uses a custom, slightly improved version of the standard F-11D that is carried by every stormtrooper in the First Order, to include an electrum finish that matches his striking gold-colored armor. The blaster also features a J20 adjustable electroscope for increased zoom and a more precise focus, as well as enlarged heat dispersal vents to prevent the gun from overheating. It is also keyed to only operate when paired with Pyre's own gloves.

The weapon's spearpoints never dull.

PHASMA'S BATON
MODEL Custom **TYPE** Melee weapon

Captain Phasma's collection of personal weapons includes a quicksilver baton that resembles the spears used on her homeworld, Parnassos. The shaft is constructed from a collapsible micromesh matrix. When not in use, the spear retracts into a small baton with a spearhead on each end, held by a containment field. When activated, it immediately extends to full length. Phasma uses the weapon in her fateful combat with former stormtrooper Finn aboard the *Supremacy*.

FIRST ORDER TIE PILOT HELMET
MANUFACTURER First Order Department of Military Research **TYPE** Flight helmet

Every First Order TIE fighter pilot wears a vac-seal helmet in case of a hull breach. The helmet connects, via tubing, to an air-filtration system and life-support control panel worn on the pilot's chest. Targeting sensors on either side of the helmet connect to a targeting interface projector that displays on the helmet's internal view-screen. The detachable chin unit contains a pilot comlink connected wirelessly to the ship's communication systems. Red marking on either side of the nose bridge denotes a Special Forces pilot.

KYLO REN'S HELMET
MODEL Custom **TYPE** Battle helmet

Kylo Ren's helmet is designed in the style of the Knights of Ren. It is also reminiscent of the infamous mask of his grandfather, Darth Vader, connecting Kylo to the dark side of his family heritage. The helmet conceals his former identity as Ben Solo (also obscured by the helmet's vocoder, which makes his voice sound more threatening), and serves to intimidate both his enemies and his subordinates in the First Order. Beyond this and the protection it affords, the helmet has no special functions. Supreme Leader Snoke is particularly unimpressed by the helmet, calling Kylo "a boy in a mask." This infuriates Kylo, especially after his many sacrifices to please Snoke, including killing his own father. In a fit of rage, Kylo smashes the helmet in the *Supremacy*'s elevator as he descends from Snoke's throne room. Now supreme leader, Kylo has the fragments of his helmet reforged. Ren chooses not to wear his helmet during interactions with Rey on Pasaana and Kef Bir. He leaves it behind entirely when he returns to the light as Ben Solo.

Helmet off
Kylo Ren ponders his helmet before he destroys it.

SPIDER PROBE DROID
MANUFACTURER Arakyd-Harch Technologies
MODEL Spider probe droid **TYPE** Sentry probe droid

Armed with numerous sensors, First Order spider probe droids watch over top-secret weapons testing grounds and other unmanned military facilities. When activated, the droids ("mothers") release smaller drones called "kids," which are equipped with blasters to dispatch detected threats. If the probe droids are destroyed or fail to eliminate the intruders, they broadcast a signal to the nearest First Order station, which scrambles a contingent of TIE fighters to their location. Poe Dameron and Kazuda Xiono encounter a spider probe droid while investigating a cataclysm caused by First Order activities, and barely escape.

Tuanul village
While on the hunt for the map to Luke Skywalker, Kylo Ren wields his lightsaber to strike down galactic explorer Lor San Tekka.

KYLO REN'S LIGHTSABER
MANUFACTURER Kylo Ren **MODEL** Custom
TYPE Crossguard lightsaber

Kylo Ren constructs a lightsaber for himself based on an antiquated design. Despite being fashioned after an ancient schematic, the crudely assembled lightsaber uses modern parts and materials. At the lightsaber's core, there is a damaged, cracked red kyber crystal, which makes the weapon unstable and barely able to contain the power generated within it. The lightsaber's two crossguards are necessary to vent the extra heat generated. The chaotic central blade emerges first, crackling and flashing in a burst of glowing red plasma energy, with the smaller quillons then emerging on either side. Kylo Ren's hands are protected by emitter shrouds at the base of the quillons. The lightsaber's unstable condition is clear evidence of Kylo Ren's inexperience in constructing such a weapon. He uses his lightsaber in battles on Starkiller Base, Crait, and Kef Bir, before throwing it into the ocean after seeing a vision of his father Han Solo.

TECHNOLOGY

REY'S QUARTERSTAFF
MANUFACTURER Rey **MODEL** Custom **TYPE** Melee staff

Rey fashions her quarterstaff from wreckage she finds while scavenging in the dunes of Jakku. A strap allows her to sling the staff over her shoulder when she is climbing, or clip it securely to her speeder. A handhold made from scraps of an old uniform gives a secure, comfortable grip. Rey uses her quarterstaff for a variety of purposes. It serves as a trusty walking stick, ideal for testing the sands of Jakku for instability and for searching for things buried underneath. It can also be used as a weapon against bandits and thugs. The skills Rey gains with her quarterstaff also help her to wield a lightsaber; however, she is so effective with her staff that she continues to use it after acquiring Luke Skywalker's legendary weapon. She uses pieces of the quarterstaff to build a new lightsaber after the Battle of Exegol.

Giving no quarter
Rey realizes that she has to be ready at all times to defend herself at Niima Outpost on Jakku.

FIRST ORDER RIOT SHIELD
MANUFACTURER Sonn-Blas Corp. **TYPE** Handheld shield

First Order riot troopers utilize lightweight composite betaplast ballistic riot shields in conjunction with Z6 riot control batons during their missions. While riot troopers are normally used to quell civil rebellions, they are also sent into battle against military targets.

GLIE-44 BLASTER PISTOL
MANUFACTURER Eirriss Ryloth Defense Tech **MODEL** Glie-44 **TYPE** Blaster pistol

The Glie-44 blaster pistol is named after Twi'lek freedom-fighter Gobi Glie. A rechargeable power cartridge slides in a front slot for convenient access. It is commonly used by Resistance members against the First Order and is also used by civilians, police, and the military throughout the galaxy.

Z6 RIOT CONTROL BATON
MANUFACTURER Sonn-Blas Corp. **MODEL** Z6 **TYPE** Riot control baton

The Z6 riot control baton is wielded by selected stormtroopers, usually against non-military personnel. Collapsible conductor contact veins are capable of delivering a powerful electric shock that can stun. The baton can also deflect lightsaber blades. The handle's adhesive grip pairs magnetically with a stormtrooper's gloves.

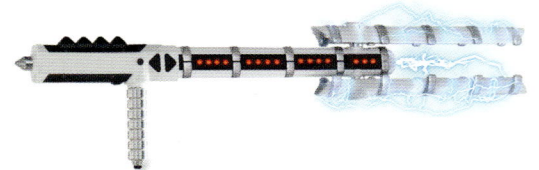

SE-44C BLASTER PISTOL
MANUFACTURER Sonn-Blas Corp. **MODEL** SE-44C **TYPE** Blaster pistol

The First Order's SE-44C is the standard-issue blaster pistol for stormtroopers. It comes with a mount for a scope and a replaceable barrel head. Some officers, such as General Armitage Hux, carry a black version made of plasteel. Captain Phasma has one finished with chromium.

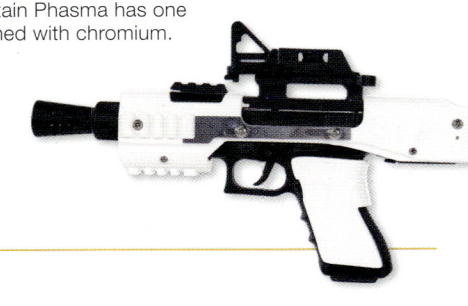

REY'S NN-14 BLASTER PISTOL
MANUFACTURER LPA **MODEL** NN-14 **TYPE** Blaster pistol

The NN-14's reinforced frame and large power core produce a powerful plasma bolt. Han Solo gives Rey an NN-14 blaster pistol before they enter Maz's castle on Takodana. While their minds are linked on the planet Ahch-To, Rey fires the blaster at Kylo Ren, but unintentionally blasts a hole in the wall of her stone hut. She uses the blaster throughout the rest of the war between the First Order and Resistance.

D-93 FLAMETHROWER
MANUFACTURER First Order Department of Military Research **MODEL** D-93 **TYPE** Flamethrower

The D-93 is used by First Order flametroopers to turn battlefields into blazing infernos, scattering the enemy, and for setting encampments alight, striking terror into their occupants. The double-barreled gun connects to a backpack containing tanks of conflagrine-14 gel, a highly volatile substance that produces a torrent of flames to a distance of up to 75 meters (246 ft). In addition to the gel, the pack also contains a smaller, central tank of pressurized propellant. A piezoelectrical ignition system fires the weapon.

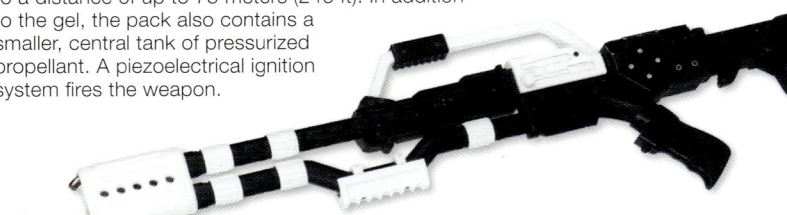

EL-16 BLASTER
MANUFACTURER BlasTech Industries **MODEL** EL-16 **TYPE** Blaster rifle

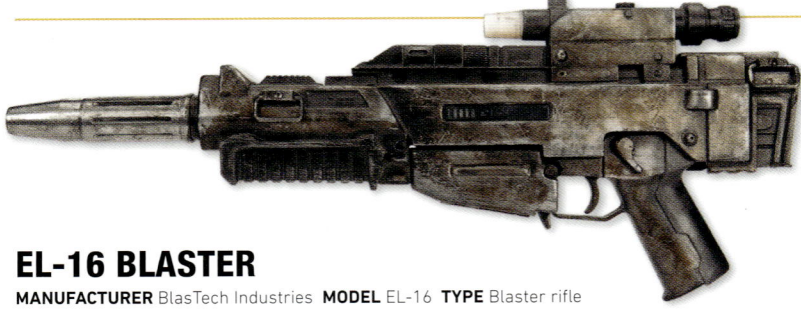

The EL-16 is the standard-issue blaster rifle of the Resistance. By the rise of the First Order it is an outdated weapon, but the Resistance is forced to make do with whatever meager munitions they can acquire from benefactors and secondhand weapons dealers. The EL-16HFE is a larger, heavy field version with a removable buttstock, designed for large-scale battles. Poe Dameron keeps one stowed aboard each of his X-wings. Both rifles are in use by the Resistance from its formation.

IT-000 INTERROGATOR DROID
MANUFACTURER First Order Department of Military Research **MODEL** IT-000 **TYPE** Interrogator droid

The First Order utilizes IT-000 interrogator droids, an advanced model of torture droid based on the Empire's old IT-O units. These droids represent a violation of the New Republic's laws. The IT-000 is a perversion of advances in medical technology. It is capable of speech and able to record answers from its victims, allowing it to conduct torture-interrogation sessions without supervision. Kylo Ren keeps one on hand for when he tires of doing his dirty work himself.

FIRST ORDER SENTRY DROID

MANUFACTURER Rebaxan Columni
TYPE Security droid

The First Order uses sentry droids to patrol Star Destroyers and bases, where they maintain security and watch out for spies. The droids appear small and docile as they roam about on their four rolling coasters. When they detect an intruder, however, they spring into action, dramatically increasing in height and relentlessly firing a pair of blasters. Poe Dameron, Kazuda Xiono, and BB-8 encounter these droids patrolling the First Order's secret Station Theta Black, just prior to the base's demolition.

RK-3 BLASTER

MANUFACTURER Merr-Sonn Munitions, Inc. and Sonn-Blas Corp. **MODEL** RK-3 (customized)
TYPE Blaster pistol

The RK-3 is popular with Imperial officers Grand Admiral Thrawn and Captain Slavin and the crime lord Azmorigan. First Order Major Elrik Vonreg owns a RK-3 blaster with a red finish to match his unique armor. Indicator lights at the back alert him to his weapon's power levels, and he can his targets with pinpoint precision.

ACP ARRAY GUN

MANUFACTURER Arakyd Industries
MODEL ACP Array Gun (customized)
TYPE Accelerated Charged Particle Array Gun

The pirate Kragan Gorr carries a custom ACP Array Gun with a modified trigger and targeting scope. It is decorated with his gang's symbol. The weapon is more suited for close-range combat against organic opponents than droids. It is also a favorite among some Trandoshans.

FLEXPOLY BACTA SUIT

MANUFACTURER Zaltin Corp.
MODEL Flexpoly bacta suit
TYPE Medical device

The flexpoly bacta suit is a temporary emergency medical device that allows severely injured patients to be transported without the need of a full-sized bacta tank. The suit has sensors and tubes to autonomously circulate bacta fluid through itself and rapidly heal injuries. Finn is placed in a medically induced coma during the evacuation of the Resistance base on D'Qar. The failing, second-hand suit begins to leak its contents of life-saving bacta shortly after Finn regains consciousness. Since the Resistance is strapped for resources, it has to settle with subpar medical equipment such as this.

SUPERLASER SIEGE CANNON

MANUFACTURER First Order Department of Military Research

The First Order's superlaser siege cannon is essentially a miniaturized Death Star laser, using technology derived from the Empire's Tarkin Initiative. The weapon is airlifted from the First Order's demolished flagship *Supremacy*, down to the surface of Crait in order to breach the old Rebel Alliance outpost where the Resistance is hiding. This devastatingly powerful cannon must be hauled along the ground by AT-HH walkers. The superlaser requires time to build up a charge between firings, during which time it is vulnerable to enemy fire.

ELECTRO-BISENTO

MANUFACTURER Praetorian Guard **TYPE** Melee vibro-weapon

Fashioned by the Praetorian Guard, electro-bisentos are used by Imperial Praetorian guards serving the Shadow Council during the New Republic era. They are also one of several weapons wielded by the elite Praetorian Guard to defend the First Order's Supreme Leader Snoke. The tempered blade vibrates at a high frequency owing to a built-in compact ultrasonic generator, making the cutting edge even more deadly. A plasma filament energizes the blade, allowing it to deflect lightsaber attacks. The near-indestructible phrik handle is similarly protected from lightsaber blows.

BILARI ELECTRO-CHAIN WHIP

MANUFACTURER Praetorian Guard **TYPE** Melee vibro-weapon

The Praetorian Guard's Bilari electro-chain whip is a solid rapier that transforms into a flexible electro-plasma chain of phrik metal. It can be used to stab, stun, flog, or restrain an opponent. On Mandalore, Paz Vizsla is killed in battle by an Imperial Praetorian Guard after being stunned and stabbed with one. The whip is designed to counter lightsabers, too, making it a formidable and versatile weapon. The Guard's gloves are insulated against the electro-pulses of the weapon. Direct contact with the skin causes burns and searing pain. Like the Guard's other weapons, the whip is proprietary and the specifications of its design are unknown even to the First Order's military engineers.

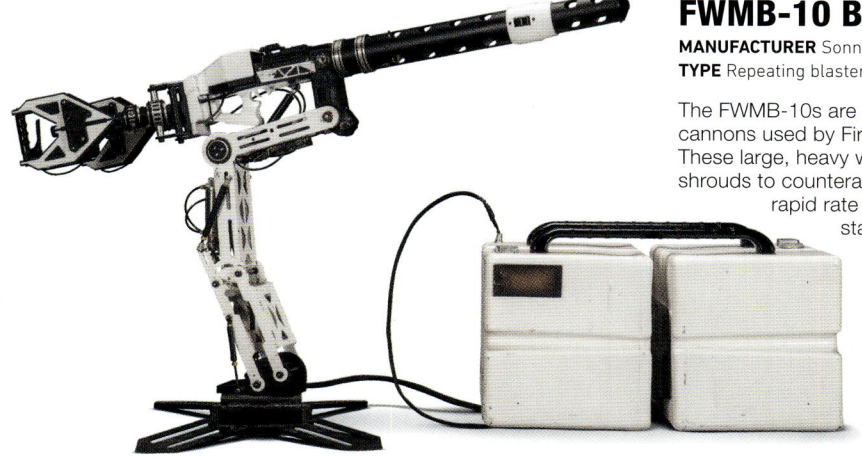

FWMB-10 BLASTER

MANUFACTURER Sonn-Blas Corp. **MODEL** FWMB-10
TYPE Repeating blaster

The FWMB-10s are a line of repeating blaster cannons used by First Order heavy stormtroopers. These large, heavy weapons feature barrel-cooling shrouds to counteract the heat generated by their rapid rate of fire, and foldout integrated stands to support their weight. The blaster requires a high input of energy to maintain its rate of fire, so it is powered by an Eksoan Class-5B1 duplex power generator. Vehicles such as the Aratech-Loratus Light Infantry Utility Vehicle carry mounted FWMB-10 blasters as their primary weapons.

LASER AX

MANUFACTURER First Order Department of Military Research
MODEL BL-155 Laser ax **TYPE** Executioner's ax

In the course of their executioner duties, First Order troopers swing the BL-155 Laser ax, which has four pairs of extendable claws forming four monomolecular energy ribbons. When the terrible laser ax falls, it causes its victim terrible, if mercifully brief, pain. First Order Commander Pyre attempts to kill Kazuda Xiono with a laser ax on the *Resurgent*-class Star Destroyer Thunderer, but CB-23 rescues him, allowing Xiono to then knock Pyre unconscious using the weapon.

TECHNOLOGY

COMMAND BRIDGE DROID
MANUFACTURER Accutronics **TYPE** Modified TDA-series droid assistant **AFFILIATION** *Colossus*

A command bridge droid is programmed to serve as part of the bridge crew aboard a vessel, running any number of operations simultaneously. The *Colossus* platform is staffed with several such droids, including 4D-M1N, who acts as a liaison for Captain Immanuel Doza while also overseeing all other command droids.

OTOGA-222 MAINTENANCE DROID
TYPE Repair droid **AFFILIATION** Various

The Otoga-222 maintenance droid can be found throughout the galaxy, acting as a repair technician. One of these droids assists podracer Ben Quadinaros during the Boonta Eve Classic. Otoga-222s are also present on the *Colossus* platform, serving various fliers.

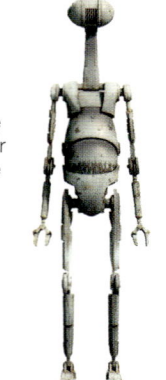

SIGNAL BEACON
MANUFACTURER Fabritech **TYPE** SB082 signal beacon

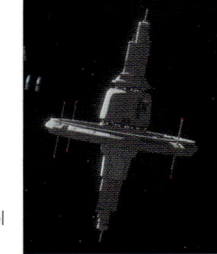

Typically the size of a starfighter, a signal beacon marks a location by sitting at a precise point in space and emitting its coordinates. Captain Immanuel Doza of the *Colossus* leaves a signal beacon for his wife, Venisa Doza of the Resistance, when she is to rendezvous with his ship. But the First Order also arrives, thwarting their plans.

FIRST ORDER SECURITY DROID
MANUFACTURER Arakyd Industries **TYPE** KXFO-series security droid **AFFILIATION** First Order

With white plating, a black exoskeleton, and piercing red sensors, the tall First Order security droid is an intimidating sight. On the *Titan* refueling station, these droids can be found stalking the corridors, making the rounds, and checking for unwanted visitors.

SITH WAYFINDER
MANUFACTURER Ancient Sith **MODEL** Custom **TYPE** Hyperspatial lodestone

Wayfinders are an exceptionally rare example of navigational technology that's still not completely understood by modern scholars. Created by the ancient Sith, without the use of modern navicomputers and hyperspace routes, the first wayfinders are inspired by the Sith's dissection of purrgil whales. They combine the species' natural faster-than-light capabilities with an infusion of the dark side of the Force.

After a location is mapped out, its hyperspace vector data is then contained within a supraluminite lodestone and a plasmatic interior, allowing the chosen user to journey safely to the destination.

Ancient technology The supraluminite lodestone is naturally attuned to certain hyperspace paths.

Plugged in The wayfinder's technology allows it to directly interface with Kylo Ren's ship, providing him with navigational support on his treacherous journey.

Darth Sidious and his apprentice Darth Vader each possess one of a pair of wayfinders, which contain the treacherous directions to the Sith planet Exegol. Decades later, Kylo Ren takes his grandfather Vader's wayfinder from its protected hiding place on Mustafar in order to track down Sidious.

The Jedi have long attempted to study this technology, with Luke Skywalker noting their mysterious history in the *Rammahgon* tome. This study gives Rey enough starting information to track down the remaining wayfinder in Sidious' antechamber.

AP'LEK'S VIBRO-AX
MANUFACTURER Ancient Mandalorians **MODEL** Custom **TYPE** Executioner's ax

Ap'lek relies on his ancient Mandalorian executioner's vibro-ax to cut down any enemy of the Knights of Ren. When turned on, the beskar steel blade becomes a conduit for pulsating energy. Harsh vibrations enhance its sharp edges to cut through almost any armor or biological material.

KURUK'S BLASTER RIFLE
MANUFACTURER Handcrafted **MODEL** Custom **TYPE** Multibarreled blaster

The sharpshooter of the Knights of Ren, Kuruk demands the most accurate and deadly of weaponry. He spends an extensive amount of time customizing his rifle to have three firing modes. This unique weapon has rapid-fire, sniping, and pump-action firing features, and it requires specialized plasma-bolt ammunition.

CARDO'S ARM CANNON
MANUFACTURER Handcrafted **MODEL** Custom **TYPE** Multi-barrel portable cannon

Cardo has long obsessed over his custom arm cannon, which he made himself. He builds out two barrels that can rapid-fire both lasers and plasma bolts, as well as serve as a crude flamethrower. The hodgepodge weapon is one of a kind and perfectly suited to its creator, turning him into a one-man arsenal during combat.

TRUDGEN'S VIBROCLEAVER
MANUFACTURER Handcrafted **MODEL** Custom **TYPE** Ultrasonic blade

The intimidating size of Trudgen's mammoth vibrocleaver often leaves his opponents filled with dread—before he even swings it. Made of crucible steel mixed with beskar shards, this vibrocleaver is equipped with ultrasonic technology that makes it even easier for the Knight of Ren to cut through flesh and bone.

USHAR'S WAR CLUB
MANUFACTURER Handcrafted **MODEL** Custom **TYPE** Kinetite-powered club

Ushar pummels any enemies of the Knights of Ren with his club, which is specially powered by kinetite—a substance able to hold and release intense energy. This energy produces enormous shock waves and concussive blows, which are able to knock out multiple combatants at once.

VICRUL'S SCYTHE
MANUFACTURER Handcrafted **MODEL** Custom **TYPE** Curved vibroblade

Like most of his fellow Knights of Ren, Vicrul has spent much time perfecting his melee weapon of choice. His scythe's sawtooth crook can catch enemy blades, thanks to its phrik-alloy composition. Its most lethal aspect, however, is its ultrasonic generator chamber, whose vibrations provide a deadly cutting power.

ALBREKH'S TOOLS
MANUFACTURER Ancient Sith **MODEL** Custom **TYPE** Sith forging equipment

The dexterous Sith alchemist Albrekh supplements his steady hands with ancient tools on a composite device known as a Sith forge. Its magnetic forceps and posable arm mechanism are perfect for delicately applying molten Sarrassian iron—a red ore that seems to scream with the Force. The device is used for repairing Kylo Ren's helmet.

ELECTROPROD
MANUFACTURER Arakyd Industries **MODEL** DX-90 electroprod **TYPE** Riot control tool

The First Order demands discipline in its controlled sectors, but it often has to rely on riot control tactics to enforce this. One of the most effective and crude tools in its arsenal is the electroprod. It allows stormtroopers to rein in any physical demonstrations before they escalate.

FIRST ORDER JET TROOPER CANNON
MANUFACTURER Sonn-Blas Corporation
MODEL G125 projectile launcher
TYPE Tri-barreled weapon

When taking to the skies, jet troopers require multiple options for aerial combat, making the G125 projectile launcher a popular weapon. Soldiers can toggle between a standard blaster and a surrounding triple-barreled projectile launcher that shoots explosive rounds.

JET TROOPER JETPACK
MANUFACTURER Nanogar Jet Products
MODEL NJP-900 integrated jetpack
TYPE Mobile propulsion unit

Each jet trooper is equipped with an agile jetpack built into their customized armor. These propulsion units were first made famous by Mandalorian warriors, but they've since been specialized for the First Order. They have complex gyroscopic technology that translates the user's movements into travel in that direction.

OCHI'S DAGGER
MANUFACTURER Ancient Sith **MODEL** Custom
TYPE Ceremonial Sith dagger

The wicked-looking Sith dagger used by Ochi of Bestoon is a mysterious relic of a past age. The dagger seems to cry out for blood to drink, and a bloodlust passes to its unknowing wielder. Ochi uses it to kill Palpatine's strandcast son and his wife, but that only temporarily satiates the knife's white-hot cries. The dagger's arrowhead-shaped blade is etched in the runic Sith language of Ur-Kittât. It also contains a recently added hidden measurement that marks the location of the Emperor's wayfinder.

Sharp words
"Old Tongue" runes and symbols brought Ochi a sense of pride.

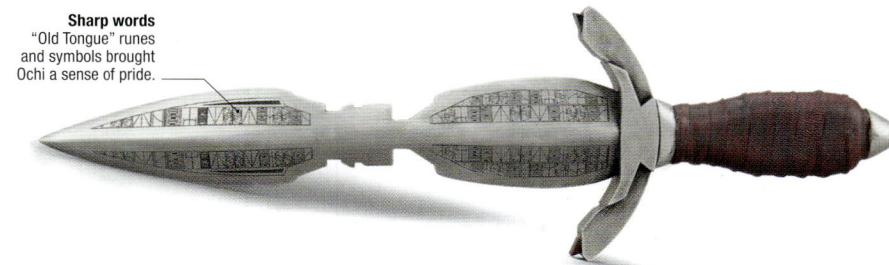

ZORII BLISS' BLASTERS
MANUFACTURER Kelvarek Consolidated Arms
MODEL E-851 blasters
TYPE Twin bronzium pistols

The E-851 blaster is the weapon of choice of many in the galaxy's underworld, thanks, in part, to its weighted style that favors only the steadiest shots. Zorii Bliss wields two such pistols, plated with bronzium like her helmet, which she uses ambidextrously as a deadly surprise during combat.

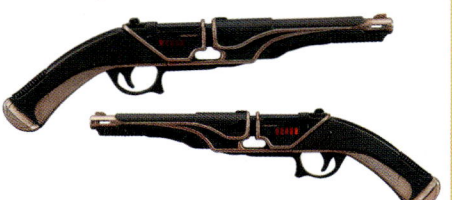

ZORII BLISS' HELMET
MANUFACTURER Custom
MODEL Custom
TYPE Bronzium life-support helmet

As a hardened criminal, Zorii Bliss needs both anonymity and intimidation, and she uses her helmet for both those purposes. Its bronzium finish denotes her leadership role within the Spice Runners of Kijimi, while its plasteel shell contains a host of technology that give her an edge in combat.

FIRST ORDER OFFICER'S TRANSIT DATA-MEDALLION
MANUFACTURER MerenData
TYPE Clearance data device

Data-medallions are used by the First Order to allow high-ranking officers to travel without cumbersome security checks. By transmitting an encrypted subspace code, the device gives a ship free passage and landing rights at any First Order facility or through any blockade that requires the highest clearance level.

SITH TROOPER BLASTER
MANUFACTURER Sith Eternal
MODEL ST-W48 blaster **TYPE** Heavy rifle

The stormtroopers of the Sith Eternal army are each given a ST-W48 blaster rifle as their standard-issue weapon. For a mass-produced heavy rifle, it's remarkably efficient and can be shifted into carbine or rifle modes quickly. Its quarrel-bolt launchers are inspired by bowcasters, but are an improvement on the explosive technology.

JANNAH'S BOW
MANUFACTURER Handcrafted
MODEL Custom
TYPE Salvaged blaster bow

After landing on Kef Bir, former stormtrooper Jannah disassembles her First Order weaponry to create makeshift powered bows for herself and her allies. Mostly constructed out of salvaged blaster parts, Jannah's personal custom-powered bow augments her physical strength, using stabilizing polarizers built into each end. In order to shoot an arrow, Jannah draws the shaft through a former blaster barrel, effectively reactivating its galven circuitry. While it may look makeshift, it proves to be an effective weapon, whether hunting on the plains of the Forest moon of Endor or fighting stormtroopers.

SITH TROOPER ARMOR
MANUFACTURER Sith Eternal
MODEL Quad-folded gammaplast armor
TYPE Armor

The red plating of the Sith troopers is meant to strike fear into the hearts of their enemies, as well as serve as a sign of their loyalty to the Sith Eternal. In nearly every respect, their crimson armor is better than that of their First Order counterparts.

Dressed to kill
Raised anisotropic bands divert enemy blasts.

LEIA'S LIGHTSABER
MANUFACTURER Handcrafted
MODEL Custom
TYPE Jedi lightsaber

When constructing her own lightsaber, Leia Organa draws on her personal history in order to craft a weapon that reflects her own life and sensibilities. Her small, artistic hilt is made of silver and gold and is fitted with pearlescent inlays that are befitting a princess of Alderaan. Leia trains with this blue blade on Ajan Kloss, eventually surrendering the weapon to Luke Skywalker when she decides to step away from her Jedi training. It's later given to her apprentice, Rey, who uses it against Darth Sidious. Rey then buries the lightsaber in the sands of Tatooine, next to the blade that belonged to Leia's father, her brother, and her apprentice.

A work of art
Leia's hilt is even more elegant and sleek than her brother's.

REY'S LIGHTSABER
MANUFACTURER Handcrafted **MODEL** Custom
TYPE Jedi lightsaber

While poring over ancient Jedi texts from the library on Ahch-to, Rey begins the complex process of creating her own lightsaber. Having carried both Luke Skywalker and Leia Organa's lightsabers for a time, she completes the construction of her own blade after the Battle of Exegol. Remaining true to her upbringing on the backwater planet of Jakku, Rey salvages hilt parts from her quarterstaff and personal clothing to create a comfortable, familiar, reflection of her journey. More rugged than either of her masters' weapons, Rey's golden-yellow, single-bladed lightsaber can be ignited by twisting a rotating gear.

VEHICLES

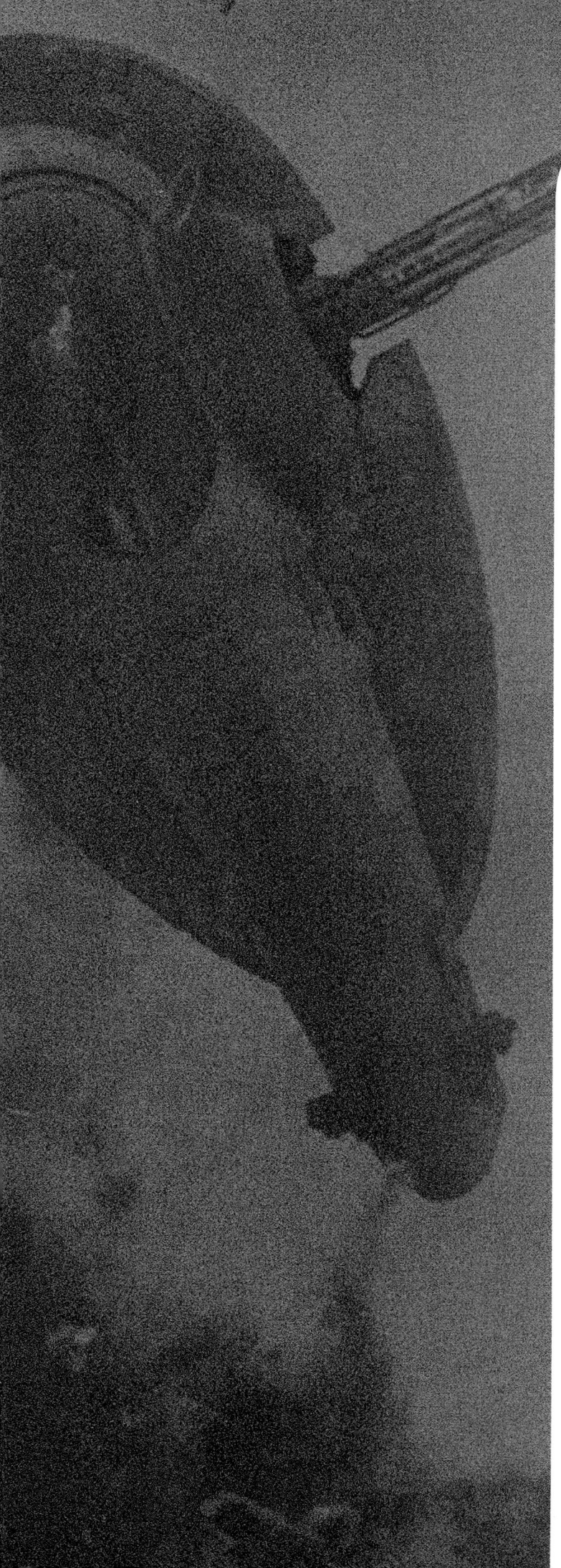

Factories produce a staggering variety of vehicles for both peaceful and warlike purposes, from starships traveling at lightspeed to transporters moving with a slow, remorseless tread.

On thousands of civilized worlds, most atmospheric-propulsion vehicles utilize repulsorlift technology, which levitates vehicles and lightweight atmosphere craft via antigravitational emanations called "repulsor fields." Some repulsorlift craft are little more than engines with padded seats that travel close to the ground, while others are large luxury vessels that can skim a planet's atmospheric ceiling. For voyages between distant star systems, starships use hyperdrive technology that enables vessels to exceed lightspeed, and sublight engines for traveling at slower speeds.

During the Clone Wars, the Galactic Civil War, and the subsequent conflict between the Resistance and the First Order, many manufacturers convert transports and freighters into combat craft, and also produce entirely new vehicles that are laden with weapons. To evade the authorities that patrol the galaxy's best-known commercial routes, pirates and smugglers outfit their own vessels with powerful engines and exotic weaponry.

VEHICLES

LEGACY RUN
MANUFACTURER Kaniff Yards **MODEL** Class A
TYPE Modular freight transport

As a modular long-haul freighter, the *Legacy Run* holds up to 144 customizable modules for cargo transportation. These take up much of its space, leaving little for the bridge and engineering section. The craft can be reconfigured to hold passenger compartments or aquatic tanks. Captain Hedda Casset commands the *Legacy Run* on a voyage to bring settlers to the Outer Rim. During that mission, a Nihil ship intercepts the transport ship and blasts it into pieces in hyperspace. Fragments and modules are thrown back into real space around the galaxy in the disastrous Emergence.

ATARAXIA
TYPE Star cruiser

The *Ataraxia* is the Jedi flagship of the High Republic era, and a large contingent of Jedi Vectors can fit in its hold. Jedi Master Jora Malli commands the star cruiser at the Battle of Kur, during which it supports the Republic cruiser *Third Horizon*. The ship is intended to be permanently stationed at Starlight Beacon, but its presence there is short-lived because it is needed in the fight against the Nihil. Lourna Dee and fellow Nihil steal the star cruiser during the fall of Starlight Beacon. Almost 100 years later, it is back in Republic control and used to transport Dooku and other Jedi initiates.

JEDI VECTOR
MANUFACTURER Valkeri Enterprises **MODEL** Vector **TYPE** Light interceptor starfighter

Jedi Vectors are one- or two-person starfighters designed to be used by Force-attuned pilots. During the High Republic era, Jedi unlock the ship's weapons by slotting their lightsaber into a specialized port on the console. Vectors' laser cannons can be dialed down to merely disable instead of kill.

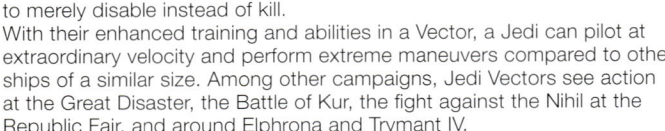

With their enhanced training and abilities in a Vector, a Jedi can pilot at extraordinary velocity and perform extreme maneuvers compared to other ships of a similar size. Among other campaigns, Jedi Vectors see action at the Great Disaster, the Battle of Kur, the fight against the Nihil at the Republic Fair, and around Elphrona and Trymant IV.

REPUBLIC LONGBEAM
MODEL Longbeam **TYPE** Cruiser

The Longbeam is a medium-size starship often used by the Republic during the era of Chancellor Lina Soh. It is typically fitted with blasters, six missiles, a suite of defensive countermeasures, and magclamps. It can be crewed by as few as three people. The *Aurora IX*, a state-of-the-art Longbeam, which shoots down debris from the *Legacy Run* above Hetzal Prime, is remarkable for its multiple distributed processors that can run its weapons and defensive systems simultaneously. The *Aurora III* also helps to stop debris from hitting the Hetzal system. Chancellor Kyong Greylark has a personal Longbeam and crew. At the Battle of Dalna, Republic Longbeams support Eirami and E'ronoh forces.

GAZE ELECTRIC
MANUFACTURER Path of the Open Hand **MODEL** Custom **TYPE** Star cruiser

Elecia Zeveron, also known as the Mother of the Path of the Open Hand, instructs her people in slowly constructing the *Gaze Electric* as a mobile base of operations during the High Republic era. When Marda Ro begins to transform the cult, she takes command of the ship as well. Eventually, it passes down to her daughter, Shalla Ro, who begins to organize the Nihil. The *Gaze Electric* is crewed primarily by enforcer droids. It moves through hyperspace in seemingly impossible twists and turns powered by the Paths provided by Mari San Tekka and a specialized Path engine.

SQUALL SPIDER
MANUFACTURER Nihil **MODEL** Spider cruiser **TYPE** Air and ground transport

The *Squall Spider* is a Nihil starship which can both fly through hyperspace and walk on a planet's surface. Even some pirates think it looks cobbled together, but its enormous size and grasping legs make it powerful in battle. The *Squall Spider* menaces Trymant IV during the Emergences. Krix Kamerat of the Path and Elder Tromak board the craft along with Marchion Ro. The Force-attuned Nihil Udi Dis pilots the *Squall Spider* through the dangerous space ice field known as the Rystan Badlands, and Marchion Ro has the *Squall Spider* with him when he encounters Vol Garat on Banchii.

STAR HOPPER
TYPE Padawan academic cruiser

Around the time of the *Legacy Run*'s destruction, Jedi Masters Yoda and Torban Buck reside on the *Star Hopper* with a class of Padawans, including Lula Talisola and Qort. The ship contains classrooms, living quarters, sparring space, and other resources to serve as a mobile temple. It can comfortably hold 18 people and requires a crew of four to fly. It is the nearest Republic ship available to stop the hyperspace debris from raining down on Trymant IV. When Zeen Mrala joins the Jedi, she spends a large portion of her time on the *Star Hopper*. The cruiser docks at Starlight Beacon shortly before the space station's destruction.

T-1 SHUTTLE
MANUFACTURER Slayn & Korpil **MODEL** T-1 **TYPE** Interplanetary shuttle

T-1 shuttles were hyperspace-capable Republic craft often used by Jedi. They are typically used to transport pairs or small groups of masters and Padawans. Jedi Master Sskeer and Padawan Keeve Trennis use a T-1 shuttle for several of their missions, including their investigation on Sedri Minor and their return to Starlight Beacon from the planet Shuraden. Jedi Master Simmix is killed when a T-1 shuttle crashes because the safety restraints were not configured to match his body shape. Orla Jareni and Cohmac Vitus, who were Padawans at the time, were also present in the crash.

VESSEL
TYPE Transport ship

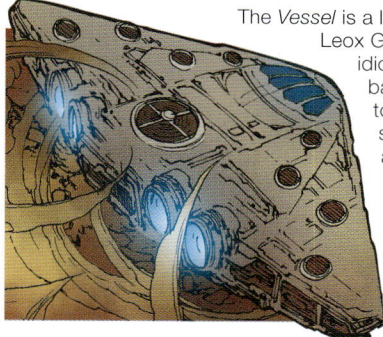

The *Vessel* is a light transport ship crewed by Affie Hollow, Leox Gyasi, and Geode. Its appearance is rather idiosyncratic, with dark-blue plating and bare-bones amenities. Leox and Affie retreat to the *Vessel* when they find themselves surrounded by an angry crowd after accidentally stealing a sacred Sun Jewel. Later, they transport a group of Jedi, including Reath Silas, to the Amaxine station. Although the *Vessel* starts out as part of the Byne Guild, Affie takes the ship as her own when she leaves the Guild. During the fall of Starlight Beacon, the *Vessel* becomes a makeshift communications center for the station, from which Affie sends a distress signal.

VOYAGER DAWN
TYPE Medium-sized cruiser

The *Voyager Dawn* is one of the vessels struck by debris during the destruction of the *Legacy Run*. The ship is a meditation retreat for elder Jedi and typically carries hundreds of occupants. Its layout includes passenger berths and large gardens. When Jedi Master Torban Buck and Captain Kardo spot the *Voyager Dawn* in distress, it is Master Kantam Sy who responds to the call for help. The ship is in danger of falling apart, but the Jedi successfully evacuate all the occupants. Later, Buck tells the story of the rescue from the *Voyager Dawn*, while baking with Ram Jomaram and other Jedi.

CRIMSON FIREHAWK
MANUFACTURER Mejson Spaceworks **MODEL** *Chellatine*-class **TYPE** Shuttle

The *Crimson Firehawk* is Nash Durango's personal shuttle. She is always ready to take Kai Brightstar, Lys Solay, and Nubs wherever they need to go. Nash's signature maneuver in space is the Throttle Buster, in which she accelerates the *Crimson Firehawk* in a circle, then stalls midair and free-falls. Nash lets Kai fly the ship when the young Jedi is first learning to fly. He pilots it into an asteroid field and performs the Throttle Buster himself.

When Princess Inaya hires Nash to transport her from Tenoo back to her home planet, Nash is very nervous. The pirate Taborr pursues the *Crimson Firehawk* in an attempt to steal Princess Inaya's gift, but Nash flies it nimbly through the trees. She loses shields and lateral controls to Taborr, forcing them to land, but she repairs the ship and asks Inaya to fly the rest of the way.

Next adventure
Alongside her Jedi friends and her astromech RJ-83, Nash has a whole galaxy to explore.

KAI'S SPEEDER
MANUFACTURER Aratech Repulsor Company **TYPE** Speeder

Kai Brightstar keeps his personal speeder bike at the Jedi temple on Tenoo. The speeder, which can carry two riders, proves useful for Kai and his friend Nash Durango on a mission to save RJ-83. When the droid tumbles off Nash's skiff and into a river, Nash calls Kai for help, and he nimbly flies his speeder to the docks in Kublop Springs, then down the river. With its heavy engine and long stabilizer fins, the speeder bike is too large to maneuver when the river enters a tangled swamp, so Kai and Nash complete their mission on foot.

IRON TALON
MANUFACTURER Corellian Engineering Corporation **MODEL** HT-150 **TYPE** Light freighter

The *Iron Talon* is the base of operations for Taborr Val Dorn's pirate gang. Taborr, Pord, and the droid EB-3 launch their raids from the ship. EB-3 steals Princess Inaya's gift from the *Crimson Firehawk* and takes it to the *Iron Talon*, but Inaya hot-wires the cargo bay doors open, allowing her and her Jedi friends to escape having retrieved the gift. The *Iron Talon* can often be found either patrolling Tenoo airspace for potential items to steal or docked at the pirate hideout of Yarrum Tower.

CRIMSON BOLT
MANUFACTURER Ubrikkian Industries **MODEL** Custom **TYPE** Racing skiff

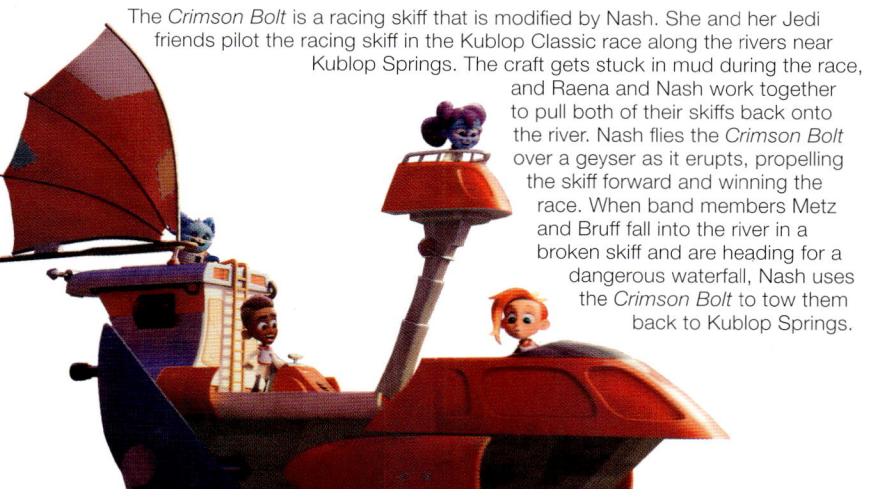

The *Crimson Bolt* is a racing skiff that is modified by Nash. She and her Jedi friends pilot the racing skiff in the Kublop Classic race along the rivers near Kublop Springs. The craft gets stuck in mud during the race, and Raena and Nash work together to pull both of their skiffs back onto the river. Nash flies the *Crimson Bolt* over a geyser as it erupts, propelling the skiff forward and winning the race. When band members Metz and Bruff fall into the river in a broken skiff and are heading for a dangerous waterfall, Nash uses the *Crimson Bolt* to tow them back to Kublop Springs.

STAR SEEKER
MANUFACTURER Koensayr **MODEL** *Renning*-class **TYPE** Shuttle

The *Star Seeker* belongs to the pilot droid OG-LC. He uses it to explore distant reaches of the galaxy while searching for information and artifacts for the Jedi Order. When the *Star Seeker* goes missing, Kai Brightstar discovers an ancient starship tracker that can lead him to the lost vessel, so Master Zia Zaldor Zanna encourages him to find it. Kai and his friends discover that OG-LC has been stranded on the planet Fobaris since two asteroids collided with the *Star Seeker*. OG has repaired the ship but is afraid to confront the asteroid field around Fobaris again. With help from the Jedi younglings, the droid successfully pilots the *Star Seeker* off the planet and through the asteroid field.

VEHICLES

Deflector shield

Jedi transport Before the dark times, red was the color of neutrality for spacecraft of the Galactic Republic.

Cockpit

Docking ring

REPUBLIC CRUISER

MANUFACTURER Corellian Engineering Corp.
MODEL *Consular*-class **TYPE** Corvette

Built in the great shipyards of the Corellian Engineering Corporation, the mighty 115-meter- (377-ft-3-in) long *Consular*-class Republic cruiser is used by the supreme chancellor, members of the Galactic Senate, and the Jedi Order for diplomatic missions. The cruiser's striking scarlet color scheme declares the ship's diplomatic immunity. Typically unarmed, the cruiser features three powerful Dyne 577 radial atomizer engines, a Longe Voltrans tri-arc CD-3.2 hyperdrive, and sturdy deflector shields as protection. The bridge is located in the cruiser's forward section, just above an interchangeable diplomatic salon pod, which can eject from the cruiser in the event of emergencies.

Converted freighter Cavernous hangar bays carry an entire invasion army.

Communications array Control signals sustain a mechanized army.

TRADE FEDERATION BATTLESHIP

MANUFACTURER Hoersch-Kessel Drive Inc.
MODEL Modified *Lucrehulk*-class LH-3210 cargo freighter **TYPE** Battleship (converted freighter)

Originally cargo freighters for the Neimoidian Trade Federation's vast commercial fleet, Trade Federation battleships are over 3 kilometers (2 miles) in diameter and hold a central sphere that contains the ship's bridge and reactor assemblies. Each battleship can carry 550 MTTs, 6,250 AATs, 1,500 troop carriers, 50 C-9979 landing craft, and 1,500 droid starfighters. Converting the freighters into warships is one of the Neimoidians' first priorities when they begin secretly building their armed forces. However, the conversion has not been entirely successful, and these immense, powerful vessels have a number of weaknesses. The addition of retractable turbolasers along the equator of the ship's hull leaves large blind spots that small, speedy enemy vessels can exploit.

The most important vessels in the Trade Federation's fleet are the Droid Control Ships, which are used to operate the droid armies. A Control Ship is distinguished from other Federation battleships by the large communications array on its dorsal hull. Neimoidian commanders typically seal themselves in the ship's bridge while their droids handle all ship operations. Destroying a Control Ship can disable every droid in the warship's service.

The Bedlam Raiders use a crashed core ship from a former Trade Federation battleship as their base of operations on Koboh during the Imperial era. Years later during the Galactic Civil War, the Rebel Alliance uses a *Lucrehulk*-class battleship as a flight training school.

Reinforced hull Irregular armor plating strengthens the ship's overall structure.

VULTURE DROID (DROID STARFIGHTER)

MANUFACTURER Xi Char Cathedral factories
MODEL Variable Geometry Self-Propelled Battle Droid, Mark I **TYPE** Droid starfighter

The Trade Federation's droid starfighters—also known as vulture droids—were designed and originally manufactured by the Xi Charrians. Like the ground-based battle droid infantry, droid starfighters are controlled by the Trade Federation's Droid Control Ship. When in starfighter mode, the droid carries four blaster cannons in its wings and two energy torpedo launchers along its forward edge, as well as buzz droid-laden discord missiles. When not in flight, the droid starfighter can transform into walking mode, allowing it to be used in surface patrols. When reconfigured for walking, the launchers are angled for anti-personnel use.

Unconventional solid fuel concentrate slugs housed in the aft fuel chamber power the droids. These slugs burn rapidly when ignited, giving the droid starfighter incredible bursts of energy but a very limited range of operation. As such, droid starfighters must operate from a nearby launch base or capital ship. When not deployed, these starfighters hang from overhead recharging racks. The Trade Federation attempts to counter any shortcomings in its automated vulture droid designs by dispatching them en masse. The Trade Federation also jealously guards its new innovations and equips the droid starfighter to protect its trade secrets. Should it lose contact with the Droid Control Ship due to a malfunction or other catastrophe, the starfighter's self-destruct mechanism is engaged, preventing it from falling into enemy hands.

Tapered claw The wings extend for walker mode.

Torpedo launchers Energy torpedoes are fired from these channels.

Laser armament Each wing houses two blaster cannons.

TRADE FEDERATION LANDING SHIP
MANUFACTURER Haor Chall Engineering
MODEL C-9979
TYPE Landing craft

With its huge wingspan and imposing loading ramp, the Trade Federation landing ship is a daunting sight. The ship can hold heavy armor, is capable of carrying a total of 28 troop carriers, 1,114 AATs, and 11 MTTs, and requires a crew of 88 droids. The wings are removable for ease of storage and docking, and when deployed, powerful tensor field generators bind the wings to the craft and strengthen the vessel's structural integrity. Additionally, large repulsorlifts keep the ship from sagging under its own weight.

TRADE FEDERATION MTT
MANUFACTURER Baktoid Armor Workshop
MODEL Multi-Troop Transport (MTT)
TYPE Repulsorcraft

A giant armored repulsorlift vehicle, the MTT is capable of depositing over a hundred battle droid soldiers into the thick of combat. The MTT's bulbous front end opens to reveal an articulated deployment rack, upon which rest dozens of compressed battle droids. The rack extends forward, releasing the droids into neatly organized rows. Upon activation from an orbiting Droid Control Ship, the droids unfold into their humanoid configuration. The hydraulically powered deployment rack can carry 112 battle droids in stowed configuration.

Landing-zone patrol
During the Naboo invasion, STAP-mounted battle droids survey the Great Grass Plains and transmit data to their Droid Control Ship.

SINGLE TROOPER AERIAL PLATFORM (STAP)
MANUFACTURER Baktoid Armor Workshop **MODEL** Single Trooper Aerial Platform
TYPE Patrol vehicle

Deployed by the Trade Federation army's battle droids, STAPs are slim, lightweight reconnaissance and patrol vehicles armed with a pair of blaster cannons. Trade Federation engineers drew inspiration for their design from similar civilian vehicles called airhooks, which they reengineered for greater performance and reliability, and to be specifically piloted by B1 battle droids. High-voltage energy cells fuel the tiny repulsorlift craft's drive turbines, which provide the STAP with impressive speed and maneuverability. The STAP's greatest weaknesses are its pilot's exposure to enemy fire and its fragility. Though the craft is highly agile, and transmissions from Droid Control Ships skillfully guide droid pilots, a lucky shot can quickly bring down a STAP or its pilot. As such, the vehicles are primarily relegated to patrol, "mopping up" missions, and the occasional foray into battle to harry enemy forces, while the brunt of combat is borne by heavier vehicles.

BONGO
MANUFACTURER Otoh Gunga Bongameken Cooperative
MODEL Tribubble bongo sub
TYPE Submarine

Organically grown through secret Gungan techniques, the bongo is a submersible vehicle used to travel the depths of Naboo's waters. Distinguished by a mantashaped hull, the bongo's hydrostatic bubble shields keep the cockpit and cargo areas dry and filled with air. A semirigid assembly of tentaclelike fins spins to provide the bongo with thrust. In emergencies, the cockpit module can eject from the sub like an escape pod.

NEIMOIDIAN SHUTTLE
MANUFACTURER Haor Chall Engineering
MODEL *Sheathipede*-class
TYPE Transport shuttle

The *Sheathipede*-class shuttle is typically used for short-range transit, either across a planetary surface or for ferrying passengers into orbital space where a larger ship or station awaits its arrival. The shuttle's curved, insectlike landing gears lower from the ship's belly, giving the craft's legs a pincer-like appearance as it touches down. Neimoidian officials prefer models with automatic pilots because the absence of a cockpit allows for an expansive passenger cabin.

Heavy bombardment
Moving slowly along city streets, AATs prompt civilians to take refuge *(above right)*. Each AAT is crewed by four battle droids: a commander, a pilot, and two gunners *(above)*.

ARMORED ASSAULT TANK (AAT)
MANUFACTURER Baktoid Armor Workshop
MODEL Armored Assault Tank (AAT) **TYPE** Repulsorlift battle tank

Studded with heavy artillery, the floating tanks known as AATs form the frontline of Trade Federation armored infantry divisions. The AAT's turret-mounted primary laser cannon has long-range destructive capability, and is bracketed by a pair of pylon-mounted secondary laser cannons. A pair of forward-facing short-range blaster cannons round out the AAT's energy-weapon complement. The tank also carries formidable additional weaponry: six energized projectile launchers that fire high-energy shells encased in a cocoon of plasma for incredible speed and penetrative power, specialized armor-piercing warheads, and high explosive "bunker-busting" shells.

Escape from Naboo
In orbit above Naboo, the Naboo Royal Starship's mirror surface reflects its planet of origin and its designers' desire to create a symbol of grace and beauty *(left)*. Sustaining damage after escaping the Trade Federation's blockade of Naboo, Amidala's ship makes an emergency landing on Tatooine *(below left)*.

NABOO ROYAL STARSHIP
MANUFACTURER Theed Palace Space Vessel Engineering Corp.
MODEL Modified J-type 327 Nubian starship
TYPE Transport

Boasting a strikingly beautiful design that embodies the craftsmanship that prevails in the peaceful years of the Republic, the Naboo Royal Starship is at Queen Amidala's disposal for formal state visits to other planetary representatives and for royal events on Naboo. The streamlined J-type 327 Nubian vessel lacks any offensive weaponry, but does feature powerful shields and a high-performance hyperdrive. Although Naboo tradition encourages the reigning monarch to personally name the royal vessel, Amidala—by the time of the Battle of Naboo—has more important concerns than the ship's name.

The Royal Starship's unique spaceframe is handcrafted at Theed but designed around the imported Nubian sublight engine and hyperdrive propulsion system. Nubian systems are often sought by discerning buyers and are easily acquired on most civilized worlds, but can be difficult to obtain on remote planets. The ship's gleaming finish is purely decorative and made of royal chromium, a substance usually reserved for vessels serving Naboo's monarch. The mirrored hull is hand-polished and crafted by fine artisans, not by automatons or factory equipment. The ship's interior is made with equal care and is quite spacious. From fore to aft, the vessel contains luxurious royal quarters; a forward hold; a main hold with tech station; the cockpit, which is accessible via turbolift; and the throne room, where Queen Amidala sits while in transit or to receive guests. Naboo citizens consider the entire ship a work of art. After Amidala's death, Darth Sidious gives the ship to Darth Vader.

Starfighter hit
Although N-1 starfighters are fast and agile, they are also prone to uncontrollable spins when the engines suffer damage.

NABOO N-1 STARFIGHTER
MANUFACTURER Theed Palace Space Vessel Engineering Corp. **MODEL** Royal N-1 **TYPE** Starfighter

Protecting the skies and space around Naboo, the N-1 starfighter—like the Royal Naboo Starship—exemplifies the philosophy of blending art and function seen throughout Naboo technology. Its twin radial J-type engines are capped in gleaming chromium and trail long delicate finials behind the ship's single-pilot compartment. Behind the pilot, a standard astromech droid plugs into a ventrally fed socket that requires the droid to compress its legs slightly and telescopically extend its domed head through a dorsal port. The fighter features twin blaster cannons, twin fire-linked torpedo launchers, and an automatic piloting system. Ahsoka Tano teaches Senator Padmé Amidala combat maneuvers in her chromium-plated personal N-1 starfighter, in acknowledgment of her former position as queen. Shortly after Death Star II is destroyed, Leia Organa, Shara Bey, and Naboo queen Sosha Soruna use N-1 starfighters to defend Theed during Operation: Cinder. Years later, mechanic Peli Motto and Din Djarin restore an N-1 starfighter after Din's ship, the *Razor Crest,* is destroyed. They add several modifications to the ship which increases its speed and allows Grogu to sit in the port that's normally used by astromech droids. N-1 starfighters continue to be used during the rise of the First Order. Several join the Resistance fleet during the Battle of Exegol.

Ready for action
Few pilots in Naboo's Space Fighter Corps have actual combat experience, but their rigorous training prepares them for the battle against the Trade Federation.

ANAKIN'S RADON-ULZER PODRACER

MANUFACTURER Radon-Ulzer (engines)
MODEL Customized repulsorlift vehicle
TYPE Podracer

Built in secret by the young Anakin Skywalker, the shiny blue-and-silver podracer is smaller and leaner than all the other competing podracers in the Boonta Eve Classic. Anakin's vehicle follows the same basic design found throughout the sport: a pod with a cockpit pulled by two high-powered engines. Energy binders lock the engines to each other, and durable Steelton control cables connect the engines to the pod. Seated in the cockpit, a pilot operates thruster bars that control power to the engines, and speeds can reach well over 800 kilometers (497 miles) per hour.

Because podracer pilots differ greatly in shape, size, and weight, the vehicles are heavily customized to match the requirements of the individual pilots. Pilots must have incredibly quick reflexes and very strong nerves. Anakin is the only known human to ever pilot a podracer and survive. Unlike other pilots, who invest in larger engines in the hopes of getting greater performance, Anakin salvages a pair of Radon-Ulzer 620C racing engines that Watto discarded, deeming them too burned out to be of any use. Anakin develops a new fuel atomizer and distribution system that sends more fuel into the Radon-Ulzer's combustion chambers, radically increasing their thrust and his podracer's top speed to almost 950 kilometers (590 miles) per hour, which is a testament to his engineering brilliance.

Race to the finish
Anakin's Radon-Ulzer engines are capped with a trio of bright yellow air scoops that provide additional control when braking and cornering. Despite the dastardly antics of his nemesis, Sebulba, Anakin remains focused on winning the Boonta Eve Classic.

SEBULBA'S PODRACER

MANUFACTURER Collor Pondrat (engines)
MODEL Customized repulsorlift vehicle **TYPE** Podracer

If reputable podracing officials were to examine Sebulba's podracer closely, they would classify it as illegal. His oversized Collor Pondrat Plug-F Mammoth Split-X engines, 7.8 meters (25 ft 7 in) in length, can achieve a top speed of 829 kilometers (515 miles) per hour. The engines are fueled by tradium power fluid pressurized with quold runium and activated with ionized injectrine. Sebulba takes pleasure in using a concealed flamethrower against competitors who dare to pass him, blasting them off course and ensuring his victory.

SITH INFILTRATOR

MANUFACTURER Republic Sienar Systems
MODEL Heavily modified Star Courier **TYPE** Armed star courier

Customized in a secret laboratory, the Sith Infiltrator, dubbed the *Scimitar*, is the personal spacecraft for Darth Maul and later Darth Sidious. The craft, 26.5 meters (86 ft 11 in) in length, with folding angular wings and a rounded bridge compartment, is equipped with many weapons and instruments of evil, including six laser cannons, spying and surveillance gear, interrogator droids, and Maul's speeder bike. Powered by a curious high-temperature ion engine sublight drive system, the craft's most impressive feature is its full-effect cloaking device, which makes it invisible. Sidious tasks the droid O-66 with protecting the *Scimitar* when he loans the ship to bounty hunter Chanath Cha for a mission.

SITH SPEEDER

MANUFACTURER Razalon
MODEL FC-20 (modified)
TYPE Speeder bike

A pared-down, crescent-shaped conveyance, Darth Maul's Sith Speeder, alias the *Bloodfin*, lacks weapons or a sensor array, so all of the vehicle's energy is devoted to speed. Maul can program his speeder to decelerate and enter a "wait mode" should he suddenly dismount.

VEHICLES

NABOO ROYAL CRUISER
MANUFACTURER Theed Palace Space Vessel Engineering Corp.
MODEL Custom-built J-type diplomatic barge
TYPE Transport

Like the Royal Starship used by the Queen of Naboo, this chrome-hulled cruiser is a J-type vessel constructed by the Theed Palace Space Vessel Engineering Corp. The shortcomings of the previous Nubian J-type 327 are addressed with improved shield generators and paired S-6 hyperdrive generators providing adequate backup for the superluminal drive. The unarmed transport often travels under escort and can function as a fighter carrier craft, carrying up to four N-1 starfighters fitted into recharge sockets along the leading edge of its wing.

ZAM'S AIRSPEEDER
MANUFACTURER Desler Gizh Outworld Mobility Corp. **MODEL** Koro-2 all-environment Exodrive
TYPE Airspeeder

A lean getaway vessel with a pressurized cabin, Zam Wesell's airspeeder features an uncommon external electromagnetic propulsion system. The forward mandibles irradiate the air around them, inducing ionization and making it conductive. Paired electrodes electrify the airstream and magnetically propel it toward the rear of the craft, resulting in the air dragging the vessel through the skies at speeds of 800 kilometers (497 miles) per hour.

ANAKIN'S AIRSPEEDER
MANUFACTURER Narglatch AirTech kit
MODEL XJ-6
TYPE Luxury airspeeder hot rod (modified)

On Coruscant, Anakin commandeers a sleek, open-cockpit airspeeder to pursue the assassin Zam Wesell. The speeder's owner, a wealthy representative of the Vorzyd sector, customized the vehicle with twin turbojet engines originally designed to function in groups of 50 aboard the gigantic bank-courier repulsor trucks of Aargau. The engines direct pressurized air through a series of thrust ducts to propel the craft.

Hyperspace booster
After the Delta-7 docks with the hyperdrive booster ring, the astromech transmits destination coordinates to the ring's navicomputer.

Enclosed cockpit
Modular options can accommodate pilots of all species.

Bow sensors
Delta-7's bow houses scanning and communications technology.

Starfighter strikeforce
During the Clone Wars, Jedi pilots and their astromechs fly Delta-7B starfighters on many missions throughout the galaxy.

DELTA-7 STARFIGHTER
MANUFACTURER Kuat Systems Engineering
MODEL Delta-7 Aethersprite-class
TYPE Light interceptor

Although Jedi generally use Republic Cruisers for missions across the galaxy, some assignments call for less conspicuous transports. For this reason, and because Jedi cannot always depend on pilots to take them to their destination, all Jedi learn how to pilot starships as part of their training. Prior to the Naboo blockade, Kuat Systems Engineering unveils the Delta-7 Jedi starfighter. A wedge-shaped, single-person craft, the Delta-7 is equipped with dual laser cannons, two secondary ion cannons, and a powerful deflector shield. Despite the craft's armaments, most Jedi pilots prefer to rely on their cunning and attunement to the Force to avoid disputes and aggression, and they use weapons as a last resort. Because the Delta-7 is too small to hold a standard navicomputer and hyperdrive, it relies on a truncated astromech droid, hardwired into the starfighter's port side, for storing navigational data, and a TransGalMeg Industries booster ring for transit through hyperspace. The astromech also provides diagnostic and repair service to the craft, as well as managing the secondary scanning and communications gear. Kuat Systems Engineering also produces a variant design of the dart-shaped starfighter: the Delta-7B Aethersprite-class interceptor. This version relocates the astromech socket from the port side to just in front of the cockpit, and has a slightly enlarged hull in order to accommodate a full-size astromech droid. Both Anakin Skywalker and Obi-Wan Kenobi pilot Delta-7Bs during the Clone Wars, and early rebels use rebuilt Delta-7s for short-range missions in the Imperial era.

BOBA FETT'S STARSHIP

MANUFACTURER Kuat Systems Engineering
MODEL Modified *Firespray-31*-class patrol and attack craft **TYPE** Pursuit vessel

Inherited by the bounty hunter Boba Fett from his father, Jango, the pursuit vessel has sophisticated anti-detection gear that ensures very few fugitives ever see their captor coming.

UNUSUAL DESIGN
An antiquated and extremely rare *Firespray-31*-class patrol and attack craft, Boba Fett's starship is a distinctive-looking vessel. A large engine cluster dominates the lower section of the ship when docked, with the cabin resting atop. Once airborne, Fett's vehicle pivots 90 degrees and its base becomes its trailing edge, while its top-mounted cockpit faces forward. The craft is armed with twin blaster cannons as well as concealed projectile launchers and a seismic charge deployer, a turret-mounted tractor beam projector, a pair of proton torpedo launchers, concussion missile tubes, and a powerful ion cannon.

FAMILY LEGACY
After an assassination assignment goes wrong for Jango Fett on Coruscant, the Jedi Obi-Wan Kenobi tracks Jango to Tipoca City on the water world Kamino. Jango and Boba board their *Firespray*-class vessel and escape to the Geonosis system, but when they realize the Jedi has pursued them, Jango launches seismic charges at Obi-Wan's starfighter. When Boba Fett eventually inherits the starship, he remembers his father's deadly tactics and learns many more.

Teaching Boba
Weaving through the asteroid belt surrounding Geonosis, Jango Fett fires the starship's laser cannons at Obi-Wan's Jedi starfighter.

PIRATE PROPERTY
Later, Boba forms an alliance with the bounty hunter Aurra Sing. On the planet Florrum, a team of Jedi captures Boba, and Sing crashes the Firespray while attempting to escape. The Weequay pirate Hondo Ohnaka salvages the vessel, repairs it, and adds it to his collection of starships. But after General Grievous and his droid army invade Florrum and capture Ohnaka, the Jedi Ahsoka Tano and a band of Jedi younglings rescue Ohnaka, and they escape in Fett's vehicle. Eventually, Boba regains ownership of his ship and modifies it to transform it into the ultimate vessel for bounty hunting.

CAPTURING HAN SOLO
On Tatooine, Boba is present when Jabba the Hutt threatens to put a bounty on the smuggler Han Solo unless he pays what he owes. Shortly after the Battle of Hoth, Darth Vader also places a bounty on Han, and Boba sees an opportunity to profit twice. Following the meeting on Vader's Super Star Destroyer, Boba sees Han's freighter jump to hyperspace and calculates its destination in the Anoat system. While tracking him there, he alerts Vader that Solo is heading for Cloud City. After securing his prize, Fett departs, making a pitstop on Nar Shaddaa to stabilize the carbonite Han is encased in. Although Crimson Dawn steals Solo from the smuggler's moon, Boba later retrieves him from the *Executor* and delivers Han to Jabba on Tatooine, finally collecting his bounty.

NEW LIFE
After escaping the belly of the Sarlacc, Fett breaks his starship out of Jabba's former palace. Fett uses the firepower of his vehicle to exact revenge on a Nikto speeder-bike gang that he believes massacred a Tusken tribe. Later, he returns to the Sarlacc to search for his missing armor, but to no avail. Fett then travels to Tython to finally retrieve his coveted gear from Din Djarin. Soon after, he takes his ship to Morak to help Djarin rescue the foundling Grogu from Moff Gideon. His debts paid, Fett returns to Jabba's palace on Tatooine with his ship and declares himself the new Daimyo of Tatooine.

Valuable cargo
Anticipating a big payout from Jabba, Boba oversees the Bespin guards who load Han onto his starship.

The end of the Kintan Striders
A vengeful Boba annihilates the Kintan Striders as they attempt to flee on their speeders. As he later discovers, the Pyke Syndicate is actually behind the Tusken massacre.

VEHICLES

NABOO YACHT

MANUFACTURER Theed Palace Space Vessel Engineering Corp.
MODEL H-type Nubian yacht (modified)
TYPE Yacht

The sleek yachts used by Padmé Amidala during the Clone Wars lack weapons, but have a powerful engine bank and a strong deflector shield generator. Padmé pilots such a vessel after a failed assassination attempt on Coruscant destroys her royal cruiser. Senator Amidala uses her new starship to travel with Anakin Skywalker to Tatooine and Geonosis, where she takes part in the opening battle between the Republic and the Separatists. Padmé's original starship is lost when she intentionally overloads its engines to disable the Separatist cruiser *Malevolence*. Later, Naboo security officers offer an H-type Nubian yacht to Jedi Master Kelleran Beq on Coruscant to help him evacuate Grogu out of harm's way during Order 66.

Staying in touch
The ship contains a communications chamber for conducting important senatorial business.

SANDCRAWLER

MANUFACTURER Various
MODEL Sandcrawler
TYPE Mobile desert base

Sandcrawlers are massive vehicles that crisscross the deserts of Tatooine on their wide treads. They are operated by tribes of glowing-eyed Jawas, who use the sandcrawlers as homes, workshops, and trash repositories. If a Jawa locates a droid that doesn't appear to have an owner, a scouting party will disable the roaming automaton while a magnetic tube sucks it inside the sandcrawler for storage. Jawa sandcrawlers frequently visit moisture farms, where they start impromptu auctions, though the merchandise is usually of questionable quality. Some Jawas reserve their finest goods—normally hidden away in their massive vehicles—for established customers only. The sandcrawler's thick armor is a reliable defense against sandstorms, but it can't stand up to sustained blaster fire from stormtroopers. The droids R2-D2 and C-3PO briefly spend time aboard a sandcrawler before the Jawas who seized the pair sell them to Owen Lars. When the Empire tracks the droids to that particular Jawa tribe, they reduce the sandcrawler to a smoking ruin, which is later discovered by Luke Skywalker and Obi-Wan Kenobi. Years later, the Mandalorian Din Djarin struggles to retrieve parts from his ship, *Razor Crest*, from a sandcrawler belonging to a group of Jawas on Arvala-7.

Scrap heap
The main hold of a sandcrawler is full of half-fixed machinery, droids, and random junk.

Sandcrawler on the horizon
For most Tatooine settlers, sandcrawlers are the only way they can replace their equipment. Jawas sometimes sell rare goods and will travel to even the most remote homesteads.

OG-9 HOMING SPIDER DROID

MANUFACTURER Baktoid Armor Workshop
TYPE OG-9 homing spider droid **AFFILIATION** Separatist

The OG-9 homing spider droid is a gigantic walker used by the Separatists throughout the Clone Wars. The homing spider droid moves slowly on four mechanical legs, with a powerful reactor situated in the heart of its spherical body. The top-mounted laser emplacement releases sustained-fire shots that quickly wear down a target's shields, while a bottom-mounted laser cannon keeps infantry at bay. Homing spider droids see action during the Battle of Geonosis, blasting away at Republic AT-TEs and formations of clone troopers.

Armored hull plating
Command bridge

Warship
The Acclamator became the Republic's premier battleship at the start of the Clone Wars.

REPUBLIC ASSAULT SHIP (ACCLAMATOR-CLASS)

MANUFACTURER Rothana Heavy Engineering
MODEL *Acclamator*-class **TYPE** Assault ship

The Republic assault ship is also known as the Acclamator. More than 700 meters (2,297 ft) long, it becomes the Republic's primary troop carrier at the start of the Clone Wars and also fills an offensive role against the Separatist Navy. Each assault ship is armed with laser cannons, turbolaser turrets, concussion missiles, and heavy torpedoes, and carries ground vehicles such as AT-TE walkers. The Acclamator is capable of both ground and water landings. After the fall of the Empire, the *Acclamator*-class ship the *Lodestar* flies for the New Republic fleet until the ship is destroyed in a battle above Troithe by Shadow Wing.

Atmospheric escort
The LAAT/i gunship fills a crucial role for the Republic military, serving as both a troop carrier and an escort for ground and aerial forces. When hovering, the LAAT/i is an elevated gun platform.

REPUBLIC LAAT/i REPULSORLIFT GUNSHIP

MANUFACTURER Rothana Heavy Engineering **MODEL** Low Altitude Assault Transport/infantry
TYPE Repulsorlift gunship

The Republic gunship is also known as the LAAT/i, or Low Altitude Assault Transport/infantry. First deployed during the Battle of Geonosis, the gunship becomes one of the most familiar Republic military vehicles during the Clone Wars. A standard gunship can carry up to 30 clone troopers and is operated by a pilot and forward gunner. Two additional clone troopers operate the bubble turrets that swing out from the troop cabin. Two more turrets are located on each wing, while three smaller laser cannons are used to scatter enemy infantry. The gunship is excellent at destroying enemy vehicles such as hailfire droids with the missiles released from the underside of each wing. A gunship can reach speeds of up to 620 kilometers (385 miles) per hour. Clone troopers grow fond of their gunships during the Clone Wars and sometimes customize them with colorful nose art.

VEHICLES

> "...make sure you get yourself to that landing zone in one piece."
> — ANAKIN SKYWALKER

Rapid deployment
The AT-TE carrier drops off its cargo and gets itself to safety as quickly as possible.

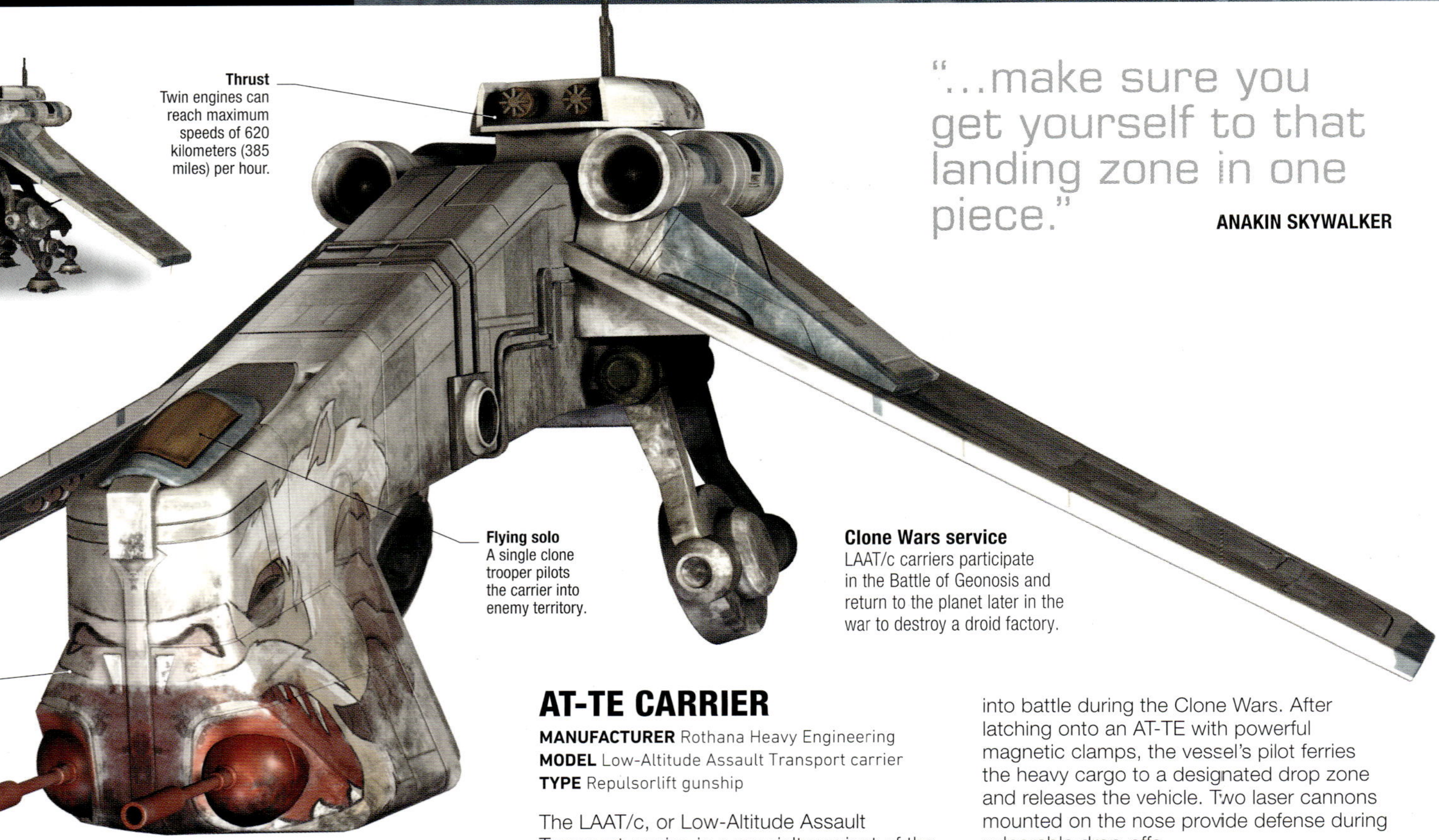

Thrust
Twin engines can reach maximum speeds of 620 kilometers (385 miles) per hour.

Flying solo
A single clone trooper pilots the carrier into enemy territory.

Clone Wars service
LAAT/c carriers participate in the Battle of Geonosis and return to the planet later in the war to destroy a droid factory.

Personalized paint job
Clone troopers often decorate carriers with colorful nose artwork.

Firepower
Swiveling laser cannons are operated from the cockpit.

AT-TE CARRIER
MANUFACTURER Rothana Heavy Engineering
MODEL Low-Altitude Assault Transport carrier
TYPE Repulsorlift gunship

The LAAT/c, or Low-Altitude Assault Transport carrier, is a specialty variant of the LAAT gunship used to transport AT-TEs into battle during the Clone Wars. After latching onto an AT-TE with powerful magnetic clamps, the vessel's pilot ferries the heavy cargo to a designated drop zone and releases the vehicle. Two laser cannons mounted on the nose provide defense during vulnerable drop-offs.

Main cannon
The AT-TE's primary weapon has its own dedicated gunner who sits above the vehicle's hull.

Tanks advance
Manufactured in great numbers during the Clone Wars, AT-TEs are the backbone of Republic ground operations from the Core to the Outer Rim.

Command center
The command cabin houses the pilot and spotter.

Firepower
Forward guns are effective against battle droids.

All terrain
Footpads can be magnetized for scaling metal walls.

AT-TE (ALL TERRAIN TACTICAL ENFORCER)
MANUFACTURER Rothana Heavy Engineering **MODEL** All Terrain Tactical Enforcer **TYPE** Walker

The All Terrain Tactical Enforcer is an early example of walker technology used to great effect on the battlefield during the Clone Wars. The six-legged tanks are both assault vehicles and transports and can carry up to 20 clone troopers. Each AT-TE is operated by a crew of seven, made up of a pilot, a spotter, four gunners, and one cannon operator. The top-mounted mass-driver cannon has a slow rate of fire, but six smaller laser cannons mounted on the AT-TE's hull provide defense against enemy infantry. Shortly after the Clone Wars, the Bad Batch hijacks an AT-TE while rescuing Senator Avi Singh. Later, Clone Commander Rex and clone troopers Wolffe and Gregor modify an AT-TE on Seelos and use it as their living quarters during the Imperial era.

Providing support
The AT-TE is excellent when used in conjunction with infantry, since it can lay down covering fire from an elevated angle.

HAILFIRE DROID

MANUFACTURER Haor Chall Engineering
MODEL IG-227 *Hailfire*-class
TYPE Droid tank

The IG-227 *Hailfire*-class droid tank is easily identified by its treaded, hooplike drive wheels. The InterGalactic Banking Clan commissioned the construction of the hailfire prior to the Clone Wars, and the units saw their first combat against Republic troops during the First Battle of Geonosis. A hailfire is an armored missile platform best used to destroy enemy vehicles. Each of the two launchers mounted on a hailfire can hold up to 15 guided missiles.

Rolling into battle
The hailfire is also called the wheel droid due to its maneuverable and speedy drive system *(below)*. Each missile from the droid leaves behind a trail of black exhaust that darkens the sky *(right)*.

SPHA-T

MANUFACTURER Rothana Heavy Engineering
MODEL Self-Propelled Heavy Artillery Turbolaser
TYPE Heavy artillery

The 12-legged SPHA-T is one of the biggest ground guns in the Republic's imposing arsenal. Each SPHA-T is operated by a crew of 30 clone troopers and only uses its legs when maneuvering between firing positions. When attacking an enemy target, the SPHA-T remains motionless to give the gunners added precision for aiming the extraordinarily heavy turbolaser beam.

GEONOSIAN STARFIGHTER

MANUFACTURER Huppla Pasa Tisc Shipwrights Collective
MODEL *Nantex*-class
TYPE Starfighter

The needle-shaped *Nantex*-class starfighter is the primary defensive craft of the insectoid inhabitants of Geonosis. A single laser cannon is mounted between the upper and lower prongs that make up the starfighter's nose, and 100 tiny tractor beam projectors aid in precision aiming and grappling with enemy vessels at close range.

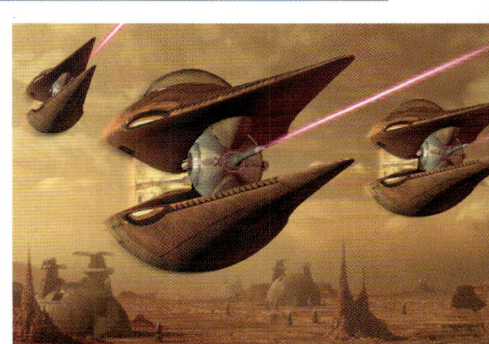

Holding the line
Republic attack cruisers, the primary defense against the Separatists, become commonly known as Jedi cruisers during the war.

SOLAR SAILER

MANUFACTURER Huppla Pasa Tisc Shipwrights Collective
MODEL *Punworcca 116*–class interstellar sloop
TYPE Star yacht

Count Dooku's unique craft relies on a retractable sail to collect stray interstellar energies, which are directed to the ship's engines to provide a near-limitless source of fuel. The main body of the ship is a luxurious sloop with a design that closely resembles that of the Geonosian starfighter—no surprise, as Dooku had the foresight to commission the vessel from his allies on Geonosis prior to the outbreak of the Clone Wars. Dooku uses an FA-4 pilot droid to handle takeoffs and landings. Within the sailer, a secure HoloNet transceiver allows the Count to communicate with his master, Darth Sidious.

REPUBLIC ATTACK CRUISER

MANUFACTURER Kuat Drive Yards
MODEL *Venator*-class
TYPE Star Destroyer

The Republic attack cruiser is also known as the *Venator*-class Star Destroyer and is one of the first examples of the triangular warships that would become a terrifying symbol of Imperial power. First deployed during the Clone Wars, Republic attack cruisers quickly become the most powerful capital ships in the Republic navy. Each vessel serves double duty as both a battleship and a starfighter carrier, with armaments including heavy turbolasers, laser cannons, proton torpedo launchers, and tractor beam projectors. The vessel's flight deck is built directly into the prow, providing a 0.5-kilometer- (550-yd-) long runway that allows starfighters to scramble into space the instant the bow doors are opened. An attack cruiser carries more than 420 starfighters, 40 gunships, and 24 AT-TEs, and operates with a crew of more than 7,400 personnel. Throughout the Clone Wars, Republic attack cruisers remain on the frontlines, keeping the space lanes free of Separatist interference and providing cover for landing parties of Jedi and clone troopers.

VEHICLES

BANKING CLAN COMMUNICATIONS FRIGATE
MANUFACTURER Hoersch-Kessel Drive
MODEL *Munificent*-class
TYPE Star frigate

The InterGalactic Banking Clan operates the *Munificent*-class frigate as both a warship and a communications vessel. It is equipped for secure ship-to-ship transmissions and also for the jamming of enemy signals.

Hangar bays for starfighters

Elongated wings support defensive weaponry

Each frigate is operated by 200 crew but can carry up to 150,000 battle droids and often skimps on life-support systems due to the small size of its crew. Laser cannons, twin turbolasers, and ion cannons allow the frigate to put up a fight against enemy capital ships.

STEALTH SHIP
MANUFACTURER Sienar Design Systems
MODEL Prototype stealth model **TYPE** Corvette

An experimental vessel developed by the Republic during the Clone Wars, the prototype stealth ship incorporates a cloaking device that renders it invisible. Additionally it is outfitted with communications antennas and gun turrets, and features an array of countermeasures to escape detection or shake missiles. During the blockade of Christophsis, the Republic deploys the stealth ship to enable a crew to reach the surface undetected and assist in Senator Bail Organa's relief mission. Anakin Skywalker decides to engage the leader of the Separatist blockade, Admiral Trench. Years later, the design of Grand Moff Tarkin's personal vessel, the *Carrion Spike*, is based on that of the stealth ship.

HYENA BOMBER
MANUFACTURER Baktoid Armor Workshop
MODEL *Hyena*-class
TYPE Bomber

Separatists use the Hyena bomber to attack warships and surface installations with high-yield explosive warheads. Hyena bombers are rarely seen during the Clone Wars, but do participate in the Battles of Christophsis and Ryloth. Like the Separatist *Vulture*-class starfighter, the Hyena bomber is controlled by a droid intelligence and is capable of splitting its wings and entering a "walking mode." The Hyena bomber carries armaments such as proton bombs, proton torpedoes, and concussion missiles, all stored in a ventral bomb bay.

Walking mode
The Hyena bomber uses its wings as limbs when taxiing from one surface location to another.

BARC SPEEDER
MANUFACTURER Aratech Repulsor Company
MODEL Biker Advanced Recon Commando speeder
TYPE Speeder bike

A swift reconnaissance vehicle, the BARC speeder is named for the specialized clone drivers who operate it. Most BARC speeders are painted in the traditional red and white colors of the Republic Army, though some bear brown or green camouflage markings. Each is equipped with a forward-facing blaster cannon and a repulsorlift engine capable of reaching speeds up to 520 kilometers (323 miles) per hour. On Saleucami, Jedi General Stass Allie pilots a BARC speeder when her escorts suddenly receive Order 66. The pursuing clone troopers blast her vehicle, killing her. BARC speeders continue to be used throughout the galaxy during the Imperial era.

Speeding away
When Emperor Palpatine enacts Order 66, Jedi Master Kelleran Beq flees the Temple with another survivor—the mysterious youngling Grogu. The pair uses a BARC speeder with a sidecar for their dangerous escape.

ALL TERRAIN RECON TRANSPORT (AT-RT)
MANUFACTURER Kuat Drive Yards
MODEL All Terrain Recon Transport
TYPE Scout walker

The AT-RT, or All Terrain Recon Transport, is a bipedal walker built for a single operator. The open cockpit offers little protection to its clone trooper driver, but the AT-RT is speedy and sure-footed as a reconnaissance vehicle. Its chin-mounted laser cannon is useful against battle droids, but too weak to damage heavy vehicles. Communications antennas allow the AT-RT to transmit battlefield intelligence. The Republic uses AT-RTs throughout the Clone Wars, including at the Battle of Ryloth and during the hunt for Master Yoda on Kashyyyk following Order 66.

Ease of use
Simple controls are similar to those of speeder bikes.

Two-legged mobility
AT-RTs are able to handle many types of planetary surfaces, ideal for Republic troopers during the galaxy-spanning Clone Wars.

Stability
A gyroscopic system allows the AT-RT to keep its balance.

TRIDENT DRILL ASSAULT CRAFT

MANUFACTURER Colicoid Creation Nest
MODEL Trident-class **TYPE** Assault ship

The Trident drill assault craft is a Separatist gunship built for underwater operation, capable of drilling through the hulls of enemy vessels and installations. In the Battles of Kamino and Mon Cala during the Clone Wars, Tridents attack with their drills and laser cannons while releasing squads of aqua droids from their holds. During the Imperial era, a modified Trident drill works on land in the deserts of Jedha, as the Empire tries to gain access to a Hidden Path sanctuary.

Armored tentacles
Mechanical limbs are equipped with magnetic grapples.

KHETANNA

MANUFACTURER Ubrikkian Industries
MODEL Luxury sail barge (modified) **TYPE** Repulsorcraft

Jabba's luxury sail barge, the *Khetanna*, is used by the Hutt crime lord whenever he leaves his palace to visit other parts of Tatooine. The vessel is driven by a repulsorlift engine in conjunction with two huge sails on the upper deck. Jabba never suffers the slightest discomfort inside the sail barge's vast interior, which is always packed with musicians, dancers, and staff serving refreshments. The *Khetanna* is protected by a large blaster cannon and several smaller blasters mounted on the side railings.

Service vehicle
From his sail barge, Jabba the Hutt watches the executions of prisoners in shaded comfort *(above)*. Jabba's luxury vessel has been in use since the Clone Wars and is always accompanied by armed guards on desert skiffs *(left)*.

DESERT SKIFF

MANUFACTURER Ubrikkian Industries
MODEL Bantha-II cargo skiff **TYPE** Repulsorcraft

Skiffs are common modes of transportation that operate using anti-gravity repulsorlifts. Most are used for moving cargo, but they can easily carry passengers. Jabba the Hutt uses a number of rugged skiffs equipped to survive the heat and sandstorms of the Tatooine deserts. The Bantha-II cargo skiffs have an elongated deck with a safety railing designed to protect passengers or cargo. The skiffs are piloted from a rear control station, and at their maximum speed, they can exceed 250 kilometers (155 miles) per hour.

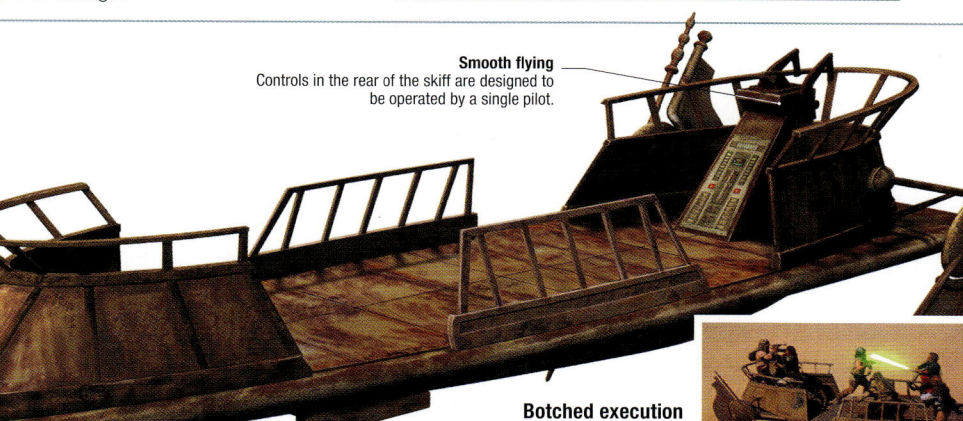

Smooth flying
Controls in the rear of the skiff are designed to be operated by a single pilot.

Reinforced bow
The armored nose is built to withstand head-on collisions.

Botched execution
At the Great Pit of Carkoon, Jabba's skiff guards make a big mistake when they try to force Luke Skywalker to walk the plank.

Deployed
During flight, the V-19 makes a three-pointed silhouette *(right)*. Clone troopers receive orders from Anakin Skywalker, with their V-19s waiting on the hangar deck *(bottom)*.

V-19 TORRENT STARFIGHTER

MANUFACTURER Slayn & Korpil **MODEL** V-19 Torrent
TYPE Starfighter

The V-19 Torrent is one of the fastest and most maneuverable starfighters used by the Republic during the Clone Wars. Its folding S-foils provide stability and a wider area of fire for its two wing-mounted blaster cannons. The V-19 is also outfitted with concussion missile launchers that can home in on targets. Though primarily flown by Republic clone pilots, V-19s are also used by Jedi commanders. During the Battle of Ryloth, Ahsoka Tano leads a squadron against the Separatists. The V-19 starfighter continues to be used by the Empire during the Imperial era.

CORPORATE ALLIANCE PERSUADER TANK DROID

MANUFACTURER Techno Union
MODEL NR-N99 Persuader-class **TYPE** Droid tank

The NR-N99 *Persuader*-class tank droid is a Separatist war vehicle. It is driven by a huge central tread and supported on either side by forward-mounted outriggers. The tank can reach speeds of up to 60 kilometers (37 miles) per hour, useful for ramming barricades. Controlled by a built-in droid intelligence, it is armed with ion cannons, heavy repeating blasters, and missile launchers. NR-N99s lead the assault against a Wookiee city during the Battle of Kashyyyk.

VEHICLES

TWILIGHT

MANUFACTURER Corellian Engineering Corp.
MODEL G9 *Rigger*-class **TYPE** Freighter

The *Twilight* serves Anakin Skywalker and other Republic heroes as a faithful transport ship throughout the Clone Wars. Originally owned by Ziro the Hutt, the G9 Rigger space freighter is found by Anakin and his Padawan Ahsoka Tano on the planet Teth. The two Jedi steal the vessel and use it to ferry Jabba the Hutt's young son, Rotta, to Tatooine. When MagnaGuards attack, Anakin is forced to crash-land the light freighter into the desert sands. He later retrieves it, and the *Twilight* sees action in the Battle of the Kaliida Nebula and the raid on Skytop Station. The vehicle meets its final fate on Mandalore, when Obi-Wan Kenobi uses it to try to escape a group of Death Watch soldiers. After the ship suffers critical hits from missile strikes, Obi-Wan and Duchess Satine Kryze must evacuate before it crashes into the surface below.

The *Twilight* is well armed for a freighter, featuring three heavy blaster cannons mounted on the wings and a rotating laser cannon operated from a periscope sight. Additionally, a concussion missile launcher provides explosive punch against large warships. The *Twilight's* most distinctive feature is its long outrigger wing, which extends from the starboard side of the main cabin and contains two secondary engines. A lower wing can be folded up during landing and extended during flight. The ship is designed to haul cargo and consequently features a tow cable and a rear-opening cargo hatch. The hold is roomy enough to accommodate a Jedi starfighter.

Escape hatch The rear cargo door can open while in flight to dump sensitive cargo.

Defensive fire Forward-mounted blaster cannons keep pirates at a distance.

Aerodynamic Large outrigger wing provides flight stability.

Old but fully armed The *Twilight's* engines don't always perform well in planetary atmospheres *(above right)*. With multiple cannons, the light freighter is able to hold its own in a fight against those who would raid its holds *(right)*.

> "Grease bucket, you're my favorite ship ever!"
> — AHSOKA TANO

TANTIVE IV

MANUFACTURER Corellian Engineering Corp.
MODEL CR90 **TYPE** Corvette

The *Tantive IV* is an Alderaan cruiser of Corellian manufacture operated by the Royal House of Alderaan. Similar ships are sometimes called blockade runners due to their powerful engine banks and ability to race past slow-moving customs vessels. Like other corvettes of its type, the *Tantive IV* sports double turbolaser cannons on both the top and bottom of the ship. The antenna dishes of the communications and sensor array are located just ahead of the drive system. Eleven ion turbine engines stacked on top of each other provide impressive sublight thrust. Within the *Tantive IV* are living quarters for the crew, dining rooms for hosting state dinners, and conference centers for sensitive negotiations with interstellar dignitaries. Escape pods give the passengers a chance to flee if the ship comes under attack.

The *Tantive IV* sees action during the Clone Wars and continues to serve Senator Bail Organa of Alderaan for nearly two decades. When Senator Organa's daughter Leia follows him into politics, the corvette becomes her ship. Princess Leia is famous for her "mercy missions" to help populations in need, but the Empire suspects she is using the ship to carry out assignments on behalf of the Rebel Alliance. After the *Tantive IV* escapes the Battle of Scarif with the plans for the Death Star, Darth Vader chases the vessel and disables it above Tatooine. The ship is drawn into a Star Destroyer's docking bay and its passengers, including Princess Leia, are captured. Years later, a senator loyal to Leia Organa finds and returns the *Tantive IV* to her. Leia takes the ship to the Resistance base on Ajan Kloss. Nien Nunb pilots the ship during the Battle of Exegol, where the ship is destroyed.

Firefight The narrow hallways of the *Tantive IV* allow its crew to set up an ambush for a stormtrooper boarding party.

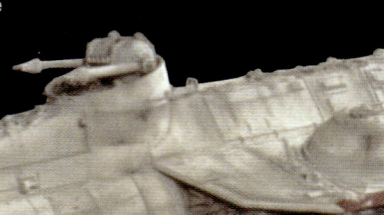

Bridge The captain of the *Tantive IV* commands the vessel from this reinforced bridge section.

> "Tear this ship apart until you've found those plans!"
> — DARTH VADER

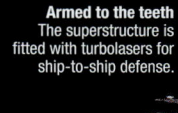

Armed to the teeth
The superstructure is fitted with turbolasers for ship-to-ship defense.

Destructive capacity
The primary ion weapon is powered by the ship's reactor.

MALEVOLENCE

MANUFACTURER Free Dac Volunteers Engineering Corp.
MODEL *Subjugator*-class
TYPE Heavy cruiser

The *Malevolence* is the flagship of General Grievous. Massive ion cannons give the ship an unprecedented destructive capacity with the release of expanding waves of energy, which disable any vessels in their path, leaving them vulnerable to the heavy cruiser's 500 turbolasers. After the *Malevolence* destroys Plo Koon's fleet, Anakin Skywalker tampers with the ship's navigation and the vehicle crashes into a moon.

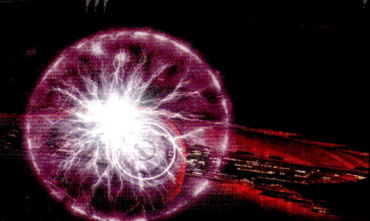

Superweapon
When fired, the *Malevolence*'s ion cannon releases a wave that interferes with electrical systems and leaves ships drifting in space.

SOULLESS ONE

MANUFACTURER Feethan Ottraw Scalable Assemblies **MODEL** Belbullab-22
TYPE Starfighter

The personal starfighter of General Grievous, the *Soulless One* is a customized Belbullab-22 starfighter designed for speed and agility when dogfighting. It is armed with two sets of triple rapid-fire laser cannons, and features a state-of-the-art hyperdrive allowing it to reach almost any location in the galaxy. Near the end of the Clone Wars, General Grievous brings the *Soulless One* to Utapau. After Obi-Wan Kenobi kills him, he uses the late general's starfighter to escape Utapau and rendezvous with Yoda and Bail Organa.

Sleek profile
The *Soulless One* is streamlined for maximum maneuverability in atmosphere.

TURBO TANK

MANUFACTURER Kuat Drive Yards
MODEL HAVw A6 Juggernaut **TYPE** Tank

The HAVw A6 Juggernaut, known as the clone turbo tank, is a heavily armed and armored Republic military transport. A single Juggernaut can carry up to 300 clone troopers and is operated by a crew of 12. The tank's superconducting armor absorbs and disperses enemy fire, and the tank retaliates with a heavy laser turret, anti-personnel cannons, a repeating laser, and projectile launchers. A clone spotter occupies a pod above the vehicle's back. A later model of the turbo tank—the HCVw A9—is used by the Empire to move prisoners on the planet Wobani.

ARC-170 STARFIGHTER

MANUFACTURER Incom Corp.
MODEL ARC-170 **TYPE** Starfighter

The ARC-170, or Aggressive ReConnaissance starfighter, functions equally well as a fighter and a bomber. Its gigantic laser cannons are capable of punching holes in capital ship armor, while twin blaster cannons operated by a tail gunner cover the rear fire arc. Explosive ordnance comes in the form of proton torpedoes. Panels on the upper and lower surfaces of the wings can open during combat to bleed off excess heat. An ARC-170 is typically operated by a crew of three plus an astromech droid.

On patrol
ARC-170s are equipped to deal with any threat they encounter.

JEDI LIGHT CRUISER

MANUFACTURER Kuat Drive Yards
MODEL *Arquitens*-class **TYPE** Light cruiser

This light warship is used by the Republic during the Clone Wars. Though not as large as other Republic ships such as the *Venator*-class Star Destroyer, the vessel is armed with four quad laser turrets and four double-barreled turbolaser batteries, as well as concussion missile launchers. Obi-Wan and other Jedi generals often take command of these ships, which results in their common name. After the Empire's formation, *Arquitens*-class cruisers continue to serve in the Imperial navy, seeing action against the Batonn rebels. A variant of the model, named the *Arquitens*-class command cruiser, is also introduced.

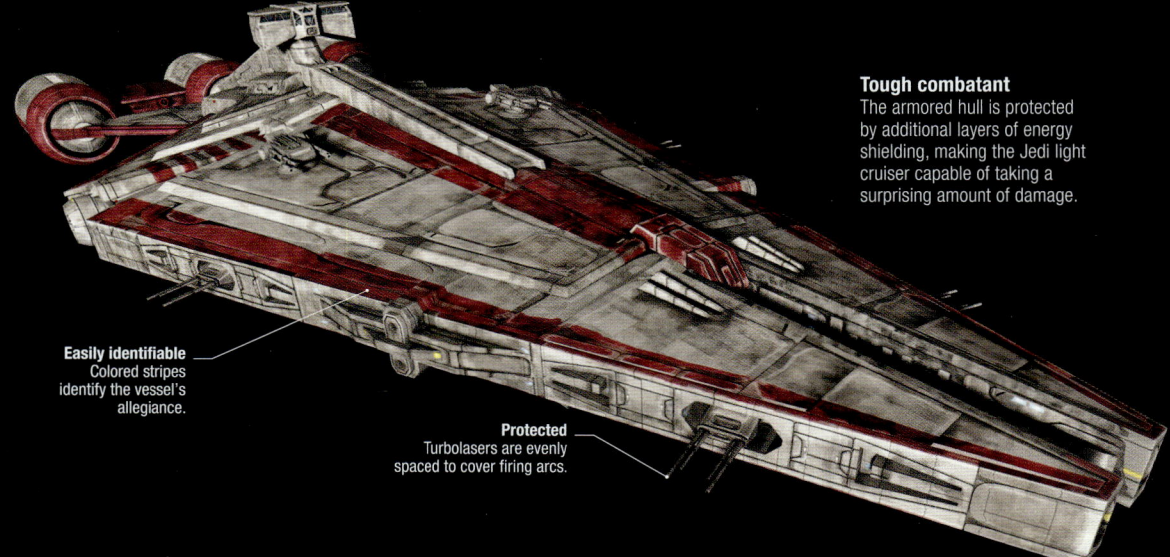

Tough combatant
The armored hull is protected by additional layers of energy shielding, making the Jedi light cruiser capable of taking a surprising amount of damage.

Easily identifiable
Colored stripes identify the vessel's allegiance.

Protected
Turbolasers are evenly spaced to cover firing arcs.

VEHICLES

TRANDOSHAN FLYING HUNTING LODGE

MANUFACTURER Ubrikkian Industries
MODEL Ubrikkian Floating Fortress
TYPE Armed hover platform

Trandoshan hunters use this platform as a mobile base when hunting live prey on the moon of Wasskah. It features a trophy room, living quarters, and a landing deck for airspeeders. During the Clone Wars, Ahsoka Tano and some Wookiees attack the lodge and the Trandoshans.

OMS DEVILFISH

MANUFACTURER Kuat Drive Yards
MODEL OMS Devilfish
TYPE Submarine

The Devilfish is a military craft designed for underwater use. It lacks armored protection, but features speedy propulsion jets and is armed with a forward-facing dual blaster cannon. During the Clone Wars, Republic troops use a swarm of Devilfish craft to fight off Separatist aqua droids on Mon Cala. When the planet later rebels against the Empire, Imperial seatroopers use Devilfish to quell the insurrection.

UMBARAN STARFIGHTER

MANUFACTURER Umbaran Militia
MODEL Zenuas 33
TYPE Starfighter

The Umbaran starfighter is operated by a single pilot, who sits in a command chair surrounded by a spherical energy shield and flies the ship using holographic controls. The command chair plugs into a spaceframe with loop-shaped wings. An Umbaran starfighter can defend itself with a single rapid-fire laser cannon and two electromagnetic pulse missile launchers.

HOUND'S TOOTH

MANUFACTURER Corellian Engineering Corp.
MODEL YV-666 (modified)
TYPE Light freighter

The Hound's Tooth is the personal starship of the bounty hunter Bossk. This highly modified Corellian freighter contains holding cells for captured prisoners and an armory for stocking up on weapons. Many sensors allow Bossk to keep an eye on the integrity of the cages. The Hound's Tooth is armed with a quad-laser turret, an ion cannon, and a concussion missile launcher.

ANAKIN'S ETA-2 JEDI STARFIGHTER

MANUFACTURER Kuat Systems Engineering
MODEL Eta-2 *Actis*-class light interceptor
TYPE Starfighter

Anakin Skywalker replaces his Delta-7B Jedi starfighter with a new Eta-2 interceptor model late in the Clone Wars. This smaller, more maneuverable ship is armed with twin laser cannons and twin ion cannons. Its forward viewport bubble features an octagonal shape that is later carried over into the Empire's TIE fighters. On the tip of each wing, S-foils can swing up and lock into a vertical position and are used during combat to safely bleed off excess heat. The ship's dual ion engines and narrow profile allow it to make tight turns while dogfighting, but it lacks sufficient engine space for a hyperdrive. Instead, the Eta-2 relies on an external hyperspace docking ring when traveling across the galaxy. A plug-in socket inside the port wing can accommodate an astromech droid for onboard repairs, and soon Anakin and R2-D2 are flying together on vital missions against the Separatists.

Anakin uses his starfighter to defend Cato Neimoidia from a Separatist attack. When a missile explodes near his ship, it releases a swarm of buzz droids, which causes extensive damage to the Eta-2. However, the ship is repaired in time for the Battle of Coruscant.

HMP DROID GUNSHIP

MANUFACTURER Baktoid Fleet Ordnance
MODEL Heavy Missile Platform
TYPE Droid gunship

The HMP droid gunship, a heavily armed repulsorlift airspeeder, is the Separatist counterpart to the Republic's LAAT/i. Operated by an advanced droid brain, the HMP's frame accommodates numerous weapons, which can easily be interchanged for different missions. The droid gunship boasts a chin-mounted cannon, two laser turrets, and two light laser cannons on the wingtips, but its real power is the payload of 14 high-explosive missiles. During the Clone Wars, droid gunships are modified to serve as troop carriers for battle droids.

Showdown
Three droid gunships fly in a tight formation *(far left)*, while laser cannons assault ground troops *(left)*.

Droid swarm
Dozens of buzz droids latch onto the hull of Anakin's starfighter.

Accompanied by Obi-Wan Kenobi in a similar interceptor, Anakin fights his way through the Separatist navy and disables the hangar shields on General Grievous' flagship *Invisible Hand*. As soon as the Eta-2 is parked inside, Anakin and R2-D2 leave the craft behind to cause trouble for Grievous.

Racing colors
Anakin painted his starfighter in a custom design inspired by his podracing past.

Y-WING STARFIGHTER

MANUFACTURER Koensayr Manufacturing
MODEL Y-wing **TYPE** Starfighter

For decades, various models of the Y-wing starfighter see combat in military conflicts. From the Galactic Republic's fleet during the Clone Wars to the Rebel Alliance's attacks on both Death Stars.

FLEET WORKHORSE

The Y-wing line of starfighters has the dubious distinction of remaining in service long enough to fly under the command of Anakin Skywalker and to be shot down by Darth Vader. During the Clone Wars, Anakin leads Shadow Squadron's BTL-B Y-wings in an attack that disables the *Malevolence*, a heavy cruiser commanded by General Grievous and armed with a massive ion cannon. Decades later, at the Battle of Yavin, eight BTL-A4 Y-wings from the Rebel Alliance's Gold Squadron take part in the assault on the Death Star. Darth Vader leads a trio of TIE fighters to confront them, personally shooting down Gold Leader and six of his wingmates; only Gold Three, piloted by Evaan Verlaine, survives. Y-wings from Gray Squadron join the attack on the second Death Star.

> *"Stay on target."*
> **GOLD FIVE**

BOMBER

The BTL-B Y-wing starfighter's cockpit has room for a pilot and gunner, as well as a socket for an astromech, while the BTL-A4 version is a single-pilot starfighter that includes a spot for a support droid positioned aft of the cockpit. Equipped with a hyperdrive for making lightspeed jumps, the ship has a pair of ion jet engines for primary propulsion. This makes the Y-wing slower and less maneuverable than other starfighters, such as the X-wing and A-wing, flying in the Rebel Alliance fleet. For defense, the pilot must count on the energy shields and the heavy armor plating around the cockpit. When dogfighting is unavoidable, the Y-wing relies on two fixed, front-mounted laser cannons and a rotating turret with anti-starfighter ion cannons. More commonly, the Y-wing operates as a bomber against capital ships in fleet battles or for ground targets in planetside action, making multiple bombing runs to deliver proton torpedoes and proton bombs from its arsenal.

FAMOUS FLYERS

In addition to Verlaine, notable Y-wing pilots and squadrons include Jon Vander; Gold Squadron, who attempts to shoot down Darth Vader over Vrogas Vas; Nora Wexley; and Nath Tensent. Jess Pava and Suralinda Javos fly an old BTL-S3 starfighter on a mission for Black Squadron and the updated BTA-NR2 Y-wing starfighter is used by the New Republic and Resistance fleets. Spice Runner Zorii Bliss flies one with Anzellan Babu Frik during the Battle of Exegol.

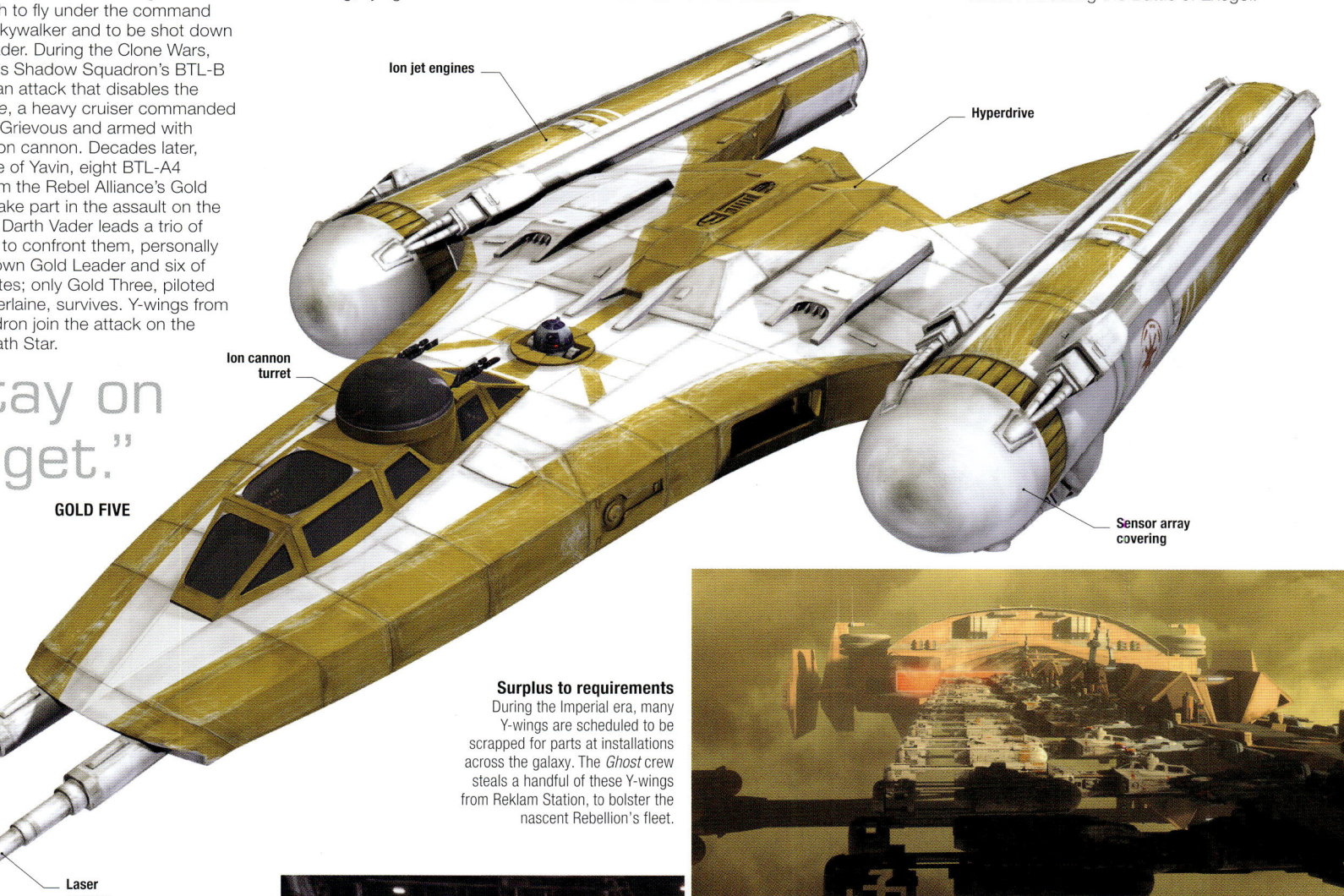

- Ion jet engines
- Hyperdrive
- Ion cannon turret
- Sensor array covering
- Laser cannon

Surplus to requirements
During the Imperial era, many Y-wings are scheduled to be scrapped for parts at installations across the galaxy. The *Ghost* crew steals a handful of these Y-wings from Reklam Station, to bolster the nascent Rebellion's fleet.

Fatal run
On the moon Yavin 4, a Y-wing is prepped for the upcoming battle with the Death Star *(right)*. Gold Leader leads a pair of Y-wings through the Death Star's narrow trench *(above)*.

VEHICLES

INVISIBLE HAND
MANUFACTURER Free Dac Volunteers Engineering Corps
MODEL *Providence*-class carrier/destroyer
TYPE Capital ship

"Get to the command ship! Get the chancellor!" OBI-WAN KENOBI

The Separatists employ a number of gargantuan warships during the Clone Wars, many of them falling under the command of the cyborg General Grievous. After Grievous loses the *Malevolence* in battle with the Republic, he claims the *Invisible Hand* as his flagship. This *Providence*-class vessel is 1 kilometer (1,094 yds) in length and is classified as both a destroyer and a carrier, a dual role that makes the Separatist dreadnought equipped for total planetary domination. It holds 20 squadrons of droid starfighters and more than 400 ground assault vehicles for use during invasions, while its numerous turbolaser turrets are capable of unleashing a surface bombardment from the safety of orbit. If threatened by Republic capital ships, the *Invisible Hand* can pummel the enemy with more than 100 proton torpedo launchers. An observation platform occupies a sensor pod high above the hull and allows commanders to get an unobstructed view of battle. The side of the ship bears the Separatist emblem of the Confederacy of Independent Systems. General Grievous uses the *Invisible Hand* during later Clone War skirmishes and soon receives orders to make a bold strike at the Republic's capital world of Coruscant. Accompanied by several Separatist warships, the *Invisible Hand* drops out of hyperspace and is soon embroiled in a space battle more intense than any conducted in the war to date. While the Republic responds to the naval threat, Grievous slips to the surface of Coruscant and kidnaps Supreme Chancellor Palpatine, bringing his captive back to the *Invisible Hand*. Anakin Skywalker and Obi-Wan Kenobi board the ship on a rescue mission. With the battle taking its toll on his ship, Grievous blasts to safety in an escape pod. As the *Invisible Hand* breaks up around him, Anakin pilots the forward section of the ship into a fiery crash landing on Coruscant.

Crash landing
As Anakin steers the wreckage of the *Invisible Hand* down to the surface, fire ships struggle to contain the damage.

Droid delegator
When General Grievous encounters Jedi Obi-Wan Kenobi and Anakin Skywalker on the bridge, he orders his IG-100 MagnaGuard to engage them.

Battle of Coruscant
The fierce space battle that rages above the Republic capital proves to be the end of the *Invisible Hand*.

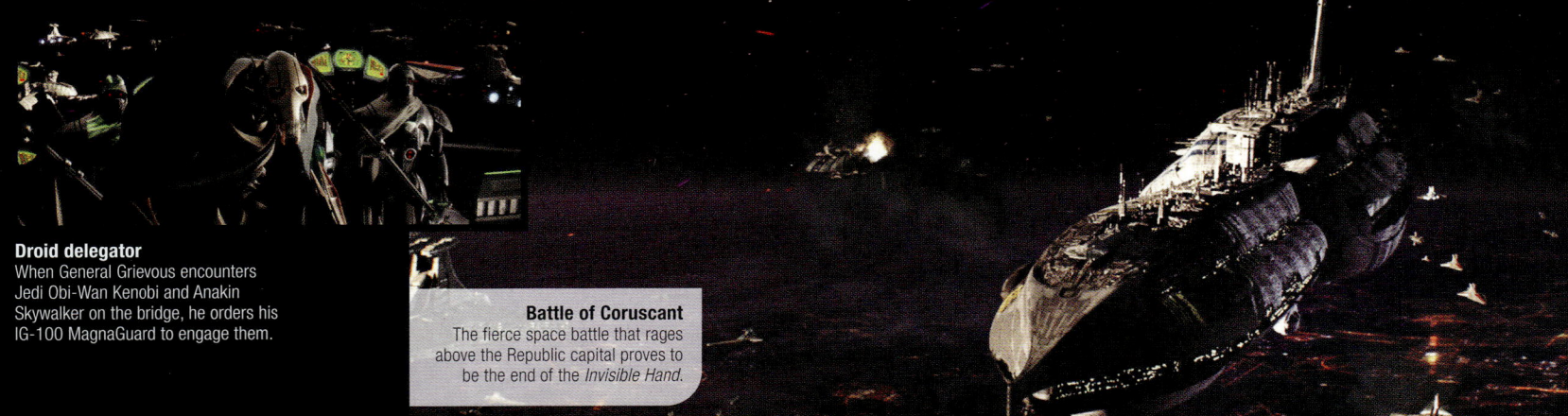

DWARF SPIDER DROID
MANUFACTURER Baktoid Armor Workshop
TYPE DSD1 dwarf spider droid **AFFILIATION** Separatist

The DSD1 dwarf spider droid is also known as the burrowing spider droid for its ability to invade narrow spaces. Frequently used by the Commerce Guild, it becomes a mainstay of Separatist ground forces during the Clone Wars. The dwarf spider droid's primary weapon is a long blaster cannon capable of both rapid-fire and high-intensity bursts. The legs of the dwarf spider droid are designed to affix securely to the sides of cliffs, and the droids are used by the Separatists during the Battle of Teth to fire at Republic AT-TE walkers trying to gain the high ground. In other engagements, dwarf spider droids provide heavy backup for squads of battle droids.

On the beach
Dwarf spider droids attack a coastal city on Kashyyyk, blasting the Wookiee defenders.

OCTUPTARRA DROID
MANUFACTURER Techno Union
TYPE Octuptarra combat tri-droid **AFFILIATION** Separatist

Octuptarra droids are found among Separatist forces during the Clone Wars. These tall, three-legged automatons have large heads containing operational software and sensory equipment. Three laser turrets are mounted equidistantly beneath the droid's three photoreceptors. Because the octuptarra looks in every direction at once, it has virtually no blind spots. Despite its omnidirectional field of fire, the droid is slow-moving and vulnerable to tripping. The Techno Union produces a number of different-sized droids during the war, some of droids are large enough to take on heavily armored Republic AT-TEs. Years later on Mustafar, Darth Vader battles and destroys a giant octuptarra droid that has been taken over by the Scourge.

Three laser cannons
The rotating turrets deliver an offensive punch.

360-degree attack
The octuptarra can swivel its head to easily cover any angle.

Three spiderlike legs

REPUBLIC ARTILLERY CANNON (AV-7)
MANUFACTURER Taim & Bak
MODEL AV-7 Anti-vehicle Artillery Cannon
TYPE Artillery cannon

The AV-7 is a self-propelled artillery unit that moves on anti-grav repulsorlifts. It can be operated by a single clone trooper who sits behind the gunnery controls located on the side of the central assembly. When an AV-7 is in position, it stabilizes itself with its four widely spaced legs. The blasts from an AV-7 can take out both tanks and battle droids.

Coward's retreat
General Grievous attempts to flee from Obi-Wan Kenobi, but is caught in a fatal duel.

GENERAL GRIEVOUS' WHEEL BIKE

MANUFACTURER Z-Gomot Ternbuell Guppat Corp. **MODEL** Tsmeu-6
TYPE Personal wheel bike

General Grievous drives a Tsmeu-6 on Utapau during the Clone Wars. This line of vehicles is also popular in mining areas, where long-distance travel underground is necessary on a variety of terrains. The Tsmeu-6 is designed for a single passenger seated beside a large central wheel. The wheel bike has a maximum speed of 330 kilometers (205 mi) per hour rolling and 10 kilometers (6 mi) per hour running on its four retractable legs, and it carries enough fuel for approximately 500 kilometers (311 mi) of travel. With a wheel diameter of 2.5 meters (8 ft 2 in) and a length of 3.5 meters (11½ ft), the Tsmeu-6 also boasts a powerful double laser cannon.

Speeder chase
Luke Skywalker and Leia Organa race to stop a biker scout from reporting their presence to the Imperials.

74-Z SPEEDER BIKE

MANUFACTURER Aratech Repulsor Company
MODEL 74-Z
TYPE Speeder bike

The 74-Z is first used by the Republic during the Clone Wars, particularly on the planet of Saleucami. The speeder is used again by the Empire to patrol forests surrounding their shield generator on Endor, and troopers with the Imperial remnant continue to use them in the following years. The bike is ideally suited for patrols and scout missions over long distances in a variety of terrains, thanks to its exceptional maneuverability and self-charging battery system. The speeder is controlled by four steering vanes, contains sensor and communications equipment between the handlebars, and a BlasTech Ax-20 blaster cannon. The 74-Z measures around 3.2 meters (10½ ft) and can reach a maximum, but inadvisable, speed of 500 kilometers (311 mi) per hour.

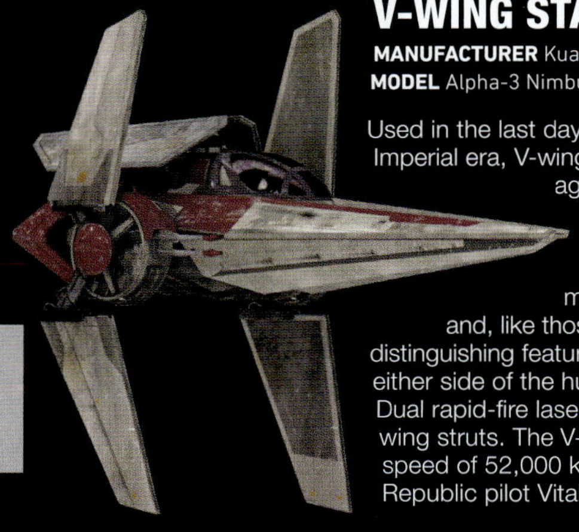

V-WING STARFIGHTER

MANUFACTURER Kuat Systems Engineering
MODEL Alpha-3 Nimbus **TYPE** Starfighter

Used in the last days of the Galactic Republic and during the Imperial era, V-wings are compact support ships ideal in battle against large numbers of enemy fighters.
V-wings are piloted by a single occupant backed by an astromech droid. The ship closely resembles various Jedi starfighter models (it is made by the same manufacturer) and, like those ships, lacks a hyperdrive. The most distinguishing feature of this craft is a pair of folding wings on either side of the hull, which extend above and below the ship. Dual rapid-fire laser cannons are situated on each of the two wing struts. The V-wing can also attain an impressive top speed of 52,000 kilometers (32,312 mi) per hour. New Republic pilot Vitale flies a V-wing fighter for a time.

No mercy mission
A trio of V-wing starfighters escorts Emperor Palpatine back to Coruscant with a critically wounded Darth Vader.

Z-95 HEADHUNTER

MANUFACTURER Incom Corporation and Subpro **MODEL** Z-95
TYPE Starfighter

The Z-95 Headhunter is a common starfighter during both the Clone Wars and Galactic Civil War. It doesn't match its successor, the X-wing, in either speed or firepower, but it is reliable and sturdy in a firefight. Most Z-95s don't have hyperdrives or space for an astromech droid, although a hyperdrive can be added. The Galactic Republic commissions a modified model of the Z-95 Headhunter for their Grand Army. Built specifically for clone troopers, it has a narrower fuselage than the standard model and is heavily armed with proton torpedoes.

YV-865 AURORE-CLASS FREIGHTER

MANUFACTURER Corellian Engineering Corporation
MODEL YV-865 **TYPE** Freighter

YV-865 *Aurore*-class freighters are often used by Zygerrian pirates. The ships' extensive cargo space and sparse but functional furnishings lend themselves to cargo hauling, both legal and illegal. Large engines on extended struts serve as supports when the ship has landed. Although large and blocky, the craft has only a single pilot. When fully staffed, it may have six crew including a comms officer, engineer, loadmaster, copilot, and gunners. Anakin Skywalker and Ahsoka Tano find themselves onboard a YV-865 *Aurore*-class freighter called the *Tecora* while trying to rescue Togruta captives from Zygerrians.

RHO-CLASS SHUTTLE

MANUFACTURER Cygnus Spaceworks
MODEL *Rho*-class shuttle
TYPE Transport shuttle

The *Rho*-class shuttle is used primarily as personnel, cargo, or medical transports during the Clone Wars. Cargo pods can be attached to the blocky cargo bay to provide even more space. The craft is capable of jumping to hyperspace and is armed with laser cannons. The Republic droid team, known as D-Squad, captures a Separatist-held *Rho*-class shuttle during the Clone Wars. Later, a young Hera Syndulla takes a *Rho*-class shuttle for a spin during the rise of the Empire. She steals it from Imperial forces who are using the craft for a mining operation.

SILVER ANGEL

MANUFACTURER Assembled by Trace Martez **MODEL** *Nebula*-class
TYPE Freighter

Cockpit floor
On a separate level from most of the ship, the cockpit has space for a pilot, copilot, and a third passenger.

The *Silver Angel* is Trace and Rafa Martez's precious freighter. Trace builds the vessel, pouring into it her hopes and dreams of leaving Coruscant. Her special modifications make the *Silver Angel* significantly faster than the base model *Nebula*-class freighter. It has at least one laser cannon for Trace and Rafa's fights against the criminal underworld and the Empire. Trace first puts the *Silver Angel* through its paces on a mission accompanying Ahsoka Tano. Later, after the Empire rises to power, Trace and Rafa leave Coruscant and live on the *Silver Angel*.

MARAUDER

MANUFACTURER Cygnus Spaceworks
MODEL *Omicron*-class
TYPE Attack shuttle

The ship begins life as a modified *Omicron*-class shuttle, which resides on Kamino for the use of the Clone Force 99, also known as the Bad Batch, during the Clone Wars. When the team flees Kamino, its members take the ship with them. It becomes a base and a warship for the Bad Batch's defense. Omega, the youngest of the clones, sleeps in a gun turret fashioned into a comfortable bunk, and the GNK-series droid Gonky also resides on board. The *Marauder* is equipped with a pulley system which can be used to lift both people or cargo.

The clone specialist Tech typically pilots the *Marauder*. Despite its angular shape, it is maneuverable enough in the right hands to survive a dogfight against V-wing starfighters. The vessel serves the Bad Batch through many of their battles, including their return to Kamino early into the Imperial era. The crew uses the *Marauder*'s laser cannons to take out Imperial weapons emplacements during a Twi'lek uprising against the Imperial occupation of Ryloth.

When the miner Benni Baro steals the *Marauder* from the Bad Batch to sell for parts, the clones journey through the caves and canyons of an inhospitable planet to attempt to get the ship back. As Omega asserts, the ship isn't just a vehicle—it's the Bad Batch's home. After the miners overthrow the cruel mine operator Mokko, Benni returns the ship to the clones who helped him escape the mines. The clones keep the *Marauder* with them during their stay in the peaceful town of Pabu. Hunter flies it to rescue Omega and her friend Lyana from a tsunami, lowering a line for them to step onto to be lifted out of danger.

Heavily armed
The *Marauder* is equipped with five light laser cannons, a single heavy laser cannon, and a rear-mounted double laser cannon.

OUTCAST
MANUFACTURER Subpro Corporation
MODEL CHM-series **TYPE** Light freighter

Bounty hunter and mercenary Fennec Shand takes her starship, the *Outcast*, to Pantora to try to capture the young clone Omega during the early years of the Imperial era. Fennec's ship is heavily armored and has two side guns. She has added a small cell in the back of the *Outcast* for her captured bounties and has upgraded the ship's computers to give her access to more starcharts. Above Bora Vio, Shand once again fails to capture Omega, and she talks to her client, Nala Se, via hologram in the cockpit of the *Outcast* before continuing her travels.

JUSTIFIER
MANUFACTURER Kuat Drive Yards **MODEL** *Justifier*-class assault transport **TYPE** Starship

Bounty hunter Cad Bane's starship, the *Justifier*, has two wings, multiple laser cannons, and a powerful hyperdrive. Its forward cockpit includes several large windows that allow Bane to see in multiple directions while he is pursuing his targets. The ship's reorienting centerpiece thruster folds back flat against the sides of the ship during takeoffs and landings. The lower level includes a cell with an energy shield that holds Omega while Bane attempts to hand her over to the Kaminoans. Fennec Shand sabotages an engine of the ship to keep Bane from delivering the young clone.

CLASS-FOUR CONTAINER VESSEL
MANUFACTURER Kuat Drive Yards **TYPE** Freighter

The Empire uses Class-Four Container Vessels to store and move cargo. The pyramid-shaped command center connects dozens of crates and cargo units, is equipped with a hyperdrive, and is staffed by officers and stormtroopers. Clone Force 99 attaches their ship, the *Marauder*, to the underside of a Class-Four Container Vessel to sneak past Corellian security sensors. Years later, the astromech droid Chopper hides in one of the freighters during a refueling mission and meets the inventory droid AP-5. Feeling mistreated by the Empire, AP-5 later helps Chopper steal the vessel.

TAY-O'S SPEEDER
MANUFACTURER TAY-O **TYPE** Speeder

Smuggler Ciddarin Scaleback finances the droid TAY-O to build a riot racing speeder for the Safa Toma racetrack. TAY-O and his pit droids retrofit a 12-series speeder to make it faster, more durable, and better shielded against other racers' weaponry. They paint it teal and orange to match TAY-O's colors. Some of Grini Millegi's riders sabotage the speeder during a race and later damage TAY-O, so Tech pilots it. He ejects its guns in order to increase its speed and maneuverability, which helps him win the race.

SKARA NAL MECH
TYPE Mech

A giant four-legged mech is awakened by the treasure hunter Phee Genoa on Skara Nal. She finds an artifact called the Heart of the Mountain—a crystallized stone that is rumored to be the key to an ancient power—from a group known as the Ancients. When Phee removes it, she rouses the metal mech. It rises from the mountain and emits a massive and destructive surge of energy, razing the ground below it. Phee is able to stop the mech by returning the Heart of the Mountain crystal, but the mech falls apart and is destroyed in the process.

TRANSPORT 904
MODEL Imperial research transport **TYPE** Transport and freighter

Despite being designed to store and transport dangerous cargo, Transport 904 crashes on Silla after a cloned zillo beast breaks free and attacks the freighter's crew. The Imperial transport ship is on its way to a cloning facility on Mount Tantiss. Ciddarin Scaleback sends Clone Force 99 to the crash site to scavenge for valuables. While searching the transport, the Bad Batch crosses paths with the zillo beast. Tech and Omega extract information about its origins from the transport's computer files.

AT-AC WALKER
MANUFACTURER Kuat Drive Yards
MODEL All Terrain Armored Cannon
TYPE Walker

The AT-AC (All Terrain Armored Cannon) is a bipedal scout and combat walker and a precursor to the later AT-ST model. The walker holds one pilot and two gunners in its cockpit. Clone Force 99 encounters AT-ACs on Ord Mantell, where they patrol the Empire-occupied streets. Echo and the droid AZI-3 capture one and turn its crew against the Imperial forces who captured his brothers-in-arms. Imperials in another AT-AC disable the captured walker by shooting its knee joints and knocking it to the ground.

REMORA
MANUFACTURER Corellian Engineering Corporation **MODEL** YG-4214 **TYPE** Mining freighter

Belonging to the clone Echo, *Remora* was once a mining vessel but has since been retrofitted for infiltration missions and combat. The vessel is capable of jumping to hyperspace and it carries a crew of four: the clones Echo, Gregor, Nemec, and Fireball. It also carries a leech vessel—a small craft that can detach from the larger ship and dock with or drill into enemy craft. Echo uses it on a mission to retrieve information and prisoners, including Howzer, from an Imperial Advanced Sciences Division cruiser.

VEHICLES

MILLENNIUM FALCON

MANUFACTURER Corellian Engineering Corp.
MODEL YT-1300f (modified)
TYPE Light freighter

Agile and swift, the *Millennium Falcon* can easily slip from a Star Destroyer's grasp or fly into the bowels of the Death Star to destroy it. Whether piloted by Lando Calrissian, Han Solo, Chewbacca, or Rey, it remains a symbol of hope for freedom fighters.

KESSEL RUN
Under the ownership of gambler Lando Calrissian, the *Millennium Falcon* is a pristine machine. The lure of profit tempts the charming rogue to shuttle a crew of smugglers to Kessel. Among the passengers is Han Solo, a talented pilot from Corellia who is familiar with the freighter design. Solo takes control of the *Falcon* when the mission goes awry. Lando is forced to upload the brain of destroyed droid L3-37 into the ship, allowing Han to plot a course through the dangerous space surrounding Kessel, enabling them to make the journey in record time. Although the crew survives the trip, the ship's interior and exterior are severely damaged. Despite no longer meeting Lando's high aesthetic standards, the light freighter loses none of its appeal to Han. He later wins the ship from Calrissian in a game of sabacc on Numidian Prime.

CAPTURED BY THE DEATH STAR
Years later, Solo is commissioned by Obi-Wan Kenobi to take him, Luke Skywalker, and two droids to the Alderaan system, which gives Han the opportunity to brag about his legendary Kessel Run (a feat he claims he did in less than 12 parsecs). Over the years, Solo has heavily modified the *Falcon* so it is optimized for smuggling. When the Death Star seizes the ship, the crew hides in secret compartments to evade capture. While Obi-Wan sabotages the Death Star's tractor beam, Han, Chewbacca, and Luke mount a prison break to rescue the captured rebel leader, Leia Organa. Obi-Wan then duels Darth Vader as a distraction while the others escape aboard Han's ship. TIE fighters give chase, but powerful cannons in the *Falcon*'s upper and lower turrets dispatch them.

REBEL SERVICE
After safely transporting Leia, Luke, and the droids to Yavin 4, Han and Chewbacca set off in the *Falcon*. However, they soon return to help during the Battle of Yavin, ensuring that Luke can fire the critical shot that destroys the Death Star. Afterward, Han and Chewbacca are handsomely rewarded for the rebel victory. During the next two years, the smugglers join the Rebel Alliance and fly the *Falcon* during many critical missions. They participate in the Dragon Void Run while rescuing rebel informants, and barely survive a dogfight with Darth Vader during the Assault on the Mako-Ta Space Docks. As Vader's forces invade Echo Base on Hoth, the *Falcon* flees the planet with a fleet of Star Destroyers on its tail. Han boldly takes cover in an asteroid field.

Looks are deceiving
The *Millennium Falcon* may not look like much, but special modifications give it exceptional speed, intelligence, and agility, making it ideal for a smuggler like Han.

Smuggler's ship
Han navigates through the Kessel Run *(top)*. After a deadly chase, Han hides the *Falcon* in a cave that turns out to be the insides of a space slug *(above)*.

SHARED OWNERSHIP
After Han is imprisoned in carbonite and delivered to Jabba the Hutt, Lando retakes his old position as the *Falcon*'s pilot, alongside Solo's copilot, Chewbacca. Together, they participate in Solo's rescue and reunite him with the *Falcon*. Faced with a new Death Star, Han offers his ship to Calrissian, who leads the assault on the space station. This time, it is the *Falcon* that delivers the destructive shot to the Empire's newest superweapon.

Death Star
The second Death Star is blown up in spectacular fashion by Lando Calrissian and his copilot Nien Nunb.

IN THE RESISTANCE
In the years following the fall of the Empire, Han Solo loses the *Falcon* to gunrunner Gannis Ducain. It then passes to the Irving Boys before ultimately being stolen by junk dealer Unkar Plutt. Plutt leaves the ship baking in the Jakku sun until it is used by Rey, a scavenger, and Finn, a First Order deserter, to escape the planet. The pair are discovered by Solo and Chewbacca, who have been searching the galaxy for their old ship. The *Falcon* and its former pilot take part in the mission to destroy yet another terrifying superweapon—Starkiller Base. When Han doesn't survive, the ship passes to Rey and Chewbacca, who use it to save the Resistance on Crait. At that battle, the very sight of the ship throws Kylo Ren, Han's son and killer, into a rage. After the battle, Chewbacca takes the *Falcon* to Black Spire Outpost on Batuu for repairs, begrudgingly leaving it in the care of an old acquaintance—businessman and former pirate, Hondo Ohnaka. After Chewbacca regains possession of the *Falcon*, Poe Dameron lightspeed skips the ship to escape the First Order during a mission to retrieve vital intel from a spy. Later on Pasaana, the First Order captures Chewbacca and takes him and the *Falcon* onto the Star Destroyer, *Steadfast*. After another daring rescue, Chewbacca and Lando Calrissian fly the *Falcon* across the galaxy to recruit Resistance supporters to join the Battle of Exegol. Rey later takes the *Falcon* to Tatooine to bury Luke and Leia's lightsabers.

Path to Exegol
Rey, Chewbacca, Finn, Poe, BB-8, and C-3PO head off in the *Falcon* to learn more about Exegol.

Final battle
During the climactic Battle of Exegol, Lando and Chewie fly the *Falcon* into battle with an enormous fleet assembled behind them.

TIE FIGHTER

MANUFACTURER Sienar Fleet Systems
MODEL TIE/ln (Twin ion engine) **TYPE** Starfighter

TIE fighters are the signature starfighter of the Imperial Navy. Their versatility and precision are a symbol of prestige for the Empire and a bane of the Rebel Alliance.

PRECISION AND SIMPLICITY
A TIE's twin ion engines provide thrust and its minute boosters are capable of quickly adjusting the ship's direction. To minimize power drain and maximize maneuverability, the vehicles lack key systems such as deflector shields and hyperdrives. A TIE fighter's central cockpit incorporates flight controls, viewscreens, targeting systems, tracking equipment, and room for a pilot, all in the central pod. The flight controls are so intuitive and easy to learn that rebel novices have been able to figure them out on the fly after stealing TIE fighters from Imperial landing fields.

STRENGTH IN NUMBERS
During the Galactic Civil War, the Imperial Navy subjugates numerous planets and orchestrates large battles. TIE fighters are the primary Imperial starfighter at the Battles of Yavin and Endor. In some cases, elite Imperial pilots are recruited into squadrons such as the 204th Imperial Fighter Wing (also known as Shadow Wing) that are tasked with disrupting the growing rebellion. In spite of this, pilots are instructed that their own well-being is secondary to their mission's objectives. Since the fighters are so fragile and the pilots expendable, TIEs achieve best results attacking in large groups. So many features are sacrificed to facilitate rapid mass production by Sienar Fleet Systems factories that the vessels can be continuously refreshed as they are lost in conflict.

Lothal TIEs
Rebel artist and weapons expert Sabine Wren sneaks into an Imperial TIE airfield, looking to create a diversion for her friends aboard the *Ghost*.

EVOLUTION OF THE TIE FIGHTER
TIE fighters display certain similarities with other, outmoded starfighter models from the old Republic era. While TIEs employ vertical wings similar in appearance to earlier V-wing starfighters, the old Jedi light interceptors are even more familiar, with a central cockpit pod, twin ion engines, common weapons technology, and vertical wings like a TIE. In their starfighter designs, Sienar Fleet Systems borrow heavily from the designs of Kuat Systems Engineering ships, thanks to acquiring key assets and engineers employed by their competitor. A variety of other models have arisen from the TIE line, including TIE interceptors and TIE bombers. Sienar factories experiment with localized improvements, producing advanced models suited to local flying conditions and incorporating secret technological breakthroughs, including the TIE avenger and TIE Advanced x1, which Darth Vader flies.

Starfights
A trio of TIE fighters returns to the Death Star after flying reconnaissance. Without a hyperdrive, TIEs are unable to travel far from base *(above, left)*. A TIE fighter pursues Luke Skywalker's X-wing and is ambushed by Wedge's fighter *(above)*.

AFTER THE EMPIRE
After the defeat of the Galactic Empire, the newly formed Sienar-Jaemus Fleet Systems builds and sells TIE fighters to the First Order and secretly to the Sith Eternal on Exegol. These vehicles have advanced flight control and include deflector shield technology. Specialty fighters include the TIE dagger and the Special Forces TIE fighter. Kylo Ren's TIE whisper has extended hyperspace and stealth modifications.

VEHICLES

STAR DESTROYER

MANUFACTURER Kuat Drive Yards **MODEL** *Imperial I*-class
TYPE Star Destroyer

Star Destroyers are the chief warships of the Imperial Navy and symbols of Imperial might. They enforce the Emperor's will by eliminating hindrances to commerce on Imperial worlds and bolstering their Imperial-backed governments. Admirals, Grand Moffs, Imperial Security Bureau officers, and other senior Imperial commanders use Star Destroyers as their personal mobile headquarters. The ship's commanding officer can be just as intimidating as the approaching ship itself—and its shadow alone can bring results.

During the Clone Wars, *Venator*-class Star Destroyers (often called "Jedi cruisers" because they served as flagships for Jedi generals) are utilized by the Republic. From this line of ships, the Empire develops the *Imperial I*-class Star Destroyers to wage war and maintain order across the galaxy.

Imperial I-class Star Destroyers measure 1,600 meters (5,250 ft) in length, nearly 460 meters (1,509 ft) longer than the *Venator*-class. They are propelled by Cygnus Spaceworks Gemon-4 ion engines and a class 2 hyperdrive. Armaments include 60 Taim & Bak XX-9 heavy turbolaser batteries and 60 Borstel NK-7 ion cannons. Tractor beams pull captured vessels into the main hangar bay, where squadrons of armed stormtroopers wait to board. In addition to a contingent of 9,700 stormtroopers, Destroyers each carry a crew of 9,235 officers and 27,850 enlisted personnel. Star Destroyers are fully equipped to engage in protracted combat on planet surfaces. A maximum contingent of auxiliary vehicles includes 8 *Lambda*-class Imperial shuttles, 20 AT-AT walkers, 30 AT-STs or AT-DPs, and 15 Imperial Troop Transports.

During the Galactic Civil War, the battleships hunt down high-priority targets, instill fear in civilian populations, and attack centers of rebel operations. At the Battle of Hoth, the Empire's fleet of Star Destroyers deploys a contingent of Imperial walkers that wages a successful ground war on the planet's surface. However, the Star Destroyers themselves exit hyperspace too close to Hoth and cost the Empire any advantage of surprise. During the rebel retreat, the Destroyers are too easily disabled, which allows rebel forces to escape. In the Battle of Endor, Star Destroyers deploy wings of 72 TIE starfighters, benefiting the war effort, but rebel fighters nonetheless exploit vulnerabilities in the Destroyers' shield generators and exposed bridges. Most Imperial Star Destroyers are wiped out during the Battle of Jakku. Years later, First Order officers command new *Resurgent*-class Star Destroyers, while *Xyston*-class Star Destroyers remain hidden away on Exegol as part of the Final Order fleet.

Overpowering the enemy
Darth Vader's Star Destroyer, *Devastator*, chases the rebel ship *Tantive IV*, which is in possession of the stolen Death Star plans. Vader orders a tractor beam to draw his quarry into the Destroyer's docking bay, where it is boarded by stormtroopers.

Battle of Scarif
When the Alliance fleet travels to Scarif to support Rogue One, Admiral Raddus orders the *Lightmaker* to ram a Star Destroyer, causing it to crash into another. The resulting debris demolishes the Scarif shield gate.

TIE/RB HEAVY STARFIGHTER

MANUFACTURER Sienar Fleet Systems
MODEL TIE/rb **TYPE** Heavy starfighter

Also known as the "TIE brute," the heavy TIE fighter is distinguished by a secondary outrigger pod with a powerful set of H-s9.3 twin laser cannons. The pilot is assisted by an MGK-300 integrated droid brain, which fulfills the role of an astromech. During his enrollment at the Carida Academy, Cadet Han Solo crashes a TIE brute in a hangar bay, leading to a tribunal and then his reassignment to the infantry on Mimban. While piloting the *Millennium Falcon*, Han is later pursued by a TIE brute through the Kessel Run.

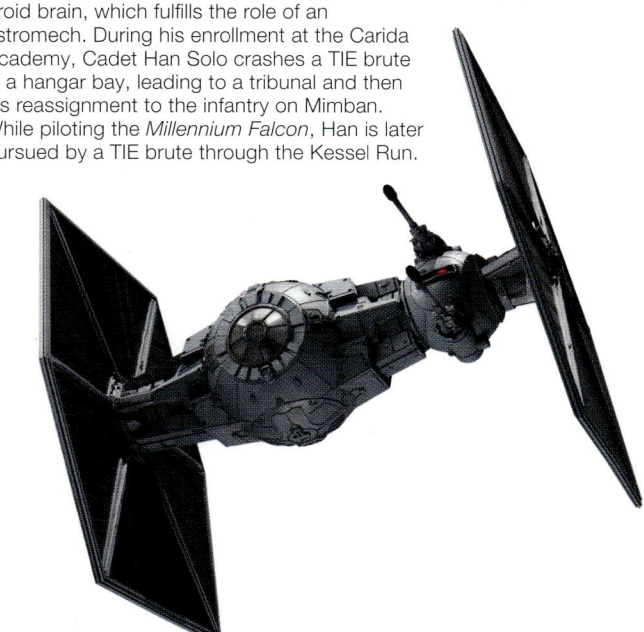

A-A4B TRUCKSPEEDER

MANUFACTURER Trast Heavy Transports
MODEL A-A4B **TYPE** Landspeeder

Moloch of the White Worms gang drives a boxy A-A4B truckspeeder through the chaotic streets of Coronet City on Corellia. The vehicle's heavy, rugged design incorporates armored cages over the driver's seat and front grille, offering its occupants protection and making the vehicle a perfect battering ram in high-speed chases. The speeder also has a holding pen that often contains Corellian hounds. Moloch chases Han and Qi'ra in his speeder from the White Worms' hideout all the way to Coronet Spaceport.

M-68 LANDSPEEDER

MANUFACTURER Mobquet Swoops and Speeders **MODEL** M-68 **TYPE** Landspeeder

Street-racing enthusiasts refer to the M-68 landspeeder as a "street blaster bolt." Available in both a hardtop and open-air version, this compact racer has air vents on its forward engine's front and dorsal surfaces to keep it cool. The rear sports a stylish spoiler above the two rear exhaust nozzles. The craft can attain speeds of 225 kilometers per hour (140 mph). Han steals and hot-wires an M-68, using it as a getaway vehicle after acquiring some illicit coaxium. When Han and his girlfriend, Qi'ra, have to escape the White Worms, Han races the speeder to Coronet Spaceport with Moloch in pursuit.

AT-HAULER

MANUFACTURER Kuat Drive Yards
MODEL Y-45 armored transport hauler
TYPE Dropship

The Empire used their Y-45 haulers to transport walkers and other military equipment into active battle zones. The ship's engines can reach an in-atmosphere speed of 125 kilometers per hour (77.7 mph). However, its hyperdrive only contains pre-set hyperspace jump destinations to specific Imperial outposts. The crane arms rotate upward during landing to conserve space in hangars. Owing to the long hours and muddy conditions crews work in on Mimban, local AT-haulers have an unusual feature: a shower stall. Tobias Beckett's crew steals an Imperial AT-hauler on Mimban for its conveyex train heist on Vandor.

CONVEYEX

MANUFACTURER Kuat Drive Yards
MODEL ATD-C45 conveyex engine
TYPE Cargo train

On frontier worlds such as Vandor, the Empire uses railcrawler conveyex transports to carry valuable cargo, such as coaxium, between high-security Imperial installations. The conveyex runs simultaneously above and below a central track with compartments on either side, and can reach a speed of 90 kilometers per hour (56 mph). In case of attack, each conveyex is armed with two repeating laser cannons and an anti-aircraft laser turret. It is often guarded by a contingent of range troopers as well.

ENFYS NEST'S BIKE

MANUFACTURER Caelli-Merced **MODEL** Skyblade-330 (modified) **TYPE** Swoop bike

Swoop bikes are essentially engines with seats, and are better suited for higher altitudes than most speeders. Enfys Nest and her Cloud-Riders launch their vehicles from a carrier ship named *Aerie* at an altitude of 400 kilometers (249 miles), and fly down to the surface on their frequent raids. While Enfys' modified Skyblade-300 can accommodate a passenger, she normally flies alone and reaches a top speed of 600 kilometers per hour (375 mph). Outriggers extend forward from her seat, with three steering vanes attached to them. Cloud-Rider bikes all feature a red-and-black color scheme to differentiate the vehicles from those belonging to other pirate swoop gangs.

FIRST LIGHT

MANUFACTURER Kalevala Spaceworks
MODEL Kalevalan star yacht **TYPE** Leisure ship

The striking *First Light* is the private yacht of Crimson Dawn leader Dryden Vos. The ship is constructed out of the finest materials and is adorned with Crimson Dawn iconography. Its amenities rival those of the best resorts and luxury liners in the galaxy. Visitors enter via the base of the ship, where security confiscates all weapons. The vast ship contains crew and guest quarters, state rooms, entertainment dens, and kitchens—where Master Chef Shrindi Meille prepares fine culinary delights. Qi'ra, Vos' lieutenant, lives and trains on the *First Light* during her time with Crimson Dawn. The main dining and party area is near the top of the ship, where live entertainment is in a continuous cycle. The largest of the six main decks is at the top of the ship and contains Vos' private residence, office, and meeting rooms. A smaller craft is housed near the *First Light*'s engine room. As the public face of Crimson Dawn, Vos acts as its leader, conducting much of his business from the ship. However, only a few trusted individuals know that Vos can contact the organization's actual leader, Maul, from his office.

ALL TERRAIN DEFENSE TURRET (AT-DT)

MANUFACTURER Kuat Drive Yards
MODEL All Terrain Defense Turret **TYPE** Walker

The All Terrain Defense Turret, or AT-DT, is one of a number of walker models produced by Kuat Drive Yards for the Imperial Army. It has a powerful main cannon that can easily neutralize enemy emplacements and vehicles, while its smaller weapons are better suited to targeting opposing infantry. The AT-DT is undoubtedly a fearsome vehicle, but it possesses notable weaknesses that can be exploited. It is slow-moving; moreover its single pilot isn't fully protected in an enclosed cockpit, so is vulnerable to a flanking attack.

Keen collector
In his private rooms, Vos keeps a collection of rare and highly valuable curiosities from around the galaxy, including a Sith holocron, ancient Mandalorian armor, and endangered species preserved in suspended animation.

KASMIRI

MANUFACTURER Corellian Engineering Corporation **MODEL** KST-100 Kestrel light executive transport **TYPE** Freighter

Named for (and by) its scoundrel owner, Janus Kasmir, the *Kasmiri* is a freighter used for smuggling and other questionable activities. Based on his homeworld of Kaller, Janus meets on-the-run Padawan Caleb Dume and allows him a night's sleep on the *Kasmiri*. The next day, as clone troopers close in on the young Jedi, Caleb steals the vessel and escapes. He soon returns the ship and accepts a job in Janus' crew, and the two become a criminal duo, with the *Kasmiri* acting as their home base.

STINGER MANTIS

MANUFACTURER Latero Spaceworks **MODEL** S-161 "Stinger" XL **TYPE** Luxury yacht

The *Stinger Mantis*, also called just the *Mantis*, is a luxury yacht used by Jedi Cere Junda and Cal Kestis as they attempt to rebuild the Jedi Order and sabotage Imperial efforts. Piloted by Greez Dritus, the interior of the *Mantis* has a cockpit, holotable, seating area, meditation space, galley, and workbench. A large, vertical fin spins around the mid-section of ship and houses the ship's outrigger engine.

Greez and Cere Junda use the *Mantis* to save Jedi Cal Kestis from the Inquisitor Second Sister on Bracca. The three then take the *Mantis* on missions to Bogano, Dathomir, Zeffo, and Kashyyyk, later adding the Nightsister Merrin to their crew. After the *Mantis* crew disbands, Kestis uses the ship along with other rebel cells. When he learns of a hidden planet named Tanalorr, he enlists the help of Greez to pilot the ship through the dangerous Koboh Array.

TRANSPORT EIGHT

MANUFACTURER SoroSuub Corporation **MODEL** TR-286 **TYPE** Transport

To help make amends for his past deceptions, Haja Estree sends Obi-Wan Kenobi and Leia Organa to *Transport Eight* to escape Daiyu. The vehicle, along with Daiyu's cargo port, is fully automated by droids, making it a perfect craft for a secret voyage. The transport uses trade routes so it moves more slowly than many starships. To escape the hands of the Third Sister, Leia uses a console to close the doors quickly and start their departure. As load-lifting and hover droids unload the cargo from *Transport Eight* on Mapuzo, Kenobi and Leia are able to sneak away.

SCYTHE

MANUFACTURER Sienar Fleet Systems **MODEL** Phi-class shuttle **TYPE** Transport

The *Scythe* shuttle transports Inquisitors from their fortress on Nur to planets across the galaxy in their hunt for Jedi. It's the Grand Inquisitor's ship of choice. The *Scythe* has secret cloaking capabilities, laser cannons, and a heavily armored command cabin. Its two wings fold up to allow the ship to land in very narrow areas. The Grand Inquisitor, Fifth Brother, and Third Sister bring the *Scythe* to Anchorhead on Tatooine while pursuing a Jedi during the height of the Imperial era.

Built for hunting The *Scythe* is equipped with an optimized hyperdrive.

ALDERAAN ROYAL SPEEDER

MANUFACTURER Thon Motors **MODEL** AM-719 **TYPE** Speeder

Alderaan royal speeders transport members of the royal family of Alderaan, their staff, and important guests from the lakeside spaceport on Aldera to the palace. The long, sleek speeders are built for comfort and include no weaponry. They have large windows so passengers can take in the breathtaking views of Alderaan during their short journey. Breha Organa's sister Celly and her family usually travel by Alderaan royal speeder when they visit Aldera for banquets and other special occasions.

TRI-WING

MANUFACTURER Incom Corporation **MODEL** Tri-wing S-91x Pegasus starfighter **TYPE** Starfighter

Developed during the Imperial era, tri-wing starfighters can hold two passengers and an astromech droid. Most are equipped with two laser cannons as well as a hyperdrive. Tri-wings are coveted by racers because they can reach high speeds in very short periods of time. As a child, Leia Organa sees a tri-wing leave the Aldera spaceport shortly before she's abducted from Alderaan. After the fall of the Empire, tri-wings are used by the New Republic. At least one is present during the Battle of Exegol.

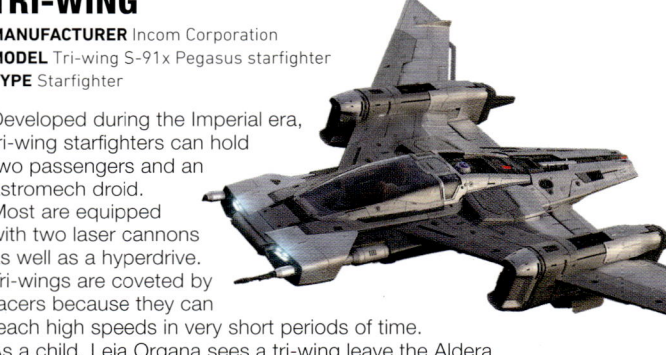

FRECK'S TRUCK

MANUFACTURER Mekuun Corporation **MODEL** FMR-385 **TYPE** Cargo speeder

A local of Mapuzo, Freck drives an Imperial transport truck to ferry stormtroopers between locations. The truck hovers above the ground, allowing it to traverse rocky terrain. Freck offers Obi-Wan Kenobi and Leia Organa a ride in the back of his truck when he discovers them on the side of the road. While driving them to the nearest port, he also picks up several stormtroopers. An Imperial flag is attached to the back of the truck, as a sign of Imperial loyalty.

JT-731 BROADHORN TRANSPORT

MANUFACTURER Corellian Engineering Corporation
MODEL JT-731 Broadhorn
TYPE Transport

To avoid Imperial detection, some early rebel cells retrofit refuse-transporting carriers into ships capable of moving large numbers of refugees to safety. Power conduits and other accessories are moved to the craft's exterior in order to maximize space inside. The Hidden Path keeps two JT-731 Broadhorn transports at its hidden base on Jabiim. One carrying Kawlan Roken, Obi-Wan Kenobi, and Leia Organa is able to depart Jabiim after Darth Vader is distracted by destroying an empty decoy ship. The ships can carry many individuals, but they can't move fast or defend themselves. When the transport ship carrying Kenobi loses its hyperdrive, he takes a shuttle off the vehicle to lure Vader away.

ANDOR FAMILY HAULER

MANUFACTURER Ferrix Field Yards **MODEL** FR-193D **TYPE** Hauler

Clem Andor and Maarva Carassi Andor, who are Cassian Andor's adoptive parents, use their hauler to search the galaxy for salvage. Natives of Ferrix, they bring their finds back to sell on their home planet, which is known for its prosperous market for scraps and parts. The hauler has a cockpit for two pilots and plenty of space for the Andors' groundmech droid, B2EMO. Multiple bins are good for storing sorted parts, and storage compartments allow the couple to hide their more precious cargo. During one salvage trip to the planet Kenari, the Andors discover a young orphan, Kassa, who they bring back to Ferrix and name Cassian.

PRE-MOR AUTHORITY CARRIER

MANUFACTURER Preox-Morlana Corporation
MODEL BTY-180 **TYPE** Carrier

Preox-Morlana maintains a fleet of starships on Morlana One to execute its role as corporate overseer of the Morlana sector. These Pre-Mor Authority Carriers patrol the sector to address any civilian unrest within the corporation's jurisdiction. They carry a squad of enforcement officials, as well as four mobile Tac-Pods for delivering Tac-Corpos troopers precisely where they're needed. Equipped with a hyperdrive and heavy laser cannons, the Authority Carrier can defend itself and accomplish goals above and beyond transportation when required.

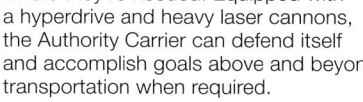

OI-CT

MANUFACTURER Kuat Drive Yards
MODEL OI-CT
TYPE Walker

The Empire utilizes different models of walker for many purposes outside the battlefield, including for construction. The OI-CT model of crane walker is put to work across the galaxy, from Mustafar and Corellia to Ferrix, for tasks like moving shipping containers and picking up ships in a salvage yard. Operators use the balanced walker to move unwieldy or heavy objects. Its four-legged construction adds stability and gives the operator room to brace and adjust the legs as needed, in order to accommodate heavy loads.

BREON DAYVAN

MANUFACTURER Koensayr
MODEL Breon HOY-39
TYPE Dayvan

In the case of the Breon Dayvan, clunkiness has value. It's the kind of civilian starship no one looks at twice, and if they do, they may confuse it with an Orlean star cab. So many of the craft were produced that it has the advantage of anonymity. Its antiquated transponder technology keeps it off the radar of traffic control systems—both Imperial and corporate. Cassian Andor borrows a battered Breon Dayvan to search for his sister on Morlana One. After Preox-Morlana tracks the ship back to Ferrix, it triggers events that result in Cassian's associates having to escape the tumultuous planet in the same Breon Dayvan.

MOBILE TAC-POD

MANUFACTURER Preox-Morlana Corporation **MODEL** RK-392
TYPE Mobile tac-pod

One of the Preox-Morlana corporation's many starships, the mobile Tac-Pod is a small craft used for transporting teams of Tac-Corpo troopers. It has limited orbital range so, over longer distances, the Tac-Pods are carried by the larger Pre-Mor Authority Carrier. A Tac-Pod can carry six Tac-Corpos to wherever Preox-Morlana needs to quell civilian trouble; it's one of the many tools the corporation uses to establish control over its holdings. Tac-Corpos, led by Sergeant Linus Mosk, take three Tac-Pods to Ferrix to search for Cassian Andor.

> **Fighting back**
> When an Imperial *Cantwell*-class Arrestor Cruiser stops Luthen Rael's Fondor above Segra-Milo, he uses his haulcraft's concealed weaponry to manipulate the tractor beam's strength against itself.

FONDOR HAULCRAFT

MANUFACTURER Fondor Yards Commercial Ventures **MODEL** V-21.1 Chevlex **TYPE** Light haulcraft

Luthen Rael is a man of two identities, and his Fondor haulcraft reflects this. It's the type of ordinary starship used to transport goods to a gallery on Coruscant—and that's all his ship appears to be. However, its unassuming surface conceals extensive modifications. Hidden laser cannons, defense mechanisms, and acceleration systems make it a formidable foe. Because Luthen trusts no one, the cockpit has only a single seat. He refuses to rely on others and instead uses a customized droid intelligence, which will respond only to his voice. Luthen wipes its memory after every trip. To help ensure no one pays any attention to the Fondor, or to his activities, Luthen typically parks it far from his destinations, sometimes using a stored speeder bike to journey the final distance.

Deployable lasers
Lethal laser beam projectors are tucked away.

VEHICLES

SHUTTLE FERRY
MANUFACTURER Ferrix Field Yards **MODEL** HFY-3920 shuttle ferry **TYPE** Repulsorcraft

Aboard Ferrix's shuttle ferries, commuting workers travel alongside those visiting on business. The shuttle ferry service has become increasingly necessary over the years as the town's footprint has expanded. The routes begin in remote valleys, where the ferry service operators charge passengers for parking their starships. A pilot operates the ferry from an elevated cockpit at the front of the vessel. Some passengers keep to themselves during the trip, while others dispense advice about how to safely navigate the streets of Ferrix. Upon arrival at the central station, passengers board and debark via droid-powered stairs.

MAX-7 RONO FREIGHTER
MANUFACTURER Sienar Fleet Systems **MODEL** Max-7 Rono **TYPE** Box freighter, rail-launched

Compared to other Imperial craft, the Max-7 Rono freighter is a cumbersome vessel. Piloting the craft takes as much determination as it does skill. It launches without acceleration compensators, making takeoffs strenuous for unaccustomed crews. In some places, the Empire has constructed a tailored launch track and overhead rail for the vessel. However, despite its bulky design, the freighter is useful for transporting cargo across long distances, thanks to its hyperdrive and a capacious interior. On Aldhani, a group of rebels load a Rono freighter with aurodium ingots that they have stolen from the Imperial garrison.

TIE BOARDING CRAFT
MANUFACTURER Sienar Fleet Systems **MODEL** TIE/SA variant **TYPE** Shuttle

Although its design is based on a TIE bomber, the TIE boarding craft is an armored shuttle. The ordnance bay of the bomber has been replaced with an area for stormtroopers; each hull can carry up to six passengers. A docking hatch facilitates the movement of troops between vessels. Elongated panels power the increased life-support systems necessary for the higher number of beings onboard. TIE boarding crafts are carried on *Cantwell*-class Arrestor Cruisers and are dispatched to board starships captured with the cruiser's tractor beams.

JPP-192 LIMOSPEEDER
MODEL JPP-192 **TYPE** Airspeeder

Navigating Coruscant's busy skylanes is considered too mundane a task for senators. Therefore, the Imperial Senate provides its members with a limousine, complete with a Senate-appointed driver, to use for business and personal travel in Imperial City. The limousine is an elevated airspeeder model that features a number of upscale touches so senators can relax while navigating their toilsome days. The enclosed vehicle has a number of windows; a plush, roomy interior; and a privacy screen so the driver doesn't overhear political secrets. The limospeeder is a place where some senators believe they can let their guard down, for however brief a time.

CANTWELL-CLASS ARRESTOR CRUISER
MANUFACTURER Kuat Drive Yards **MODEL** *Cantwell*-class Arrestor Cruiser **TYPE** Patrol and detainment cruiser

The Imperial Navy and the Department of Imperial Justice commissioned the *Cantwell*-class Arrestor Cruiser for a singular purpose: to stop suspicious vessels and prevent them from being where they are not supposed to be. Named for starship designer Walex Cantwell Blissex I, the streamlined vessel sends a message of security and enforcement. With a triple tractor beam array, the vessel typically captures other starships easily. Next, it can fire its twin ion cannons or heavy turbolasers, reel its quarry into its holding bays, or simply keep the starship immobilized until reinforcements arrive.

PHANTOM
MANUFACTURER Corellian Engineering Corp. **MODEL** Modified VCX-series auxiliary starfighter **TYPE** Short-range Corellian shuttle fighter

The *Phantom* docks in the aft section of the *Ghost*, where it acts as the ship's third laser emplacement (when facing outward). A single-pilot cockpit is located at the front, with a small cargo section and fold-down seats situated in the rear. The *Phantom* is an ideal shuttle for short-range supply runs and transporting members of the growing crew on secondary missions. Unfortunately, the *Phantom* is destroyed on a mission to Reklam Station on the planet Yarma. Ezra Bridger's miscalculation sends the ship crashing into Yarma and leaves the crew of the *Ghost* without a secondary craft until they acquire a replacement, the *Phantom II*.

Stealth fighter
As a small ship, the *Phantom* can quietly maneuver through Imperial territory, yet it is capable of taking on TIEs and other small fighters in dogfights.

WINDFALL
MANUFACTURER Subpro Corporation **MODEL** STE-series **TYPE** Light freighter

The *Windfall* is the ship of choice for droid Z0-E3 and her smuggler captain. Although the vessel isn't acquired legally, it becomes something of a home for the pair. During one of their jobs, the *Windfall* is ripped from hyperspace by an Imperial *Interdictor*-class Star Destroyer. The smuggler, who is unknowingly Force-attuned and a descendant of Lord Corvax, is needed by Darth Vader to restore the mystical Aeon Engine. They thwart the Sith Lord's efforts, however, and recover the *Windfall* before making their escape and heading off on another adventure.

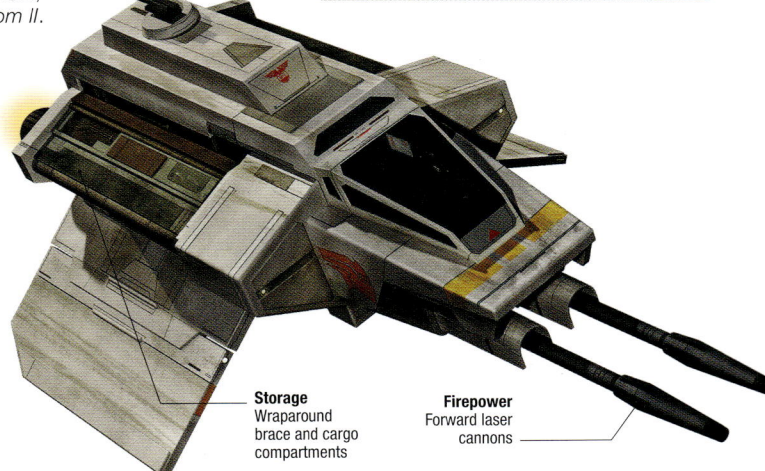

Storage Wraparound brace and cargo compartments

Firepower Forward laser cannons

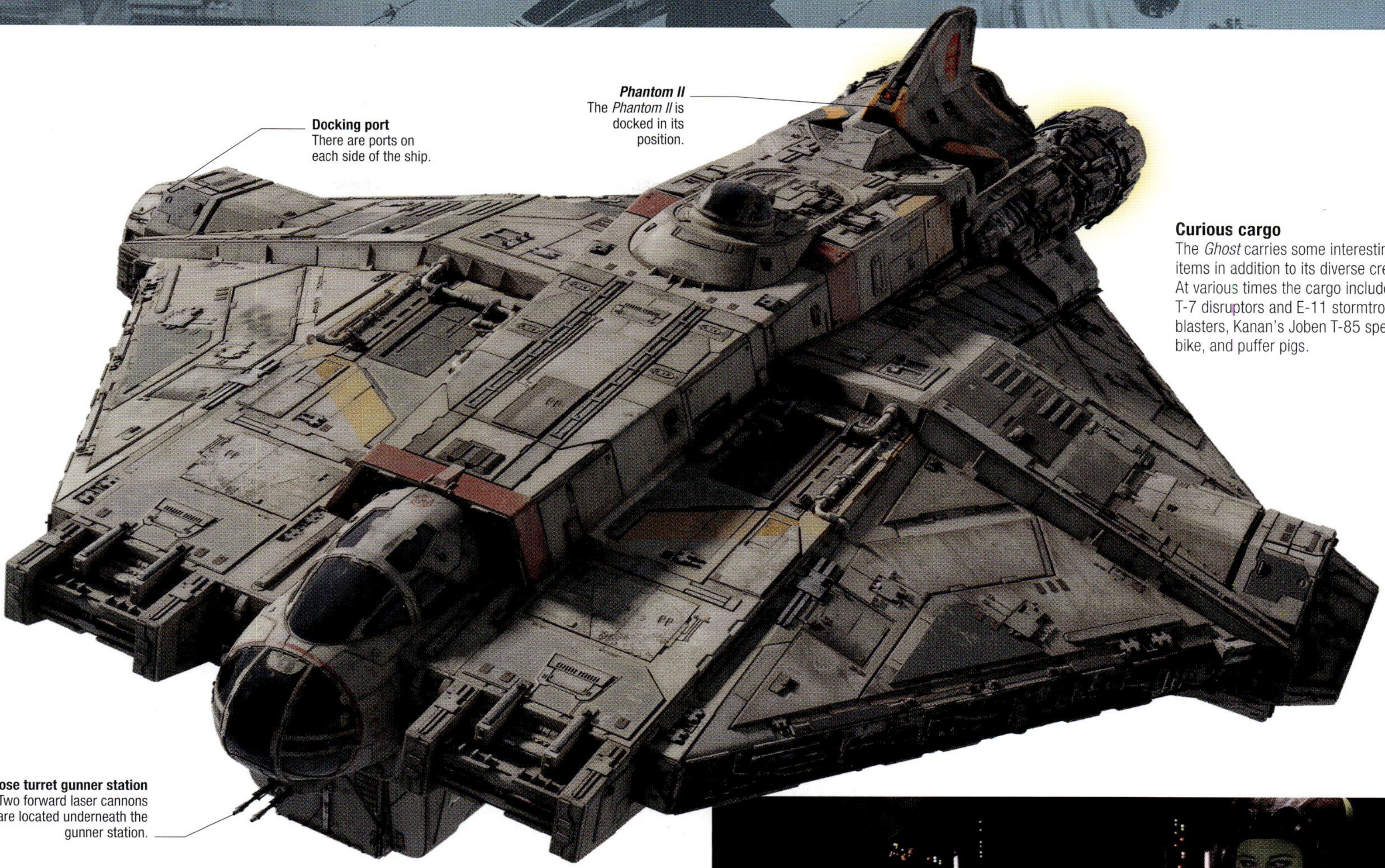

Docking port
There are ports on each side of the ship.

Phantom II
The *Phantom II* is docked in its position.

Curious cargo
The *Ghost* carries some interesting items in addition to its diverse crew. At various times the cargo includes T-7 disruptors and E-11 stormtrooper blasters, Kanan's Joben T-85 speeder bike, and puffer pigs.

Nose turret gunner station
Two forward laser cannons are located underneath the gunner station.

GHOST

MANUFACTURER Corellian Engineering Corp.
MODEL VCX-100 (modified)
TYPE Light freighter

Piloted by Hera Syndulla, the *Ghost* is named for its ability to evade Imperial sensors. The vehicle is not only a starfighter, but also a freighter and home to its misfit crew. A smaller auxiliary fighter makes the *Ghost* particularly adaptable.

HERA'S SHIP
Hera is the owner of the *Ghost*, so she is naturally protective of her ship. When things get out of hand, or if other crew members—namely Ezra Bridger, Zeb Orrelios, and Chopper—become too rambunctious, she sends them on novelty errands (like shopping for meiloorun fruit) to get them away from the ship. The *Ghost* is an old vessel with a few scars from battles with Imperial freighters and TIE fighters, but it still performs reliably. Nonetheless, Chopper makes a lot of unusual modifications himself, to the extent that he might be the only one who knows how to fully repair it.

MISSION READY
While the *Ghost* doesn't have a cloaking device, its countermeasure systems, such as jamming signals and transmitting false information, easily elude Imperial scanners. The *Ghost* is also a fast ship—it outruns Imperial starships, and not just *Gozanti*-class cruisers. Its hyperdrive helps the crew escape Imperial entanglements on more than one occasion. Though most of the crew's early missions are on Lothal, the *Ghost* takes members to far-flung worlds like Ryloth, Gorse, Garel, Kessel, and Stygeon Prime. When Jedi Kanan Jarrus is captured by the Empire, the *Ghost* takes part in his rescue and the destruction of Grand Moff Wilhuff Tarkin's Star Destroyer, *Sovereign*.

REBEL ALLIANCE
The *Ghost* crew does not operate solo for long and joins up with a larger rebel cell named Phoenix Squadron. One of their most high-profile missions involves a rendezvous with Senator Mon Mothma. After an attempt to refuel Mothma's shuttle is interrupted by the Empire, the senator boards the *Ghost* to escape. From the ship's cockpit, Mothma later makes a declaration announcing the formation of the Rebel Alliance to the entire galaxy. During the Liberation of Lothal, the *Ghost* is key to Ezra's plan to break the Star Destroyer blockade surrounding the planet. From the ship, the rebels transmit a message on frequency zero that signals a pod of purrgil to join the battle and crash into the Imperial ships. While Hera continues to ascend the Alliance hierarchy (coming to command a Mon Calamari cruiser at one point), she still keeps her beloved freighter, and pilots the *Ghost* during the Battle of Scarif and Endor.

POST EMPIRE
During the New Republic era, General Syndulla and Chopper fly the *Ghost* on behalf of the New Republic fleet. Hera's son Jacen regularly serves as her copilot. Without permission from the New Republic, Hera takes the *Ghost* to Seatos to assist Sabine Wren and Ahsoka Tano. The *Ghost* later leads a successful search party for Tano over the planet's ocean.

Continuing adventures
Now a general, Hera, with Chopper and Jacen, continues to pilot her ship on missions against the Imperial remnant.

Historic proclamation
From the *Ghost*'s cockpit, Mon Mothma announces the creation of the Rebel Alliance. Chopper transmits her words across the galaxy.

Purrgil attack
Piloted by clone trooper Wolffe and rebel Mart Mattin, the *Ghost* leads a pod of purrgil into battle.

VEHICLES

LAMBDA-CLASS IMPERIAL SHUTTLE

MANUFACTURER Sienar Fleet Systems
MODEL *Lambda*-class T-4a **TYPE** Shuttle

The *Lambda*-class Imperial shuttle transports high-ranking officers and dignitaries, from Captain Rae Sloane and Count Vidian to Darth Vader and Governor Tarkin. It can also be configured for sizable cargo shipments and troop deployments. The ship works well in both the vacuum of space and planetary atmospheres. Its heavy shielding and reinforced hull make it safe for important officials, and its cockpit can be jettisoned as a lifeboat and travel at sublight speed for short distances. The cockpit lacks room for the shuttle's full quota of 20 passengers, so priority is given to the highest ranks.

In the last days of the Empire, Emperor Palpatine travels to the second Death Star aboard his *Lambda*-class shuttle. The heavily modified ship also carries his Royal Guard and advisers such as Sim Aloo and Janus Greejatus. At about the same time, Leia and a team of rebels, including Nien Nunb, find themselves aboard a Star Destroyer called the *Shieldmaiden*. One of the team members sacrifices themself and Nunb's ship, the *Mellcrawler*, creating a path for Leia and her team to escape in a stolen Imperial shuttle, named the *Tydirium*. Using a stolen access code, Han Solo leads a strike team in this shuttle past an Imperial blockade and on to the moon of Endor, where they destroy the Death Star's shield generator.

At the end of the Battle of Endor, Luke Skywalker evacuates the Death Star on board Darth Vader's own Imperial shuttle. All three ships play vital roles in the final moments of the Galactic Civil War. After the Battle of Jakku, *Lambda*-class shuttles are used by both the Imperial remnant and the New Republic. At one point, Moff Gideon escapes from a New Republic shuttle being used as a prison transport.

Imperial shuttles are 20 meters (65½ ft) long and can carry a maximum cargo of 80 metric tons (176,370 lbs). They are equipped with two sublight ion engines and a hyperdrive engine for long-distance travel. Forward armaments include two double blaster cannons and two double laser cannons. Aft, there is also a retractable double laser cannon. Military shuttles boast additional weaponry.

The Dark Lord arrives
Darth Vader arrives on the Death Star to oversee its final construction and is greeted by Moff Jerjerrod.

Shuttle *Tydirium*
Han Solo and Chewbacca sit in the cockpit of a stolen Imperial shuttle, on their way to Endor with other rebels operatives.

Later uses
Imperial remnant troopers commanded by Moff Gideon surround Din Djarin, Cara Dune, and Greef Karga on Nevarro.

IMPERIAL TROOP TRANSPORT

MANUFACTURER Ubrikkian Industries
MODEL K79-S80 **TYPE** Armored troop transport

Imperial Troop Transports (ITTs) are some of the army's most dependable vehicles. Their sturdy construction and heavy armaments make them an ideal mobile stronghold for soldiers in minor conflicts. As ITTs are designed to move stormtroopers between important locations, citizens of the Empire steer clear when they hear the transport's loudspeakers approaching their neighborhood. It always means one of two things: either stormtroopers are moving in or Imperials are moving locals out. Despite not being specifically designed for combat, the ITTs have protective laser guns. When the Empire seizes land from uncooperative farmers on Lothal, it uses ITTs to forcibly relocate them. When Ezra Bridger and Zeb Orrelios try to rescue Morad Sumar and other settlers with a stolen TIE fighter, they learn how tough ITTs are.

TIE BOMBER

MANUFACTURER Sienar Fleet Systems
MODEL TIE/sa bomber **TYPE** Starfighter

TIE bombers are robust Imperial crafts for planetary and ship bombardment. As with standard TIE fighters, solar panels supplement fuel tanks to power twin ion engines, but the ship lacks a hyperdrive, which limits its flight range. However, bombers are deployed for longer use than fighters, so they carry a two-day supply of air and rations. Bombers not only have a complete life-support system, but also cockpit ejector seats. Armaments include a pair of laser cannons and payloads of concussion missiles, orbital mines, and proton bombs.

Imperial destruction
TIE bombers wreak havoc during Operation: Cinder and on Mandalore during the Night of a Thousand Tears.

Surplus
Model 614-AvA speeders are used by Imperials. Older models are sold to civilians. Ezra has an orange-and-green speeder.

Load haulers
Ezra watches from above as officers prepare to deliver a shipment of E-11 blasters on their Imperial speeder bikes.

Air intake cooling vents
Brake pedal
Altitude adjustment vane
Blaster cannon
Steering vane

LOTHAL IMPERIAL SPEEDER BIKE

MANUFACTURER Aratech Repulsor Company
MODEL 614-AvA **TYPE** Speeder bike

The 614-AvA speeder bike is a popular Imperial model on Lothal. Fitted with twin BlasTech JB-37 blaster cannons, Imperial speeder bikes are indispensable to the military. Working in tandem with AT-DPs and TIE fighters, the bikes form a surgical strike team to take on rebel forces. They are more maneuverable than landspeeders, allowing stormtroopers to cover diverse terrain. Their ease of use for pilots and minimal fuel consumption make speeders the ideal vehicles for distant reconnaissance missions and patrolling large areas. Pilots steer their speeders using handlebars and foot pedals that control three steering vanes attached at the front of the bike. The rebels on Lothal are often chased by Imperial speeders, but occasionally manage to steal one of the bikes. Novices like Ezra Bridger may require lessons, but Zeb Orrelios and Kanan Jarrus find the 614-AvA easy to drive.

New crew
During the New Republic era, Bo-Katan Kryze leads a team that takes control of a freighter, which is being used by the Imperial remnant.

Cargo ship
Imperial freighters carry crucial supplies to Imperial bases throughout the Outer Rim. They are protected by a complement of TIE fighters and laser cannons, lest they are attacked along hyperspace routes like the Kessel Run.

Shield projector

Heavy laser cannon
The weapon easily destroys speeders.

Terrain-sensing stabilizer pad
The walker's "feet" bear half of the AT-DP's 11,200-kg (24,692-lb) weight.

ALL TERRAIN DEFENSE POD (AT-DP)

MANUFACTURER Kuat Drive Yards
MODEL AT-DP **TYPE** Imperial walker

One of several walker models used by the Empire, AT-DPs are an improvement over the AT-RTs used by the Republic during the Clone Wars. AT-DPs are essentially high-speed tanks on legs that carry two officers: a pilot seated in front and a gunner behind, who controls the Kyuzo Maad-38 heavy laser cannon. The Lothal garrison finds them very effective when clearing out squatting farmers from land appropriated for mines and factories. AT-DPs patrolling the streets of Lothal are an intimidating sight, meant to discourage rebel uprisings, and they are also ideal for patrols and short scouting missions. Like speeders, they allow a limited number of troopers to patrol large areas. While AT-DPs can chase suspicious vehicles, they lack the firepower of AT-STs required for substantial combat, and as such are often relegated to defensive roles like sentry duty or policing.

IMPERIAL FREIGHTER

MANUFACTURER Corellian Engineering Corp.
MODEL Imperial *Gozanti*-class cruiser
TYPE Armored freighter

Gozanti-class cruisers are heavily armored to deter pirates and rebels (for example, the crew of the *Ghost*). The freighters have been used by a variety of factions, but the Imperial model employs heavier shielding, faster engines, and superior weaponry. Imperial freighters are used to carry important payloads, such as weapons and prisoners, or to transport AT-DPs. These transports carry their own TIE fighter escorts and a rotating crew of stormtroopers to defend their cargo. The ships are fitted with large brigs containing multiple cell blocks to transport their prisoners to Imperial prisons and labor camps, such as the spice mines of Kessel or the Spire on Stygeon Prime.

VEHICLES

C-ROC CARRIER SHIP
MANUFACTURER Corellian Engineering Corp.
MODEL Modified *Gozanti*-class **TYPE** Cruiser

The ore mined on Lothal is so valuable to the Empire that an Imperial Star Destroyer is permanently stationed above the planet. The ore is equally valuable to smugglers, who try to outrun the Imperial blockade. Modified from a Gozanti freighter frame, the C-ROC carrier ship has expanded open-bed cargo capacity to maximize the number of secured ore containers it can convey in one flight. The ship's five engine pods provide enough power to propel the C-ROC to high speeds quickly and evade the Imperial Navy's forces. Cikatro Vizago's ship *Broken Horn* is a modified C-ROC carrier ship.

Blockade runner
The C-ROC's cargo capacity is modified to haul as much valuable Lothal ore as possible.

- Engine pods
- Ore containers

IMPERIAL LANDING CRAFT
MANUFACTURER Sienar Fleet Systems
MODEL *Sentinel*-class landing craft
TYPE Shuttle

The primary function of the Imperial landing craft is to shuttle the Empire's military forces from a Star Destroyer in orbit to planetside operations. These heavily armored landing craft come equipped with laser cannons and concussion missiles and can undertake missions such as short-range scouting, transporting cargo, and providing air support for ground troops. When Darth Vader dispatches sandtroopers to track down the missing escape pod discharged by Princess Leia Organa's *Tantive IV* during its capture over Tatooine, these landing craft ferry them down to the planet's surface.

TIE ADVANCED V1 PROTOTYPE
MANUFACTURER Sienar Fleet Systems
MODEL TIE Advanced v1 (prototype) **TYPE** Starfighter

Compared to standard TIE fighters, the prototype TIE Advanced v1 vehicles used by members of the Inquisitorius have faster engines, stronger laser cannons, and projectile launchers, which can fire tracking devices at ships. The ship's foldable S-foils have solar panels for keeping the starfighter fully charged in most field conditions. Even the swift freighter *Ghost* has difficulty evading a TIE Advanced v1 prototype. Lindon Javes—before he defects to the Rebellion—flies a TIE Advanced v1 fighter.

Latest tech
The Inquisitorius have access to the Empire's very best technological developments, including ships like the TIE Advanced prototype.

- Extended S-foil wings
- Cockpit canopy

Blasting rebels
The prototype TIE Advanced has two powerful laser cannons for eliminating traitorous ships.

STAR COMMUTER 2000
MANUFACTURER Sacul Industries **TYPE** Passenger shuttle

Star Commuters ferry passengers between nearby worlds, running regular commuter lines for tourists, businesspeople, low-level government officials, and dignitaries. Each is piloted by an RX-series droid and can carry up to 24 passengers. With the exception of the pilot, droids are required to remain in the back of the ship during flights as per Imperial regulations. However, Star Commuters are used throughout the galaxy and are common during the Republic, Imperial, and New Republic eras.

EZRA BRIDGER'S SPEEDER BIKE
MANUFACTURER Aratech Repulsor Company
MODEL 614-AvA **TYPE** Speeder bike

Ezra Bridger steals an Imperial military speeder bike on Lothal and repaints it. This isn't the first time Ezra has stolen an Imperial speeder—though the young driver usually crashes them soon after. The 614-AvA speeder is rugged and versatile. It can even telescope to compact for easier storage. The speeder can attain speeds of 375 kilometers per hour (233 mph) and is armed with a BlasTech JB-37 blaster cannon. Ezra uses Loth-rats for target practice while riding across the plains of Lothal.

POLICE GUNSHIP
MANUFACTURER Rothana Heavy Engineering
MODEL Low Altitude Assault Transport (LAAT/le)
TYPE Gunship

The police variant of the Low Altitude Assault Transport (LAAT/le) is well armed, with two turret laser cannons, one tail laser cannon, and two missile launchers. During the Republic era, the LAAT/le is initially used for law enforcement efforts on Coruscant, and is used in a similar fashion on other planets after the Empire's formation. The ships usually carry police officers or stormtroopers and become synonymous with Imperial subjugation of indigenous populations. Their searchlights are often seen shining into city neighborhoods at night, looking for rebels or criminals. Years later, these transports are used by New Republic police forces and Grand Admiral Thrawn's night troopers on Peridea.

PHOENIX HOME
MANUFACTURER Kuat Drive Yards **MODEL** *Pelta*-class **TYPE** Frigate

During the Clone Wars, the Republic uses *Pelta*-class frigates as medical vessels. They deliver medical supplies and transport injured clone troopers to military hospitals. Prior to the Battle of Yavin, Jun Sato—leader of the rebel cell named Phoenix Squadron—commands the *Pelta*-class frigate Phoenix Home. The ship can defend itself thanks to onboard turbolasers and laser cannons, as well as the cell's small complement of A-wing starfighters. However, Phoenix Home cannot survive an attack by Darth Vader himself. The ship is destroyed along with six A-wings.

REX'S AT-TE

MANUFACTURER Rothana Heavy Engineering
MODEL All Terrain Tactical Enforcer (modified)
TYPE Mobile residence

After the Clone Wars, clone troopers Rex, Wolffe, and Gregor retire to the planet Seelos, where they live in a modified AT-TE and spend their days relaxing. The AT-TE interior is emptied of military hardware to make room for bunk beds and a kitchen. Outside, handrails and ladders have been installed to make balconies, walkways, and decks. The main cannon is converted into a rod and reel for catching joopas—large, wormlike creatures native to Seelos. The AT-TE is still otherwise functional, until the clones and their rebel visitors are forced to do battle with Imperial AT-ATs. Afterward, Gregor and Wolffe move into an AT-AT.

BLADE WING

MANUFACTURER Quarrie **MODEL** B-wing prototype
TYPE Starfighter

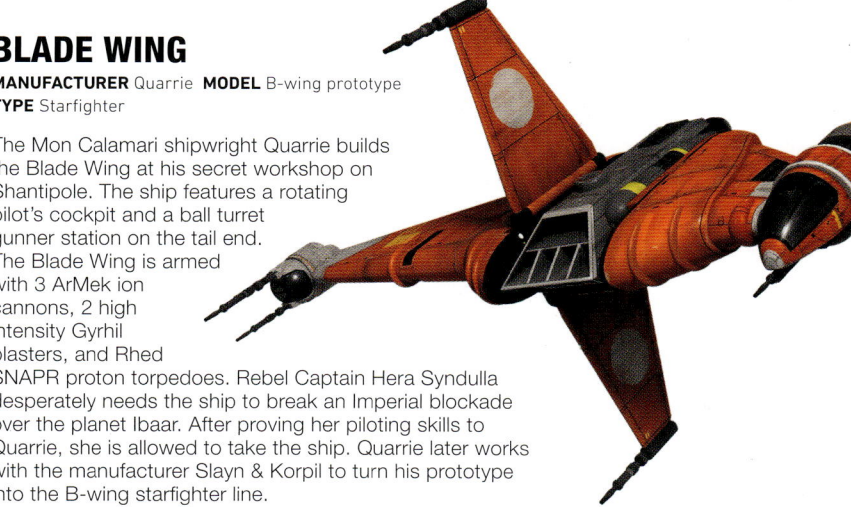

The Mon Calamari shipwright Quarrie builds the Blade Wing at his secret workshop on Shantipole. The ship features a rotating pilot's cockpit and a ball turret gunner station on the tail end. The Blade Wing is armed with 3 ArMek ion cannons, 2 high intensity Gyrhil blasters, and Rhed SNAPR proton torpedoes. Rebel Captain Hera Syndulla desperately needs the ship to break an Imperial blockade over the planet Ibaar. After proving her piloting skills to Quarrie, she is allowed to take the ship. Quarrie later works with the manufacturer Slayn & Korpil to turn his prototype into the B-wing starfighter line.

IMPERIAL INTERDICTOR

MANUFACTURER Sienar Fleet Systems
MODEL *Interdictor*-class **TYPE** Star Destroyer

The Imperial Interdictor is an experimental vessel equipped with four dome-shaped gravity well projectors capable of pulling enemy ships out of hyperspace. The ship is 1,129 meters (3,704 ft) long, armed with 20 quad laser cannons, and can carry up to 20 TIE fighters. Admiral Brom Titus uses his ship to pull the rebel vessel *Liberator* from hyperspace, capturing Ezra Bridger and Commander Jun Sato. The rebels' allies mount a rescue mission and manage to destroy the Interdictor. The prototype leads to a line of Star Destroyers named the *Interdictor*-class with the same capabilities. Two of these ships are used by the Empire to battle the rebels over Atollon, but both are likewise destroyed and the surviving rebels flee. One of the last Imperial Interdictors is destroyed at the Battle of Jakku.

Chain reaction
Thanks to rebel sabotage, the Interdictor malfunctions, drawing in other Imperial ships, which crash into the vehicle and destroy it.

SHADOW CASTER

MANUFACTURER MandalMotors
MODEL *Lancer*-class
TYPE Black Sun pursuit craft

Belonging to Black Sun bounty hunter Ketsu Onyo, the *Shadow Caster* is a *Lancer*-class vessel that is originally designed to chase down cargo vessels and raid them. The model is a favorite of the underworld because it requires very little maintenance or upkeep due to its sturdy construction and redundant systems. After rekindling her friendship with Sabine Wren, Ketsu uses the *Shadow Caster* to help her rebel friends escape an Imperial fleet and flee to safety.

HAMMERHEAD CORVETTE

MANUFACTURER Corellian Engineering Corp.
MODEL *Sphyrna*-class
TYPE Corvette

The *Sphyrna*-class corvette, also known as the Hammerhead corvette, is an ancient line of ships. These vehicles are 315 meters (1,033 ft) long and can attain a speed of 900 kilometers per hour (559 mph). They are armed with two forward dual laser cannons and one rear dual laser cannon. During the Imperial era, Hammerheads are used by rebel cells and later by the Rebel Alliance. The vessels serve many roles—as scout ships, transports, tugs for inoperative craft, and even as battleships. During the Battle of Scarif, the Hammerhead corvette *Lightmaker* (under the command of Kado Oquoné) rams the Imperial Star Destroyer *Persecutor*, which crashes into the Star Destroyer *Intimidator*, and then smashes into the Scarif shield gate. The *Lightmaker*'s sacrifice changes the course of the battle in favor of the Rebel Alliance. The starships continue to be used by the New Republic and Resistance fleets.

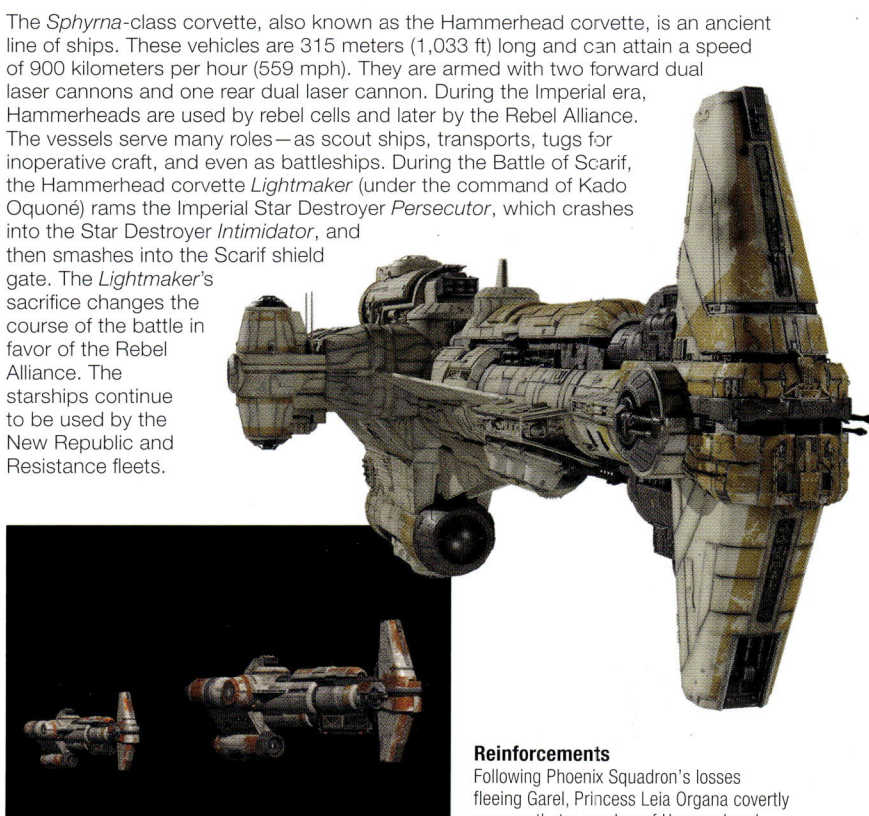

Reinforcements
Following Phoenix Squadron's losses fleeing Garel, Princess Leia Organa covertly ensures that a number of Hammerhead corvettes can reinforce their fleet.

TAYLANDER SHUTTLE

MANUFACTURER Gallofree Yards, Inc. **TYPE** Shuttle

Common throughout the galaxy, Taylander shuttles are popular civilian craft used to transport passengers and cargo. They are frequently seen on worlds like Coruscant, where levels of commerce and tourism are high. They are relatively small transport shuttles, measuring only 43.5 meters (143 ft) long. Their engines reach a maximum speed of 950 kilometers per hour (590 mph), and they possess a Class 2 hyperdrive. Taylanders are also commonly used by rebels for covert missions, making them a target for Imperial searches over time. Rebel leader Mon Mothma travels in a Taylander named the *Chandrila Mistress*.

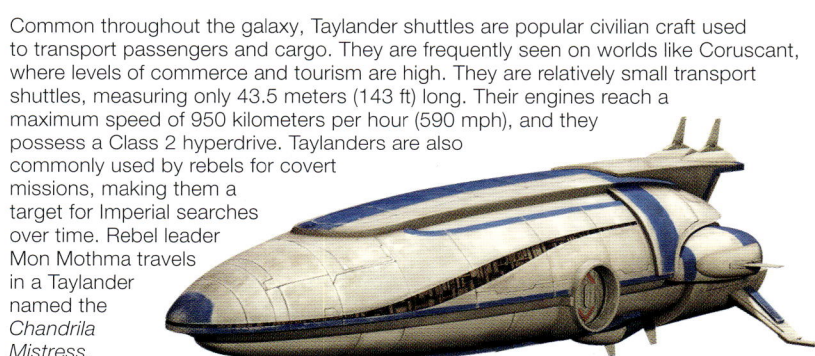

406 VEHICLES

FANG FIGHTER
MANUFACTURER SoroSuub Corp. and MandalMotors
MODEL *Fang*-class **TYPE** Starfighter

Designed for space and aerial battles, Fang fighters are fast, maneuverable, and deadly. The Fang pilots of the Mandalorian Protectors of Concord Dawn have all been personally trained by their leader, Fenn Rau. The vehicles are armed with powerful weapons, including two wing-mounted laser cannons and one ventral proton torpedo launcher. The ships' small profiles make them difficult for the opposition to target, and they prove deadly adversaries for A-wing fighters when the rebels first attempt to traverse the Concord Dawn system. Some of the Mandalorian fleet, assembled by Bo-Katan Kryze during the New Republic era, includes Fang fighters.

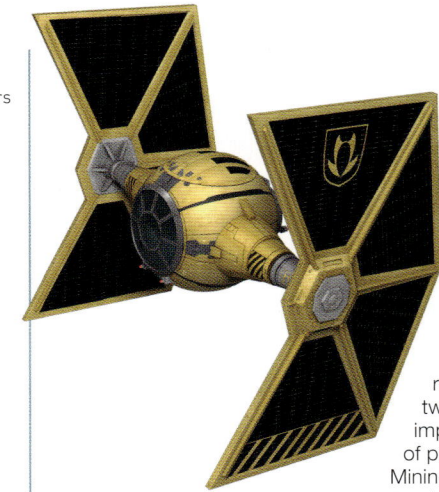

MINING GUILD TIE FIGHTER
MANUFACTURER Sienar Fleet Systems
MODEL TIE/ln (modified)
TYPE Starfighter

The Empire supplies the Mining Guild with modified TIE fighters as recompense for the critical resources they provide. The Mining Guild starfighter is painted yellow to distinguish it from Imperial TIEs. It also has two solar collector panels removed on each stabilizer wing, reducing the total number of panels from twelve to eight. While this alteration improves pilot visibility, it comes at the cost of power refresh rate and maneuverability. Mining Guild TIE fighters are armed with two standard L-s1 laser cannons.

NU-CLASS SHUTTLE
MANUFACTURER Cygnus Spaceworks **MODEL** *Nu*-class **TYPE** Transport shuttle

Republic attack shuttles, otherwise known as *Nu*-class shuttles, are used during the Clone Wars. They are forerunners to later models, such as the *Lambda*-class, *Sentinel*-class, and *Theta*-class shuttles. *Nu*-class shuttles have room for eight seated passengers, and more if standing, and are equipped with two double rotary blaster cannons and two double laser cannons. *Nu*-class shuttles are also used during the early Imperial era where many are painted completely gray. One shuttle also falls into the hands of the Free Ryloth Movement.

Custom job
The Free Ryloth Movement have adorned their shuttle with rebel markings.

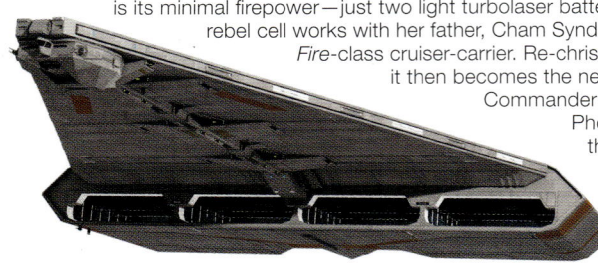

PHOENIX NEST
MANUFACTURER SoroSuub Corp. **MODEL** *Quasar Fire*-class
TYPE Cruiser-carrier

Quasar Fire-class cruiser-carriers, also known as Imperial light carriers, orbit occupied worlds and deploy squadrons of TIE bombers to quell local rebellions. The ship's strength is its four open bays, allowing multiple fighters to launch simultaneously. Its weakness is its minimal firepower—just two light turbolaser batteries. Hera Syndulla's rebel cell works with her father, Cham Syndulla, to steal a *Quasar Fire*-class cruiser-carrier. Re-christened *Phoenix Nest*, it then becomes the new flagship for rebel Commander Jun Sato and his Phoenix Squadron. During the Battle of Atollon, Sato sacrifices himself and *Phoenix Nest* so that Ezra Bridger can get help.

TRAINING A-WING
MANUFACTURER Kuat Systems Engineering
MODEL RZ-1T **TYPE** Starfighter trainer

The RZ-1T is a modified A-wing starfighter used by rebel cells to train new pilots. The ship is fitted with an extra seat for an instructor in the rear of the cockpit. In most other ways the RZ-1T is a conventional A-wing, though some systems, such as the missile launchers, may be disabled until the student is ready to handle them. Ezra Bridger takes the Phoenix cell's RZ-1T from Chopper Base on Atollon to Tatooine in search of Maul. Once he lands, the ship is quickly destroyed by Tuskens.

GAUNTLET STARFIGHTER
MANUFACTURER MandalMotors
MODEL *Kom'rk*-Class **TYPE** Starfighter

The violent Mandalorian splinter group known as Death Watch flies in Gauntlet starfighters. These ships are similar to the Fang fighters of the Mandalorian Protectors, but they are far more powerful, possessing four laser cannons, and they are even faster. Gauntlet starfighters also have a large hold for 24 soldiers, thus they can act as troop transports. Maul owns a modified Gauntlet starfighter named the *Nightbrother*, which passes to Ezra Bridger after Maul's death. Years later, after the fall of the Empire, Bo-Katan Kryze flies a Gauntlet starfighter. Kryze drops two teams of Mandalorian warriors above Nevarro to help protect its citizens from an invasion by Gorian Shard's pirates. Mercenary Bazine Netal also uses a Gauntlet ship during some of her jobs.

PHANTOM II
MANUFACTURER Haor Chall Engineering
MODEL *Sheathipede*-class (modified)
TYPE Transport shuttle

After the first *Phantom* is destroyed, the *Ghost* crew soon finds a replacement. While scavenging on Agamar, the team acquires a former Separatist shuttle. Renamed *Phantom II* for its service in the Rebellion, the ship is heavily modified by the *Ghost* crew. They add blaster cannons and turrets to the previously unarmed vessel, give it a new paint job, and add an astromech socket for Chopper. Much like its predecessor, the *Phantom II* docks in the aft section of the *Ghost*. During the New Republic era, Hera Syndulla flies the *Phantom II* above Corellia where Chopper attaches a homing beacon on Shin Hati and Marrok's transport ship.

SATO'S HAMMER
MANUFACTURER Corellian Engineering Corp.
MODEL YT-2400
TYPE Light freighter

Sato's Hammer belongs to a tiny and innovative rebel cell called Iron Squadron, which is comprised of Mykapo natives Jonner Jin, Gooti Terez, Mart Mattin, and their droid, R3-A3. Their freighter shares many design similarities with the *Millennium Falcon* and is a popular ship model among pirates and cargo haulers alike. It features two double laser turrets (one each on the dorsal and ventral sides) and concussion missile launchers. It is also a fast and highly maneuverable ship. The Iron Squadron use *Sato's Hammer* to conduct attacks on the Imperial forces occupying Mykapo.

TIE DEFENDER

MANUFACTURER Sienar Fleet Systems
MODEL Twin Ion Engine/d defender **TYPE** Starfighter

Enamored with Morgan Elsbeth's brilliant designs, Grand Admiral Thrawn pushes forward the TIE defender's development at the Sienar factories on Lothal. In comparison to the majority of the TIE fighter line (which is manufactured to be easily replaceable), the TIE defender is superior and designed to outclass any rebel ships in battle. As well as being exceptionally fast, the defender includes a hyperdrive (Class 2), deflector shields, and six wing-tip laser cannons. Thrawn deploys his TIE defenders against Hera Syndulla and her crew, attempting unsuccessfully to capture Senator Mon Mothma in the Archeon Nebula, and also in a conflict with the Grysk Hegemony. Officially, the TIE defender program never makes it past the prototype stage, as the destruction of the fuel depot in Lothal's capital city seems to bring the TIE defender program to an end. However, some vehicles remain in action during the Galactic Civil war, including fighters from the Imperial starfighter group Dark Squadron.

Defenseless Y-wings
The Y-wings of Gold Squadron are picked off by a single TIE defender in the Archeon Nebula—only Gold Squadron leader Jon Vander and Ezra Bridger survive.

Solar collectors
TIE defenders have three solar collector wings, enabling the vessel to accumulate far more solar energy than other two-winged TIE fighter models.

Reklam Station
A modified Imperial Construction Module named Reklam Station is based in the atmosphere of the planet Yarma. The Empire uses the station to scrap outdated starfighters, until the *Ghost* crew steal a number of fighters from the base and then cause it to crash toward Yarma's surface.

IMPERIAL CONSTRUCTION MODULE

MANUFACTURER Huppla Pasa Tisc Shipwrights Collective **MODEL** ICM-092792 **TYPE** Space station

Orbital command habitats, also known as Imperial construction modules, are mobile space stations designed to oversee large construction projects. They house all the data concerning the projects and serve as a base of operations for personnel involved in them. The modules also contain cranes and mechanical arms, so can act as giant construction droids, of sorts. The Imperial command center in Lothal's capital city is an Imperial construction module, positioned to oversee the local Imperial factories, harvesting of local resources, and the subjugation of the Lothal population.

IGV-55 SURVEILLANCE VESSEL

MANUFACTURER Corellian Engineering Corp.
MODEL Modified *Gozanti*-class **TYPE** Espionage ship

The Empire uses IGV-55 surveillance vessels to uncover subversive activities. The ships are modified *Gozanti*-class cruisers with a wide array of sensors and communications dishes installed. They use this equipment to monitor civilian and government communications, as well as to sift through other forms of data. While they are often stationed far away from hyperspace lanes, the vessels are equipped with two heavy laser cannons in case they are found and attacked. Its crewmembers are equipped with Lobot-Tech headgear to make them more efficient.

BRAHA'TOK-CLASS GUNSHIP

MANUFACTURER Braha'ket Fleetworks Conglomerate
MODEL *Braha'tok*-class **TYPE** Gunship

Also known as Dornean gunships, *Braha'tok*-class gunships are designed to protect Dornea from the Empire, and later serve in the Rebel Alliance during the Galactic Civil War. The ships excel at combating great numbers of enemy starfighters due to their eight double turbolaser cannons and eight concussion missile launchers. They can also carry two starfighters into battle. *Braha'tok*-class gunships see action during the Battle of Atollon, the Battle of Scarif, and the Battle of Endor. Years after the Galactic Civil War, the vessels are still used by the Dorneans to protect their homeworld. Several Braha'tok gunships fight with the Resistance during the Battle of Exegol.

IMPERIAL SUPPORT VESSEL

MANUFACTURER Rendili StarDrive
MODEL *Dreadnought*-class **TYPE** Heavy cruiser

Imperial support vessels are mid-sized capital ships that have 12 sublight engines and a Class 2 hyperdrive. They are versatile vessels designed to support multiple weapon configurations. Prior to the Battle of Yavin, insurgents from Batonn use a contingent of Imperial support vessels in an attack against Grand Admiral Thrawn's forces, but they are defeated. Thrawn later employs the vessels in his blockade of Lothal, but many are destroyed when they crash into a pod of purrgil that unexpectedly arrives out of hyperspace. The blockade is destroyed and Lothal is liberated.

Ejector seats
If necessary for safety, the seats (and their occupants) can be ejected from the cockpit.

T-6 SHUTTLE

MANUFACTURER Slayn & Korpil **MODEL** T-6 **TYPE** Shuttle

Designed to be ambassadorial craft for the Jedi, T-6 shuttles do not have any weapons. They are manufactured by Slayn & Korpil of the Verpine Hives. Unusually, when in flight, the T-6's wing blades rotate around the cockpit, passenger hold, and engines, which remain in a level position. This innovative feature inspires the later Rebel Alliance B-wing starfighter. T-6s become a rarer sight following the Jedi Order's destruction. However, Ahsoka Tano and Sabine Wren depart Lothal in one such shuttle after the Battle of Endor.

VEHICLES

U-WING
MANUFACTURER Incom Corp.
MODEL UT-60D U-wing starfighter/support craft **TYPE** Troop transport

U-wings are dropships with large interior holds, used by the Rebel Alliance to transport soldiers into battle. The vehicles can also function as starfighters, should the need arise. Their weaponry includes two Taim & Bak KX7 laser cannons and two optional heavy weapon installation points behind the main doors, for greater versatility in battle. U-wings are fitted with an Incom 4J.7 fusial thrust engines capable of reaching 950 kilometers per hour (590 mph), and impressive Class 1 hyperdrives. Their wings have two configurations: they can face backward to prioritize shield strength and engine heat dissipation or face forward to lessen atmospheric friction. The vehicles are notably flown by Saw Gerrera, as well as Cassian Andor during the search for Galen Erso. They also provide support for Rebel Alliance fighters at the Battle of Scarif. During the New Republic era, Kierah Koovah pilots a U-wing with Vanguard Squadron, and Kairos flies one with Alphabet Squadron. They are also used at the Battle of Exegol.

Rare ships
The Alliance owns a small number of U-wings sourced by Bail Organa, who ensured a consignment was lost in transit.

Imposing passengers
Wherever Director Krennic travels in his shuttle, he is always accompanied by a contingent of death troopers. These troops instill fear in whoever Krennic is visiting.

DELTA-CLASS T-3C SHUTTLE
MANUFACTURER Sienar Fleet Systems
TYPE Personnel transport shuttle

The *Delta*-class T-3c shuttle is part of the Abecederian line of executive shuttles first manufactured by Cygnus Spaceworks and later by Sienar Fleet Systems. Imperial Director Orson Krennic commissions production of the craft and acquires ship ST 149 (nicknamed the *Pteradon*) as his personal shuttle. The craft has a minimalist interior with very basic seating. It is armed with twin KX9 laser cannons and three wingtip KX3 laser cannons. Captain Magna Tolvan also commands a *Delta*-class T-3c shuttle that she uses to travel to Skako Minor in pursuit of Doctor Chelli Aphra.

TX-225 COMBAT ASSAULT TANK
MANUFACTURER Rothana Heavy Engineering
MODEL TX-225 GAVw "Occupier" combat assault tank **TYPE** Ground assault vehicle

The Empire deploys combat assault tanks to patrol the streets of the Holy City of Jedha and to transport any kyber crystals that they've commandeered from its inhabitants. The tanks' segmented tracks give them the maneuverability they need to navigate the tight streets of Old City. They are armed with three Dymek MK 2e/w medium laser cannons. Each tank typically requires a crew of three: a commander, driver, and gunner. They can reach speeds of up to 72 kilometers per hour (45 mph) on open roads. The Empire also possesses a hovering variant of the tank, the TX-225 GAVr, that sees action during Lothal's occupation.

AT-ACT
MANUFACTURER Kuat Drive Yards
MODEL All Terrain Armored Cargo Transport
TYPE Walker

The AT-ACT is a much taller version of the Empire's AT-AT walker. However, instead of being deployed on the battlefield, it is designed to haul cargo at Imperial construction projects and research facilities. The AT-ACT's central containers hold 550 cubic meters (19,423 cubic ft) of cargo; stevedore droids load and unload the freight. Despite its ostensible non-combat purpose, the AT-ACT is heavily armored and fitted with advanced weaponry to combat rebel attackers and pirates. Several AT-ACTs are present during the Empire's attack on a Hidden Path base on Jedha. Later, the imposing vehicle's twin Taim & Bak MS-2 heavy laser cannons pose a significant threat to Rebel Alliance fighters during the Battle of Scarif.

TIE STRIKER
MANUFACTURER Sienar Fleet Systems
MODEL TIE/sk x1 experimental air superiority fighter **TYPE** Starfighter

TIE strikers are utilized by both the Imperial Army and Navy. They are primarily designed for in-atmosphere flight, although they are also capable of limited space flight. TIE strikers are heavily armed with four fire-linked L-s9.3 laser cannons, two H-s1 heavy laser cannons, and a payload of proton bombs. The cockpit typically carries a pilot and gunner, but may be enlarged to carry extra passengers and cargo. T E strikers form the main air support on Scarif, and are key players in the battle against the Rebel Alliance.

TIE REAPER
MANUFACTURER Sienar Fleet Systems
MODEL TIE/rp reaper attack lander **TYPE** Troop transport

Similar in design to the TIE striker, the TIE reaper is a dropship used to ferry troops into the center of active battlefields. The transports can reach a maximum speed of 950 kilometers per hour (590 mph) and are armed with two laser cannons. The Empire also uses TIE Reapers in search and rescue missions. A Reaper patrolled the skies of Narkina 5 after a mass prison break. During the Battle of Scarif, a TIE reaper transports Director Orson Krennic's squad of death troopers. Darth Vader later takes TIE reapers to Tython, searching for a Rebel base. In the years following the fall of the Empire, the ships fall into the hands of criminal organizations, including the Ranc gang.

PROFUNDITY
MANUFACTURER Mon Calamari Shipyards **MODEL** MC75 (modified)

The *Profundity* is a large ship, 1,204 meters (3,951 ft) in length. It is the former Civic Governance tower of the city of Nystullum and is flown under the command of the city's Mayor Raddus during the Mon Calamari exodus. Raddus continues to command the ship as an admiral in the Rebel Alliance. After being modified into a warship, the *Profundity* operates with a crew of 3,225 and is heavily armed, with 20 point-defense laser cannons, 12 turbolaser cannons, 4 ion cannons, 12 proton torpedo launchers, and 6 tractor beam projectors. Raddus leads the Alliance fleet during the Battle of Scarif, and his ship receives the Death Star plans from Jyn Erso on the planet's surface below. The plans are then transferred to Princess Leia aboard the *Tantive IV*, which has docked inside the *Profundity*. While the *Tantive IV* escapes Scarif, the *Profundity*'s hyperdrive isn't operational, and it is destroyed.

ZETA-CLASS SHUTTLE
MANUFACTURER Telgorn Corp.
TYPE Cargo shuttle

The Empire uses *Zeta*-class shuttles to transport kyber crystals and other materials between Jedha, Eadu, and Scarif for the Death Star's construction. The pilot and copilot fly the ship from the cockpit, located in the upper deck's bow. The central deck carries the bulk of the cargo and may be detached at the delivery point. The ship is powered by a Class 3 hyperdrive with a very slow Class 12 as backup and armed with two wing-mounted KV22 heavy laser cannons and three hull-mounted KX7 laser cannons. Rogue One uses a *Zeta*-class shuttle to infiltrate Scarif and steal the Death Star plans.

Headquarters
Up to the Battle of Scarif, the *Profundity* serves as the Alliance's flagship. It is eventually replaced by Admiral Ackbar's *Home One*.

LUKE SKYWALKER'S X-34 LANDSPEEDER
MANUFACTURER SoroSuub Corp. **MODEL** X-34
TYPE Landspeeder

A civilian vehicle of mundane design, the X-34 landspeeder has neither weapon mounts, nor armor, nor any other combat capability. Levitating no higher than 1 meter (3 ft 3 in) above the ground on its repulsorlifts and propelled by three turbine engines, a landspeeder can travel smoothly over even the roughest terrain. With either an open-air or sealed cockpit to choose from, the landspeeder is perfect for Tatooine's harsh desert climate.
In the years before he leaves his homeworld and joins the Rebel Alliance, Luke puts his landspeeder to extensive use.

An old friend
Obi-Wan Kenobi gives Luke Skywalker a model T-16 skyhopper as a gift when he is a child.

Low trade-in value
After discovering his aunt and uncle murdered *(above right)*, Luke Skywalker takes Obi-Wan Kenobi, C-3PO, and R2-D2 to Mos Eisley *(right)*. He sells his landspeeder to help fund the cost of passage to Alderaan.

T-16 SKYHOPPER
MANUFACTURER Incom Corp.
MODEL T-16 **TYPE** Airspeeder

Recognizable by its distinctive tri-wing design, the T-16 skyhopper airspeeder is a popular civilian vehicle across the galaxy, providing stable and reliable transportation on almost any world. Reaching speeds of up to 1,200 kilometers per hour (745 mph) from its ion drive and altitudes of 300 meters (984 ft) from its repulsors, the T-16 provides many youngsters with their first flight-training opportunity. On Tatooine, Luke Skywalker flies his T-16 through the dangerous twists of Beggar's Canyon, taking potshots at womp rats with the craft's pneumatic cannon. On one occasion, Luke in in his T-16 saves his falling Uncle Owen Lars by catching him on one of the ship's wings. When he joins the Rebel Alliance, Luke benefits from the similarities between the controls of the T-16 and the X-wing starfighter, which is also manufactured by Incom.

RED FIVE

MANUFACTURER Incom Corp.
MODEL T-65 X-wing **TYPE** Starfighter

Red Five is Luke Skywalker's pilot designation when he destroys the first Death Star. The name becomes synonymous with the actual X-wing fighter he flies.

BATTLE OF YAVIN
Luke's experience on Tatooine flying T-16 skyhoppers, made by the same manufacturer as the X-wing, gives him enough familiarity with Incom flight controls to be assigned pilot duties in Red Squadron as the Death Star approaches the Rebel Alliance base on Yavin 4. Red Leader Garven Dreis assigns Luke the position of Red Five, a callsign open after the death of Pedrin Gaul during the Battle of Scarif. The more experienced pilots Wedge Antilles and Biggs Darklighter round out the trio as Red Two and Red Three, respectively. During their run down the trench, Luke hears the ethereal voice of Obi-Wan Kenobi telling him to "use the Force." He turns off Red Five's targeting computer and fires his torpedoes into the Death Star's exhaust port, sealing the Rebel Alliance victory.

DARING MANEUVERS
Now a member of the Alliance, Luke participates in a bold rebel plan to capture an Imperial Star Destroyer called *Harbinger*. Thanks to a hull breach made by the *Millennium Falcon*, Luke flies directly into the *Harbinger* and through its primary reactor, causing it to start overloading. The stunt causes the Imperial crew to abandon ship, allowing it to be commandeered and then repaired by a rebel crew. The mission is one of the first major victories after the Battle of Yavin for the rising Rebel Alliance. After the Battle of Hoth, Luke takes his ship to Dagobah, where Yoda teaches Luke an important lesson about the Force when he lifts the X-wing out of a swamp.

Perfect shot
Red Five careens down the Death Star trench, heading for the exhaust port.

Blaster cannon
When firing synchronized blasts, the X-wing's guns easily vaporize TIE fighters.

Attack position
The X-wing's S-foils remain closed for swifter flight, then spread open for combat.

Fusial thrust engines
These powerful and efficient engines provide top-notch speed and acceleration.

Cockpit
Luke flies his single-pilot starfighter with assistance from R2-D2.

Faithful copilot
Even though Luke is a starfighter rookie at the Battle of Yavin, seasoned astromech R2-D2 is ready to back him up. During the attack run on the Death Star, R2-D2 keeps Red Five functional by making on-the-fly repairs until he is disabled by Darth Vader's laser blast. Rebel technicians are able to repair the droid, and he continues his legendary partnership with Luke.

Controlled crash
Only a pilot as skilled as Luke could avoid the numerous trees rising out of the Dagobah swamp. Despite surviving the crash, he is still wary of the many unseen perils waiting for him (left).

FIGHTING THE EMPIRE
Luke spends his time flying Red Five to many locations including Bespin, Serelia, Tempes, and Tatooine as he helps lead the Rebel Alliance in its fight against the Empire. After the regime falls, Luke's journeys take him to Pillio, where he finds a compass, and later Ossus, where he forms a new Jedi Academy. Luke also takes Red Five to Moff Gideon's light cruiser in order to rescue Grogu from the Imperial remnant and his dark troopers. When Grogu later decides to abandon his Jedi training to return to Din Djarin, Luke sends him back to Tatooine on Red Five, with R2-D2 serving as his chaperone.

IN EXILE
When Luke's attempt to train another generation of Jedi fails, he pilots his X-wing to Ahch-To: one of the most remote parts of the galaxy. The starfighter lies in the shallow seawater around the ancient village Luke calls home, largely out of his sight, as he seeks to live out his final days alone. Years later, Luke raises Red Five from the sea so Rey can use the ship to travel to Exegol.

> "This is Red Five; I'm going in." — LUKE SKYWALKER

Proving a point
For Jedi apprentice Luke, Yoda's chief admonishment, "Do or do not, there is no try," can be a difficult concept to grasp. After Luke gives up on levitating his crashed X-wing, Jedi Master Yoda proves to Luke it is possible.

Back from the Depths
After being lifted out of the waters of Ahch-To, Rey flies Red Five to Exegol to confront the Emperor.

TIE ADVANCED FIGHTER X1

MANUFACTURER Sienar Fleet Systems
MODEL TIE Advanced x1 **TYPE** Starfighter

Darth Vader only flies the best. His starfighter is a modified early prototype of the TIE Advanced x1 line. Unlike most TIE models, the Advanced x1 has a hyperdrive and deflector shield generator. Vader's fighter is fast and heavily armed, featuring fixed-mounted twin blaster cannons and cluster missiles. The custom cockpit matches Vader's exacting specifications and accommodates the unique features of his suit. Vader displays his prowess at the controls of his starfighter at many points, including single-handedly laying waste to the rebel A-wing pilots of Phoenix Squadron several years before the Battle of Yavin. At the Battle of Vrogas Vas, he successfully defeats two squadrons of rebel X-wings before he is stopped by a head-on collision with Luke Skywalker.

Rebel pursuit
In the Death Star's meridian trench, Darth Vader chases rebel fighters intent on destroying the battle station (above).

Star power High performance solar cells.

Deadly weapons Two L-s9.3 laser cannons.

MOBILE PRISON FACILITY

MODEL Custom Built
TYPE Mobile Prison Facility

The mobile prison facility is run by the Empire. It consists of 80,000 tons of wrecked starships held together with an attractor node, hauled by a cruiser on plasma strings. Inmates are injected with a micro-explosive, which will detonate should they not follow orders. When Gundravian hookspores are discovered in the jail, it is commissioned for destruction. Darth Vader boards the jail looking for inmate Doctor Chelli Aphra, but allows it to be destroyed when his search is unsuccessful.

LUCREHULK PRIME

MANUFACTURER Hoersch-Kessel Drive Inc.
MODEL *Lucrehulk*-class
TYPE Battleship

Once a Droid Control Ship used by the Trade Federation, the *Lucrehulk Prime* is repurposed as a base and flight school by the Rebel Alliance. General Hera Syndulla oversees operations on the station and approves all recruits who partake in flying drills in the *Lucrehulk Prime*'s immediate vicinity. Doctor Chelli Aphra and her crew track the ship, taking Syndulla hostage. The battleship follows, and Aphra takes remote control of the vessel, using it to steal a datacore from the Imperial facility Hivebase-1. Though it sustains damage in the escapade, the *Lucrehulk Prime* survives and Syndulla returns to the ship.

ARK ANGEL

MANUFACTURER Hoersch-Kessel Drive Inc.
MODEL *Bellicose*-class (modified)
TYPE Heavy duty lifter

The *Ark Angel* is the first in a series of ships with the same name by Doctor Chelli Aphra, and used by the treasure hunter for various schemes, missions, and misadventures. The vessel has a decidedly unique profile, with a disk-shaped top and elongated vertical section leading to the entry ramp, along with heavy weaponry. When Darth Vader battles Mon Calamari cyborg Commander Karbin on the rocky world of Vrogas Vas, he orders Aphra to fly the *Ark Angel* into his opponent. She obeys, killing Karbin and ejecting before her ship crashes into the mountainous landscape.

BROKEN WING

MANUFACTURER Corellian Engineering Corporation
MODEL Modified YV-580
TYPE Light freighter

Beilert Valance's ship the *Broken Wing* is modified to suit the cyborg bounty hunter's needs. It features a central raised cockpit, which is part of a small middle section that can separate from the main vehicle in times of emergency. Two prongs flank and extend past the cockpit, which is sitting on a dish-shaped hull, with laser cannons mounted on the inner and outer sides. Valance flies the ship for many jobs, including the Hidden Hand's mission to destroy Darth Vader, before detaching the mid-section and landing inside a rebel cruiser during a pirate attack.

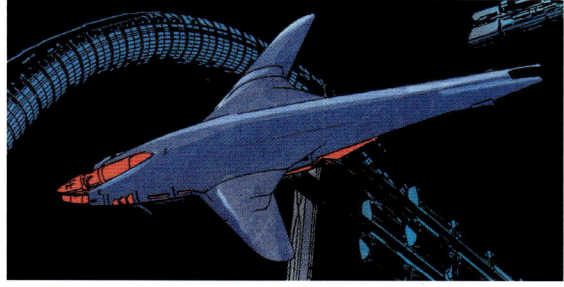

IMPERIALIS

MANUFACTURER Republic Sienar Systems
MODEL *Cosinga*-class heavy corvette **TYPE** Yacht

The *Imperialis* is an advanced pleasure cruiser belonging to Emperor Palpatine. The sleek ship, predominantly silver-blue and red with large, finlike wings, features sharp handling and automatic defenses that can destroy threats such as gravity mines. Significantly, the *Imperialis* is home to some of Palpatine's treasures, including the mask of Lord Momin. Lando Calrissian and his friend Lobot steal the *Imperialis* for crime lord Toren—unaware of who actually owns it. In response, the Emperor launches a hunt for the thieves, charging bounty hunter Chanath Cha with finding the ship. She eventually lets Lando and Lobot go, but follows orders in exploding the *Imperialis*.

VOLT COBRA

MANUFACTURER Corellian Engineering Corporation
MODEL Custom YT-1010
TYPE Light freighter

The *Volt Cobra* belongs to scoundrel and smuggler Sana Starros. With speed on a par with the *Millennium Falcon*, it features a round main body with a separate forward cockpit, and two laser cannons mounted topside with 360-degree functionality. Starros agrees to take Han Solo, Luke Skywalker, and Leia Organa in search of Chewbacca, but comes upon a Star Destroyer in the Dene Gois Cluster. Starros decides the group will stow aboard an escape pod and abandon the *Volt Cobra* in space in an effort to survive.

CORVUS

MANUFACTURER Kuat Drive Yards
MODEL *Raider II*-class
TYPE Corvette

The *Corvus* is a *Raider II*-class corvette—an agile and quick Imperial vessel that serves as a base of operations for the elite Inferno Squad. The ship is outfitted with turbolasers and a hyperdrive, and sees action in several memorable clashes, including the Battle of Endor. Following Iden Versio and Del Meeko's defection from the Empire, the *Corvus* is refitted as a New Republic ship, and later serves the Resistance. Meeko takes the craft in his search for the map that leads to Luke Skywalker, only to be captured by ex-teammate Gideon Hask. Finally, the *Corvus* is destroyed by the First Order at Vardos in a failed effort to kill Iden's daughter, Zay Versio.

T-47 AIRSPEEDER

MANUFACTURER Incom Corp.
MODEL T-47
TYPE Airspeeder (modified)

T-47 airspeeders include controls that are similar to those in starfighters, but can only be used in low altitudes. Many are modified by rebel troops to meet their needs on Hoth, in the frigid cold. The Hidden Path uses two such vehicles to pick up Obi-Wan Kenobi, Tala Durith, and Leia Organa from Fortress Inquisitorius during Organa's rescue. One of them, piloted by Wade Resselian, is destroyed by Imperial fire.

Years later on Hoth, the extreme cold creates a unique set of operational issues that threaten to permanently ground the Rebel Alliance's force of airspeeders. Ingenuity overcomes the bitter Hoth elements: the rebels modify their T-47s to become snowspeeders. The craft is a wedge-shaped, two-person vessel armed with two forward laser cannons and a rear harpoon gun. It is designed to be flown by a single pilot, backed up by a rear-facing tail gunner.

The Imperial assault force that lands on Hoth is led by AT-AT walkers, which are tasked with destroying Echo Base's main power generator. Spearheading the defense of the generator is the elite Rogue Squadron, piloting the newly operational snowspeeders. As Rogue Squadron does not possess the necessary firepower to bring down the walkers, its commander, Luke Skywalker, suggests an alternative tactic: trip up the massive assault vehicles using their ships' harpoons and tow cables. Dak Ralter, Luke's gunner, is killed before he can take a shot, and a short time later their snowspeeder crashes into the snow after absorbing an explosive blast from an attacking AT-AT. Luke is nearly crushed by the walker's foot while retrieving the speeder's unused harpoon gun.

Wedge Antilles and Wes Janson have better luck, harpooning a walker and tripping it up, per Luke's recommendation. Precision firing from Antilles finishes the job, as he hits the downed AT-AT's vulnerable neck. Nonetheless, the rebels' power generator is destroyed, leaving the base vulnerable to invasion.

Fortress Inquisitorius
During the dangerous missions to Nur, the brave pilots of the Hidden Path risk everything to help someone in need.

Rogue pilot
A snowspeeder from Rogue Squadron barely evades enemy fire as it rapidly closes in on the invading Imperial AT-AT walkers.

EXECUTOR (SUPER STAR DESTROYER)

MANUFACTURER Kuat Drive Yards
MODEL *Executor*-class Star Dreadnought
TYPE Super Star Destroyer

The Super Star Destroyer is one of the largest, most powerful Imperial vessels in the galaxy and signifies the might of the Empire. Viewed from above, it presents an arrowhead-shaped silhouette, and boasts more than 1,000 weapons, including turbolasers, ion cannons, and concussion missile tubes. The main hangar bay is situated ventrally and forward and houses a mix of TIE fighters, TIE bombers, and TIE interceptors. The gargantuan craft is propelled through space by 13 colossal engine thrusters. The command tower rises from the aft of the central habitable island and is capped with two geodesic communication and deflection domes.

The first Super Star Destroyer, the *Executor*, is given to Darth Vader as his personal flagship after he successfully stops an attempt by a rogue Imperial scientist, Doctor Cylo, to commandeer the ship. The *Executor* is then specifically modified to Vader's needs, including a meditation chamber much like the one in his castle on Mustafar. While Vader has control over the entire Imperial fleet, he often leads the Death Squadron from the *Executor,* for example during the Imperial assaults on the Rebel Alliance's Mako-Ta Space Docks and Echo Base on Hoth. During the attack on Echo Base, Vader is displeased when Admiral Kendal Ozzel brings the fleet out of hyperspace near Hoth rather than stealthily using a wider approach from the system's outskirts. The tactical blunder buys the Alliance time to raise their base's energy shield. Having tired of Ozzel's incompetence, Vader telekinetically executes the admiral, but cannot prevent much of the rebel fleet from escaping. When the Crimson Dawn criminal syndicate holds an auction for Han Solo, Vader travels to the event in the *Executor*. Following the auction, Vader offends the Hutt Council. The group orders its armada to attack the *Executor*, but the Super Star Destroyer emerges victorious. Serving as the Imperial command ship during the Battle of Endor, the vehicle is finally destroyed when a rebel A-wing starfighter crashes into its command bridge, causing it to lose control and smash into the second Death Star.

REBEL TRANSPORT

MANUFACTURER Gallofree Yards, Inc.
MODEL GR-75   **TYPE** Medium transport

The GR-75 is a sister design to the civilian GR-45, which is used by shipping firms to haul cargo. The transport's outer hull is a thick shell with the interior entirely open for cargo pods. To maximize space, the GR-75 is minimally armed with four twin laser cannons and a deflector shield. Inexpensive to produce, the GR-75 is known for keeping maintenance personnel on their toes. Some of these transports are used as shuttles for high-ranking rebel personnel when the Alliance flees its base on Hoth. The Alliance also use GR-75s in the battles of Atollon, Scarif, Endor, and Jakku.

Fleeing Hoth
GR-75 transports play a crucial role in the Rebel Alliance *(above)*. The last transport, *Bright Hope*, leaves Echo Base during the Battle of Hoth with the help of starfighter pilots Wedge Antilles, Tarrin Datch, and Wes Janson *(right)*.

ALL TERRAIN ARMORED TRANSPORT (AT-AT)

MANUFACTURER Kuat Drive Yards
MODEL All Terrain Armored Transport
TYPE Walker

The All Terrain Armored Transport, commonly known as the AT-AT, is a four-legged combat vehicle used by Imperial ground forces. The cockpit is located in the "head," while dual fire-linked, medium-repeating blasters protrude from the "temples," and two heavier Taim & Bak MS-1 fire-linked laser cannons are mounted under the "chin." The armor plating is impervious to blaster bolts, rendering the AT-AT nearly unstoppable.

At over 22 meters (72 ft) tall, the AT-AT's size gives it a powerful psychological advantage, creating fear in its opponents as it marches forward like an armored behemoth. However, the AT-AT is not without its weaknesses. Its neck, especially, is vulnerable to blaster barrages. Unstable legs and the AT-AT's high center of gravity also make it susceptible to tripping. This tactic is employed by Rogue Group snowspeeders defending Echo Base on Hoth as key personnel flee the planet. When pilot Wedge Antilles makes a close pass on an AT-AT, his gunner Wes Janson fires an ace shot, harpooning the AT-AT with the tow cable. Antilles loops the speeder around the walker's legs until it tumbles to the snow. With the machine's neck better exposed, Antilles' next shot destroys the fallen AT-AT.

The walker also lacks armor covering on its underbelly, leaving the area open to mounted guns or portable missile launchers. For this reason, AT-STs are usually stationed around the flanks of the walker to protect the AT-AT's weak underside. The Empire never anticipates an attack as bold as Luke Skywalker's—he uses a harpoon gun to reach an AT-AT's underbelly and throws a grenade up through the floor into its interior.

Target eliminated
On Hoth, an AT-AT approaches the shield generator, targeting the fleeing Alliance soldiers in its path.

Sneak attack
After his snowspeeder is downed by an Imperial AT-AT and his gunner Dak Ralter is killed, Luke Skywalker attempts to disable the walker another way. He ascends to the belly section, where he leaves behind a concussion grenade, destroying the walker's interior.

Walking death
Rebel ground troops on Hoth do not stand a chance against the Imperial invasion forces led by AT-ATs under the command of General Maximilian Veers. The walkers advance on the shield generator, decimating rebel troops in their trenches.

VEHICLES

ALL TERRAIN SCOUT TRANSPORT (AT-ST/SCOUT WALKER)

MANUFACTURER Kuat Drive Yards
MODEL All Terrain Scout Transport **TYPE** Walker

A quick-strike companion to the larger and more formidable AT-AT walker, the AT-ST's lightweight bipedal design enables swift movement across most types of terrain. Its speed and agility make the AT-ST well suited for patrol and reconnaissance duties supporting Imperial ground operations, and lead to its moniker "scout walker." The Empire deploys AT-STs in vastly different environments. AT-STs are used against Saw Gerrera's partisans in the crowded streets of Jedha, but also take on the Rebel Alliance in remote ground battles. While the scout walkers help defeat the rebel forces at Hoth, the AT-STs are soundly defeated at Endor and Jakku.

For all its advantages in speed and size over the AT-AT, the AT-ST's offensive and defensive power is significantly compromised. The pair of chin-mounted medium blaster cannons offer a range of just 2 kilometers (1 mi 427 yds), while the concussion grenade launcher and light blaster cannon fitted on either side of the head are effective only at close range against infantry. Similarly, its much lighter armor can repel attacks from blasters and other small arms, but cannot withstand laser cannons, missiles, or other heavy weapons. The AT-ST is also vulnerable to a variety of other short-range attacks, exploited to great effect by the Ewoks in the Battle of Endor. Thick ropes slung across its lower legs like a tripwire can topple the walker, while rocks or other debris dropped from hang gliders can destabilize its footing. The Ewoks also discover that ramming logs that are suspended from trees into the sides of the walker's head will strike with enough force to smash through the light armor, destroying the cockpit.

Perhaps the scout walker's greatest weakness, though, is its susceptibility to hijacking. After swinging on a rope to land on top of an AT-ST, Chewbacca uses his mighty arms to rip open the roof hatch, and then reach inside to grab the pilots and hurl them out of the cockpit. The Wookiee then uses the commandeered walker's cannons to destroy other AT-STs in the battle, as well as wreak havoc on the unsuspecting stormtrooper infantry. After the defeat of the Empire, many AT-STs fall into the hands of pirates and criminals. Din Djarin and Cara Dune help take down an AT-ST that's controlled by a group of raiders, in a village on the planet Sorgan.

EDGEHAWK

MANUFACTURER SubPro
MODEL Modified *Eskherf*-class shuttle
TYPE Transport

Active in the galactic underworld, bounty hunter T'onga flies the *Edgehawk*. The silver ship can fit a small crew, including T'onga's wife, Losha Tarkon, and has four wings that point downward from the hull. On a job to find a young girl named Cadeliah, heir to the Unbroken Clan and Mourner's Wail syndicate criminal organizations, the *Edgehawk* sees action against the Empire, including a pursuit through an asteroid field by the elite Inferno Squad. Though T'onga finds safe harbor and gets the *Edgehawk* repaired, she ultimately sells the ship to pay and keep her crew.

ACQUISITOR

MANUFACTURER TaggeCo.
MODEL Custom

The *Acquisitor* is the luxurious vessel of Lady Domina Tagge, head of the Tagge Dynasty. It serves as her home and headquarters for the Tagge Corporation. The *Acquisitor*'s unique structure has several forward viewports with a central bridge. The interior design is minimalist, with most rooms being blue-silver, yet the large craft is fit with an array of high-end technological features, including ray shields. In addition, the *Acquisitor* houses a full garden, kitchen, medical facility, and more amenities, giving Tagge more than enough at her disposal to enjoy life and manage her various operations.

VERMILLION

MODEL Unique
TYPE Flagship-fortress

The mobile base of operations for the Crimson Dawn crime syndicate, the *Vermillion* is a versatile ship, that is both luxurious and deadly. It has a daggerlike shape, with lower wings that fold out for landing, and an eye-catching red and silver color scheme. The *Vermillion*'s main feature is a grand ballroom, complete with a bar. It becomes the site of an auction for rebel pilot Han Solo, who is frozen in carbonite and comes into the possession of Qi'ra, Crimson Dawn's leader. On the ship, she hosts some of the galaxy's most powerful, from the Hutts to Darth Vader himself. The ship later falls in battle to Imperial forces.

SCOURGE ONE

MANUFACTURER Kuat Drive Shipyards
MODEL *Imperial I*-class (modified)
TYPE Star Destroyer

Emperor Palpatine sends the Star Destroyer *Chelator* to clear out the Amaxine station, where a KX-series security droid encounters the Scourge: an artificial intelligence of unimaginable power. The Scourge quickly imprints itself on the droid and spreads across the ship, slaughtering the human crew and taking over the vessel. Soon, the Imperial craft is rechristened *Scourge One*, and augmented with new tech and coverings. Purple lights glow from the viewports, a sign of the Scourge's control, and it launches droid-piloted TIE fighters when attacked. The nightmarish vessel stands as flagship and home to one of the galaxy's greatest threats until the Scourge is defeated.

TWIN-POD CLOUD CAR

MANUFACTURER Bespin Motors
MODEL Storm IV twin-pod **TYPE** Atmospheric repulsorcraft

A familiar sight over the skies of Cloud City, the bright orange twin-pod cloud car polices the surrounding airspace. Specifically designed for patrol purposes, the vehicle is powered by an ion engine and a repulsorlift drive. The port-side pod houses the pilot, while the gunner in the starboard pod controls a pair of blaster cannons. When the *Millennium Falcon* seeks refuge in Cloud City for repairs, Han Solo nearly provokes a confrontation with a cloud car before receiving landing clearance from his old friend Lando Calrissian.

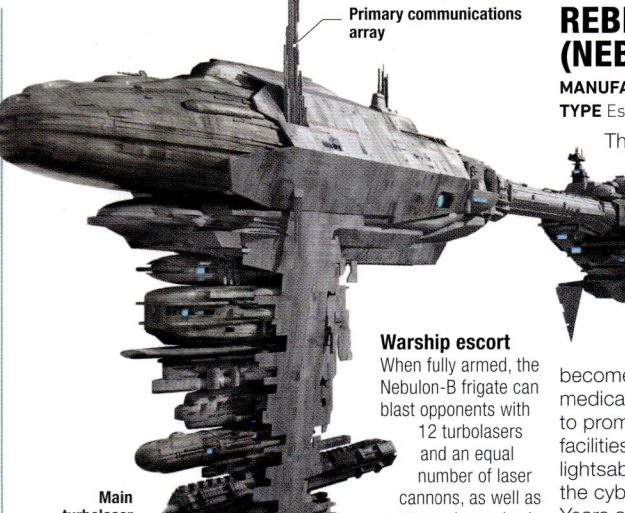

Primary communications array

Warship escort
When fully armed, the Nebulon-B frigate can blast opponents with 12 turbolasers and an equal number of laser cannons, as well as capture adversaries in its dual tractor beams.

Main turbolaser

Main laser cannon

REBEL CRUISER (NEBULON-B FRIGATE)

MANUFACTURER Kuat Drive Yards **MODEL** EF76 Nebulon-B
TYPE Escort frigate

The Rebel Alliance deploys Nebulon-B frigates, with their highly versatile design platform, in several different capacities across its fleet. Equipped with heavy armament and powerful tractor beams, they escort convoys to protect transport ships against Imperial attacks and pirate raids. While some frigates are modified for deployment on long-range scouting missions or search-and-rescue operations, Nebulon-Bs become most famous for their use by the Rebel Alliance as medical frigates. These ships are equipped with bacta tanks to promote healing, medical droids, and full-service hospital facilities. When Luke Skywalker's hand is amputated in a lightsaber duel with Darth Vader, a surgical droid attaches the cybernetic replacement in a Nebulon-B medical frigate. Years after the Battle of Jakku, Jinata Security uses repainted Nebulon-B frigates while kidnapping children for the First Order as part of Project: Resurrection at Exegol.

TIE INTERCEPTOR

MANUFACTURER Sienar Fleet Systems
MODEL TIE/in interceptor **TYPE** Starfighter

Easily recognized by its sharply pointed solar panels, the TIE interceptor is a far deadlier opponent than a standard TIE fighter. Although it also lacks shields and a hyperdrive, the interceptor has four laser cannons mounted on its wingtips, as well as upgraded engines providing considerably improved maneuverability and speed. The Empire places its elite pilots in interceptor cockpits to maximize the craft's effectiveness. With these advantages, interceptors are ideally suited for their main function: chasing down and eliminating rebel starfighters. During the New Republic, Imperial remnant leader Moff Gideon uses TIE interceptors to draw Din Djarin and Bo-Katan Kryze away while his TIE bombers destroy Kryze Castle on Kalevala.

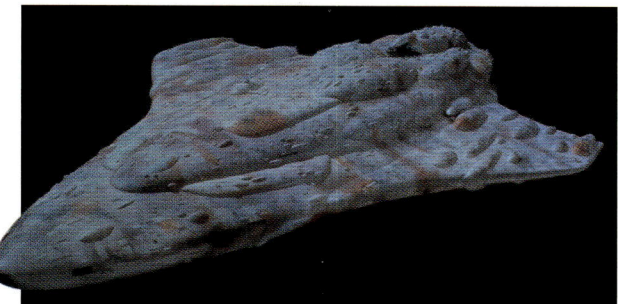

MON CALAMARI MC80 STAR CRUISER

MANUFACTURER Mon Calamari Shipyards
MODEL MC80 **TYPE** Star cruiser

The MC80 star cruisers in the Rebel Alliance fleet operate as command ships or battleships capable of direct engagement with an Imperial Star Destroyer. Each MC80 has a unique design, though common features include a tapered bow, bulbous hulls, hangar bays, heavy armor and shielding, and 10 sublight thrusters. With over 5,000 crew at full strength, it can deploy as many as 10 squadrons of starfighters into a space battle. The MC80's own powerful weapons include dozens of turbolasers and ion cannons. MC80 star cruisers are also a part of the New Republic and Resistance fleets.

HOME ONE

MANUFACTURER Mon Calamari Shipyards
MODEL MC80A **TYPE** Star cruiser

Originally a civilian Mon Calamari vessel intended for long missions exploring deep space, *Home One* is retrofitted for military service and can function as a flagship, battleship, or carrier. With heavy hull plating and triple-strength shields, the ship carries extensive offensive weaponry and boasts 20 hangars for bearing other warships or starfighter squadrons. It is sometimes called the Headquarters Frigate because it houses the command and control center for Admiral Ackbar. At the Battle of Endor, *Home One* is the most celebrated of the MC80 star cruisers in the Rebel Alliance fleet. *Home One* remains central to the New Republic fleet for many years. Decades later, this legendary vessel becomes part of the Resistance fleet.

Admiral's flagship
The largest, most advanced capital ship in the fleet, *Home One* brings pride to the Rebel Alliance whenever it joins the battle. From the bridge, Admiral Ackbar leads the Rebel Alliance fleet at the Battle of Endor (above).

Spy craft
Using its full suite of sensor, tracking, and imaging systems, the A-wing exploits its speed and maneuverability on highly effective intelligence-gathering missions.

A-WING STARFIGHTER

MANUFACTURER Kuat Systems Engineering
MODEL RZ-1 A-wing
TYPE Starfighter

The A-wing is one of the fastest starfighter models in the galaxy. Essentially a cockpit attached to two large engines, it requires precision manipulation of the dorsal and ventral stabilizers without assistance from an astromech. As a result, only the best pilots can fly an A-wing without losing control. The A-wing possesses superior speed, defensive shields, and a hyperdrive, and is armed with two laser cannons and 12 concussion missiles. During the Battle of Endor, an A-wing crashes into and demolishes the bridge of the Imperial flagship *Executor*.

B-WING STARFIGHTER

MANUFACTURER Slayn & Korpil
MODEL A/SF-01 B-wing starfighter
TYPE Starfighter

The B-wing starfighter is designed by Mon Calamari engineer Quarrie, and is among the most heavily armed assault starfighters in the Rebel Alliance fleet. The cockpit's gyroscopic mounting, with full 360-degree rotation, ensures the pilot remains sitting upright regardless of the fighter's orientation. The center of the primary airfoil houses the engines, while the fighter's far end holds the heavy weapons pod, which includes ion cannons and proton torpedoes. When extended, the smaller S-foils broaden the firing arc of the B-wing's twin laser cannons. Specializing in attacking Imperial capital ships, squadrons of B-wings play a major role in the Battle of Endor.

Quick strikes
Powered by an ionization reactor that fuels four high-performance engines, the B-wing races swiftly across the battlefield to engage enemy capital ships (right).

VEHICLES

RAZOR CREST

MANUFACTURER Corellian Engineering Corporation
MODEL ST-70 M-111 Razor Crest series
TYPE Gunship

Quick getaways
The *Razor Crest* is boarded via a retractable telescopic gangway on the port side. Din has replaced the original twin laser cannons with more powerful ones.

The *Razor Crest* is a former military craft used for patrolling local territories before the Empire placed a stronghold over the galaxy. The vessel comes into the possession of the bounty hunter Din Djarin, who uses the reliable spacecraft as transportation and living quarters. After Din rescues Grogu and makes it his mission to keep the child safe, Grogu begins living on board the *Razor Crest* as well.

The ship is equipped for battle via two front Mk 3e/W heavy laser cannons, two large engines on each wing, and sensors at the back of the vehicle. The *Razor Crest* may be piloted by one individual, but it has substantial room for two other passengers in the cockpit. As with most intergalactic vessels, it contains a hyperdrive and shields. However, unlike many starships, it contains a small carbon-freezing chamber for Din to transport multiple bounties.

In addition to the portable chamber, Din has a small armory of blasters and other weapons for him and his allies as they traverse the galaxy or find themselves pursued by bounty hunters hired by the Imperial remnant. The *Razor Crest* has other defensive capabilities, too, such as ground security protocols for when the vessel is docked.

The classic starship is a mainstay of Din Djarin's early adventures with Grogu as they evade Imperial detection and continue their quest to reunite Grogu with his kind, the Jedi. Grogu's innate Force abilities make him a maximum priority target for former ISB agent Moff Gideon, who obsessively hunts the *Razor Crest* for his nefarious purpose.

The duo travels to Tython so Grogu can sit on top of the Seeing Stone and reach out through the Force to find other Jedi. However, the mission is cut short when Gideon tracks them down, thanks to a tracker placed by an Imperial agent while the ship is being repaired on Nevarro. With a single blast from Gideon's light cruiser, the powered-down *Razor Crest* is incinerated into thousands of pieces, with only Din's beskar spear remaining intact. In one fell swoop, Din loses his home, transportation, and temporarily his ability to rescue Grogu, whom Gideon's dark troopers take to places unknown.

Over countless adventures, the *Razor Crest* has gone through multiple modifications, damage, and repairs. Still, its final destruction on Tython doesn't dampen Din's resolve as he teams up with Boba Fett and Fennec Shand to rescue his companion.

Weapons locker
The *Razor Crest* (above) is heavily stocked with blaster pistols, sniper rifles, explosives, and other weaponry. There are ample munitions available for Din's comrades, too.

HOVER PRAM

TYPE Hover pram

The hover pram is a multifunctional tool for transportation, safety, and security for a young child. The traveling armored bassinet is a source of comfort for Din Djarin while he and Grogu find a safe place to evade detection from wayward scum and villainy. An accompanying wrist device keeps the hover pram near its wearer and has a feature that can close the lid via a special screen to protect Grogu from attack or provide a calm atmosphere so the little one can rest up for the next adventure.

712-AVA SPEEDER BIKE

MANUFACTURER Aratech Repulsor Company
MODEL 712-Ava
TYPE Speeder bike

The 712-Ava speeder bike is a reliable, low-to-the-ground vehicle known for its speed and sturdy engineering. It is manufactured by the Aratech Repulsor Company, which builds several repulsorlift vehicles used throughout the galaxy. The inexperienced and untrustworthy bounty hunter Toro Calican uses a 712-Ava speeder bike to hunt down a bounty for the dangerous Fennec Shand on the dusty plains of Tatooine. He is overly impressed with the speeder bike, and with himself. He hopes that Din Djarin will share his appraisal of the vehicle, and of him, too, as they team up to go on the hunt.

AT-ST RAIDER

MANUFACTURER Kuat Drive Yards
MODEL All Terrain Scout Transport
TYPE Walker

The lumbering AT-ST Raider is a heavily modified variant of the Imperial walker used by Klatooinian bandits on Sorgan. Sparsely covered with streaks of red war paint to match its occupants' livery, it also features two view ports with ominous red light shining out of them, giving the marching weapon a monstrous appearance. The Raider helps keep the Sorgan villagers terrified and in desperate need of assistance from the itinerant warriors Din Djarin and Cara Dune. The two, along with the Sorgan people, dig a massive water hazard and lure the AT-ST Raider into the trap, rendering it partially submerged and useless. Din attaches a grav charger to the two-legged transport, blowing it up and taking away the Klatooinians' advantage over the villagers.

ZEPHYR-J SPEEDER BIKE

MANUFACTURER Mobquet Swoops and Speeders **MODEL** Zephyr-J **TYPE** Speeder bike

The Zephyr-J speeder bike is a highly maneuverable and frequently used single-rider transport. On more rugged terrain environments such as Tatooine, these vehicles are typically run down, due to the intense heat, dust, and other mechanically hazardous conditions. Nevertheless, due to their engineering, the crafts' speed is never a concern for the rider. Kelleran Beq uses a version of the Zephyr-J when he rescues the infant Grogu from the terror of Order 66. Later, Din Djarin borrows a stripped-down version from Peli Motto and uses it to pursue a bounty on Fennec Shand.

RIOT MAR'S STARFIGHTER

MODEL Helix J-104 starfighter (modified)
TYPE Combat starfighter

The bounty hunter Riot Mar flies a customized starfighter with a yellow nose and striped markings across the top of its twin engines. The cockpit snugly fits one pilot, and the ship has a dual set of laser cannons (one set at the front and one cannon per wing). The ship contains a small hyperdrive in the rear and a communications antenna toward the front. There are signs of rust sporadically located on the hull of the craft. Rio Mar skillfully pilots the craft in pursuit of Din Djarin, but the Mandalorian artfully evades capture and blasts Riot's starship into pieces above Tatooine.

BOTHAN-5

MANUFACTURER New Republic Correctional Transport **TYPE** Prison ship

The Bothan-5 is one of several New Republic prison ships designed to take sentenced individuals from place to place, often picking up new residents and depositing others at work sites. The Bothan-5's crew consists primarily of droids, including R1 security droids, N5 security droids, and mouse droids. A single human, Lant Davan, supervises the entire ship. Most of the space on board the Bothan-5 is dedicated to prison cells. Only the droids can open the cells manually. In the case of an emergency, blast doors

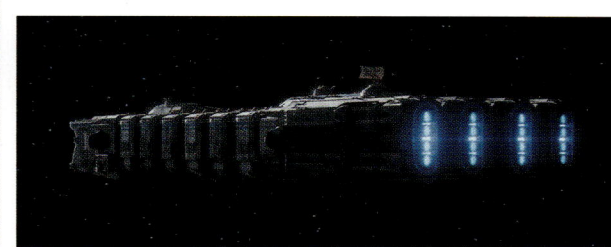

seal off the affected sections of the ship. Din Djarin boards the Bothan-5 on his mission to release the mercenary Qin.

OUTLAND TIE FIGHTER

MANUFACTURER Sienar Fleet Systems **MODEL** Outland **TYPE** Fighter

The Outland TIE Fighter sets itself apart from a very similar model, the basic TIE/ln, by having foldable wings and built-in, rugged landing gear. On rough terrain, the Outland TIE Fighter can land and take off of its own accord, thanks to it having landing gear, as opposed to wings that fit into a docking rack in a larger starfighter. The Empire begins manufacturing Outland TIE Fighters toward the end of its reign. Moff Gideon flies an Outland TIE Fighter during his attack on Nevarro. Din Djarin subsequently destroys that ship by adhering explosives to the craft's wing joints.

COBB VANTH'S SPEEDER

MANUFACTURER Radon-Ulzer (engine) with custom additions **MODEL** 620C (engine)
TYPE Speeder

Although this speeder packs the power of the podracer engine it's built on, Cobb Vanth has modified the engine to serve as a vehicle in his daily work as the marshal of Mos Pelgo. Cobb uses this speeder to travel around the inhospitable desert wastes between

towns on Tatooine. He rides his speeder to the site of a krayt dragon's lair, where he teams up with Din Djarin and is able to outpace Din's speeder. He then uses this speeder to return to Mos Pelgo during the effort to kill the krayt dragon.

HI-CT WALKER

MODEL Heavy industrial crane transport
TYPE Cargo lifter

The HI-CT walker towers over seaside loading docks on the watery moon of Trask. Each vehicle has four sturdy legs and feet, a crew deck and command bridge, and a crane. The walker's legs are sealed thoroughly against the salt water. At the time of Din Djarin and Grogu's journey to Trask, dock workers at a criminal market port use this walker to carry cargo and, occasionally, to lift ships out of the ocean. Din experiences this firsthand after a crane pulls the damaged Razor Crest out of the water next to the landing pads the bounty hunter was attempting to reach.

QUARREN FISHING VESSEL

MANUFACTURER United Dac Engineering Corps **MODEL** Pammant Prowler-250 **TYPE** Fishing ship

The fishing vessel used by a group of Quarren sailors on Trask is sturdy and weather-beaten. A crew of about six Quarren work on the ship, which has two large engines above the water and more below. Light tubes along the sides of the main deck illuminate the ship at night. The deck is strewn with nets, buoys, and other fishing equipment. The Quarren keep a mamacore—a large aquatic predator—in a cage in the middle of the ship. The crew attempts to feed Grogu to the creature and steal Din Djarin's beskar, but Bo-Katan and her Nite Owls fly out to the ship to rescue Grogu and Din.

MYTHROL'S SPEEDER

MANUFACTURER Mobquet Swoops and Speeders **MODEL** M-350 landspeeder
TYPE Landspeeder

The Mythrol's speeder is a standard Nevarro speeder used for transportation and recreation. It utilizes repulsorlift technology to propel itself as it hovers above the

surface of the planet. The speeder seats four passengers (two in the front and two in the back) and features four large propulsion units in the rear, giving it a more modern look as well as faster speeds than a standard model. The vehicle is bluish-gray and also has a bit more legroom than other speeders. It's destroyed when Cara Dune drives a Trexler Marauder off an Imperial remnant base's landing platform in a frenetic escape.

TREXLER MARAUDER

MANUFACTURER Trexler **MODEL** 906
TYPE Armored tank

The Trexler Marauder is an Imperial armored tank designed to engage other vehicles in battle. It is much more equipped for combat than the Imperial troop transport, which the Marauder's design is heavily influenced by. In addition to the strong armor, the tank has multiple fixed laser cannons at the front and a 360-degree laser turret perched at the rear. The targeting computer for the turret is similar to those on starships, meaning a high likelihood of accuracy from its laser. However, it's extremely rare to find a Trexler Marauder since so few were made by the Empire.

418 VEHICLES

MOFF GIDEON'S LIGHT CRUISER
MANUFACTURER Kuat Drive Yards
MODEL Class 546 **TYPE** Battle cruiser

Moff Gideon leads his Imperial remnant forces from an *Arquitens*-class command cruiser of a type commonly found in the Imperial Navy. This hyperspace-capable ship can carry up to 250 crew members, including communications officer Elia Kane, and 100 passengers. Its laser cannons, missiles, and deflector shield make it a formidable war machine. The light cruiser is home to platoons of stormtroopers and dark troopers, plus the equipment needed to house and arm them. The ship also contains docking bays, prison cells, a combat information center with a holoprojector, and other facilities. After Gideon's troops capture Grogu on Tython, they bring the infant to the light cruiser and leave the planet's orbit. Having tracked down the vehicle, Din Djarin and Bo-Katan Kryze lead a rescue mission, battling through corridors and elevators to reach the bridge. When they successfully capture the ship, Bo-Katan keeps command of the vessel until Axe Woves takes over her Mandalorian group. When Axe agrees to help retake Mandalore, he crashes it into Gideon's hidden base on planet, destroying both the base and the ship.

Rescue mission
Aboard Moff Gideon's captured cruiser, Din Djarin lovingly cradles Grogu in his arms for what may be the last time. Grogu will now resume his Jedi training but wants Din's permission before this next step.

TATOOINE REPULSOR TRAIN
TYPE Repulsor train

The massive Tatooine repulsor train incorporates hovercraft technology to speed across the dusty dunes of Tatooine. During the Pyke Syndicate's temporary occupation of Jabba the Hutt's former criminal empire, the spice dealers routinely open fire on unsuspecting Tusken tribes to help ensure no interference in their criminal dealings. An engineer droid pilots the repulsor train with its multiple mechanical limbs and can be relied upon for efficiency and discretion, while the Pykes operate in several towns across the planet. Boba Fett helps a Tusken clan seize the train, ending the Pyke's murderous route through the territory and cementing his place as a member of the group.

MOD SCOOTER
TYPE Grav scoot (modified)

The Mod gang cruises through the streets of the Worker's District in Mos Espa. Although the gang members aren't inclined to steal, and only want to be left alone, they're forced to take water from Lortha Peel. After taking the water, they use their open-air repulsorlift speeders to race away. Each person rides a different color scooter, from red, blue, yellow, or green. The chassis resembles a bike more than it does a speeder, but the bulky nature of each vehicle, combined with its slower speeds, aligns it more with a classic speeder.

IMPERIAL TROOP TRANSPORT
MANUFACTURER Ubrikkian Industries **TYPE** Troop transport

The Imperial Troop Transport (ITT) is developed to move the Empire's stormtroopers and other personnel from site to site. The heavily armored vehicle can also be relied upon for forcibly restraining prisoners for easy relocation. While not manufactured specifically for combat, the ITT is well armed so its presence is likely to increase anxiety for those opposed to Imperial occupation. Stormtroopers marching down the exit ramp is an alarming sight. A modified version of the Imperial Troop Transport hauls Cassian Andor to a massive prison complex on Narkina 5 after his arrest on Niamos. Years later, two ITTs loaded with armed stormtroopers also attempt to capture Din Djarin and Grogu, but they are destroyed by a blast from Boba Fett's jetpack.

JUGGERNAUT TRANSPORT
MANUFACTURER Kuat Ship Yards **MODEL** HCVw A9.2 **TYPE** Juggernaut transport

The HCVw A9.2 juggernaut transport is a large ground assault vehicle composed of four individual segments and the driver's twin cockpit. Each individual section has two heavy-duty wheels, which allow for the transport to traverse over any rough terrain, including mud, rock, and sand. The vehicle isn't armed but has a thick armored hide to keep its crew safe. On Morak, Din Djarin and Migs Mayfeld hijack an HCVw A9.2 and plan to drive into an Imperial refinery undetected. A group of Shydopp pirates tries to besiege the ground vehicle but is defeated by Din before they can destroy the transport.

MAYOR MOK SHAIZ'S LUXURY SPEEDER
TYPE Luxury speeder

The Mayor of Mos Espa, Mok Shaiz, has a luxury top-of-the-line vehicle with ample space, befitting his powerful position. The vehicle's normal leisurely style of travel is dramatically altered when the mayor's majordomo takes the speeder and is chased by Drash, the leader of the Mods. He weaves frenetically through the city to avoid capture and is shocked to discover that Drash's speeder has fallen out of the sky and onto his hood. Her daring jump over a building and subsequent crash landing causes the luxury craft to smash into a fruit stand full of meiloorums.

INTERPLANETARY STARLINER
TYPE Passenger transport

The passenger starliner is an enormous spacecraft with several different models in continual use throughout the galaxy. The vessels transport countless travelers from planet to planet each rotation and can be booked in advance for business, leisure, or necessity. The exact specifications for the three engines on each passenger craft aren't known, but due to popularity, ease of travel, and availability, they're advantageous for long journeys. Din Djarin books a passage on the starliner from Glavis Ringworld to Mos Eisley, but due to strict travel regulations, he must leave his substantial arsenal in a secure locked case with a travel droid.

DIN DJARIN'S N-1 STARFIGHTER

MANUFACTURER Theed Palace Space Vessel Engineering Corps
MODEL N-1 **TYPE** Starfighter

A range of modifications
Din and Peli undertake a range of modifications to the ship, causing lots of chaos along the way.

This classic, hyperspace-worthy Naboo N-1 starfighter sits partially disassembled in Peli Motto's shop until it's rebuilt for Din Djarin. The starfighter is smaller than Din's previous ship, the *Razor Crest*, and at first, he protests that it's not what he wants. Once Din flies the N-1, though, he's won over by the speed and maneuverability of its J-type engines. Critically, the modified astromech pod is now a seat for Grogu. Peli points out that all the parts are handmade, without the use of droids. Because the ship was made before the rise of the Empire, it's hard to trace.

Din and Peli remove the N-1's distinctive yellow paint to reveal more of the chromium hull beneath. Some parts are sourced from Peli's Jawa contacts, including a turbonic venturi power assimilator. Din also asks for bolt-on aftermarket speed mods and vintage hyperware, concerned it will be difficult to find parts for such a classic ship. The vapor manifold is missing, but Peli tells Din not to worry because the manifold will just strangle the thrust capacity. Peli fabricates an induction intake charger and reinforces the compression housing so Din can use a Kineso switch to supercharge the sublight thrusters. That combination turns out to be powerful enough for the ship to quickly outpace New Republic X-wings. Along with souped-up twin blaster cannons and the original automatic piloting system, Din's N-1 also has the original twin fire-linked torpedo launchers.

Din tests the N-1 on Tatooine, speeding through Beggar's Canyon and up out of the atmosphere. A Republic patrol intercepts him, but Din rockets away too fast for them to pursue. He uses the N-1 to travel to distant locations such as Luke Skywalker's Jedi academy on Ossus, ruined Mandalore, Nevarro, and the hidden Mandalorian covert.

In the cockpit
Din can access a range of readings from the cockpit of his starfighter, including about the location of nearby vehicles.

GORIAN SHARD'S PIRATE CORSAIR

MODEL *Cumulus*-class **TYPE** Corsair

Pirate King Gorian Shard's pirate Corsair is his primary warship and location of operations during his invasion of Nevarro. The impressive ship holds at least ten pirate snub fighters in its launch bay and is protected by a deflector shield generator. Gorian's warship is certain to overwhelm innocent planets with 14 ventral ball-shaped turret missile launchers and four quad laser cannons. The Corsair hovers above the atmosphere of Nevarro to remind people of their occupation and helplessness. However, Din Djarin returns to Nevarro with Bo-Katan Kryze and other Mandalorians to help liberate the planet and destroy the pirate menace. Gorian's Corsair is no match for the aerial agility of Din Djarin's N-1 starfighter and the pirate vessel is destroyed, along with the pirate king and the rest of the occupants.

PIRATE SNUB FIGHTER

MODEL *Cumulus*-class **TYPE** Corsair

Pirate snub fighters are the primary attack vehicles of the pirates working for Pirate King Gorian Shard. They're stocked with four front-facing laser cannons and only room for a single pilot in the cockpit. Led by Vane, who is Gorian's second-in-command, these highly maneuverable starfighters swarm Din Djarin's N-1 starfighter as he attempts to leave Nevarro. They follow him through an asteroid field, and many are lost in the fruitless chase. During the emancipation of Nevarro, all the pirate snub fighters are destroyed in the aerial battle, except for Vane, who escapes once Gorian Shard's pirate Corsair has exploded.

SPIDER TANK

TYPE Droid mech

The mysterious spider tank is a hulking, remote-control droid manually operated by an equally enigmatic cyborg beneath the surface of Mandalore. The spider tank lies dormant beneath the soil in a dark tunnel and springs forth to sedate and capture a surprised Din Djarin. The underbelly of the loathsome murder bot has a cage of ribs, which contains its fresh catch of the day. Bo-Katan Kryze ambushes the spider droid and its pilot before they can make a meal of Din. Bo-Katan penetrates the tank's armored hide with the Darksaber and destroys it.

HYPERLOOP POD

TYPE Hyperloop pod

The fastest and most efficient way to travel across Plazir-15 is on the high-speed monorail named the Hyperloop. Used for public transportation, it operates on a track through an elongated plastic tube that serves most of the planet. When Din Djarin and Bo-Katan Kryze are hired to investigate a series of disturbing events, they're instructed by a protocol droid to proceed to a Hyperloop pod. Its top speed is not known to the public, but due to the brief amount of time it takes to travel long distances, the force must be significant. Because it's a popular way for citizens and guests to travel, it's ornate and comfortable.

VEHICLES

LANGSKIB
MODEL Custom-built

A Mandalorian captain leads his people across the desolate terrain of his home planet aboard a langskib land boat, which serves as a resting place in addition to transportation. Two extended thin arms stretch out on port and starboard and connect to skids. The bow also has a skid, but it is much closer to the langskib than the others. Two huge sails on a tall mast can be used whenever wind power is needed. However, the Mandalorian vehicle is obliterated by a trinitaur that thrusts its scaly serpentine neck through the hull.

VESPER
MANUFACTURER Mon Calamari Shipyards **MODEL** *Defender*-class **TYPE** Cruiser

A reliable *Defender*-class cruiser in the service of the New Republic, the *Vesper* carries out missions and patrols as instructed by the fleet's leaders. Captain Hayle commands the vessel and oversees the transportation of prisoner Morgan Elsbeth before her planned transfer to *Home One*. Hayle permits Baylan Skoll and his apprentice Shin Hati to board the ship, to call their bluff about being Jedi. The devious pair, there to free Morgan, kills the crew before they can raise a defense. Baylan and Shin leave the *Vesper* adrift in space.

AHSOKA'S T-6 JEDI SHUTTLE
MANUFACTURER Slayn & Korpil **MODEL** T-6 **TYPE** Shuttle

After the end of the Galactic Civil War, Ahsoka Tano travels in a T-6 Jedi shuttle. Known as T-6 1974, the nimble starship features a rotating engine block and cockpit, allowing the shuttle to land on varying planetary surfaces with flexibility. A single pilot can operate the shuttle, but Ahsoka has the droid Huyang at her side as a navigator and experienced copilot. The droid uses one area of the T-6's capacious interior as a workshop, storing his inventory of lightsaber components accumulated across his decades of teaching and overseeing lightsaber construction. Ahsoka has another area dedicated to lightsaber training, keeping it stocked with practice bokken sabers and helmets.

Ahsoka and Huyang travel in the T-6 1974 to another galaxy, courtesy of a purrgil. Huyang pilots the ship inside the creature's mouth before it jumps into hyperspace and follows an ancient migration route to Peridea. Once there, the T-6 shuttle engages in a number of attacks, revealing the ship's resilience that once served the Jedi well during the Clone Wars.

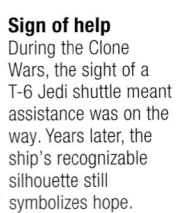

Sign of help
During the Clone Wars, the sight of a T-6 Jedi shuttle meant assistance was on the way. Years later, the ship's recognizable silhouette still symbolizes hope.

QUARREN FREIGHTER
TYPE Freighter

Shuggoth is the Quarren captain of a ship, who falls deeply in love with a Mon Calamari prince. The star-crossed lovers attempt to flee detection from both their families on the ship, which is small and only needs a tiny crew. Shuggoth passes the time soaking her amphibious body in her personal saltwater tank on the ship's bridge. However, the lovers' escape is short-lived once they are hailed on board a captured Imperial light cruiser, which is commanded by Mandalorian leader Axe Woves.

ETA-CLASS SHUTTLE
MANUFACTURER Cygnus Spaceworks **MODEL** *Eta*-class **TYPE** Shuttle

Eta-class shuttles serve different groups over the years. Before the Clone Wars, the Galactic Senate and Republic Ambassadorial Corps use the starships for diplomatic missions. Later, the Jedi Order and Grand Army of the Republic press the shuttles into service, particularly for Jedi generals. The ships are modified with weapons and hidden systems to make them more functional for war. The vessels can carry up to ten passengers and plentiful rations and supplies. Years after the fall of the Jedi, *Eta*-class shuttles find new owners. Former Jedi Baylan Skoll and his apprentice Shin Hati travel in one as they carry out their work for Morgan Elsbeth.

Laser cannons
Three laser cannons give this ambassador shuttle a fighting chance if it is caught in crossfire.

E-WING
MANUFACTURER FreiTek Inc. **MODEL** E-wing **TYPE** Starfighter

The New Republic Defense Fleet encompasses a variety of starships, including the E-wing. An advanced combat starfighter, the ship can carry one astromech droid and one pilot. The New Republic strategically deploys E-wings across its bases in the galaxy to bolster established fleets. One E-wing squadron is stationed on Lothal. Governor Ryder Azadi uses the ships to complete patrols around Capital City, ensuring protection for the citizens of the formerly Imperial-occupied city. Years later, Resistance pilot Poe Dameron sees an E-wing in Baron Paw Maccon's collection of starfighters.

SHIPYARD TOUR PERSONNEL CARRIER
MANUFACTURER Santhe Corporation **MODEL** REV-2K **TYPE** Personnel carrier

When General Hera Syndulla and Ahsoka Tano visit the Corellian shipyards to investigate why one of Morgan Elsbeth's HK-87 assassin droids has been there, regional supervisor Myn Weaver provides a tour of the facility. He uses a repurposed speeder to ferry them round the extensive shipyards. Myn goes to great lengths to demonstrate to his New Republic visitors that his workers are indeed dismantling Imperial starships and rebuilding equipment for the New Republic. Bureaucrat Myn pilots the speeder to only the busiest areas of the facility that show no evidence of Imperial collusion.

CT-05
TYPE Transport ship

The New Republic uses heavy transports to haul ship parts from shipyards on Corellia to wherever they are needed in the galaxy. Equipped with hyperdrive units, the transports move their unwieldy loads with speed and efficiency. Crew can defend themselves with turrets on the wings and rear of the crafts. Imperial sympathizers in the Santhe shipyards appropriate one of these transports, call sign CT-05, to deliver a hyperdrive core from a Super Star Destroyer to Morgan Elsbeth and the waiting *Eye of Sion* in the Denab system. Ahsoka Tano and Hera Syndulla track the ship to find Morgan.

SCION SHUTTLE
MODEL Custom **TYPE** Shuttle

Imperial loyalist and Dathomirian witch Morgan Elsbeth travels in a golden-hued shuttle with two of her scout guards. She uses the distinctive starship after Baylan Skoll and his apprentice Shin Hati free her from New Republic imprisonment. A star navigator droid pilots the ship from a triangular cockpit that can accommodate a small group of individuals. Morgan uses the streamlined and swift vessel as a shuttle, taking it back and forth between the henge at Seatos and the *Eye of Sion*, and then between the extragalactic hyperspace ring vessel and Peridea.

EYE OF SION
MODEL Custom **TYPE** Extragalactic hyperspace transport ring

Hyperspace transport
Hyperspace transport rings aren't uncommon, but one capable of traveling between galaxies is unique. Its construction is an impressive feat.

Needing a way to travel to the far galaxy, Morgan Elsbeth works with Imperial sympathizers to construct the *Eye of Sion* transport ring. Although Morgan doesn't know the exact location of the Great Mothers and Grand Admiral Thrawn when she commissions the vessel, she knows she needs an expansive hyperspace transport ring that can send an *Imperial I*-class Star Destroyer on an extragalactic journey to reach them. Using the network she formed when overseeing the Santhe Shipyards on Corellia, Morgan is able to leverage suppliers and loyal supporters for the parts the unique starship needs. Three clusters of hyperdrive engines along the *Eye of Sion*'s circular chassis power the ship, giving it an incredibly potent hyperdrive system, while turbolaser cannons provide defense. Morgan commands the *Eye of Sion* from its gold bridge, which is equipped with advanced navigation computers for calculating the hyperspace route to Peridea. Launching into hyperspace, the starship's forceful engines generate an X-wing-destroying shock wave, but it makes the voyage to another galaxy successfully. On its return trip, the *Eye of Sion* transports Thrawn's *Imperial I*-class Star Destroyer, the *Chimaera*, in its ring.

The *Chimaera*
Grand Admiral Thrawn's modified *Imperial I*-class Star Destroyer docked with the transport ring.

RP82 FIEND FIGHTER
MODEL RP82 Fiend fighter
TYPE Starfighter

Morgan Elsbeth engages a number of mercenaries and guards to help her locate the map to Peridea and ensure the journey happens without external interference. She uses her Imperial connections to ensure those in her employ are well-equipped and prepared to defend her and the *Eye of Sion*. Two of Morgan's mercenaries, Shin Hati and Marrok, fly RP82 Fiend fighters. Agile and compact, though not as small as other starfighters in Morgan's arsenal, the Fiend fighters are built for high performance. In the hands of a talented pilot, the Fiend fighters' maneuverability makes them an optimal assault craft.

CHIMAERA
MANUFACTURER Kuat Drive Yards
MODEL *Imperial I*-class **TYPE** Star Destroyer

Grand Admiral Thrawn commands the *Chimaera*, which is a modified *Imperial I*-class Star Destroyer. The depiction of a chimaera on the ship's hull makes the ship stand apart. Thrawn takes over command of the vessel early in his Imperial career, directing it across the galaxy to attack rebels, particularly those based on Lothal. The *Chimaera* is part of attacks on Botajef, Batonn, Atollon, and Lothal. It is from Lothal that purrgil, at Ezra Bridger's bidding, transport the *Chimaera* to the far galaxy. The battered warship remains in exile there with Thrawn, until Morgan Elsbeth finds a path to Peridea, and Thrawn is able to return to the known galaxy aboard the *Chimaera*.

NOTI PODS
MANUFACTURER Noti
MODEL Custom
TYPE Repulsorlift pod

A nomadic species, the Noti spend their existence on the move, traveling between different locations on Peridea. They develop a unique and efficient vehicle for their journeys, which functions as a modest home as well as transportation. The Noti park their pods in defensive circles, creating temporary settlements for them to live in; the pods have doors and a window and provide all the shelter the Noti need. Ezra Bridger lives in a custom-built Noti pod for a time. When the Noti are ready to move on to a new location in Peridea's plains or flee danger, repulsorlift technology enables the pods to lift from the ground and slowly travel.

STARHAWK
MANUFACTURER Nadiri Dockyards
MODEL *Starhawk*-class
TYPE Battleship

A top-secret New Republic initiative, the *Starhawk* is a prototype battleship assembled from salvaged Imperial Star Destroyers. Constructed at the Nadiri Dockyards in the waning days of the Galactic Civil War, the ship is meant to level the playing field against the Empire's capital ships. It features heavy durasteel armor, deflector shields, turbolaser batteries, and a tractor beam array. The *Starhawk* is ultimately sacrificed by Hera Syndulla, who sends it into the Galitan moon in order to eliminate an Imperial threat. Seeing the ship's potential, however, the New Republic continues to develop versions of the battleship and a number of the ships see action during the Battle of Jakku.

VEHICLES

T-85 X-WING

MANUFACTURER Incom-FreiTek **MODEL** T-85 X-wing **TYPE** Starfighter

After the Battle of Endor, the New Republic Defense Fleet flies T-85 X-wings, which are among the most innovative starfighters created by Incom-FreiTek. The ships are more advanced than the Rebel Alliance's T-65B and T-65C X-wings, as well as the Resistance's T-70s. Flown by New Republic pilot Kazuda Xiono on his first encounter with Captain Poe Dameron, the blue-and-silver New Republic T-85s have the words "Republic Navy" written in Aurebesh across the ships' bow. Most are destroyed during the Hosnian cataclysm, but a few remain active in the Resistance fleet.

RESISTANCE BLOCKADE RUNNER

MANUFACTURER Corellian Engineering Corp. **MODEL** CR90 **TYPE** Corvette

The Resistance flies old but trusty ships that are both familiar and comfortable to its former Rebel Alliance members, especially its leader, General Leia Organa. Much like the *Tantive IV*, this CR90 participates in the Battle of Scarif. The corvette later serves as Leia's mobile operations center for the Resistance prior to the destruction of Hosnian Prime. After their dogfight with Major Elrik Vonreg, Poe Dameron and Kazuda Xiono dock with the ship to contact her via hologram. Following this conversation, they return to the ship and are briefed by Leia in person regarding a new mission.

TIE BARON

MANUFACTURER Sienar-Jaemus Fleet Systems **MODEL** TIE/in interceptor **TYPE** Starfighter

All-red
The fact that Vonreg flies in an all-red TIE suggests that his skills far surpass those of the Special Forces TIE pilots, who fly in ships adorned with a red stripe only.

Major Elrik Vonreg is one of the First Order's most skilled pilots, and flies a crimson First Order TIE interceptor. The starfighter's twin ion engines are powered by two ion reactors with pre-charged deuterium power cells which are capable of achieving an atmospheric speed of 1,250 kilometers per hour (777 mph). The ship's weaponry includes four wingtip L-s9.7 laser cannons and projectile launchers capable of firing ST7 concussion missiles and mag-pulse warheads. The TIE interceptor is well-protected with shielding and it contains an ejection seat if all else fails. The ship is also managed by an experimental Torplex flight computer and is equipped with a class 2 hyperdrive. In his advanced ship, Vonreg is can easily annihilate most enemy starfighters. During the Battle at Castilon, Kazuda Xiono destroys the TIE Baron while defending the *Colossus*.

Hasty retreat
When facing Poe Dameron and Kazuda Xiono in a dogfight, Vonreg is outmatched and has to flee.

BLACK ONE

MANUFACTURER Incom-FreiTek **MODEL** T-70 X-wing **TYPE** Starfighter

Poe Dameron flies a customized T-70 X-wing for the Resistance, code-named *Black One*. Poe leads Black Squadron but is also in command of Red and Blue Squadrons. He flies *Black One* during many skirmishes and battles—including the mission to Ovanis, the Battle of Takodana, and the assault on Starkiller Base.

The orange-and-black livery covering Poe's X-wing differentiates it from the other Resistance X-wings and scatters First Order sensors, allowing Poe to run covert missions undetected. The astromech slot behind Poe's cockpit is specially fitted for BB-8, allowing for his unique shape and internal toolset.

Unlike the Rebel Alliance, which historically manufactures its T-65 X-wings in secret, the New Republic can build its X-wings openly. The Resistance lacks such resources, so relies on donations of surplus assets from powerful people and governments. The organization must ration supplies and conserve finances in order to maintain its humble fleet.

The T-70 X-wings are faster and carry better weapons than the older T-65s of the Rebel Alliance. T-70s owe their sleeker, slighter design to new technological breakthroughs in miniaturization of ship components. They are, however, a downgrade from the New Republic's cutting-edge T-85s.

Though these X-wings are more expensive to buy and maintain than the First Order's TIE fighters, they are more versatile and can perform in a range of combat situations. The wingtip laser cannons can fire in single, dual, and quad modes. Interchangeable magazines allow pilots to swap payloads of eight proton torpedoes with mag-pulse warheads, concussion missiles, and other ordnances.

During the evacuation of D'Qar, *Black One* is outfitted with an experimental accelerator pod that greatly increases its speed, allowing Poe to launch an assault on the First Order fleet preparing to attack the Resistance base. After fleeing the planet, *Black One* is in the *Raddus*' main hangar when it is destroyed during an attack by Kylo Ren's TIE fighter squadron. The resulting carnage is devastating to the Resistance's already depleted starfighter corps.

Poe to the rescue
When C-3PO's droid contact alerts the Resistance to BB-8's location, Poe races to retrieve him.

Local support
The *Fireball*'s first sponsor is local Gorg seller Bolza Grool.

FIREBALL
TYPE Racing starfighter

The *Fireball* is an aging starfighter that belongs to Jarek Yeager, who runs a repair shop on the *Colossus* refueling station. It's called *Fireball* because of its unfortunate tendency to erupt in flames during flight. Rumor has it that Jarek Yeager used to race it himself, and that he cobbled it together from an old rebel X-wing and a Z-75 Headhunter that he inherited from family members. It has impressive weaponry, and is armed with two wingtip Taim & Bak KX11C laser cannons and a pair of missile launchers which are able to fire miniaturized Krupx MG7-A proton torpedoes and concussion missiles. Yeager promises the ship to his employee Tam Ryvora if she can get it fixed up. Tam is not happy at all when the Resistance spy Kazuda Xiono arrives on the *Colossus* and Yeager lets Kaz fly it in a race against Torra Doza. Nonetheless, Team *Fireball* (which is named after the ship itself) work together to acquire parts and get the ship in working order. Most of the used parts come from Flix and Orka at the *Colossus* Office of Acquisitions. Kaz must do several favors for them in exchange for the parts he needs. Kaz nearly finishes the race, but pushes the ship too far and crashes into the sea toward the end of the event. Afterward, Team *Fireball* spends a lot of time and work repairing and improving the ship. Though Kaz and Tam grow to be friends, they experience occasional friction over the *Fireball*. Clumsy Kaz breaks the ship's newly repaired acceleration compensator at one point, so Tam makes him fix it. He accomplishes this with the help of some new Chelidae friends. Kaz also learns a valuable lesson when he tries to sneak away with the ship to meet Poe Dameron without telling Tam. It is not until he is far from the *Colossus* that he realizes she was in the middle of fixing the ship's stabilizers, and the ship is once again in danger of crashing.

During the First Order's occupation of the *Colossus*, Tam feels betrayed by her friends and joins the group, leaving them and the *Fireball*. When the station's residents rise up to free their home from the occupiers, Kaz flies the *Fireball* alongside the Aces and Yeager, and shoots down Major Vonreg. After joining Ace Squadron, Kaz pilots the ship while the *Colossus* is on the run from the First Order, and later flies it during the Battle of Exegol.

CARRION SPIKE
MANUFACTURER Sienar Fleet Systems
MODEL IPV-2C (modified) **TYPE** Stealth corvette

The personal ship of Grand Moff Wilhuff Tarkin, the *Carrion Spike* is used by the cunning leader for missions as well as transportation. It eventually falls into the possession of Agent Terex of the First Order Security Bureau. The dagger-shaped craft is formidable, with myriad weaponry and defenses. Terex installs several personal upgrades, including a trophy case displaying various bits of armor. He uses the ship in his voracious pursuit of Resistance hero Poe Dameron, which becomes his beloved ship's downfall. After Terex disobeys Captain Phasma's orders not to engage the Resistance, she dispatches a Star Destroyer to hunt him down, resulting in the fast destruction of the *Carrion Spike*.

ROMARY
MANUFACTURER Rendili StarDrive **MODEL** *Phelarion*-class **TYPE** Fuel tanker

The *Romary* is a fuel tanker under the stewardship of Captain Perrili, a Xexto smuggler and one of the Resistance's underworld contacts for resources. One scheduled drop turns to tragedy when the First Order arrives before Poe Dameron's Black Squadron, killing Perrili and her small crew, stealing the fuel, and sabotaging the *Romary*. When Dameron arrives and discovers what has happened, he decides to fly the freighter back to the thieves. He eventually makes a deal for the First Order's fuel ship, allowing the officers to evacuate before the *Romary* finally explodes.

BLUE ACE
MANUFACTURER Joben and Sons
MODEL Customized
TYPE Racing starfighter

Torra Doza, daughter of the administrator of *Colossus*, flies a luxurious custom racer. Torra spares no expense to create an aerodynamic, state-of-the-art ship to suit her unique flying style and aesthetic tastes. A lavish racer that would have fit right in among Coruscant's airspeeders during the golden age of the Old Republic, the *Blue Ace* is a stylish starfighter with more than a few tricks up its sleeves. It's much faster and sleeker than most of the old Resistance ships and has enough firepower to take on First Order TIE fighters. Torra flies the *Blue Ace* throughout her missions for the Resistance including the Battle of Exegol.

RED ACE
MANUFACTURERS Kuat Systems Engineering and Freya Fenris
MODEL Customized **TYPE** Racing starfighter

Taking inspiration from Kuat Systems' legendary line of A-wings, Freya Fenris comes up with a starfighter design incorporating added wings with laser cannons for additional stability and extra firepower. Her *Red Ace* is an achievement in precision design, technological advancement, and speed. Her ship is propelled by a pair of Novaldex K-99 Event Horizon sublight engines. Weaponry includes a pair of wingtip Zija Valkyr-2 laser cannons, and at the bow are a pair of Zija Asgar-4 lasers. In her *Red Ace*, Fenris often leads the other Aces from the front when they must defend the *Colossus* from attack.

GREEN ACE
MANUFACTURER Incom-FreiTek
MODEL G30 (modified) **TYPE** Racing starfighter

Bearing some similarities to Incom-FreiTek's classic X-wings, Hype Fazon's flashy *Green Ace* is covered in sponsor names and logos, many of them from businesses that have been around since the Clone Wars. The ship's S-foil wing positions can be adjusted for speed and maneuverability as well as for aiming the ship's two wingtip Taim & Bak KX10B laser cannons. The left wing carries an advertisement for "Outer Rim Supply Co.," while the right advertises "Craft Repair and Maintenance." The ship is also equipped with missile launchers.

YELLOW ACE
MANUFACTURER Ravager Mechanics **MODEL** Mark 71NB (customized "Changeling")
TYPE Racing starfighter

Colossus Ace pilot Bo Keevil's ship is customized for speed and agility. The *Yellow Ace*'s wings change configurations to facilitate his many dangerous flight acrobatics. This maneuverability comes at a price—the ship is exceptionally difficult to handle and the controls are highly sensitive. Bo installs extra countermeasures for likely crash-landings. The "Primeval" Keevil has flown his ship in countless significant races, including the Platform Classic and the All Aces Battle Royale on the *Colossus*, and the Cloud City Grand Prix.

VEHICLES

BLACK ACE
MANUFACTURER Sienar Fleet Systems and Griff Halloran **MODEL** Customized
TYPE Racing starfighter

Griff Halloran builds his own customized vehicle from an old TIE fighter, but tricks it out with many extras. It is barely recognizable as a former Imperial craft, apart from the signature TIE forward viewport. Some believe that the fighter resembles an old Eta-2 *Actis*-class interceptor more than a TIE. Not only is his ship sleek and fast, its Imperial style intimidates Griff's competitors. The *Black Ace* is heavily damaged during the Platform Classic race, but Halloran has it up and running in time to help with the giant rokkna attack on *Colossus* station. During the *Colossus'* battle against the First Order on Castilon, Griff's ship is hit, but Kaz saves both him and *Black Ace* from destruction. The vehicle goes on to face the First Order in many other entanglements.

THE GALLEON
MANUFACTURER Warbirds **MODEL** Customized **TYPE** Pirate ship

The *Galleon* is the flagship of Kragan Gorr's Warbirds—a gang of pirates operating on Castilon. The ship is built and modified by Kragan's gang over decades, gradually incorporating Imperial ship components and scavenged parts and cannons onto the original Ubrikkian barge hull. An AT-AT makes up the main cabin, and an upside-down AT-AT foot and leg forms the crow's nest. *Lambda*-class shuttle wings stabilize the vessel. The stern hosts a landing platform for large ships. When the *Colossus* needs help against the First Order, the Warbirds assist them, joining the battle in the *Galleon* and docking with the station before it escapes to hyperspace. However, it isn't a permanent berth, and the ship is cast out with most of its crew when Gorr attempts to mutiny against the *Colossus'* captain, Imanuel Doza.

WARBIRD SKIFF
MANUFACTURER Warbirds **MODEL** Customized **TYPE** Skiff

Kragan Gorr's Warbirds gang uses a number of heavily modified repulsorlift skiffs as mobile platforms on Castilon. The custom-built skiffs are ramshackle combinations of Imperial parts and other scavenged pieces. When the Warbird pirates sneak aboard the *Colossus* and kidnap Ace pilot Torra Doza, they initially escape on a pair of swoop bikes. Then they rendezvous with a pirate skiff. Pilot Kazuda Xiono tries to follow them from his ship, the *Fireball*, as the pirates fire at him from a cannon turret at the stern of the skiff. He is forced to fall back however, lest he hurt Torra aboard the tiny skiff.

KRAGAN GORR'S SHUTTLE
MANUFACTURER Warbirds **MODEL** Customized **TYPE** Shuttle-fighter

The Warbird leader Kragan Gorr's personal shuttle is a unique vessel that clearly derives some of its parts from scavenged Imperial *Lambda*-class shuttles. The ship is covered in lasers and ion cannons, which are taxing on the ship's power reserve. Though the vehicle is fast and maneuverable in-atmosphere, the shields are minimal and the hyperdrive is unreliable. Still, the shuttle has ample cargo space for stolen loot—a quality necessary for any true pirate ship. Synara San flies Gorr's shuttle in the Battle of Barabesh against the First Order Star Destroyer *Thunderer*.

WARBIRD STARFIGHTER
MANUFACTURER Warbirds **MODEL** Customized **TYPE** Starfighter

The Warbirds' starfighters are a hodgepodge of several different ships—including parts from A-wings, Eta-2 *Actis*-class interceptors, and Imperial TIE interceptors. Although they look like they could fall apart or explode at any moment, these ships are actually highly maneuverable, and well armed with precision targeting systems. Kragan Gorr's pirate gang uses the ships to raid the *Colossus* station and other vulnerable targets on Castilon. While the pirates' piloting skills may not be as celebrated as the Aces, they are experts at operating their deadly and speedy ships.

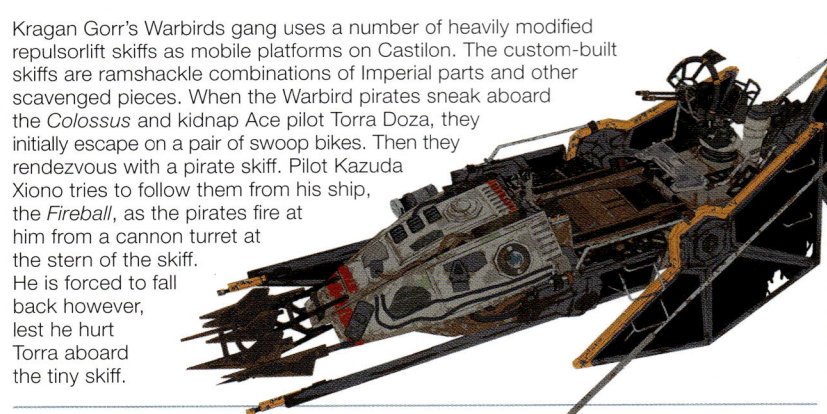

GALAXY'S GLORY
TYPE Racing starfighter

Famous across the galaxy, Marcus Speedstar is a renowned racing pilot who arrogantly names his custom racer *Galaxy's Glory*. Speedstar's ship is designed to win races rather than fight in big space battles. His racer has a pair of laser cannons, but they are more for aesthetics than heavy combat. The ship has a distinctive black, purple, and silver color scheme that matches both Speedstar's flight suit and his droid copilot R4-D12.

RUCKLIN'S RACER
TYPE Racing starfighter

Racing fanatic Jace Rucklin spends his life savings and countless hours working on his ship in an effort to make it as light and fast as possible. He removes everything from the ship that he considers to be unnecessary weight, including the ejection seat parachute. Rucklin steals hyperfuel from Jarek Yeager's garage to get an edge on his upcoming race, but as a result, he unknowingly turns his ship into a flying bomb. Rucklin is nearly killed, but Kazuda Xiono saves him just before the ship explodes. Nonetheless, the ungrateful wretch blames everything on Kaz.

JAREK YEAGER'S RACER
TYPE Racing starfighter

Jarek Yeager's personal starfighter is a fast and powerful vehicle, and during his career he competes in and wins many races in it. When he first arrives on the *Colossus*, he continues to race in the ship, but soon gives up and opens a garage instead. His starfighter remains grounded for years until his brother, Marcus Speedstar, arrives. Yeager agrees to race against Speedstar in the Platform Classic. At first, Jarek is intent on victory, but he realizes that his brother must win to save a friend's life, so lets Marcus beat him. Yeager flies in the ship during the *Colossus'* fight with the First Order, where Kazuda Xiono saves him by shooting down Major Vonreg, allowing both Kaz and Jarek to board *Colossus* before it jumps to hyperspace. Yeager soon becomes head of Ace Squadron, and sees more time in the cockpit of his racer. Kaz is even allowed to pilot the ship during the Battle of Aeos Prime. Alongside Kaz, Yeager is one of the hundreds of pilots that travels to Exegol, answering Lando Calrissian's call to assist the Resistance.

DARIUS G-CLASS FREIGHTER

MANUFACTURER Darius **MODEL** G-Class **TYPE** Freighter

Common across the galaxy, Darius G-class freighters are a spacious line of cargo ships with chin-mounted loading ramps. They are often equipped with eighteen single-occupant escape pods which launch from the ventral surface of the hull. The First Order's Major Elrik Vonreg delivers a fuel shipment to Colossus station aboard one such freighter. Kazuda Xiono and Poe Dameron later rescue pirate Synara San aboard a derelict Darius freighter overrun by Kowakian monkey-lizards. Another Darius freighter is owned by a Keteerian named Teroj Kee, who claims to work for the Mining Guild but is actually a secret agent for the First Order. After Teroj steals a phase connector from the Colossus Department of Acquisitions, Kazuda sabotages his ship, forcing Teroj and his crew to abandon it. Meanwhile, the stowaway Kazuda (with the pet gorg Bitey) returns to the Colossus in an escape pod.

FIRST ORDER TIE FIGHTER

MANUFACTURER Sienar-Jaemus Fleet Systems
MODEL TIE/fo space superiority fighter
TYPE Starfighter

While the Empire considered its pilots expendable, the First Order values its pilots. First Order TIE fighters may resemble their Imperial predecessors, but its engineers have made many technological advances on the original design. These TIE fighters have more robust weaponry, more efficient solar energy collector arrays in their wing panels, and the crucial addition of shield generators. Standard First Order TIEs still lack hyperdrives however, limiting them to short-range missions. The TIE is the First Order's standard starfighter, and squadrons are stationed aboard all Star Destroyers in addition to Starkiller Base.

FIRST ORDER SF TIE FIGHTER

MANUFACTURER Sienar-Jaemus Fleet Systems **MODEL** TIE/sf space superiority fighter **TYPE** Starfighter

Unlike standard TIEs, the Special Forces model has the capacity for an additional crew member—a gunner. Designed for long-range missions, it is equipped with a hyperdrive. Thanks to banks of high-yield deuterium cells, each fighter has additional power devoted to engines, shields, and weapons systems. The TIE/sf is equipped with forward-facing laser cannons, as well as 360-degree coverage via a heavy weapon turret and warhead launcher. The rear-facing gunner is best suited to control the turret, though the pilot can manage if required. The extra systems mean that the ship has a tendency to overheat.

KYLO REN'S SHUTTLE

MANUFACTURER Sienar-Jaemus Army Systems
MODEL Upsilon-class shuttle
TYPE Transport

Sensors
Upper wings contain hyperwave scanners and subspace communications.

Designed to intimidate
The threatening look of the Upsilon-class ship contrasts with the unassuming Lambda and Sentinel shuttles used by Imperial dignitaries.

Protection
Lower wings are protected by durasteel armor and deflector shields.

Firepower
Twin laser cannons easily cut through Resistance X-wings.

Kylo Ren commands First Order military forces from aboard the Finalizer, but he requires smaller craft to shuttle down to planet surfaces. Like other high-level First Order officers and dignitaries, Kylo Ren terrorizes approaching worlds from an elite Upsilon-class shuttle. The ship's features are developed in part thanks to classified Imperial research and continued in top secret labs by the First Order within the Unknown Regions of the galaxy.

Supreme leader
After killing Snoke, Kylo Ren becomes the First Order's supreme leader. Flying above the battleground in his shuttle, Kylo personally oversees the attack on the Resistance base on Crait.

During flight, the craft's batlike wings tilt outward and nearly double in length, exposing long-range sensor arrays in the upper extensions. When landing, the 37.2-meter (122.04-ft) wings retract and the sensitive technology is protected by the wing bases' armor. Shield generators located also protect the passenger cabin and its very important occupants.

While it is normally accompanied by a TIE fighter escort, each shuttle possesses two twin heavy laser cannons (a pair on each wing). A countermeasures system at each wingtip is capable of deflecting incoming projectiles with ghost signals that confuse warhead sensors. The upper wings carry long-range scanners to detect approaching ships, while the lower wings contain jammers to wipe out enemy communications. Upsilon-class shuttles are capable of sweeping star systems for errant communications and pinpointing Resistance spies' transmissions. Kylo Ren's command shuttle can easily isolate a lone ship and eliminate it before it even detects the shuttle's imminent approach—let alone gets out a distress call.

Kylo's shuttle accommodates five crew with space for 10 additional passengers. A pilot and copilot remain ready on board at all times, awaiting Kylo's return. Upon landing, Kylo descends a ramp underneath the main cabin as stormtroopers stand guard to bar any unauthorized access to the vessel and defend it from any enemy assault.

VEHICLES

FINALIZER

MANUFACTURER Kuat-Entralla Engineering
MODEL *Resurgent*-class
TYPE Star Destroyer

The *Finalizer* is a flagship of the First Order's fleet and the command seat of both Kylo Ren and General Armitage Hux. The *Resurgent*-class Star Destroyers are a symbol of the First Order's power and are well staffed. The *Finalizer* maintains an entire legion of more than 8,000 stormtroopers, 55,000 enlisted crew, 19,000 officers, and pilots of all levels. The stormtroopers aboard have been trained since birth to be loyal to Snoke and the First Order. They consider the *Finalizer* their only true home.

As a military carrier, the *Finalizer* hosts two wings of TIE fighters and more than a hundred assault vehicles, including walkers. A refined design means that starfighters are more easily launched from the dorsal flight decks and side hangars than from Imperial Star Destroyers. Approaching enemy ships find themselves surrounded by squadrons of TIE fighters before they've even detected that the starfighters have left the *Finalizer*'s bays. The command bridge is much more efficiently defended than those on the older Imperial warships as it is no longer set so far apart from the rest of the vessel, and its deflector shield generators are not the large, obvious, and relatively undefended targets they once were.

As a mobile weapons platform, the *Finalizer* is fitted with more than 3,000 turbolasers and ion cannons, as well as tractor beams and projectile launchers situated in multiple locations. These provide more than adequate munitions for ship-to-ship combat and planetary bombardment. Smaller defensive missile launchers and laser turrets are located at key areas of strategic importance.

The *Finalizer*'s weapons capabilities and size violate the treaties between the First Order and the New Republic. For a time, *Resurgent*-class Star Destroyer development is kept secret by the First Order, yet General Leia Organa is well aware of the ships' existence. The Resistance does its best to track sightings and the movements of these ships. Nonetheless, reports made to senators in the New Republic have largely fallen on deaf ears. Branding Leia as a warmonger, few in the Senate heed her warnings until it is much too late.

Kylo Ren watches the destructive blast generated by Starkiller Base that destroys Hosnian Prime from the bridge of the *Finalizer*. The Star Destroyer later razes the planet Tah'Nuhna after the crew traces the Resistance from that location. Kylo Ren transfers his command from the capital ship to the *Steadfast* once it sustains significant damage from the Resistance fleet on Batuu.

FIRST ORDER SNOW SPEEDER

MANUFACTURER Aratech-Loratus Corp.
MODEL Light Infantry Utility Vehicle (LIUV) **TYPE** Speeder

The First Order relies on repulsorlift snow speeders as its primary mode of ground transportation on Starkiller Base. The craft has capacity for two seated occupants, but an additional passenger can crouch in the front. A FWMB-10 repeating blaster turret is mounted on the bow, with wide firing arcs to spray enemy fortifications with horizontal blaster fire or aim for the skies above to take out incoming fighters. The blaster can be easily disassembled to make room for large cargo loads at the front of the speeder. Compared to civilian models, the First Order snow speeder has a bigger power source and upgraded power converters. The driver and gunner are both exposed to the elements and rely on heated seats to stay warm. Without any protective barriers, they must also take care at high speeds not to be dislodged should the vehicle hit a snow bank.

ERAVANA

MANUFACTURER Corellian Engineering Corp.
MODEL *Baleen*-class
TYPE Freighter

After Han Solo and Chewbacca lose their beloved *Millennium Falcon*, they are forced to find a new ship. The legendary pair end up with the *Eravana*—a giant, sluggish, and unwieldy vessel that is quite a contrast to the small, fast, and agile *Falcon*. Bulk freighters like the *Eravana* are often manufactured in space. They rarely enter planetary atmospheres, and instead they tend to dock at space stations and orbital platforms to load and unload cargo. Few of these expensive ships are owned by private individuals, and most belong to guilds, corporations, or governments. The *Eravana* possesses a labyrinth of shipping containers that are attached externally between the docking bay and the engines. This large docking bay is used for more delicate cargo, requiring special attention. At 426 meters (1,398 ft) long, this *Baleen*-class ship can carry a large amount of cargo. Indeed, Han and Chewie typically carry diverse loads—from kiirium ingots to Aldo Spachian comet dust—bound for different buyers. When Rey and Finn encounter the *Eravana*, the ship's current cargo includes a shipment of three dangerous rathtars for King Prana. The ship's size makes it difficult for Han and Chewie to monitor, so they are not immediately aware that a couple of gangs have boarded the ship and that Rey has accidentally released the rathtars.

STORMTROOPER TRANSPORT

MANUFACTURER Sienar-Jaemus Army Systems
MODEL Atmospheric Assault Lander (AAL) **TYPE** Troop transport

The stormtrooper transport is a mainstay of the First Order's arsenal. Each transport can transfer two squads of stormtroopers quickly and directly into battle from orbiting command ships. When landing, each ship uses searchlights to dazzle the enemy and then a dorsal gunner covers the soldiers with a 240-degree range of fire. An AAL may leave its soldiers on the ground for the operation, return with reinforcements, or wait back at its base until the battle is over and return to pick up surviving troops later. Shields and heavy armor protect the AAL from danger as it moves in and out of combat. The isolated cockpit is a key weakness. It is conceivable that a well-targeted weapon could take out the pilot mid-flight. While the lander possesses a secondary set of controls, these are far less precise than the primary system.

QUADJUMPER

MANUFACTURER Subpro
MODEL Quadrijet transfer spacetug **TYPE** Hauler

A quadjumper pilot uses magnetic clamps to attach the ship to heavy cargo containers, then uses its four powerful and oversize thrusters to move the loads across shipping yards. Around the pilot's seat are 180-degree viewports in all directions, allowing the pilot to keep track of the other spacetugs, loader droids, and personnel working alongside them. While designed for planetary cargo transport, the craft can also operate in space. The vessel's versatility makes it desirable to smugglers, prospectors, and pirates. Cassian Andor and Ruescott Melshi convince anglers on Narkina 5 to let them use their quadjumper after the two escape an Imperial prison. Years later, Rey rushes toward a quadjumper on Jakku until a pursuing TIE fighter blows it up.

REY'S SPEEDER

MANUFACTURER None **MODEL** Customized
TYPE Repulsor bike

Rey's speeder is a custom repulsorlift vehicle made from a range of parts. Part speeder, part swoop, it does not quite fit into either category—technically it is something in between. Rey is incredibly proud of her treasured vehicle that is uniquely suited to her abilities. Her Jedi-like piloting skills and reflexes make it easy for Rey to drive her speeder at near podracing speeds when other drivers would surely crash into the dunes.

The speeder's propulsion comes from twin turbojet engines from a wrecked cargo-hauler, customized with racing-swoop afterburners and repulsorlifts from crashed X-wing starfighters for lift. A primary heat exchanger keeps the powerful engines from overheating, and a strategically-positioned heat sink keeps Rey from burning herself on the rear afterburner assembly. Vertical stabilizers help keep the speeder upright, and a tractor web holds Rey to the seat. With these modifications, Rey can attain the elevations of a typical airspeeder—and when nobody is looking, she takes flight.

While her speeder can carry large loads, Rey knows that this will attract unwanted attention. She tends to carry a small load of salvaged scrap that hangs on each of the speeder's sides in nets and make more frequent trips at higher speeds on her way to Niima Outpost.

Rey's speeder is not equipped with any weapons, but has other defenses. If someone tries to steal her salvage or speeder, Rey can electrify the chassis to incapacitate the prospective thief, and the engine will not start without her fingerprint. The speeder simply is not worth the trouble for most thugs to tamper with.

RESISTANCE TRANSPORTER

MANUFACTURER Slayn & Korpil
MODEL Customized Resistance ship **TYPE** Transport

Resistance transporters are a hodgepodge of components assembled from a variety of vessels—most notably the B-wing Mark II, but also from Republic-era *Montura*-class shuttles. The transporters are difficult to maneuver and their cockpits have poor visibility, so they are normally accompanied by X-wing escorts for defense. If the transporter is caught without an escort, it can utilize a full array of weapons adapted from B-wing fighters. Two seating compartments in the middle of the ship provide space for up to 20 passengers, droids, and equipment. The transporters are subject to frequent malfunctions due to the nature of their custom construction with used parts. Astromechs are usually stationed on board to make repairs on the fly and restore backups of ship computer systems.

B/SF-17 HEAVY BOMBER

MANUFACTURER Slayn & Korpil
MODEL MG-100 Starfortress SF-17
TYPE Bomber

The Resistance's potent heavy bombers require significant hands-on management from their crew, which includes one pilot, two gunners, one flight engineer, and one bombardier. The ships are armed with three Merr-Sonn Munitions EM-1919 paired repeating laser cannons and six medium laser cannons, but the truly important payload is composed of a modular bombing magazine containing up to a total of 1,048 proton bombs. During the evacuation of D'Qar, the Resistance sends its entire fleet of heavy bombers to attack the First Order's Dreadnought *Fulminatrix*. Though Paige Tico's bomber successfully destroys its target, all of the Resistance's bombers are lost in the effort.

FULMINATRIX

MANUFACTURER Kuat-Entralla Engineering **MODEL** *Mandator IV*-class
TYPE Siege Dreadnought

When Iden Versio steals Imperial data about Project: Resurrection, she also acquires the blueprints for the First Order's *Mandator IV*-class Siege Dreadnought. The warship is armed with two orbital autocannons, 26 dorsal point-defense turrets, a myriad of TIE fighters, and six tractor beams. Iden Versio's information is passed on to Captain Poe Dameron, who uses it to destroy the Dreadnought *Fulminatrix*, as it bombards the Resistance base on D'Qar. The destruction of the *Fulminatrix* is a huge blow to the First Order, but also comes at a cost to the Resistance. Shortly after its destruction, some crew members from the *Colossus* board the remains of the *Fulminatrix* searching for coaxium fuel.

RZ-2 A-WING

MANUFACTURER Kuat Systems Engineering
MODEL RZ-2 A-wing
TYPE Starfighter

Capitalizing on the popularity of the original A-wing starfighter flown by the Rebel Alliance during the Galactic Civil War, Kuat Systems creates a new version soon after the war's end. The RZ-2 A-wing incorporates the best upgrades made by rebel cells in the field while also elongating the bow of the ship for increased speed. These second-generation A-wings are armed with two Zija GO-4 laser cannons and two concussion missile launchers. A number of A-wings accompany the Resistance fleet during the evacuation of D'Qar, including one piloted by Blue Leader Tallissan Lintra. When Kylo Ren attacks the Resistance flagship, Tallissan is killed and her A-wing is destroyed.

VEHICLES

U-55 ORBITAL LOADLIFTER

MANUFACTURER Sienar Fleet Systems **MODEL** U-55 **TYPE** Personnel transport

The U-55 is a basic shuttle craft found throughout the galaxy. The Resistance versions lack weapons or hyperdrives but are equipped with simple cloaking systems devised by technician Rose Tico. They are capable of transporting an average of 60 passengers and are normally used to transport dignitaries and Resistance members to and from secret meetings. When the Resistance is forced to leave the *Raddus*, its personnel escape aboard 30 U-55 "lifeboats" docked inside the flagship. Sadly, they are betrayed, and 24 U-55s are destroyed by the First Order before they can reach Crait.

NINKA

MANUFACTURER Corellian Engineering Corp. **MODEL** Free *Virgillia*-class Bunkerbuster **TYPE** Corvette

The *Ninka* is a heavily armed blockade-runner (officially known as a "Bunkerbuster"), designed to break through planetary sieges and other obstacles. Its weapons include two heavy turbolaser turrets, four point-defense laser cannon turrets, three heavy plasma bombs, and eight ordnance pods. The *Ninka* is initially under the command of Vice Admiral Amylin Holdo and is one of the four large Resistance ships to escape during the evacuation of D'Qar. It is destroyed by the First Order flagship *Supremacy* soon after.

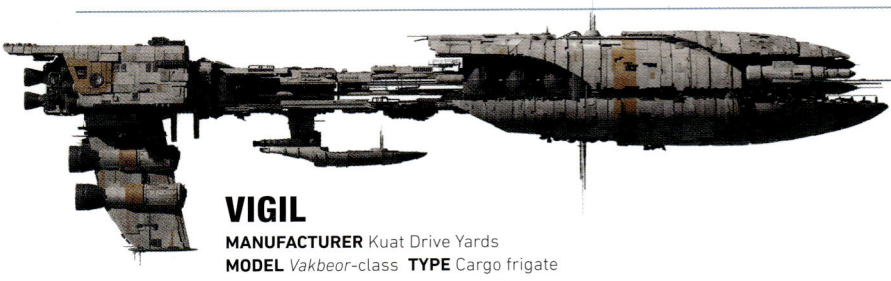

VIGIL

MANUFACTURER Kuat Drive Yards **MODEL** *Vakbeor*-class **TYPE** Cargo frigate

The *Vigil* is captured by the Resistance from pirates during the Battle at the Chasidron Shoals. It has only light weapons systems, with four laser cannons and two tractor beam projectors, and it is supported by a crew of twenty-six. The *Vigil* falls under the command of Resistance Vice Admiral Jotis, and is one of four large ships that evacuate from D'Qar following the destruction of Starkiller Base. It is carrying vital Resistance supplies but is soon destroyed by the *Supremacy*.

LIBERTINE

MANUFACTURER Guild d'Lanseaux **MODEL** Custom **TYPE** Star Yacht

The *Libertine* is a star yacht stolen by the droid BB-8 and slicer DJ, who use it to rescue Resistance fighters Finn and Rose. They then fly from Canto Bight to the First Order Flagship *Supremacy*. The *Libertine* is formerly owned by Sienar-Jaemus Corporation manager, Korfé Bennux-Ai, a weapons dealer who sells his products to all sides in the fight between the First Order, and the New Republic and Resistance. The luxury craft is used by Bennux-Ai to host guests and strike business deals.

RADDUS

MANUFACTURER Mon Calamari Shipyards and Corellian Engineering Corp. **MODEL** MC85 **TYPE** Star Cruiser

The *Raddus* is the flagship of the Resistance and the mobile command center of General Leia Organa. Originally named the *Dawn of Tranquility*, it was decommissioned by the New Republic and then acquired by the Resistance. Admiral Ackbar successfully petitioned to have the ship renamed after the valiant Admiral Raddus, who gave his life at the Battle of Scarif to secure the Death Star plans.

The immense ship measures 3,438 meters (11,280 ft) in length, with a width of 707 meters (2,319 ft) and a height of 462 meters (1,515 ft). Its durasteel hull is heavily armored and it is protected by experimental deflector shields. The *Raddus* is a speedy ship for its size, with 11 sublight ion drives and a Class 1 hyperdrive. It is also powerfully armed, with 18 heavy turbolasers, 18 heavy ion cannons, 12 point-defense laser cannons and six proton torpedo launchers.

Following the destruction of the First Order's Starkiller Base, the Resistance is forced to evacuate their base on D'Qar. Four capital ships escape and successfully jump to hyperspace. However the First Order continues to track the Resistance and emerges with them in realspace. The other three capital ships are soon destroyed, leaving only the *Raddus*. All of the senior Resistance leaders are killed in an attack by Kylo Ren—barring Leia, who is rendered comatose—leaving Vice Admiral Holdo in command.

Holdo devises a plan to evacuate the surviving Resistance to the nearby planet Crait, fleeing aboard a small fleet of U-55 lifeboats. She elects to remain behind to pilot the *Raddus* alone, as a distraction to the First Order. Unbeknownst to Holdo, the traitor DJ informs the First Order of her plans, and they begin destroying the Resistance lifeboats. In an effort to save the remaining ships, Holdo sacrifices herself. She turns the *Raddus* toward the First Order's pursuing flagship *Supremacy* and jumps to hyperspace. The resulting collision tears the *Supremacy* in half, but also destroys the *Raddus*.

Destruction
Vice Admiral Holdo's final attack with the *Raddus* devastates the First Order fleet.

TIE SILENCER

MANUFACTURER Sienar-Jaemus Fleet Systems **MODEL** TIE/vn space superiority fighter **TYPE** Starfighters

The TIE silencer is Kylo Ren's personal starfighter. It is exceptionally agile, making it a difficult craft to fly for even the most skilled pilots, however Kylo's connection to the Force makes him a natural pilot. The TIE silencer is 10.7 meters (35 ft) longer than a standard First Order TIE fighter. It is potently armed, with SJFS heavy laser cannons and missile launchers equipped with Arakyd ST7 concussion missiles, mag-pulse warheads, and proton torpedoes. This makes it ideally suited for attacking capital ships—something Kylo demonstrates when his attack on the *Raodus* destroys the ship's main hanger and wipes out the entire Resistance starfighter corps.

SKI SPEEDER
MANUFACTURER Roche Machines
MODEL V-4X-D ski speeder **TYPE** Airspeeder

Ski speeders are distantly related to B-wing starfighters, as both ship types are inspired by Verpine designs. The V-4 series is originally created for asteroid slalom racing, but after the sport loses popularity, the design becomes a favorite craft of explorers. The Rebel Alliance brings a small contingent of ski speeders to Crait but abandons them there. When the Resistance flees to Crait decades later, it uses the decrepit old speeders to face the First Order. Led by Poe Dameron, they charge at the enemy's siege cannon, but are forced to turn back by the overwhelming firepower of the enemy walkers.

AT-M6
MANUFACTURER Kuat-Entralla Drive Yards
MODEL All Terrain MegaCaliber Six
TYPE Walker

The AT-M6 is the First Order's most powerful combat walker. A contingent of them is deployed to the surface of Crait to pursue the Resistance remnant. The AT-M6s are each armed with two heavy fire-linked dual laser cannons, two medium anti-ship laser cannons, and one MegaCaliber Six turbolaser cannon—the source of the vehicle's name—which is mounted on its back. The cannon is powerful enough to penetrate shields rated to resist orbital bombardment. The front legs are modified to support the immense additional weight of the cannon, as well as stabilize the walker to withstand the cannon's considerable recoil.

SUPREMACY
MANUFACTURER Kuat-Entralla Engineering **MODEL** *Mega*-class
TYPE Star Dreadnought

The *Supremacy* is the flagship of the First Order and effectively its capital, serving as the mobile headquarters of Supreme Leader Snoke. The vast ship is more than 60 km (37 mi) wide, with a crew of 2,225,000 First Order personnel. The majority of the crew are adolescents still in training to become officers and stormtroopers. The *Supremacy* is protected by heavy turbolasers and ion cannons, anti-ship missile batteries, and multiple tractor beam projectors. The ship is also a gigantic weapons factory, able to produce AT-M6s, AT-ATs, AT-STs, and TIE fighters. Two *Resurgent*-class Star Destroyers can be docked internally and six more externally.

After the *Supremacy* joins the vessels commanded by General Hux, Snoke directs the attack on the Resistance fleet. Though the Resistance escapes, a tracker aboard the *Supremacy* traces them as they flee through hyperspace. Emerging back into realspace in front of the Resistance and commencing its attack, the *Supremacy* quickly destroys three of the four Resistance capital ships.

A short while later, Rey arrives aboard the ship, and is brought before Snoke. Kylo Ren suddenly turns on and kills his master, and both Rey and Kylo team up to defeat Snoke's Praetorian Guard—before Rey escapes alone. At the same time, Finn, Rose, and DJ board the ship.

Finn and Rose believe DJ is helping them deactivate the First Order's hyperspace tracker, however he betrays them for a large sum of money. DJ informs the First Order of the Resistance's plans to flee to nearby Crait, and the First Order begin shooting down the defenseless Resistance U-55s.

With no other options left, Resistance Vice Admiral Holdo turns the Resistance flagship *Raddus* on the *Supremacy* and splits it apart in a cataclysmic collision. The Resistance remnant escapes to Crait, but are followed by Kylo Ren and the First Order, who depart the *Supremacy*'s wreckage and continue their pursuit of the Resistance to the planet's surface below.

War machine
Huge hangars serve as assembly areas for legions of stormtroopers, as ground vehicles are loaded onto dropships in readiness for a planetary invasion.

KYLO REN'S TIE FIGHTER
MANUFACTURER Sienar-Jaemus Fleet Systems
MODEL TIE/wi modified interceptor
TYPE Starfighter

Supreme Leader Kylo Ren speeds into battle aboard a TIE whisper modified to his exacting specifications, boasting increased range, speed, and firepower than the standard model. The whisper carries sensor-confusing technology that allows Ren to avoid enemy detection. When Kylo arrives on Pasaana to confront Rey, she slices off one of the starfighter's wings. Kylo later takes a similar ship to Kef Bir, and Rey takes this TIE to Ahch-To, where she sets it on fire.

TIE DAGGER
MANUFACTURER Sienar-Jaemus Fleet Systems
MODEL TIE/dg
TYPE Starfighter

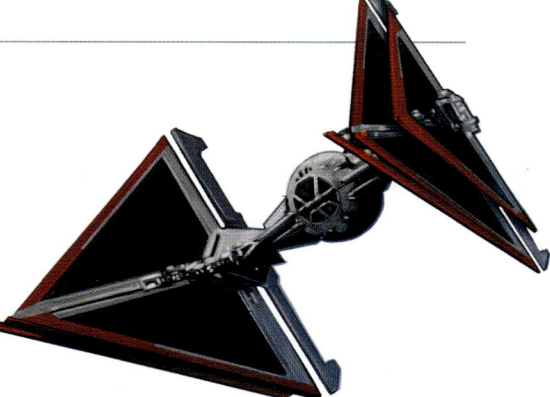

Forged in secret by sinister forces, this new generation of TIE fighter swoops into action, with triangular wings that give the sleek Sith vessel a menacing profile. The TIE dagger sees action during the Battle of Exegol, where it engages the Resistance forces.

BTA-NR2 Y-WING STARFIGHTER
MANUFACTURER Koensayr
MODEL BTA-NR2
TYPE Starfighter

The BTA-NR2 is the latest version of a venerable starfighter design dating all the way back to the Clone Wars. Its unusually large ordnance bay and powerful forward-firing laser cannons make it a formidable attack ship, but as with all Y-wing variants, that hitting power comes at the price of reduced speed and agility. Zorii Bliss flies a BTA-NR2 Y-wing starfighter in the Battle of Exegol.

FIRST ORDER LIGHT CRUISER

MANUFACTURER Kuat-Entralla Engineering **MODEL** First Order light cruiser
TYPE Shuttle, troop transport

Multifaceted and powerful, the First Order light cruiser can dock onto a *Resurgent*-class Star Destroyer and carry up to 24 TIE fighters along with a *Xi*-class shuttle. Poe Dameron's Black Squadron makes use of a design flaw in the ship to cripple one in battle.

DROID RACER

TYPE Racer

As fast as the best racing ships, droid racers are a good bet on any track. Vranki the Hutt, proprietor of Vranki's Hotel and Casino, uses droid racers in the competitions at his own resort. On Vranki's orders, droid racers don't necessarily follow the rules. They fire live weapons at opponents and use their four movable wings to grab competitors, slowing them down or damaging their craft. Droid racers prove near unbeatable to the *Colossus* Aces, until Neeku Vozo discovers a weakness: the course and the droids share programming with a casino holo game. By hacking in, Neeku is able to shut down the unfair obstacles and give Kazuda Xiono a chance to win.

TITAN

MANUFACTURER Kuat Drive Yards
MODEL *Trantor*-class
TYPE Supertanker fuel depot

A huge refueling station similar in design to the *Colossus*, the *Titan* is important to the First Order's fleet operations. Unlike the *Colossus*, however, the *Titan* is new and in excellent condition. Because of this, it becomes a target. Kazuda Xiono, Neeku Vozo, and astromech CB-23 sneak onto the tanker to steal a device for the ailing *Colossus*. The trans binary deflector, located in the engineering room, prevents deadly cosmic radiation from leaking out. With the help of old friend and First Order cadet Tam Ryvora, the team from the *Colossus* escapes, using cranes in the *Titan*'s hangar to avoid detection.

X-WING DRONE

MANUFACTURER First Order Department of Military Research **MODEL** *Microraptor*-class
TYPE Target drone

Built for First Order training exercises, X-wing drones are pared down, cockpit-less replicas of the famous Rebel Alliance and Resistance fighters. This tech is used for both target practice and combat development, as the drones fire live blasts capable of destroying trainees' craft. They feature interesting design elements, including four additional smaller wings reminiscent of the Clone Wars–era ARC-170. Lieutenant Galek of the First Order uses X-wings to test her cadets, awarding the rank of squad leader to the pilot who eliminates the most—and survives.

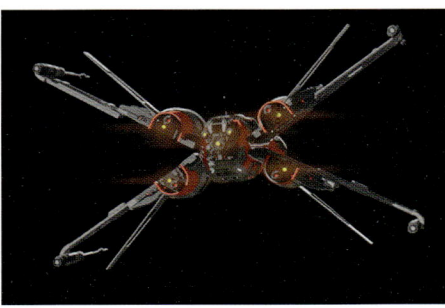

GUAVIAN DEATH GANG SHIP

MANUFACTURER Incom-FreiTek **MODEL** *Avandor*-class **TYPE** Fighter/transport

The Guavian Death Gang ship is a sleek, powerful fighter. Sporting a threatening red-and-black color scheme, the craft matches Guavian armor, creating a uniform that extends from members to vehicle. The Guavian Death Gang uses its ships for both scouting and patrol, monitoring its occupied space for any unwelcome visitors. One such instance occurs when the *Colossus* unknowingly enters Guavian territory. The gang demands a ransom for passage and later hides its ships inside an asteroid field, waiting to attack the refueling station's Aces.

DALKOR DAGGER

MANUFACTURER Sabaoth Industries
MODEL *Novahawk*-class
TYPE Assault transport

The ship of choice for fearsome bounty hunter Ax Tagrin, the *Dalkor Dagger* is heavily armored and outfitted with an impressive array of weaponry. It also has storage compartments that can hold captives. When Tagrin traps several members of the *Colossus* and the Resistance, including Kazuda Xiono, he prepares to transport them to the First Order in the *Dalkor Dagger*. However, Xiono's droid, CB-23, overrides the craft's onboard computer system, shorting an engine and bringing the *Dalkor Dagger* crashing down onto the rocky Varkana landscape.

HALCYON

MANUFACTURER Corellian Engineering Corporation
MODEL MPO-1400 **TYPE** *Purrgil*-class star cruiser

Chandrila Star Line operates the luxurious *Halcyon*. The jewel of their company, the sprawling star cruiser has unparalleled amenities for its passengers. Shug Drabor oversees its construction on Corellia at the Santhe Shipyards in the days of the High Republic.

Designed for maximum comfort and style, the *Halcyon* ferries passengers around the galaxy in the spirit of exploration. Its maiden voyage goes to the Outer Rim planet of Batuu. Although the *Halcyon* is built for luxury travel, the star cruiser has twelve turbolasers and shields for protection because it travels in a turbulent galaxy.

During more than 200 years of service, various groups use the vessel, leaving behind remnants that contribute to the *Halcyon*'s colorful legacy. Nihil pirates attack, the Hutt clan purchases the star cruiser to use as a mobile casino, and the Empire seizes the ship as a retreat for Imperial officers. The *Halcyon*'s guest log notes distinguished visitors over the decades, such as Jedi Knight Anakin Skywalker and Rebellion heroes Han Solo and Leia Organa. Today, having been restored to its early glory, it takes passengers on chartered voyages around the galaxy.

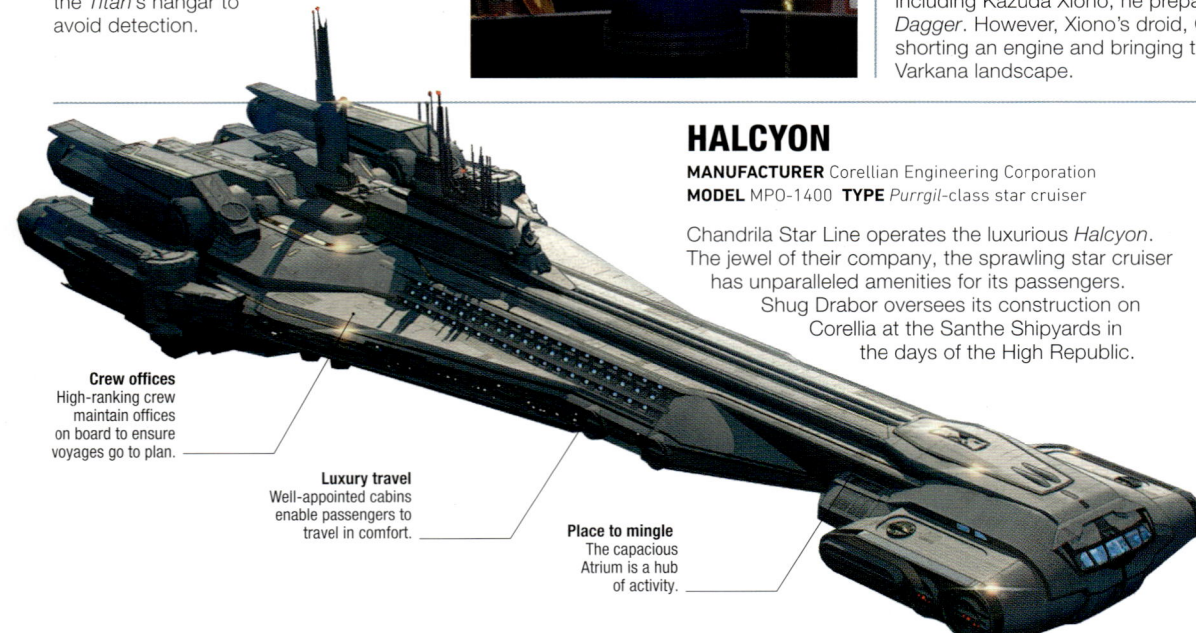

Crew offices High-ranking crew maintain offices on board to ensure voyages go to plan.

Luxury travel Well-appointed cabins enable passengers to travel in comfort.

Place to mingle The capacious Atrium is a hub of activity.

MESON MARTINET
MANUFACTURER Corellian Engineering Corporation
MODEL Modified CSS-1 Corellian Star Shuttle **TYPE** Pirate ship

The *Meson Martinet* belongs to the arms dealer and pirate Sidon Ithano. A modified CSS-1 Corellian Star Shuttle, the ship is heavily fortified and weaponized. Sidon flies it to a meeting with Kragan Gorr of the Warbird gang to sell some hard-to-find weaponry: super battle droids left over from the Clone Wars. The ship is later seen outside Maz Kanata's castle on Takodana, where its captain recruits defected stormtrooper Finn to his crew—though the former soldier quickly takes his leave, returning to his Resistance friends.

TIE ECHELON
MANUFACTURER Sienar-Jaemus Fleet Systems **MODEL** Twin Ion Engine Transport
TYPE Cargo and troop transport

The First Order uses the TIE Echelon, part of the ever-evolving TIE series, for transporting small loads of cargo and up to 12 crew members. While its primary purpose is transportation, the TIE Echelon includes a number of elements that make it battle-ready: advanced sensors, twin clusters of three ion engines on each side, heavy laser cannons, a cockpit turret, and a shield generator. The First Order uses a TIE Echelon to bring stormtroopers of the 709th legion, and later Kylo Ren, to Batuu to search for Rey and the Resistance base.

INTERSYSTEM TRANSPORT SHIP
MANUFACTURER Corellian Engineering Corporation **TYPE** Transport

The Resistance relies on the hyperdrive-equipped Intersystem Transport Ship (I-TS) to move troops between bases. With a spacious interior for hauling cargo and crew, the I-TS also has forward and rear guns for protection. Nien Nunb pilots one such transport, designation Cargo vessel TR-141, under the command of Lieutenant Bek. It transfers Resistance recruits from Batuu to a secret base on Pacara. The First Order captures the I-TS above Batuu, but Nunb makes a daring escape, returning the transport and Bek to the Resistance base on Batuu.

POE DAMERON'S NEW X-WING
MANUFACTURER Incom-FreiTek **MODEL** T-70 X-wing **TYPE** Starfighter

After his beloved *Black One* starfighter is destroyed during the evacuation of D'Qar, Poe Dameron flies a new X-wing, this time one painted in a striking orange-and-gray livery. Like Poe's previous ship, this model of X-wing has been carefully updated by Incom-FreiTek to reflect the preferences (and address the complaints) of Rebel Alliance veterans. The resulting T-70 model is more complex than First Order TIE Fighters but is also more versatile. Its excellent maneuverability proves to be an important feature for Dameron during the Battle of Exegol, as he leads the Citizens' Fleet, with R2-D2 in the astromech socket.

FIRST ORDER TIE BRUTE
MANUFACTURER Sienar Fleet Systems **MODEL** Twin Ion Engine Transport **TYPE** Starfighter

Much like their Imperial predecessors, the First Order uses the First Order TIE/rb heavy starfighter when they need extra firepower. In comparison to the standard TIE, the Brute has heavier armor and armaments and pivoting twin laser cannons that sit in an outrigger pod that can bear their weight. A crew of smugglers piloting the *Millennium Falcon* encounters a First Order iteration of the Brute while on a supply run to Corellia for former pirate lord turned legitimate businessperson Hondo Ohnaka.

KATOONI
MANUFACTURER Starfeld Industries
MODEL ZH-40 *Tribune*-class
TYPE Light freighter (modified)

The Weequay pirate Hondo Ohnaka has made a number of modifications to his ship, *Katooni*, to suit his "entirely legitimate" business operations at Ohnaka Transport Solutions. The freighter has JV-74 engines and seven laser cannons, four of which can be fire-linked to quad-fire, increasing the weapons' output. With additional components for handling and storing 85 metric tons (83.5 imperial tons) of cargo, the *Katooni* is uniquely suited for supply runs. Hondo seems to have a soft spot for the ship, which may have to do with its name, chosen in honor of a Tholothian youngling who makes an impression upon Hondo.

MC95 STAR CRUISER
MANUFACTURER Mon Calamari Shipyards
MODEL MC95 **TYPE** Star cruiser

Seeing the success of the MC80 and MC85 star cruisers, the Mon Calamari develop the MC95 with five sub-models. A sleek vessel with the fluid lines characteristic of Mon Calamari design, the MC95 star cruiser is armed with laser cannons powerful enough for it to serve as a flagship. Following the Battle of Crait, Aftab Ackbar commands an MC95 and leads a fleet of cruisers away from a First Order attack on Mon Cala. Ackbar and his ship help rebuild the Resistance fleet, and MC95 star cruisers play key roles in the Battle of Batuu and the Battle of Exegol.

RESISTANCE B-WING FIGHTER
MANUFACTURER Slayn & Korpil **MODEL** B-wing Mark III
TYPE Starfighter

As the newest addition to the "blade wing" line, the Resistance B-wing fighter Mark III may lack the speed and maneuverability of its contemporaries, but it has the raw firepower needed to take on the Sith Eternal fleet. Originally spearheaded by Mon Calamari ship builder Quarrie, the B-wing has often been the most heavily armed starfighter in the skies, taking design inspiration from the T-6 Jedi shuttle and V-19 fighter. Pattros Navesh, a pilot from Lantillies, fights for the Resistance during the Battle of Exegol in one of several B-wings, which are all armed with the fearsome Gyrhil R-9X heavy laser cannon.

432 VEHICLES

NIGHT BUZZARD
MANUFACTURER Osseriton Assemblages **MODEL** Modified *Oubliette*-class transport
TYPE Converted prison ship

During a raiding mission to the penal world of Osseriton, the Knights of Ren successfully liberate the prisoners, as they had been hired to do. They also "liberate" one of the planet's prison transports. This stolen ship becomes their own permanent craft, the *Night Buzzard*, and is eventually customized to accommodate the Knights' dark machinations. It's modified to have a more powerful (and cruder) engine system, and its heavy weaponry arsenal is significantly upgraded. The converted dungeon ship is piloted by Kuruk, and it makes a perfect flying headquarters for the vicious band of warriors.

TRANSPORT SKIMMER
MANUFACTURER GoCorp
MODEL Modified Arunskin 75D
TYPE Transport skimmer

An essential tool for the farmers of Pasaana, the modified Arunskin 75D skimmer is a basic, lightweight cargo carrier with a simple but sturdy construction. The vehicle's controls are so simple that even fifth-degree labor droids can operate them on farms. Poe Dameron is able to hot-wire a transport skimmer that belongs to Jo-Dapshi Gorobunn. A Pasaana farmer, he had used it to bring supplies to the Festival of the Ancestors. His skimmer has been specially modified by his thrill-seeking grandson, who decoupled the governors that limit the 75fw turbine thruster's top speed.

LOAD SKIMMER
MANUFACTURER SoroSuub Corporation
MODEL HS-19 **TYPE** Cargo loading skimmer

A snub-nosed utility vehicle, the HS-19 is an open-air skimmer typically used to haul cargo across the sands of Pasaana. The stripped-down, simple transport can carry up to 120 metric tons (118 imperial tons) of cargo, often seeds or supplies. The skimmer's raw repulsorlift power can also be used for velocity, allowing it to travel long distances across the vast desert planet, at speeds of up to 250 kilometers (155 miles) per hour. Using skills he acquired in his youth on Kijimi, Poe Dameron hot-wires an HS-19 skimmer that belongs to a Pasaana resident, while attempting to escape the First Order.

TREADABLE
MANUFACTURER Pasaana Kitha-Garra-du ("Heavy Works")
MODEL DN-25 treadable **TYPE** Sandcrawler

DN-25 treadables are lumbering transports with long, continuous treads that successfully journey across Pasaana's variety of desert landscapes. The Aki-Aki, an indigenous species on the planet, base the design for their treadables on crawlers that have been left behind by offworlders visiting the Festival of the Ancestors celebration that's held every 42 years. The multipurpose use of such a simple vehicle, as well as its need for only one pilot, makes the treadable a popular choice for merchants and haulers. One such vehicle is piloted by the eager Kalo'ne. She carries many tempting items for sale, as well as a mysterious hermit—Lando Calrissian–and his Resistance friends fleeing the First Order.

TREADSPEEDER
MANUFACTURER Aratech-Loratus
MODEL 125-Z **TYPE** Treadspeeder bike

The 125-Z treadspeeder is a rugged, shielded patrol bike specially designed by the First Order to counter technology that jams traditional repulsorcraft. The vehicle features a forward tread that grabs the ground and pulls the vehicle forward, making it the perfect choice for scouting expeditions across unfamiliar terrain. Rugged and reliable, the craft is also surprisingly agile, able to reach speeds of up to 200 kilometers (124 miles) per hour, thanks to its powerful rear Aratech thrusters. With a well-timed brake, the driver can use the bike to launch jet troopers off the back and into the sky.

BESTOON LEGACY
MANUFACTURER Subpro Corporation **MODEL** Modified WTK-85A **TYPE** Interstellar transport

The infamous Sith assassin Ochi of Bestoon hunts prey across the galaxy in his heavily customized ship, the aptly named *Bestoon Legacy*. Originally manufactured during the last days of the Republic, the ship is designed particularly for those who prefer flying with a minimal crew—something the hot-tempered Ochi appreciates. It's equipped with a state-of-the-art navicomputer and distinctive twin back engines.

Ochi's ship is stolen by Dathan—the strandcast son of Palpatine—and Dathan's wife Miramir, in order to escape Jakku and lead Ochi away from their daughter, Rey. The ploy works and saves Rey, but Ochi still manages to kill the couple. Reclaiming his legacy, the assassin follows a clue and heads to Pasaana, where he perishes. His ship and much-maligned droid, D-O, are abandoned, parked on a bluff beyond Lurch Canyon.

When the *Bestoon Legacy* is discovered by the Resistance, it has been neatly preserved by the desert and is ready to fly, even after more than a decade of inactivity.

UA-TT WALKER

MANUFACTURER Kuat-Entralla Engineering
MODEL Urban assault triped transport walker **TYPE** Triped walker

Unlike the larger AT-M6 walker, the Urban Assault Triped Transport (UA-TT) walker is small and has three, rather than four, legs. It's specifically used for the First Order's "pacification" purposes and is preferred for city operations. On narrow streets, like those on Kijimi, it can demonstrate significant riot control without demolishing its surroundings. The walker is ideal for the surgical removal of entrenched rebel cells. Its manipulator claw can either hold victims captive or effortlessly crush them. It also has significant firepower, with a scorching chin-mounted double laser cannon and a turret cluster with a heavy blaster cannon.

Fire away
The ion engines of the *Bestoon Legacy* pack a surprising punch, thrust through the articulated fuel exhaust nozzles.

FORTITUDE

MANUFACTURER Corellian Engineering Corporation
MODEL YC-123B
TYPE Transport hauler

One of the most dependable Resistance ships, the *Fortitude* is a hyperdrive-equipped transport hauler nicknamed the "lucky lander" because of its track record. Finn and members of the Resistance have successfully used it for many unconventional missions.

The *Fortitude* is a sturdy ship with decent shields, although it requires a deft touch from a pilot. With space for more than 100 passengers, it can weather most rough rides, including its journey through the Red Honeycomb Zone. Piloted by Captain Dreanna Conunda during the Battle of Exegol, the *Fortitude* drops a ground crew onto a Star Destroyer.

SEA SKIFF

MANUFACTURER Custom **MODEL** Sea skiff number one **TYPE** Skimmer

Cobbled together by the former First Order stormtroopers of Ccmpany 77, sea skimmers are used for fishing and scouting expeditions over the rough seas of Kef Bir. The skiffs are actually a marvel of recycling ingenuity, having been constructed from pieces of crashed Rebel Alliance ships and parts of repulsorlift utility vehicles used during the construction of the second Death Star. With the right handler, the two sea skiffs can expertly cut through the tall waves and dark waters of the ocean moon of Endor, only needing the slightest touch of the rudder to successfully navigate to a destination.

SITH STAR DESTROYER

MANUFACTURER Kuat-Entralla Engineering
MODEL *Xyston*-class **TYPE** Star destroyer

Emerging from the barren firmament of Exegol, hundreds of Sith Star Destroyers make up the spine of the Sith Eternal fleet. Each is equipped with deadly technology that's been perfected during years of trial and error. The new Star Destroyers are based on the original *Imperial II*-class model, as well as elements of the First Order Dreadnought, but have been further scaled up and made with automation systems in order to reduce the size of the crew.

The hidden warships have been in the works since the time of the Empire, with Darth Sidious secretly building up his forces on the ancient Sith planet of Exegol, bleeding kyber crystals on the secret world to further supplement his terrible weaponry. Darth Vader and Sith assassin Ochi of Bestoon catch a glimpse of these devious plans when they journey to Exegol, but they don't grasp the full extent of Sidious' contingency machinations.

The presence of Sith loyalists on the executive boards of several ship manufacturers, including Sienar-Jaemus and Kuat-Entralla, make it possible for the covert funneling of designs and supplies over many quietly seething years. The building of these warships requires time and patience, but the final result is seemingly devastating to the people of the galaxy.

Adorned with the red markings of the Sith Eternal fleet, each newly minted *Xyston*-class warship has enough firepower to destroy a planet a long way from its orbit, thanks to its reactor-fed axial superlaser. Allegiant General Pryde is ordered by Sidious to finally deploy the fleet across the known galaxy. The first warship to emerge from the Unknown Regions, the *Derriphan*, destroys the icy world of Kijimi as an example of the First Order's new might. Its devastating launch of further warships is prevented by the Citizens' Fleet and Resistance's victory at the Battle of Exegol, inspiring peace across the galaxy.

Children of the Sith
The bridge is made up of resolute officers and technicians, nearly all children of Sith Cultists, who have trained their entire life to operate these devastating machines.

Fleet of darkness
The enormous Sith Fleet rises above the atmosphere of Exegol, ready to travel out of their hidden homeworld and finally attack the New Republic.

INDEX

Page numbers in **bold** refer to main entries

1.4 FD P-Tower **354**
2-1B **350**
2X-3KPR **109**
4-LOM **158**
4D-M1N **198**
8D-J8 **224**
8D8 **164**
41st Elite Corps trooper **81**
74-Z speeder bike **391**
79's **272**
80-M **164**
99 **81**
712-Ava speeder bike **416**
773 firepuncher sniper rifle **339**

A

A-A4B truckspeeder **397**
A-wing starfighters **415**
  RZ-2 A-wing **427**
  training A-wing **406**
A280 blaster rifle **354**
A300 blaster rifle **350**
Ab Dalis **238**
Abafar **265**
Abersyn symbiote **154**
Acclamator-class ship **381**
Ace Squadron 197, 198, 199, 201, 307
Ackbar, Admiral Gial **76**, 227, 415, 428
Ackbar, Aftab **227**, 431
acklay **57**, 256
ACP array gun **365**
Acquisitor **414**
AD-4M **226**
Adelhard, Ubrik 294
Adell, Romar **93**
Adelphi **303**
Adema, Lieutenant **145**
adventurer slugthrower rifle **325**
Aeon Engine 139, 288, 343, 400
Aeos Prime **314**
Aeosian Queen **223**
Agate, Kyrsta **169**
aggrocrabs **93**
Agira **109**
Agnon **224**
Ahch-To 40, 87, 209, 218, **312**, 410
  first Jedi temple **312**
airspeeders **378**
AJ^6 cyborg construct **351**
Ajan Kloss 74, 88, 195, 209, 226, 227, **315**
Akaris, Iskat *see* Thirteenth Sister
Aki-Aki **229**, 316
Akkani **108**
Akuna, Bode **112**
Akuna, Kata **112**
AL **198**
AL-42 **184**
Alamite **186**
Alazmec of Winsit **226**
Albrekh **227**
  tools **366**
Alcida-Auka **218**
Alderaan **261**
  Alderaanian Guard **109**
  destruction of 73, 76, 83, 287
  Royal speeder **398**
Aldhani **277**
All Terrain Armored Transport (AT-AT) **413**
All Terrain Defense Pod (AT-DP) **403**
All Terrain Defense Turret (AT-DT) **397**
All Terrain Recon Transport (AT-RT) **384**
All Terrain Scout Transport (AT-ST/Scout Walker) **414**
Allie, Stass 43, **58**, 81, 259, 384
Almec, Prime Minister **68**
Aloo, Sim 402
Alphabet Squadron 168, 169
Amaxine space station 105, **238**
Amedda, Mas **45**, 247, 248, 330
Ames, Tawni **93**
Amidala, Padmé 23, **25**, 27, 28, 31, 33, 45, 48, 49
  and Anakin Skywalker 24, 25, 54, 68, 252, 306
  assassination attempt 62, 63, 252, 380
  Battle of Naboo 240, 242
  Coruscant Apartment **250**
  and Darth Vader 32, 258, 288, 343
  death 83, 241, 250, 258, 261, 270
  Galactic Senate Chamber 249
  Geonosis Execution Arena 57, 256
  handmaidens 25, 28, 29, 32, 46, 109, 159, 162, 242, 295, 326
  and Palpatine 24, 25
  and R2-D2 30
  Royal Palace Throne Room 242
  vehicles 376, 380
  weapons 326
Anaxes **282**
Andor, Cassian **113**, 114, 117, 142, 277, 278
  Death Star 113, 140, 141, 142, 285, 289
  Narkina 5 119, 141, 279
  Pre-Mor Tac-Corpos 115
  vehicles 399, 408
  weapons 342
Andor, Clem 113, 114, 115, **117**, 342, 399
  blaster pistol **342**
Andor, Maarva Carassi 113, 114, **115**, 117, 121, 278, 399
Andor family hauler **399**
Anno, Loo Re **150**
ant droid **358**
Anthan Prime **290**
Antilles, Captain Raymus **83**
Antilles, Wedge 148, 157, 410, 412, 413
AP-5 **134**, 347, 393
AP-1982 **178**
Aphra, Doctor Chelli **152**, 154, 155, 324
  and Bossk 69
  and Darth Vader 32, 152, 153, 255, 290, 293, 301, 333, 411
  and Just Lucky 152, 161
  and Triple-Zero 146, 152, 153, 290, 291, 328
Aphra, Korin **154**
Aphra, Lona **155**, 291
Ap'lek **227**
Ap'lek's vibro-ax **366**
Apruk, Niv Drendow 17
Aq Vetina **298**
aqua droids 335, 388
arakurth **226**
Ar'alani, Admiral **97**
Arbiflux **291**
ARC troopers **80**
ARC-170 starfighters **387**
Arcana **303**
Arcana Star Map **360**
Archium **273**
Archivist **161**
Aresko, Cumberlayne **128**, 280
Argente, Passel **55**
Ark Angel **411**
Arkoff **13**, 15, 239
armor
  Boba Fett's **351**
  Captain Phasma's **362**
  Commander Pyre's **362**
  Darth Vader's **350**
  death troopers' **347**
  Din Djarin's **356**
  First Order stormtroopers' **362**
  Gideon's dark troopers' **359**
  Grogu's **359**
  Imperial supercommandos' **360**
  Katarn-class commandos' **339**
  Mandalorian **336**
  Phase I clone troopers' **327**
  Phase II clone troopers' **336**
  Phase II purge trooper' **342**
  Sabine Wren's **344**
  Sith troopers' **367**
  stormtroopers' **340**, 362
  TK troopers' **339**
Armored Assault Tank (AAT) **375**
the Armorer 75, 172, **174**, 186, 301
Armorer's planet **301**
Arpagion, Tunga **155**
array guns, ACP **365**
artillery stormtroopers **181**
Arvala-7 **298**
Ashas Ree **314**
assassin droids
  HK-87 assassin droids 332, **358**
  IG-series assassin droids **336**
  SD-K4 assassin droids **335**
Astarte, Aiolin **151**
Astarte, Morit **151**
astromech droids
  R-series astromechs **329**
  R2-D2 **30**
  R4-P17 **51**
Asty, Ello **215**
AT-AC Walkers **393**
AT-ACT **408**
AT-haulers **397**
AT-M6 **429**
AT-ST Raiders **416**
AT-TE (All Terrain Tactical Enforcer) **382**
  Rex's AT-TE **405**
Ataraxia **372**
Atollon **282**
  Battle of Atollon 126, 132, 136, 137, 406, 407
  Chopper Base **283**
Atrius, Darth 346
Attichitcuk **171**
Attsmun, Yasto **220**
Aunt Z **200**
  Aunt Z's Tavern 202, **306**
Aurore-class freighter **392**
autonomous translator module, Mark II **353**
Averross, Rael 56
Axis Base **272**
Axis droid leader **94**
Aynaboni **271**
Azadi, Ryder **133**
AZI-3 **77**
Azmorigan **132**

B

B-U4D **216**
B-wing starfighter **415**
  Resistance B-wing fighter **431**
B/SF-17 heavy bomber **427**
B1 battle droids 26, 55, 254, **323**, 375
B2 battle droids 254, **328**
B2EMO **114**
Baba, Ponda 146
bacta pods **358**
bacta spray **357**
bacta suits, flexpoly 365
bacta tanks **351**
Bad Batch *see* Clone Force 99 (Bad Batch)
Bagnoro, Gwellis **215**
Baiz, Kaba **184**
Bala-Tik **212**
Balmorra **273**
Banai, Kitster **36**
Banchii **239**
Bane, Cad 34, 37, 38, 51, 53, 63, **65**, 66, 258
  holocrons 334
  Justifier **393**
  weapons 339
Bane, Darth **79**
Banking Clan communications frigate **384**
Bansee **103**
banthas **35**, 39, 243
Barada **165**
BARC speeders **384**
BARC troopers **81**
Barcona, Taramyn **118**
Bardotta **265**
Bar'leth **291**
BARM-ST12 scattergun **357**
Baro, Benni **94**, 392
Barodai, Ardo **170**
Barr, Ferren 83, **96**
Barso, Woan **144**
Barton IV 95, **273**
  the Outpost **273**
battle droids 253, 254, **323**
  B1 battle droids 26, 55, 254, **323**, 375
  B2 battle droids 254, **328**
Batuu **306**
  Battle of Batuu 306, 431
Baysee, Lieutenant **190**
BB-8 194, **195**, 205, 211, 217, 220, 308, 309, 310, 361, 422, 428
BB-9E **221**
BB-series droids **361**
BD-1 **99**
BD-72 **185**
BD-Unit **359**
Beckett, Tobias 38, 74, 100, **104**
  blasters **340**
  coaxium 274, 275
  and Han Solo 100, 104
  and Val 103, 104
  weapons 352
Bedlam Raiders 112, 277, 333, 374
Beed **36**
Beehaz, Jayhold **119**
Bendu **135**, 282
Benthic "Two Tubes" **141**
Beq, Kelleran **187**, 416
beskar spear **358**
Bespin **293**
  Bespin wing guards **157**
  carbon-freezing chamber **294**
  Cloud City **294**
Bestoon Legacy **432**
Bevelyn **162**
Bey, Shara **159**, 194, 292, 376
Beyta, Lieutenant **190**
Bibble, Sio **26**
Bibo **204**
bilari electro-chain whip **365**
Billaba, Depa 41, 43, **44**, 47, 271
Binks, Jar Jar 23, **27**, 28, 33, 76, 265
Birnok **120**
Bitey **204**
Black Ace **424**
Black Mask **109**
Black One **422**
Black Spire Outpost 224, 225, 306
Black Squadron 192, 193, 194, 195, 206, 212, 215, 304, 311, 422
Black Sun syndicate 78, 133, 158, 162, 267
Blade of Talzin 188, 191, **361**
Blade Wing **405**
Blagg, Temiri **221**
blaster pistols
  Clem's blaster pistol **342**
  DH-17 blaster pistol **348**
  DL-18 blaster pistol **343**
  Glie-44 blaster pistol **364**
  LL-30 blaster pistol **339**
  NN-14 blaster pistol **364**
  SE-44C blaster pistol **364**
  WESTAR-34 blaster pistol **327**
blaster rifles
  A280 blaster rifle **354**
  A300 blaster rifle **350**
  Captain Phasma's **362**
  Corpo rifle **342**
  DC-15 blaster rifle **327**
  DLT-19 heavy blaster rifle **349**
  E-11 blaster rifle **350**
  EE-3 blaster rifle **353**
  KA74 blaster rifle **357**
  Kuruk's **366**

M-32 light repeating blaster rifle **357**
stormtroopers' **337**
blasters
Commander Pyre's **362**
Corpo blasters **342**
DC-15A blasters **330**
DC-17 blasters **330**
defender sporting blasters **348**
Din Djarin's **356**
E-5 droid blaster **324**
E-Web repeating blaster **354**
EL-16 blaster **364**
FWMB-10 blaster **365**
Geonosian sonic blaster **327**
Hera Syndulla's **343**
ionization blaster **349**
RK-3 blaster **365**
scout troopers' **354**
Sith troopers' **367**
T-21 light repeating blaster **341**
Tobias Beckett's **340**
WESTAR-35 twin blasters **345**
Zorii Bliss' **367**
Blevin **117**
Bliss, Zeva 144, **163**
Bliss, Zorii 194, **230**, 231, 389, 429
blasters **367**
helmet **367**
Blizzard One 156, **157**
Blue Ace **423**
Blue Squadron 142, 422
bluevev glider **111**
blurrg **176**
Bly, Commander 50, **330**
Blythe, Captain **163**, 295
bo-rifles **344**
Bobbajo **211**
Bog, Caysin **144**
Boga **79**
Bogano **273**
Bokken saber, Sabine Wren's **360**
Boll, Sionver **66**
Bolo **91**
B'omarr monks **184**
Bombardier, Lord **187**
Bongo **375**
Bonteri, Lux **70**
Bonteri, Mina 25, **70**, 265
bonzami **134**
Boolan, Baron **17**
Boolio **226**
Boonta Eve Classic 34, 36, 37, 38, 246, 366, 377
Bora Vio **271**
Bosh, Draiven **20**
Bossk 53, **69**, 227, 388
Bothan-5 357, **417**
Bounty Hunters Guild 172, 173, 299, 339, 356
Boushh 107, **158**, 214, 267
bowcaster, Chewbacca's **349**
the Box **265**
Bracca **271**
Bragg, Captain **92**
Braha'tok-class gunship **407**
Brasso **114**
Braygh **20**
Brebtin, Jeela **168**
Brenne, Colonel Alva **288**
Breon Dayvan **399**
brezak **77**
Bridger, Ephraim 127, 280
Bridger, Ezra 31, 32, 39, 44, 64, **127**, 128, 324, 345
and Ahsoka Tano 62, 127
and Darth Maul 126, 127, 283
and Darth Vader 345, 346
Dathomir 263
Ezra's Roost **281**
Ghost 401
and the Grand Inquisitor 130
holocron 343
and Kanan Jarrus 122, 127, 343, 345
lightsaber 345, 346, **361**
Loth-cats 133
Loth-wolves 284
Nightsisters 338
Phantom 400
Phoenix Squadron 406
and Sabine Wren 126, 127, 191, 360, 361

slingshot **344**
speeder bike **404**
and Thrawn 136
weapons 344, 352
the world between worlds 284
Bridger, Mira 127, 280
the Bright Star 139, 288, **343**
Brightstar, Kai 17, **18**, 19, 20, 21, 40, 239, 322
speeder **373**
Broken Horn Syndicate 344
Broken Wing **411**
Broosh, Teso **167**
Brother Viscus **72**
BT-1 152, **153**
BTA-NR2 Y-wing starfighter **429**
Buck, Torban **15**, 372, 373
Buggles **204**
Buran, Rok **12**
Burg **178**
burrowberry birds **19**
Burryaga **15**, 322, 346
Burtoni, Halle **94**
buzz droids **337**
Bynar, Ooris **160**

C

C-3PO **33**, 254, 287, 294
and Anakin Skywalker 33, 329
and the Ewoks 33, 166, 296, 297
and Leia Organa 30, 33
and Luke Skywalker 87, 255
and R2-D2 30, 33, 48, 225, 348
C-21 Highsinger **77**
C-ROC carrier ship **404**
C1-D1 **189**
Cadeliah **160**
Calamari, Mon Cala **265**
Caleen, Bix 114, **115**
Calican, Toro **177**, 263, 416
Calip, Warba **155**
Callahan, Lieutenant **189**
Calrissian, Kadara **107**
Calrissian, Lando 37, **107**, 157, 158, 294, 424
and the Death Star 76, 297
Imperialis 411
and L3-37 106, 107, 394
Millennium Falcon 74, 100, 102, 107, 275, 297, 340, 341, 394
puffer pigs 107, 132
SE-14R **341**
CAM **224**
CAM-E 19, **224**
Canady, Moden **218**
cannons
Cardo's arm cannon 366
E-HOB heavy repeating laser cannon **357**
First Order jet trooper cannon **367**
MWC-35C repeating cannon **347**
superlaser siege cannon **365**
Cantaros, Imri 15, 17
Canto Bight (Cantonica) **313**
Canto Casino (Cantonica) **313**
Cantonica **313**
Cantwell-class arrestor cruiser 122, **400**
Caphtor, Emerick **15**, 17
Capital City, Lothal **281**
carbon-freezing chamber **294**
Card, Nix **70**
Cardinal **192**
Cardo **227**
arm cannon 366
Cardovyte **315**
Carida **270**
Carrion Spike 73, 351, 384, **423**
Cassamam, Dava **105**
Casset, Captain Hedda **372**
Castas 53
Castilon **306**
Catacombs of Cadera **285**
Cathley, Matthea **12**, 13
Cato Neimoidia **259**
Cator **86**
Cave of Evil, Dagobah 213, 266, **267**
CB-23 **205**, 361, 430

CC-420 pistol **358**
Ceeli 17
Celsor 3 **314**
Ceret **15**
CH-33P **86**
Cha, Chanath **96**, 377, 411
Chadic, Chass na 168, **169**
chain code **339**
Chalis, Everi **160**
Champion, Dar **155**
Chandrila Star Line **430**
Chandrilan Embassy **278**
Char-Ryl-Roy **12**
Chava **134**
Chelidae **205**
chell **94**
Chettkap, Elder **176**
Chewbacca 30, 38, 40, **74**, 106, 170, 292
AT-ST 414
bowcaster **349**
Death Star 287
Eravana 100, 426
and Han Solo 74, 100
Kashyyyk 269
and the *Millennium Falcon* 74, 262, 263, 394
Chigg **19**
Children of the Path 13
Children of the Watch 172, 174, 176, 186, 336, 356
Chimaera 127, 191, **421**
Chireen, Aarton **226**
Chireen, Nimi **232**
chirodactyl **99**
Chirpa, Chief **166**
Chopper (C1-10P) 39, 123, **124**, 347, 393, 401
Chopper Base **283**
Christophsis **264**
Battle of Christophsis 52, 58, 264, 384
Chuan, Sowa **193**
Chuchi, Riyo 48, 62, **64**, 271
Cid's Parlor **271**
Cimina **225**
the Citadel (Lola Sayu) **264**
the Citadel of Ktath'atn **291**
Citadel Tower (Scarif) **289**
Class-A thermal detonator **355**
Class-Four Container Vessel **393**
The Client **173**, 174
Clone 99 **81**
clone army 251, 252
Clone Force 99 (Bad Batch) 64, 65, 73, 82, 89, 90, 93, 94, 95, 259, 264, 265, 267, 271, 282, 323, 336, 339, 382, 392, 393
clone pilots **80**
clone scuba troopers **80**
clone troopers **52**, 55
gunships 381
Phase I clone trooper armor **327**
Phase II clone trooper armor **336**
weapons 327, 330
see also individual characters
Clone Wars 24, 42, 43, 47, 49, 52, 59, 251, 253, 261, 382, 388
Clone X **94**
Closed faction 45
Cloud City **294**
Cloud-Riders 34, 104, 141, 275
Clovis, Rush 66, **68**, 259
coaxium **340**
Cobalt Squadron 217
Coburn, Barton **95**
code cylinders **350**
Cody, Clone Commander 52, **58**, 324
cold assault clone trooper **81**
colo claw fish **29**
Colony of Kezarat **295**
Colossus platform 196, 197, 198, 199, 200, 201, 202, 204, 205, 222, 306, 307, 314, 323, 328, 366, 422, 423, 430
Aunt Z's Tavern **306**
command bridge droids **366**
commando droids **333**
Commerce Guild **390**
Concord Dawn **282**
Concordia **302**
Connix, Kaydel Ko **216**
constable droids **359**
Conunda, Dreanna **233**, 433
conveyex **397**

INDEX

convor 80
Corbyt, Jensen 189
Cordova, Eno 23, 47, **99**, 334, 359
Corellia **274**
   Corellian hounds 103
   Den of the White Worms 274
   Santhe Shipyards 303
Corellian Engineering Corporation 374
Coronet 335
Corpo blasters 342
Corpo rifles 342
Corporate Alliance *Persuader* tank droids **385**
Corran **109**, 110
Coruscant **247**
   79's **272**
   Chancellor Palpatine's Office **250**
   Chandrilan Embassy **278**
   Coruscant Eastern Spaceport **279**
   Coruscant Underworld **250**
   Dex's Diner **250**
   Galactic Antiquities and Objects of Interest **278**
   Galactic Senate Chamber **249**
   Galaxies Opera House **268**
   Inquisitor Base **270**
   ISB Central Office **278**
   Jedi Temple **248**
   Karn household **279**
   Level 1313 **270**
   Martez Sisters' Repair Shop **270**
   Monument Plaza **302**
   Outlander Gambling Club **250**
   Padmé's Coruscant Apartment **250**
   Palpatine's apartment **254**
   Republic Executive Building **250**
Corvax, Dorwin **139**
   lightsaber **343**
Corvax, Lady **139**, 226, 258, 288, 343
Corvax Sentinels **343**
Corvus **300**
Corvus (*Raider II*-class) **411**
the Countess **220**
crab droids, LM-432 "Muckraker" **333**
Cracken, Airen **167**
Crait **313**
Crèche cult **192**
Crimson Bolt 17, **373**
Crimson Dawn 29, 32, 37, 46, 53, 263, 288, 341
   coaxium 275
   Dryden Vos 31, 102, 104, 146, 397
   Han Solo 295, 379, 412, 414
   Qi'ra 31, 64, 100, 102, 104, 105, 158, 161, 227, 231, 353, 397
Crimson Firehawk **373**
crossguard lightsabers **346**
Crosshair 58, **89**, 91, 95, 272, 273, 324, 339
Crumb, Salacious B. **164**
Cryar, Cassie 68
cryo-furnace **356**
cryogenic density combustion booster **358**
CT-05 **421**
cyborg mech **186**
Cylo 32, **151**, 333, 350, 412
Cymoon 1 **290**
Czerka Corporation 324, 352

D

D-0 **230**
D-72W oppressor **357**
D-93 flamethrower **364**
D-wing droid **339**
D'Acy, Larma **218**, 227
daggers, Ochi of Bestoon's **367**
Dagobah 213, **266**
   Cave of Evil 213, 266, **267**
   Yoda's Hut **293**
Dagonet **21**
Daiyu **276**
Dalkor Dagger **430**
Dalna **238**
Dameron, Kes **159**, 194, 292
Dameron, Poe 30, **194**, 196, 219, 348, 363, 394, 423
   and BB-8 194, 195, 205
   Black One 422, **431**
   Black Squadron 192, 193, 194, 195, 212, 304, 311

Cardovyte 315
Castilon 306
and Finn 207
and Kylo Ren 309
and Lor San Tekka 87, 153, 192, 194, 195, 206, 215
Millennium Falcon 194, 226, 315
   new X-wing **431**
   skimmers 432
   Starkiller Base 305
   and Zorii Bliss 230, 231
D'an, Figrin **146**
Dand, Ibdun **227**
Dand, Vober **216**, 227
Dantooine **283**
Darius G-class freighter **425**
dark troopers **357**
   Gideon's dark trooper armor **359**
darkghast **139**
Darklighter, Biggs **147**, 410
the Darksaber 75, 126, 137, 172, 176, 179, 184, **338**
Daro **271**
Darrb **223**
Darth Maul *see* Maul
data visor **339**
datapad **330**
Dathan 24, 209, **231**, 308, 316
Dathomir **263**
Datoo, Colonel **212**
the Daughter **72**
DC-15 blaster rifle **327**
DC-15A blaster **330**
DC-17 blaster **330**
DD-BD **105**
Death Squadron 412
Death Star I 24, 30, 146, **287**
   construction of 73, 138, 253, 355
   destruction of 58, 76, 87, 147, 394, 410
   destruction of Alderaan 48, 83, 261
   destruction of Jedha 73, 84, 138, 140, 141, 142, 143, 285, 287
   panel joins 342
   plans 32, 87, 88, 113, 140, 141, 142, 143, 144, 262, 286, 287, 289, 348, 409, 428
   weapons 335, 337
Death Star II 24, 32, 97, 100, 296, **297**
   attack on 389
   construction of 165, 300, 317, 433
   destruction of 165, 166, 412
   Emperor's throne room **297**, 317
death troopers **141**, 350
   armor **347**
Death Watch 68, 69, 260, 301, 302, 336, 338, 345, 406
Deathstick **161**
decimator droid **339**
Dee **19**
Dee, Lourna 14, **16**, 17, 44, 239, 372
defender sporting blaster **348**
Defender-class **420**
Dejarik table **336**
Dek-[Nil] **154**
Delta-7 starfighter **378**
Delta-class T-3C shuttle **408**
Den of the White Worms **274**
Dendra, Doma **112**
Deng, Rothgar **229**
Dengar **77**
Derlin, Major Bren **157**
Derrown **77**
desert skiff **385**
Desix **272**
dewbacks **35**, 243
Dex's Diner **250**
DH-17 blaster pistol **348**
dianoga **147**
Dibs, Prosset *see* Tenth Brother
Dinnes, Zal **145**
Dipterz, Vazzet **227**
dismantler droid **346**
Diss, Carib **231**
Ditcher, Groff **109**
DJ **219**
DJ R-3X **225**
Djarin, Din 30, 39, 53, **172**, 181, 263, 298, 301, 323, 339, 379
   and Ahsoka Tano 172, 175, 300, 302

armor 336, **356**
and the Armorer 172, 174
blaster **356**
and Bo-Katan Kryze 75, 172, 175, 176, 185, 186, 187, 301, 302
and Carson Teva 180
Darksaber 172, 176, 179, 184, 338
and Grogu 87, 172, 173, 174, 175, 176, 178, 179, 219, 299, 301, 302, 356, 357, 359, 360, 416, 418
Mandalore 260
N-1 starfighter **419**
Razor Crest 176, 177, 298, 376, 380, 416, 417, 419
rifle **356**
technology 351, 352, **356**, 358
vehicles 417, **419**
DL-18 blaster pistol **343**
DL-44 heavy blaster pistol, Han Solo's modified **352**
DLT-19 heavy blaster rifle **349**
Dobbs, Radicaz "Sunshine" **13**
Dod, Lott **45**
Dodger, Jib **178**
Dodibin **220**
Dodonna, Jan **147**, 286
Dogma **81**
Dok-Ondar **224**
Domadi, Kier **134**
Dooku, Count *see* Tyranus, Darth (Count Dooku)
Dormé **46**
Dorn, Taborr Val **19**, 21, 239, 332, 373
Doza, Captain Imanuel 196, 197, 199, **201**, 205, 223, 307, 314, 366, 424
Doza, Torra **199**, 201, 202, 204, 205, 307, 423
Doza, Venisa 222, **223**, 352, 366
D'Qar 195, 210, 212, 213, 216, 217, **309**, 422, 428
   Resistance base 311, 427
Drabor, Shug 430
Dragus, Daq **171**
Drahgor III **314**
Drash **184**
Draven, Davits **142**
the Dreamers 70
Dree, Lyttan **97**
Dree, Tamu **97**
Dreis, Garven **147**, 410
Drell **202**
Drengir 14, **16**, 238, 239
Drezzer, Kravas **114**
Dritus, Greez **98**, 398
Droid Crush Pirates of Bestoon **159**
droid racers **430**
droid starfighters **374**
droideka (a.k.a. destroyer droid) **324**
droids see individual droids and types of droid
Duaba, Trinto **214**
Ducain, Gannis **394**
the Duchess **187**
Dudge, Wolentic **231**
Duloks **296**
Dume, Caleb *see* Jarrus, Kanan
Dune, Cara **177**, 299, 300, 416, 417
   blaster **357**
Durand, Roland **92**
Durango, Nash **17**, 18, 19, 20, 21, 239, 373
   Nash's Moms **17**, 20
Durant, Rio **104**
Durd, Lok 50, 59, 254
Durge **161**
Durith, Tala **110**, 276
dwarf spider droids **390**
Dyun, Gandris **233**

E

E-5 droid blasters **324**
E-11D **350**
E-22 rifles **341**
E-HOB heavy repeating laser cannons **357**
E-Web repeating blasters **354**
E-wings **420**
E-XD infiltrator droids **347**
Eadu **289**
   Imperial Kyber Refinery **289**
EB-3 **21**, 373
Echo, clone trooper 55, 59, **65**, 80, 89, 393
Echo Base **292**, 412

Edgehawk **414**
Edrio "Two Tubes" **141**
EE-3 blaster rifle **353**
Eekway, Chi 69, 263
EG-series droid **351**
   EG-86 **133**
Egdir **202**
Eighth Brother **135**
Eila **201**
Eiram **238**
Eirriss family **343**
Eirtaé **29**
Ekwesh, Ishbul 19, 20, 322
EL-16 blaster **364**
electro-bisento **365**
electroprod troopers, First Order **229**
electroprods **366**
electrostaff **332**
Elee **202**
Eleventh Brother **96**
Elite Squad troopers **91**
Elk **121**
Elsbeth, Morgan 62, **188**, 274, 300, 332, 346, 420
   Blade of Talzin 188, 191
   and Captain Hayle 189
   Scion shuttle **421**
   scout guards 181
   Seatos 303
   technology 358, 360, 361
   TIE defender 407
Emari, Jas 66, **169**
Ematt, Caluan 216
Embo **66**
Emergences 238
Emperor's Throne Room (Death Star II) **297**, 317
Endor 165, **296**, 355
   Battle of Endor 166, 296, 297, 395, 412
   Death Star II **297**
   Endor bunker secret entrance **297**
   Ewok Village **297**
   Kef Bir **317**
Endurance 38, 53
energy balls (booma) **326**
energy shields **358**
Enforcer droids **322**
Engell, Amret **228**
Engle, Porter **12**, 14, 16, 68
Enoch, Captain **191**
eopie **36**
Epikonia **295**
Eravana 74, 100, 212, **426**
Eriadu **295**
E'ronoh **238**
Erso, Galen Walton 84, 113, **138**, 140
   Death Star 67, 138, 142, 145, 287, 289
   kyber crystals 287, 289, 335
Erso, Jyn 138, **140**, 287
   Death Star 67, 113, 140, 141, 142, 143, 144, 289, 409
   and Saw Gerrera 84, 140, 141
Erso, Lyra 84, **138**, 140
Erso homestead **284**
ES-01 **91**
ES-02 **91**
ES-03 **91**
ES-04 **91**
escape pods **348**
Estree, Haja 109, **110**, 276, 398
Eta-class shuttle **420**
EV-9D9 **164**
Eval, Moralo 65, **77**, 265
Evazan, Doctor **146**
Ewok Village **297**
Ewoks 33, 100, 166, 167
   Battle of Endor 166, 414
   and C-3PO 166, 296, 297
   Endor **296**, 297
   Ewok Village **297**
EX Communication droids **322**
Executor (Super Star Destroyer) 105, 156, **412**, 415
Exegol **316**
   Battle of Exegol 195, 207, 217, 228, 316, 394, 433
extragalactic navicomputer **360**
Eye of Sion 136, 190, 191, 360, **421**
Eye of Webbish Bog **226**
Eyta, Pan **322**

F

F'alma, Vylip 139
Fang fighter 406
Faraz 20
Farkiller 353
farmer droid 357
Farr, Onaconda 57
Farrus, Kho Phon 162
the Father 72
fathier 221
Fazon, Hype 199, 423
FD3-MN 106
Fenris, Astrid 105
Fenris, Freya 199, 423
fermata cage 102, 161, 353
Ferrix 277
Fertha, Perrin 119, 278
Festival of Light 240, 241
Fett, Boba 42, 49, 51, **53**, 92, 181, 379, 416
   armor 351, 356
   and Aurra Sing 38, 53, 379
   and Cad Bane 65
   as Daimyo 164, 165, 182, 183, 184, 244, 257, 301, 351, 379
   gaderffii stick 357
   Gamorrean guards 335
   and Han Solo 37, 53, 100, 102, 106, 107, 158, 257, 294, 379
   and Jabba the Hutt 37, 53, 182
   jetpack 352
   Krayt's Claw 53, 66, 69, 77
   and Luke Skywalker 293
   and Mace Windu 41, 69
   Mos Espa 244
   rancors 184, **185**
   and the Sarlacc 165, 351, 358, 379
   starship 379
   technology 325, 327, 349, 352, 353, 357
   and the Tuskens 39, 182, 183, 184, 349, 357, 358, 418
   wrist gauntlets 352
Fett, Jango 41, **49**, 50, 51, 57
   apartment 252
   clones 52, 53, 56, 90, 251, 252, 327
   and Count Dooku 49, 256
   and Mace Windu 49, 53
   starship 379
   technology 327, 336, 351
Fife 85
Fifth Brother **133**, 398
Figg, Lord Ecclessis 294
Final Order fleet technician 233
Finalizer 194, 207, **426**
Finn 194, 195, 200, 206, **207**, 394
   and Captain Phasma 203, 207
   and Kylo Ren 209, 331
   and Rey 206, 207
   and Rose Tico 210, 217, 219, 220, 221
Fireball (former clone trooper) 95
Fireball (racing starfighter) 423
First Light 104, 105, **397**
First Order
   AT-M6 **429**
   Colossus **307**, 423
   Finalizer **426**
   First Order electroprod troopers 229
   First Order flametroopers 206
   First Order fleet gunner 218
   First Order heavy troopers 206
   First Order jet trooper cannons 367
   First Order jet troopers 229
   First Order light cruisers **430**
   First Order officer's transit data-medallions 367
   First Order Raiders 222
   First Order riot shields 364
   First Order scuba troopers 222
   First Order security droids 366
   First Order sentry droids 365
   First Order SF TIE fighters 425
   First Order shuttle pilots 218
   First Order snow speeders **426**
   First Order snowtroopers 206
   First Order Special Forces TIE pilots **206**
   First Order stormtroopers 200
   First Order stormtroopers' armor 362
   First Order TIE brute 431
   First Order TIE fighter pilots 206
   First Order TIE fighters 425
   First Order TIE pilots' helmet 363
   First Order treadspeeder pilots 229
   stormtrooper transport 426
   superlaser siege cannons 365
   TIE Echelon 431
   Titan 430
   treadspeeders 432
Fisto, Kit 41, 43, **46**, 61
Fives, clone trooper **63**, 65, 77, 80, 272
flamethrowers, D-93 364
flametroopers 362, 364
   First Order flametroopers 206
Flanx 222
the Fledgling Mythrol 173
flexpoly bacta suit 365
Flix 201, 204, 222
Florrum 264
FN-2003 206
FN-2199 206
Fode 36
Fondor haulcraft 399
force pike 351
Force priestesses 79
Forest Moon of Endor 165
forest walker 181
Fort Ypso 274
Forte, Aida 12
Fortitude **433**
Fortress of Garn 291
Fortuna, Beezer 142
Fortuna, Bib 37, **38**, 53, 69, 164, 165, 257
Forvan 163
Fourth Sister 110
Fox, Commander 63
Freck 111
   truck 398
Free Ryloth Movement 80, 82, 92, 93, 254, 337, 406
Frell 159
Frezno 279
Frik, Babu 231, 389
Frisk 170
Frog babies 181
Frog Lady 177
Frog Man 180
Fulminatrix 194, 210, 216, **427**
Furball 160
Fwip, Garsa 183
   Garsa's Sanctuary **301**
FWMB-10 blaster 365
FX-series 350
fyrnock 131

G

G-90 162
GA-97 212
Gaava, Lin 202
Gabredor III 295
gaderffii (gaffi) stick 349
Galactic Antiquities and Objects of Interest 278
Galactic Civil War 219, 247, 395, 396
Galactic Concordance 67, 247
Galactic Senate Chamber 249
Galactic Society of Creature Enthusiasts 224
Galaxies Opera House 268
Galaxy's Glory **424**
Galek, Lieutenant 222, 430
Galleon **424**
Gallia, Adi **43**, 44
Gamorrean ax 335
Gamorrean guard 165
Ganodi 85
Gar 86
Garan, Lanzora 231
Garat, Vol 13
Garel 282
Garfalaquox 182
Garganchie 20
Garindan 147
Garma 202
Garra, Oga 224
Garro 154
Gascon, Meebur 78
Gasgano 36
Gauge 225
Gauntlet starfighter **406**
Gavi 17
Gaze Electric 322, **372**
Gazian 162
Gedonian ground weevil 19
Genoa, Phee 93, 272, 393
Geode 17, 373
Geonosian starfighter **383**
Geonosis 68, 151, **253**
   Battle of Geonosis 52, 253, 256
   Geonosian sonic blaster 327
   Geonosis droid factory 254
   Geonosis Execution Arena 256
Gera, Dagan **112**, 277, 351
Gerrera, Saw 26, **84**, 253, 265, 287, 346
   and Jyn Erso 84, 140, 141
   partisan group 84, 104, 120, 140, 141, 142, 143, 265, 279
   suit 347
   vehicles 408
Gerrera, Steela 78, 84, 265
Ghima, Nambi 229
ghoat 118
Ghost **401**
Gideon, Moff 30, 53, **179**, 260, 356, 402
   dark troopers 357, **359**
   the Darksaber 338
   death 181
   Dr. Pershing 173, 174, 175, 182
   droids 352
   light cruiser **418**
   Nevarro 299
   vehicles 415
Gios, Stellan **14**, 15, 37, 238, 346
Girard, Captain 191
Gita 137
Glavis Ringworld **301**
Glem 202
Glie, Gobi **80**, 364
Glie-44 blaster pistol 364
Glitch 200
Go, Rexa 154
Gol 163
Golan arms DF.9 anti-infantry battery 353
Gonky 91
Gork 222
Gorn 119
Gorr, Kragan 196, 198, **201**, 202, 204, 222, 307, 328, 365
   shuttle 424
Gorr, Lieutenant 159
Gorst 120
Gozanti-class cruisers 401, 403, 407
GR-75 **413**
Graf, Auric 96
Graf, Lina 96
Graf, Sky 13
Graf family 96
Grammus sisters 220
the Grand Inquisitor 47, 50, 108, **130**, 131, 267, 295
   lightsaber 345
   vehicles 398
Great Mothers 101, 188, **191**, 303, 361
   Great Mothers' orbs 360
Great Mountain 154
Greatstorm, Loden 12, **14**, 15, 17
Greedo 37, 69, **70**, 165, 263
Green Ace **423**
Gregor **78**, 382, 405
Grek 159
Gremm, Aemon 105
Gretta 163
Grevel 202
Grey 86
Grey, Mika 222, 314
Grey, Varko **170**
Greylark, Axel 12, **14**
Greylark, Kyong **13**, 14, 372
Grievous, General 25, 28, 42, 43, 44, **61**, 251
   and Count Dooku 56, 61
   death 79
   kyber crystals 268
   MagnaGuards 332, 344

INDEX

MagnaGuards 332, 344
Mustafar 258
Nightsisters 71
  and Obi-Wan Kenobi 61, 268, 387
  and Palpatine 49, 390
  vehicles 387, 388, 389, 390, 391
    wheel bike 391
Grig, Tetha **109**
Grint, Myles **128**, 280
Griss, Frantis **228**
Grogu 30, 53, 75, **175**, 180, 187, 330, 338, 355, 380, 410
  armor 358, **359**
  and Din Djarin 87, 172, 173, 174, 175, 176, 178, 179, 299, 301, 302, 356, 357, 359, 360, 416, 418
  and Luke Skywalker 87, 175, 301, 302
  Mandalore 260
  and Peli Motto 177
  stone crabs 186
Grool, Bolza **200**
Grozz **171**
Grummgar **215**
Grysk 306
Guavian Death Gang 196, 204, 212, 225
  Guavian Death Gang enforcer **212**
  Guavian Death Gang ship **430**
Guavian Death Space **314**
Gullet, Bor **141**
gundark **64**
Gundravian Hookspores **154**
Gungans 27, 242
  atlatl **326**
  Gungan Grand Army 26, 27, 76, 326
  Gungan Sacred Place **240**
  personal energy shield **326**
Gungi **85**, 94
Gunny **170**
Gunray, Nute **26**, 47, 49, 57, 240, 241
Gurtyl **155**
Gwarm **66**
GX-8 water vaporator **325**
Gyuti, Lord **162**

H

Hailfire-class droid **383**
Halcyon 49, **430**
Halloran, Griff **199**
  Black Ace **424**
Ham **120**
Hammerhead corvette **405**
Hap **21**
happabore **211**
Harbinger 74, 188, 410
Hask, Gideon (Gid) 149, **150**, 221, 411
Hati, Shin **189**, 420
Hawkins, Vic **190**
Haydenn, Jyala **162**
Hayle, Captain **189**, 420
Hays Minor **304**
Hazard, Lyana **95**
Hazard, Shep **95**
heavy troopers, First Order **206**
Heert **117**
Helgait, Commissioner **187**
helmets
  Enfys Nest's **341**
  Fennec Shand's **339**
  First Order TIE pilot's **363**
  Kylo Ren's 227, **363**
  Luke Skywalker's **353**
  Marchion Ro's **322**
  TIE fighter pilot's **345**
  Zorii Bliss' **367**
Hemlock, Royce 24, 63, 90, **95**, 272
the Herald (Werth Plouth) 12, **13**
Hess, Valin **182**
Hetzal Prime **238**
Hevy **80**
HI-CT walker **417**
Hidden Hand 411
Hidden Path 22, 99, 110, 111, 130, 276, 277, 399, 408, 412
Hill, San **55**
HK-87 assassin droid 332, **358**

HMP droid gunship **388**
Holdfast, Clegg **36**
Holdo, Vice Admiral Amilyn **219**, 428
Hollow, Affie **17**, 373
holo puck **356**
Holocron Vault 334
holocrons
  Jedi 248, **334**
  Sith **343**
hologram target hilt **360**
Holowan Laboratories **336**
Holt, Sian **17**
Holy City, Jedha 138, 140, 141, 142, 143
Home One 158, **415**
homing spider droid, OG-9 **381**
horned gekko **184**
Hosnian Prime **311**
Hoth 292, 301, 412
  Battle of Hoth 156, 157
  Echo Base 292
Hoth Asteroid Belt **293**
Hound's Tooth **388**
hover pram **416**
howlers **190**
Howzer **93**
Hubin **291**
Hunter **82**, 89, 272, 339
Hunters of the Outer Rim **171**
Hush-98 comlink **325**
Hutt, Balada the **171**
Hutt, Bokku the **159**
Hutt, Gardulla the 35, 36, **38**
Hutt, Grakkus the 142, **153**, 290, 304, 332, 334
Hutt, Jabba the **37**, 38, 53, 63, 65, 246
  death 164, 165
  and Han Solo 37, 38, 69, 100, 107, 214, 257, 294, 379, 394
  Jabba's Palace **257**
  Khetanna **385**
  and Leia Organa 107, 158, 257, 355
  pets 164, 165
  technology 332
Hutt, Niima the **309**
Hutt, Rotta the 37, 56, 60, **63**, 254, 386
Hutt, Sutha the **86**
Hutt, Vranki the 199, **223**, 314, 430
  Vranki's Hotel and Casino **314**
Hutt, Ziro the 34, 37, 38, **63**, 65, 70, 254, 386
Hutt family 243, 244, 246, 254, 290
Hux, Armitage 200, 205, **210**, 231, 233, 305, 364, 426
Hux, Brendol **188**, 192, 200, 210
Huyang, Professor **189**, 343, 360, 361
Hydan, Veris **138**, 284
hydroid medusa **76**
Hyena bombers **384**
Hyne **114**
hyperloop pods **419**

I

ice vultures **95**
ID9 seeker droid **346**
IG-11 **174**, 336
IG-12 **359**, 360
IG-88 64, **158**, 336, 357
IG-RM droid **344**
IG-series assassin droid **336**
IGV-55 surveillance vessel **407**
lit, Naka **221**
Ikkrukk **304**
imagecaster **324**
Imperial
  AT-DPs **403**
  Cantwell-class Arrestor Cruiser **400**
  Class-Four Container Vessels **393**
  Imperial cadets **133**
  Imperial combat pilots **128**
  Imperial construction droids **342**
  Imperial construction modules **407**
  Imperial deck technician **145**
  Imperial fleet troopers **145**
  Imperial freighters **403**
  Imperial incinerator troopers **179**

Imperial Interdictor **405**
Imperial Kyber Refinery **289**
Imperial landing craft **404**
Imperial N-S9 starpath unit **342**
Imperial probe droids **352**
Imperial Royal Guard 52, **83**, 233, 351
Imperial Security Bureau (ISB) 58, 129, **278**, 342, 349
Imperial security troopers **121**
Imperial sentry droids **347**
Imperial super commandos **135**
Imperial super commandos' armor **360**
Imperial support vessel **407**
Imperial tank pilots **144**
Imperial troop transport **402**, 418
Imperial turbolasers **337**
Imperial weapons technicians **142**
Lambda-class Imperial shuttles **402**
Lothar Imperial Speeder Bike **403**
Star Destroyers **396**
TIE fighters **395**
TIE reapers **409**
TIE strikers **408**
Imperial I-class Star Destroyers 396, **421**
Imperial Security Bureau (ISB) 58, 129, **278**, 342, 349
  ISB Central Office **278**
Imperialis 158, **411**
Îmwe, Chirrut 142, **143**
  lightbow **347**
  staff **347**
Inaya, Princess 17, **20**, 21, 373
Infil'a, Kirak **86**, 272, 348
inhibitor chips **336**
Inquisitor Base **270**
Interdictor-class Star Destroyer 400, 405
InterGalactic Banking Clan 259, 383, 384
interplanetary starliner **418**
interrogator droids **349**
  IT-000 interrogator droid **364**
Intersystem Transport Ship **431**
Invisible Hand 56, 61, 330, 331, 332, **390**
ionization blaster **349**
Ipsidon **273**
  Ipsidon buck **94**
Ipsium **339**
irling **92**
Iron Squadron 135, 406
Iron Talon **373**
IT-000 interrogator droid **364**
Ithano, Sidon **214**, 328, 431
Ivexia **315**

J

J-3DI **171**
J-19 Bo-rifle **346**
J-Squadron **193**
Jabiim **276**
  Unnamed Jabiim Moon **276**
Jakku **308**, 309
  Niima Outpost **309**
  Rey's home **309**
jakoosk **222**
Jamillia, Queen **51**
Jannah 207, **232**
  Jannah's bow **367**
Janson, Wes 148, **157**, 412, 413
Jarrus, Kanan (Caleb Dume) 31, 32, 44, 59, **122**, 126, 271, 338, 345, 349
  and Ezra Bridger 122, 127, 345
  Ghost 280
  and the Grand Inquisitor 130, 267
  and Hera Syndulla 122, 123, 138
  lightsaber **343**
  Lothal 282, 284
  Mustafar 258
  vehicles 403
Javes, Lindon **169**, 404
Javos, Suralinda **193**, 389
Jawas 33, 34, **35**, 243, 245
  sandcrawlers **380**
  weapons 349
Jayco **109**

Jebel, Nower **144**
Jedha **285**
  Catacombs of Cadera **285**
  Jedha City 73, 84, 138, 140, 141, 142, 143, **285**, 287
  spamels **14**
  Temple of the Kyber **285**
Jedi Order
  Delta-7 Starfighter **378**
  first Jedi temple **312**
  Jedi Academy **358**
  Jedi Archives 86, **248**, 251, 283, 334
  Jedi High Council 248
  Jedi holocron **334**
  kyber crystals **335**
  light cruiser **387**
  Order 66 31, 44, 47, 49, 50, 52, 59, 62, 65, 79, 269, 336
  technology 324, 325, 327, 329
  Vectors **372**
Jedi temples
  Coruscant 248, 334
  Lothal **282**, 284
  Tanalorr 277
Jedi Temple Guard **81**
Jekara **295**
Jemboc **120**
Jensu, Lieutenant **190**
Jerjerrod, Moff **162**
Jesse **81**
jet troopers
  cannons **367**
  First Order jet troopers **229**
  jetpacks **367**
  Sith jet troopers **233**
jetpacks **367**
  Z-6 jetpack **352**
Jettster, Dexter 12, **50**
  Dex's Diner **250**
Jezzi **121**
JG-1 **19**
Jin, Jonner **135**, 406
Jinara, Marlaa 18, **19**
Jinn, Qui-Gon **23**, 33, 39, 56, 240
  and Anakin Skywalker 23, 32, 35, 42
  holoprojectors 324
  and Jar Jar Binks 23, 27
  and Maul 31, 249, 326
  and Obi-Wan Kenobi 22, 23, 27
  and Yoda 40, 266, 278
Jo **180**
Jomaram, Ram **15**, 17, 322
Jooks **202**
joopa **133**
JPP-192 limospeeder **400**
JS-1975 **179**
JT-12 jetpack **336**
JT-731 Broadhorn transport **399**
juggernaut transport **418**
Julia, Queen 27, **79**, 265
Junda, Cere 32, **99**, 248, 334, 342, 348, 398
Jung, Lonni **117**
Just Lucky 152, **161**
Justifier **393**

K

K-2SO **142**, 143
KA74 blaster rifle **357**
kaadu **26**
Kachirho **270**
Kaddak **304**
Kairos **169**
Kaitis, Eldra **21**, 31, 326
Kakra **291**
Kakrans **155**
Kalani, General **83**, 323, 337
Kalevala **301**
Kaller **271**
Kallisto, Ace 18, **20**
Kallus, Alexsandr 58, 125, **129**, 265, 280, 281, 346
Kalo'ne **229**, 432
Kalonia, Harter **216**
Kamerat, Krix 12, 17

Kamino **251**
   Jango's apartment **252**
   Kaminoan saberdarts **326**
   Tipoca City **252**
Kamo, Lens **225**
Kanata, Maz 12, 14, **214**, 331
   Maz Kanata's Castle 214, 215, **310**
Kanchar **154**
Kandia, Tishra **229**
Kane, Elia **182**
Karbin **151**, 411
Karga, Greef **173**, 174, 175, 177, 299, 356, 359
Karina the Great (Geonosian affiliation) **151**
Karina the Great (Separatist affiliation) **68**
Karius, Gable **139**
Karlo, Timm **114**
Karn, Eedy **119**, 279
Karn, Syril **114**, 279
Karn household **279**
karnex dragon **222**
Karr, Emerie **95**
Karthon **300**
Kashyyyk 74, 94, **269**
   Battle of Kashyyyk **269**
   Kachirho **270**
   Wasskah **270**
Kasmir, Janus **96**, 398
Kasmiri **398**
Kast, Rook **85**
Katarn-class commando armor **339**
Katooni (light freighter) **431**
Katooni (Tholothian) **85**
Katuunko, King 48, **63**
Kaz, Cinta **118**
Kcaj, Coleman **79**
Keen, Enya **12**
keeradak **85**
Keevan, Riyola **225**
Keevil, Bo **198**, 423
Kef Bir **317**
Keize, Soran **168**
Kel **201**
Kelen, Nakari **150**
Kell, Jai **132**
Kenari **278**
Kendoh Gang **224**
Kenobi, Obi-Wan **22**, 25, 38, 41, 51, 58, 77, 100
   and Anakin Skywalker 22, 25, 32, 42, 43
   and Asajj Ventress 60, 259
   Battle of Geonosis 253
   Battle of Naboo 240
   clone army 53, 250, 251
   Clone Wars 49, 52, 59, 378
   and Count Dooku 56, 254, 270, 330
   and Darth Vader 22, 32, 110, 258, 276, 287, 331, 348, 350, 394
   death 293
   Death Star 287, 394
   and Duchess Satine Kryze 68, 69
   escape from Daiyu 398
   and General Grievous 61, 268, 387
   Geonosis Execution Arena 57, 256
   Haja Estree 109, 110
   home 293
   and Kanan Jarrus 122
   kyber crystals 268
   and Leia Organa 48, 54, 88, 111, 255, 276, 324, 342
   lightsaber **324**, 355
   and Luke Skywalker 22, 31, 54, 87, 255, 266, 331
   and the MagnaGuards 332
   and Maul 22, 31, 43, 71, 240, 249, 324, 326
   and Qui-Gon Jinn 22, 23, 27
   and Quinlan Vos 34
   and R4-P17 51
   and Reva 108, 109
   and the Trade Federation 39
   Twilight 386
   and Zam Wesell 250
Kerri **114**
Kerrill, Terisa **169**
Kessel **275**
   Kessel Spice Mines **275**
   Oba Diah **270**
Kessel Run 74, 106, **275**
Kestis, Cal 53, **98**, 99, 324, 334, 335, 348, 398

BD-1 359
and Bode Akuna 112
Bogano 273
Bracca 271
Dathomir 263
Level 2046 247
lightsaber **342**, 346
Zeffo 273
Ketch 92
Ketter, Sash **178**
Kev, Norath **223**
Keysax, Merzin **120**
Khetanna 37, 257, **385**
Khri, Santari **112**
Ki-Adi-Mundi **42**, 45
Kijimi **317**
Kimzi **119**
Kin, Beaumont 216, **227**
Kintan Striders **183**
Kix **80**
Klaatu **165**
Klam, Vulaada 152, **155**
Klatooinian marauders **177**
Klaud **226**
Kleeve, General **96**
Kligson's Moon **295**
Klik-Klak **137**, 253
Klivian, Derek "Hobbie" **157**
Klorri-Clan battle shield **342**
Kloris, Exmar **119**
Kneesaa **167**
Knights of Ren 102, 161, 208, 227, 228, 288, 366, 432
Koboh **277**
   Tanalorr **277**
Kolara **45**
Kolma, Tay **120**
Kondra **160**
Konstantine, Admiral Kassius **132**
Koon, Plo **42**, 43
Koresh, Gor **179**
   Gor's Koresh's Honky Tonk **300**
Koth, Eeth 32, 43, **44**, 61
kouhun 49
Kowakian ape **204**
Krail, Davish "Pops" **148**
krakavora **223**
krayt dragons **180**
Krayt's Claw 53, 66, 69, 77
Kreel **153**
Krell, Pong 43, 58, **76**
Krennic, Orson Callan 55, **138**, 140, 287, 289, 408
krill **176**
Krim, Marg **85**
Kriss, Avar 14, 15, 16, 17, 238
Kristiss **97**
Krownest **283**
Krrsantan 54, **183**
krykna **134**
Kryze, Bo-Katan **75**, 323, 339, 356, 359, 419
   the Darksaber 338
   and Din Djarin 75, 172, 175, 176, 185, 186, 187, 301, 302
   Kryze Fortress **302**
   Lafete 301
   Mandalore 260
   Nite Owls 181
   technology 345, 352
   vehicles 406, 418
Kryze, Duchess Satine 22, 62, **68**, 69, 75, 260, 301, 302, 335
Kryze, Korkie **69**
Kryze Fortress **302**
Ktath'atn, Queen of **154**
the Ku-Bops **20**
Kuat Systems Engineering 378, 395, 427
Kuiil **174**
Kun, Karé **192**
Kuruk **228**
   blaster rifle **366**
KX-series droid **350**
kyber crystals 85, 138, 268, 285, 305, 316, **335**, 409
Kyrell, Thane **97**
Kryelle, Teega **111**

L

L0-LA59 **109**
L3-37 **106**, 394
Lafete **301**
Lagret **117**
Lah'mu **284**
   Erso homestead **284**
Lake Country **252**
lake monster **185**
Lambda-class Imperial shuttle **402**
L'ampar, L'ulo **192**
Lander, Lieutenant **190**
Lang **181**
langskib **420**
Larik **21**
Lark, Wyl **168**
Lars, Beru Whitesun 22, 35, **54**, 255
Lars, Cliegg 35, **54**, 255
Lars, Owen 22, 33, 35, **54**, 87, 255, 380, 409
Lars moisture farm **255**
laser ax **365**
Lash, Nakano 69, **159**
lava meerkats **181**
Lawquane, Cut **81**, 259
Lawquane, Jek **81**
Lawquane, Shaeeah **81**
Lawquane, Suu **81**
Lechee **223**
Lee-Char, Prince 46, 76, 82, **83**, 265
Leebon 12, **13**
Leech, Tasu **212**
Leffbruk, Dass **13**
Legacy Run 14, 15, 238, **372**, 373
Lenwith, Milon **233**
Leonis, Zare **131**, 132
Leoz **202**
LEP service droid **358**
Level 1313 **270**
Level 2046 **247**
Libertine **428**
light cruisers
   First Order's **430**
   Moff Gideon's **418**
lightsabers 189
   Ahsoka Tano's 68, **332**, 346, 361
   Anakin Skywalker's 45, 254, 331
   Asajj Ventress' **330**
   Cal Kestis' **342**
   Count Dooku's **330**
   Crossguard **346**
   the Darksaber 75, 126, 137, 172, 176, 179, 184, **338**
   Darth Sidious' **337**, 345
   Darth Vader's 32, 288, 332, **348**
   Ezra Bridger's **345**, 361
   Grand Inquisitor's **345**
   Kanan Jarrus' **343**
   kyber crystals **335**
   Kylo Ren's 346, **363**
   Leia Organa's 88, 255, 331, **367**, 394
   lightsaber analysis device **360**
   lightwhip **322**
   Lord Corvax's **343**
   Luke Skywalker's 255, 330, 331, **353**, 355, 367, 394
   Mace Windu's **327**, 361
   Maul's 31, **326**
   Obi-Wan Kenobi's **324**, 355
   Reva's **342**
   Rey's 214, 331, 364, **367**
   Sabine Wren's **346**
   Skywalker lightsaber **331**
   Yoda's 45, **330**
lightwhip lightsaber **322**
Lintra, Tallissan **216**
Lira San **282**
Living Waters of Mandalore **302**
LL-30 blaster pistols **339**
LM-432 "Muckraker" crab droids **333**
Lo, Slowen **220**
load skimmers **432**
Loathsom, General Whorm **58**
Lobot 96, **158**, 295, 351, 411
locations **236–317**

INDEX

Lograay **166**
Lola Sayu **264**
 the Citadel **264**
Lompop, Deva **161**
Loneozner, Laze "Fixer" **183**, **184**
Longbeam **372**
Loriach **162**
Loth-cats **132**, 189
 white Loth-cat **133**
Loth-wolves **137**
 Loth-wolf den **284**
 white Loth-wolf **137**
Lothal **67**, **280**
 Atollon **282**
 Capital City **281**
 Ezra's Roost **281**
 Garel **282**
 Loth-cats **132**, 189
 Loth-wolf den **284**
 Lothal Imperial speeder bike **403**
 Lothal Jedi temple **282**
 Lothal Resistance Camp **284**
 Old Jho's Pit Stop **282**
Loy, Kino **120**
LT-514 **170**
Lucrehulk Prime **411**
luggabeast **212**
Lumpawaroo **170**
Lyonie, Boss **76**
Lyste, Yogar **128**

M

M1-RE **224**
M-32 light repeating blaster rifle **357**
M-68 landspeeder **397**
MA-13 **179**
Mac, Vildar **12**, 13
McCool, Droopy **164**, 165
Madine, General Crix **165**
MagnaGuards 61, **332**, 344, 386
Mai, Shu **55**
maintenance droid, Otoga-222 **366**
majordomo, Mok Shaiz's **182**
Mako-Ta Space Docks **291**
Malachor **283**
 Malachor Sith temple **283**
Malagán, Sav **12**, 14, 68, 214, 310
Malarus **193**
Malastare **259**
Malbus, Baze 142, **143**, 347
Maldo Kreis **300**
Maldo Kreis ice spiders **180**
Malevolence 42, 63, 333, **387**, 389, 390
Malicos, Taron 72, **99**
Malk, Ranzar 177, **300**
Malla **170**
mamacore **180**
Manaroo **163**
Mandalore **260**
 Concordia **302**
 the Darksaber **338**
 Kalevala **301**
 Kryze Fortress **302**
 Living Waters of Mandalore **302**
 Mandalorian armor **336**
 Mandalorian captain **188**
 Mandalorian judge **186**
 Mandalorian vault **339**
 Sundari **260**
 weapons **345**
Mandible, Doctor **177**
Mandrell, Ody **36**
Mann, Elzar 14, **15**, 16, 238
Mapuzo **276**
Mar, Riot 177, **417**
 starfighter **417**
Marauder 91, 94, 132, 141, **392**
Margo **105**
Maridun **254**
Mark IV patrol droid **360**
Marki, Kleya **118**, 278
Markona, Thane **155**, 291, 331
Markona, Tula **155**

Marrok **190**
Marstrap, Camie **183**, 184
Martez, Rafa **86**, 392
Martez, Trace **86**, 392
Martez Sisters' Repair Shop **270**
Maru, Estala **15**, 238
the Mask of Momin **339**
massifs **55**
Mattin, Mart **135**, 406
Maul 21, **31**, 38, 65, 68, 263, 341
 and Ahsoka Tano 270, 339
 and Count Dooku 50, 263
 the Darksaber 126, **338**
 and Darth Sidious 31, 263, 267, 326
 and Ezra Bridger 126, 127, 283
 holocron 343
 and Kanan Jarrus 122, 343
 lightsaber 31, **326**
 and Obi-Wan Kenobi 22, 31, 43, 71, 240, 249, 324, 326
 and Qi'ra 102, 263
 and Qui-Gon Jinn 31, 249, 326
 and Savage Opress 31, 43
 Shadow Collective 37, 69, 71, 85, 257, 260, 270
 vehicles 377, 406
Mawood, Lorrin **190**
Max-7 Rono freighter **400**
Maxa, Moda **105**
Mayday 89, **95**
Mayfeld, Migs **178**, 300, 325, 357, 418
Maz Kanata's castle 214, 215, **310**
MB-13 **202**
MC95 star cruiser **431**
ME-8D9 **214**
Medon, Tion **79**
Meeko, Del **149**, 150, 168, 221
Meero, Dedra **116**, 117
Megadroid **334**
Megalox Beta **304**
MEL-221 **93**
Melch **135**
Melshi, Ruescott **141**
Melton, Jon **162**
memory search device **360**
Meorti **155**
Merrick, Antoc **142**
Merrin 98, **99**
Meson Martinet **431**
Miak, Tarna **13**
Military Creation Act 249, 250
Millegi, Grini **93**, 272
Millennium Falcon 53, 149, 211, 214, 262, 263, **394**
 and the Death Stars 87, 287, 297, 410
 and Han Solo 100, 157, 158, 195, 340, 341
 Hoth Asteroid Belt 293
 Kessel Run 74, 106, 275
 and Lando Calrissian 74, 100, 107
 and Nien Nunb 167
 and Poe Dameron 194, 226, 315
 and Rey 195, 206, 308
Milvayne **291**
Mimban **274**
Mining Guild 132, 275, 335, 344
 Mining Guild TIE fighter **406**
Minst, Kradon **13**
Mira 44, **96**
Miramir 209, **231**, 308
Miril **163**
mobile prison facility **411**
mobile Tac-Pod **399**
Mod scooter **418**
the Modal Nodes **146**
Model 201 mortar **358**
the Modifier **185**
Moj, Ziton **78**
Mokko 95, **273**
Mollo, Orlen **13**
Moloch **103**, 397
Momin, Darth **97**, 288, 339, 353, 411
Mon Cala **265**
Mon Calamari MC80 Star Cruiser **415**
Monument Plaza **302**
Monument to the Ones **304**
moonyo **95**
Moore, Sly **46**
Moradi, Vi **192**

Morai **134**
Morak **300**
Morlana, Ferrix **277**
Morlana One **277**
Mortis **264**
Mos Eisley
 Mos Eisley Cantina 146, **263**
 Mos Eisley Spaceport **262**
Mos Espa **244**
 Battle of Mos Espa 184, 185
 Mos Espa City Hall **301**
 Mos Espa Grand Arena **246**
 Watto's Shop **245**
Mos Pelgo **300**
Mosk, Linus **118**, 399
Mother of the Path (Elecia Zeveron) 13
Mothma, Leida **119**, 278
Mothma, Mon 48, **67**, 123, 286, 401, 405
 family 119, 278
Motti, Admiral **146**
Motto, Peli **177**, 325, 358, 359, 376, 419
mouse droids **351**
Mowaat, Lieutenant **190**
Mrala, Zeen 16, **17**, 372
Mubo **225**
mud yak **185**
mudhorn **176**
mudtroopers **104**, 341
Murley **189**
Mustafar **258**
 Darth Vader's fortress **288**
Mustafarian Priestess **139**
Musters, Oolin **141**
Muva, Oddy **192**, 193
MWC-35C repeating cannon **347**
Myarga the Merciless **17**
mylaya **94**
mynock **157**
Mythosaur **186**
Mythrol's speeder **417**

N

N1-ZX **193**, 333
N5 sentry droids **357**
Naboo **240**
 Battle of Naboo **240**, 241, 242, 249
 Lake Country **252**
 N-1 starfighter **376**
 Naboo Lake Retreat **252**
 Naboo Palace Guard 241
 Otoh Gunga **242**
 Royal cruisers **378**
 Royal pistols **326**
 Royal starship 30, **376**
 Theed **241–2**
 Theed Power Generator **249**
 yachts **380**
Nadon, Momaw **146**
Nak-II **21**
Nalor, Nenavakasa "Nena" **222**
the Nameless 12, 13, **16**, 17
 Nameless control rods **322**
Nar Shaddaa **290**
Narb **202**
narglatch **64**
Nari **108**
Nark, Hallion **201**
Narkina 5 119, 120, **279**, 342
Nass, Boss 27, **28**, 242
Nattai, Gella **12**, 14
Nax **109**
ND-5 **164**
NED-B **110**
Needa, Captain Lorth **157**
Needle **159**
Neeva **225**
Neimoidian shuttle **375**
Nemec **95**
Nemik, Karis **118**, 279
nerf **154**
Nest, Enfys 34, **104**
 bike **397**
 helmet **341**
 shields **341**

staff **341**
Netal, Bazine **214**, 310, 406
netcaster **94**
Nevarro **299**
New Republic 247, 339, 421, 422
nexu **57**, 256
Niamos **279**
Nico, Kanina **97**
Night Buzzard **432**
Night of a Thousand Tears 75, 188, 338, 352
night troopers **191**, 350
Night Wind assassin **182**
Nightbrothers **31**, 43, 71, 72
Nightsisters 56, 60, 71, 77, 263, 264
 crystal balls **335**
 energy bow **335**
nightwatcher worm **211**
the Nihil 14, 15, 16, **322**, 372
Ninka **428**
Ninth Sister **86**
Nitani, Rooper **12**, 13, 322
Nix **164**
No-Space **239**
Nod **202**
Nokk **155**
Nokru, Vect **109**
Nolan **95**, 273
Noti **191**, 361
 Noti pods **421**
 Noti slingshot **361**
Nu, Jocasta 32, **50**, 63, 66, 86, 130, 334, 348
Nu-class shuttles **406**
Nubs **18**, 19, 20, 21, 40, 239, 322
Numa **80**
Numidian Prime **275**
Nunb, Nien **167**, 219, 386, 42
Nur **276**
Nuress, Shakara **168**
Nyche **110**

O

O-MR1 **193**
Oba Diah **270**
Ochi of Bestoon 44, 107, 159, 230, **231**, 258, 316, 432
 dagger **367**
octuptarra droids **390**
Offee, Barriss **47**, 62, 110, 330
OG-9 homing spider droid **381**
OG-LC **19**, 322, 373
Ohnaka, Hondo 38, 43, 53, 56, **64**, 224, 264, 274, 306, 332, 379, 394, 431
Ohnaka Gang 64, 66
OI-CT **399**
Oki-Poki **229**
Okka, Eustacia **160**
Old Daka **77**
Old Jho **131**
 Old Jho's Pit Stop **282**, 306
Olié, Ric **29**
Omega 65, 77, 82, 89, **90**, 95, 271, 272, 339, 392, 393
Omera **176**
Ommlen, Praster **215**
OMS Devilfish **388**
Onderon **265**
Onyo, Ketsu **133**, 405
 staff **346**
Oola **165**
OOM-9 **26**
opee sea killer **28**
Opeepit **198**
Operation: Cinder 24, 149, 150, 168, 178, 182, 240, 241, 298
Opress, Savage 31, 43, 56, 60, 63, **71**, 257, 335
 and Asajj Ventress 71, 72, 263
 and Count Dooku 71, 263
orbak **232**
orbital mines **361**
Ord Mantell **267**
 Cid's Parlor **271**
Order 66 31, 44, 47, 49, 50, 52, 59, 62, 65, 79, 269, 336
Order of the Night Wind **358**

Organa, Bail 30, 33, **48**, 83, 261, 313, 324, 386
Organa, Breha 48, **83**, 109, 261, 324
Organa, Celly **109**
Organa, Kayo **109**
Organa, Leia (Princess Leia; General Organa) 22, 26, **88**, 134, 334
   Alderaan 261
   and Amilyn Holdo 219
   and Bail and Breha Organa 48, 83, 88
   and Ben Solo 208
   and C-3PO 30, 33
   and Chewbacca 74
   Crait 313
   and Darth Vader 88, 167, 349
   death 88, 209, 214, 218, 283
   and the Death Star 76, 88, 286, 287, 358, 409
   escape from Daiyu 398
   and the Ewoks 166, 297
   and Han Solo 88, 100, 107, 195, 214, 297, 311
   and Jabba the Hutt 37, 107, 158, 257, 355
   kidnapping of 276, 324
   L0-LA59 109
   lightsaber 88, 255, 331, **367**, 394
   and Luke Skywalker 88, 315, 355
   and Mon Mothma 67
   and Obi-Wan Kenobi 48, 54, 88, 111, 255, 276, 342
   Operation: Cinder 376
   and Poe Dameron 194
   and R2-D2 30, 87, 88
   Raddus 428
   and the Rebel Alliance 290
   and the Resistance 76, 88, 311
   Tantive IV 83, 88, 386, 409
   toy droids 342
   weapons 348
   Wobani 285
Organa, Niano **109**
Ori **21**
Orka **201**, 204
orray **57**
Orrelios, Garazeb "Zeb" **125**, 126, 129, 282, 347, 401
   bo-rifle **344**
   vehicles 402
Ossus **302**
Otoga-222 maintenance droid **366**
Otoh Gunga **242**
Outcast **393**
Outland TIE fighter **417**
Outlander Gambling Club **250**
the Outpost **273**
Ovanis **304**
Ovanis Crèche Elder **192**
Ozzel, Admiral Kendal **156**, 412

P

Paak, Salman **115**
Paak, Wilmon **115**
Pabu **273**
   Archium **273**
Pagalies, Teemto **36**
Pagodon **298**
Palpatine, Sheev *see* Sidious, Darth
Pamlo, Tynnra **144**
Panaka, Quarsh **26**
Panisia **295**
Panox, Argus **105**
Pantora **271**
Papanoida, Baron 37, **69**, 263
Paploo **166**, 297
Parasitti, Cato 50, **66**, 334
Parnadee, General **228**
parole droid **359**
Partagaz, Lio **117**
Pasaana **316**
Pastoria **304**
Pateesa **164**
Path engine **322**
Path of the Open Hand 12, 13, 17, 40, 45, 238, **322**
patrol droids, Mark IV **360**
patrol troopers **103**
Pav-Ti **21**

Pava, Jessika **215**, 389
Peavey, Edrison **218**
Peekpa **167**
Peel, Lortha **184**
Pellaeon, Gilad **188**
Peridea **303**
   Monument to the Ones **304**
   Peridea Fortress **303**
Peridea bandits **191**
Pershing, Dr. Penn **174**, 182, 186, 268, 359
Persuader-class tank droids **385**
Petro **85**
Phaedra **111**
Phantom **400**
Phantom II **406**
Phase I clone trooper armor **327**
Phase II clone trooper armor 52, **336**
Phase II purge trooper armor **342**
Phasma, Captain 188, 192, 200, **203**, 221, 305
   armor **362**
   baton **363**
   blaster rifle **362**
Phoenix Home **404**
Phoenix Nest **406**
Phoenix Squadron 67, 123, 124, 148, 282, 283, 286, 401, 411
Pidys, Derla **220**
Piell, Even 42, 43, **44**, 58, 73, 323
Piett, Admiral Firmus **156**
Pillio **298**
pilots
   clone pilots **80**
   First Order shuttle pilots **218**
   First Order Special Forces TIE pilots **206**
   First Order TIE fighter pilots **206**
   First Order treadspeeder pilots **229**
   Imperial combat pilots **128**
   Imperial tank pilots **144**
pirate Corsair, Gorian Shard's **419**
pirate snub fighter **419**
pistols
   CC-420 pistol **358**
   Naboo Royal pistol **326**
   see also blaster pistols
pit droids **325**
Plank, Sarco **211**
plasma pike **358**
Plazir-15 **303**
Plouth, Werth (the Herald) **13**
pluripleq **155**
Plutt, Unkar **211**, 308, 309, 394
podracing 245, 246
   Radon-Ulzer podracer **377**
   Sebulba's podracer **377**
Poggle the Lesser 47, **55**, 68, 253, 256
police gunship **404**
Polis Massa **270**
Poof, Yarael **45**
Pord **21**
porg **218**
Porkins, Jek **147**
Porter, Captain **189**
Posla, Tam **144**
Praetorian Guard 213, **219**, 331
   weapons **365**
Prauf **98**
Pre-Mor authority carrier **399**
Primoc, Luleo **105**
probe droids, spider **363**
Profundity 144, 348, **409**
protocol droids **329**
   see also individual droids
Proxima, Lady **103**, 274
Pryce, Arihnda 73, **135**, 280, 343
Pryde, General 210, **228**, 233
puffer pigs **132**
purge troopers **111**, 350
   Phase II purge trooper armor **342**
purrgil **134**
Pyke, Lom **78**
Pyke Boss **184**
Pyke Syndicate 53, 56, 78, 79, 106, **418**
   Cad Bane 65
   Kessel 275
   Mos Espa 244
   Mos Pelgo 300

Oba Diah **270**
   and the Tuskens 182, 183
   weapons 350, 358
Pyloon's Saloon regulars **112**
Pyre, Commander **205**, 365
   armor **362**
   blaster **362**
PZ-4CO **216**

Q

Q9-0 **178**, 353
qartuum **178**
Qin **178**
Qi'ra **102**, 334, 340, 341, 353, 397
   Crimson Dawn 31, 64, 100, 102, 104, 105, 158, 161, 227, 231, 353, 397
   and Darth Maul 102, 263
   and Han Solo 100, 102, 103, 104, 295
   Vermillion 414
QT-KT **85**
Quadinaros, Ben **36**, 366
quadjumper **427**
Quadpaw, Doctor **119**, 279
Quarantine World III **290**
Quarren 180
   fishing vessel **417**
   freighter **420**
Quarrie **133**, 405, 415
Quell, Yrica **168**
Quiggold **215**
Quinn, Domaric **229**

R

R-series astromech **329**
R1 security droid **357**
R1-J5 **197**
R2-C4 **196**
R2-D2 **30**, 287, 323, 410
   and C-3PO 30, 33, 48, 225, 348
   and Leia Organa 30, 87, 88
   and Luke Skywalker 30, 87, 145, 255, 355, 410
R3-T2 **108**
R4-D12 **204**
R4-G77 **199**
R4-M1 **85**
R4-P17 **51**
R5-D4 **145**
R5-G9 **199**
R5-P8 **224**
R7-A7 **63**
R23-X9 **199**
Rabé **29**
Raddus 195, 217, 219, 348, **428**
Raddus, Admiral 76, **144**, 409
Rael, Luthen 67, 84, 113, **116**, 117, 118, 278, 279, 326, 342, 399
Ragnar **185**
Ralter, Dak **157**, 412
Ramda, General Sotorus **145**, 289
Rampart, Edmon 24, **91**, 252
Rancisis, Oppo **44**
rancors 184, 257
   Boba's rancor **185**
   rancor keepers **184**
range troopers **105**
   boots **340**
raptor **187**
Rashin, Tara **225**
rathtar **212**
Rau, Fenn **134**, 282, 406
Rax, Gallius 45, 149, 169, 200
Raxlo 18, **20**
raxshir **21**
Raxus Secundus **265**
Ray, Eneb **151**, 344
Rayvis **112**
Razor Crest 172, 173, 176, 356, 358, **416**
Razzi, Latts **77**
RD-3 **189**
Re-Integration technician **186**
Rebel Alliance 156, 167, 261, 263

INDEX

on Dantooine 283
Death Star 73
Echo Base 292
formation of 283, 286
on Hoth 301
Lightmaker 405
Lucrehulk Prime 411
Panisia 295
Resistance base 311
technology 329, 350
vehicles 408, 412, 422
Rebel cruiser (Nebulon-B Frigate) 414
Rebel transport 413
Rebo, Max 164, **165**
Rebolt 103
Red Ace 423
Red Five 353, 410
Red Honeycomb Zone 314
Red Squadron 147, 148, 410, 422
Ree, Ciena **97**
Reed 185
reek **57**, 256
Reeves, Koska 180, **181**, 301
Réillata, Queen 25, 51
Rell, Azlin 13, **16**, 40
Remora 393
remote 327
Ren 161
Ren, Kylo (Ben Solo) 30, 40, 57, 88, 100, 161, 203, 206, **208**, 210, 228, 330, 394
  Cave of Evil 213, 266, 267
  and Darth Sidious (Palpatine) 24, 208, 226, 366
  Finalizer 425, 426
  and Han Solo 74, 100, 208, 209, 213, 363
  helmet 227, **363**
  lightsaber 346, **363**
  and Lor San Tekka 309
  and Luke Skywalker 87, 192, 208, 302, 312, 313, 355
  on Mustafar 226, 258
  and Rey 24, 195, 208, 209, 213, 219, 229, 297, 312, 331, 348, 363, 364
  shuttle 425
  and Snoke 208, 209, 213, 363, 429
  TIE fighter **429**
  vehicles 395, **425**, 428, **429**
reptavian 178
Republic 391
  artillery cannon (AV-7) **390**
  Assault ship (*Acclamator*-class) **381**
  attack cruiser **383**
  Jedi light cruiser **387**
  LAAT/i repulsorlift gunship **381**
  Longbeam **372**
  Republic Cruiser **374**
  Republic Executive Building **250**
  V-19 Torrent Starfighter **385**
Republic (ship) 147, 155
Resistance 167
  B-wing fighter **431**
  blockade runner **422**
  heavy bombers **427**
  Intersystem Transport Ship **431**
  Resistance base 311
  technology 329, 364
  transporter **427**
Resselian, Wade 111, 412
Reva 22, 48, 54, **108**, 109, 130, 255, 276, 342, 398
  lightsaber **342**
the Revengers **162**
Rex, Captain 31, 32, 52, 58, **59**, 63, 323, 405
  AT-TE 382, **405**
  and Echo 65
  and Lawquane family 81
  Order 66 86
  weapons 330
Rey 22, 30, 40, 195, **209**, 231, 255
  Ancient Rite of Challenge 335
  and Darth Sidious (Palpatine) 24, 33, 41, 43, 50, 208, 209, 230, 366, 367
  and Finn 206, 207
  helmets 353
  on Jakku 209, 211, 212, 308
  and Kylo Ren (Ben Solo) 24, 195, 208, 209, 213, 219, 229, 297, 312, 331, 348, 363, 364
  lightsaber 214, 310, **331**, 364, **367**

and Luke Skywalker 87, 207, 209, 214, 255, 310, 312, 331
  Millennium Falcon 195, 206, 308, 394
  NN-14 blaster pistol **364**
  quarterstaff **364**
  Rey's home **309**
  speeder **427**
RG-G1 **86**
Rhasiv 121
Rho-class shuttle **392**
Ri, Nossor **83**
RIC-series droid **358**
Rieekan, General Carlist **156**, 292
Rieve 171
rifles
  773 firepuncher sniper rifle **339**
  adventurer slugthrower rifle **325**
  Corpo rifle **342**
  Din Djarin's **356**
  E-11D rifle **350**
  E-22 rifle **341**
  Fennec's sniper rifle **339**
  J-19 Bo-rifle **346**
  Tusken rifles **325**
  see also blaster rifles
Ring of Kafrene 285
Rings of Vaale 353
Rishi Station **254**
Rivas, Sol 221
River Moon of Al'doleem 272
RJ-83 17, **18**, 20, 322, 373
RK-3 blaster **365**
Ro, Bansu 168
Ro, Marchion 14, **16**, 322, 372
  helmet **322**
Ro, Marda **13**, 372
Ro, Yana 12, **13**
Robonino **70**
Rodrigo, Senator **190**
Rogue One 141, 144, 286, 409
Rogue Squadron 148, 156, 157, 412
Roken, Kawlan **111**, 399
rokkna 204, 306
Romary **423**
Romodi, General **145**
rontos 34, 243
Rook, Bodhi **141**, 142, 287
the Roost **300**
Royal Naboo Security Forces 242, 249
RP82 Fiend Fighter **421**
Ruby 92
Rucklin, Jace **201**, 202
  racer **424**
Rudor, Baron Valen **128**
Rukh 138, **332**
Rur **154**
Rwoh, Vernestra 14, **15**, 17, 37, 45, 322
RX-series droid **358**
Ryloth **254**
  Syndulla residence **283**
Ryvora, Tamara "Tam" **198**, 205, 423
RZ-2 A-wing **427**

S

Sabacc **341**
Sabé 25, 28, **29**, 32, 36, 270, 295
saberjowl **93**
Sabrond, Chesille **233**
Saché **29**
Safa Toma 272
Sage, Zerelda **170**
Sagwa **106**
Saifir **187**
Saleucami **259**
Salju **224**
San, Synara 196, **204**, 307, 424
sand beasts **183**
sandcrawlers **380**
sando aqua monsters **28**
sandtroopers **145**, 349
Sanjay Rash, King **78**
Santhe Shipyards **303**
the Sarlacc 53, **165**, 351, 358, 379

Sartha, Vel 117
Sato, Jun **132**, 405
Sato's Hammer **406**
Savareen 275
Saxon, Gar 79, **135**, 260, 282, 338
SC-X2 **198**
Scalder, Doctor **93**
Scaleback, Ciddarin "Cid" **91**, 93, 267, 271, 272, 273, 393
Scarif 289
  Battle of Scarif 144, 289
  Citadel Tower **289**
  Death Star 67, 73, 113, 140, 141, 142, 143, 144
scattergun, BARM-ST12 **357**
Scav droids **322**
Scay, Dobbu **220**
Scintel, Miraj **76**, 335
Scion shuttle **421**
Scipio **259**
Scissorpunch, Therm **105**
Scorch 93
Scott **185**
the Scourge 158, **163**
Scourge One **414**
scout guard **181**
scout troopers **165**
  blasters **354**
scuba troopers 80, **362**
  First Order scuba troopers **222**
Sculdun, Davo **121**
Scythe **398**
SD-K4 assassin droids **335**
Se, Nala 51, **63**, 393
SE-44C blaster pistol **364**
sea skiffs **433**
Seatos **303**
Sebulba **34**, 36, 246
  podracer **377**
Second Sister **98**, 99, 348
Secura, Aayla 34, 49, **50**
security droids
  First Order security droids **366**
  R1 security droids **357**
Seevor **137**
Seezelslak **225**
Segra-Milo **279**
Sella, Korr **212**
Semage **21**
Senate Guard **80**
Senesca, Zev **156**
Senna **106**
Sentinel **171**
sentinel droids **343**
sentry droids
  First Order sentry droids **365**
  Imperial sentry droids **347**
  N5 sentry droids **357**
Separatists
  aqua droids **335**
  battle droids **323**
  crab droids **333**
  droids **390**
  Hyena bomber **384**
  Invisible Hand **390**
  Trident drill assault craft **385**
Serenno **264**
  the Box **265**
  Dooku's Castle **264**
Seripas **66**
Serolonis, Safa Toma 272
Seventh Sister **133**, 346
SF-R3 19, **224**
Shaa, Darth **97**
Shadow Caster **405**
Shadow Collective 31, 37, 61, 69, 71, 85, 257, 260, 270, 336
Shadow Council **188**
Shaiz, Mok **183**, 301
  luxury speeder **418**
  majordomo **182**
Shand, Fennec 51, 53, 65, **92**, 185, 257, 263, 393, 416
  helmet **339**
  sniper rifle **339**
Shard, Gorian **185**, 406
  pirate Corsair **419**

Sharest, Falthina **103**
Shen **170**
shields
  energy shields **358**
  Enfys Nest's shield **341**
  First Order riot shields **364**
  Gungan personal energy shields **326**
  Klorri-Clan battle shields **342**
  Silandra Sho's shield **322**
  Zaly shields **354**
shipyard tour personnel carrier **420**
Sho, Silandra **12**, 322
  shield **322**
shock troopers **81**
Shoklop, Kedpin **220**
shoretroopers **145**, 341
Shryke, Melis **17**
Shu-Torun **290**
Shuggoth **187**, 420
shuttle ferry **400**
Shydopp pirates **181**
Sidious, Darth (Sheev Palpatine) **24**, 48, 56, 60, 65, 67, 251, 258, 326
  and Anakin Skywalker 24, 32, 331
  apartment **254**
  clone troopers 52
  and Count Dooku 45, 56, 251, 383
  and Darth Vader 32, 151, 258, 288, 348, 350
  death 226, 247
  the Death Stars 24, 287, 297, 402
  death troopers 141
  droids 55
  Emperor's Throne Room **297**, 317
  Exegol 316, 433
  Festival of Light 65
  Galactic Senate Chamber 249
  Galaxies Opera House 268
  and General Grievous 49, 390
  and the Grand Inquisitor 130
  and Grand Moff Tarkin 73
  Inquisitor Base 270
  Jakku 308
  and Jar Jar Binks 27
  Jedi temple killing mission 248
  and Kylo Ren 24, 208, 226, 366
  lightsabers 337, 345
  and Mace Windu 41, 43, 46
  Malachor 283
  and Mas Amedda 45
  and Maul 31, 263, 267, 326
  and Mother Talzin 71
  and Nute Gunray 26
  office **250**
  Operation: Cinder 240
  Order 66 42, 47, 52, 59, 62, 65, 79, 269, 336
  and Padmé Amidala 24, 25
  and Qi'ra 353
  and Rey 24, 33, 41, 43, 50, 208, 209, 230, 366, 367
  Royal Guards 80, **83**, 219
  Scimitar **377**
  Sith Cultists 226
  and Sly Moore 46
  and Snoke 213
  the Spire 267
  stormtroopers 101
  vehicles 411
  the world between worlds 284
  and Yoda 40, 249, 330
Sienar, Grace **170**
Sienar Fleet Systems 274, 395, 408
Sifo-Dyas 39, 51, 56, 78, **79**, 251, 270, 336
Sigma, Ajax **163**, 295
signal beacon **366**
Silas, Reath **15**, 16, 17
Silvain, Barash **12**
Silver Angel 63, **392**
Sin, Karr Nuq **193**
Sing, Aurra **38**, 49, 53, 104, 261, 379
Singh, Avi **92**, 265, 382
Single Trooper Aerial Platform (STAP) **375**
Sinta Glacier Colony **315**
Sinube, Tera **68**, 276
Sion, Hugh **223**
Sirrek, Tey 12, **13**
Sister Six **154**

Sith
  Sith Cultists **226**, 233
  Sith holocron **343**
  Sith Infiltrator **377**
  Sith jet troopers **233**
  Sith speeders **377**
  Sith star destroyers **433**
  Sith troopers **233**
  Sith troopers' armor **367**
  Sith troopers' blasters **367**
  Sith wayfinder 258, **366**
Siv **192**
Sixth Brother **86**
Skad **184**
Skako Minor **270**
Skara Nal **272**
  Skara Nal compass **339**
  Skara Nal Mech **393**
Skeen, Arvel **118**
Skerris, Vult **135**
ski speeder **429**
Skiff, Verlo **114**
Skoll, Baylan **188**, 304, 420
Skora **171**
Skreek **202**
skriffles **20**
Skywalker, Anakin see Vader, Darth (Anakin Skywalker)
Skywalker, Luke 30, 50, **87**, 257, 351
  Ahch-To 312
  and Boba Fett 293
  and C-3PO 87, 255
  and Darth Vader 24, 32, 37, 53, 87, 255, 290, 293, 294, 295, 297, 331, 348, 350, 355, 414
  and the Death Star 286, 287, 353, 410
  flight helmet **353**
  Geonosis Execution Arena 153
  and Grakkus the Hutt 153, 290
  and Grogu 87, 175, 301, 302
  and Han Solo 37, 38, 87, 100, 156
  holocron library 334
  on Hoth 292, 412
  and Kylo Ren (Ben Solo) 87, 192, 208, 302, 312, 313, 355
  and Leia Organa 88, 315, 355
  lightsabers 255, 330, **331**, **353**, **355**, 367, 394
  and Obi-Wan Kenobi 22, 31, 54, 87, 255, 266, 331
  Ossus 302
  Pillio 298
  and R2-D2 30, 87, 145, 255, 355, 410
  and Reva 108, 109, 342
  and Rey 87, 207, 209, 214, 310, 312, 331
  X-34 landspeeder **409**
  and Yoda 40, 87, 266, 267, 293, 410
Skywalker, Shmi 25, 29, 32, 33, **35**, 38, 39, 54, 255
Slaygh **20**
SLD-26 planetary shield generator **355**, 391
Slingshot**171**
Slip **94**, 206
Sloane, Rae **149**, 402
Smyth, Freyta **160**
Snarl **202**
Snoke 210, **213**, 219, 331
  Cave of Evil 266, 267
  and Kylo Ren 208, 209, 213, 363, 429
  Snoke's navigators **218**
  Starkiller Base 305
  Supremacy 429
Snootles, Sy 37, 63, **70**, 254
snow speeders **426**
snowtroopers **157**
  armor 362
  First Order snowtroopers **206**
Snu, Gorvin **176**
Sobeck, Osi **72**, 264
Soh, Lina 14, **16**, 45, 238, 351
Sokoli, Tarl **162**
Sol, Rella **170**
solar sailer **383**
Solay, Lys 17, **18**, 19, 20, 40, 239, 322
Solo, Ben see Ren, Kylo (Ben Solo)
Solo, Han 30, 70, 97, **100**, 269, 292, 412, 414
  and Boba Fett 37, 53, 100, 102, 106, 107, 158, 257, 294, 379
  in carbonite 69, 74, 100, 102, 106, 107, 294
  and Chewbacca 74, 100

and Darth Vader 46, 53, 100, 102, 159, 294, 379
death 76, 167
and the Death Stars 76, 100, 287, 296, 358, 402
dice **340**
Eravana 100, 212, 426
and Jabba the Hutt 37, 38, 69, 100, 107, 214, 257, 294, 379, 394
Kessel Run 106, 275
and Kylo Ren 74, 100, 209, 213, 363
and Leia Organa 88, 100, 107, 195, 214, 297, 311
and Luke Skywalker 37, 38, 87, 100, 156
and Maz Kanata 214, 310
Millennium Falcon 157, 195, 262, 275, 340, 341, 394, 396, 414
modified DL-44 heavy blaster pistol **352**
and Qi'ra 100, 102, 103, 104, 295
Starkiller Base 100, 305
and Tobias Beckett 100, 104
the Son **72**
Son-Tuul **290**
Sooger, Lexo **220**
Sorgan frog **176**
Soulless One **387**
Sovereign 345, 401
Sovereign Protector **233**
space slug **157**
Spalex **304**
spamel **14**
Spanjaf, Merei **131**
Spark Eternal 152, **153**, 163
Sparkburn, Jordanna **17**
speagull **205**
speeder bikes
  712-Ava speeder bike **416**
  Zephyr-J speeder bike **416**
speeders
  Cobb Vanth's **417**
  Kai Brightstar's **373**
  Mayor Mok Shaiz's luxury **418**
  Mythrol's **417**
  Rey's **427**
  TAY-0's **393**
Speedstar, Marcus 197, **204**
  Galaxy's Glory **424**
Sperado, Kullbee **121**
SPHA-T **383**
Spice Runners 194, 230, 231
spider droids
  OG-9 homing spider droid **381**
  spider probe droid **363**
spider tank **419**
the Spire **267**
Sprocket **171**
Squall Spider **372**
Sskeer **14**, 372
Star Commuter 2000 **404**
Star Destroyers 337, **396**
  Sith Star Destroyer **433**
Star Hopper **372**
star navigator droid **360**
Star Seeker **373**
starfighters
  A-wing starfighter **415**
  ARC-170 starfighter **387**
  B-wing starfighter **415**
  BTA-NR2 Y-wing starfighter **429**
  Delta-7 starfighter **378**
  Din Djarin's N-1 starfighter **419**
  ETA-2 Jedi Starfighter **388**
  Gauntlet starfighter **406**
  Geonosian starfighter **383**
  Riot Mar starfighter **417**
  training A-wing starfighter **406**
  Umbaran starfighter **388**
  V-19 Torrent starfighter **385**
  V-wing starfighter **391**
  Warbird starfighter **424**
  Y-wing starfighters **389**
Starhawk **421**
Stark, Sully **111**
Starkiller Base 100, **305**, 311, 426
Starlight Beacon 14, 15, 16, 45, **238**, 348, 372, 373
Starros, Aryssha **163**
Starros, Avon 15, **17**
Starros, Ghirra **16**
Starros, Mevera **163**

Starros, Phel **163**
Starros, Sana 37, **150**, 152, 161, 163, 310, 346, 411
Starros, Thea **163**
Starweird **163**
Statura, Ushos O. **216**
Steadfast 44, 74, 228, 229, 232
stealth ship **384**
steelpecker **211**
Stinger Mantis 98, 99, **398**
stone crabs **186**
Stormseed **322**
stormtrooper executioner **221**
stormtroopers 52, **101**
  armor **340**, 362
  blaster rifle **337**
  First Order stormtrooper armor **362**
  First Order stormtroopers **200**
  stormtrooper transport **426**
  TK trooper armor **339**
  weapons 337, 341, 349, 364, 367
Strassi, Dokk **182**
Strung, Ansen 19, **20**, 21
Strung, Senna **21**
Stygeon Prime **267**
  the Spire **267**
Su, Prime Minister Lama **51**, 65, 251, 252, 272
Suduri, Trilla see Second Sister
Sugi **66**, 353
summa-verminoth **106**
Sun, Creighton **12**, 346
Sundari **260**
Sunspot Prison **290**
Sun'Zee, Ady **13**
super battle droids **328**
super tactical droids **337**
superlaser siege cannon **365**
Supremacy 195, 207, 210, 217, 218, 219, 331, 365, 428, **429**
Suurgav, Shriv **168**
Syke **103**
Syndulla, Cham 41, 46, 80, **82**, 93, 123, 254, 283, 343, 406
Syndulla, Eleni **92**
Syndulla, Hera 33, **123**, 126, 180, 190, 254, 392, 411
  blaster **343**
  Chopper 123, 124
  Ghost 280, 401
  and Kanan Jarrus 122, 123, 138
  mission to Seatos 190, 191
  Syndulla residence 82, 283
  vehicles 405, 406
Syndulla, Jacen 121, 123, 124, **138**, 401
Syndulla residence **283**
Syphacc **160**

T

T-1 shuttles **372**
T3-K10 **199**
T-6 Jedi shuttle **420**
T-6 shuttle **407**
T-14 hyperdrive **324**
T-16 skyhopper **409**
T-21 light repeating blaster **341**
T-47 airspeeder **412**
T-85 X-wing **422**
T-series tactical droids **330**
Taa, Orn Free **46**, 254
Taanti **180**
Taborr 21, **239**, 373
Taga **120**
Tagge, Domina **161**, 414
Tagge, General Genera 32, **146**
Tagge, Lapin **161**
Tagge, Ronen **160**, 161
Tagrin, Ax **223**, 314, 430
Tak **105**
Takodana **309**
  Maz Kanata's Castle 214, 215, **310**
Tal, Aran **171**
Talisola, Lula **15**, 372
Talzin, Mother 31, 61, **71**, 263, 335, 338, 361
Tambor, Jul **162**
Tambor, Wat **55**, 65, 254, 270

INDEX

Tamson, Riff **82**
Tanalorr **277**
Tandin, General **78**
Tanna, Khel **111**
Tano, Ahsoka 21, 38, 42, 47, 48, 50, 58, 61, **62**, 85, 303, 326
  and Anakin Skywalker 62, 63, 72, 264, 284, 332
  and Asajj Ventress 60, 62, 330
  and Captain Rex 59, 63
  Clone Wars 59, 388
  and Darth Vader 32, 62, 127, 283, 284, 346, 348
  and Din Djarin 172, 175, 300, 302
  and Ezra Bridger 62, 127
  and Hera Syndulla 180
  Jedi temple explosion 47
  lightsaber 68, **332**, **346**, 361
  and Luke Skywalker 87
  and Maul 31, 270, 339
  and Padmé Amidala 261, 376
  and Sabine Wren 62, 189, 360
  T-6 Jedi shuttle **420**
  technology 360, 361
  vehicles 407, 420
  Wasskah 264
Tantive IV 83, 88, 144, 167, 226, 348, **386**, 409, 422
Tapal, Jaro **99**, 342
Tarfful, Chief 74, **83**
Tarkin, Grand Moff 44, 48, **73**, 101, 145, 283, 423
  and Darth Vader 73, 138, 253
  Death Star 261, 287
Tarkin Initiative 24
Tarkintown **280**
Tarkon, Losha **160**
Tarpals, Captain **28**
Task Force 99 (SCAR Squadron) **154**, 155
Tatooine **243**
  Ben Kenobi's home **293**
  Garsa's Sanctuary **301**
  Jabba's Palace **257**
  Lars moisture farm **255**
  Mos Eisley Cantina **263**
  Mos Eisley Spaceport **262**
  Mos Espa **244**
  Mos Espa City Hall **301**
  Mos Espa Grand Arena **246**
  Mos Pelgo **300**
  repulsor train **418**
  Watto's Shop **245**
tauntaun **156**
Tauntaza **162**
TAY-0 **93**
  TAY-0's speeder **393**
Taylander shuttle **405**
Tayshin **105**
Tech 73, 85, **89**, 90, 272, 392, 393
Techno Union 254, 258, 270, 328, 339, 390
technology **320–67**
Teebo **166**
Teedo **212**
Teeka **108**
Tekka, Lor San **206**, 259, 309, 311
  and Poe Dameron 87, 153, 192, 194, 195, 206, 215
Tekka, Mari San 322, 372
Tempes **295**
Temple of the Kyber **285**, 335
Tenoo **239**, 322
Tensent, Nath **169**, 389
Tenth Brother **77**
Tenza, Leevan **121**
Terec **15**
Terex **193**, 304, 423
Terez, Gooti **135**, 406
Teth **254**
Teva, Carson 180, 303
thala-siren **218**
Thamm **220**
Thanoth, Inspector **153**
Tharnakan story stone 19, 20, **322**
Theed **241**
  Royal Palace Throne Room **242**
  Theed Hangar **242**
  Theed Power Generator **249**
  Theed Royal Palace 241, **242**
Thi-Sen **64**
Third Sister *see* Reva

Thirteenth Sister 43, 50, **96**
Thodibin **220**
thought dowser **353**
Thrawn 58, 62, 123, 129, **136**, 138, 188, 191
  and Arihnda Pryce 135, 136
  Chimaera 421
  Dathomir 263
  droids 337, 360
  and Hera Syndulla 190
  Peridea 136, 191, 303
  Seventh Fleet 358
  Thrawn's undead troopers **191**
  TIE defender 407
Threnalli, C'ai **216**
Ti, Shaak **49**, 50
tibidee **132**
Tico, Hue **192**
Tico, Paige 192, **216**, 217, 304, 427
Tico, Rose 192, 194, 216, **217**, 304, 428
  and Finn 207, 210, 217, 219, 220, 221
Tico, Thanya **192**
Tidian, Amuncie **229**
TIE advanced fighter X1 **411**
TIE advanced V1 prototype **404**
TIE baron **422**
TIE boarding craft **400**
TIE bomber **402**
TIE brute
  First Order TIE brute **431**
  TIE/RB heavy starfighter **396**
TIE dagger **429**
TIE defender **407**
TIE Echelon **431**
TIE fighter pilots **121**
  First Order **363**
  helmets 345, **363**
TIE fighters **395**
  First Order SF TIE fighter **425**
  First Order TIE fighter **425**
  Kylo Ren's **429**
TIE interceptor **415**
TIE/RB heavy starfighter **396**
TIE reaper **409**
TIE silencer **428**
TIE striker **408**
Tierny, Agent 198, **205**
Tigo, Vanis **119**
Tiin, Saesee 41, 42, **43**, 46
Tikkes, Senator **45**
Tills, Senator Meena **76**
Time Grappler **115**
Tipoca City **252**
  Jango's apartment **252**
Tiree, Dex **148**
Titan **430**
Titus, Brom **132**, 405
TK troopers **93**
  armor **339**
Todo 360 **66**
Tolsite, Quay **106**, 275
Tolvan, Magna 152, **154**, 289, 408
Tomasso **163**
Tomder, Bargwill **221**
T'onga 69, 158, **159**, 160, 414
T'ongor **159**
Tonra, Sergeant **29**
Tora-Asi, Lily 13, **15**, 16
Torch **222**
Toren, Papa **150**
toy droid **342**
Trach, Masir **233**
tracking fob **356**
tractor beam **333**
Trade Federation 253
  Armored Assault Tank (AAT) **375**
  battle droids 323, 328
  battleships **374**
  landing ship **375**
  MTT **375**
  Naboo blockade 241, 242, 249
  Single Trooper Aerial Platform (STAP) **375**
  technology 324
  vulture droids **374**
training A-wing **406**
training darts **359**
training droids **322**

training remote **327**
Trandoshan flying hunting lodge **388**
Transport Eight **398**
transport skimmers **432**
Transport 904 **393**
Trask **300**
Trayvis, Gall **131**
treadable **432**
treadspeeder **432**
Trebor, Coleman 45, **50**
Trench, Admiral **58**, 337
Trennis, Keeve **14**, 16, 372
Tres, Oma **231**
Trexler Marauder **417**
tri-wing **398**
Trident drill assault craft **385**
Trinia **161**
trinitaur **188**
Trios 76, **151**, 290, 291
Triple-Zero 152, **153**, 154, 290, 291
Trudgen **228**
  vibrocleaver **366**
TT-8L/Y7 **332**
Tua, Maketh **131**, 280
Tuanul Village **309**
Tuggs, Strono **215**
Tup 49, **80**
turbo tank **387**
Tuskens 35, **39**, 53, 55, 183, 184, 243, 255
  ballista **357**
  krayt dragons 180
  rifles **325**
  Tusken chieftain **182**
  Tusken warrior **182**
  weapons **325**, 349, 357
Tuttle **187**
Twi'leks 254, 330
Twilight **386**
twin-pod cloud car **414**
the Twins **183**
TX-225 combat assault tank **408**
Tyce, Wrobie **227**
Tyerell, Ratts **39**
Typho, Gregor **46**
Typhonic Nebula **315**
Tyra, Corbus **111**
Tyranus, Darth (Count Dooku) 21, 45, 49, 50, 51, 52, **56**, 64, 78, 214, 287
  and Anakin Skywalker 32, 56, 270, 330, 331
  and Asajj Ventress 34, 56, 60, 71, 263, 264, 265, 330
  and Darth Maul 50, 263
  and Darth Sidious 45, 56, 251, 383
  Dooku's Castle **264**, 265
  and General Grievous 56, 61
  Geonosis Execution Arena 256
  lightsaber **330**
  and Mace Windu 41
  and Master Mundi 42
  and Obi-Wan Kenobi 56, 254, 270, 330
  and Qui-Gon Jinn 23, 56
  rise of the Separatist movement 253
  and Sifo-Dyas 78, 79, 336
  solar sailor **383**
  and Yoda 60, 56, 253, 330
Tython **301**
TZ-2 **155**

U

U-55 orbital loadlifter **428**
U-wing **408**
UA-TT walker **432**
Ugnaughts **294**
Ulaf **120**
Umbara **265**
  Umbaran starfighter **388**
Unamo, Chief Petty Officer **212**
Unduli, Luminara 47, 60, 330
Unkar's thugs **211**
Unnamed Jabiim Moon **276**
Urtya, Dors 76, **155**, 265
Ushar **228**
  war club **366**
Utapau **268**
Utooni **171**

V

V-19 Torrent starfighter **385**
V-150 planet defender **354**
V-wing starfighter **391**
Vader, Darth (Anakin Skywalker) 26, 28, 44, 58, **226**, 231, 334, 343
  and Ahsoka Tano 32, 62, 63, 64, 72, 127, 264, 283, 284, 332, 346, 348
  airspeeder **378**
  armor **350**, 363
  and Asajj Ventress 259
  Battle of Naboo 240
  Battle of Yavin 389
  and C-3PO 33, 329
  Clone Wars 49, 50, 52, 59, 254, 323, 378, 388, 389
  commando droids 333
  and Count Dooku 32, 56, 270, 330, 331
  and Darth Sidious (Palpatine) 24, 25, 32, 54, 151, 258, 288, 331, 348, 350
  and Doctor Chelli Aphra 32, 152, 153, 255, 290, 293, 301, 333, 411
  droids 347
  and Eeth Koth 44
  ETA-2 Jedi starfighter **388**
  and Ezra Bridger 345, 346
  fortress 97, 276, 285, **288**
  Geonosis 253
  Geonosis execution arena 57, 256
  and the Grand Inquisitor 130, 345
  and Grand Moff Tarkin 73
  and Han Solo 46, 53, 100, 102, 159, 294, 379
  and IG-88 158
  Inquisitors 96
  Invisible Hand **390**
  and Jabba the Hutt 37
  Jedi training 248
  kyber crystals 268
  and Leia Organa 88, 167, 349
  lightsaber 32, 45, 254, 288, **331**, 332, 348
  and Luke Skywalker 24, 32, 37, 53, 87, 255, 290, 293, 294, 295, 297, 331, 348, 350, 355, 414
  and the MagnaGuards 332
  mechno-arm **330**
  meditation chamber **351**
  and Obi-Wan Kenobi 22, 25, 30, 32, 42, 43, 110, 258, 276, 287, 331, 348, 350, 394
  and Padmé Amidala 29, 32, 68, 252, 258, 288, 306, 343
  podracing 34, 35, 36, 37, 38, 246, 377
  and Qui-Gon Jinn 23, 32, 35, 42
  Radon-Ulzer podracer **377**
  and R2-D2 30
  river moon of Al'doleem 272
  and Sabé 29, 32, 36, 270, 295
  and Shmi Skywalker 35, 39, 54, 255
  Tantive IV **386**
  Tarkintown 280
  and the Tuskens 39
  Twilight **386**
  vehicles 395, 409, 411, 412
  Watto's shop 245
  and Yoda 40
  Zaly shield 354
Val **103**
Valance, Beilert **97**, 137, 270, 282, 411
Valik **202**
Valo **239**
Valorum, Supreme Chancellor 24, **39**, 45, 55, 249, 261
Vancto, Marshal Buck **111**
Vander, Jon **147**, 389
Vandor **274**
  Fort Ypso **274**
Vane **185**, 419
Vanik, Seftin **232**
Vann, Feyn **144**
Vanth, Cobb 53, 65, **179**, 180, 185, 300, 339, 351, 356, 357
  speeder **417**
Vanto, Eli **96**
Var-Shaa **298**
varactyl **79**
Vardos **298**
Varish **21**

Varkana 314
Vaspar, Vasp 144
Vebb, Nahdar 46, 61
Vectors 372
Veers, General Maximilian 156, 292
Vega, Yuralla 137
vehicles 370–433
Velti, Minas 108
Venator-class Star Destroyer 147, 252, 383, 396
Venim, Jet 93
Venomor, Babwa 94
Ventafoli, Aurodia 105
Ventress, Asajj 31, 47, **60**, 63, 259
    and Ahsoka Tano 60, 62, 330
    Clone Wars 49, 50
    and Count Dooku 34, 56, 60, 71, 263, 264, 265, 330
    Kamino 251
    lightsaber 330
    and Obi-Wan Kenobi 60, 259
    and Quinlan Vos 34, 56, 60, 263, 264
    and Savage Opress 71, 72, 263
Venzee, Keo 170
Verla 96
Verlaine, Evaan 149, 389
Vermillion 153, 414
Versio, Garrick 149, **150**
Versio, Iden **149**, 150, 168, 221, 346, 427
Versio, Zay 221
Vespaara 298
Vesper 420
Vess, Kay 164
Vessel 373
Vetch 115
Vex, Imara 171
vexis 229
Vicrul 228
    scythe 366
Viess, Abediah 12, **16**, 17
Vigil 428
Vil'pak 202
Vindi, Dr. Nuvo 64
Vish, Dara 177
Vitus, Cohmac 15, 372
Vizago, Cikatro **128**, 344, 404
Vizsla, Paz **176**, 219, 301, 302, 365
Vizsla, Pre 68, **69**, 338
Vizsla, Tarre **137**, 338
Voe 192
Voidgazer, Tulon 43, **151**
Volk, Tredgar 110
Volt Cobra 411
Von, Arkik 14
Vonreg, Havina 170
Vonreg, Major **196**, 205, 365, 422, 425
Voor, Pitina Mar-Mar 155
Vos, Dryden 31, **104**, 105, 341
    Crimson Dawn 31, 102, 104, 146, 397
    Kyuzo petars 341
    signet ring 341
Vos, Quinlan **34**, 38, 50, 56, 265
    and Asajj Ventress 34, 56, 60, 263, 264
Voyager Dawn 373
Vozo, Neeku **197**, 204, 205, 223, 430
Vranki's Hotel and Casino 314
Vrogas Vas 290
Vukorah 160
vulptex 221
Vulture droid 374

W

W1-LE **132**
WAC-47 **78**
Wald 34
wampas **156**, 292
Wannek 139
Warbirds 202, 204, 424
    skiff 424
    starfighter 424
Warrick, Pommet 233
Warrick, Wicket W. 88, **166**, 233, 297
Wasskah 264
Watto 32, 33, **35**, 38, 54, 246, 377
    Watto's Shop 245

Waxer, clone trooper **66**
wayfinders, Sith 258, **366**
Wayland 272
Waylin, Willard 170
We, Taun 51
Weaver, Myn **190**, 420
Weazel 34
WED Treadwell droid 349
Weebo 19
Weeteef Cyu-Bee 142
wellagrins 19
Wesell, Zam **49**, 250
    airspeeder 378
WESTAR-34 blaster pistol 327
WESTAR-35 twin blasters **345**
Wexley, Norra 148, 149, **169**, 215, 389
Wexley, Temmin "Snap" 169, 192, **215**, 323
WG-22 **106**
whale-sg constructhip 151
Whip of Sorrows 353
white Loth-cat 133
white Loth-wolf **137**
White Worms 100, 102, 103, 397
    den of the **274**
Wilco 93
Wiles, Gorrak 202
Windfall 343, **400**
Windu, Mace 21, 40, **41**, 43, 44, 69
    on Dantooine 283
    Geonosis Execution Arena 256
    and Jango Fett 49, 53
    lightsaber **327**, 361
    and Luminara Unduli 47
    and Padmé Amidala 27
    and Palpatine 41, 43, 46, 250
    and Queen Julia 265
    Ryloth 254
Wing 181
Winloss 155
Winta 176
Wobani 285
Wodibin 220
Wolf, Trapper **178**, 303
Wolffe, Commander 42, **63**, 382, 405
Wollivan 215
Wookiees 94, 170, 171, 275, 336, 342
    Kashyyyk 269
    weapons 349
the world between worlds 284
worrt rooster 185
Woves, Axe 75, **181**, 187, 345
Wrecker **90**, 91
Wren, Alrich **137**
Wren, Sabine 79, **126**, 133, 189, 324, 345
    and Ahsoka Tano 62, 189, 360
    airbrushes 343
    armor **336**, **344**
    Bokken saber **360**
    Darksaber 126, 338
    and Ezra Bridger 126, 127, 191, 360, 361
    lightsaber **346**
    scanning device **360**
    and Shin Hati 189
    Sundari 260
    technology 360
    vehicles 407
Wren, Tristan **137**
Wren, Ursa **137**
Wren Clan 126, 137, 283, 284
    Wren stronghold 284
Wuher 146

X

X-34 landspeeder **409**
X-wing, Poe Dameron's **431**
X-wing drone 430
Xane, Utani 290, 328
Xaul 120
Xi'an 178
Xiono, Hamato **190**
Xiono, Kazuda **196**, 197, 198, 199, 201, 202, 204, 205, 222, 223, 306, 307, 314, 363, 365, 422, 423, 424, 425, 430
Xrexus Cartel 21, 324

Y

Y-wing starfighter 389
Yaddle 12, **45**, 56, 270
Yaluna, Tualon **96**
Yamradi 239
Yanna 94
Yao, Detta 160
Yarrow, Chancey 15, 17, 322
Yarrow, Sylvestri 17
Yarrum 239
Yavin 4 **286**, 291, 292
    Battle of Yavin 389, 395
Yazal, Qin 85
Yeager, Jarek 196, **197**, 204, 307, 423
    racer 424
Yellow Ace 423
Yoda 13, 39, **40**, 41, 43, 45, 47, 62, 312
    Battle of Kashyyyk 269
    clone troopers 52
    and Count Dooku 40, 56, 253, 330
    on Dagobah **293**
    Geonosis Execution Arena 256
    Golatha droid factory 334
    and the Great Mountain 154
    Jedi training 248
    and Kanan Jarrus 122
    lightsaber 45, **330**
    and Luke Skywalker 40, 87, 266, 267, 293, 410
    Order 66 269
    and Palpatine 40, 249, 330
    and Qui-Gon Jinn 40, 266, 267
    Star Hopper 372
    Yoda's Hut **293**
Yorrick, Ty 16
Yu, Ariole 161
Yularen, Admiral Wullf **58**, 129
YV-865 *Aurore*-class freighter 392

Z

Z0-E3 **139**, 400
Z-6 jetpack **352**
Z6 Riot control baton **364**
Z-95 headhunter 392
Zahra, Ellian 73, **159**
Zaina 171
Zala, Mycho 20
Zaly shield **354**
Zanna, Zia Zaldor **18**, 20
Zarro **150**
Zatt 85
Zavor, Anj 144
ZED-6-7 **159**
Zeffo 273
Zepher 20
Zephyr-J speeder bike **416**
Zess, Raena 17, **19**, 20, 325
Zeta-class shuttle **409**
Zettifar, Bell 12, 14, **15**
Zeveron, Elecia (the Mother) **13**, 372
Zeveron, Oliviah **12**, 13
zillo beast 50, **66**, 93, 259, 393
Zin, Chilla 162
Zinska 120
ZN-A4 **112**
Zuckuss 158
Zygerrian electro-whip **335**
Zygerrian energy bow **339**
zymod 226

Senior Editor Matt Jones
Editor Frankie Hallam
Senior Designers Clive Savage and Nathan Martin
Project Art Editors Stefan Georgiou, Chris Gould, and Jon Hall
Designers James McKeag and Izzy Merry
Production Editor Marc Staples
Senior Production Controller Laura Andrews
Managing Editor Emma Grange
Managing Art Editor Vicky Short
Publisher Paula Regan
Art Director Charlotte Coulais
Managing Director Mark Searle

Edited by Elly Dowsett and Catherine Saunders
Designed by Jim Green, Simon Murrell, Lisa Robb, and Rob Perry
Cover Illustration Brian Rood

For Lucasfilm
Senior Editor Brett Rector
Creative Director Michael Siglain
Art Director Troy Alders
Story Group James Waugh, Pablo Hidalgo, Leland Chee, Matt Martin, Phil Szostak, Emily Shkoukani, and Kate Izquierdo
Asset Management Steve Newman, Gabrielle Levenson, Tim Mapp, Bryce Pinkos, Erik Sanchez, Nicole LaCoursiere, Kelly Jensen, and Shahana Alam

Dorling Kindersley would like to thank: Chelsea Alon, Angela Grief, Shana Highfield, Rima Simonian, and Thomas Wang at Disney; Ruth Amos, Alastair Dougall, David Fentiman, Romi Chakraborty, Upamanyu Das, Kingshuk Ghoshal, and Nehal Verma for editorial and design assistance; Adam Bray, Cole Horton, Patricia Barr, Daniel Wallace, Ryder Windham, David Fentiman and Emma Grange for additional text on previous editions; Alex Evangeli for picture research; Beth Davies, Emma Grange, Shari Last, Lisa Stock, Lauren Nesworthy, Nicole Reynolds, and Cefn Ridout for editorial work on the previous editions; Anna Formanek, Lisa Lanzarini, Lynne Moulding, Anne Sharples, Jess Tapolcai, and Toby Truphet for design work on the previous editions; Cameron + Company for their work on the original edition; Maxine Pedliham for initial design concept; Megan Douglass for providing an initial proofread; Victoria Taylor for proofreading, and Vanessa Bird for indexing.

First published in Great Britain in 2024 by
Dorling Kindersley Limited
20 Vauxhall Bridge Road,
London SW1V 2SA

The authorised representative in the EEA is Dorling Kindersley Verlag GmbH. Arnulfstr. 124, 80636 Munich, Germany

First published in 2015 and 2019 as *Ultimate Star Wars*

Page design copyright © 2024
Dorling Kindersley Limited
A Penguin Random House Company

© & TM 2024 LUCASFILM LTD.

10 9 8 7 6 5 4 3 2
003–339705–Nov/24

All rights reserved.
No part of this publication may be reproduced, stored in or introduced into a retrieval system, or transmitted, in any form, or by any means (electronic, mechanical, photocopying, recording, or otherwise), without the prior written permission of the copyright owner.

A CIP catalogue record for this book is available from the British Library.
ISBN: 978-0-2416-6162-8

Printed and bound in China

www.dk.com
www.starwars.com

This book was made with Forest Stewardship Council™ certified paper – one small step in DK's commitment to a sustainable future.
Learn more at www.dk.com/uk/information/sustainability

Includes the characters Del Meeko, Garrick Versio, Gideon Hask, Iden Versio, sentinel droid, Shriv Suurgav, and Zay Versio from *Star Wars:* Battlefront II (2017)

Includes the characters Dorwin Corvax, Gable Karius, Lady Corvax, Mustafarian Priestess, Vylip F'alma, Wannek, and ZO-E3 from *Star Wars:* Vader Immortal (2019)

Includes the characters BD-1, Cal Kestis, Cere Junda, Eno Cordova, Greez Dritus, Jaro Tapal, Ninth Sister (Masana Tide), Merrin, Second Sister (Trilla Suduri), Taron Malicos, and Prauf from *Star Wars:* Jedi Fallen Order (2019)

Includes the characters Ardo Barodai, Frisk, Grace Sienar, Gunny, Havina Vonreg, Keo Venzee, Lindon Javes, LT-514, Rella Sol, Shen, Terisa Kerrill, Varko Grey, Willard Waylin, and Zerelda Sage from *Star Wars:* Squadrons (2020)

Includes the characters Ady Sun'Zee, Gauge, Lens Kamo, Mubo, Neeva, Seezelslak, and Tara Rashin from *Star Wars:* Tales from the Galaxy's Edge (2020)

Includes the characters BD-1, Bode Akuna, Bhima Ook, Cal Kestis, Cere Junda, Eno Cordova, Dagan Gera, Doma Dendra, Greez Dritus, Kata Akuna, Merrin, Ninth Sister (Masana Tide), Pili Walde, Rayvis, Santari Khri, Tulakt, Tulli M'u, Turgle, and ZN-A4 from *Star Wars:* Jedi Survivor (2023)

Includes the characters Aran Tal, Balada the Hutt, Daq Dragus, Grozz, Imara Vex, J-3DI, Rieve, Sentinel, Skora, Slingshot, Sprocket, Utooni, and Zaina from *Star Wars:* Hunters (2024)

Includes the characters Kay Vess, ND-5, and Nix from *Star Wars:* Outlaws (2024)